Cooper's Comprehensive Environmental Desk Reference

Cooper's Comprehensive Environmental Desk Reference

Compiled and Edited by

ANDRÉ R. COOPER, SR.

VAN NOSTRAND REINHOLD

I(T)P® A Division of International Thomson Publishing Inc.

New York • Albany • Bonn • Boston • Detroit • London • Madrid • Melbourne
Mexico City • Paris • San Francisco • Singapore • Tokyo • Toronto

116084

Copyright © 1996 by André R. Cooper, Sr.

I(T)P® A division of International Thomson Publishing, Inc.
The ITP logo is a registered trademark.

Printed in the United States of America

For more information, contact:

Van Nostrand Reinhold
115 Fifth Avenue
New York, NY 10003
USA

Chapman & Hall GmbH
Pappelallee 3
69469 Weinheim
Germany

Chapman & Hall
2-6 Boundary Row
London SEI 8HN
United Kingdom

International Thomson Publishing Asia
221 Henderson Road #05-10
Henderson Building
Singapore 0315

Thomas Nelson Australia
102 Dodds Street
South Melbourne 3205
Victoria, Australia

International Thomson Publishing Japan
Hirakawacho Kyowa Building, 3F
2-2-1 Hirakawacho
Chiyoda-ku, 102 Tokyo
Japan

Nelson Canada
1120 Birchmount Road
Scarborough, Ontario
Canada M1K 5G4

International Thomson Editores
Campos Eliseos 385, Piso 7
Col. Polanco
11560 Mexico D.F. Mexico

1 2 3 4 5 6 7 8 9 10 QEB-KP 01 00 99 98 97 96

Library of Congress Cataloging-in-Publication Data

Cooper, André R.
    Cooper's comprehensive environmental desk reference: with supplemental spell check disk / compiled and edited by André R. Cooper, Sr.
        p.   cm.
    ISBN 0-442-02159-3 (hardcover)
    1. Environmental sciences--Handbooks, manuals, etc. 2. Environmental sciences--Dictionaries 3. Environmental protection--Handbooks, manuals, etc. 4. Environmental protection--Dictionaries. I. Title.

GE123.C64   1995
363.7--dc20
                                                                                        95-38571
                                                                                        CIP

To André R. Cooper, Jr.

— may his environmental and engineering knowledge continue to expand, so that he may edit the many future editions of "Cooper's Comprehensive Environmental Desk Reference" to come.

And special thanks, once again, to N.L. Montgomery, who conducted the laborious technical edit for this project.

CONTENTS

INTRODUCTION

Cooper's Comprehensive Environmental Desk Reference was designed to unlock the door to environmental jargon! It is a specialized reference to the standard jargon used by environmentalists, planners, compliance officers, bureaucrats, professionals and other participants in the environmental field.

Cooper's Comprehensive Environmental Desk Reference is presented in eight sections — Section I, provides instant access to thousand's of environmental terms and terminology (from A to Z) — Section II, provides a quick reference listing of over hundreds of environmental acronyms and abbreviations. Together sections I and II provide over 10,000 environmental terms, acronyms, and abbreviations — Section III, provides a Sample Phase I Environmental Site Assessment that can be used for student instruction or professional reference in conducting Phase I ESAs — Section IV, provides quick reference to the Hazardous Air Pollutants (HAPs) List found in the Clean Air Act, — Section V, provides one of the most comprehensive sets of environmental data conversion tables available — Section VI, provides a listing of chemical elements and abbreviations — Section VII, provides information on EPA Offices and Programs, and — Section VIII, is the Environmental Jargon Finder, a topical index of selected terms included in the book.

Cooper's Comprehensive Environmental Desk Reference is an expanded version of a self-published work (*Cooper's Pocket Environmental Reference*) started in 1991. This environmental data has been used by practitioners in the field as a quick reference tool; by students in environmental programs; by realtors, bankers, and appraisers; and by the Department of Energy as a skill building tool leading to competence in the language of the environmental profession.

A wide variety of references were consulted in the preparation of this book. For the most part the following acts, as amended, were referred to frequently in compiling this first edition: NEPA; CAA; CERCLA; SARA: FWPCA; CWA; TSCA; SWDA; RCRA; ESA; PHSA; EPCRTKA; Title 40 of the CFR; CEQA; NHPA; and other environmental legislation and deliverables prepared and reviewed over a ten year span in the environmental field. Every reasonable effort has been made to ensure data accuracy, but the author and publisher cannot assume responsibility for third party (government) information.

Cooper's Comprehensive Environmental Desk Reference is being sold with the understanding that neither the publisher nor the editors are engaged in rendering legal advice or services, of any kind, and no endorsement by DOE, DOD, EPA, or any other agency, on the information herein, implicit or explicit, has been received.

André R. Cooper, Sr., R.E.A.

Section I

Environmental Terms and Terminology

A

A/E Services
See Architectural and Engineering Services.

A-95 Clearinghouse
A multijurisdictional agency that operates in coordination with cities and counties to carry out the review provided for under the Office of Management and Budget's Circular A-95. Three types of clearinghouses exist: state; regional; and metropolitan.

A-95 Review
A review administered by the Federal Office of Management and Budget whose purpose is to assure review and comment by both public and private interests that might be impacted by federally funded real estate development programs.

A-Scale Sound Level
A measurement of sound approximating the sensitivity of the human ear, used to define the annoyance of sounds or intensity of noise pollution.

A-Stage
An early stage of polymerization of thermosetting resins in which the material is still soluble in certain liquids and is fusible.

AA
An acronym for the Agriculture Act of 1970; and the Antiquities Act of 1906.

AACS
An acronym for Airborne Activity Confinement Systems.

Abandoned Areas
Deserted mine areas in which work has ceased and in which further work is not intended. Areas that function as escapeways and areas formerly used as lunchrooms, shops, and transformer or pumping stations are not considered abandoned areas.

Abandoned Well
A well whose use has been permanently discontinued due to lack of resources, need, or one that is in a state of disrepair to the extent that it cannot be used for its intended purpose.

Abatement
Reducing the degree or intensity of, or sometimes eliminating, a pollutant or the condition generating the pollution.

Abatement Date
The date by which an owner/operator is allowed, and required, to correct the condition constituting noncompliance with environmental order, regulation, policy, ordinance, or act.

ABEL
EPA's computer model for analyzing a responsible party's, or violator's, ability to pay a civil

penalty for noncompliance with environmental laws.

Abiotic
A term meaning nonbiological.

Ablation
The removal of loose surface material by wind; the melting and evaporation of surface ice.

Ablative
A material that absorbs heat through a decomposition process called pyrolysis at or near the exposed surface.

ABOSFN
An acronym for Nominal Automatic Burnout Safety Factor.

Aboveground Releases
Releases to the surface of the land or to surface water. This includes, but is not limited to, releases from the aboveground portion of an underground storage tank (UST) system and aboveground releases associated with overfills and transfer operations as the regulated substance moves to or from a UST system, tank, or facility.

Aboveground Storage Facility
A tank or other holding container, which is no more than 6 inches below its surrounding surface area.

Aboveground Storage Tank (AST)
A tank device situated in such a way that the entire surface area of the tank is completely above the plane of the adjacent surrounding surface and the entire surface area of the tank can be visually inspected.

Abrasion
1) The wearing away of surface materials by the abrasive action of moving solids, liquids, and/or gases. 2) In photography, a scratch or mark produced mechanically on an emulsion surface or film base.

Abrasive
A substance used to erode or polish a surface by friction, via liquid and solid materials such as emery, sand, and diamonds.

ABS-SC
An acronym for Automatic Backup Shutdown of the Safety Computer.

Absolute Age
The age of rock, mineral, or fossils in years; usually determined by radiometric dating.

Absolute Dud
A nuclear weapon which, when launched at or emplaced on a target, fails to explode.

Absolute Filter
A filter capable of cutting off 100% by weight of solid particles greater than a stated micron size.

Absolute Pressure (psia)
The sum of the atmospheric pressure and gauge pressure (psig).

Absorb
To transform radiant energy into a different form, with a resultant rise in temperature.

Absorbed Dose
1) The amount of a substance penetrating across the exchange boundaries of an organism, via either physical or biological processes, after contact (exposure). 2) The amount of energy imparted by nuclear (or ionizing) radiation to unit mass of absorbing material.

Absorbed Dose Rate
The energy from ionizing radiation absorbed per unit mass. The unit of absorbed dose is the gray (1 joule/kg) or, historically, the rad which is equal numerically to 10^{-2} joule/kg (100 erg/g).

Absorption
1) The incorporation of liquids or gases into the body. 2) The process by which liquid hazardous

materials are soaked up by sand, sawdust, or other material to limit the spread of contamination.

Absorption, Chemical

1) Adhesion of molecules of gas, liquid or dissolved solids to a surface. 2) The passage of one substance into or through another (e.g., an operation in which one or more soluble components of a gas mixture are dissolved in a liquid).

Absorption, Human

To take in a substance through a body surface such as the lungs, gastrointestinal tract, or skin and, ultimately, into body fluids and tissues.

Absorption, Radiation

The phenomenon by which radiation imparts some or all of its energy to any material through which it passes.

Absorption, Waste

An advanced method of treating wastes in which activated carbon removes organic matter from wastewater.

Absorption Coefficient

In acoustics, the ratio of sound waves absorbed by a material's surface to the total sound energy that strikes it. If the absorption coefficient = 1, then 100% of the sound energy is absorbed.

Absorption Hazards

Hazards where exposure to materials that can be absorbed through the skin or which can cause a skin effect (e.g., dermatitis) where appropriate personal protective equipment (clothing) is necessary but not worn. Such hazards do not depend on measurements of airborne concentrations. If a serious skin absorption or dermatitis hazard exists that cannot be eliminated with protective clothing, engineering or administrative controls should be utilized to minimize or prevent the hazard.

Absorption Unit

A factory-built assembly of component parts designed to produce refrigeration for comfort cooling or comfort heating by the application of heat.

Absorptive Capacity

A measure of the total amount of waste that can be dispersed in a particular environment without causing an adverse ecological or aesthetic impact.

Abstract of Title

A summary or condensation of the essential parts of all recorded instruments that affect a particular piece of real estate, arranged in the order they were recorded.

Abut

To border on. When two adjacent properties share a common public easement, such as a highway, they are called "abutting" properties. Properties that share a common property line are adjoining or adjacent sites.

AC

An acronym for Alternating Current.

ACAA

See Agricultural Conservation and Adjustment Administration of World War II.

Acaricide

Chemicals, pesticides, and organochlorines used to kill ticks and mites.

Acaulescent

Stemless or nearly stemless.

ACC

An acronym for Abnormal Condition Control.

Acceleration

The rate of change of velocity with time. According to Newton, acceleration x mass = force = rate of change of momentum.

Acceleration Clause

A clause in a contract by which the time for payment of a debt is advanced, usually making the balance of the obligation due.

Accelerator

In the field of nuclear energy, a device used to speed up small particles for bombarding the nuclei of atoms. A device used to increase the kinetic energy of charged elementary particles.

Acceptability of Plan Review Criterion

In planning, the determination of whether a contemplated course of action is worth the cost in manpower, material, and time involved. *See* Adequacy of Operation Plan Review Criterion.

Acceptable Daily Intake

An estimate similar in concept to the Reference Dose (RfD), however, derived using a less rigorously defined methodology. RfDs have replaced the ADI as EPA's preferred value for use in evaluating potential noncarcinogenic health effects resulting from exposure to a chemical.

Acceptable Quality Level (AQL)

Maximum amount of laboratory failings considered satisfactory in a process average; expressed as a percentage.

Acceptable Risks

Residual risks remaining after controls have been applied to associated hazards that have been identified, quantified, analyzed, communicated to the proper level of management, and accepted after cost/benefit evaluations.

Acceptance

1) The indication or manifestation by the offeree that he/she is willing to be bound by the terms of the offer. 2) In real estate, the consent by a person receiving an offer to enter into a binding agreement with the offeror.

Access Agreement

1) An agreement allowing public access to privately owned land. 2) An agreement allowing a contractor/consultant access to a site throughout the course of a specific project period.

Access to Classified Information

The ability and opportunity to obtain knowledge of classified information. Persons have access to classified information if they are permitted to gain knowledge of the information or if they are in a place where they would be expected to gain such knowledge. Persons do not have access to classified information by being in a place where classified information is kept if security measures prevent them from gaining knowledge of the information.

Accessible Emission Level

1) The maximum accessible emission level. 2) The magnitude of accessible laser (or collateral) radiation of a specific wavelength or emission duration at a particular point as measured by appropriate methods and devices. 3) Radiation to which human access is possible in accordance with the definition of the laser's hazard classification.

Accessible Environment

The atmosphere, land surface, surface water, oceans, and the portion of the lithosphere that is outside the controlled area.

Accessible Location

A location that can be reached by an individual standing on the floor, platform, runway, or other permanent work area.

Accession

A transaction whereby one or more objects are acquired in the same manner from one source at one time for a museum collection. Types of accessions include gifts, exchanges, loans, and transfers.

Accessory Attachment/Improvement

Any additional structure, air-conditioning unit, driveway, landscaping, skirting, awning, carport, shed, porch, or other items contracted for and included in the purchase document for the purchase or lease of a manufactured home, mobile home, and/or its installation site.

Accessory Structure

A structure on a site that is detached from the main facility and that has a use related, but incidental to that of the main facility.

Accessory Use

In zoning, a use of land incidental to the major zoning classification for the property, such as parking lots in commercial zones and swimming pools in residential zones.

Accident

1) Any unexpected, undesirable event that adversely affects human health, welfare, or the environment. 2) A deviation from normal operations or activities associated with a hazard that has the potential to result in an emergency. 3) Unwanted transfers of energy or environmental conditions which, due to the absence or failure of barriers and/or controls, produces injury to persons, property, or process. In the context of nuclear safety or radiation protection, events which lead or could lead to abnormal exposure conditions.

Accident Prevention Measures for Regulated Substances (APMRS)

Measures adopted for release prevention, detection, and correction requirements that may include monitoring, record-keeping, reporting, training, vapor recovery, secondary containment, including other design, equipment, work practice, and operational requirements.

Measures should make distinctions between various types, classes, and kinds of facilities, devices and systems taking into consideration factors including, but not limited to, the size, location, process, process controls, quantity of substances handled, potency of substances, and response capabilities present at any stationary source.

Prevention measures typically cover the use, operation, repair, replacement, and maintenance of equipment to monitor, detect, inspect, and control such releases, including training of persons in the use and maintenance of such equipment and in the conduct of periodic inspections.

Accident Prevention Program (APP)

A program for preventing accidental releases of regulated substances, including safety precautions, maintenance, monitoring, and employee training measures.

Accident Prevention Regulations for Hazardous Substances (APRHS)

The regulations that require owners or operators of stationary sources at which a regulated substance is present in more than a threshold quantity to prepare and implement a risk management plan to detect and prevent or minimize accidental releases of such substances from the stationary source, and to provide a prompt emergency response to any such releases in order to protect human health and the environment. These regulations cover storage, as well as operations. The regulations, as appropriate, recognize differences in size, operations, processes, class and categories of sources, and the voluntary actions of such sources to prevent such releases and respond to such releases.

Accident Prevention Risk Management Plan

A plan that provides for compliance with the requirements of the CAA that includes each of the following: a) a hazard assessment to assess the potential effects of an accidental release of any regulated substance. This assessment includes an estimate of potential release quantities and a determination of downwind effects, including potential exposures to affected populations. Such assessment shall include a previous release history of the past 5 years, including the size, concentration, and duration of releases, and shall include an evaluation of worst case accidental releases; b) a program for preventing accidental releases of regulated substances, including safety precautions and maintenance, monitoring and employee training measures to be used at the source; and c) a response program providing for specific actions to be taken in response to an accidental release of a regulated substance so as to protect human health and the environment, including procedures for informing the public and local agencies responsible for responding to accidental releases, emergency health care, and employee training measures. Owners and/or operators stationary sources covered by certain provisions of the CAA are required to submit risk management plans to the Administrator, the Chemical Safety and Hazard Investigation Board (CSHIB), the state in which the stationary source is located, and to any local agency or entity having responsibility for planning for or responding to accidental releases that may occur at the source.

Accident Prone Situation
A condition in which accidents are predisposed to happen due to the existence of unwanted energy flows around potential targets in the absence of adequate barriers.

Accident Response Capabilities Coordinating Committee (ARCCC)
An advisory body that assists the manager of the Albuquerque Operations Office in matters relating to the overall management and coordination of DOE's nuclear weapons accident response.

Accident Response Groups (ARG)
Groups of technical and scientific experts composed of DOE and DOE-contractor personnel assigned responsibility for providing DOE assistance to peacetime accidents and significant incidents involving nuclear weapons anywhere in the world.

Accident Scenario
A simulation of an imagined disaster to test the responsiveness of an emergency preparedness team and to help quantify the potential, or actual, extent of damage to life and property.

Accident Site
The geographic location of an unexpected, inadvertent occurrence. A system failure or release at a facility or along a transportation route, where a release of hazardous materials has occurred.

Accident Types
Classification of accidents according to cause, such as the energy or environmental conditions involved (e.g., electrical accidents, radiation accidents).

Accidental Occurrences
Accidents, including continuous or repeated exposure to conditions, that result in bodily injury or property damage that are neither expected nor intended from the standpoint of the insured.

Accidental Release
An unanticipated emission of a regulated substance or other extremely hazardous substance into the ambient air from a stationary source.

Accidents, Explosive
Incidents or occurrences that result in an uncontrolled chemical reaction involving explosives.

Acclimation
Behavioral or physiological adaptation of organisms to external environmental conditions.

Acclimatization
The physiological and behavioral adjustments of an organism to changes in its environment.

Accountability
The obligation imposed by law or lawful order or regulation on an officer or other person for keeping accurate record of property, documents, or funds. The person having this obligation may or may not have actual possession of the property, documents, or funds. Accountability is concerned primarily with records, while responsibility is concerned primarily with custody, care, and safekeeping. *See* Responsibility.

Accreditation
1) The DOE process of evaluating a program which, through the use of radiation dosimeters, measures and records dose equivalents received by radiation workers. 2) A DOE process to formally recognize reactor and nonreactor facility training programs as meeting established accreditation objectives and criteria.

Accreditation Coordinators

DOE personnel appointed within the program office and the field organization who are responsible for reviewing accreditation documents and maintaining the communication between DOE and the contractor concerning all accreditation activities associated with the office.

Accreditation Maintenance Report (AMR)

DOE reports written 2 years after accreditation or renewal of accreditation that describe changes in the accredited training programs since the last accreditation review.

Accreditation Review Team (ART)

DOE groups and individuals representing the Training Accreditation Program with collective expertise in nuclear facility or reactor operations, nuclear facility training, instructional processes, and training program evaluation. These teams review the facility's Contractor Self-Evaluation Report (CSER), visit the facility, evaluate training, and prepare a report of conclusions and recommendations.

Accredited

The status conferred upon DOE and DOE contractor dosimetry programs that have undergone the accreditation process and met or exceeded the applicable criteria of DOE/EH-0026 and DOE/EH-0027. Programs are accredited for a period of 2 years from the date of notification.

Accrediting Boards

Independent groups of individuals responsible for making the decision to award or deter accreditation.

Accretion

An increase in the area of riparian land due to the gradual deposit of solid materials by the water (alluvion), or due to the gradual but permanent receding of a waterway (dereliction).

Accuracy

The relationship of a result or the mean of a set of results to the true value. Accuracy is assessed by means of measuring divergence from a reference sample and deducting for error percentages.

Acetic Acid ($C_2H_4O_2$)

Ethanoic acid, the acid in vinegar, an important industrial material obtained by fermentation from ethanol.

Acetone (C_3H_6O)

Propanone; a laboratory and industrial solvent used for making plastics. It is mixable with water and often used as a cleaning agent.

Acetylcholine

A substance in the human body having important neurotransmitter effects on various internal systems; often used as a bronchoconstrictor.

ACH

An acronym for Air Changes per Hour.

Achene

A small, thin drywalled fruit, such as those of buttercups or dandelions, that do not split when ripe.

Acicular

A needlelike bristle, spine or crystal.

Acid

1) A compound consisting of hydrogen plus one or more other elements and which, in the presence of certain solvents or water, reacts with the production of hydrogen ions. Acid reacts with alkali to form a salt water, has a sour taste, and turns blue litmus red. 2) A term applied to water with a pH less than 5.5. 3) A corrosive solution with a pH less than 7. *See* pH.

Acid Deposition

A complex chemical and atmospheric process whereby recombined emissions of sulfur and nitrogen compounds are redeposited on earth in wet or dry form. *See* Acid Rain; Particulates.

Acid Deposition Report (ADR)

A biennial report to Congress describing technical information about acid deposition to facilitate communication with policymakers and the public. The report includes, a) actual and projected emissions and acid deposition trends; b) average ambient concentrations of acid deposition precursors and their transformation products; c) the status of ecosystems (including forests and surface waters), materials, and visibility affected by acid deposition; d) the causes and effects of such deposition, including changes in surface water quality and forest and soil conditions; e) the occurrence and effects of episodic acidification, particularly with respect to high elevation watersheds; and f) the confidence level associated with each conclusion to aid policymakers in use of the information.

Acid Dipping

The immersion of metal-based equipment into a tank of acid-based cleaning solvents to remove debris and clean the object.

Acid Precipitation Research Program (APRP)

A program carried out by the Acid Precipitation Task Force for coordinating, augmenting, monitoring, and sponsoring additional research in the scientific community as necessary to ensure the availability and quality of data and methodologies needed to evaluate the status and effectiveness of acid deposition control programs. Research and monitoring efforts include, but are not limited to, a) continuous monitoring of emissions of precursors of acid deposition; b) maintenance, upgrading, and application of models, such as the Regional Acid Deposition Model, that describe the interactions of emissions with the atmosphere, and models that describe the response of ecosystems to acid deposition; c) analysis of the costs, benefits, and effectiveness of the acid deposition control program; and d) publication and maintenance of a National Acid Lakes Registry that tracks the condition and change over time of a statistically representative sample of lakes in regions that are known to be sensitive to surface water acidification.

Acid Precipitation Task Force (APTF)

A task force comprised of the Administrator of the Environmental Protection Agency, the Secretary of Energy, the Secretary of the Interior, the Secretary of Agriculture, the Administrator of the National Oceanic and Atmospheric Administration, the Administrator of the National Aeronautics and Space Administration, and such additional members as the president may select. The responsibilities of the Task Force shall include reviewing the status of research activities conducted to date under the comprehensive research plan developed pursuant to the Acid Precipitation Act of 1980 (42 USC 8901 et seq.) and developing plans that identify significant research gaps and establish a coordinated program to address current and future research priorities.

Acid Rain

Rainwater that has an acidity content greater than the postulated natural pH of about 5.6. It is formed when sulfur dioxides and nitrogen oxides, as gases or fine particles in the atmosphere, combine with water vapor and precipitate as sulfuric acid or nitric acid in rain, snow, or fog. The dry forms are acidic gases or particulates. *See* Acid Deposition.

Acid Suit

See Anticontamination Clothing, Personal Protective Equipment.

Acknowledgment

1) A declaration made by a person to a notary public, or other public official, authorized to take acknowledgments, that a written instrument was executed by the individual and that it is was done as a free and voluntary act. 2) A message from the addressee informing the originator that his or her communication has been received and is understood.

Aclinic Line

See Magnetic Equator.

ACLs

An acronym for Alternate Concentration Limits.

ACOE
An acronym for Army Corps of Engineers.

Acoustic
A term used to describe the qualities and characteristics associated with sound transmissions.

Acoustic Intelligence
Intelligence derived from the collection and processing of acoustic phenomena.

Acoustical Surveillance
Employment of electronic devices, including sound-recording, -receiving, or -transmitting equipment, for the collection of information.

Acquired Character
A change in an organism resulting in response to an outside environmental influence.

Acquisition
The act or process of acquiring fee title or interest other than fee title to real property, including acquisition of development rights; obtaining ownership or possession of property by lawful means.

Acquisition of the Equivalent
The substitution of one resource for another resource that provides the same or substantially similar services, when such substitutions are in addition to any substitutions made, or anticipated, as part of response actions and when such substitutions exceed the level of response actions determined appropriate to the site pursuant to the National Contingency Plan (NCP).

Acre Foot
A term used in measuring the volume of water, equal to the quantity of water required to cover 1 acre of a level area 1 foot in depth (e.g., 43,560 cubic feet, 1232.73 cubic meters).

Acronyms
Alphanumeric abbreviations for complex terms, names, programs, procedures, or concepts. There are over 10,000 terms and acronyms in this edition of *Cooper's Comprehensive Environmental Desk Reference*. Acronyms, and their corresponding phrases, are found in their correct alphabetical position in the main body of the text. A comprehensive listing of all acronyms mentioned in the book and their corresponding meanings are included in their own section.

ACRR
An acronym for Annular Core Research Reactor.

ACRS
An acronym for the Advisory Commitment on Reactor Safety.

Acrylic Fiber
A manufactured synthetic material made of any long-chain synthetic polymer composed of a minimum 85%, by weight, of acrylonitrile units.

Acrylic Resins
A widely used group of synthetic resins, obtained from the polymerization of monomers derived from acrylic acid.

ACS
An acronym for Alternative Control Strategies.

Act of God
An unanticipated grave natural disaster or physical phenomenon of an extraordinary, fated, and compelling character, the effects of which could not have been foreseen or avoided.

Act of Nature
An act exclusively by violence of nature and without the interference of any human agency. A natural occurrence that cannot be foreseen or prevented. Also called an Act of God.

Actinmycetes
A group of moldlike bacteria that smell like very rich earth and are significant in the stabilization of organic solid waste by composting.

Actinoids
The radioactive elements from the periodic table ranging from actinium to lawrencium, including:

actinium (89); thorium (90); protactinium (91); uranium (92); neptunium (93); plutonium (94); americium (95); curium (96); berkelium (97); californium (98); einsteinium (99); fermium (100); mendelevium (101); nobelium (102); and lawrencium (103).

Actinomorphic
Having radial symmetry.

Action Areas
All areas to be affected directly or indirectly by the federal action and not merely the immediate area involved in the action.

Action Charlie
Procedural shutdown, manual scram.

Action Description Memoranda (ADM)
An internal DOE document (normally, not more than 6 pages) containing a concise description of a proposed action and discussion of relevant potential environmental issues, to assist DOE in determining the appropriate level of NEPA document for a proposed action.

Action Levels
1) Regulatory levels recommended by EPA, for enforcement by FDA and USDA, when pesticide residues occur in food or feed commodities for reasons other than the direct application of the pesticide. As opposed to "tolerances" which are established for residues occurring as a direct result of proper usage, action levels are set for inadvertent residues resulting from previous legal use or accidental contamination. 2) In the Superfund program, the existence of a contaminant concentration in the environment high enough to warrant action or trigger a response under SARA and the National Oil and Hazardous Substances Contingency Plan. The term can be used similarly in other regulatory programs. *See* Tolerance.

Action Plans
DOE plans intended to set forth specific actions that the site will undertake to remedy deficiencies noted in a Tiger Team Assessment Report. The plans include timetables and funding requirements for the implementation of planned actions.

Action Propensity
The ability to make things happen. In an organization, the general manager has a much higher action propensity, than those in staff positions regarding safety, for example.

Actions
All activities or programs of any kind authorized, funded, or carried out, in whole or in part, by federal agencies in the United States or upon the high seas. Examples include, but are not limited to, a) actions intended to conserve listed species or their habitat; b) the promulgation of regulations; c) the granting of licenses, contracts, leases, easements, rights-of-way, permits, or grants-in-aid; or d) actions directly or indirectly causing modifications to the land, water, or air.

Activate
1) To put into existence by official order a unit, post, camp, station, base, or shore activity that has previously been constituted and designated by name or number, or both, so that it can be organized to function in its assigned capacity. 2) To prepare for active service a naval ship or craft that has been in an inactive or reserve status.

Activated Carbon
A form of carbon with a high adsorptive capacity for gases, vapors, and colloidal solids; it is made by heating carbon to 900°C with steam and/or carbon dioxide which gives it a porous particulate structure. It is used to control odors, fumes, and other types of pollution, and is also used as the primary filter material in gas masks. In waste treatment it is used to remove dissolved organic matter from wastewater. It is also used in motor vehicle evaporative control systems. *See* Carbon Absorption.

Activated Sludge
1) The biologically active material used to purify sewage, in the third level of treatment. When added to aerated sewage the organisms break down the organic matter that is present, using it as

food, multiplying, creating more activated sludge. This speeds breakdown of organic matter in raw sewage undergoing secondary waste treatment. 2) Sludges that result when primary effluent is mixed with bacteria-laden sludge and then agitated and aerated to promote biological treatment.

Activated Sludge Process
A sewage treatment process by which bacteria that feed on organic wastes are continuously circulated and put in contact with organic waste in the presence of oxygen to increase the rate of decomposition.

Activation
Notification by phone or other expeditious manner or, when required, the assembly of some or all of the appropriate members of the Regional or National Response Teams.

Activation Detector
A device used to determine neutron flux or density by virtue of the radioactivity induced in it as a result of neutron capture.

Active Communications Satellite
See Communications Satellite.

Active Immunity
The immunity built up by the body to combat a toxin.

Active Ingredient
In any pesticide product, the component that kills or otherwise controls targeted pests. Pesticides are primarily regulated by their active ingredients. 1) In the case of a pesticide other than a plant regulator, defoliant, or desiccant, ingredients that will prevent, destroy, repel, or mitigate any pest. 2) In the case of a plant regulator, ingredients that, through physiological action, accelerate or retard the rate of growth or rate of maturation or otherwise alter the behavior of ornamental or crop plants or product thereof. 3) In the case of a defoliant, ingredients that will cause the leaves or foliage to drop from a plant. 4) In the case of

desiccant, ingredients that will artificially accelerate the drying of plant tissue.

Active Institutional Control
1) Restricting access to a disposal site through active controls such as guards and gates. 2) Performing maintenance and monitoring related to a disposal system's operating efficiency. 3) Performing site clean-up and remedial action tasks at an institution.

Active Life of a Facility
The period from the initial receipt of hazardous waste at the facility until the Regional Administrator receives certification of final closure.

Active Maintenance
Any significant remedial activity need during the period of institutional control to maintain a reasonable assurance that the performance objectives in 10 CFR 61.41 and 61.42 are met.

Active maintenance includes ongoing activities such as the pumping and treatment of water from a disposal unit or one-time measures such as replacement of a disposal unit cover. Active maintenance does not include custodial activities such as repair of fencing, repair or replacement of monitoring equipment, revegetation, minor additions to soil cover, minor repair, and general disposal site upkeep.

Active Material
Material, such as plutonium and certain isotopes of uranium, which is capable of supporting a fission chain reaction.

Active Mines
Underground uranium mines from which ore or waste material is currently removed by conventional methods.

Active Nest
A bird nest site where breeding efforts have recently occurred, as determined by a state's department of fish and game, or the U.F.W.S.

Active Portion

That portion of a facility where treatment, storage, or disposal operations are being, or have been, conducted and that are not closed portions.

Activities

Natural or normal functions or operations; an occupation, pursuit, or recreation in which an individual participates.

Activity

1) The total flow of energy through an ecological system in a unit of time; an all-inclusive term describing a specific set of operations or tasks to be conducted, either serially or in parallel (e.g., research and development, field sampling, analytical assessments, equipment installation), that, in total, result in a service or product. 2) A specific line of work carried on by an agency in order to perform its functions. 3) A function or mission.

Activity, Nuclear

The number of nuclear disintegrations occurring in a given quantity of material per unit time. Sometimes the former special unit curie (Ci) is still used. A special name for the unit of activity is becquerel (Bq).

Activity Mapping

A method of recording and displaying performance data in relation to an environmental setting. The planner notes activities and their frequencies on site and on facility maps that, when completed, show operational behaviors; location of storage, treatment, shipping, disposal, and other activities; frequency of the storage, treatment, shipping, disposal, and other activities at varying locations; waste movement; relation of people to facilities and projects; and people movement.

Activity Types

A general term denoting specific lines of work carried on in order to complete a function or category of tasks, such as building/equipment maintenance and repair activity; classified activity; construction activity; decommissioning activity; decontamination activity; emergency response activity; equipment installation activity; food service activity; fuel handling activities; ground maintenance activity; inspection/monitoring activity; material handling activity; mining/drilling activity; office activity; other nontask activity; physical fitness training activity; pre-startup/calibration activity; production/operation activity; reactor refueling activity; recreation/break activity; research/testing activity; security activity; training/education activity; transportation activity; travel activity; vehicle maintenance and repair activity.

Acts

The formal Statutes and Regulations of a legislative body, such as the Administrative Procedures Act; Archaeological Resources Protection Act of 1979; Atomic Energy Act; Clean Air Act; Clean Water Act; Comprehensive Environmental Response, Compensation, and Liability Act; Endangered Species Act; National Environmental Policy Act; Nuclear Waste Policy Act; Resource Conservation and Recovery Act; Safe Drinking Water Act; Solid Waste Disposal Act; Superfund Amendments and Reauthorization Act of 1986; Toxic Substances Control Act; Public Health Service Act.

Actual Cash Value

Replacement cost of property at the time of loss, less depreciation based on age, condition, time in use, and obsolescence.

Actual Ground Zero

The point on the surface of the earth at, or vertically below or above, the center of a nuclear detonation. *See* Desired Ground Zero; Ground Zero.

Actuarial

Data from actual past experience used to project future performance.

Actuator

A power mechanism that converts electrical, hydraulic, or pneumatic energy into motion.

Acuminate

Tapering to a sharp point.

Acute

Any event occurring over a short period of time resulting in biological effects shortly after exposure to a hazardous substance.

Acute Dermal LD 50

A single dermal dose of a substance, expressed as milligrams per kilogram of body weight, that is lethal to 50% of the test population of animals under test conditions as specified in government guidelines (e.g., OSHA). *See* Lethal Dose.

Acute Effect

1) An adverse effect on any living organism in which severe symptoms develop rapidly and often subside after the exposure stops. 2) A pathologic process caused by a single substantial exposure. 3) A short-term symptom of exposure to a hazardous material.

Acute Exposure

A single exposure to a toxic substance, or multiple encounters over a short period of time, usually a day or less, which results in severe biological harm and/or death.

Acute LD 50

A concentration of a substance, expressed as parts per million parts of medium, that is lethal to 50% of the test population of animals under test conditions as specified in government guidelines (e.g., OSHA). *See* Lethal Dose.

Acute Lobe

A rounded projection ending on a short point.

Acute Oral LD 50

A single orally administered dose of a substance, expressed as milligrams per kilogram of body weight, that is lethal to 50% of the test population of animals under test conditions as specified in government guidclines (e.g., OSHA). *See* Lethal Dose.

Acute Radiation Dose

Total ionizing radiation dose received at one time and over a period so short that biological recovery cannot occur.

Acute Toxicity

1) The ability of a substance to cause poisonous effects that result in severe biological harm or death soon after a single exposure or dose. 2) Any severe poisonous effect resulting from a single short-term exposure to a toxic substance. 3) Any poisonous effect produced within a short period of time, usually less than 96 hours. *See* Chronic Toxicity; Toxicity.

ACV

An acronym for Air Cushion Vehicle.

Ad Valorem

Latin, meaning "according to value"; normally used to describe a tax based on the assessed value of real property.

Adaptation

A biological quality or structure that helps a living organism survive in its environment; a change in an organism's structure or habit that help it adjust to its surroundings; the tendency of certain receptors to become less responsive or cease to respond to repeated or continued stimuli.

Adaptive Reuse

The act or process of adapting a structure for a use other than its originally designed purpose.

Adaxial

Relating to or being positioned on the side toward a plant's stem.

ADCP

An acronym for Acid Deposition Control Program (CAA).

Add-On Control Device

An air pollution control device such as a carbon adsorber or incinerator that reduces the pollution in an exhaust gas. The control device usually does not affect the process being controlled and thus is "add-on" technology as opposed to a scheme to control pollution through making some alteration to the basic process.

Addition, Building

An increase in floor area or volume of enclosed space that is physically attached to an existing building by connections that are required for transmitting vertical or horizontal loads between units.

Additive

A chemical substance that is intentionally added to another chemical substance to improve its stability or impart some other desirable quality.

Additive and Synergistic Effects

Substances that have a known additive effect and, therefore, result in a greater probability/severity of risk when found in combination. These combined substances are evaluated based upon the exposures' additive effect on the same body organ or system. If it is decided that there is a synergistic effect of the substances found together, the violations are grouped, when appropriate, for purposes of increasing the violation classification severity and/or the penalty.

Additivity

A pharmacologic or toxicologic interaction in which the combined effect of two or more chemicals is approximately equal to the sum of the effect of each chemical alone.

Adenoma

A benign tumor originating in the covering tissue (epithelium) of a gland.

Adequacy of Operation Plan Review Criterion

The determination as to whether the scope and concept of a planned operation are sufficient to accomplish the task assigned. *See* Acceptability of Plan Review Criterion.

Adequately Wetted

Sufficiently mixed or coated with water or an aqueous solution to prevent dust emissions.

Adhesion

Molecular attraction that holds the surfaces of two substances in contact.

ADI

See Acceptable Daily Intake.

Adjoining Flood Plain

That portion of a flood plain contiguous to a particular river, stream, watercourse, or other body of water that might reasonably be expected to flood at depths or velocities that could endanger life or where encroachment upon that could significantly restrict the carrying capacity of the floodway under conditions resulting from a design flood. For streams traversing alluvial cones, the adjoining flood plain is construed to refer only to the existing active stream channel area and the immediately adjoining active overflow area.

Adjudication

An agency process for the formulation of an order.

ADM

See Action Description Memoranda.

Administered Dose

The amount of a substance given to a human or test animal in determining dose-response relationships, especially through ingestion or inhalation (*See* Applied Dose). Administered dose is actually a measure of exposure, because even though the substance is "inside" the organism once ingested or inhaled, administered dose does not account for absorption (*See* Absorbed Dose).

Administration

1) The management and execution of all military matters not included in strategy and tactics. 2) Internal management of units.

Administrative Procedures Act

A law that spells out procedures and requirements related to the promulgation of regulations.

Administrative Assessment of Civil Penalties

An administrative order against a person assessing a civil penalty of up to $25,000, per day of violation, whenever, on the basis of any available information, the Administrator finds that such person has a) violated or is violating any requirement or prohibition of an applicable implementation plan during any period of federally assumed enforcement, or 30 days following the date of the Administrator's notification; b) violated or is violating any other requirement or prohibition, including, but not limited to, a requirement or prohibition of any rule, order, waiver, permit, or plan promulgated, issued, or approved under the CAA, or for the payment of any fee owed the United States; or c) attempted to construct or modify a major stationary source in any nonattainment area. The Administrator's authority is limited to matters where the total penalty sought does not exceed $200,000 and the first alleged date of violation occurred no more than 12 months prior to the initiation of the administrative action, except where the Administrator and the Attorney General jointly determine that a matter involving a larger penalty amount or longer period of violation is appropriate for administrative penalty action. Determinations by the Administrator and the Attorney General are not to be subject to judicial review.

Administrative Lead Time

The interval between initiation of a procurement action and the letting of contract or the placement of an order.

Administrative Map

A map containing graphically recorded information pertaining to administrative matters, such as supply and evacuation installations, personnel installations, medical facilities, collection points for stragglers, service and maintenance areas, main supply roads, traffic circulation, boundaries, and other details necessary to show the administrative situation. *See* Map.

Administrative Order (AO)

1) An enforceable order between the EPA and a potentially responsible party (PRP), whereby the PRP agrees to take corrective action or refrain from a pollutant-emitting activity. The order describes actions to be taken at a site, time frames for compliance, and may include provisions for a public comment and review period. 2) An order covering traffic, supplies, maintenance, evacuation, personnel, and other administrative details. Unlike a consent decree, an administrative order does not have to be approved by a judge. This order may be issued, for example, as a result of an administrative complaint whereby the respondent is ordered to pay a penalty for violations of a statute.

Administrative Order on Consent (AOC)

A legal and enforceable agreement signed between EPA and a potentially responsible party, whereby the PRP agrees to perform or pay the cost of site cleanup. The agreement describes actions to be taken at a site, time frames for compliance, and may include provisions for a public comment and review period. Like an administrative order, an administrative order on consent does not have to be approved by a judge, applies to civil actions, and can be enforced in court.

Administrative Record

All documents that EPA considered or relied upon in selecting the remedy at a Superfund site, culminating in the record of decision for remedial action, or an action memorandum for removal actions.

Administrator

1) The Administrator of EPA, or any office or employee of the Agency to whom authority to act in his/her stead has been delegated. 2) In real estate, a person appointed by the court to administer the estate of a deceased person who died without leaving a will; that is, who died intestate.

Administrator's Periodic Report, Accident Prevention

The annual comprehensive report on the measures taken by the EPA and by the states to implement the provisions of the CAA, with respect to accident prevention. The report includes, but is not limited to: a) a status report on standard-setting; b) information with respect to compliance with such standards including the costs of compliance experienced by sources in various categories and subcategories; c) development and implementation of the national urban air toxics program; and d) recommendations of the Chemical Safety and Hazard Investigation Board (CSHIB) with respect to the prevention and mitigation of accidental releases. Also included in the report is information from the Administrator's database on pollutants and sources.

ADR
See Acid Deposition Report (CAA).

ADS
An acronym for Automatic Depressurization System.

Adsorption
1) Physical or chemical bonding of molecules of gas, liquid, or a dissolved substance to the inner surface of a porous material, or the outer surface of a solid. 2) An advanced method of treating wastes in which activated carbon removes organic matter from wastewater.

Adulterants
Chemical impurities and substances found in food, animals, plants, or pesticide formulas.

Adulteration
Adding impurities or other foreign elements to a substance, altering or contaminating it.

Advanced Wastewater Treatment
Any treatment of sewage that goes beyond the secondary or biological water treatment stage and includes the removal of nutrients such as phosphorus and nitrogen and a high percentage of suspended solids. *See* Primary Treatment; Secondary Treatment.

Advection
A process where solutes are transported by the mass motion of flowing groundwater, or other flowing fluids.

Adventitious
Appearing in an unusual place or in an irregular or sporadic manner.

Adverse Affect
A reasonable likelihood of more than moderate adverse consequences for the scenic, cultural, recreation or natural resources of the scenic area, the determination of which is based on a) the context of a proposed action; b) the intensity of a proposed action, including the magnitude and duration of an impact and the likelihood of its occurrence; c) the relationship between a proposed action and other similar actions that are individually insignificant but that may have cumulatively significant impacts; and d) proven mitigation measures that the proponent of an action will implement as part of the proposal to reduce otherwise significant affects to an insignificant level.

Adverse Effect
A biochemical change, functional impairment, or pathological lesion that either singly or in combination adversely affects the performance of the whole organism, or reduces an organism's ability to respond to an additional environmental challenge.

Adverse Environmental Effect
The result of an action that is anticipated to be detrimental to the environmental health of human, animal, or aquatic lifeforms (and their habitat), or to the existence of other natural or cultural resources; a significant degradation of environmental quality over a widespread area or a cumulative period of time. *See* Significant Adverse Environmental Impact.

Adverse Impact on Visibility
Denotes visibility impairment that interferes with the management, protection, preservation, or enjoyment of the visitor's visual experience of the

Federal Class I area. This determination must be made on a case-by-case basis taking into account the geographic extent, intensity, duration, frequency and time of visibility impairments, and how these factors correlate with a) times of visitor use of the Federal Class I area; and b) frequency and timing of natural conditions that reduce visibility. This term does not include effects on integral vistas.

Adverse Modifications
Direct or indirect alterations that appreciably diminish the value of the critical habitat for both the survival and recovery of a listed species. Such alterations include, but are not limited to, alterations adversely modifying any of those physical or biological features that were the basis for determining the habitat to be critical.

Adverse Possession
The right of an occupant of land to acquire a superior title to the real estate against the record owner, where such possession has been actual, notorious, hostile, visible, and continuous for the required statutory period (in Colorado, 13 years). The purpose behind this concept is to promote the productive use of land and to give title to the one putting the land to use.

Adverse Weather
Weather in which military operations are generally restricted or impeded. *See* Marginal Weather.

Advisory
1) A nonregulatory document that communicates risk information to persons who may have to make risk management decisions. 2) A public announcement (PA). *See* Public Notification.

Advisory Council on Historic Preservation (ACHP)
A federal agency established by Section 201 of the National Historic Preservation Act of 1966 (as amended). The Council reviews and comments on all federal actions affecting cultural resources under the authority of Section 106 of the National Historic Preservation Act. It also advises the President and the Congress on historic preserva-

tion matters; recommends measures to coordinate activities of federal, state, and local governments; and advises on the dissemination of information pertaining to such activities.

AEA
See Atomic Energy Act of 1954.

Aegis
A totally integrated shipboard weapon system that combines computers, radars, and missiles to provide a defense umbrella for surface shipping. The system is capable of automatically detecting, tracking, and destroying airborne, seaborne, and land-launched weapons.

Aeolian Deposits
Windblown particulate and sediment deposits.

Aeration
To mix oxygen with a substance (e.g., as in wastewater) to aid in its purification; a process that promotes biological degradation of organic water. The process may be passive (as when waste is exposed to air), or active (as when a mixing or bubbling device introduces the air).

Aeration Lagoon
A basin for the secondary treatment of water pollution. Aerators in the basin mix oxygen with wastewaters, which encourages the growth of bacteria to consume organic waste deposits.

Aeration Pond
See Aeration Lagoon.

Aeration Tank
A chamber used to inject air into water.

Aeration Zones
The zones between the land surface and the water table.

Aerial Measuring Systems
Aerial detection systems with the capability of measuring extremely low levels of gamma radia-

tion and locating and tracking multi-spectral sensing capabilities.

Aerial Plankton

Spores, bacteria, and other microorganisms floating in the air.

Aerobic

Life or processes requiring air (oxygen) to survive. A biological process that occurs in the presence of oxygen. *See* Anaerobic.

Aerobic Treatment

A process in which microbes decompose complex organic compounds in the presence of oxygen and recycle the expended energy for additional reproduction and growth. Types of aerobic processes include extended aeration, trickling filtration, and rotating biological contractors.

Aerodynamic Diameter

A measurement of the diameter of a particle expressed as the diameter of a unit density sphere with identical inertial properties.

Aeromedical Evacuation

The movement of patients under medical supervision to and between medical treatment facilities by air transportation.

Aeromedical Evacuation Control Center (AECC)

The control facility established by the commander of an air transport division, air force, or air command. It operates in conjunction with the command movement control center and coordinates overall medical requirements with airlift capability. It also assigns medical missions to the appropriate aeromedical evacuation elements in the system and monitors patient movement activities.

Aeromedical Evacuation Control Officer (AECO)

The officer of the air transport force or air command responsible for controlling the flow of patients by air.

Aeromedical Evacuation System

A system that provides a) control of patient movement by air transport; b) specialized medical attendants and equipment for in-flight medical care; c) facilities on or in the vicinity of air strips and air bases, for the limited medical care of in-transit patients entering, en route via, or leaving the system; and d) communication with originating, destination, and en route medical facilities concerning patient transportation.

Aeromedical Evacuation Unit

An operational medical organization concerned primarily with the management and control of patients being transported via an aeromedical evacuation system or system echelon. *See* Forward Aeromedical Evacuation.

Aeronautical Chart

A specialized representation of mapped features of the earth, or some part of it, produced to show selected terrain, cultural, and hydrographic features, and supplemental information required for air navigation, pilotage, or for planning air operations.

Aerosol

1) Fine liquid droplets of solid particles that remain dispersed in the air for a period of time. 2) A suspension of liquid or solid particles in a gaseous medium.

Aerospace

Of, or pertaining to, earth's envelope of atmosphere and the space above it; two separate entities considered as a single realm for activity in launching, guidance, and control of vehicles that will travel in both entities.

Aetiology

The science of the causes and origins of disease.

Affected Facilities

With reference to the CAA and a stationary source, apparatuses to which a New Source Performance Standard is applicable. *See* New Source Performance Standards.

Affected Indian Tribe

Any Native American Indian tribe that a) within whose reservation boundaries a monitored retrievable storage facility, test and evaluation facility, or a repository for high-level radioactive waste or spent fuel is proposed to be located; b) whose federally defined possessory or usage rights to other lands outside of the reservation's boundaries arising out of congressionally ratified treaties may be substantially and adversely affected by the locating of such a facility, provided that the Secretary of the Interior finds, upon the petition of the tribe, that such effects are both substantial and adverse to the tribe.

Affected Persons

Individuals who have been exposed and/or injured as a result of an accident involving any type of hazardous material, to a degree requiring special attention (i.e., decontamination, first aid, or medical service).

Affected Tribal Council

The governing body of any Native American Indian tribe within whose reservation boundaries there is located a potentially acceptable site for interim storage capacity of spent nuclear fuel from civilian nuclear power reactors, or within whose boundaries a site for such capacity is selected by the Secretary of the Interior, or whose federally defined possessory or usage rights to other lands outside of the reservation's boundaries arising out of congressionally ratified treaties, as determined by the Secretary of the Interior pursuant to a petition filed with him/her by the appropriate governmental officials of such tribe, may be substantially and adversely affected by the establishment of any such storage capacity.

Affidavit

A statement or declaration made in writing and sworn to or affirmed before an officer who has the authority to administer such an oath or affirmation.

Affiliate

1) Any person directly or indirectly controlling, controlled by, or under common control with another person. 2) A person owning or controlling 10% or more of the outstanding voting securities of such other person. 3) Any officer or director of such other person. 4) If such other person is an officer or director, any company for which such person acts in any such capacity.

Affiliate or Commonly Owned Organization

Two or more firms and/or service offerings that are owned by the same person, corporation, or entity.

Affiliated with Department of Defense

Persons, groups of persons, or organizations that are a) employed by, or contracting with, the Department of Defense or any activity under the jurisdiction of the Department of Defense, whether on a full-time, part-time, or consultative basis; b) members of the Armed Forces on active duty, National Guard members, or those in a reserve or retired status; c) residing on, authorized access to, or conducting or operating any business or other function at any DOD installation or facility; d) authorized access to defense information; e) participating in other authorized DOD programs; or f) applying or being considered for any status described above.

Affirmative Defense

Any matter that, if established by an employer or facility owner/operator, will excuse him or her from a violation that has otherwise been proved by an agency inspector.

Afterburner

An internal or external incinerator burner located such that gases from combustion are forced through the flame to remove smoke and odors. It may be attached to or be separated from the incinerator proper.

Afterburning

1) The characteristic of some rocket motors to burn irregularly for some time after the main burning and thrust has ceased. 2) The process of fuel injection and combustion in the exhaust jet of a turbojet engine (aft or to the rear of the turbine).

Afterwinds

Wind currents set up in the vicinity of a nuclear explosion directed toward the burst center, resulting from the updraft accompanying the rise of the fireball.

AFW

An acronym for Auxiliary Feedwater.

AG

See Air-Gap Separation.

Agamospermy

A phenomenon found in plants in which the asexual development of diploid (genetically similar chromosomes) cells is incomplete due to the abnormal development of the pollen and the embryo sac.

Age of Moon

The elapsed time, usually expressed in days, since the last new moon.

Agency

1) In real estate, a legal relationship resulting from an agreement or contract, either expressed or implied, written or oral, whereby one person, called the agent, is employed by another, called the principal, to do certain acts in dealing with a third party.
2) A department of a federal, state, or local government.
3) An executive department as defined in Title 5 of the United States Code, Section 101.
4) The Environmental Protection Agency. Agency does not include: a) the Congress; b) the courts of the United States; c) the governments of the territories or possessions of the United States; d) the government of the District of Columbia; e) agencies composed of representatives of the parties or of representatives of organizations of the parties to the disputes determined by them; f) courts-martial and military commissions; or g) military authority exercised in the field in time of war or in occupied territory.

Agency Action

The whole or a part of a federal agency rule, order, permit, license, sanction, relief, or the equivalent or denial thereof.

Agency for Toxic Substances and Disease Registry (ATSDR)

ATSDR conducts research focused on toxic substances and their effects on public health. Programs include health studies, substance-specific research, and maintaining various disease registries.

Agency Lead Officials

The designated officials in each participating agency authorized to direct that agency's response to emergencies.

Agency Working Days

Weekdays, Mondays through Fridays, not including Saturday, Sunday, or holidays. In computing working days, the day of receipt of any notice should not be included.

Agent

Any person, partnership, association, or corporation authorized or employed by another, called the principal, to act for, on behalf of, and subject to the control of the latter.

Agent Orange

A toxic herbicide and defoliant that was used in the Vietnam conflict. It contains 2,4,5-trichlorophenoxyacitic acid (2,4,5-T) and 2-4 dichlorophenoxyacetic acid (2,4-D) with trace amounts of dioxin.

Agglomeration

The process by which precipitation particles grow larger by collision or contact with cloud particles or other precipitation particles.

Agglutination

The process of uniting solid particles coated with a thin layer of adhesive material or of arresting solid particles by impact on a surface coated with an adhesive.

Aggradation

The raising of the land's surface by the accumulation of deposited materials.

Aggregate

Crushed rock and/or gravel sorted in various sizes for use in concrete, cement, or bituminous mixes for ultimate use as road and construction-related materials.

Aggregate Risk

The sum of individual increased risks of an adverse health effect in an exposed population.

Aggressive Biological Treatment Facility (BTF)

A system of surface impoundments in which the initial impoundment of the secondary treatment segment of the facility utilizes intense mechanical aeration to enhance biological activity to degrade wastewater pollutants, and a) the hydraulic retention time in such initial impoundment is no longer than 5 days under normal operating conditions, on an annual average basis; b) the hydraulic retention time in such initial impoundment is no longer than 30 days under normal operating conditions, on an annual average basis, provided that the sludge in such impoundment does not constitute a hazardous waste, as identified by the extraction procedure toxicity characteristic in effect on November 8, 1984; or c) such system utilizes activated sludge treatment in the first portion of secondary treatment.

Agonic Line

A line drawn on a map or chart joining points of zero magnetic declination for a specified year date. *See* Magnetic Declination.

Agreement States

States with which the Atomic Energy Commission or the Nuclear Regulatory Commission has entered into an effective agreement under Subsection 274(b) of the Atomic Energy Act of 1964, as amended.

Agreements

Signed documented statements of the actions to be taken by the state(s) and the Director in furthering certain purposes of the Endangered Species Act. They include: a) a Cooperative Agreement entered into pursuant to Section 6(c) of the Act and, where appropriate, containing provisions found in Section 6(d)(2) of the Act; b) a Grant-in-Aid Award that includes a statement of the actions to be taken in connection with the conservation of endangered or threatened species receiving federal financial assistance, objectives and costs of such action, and costs to be borne by the federal government and by the state(s). *See* Endangered Species Act.

Agricultural Commodity

1) An unprocessed product of farms, ranches, nurseries and forests (except livestock, poultry and fish). 2) Any agricultural commodity planted and produced by annual tilling of the soil, including tilling by one-trip planters. Agricultural commodities include fruits and vegetables; grains, as wheat, barley, oats, rye, triticale, rice, corn, and sorghum; legumes, such as field beans and peas; animal feed and forage crops; rangeland and pasture; seed crops; fiber crops, such as cotton; oil crops, such as safflower, sunflower, corn, and cottonseed; trees grown for lumber and wood product nurse stock grown commercially; Christmas trees; ornamental and cut flowers; and turf grown commercially for sod.

Agricultural Conservation and Adjustment Administration (ACAA)

The consolidated agency established during World War II, which combined several agricultural agencies with the Soil Conservation Service into a single entity for the duration of the war.

Agricultural Engineering

The branch of professional engineering that requires such education and experience as is necessary to understand and apply engineering principles to the design, construction, and use of specialized equipment, machines, structures, and materials relating to the agricultural industry and economy. It requires knowledge of the engineering sciences relating to physical properties and biological variables of foods and fibers; atmospheric phenomena as they are related to agricultural operations; soil dynamics as related to traction, tillage, and plant-soil-water relationships; and human factors relative to safe design and use of agricultural machines. The safe and proper application and use of agricultural chemicals and their effect on the environment are also concerns of agricultural engineers.

Agricultural Land Rental Payment

A payment made by the Secretary to an owner or operator of a farm or ranch containing highly erodible cropland to compensate the owner or operator for retiring such land from crop production and placing such land in the conservation reserve in accordance with the Erodible Land and Wetland Conservation and Reserve Program.

Agricultural Pollution

The liquid and solid wastes from farming, including runoff and leaching of pesticides and fertilizers; erosion and dust from plowing; animal manure and carcasses; and crop residues and debris.

Agricultural Solid Wastes

The solid waste that is generated by the rearing of animals and the producing and harvesting of crops or trees.

Agricultural Waste

Poultry and livestock manure, and residual materials in liquid or solid form, generated from the production and marketing of poultry, livestock, forbearing animals, and their products. Also includes grain, vegetable, and fruit harvest residue.

Agricultural Water Quality Protection Practice

A farm-level practice or a system of practices designed to protect water quality by mitigating or reducing the release of agricultural pollutants, including nutrients, pesticides, animal waste, sediment, salts, biological contaminants, and other materials, into the environment.

Agroecosystem

The community of organisms, plants, crops and animals, and the abiotic environs that occur on farmed agricultural lands.

Agronomy

The study of rural economies and animal husbandry.

AIA

An acronym for American Institute of Architects, Asbestos Information Act of 1988. *See* Automatic Incident Actions.

AIC

An acronym for Acceptable Intake for Chronic Exposure.

AIF

An acronym for Atomic Industrial Forum.

Air

1) A mixture of inert gases, water vapor, and emission-related pollutants. In its purest form, air is comprised of approximately 78% nitrogen, 21% oxygen, including minute percentages of carbon dioxide, argon, varied inert gases, and water vapors. 2) Those naturally occurring constituents of the atmosphere, including those gases essential for human, plant, and animal life.

Air-Breathing Missile

A missile with an engine requiring the intake of air for combustion of its fuel, as in a ramjet or turbojet. To be contrasted with the rocket missile, which carries its own oxidizer and can operate beyond the atmosphere.

Air Cartographic Camera

A camera having the accuracy and other characteristics essential for air survey or cartographic photography. Also called mapping camera.

Air Cartographic Photography

The taking and processing of air photographs for mapping and charting purposes.

Air Changes per Hour (ACH)

The movement of a volume of air in a given period of time; if a house has one air change per hour, it means that all of the air in the house will be replaced in a one-hour period.

Air Contaminants

Particulate matter, gases, or combination thereof, other than water vapor or natural air. *See* Air Pollutant.

Air Curtain

A method of containing oil spills. Air bubbling through a perforated pipe causes an upward water flow that slows the spread of oil. It can also be used to stop fish from entering polluted water.

Air Cushion Vehicle (ACV)

A vehicle capable of being operated so that its weight, including its payload, is wholly or significantly supported on a continuously generated cushion or "bubble" of air at higher than ambient pressure.

Air Force Component Headquarters

The field headquarters facility of the Air Force commander charged with the overall conduct of Air Force operations. It is composed of the command section and appropriate staff elements.

Air-Gap Separation (AG)

A physical break between a physical supply line and a receiving tank or vessel.

Air-Handling Unit

A blower or fan used for the purpose of distributing conditioned air to a room or other space.

Air-line Respirator

A respirator attached to an air-line or hose whereby respirable air is supplied to the wearer by means of a flow control valve, orifice, or diaphragm to govern the rate of air flow.

Air Lock, Personnel

A chamber through which employees pass from one air pressure environment into another.

Air Mass

A widespread body of air that gains certain meteorological or polluted characteristics, e.g., a heat inversion or smogginess while set in one location. The characteristics can change as it moves away.

Air Mobility Command (AMC)

The Air Force Component Command of the U.S. Transportation Command.

Air Monitoring

Periodic or continuous surveillance or testing of air to determine the level of compliance with statutory requirements and/or pollutant levels in the atmosphere. *See* Monitoring.

Air Photographic Reconnaissance

The obtaining of information by air photography, divided into three types: a) strategic photographic reconnaissance; b) tactical photographic reconnaissance; and c) survey/cartographic photography or air photography taken to survey/cartographic standards of accuracy.

Air Pollutant

1) Any substance in air that could, if in high enough concentration, harm humans, other animals, vegetation, or material. Pollutants may include almost any natural or artificial composition of matter capable of being airborne. They may be in the form of solid particles, liquid droplets, gases, or in combinations of these forms. Generally, they fall into two main groups: a) those emitted directly from identifiable sources and b) those produced in the air by interaction between two or more primary pollutants or by reaction with normal atmospheric constituents, with or without photoactivation. 2) Any air pollution agent or combination of such agents, including any physical, chemical, biological, radioactive (including source material, special nuclear material, and byproduct material) substance or matter that is emitted into or otherwise enters the ambient air. Exclusive of pollen, fog, and dust (which are of natural origin), about 100 contaminants have been identified and fall into these categories: solids, sulfur compounds, volatile organic chemicals, ni-

trogen compounds, oxygen compounds, halogen compounds, radioactive compounds, and odors.

Air Pollution

The existence of contaminants in the air in concentrations too high to allow the normal dispersal ability of the air and that interfere directly, or indirectly, with human health, safety, welfare, or comfort, and/or inhibit the full use and enjoyment of property.

Air Pollution Control Agency (APCA)

1) A single state agency designated by the governor of that state as the official state air pollution control agency for purposes of this chapter. 2) An agency established by two or more states and having substantial powers or duties pertaining to the prevention and control of air pollution. 3) A city, county, or other local government health authority, or, in the case of any city, county, or other local government in which there is an agency other than the health authority charged with responsibility for enforcing ordinances or laws relating to the prevention and control of air pollution, such other agency. 4) An agency of two or more municipalities located in the same state or in different states and having substantial powers or duties pertaining to the prevention and control of air pollution. 5) An agency, similar to the aforementioned, under authority of a Native American Indian tribe.

Air Pollution Control Technology Information

Control technology information compiled from permits issued under the CAA for purposes of making such information available through the RACT/BACT/LAER clearinghouse to other states and to the general public.

Air Pollution Episode

A period of abnormally high concentrations of air pollutants, often due to low winds and temperature inversion, that can cause illness and death.

Air Pollution Planning and Control Grants

EPA grants to air pollution control agencies, in an amount up to three-fifths of the cost of implementing programs for the prevention and control of air pollution or implementation of national primary and secondary ambient air quality standards.

Air Priorities Committee

A committee set up to determine the priorities of passengers and cargo.

Air-Purification Devices

Respirators or filtration devices that remove particulate matter, gases, or vapors from the atmosphere. These devices range from full-facepiece, dual-cartridge respirators with eye protection to half-mask, facepiece-mounted cartridges with no eye protection.

Air Quality

The condition and degree to which air is polluted. Standards have cultural and environmental variations.

Air Quality Control Region (AQCR)

Area designated by the federal government in which two or more communities situated in the same or different states share a common air-pollution problem.

Air Quality Criteria

The levels of pollution and lengths of exposure above which adverse health and welfare effects may occur.

Air Quality Maintenance Area (AQMA)

Areas in the U.S. that have the potential for exceeding national air quality standards within the next two decades. Each state is required to submit an analysis, to EPA, of how projected growth and development will impact air quality in these areas.

Air Quality Maintenance Plan (AQMP)

A plan required by EPA under the Clean Air Act for maintenance of national air standards in AQMAs. Plans are developed and implemented by states that may delegate responsibility to local and/or regional government entities. The plan must provide for the maintenance of the national primary ambient air quality standard for such air pollutant in the area concerned for at least 10 years after the redesignation. The plan typically contains additional measures necessary to ensure such maintenance.

Each plan revision should contain contingency provisions as the Administrator deems necessary to assure that the state will promptly correct any violation of the standard that occurs after the redesignation of the area as an attainment area. Such provisions shall include a requirement that the state will implement all measures with respect to the control of the air pollutant concerned that were contained in the state implementation plan for the area before redesignation of the area as an attainment area.

Air Quality Monitoring
The sampling for, and measuring of, contaminants in the air.

Air Quality Monitoring Program
The monitoring component of a program conducted under this section shall identify and determine sources of pollutants for which national ambient air quality standards (NAAQS) and other air quality goals have been established.

Monitoring components of the program include, but are not limited to, the collection of meteorological data, the measurement of air quality, the compilation of an emissions inventory, and shall be sufficient to the extent necessary to successfully support the use of a state-of-the-art mathematical air modeling analysis. Any such monitoring component of the program shall collect and produce data projecting the level of emission reductions necessary to bring about attainment of both primary and secondary NAAQS, and other air quality goals.

Air Quality Planning
Planning procedures for any ozone, carbon monoxide, or PM-10 nonattainment areas, set forth by a state, or states, containing such area and elected officials of affected local governments.

Air Quality Remediation Program
Remediation measures to reduce the level of airborne pollutants to achieve and maintain primary and secondary NAAQS, and other air quality goals. Measures may include, but not be limited to measures included in the Environmental Protection Agency's Control Techniques and Control Technology documents.

Air Quality Standard
The prescribed level of pollutants in the outside air that cannot be legally exceeded during a specified time, within a specific geographical area. Used to determine the amount of pollutants that may be emitted by industry.

Air Reconnaissance
The acquisition of intelligence information by employing visual observation and/or sensors in air vehicles.

Air Resources
Those naturally occurring constituents of the atmosphere, including those gases essential for human, plant, and animal life.

Air Stripping
A treatment system that removes volatile organic compounds (VOCs) from contaminated ground, or surface water by forcing an airstream through the water and causing the compounds to evaporate.

Air-Supplied Respirators
A device that provides the user with compressed air for breathing.

Air Survey Camera
See Air Cartographic Camera.

Air Survey Photography
See Air Cartographic Photography.

Air Tank
A pressure vessel used for the storage or accumulation of air under pressure. This definition is not intended to include utilization equipment, includ-

ing such devices as grease tanks, fire extinguishers, or paint sprayers, where the tank is partly filled with a product and the air pressure is used only for a cushion or to eject the product from the tank, or such devices as strainers, scrubbers, separators, that are a part of the piping system.

Air Target Materials Program
A DOD program under the management control of the Defense Mapping Agency established for and limited to the production of medium- and large-scale map, chart, and geodetic products that support worldwide targeting requirements of the unified and specified commands, the military departments, and allied participants. It encompasses the determination of production and coverage requirements, standardization of products, establishment of production priorities and schedules, and the production, distribution, storage, and release/exchange of products included under it.

Air Target Mosaic
A large-scale mosaic providing photographic coverage of an area and permitting comprehensive portrayal of pertinent target detail. These mosaics are used for intelligence study and in planning and briefing for air operations.

Airborne Particulates
Total suspended particulate matter found in the atmosphere as solid particles or liquid droplets. Chemical composition of particulates varies widely, depending on location and time of year. Airborne particulates include windblown dust, emissions from industrial processes, smoke from the burning of wood and coal, and the exhaust of motor vehicles.

Airborne Radioactive Material
Any radioactive material dispersed in the air in the form of dusts, fumes, mists, vapors, or gases.

Airborne Release
Release of any chemical into the air.

Airborne Response Teams
Groups of one or more armed security inspectors who are specially trained in airborne tactics and equipment to respond to emergency/security incidents.

Airborne Tactical Data System
An airborne early warning system capable of integration into the tactical data system environment. It provides an automated, operator-controlled capability for collecting, displaying, evaluating, and disseminating tactical information via tactical digital information links. It is part of the Naval Tactical Data System (NTDS).

Aircraft Accident
An occurrence associated with the operation of an aircraft that takes place between the time a person boards the aircraft with the intention of flight until such time as all persons have disembarked and in which any person suffers death or serious injury as a result of being in or on the aircraft or anything attached thereto, or in which the aircraft receives substantial damage.

Aircraft Incidents
Deviations from the normal, planned, or expected aviation operation, if deviations have adverse safety, health, or environmental effects or potential effects and are not classified as accidents.

Airshed
The air overlying any geographical region; the region may combine adjacent cities or areas that share similar air pollution problems.

Airway
Any conducting segment of the respiratory tract through which air passes during breathing. The bronchial tubes are examples of airways.

Airway Resistance
The functional resistance to air flow afforded by the airways between the mouth and the alveoli.

AIS

An acronym for Acceptable Intake for Subchronic Exposure.

Alachlor

A herbicide, marketed under the trade name Lasso, used mainly to control weeds in corn and soybean fields.

Alanine ($CH_3CH(NH_2)COOH$)

An amino acid with a molecular weight of 89.1 atomic mass units.

ALAP

An acronym for As Low as Practicable. This DOE guideline limited personnel exposures to ionizing radiation to ALAP levels, which considered economic and technical feasibility. This has been replaced by "As Low as Reasonably Achievable (ALARA)."

Alar

Trade name for daminozide, a pesticide that makes apples redder, firmer, and less likely to drop off trees before growers are ready to pick them. It is also used to a lesser extent on peanuts, tart cherries, concord grapes, and other fruits.

ALARA

See As Low as Reasonably Achievable.

Alarms

A series of alerting devices that may include effluent or stack monitor alarms, duress alarms, vault alarms, gas alarms, entry alarms, radiation monitor alarms, or other alarms.

Alaska Power Administration (APA)

The APA is responsible for operating and marketing power for two federal hydroelectric projects in Alaska. Power operations and marketing functions involving the Eklutna and Snettisham Hydroelectric Projects include the projects' transmission systems serving the Anchorage and Juneau areas.

Alaskan Native

A person defined in the Alaska Native Claims Settlement Act (43 USC 1603(b); 85 Stat. 588) as a citizen of the United States who is of one-fourth degree or more Alaskan Indian (including Tsimshian Indians enrolled or not enrolled in the Metlaktla Indian Community), Eskimo, or Aleut blood, or combination thereof. The term includes any Native, as so defined, either or both of whose adoptive parents are not Natives. It also includes, in the absence of proof of a minimum blood quantum, any citizen of the United States who is regarded as an Alaskan Native by the Native village or town of which he/she claims to be a member and whose father or mother is (or, if deceased, was) regarded as Native by any Native village or Native town.

Albumin

Any of several simple, water soluble proteins that are coagulated by heat and are found in egg white, blood serum, milk, animal tissues, and many plant juices.

Albuminuria

The presence of protein (primarily alburnin) in the urine; usually indicative of transient dysfunction or disease.

Albuquerque Operations Office

A DOE Research and Development Field Facility whose principal mission was national security. Established in 1946, AL operated an extensive weapons laboratory and production complex from Florida to California. AL directed weapons research, development and production, and provided program execution and project management functions for assigned energy research and development activities. AL also operated a system for safe and secure transport of all government-owned Special Nuclear Material of strategic quantities, coordinated and administered nuclear test detection activities and maintained capabilities for radiological assistance and nuclear weapons accident response.

Alcohol

An organic compound synthesized either from petroleum or natural products or derived from a fermentation process. Widely used as a solvent and for chemical syntheses. A mixture containing 85% or more by volume methanol, ethanol, or other alcohols, in any combination.

Aldicarb

An insecticide sold under the trade name Temik. It is made from ethyl isocyanate.

Aldrin

An organochlorine insecticide whose use is now very restricted due to its poisonous effect on vertebrates.

Alert

1) An emergency response level that represents an event in progress, or having occurred, that involves an actual or potential substantial reduction of the level of safety of the facility. 2) Readiness for action, defense, or protection against any release of hazardous materials (radiological or non-radiological). 3) A warning signal of a real or threatened danger, such as an air attack. 4) The period of time during which troops stand by in response to an alarm. 5) To forewarn; to prepare for action.

Alert Signals

Three- to five-minute steady tones, sounded strictly at the option of and on the authority of local government officials. The signals may be activated for natural or manmade disasters as local authorities may determine and may also be used to call attention to essential emergency information. Use of the attention or alert signals should always be accompanied by a public explanation and instructions to TV viewers over local broadcast stations or by other means.

Algae

Simple rootless plants that grow in sunlit waters in relative proportion to the amounts of nutrients available. They can affect water quality adversely by lowering the dissolved oxygen in the water.

They are microscopic, single-celled plants and serve as food for fish and small aquatic animals.

Algal Blooms

Sudden spurts of algal growth, which can affect water quality adversely and indicate potentially hazardous changes in local water chemistry.

ALI

See Annual Limit on Intake.

Alienation

The transfer of real property by one person to another.

Aliouots

Fractions of a field sample taken for complete processing through an analytical procedure (a "laboratory sample" of a field sample).

Alkali

A basic substance (pH greater than 7) that has the capacity to neutralize an acid and form a salt; soluble mineral salts found in natural water and arid soils. *See* Base.

Alkaline

The condition of wastewater or soil that contains a sufficient amount of alkali substances to raise the pH above 7.0; containing soluble mineral salts; opposite of acidic. *See* Acid; pH.

Alkalinity

Having the properties of a base with a pH of more than 7. A common alkaline is baking soda.

Alkylation

The substitution of an alkyl radical for a hydrogen atom in a chemical molecule. Alkylation is viewed as an event that may lead to toxicity.

All Clear

The term used at a Site that means a Tornado Warning is no longer in effect for the Site. A Tornado Watch may remain in effect if All Clear follows a Tornado Warning. This term is not synonymous to that used by news forecasters who cancel watches and warnings or allow them to expire. *See* Site.

Allegations
Statements, made without formal proof or regard for evidence, that a chemical substance or mixture has caused a significant adverse reaction to health or to the environment.

Allergen
An antigenic substance capable of eliciting an allergic response.

Alley Cropping
The practice of planting rows of trees bordered on each side by a narrow strip of groundcover, alternated with wider strips of row crops or grain.

Allochthonous
Originating elsewhere, or living in a different habitat.

Allotment Management Plan
A document prepared in consultation with the lessees or permittees involved that applies to livestock operations on public lands or on lands within National Forests in the eleven contiguous Western States and that a) prescribes the manner in, and extent to, which livestock operations will be conducted in order to meet the multiple-use, sustained-yield, economic and other needs and objectives as determined for the lands by the Secretary concerned; b) describes the type, location, ownership, and general specifications for the range improvements to be installed and maintained on the lands to meet the livestock grazing and other objectives of land management; and c) contains such other provisions relating to livestock grazing and other objectives found by the Secretary concerned to be consistent with applicable law.

Allowable Emissions
The emissions rate of a stationary source calculated using the maximum rated capacity of the source (unless the source is subject to federally enforceable limits that restrict the operating rate,

or hours of operation, or both) and the most stringent of the following: a) The applicable standards set forth in 40 CFR 60 or 61; b) any applicable state implementation Plan emissions limitation including those with a future compliance date; or c) the emissions rate specified as a federate enforceable permit condition, including those with a future compliance date.

Allowable Load
The total load that an aircraft can transport over a given distance, taking into account weight and volume. *See* Load; Payload.

Allowable Soil Bearing Capacity
The maximum permissible pressure on foundation soils under which the settlements of various footings will not exceed a reasonable value.

Allowable Working Pressure
The pressure for which an air tank was constructed, or if conditions have changed, the maximum pressure permitted at the last inspection by a certified inspector or qualified safety engineer.

Alluvial
Pertaining to or composed of alluvium or water.

Alluvial Deposits
Sediment deposited by flowing water.

Alluvial Plain
The plain created by accumulation of soil and other materials where a river emerges from a steep course onto flatland.

Alluvion
The flow of water against a shore or bank.

Alluvium
1) Sediment transported and deposited by a flowing river. 2) General term for clay, silt, and sand material deposited during comparatively recent geologic time by a stream or other body of running water as a sorted or semisorted sedimentary floodplain or delta, or as a cone or fan at the base of a mountain slope. *See* Alluvial Deposits.

ALPHA

A maximum alert action that shall be effected when the head of a field office determines that conditions warrant maximum security measures at U.S. Department of Energy (DOE) or DOE contractor facilities. *See* Operational Emergency Response Levels.

Alpha Particles

1) Positively charged particles composed of two neutrons and two protons released by some atoms undergoing radioactive decay. The particles are identical to the nucleus of a helium atom. 2) A strongly ionizing particle emitted from the nucleus during radioactive decay having a mass and charge equal in magnitude to a helium nucleus, consisting of two protons and two neutrons with a double positive charge. The nucleus of a helium atom that is ejected from some radionuclides during radioactive decay.

Alpha Rays

Streams of fast-moving helium nuclei (alpha particles), a strongly ionizing and weakly penetrating radiation.

Altered Growth

A change in offspring, organ, or body weight or size. Altered growth can be induced at any stage of development, may be reversible, or may result in a permanent change.

Alternate Emergency Operations Center

An alternate facility to the designated DOE Emergency Operations Center from which the emergency management team can carry out emergency response activities in the event the designated primary Emergency Operations Center cannot be used.

Alternate Method

Any method of sampling and analyzing for an air pollutant that is not a reference or equivalent method but that has been demonstrated in specific cases to EPA's satisfaction to produce results adequate for compliance.

Alternative Courses of Action

All reasonable and prudent alternatives, including both no action and alternatives extending beyond original project objectives and the acting agency's jurisdiction.

Alternative Dispute Resolution (ADR)

A term used to denote methods (e.g., such as arbitration, mediation) for resolving disputes other than litigation.

Alternative Energy

Energy derived from nontraditional sources (e.g., compressed natural gas, solar, hydroelectric, wind).

Alternative Fuels

Gaseous, liquid, or solid fuels and chemical feedstocks derived from coal, shale, tar sands, lignite, peat, biomass, solid waste, unconventional natural gas, and other minerals or organic materials other than crude oil or any derivative thereof.

Alternative System

Any method for the management of sewage sludge or industrial waste that does not require a permit under the Ocean Dumping Act.

Alternative Water Supplies

Includes, but is not limited to, drinking water and household water supplies.

Altitude

The vertical distance of a level, a point or an object considered as a point, measured from mean sea level. *See* Density Altitude; Elevation; Pressure Altitude.

Altitude Acclimatization

A slow physiological adaptation resulting from prolonged exposure to significantly reduced atmospheric pressure.

Altitude Chamber

See Hyperbaric Chamber.

Altitude Datum
The arbitrary level from which vertical displacement is measured. The datum for height measurement is the terrain directly below some specified datum; for pressure altitude, the level at which the atmospheric pressure is 29.92 inches of mercury (1013.2 m.bs); and for true altitude, mean sea level. *See* Altitude.

Altitude Sickness
The syndrome of depression, anorexia, nausea, vomiting, and collapse, due to decreased atmospheric pressure, occurring in an individual exposed to an altitude beyond that to which acclimatization has occurred.

Alveolar
Pertaining to the air sacs (alveoli) of the lung where gas exchange occurs.

Alveolar Ducts
The smallest of the lungs' airways that connect terminal bronchioles and alveolar sacs. Sometimes called bronchioles.

Alveolar Macrophage
A cell within the lung that contributes to immunological activities of the lung by phagocytosing (engulfing) and killing microbes, phagocytosing inhaled particles, secreting/excreting antimicrobial substances, and performing other activities. Under some conditions, it also can secrete/excrete enzymes capable of digesting lung tissue.

Alveolar Ventilation
The volume of air entering the alveoli each minute.

Alveoli (singular alveolus)
Microscopic air sacs in which gas exchange between the blood and the lungs occurs.

Ambient
1) Any unconfined portion of the atmosphere. 2) Encompassing or surrounding environmental conditions.

Ambient Air
Any unconfined portion of the atmosphere; the outside air; open air or surrounding air. That portion of the atmosphere, external to buildings, to which the general public has access.

Ambient Air Quality Standards
Air quality standards established by EPA that specify concentrations and durations of air pollutants that reflect the relationship between the intensity and composition of pollution to undesirable effects. *See* Criteria Pollutants; National Ambient Air Quality Standards.

Ambient Air Standard
Federal standard regarding the maximum permissible concentrations of pollutants in the air of a basin or region, as distinguished from permissible concentrations of pollutants resulting from emissions from various point sources.

Ambient Noise
The background and prevailing noises.

Ambient Pressure
Encompassing pressure surrounding all sides.

Ambient Temperature
The temperature of the surrounding air.

Amblyopsids
Cave fish or ray fish distinguished by the structure of the paired fins, supported by the dermal rays.

Ambulatory Patient
See Walking Patient.

AMC
See Air Mobility Command.

Amelioration
Those things that are done immediately following an accident to limit its consequences and to reduce the sensitivity of those consequences.

Amenities

In real estate, amenities refer to such circumstances (e.g., location, outlook, or access to a park, lake, highway, river) that enhance the location, aesthetic environs, or desirability of a particular site and that contribute to the enjoyment of the occupants.

American Indian

Any person who is a member of a Native American Indian tribe or band recognized by the Federal Bureau of Indian Affairs; or has at least one-quarter American Indian blood quantum of tribes or bands indigenous to the United States and/or Canada.

American National Metric Council (ANMC)

A private nonprofit organization that serves as a planning, coordinating, and information center for metric use in the United States.

Ames Test

An in vitro bacterial test for detecting point mutations in a group of histidine-requiring strains of *Salmonella typhimurium*. An Ames test is usually conducted with an erogenous source of metabolic activation by adding, for example, enzymes obtained from mammalian liver cells to the *S. typhimurium* assay system.

Amino Acids

Organic compounds containing a carboxyl group (-COOH) and an amino group ($-NH_2$). About 30 amino acids are known to exist. They are fundamental constituents of living matter.

Ammunition

As associated with small arms, is the assembled cartridge, including primer, powder, case, and projectile.

Ammunition Lot

A quantity of homogeneous ammunition, identified by a unique lot number, that is manufactured, assembled, or renovated by one producer under uniform conditions and that is expected to function in a uniform manner.

Ammunition and Toxic Material Open Space

An area especially prepared for storage of explosive ammunition and toxic material. For reporting purposes, it does not include the surrounding area restricted for storage because of safety distance factors. It includes barricades and improvised coverings. *See* Storage.

Amorphous

A term that describes polymers that have no order to their molecules, thus no crystalline component.

Amortization

The liquidation or gradual retirement of a financial obligation by periodic installments.

Amphibian

Animals capable of living in both water and land habitats.

Amphipod

A small crustacean of the order Amphipoda, including sand fleas.

Anadromous

Fish that spend their adult life in the sea but swim upriver to fresh-water spawning grounds to reproduce.

Anaerobic

A life or process that occurs in, or is not destroyed by, the absence of oxygen.

Anaerobic Digestion

Biological stabilization of domestic wastewater sludge by microorganisms that function in the absence of oxygen.

Analyses

The use of methods and techniques of arranging data to a) assist in deciding what additional facts are needed; b) establish consistency, validity, and logic; c) establish necessary and sufficient events for causes; and d) guide and support inferences and judgments.

Analysis

A step in the processing phase of the information cycle in which primary and secondary data is subjected to review in order to identify significant facts for subsequent interpretations.

Analysis of Variance

In statistics, the method of attributing amounts of variation to differing causal factors.

Analytes

The chemicals for which a sample is analyzed.

Analytical Batches

Samples that are analyzed together with the same method sequence and the same lots of reagents and with the manipulations common to each sample within the same time period or in continuous sequential time periods. Samples in each batch should be of similar composition.

Analytical Logic Trees

Diagrams, in the shapes of trees, using different geometrical symbols to aid a user in systematically portraying information in a logical sequence and showing relationships between elements of the tree. Trees may be positive or negative (fault tree).

Analytical Model

A manual or computerized model that provides approximate or exact solutions to forms of the differential equations for water movement and solute transport.

Anaphylaxis

An exaggerated reaction to an antigen to which an organism has been previously sensitized.

Ancillary Equipment

Any device including, but not limited to, piping, fittings, flanges, valves, and pumps that is used to distribute, meter, or control the flow of hazardous waste from its point of generation to a storage or treatment tank(s), between the hazardous waste storage and treatment tanks to a point of disposal on-site, or to a point of shipment for disposal offsite.

ANCSA

An acronym for Alaska Native Claims Settlement Act.

And Gate

A logic gate that produces an output only when all input events occur. May contain the identifying word "AND."

Andepts

Soils with a low bulk density that are susceptible to becoming acidic.

Anders Celsius

Mr. Celsius was a Swedish astronomer who defined the base of ten temperature scale used in the metric system for temperature measures. The point at which water freezes or becomes a solid is 0° Celsius and the point of transition of water from a liquid to a gas is at 100° Celsius. This definition assumes that the atmospheric pressure is at a standard of 760 millimeters of mercury pressure.

Anemia

Any condition in which the number of red blood cells, the amount of hemoglobin, and the volume of packed red blood cells per 100 milliliters of blood are less than normal.

Anemometer

An instrument used to measure wind speed and produce anemographs — graph-type records of the wind speeds detected by the instrument over time.

Anergy

Diminished reactivity to specific antigens.

Aneuploidy

A condition in which the chromosome number is not an exact multiple of the usual number of chromosomes for that species. For example, a "normal" human has 46 chromosomes; an individual with 47 chromosomes would be described as aneuploid.

Angle of Convergence
The angle subtended by the eyebase of an observer at the point of focus.

Angle of Depression
1) The angle in a vertical plane between the horizontal and a descending line. 2) In air photography, the angle between the optical axis of an obliquely mounted air camera and the horizontal. Also called depression angle.

Angle of View
1) The angle between two rays passing through the perspective center (rear nodal point) of a camera lens to two opposite corners of the format. 2) In photogrammetry, twice the angle whose tangent is one-half the length of the diagonal of the format divided by the calibrated focal length.

ANGTS
An acronym for Alaska Natural Gas Transportation System.

Anhydrous
Containing no water.

ANILCA
An acronym for Alaska National Interest Lands Conservation Act.

Animals
All vertebrate and invertebrate species, including but not limited to man and other mammals, birds, fish, and shellfish.

Anisocytosis
Considerable variation in the size of blood cells.

Anisotropic
The tendency of a material to exhibit different properties in response to stresses applied along axes in different directions.

Anisotropy
A condition in which one or more of the hydraulic properties of an aquifer vary according to the direction of flow.

ANL-E
An acronym for Argonne National Laboratory (East). *See* Argonne National Laboratory.

ANL-W
An acronym for Argonne National Laboratory (West). *See* Argonne National Laboratory.

Annex
A document appended to an operation order or other document to make it clearer or to give further details.

Annihilation, Electron
An interaction between a positive and negative electron; their energy, including rest energy, being converted into electromagnetic radiation (annihilation radiation).

Annotated Print
A photograph on which interpretation details are indicated by words or symbols.

Annotation
A marking placed on imagery or drawings for explanatory purposes or to indicate items or areas of special importance.

Annual Document Logs
Detailed information maintained by a facility on the PCB waste handling at that facility.

Annual Dose Equivalent
The dose equivalent received in a year. Annual dose equivalent is expressed in units of rem (or sievert).

Annual Dose Equivalent Limit
The value of the annual dose equivalent that must not be exceeded, it is regarded as the lower boundary of an unacceptable dose region.

Annual Effective Dose Equivalent
The effective dose equivalent received in a year, expressed in units of rem (or sievert).

Annual Fuel Utilization Efficiency
The efficiency descriptor for furnaces and boilers, determined using test procedures and based on the assumption that all a) weatherized warm air furnaces or boilers are located out-of-doors; b) warm air furnaces that are not weatherized are located indoors and all combustion and ventilation air is admitted through grills or ducts from the outdoors and does not communicate with air in the conditioned space; and c) boilers that are not weatherized are located within the heated space.

Annual Incidence
The number of new cases of a disease occurring or predicted to occur in a population over a year.

Annual Limit on Intake (ALI)
The quantity of a single radionuclide which, if inhaled or ingested in 1 year, would irradiate a person, represented as a limiting value for control of workplaces.

Annual Reports
Written documents submitted each year by commercial disposers and storers of PCB waste to the appropriate EPA Regional Administrator. The annual report is a brief summary of the information included in the annual document log.

Annual Site Environmental Reports
Reports that present summary environmental data so as to characterize site environmental management performance, confirm compliance with environmental standards and requirements, and highlight significant programs and efforts. Reports shall be prepared for all sites that conduct significant environmental protection programs. The breadth and detail should reflect the size and extent of any environmental programs conducted at a particular site.

Annular Injection
The reinjection of brines associated with the production of oil or gas between the production and surface casings of a conventional oil or gas producing well.

Anoxia
Lack of oxygen in inspired air, blood, tissues, or significant reduction in oxygen.

ANS
An acronym for American Nuclear Society.

ANSI
An acronym for the American National Standards Institute — an accreditation and standards setting organization located at 1430 Broadway, New York, N.Y., 10017.

ANSI Standard
A standard developed by a committee accredited by the American National Standards Institute (ANSI).

ANSP
See Aquatic Nuisance Species Program.

ANSTF
See Aquatic Nuisance Species Task Force.

Antagonism
1) A pharmacologic or toxicologic interaction in which the combined effect of two chemicals is less than the sum of the effect of each chemical alone; the chemicals either interfere with each other's actions or one interferes with the action of the other. 2) The interaction of two chemicals having an opposing, or neutralizing, effect on each other, or — given some specific biological effect — a chemical interaction that appears to have an opposing or neutralizing effect over what might otherwise be expected. *See* Synergism.

Antarctic "Ozone Hole"
Refers to the seasonal depletion of ozone in a large area over Antarctica.

Antennae, Wildlife Species
A species descriptor that refers to the head appendages in invertebrates.

Anterior
To the front of something.

Anterior Chamber of the Eye
The fluid-filled front portion of the eye between the cornea and the lens.

Anterior Margin
1) In zoology, means toward the forward or ventral end. 2) In botany, means inferior or lower; facing away from the axis.

Anthesis
The blooming of a flower or the time the flower is in full bloom.

Anthracite
A hard, black, lustrous coal that burns efficiently and is therefore valued for its heating quality.

Anthropogenic
The impact of people and their activities on the natural environment.

Anthropology
The scientific study of the human condition, including cultural, biological, and physical adaptations over time and under various natural and socio-environmental conditions. It is broad in scope in that it describes and interprets the human situation in terms of the interrelationships of culture, natural environments, and biological facts. It is a discipline that describes and interprets human existence over time. Specializations include: archaeology, cultural anthropology, ethnography, ethnology, linguistics, applied and physical anthropology.

Anti-Flooding Device
A primary safety control that causes the liquid fuel flow to be shut off upon a rise in fuel level or upon receiving excess fuel, and that operates before a hazardous discharge of fuel can occur.

Anti-G Suit
A device worn by aircrew to counteract the effects on the human body of positive acceleration.

Anti-Microbial Agents
Includes all substances or mixtures of substances intended for inhibiting the growth of, or destroying any, bacteria, fungi pathogenic to man and other animals, or viruses declared to be posts. These include but are not limited to: disinfectants, bacteriostats, sterilizers, fungicides and fungistats, and commodity preservatives and protectants. These do not include a) substances or mixtures of substances intended to inhibit the growth of, inactivate, or destroy fungi, bacteria, or viruses in or on living man or other animals; or b) substances or mixtures of substances intended to inhibit the growth of, inactivate, or destroy fungi, bacteria, or viruses in, or on, processed food, beverages, or pharmaceuticals, including cosmetics.

Antibodies
1) Proteins produced in the body by immune system cells in response to antigens, and capable of combining with antigens. 2) Protein substances developed in response to, and interacting specifically with, an antigen. The antibody-antigen reaction forms a major basis for immunity.

Anticipated Operational Occurrences
Abnormal events that are expected to occur.

Anticipated Processes and Events
Those natural processes and events that are reasonably likely to occur during the period the intended performance objective must be achieved. To the extent reasonable in the light of the geologic record, it shall be assumed that those processes operating in the geologic setting during the Quaternary Period continue to operate but with the perturbations caused by the presence of emplaced radioactive waste superimposed thereon.

Anticontamination Clothing
Personal Protective Equipment (PPE) and clothing such as acid suits, lab coats, or radiation suits. *See* Personal Protective Equipment.

Anticrop Agent
A living organism or chemical used to cause disease or damage to selected food or industrial crops.

Anticrop Operation
The employment of anticrop agents in military operations to destroy the enemy's source of selected food or industrial crops. *See* Antiplant Agent; Herbicide.

Antidegradation Clause
A provision, included in environmental legislation regulating air and water quality, whose purpose is to prevent deterioration of environmental quality in areas where current pollutant levels are below the allowable rates.

Antidote
An agent that neutralizes a poison or counteracts its effects.

Antigen
1) A substance that causes production of antibodies when introduced into animal or human tissue. 2) A substance that induces the formation of antibodies and interacts with its specific antibody. Antigens may be introduced into the body or may be formed within the body. The antigen-antibody reaction forms a basis for immunity. *See* Antibodies.

Antimateriel Agent
A living organism or chemical used to cause deterioration of, or damage to, selected material.

Antiplant Agent
A microorganism or chemical that will kill, disease, or damage plants. *See* Anticrop agent; Herbicide.

Antitrust Laws
Includes a) the Act entitled "An Act to protect trade and commerce against unlawful restraints and monopolies", approved July 2, 1890 (15 USC 1, et seq.); b) the Act entitled "an Act to supplement existing laws against unlawful restraints and monopolies, and for other purposes," approved October 15, 1914 (15 USC 12, et seq.); c) the Federal Trade Commission Act (15 USC 41, et seq.); d) Sections 73 and 74 of the Act entitled "an Act to reduce taxation, to provide revenue for the government, and for other purpose," approved August 27, 1894 (15 USC 8 and 9); and e) the Act of June 19, 1936, Chapter 592 (15 USC 13, 13a, 13b, and 21A).

Antivignetting Filter
A filter bearing a deposit that is graduated in density to correct the uneven illumination given, by certain lenses, particularly wide-angle types.

Anuria
Absence of urine production.

AO
An acronym for Auxiliary Offices.

AOC
See Administrative Order of Consent.

AOT
An acronym for Allowable Outage Time.

APA
An acronym for Acid Precipitation Act of 1980.

Apatite ($Ca_5(OH,F,C_1)(PO_4)_3$)
Group of minerals found in igneous rocks and metamorphosed limestones. It is the main source of phosphate.

Aperture
An opening through which radiation can pass.

Apex
1) With respect to the Marine Protection, Research, and Sanctuaries Act (MPRSA), a site within the New York Bight Apex, at which the dumping of municipal sludge occurred before October 1, 1983. 2) With respect to the Endangered Species Act, means the tip. *See* New York Bight Apex.

API
An acronym for American Petroleum Institute.

API Scale
An arbitrary measuring system adopted by the American Petroleum Institute for use with crude oil. Gravity values are expressed in degrees, resulting from the formula: degrees API = (141.5 to 131.5)/specific gravity at 600°F. Most Arab crude oils fall within the range 27.0 to 43.0° API.

Apical
Pertaining to or located at the apex (tip).

Apiculate
Ending with a sharp, abrupt tip.

Aplastic Anemia
A condition characterized by a decrease in the amount of hemoglobin in the blood due to incomplete or defective development of red blood cells; usually accompanied by defective regeneration of white blood cells and platelets.

APM
An acronym for Axial Power Monitors.

APMRS
See Accident Prevention Measures for Regulated Substances (CAA).

Apnea
Temporary cessation of breathing.

Apogee
The point at which a missile trajectory or a satellite orbit is farthest from the center of the gravitational field of the controlling body or bodies.

Apomixis
The rare reproductive process in which a new individual is produced from a female cell other than an egg cell.

APP
See Accident Prevention Program (CAA).

Apparent Horizon
The visible line of demarcation between land/sea and sky.

Apparent Precession
The apparent deflection of the gyro axis, relative to the earth, due to the rotating effect of the earth, and not due to any applied force. Also called "apparent wander".

Appeal
A request made by a complainant for reconsideration or reinvestigation of a complaint at a level higher than the source of a preceding decision unsatisfactory to the complainant, and includes applications, petitions, protests, and complaints.

Appellant
A person, or organization, filing any appeal.

Appendix
A subsidiary addition to a main paper. Details essential to the main paper but too bulky or numerous to include therein are usually embodied in appendices.

Appliance
Any article, such as a room air-conditioner, refrigerator-freezer, or dishwasher, that the EPA classifies as an appliance.

Applicable or Relevant and Appropriate Requirement (ARAR)
Requirements, including cleanup standards, standards of control, and other substantive environmental protection requirements and criteria for hazardous substances as specified under federal and state law and regulations, that must be met when complying with the Comprehensive Environmental Response, Compensation, and Liability Act (from the Superfund Amendments and Reauthorization Act).

Applicable Requirements
Federal requirements that would be legally applicable, whether directly or as incorporated by a federally authorized state program, if the response

actions were not taken pursuant to CERCLA Sections 104 or 106.

Applicable Standards and Limitations

All state, interstate, and federal standards and limitations to which a "discharge," a "sludge use or disposal practice" or a related activity is subject under the CWA (Clean Water Act), including "standards for sewage sludge use or disposal," "effluent limitations," water quality standards, standards of performance, toxic effluent standards or prohibitions, "best management practices," and pretreatment standards under Sections 301, 302, 303, 304, 306, 307, 308, 403, and 406 of the Clean Water Act.

Application

1) The system or problem to which a computer is applied. Reference is often made to an application as being either of the computational type, wherein arithmetic computations predominate, or of the data processing type, wherein data handling operations predominate. 2) In the intelligence context, the direct extraction and tailoring of information from an existing foundation of intelligence and near real time reporting. It is focused on and meets specific, narrow requirements, normally on demand.

Application for Federal Assistance

A description of work to be accomplished, including objectives and needs, expected results and benefits, approach, cost, location, and time required for completion. *See* Code of Federal Regulations.

Application Program

The set of instructions that defines the specific intended tasks of robots and robot systems. This program may be originated and modified by the robot user.

Applied Dose

The amount of a substance given to a human or test animal in determining dose-response relationships, especially through dermal contact. Even though this term is encountered in the literature, applied dose is actually a measure of exposure,

since it does not take absorption into account. *See* Administered Dose.

Applied Research

1) Research concerned with the practical application of knowledge, material, and/or techniques directed toward a solution to an existent or anticipated requirement. 2) Systematic study directed toward a greater scientific knowledge or understanding for direct use in fulfilling specific energy requirements. *See* Research.

Apportionment

In the general sense, distribution for planning of limited resources among competing requirements.

Appraisal

1) An estimate or opinion of value. In the real estate business, the highest level of appraisal activity is conducted by professional real estate appraisers who are recognized for their knowledge, training, skill, and integrity in this field. Formal appraisal reports are relied upon in important decisions made by mortgage lenders, investors, public utilities, governmental agencies, businesses, and individuals. *See* Value. 2) A personal conclusion, official estimate, and assumption about another party's intent, capability, and activities; used in planning and decisionmaking.

Appropriate Act and Regulations

Applicable regulations promulgated under such statutes as the Clean Water Act (CWA); the Solid Waste Disposal Act (SWDA), as amended by the Resource Conservation Recovery Act (RCRA); or Safe Drinking Water Act (SDWA). In the case of an "approved state program," appropriate act and regulations would also include those program requirements.

Appropriate Committees

The Committee on Merchant Marine and Fisheries in the House of Representatives and the Committee on Environment and Public Works and Committee on Commerce, Science, and Transportation in the Senate.

Appropriate Public Agency

Appropriate public agency, as that term is used in Water Code Section 8411, means any city, city and county, county, or other public agency organized, existing, and acting pursuant to the laws of the state, that is authorized under the laws of the state to exercise the police power to establish flood plain regulations within its jurisdiction.

Appropriator

One who diverts and puts to beneficial use the water of a stream or other body of water, under a water right obtained through appropriation.

Approval

The decision an agency or department makes that commits the department to a definite course of action with regard to a project. With respect to activities to be carried out by other agencies or persons, approval occurs when the department contracts or commits to issue a grant, loan, permit, certificate, or other entitlement for use of the project.

Approvals Necessary to Begin Construction

Permits and approvals required under federal, state or local hazardous waste control statutes, regulations or ordinances.

Approved Laboratory, Sound

An "approved" laboratory has facilities and equipment for testing sound measuring equipment to American National Standards Institute Standard S1.4-1971.

Approved Medical Practitioners

Medical practitioners responsible for the medical surveillance of occupationally exposed workers whose capacity to act in this capacity is recognized by the competent authority.

Approved Plans and Specifications

Plans, specifications, addenda and change orders that have been duly approved by a local enforcing agency and that are identified by a stamp bearing the approving official's name, the application number, date, and signature.

Approved Programs

State implementation plans that have been approved or authorized by EPA under 40 CFR 271, providing for issuance of PSD permits that have been approved by EPA under the Clean Air Act and 40 CFR 51.

Approved State Primacy Program

Those program elements listed in 40 CFR 142.11(a) that were submitted with the initial state application for primary enforcement authority and approved by the EPA Administrator and all state program revisions thereafter that were approved by the EPA Administrator.

Approved States

States having programs that have been approved or authorized by EPA under 40 CFR 271.

Approved Storage Containers

Containers that are fabricated from any combustible material(s) that satisfy container integrity criteria developed from the safety analysis for the particular form(s) of stored material under normal storage conditions, design basis fire and other design basis accident conditions, and that are approved for their intended use by the responsible DOE operating contractor and the responsible DOE field organization.

Approved Water Supply (SDWA)

A water supply whose potability is regulated by a state or local health agency.

Appurtenance

1) That which belongs to something else; something adapted to the use of the real property to which it is connected or belongs, and which was intended to be a permanent addition to the land, such as a house, a fence, or a right of way. 2) A device installed on, and used in the normal operation of, a vessel or tank system. This includes, but is not limited to, pumps, safety relief devices, liquid level gaging devices, valves, pressure gages, and piping between the vessel and device. It does not usually include piping beyond that point.

APRHS
See Accident Prevention Regulations for Hazardous Substances.

APRMP
See Accident Prevention Risk Management Plan.

Apron
A defined area, on an airfield, intended to accommodate aircraft for purposes of loading or unloading passengers or cargo, refueling, parking, or maintenance.

APRP
See Acid Precipitation Research Program.

APTF
See Acid Precipitation Task Force.

AQEL
An acronym for Air Quality and Emission Limitations.

Aquatic
Means living, growing, or taking place in or on water.

Aquatic Environment
Waters of the United States, including wetlands, that serve as habitat for interrelated and interacting communities and populations of plants and animals.

Aquatic Nuisance Prevention and Control Act (ANPCA)
Under 16 USC Chapter 67, the act established to a) prevent unintentional introduction and dispersal of nonindigenous species into waters of the United States through ballast water management and other requirements; b) coordinate federally conducted, funded, or authorized research, prevention control, information dissemination, and other activities regarding the zebra mussel and other aquatic nuisance species; c) develop and carry out environmentally sound control methods to prevent, monitor, and control unintentional introductions of nonindigenous species from pathways other than ballast water exchange; d) understand and minimize economic and ecological impacts of nonindigenous aquatic nuisance species that become established, including the zebra mussel; and e) establish a program of research and technology development and assistance to states in the management and removal of zebra mussels.

Aquatic Nuisance Species
A nonindigenous species that threatens the diversity or abundance of native species or the ecological stability of infested waters, or commercial, agricultural, aquacultural, or recreational activities dependent on such waters. *See* Aquatic Nuisance Prevention and Control Act.

Aquatic Nuisance Species Control
Cooperative efforts to control established aquatic nuisance species and to minimize the risk of harm to the environment and the public health and welfare. Control efforts include eradication of infestations, reductions of populations, development of means of adapting human activities and public facilities to accommodate infestations, and prevention of the spread of aquatic nuisance species from infested areas. Control efforts are typically developed in consultation with affected federal agencies, states, Native American Indian tribes, local governments, interjurisdictional organizations, and other appropriate entities. Control actions are based on the best available scientific information and are conducted in an environmentally sound manner. In determining whether a control program is warranted, the Task Force evaluates the need for control (including the projected consequences of no control and less than full control); the technical and biological feasibility and cost-effectiveness of alternative control strategies and actions; whether the benefits of control, including costs avoided, exceed the costs of the program; the risk of harm to nontarget organisms and ecosystems, public health and welfare; and such other considerations the Task Force determines appropriate. The Task Force shall also determine the nature and extent of control of target aquatic nuisance species that is feasi-

ble and desirable. *See* Aquatic Nuisance Prevention and Control Act.

Aquatic Nuisance Species Monitoring (ANPCA)

Monitoring measures implemented by the Aquatic Nuisance Species Task Force to: a) detect unintentional introductions of aquatic nuisance species; b) determine the dispersal of aquatic nuisance species after introduction; and c) provide for the early detection and prevention of infestations of aquatic nuisance species in unaffected drainage basins. *See* Aquatic Nuisance Prevention and Control Act.

Aquatic Nuisance Species Prevention

Measures, within the Aquatic Nuisance Species Program (ANSP) developed to minimize the risk of introduction of aquatic nuisance species to waters of the United States, including: a) identification of pathways by which aquatic organisms are introduced to waters of the United States; b) assessment of the risk that an aquatic organism carried by an identified pathway may become an aquatic nuisance species; and c) evaluation of whether measures to prevent introductions of aquatic nuisance species are effective and environmentally sound. Whenever the Task Force determines that there is a substantial risk of unintentional introduction of an aquatic nuisance species by an identified pathway and that the adverse consequences of such an introduction are likely to be substantial, the Task Force, acting through the appropriate federal agency, and after an opportunity for public comment, is charged with carrying out cooperative, environmentally sound efforts with regional, state and local entities to minimize the risk of such an introduction. *See* Aquatic Nuisance Prevention and Control Act.

Aquatic Nuisance Species Program (ANSP)

A program developed and implemented by the Aquatic Nuisance Species Task Force (ANSTF) for waters of the United States to prevent introduction and dispersal of aquatic nuisance species; to monitor, control and study such species; and to disseminate related information. The program's purpose is to a) identify the goals, priorities, and approaches for aquatic nuisance species prevention, monitoring, control, education and research to be conducted or funded by the federal government; b) describe the specific prevention, monitoring, control, education and research activities to be conducted by each Task Force member; c) coordinate aquatic nuisance species programs and activities of Task Force members and affected state agencies; d) describe the role of each Task Force member in implementing the elements of the program; e) include recommendations for funding to implement elements of the program; and f) develop a demonstration program of prevention, monitoring, control, education and research for the zebra mussel, to be implemented in the Great Lakes and any other waters infested, or likely to become infested in the near future, by the zebra mussel. *See* Aquatic Nuisance Prevention and Control Act; Aquatic Nuisance Species Task Force.

Aquatic Nuisance Species Research Priorities

Research concerning a) the environmental and economic risks associated with the introduction of aquatic nuisance species into the waters of the United States; b) the principal pathways by which aquatic nuisance species are introduced and dispersed; c) possible methods for the prevention, monitoring, and control of aquatic nuisance species; and d) the assessment of the effectiveness of prevention, monitoring, and control methods. *See* Aquatic Nuisance Prevention and Control Act.

Aquatic Nuisance Species Task Force (ANSTF)

A task force established under Section 4721 of the Aquatic Nuisance Prevention and Control Act, (ANPCA) 16 USC Chapter 67.

Task force members include: a) the Director and Under Secretary of Commerce for Oceans and Atmosphere; b) the Administrator of the Environmental Protection Agency; c) the Commandant of the United States Coast Guard; d) the Assistant Secretary; and e) the head of any other federal agency that the chairpersons deem appropriate. The ANSTF may also include ex officio members/representatives of the Great Lakes Commission, state agencies, and other governmental entities the chairpersons deem appropriate. *See* Aquatic Nuisance Prevention and Control Act; Aquatic Nuisance Species Task Force.

Aquatic Nuisance Task Force Objectives
Guidelines to ensure that research activities carried out do not result in the introduction of aquatic nuisance species to waters of the United States; allocate funds for competitive research grants to study all aspects of aquatic nuisance species, which shall be administered through the National Sea Grant College Program and the Cooperative Fishery and Wildlife Research Units; provide technical assistance to state and local governments and persons to minimize the environmental, public health, and safety risks associated with aquatic nuisance species, including an early warning system for advance notice of possible infestations and appropriate responses; establish and implement educational programs through Sea Grant Marine Advisory Services and any other available resources that it determines to be appropriate to inform the general public, state governments, governments of political subdivisions of states, and industrial and recreational users of aquatic resources in connection with matters concerning the identification of aquatic nuisance species, and control methods for such species, including the prevention of the further distribution of such species. *See* Aquatic Nuisance Prevention and Control Act; Aquatic Nuisance Species Task Force.

Aqueous
Of, relating to, or resembling, water; made from, with, or by, water.

Aquifer
An underground rock formation composed of materials such as sand, soil, or gravel that can store and supply groundwater to wells and springs; a geologic formation, group of formations, or part of a formation. Most aquifers used in the United States are within about 1000 feet of the earth's surface.

Aquifer Recharge Area
The portion of an aquifer that is exposed at ground level.

Aquifer System
A body of permeable and relatively impermeable materials that functions regionally as a water-yielding unit. Usually comprises two or more permeable units separated at least locally by confining units that impede groundwater movement but does not greatly influence the regional hydraulic continuity of the system. The permeable materials can include both saturated and unsaturated sections.

Aquifer Test
A test to determine hydrologic properties of an aquifer that involves the withdrawal of measured quantities of water from, or addition of water to, a well — as well as the measurement of resulting changes in head in the aquifer both during and after the period of discharge or addition.

Arachnids
The classes of species that include spiders, scorpions, mites, and ticks.

ARARs
See Applicable or Relevant and Appropriate Requirement.

Arbitration
A process for the resolution of disputes. Decisions are made by an impartial arbitrator selected by the parties. These decisions are usually legally binding.

Arboriculture
The cultivation of trees.

Arborist
A person who studies trees.

Archaeological Clearance
A memorandum that documents that an undertaking (e.g., an action or project) has complied with environmental and historic preservation guide-

lines and requirements with respect to the archae-ological value of cultural resources. Usually is-sued when a) there are no significant archaeological resources within the project's area of impact; b) significant archaeological resources within the project area will not be adversely im-pacted; c) significant archaeological values within a project's area of impact that will be ad-versely affected have been salvaged in accord-ance with an approved data recovery plan under National Park Service standards; and d) required for a determination of no effect.

Archaeological Excavation and Removal Permit

A permit issued pursuant to an application under the Archaeological Resources Protection Act of 1979 (ARPA) pursuant to uniform regulations un-der the act that indicate a) the applicant is quali-fied to carry out the permitted activity; b) the activity is undertaken for the purpose of further-ing archaeological knowledge in the public inter-est; c) the archaeological resources that are excavated or removed from public lands will re-main the property of the United States, and such resources and copies of associated archaeological records and data will be preserved by a suitable university, museum, or other scientific or educa-tional institution; and d) the activity to be permit-ted is not inconsistent with any management plan applicable to the public lands concerned. If a per-mit may result in harm to, or destruction of, any religious or cultural site, as determined by the federal land manager, before issuing such permit, the federal land manager shall notify any Native American tribe that may consider the site as hav-ing religious or cultural importance.

Archaeological Resource

Any tangible remains of past human life or activi-ties that are of archaeological interest, including, but not limited to: pottery, basketry, bottles, weapons, weapon projectiles, tools, structures or portions of structures, pit houses, rock paintings, rock carvings, intaglios, graves, human skeletal materials, or any portion or piece of any of the foregoing items. Nonfossilized and fossilized pa-leontological specimens, or any portion or piece

thereof, are not considered archaeological re-sources, unless found in archaeological context. An item is not treated as an archaeological re-source unless such item is at least 50 years of age.

Archaeological Resources Protection Act of 1979 (ARPA)

The act established by Congress based upon the findings that a) archaeological resources on pub-lic lands and Native American lands are an acces-sible and irreplaceable part of the nation's heritage; b) these resources are increasingly en-dangered because of their commercial attractive-ness; c) existing federal laws do not provide adequate protection to prevent the loss and de-struction of these archaeological resources and sites resulting from uncontrolled excavations and pillage; and d) there is a wealth of archaeological information that has been legally obtained by pri-vate individuals for noncommercial purposes and that could voluntarily be made available to pro-fessional archaeologists and institutions. The purpose of the act is to secure, for the present and future benefit of the American people, the protec-tion of archaeological resources and sites that are on public lands and Native American lands, and to foster increased cooperation and exchange of information between governmental authorities, the professional archaeological community, and private individuals having collections of archae-ological resources and data that were obtained before October 31, 1979.

Archaeological Sites

Sites evidencing ancient living areas or ancient farming, hunting and gathering activities, or of burials and funerary remains, artifacts, and struc-tures of all types. These sites usually date from prehistoric or aboriginal periods, or from historic periods of which only vestiges remain.

Archaeology

The scientific study, interpretation, and recon-struction of past human cultures based on the in-vestigation of the surviving physical evidence of human activity and the reconstruction of related past environments. An archaeologist is a scientist professionally trained to conduct such tasks.

Architectural and Engineering Services

Services rendered by an architect or engineer, but may include ancillary services logically or justifiably performed in connection therewith.

Architectural Conservation

The science of preserving architecture and its historic fabric by observing and analyzing the evolution, deterioration, and care of structures. The conducting of investigations to determine cause, effect, and remedies for structural problems. The directing of remedial interventions focused on maintaining the integrity and quality of the historic context.

Architectural Conservator

A specialist in scientific analysis of structural materials and systems. An Architectural Conservator has knowledge of the causes of deterioration and treatment of the structural materials used in historic buildings.

Architectural Design

The preparation of architectural drawings and specifications. It includes preliminary plans, plans at intermediate stages, models, final working drawings, specifications, and engineering.

Architectural Historian

A historian concentrating on the study of architecture through written records and the examination of structures, sites, and objects in order to determine their relationship to preceding, contemporary, and future architectural events.

Architecture

A framework or structure that portrays relationships among all the elements of the subject system, activity, or structure.

Archives

The nonrecurrent records of an organization or institution preserved for their historic value. Term used to refer to the repository where archives and other historic documents are stored.

Archivist

A person trained in the management of archives and historic documents, including their collection, appraisal, disposition, cataloging, preservation, arrangement, description, reference service, exhibition, and publication.

Area Affected by Outer Continental Shelf Activities

Any geographic area a) that is under oil or gas lease on the Outer Continental Shelf; b) where Outer Continental Shelf exploration, development, or production activities have been permitted, with the exception of geophysical activities; c) where pipeline rights-of-way have been granted; or d) otherwise impacted by such activities including but not limited to expired lease areas, relinquished rights-of-way and easements, Outer Continental Shelf supply vessel routes, or other areas as determined by the Secretary.

Area Assessment

The prescribed collection of specific information that commences upon employment and is a continuous operation. It confirms, corrects, refutes, or adds to previous intelligence acquired from area studies and other sources prior to employment.

Area Coordination Group

A composite organization, including representatives of local military, paramilitary, and other governmental agencies and their U.S. counterparts, responsible for planning and coordinating internal defense and development operations.

Area Damage Control

Measures taken before, during, or after hostile action or natural or manmade disasters, to reduce the probability of damage and minimize its effects. *See* Damage Control; Disaster Control.

Area of Influence

An area surrounding a pumping or recharging well within which the water table or potentiometric surface has been altered due to the well's pumping or recharge.

Area of Militarily Significant Fallout

Area in which radioactive fallout affects the ability of military units to carry out their normal mission.

Area of Review (UIC)

1) In the Underground Injection Control program, the area surrounding an injection well that is reviewed during the permitting process to determine whether the injection operation will induce flow between aquifers. 2) The area surrounding an injection well described according to the criteria set forth in 40 CFR 146.06 or in the case of an area permit, the project area plus a circumscribing area the width of which is either 1/4 of a mile or a number calculated according to the criteria set forth in Section 146.06.

Area Source

1) Any small source of nonnatural air pollution that is released over a relatively small area but which cannot be classified as a point source. Such sources may include vehicles and other small fuel combustion engines. 2) Any stationary source of hazardous air pollutants that is not a major source. 3) Any small residential, governmental, institutional, commercial, or industrial fuel combustion operations; onsite solid waste disposal facility; motor vehicles, aircraft vessels, or other transportation facilities or other miscellaneous sources identified through inventory techniques similar to those described in EPA's AEROS Manual series.

Area Source Program

A research program on sources of hazardous air pollutants in urban areas and shall include within such program a) ambient monitoring for a broad range of hazardous air pollutants (including, but not limited to, volatile organic compounds, metals, pesticides, and products of incomplete combustion) in a representative number of urban locations; b) analysis to characterize the sources of such pollution with a focus on area sources and the contribution that such sources make to public health risks from hazardous air pollutants; and c) consideration of atmospheric transformation and other factors that can elevate public health risks from such pollutants. Health effects considered under this program shall include, but not be limited to, carcinogenicity, mutagenicity, teratogenicity, neurotoxicity, reproductive dysfunction and other acute and chronic effects including the role of such pollutants as precursors of ozone or acid aerosol formation.

Areas of Critical Environmental Concern

Areas within the public lands where special management attention is required (when such areas are developed or used or where no development is required) to protect and prevent irreparable damage to important historic, cultural, or scenic values, fish and wildlife resources or other natural systems or processes, or to protect life and safety from natural hazards.

Areawide Wastewater Treatment Management

A program established by Section 208 of the Federal Water Pollution Control Act Amendments of 1972 requiring areawide wastewater treatment, management, planning, and implementation, with emphasis on land-use criteria and nonpoint source pollution control systems.

Areodesy

The branch of mathematics that determines, by observation and measurement, the exact positions of points and the figures and areas of large portions of the surface of the planet Mars, or the shape and size of the planet Mars.

Areodetic

Of or pertaining to, or determined by, areodesy.

Areoles

The small space between veins in leaves or insect wings.

Argiustoll

A soil that is darkly colored with an accumulation of silicate clay layers with an average temperature between 5° and 8°C.

Argon
A gas used as a laser medium. It emits blue/green light primarily at 448 and 515 nanometers.

Argonne National Laboratory (ANL)
A DOE Research and Development and Field Facility, established by the Atomic Energy Act of 1946, that conducts applied research and engineering development in nuclear fission and other energy technologies and scientific research in basic physical and life sciences. R&D at ANL links technology base research with engineering development, from concept stages to application. ANL's role is to develop and operate research facilities for members of the scientific community, maintain close interaction with personnel in universities and industry, and aid in the education of scientists and engineers.

Arid
Parched with heat; dry, barren, desertlike.

Arid Zone
A zone at 15° to 30° latitude in both hemispheres, of limited rainfall, which contains most of the world's deserts.

Armed Forces of the United States
A term used to denote collectively all components of the Army, Navy, Air Force, Marine Corps, and Coast Guard. *See* United States Armed Forces.

Armed Services Medical Regulating Office (ASMRO)
A joint activity reporting directly to the Commander in Chief, U.S. Transportation Command. The Armed Services Medical Regulating Office authorizes transfers to medical treatment facilities of the Military Departments or the Department of Veterans Affairs and coordinates inter-theater and inside continental United States patient movement requirements with the appropriate transportation component commands of U.S. Transportation Command.

Arms Control
1) Any plan, arrangement, or process, resting upon explicit or implicit international agreement, governing any aspect of the following: the numbers, types, and performance characteristics of weapon systems (including the command and control, logistics support arrangements, and any related intelligence-gathering mechanism); and the numerical strength, organization, equipment, deployment, or employment of the Armed Forces retained by the parties (it encompasses disarmament). 2) On some occasions, those measures taken for the purpose of reducing instability in the military environment.

Arms Control Agreement
The written or unwritten embodiment of the acceptance of one or more arms control measures by two or more nations.

Arms Control Agreement Verification
The collection, processing, and reporting of data indicating testing or employment of proscribed weapon systems, including country of origin and location, weapon and payload identification, and event type.

Arms Control Measure
Any specific arms control course of action.

Army Base
A base or group of installations for which a local commander is responsible, consisting of facilities necessary for support of Army activities including security, internal lines of communication, utilities, plants and systems, and real property for which the Army has operating responsibility.

Aromatic
Applied to a group of hydrocarbons and their derivatives characterized by the presence of the benzene nucleus (molecular ring structure).

ARPA
See the Archaeological Resources Protection Act of 1979.

Arrhythmia
Any variation from the normal rhythm of the heartbeat.

Arroyo
A steep-sided, flat-floored stream channel; a landform found in arid regions.

Arsenic Containing Glass Types
Any glass that is distinguished from other glass solely by the weight percent of arsenic added as a raw material and by the weight percent of arsenic in the glass produced. Any two or more glasses that have the same weight percent of arsenic in the raw materials as well as in the glass produced shall be considered to belong to one arsenic-containing glass type, without regard to the recipe used or any other characteristics of the glass or the method of production.

Arsenic Kitchens
Baffled brick chambers where inorganic arsenic vapors are condensed and removed in a solid form.

Artesian Aquifer
A commonly used expression, synonymous with confined aquifer. *See* Aquifer.

Artesian Well
A well deriving its water from a confined aquifer.

Arthropod
An invertebrate organism with a horny, segmented external covering and jointed limbs; includes insects, crustaceans, arachnids (such as spiders), and myriapods (such as centipedes).

Articles
Manufactured items that a) are formed to a specific shape or design during manufacture; b) have use functions dependent in whole or in part upon their shape or design during end use; and c) do not release a toxic chemical under normal conditions of processing or use of those items at the facility or establishments.

Artifact
Portable object resulting from human activity, usually applied to objects found in or removed from archaeological sites, whether historic or pre-historic.

Artificial Heat
Any heat other than solar or atmospheric heat.

Artificial Reefs
Structures that are constructed or placed in the navigable waters of the United States or in the waters overlying the outer continental shelf for the purpose of enhancing fishery resources and commercial and recreational fishing opportunities. The term does not include activities or structures such as wing deflectors, bank stabilization, grade stabilization structures, or low flow key ways, all of which may be useful to enhance fisheries resources.

As Expeditiously as Practicable (AEAP)
As it refers to the CAA, the term means as expeditiously as practicable but in no event later than five years after the date of approval of a plan revision.

As Low as Reasonably Achievable (ALARA)
A phrase used to describe an approach to radiation protection to control or manage exposures (both individual and collective to the work force and the general public) and releases of radioactive material to the environment as low as social, technical, economic, practical, and public policy considerations permit. ALARA is not a dose limit, but rather it is a process that has as its objective the attainment of dose levels as far below applicable limits as practicable. This includes keeping worker and public exposures to ionizing radiation as low as reasonably achievable by various techniques outlined by the DOE.

Asbestos
1) A noncombustible fibrous mineral used for fireproofing in industrial and construction applications. Prolonged exposure to airborne asbestos fibers through inhalation has been deemed to be extremely hazardous and can cause various forms

of cancer and respiratory diseases. 2) Asbesti-form varieties of chrysotile (serpentine), croci-dolite (riebeckite), amosite (cummingtonite-grunerite), anthophylite, tremolite, or actinolite. 3) A naturally occurring mineral, that because of its properties of incombustibility, noise absorp-tion, and resistance to electrical current, corro-sion, and bacterial attack, was used in a large number of building products intended for fire-proofing, acoustical soundproofing, and heating and cooling system insulation.

In 1973, EPA banned the use of sprayed-on or trowled-on friable materials. By 1979, sprayed-on ACMs were no longer allowed in building construction. Asbestos-containing materials (ACM) have been used extensively in many schools, public buildings, and private residences. Over three thousand products have been identi-fied as asbestos-containing materials. The Envi-ronmental Protection Agency (EPA) recently estimated that friable (easily crumbled with hand pressure) asbestos could be found nationally in approximately 31,000 schools and 733,000 other public and private buildings. Three forms of as-bestos are typically found in buildings. They are: a) surfacing materials; b) thermal system insula-tion; and c) miscellaneous forms. The quality that made asbestos desirable as a construction ma-terial is that it is virtually indestructible. Asbestos exposure has been linked to several diseases, such as lung cancer, the debilitating asbestosis, cancers of the esophagus, stomach, colon, and the rare chest cancer called mesothelioma. *See* Asbestos Surfacing Material; Asbestos Thermal System In-sulation; and Asbestos, Miscellaneous Material.

Asbestos, Emergency Repair
A repair in a building that was not planned and was in response to a sudden, unexpected event that threatens either a) the health or safety of building occupants; or b) the structural integrity of the building.

Asbestos, EPA Information or Advisory
The information or advisory guidance distributed to all local education agencies and state governors to a) facilitate public understanding of the com-parative risks associated with in-place manage-ment of asbestos-containing building materials and removals; b) promote the least burdensome response actions necessary to protect human health, safety, and the environment; and c) de-scribe the circumstances in which asbestos re-moval is necessary to protect human health.

Asbestos, Miscellaneous Material
Asbestos-containing materials on building or structural components, structural members, or fix-tures. This group includes vinyl asbestos floor tile, ceiling tiles, cement-asbestos board (transite), linoleum, heat resistant gaskets, and roofing ma-terials. The term does not include surfacing mate-rial or thermal system insulation.

Asbestos, Operations and Maintenance
Operations, maintenance, and repair programs as described in the *Guide for Controlling Asbestos-Containing Materials in Buildings* for all friable asbestos-containing material in a school building under the authority of a local educational agency.

Asbestos, Periodic Surveillance
The Administrator's regulations to require the fol-lowing: a) an identification of the location of friable and nonfriable asbestos in a school build-ing under the authority of a local educational agency; b) provisions for surveillance and peri-odic reinspection of such friable and nonfriable asbestos, c) provisions for education of school employees, including school service and mainte-nance personnel, about the location of and safety procedures with respect to such friable and non-friable asbestos.

Asbestos, Post-Response Action
Any periodic reinspection of asbestos-containing material and long-term surveillance activity.

Asbestos, Preventive Measures
Actions that eliminate the reasonable likelihood of asbestos-containing material becoming dam-aged, deteriorated, or delaminated, or signifi-cantly damaged, deteriorated, or delaminated (as the case may be), or that protect human health and the environment.

Asbestos, Response Action

Methods that protect human health and the environment from asbestos-containing material. Such methods include methods described in the Environmental Protection Agency's *Guide for Controlling Asbestos-Containing Materials in Buildings.*

Asbestos Abatement Project

An activity involving the mitigation (removal, enclosure, or encapsulation) of friable asbestos materials.

Asbestos or Asbestos-Containing Materials, Identifying Characteristics

A description of: a) the mineral or chemical constituents (or both) of the asbestos or material by weight or volume (or both); b) the types or classes of the product in which the asbestos or material is contained; c) the designs, patterns, or textures of the product in which the asbestos or material is contained; and d) the means by which the product in which the asbestos or material is contained may be distinguishable from other products containing asbestos or asbestos-containing material.

Asbestos Disposal

The Administrator's regulations that prescribe standards for transportation and disposal of asbestos-containing waste material to protect human health and the environment. Regulations include provisions related to the manner in which transportation vehicles are loaded and unloaded as will ensure the physical integrity of containers of asbestos-containing waste material.

Asbestos Guidance Document

The Environmental Protection Agency as in effect on March 31, 1986, entitled *Guidance for Controlling Asbestos-Containing Material in Buildings.* Most current guidance document means the guidance document as modified by the Environmental Protection Agency after March 31, 1986.

Asbestos Inspection

Conducting physical site reconnaissance tasks, to: identify, quantify, characterize, and delineate the presence of asbestos-containing materials at a building or facility. *See* Asbestos Survey, Comprehensive.

Asbestos Management Plan

An asbestos plan that includes the following elements, wherever relevant, a) an inspection statement describing inspection and response action activities; b) a description of the results of the inspection conducted pursuant to regulations under TSCA, including a description of the specific areas inspected; c) a detailed description of measures to be taken to respond to any friable asbestos-containing material pursuant to the regulations promulgated under TSCA and AHERA, including the location or locations at which a response action will be taken, the method or methods of response action to be used, and a schedule for beginning and completing response actions; d) a detailed description of any asbestos-containing material that remains in the building inspected, once response actions are undertaken; e) a plan for periodic reinspection and long-term surveillance activities, and a plan for operations and maintenance activities developed; f) with respect to the person or persons who inspected for asbestos-containing material and who will design or carry out response actions with respect to the friable asbestos-containing material, copies of a state and/or AHERA Certification, covering the work to be performed; g) a list of the laboratories that analyzed any bulk samples of asbestos-containing material found in the school building or air samples taken to detect asbestos in the school building and a statement that each laboratory has been accredited; h) an evaluation of resources needed to successfully complete response actions and carry out reinspection, surveillance, and operation and maintenance activities.

Asbestos Materials

Any materials containing asbestos.

Asbestos Mills (CAA; CFR)

Facilities engaged in converting, or in any intermediate step in converting, asbestos ore into commercial asbestos. Outside storage of asbestos material is not considered a part of the asbestos mill.

Asbestos Protocol

Any procedure for taking, handling, and preserving samples of asbestos and asbestos-containing material and for testing and analyzing such samples for the purpose of determining the person who manufactured or processed for sale such samples and the identifying characteristics of such samples.

Asbestos Standards

Regulations promulgated by the U.S. Occupational Safety and Health Administration (OSHA) in 1986 that require major reductions in the level of airborne asbestos fibers in work places, and that also prescribe a system of engineering controls and work practices related to asbestos. Actually two standards exist, one for general industry, and one for the construction industry, with somewhat differing requirements.

Asbestos Surfacing Material

Material in a building that is sprayed on surfaces, trowled on surfaces, or otherwise applied to surfaces for acoustical, fireproofing, or other purposes, such as acoustical plaster on ceilings and fireproofing material on structural members. Included in this category are decorative, sprayed ceiling material, some plasters, and structural fireproofing.

Asbestos Survey, Comprehensive

A survey and inspection that includes a) conducting visual inspections of the building units to determine the presence of suspect asbestos-containing building materials either friable or nonfriable; b) identifying locations of homogeneous areas of suspect asbestos-containing materials from which samples were to be obtained; c) collecting bulk samples of suspect ACMs; d) preparing diagrams of the inspected buildings that illustrate sample collection locations; e) taking photographs of the types of suspect materials sampled; f) having bulk-samples tested and analyzed by an EPA or NVLAP Certified Laboratory; and g) preparing a written report of findings, recommendations, and the related costs for maintenance and/or abatement, if necessary.

Asbestos Tailings

Solid wastes that contain asbestos and are products of asbestos mining or milling operations.

Asbestos Thermal System Insulation

Material in a building applied to pipes, fittings, boilers, tanks, ducts, or other structural components to minimize or prevent heat loss or gain or water condensation, or for other purposes.

Asbestos Waste from Control Devices

Any waste material that contains asbestos and is collected by a pollution control device.

Asbestos-Containing Materials

Materials that contain more than 1% asbestos by weight.

Asbestos-Containing Waste Materials

Any waste that contains commercial asbestos and is generated by a source subject to an AHERA regulated abatement project. The term includes asbestos mill tailings, asbestos waste from control devices, friable asbestos waste material, and bags or containers that previously contained commercial asbestos. However, as applied to demolition and renovation operations, this term includes only friable asbestos waste and asbestos waste from control devices.

Asbestosis

1) A disease associated with chronic exposure to and inhalation of asbestos fibers. The disease makes breathing progressively more difficult and can lead to death. 2) A dust-related disease caused by continued inhalation of asbestos fibers; reduces lung functioning and leads to chronic shortness of breath.

ASE

An acronym for Automotive Service Excellence.

Ash

The mineral content of a product remaining after complete combustion.

ASHRAE

An acronym for the American Society of Heating, Refrigeration and Air-Conditioning Engineers, 345 East 47th Street, New York, N.Y. 10017.

ASME

An acronym for the American Society of Mechanical Engineers.

ASME Code

The American Society of Mechanical Engineers' Boiler and Pressure Vessel Code, 1986 edition. 1) Power Boilers, Section I. 2) Materials Specifications, Section II. 3) Nuclear Power Plant Components, Section III, Division 1 and 2. 4) Heating Boilers, Section IV.(5) Nondestructive Examination, Section V. 6) Recommended Rules for Care and Operation of Heating Boilers, Section VI. 7) Recommended Rules for Care of Power Boilers, Section VII. 8) Pressure Vessels, Section VIII, Division 1 and 2. 9) Welding and Brazing Qualifications, Section IX. 10) Fiberglass-Reinforced Plastic Pressure Vessels, Section X. 11) Rules for Inservice Inspection of Nuclear Power Plant Components, Section XI.

ASMFC

An acronym for Atlantic States Marine Fisheries Compact.

Aspect Ratio

The ratio of length to diameter of a fiber.

Asphalt

Crude asphalt and finished products such as cements fluxes.

Asphyxia

A condition in which the exchange of oxygen and carbon dioxide in the lungs is absent or impaired.

Asphyxiants

Chemical vapors or gases that replace the oxygen in air and can cause death by suffocation. Asphyxiants are especially hazardous when present in confined spaces.

Asphyxiation

Human deprivation of oxygen by chemical or physical means. Chemical asphyxiants prevent oxygen transfer from the blood to body cells. Physical asphyxiants prevent oxygen from reaching the blood.

Aspiration Pneumonia

Inflammation of the lungs due to inhalation of foreign material, usually food or vomitus, into the bronchi.

Assembly

In logistics, an item forming a portion of a piece of equipment, that can be provisioned and replaced as an entity and that normally incorporates replaceable parts or groups of parts. *See* Components.

Assembly Area

1) An area in which a response team is assembled preparatory to further action. 2) In a supply installation, the gross area used for collecting and combining components into complete units, kits, or assemblies.

Assessed Valuation

The estimate of value placed on real estate property for taxation purposes.

Assessment

1) In environmental planning, the evaluation and appraisal of a project or property for the purpose of approximating and planning for the mitigation of adverse effects upon the surrounding environs. Also, used as a primary means of developing alternative approaches of completing a project, while simultaneously minimizing or avoiding negative impacts. 2) In property taxation, the procedure for determining the value of property, real or personal, for the purpose of determining an ad valorem tax, as well as a valuation. 3) In military science, analysis of the security, effectiveness, and potential of an existing or planned intelligence activity. 4) Judgment of the motives, qualifications, and characteristics of present or prospective employees or "agents."

Assessment Actions
Those actions taken during or immediately after an incident or emergency to gather and process the information necessary to make decisions and to implement specific emergency measures.

Assessment Area
The area or areas within which natural resources have been affected directly or indirectly by the discharge of oil or release of a hazardous substance and that serves as the geographic basis for the injury assessment.

Assessment of International Air Pollution Control Technologies (IAPCT)
An EPA study that compares international air pollution control technologies of selected industrialized countries to determine if there exist air pollution control technologies in countries outside the United States that may have beneficial applications to this nation's air pollution control efforts. With respect to each country studied, the study shall include the topics of urban air quality, motor vehicle emissions, toxic air emissions, and acid deposition.

Assessment of Risk
A planning method used in evaluating the relative costs, benefits, and environmental impacts of a proposed project. This process compares precedents set for similar projects regarding the health and welfare impacts to a population over a long-range timeframe and is based on statistical facts that do not account for special interest groups who may have specific perceived risks.

Assessment Plan
A plan that outlines key issues, general approaches, and specific on-site activities to be conducted. The plan should include a) issue identification; b) an implementation strategy; c) review and compilation of a list of historic studies, files, and other documents that pertain to the site; and d) a determination of the presence of classified hazardous wastes, and the adequacy of operations and maintenance oversight.

Assessment Team Leaders
Individuals primarily responsible for the detailed technical conduct and results of their respective assessment teams and tasks. These individuals provide direct supervision of the day-to-day activities of their individual team members.

Assessments
The processes of collecting, compiling, and analyzing information, statistics, or data through prescribed methodologies.

Assets
1) All existing and all probable future economic benefits obtained or controlled by a particular entity. 2) Any resource, person, group, relationship, instrument, installation, or supply at the disposition of an organization for use in an operational or support role.

Assign
1) To place units or personnel in an organization where such placement is relatively permanent, and/or where such organization controls and administers the units or personnel for the primary function, or greater portion of the functions, of the unit or personnel. 2) To detail individuals to specific duties or functions where such duties or functions are primary and/or relatively permanent.

Assigned Risks
Risks that are assigned, by state law, to an insurer from a pool of insurers (usually all those licensed in the state) who would not otherwise accept it.

Assignee
The party to whom a legal right has been assigned or transferred.

Assignment
The transfer of a legal right to another.

Assignor
The party who assigns or transfers a legal right.

Assimilation
The ability of a body of water to purify itself of pollutants.

Assimilative Capacity
The ability of a natural body of water to receive wastewaters or toxic materials without adverse effects, such as damage to aquatic life, etc.

Assistant Administrator for Fisheries
The Assistant Administrator for Fisheries, National Oceanic and Atmospheric Administration, Department of Commerce, or his/her authorized delegate. The Assistant Administrator for Fisheries is in charge of the National Marine Fisheries Service.

Associated Support
Assistance provided by an organization (public or private) or individual to another organization that is depending on the support tasks and neither one is subordinate to the other.

Association
A group of species that are dependent on one another.

Assumed Azimuth
The assumption of azimuth origins as a field expedient until the required data are available.

Assumed Grid
A grid constructed using an arbitrary scale superimposed on a map, chart, or photograph for use in point designation without regard to actual geographic location. *See* Grid.

Assumed Risks
Specific, analyzed residual risks accepted at an appropriate level of management. Ideally, the risk has been analyzed for alternative means of increasing control and evaluated for the significance of inherent secondary impacts.

Assumption
A supposition on the current situation or a presupposition on the future course of events, either or both assumed to be true in the absence of positive proof, necessary to enable the process of planning to complete an estimate of the situation, develop alternatives, and make a decision on the course of action.

Assumption of Liability
As applied to the waste business, assumption of liability occurs when a licensed transporter facility automatically assumes responsibility, and accordingly, risk and liability for a generator's waste when the waste is accepted for transportation, storage, treatment, or other handling. This assumption does not, however, reduce or remove the generator's liability or responsibility.

Assurgent
Slanting or curving upward.

Astern Fueling
The transfer of fuel at sea during which the receiving ship keeps a position astern of the delivering ship.

Asthma
A condition marked by recurrent attacks of difficult or labored breathing and wheezing resulting from spasmodic contraction and hypersecretion of the bronchi resulting from exposure to allergens such as drugs, foods, environmental pollutants, or other intrinsic factors.

ASTM
An acronym for American Society for Testing and Materials.

Ataxia
A lack of coordination of voluntary movements, especially affecting gait and speech.

Atelectasis
Lung collapse.

Atmosphere
1) The whole mass of air surrounding the earth, composed largely of oxygen and nitrogen. 2) A standard unit of pressure representing the pressure

exerted by a 29.92-inch column of mercury at sea level at 45° latitude and equal to 1000 grams per square centimeter. *See* Ionosphere; Stratosphere; Tropopause; Troposphere.

Atmosphere Gases
Gases that are commercially derived through an air separation process.

Atmospheric Dispersion
The dilution of gases, smoke, and particulates by a progressive diminution of airborne concentrations.

Atmospheric Environment
The envelope of air surrounding the earth, including its interfaces and interactions with the earth's solid or liquid surface.

Atmospheric Half-Life
The time required for one half of the quantity of an air pollutant to react and/or break down in the atmosphere.

Atmospheric Pressure
The pressure of air at sea level, usually 14.7 pounds per square inch absolute (psia) (one atmosphere), or 0 pounds per square inch gauge (psig).

Atmospheric Release Advisory Capability
A computer-based system that provides rapid predictions of the transport, diffusion, and deposition of radioactive nuclides or other toxic materials released to the atmosphere and dose projections to people and the environment.

Atmospheric Residence Time
The time required for removal of a substance from the atmosphere to the extent that approximately 37% of the original material remains.

Atom
The smallest particle of an element that is capable of entering into a chemical reaction; atoms are the chemical units from which all matter is made.

Atomic Energy Act of 1954 (AEA)
The Act that placed production and control of nuclear materials within a civilian agency, originally the Atomic Energy Commission (AEC). *See* Atomic Energy Commission.

Atomic Energy Act Facilities
DOE facilities operated under authority of the Atomic Energy Act of 1954 as amended.

Atomic Energy Commission (AEC)
Federal agency created after World War II (1946) to manage the development, use, and control of nuclear energy for military and civilian application. The AEC was abolished by the Energy Reorganization Act of 1974 and succeeded by the Energy Research and Development Administration (now part of DOE) and the U.S. Nuclear Regulatory Commission.

Atomic Energy Defense Activity
Any activity of the Secretary of the DOE performed in whole or in part in carrying out any of the following functions: a) naval reactors development; b) weapons activities including defense inertial confinement fusion; c) verification and control technology; d) defense nuclear materials production; e) defense nuclear waste and materials by-products management; f) defense nuclear materials security and safeguards and security investigations; and g) defense research and development.

Atomic Mass
The mass of an atom of an element compared with 1/16 the mass of an oxygen 16 atom.

Atomic Number
The number of protons in the nucleus, and hence the number of positive charges on the nucleus. Also, the number of electrons outside the nucleus of a neutral atom.

Atomic Radiation
Radiation produced by energy changes in atomic nuclei or atomic electron clouds; ionizing radiation.

Atomic Weapon

Any device utilizing atomic energy, exclusive of the means for transporting or propelling the device (where such means are a separable and divisible part of the device), the principal purpose of which is for use as, or for development of, a weapon prototype, or a weapon test device.

Atomic Weight

The average weight (or mass) of all the isotopes of an element, as determined from the proportions in which they are present in a given element, compared with the mass of the 12 isotope of carbon (taken as precisely 12.000), that is the official international standard; measured in daltons.

Atomize

To divide a liquid into extremely minute particles, either by impact with a jet of steam or compressed air, or by passage through some mechanical device.

Atopy

A tendency or predisposition to allergic reactions.

Atrophy

Reduction in the size of a structure or organ resulting from lack of nourishment or functional activity, death and reabsorption of cells, diminished cellular proliferation, pressure, ischemia, or hormone changes.

ATSDR

See Agency for Toxic Substances and Disease Registry.

Attachment

A type of encumbrance, permitted only under special circumstances, that is placed against the real estate of a defendant in a pending lawsuit for monetary damages.

Attack Warning Signals

Three- to five-minute wavering tones on sirens or short blasts on horns or other devices, repeated as deemed necessary. It means that an actual attack against the U.S. has been detected and that pro-

tective action should be taken immediately. As a matter of national civil defense policy, attack warning signals are used for no other purposes and have no other meanings.

Attainment Area

Areas considered to have air quality as good as or better than the national ambient air quality standards as defined in the Clean Air Act. An area may be an attainment area for one pollutant and a nonattainment area for others.

Attainment Demonstration

A demonstration that a State Implementation Plan (SIP), as revised, will provide for attainment of the national ambient air quality standard for ozone by the applicable attainment date. This attainment demonstration must be based on photochemical grid modeling or any other analytical method determined by the Administrator, in the Administrator's discretion, to be at least as effective. *See* State Implementation Plan (SIP).

Attainment of Carbon Monoxide Levels

Means that a state has established to the satisfaction of the Administrator that, with respect to a carbon monoxide nonattainment area in such state, such state has attained the national ambient air quality standard for carbon monoxide by the applicable attainment date, excluding emissions emanating from outside the United States.

Attainment of Ozone Levels

Means that a state has established to the satisfaction of the Administrator that, with respect to an ozone nonattainment area in such state, such state has attained the national ambient air quality standard for ozone by the applicable attainment date, excluding emissions emanating from outside the United States.

Attainment of PM-10 Levels

Means that a state has established to the satisfaction of the Administrator that, with respect to a PM-10 nonattainment area in such state, such state would have attained the national ambient air quality standard for carbon monoxide by the applicable attainment date, but for emissions emanating from outside the United States.

Attention Signals

Three- to five-minute steady tones, sounded strictly at the option of and on the authority of local government officials. The signals may be activated for natural or manmade disasters as local authorities may determine and may also be used to call attention to essential emergency information. Use of the attention or alert signals should always be accompanied by a public explanation and instructions to the public over local broadcast stations or by other means.

Attenuation

1) The process of diminishing contaminant concentrations in groundwater, due to filtration, biodegradation, dilution, sorption, volatilization, and other processes. 2) The process by which a compound is reduced in concentration over time, through adsorption, degradation, dilution, and/or transformation. 3) The decrease in energy (or power) as a beam passes through an absorbing or scattering medium.

Attenuation Factor

The ratio of the incident radiation dose or dose rate to the radiation dose or dose rate transmitted through a shielding material. This is the reciprocal of the transmission factor.

Attitude

1) The position of a body as determined by the inclination of the axes to some frame of reference. If not otherwise specified, this frame of reference is fixed to the earth. 2) The grid bearing of the long axis of a specific target area.

Attitude Indicator

An instrument that displays the attitude of the aircraft by reference to sources of information that may be contained within the instrument or be external to it. When the sources of information are self-contained, the instrument may be referred to as an artificial horizon.

Attorney's Opinion

In real estate, the written opinion of an attorney-at-law regarding the marketability of title to real property based upon an examination of the abstract of title or the records in the county clerk and recorder's office.

Attractant

Chemicals or agent that lure insects or other pests by stimulating their sense of smell.

Attractive Nuisance

An insurance term applicable to any existing or visible condition that may attract attention and the desire to inspect the condition or circumstance. An example would be a construction site containing interesting or unusual machinery, devices, sand piles, or structures that can be climbed on and might attract children or others for closer investigation, thereby risking harm or damage to persons or property. Fencing and/or other security may be ways to control an attractive nuisance, although they may not always be sufficient. Owners must take reasonable precautions to protect children, even though they illegally trespass on the property.

Attrition

1) Wearing or grinding down of a substance by friction. A contributing factor in air pollution, as with dust. 2) The reduction of the effectiveness of a force caused by loss of personnel and material.

Attrition Rate

A factor, normally expressed as a percentage, reflecting the degree of losses of personnel or material due to various causes within a specified period of time.

Audit

1) Planned and documented investigations of a facility, item, or process to determine its adequacy and effectiveness, as well as compliance standing with established regulations, policies, specifications, and/or other pertinent documents. 2) Reviews and evaluations by an organization of its own internal safety/loss control program, pro-

gram plan implementation, and operations under its direct control. They may consist, for example, of management audits, functional audits, comprehensive audits.

Auricular
The feathers covering the opening of a bird's ear; pertaining to hearing.

Autecology
The study of the relationships between a single species and its environment.

Authentic Native Articles of Handicrafts and Clothing
Items composed wholly or in some significant respect of natural materials, and which are produced, decorated, or fashioned in the exercise of traditional native handicrafts without the use of pantographs, multiple carvers, or other mass copying devices. Traditional native handicrafts include, but are not limited to, weaving, carving, stitching, sewing, lacing, beading, drawing, and painting.

Authentication
1) A security measure designed to protect a communications system against acceptance of a fraudulent transmission or simulation by establishing the validity of a transmission, message, or originator. 2) A means of identifying individuals and verifying their eligibility to receive specific categories of information. 3) Evidence by proper signature or seal that a document is genuine and official.

Authorized Agency Representative
A person authorized to act on behalf of a public agency by law, by court order, or by a written agreement.

Authorized Inspectors, Boiler
Inspectors who are currently commissioned by the National Board of Boiler and Pressure Vessel Inspectors and employed as an Inspector by an authorized inspection agency.

Authorized Limits
Limits of any quantity specified by the competent authority for a given radiation practice or source pollutant. These are generally lower than the primary, secondary, or derived limits.

Authorized Officers
Any commissioned, warrant, or petty officer of the United States Coast Guard, or any officer or agent designated by the Director of the U.S. Fish and Wildlife Service, the Secretary of the Interior, the Secretary of Commerce, or the Secretary of the Treasury, or any officer designated by the head of a federal or state agency that has entered into an agreement with the Secretary of the Interior, Secretary of Commerce, Secretary of the Treasury, or Secretary of Transportation to enforce the Acts, or any Coast Guard personnel accompanying and acting under the direction of a person included above in this definition.

Authorized Officials
Federal or state officials with the delegated authority to act on behalf of the federal or state agency designated, or officials designated by Native American Indian tribes, pursuant to Section 126(d) of CERCLA, to perform a natural resource damage assessment.

Authorized Representatives
People responsible for the overall operation of a facility or an operational unit (i.e., part of a facility); for example, plant managers, superintendents, or people of equivalent responsibility.

Authorized Weapons
Weapons authorized by the DOE and issued by the responsible contractor or departmental element to be used by protective force personnel in the performance of their duties.

Autoignition Temperature
The lowest temperature at which a gas or vapor-air mixture will ignite from its own heat source or a contacted heated surface without a spark or flame.

Automatic Data Handling
A generalization of automatic data processing that includes the aspect of data transfer.

Automatic Data Processing
The branch of science and technology concerned with methods and techniques relating to data processing performed by automatic means; data processing largely performed by automatic means.

Automatic Guided Vehicle Systems
Advanced material-handling or conveying systems that involve a driverless vehicle that follows a guidepath.

Automatic Incident Actions
The automatic mitigation of large process water leaks.

Automatic Message Processing System
Any organized assembly of resources and methods used to collect, process, and distribute messages by computerized or automatic means.

Automatic Operation
The time during which robots are performing programmed tasks through unattended program execution.

Automatic Rifles
Firearms that employ either gas pressure or recoil force and mechanical spring action in ejecting the empty cartridge case after the first shot, loading the next cartridge from the magazine, firing and ejecting that cartridge, and repeating the above cycle as long as the pressure on the trigger is maintained or until the ammunition is exhausted.

Automatic Safety Shutdown Devices
Safety controls (other than operating controls) that monitor certain essential operating conditions of a fired boiler and that will shut down the boiler in the proper sequence when any of the essential conditions vary from set limits and require the services of the attendant to place the boiler back in operation.

Automatic Storage and Retrieval Systems
Storage racks linked through automatically controlled conveyors and an automatic storage/retrieval machine or machines that ride on floor mounted guiderails and power driven wheels.

Automatically Controlled Boiler
A boiler equipped with devices to maintain the burner firing conditions, the pressure and/or temperature, and the water level or water content within the predetermined limits without manual manipulation.

Autoradiographies
Records of radiation from radioactive material in an object, made by placing the object in close proximity to a photographic emulsion.

Autotrophic
An organism that produces food from inorganic substances; producing food from inorganic substances.

AUVs
An acronym for Autonomous Undersea Vehicles.

Auxiliary Feedwater
Backup feedwater supply used during nuclear plant start-up and shutdown; also know as emergency feedwater.

Auxiliary Water Supply
Any water supply other than that received from a public water system.

AV
An acronym for Adjusted Volume for refrigerators, refrigerator-freezers, and freezers, as defined in the applicable test procedure.

Available Payload
The passenger and/or cargo capacity expressed in weight and/or space available to the user.

Average Annual Energy Use
The estimated aggregate (per household) annual energy use (in kilowatt-hours or Btu equivalent)

of electronic consumer products used by households in the United States, divided by the number of households that use the products.

Average Annual Net Earnings
One half of any net earnings of a business or farm operation before federal, state, and local income taxes during the two taxable years immediately preceding the taxable year in which the business or farm operation moves from the real property acquired. If the two taxable years immediately preceding displacement are not representative, a more representative two-year period, beginning with the two tax years prior to the initiation of negotiations on the project is used. In the case of a corporate owner, earnings shall include any compensation paid to the spouse or dependents of the owner of a majority interest in the corporation. For the purpose of determining majority ownership, stock held by a husband, his wife, and their dependent children shall be treated as one unit.

Average Load
The midpoint between the minimum and maximum instantaneous load for a given month.

Average Throughput
The liquid volume transported by a pipeline during a period divided by the number of days in the period.

Averaging Time
The time period over which a function (e.g., average concentration of an air pollutant) is measured, yielding a time-weighted average.

Aversion Response
Movement of the eyelid, the head, or other part of the body to avoid an exposure to a noxious stimulant, bright light, etc. It can occur within 0.25 seconds, and it includes the blink reflex time.

Aviation Fuels
Aviation gasoline, naphtha jet fuels, and kerosene jet fuel.

Aviation Gasoline
All special grades of gasoline for use in aviation reciprocating engines, as given in ASTM Specification D910, including all refinery products within the gasoline range that are to be marketed straight or in blends as aviation gasoline without further processing, and also including finisher components in the gasoline range that will be used for blending or compounding aviation gasoline.

Aviation Medicine
The special field of medicine that is related to the biological and psychological problems of flight.

Aviation Operations
Any operations of aircraft or airports, or the provision of any aviation support services thereto.

Aviation Safety
Established procedures that provide guidance to ensure that DOE and DOE contractor aviation operations are conducted in the safest manner possible, and that, to the extent possible, passenger and hazardous cargo air carrying operations maintain a level of safety equivalent to that attained by United States air carriers operating under 14 CFR 121.

Awareness Barrier, Physical and/or Visual
Signs, fences, roping, and other types of barriers that warn a person of an approaching or present hazard.

Awareness Signal
A device that warns a person of an approaching or present hazard by means of audible sound or visible light.

AWS
An acronym for the American Welding Society.

AWWA Standard
An official standard developed and approved by the American Water Works Association (AWWA).

Axial Route

A route running through the rear area and into the forward area.

Axil

The angle between the upper surface of a stalk and its stem or between a branch and its trunk.

Axis

The line about which a rotating body, such as a tool, turns.

Axon

The part of a nerve cell that conducts nervous impulses away from the nerve cell body to the remainder of the cell (i.e., dendrites); large number of fibrils enveloped by a segmented myelin sheath.

Axonal

Pertaining to an axon.

Azimuth Angle

An angle measured clockwise in the horizontal plane between a reference direction and any other line.

B

B&RC
An acronym for Budget and Reporting Code.

BAAQMD
An acronym for Bay Area Air Quality Management District.

Backfit Reviews
Safety reviews of a system, process, procedure, or plant already in existence or in process. Such reviews may be conducted due to changing conditions or requirements or, due to the fact that an adequate system safety review had not been conducted previously.

Background Count
The evidence or effect on a detector of radiation, other than that which it is desired to detect, caused by any agent. In connection with health protection, the background count usually includes radiations produced by naturally occurring radioactivity and cosmic rays.

Background Level
In air pollution control, the concentration of air pollutants in a definite area during a fixed period of time prior to the starting up or the stoppage of a source of emission under control. In toxic substances monitoring, the average presence in the environment, originally referring to naturally occurring phenomena.

Background Radiation
1) Nuclear (or ionizing) radiations arising from within the body and from the surroundings to which individuals are always exposed. 2) Ionizing radiation arising from radioactive material other than the one directly under consideration. Background radiation due to cosmic rays and natural radioactivity is always present. There may also be background radiation due to the presence of radioactive substances in other parts of the building, in the building material itself, for example.

Background Research
A preliminary investigation of facility/project needs, relevant permit issues, and existing information for establishing compliance goals and objectives prior to further investigation. This data has often already been compiled by the owner/operator; if so, that data should be verified and included. The scope and nature of environmental background data depends on the perceived impacts of the project to public health, welfare, and the environment. The objective is to obtain and organize as much useful (factual) information as possible on a facility or project's environmental impacts and to analyze existing data by prioritizing future research needs. This data helps to: define information needs and compliance tasks; identify sources of information; familiarize the planner with the facility/project objectives, compliance philosophy, management, and operations; and create an environmental database for future reports and further analysis.

Background Soil pH
The pH of the soil prior to the addition of substances.

Backup
In cartography, an image printed on the reverse side of a map sheet already printed on one side. Also the printing of such images.

Backup Systems
Systems that are in backup status when a malfunction is detected.

BACT
An acronym for Best Available Control Technology. An emission limitation based on the maximum degree of emission reduction that (considering energy, environmental, and economic impacts, and other costs) is achievable through application of production processes and available methods, systems, and techniques. In no event does BACT permit emissions in excess of those allowed under any applicable Clean Air Act provisions. Use of the BACT concept is allowable on a case by case basis for major new or modified emissions sources in attainment areas and applies to each regulated pollutant. *See* Best Available Control Technology.

Bacteria
Microscopic living organisms that can aid in pollution control by consuming or breaking down organic matter in sewage or by similarly acting on oil spills or other water pollutants. Bacteria in soil, water, or air can also cause human, animal, and plant health problems. The singular form of bacteria is bacterium.

Bactericide
A pesticide used to control or destroy bacteria, typically in homes, schools, or in hospitals.

Baffle
A plate, grating, or refractory wall used to block, hinder, or divert a flow, or to redirect the path of a substance.

Baffle Chamber
In incinerator design, a chamber designed to promote the settling of fly ash and coarse particulate matter by changing the direction and/or reducing the velocity of the gases produced by the combustion of the refuse or sludge.

Baghouse Filters
Large fabric bags, usually made of glass fibers, used to eliminate intermediate and large (greater than 20 microns in diameter) particles. These devices operate in a way similar to the bag of an electric vacuum cleaner, passing the air and smaller particulate matter, while entrapping the larger particulates.

Balance Station Zero
See Reference Datum.

Baleen
A species descriptor that refers to plates located in the upper jaws of whales that filter plankton from sea water.

Balers
Machines used to compress solid waste, primary material, or recoverable material, with or without binding, to a density or form that will support handling and transportation as a material unit rather than requiring a disposable or reusable container. This specifically excludes briquatters and stationary compaction equipment that are used to compact materials into disposable or reusable containers.

Baling
Compacting solid waste into blocks to reduce volume and simplify handling.

Ballast, Railroads
Crushed stone used in a railroad bed to support the ties, hold the track in line, and help drainage.

Ballast Efficacy Factor
The relative light output divided by the power input of a fluorescent lamp ballast, as measured

under test conditions specified in ANSI standards, or as may be prescribed by the Secretary.

Ballast Input Voltage
The rated input voltage of a fluorescent lamp ballast.

Ballast Water
Any water and associated sediments used to manipulate the trim and stability of a vessel.

Ballistic Separator
A machine that sorts organic from inorganic matter for composting.

Ballistics
The science or art that deals with the motion, behavior, appearance, or modification of missiles or other vehicles acted upon by propellants, wind, gravity, temperature, or any other modifying substance, condition, or force.

Balut
Shell eggs from any species of fowl, removed from incubation after partial embryo development and intended for human consumption.

Band Application
In pesticides, the spreading of chemicals over, or next to, each row of plants in a field.

Bank
A mass of soil rising above a digging level.

Banking
A system for recording qualified air emission reductions for later use in bubble, offset, or netting transactions. *See* Emissions Trading.

Banned Hazardous Substance
1) Any toy, or other article intended for use by children, that is a hazardous substance, or that bears or contains a hazardous substance in such manner as to be susceptible of access by a child to whom such toy or other article is entrusted. 2) Any hazardous substance intended, or packaged in a form suitable, for use in the household, that the Commission by regulation classifies as a banned hazardous substance on the basis of a finding that, notwithstanding such cautionary labeling as is or may be required under this chapter for that substance, the degree or nature of the hazard involved in the presence or use of such substance in households is such that the objective of the protection of the public health and safety can be adequately served only by keeping such substance, when so intended or packaged, out of the channels of interstate commerce; provided that the Commission, by regulation, (i) shall exempt from Clause 1) of this paragraph articles, such as chemical sets, which by reason of their functional purpose require the inclusion of the hazardous substance involved or necessarily present an electrical, mechanical, or thermal hazard, and which bear labeling giving adequate directions and warnings for safe use and are intended for use by children who have attained sufficient maturity, and may reasonably be expected, to read and heed such directions and warnings, and (ii) shall exempt from clause 1), and provide for the labeling of, common fireworks (including toy paper caps, cone fountains, cylinder fountains, whistles without report, and sparklers) to the extent that it determines that such articles can be adequately labeled to protect the purchasers and users thereof.

Bar
An elongated landform generated by waves and currents, usually running parallel to the shore, composed predominantly of unconsolidated sand, gravel, stones, cobbles, or rubble and with water on two sides.

Bar Screen
In wastewater treatment, a device used to remove large solids.

Barbel
A species descriptor that means a slender, whiskerlike sensory organ on the head of a fish or other aquatic animal.

Barges
Vessels that are not self-propelled.

Barometer
An instrument used for measuring atmospheric pressure.

Barometric Altitude
The altitude determined by a barometric altimeter by reference to a pressure level and calculated according to the standard atmosphere laws. It corresponds to the difference in altitude between the altimeter pressure level and the mean sea level pressure.

Barred
A species descriptor that means white or light colored lines; typically refers to barring on the dorsal side of a fish or the breast/belly of a bird.

Barrel (bbl)
A liquid-volume measure equal to 42 United States gallons at 60° Fahrenheit; used in expressing quantities of petroleum-based products.

Barrier
1) A physical means of separating persons from a restricted envelope (space). 2) Anything used to control, prevent, or impede energy flows. Types of barriers include physical, equipment design, warning devices, procedures and work processes, knowledge and skills, and supervision. Barriers may be control or safety barriers or act as both. 3) A coordinated series of obstacles designed or employed to channel, direct, restrict, delay, or stop the movement of an opposing force and to impose additional losses in personnel, time, and equipment on the opposing force. Barriers can exist naturally, be manmade, or a combination of both.

Barrier Coating(s)
Layers of a material that act to obstruct or prevent passage of something through a surface that is to be protected, e.g., grout, caulk, or various sealing compounds. Sometimes used with polyurethane membranes to prevent corrosion or oxidation of metal surfaces, chemical impacts on various materials, or, for example, to prevent soil-gas-borne radon from moving through walls, cracks, or joints in a house.

BART
An acronym for Best Available Retrofit Technology.

Basal
A species descriptor that means located at or pertaining to the base.

Basal Application
In pesticides, the application of a chemical on plant stems or tree trunks just above the soil line.

Basalt
A fine-grained igneous rock, composed of calcium-rich plagioclase feldspar and a pyroxene, with or without olivine.

Base
A compound that reacts with an acid to form a salt; another term for alkali. It turns litmus paper blue.

Base Benefits
The benefits of the project used in the computation of economic justification.

Base Course
The first layer of underlying material installed prior to the placement of a roadway pavement wearing surface.

Base Development Plan
A plan for the facilities, installations, and bases required to support military operations.

Base Element
See Base Unit.

Base Files
Files containing the base data from a compliance agreement. These are a) OSHA CSA Tracking System files containing specific information about the corporation and each plant or facility covered by the CSA, and milestone data from the agreement; and, b) information on the initiating violation(s) provided by OFP with revised abatement dates as reflected in the compliance agree-

ment and the dollar amount of penalties to be imposed if necessary.

Base Flow

That part of stream discharge not attributable to direct runoff from precipitation or snowmelt, usually sustained by groundwater discharge.

Base Line

1) In surveying, a line established with more than usual care, to which surveys are referred for coordination and correlation. 2) In photogrammetry, the line between the principal points of two consecutive vertical air photographs. It is usually measured on one photograph after the principal point of the other has been transferred. 3) In radio navigation systems, the shorter arc of the great circle joining two radio transmitting stations of a navigation system. 4) In triangulation, the side of one of a series of coordinated triangles the length of which is measured with prescribed accuracy and precision and from which lengths of the other triangle sides are obtained by computation.

Base Load Unit

A generating unit that is normally operated during a given month to provide all or part of the base load of an electric utility system and that, consequently, is operated essentially at a constant output.

Base Map

A map or chart showing certain fundamental information, used as a base upon which additional data of specialized nature are compiled or overprinted. Also, a map containing all the information from which maps showing specialized information can be prepared. *See* Chart Base; Map.

Base Period

That period of time for which factors were determined for use in current planning and programming.

Base Shear

The total design lateral force or shear at the base of a structure.

Base Surge

A cloud that rolls out from the bottom of the column produced by a subsurface burst of a nuclear weapon. For underwater bursts, the surge is, in effect, a cloud of liquid droplets that has the property of flowing almost as if it were a homogeneous fluid. For subsurface land bursts the surge is made up of small solid particles but still behaves like a fluid.

Baseline

The condition or conditions that would have existed at an assessment area had the discharge of oil or release of the hazardous substance under investigation not occurred.

Baseline Concentration

With respect to a pollutant, the ambient concentration levels that exist at the time of the first application for a permit in an area subject to this part, based on air quality data available in the Environmental Protection Agency or a state air pollution control agency and on such monitoring data as the permit applicant is required to submit. Such ambient concentration levels shall take into account all projected emissions in, or that may affect, such area from any major emitting facility on which construction commenced prior to January 6, 1975, but which has not begun operation by the date of the baseline air quality concentration determination. Emissions of sulfur oxides and particulate matter from any major emitting facility on which construction commenced after January 6, 1975, shall not be included in the baseline and shall be counted against the maximum allowable increases in pollutant concentrations established under this part.

Baseline Data

A collection of information regarding the existing conditions of a specific and geographically defined environmental area, usually taking into account the built, natural, wildlife, human, cultural, and economic environmental characteristics.

Baseline Emissions

The total amount of actual VOC or NOx emissions from all anthropogenic sources in the area during the calendar year 1990, excluding emissions that would be eliminated under the new regulations.

Baseline Vehicles

Representative model year 1990 vehicles.

Baseload

The minimum load of an electric (or gas) utility over a given period of time. Units in baseload service are operated at full capacity all the time.

Bases

The level at which the earthquake motions are considered to be imparted to the structure or tho level at which the structure as a dynamic vibrator is supported.

BASI

An acronym for Best Available Scientific Information.

Basic Causes

Root causes.

Basic Psychological Operations Study

A document that describes succinctly the characteristics of a country, geographical area, or region that are most pertinent to psychological operations, and that can serve as an immediate reference for the planning and conduct of psychological operations.

Basic Research

1) Research directed toward the increase of knowledge, the primary aim being a greater knowledge or understanding of the subject under study. 2) Systematic, fundamental study directed toward a greater scientific knowledge or understanding of subjects bearing on national energy needs. *See* Applied Research; Research.

Basic Undertakings

The essential things, expressed in broad terms, that must be done in order to implement an implementation task or concept successfully. These may include review of historic documents on regulatory standing, environmental and socioeconomic issues, and other measures.

Basin

An area drained by the main stream and tributaries of a major river; includes rivers and their tributaries, lakes, and other bodies of water or portions thereof.

Basis of Issue

Authority that prescribes the number of items to be issued to an individual, a unit, a military organization, or for a unit piece of equipment.

BAT

An acronym for Best Available Technology.

Batches

Specific quantities or lot of test or control substances that have been characterized according to 40 CFR 792.105(a).

Bathymetric Contour

See Depth Contour.

Battle Damage Assessment (BDA)

The timely and accurate estimate of damage resulting from the application of military force, either lethal or nonlethal, against a predetermined objective. Battle damage assessment can be applied to the employment of all types of weapon systems (air, ground, naval, and special forces weapon systems) throughout the range of military operations. Battle damage assessment is primarily an intelligence responsibility with required inputs and coordination from the operators. Battle damage assessment is composed of physical damage assessment, functional damage assessment, and target system assessment. *See* Bomb Damage Assessment.

Battle Damage Repair
Essential repair, which may be improvised, carried out rapidly in a battle environment in order to return damaged or disabled equipment to temporary service.

BBC
An acronym for Balanced Biological Communities.

BCL
An acronym for Battelle Columbus Laboratories.

BDAT
An acronym for Best Demonstrated Available Technology.

Beach
1) A sloping landform on the shore of larger water bodies, generated by waves and currents and extending from the water to a distinct break in landform or substrate type (e.g., a foredune, cliff, or bank). 2) The area extending from the shoreline inland to a marked change in physiographic form or material, or to the line of permanent vegetation (coastline). 3) In amphibious military operations, that portion of the shoreline designated for landing of a tactical organization.

Beach Capacity
An estimate, expressed in terms of measurement tons, or weight tons, of cargo that may be unloaded over a designated strip of shore per day. *See* Clearance Capacity; Port Capacity.

Beachhead
A designated area on a hostile or potentially hostile shore that, when seized and held, ensures the continuous landing of troops and material, and provides maneuver space requisite for subsequent projected operations ashore.

Beak or Bill
A species descriptor for the appendage birds use to gather food; beak also refers to the cone-shaped structure in mussels.

Beak Cavities
A species descriptor for the hollow portion in the tip of the umbo of a bivalve mollusk shell.

Beam
A collection of rays that may be parallel, convergent, or divergent.

Beam Diameter
The distance between diametrically opposed points in the cross section of a circular beam.

Bearing
The horizontal angle at a given point measured clockwise from a specific datum point to a second point. *See* Grid Bearing; Relative Bearing; True Bearing.

Bearing Capacity
A loading intensity that the bearing materials can sustain without such deformation as would result in settlement damaging to the structure.

Bearing Strength
The maximum bearing stress that will not fail a composite when applied through a cylindrical fastener surface.

Bearing Stress
Applied load divided by bearing area (hole diameter times thickness).

Bearing Wall Systems
Structural systems without complete vertical load carrying space frames.

Beaten Zone
The area on the ground upon which the cone of fire falls.

Becquerel (Bq)
A unit of radioactivity. One becquerel is one nuclear transformation per second.

Bedrock
A general term for the rock, usually solid, that underlies soil or other unconsolidated material.

Beetles
Tank top leak detectors.

Behavioral Stereotypes
The "normal" or fixed patterns in which a person thinks and acts or reacts in a given situation. These patterns may be altered through practice, but under stress a person will likely return to the original pattern of behavior. An example of a behavioral stereotype is the way in which a person crosses his/her arms. We consistently place the same arm on top of the other and it takes a conscious effort to cross the arms with the other one on top.

Bell Hole
An additional excavation made into the sides or bottom of a trench to provide additional work space.

Belled Excavation
A part of a shaft or footing excavation, usually near the bottom and bell-shaped, that makes the cross-sectional area at that point larger than that above.

Below Regulatory Concern
A definable amount of low level waste that can be deregulated with minimal risk to the public.

Belowground Releases
Releases to the subsurface of the land and to groundwater. This includes, but is not limited to, releases from the belowground portions of an underground portion of an underground storage tank, as well as belowground releases associated with overfills and transfer operations as the regulated substance moves to or from an underground storage tank.

BEN
An abbreviation for benefit; the name of EPA's computer model for analyzing a violator's economic gain from not complying with the law.

Bench Marks
Survey control monuments installed to provide vertical control for construction purposes. Official elevation marker used in topographic surveys by the USGS (United States Geological Survey).

Benching
A method of excavation whereby the faces of an excavation or trench are widened progressively outward with respect to the bottom by a specific series of horizontal and vertical cuts to provide protection against the hazard of moving ground.

Benchmarking
The use of plant or animal species to measure pollution based on assessments (or benchmark) of population level and growth characteristics, against which changes can be monitored and evaluated.

Benefaction
Preliminary conditioning of an ore for refinement.

Beneficial Organisms
Any pollinating insect or any post predator, parasite, pathogen, or other biological control agent that functions naturally or as part of an integrated pest management program to control another pest.

Beneficial Use
A use of the environment that benefits a population, mitigates any adverse environmental impacts, and/or enhances built or natural environs.

Beneficiary
1) The person who receives or is to receive the benefits resulting from certain acts. 2) One receiving profits or advantages. 3) One for whose benefit a trust is created.

Benign

A condition of a neoplasm (tumor) in which the morphological and behavioral characteristics of the tumor differ minimally from the tissue from which it originates. A benign neoplasm (as distinct from malignant) may expand, but remains encapsulated, and has limited potential to invade local structure and proliferate.

Benthic

A species descriptor that means pertaining to organisms living on the bottom of a lake or the sea.

Benthic Organisms (Benthos)

Forms of aquatic plant or animal life that is found on or near the bottom of a stream, lake, or ocean. The presence or absence of certain benthic organisms can be used as an indicator of water quality.

Benthic Region

The bottom layer of a body of water.

Bentonite

A fine clay formed by the alteration of volcanic ash deposits; these particular types of colloidal clays swell when wet and form a gel membrane.

Benzene (C_6H_6)

A highly flammable narcotic liquid carcinogen. It is the simplest aromatic hydrocarbon found in coal tar; used extensively as an industrial solvent, in labs, and in the manufacture of styrene, lacquers, varnishes, and paints.

Berm

A curb or dike constructed to control water and prevent roadway runoff waters from discharging onto roadside slopes and/or to provide material for subsequent road maintenance.

Bernoulli's Equation

Under conditions of steady flow of water, the sum of the velocity head, the pressure head, and the head due to elevation at any given point is equal to the sum of these heads at any other point plus or minus the head losses between the points due to friction or other causes.

Beryllium

1) A poisonous metallic element used in the production of corrosion-resistant, nonferrous alloys, in X-ray tubes, and as a moderator at nuclear plants. 2) An airborne metal that can be hazardous to human health when inhaled. It is discharged by machine shops, ceramic and propellant plants, and foundries. 3) The element beryllium. Where weights or concentrations are specified, such weights or concentrations apply to beryllium only, excluding the weight or concentration of any associated elements.

Beryllium Alloys

Metals to which beryllium has been added in order to increase its beryllium content and that contain more than 0.1% beryllium by weight.

Beryllium Containing Wastes

Materials contaminated with beryllium and/or beryllium compounds used or generated during any process or operation performed by a source subject to the CAA and 40 CFR 61.31.

Beryllium Ores

Any naturally occurring materials mined or gathered for their beryllium content.

Beryllium Propellants

Propellants incorporating beryllium.

Best Available Controls (BAC)

The degree of emissions reduction that the Administrator determines, on the basis of technological and economic feasibility, health, environmental, and energy impacts, is achievable through the application of the most effective equipment, measures, processes, methods, systems or techniques, including chemical reformulation, product or feedstock substitution, repackaging, and directions for use, consumption, storage, or disposal.

Best Available Control Technology (BACT)

1) An emission limitation based on the maximum degree of emission reduction that (considering energy, environmental, and economic impacts and

other costs) is achievable through application of production processes and available methods, systems, and techniques. In no event does BACT permit emissions in excess of those allowed under any applicable Clean Air Act provisions.

2) Treatment technologies that have been shown through actual use to yield the greatest environmental benefit among competing technologies that are practically available.

The determination of BACTs takes into account energy, environmental and economic effects, and other costs. Use of the BACT concept is allowable on a case-by-case basis for major new or modified emissions sources in attainment areas and applies to each regulated pollutant. *See* 42 USC 7491 Section 169.

Best Available Retrofit Technology (BART)
An emission limitation based on the degree of reduction achievable through the application of the best system of continuous emission reduction for each pollutant that is emitted by an existing stationary facility. The emission limitation must be established, on a case-by-case basis, taking into consideration the technology available, the costs of compliance, the energy and nonair quality environmental impacts of compliance, any pollution control equipment in use or in existence at the source, the remaining useful life of the source, and the degree of improvement in visibility that may reasonably be anticipated to result from the use of such technology.

Best Available Technology (BAT)
The preferred technology for treating a particular process liquid waste, selected from among others after taking into account factors related to technology, economics, public policy, and other parameters. As used in this definition, BAT is not a specific level of treatment, but the conclusion of a selection process that includes indepth analyses of several treatment alternatives.

Best Available Technology Economically Achievable (BATEA)
Originally described under Section 304(b)(2)(B) of the Clean Water Act, this level of control is generally described as the best technology currently in use and includes controls on toxic pollutants.

Best Management Practices (BMP)
1) Procedures or controls other than effluent limitations to prevent or reduce pollution of surface water (includes runoff control, spill prevention, and operating procedures). 2) Methods, measures, or practices selected by an agency to meet its nonpoint source control needs. BMPs include, but are not limited to, structural and nonstructural controls and operation and maintenance procedures applied before, during, or after pollution-producing activities to reduce or eliminate the introduction of pollutants into receiving waters. Within a Tiger Team Assessment, BMP findings are derived from regulatory agency guidance, DOE draft orders, accepted industry practices, and professional judgment.

Beta Decay
Radioactive decay in which a beta particle is emitted or in which orbital electron capture occurs.

Beta-Minus Decay Radioisotopes
Hazardous radionuclide substances such as: antimony-125; cerium-144; cerium-141; cesium-137; cesium-134; cobalt-60; cobalt-58; iodine-131; radium-228; ruthenium-103; strontium-90; tellurium-132; thorium-232; tritium (hydrogen-3); zinc-65; and zirconium-96.

Beta-Particles
1) Electrons emitted by radioactive decay; moderate penetrative powers and can damage living tissue. 2) Elementary particles emitted by radioactive decay that may cause skin burns. They are halted by a thin sheet of paper. 3) Charged particles emitted from the nucleus of an atom, having mass and charge equal in magnitude to electrons. An electron, of either positive or negative charge, that has been emitted by an atomic nucleus or neutron in a nuclear transformation.

Beta Rays

Streams of high speed electrons or positrons of nuclear origin more penetrating but less ionizing than alpha rays.

BExC

An acronym for Benefits (of control) Exceed Costs (of control).

BFA

An acronym for Blank Fire Adapter.

BFI

An acronym for Bottom Fitting Insert.

BG

An acronym for Blanket Gas; Burial Ground.

BIA

An acronym for the Bureau of Indian Affairs, of the United States Department of Interior.

Bicuspid

A species descriptor that means having two points at the cusp; a tooth with two points.

Biennial-Monocarpic

A species descriptor that means producing a single fruit every other year.

BIF

An acronym for Boiler/Industrial Furnaces.

Bilirubin

A red pigment that results from normal and abnormal destruction of red blood cells.

Bin Storage

Storage of small hazardous and nonhazardous items, materials and equipment in an individual compartment or subdivision of a storage unit in less than bulk quantities. *See* Bulk Storage; Storage.

Binary Chemical Munition

A munition in which chemical substances, held in separate containers, react when mixed or combined as a result of being fired, launched, or otherwise initiated to produce a chemical agent. *See* Munition.

Binary Cycle

An energy-recovery system that results in heat exchange between two separate fluid-circulation systems. The purpose of a binary cycle is to obtain higher efficiencies from the energy source.

Binding

The fastening or securing of items to a movable platform called a pallet. *See* Palletized Unit Load.

Bioaccumulation

A process where chemicals are retained in fatty body tissue and increase in concentration over time because the rate of intake exceeds the organism's ability to remove the substance from the body.

Bioaccumulative

Substances that increase in concentration in living organisms (that are very slowly metabolized or excreted) as they breathe contaminated air, drink contaminated water, or eat contaminated food. *See* Biomagnification.

Bioassay

1) The quantification, under controlled conditions, of the effects of a substance on an organism or part of an organism. 2) A test conducted in living organisms to determine the hazard or potency of a chemical by its effect on animals, isolated tissues, or microorganisms. 3) Using living organisms to measure the effect of a substance, factor, or condition by comparing before-and-after data. The term is often used to mean cancer bioassays. 4) (NCRP) Procedures used to determine the kind, quality, location and/or retention or radionuclides in the body by direct (in vivo) measurements or by in vitro analysis of material excreted or removed from the body.

Bioavailability

1) A measure of the degree to which a dose of a substance becomes physiologically available to the body tissues depending upon absorption, distribution, metabolism, and excretion rates. 2) Refers to the rate and extent to which the administered compound is absorbed, i.e., reaches the systemic circulation.

Biochemical(s)

1) Chemical processes or substances produced by, or related to, the activity of living organisms. 2) Chemicals that are either naturally occurring or identical to naturally occurring substances. Examples include hormones, pheromones, and enzymes. Biochemicals function as pesticides through nontoxic, nonlethal modes of action, such as disrupting the mating pattern of insects, regulating growth, or acting as repellents. Biochemicals tend to be environmentally compatible and are thus important to integrated pest management programs.

Biochemical Oxygen Demand

1) The amount of oxygen used for biochemical oxidation by a unit volume of water, at a given temperature, over a specific time frame, and under specified conditions.

Biocides

Agents that kill living organisms.

Bioclimatology

The scientific study of the relationship between living organisms and the effects of climate.

Bioconcentration

Same as bioaccumulation; refers to the increase in concentration of a chemical in an organism.

Bioconversion

A general term describing the conversion of one form of energy into another by plants or microorganisms. Synthesis of organic compounds from carbon dioxide by plants is bioconversion of solar energy into stored chemical energy. Similarly, digestion of solid wastes or sewage by microorganisms to form methane is bioconversion of one form of stored chemical energy into another, more useful, form.

Biodegradable

1) The ability of a substance to be broken down physically and/or chemically by microorganisms. 2) The ability to break down or decompose rapidly under natural conditions and processes. Many chemicals, food scraps, cotton, wool, and paper are biodegradable; plastics and polyester generally are not.

Biodiversity

The number and variety of different organisms in the ecological complexes in which they naturally occur. Organisms are organized at many levels, ranging from complete ecosystems to the biochemical structures that are the molecular basis of heredity. Thus, the term encompasses different ecosystems, species, and genes that must be present for a healthy environment. A large number of species must characterize the food chain, representing multiple predator-prey relationships.

Bioecology

A collective term relating to plant and animal ecology as a single discipline.

Bioengineering

The employment of biochemical processes on an industrial level, to produce drugs or foodstuffs for humans or livestock; including the means to exploit the recycling processes thereof.

Biogeographical Province

An area of the earth's surface identified by the species of flora and fauna that inhabit it.

Biogeography

The study of geographical distribution of plants and animals and the factors influencing distribution.

Biological Additives

Microbiological cultures, enzymes, or nutrient additives that are deliberately introduced into an oil discharge for the specific purpose of encouraging biodegradation to mitigate the effects of the discharge.

Biological Agent

A microorganism that causes disease in personnel, plants, or animals or causes the deterioration of material. *See* Biological Operation; Biological Weapon; Chemical Agent.

Biological Ammunition

A type of ammunition, the filler of which is primarily a biological agent.

Biological Assessments

Information prepared by or under the direction of the federal agency concerning listed and proposed species and designated and proposed critical habitat that may be present in the action area and the evaluation potential effects of the action on such species and habitat.

Biological Clearance Rate

The fractional change per unit time in the number of atoms of a stable chemical element in a tissue, an organ, or the whole body occurring when the removal of that element follows an approximately exponential function.

Biological Control

The control of pests and contamination using natural means; the use of animals and organisms that eat or otherwise kill or out-compete pests.

Biological Defense

The methods, plans, and procedures involved in establishing and executing defensive measures against attacks using biological agents.

Biological Environment

Conditions found in an area resulting from direct or persisting effects of biological weapons.

Biological Half-Life

The time required for the concentration of a chemical present in the body or in a particular body compartment to decrease by one-half

through biological processes such as metabolism and excretion.

Biological Half-Time

The time required for a biological system to eliminate, by natural processes, half the amount of a substance (e.g., radioactive material) that has entered it. Same as biological half-life.

Biological Magnification

The process whereby certain substances such as pesticides or heavy metals move up the food chain, work their way into a river or lake, and are eaten by aquatic organisms such as fish that in turn are eaten by large birds, animals, or humans. The substances become concentrated in tissues or internal organs as they move up the chain. *See* Bioaccumulative.

Biological Monitoring

1) Periodic examination of blood, urine, or any other blood substance to determine the extent of body absorption and retention of toxic materials. 2) Monitoring chemicals or their metabolites in biological materials (e.g., blood, urine, breath) to estimate exposure or to detect biochemical changes in the exposed subject before or during the onset of adverse health effects. Sometimes refers to a specific indicator for a particular disease/functional disturbance.

Biological Operation

Employment of biological agents to produce casualties in personnel or animals and damage to plants or material; or defense against such employment.

Biological Opinion

A document that states an opinion as to whether or not a federal action is likely to jeopardize the continued existence of listed species or result in the destruction or adverse modification of critical habitat.

Biological Oxidation

The way bacteria and microorganisms feed on and decompose complex organic materials. Used in self-purification of water bodies and in activated sludge wastewater treatment.

Biological Oxygen Demand (BOD)

1) A measure of the oxygen required to break down organic materials in water. Higher organic loads require larger amounts of oxygen and may reduce the amount of oxygen available for fish and aquatic life below acceptable levels. The greater the BOD, the greater the degree of pollution. 2) A standard test used in assessing wastewater strength.

Biological Pesticides

Certain microorganisms, including bacteria, fungi, viruses, and protozoa that are effective in controlling target pests. These agents usually do not have toxic effects on animals and people and do not leave toxic or persistent chemical residues in the environment.

Biological Processes

A general term that refers to various processes, including, but not limited to, the following: aeration, diffused air process, mechanical aeration, bioassays, biological magnification, biological oxidation, composting, decomposition, denitrification, destruction, differentiation, evapotranspiration, genetic engineering, infiltration, natural selection, osmosis, reverse osmosis, photosynthesis, regeneration, sterilization, transpiration.

Biological Resources

Natural resources referred to in CERCLA as fish and wildlife and other biota. Fish and wildlife include marine and freshwater aquatic and terrestrial species; game, nongame, and commercial species; and threatened, endangered, and state sensitive species. Other biota encompass shellfish, terrestrial and aquatic plants, and other living organisms not otherwise listed in this definition.

Biological Treatment

A treatment technology that uses bacteria to consume waste. This treatment breaks down organic materials.

Biological Warfare

See Biological Operation.

Biological Weapon

An item of material that projects, disperses, or disseminates a biological agent including arthropod vectors.

Biologically Significant Effect

A response in an organism or other biological system that is considered to have a substantial or noteworthy effect (positive or negative) on the well-being of the biological system. Used to distinguish statistically significant effects or changes, which may or may not be meaningful to the general state of health of the system.

Biology

The study of all organisms; includes paleontology.

Biomagnification

The increase of tissue accumulation in species higher in the natural food chain as contaminated food species are eaten.

Biomass

The total quantity of living organisms of one or more species per unit of space; all of the living material in a given area; often refers to vegetation. Also called "biota."

Biometeorology

The study of the relationship between living things and the weather.

Biometrics

The implementation of measurement and statistics to biological studies.

Biomonitoring

1) The use of living organisms to test the suitability of effluents for discharge into receiving waters and to test the quality of such waters downstream from the discharge. 2) Analysis of blood, urine, tissues, etc., to measure chemical exposure in humans. Same as Biological Monitoring.

Bioremediation

The use of living organisms (e.g., bacteria) to clean up oil spills or remove other pollutants from soil, water, and wastewater.

Biosphere

The portion of earth and its atmosphere that can support life.

Biostabilizers

Machines that convert solid waste into compost by grinding and aeration.

Biota

Combined fauna and flora of any area or geological period; all of the living material in a given area; often refers to vegetation.

Biotechnology

Techniques that use living organisms or parts of organisms to produce a variety of products (from medicines to industrial enzymes) to improve plants or animals or to develop microorganisms for specific uses such as removing toxics from bodies of water, or as pesticides.

Biotic Communities

Naturally occurring assemblages of plants and animals that live in the same environment and are mutually sustaining and interdependent.

Biotic Factors

Environmental influences, such as predator-prey relationships and species competition, that impact the activities of living organisms.

Biotic Index

A rating used to assess the quality of the environment in ecological terms. Unpolluted fresh water areas have a high index rating. As pollution increases, oxygen levels in lakes and rivers decrease, and the more sensitive organisms disappear; and the rating decreases. Severely polluted water, in which only a few persistent species can survive, gets very low ratings.

Biotic Potential

An estimate of the maximum rate of species growth in the absence of competition from predators.

Biotic Pyramid

1) Communities of living organisms (with size groups on the vertical coordinate and numbers of organisms on the horizontal coordinate) that describe a pyramid when plotted. 2) Large numbers of living organisms of small size with a somewhat progressively decreasing number of large organisms balancing out the ecology of the community.

Biotransformation

An enzymatic chemical alteration of a substance within the body that generally leads to a more excretable metabolite, sometimes producing a more toxic form of the substance.

Bipinnately

A species descriptor that means having leaflets, lobes, or divisions in a featherlike arrangement on every other side of a common axis.

Bird Strike

An airspace conflict between aircraft flight patterns and birds or waterfowl.

Bismaleimide

A type of polyimide that cures by an addition reaction, avoiding formation of volatiles, and has temperature capabilities between those of epoxy and polyimide.

Bituminous Coal

A coal ranking, between lignite and anthracite, that burns with a smoky, luminous flame.

Bivalve Mollusk

A species descriptor that means a mollusk, such as a clam, whose shell consists of two hinged halves.

Black Lung

A disease of the lungs caused by habitual inhalation of coal dust.

Blackwater
Water that contains animal, human, or food wastes.

Blank Ammunition
A cartridge loaded with powder but containing no projectile or ammunition that is deemed by the manufacturer to be incapable of firing a projectile that will kill, wound, or otherwise harm any individual at a distance greater than 10 feet.

Blank Fire Adapter
A mechanical device attached to a firearm for the purpose of adapting it for use with blank ammunition.

Blanket Assembly
Natural convection cooled; reduces neutron irradiation to the reactor walls; lithium assemblies.

Blanks
Artificial samples designed to monitor the introduction of artifacts into the process. For aqueous samples, reagent water is used as a blank matrix; however, a universal blank matrix does not exist for solid samples, and therefore, no matrix is used. The blank is taken through the appropriate steps of the process.

Blast
The brief and rapid movement of air, vapor, or fluid away from a center of outward pressure, as in an explosion or in the combustion of rocket fuel; the pressure accompanying this movement. This term is commonly used for "explosion," but the two terms may be distinguished.

Blast Effect
Destruction of or damage to structures and personnel by the force of an explosion on or above the surface of the ground. Blast effect may be contrasted with the cratering and ground-shock effects of a projectile or charge that goes off beneath the surface.

Blast Line
A horizontal radial line on the surface of the earth originating at ground zero on which measurements of blast from an explosion are taken.

Blast Wave
A sharply defined wave of increased pressure rapidly propagated through a surrounding medium from a center of detonation or similar disturbance.

Blast Wave Diffraction
The passage around and envelopment of a structure by the nuclear blast wave.

Blasting Agents
Materials designed for blasting and found to be so insensitive that there is very little probability of accidental initiation to explosion. Ammonium nitrate fuel oil mixtures, containing only pulled ammonium nitrate and fuel oil, are examples of blasting agents.

Bleeding Edge
That edge of a map or chart on which cartographic detail is extended to the edge of the sheet.

Blepharospasm
Involuntary spasmodic blinking or closing of the eyelids due to severe irritation.

Blister Agent
A chemical agent that injures the eyes and lungs, and burns or blisters the skin. Also called vesicant agent.

Blizzard Warning
An alert given when heavy falling or blowing snow will combine with sustained wind or gusts of 35 miles per hour (mph) or greater to reduce visibility to 1/4 mile or less. The winds and cold temperature may combine to produce life-threatening wind chills. These conditions are considered imminent or expected with near certainty, and will persist for 3 hours or longer.

Block Group/Enumeration District (BG/ED)
The smallest geographic areas used by the Bureau of Census in conducting the population census. Block groups are designated for urban areas, while enumeration districts are designated for rural areas. BG/EDs data are frequently incorporated into exposure models to estimate population exposure to environmental pollutants.

Blood Agent
A chemical compound, including the cyanide group, that affects bodily functions by preventing the normal utilization of oxygen by body tissues.

Bloom
A proliferation of algae and/or higher aquatic plants in a body of water; often related to pollution, especially when pollutants accelerate growth.

Blowhole
A species descriptor that means the breathing hole located on the head of a whale.

Blowing
The injection of air or oxygen-enriched air into a molten converter bath.

Blowing Snow Advisory
An alert given when conditions are expected where wind-blown snow will intermittently reduce visibility to 1/4 mile or less, or produce significant drifting over roads, sidewalks, and parking lots.

BLVR
An acronym for Building Power Low Voltage Relay.

BMP
An acronym for Best Management Practices.

BNL
An acronym for Brookhaven National Laboratory.

Boards
A group of persons having managerial, supervisory, or investigatory powers.

Boattail
The conical section of a ballistic body that progressively decreases in diameter toward the tail to reduce overall aerodynamic drag.

BOD
An acronym for Biological Oxygen Demand.

BOD (Biological Oxygen Demand) Load
The BOD content, in pounds per unit of time, of wastewater passing into a waste treatment system or to a body of water.

BOD 5
The amount of dissolved oxygen consumed in 5 days by biological processes breaking down organic matter.

Body Content
The total amount (which may be expressed as activity) of a specified radionuclide in a human or animal body (formerly called body burden).

Body System(s)
A term that includes, but is not limited to, the circulatory system, digestive system, excretory system, nervous system, brain, and respiratory system.

Body Wave Magnitude
Measure of seismic body waves, primary (P) and secondary (S), which have periods usually from 1 to 10 seconds.

Bog
A type of wetland that accumulates appreciable peat deposits. Bogs depend primarily on precipitation for their water source, are usually acidic, and are rich in plant residue with a conspicuous mat of living green moss.

Boiler
1) An enclosed device using controlled flame combustion and having the following characteristics: a) the unit must have physical provisions for recovering and exporting thermal energy in the form of steam, heated fluids, or heated gases; b) the unit's combustion chamber and primary energy recovery section(s) must be of integral design. 2) A fired or unfired pressure vessel used to generate steam pressure by the application of heat. This definition is intended to include steam generators and forced-circulation boilers but excludes unfired evaporators.

Boiling Point
The temperature at which the vapor pressure of a liquid equals the atmospheric pressure and the liquid becomes vapor.

Boiling Water Reactor
A reactor in which water, used as both coolant and moderator, is allowed to boil in the core. The resulting steam can be used directly to drive a turbine and electrical generator.

Bomb Damage Assessment (BDA)
The determination of the effect of all air attacks on targets (i.e., bombs, guided missiles, rockets).

Bomb Disposal Unit
See Explosive Ordnance Disposal Unit.

Bomb Incidents
Incidents involving the threatened, attempted, or actual use of conventional explosives in a malevolent manner (including threatened, attempted, or actual use of flammable, corrosive, or hazardous substances).

Bomb Threats
Expressions of intention to destroy or damage facilities by use of explosives.

Bona Fide Association
An organization of employees and former employees of an organization including affirmative action advocacy groups and professional organizations that do not have as one of their purposes the representation of employees in their relations with the organization.

Bond Strength
As measured by load/bond area, the stress required to separate a layer of material from that to which it is bonded. The amount of adhesion between bonded surfaces.

Bonding
In electrical engineering, the process of connecting together metal parts so that they make low resistance electrical contact for direct current and lower frequency alternating currents. *See* Earthing.

Bone Seekers
Any radionuclides that are incorporated more readily into bone than into other living tissue.

Bonneville Power Administration (BPA)
The BPA markets electric power and energy from federal hydroelectric projects in the Pacific Northwest. Through interregional connections, it sells surplus power to areas outside the Pacific Northwest region and participates in exchanges of power. The BPA is responsible for energy conservation, renewable resource development, and fish and wildlife enhancement under the provisions of the Pacific Northwest Electric Power Planning and Conservation Act of 1980. In cooperation with the Corps of Engineers, it represents the United States in implementing the provisions of the Columbia River Treaty with Canada. States served include Washington, Oregon, Nevada, Idaho, Montana, and Wyoming.

Booms
1) Floating devices used to contain oil on a body of water. 2) Pieces of equipment used to apply pesticides from ground equipment such as a tractor or a truck.

Boost Phase
That portion of the flight of a ballistic missile or space vehicle during which the booster and sustainer engines operate.

Booster
1) A high-explosive element sufficiently sensitive so as to be actuated by small explosive elements in a fuze or primer and powerful enough to cause detonation of the main explosive filling. 2) An auxiliary or initial propulsion system that travels with a missile or aircraft and that may or may not separate from the parent craft when its impulse has been delivered. A booster system may contain, or consist of, one or more units. *See* Fuze.

BOP
An acronym for Balance of Plant.

BOR
An acronym for Burnout Risk.

Border
In cartography, the area of a map or chart lying between the neatline and the surrounding framework.

Border Break
A cartographic technique used when it is required to extend a portion of the cartographic detail of a map or chart beyond the sheetlines into the margin.

Border Crosser
An individual, living close to a frontier, who normally has to cross the frontier frequently for legitimate purposes.

Boresafe Fuze
A type of fuze having an interrupter in the explosive train that prevents a projectile from exploding until after it has cleared the muzzle of a weapon. *See* Fuze.

Borings
Boreholes drilled to collect soil samples as part of subsurface investigations conducted for the purpose of structural foundation design.

Boron Fiber
A fiber usually of a tungsten-filament core with elemental boron vapor deposited on it to impart strength and stiffness.

BOSF
An acronym for Burnout Safety Factor.

Botanical Pesticides
Pesticides whose active ingredient is a plant-produced chemical such as nicotine or strychnine.

Bottle Bill
Proposed or enacted legislation that requires a returnable deposit on beer or soda containers and provides for retail store or other redemption centers. Such legislation was designed to discourage use of throwaway containers.

Bottles
Containers having a neck of relatively smaller cross section than the body and an opening capable of holding a closure for retention of the contents.

Bottom Ash
The solid material that remains on a hearth or falls off the grate after thermal processing is complete.

Bottomland
Land, usually flood plains, adjacent to a river or watercourse.

Bottomland Hardwoods
Forested freshwater wetlands adjacent to rivers in the southeastern United States. They are especially valuable for wildlife brooding and nesting and habitat areas.

Boulders
Rock fragments larger than 60.4 cm (24 inches) in diameter.

Boundary
A line that delineates surface areas for the purpose of facilitating coordination and deconfliction of operations between adjacent units, formations, or areas.

Boundary Elements
Elements at edges of openings or at perimeters of shear walls or diaphragms.

BPT
An acronym for Best Practical Technology.

Bq
See Becquerel.

BRAC
An acronym for Base Realignment and Closure.

BRACC
An acronym for Base Realignment and Closure Commission.

Braced Frame
An essentially vertical truss system of the concentric or eccentric type that is provided to resist lateral forces.

Braces for Excavations
The horizontal members of the shoring system the ends of which bear against the uprights or stringers.

Brackish Areas
Bays, mouths of rivers, salt marshes, and other areas where tidal action and river flow create a mixing of fresh and salt water.

Brackish Waters
1) River and near-shore ocean waters where tidal action and river flow create a mixing of fresh and salt water. Brackish water ecosystems shelter and feed marine life, birds, and wildlife. 2) Marine and estuarine waters with mixohaline salinity; a mixture of fresh and salt water.

Bract
A species descriptor that refers to the lifelike part of a plant located below the flower, usually small and sometimes brightly colored; leaves that bracket the flower of a plant.

Bradycardia
Slow heart rate, usually under 60 beats per minute.

Branch
1) A subdivision of any organization. 2) A geographically separate unit of an activity that performs all or part of the primary functions of the parent activity on a smaller scale. Unlike an annex, a branch is not merely an overflow addition. 3) An arm or service of the Army. 4) An organizational level having functional/geographic responsibility for major segments of incident operations. 5) The limb of a tree.

Branchia
A species descriptor that means a gill or similar breathing organ.

BRAVO
A substantial alert action put into effect when the head of a field office determines that conditions or information received warrants more than the preparatory safeguards actions dictated under Safeguards and Security Alert III. *See* Operational Emergency Response Levels.

BRC
An acronym for Below Regulatory Concern.

Break-Bulk
Packages of hazardous materials that are handled individually, pelletized, or unitized for purposes of transportation as opposed to bulk and containerized freight.

Break-Up
In imagery interpretation, the result of magnification or enlargement that causes the imaged item to lose its identity and the resultant presentation to

become a random series of tonal impressions. Also called split-up.

Breakaway
The onset of a condition in which the shock front moves away from the exterior of the expanding fireball produced by the explosion of a nuclear weapon.

Breakthrough
The process of developing and attaining a now high standard for control of anything.

Breakthrough Curve
A plot of relative concentration versus time, where relative concentration is defined as a point in the groundwater flow domain (C) divided by the source concentration (C_0)[equation C/C_0].

Breathing Tube
A tube through which air or oxygen flows to the facepiece, helmet, or hood.

Breeder
A nuclear reactor that produces more fuel than it consumes. This is possible because of two facts of nuclear physics: a) fission of atomic nuclei produces on average more than two neutrons for each nucleus undergoing reaction. These excess neutrons can then be used to create more fuel while the initial neutron sustains the fission chain reaction; b) some nonfissionable nuclei can be converted into fissionable nuclei by capturing a neutron of proper energy.

Bremsstrahlung
Electromagnetic (X-ray) radiation associated with the deceleration of charged particles passing through matter. Usually associated with energetic beta emitters, e.g., phosphorus-32.

Briefing
The act of giving in advance specific instructions or information.

Brightness
The visual sensation of the luminous intensity of a light source. The brightness of a laser beam is most closely associated with the radio-metric concept of radiance.

British Thermal Unit (Btu)
The quantity of heat necessary to raise the temperature of 1 pound of water 1 degree Fahrenheit. 1btu = 252 calories = 778 foot lbs = 1055 joules = 0.293 watt/ hrs.

Broad-Leaved Deciduous
Woody angiosperms (trees or shrubs) with relatively wide, flat leaves that are shed during the cold or dry season.

Broad-Leaved Evergreen
Woody angiosperms (trees or shrubs) with relatively wide, flat leaves that generally remain green and are usually persistent for a year or more.

Broadcast Application
In pesticides, the spreading of chemicals over an entire area.

Bronchi
Large divisions of the trachea that convey air to and from the lungs.

Bronchial
Pertaining to the airways of the lung below the larynx that lead to the alveolar region of the lungs. Bronchial airways provide a passageway for air movement.

Bronchial Epithelium
The surface layer of cells lining the conducting airways.

Bronchiectasis
Pathological dilation of a bronchus or of the bronchial tubes.

Bronchiole
A small-diameter airway branching from a bronchus.

Bronchitis
Inflammation of the mucous membrane of the bronchial tubes, usually associated with a persistent cough and sputum production.

Bronchorrhea
Increased bronchial secretions.

Bronchospasm
Contraction of the smooth muscle of the bronchi, causing narrowing of the bronchi. This narrowing increases the resistance of air flow into the lungs and may cause a shortness of breath, typically associated with wheezing.

Brood Parasitism
A species descriptor referring to a situation in which a bird of one species lays eggs in the nest of a different species to the detriment of the host bird's own young.

Brookhaven National Laboratory (BNL)
A DOE Research and Development and Field Facility, established in 1947. BNL conceives, develops, constructs, and operates complex research facilities for the study of fundamental properties of matter. BNL conducts basic and applied research in technology base areas, supports research facilities, and establishes important new directions for research. Major disciplinary strengths at BNL are high energy, nuclear and solid state physics, chemistry, and biology. Research programs include the exploration of the fundamental constituents of matter, properties, and interactions.

Brown Tree Snake Control Program (BTSCP)
A comprehensive, environmental program headed by the ANSTF in coordination with regional, territorial, state, and local entities to control the brown tree snake (*Boiga irregularis*) in Guam and other areas where the species is established outside of its historic range.

Brush Treated
A material to be burned has been felled, crushed or uprooted with mechanical equipment, has been desiccated with herbicides, or is dead.

BS&W
An acronym for Basic Sediment and Water.

BTDR
An acronym for Building Time Delay Relay.

BTF
An acronym for Biological Treatment Facility.

BTSCP
See Brown Tree Snake Control Program.

Btu
See British Thermal Unit.

Btu Equivalent
The Btu equivalent for kilowatt-hours; 1 kilowatt-hour (kwH) = 3,412 British thermal units (Btus).

Btuh
An abbreviation for British Thermal Units per Hour.

BTW
An acronym for Boundary Waters Treaty of 1909.

Bubble Policy
1) Use of alternative emission limits to meet SIPs/NSPS air quality requirements. 2) EPA policy that allows a plant complex with several facilities to decrease pollution from some facilities while increasing it from others, so long as total results are equal to or better than previous limits. Facilities where this is done are treated as if they exist in a bubble in which total emissions are averaged out. Complexes that reduce emissions substantially may "bank" their "credits" or sell them to other industries. *See* Emissions Trading.

Buckled Zones

Regions of highest neutron flux.

Buckling, Composite

A failure mode usually characterized by fiber deflection rather than breaking because of compressive action.

Buddy System

A system of organizing employees into work groups in such a manner that each employee of the work group is designated to be observed by at least one other employee in the work group. The purpose of the buddy system is to provide rapid assistance to employees in the event of an emergency.

Buffer

Any of certain combinations of chemicals used to stabilize the pH values or alkalinities of solutions.

Buffer Distance

1) In nuclear warfare, the horizontal distance that, when added to the radius of safety, will give the desired assurance that the specified degree of risk will not be exceeded. The buffer distance is normally expressed quantitatively in multiples of the delivery error. 2) The vertical distance that is added to the fallout safe-height of burst in order to determine a desired height of burst that will provide the desired assurance that militarily significant fallout will not occur. It is normally expressed quantitatively in multiples of the vertical error.

Buffer Strips

Strips of grass or other erosion-resisting vegetation between or below cultivated strips or fields.

Buffer Zone

1) A strip of land separating one type of land use from another, as a residential area is separated or shielded from a highway corridor. This type of buffer is intended to partially insulate the residential area from the noise and emissions emanating from the highway. 2) The area of protection surrounding a nest tree in which timber operations must be conducted in accordance with the provisions set forth in these regulations. In this definition a buffer zone does not constitute a special treatment area. 3) The smallest region beyond the disposal unit that is required as controlled space for monitoring and for taking mitigative measures, as may be required.

Builae

Large fluid-filled blisters.

Building

1) A roofed structure that is suitable for housing people, material, or equipment. 2) Any permanent structure built for the support, shelter, or enclosure of persons, animals, chattels, or property of any kind. Also included are sheds and other roofed structures that provide partial protection from the weather.

Building Acquisitions

New pre-engineered metal buildings, other semipermanent or temporary facilities such as in-plant fabricated modular-relocatable buildings and trailer units, and other buildings to be acquired.

Building Arts

The study of all practical and scholarly aspects of prehistoric, historic, and contemporary architecture, archaeology, construction, building technology and skills, landscape architecture, preservation and conservation, building and construction, engineering, urban and community design and renewal, city and regional planning, and related professions, skills, trades, and crafts.

Building Code

A legal instrument that is in effect in a state or unit of local government, that must be adhered to if a building is to be considered to be in compliance with local laws and ordinances for suitable occupancy and use.

Building Drill
A planned event simulating emergency conditions for purposes of evaluating the building and the personnel in emergency responses.

Building Emergency Support Team (BEST)
The response personnel that provide initial response to an emergency situation prior to arrival of the fire department and the incident commander (IC) on the scene.

Building Emergency Program Administrator (BEPA)
The person appointed by the Building Operations Manager who is responsible for the EP Program in a specific building or area.

Building Emergency Plan (BEPLAN)
Plans prepared to guide emergency response to specific building or facility events.

Building Frame Systems
Essentially complete space frames that provide support for gravity loads.

Building Materials
Construction materials used in walls, ceilings, roofs, and floors of buildings.

Building Permit
An electrical, plumbing, mechanical, building, or other permit or approval, that is issued by a governmental or quasi-governmental enforcement agency, and that authorizes any construction in the subject jurisdiction.

Buildup
The process of attaining prescribed levels of personnel and resources, including, but not limited to vehicles, equipment, stores, and supplies. Also may be applied to the means of accomplishing this process.

Buildup Factor
A dimensionless coefficient equal to the ratio of a given radiation quantity charactcrizing the total scattered and unscattered diation field at some point in a medium through which the radiation is passing to the quantity characterizing the unscattered field along at that point.

Bulk Cargo
That which is generally shipped in volume where the transportation conveyance is the only external container; such as liquids, ore, or grain.

Bulk Container
A large container that can either be pulled or lifted mechanically onto a service vehicle or emptied mechanically into a service vehicle.

Bulk Liquid Load
A nonsolid, nongaseous solution, mixture, suspension, or wetted solid in mixture or suspension that is subject to surge during transport within a structure designed to contain such materials having a volumetric capacity of more than 1000 gallons. Examples of liquids are milk, gasoline, ketchup, molasses, cherries in syrup, and liquid petroleum gas.

Bulk Packaging
A packaging, other than a vessel or a barge, including a transport vehicle or freight container, in which hazardous materials are loaded with no intermediate form of containment and that has a) an internal volume greater than 450 liters (118.9 gallons) as a receptacle for a liquid; b) a capacity greater than 400 kilograms (881.8 pounds) as a receptacle for a solid; or c) a water capacity greater than 1000 pounds (453.6 kilograms) as a receptacle for a gas.

Bulk Petroleum Product
A liquid petroleum product transported by various means and stored in tanks or containers having an individual fill capacity greater than 250 liters.

Bulk Plant
An installation other than a dispensary, used to store a product for further transfer, or resale, via tank delivery truck.

Bulk Resins
Resins that are produced by a polymerization process in which no water is used.

Bulk Storage
1) Storage in a warehouse of supplies and equipment in large quantities, usually in original containers, as distinguished from bin storage. 2) Storage of liquids, such as petroleum products in tanks, as distinguished from drum or packaged storage. 3) Storage in vessels other than DOT cylinders. *See* Bin Storage; Storage.

Bulk Terminal
A storage and distribution facility that is primarily used for the wholesale marketing of petroleum products and that has total storage capacity of 50,000 barrels or receives its petroleum products by tanker, barge, or pipeline, and is not a public storage facility.

Bulkhead
1) An airtight structure separating the working chamber from free air or from another chamber under a different pressure than the working pressure. 2) Air-restraining barriers constructed for long-term control of radon-222 and radon-222 decay product levels in mine air.

Bulky Wastes
Large items of solid waste such as household appliances, furniture, large auto parts, trees, branches, stumps, and other oversize wastes whose large size precludes or complicates their handling by normal solid wastes collection, processing, or disposal methods.

Bullet Containment Device
A device used to point a weapon at or into during the loading or unloading process that will contain any inadvertently discharged round.

Bump Cap
1) A DOE term for the smallest region beyond the disposal unit that is required as controlled space for monitoring and for taking mitigative measures, as may be required. 2) Head protection and/or personal protective equipment.

Buoyancy
The total upward forces, exerted by the water on a submerged or floating mass, equal to the weight of the water displaced by the mass.

Burden of Proof
The burden on an owner/operator petitioning for costs to establish by a preponderance of the evidence that the issuance of a citation was the result of arbitrary or capricious action or conduct by the Division. *See* Division.

Bureau
The Bureau of Land Management.

Burial Ground (BG)
A disposal site for radioactive waste materials that uses earth or water as a shield. Also known as the Graveyard.

Burial Operations
Any method, technique, or process, including storage for radioactive decay, designed to change the physical, chemical, or biological characteristics or composition of any waste in order to render the waste for transport, storage, or disposal, amendable to recovery, convertible to another usable material, or reduced in volume.

Burning Agents
Those additives that, through physical or chemical means, improve the combustibility of the materials to which they are applied.

Bursa Copulatrix
A species descriptor that means a saclike, bodily cavity used in copulation.

Bus
A vehicle that is designed to transport 30 individuals or more.

Business

Any lawful activity, except a farm operation, conducted primarily for a) the purchase, sale, lease, or rental of personal and real property, and for the manufacture, processing, or marketing of products, commodities, or any other personal property; or b) the sale of services to the public.

Business Confidentiality

A term that includes the concept of trade secrecy and other related legal concepts that give (or may give) a business the right to preserve the confidentiality of business information and to limit its use or disclosure by others in order that the business may obtain or retain the business advantages it derives from its right to this information. The definition is meant to encompass any concept that authorizes a federal agency to withhold business information under 5 USC 552(b)(4), as well as any concept that requires EPA to withhold information from the public for the benefit of a business under 18 USC 1905.

Butt Joint

A joint in which parts are joined with no overlap.

BWR

An acronym for Boiling Water Reactor.

BWST

An acronym for Borated Water Storage Tank.

By-Product Materials

1) Radioactive materials (except special nuclear material) yielded in or made radioactive by exposure to the radiation incident to the process of producing or utilizing special nuclear material. 2) The tailings or wastes produced by the extraction or concentration of uranium or thorium from any ore processed primarily for its source material content.

By-Products

1) Materials, other than the principal products, that are generated as a consequence of an industrial process. 2) Chemical substances produced without separate commercial intent during the manufacturing or processing of another chemical substance(s) or mixture(s).

Bypasses

Applies to electric circuits as well as cooling circuits.

BZ

An acronym for Buckled Zones; Buffer Zone.

C

C&D
An acronym for Charge and Discharge.

CO₂
See Carbon Dioxide.

Ca
An abbreviation for Calcium.

CA
An acronym for the Classification Act of 1949.

CAA
An acronym for Clean Air Act.

Cable Roads
The path followed by logs being yarded by a cable system.

Cable Yarding
The system of skidding or transporting logs by means of cable (wire rope) to the yarding machine (yarder) or a landing while the yarder remains stationary.

CAD
An acronym for Computer-Aided Drafting and Computer-Assisted Design; an approach to drafting engineering or architectural plans, schematics, diagrams, and other documents required to be "to scale" utilizing a computer, an output device (usually a plotter), and software specifically designed for drafting purposes.

Cadastre
The official inventory of the real property in a community, used for determining taxes and its appraised value.

Cadmium (Cd)
1) An element found associated with zinc ores, that is used for the manufacture of fusible alloys, in electroplating, and for making control rods in nuclear reactors. 2) A heavy metal element that accumulates in the environment.

Caduceus
Dropping off or shedding at an early stage of development, as in the gills of amphibians or the leaves of plants.

Caespitose
Growing in dense tufts or clumps.

CAF
See Clean Alternative Fuels (CAA).

CAIRS
See Computerized Accident/Incident Reporting System.

Caissons
Shafts of concrete placed under a building column or wall that extend down to rock or solid substratum (also known as pier foundations).

Calcareous

Formed of calcium carbonate or magnesium carbonate by biological deposition or inorganic precipitation in sufficient quantities to effervesce carbon dioxide visibly when treated with cold, 0.1 normal hydrochloric acid. Calcareous sands are usually formed of a mixture of fragments of mollusk shells, echinoderm spines and skeletal material, coral, and algal platelets (e.g., *Halimeda*).

Calciners

Units in which phosphate rock is heated to high temperatures to remove organic material and/or to convert it to nodular form. Calciners and nodulizing kilns are considered to be similar units.

Calcium (Ca)

An element that tarnishes quickly with air contact. It occurs widely as calcium carbonate (CO_3Ca) and has numerous industrial uses.

Calendar Quarter

Means not fewer than 12 consecutive weeks nor more than 14 consecutive weeks. The first calendar quarter of each year shall begin in January. Calendar quarters should be arranged so that no day in any year is omitted from inclusion within a calendar quarter.

Calibration

1) The determination, checking, or rectifying of the graduation of any instrument giving quantitative measurements. 2) The process of taking measurements or of making observations to establish the relationship between two quantities. 3) A quality control maintenance measurement. 4) The adjustment of input data until computed heads match the field values.

California Tidelands

All tidal waters under state jurisdiction pursuant to 43 USC Section 1311.

California Standard Tank

A tank built in accordance with the requirements for California standard tanks as set forth in the Air Pressure Tank Safety Orders in force at the time the tank was constructed.

Calyx

The outer protective covering of a flower consisting of leaflike, usually green, segments called sepals.

Camera Axis Direction

Direction on the horizontal plane of the optical axis of the camera at the time of exposure. This direction is defined by its azimuth expressed in degrees in relation to true or magnetic north.

Camera Calibration

The determination of the calibrated focal length, the location of the principal point with respect to the fiducial marks and the lens distortion effective in the focal plane of the camera referred to the particular calibrated focal length.

Camera Cycling Rate

The frequency with which camera frames are exposed, expressed as cycles per second.

Camouflet

The resulting cavity in a deep underground burst when there is no rupture of the surface. *See* Crater.

Campanulate

A term meaning bell shaped.

CAM

An acronym for Continuous Air Monitor.

Canalize

To restrict operations to a narrow zone by use of existing or reinforcing obstacles or by fire or bombing.

Cancellation

Refers to Section 6 (b) of the Federal Insecticide, Fungicide and Rodenticide Act (FIFRA) that authorizes cancellation of a pesticide registration if unreasonable adverse effects to the environment and public health develop when a product is used according to widespread and commonly recognized practice, or if its labeling or other material required to be submitted does not comply with FIFRA provisions.

Cancer

A malignant new growth. Cancers are divided into two broad categories, carcinoma and sarcoma.

Candidate Site

An area, within a geologic and hydrologic system, that is recommended by the Secretary of the responsible agency or the Administrator of EPA for site characterization. *See* Administrator; Secretary.

Candidates

Species being considered for listing as an endangered or a threatened species, but not yet the subject of a proposed rule.

Cannibalize

To remove serviceable parts from one item of equipment in order to install them on another item of equipment.

Canthal

A term referring to either of two angles formed by the junction of the eyelids.

Cantilever Footings

Footings used to support a wall column near its edge without causing nonuniform soil pressure.

Cap

A highly impermeable seal, usually composed of clay-type soil or a combination of clay soil and synthetic liner, that is installed over the top of a closed landfill to prevent entry of rainwater. The cap serves to minimize leachate volume during biodegradation of the waste by keeping precipitation from percolating through the landfill. The cap also keeps odors down and animal scavengers from gathering.

CAP

See Capacity Assurance Plan; Crisis Action Planning.

Capability

The ability to execute a specified course of action.

Capable Fault

A fault that has exhibited one or more of the following characteristics: a) movement at or near the ground surface at least once within the past 35,000 years, or b) movement of a recurring nature within the past 5,000,000 years.

Capacitor

A device for accumulating and holding a charge of electricity and consisting of conducting surfaces separated by a dielectric. Types of capacitors are a) small capacitor (a capacitor that contains less than 1.36 kg (3 lbs) of dielectric fluid); b) large high-voltage capacitor (a capacitor that contains 1.3 kg (3 lbs) or more of dielectric fluid and that operates at 2,000 volts (AC or DC) or above); and c) large low-voltage capacitor (a capacitor that contains 1.36 kg (3 lbs) or more of dielectric fluid and that operates below 2,000 volts).

Capacity

1) The gross capacity of a pressure vessel (tank) in U.S. Gallons. 2) The maximum quantity of all supplies (ammunition; petroleum, oils, and lubricants; rations; general stores; maintenance stores; etc.) that each vessel can carry in proportions prescribed by proper authority.

Capacity Assurance Plan (CAP)

A plan that ensures that a state has the ability to treat and dispose of hazardous wastes generated within its borders over the next 20 years. Section 104 of SARA required the first plan to be submitted to EPA in October 1989. But even though capacity has been certified, the state is not required to treat or dispose of hazardous wastes at home, and many are exporting to other states that have commercial facilities, permitted landfills, and incinerators.

Capacity Factor, Electric

The ratio between the actual electric output from a unit and the potential electric output from that unit.

Capillary Action

The movement of water within the interstices of a porous medium due to the forces of adhesion, cohesion, and surface pressure acting in a liquid that is in contact with a solid. Synonymous with capillarity, capillary flow, and capillary migration.

Capillary Fringe

1) The zone at the bottom of the vadose zone where groundwater is drawn upward by capillary force. 2) The zone immediately above the water table, where water is drawn upward by capillary action.

Capillary Rise

The height above a free water surface to which water will rise by capillary action.

Capillary Water

1) Water held in the soil above the phreatic surface by capillary forces, or soil water above hygroscopic moisture and below the field capacity. 2) Soil moisture held as a continuous adsorbed film around soil particles and in interstices between the soil particles due to surface attraction.

Capital Expenditure

An expenditure for a physical or operational change to a stationary source that exceeds the product of the applicable annual asset guideline repair allowance percentage specified in the latest edition of Internal Revenue Service (IRS) Publication 534 and the stationary source's basis, as defined by Section 1012 of the Internal Revenue Code. However, the total expenditure for a physical or operational change to a stationary source must not be reduced by any "excluded additions" as defined for stationary sources constructed after December 31, 1981, in IRS Publication 534, as would be done for tax purposes. In addition, the annual asset guideline repair allowance may be used even though it is excluded for tax purposes in IRS Publication 534.

Capital Improvement Plan

A plan that coordinates capital improvements and expenses over a specified time period to ensure proper timing, location, and financing.

Capital Improvements

Items, including renovation and construction modifications, ordinarily treated as capitalized long-term investments because of their substantial value and life span.

Caps

Layers of clay, or other highly impermeable materials, installed over the top of a closed landfill to prevent entry of rainwater and minimize production of leachate.

Capsule

1) A sealed, pressurized cabin for extremely high altitude or space flight that provides an acceptable environment for man, animal, or equipment. 2) An ejectable sealed cabin having automatic devices for safe return of the occupants to the surface.

Captain of the Port

The officer of the Coast Guard, under the command of a District Commander, so designated by the Commandant for the purpose of giving immediate direction to Coast Guard law enforcement activities within his/her assigned area or, with respect to remaining areas in his/her district not assigned to officers designated by the Commandant, or the District Commander.

Captivity

Refers to wildlife held in a controlled environment that is intensively manipulated by man for the purpose of producing wildlife of the selected species, and that has boundaries designed to prevent animal, eggs, or gametes of the selected species from entering or leaving the controlled environment. General characteristics of captivity may include, but are not limited to, artificial housing, waste removal, health care, protection from predators, and artificially supplied food.

Captivity-Bred

Refers to wildlife, including eggs, born or otherwise produced in captivity from parents that mated or otherwise transferred gametes in captivity, if reproduction is sexual, or from parents that were in captivity when development of the progeny began, if development is asexual.

Capture Efficiency

The fraction of all organic vapors generated by a process that is directed to an abatement or recovery device.

CAR

An acronym for Corrective Action Reporting.

Carapace

A hard structure covering all or part of the body, such as a turtle's shell.

Carbamates

Esters of N-methyl carbamic acid that inhibit cholinesterase.

Carbon Absorbers

Added-on control devices that use activated carbon to absorb volatile organic compounds (VOCS) from a gas stream. The VOCs are later recovered from the carbon.

Carbon Absorption

A treatment system where contaminants are removed from groundwater or surface water when the water is forced through tanks containing activated carbon, a specially treated material that attracts the contaminants.

Carbon Dioxide (CO_2)

1) A minor atmospheric constituent comprising about 0.4% of the atmosphere; a compound essential to living organisms. The atmospheric content has steadily increased since the widespread burning of coal, oil, and gas began. 2) A colorless, odorless, nonpoisonous gas, that results from fossil fuel combustion and is normally a part of the ambient air. 3) A molecule used as a laser medium. Emits far energy at 10,600 nanometers.

Carbon Dioxide Spaces

Annular spaces between main tanks and carbon steel liners filled with carbon dioxide.

Carbon Fiber

An important reinforcing fiber known for its light weight, high strength, and high stiffness that is produced by pyrolysis of an organic precursor fiber in an inert atmosphere at temperatures above 180°F. The material may also be graphitized by heat treating above 300°F.

Carbon Monoxide (CO)

A colorless, odorless, poisonous gas found in the atmosphere, produced by incomplete combustion, primarily from motor vehicles and to a lesser degree from cigarettes. Carbon monoxide is harmless in small doses and lethal in large quantities.

Carbon Monoxide Nonattainment Areas, Additional Provisions

The designations for each carbon monoxide nonattainment area. Designations include Moderate Area or a Serious Area based on the design value for the area: Moderate Area design value of 9.1-16.4 ppm with an attainment date of December 31, 1995; and Serious Area design value of 16.5 ppm and above with an attainment date of December 31, 2000.

Carbonate Rock

Rock consisting chiefly of carbonate minerals, such as limestone and dolomite.

Carbonate

Sediment formed by the organic or inorganic precipitation from aqueous solutions of carbonates of calcium, magnesium, or iron.

Carboxyhemoglobin

Hemoglobin in which the iron is associated with carbon monoxide (CO). The affinity of hemoglobin for CO is about 300 times greater than for oxygen.

CARC

An acronym for Containment Air Recirculation and Cooling.

Carcinogen

Any cancer-producing substance or agent. In many cases the carcinogen does not cause the cancer directly, but is the impetus for a chain of aberrant cell behavior that, at maturity, is cancer. Suspect carcinogens are substances that may cause cancer in humans or animals but for which the evidence is not conclusive. Standards have been adopted for the following carcinogens, recognized as cancer-causing substances, including, but not limited to any of the following substances (and any compound, mixture, or product containing such substances):

- 2-acetylaminofluorene; 4-aminodiphenyl; benzidine and its salts; bis (chloromethyl) ether; 3,3-dichlorobenzidine and its salts; 4-dimethylaminoazobenzene; beta-naphthylamine; 4-nitrobiphenyl; N-nitrosodimethylamine; beta-proppriolactone; methyl chloromethyl ether; alpha-naphthylamine; 4,4-methylenebis (2-chloroaniline); and ethyleneimine

- asbestos, including chrysotile, amosite, crocidolite, tremolite, anthophyllite, and actinolite

- vinyl chloride

- 1,2-dibromo-3 chloropropane (DBCP)

- coke oven emissions

- acrylonitrile

- inorganic arsenic

- ethylene dibromide (EDB)

- ethylene oxide

The above list also includes any other substance for which standards are adopted and in effect due to cancer causing properties and any compound, mixture, or product containing such a substance, except as specifically exempted.

Carcinogen Risk Assessment Verification Workgroup

An EPA workgroup formed to validate Agency carcinogen risk assessments and resolve conflict-

ing potency values among various program offices.

Carcinogenic

Able to produce malignant tumor growth. Cancer-producing. Operationally includes most benign tumors as well.

Carcinogenic Process

A series of stages at the cellular level after which cancer will develop in an organism. Some believe there are at least three stages (initiation, promotion, and progression). While hypothesized as a staged process, little is known about specific mechanisms of action.

Carcinoma

A malignant tumor of epithelial cell origin (e.g., skin, lung, breast), tending to infiltrate the surrounding tissue and giving rise to metastases.

Cardiac Dysrhythmia

Abnormality in the rate, regularity, or sequence of the heart beat. Formerly referred to as cardiac arrhythmia.

Caretaker Status

A nonoperating condition in which the installations, material, and facilities are in a "care and limited preservation" status. Only a minimum of personnel is required to safeguard against fire, theft, and damage from the elements.

Cargo

Commodities and supplies in transit. *See* Dangerous Cargo; Loading; Chemical Ammunition Cargo; General Cargo; High Explosive Cargo; Special Cargo; Vehicle Cargo.

Cargo Aircraft Only

An aircraft that is used to transport cargo and is not engaged in carrying passengers.

Cargo Carrier

Highly mobile, air transportable, unarmored, full-tracked cargo and logistic carrier capable of swimming inland waterways and accompanying and resupplying self-propelled artillery weapons.

Cargo Sling
A strap, chain, or other material used to secure cargo items that are to be hoisted, lowered, or suspended.

Cargo Tank
Any tank permanently attached to or forming a part of any motor vehicle or any bulk liquid or compressed gas packaging not permanently attached to any motor vehicle by reason of its size, construction, or attachment to a motor vehicle. Any packaging fabricated under specifications for cylinders is not a cargo tank.

Cargo Tie-Down Point
A point on material shipments designed for attachment of various means for securing the item for transport.

Cargo Transporter
A reusable metal shipping container designed for worldwide surface and air movement of suitable supplies and equipment through the cargo transporter service.

Cargo Vessels
1) Vessels other than passenger vessels. 2) Ferries being operated under authority of a "change of character certificate" issued by a Coast Guard Officer-in-Charge, Marine Inspection.

Carinameans
A keel-shaped ridge, such as that on the breastbone of a bird or the petals of certain flowers.

Carnet (Fr)
A document of international customs that permits temporary duty-free importation for specific items into certain nations.

Carpel
The central, ovule-bearing, female organ of a plant.

Carrier
1) Any person engaged in the transportation of passengers or property as common, contract, or private charter, or freight forwarder, as those terms are used in the Interstate Commerce Act, as amended, or by the U.S. Postal Service. 2) Any person engaged in the transportation of passengers or property by land or water as a common-, contract-, or private-carrier, or by civil aircraft.

Carryall
A self-loading and unloading vehicle pulled by a tractor or powered attachment that is used for movement and placement of earth or other materials.

Carrying Capacity
1) The maximum population of a species possible without damaging the environmental resources; the maximum number of animals an area can support during a given period of the year. 2) Maximum uses of a site/facility without negatively impacting operations. 3) In recreation management, the amount of use a recreation area can sustain without deterioration of its quality.

Cartage
The charge for pickup and delivery of a shipment.

Cartridge
A small circular canister. Cartridges are approved for use in concentrations of contaminants less than 0.1% or 1000 parts per million, by volume.

CARVER
An acronym for the criteria used by special operations forces throughout the targeting and mission planning cycle to assess mission validity and requirements. The acronym stands for "criticality, accessibility, recuperability, vulnerability, effect, and recognizability."

Caryopsis
A one-celled, one-seeded dry fruit, such as wheat, that has its outer covering fused to its surface.

CAS
See Chemical Abstract Service; Comprehensive Asbestos Survey; Condition Assessment Surveys.

Case-Control Study
A retrospective epidemiologic study in which individuals with the disease under study (cases) are compared with individuals without the disease (controls) in order to contrast the extent of exposure in the diseased group with the extent of exposure in the controlled group.

Cased Explosives
Explosives that are enclosed in a physical protective covering that will retain the explosives securely and will offer significant protection against accidental detonation during approved handling and intraplant transportation operations.

Cash or Cash Equivalent
Includes, but is not limited to, a) cash, checks, money orders, or drafts; b) promissory notes, bills of sale, or certificates of ownership, or other intangible property; c) assignments of funds, proceeds, contracts, rights, or other negotiable instruments; and d) any real or personal property.

Casings
Pipes or tubing of appropriate material, of varying diameter and weight, lowered into a borehole during or after drilling in order to support the sides of the hole and thus prevent the walls from caving. Also used to prevent loss of drilling mud into porous ground, or to prevent water, gas, or other fluid from entering or leaving the hole.

Cask
A thick-walled container (usually lead) used to transport radioactive material. Also called a coffin.

Casualty
Any person who is lost to an organization by having been declared "dead," "status—whereabouts unknown," "missing," "ill," or "injured." *See* Casualty Status.

Casualty Category
A term used to specifically classify a casualty for reporting purposes based upon the casualty type and the casualty status.

Casualty Status
A term used to classify a casualty for reporting purposes. There are seven classifications: a) deceased, b) status—whereabouts unknown, c) missing, d) very seriously ill or injured, e) seriously ill or injured, f) incapacitating illness or injury, and g) not seriously injured. *See* Casualty; Casualty Category; Incapacitating Illness or Injury; Not Seriously Injured; Seriously Ill or Injured; Very Seriously Ill or Injured.

Cataloging
The process of assigning a unique identifying number to a museum object and recording descriptive and documentary data on the Museum Catalog Record, Form 10-254 or 10-254B.

Catalogs
In computer usage, lists of vocabulary words that are systematically grouped.

Catalytic Converter
An air pollution abatement device attached to a motor vehicle's exhaust system to reduce emissions of unburnt hydrocarbons, carbon monoxide (CO) and nitrogen oxides (NO_X), by catalyzing chemical reactions and trapping pollutants that either oxidize them into carbon dioxide and water or reduce them to nitrogen and oxygen.

Catalytic Incinerator
A control device that oxidizes volatile organic compounds (VOCs) by using a catalyst to promote the combustion process. Catalytic incinerators require lower temperatures than conventional thermal incinerators, with resultant fuel and cost savings.

Catanadramous
Fish that swim downstream to spawn.

Cataract
Loss of transparency (clouding) of the lens of the eye.

Catastrophic Collapses
Sudden major failures of overlying strata caused by removal of underlying materials.

Catch Basin
A chamber or well, usually built at the curbline of a street, that admits surface water for discharge into a stormwater drain.

Catchment Area
An area where a river or lake derives its water. Catchments are separated from one another by watersheds.

Catecholamines
Substances of a specific chemical nature (pyrocatechols with an alkylamine side chain). Catecholamines of biochemical interest are those produced by the nervous system (e.g., epinephrine [adrenaline] or dopamine) to increase heart rate and blood pressure, or medicines with the same general chemical structure and effect.

Categorical Exclusion
1) A class of actions that either individually or cumulatively would not have a significant effect on the human environment and therefore would not require preparation of an environmental assessment or environmental impact statement under the National Environmental Policy Act (NEPA). 2) A category of actions, as defined at 40 CFR 1508.4 and listed in Section D of the DOE NEPA Guidelines, that do not individually or cumulatively have a significant effect on the human environment and for which neither an environmental assessment (EA) nor an environmental impact statement (EIS) is normally required.

Categorical Pretreatment Standards
Technology-based effluent limitation for an industrial facility that discharges into a municipal sewer system. Analogous in stringency to Best Available Technology (BAT) for direct dischargers.

Category A Reactors
A DOE designation based on power level (e.g., 20 megawatt steady state), potential fission product inventory, and experimental capability. Other DOE-owned reactors (excluding reactors assigned to the Deputy Assistant Secretary for Naval Reactors, Nuclear Engineering-60) are designated Category S.

Category I Seriousness
A DOE situation for which a clear and present danger exists to workers or members of the public. A concern in this category is to be immediately conveyed to the managers of the facility for action. At this point, consideration shall be given to whether a "clear and present danger" exists such that the facility shutdown authority of the Assistant Secretary should be exercised. If so, the Assistant Secretary or his/her designee is informed immediately.

Category II Seriousness
A significant risk (but does not involve a situation for which a clear and present danger exists to workers or members of the public) or substantial noncompliance with DOE Orders. A concern in this category is to be conveyed to the manager of the facility no later than the appraisal closeout meeting for immediate attention. Category II concerns have a significance and urgency such that the necessary field response should not be delayed until the preparation of a final report and the routine development of an action plan. Any issues surrounding the concern or the suggested response should be addressed during the appraisal or immediately thereafter. Again, consideration should be given to whether facility shutdown is warranted under the circumstances.

Category III Seriousness
Indicates significant noncompliance with DOE Orders or suggests significant improvements are required to the margin of safety, but without the urgency to require immediate attention.

Category of Chemical Substances
A group of chemical substances the members of which are similar in molecular structure, in physical, chemical, or biological properties, in use, or in mode of entrance into the human body or into the environment, or the members of which are in some other way suitable for classification as such, except that the term does not mean a group of chemical substances that are grouped together solely on the basis of their being new chemical substances.

Category of Mixtures
A group of mixtures, the members of which are a) similar in molecular structure; in physical, chemical, or biological properties; in use; in the mode of entrance into the human body or into the environment; b)in some other way suitable for classification.

Cathodic Protection
A technique to prevent corrosion of a metal surface by making that surface the cathode of an electrochemical cell. For example, a tank system can be cathodically protected through the application of either galvanic anodes or impressed current.

Cathodic Protection Testers
People who demonstrate an understanding of the principles and measurements of all common methods of cathodic protection systems as applied to buried or submerged metal piping and tank systems. At a minimum, such persons must have education and experience in soil resistance, stray current, structure-to-soil potential, and component electrical isolation measurements of buried metal piping and tank systems.

Cation Exchange Capacity
The sum of exchangeable cations a soil can absorb expressed in milli-equivalents per 100 grams of soil as determined by sampling the soil to the depth of cultivation or solid waste placement, whichever is greater, and analyzing by the summation method for distinctly acid soils or the sodium acetate method for neutral, calcareous, or saline soils.

CATS
An acronym for Computer Assisted Tracking System.

Calibration
Determination of variation from standard, or accuracy, of a measuring instrument to ascertain necessary correction factors.

Caudal
A species descriptor that means near the tail or hind parts.

Caudal Fin
A species descriptor that means the tail fin of a fish.

Caudex
1) The woody trunklike stem typical of some trees. 2) The thickened base of the stem in some perennial plants.

Caulescent
A species descriptor that means having a stem showing above the ground.

Cauline
A species descriptor that means growing on a stem.

Cause and Effect Diagram
A graphic method used to identify factors that influence a problem or a goal, and aid in determining the various impacts of these factors.

Cause of Action
Intrusion on a person's legal right by a breach of contract; breach of a legal duty toward a person or property.

Causes
In system safety, causes are anything that contributes to an accident or incident. In analysis or investigation, avoid the use of cause as a singular term; prefer, causal factors. Any "probable cause" statement required in an investigation report should be the immediate, proximate cause of the

primary, major damage and should be accompanied by succeeding statements of contributing causes of energy buildup and release and of inadequacies of plans, operations, detection, and control.

Caustic
1) A class of substances, also known as bases or alkalies. Strong caustics are corrosive. 2) A substance that strongly irritates, burns, corrodes, or destroys living tissue.

Caustic Scrubbing
A process for removing sulfur dioxide from flue gases by passing them through a solution of sodium hydroxide.

Caustic Soda
Sodium hydroxide, a strong alkaline substance used as the cleaning agent in some detergents.

Caveat Emptor
New Latin legal phrase for "let the buyer beware." The buyer is duty bound to examine the property he/she is purchasing and he/she assumes all environmental conditions that are readily apparent upon inspection.

CBIA
An acronym for Coastal Barrier Improvement Act of 1990.

CBOD 5
The amount of dissolved oxygen consumed in 5 days from the carbonaceous portion of biological processes breaking down in an effluent. The test methodology is the same as for BOD5, except that nitrogen demand is suppressed. *See* BOD 5.

CBRA
An acronym for Coastal Barrier Resources Act.

CBRS
See Coastal Barrier Resources System.

CCDF
An acronym for Complementary Cumulative Distribution Function.

CCF
An acronym for Common Cause Failure.

CCW
An acronym for Component Cooling Water.

Cd
See Cadmium.

CD
See Counterdrug.

CDC
See Centers for Disease Control and Prevention.

CEARP
An acronym for Comprehensive Environmental Assessment and Response Program.

Cease and Desist Order
A demand by a court or governmental agency that a firm or individual cease a specific, usually environmentally hazardous, activity.

CEC
An acronym for Committee on Energy and Commerce.

Ceiling
The height above the earth's surface of the lowest layer of clouds or obscuration phenomena that is reported as "broken," "overcast," or "obscured" and not classified as "thin" or "partial."

Ceiling Limit
A concentration limit in the workplace that should not be exceeded, even for a short time, to protect workers against frank health effects.

CEL
An acronym for Channel Effluent Limit.

Celestial Guidance
The guidance of a missile or other vehicle by reference to celestial bodies.

Celestial Sphere
An imaginary sphere of infinite radius concentric with the earth, on which all celestial bodies except the earth are imagined to be projected.

Cell Rooms
Structure(s) housing one or more mercury electrolytic chlor-alkali cells.

Cells
1) In solid waste disposal, holes where waste is dumped, compacted, and covered with layers of dirt on a daily basis. 2) The smallest structural part of living matter capable of functioning as an independent unit.

Celsius
See Anders Celsius.

Cementing
The operation whereby a cement slurry is pumped into a drilled hole and/or forced behind the casing.

Censorship
All types of censorship conducted by personnel of the government and Armed Forces of the United States, to include armed forces censorship, civil censorship, prisoner of war censorship, and field press censorship.

Center of Burst
See Mean Point of Impact.

Centers
Places, areas, people, groups, or concentrations marked significantly or dominantly by an indicated activity, pursuit, interest, or appeal.

Centers for Disease Control and Prevention (CDC)
The CDC track and evaluate incidents of disease and perform epidemiological studies. 1600

Clifton Road, N.E., Building 1, Atlanta, GA 30333, 404/639-2888.

Centigray
A unit of absorbed dose of radiation (one centigray equals one rad).

Central Alarm Stations
Physical locations to which security system alarms, radiation alarms, fire alarms, and hazardous substance alarms are electronically communicated.

Central Business District (CBD)
An urbanized area containing the core of economic, employment, and entertainment activity in a city; downtown.

Central Nervous System
The portion of the nervous system that includes the brain and spinal cord, and their connecting nerves.

Central Procurement
The procurement of material, supplies, or services by an officially designated agency with funds specifically provided for such procurement for the benefit and use of the entire component, or, in the case of single managers, for the military departments as a whole.

Central Training Academy (DOE)
Located at Kirkland Air Force Base East, Albuquerque, New Mexico. Program responsibility is to the Director of Safeguards and Security.

Centrally Managed Item
An item of material subject to inventory control point (wholesale level) management.

Centrifugal Collector
A mechanical system using centrifugal force to remove aerosols from a gas stream or to dewater sludge.

Centrifuge

A mechanical device in which centrifugal force is used to separate solids from liquid and/or to separate liquids of different densities.

CEPW

An acronym for Committee on Environment and Public Works.

CEQ

See Council on Environmental Quality.

Cerambycid

A species descriptor for a member of the longhorn beetle family.

CERCLA (Comprehensive Environmental Response, Compensation, and Liability Act of 1980, 42 USC 9601 et seq.)

CERCLA provides a federal "Superfund" to clean up uncontrolled or abandoned hazardous waste sites as well as accidents, spills, and other emergency releases of pollutants and contaminants into the environment. Through the Act, EPA was given power to seek out those parties responsible for any release and ensure their cooperation in the cleanup. EPA cleans up orphan sites when potentially responsible parties (PRPs) cannot be identified or located, or when they fail to act. Through various enforcement tools, EPA obtains private party cleanup through orders, consent decrees, and other small party settlements.

EPA also recovers costs from financially viable individuals and companies once a response action has been completed. EPA is authorized to implement the Act in all 50 states and U.S. territories. Superfund site identification, monitoring, and response activities in states are coordinated through the state environmental protection or waste management agencies. *See* Comprehensive Environmental Response, Compensation and Liability Act of 1980.

CERCLA Hazardous Substances

As defined by Section 101(14) of CERCLA, a hazardous substance is: a) any substance designated Pursuant to Section 31(b)(2)(A) of the Clean Water Act (CWA); b) any element, compound, mixture, solution, or substance designated Pursuant to Section 31(b)(2)(A) of the CWA pursuant to Section 102 of CERCLA; c) any hazardous waste having the characteristics identified under or listed pursuant to Section 3001 of the Solid Waste Disposal Act (but not including any waste the regulation of which under the Solid Waste Disposal Act has been suspended by Act of Congress); d) any toxic pollutant listed under Section 307(a) of the Federal Clean Water Act; e) any hazardous air pollutant listed under Section 112 of the Clean Air Act; and, f) any imminently hazardous chemical substance or mixture with respect to which the Administrator has taken action pursuant to Section 7 of the Toxic Substances Control Act.

This typically includes hazardous substances and materials considered toxic, corrosive, an irritant, a strong sensitizer, flammable or combustible, or one that generates pressure through decomposition, heat, or other means, if such substances or mixture of substances may cause substantial personal injury or substantial illness during or as a result of any reasonably foreseeable handling or use, including reasonably foreseeable ingestion by children. "Hazardous substance" includes any toy or other article intended for use by children which has been determined to present an electrical, mechanical, or thermal hazard.

The term does not include petroleum, crude oil, or any fraction thereof which is not otherwise specifically listed or designated as a hazardous substance under the Clean Water Act, and the term does not include natural gas, natural gas liquids, liquefied natural gas, or synthetic gas usable for fuel (or mixtures of natural gas and such synthetic gas). Other exclusions include pesticides subject to the Federal Insecticide, Fungicide, and Rodenticide Act (7 USC 136 et seq.); foods, drugs, and cosmetics subject to the Federal Food, Drug, and Cosmetic Act (21 USC 301 et seq.); substances intended for use as fuels when stored in containers and used in the heating, cooking, or refrigeration system of a house; tobacco and tobacco products; any source material, special nuclear material, or byproduct material as defined in the Atomic Energy Act of 1954, as amended. *See* Hazardous Substances.

CERCLIS (Comprehensive Environmental Response, Compensation, and Liability Information System)

The EPA database that includes all sites that have been nominated for investigation by the Superfund program and the actions that have been taken at these sites. If the site investigation reveals contamination, the site is ranked and may be included on the National Priorities List for Superfund cleanup. Inclusion in the CERCLIS database does not necessarily mean that a property is a hazardous waste site. An emergency action may have been conducted there or a simple investigation that concluded that no further action was required.

Cerebellar Abnormalities

Any irregularity in the cerebellum of the brain.

Cerebellum

The large brain mass located at the posterior base of the brain, responsible for balance and coordination of movement.

Cerebral Infarctions

Death of tissue in the cerebrum due to lack of blood flow to the area.

Cerebrum

The largest portion of the brain; includes the cerebral hemispheres (cerebral cortex and basal ganglia).

Chemexfoliation

Chemical skin peeling; use of chemicals to remove scars or pigmentation defects.

Certificate of Disposal/Certificate of Destruction (COD)

A document that verifies destruction, the receipt for destruction, or successful delivery of wastes to an ultimate or intermediary location. While these documents are considered by some transporters and generators legal proof of the end of their liability for contamination, they may only serve to prove responsibility for contribution to a site that is later identified by EPA as a Superfund site.

Certificate of Taxes

A written statement or guaranty of the condition of the taxes on a certain property, made by the county treasurer of the county where the property is located.

Certification

The recognition by a certifying agency that a person is competent and thus authorized to use or supervise the use of restricted-use pesticides.

Certified Applicators

Individuals who are certified under Section 4 (7 USC 136) as authorized to use or supervise the use of any pesticide that is classified for restricted use. Any applicator who holds or applies registered pesticides, or uses dilutions of registered pesticides consistent with the Act, only to provide a service of controlling posts without delivering any unapplied pesticide to any person so served is not deemed to be a seller or distributor of pesticides under the Act.

Certified Wastes

Waste that has been confirmed to comply with disposal site waste acceptance criteria (e.g., the Waste Acceptance Criteria for transuranic waste at the Waste Isolation Pilot Plant) under an approved certification program.

Cesium (Cs)

A silver-white, soft ductile element of the alkali metal group that is the most electropositive element known. Used especially in photoelectric cells.

Cespitose

A species descriptor that means growing in dense tufts or clumps; or matted.

CExB

An acronym for Costs (of control) Exceed Benefits (of control).

CFCs

See Chlorofluorocarbons.

CFR
An acronym for Code of Federal Regulations.

CFV
See Clean Fuel Vehicle.

CFWRU
An acronym for Cooperative Fishery and Wildlife Research Unit.

CFWSRDA
An acronym for Clarks Fork Wild and Scenic River Designation Act of 1990 (WSRA).

Chain of Command
The succession of commanding officers, from a superior to a subordinate, through which command is exercised. Also called command channel. *See* Operational Chain of Command.

Chain Reaction
1) A situation where one event causes another event, which then leads to a third, and so on; domino effect. 2) In a nuclear reactor the release of neutrons from the fuel causes neutron bombardment of other fuel, which in turn releases more neutrons that cause further fuel bombardment, and so on.

Chairman of the Joint Chiefs of Staff Instruction
A replacement document for all types of correspondence containing Chairman of the Joint Chiefs of Staff (CJCS) policy and guidance that does not involve the employment of forces. An instruction is of indefinite duration and is applicable to external agencies or both the Joint Staff and external agencies. It remains in effect until superseded, rescinded, or otherwise canceled. CJCS Instructions, unlike joint publications, will not contain joint doctrine and/or joint tactics, techniques, and procedures.

Chairman of the Joint Chiefs of Staff Memorandum of Policy
A statement of policy approved by the Chairman of the Joint Chiefs of Staff and issued for the guidance of the Services, the combatant commands, and the Joint Staff.

Change of Operational Control (CHOP)
The date and time at which the responsibility for operational control of a force or unit passes from one operational control authority to another.

Changed Use Pattern
A significant change from a use pattern approved in connection with the registration of a pesticide product. Examples of significant changes include, but are not limited to, changes from non-food to food use, outdoor to indoor use, ground to aerial application, terrestrial to aquatic use, and nondomestic to domestic use.

Channel
1) An open conduit either naturally or artificially created that periodically or continuously contains moving water, or that forms a connecting link between two bodies of standing water. 2) The bed or deeper part of a stream, river, or harbor.

Channel Bank
The sloping land bordering a channel. The bank has steeper slope than the bottom of the channel and is usually steeper than the land surrounding the channel.

Channelization
1) Straightening and deepening streams so water will move faster, a flood-reduction or marsh-drainage tactic that can interfere with waste assimilation capacity and disturb fish and wildlife habitats. 2) The process of deepening a river bed.

Chaparral
A species descriptor that means a dense thicket of shrubs and small trees.

Characteristic, Waste
Any one of the four categories used in defining hazardous waste: a) ignitability, b) corrosivity, c) reactivity, and d) toxicity.

Characterization, Evaluation
A biographical sketch of an individual or a statement of the nature and intent of an organization or group.

Charge
1) The amount of propellant required for a fixed, semifixed, or separate loading projectile, round or shell. It may also refer to the quantity of explosive filling contained in a bomb, mine or the like. 2) In combat engineering, a quantity of explosive, prepared for demolition purposes.

Charged Particle Equilibrium
The condition existing at a point within a medium under irradiation, when, for every charged particle leaving a volume element surrounding the point, another particle of the same kind and energy enters.

Charged Particles
A particle whose charge is not zero; the charge of a particle is added to its designation as a superscript, with particles of charge +1 and -1 (in terms of the charge of the proton) denoted by + and - respectively.

CHARLIE
In military science, a preparatory alert action that shall be effected when the head of a field office determines that existing preemergency conditions warrant increased safeguards and security measures at facilities under his/her jurisdiction; however, the Office of the Assistant Secretary for Defense Programs may establish a general U.S. Department of Energy-wide or a locally confined Safeguards and Security Alert III without prior consultation with the head of field offices. *See* Operational Emergency Response Levels.

Chart Base
A chart used as a primary source for compilation or as a framework on which new detail is printed. Also called topographic base. *See* Base Map.

Chart Index
See Map Index.

Chart Series
See Map; Map Series.

Chart Sheet
See Map; Map Sheet.

Chasmogamous
A term referring to pollination in open flowers.

Chattel
Any item of property other than real estate, usually referred to as personal property. An item of movable property.

Check Samples
Artificial samples that have been spiked with the analyte(s) from an independent source in order to monitor the execution of the analytical method are called check samples. The level of the spike shall be at the regulatory action level when applicable, otherwise, the spike shall be at five times the estimate of the quantification limit. The matrix used shall be phase-matched with the samples and well characterized; for example, reagent grade water is appropriate for an aqueous sample.

Check Valves
Valves that prevent moderator backflow from a reactor.

Checkpoint
1) A predetermined point on the surface of the earth used as a means of controlling movement, a registration target for fire adjustment, or reference for location. 2) Center of impact; a burst center. 3) Geographical location on land or water above which the position of an aircraft in flight may be determined by observation or by electrical means. 4) A place where military police check vehicular or pedestrian traffic in order to enforce circulation control measures and other laws, orders, and regulations.

Chela
A pincherlike claw of a crustacean, like those of a crab or lobster.

Chelicerae

Two pincherlike appendages near the mouth of an arachnid used for grasping.

Chelonian

Belonging to the order of Chelonia, that includes turtles and tortoises.

Chemical Abstract Service (CAS)

Since the 1890s, CAS has been assigning identification numbers to chemicals that companies register with them. Every year, CAS updates and writes new chemical abstracts on over a million different chemicals, including their composition, structure, characteristics, and all the different names of that chemical. CAS On-Line is a computer network available to individual and business account holders to receive information about specific chemicals of concern. Each abstract is accompanied by the CAS number.

Chemical Agent

1) In general, chemical substances, compounds, or mixtures that coagulate, disperse, dissolve, emulsify, foam, neutralize, precipitate, reduce, solubilize, oxidize, concentrate, congeal, entrap, fix, make the pollutant mass more rigid or viscous, or otherwise facilitate the mitigation of deleterious effects or removal of the pollutant from the water. 2) A chemical substance intended for use in military operations to kill, seriously injure, or incapacitate personnel through its physiological effects. Excluded from consideration are riot control agents, herbicides, smoke, and flame. *See* Biological Agent.

Chemical Agent Cumulative Action

The building up, within the human body, of small ineffective doses of certain chemical agents to a point where eventual effect is similar to one large dose. Conditions found in an area resulting from direct or persisting effects of chemical weapons.

Chemical Ammunition

1) A type of ammunition, the filler of which is primarily a chemical agent. 2) All shells, bombs, grenades, etc., loaded with toxic, tear, or other gas, smoke or incendiary agent, also such miscellaneous apparatus as cloud-gas cylinders, smoke generators, that may be utilized to project chemicals.

Chemical Ammunition Cargo

Cargo such as white phosphorous munitions (shell and grenades).

Chemical, Biological, and Radiological Operation

A collective term used only when referring to a combined chemical, biological, and radiological operation.

Chemical Cartridge Respirator

A respirator usually consisting of a half mask facepiece connected to one or two cartridges. A half-mask may be used in conditions not immediately dangerous to life or health, provided no skin or eye hazard exists, and the concentration of the air contaminant does not exceed 10 times the hazard level.

Chemical Defense

The methods, plans, and procedures involved in establishing and executing defensive measures against attack utilizing chemical agents. *See* NBC Defense.

Chemical Dose

The amount of chemical agent, expressed in milligrams, that is taken or absorbed by the body.

Chemical Engineering

The branch of engineering concerned with the manufacture of chemical products, conversion of raw materials, production of food-related products, and other process-type chemical manufacturing environments. It is concerned with the research, design, production, operational, organizational, and economic aspects of the above.

Chemical Formula

The collection of atomic symbols and numbers that indicates the chemical composition of a pure substance.

Chemical Hazards Emergency Management System

The system developed for DOE by the Center for Assessment of Chemical and Physical Hazards at Brookhaven National Laboratory. The purpose of the database is to provide health, safety, and environmental information to DOE and its contractors for chemicals and materials of interest to them.

Chemical Lot

A quantity of a homogeneous chemical, identified by a unique lot number, that is manufactured, by one producer under uniform conditions and that is expected to function in a uniform manner.

Chemical Mixture

1) Any combination of two or more chemical substances if the combination does not occur in nature and is not, in whole or in part, the result of a chemical reaction; except that such term does include any combination that occurs, in whole or in part, as a result of a chemical reaction if none of the chemical substances comprising the combination is a new chemical substance and if the combination could have been manufactured for commercial purposes without a chemical reaction at the time the chemical substances comprising the combination were combined. 2) Any combination of two or more substances regardless of source or of spatial or temporal proximity.

Chemical Monitoring

The continued or periodic process of determining whether or not a chemical agent is present. *See* Chemical Survey.

Chemical Operations

Employment of chemical agents to kill, injure, or incapacitate for a significant period of time, personnel or animals, and deny or hinder the use of areas, facilities, or material; or defense against such employment.

Chemical Oxygen Demand (COD)

A measure of the amount of oxygen required to oxidize organic and oxidizable inorganic compounds in water or wastewater; the amount of oxygen consumed from a chemical oxidant in a specific test. The COD test is used to determine the degree of pollution in an effluent.

Chemical Processes

Those processes including, but not limited to: chemical absorption, corrosion, dechlorination, degradation, desalinization, fermentation, hydrolysis, in situ volatization, in situ extraction, neutralization, oil fingerprinting, oxidation, combustion, precipitation, pyrolysis, reduction, or sorption.

Chemical Processing

The preparation of a chemical substance or mixture, after its manufacture, for distribution in commerce: a) in the same form or physical state as, or in a different form or physical state from, that in which it was received by the person so preparing such substance or mixture; or b) as part of an article containing the chemical substance or mixture.

Chemical Processor

Any person who processes a chemical substance or mixture.

Chemical Protective Clothing

Clothing specifically designed to protect the skin and eyes from direct chemical contact. Descriptions of chemical-protective apparel include nonencapsulating and encapsulating (referred to as liquid-splash protective clothing and vapor-protective clothing, respectively).

Chemical Reaction

A change in the arrangement of atoms or molecules to yield substances of different composition and properties.

Chemical Safety and Hazard Investigation Board (CSHIB)

See Chemical Safety Board.

Chemical Safety Board (CSB)

The 5 member independent safety board known as the Chemical Safety and Hazard Investigation Board (CSHIB), appointed for 5 year terms, on the basis of technical qualification, professional standing, and demonstrated knowledge in the fields of accident reconstruction, safety engineering, human factors, toxicology, or air pollution regulation.

The responsibilities of CSHIB, include, but are not limited to, the following:

- i) investigating (or cause to be investigated), determine and report to the public in writing the facts, conditions, and circumstances and the cause or probable cause of any accidental release resulting in a fatality, serious injury, or substantial property damages;

- ii) issuing periodic reports to the Congress, federal, state and local agencies, including the Environmental Protection Agency and the Occupational Safety and Health Administration, concerned with the safety of chemical production, processing, handling, and storage, and other interested persons recommending measures to reduce the likelihood or the consequences of accidental releases and proposing corrective steps to make chemical production, processing, handling and storage as safe and free from risk of injury as is possible and to include in such reports proposed rules or orders to prevent or minimize the consequences of any release of substances that may cause death, injury, or other serious adverse effects on human health or substantial property damage as the result of an accidental release; and

- iii) establishing regulatory requirements binding on persons for reporting accidental releases into the ambient air subject to the Board's investigatory jurisdiction.

Reporting releases to the National Response Center, in lieu of the Board directly, typically satisfies regulations.

To ensure coordination of functions and to limit duplication of activities the Board enters into memoranda of understanding with the National Transportation Safety Board, the Occupational Safety and Health Administration; or conducts studies in cooperation with federal agencies involving emergency response authorities, state and local governmental agencies, and associations and organizations from the industrial, commercial, and nonprofit sectors.

Chemical Standards for the Development of Test Data

A prescription of health and environmental effects, and information relating to toxicity, persistence, and other characteristics that affect health and the environment, for which test data for a chemical substance or mixture are to be developed and any analysis that is to be performed on such data. This includes analyzing a) the extent necessary to ensure that data respecting such effects and characteristics are reliable and adequate; b) the manner in which such data are to be developed, c) the specification of any test protocol or methodology to be employed in the development of such data, and d) other requirements necessary to provide such assurance.

Chemical Substance

1) Any organic or inorganic substance of a particular molecular identity, including any combination of such substances occurring in whole or in part as a result of a chemical reaction or occurring in nature, and any element or uncombined radical. It does not include any mixture of separable chemicals. 2) Any pesticide (as defined in the Federal Insecticide, Fungicide, and Rodenticide Act) when manufactured, processed, or distributed in commerce for use as a pesticide for tobacco or any tobacco product. 3) Any source material, special nuclear material, or by-product material (as defined in the Atomic Energy Act of 1954 and regulations issued under such Act). 4) Any article, the sale of which is subject to the tax imposed by the Internal Revenue Code of 1954 (determined without regard to any exemptions from such tax provided by Section 4182 or Section 4221 or any provisions of such Code). 5) Any food, food additive, drug, cosmetic, or device (as defined in Section 201 of the Federal Food, Drug, and Cosmetic Act) when manufactured, processed, or distributed in commerce for use as a food, food additive, drug, cosmetic, or device. The term includes, but is not limited to: chemical and biological additives, burning agents, sinking agents, adulterants, inorganic chemicals, intermediates, nitrites, organic chemicals, chlorinated hydrocarbons, volatile organic compounds, and other listed hazardous substances.

Chemical Survey

The directed effort to determine the nature and degree of chemical hazard in an area and to delineate the perimeter of the hazard area.

Chemical Treatment

Any one of a variety of technologies that use chemicals or a variety of chemical processes to treat waste.

Chemical Vapor Deposition (CVD)

A process in which desired reinforcement material is deposited from vapor phase onto a continuous core; boron on tungsten, for example.

Chemical Warfare Agent

See Chemical Agent.

Chemical Warfare Weapons

Lethal and incapacitating munitions and agents of chemical or biological origin.

Chemical Warfare

All aspects of military operations involving the employment of lethal and incapacitating munitions/agents and the warning and protective measures associated with such operations. Riot control agents and herbicides are not considered to be chemical warfare agents.

Chemical Waste Landfill

A landfill at which protection against risk of injury to health or the environment from migration of PCBs to land, water, or atmosphere is provided by locating, engineering, and operating the landfill as specified in 40 CFR 761.75 (TSCA).

Chemicals of Potential Concern

Chemicals that are potentially site-related and whose data are of sufficient quality for use in the quantitative risk assessment.

Chemoreception

The reaction of a sense organ to a chemical stimulus.

Chemosterilant

A chemical that controls pests by preventing reproduction.

CHEMS

An acronym for Chemical Hazards Emergency Management System.

Chesapeake Bay and Lake Champlain Monitoring

1) The program established by EPA to determine the role of air deposition in the pollutant loadings of the Chesapeake Bay and Lake Champlain, investigate the sources of air pollutants deposited in the watersheds, evaluate the health and environmental effects of such pollutant loadings, and sample pollutants in biota, fish and wildlife within the watersheds, as necessary to characterize such effects. 2) EPA's operation of atmospheric deposition stations to monitor deposition of hazardous air pollutants (and other air pollutants) within the Chesapeake Bay and Lake Champlain watersheds.

CHESS

An acronym for Community Health and Environmental Surveillance System.

Chi-Square *(x)*

A means of estimating whether a given set of data differs from expected values to such an extent that it could be statistically significant of nonchance factors. It is the sum of the quotients obtained by dividing the square of each difference between an actual and an expected frequency by the expected frequency.

Chicago Operations Office (COO)

The DOE Research and Development and Field Facility, established in 1946 as one of the Atomic Energy Commission's first field offices. In 1977, as part of the newly established DOE, the Office focused its efforts on long-term, high-risk research and development in conjunction with business and industry as well as the academic community. Major missions include institutional management of major government-owned, contractor-operated laboratories and facilities; scientific and technical management of programs and projects including nuclear waste management, magnetic fusion, and coal gasification; and business and technical management of contracts and grants, including fiscal and construction management as well as responsibilities for safety, environmental protection, and quality assurance.

Chief

A title for the individual responsible for command of functional areas, or tasks, such as operations, planning, logistics, and administration.

Chief of Staff

The senior or principal member or head of a staff, or the principal assistant in a staff capacity to a person in a command capacity; the head or controlling member of a staff, for purposes of the coordination of its work.

Chilling Effect

The lowering of the earth's temperature because of increased particles in the air blocking the sun's rays. *See* Greenhouse Effect.

Chitin

A semitransparent horny substance forming the principal component of crustacean shells, insect exoskeletons, and the cell walls of certain fungi.

Chloramines

Compounds of organic or inorganic nitrogen and chlorine.

Chlorinated Hydrocarbons

A class of persistent, broadspectrum insecticides that linger in the environment and accumulate in the food chain. Among them are DDT, aldrin, dieldrin, heptachlor, chlordane, lindane, endrin, mirex, hexachloride, and toxaphene. Other examples include TCE, used as an industrial solvent.

Chlorinated Solvent

An organic solvent containing chlorine atoms, e.g., methylene chloride and 1,1,1-trichloromethane that is used in aerosol spray containers and in road paint.

Chlorination

Adding chlorine to drinking water, sewage, or industrial wastewater, for the purpose of disinfection, oxidation, or other biological or chemical results. Chlorine also is used almost universally in manufacturing processes, particularly for the plastics industry.

Chlorination Chamber

See Chlorine Contact Chamber.

Chlorinators

Devices that add chlorine, in gas or liquid form, to water or sewage to kill infectious bacteria.

Chlorine (Cl_2)

An essential ingredient in many industrial chemicals; it is an extremely toxic gas, heavier than air and it combines with water to produce hydrochloric acid (HCl) and hypochlorite. An element ordinarily existing as a greenish-yellow gas about 2.5 times as heavy as air. At atmospheric pressure and a temperature of 30.1°F, the gas becomes an amber liquid about 1.5 times as heavy as water. The atomic weight of chlorine is 35.457; its molecular weight is 70.914.

Chlorine Contact Chamber

1) A detention basin provided primarily to secure diffusion of chlorine through the liquid. 2) That part of a water treatment plant where effluent is disinfected by chlorine. Also called chlorination chamber.

Chlorofluorocarbons (CFCs)

A family of inert, nontoxic, and easily liquefied chemicals used as coolants in refrigeration, air conditioning, packaging, insulation, or as solvents and aerosol propellants. Because CFCs are not destroyed in the lower atmosphere they drift into the upper atmosphere where their chlorine components destroy ozone. CFCs are thought to be a major cause of the ozone hole over Antarctica.

Chlorophyllous Leaves
Leaves containing chlorophyll (green pigment), which enables the photosynthesis process to occur.

Chlorosis
Discoloration of normally green plant parts, that can be caused by disease, lack of nutrients, or various air pollutants.

CHOP
See Change of Operational Control.

CHR
An acronym for Confinement Heat Removal.

Chromatophore
A pigment producing cell, or a pigmented animal cell that can change the color of the skin, as in some lizards.

Chromium (Cr)
A heavy metal. *See* Heavy Metals.

Chromosome
A very long molecule of DNA completed with protein, containing genetic information arranged in a linear sequence.

Chromosome Abnormality
A group of conditions associated with abnormalities in the number or structure of chromosomes. These can be produced by insertion, deletion, or rearrangement of chromosomal segments.

Chronic Effect
1) Effects of exposure to a hazardous material on any living organism in which symptoms develop slowly after many exposures or recur frequently. 2) A pathologic process caused by repeated exposures over a period of long duration.

Chronic Exposure
Repeated exposures or contact with a toxic substance over a long period of time, usually lasting over six months to a lifetime.

Chronic Obstructive Pulmonary Disease (COPD)
A disease of the lung, involving increased resistance to air flow in the bronchial airways and loss of tissue elasticity, that leads to decreased ability of the lungs to perform ventilation. The pathological changes that lead to COPD can be caused by chronic bronchitis, pulmonary emphysema, chronic asthma, and chronic bronchiolitis.

Chronic Radiation Dose
A dose of ionizing radiation received either continuously or intermittently over a prolonged period of time. A chronic radiation dose may be high enough to cause radiation sickness and death but if received at a low dose rate a significant portion of the acute cellular damage will be repaired. *See* Acute Radiation Dose; Radiation Dose; Radiation Dose Rate.

Chronic Reference Dose Value (RfD)
An estimate of a lifetime daily exposure level for the human population, including sensitive subpopulations, that is likely to be without an appreciable risk of deleterious effects. A chronic RFD is specifically developed to be protective for long-term exposure to a compound (7 years to a lifetime).

Chronic Toxicity
The capacity of a substance to cause long-term poisonous human health effects. *See* Acute Toxicity.

CIFC
An acronym for Committee on Interstate and Foreign Commerce.

CIIA
An acronym for Committee on Interior and Insular Affairs.

Ciliate
A species descriptor meaning having microscopic, hairlike appendages extending from a cell and often capable of rhythmical motions.

Ciliated Epithelial Cell
A cell with cilia that lines the tracheobronchial region of the lung. The beating of the cilia moves mucus and substances (such as inhaled particles trapped on/in the mucus) upwards and out of the lung, thereby contributing significantly to lung clearance.

Cilium
See Ciliate.

CILRT
An acronym for Containment Integrated Leak Rate Test.

CIP
An acronym for Capital Improvement Project; Catalog in Publication.

Cipher
Any cryptographic system in which arbitrary symbols or groups of symbols, represent units of plain text of regular length, usually single letters, or in which units of plain text are rearranged, or both, in accordance with certain predetermined rules.

Circumneutral
A term applied to water with a pH of 5.5 to 7.4.

Circumscissile
A term meaning splitting or opening along a transverse circular line.

Cirolanid Facies
A species descriptor referring to the characteristics or appearance of a population of isopod crustaceans.

Cirrhosis
A liver disease characterized by increased fibrous tissue, accompanied by other abnormal physiological changes. Clinical signs of cirrhosis include the loss of functional liver cells and increased resistance to blood flow through the liver.

Cirri
A term pertaining to cirrus clouds.

CIRVIS
An acronym for Communications Instructions for Reporting Vital Intelligence Sightings.

CIT
See Critical Incident Technique.

Citable Program Elements
Specific program elements in 29 CFR Part 1960 that may be cited when found not in compliance during inspections or evaluations.

CITES
An acronym for the Convention on International Trade in Endangered Species. *See* Convention on International Trade in Endangered Species of Wild Fauna and Flora.

Civil Defense
All those activities and measures designed or undertaken to a) minimize the effects upon the civilian population caused or that would be caused by an enemy attack on the United States; b) deal with the immediate emergency conditions that would be created by any such attack; and c) effectuate emergency repairs to, or the emergency restoration of, vital utilities and facilities destroyed or damaged by any such attack.

Civil Defense Emergency
See Domestic Emergencies.

Civil Nuclear Power
A nation that has potential to employ nuclear technology for development of nuclear weapons but has deliberately decided against doing so.

Civil Transportation
The movement of persons, property, or mail by civil facilities, and the resources necessary to accomplish the movement. The term does not include transportation operated or controlled by the military, and petroleum and gas pipelines.

Civilian Nuclear Activity
Any atomic energy activity other than an atomic energy defense activity.

CJCS
An acronym for Chairman of the Joint Chiefs of Staff.

Cladding
The thin-walled metal tube that forms the outer jacket of a nuclear fuel rod. It prevents corrosion of the fuel by the coolant and the release of fission products into the coolant. Aluminum, stainless steel and zirconium alloys are common cladding materials.

Claim
A demand in writing for a certain sum.

Claimant
1) Any person who presents a claim for compensation under CERCLA. 2) A person submitting a claim of trade secrecy to EPA in connection with a chemical otherwise required to be disclosed in a report or other filing made under the Superfund Amendments and Reauthorization Act of 1986.

Clandestine Operation
An operation sponsored or conducted by governmental departments or agencies in such a way as to ensure secrecy or concealment. A clandestine operation differs from a covert operation in that emphasis is placed on concealment of the operation rather than on concealment of identity of the sponsor. In special operations, an activity may be both covert and clandestine and may focus equally on operational considerations and intelligence-related activities. *See* Covert Operation; Overt Operation.

Clarification
1) Any process or combination of processes whose primary purpose is to reduce the concentrations of suspended matter in a liquid. 2) Clearing action that occurs during wastewater treatment when solids settle out. This is often aided by centrifugal action and chemically induced coagulation in wastewater.

Clarifier
A unit whose primary purpose is to secure clarification. Accomplished in a tank in which solids are settled to the bottom and subsequently removed as sludge. The term is usually applied to sedimentation tanks or basins.

Class
1) The category by which most animals are referred to, such as birds, reptiles, insects, crustaceans, arachnids, amphibians, snails, and mammals, or classes of plants, such as ferns, mosses, and mushrooms. 2) The taxonomic classification of organisms belonging to related orders.

Class A Equipment
A DOE term for active or passive safety devices/systems or primary environmental monitors.

Class A Explosives
Explosives that are detonating or otherwise a maximum hazard. Black powder, explosive boosters, blasting caps, and explosive bombs are examples of Class A Explosives.

Class A Fires
Fires in ordinary combustible materials.

Class B Equipment
A DOE term for devices/systems that, although not primarily safety related, will result in facility shutdown or degradation of operating parameters, or any secondary environmental monitors.

Class B Explosives
Explosives that function by rapid combustion, rather than detonation. Special fireworks, jet thrust units, rocket ammunition with solid projectile are examples of Class B Explosives.

Class B Fires
Fires in flammable liquids.

Class C Explosives

Explosives that include certain types of manufactured articles that contain Class A or Class B explosives, or both, as components, but in restricted quantities. This class of explosive also includes certain types of fireworks specifically identified as Class C explosives. Explosive release devices, fuse igniters, time fuses, and igniter cords are examples of these types of explosives.

Class C Fires

Fires involving energized electrical equipment.

Class C Wastes

Waste that will not decay to levels that present an unacceptable hazard to an intruder within 100 years.

Class D Fires

Fires in combustible metals.

Class I and Class II Substances

Hazardous substances used as refrigerants, solvents, fire retardants, foam blowing agents, and other commercial applications that are being replaced by chemicals, product substitutes, or alternative manufacturing processes that reduce overall risks to human health and the environment.

Class I Area, Maximum Allowable Increases in Concentrations (MAIC)

The maximum allowable increase in concentrations over baseline concentrations for particulate matter and sulfur dioxide in micrograms per cubic meter (mgcm). Class I MAICs are as follows: a) for particulate matter — annual geometric mean = 5 mgcm, 24-hour maximum = 10 mgcm; b)for sulfur dioxide — annual arithmetic mean = 2 mgcm; 24-hour maximum = 5 mgcm; and 3-hour maximum = 25 mgcm.

Class I Attainment Area

Areas such as a) international parks; b) national wilderness areas that exceed 5,000 acres in size; c) national memorial parks that exceed 5,000 acres in size; and d) national parks that exceed 6,000 acres in size, and that were in existence on August 7, 1977.

Class II Area, Maximum Allowable Increases in Concentrations (MAIC)

The maximum allowable increase in concentrations over baseline concentrations for particulate matter and sulfur dioxide in micrograms per cubic meter (mgcm). Class II MAICs are as follows: a) for particulate matter — annual geometric mean = 19 mgcm, 24-hour maximum = 37 mgcm; b) for sulfur dioxide — annual arithmetic mean = 20 mgcm; 24-hour maximum = 91 mgcm; and 3-hour maximum = 512 mgcm.

Class II Attainment Areas

All areas in a state designated pursuant to Section 7407(d) of the CAA as attainment or unclassifiable that are not established as a Class I Area. *See* Class I Attainment Area.

Class II Wells

Wells that inject fluids a) brought to the surface in connection with conventional oil or natural gas production and may be commingled with waste waters from gas plants that are an integral part of production operations, unless those waters would be classified as a hazardous waste at the time of injection; b) for enhanced recovery of oil or natural gas; and c) for storage of hydrocarbons that are liquid at standard temperature and pressure.

Class III Area, Maximum Allowable Increases in Concentrations (MAIC)

The maximum allowable increase in concentrations over baseline concentrations for sulfur dioxide and particulate matter in micrograms per cubic meter. Class III MAICs are as follows: a) for particulate matter — annual geometric mean = 37 mgcm, 24-hour maximum = 75 mgcm; b)for sulfur dioxide — annual arithmetic mean = 40 mgcm; 24-hour maximum = 182 mgcm; and 3-hour maximum = 700 mgcm.

Class of Covered Products

A group of products, whose functions, characteristics, and/or intended uses are similar.

Classification, Emergencies

The grouping of emergencies into one of three specific classes that have predetermined response actions for each class in support of requirements outlined in DOE's Emergency Response, Planning, and Preparedness for Operational Emergencies guidelines. These classes include: a) Alert; b) Site Area Emergency; and c) General Emergency.

Classification, Information

A means of identifying information concerning the national defense and foreign relations of the United States that in the interests of national security, requires protection against unauthorized disclosure. *See* Security Classification.

Classified Contract

Any contract that requires or will require access to classified information by the contractor or the employees in the performance of the contract. A contract may be classified even though the contract document itself is not classified.

Classified Information

Official information that has been determined to require protection against unauthorized disclosure and that has been designated Top Secret, Secret, Confidential Restricted Data, Formerly Restricted Data, and/or National Security Information, that requires safeguarding in the interest of national security and defense.

Classified Interests

Classified documents, information, or material including classified special nuclear material possessed by the department, a contractor of the department, a departmental facility, or any other facility under the department's jurisdiction.

Classified Matter

Official information, documents, parts components, or other matter in any form or of any nature that requires protection in the interests of national security. *See* Unclassified Matter.

Classified Telecommunications Facilities

Facilities that contain both crypto equipment and input/output equipment for the electronic transmission, receipt, or processing of classified information. The crypto equipment and input/output equipment may either be installed in the same area and share common security measures or be installed in different parts of the same security area connected by a protected distribution system, with each area having its own security measures.

Classified Wastes

Waste material that has been given security classification in accordance with 50 USC 401 and Executive Order 11652.

Clastic

A term pertaining to a rock or sediment composed primarily of broken fragments that are derived from preexisting rocks or minerals and that have been transported from their places of origin.

Clastogenic

Able to break chromosomes and thereby produce chromosome abnormalities, a form of genotoxicity. This results in the gain, loss, or rearrangement of pieces of chromosomes.

CLDTMP

A computer code to calculate cladding temperature limit.

Clean Air Act of 1970 (CAA; 42 USC 7401 et seq.)

The comprehensive federal law that regulates air emissions from area, stationary, and mobile sources. The Act establishes federal policy for the attainment and maintenance of national air quality standards under which an integral means for obtaining compliance is land-use regulation. CAA gives EPA authority for establishing standards for primary and secondary ambient air quality; performance for new stationary sources; and emission standards for hazardous air pollutants.

The purpose of the Clean Air Act is to:

- a) protect and enhance the quality of the nation's air resources so as to promote the public health and welfare and the productive capacity of its population;

- b) initiate and accelerate a national research and development program to achieve the prevention and control of air pollution;

- c) provide technical and financial assistance to state and local governments in connection with the development and implementation of their air pollution prevention and control programs; and

- d) encourage and assist the development and operation of regional air pollution control programs.

The CAA authorizes EPA to establish National Ambient Air Quality Standards (NAAQS) to protect public health and the environment. The goal of the Act was to set and achieve NAAQS in every state by 1975. This setting of maximum pollutant standards was coupled with directing the states to develop state implementation plans (SIPs) applicable to appropriate industrial sources in the state. The Act was amended in 1977 primarily to set new goals (i.e., dates) for achieving attainment of NAAQS since many areas of the country had failed to meet the deadlines. The 1990 amendments to the Clean Air Act in large part were intended to meet unaddressed or insufficiently addressed problems such as acid rain, ground level ozone, stratospheric ozone depletion, and air toxics.

Clean Alternative Fuels (CAF)

Any fuel (including methanol, ethanol, or other alcohols and any mixture thereof) containing 85% or more by volume of such alcohol with gasoline or other fuels (such as reformulated gasoline, diesel, natural gas, liquefied petroleum gas, and hydrogen) or power sources (including electricity) used in a clean-fuel vehicle that complies with the standards and requirements applicable to such vehicle.

Clean Alternative Fuels Program (CAFP)

An EPA research program to identify, characterize, and predict air emissions related to the production, distribution, storage, and use of clean alternative fuels to determine the risks and benefits to human health and the environment relative to those from using conventional gasoline and diesel fuels.

Clean Fuel Vehicle (CFV)

A vehicle in a class or category of vehicles that has been certified to meet for any model year the clean fuel vehicle standards applicable under the CAA for that model year to clean fuel vehicles in that class or category.

Clean Oceans Fund

Interest-bearing accounts established by each state that is a party to a compliance agreement or an enforcement agreement. *See* Marine Protection, Research, and Sanctuaries Act (MPRSA); Ocean Dumping Compliance/Enforcement Agreements.

Clean Rooms

An uncontaminated room having facilities for the storage of employees' street clothing and uncontaminated materials and equipment.

Clean Water Act of 1977 (CWA; 33 USC 121 et seq.)

The 1977 amendments to the Federal Water Pollution Control Act of 1972, which set the basic structure for regulating discharges of pollutants to waters of the United States. This law gave EPA the authority to set effluent standards on an industry-by-industry basis (technology-based) and continued the requirements to set water quality standards for all contaminants in surface waters. The CWA makes it unlawful for any person to discharge any pollutant from a point source into navigable waters unless a permit (NPDES) is obtained under the Act. The 1977 amendments focused on toxic pollutants. In 1987, the CWA was reauthorized and again focused on toxic substances, authorized citizen suit provisions, and funded sewage treatment plants (POTWs) under the Construction Grants Program. The CWA provides for the delegation by EPA of many permitting, administrative, and enforcement aspects of the law to state governments. In states with the authority to implement CWA programs, EPA still retains oversight responsibilities. *See* Federal

Water Pollution Control Act (FWPCA); Publicly Owned Treatment Works (POTW).

Cleanup
Actions taken to deal with a release or threatened release of hazardous substances that could affect the public health, welfare, and/or the environment. The term "cleanup" is often used generally to describe various implementation actions or phases of remedial responses, such as remedial action, removal action, response action, or corrective action, remedial investigation.

Cleanup Operation
An operation where hazardous substances arc removed, contained, incinerated, neutralized, stabilized, cleared up, or in any other manner processed or handled with the ultimate goal of making the site safer for people or the environment.

Cleansing Station
See Decontamination Station.

CWA
See Clean Water Act of 1977.

Clear
1) To approve or authorize, or to obtain approval or authorization for: a) a person or persons with regard to their actions, movements, duties, etc.; b) an object or group of objects, such as equipment or supplies, with regard to quality, quantity, purpose, movement, or disposition; and c) a request, with regard to correctness of form, validity, etc. 2) To give one or more aircraft a clearance to land or takeoff. 3) To give a person a security clearance. 4) To pass a designated point, line, object, etc.

Clear Cut
1) An area from which all trees and natural vegetation have been removed, exposing the area to erosion by wind and/or rain. 2) A forest management technique that involves harvesting all the trees in one area at one time, a practice that can destroy vital habitat and biodiversity and encour-

ages rainfall or snowmelt runoff, erosion, sedimentation of streams and lakes, and flooding.

Clearance
The disappearance of a compound from a specific organ or body compartment or the whole body. In pulmonary toxicology, clearance refers specifically to removal of an inhaled substance that deposits on the lung surface.

Clearance Capacity
An estimate expressed in terms of measurement or weight tons per day of the cargo that may be transported inland from a beach or port over the available means of inland communication, including roads, railroads, and inland waterways. The estimate is based on an evaluation of the physical characteristics of the transportation facilities in the area.

Cleistogamous
A term meaning characterized by self-fertilization in an unopened, budlike state.

Climate Change
A term that refers to the buildup of manmade gases in the atmosphere that trap the sun's heat, causing changes in weather patterns on a global scale. The effects include changes in rainfall patterns, sea level rise, potential droughts, habitat loss, and heat stress. The greenhouse gases of most concern are carbon dioxide, methane, and nitrous oxides. If these gases in our atmosphere double, the earth could warm up by 1.5°F to 4.5°F by the year 2050, with changes in global precipitation having the greatest consequences. *See* Global Warming; Greenhouse Effect.

Climatic Hazards
Environmental hazards associated with weather impacts, such as soil erosion by wind and/or rains; crop loss due to excessive heat and/or droughts.

Climatology
The scientific study of climates over long periods of time.

Climax

The fully developed stage of an ecosystem.

Clinic

A medical treatment facility primarily intended and appropriately staffed and equipped to provide outpatient medical service for nonhospital type patients. Examination and treatment for emergency cases are types of services rendered. A clinic is also intended to perform certain nontherapeutic activities related to the health of the personnel served, such as physical examinations, immunizations, medical administration, and other preventive medical and sanitary measures necessary to support a primary military mission. A clinic will be equipped with the necessary supporting services to perform the assigned mission. A clinic may be equipped with beds (normally fewer than 25) for observation of patients awaiting transfer to a hospital and for care of cases that cannot be cared for on an outpatient status, but which do not require hospitalization. Patients whose expected duration of illness exceeds 72 hours will not normally occupy clinic beds for periods longer than necessary to arrange transfer to a hospital.

Cloning

In biotechnology, obtaining a group of genetically identical cells from a single cell; making identical copies of a gene.

Close Reflection by Water

Immediate contact by water of sufficient thickness to reflect a maximum number of neutrons.

Closed Area

A designated area in or over which passage of any kind is prohibited.

Closed Container

A container sealed by means of a lid or other device that will not let liquid or vapor escape from it at ordinary temperatures.

Closed Installation

Any location where lasers are used that will be closed to unprotected personnel during laser operation.

Closed Portions

Portions of a facility that an owner or operator has closed in accordance with the approved facility closure plan and all applicable closure requirements.

Closed System

A procedure for removing a hazardous substance from its original container, rinsing the emptied container and transferring the substance, mixtures, and dilutions and rinse solution through connecting hoses, pipes, and couplings that are sufficiently tight to prevent exposure of any person to the substance or rinse solution. Rinsing is not required when the substance is used without dilution, and the container is disposed in accordance with applicable regulations. The system's design and construction must meet the state enforcing agency's closed system criteria.

Closed Vent Systems

Systems that are not open to the atmosphere and that are composed of piping, connections, and, if necessary, flow-inducing devices that transport gas or vapor from a piece or parts of equipment to a control device.

Closed-Loop Recycling

Reclaiming or reusing wastewater for nonpotable purposes in an enclosed process.

Closure, Landfill

The act of securing a solid waste landfill or hazardous waste management facility according to specific EPA requirements. Closure is the procedure an operator must go through when a landfill reaches the legal capacity for solid waste. No more waste can be accepted and a cap usually is placed over the site. The cap is then planted with grasses and other ground covers. Post-closure care includes monitoring ground water, landfill gases, and leachate collection systems, sometimes for as long as 30 years.

Closure, Logistics
In transportation, the process of a unit arriving at a specified location. It begins when the first element arrives at a designated location, e.g., port of entry/port of departure, intermediate stops, or final destination, and ends when the last element does likewise. For the purposes of studies and command post exercises, a unit is considered essentially closed after 95% of its movement requirements for personnel and equipment are completed.

Closure Period
The period of time beginning with the cessation, with respect to waste impoundment of uranium ore processing operations, and ending with completion of requirements specified under a closure plan.

Closure Plans
1) Documentation prepared to guide the deactivation, stabilization, and surveillance of a waste management unit or facility under the Resource Conservation and Recovery Act. 2) The closure of a DOE operating facility. The plans contain a complete survey of the environmental problems at a DOE facility, budget data that indicate the cost of environmental restoration and remediation at the facility, and a discussion of the proposed cleanup schedule.

Closure Shortfall
The specified movement requirement or portion thereof that did not meet scheduling criteria and/or movement dates.

Clothing, Protective
A term referring to anticontamination clothing such as acid suits, lab coats, radiation suits, flame retardant clothing, and other personal protective clothing items.

Cloud Amount
The proportion of sky obscured by cloud, expressed as a fraction of sky covered.

Cloud Chamber Effect
See Condensation Cloud.

Cloud Cover
See Cloud Amount.

Cloud forest
A high-altitude forest with a dense undergrowth of dwarf trees, ferns, mosses, and other plants that grow on the trunks of the trees.

Cloud Top Height
The maximal altitude to which a nuclear mushroom cloud rises.

CLP
An acronym for Contract Laboratory Program.

Clump
A thick grouping of plants or trees.

Cluster
A group of similar elements, such as flowers on a plant, occurring closely together.

Clutch
The number of eggs laid in one breeding.

CM
An acronym for Core Melt.

cm/sec
An abbreviation for centimeters per second.

CMMF
An acronym for Committee on Merchant Marine and Fisheries.

CMPPA
An acronym for Computer Matching and Privacy Protection Amendments.

CMS
An acronym for RCRA Corrective Measures Study.

CMT
See Control Methods and Technologies (CAA); Crisis Management Team.

Compressed Natural Gas (CNG)
Natural gas that has been compressed for storage in tanks or cylinders.

CNHR
An acronym for Containment Atmosphere Heat Removal.

CNPWP
See Convention on Nature Protection and Wildlife Preservation.

CNRR
An acronym for Containment Radioactivity Removal.

CO Milestone Demonstration Date
The March 31, 1996, deadline, by which each state in which all or part of a Serious Area is located shall submit, to the Administrator of EPA, a demonstration that the area has achieved a reduction in emissions of carbon monoxide (CO) equivalent to the total of the specific annual emission reductions required by December 31, 1995.

CO_2 Sublaser
A widely used laser in which the primary lasing medium is carbon dioxide gas. The output wavelength is 10.6 micrometers (m) (i.e., 10,600 nanometers) in the far infrared spectrum. It can be operated in either continuous wave (CW) or pulsed wave.

COA
See Course of Action.

Coagulation
1) A clumping of particles in wastewater to settle out impurities. It is often induced by chemicals such as lime, alum, and iron salts. 2) A process using coagulant chemicals and mixing by which colloidal and suspended materials are destabilized and agglomerated into flocs (i.e., the product flocculation).

Coal
All solid fuels classified as anthracite, bituminous, subituminous, or lignite by the American Society and Testing and Materials, Designation D388-77.

Coal Laboratory
A university coal research laboratory established and operated pursuant to a designation made under the Surface Mining Control and Reclamation Act.

Coal Refuse
Waste-products of coal mining, cleaning, and coal preparation operations (e.g., culm, gob) containing coal, matrix material, clay, and other organic and inorganic material.

Coassembly
With respect to exports, a cooperative arrangement (e.g., U.S. Government or company with foreign government or company) by which finished parts, components, assemblies, or subassemblies are provided to an eligible foreign government, international organization, or commercial producer for the assembly of an end-item or system. This is normally accomplished under the provisions of a manufacturing license agreement per the U.S. International Traffic in Arms Regulation (ITAR) and could involve the implementation of a government-to-government memorandum of understanding.

Coastal Barrier Management Report
The Coastal Barriers Task Force (CBTF) report regarding the Coastal Barrier Resources System. The report includes, but is not limited to, the following

- an analysis of the effects of any regulatory activities of the federal government on development within units of the System, for the period from 1975 to 1990;
- an analysis of the direct and secondary impacts of tax policies of the federal government on

development within units of the System, for the period from 1975 to 1990;

- c) an estimate and comparison of the costs to the federal government with respect to developed coastal barriers on which are located units of the System, for the period from 1975 to 1990, that includes costs of shore protection activities, beach renourishment activities, evacuation services, disaster assistance, and flood insurance subsidies under the national flood insurance program; and

- d) a determination of the number of structures for which flood insurance under the national flood insurance program has been unavailable since the enactment of the National Flood Insurance Act of 1968 (Aug. 1, 1968) because of the prohibition, under Section 1321 of such Act (42 USC 4028), of the provision of insurance for structures located on coastal barriers within the System.

Coastal Barrier Resources System

The system consisting of undeveloped coastal barriers and other areas located on the coasts of the United States that are identified and generally depicted on the maps "Coastal Barrier Resources System," dated October 24, 1990, as such maps may be revised under Section 4 of the Coastal Barrier Improvement Act of 1990.

Coastal Barrier System Maps

The maps prepared under the Coastal Barrier Improvement Act of 1990 (CBIA), and any modification to those maps under that act.

Coastal Barrier System Unit

Any undeveloped coastal barrier, or combination of closely related undeveloped coastal barriers, included within the Coastal Barrier Resources System established by Section 3503 of the Coastal Barrier Resources Act.

Coastal Barriers Task Force (CBTF)

The special purpose interagency task force composed of 11 members, one each from the following departments: Agriculture, Commerce, Defense, Energy, Housing and Urban Development, Interior, Transportation, Treasury, Environmental Protection Agency, Federal Emergency Management Agency, and the Small Business Administration. The Task Force was charged with preparing a coastal barrier management report and terminated 90 days after submission of the report. *See* Coastal Barrier Management Report.

Coastal Commission Special Treatment Areas (STAs)

Those areas that have been designated so based upon the following criteria: scenic view corridors; sites of significant scenic value; wetlands, lagoons, streams, estuaries, and marine environments; significant animal and plant habitat areas; and recreation areas.

Coastal Convoy

A convoy whose voyage lies in general on the continental shelf and in coastal waters.

Coastal Frontier

A geographic division of a coastal area established for organization and command purposes in order to ensure the effective coordination of military forces employed in military operations within the coastal frontier area.

Coastal Refraction

The change of the direction of travel of a radio ground wave as it passes from land to sea or from sea to land. Also called land effect or shoreline effect.

Coastal Region Management Plans

Waste disposal plans developed by the Administrator, in cooperation with other officials of appropriate federal, state, and local agencies, to assess the feasibility of regional management plans for the disposal of waste materials in coastal areas. Plans typically integrate all waste disposal activities into a comprehensive regional disposal strategy, and address: a) the sources, quantities, and types of materials that require and will require disposal; b) the environmental, economic, social, and human health factors (and the methods used to assess these factors) associated with disposal alternatives; c) the improvements in production processes, methods of disposal, and recycling to reduce the adverse effects associated with such disposal alternatives; d) the applicable laws and regulations governing waste disposal; and e) improvements in permitting processes.

Coastal Resource
Any coastal wetland, beach, dune, barrier island, reef, estuary, or fish and wildlife habitat, determined by a coastal state to be of substantial biological or natural storm protective value.

Coastal Special Treatment Area
An identifiable and geographically bounded forest area designated within the Coastal Zone that constitutes a significant wildlife and/or plant habitat area, area of special scenic significance, and any land where timber operations could adversely affect public recreation areas or the biological productivity of any wetland, estuary, or stream especially valuable because of its role in a coastal ecosystem.

Coastal State
1) A state of the United States that is in, or bordering on, the Atlantic Ocean, Pacific Ocean, or Arctic Ocean, the Gulf of Mexico, Long Island Sound, or one or more of the Great Lakes. 2) Any one of the states of Alabama, Alaska, California, Connecticut, Delaware, Florida, Georgia, Hawaii, Louisiana, Maine, Maryland, Massachusetts, Mississippi, New Hampshire, New Jersey, New York, North Carolina, Oregon, Rhode Island, South Carolina, Texas, Virginia, and Washington. Includes Puerto Rico, the Virgin Islands, Guam, the Commonwealth of the Northern Mariana Islands, and the Trust Territories of the Pacific Islands, and American Samoa.

Coastal System
The Coastal Barrier Resources System established by the Coastal Barrier Resources Act, as amended by the Coastal Barrier Improvement Act of 1990.

Coastal System Report
The report prepared in consultation with the governors and the coastal zone management agencies of states in which system units are located on:
a) recommendations for the conservation of the fish, wildlife, and other natural resources of the System based on an evaluation and comparison of all management alternatives, and combinations thereof, such as state and local actions, federal actions, and initiatives by private organizations and individuals;
b) recommendations for additions to, or deletions from, the Coastal Barrier Resources System, and for modifications to the boundaries of system units;
c) a summary of the comments received from the governors of the states, state coastal zone management agencies, other government officials, and the public regarding the system; and
d) an analysis of the effect, if any, that general revenue sharing grants have had on undeveloped coastal barriers.

Coastal Waters
1) The territorial sea of the United States. 2) The waters of the coastal zone except for the Great Lakes and specified ports and harbors on inland rivers. 3) The marine and estuarine waters of the United States up to the head of tidal influence. 4) The Exclusive Economic Zone established by Presidential Proclamation Number 5030, March 10, 1983.

Coastal Zone
1) All U.S. waters subject to the tide, U.S. waters of the Great Lakes, specified ports and harbors on the inland rivers, waters of the contiguous zone, other waters of the high seas subject to the National Contingency Plan, and the land or land substrata, groundwater, and ambient air proximal to those waters. 2) Lands and waters adjacent to the coast that exert an influence on the uses of the sea and its ecology, or, inversely, whose uses and ecology are affected by the sea. The term coastal zone delineates an area of federal responsibility for response action. Precise boundaries are determined by EPA/USCG agreements and identified in federal regional contingency plans.

Coastal Zone Management Act (CZMA)
A law adopted by Congress in 1972 authorizing the establishment of a national policy to preserve, protect, develop, and where possible, restore

coastal resources through a partnership between states and the federal government. The Act encourages the preparation of special area management plans that provide for increased specificity in protecting significant natural resources, reasonable coastal-dependent economic growth, improved protection of life and property in hazardous areas, and improved predictability in governmental decisionmaking. Administered by the Office of Coastal Zone Management of the Department of Commerce.

Coastwise Traffic
Sea traffic between continental United States ports on the Atlantic coast, Gulf coast, and Great Lakes, or between continental United States ports on the Pacific coast.

Cobalt-58
A radionuclide and listed CERCLA Hazardous Substance.

Cobalt-60
A radionuclide and listed CERCLA Hazardous Substance.

Cobbles
Rock fragments 7.6 cm (3 inches) to 25.4 cm (10 inches) in diameter.

COBOL
See Common Business Oriented Language.

COCA
An acronym for Consent Order and Compliance Agreement.

Cocoon
The tough protective covering wherein insect larvae pupate (take their adult form).

COD
See Chemical Oxygen Demand.

Code of Federal Regulations (CFR)
A periodic publication of the regulations established by U.S. law.

Codes, Standards, and Regulations
Nonspecific terminology for all guidelines, requirements, and laws of federal, state, or local origin by which a company, organization, or individual is controlled in their operations. These could include all aspects, such as specifications of materials, performance, design, or operations; measurements of quality control; permitting and documentation requirements; and qualifications of personnel.

CODF
An acronym for Complementary Cumulative Distribution Function.

Codominant
1) Two or more species providing about equal area cover that in combination control the environment. 2) Trees with crowns forming the general level of the crown cover and receiving full light from above, but comparatively little from the sides; usually with medium sized crowns more or less crowded on the sides.

COE
An acronym for Army Corps of Engineers.

Coefficient of Haze (COH)
A measurement of visibility interference in the atmosphere.

Coefficient of Storage
The volume of water an aquifer releases from or takes into storage per unit surface area of the aquifer per unit change in head.

Coefficient of Thermal Expansion
A material's fractional change in length for a given unit change of temperature.

Coefficient of Transmissivity
See Transmissivity.

COG
An acronym for Council of Governments.

COGEMT

An acronym for Continuity of Government Emergency Management Teams.

Cognitive Function

The ability to think.

Cognizant Federal Agency Officials

The senior government official with jurisdiction over the facility, program, or activities involved in an accident.

Cognizant Federal Agencies

The federal agency that owns, authorizes, regulates, or is otherwise deemed responsible for an emergency causing activity and that has the authority to take whatever steps necessary to stabilize the accident.

COH

See Coefficient of Haze.

Coherence

A term describing light as waves that are in phase in both time and space. Monochromaticity and low divergence are two properties of coherent light.

Cohort Study

A study of a group of persons sharing a common experience (e.g., exposure to a substance) within a defined time period; this experiment is used to determine if an increased risk of a health effect (disease) is associated with that exposure.

Coke Oven Production Technology, Study

The study jointly conducted by the Secretary of the Department of Energy and the Administrator to assist in the development and commercialization of technically practicable and economically viable control technologies that have the potential to significantly reduce emissions of hazardous air pollutants from coke oven production facilities. In identifying control technologies, the Secretary and the Administrator consider the range of existing coke oven operations and battery design and the availability of sources of materials for such coke ovens as well as alternatives to existing coke oven production design.

Cold CO Standard

The regulations applicable to emissions of carbon monoxide from 1994 and later model year light-duty vehicles and light-duty trucks when operated at 20° Fahrenheit. The regulations contain standards that provide that emissions of carbon monoxide from a manufacturer's vehicles when operated at 20° Fahrenheit may not exceed, in the case of light-duty vehicles, 10.0 grams per mile, and in the case of light-duty trucks, a level comparable in stringency to the standard applicable to light-duty vehicles. The standards take effect after model year 1993, according to a phase-in schedule that requires a percentage of each manufacturer's sales volume of light-duty vehicles and light-duty trucks to comply with applicable standards after model year 1993. The Phase-In Schedule for Cold Start Standards is as follows: 1994 — 40%; 1995 — 80%; and 1996 and thereafter — 100%. Not later than June 1, 1997, the Administrator of EPA is supposed to complete a study assessing the need for further reductions in emissions of carbon monoxide and the maximum reductions in such emissions achievable from model year 2001, and later model year light-duty vehicles and light-duty trucks when operated at 20° Fahrenheit.

Cold War

A state of international tension wherein political, economic, technological, sociological, psychological, paramilitary, and military measures short of overt armed conflict involving regular military forces, are employed to achieve national objectives.

Coleopteran

An insect, such as a beetle, characterized by fore wings modified to form tough protective covers for the hind wings.

Coliform Index

A rating of the purity of water based on a count of fecal bacteria.

Coliform Organisms

Microorganisms found in the intestinal tract of humans and animals. Their presence in water indicates fecal pollution and potentially dangerous bacterial contamination by disease-causing microorganisms.

Collaborative Purchase

A method of purchase whereby, in buying similar commodities, buyers for two or more departments exchange information concerning planned purchases in order to minimize competition between them for commodities in the same market.

Collate

1) The grouping together of related items to provide a record of events and facilitate further processing. 2) To compare critically two or more items or documents concerning the same general subject. 3) To place in order.

Collateral Task

A task other than those for which a person, or group, is primarily organized, trained, and equipped, that the person, or group, can accomplish by virtue of the inherent capabilities of that individual, or group of individuals.

Collecting Point

A point designated for the assembly of personnel casualties, stragglers, disabled material, salvage, etc., for further movement to collecting stations or rear installations.

Collection Operations Management (COM)

The authoritative direction, scheduling, and control of specific collection operations and associated processing, exploitation, and reporting resources. *See* Collection Requirements Management.

Collection Requirement

An established intelligence need considered in the allocation of resources to fulfill the essential elements of technical information needs.

Collection Requirements Management (CRM)

The authoritative development and control of collection, processing, exploitation, and/or reporting requirements that normally result in either the direct tasking of assets over which the collection manager has authority, or the generation of single-discipline tasking requests to collection management authorities at a higher, lower, or lateral echelon to accomplish the collection mission. *See* Collection Operations Management.

Collective Effective Dose Equivalent

1) The sum of the dose equivalents or effective dose equivalents of all individuals in an exposed population within an 80-km radius, expressed in units of person-rem (or person-sievert). When the collective dose equivalent of interest is for a specific organ, the units would be organ-rem (or organ-sievert). The 80-km distance shall be measured from a point located centrally with respect to major facilities or DOE program activities. 2) The sum of the effective dose equivalents of all individuals in an exposed population within 50 miles. It is expressed in units of person-rem or person-sieverts (1 person = 100 person-rem). *See* rem; Sievert.

Collective Effective Dose Equivalent Rate

1) The total collective effective dose equivalent rate from a given source obtained by including all individuals irradiated by the source, over a specified time. 2) The integrated product of the effective dose equivalent rate and the number of individuals in the population.

Collective Nuclear, Biological, and Chemical Protection (CNBCP)

Protection provided to a group of individuals in a nuclear, biological, and chemical environment that permits relaxation of individual nuclear, biological, and chemical protection.

Collectors, Structural

Members or elements provided to transfer lateral forces from a portion of a structure to vertical elements of the lateral force resisting system.

Collimated Light
Light rays that are parallel. Collimated light is emitted by many lasers. Diverging light may be collimated by a lens or other device.

Collimation
Ability of the laser beam to focus with little, or no, divergence over long distances.

Collocation
The physical placement of two or more response teams, units, agencies, or facilities at a specifically defined location.

Colloids
1) Finely divided solids that will not settle but may be removed by coagulation or biochemical action or membrane filtration; they are intermediate between true solutions and suspensions. 2) In general, colloidal particles are distinguished from ordinary molecules by their inability to diffuse through membranes that allow ordinary molecules and ions to pass freely.

Colonial
A term meaning forming colonies; an inhabitant of a colony.

Colonize
To establish a population in a new territory.

Colony
A term referring to groups of the same species living and growing together.

COM
See Collection Operations Management.

Combined Operation
An emergency response operation conducted by a team of two or more allied agencies or entities acting together for the accomplishment of a single response effort.

Combined Residual Chlorination
The application of chlorine to water or wastewater to produce, with the natural or added ammonia or with other certain organic nitrogen compounds, a combined chlorine residual.

Combined Response Team
An emergency response team composed of elements of two or more agencies or entities (e.g. police, fire, medical, and government personnel).

Combined Sewers
A sewer system that carries both sewage and stormwater runoff. Normally, its entire flow goes to a waste treatment plant, but during a heavy storm, the storm water volume may be so great as to cause overflows. When this happens, untreated mixtures of storm water and sewage may flow into receiving waters. Stormwater runoff may also carry toxic chemicals from industrial areas or streets into the sewer system.

Combustible Liquid
A liquid having a flash point at or above 100°F (37.8°C). Combustible liquids shall be subdivided as follows: a) Class II liquids shall include those having flash points at or above 100°F (37.8°C) and below 140°F (60°C); b) Class IIIA liquids shall include those having flash points at or above 140°F (60°C) and below 200°F (93.4°C); and c) Class IIIB liquids shall include those having flash points at or above 200°F (93.4°C).

Combustible Material
Materials made of or surfaced with wood, compressed paper, plant fibers or other materials that will ignite and burn, even though flameproofed, fire-retardant treated or plastered.

Combustion
Burning, or rapid oxidation, accompanied by release of energy in the form of heat and light. A basic cause of air pollution.

Combustion of Contaminated Used Oil
An EPA study evaluating the health and environmental impacts of the combustion of contaminated used oil in ships, the reasons for using such oil for such purposes, the alternatives to such use,

the costs of such alternatives, and other relevant factors and impacts.

Combustion Product
A substance produced during the burning or oxidation of a material.

Command
The act of directing, ordering, and/or controlling resources by virtue of explicit legal, agency, or delegated authority.

Command Center
A facility from which an authorized first responder and his/her representatives direct operations and control emergency response team personnel. It is organized to gather, process, analyze, display, and disseminate planning and operational data and perform other related tasks.

Command Channel
See Chain of Command.

Command, Control, Communications, and Computer Systems
Integrated systems of doctrine, procedures, organizational structures, personnel, equipment, facilities, and communications designed to support the supervising first responder's exercise of command and control, through all phases of the hazard response continuum.

Command Post
Facilities located at a safe distance upwind from an accident site, where the on-scene coordinator, responders, and technical representatives can make response decisions, deploy manpower and equipment, maintain liaison with news media, and handle communications.

Comment Period
1) A time period during which the public can review and comment on certain documents and EPA actions. For example, a comment period is provided when EPA proposes to add sites to the National Priorities List (NPL). 2) A minimum 3-week comment period held to allow community members to review and comment on a draft project feasibility study. 3) Time provided for the public to review and comment on a proposed EPA action or rulemaking after it is published in the Federal Register.

Commerce
Trade, traffic, commerce, or transportation a) between a place in a state and any place outside thereof, or b) that affects trade, traffic, commerce, or transportation.

Commercial Activity
All activities of industry and trade, including, but not limited to, the buying or selling of commodities and activities conducted for the purpose of facilitating such buying and selling; provided, however, that it does not include exhibition of commodities by museums or similar cultural or historical organizations.

Commercial Applicator
An applicator (whether or not he/she is a private applicator with respect to some uses) who uses or supervises the use of any pesticide that is classified for restricted use for any purpose other than as provided by regulation.

Commercial Areas
Those areas where people work in other than manufacturing or forming industries. Commercial areas are typically accessible to both members of the general public and employees and include public assembly properties, institutional properties, stores, office buildings, and transportation centers.

Commercial Arsenic
Any form of arsenic that is produced by extraction from any arsenic-containing substance and is intended for sale or for intentional use in a manufacturing process. Arsenic that is a naturally occurring trace constituent of another substance is not considered "commercial arsenic."

Commercial Asbestos
Any asbestos that is extracted from asbestos ore.

Commercial Building

Any building other than a residential building, including any building developed for industrial or public purposes.

Commercial Fisherman

Any citizen of the United States who owns, operates, or derives income from being employed on a commercial fishing vessel.

Commercial Fishing Vessel

Any vessel, boat, ship, or other craft that is a) documented under the laws of the United States or, if under 5 net tons, registered under the laws of any state, and b) used for, equipped to be used for, or of a type that is normally used for commercial purposes for the catching, taking, or harvesting of fish or the aiding or assisting of any activity related to the catching, taking, or harvesting of fish, including, but not limited to, preparation, supply, storage, refrigeration, transportation, or processing.

Commercial Loading

See Loading.

Commercial Product

Any substance, product (including paints, coatings, and solvents), or article (including any container or packaging) held by any person, the use, consumption, storage, disposal, destruction, or decomposition of which may result in the release of volatile organic compounds. The term does not include fuels or fuel additives regulated under Section 7545 of the CAA, or motor vehicles, nonroad vehicles, and nonroad engines as defined under Section 7550 of the CAA.

Commercial Solid Wastes

All types of solid wastes generated by stores, offices, restaurants, warehouses, and other non-manufacturing activities, excluding residential and industrial wastes.

Commercial Standards

Standards that are generally established by private sector organizations and are available for use by any person or entity, private or governmental. Voluntary standards are also referred to as "industry standards" as well as "consensus standards," but do not include professional standards of personal conduct, private standards of individual firms, standards mandated by law, or standards of individual organizations for their internal use.

Commercial Storers of PCB

The owner or operator of each facility that is subject to the polychlorinated biphenyl (PCB) storage facility standards of 40 CFR 761.66, and who engages in storage activities involving PCB waste generated by others, or PCB waste that was removed while servicing the equipment owned by others and brokered for disposal. The receipt of a fee or any other form of compensation for storage services is not necessary to qualify as a commercial storer of PCB waste. It is sufficient under this definition that the facility stores PCB waste generated by others or the facility removed the PCB waste while servicing equipment owned by others. A generator who stores only the generator's own waste is subject to the storage requirements of 40 CFR 761.65, but is not required to seek approval as a commercial storer. If a facility's storage of PCB waste at no time exceeds 500 gallons of PCBs, the owner or operator is not required to seek approval as a commercial storer of PCB waste.

Commercial Timberland

Forest land that is capable of and available for producing successive crops of commercial tree species and is generally capable of producing an annual growth of wood fibre in excess of 20 cubic feet/acre.

Commercial Waste

All solid waste from businesses. This category includes, but is not limited to, solid waste originating in stores, markets, office buildings, restaurants, shopping centers, and theaters.

Commercial Waste Management Facility

A treatment, storage, disposal, or transfer facility that accepts wastes from a variety of sources for profit. A commercial facility manages a broader spectrum of wastes than a private facility, that normally manages a limited volume or type of waste.

Commercially Available Items

Articles of supply readily available from established commercial distribution sources that an agency or inventory managers in the military services have designated to be obtained directly or indirectly from such sources.

Comminuter

A machine that shreds or pulverizes solids to make waste treatment easier.

Comminution

1) The process of cutting and screening solids contained in wastewater flow before it enters the flow pumps or other units in a waste treatment facility. 2) Mechanical shredding or pulverizing of waste. Used in both solid waste management and wastewater treatment.

Commission on Population Growth and the American Future (CPGAF)

The commission established to conduct and sponsor research studies regarding a broad range of problems associated with population growth and their implications for America's future.

Commission Proceeding

An application, complaint, investigation, or rule-making before a governmental board or commission.

Commissure

In botany, a surface by which adhering carpels (female organ of a plant) are joined.

Committed Dose Equivalent

The predicted total dose equivalent to a tissue or organ over a 50-year period after a known intake of a radionuclide into the body. It does not include contributions from external dose. Committed dose equivalent is expressed in units of rem (or sievert).

Committed Effective Dose Equivalent

1) The sum of the committed dose equivalents to various tissues in the body, each multiplied by the appropriate weighting factor. Committed effective dose equivalent is expressed in units of rem (or sievert). 2) The effective dose equivalent in an individual that will be accumulated during the 50 years following an intake of radioactive material into the body.

Committed Uses

Either current public uses or planned public uses of a natural resource for which there is a documented legal, administrative, budgetary, or financial commitment established before the discharge of oil or release of a hazardous substance is detected.

Commodity Manager

An individual within the organization of an inventory control point or other such organization assigned management responsibility for homogeneous grouping of material items.

Common Business Oriented Language (COBOL)

A specific language by which business data-processing procedures may be precisely described in a standard form. The language is intended not only as a means for directly presenting any business program to any suitable computer for which a compiler exists, but also as a means of communicating such procedures among individuals. It is a flexible language, compatible with most computers in use today, and easily understood upon practice.

Common Exposure Routes

Likely ways in which contaminants may reach and/or enter an organism. These include: ingestion, inhalation, dermal absorption, and ocular pathways.

Common Laboratory Contaminants

Certain organic chemicals (considered by EPA to be acetone, 2-butanone, methylene chloride, toluene, and the phthalate esters) that are commonly used in the laboratory and thus may be introduced into a sample from laboratory cross-contamination, not from the site.

Common Use

Services, materials, or facilities provided by a Department of Defense agency or a military department on a common basis for two or more Department of Defense agencies.

Common Use Alternatives

Systems, subsystems, devices, components, and materials, already developed or under development, that could be used to reduce the cost of new systems acquisition and support by reducing duplication of research and development effort and by limiting the addition of support base.

Common-User Item

An item of an interchangeable nature that is in common use by two or more nations or services of a nation.

Common-User Lift

U.S. Transportation Command-Controlled Lift. The pool of strategic transportation assets, either government-owned or -chartered, that are under the operational control of Air Mobility Command, Military Sealift Command, or Military Traffic Management Command for the purpose of providing common-user transportation to the Department of Defense across the range of military operations. These assets range from common-user organic or chartered pool of common-user assets available day to day to a larger pool of common-user assets phased in from other sources.

Commonality

A quality that applies to material or systems a) possessing like and interchangeable characteristics enabling each to be utilized, or operated and maintained, by personnel trained on the others without additional specialized training; b) having interchangeable repair parts and/or components; c) applying to consumable items interchangeably equivalent without adjustment.

Communications

A method or means of conveying information of any kind from one person or place to another. *See* Telecommunication.

Communications Center

An agency charged with the responsibility for handling and controlling communications traffic. The center normally includes a message center, transmitting, and receiving facilities. *See* Telecommunications Center.

Communications Satellite

An orbiting vehicle, that relays signals between communications stations. There are two types: a) Active Communications Satellite, a satellite that receives, regenerates, and retransmits signals between stations; and b) Passive Communications Satellite, a satellite that reflects communications signals between stations.

Communications Security (COMSEC)

The protection resulting from all measures designed to deny unauthorized persons information of value that might be derived from the possession and study of telecommunications, or to mislead unauthorized persons in their interpretation of the results of such possession and study. Communications security includes the following:

- cryptosecurity
- transmission security
- emission security
- physical security

1) *Cryptosecurity* — the component of communications security that results from the provision of technically sound cryptosystems and their proper use.

2) *Transmission security* — the component of communications security that results from all measures designed to protect transmissions from interception and exploitation by means other than cryptanalysis.

3) *Emission security* — the component of communications security that results from all measures taken to deny unauthorized persons

information of value that might be derived from intercept and analysis of compromising emanations from cryptoequipment and telecommunications systems.

4) *Physical security* — the component of communications security that results from all physical measures necessary to safeguard classified equipment, material, and documents from access thereto or observation thereof by unauthorized persons.

Communications Security Material

All documents, devices, equipment, or apparatus, including cryptomaterial, used in establishing or maintaining secure communications.

Communications Zone

Rear part of an emergency operations (behind but contiguous to the containment zone) that contains the lines of communications, establishments for supply and evacuation, and other agencies required for the immediate support and maintenance of the field emergency response team(s).

Communicators

Individuals who provide for the timely and accurate flow of information among emergency response staffs. These individuals are normally found at emergency control centers but may also be located in control rooms or field command posts, as needed. Communicators shall maintain staff journals that contain a chronology of events involving their areas or facilities.

Community

Any naturally occurring group of organisms that occupy a common environment.

Community Awareness And Emergency Response Program (CAERP)

Programs developed by the Chemical Manufacturers Association (CMA) to assist chemical plant managers in taking the initiative in cooperating with local communities to develop integrated community or industry plans for responding to releases of hazardous materials.

Community Development Element

Part of a conservation area plan under the Resource Conservation Act that sets forth measures for the development of natural resources based industries, protection of rural industries from natural resource hazards, development of aquaculture, development of adequate rural water and waste disposal systems, improvement of recreation facilities, improvement in the quality of rural housing, provision of adequate health and education facilities, and the satisfaction of essential transportation and communication needs. *See* Conservation Area Plan.

Community Relations

1) EPA's program to inform and involve the public in the Superfund process and respond to community concerns. Specific community relations activities such as holding public meetings and comment periods and opening information repositories are required at Superfund sites. 2) The EPA effort to establish two-way communication with the public to create understanding of EPA programs and related actions, to ensure public input into decision-making processes related to affected communities, and to make certain that the Agency is aware of and responsive to public concerns. 3) The relationship between government and citizen communities.

Community Relations Program

That function that evaluates public attitudes, identifies the mission of organizations with the public interest, and executes a program of action to earn public understanding and acceptance. Community relations programs are conducted at all levels of government, both in the United States and overseas. Community relations programs include, but are not limited to, such activities as liaison and cooperation with associations and organizations and their local affiliates at all levels; government participation in international, national, regional, state, and local public events; people-to-people and humanitarian acts; cooperation between government officials and community leaders; and encouragement of armed forces personnel and their dependents to participate in activities of local schools, churches, fraternal, social, and civic organizations, sports, and recreation programs, and other aspects of community life to the extent feasible and appropriate, regardless of where they are located.

Community-Right-to-Know

The shortened name for the Emergency Planning and Community-Right-to-Know Act of 1986 (EPCRA), also known as Title III of the Superfund Amendments and Reauthorization Act of 1986 (SARA). The act covers facilities that keep specified quantities of extremely hazardous chemicals on site; contains reporting and emergency planning requirements.

Community Water Systems

Public water systems that serve at least 15 service connections used year-round by residents or regularly serve at least 25 year-round residents.

Compaction

Reduction of the bulk of solid waste by rolling and tamping.

Company Compliance Standardization

A management technique for defining, developing, and/or maintaining the optimum utilization of resources with the formal creation of the most appropriate predetermined solutions to recurring environmental compliance problems.

Compartmentalized Vehicles

A collection vehicle that has two or more compartments for placement of solid wastes or recyclable materials. The compartments may be within the main truck body or on the outside of that body as in the form of metal racks.

Compass Direction

The horizontal direction expressed as an angular distance measured clockwise from compass north.

Compass North

The uncorrected direction indicated by the north seeking end of a compass needle. *See* Magnetic North.

Compass Rose

A graduated circle, usually marked in degrees, indicating directions and printed or inscribed on an appropriate medium.

Compatibility

1) Capability of two or more items or components of equipment or hazardous materials, to exist or function in the same environment without mutual interference. 2) The ability of two or more substances to maintain their respective physical and chemical properties upon contact with one another for the design life of the tank system under conditions likely to be encountered in the underground storage tank (UST).

Compensation and Liability

A legal phrase that embraces the idea of placement of fault for an unwanted occurrence, including appropriate restitution by the party or parties responsible for the unwanted occurrence.

Competency

The prescribed performance level for a skill, knowledge, and attitude necessary to accomplish a job task.

Competent Authorities

1) Authorities designated or otherwise recognized by a government for specific purposes in connection with radiation protection and/or nuclear safety. 2) A national agency responsible under its national law for the control or regulation of a particular aspect of the transportation of hazardous materials.

Competition

The interaction between different species vying for the same ecological niche, habitat, or food supply.

Complainant

Any person who files a complaint, alleging the violation of any environmental regulation, order, decision, or statute adopted, administered, or enforced by a public, or quasi-public, entity.

Complaint

1) A written and signed expression of discontent, disagreement, objection, or disapproval alleging a violation of state or federal law or regulations. 2) With regard to OSHA, a notice of a hazard or a violation believed to exist in a workplace given by an employee, a representative of employees, or any other source. To constitute a complaint the notice must allege that a hazard exists or that a regulatory act (meaning a standard or the general duty clause) is being violated. If, as a result of a recent inspection or on the basis of other objective evidence, an agency inspector determines that the hazard that is the subject of the notice is not present (e.g., it has already been corrected)such a notice is not a valid complaint. 3) Oral or written communications by an employee or representative thereof, alleging that there are conditions in the work environment that are in violation of the OSHA standards or that pose safety or health hazards to employees.

Complete Carcinogen

Chemicals that are capable of inducing tumors in animals or humans without supplemental exposure to other agents. Complete refers to the three stages of carcinogenesis, initiation, promotion, and progression that need to be present in order to induce a cancer.

Complete Round

A term applied to an assemblage of explosive and nonexplosive components designed to perform a specific function at the time and under the conditions desired. Examples of complete rounds of ammunition are as follows: a) separate loading, consisting of a primer, propelling charge, and, except for blank ammunition, a projectile and a fuse; b) fixed or semifixed, consisting of a primer, propelling charge, cartridge case, a projectile, and, except when solid projectiles are used, a fuse; c) bomb, consisting of all component parts required to drop and function the bomb once; d) missile, consisting of a complete warhead section and a missile body with its associated components and propellants; and e) rocket, consisting of all components necessary to function.

Completeness, Operation Plan Review Criterion

The determination that each course of action taken in response to a hazardous situation must be complete and answer the questions: who, what, when, where, and how. *See* Acceptability of Plan Review Criterion; Adequacy of Plan Review Criterion.

Compliance Audit

An independent assessment of the current compliance status with applicable environmental statutes and regulatory requirements. This type of audit includes, but is not limited to, review and analysis of: a) formal corporate environmental compliance agendas, and means of implementation; b) environmental training programs; c) condition of equipment, facilities, budgets, and plans for efficient compliance measures, including ongoing monitoring, recordkeeping, and reporting systems; d) operational procedures and maintenance programs; e) internal and community emergency contingency plans; and f) hazard identification, and risk assessment methodologies.

Compliance Coatings

Coatings whose volatile organic compound content do not exceed that allowed by regulation.

Compliance Findings

Conditions that, in the judgment of an assessment team, may not satisfy applicable environmental or safety and health regulations, DOE Orders (including internal DOE memoranda, where referenced), enforcement actions, agreements with regulatory agencies, or permit conditions.

Compliance Inspections

Documented visits to and evaluations of a facility, to include an examination of the equipment, physical plant, methods, operations, procedures, and processes, and to assess and ensure conformance with prescribed environmental, health, and safety standards, and/or other regulations.

Compliance Plan

1) A statement that the source will comply with all applicable regulatory requirements. 2) Where

applicable, a schedule and description of the method or methods for compliance and certification by the owner or operator that the source is in compliance.

Compliance, Pulmonary

The volume change per unit of pressure change for the lungs, the thorax, or the lungs-thorax system. The distensibility of the lungs or thorax.

Compliance Report and Plan (CRP)

A document submitted by a defendant/respondent to EPA, pursuant to a decree/agreement, that: a) describes in full detail every corrective action taken in response to an Environmental Audit Report; b) in case of violations not corrected within 60 days of the Facility Audit Report, describes every action to be taken; c) certifies the accuracy of information contained in the CRP.

Compliance Schedule

1) Negotiated agreements between a pollution source and a government agency that specify dates and procedures by which a source will reduce emissions and, thereby, comply with a regulation. 2) The date or dates by which a source or category of sources is required to comply with specific emission limitations contained in an implementation plan and with any increments of progress toward such compliance.

Components

1) Any constituent parts of a unit or any group of constituent parts of a unit that are assembled to perform a specific function (e.g., a pump seal, pump, kiln liner, kiln thermocouple). 2) The tank or ancillary equipment of a tank system. 3) An assembly or any combination of parts, subassemblies, and assemblies mounted together.

Composite Aerial Photography

Aerial photographs made with a camera having one principal lens and two or more surrounding and oblique lenses.

Composite Sample

A combination of individual samples of water or wastewater taken at selected intervals, generally hourly over some specified period, to minimize the effect of the variability of the individual sample.

Compost

1) A mixture of various substances such as dung or dead leaves, used primarily as fertilizer. 2) Decomposed organic material that is produced when bacteria in soil break down mixtures of garbage and biodegradable trash. Making compost requires turning and mixing and exposing the materials to air. Gardeners and farmers use compost for soil enrichment. *See* Urea.

Composting

The natural biological decomposition of organic material in the presence of air to form a humus-like material. Controlled methods of composting include mechanical mixing and aerating, ventilating the materials by dropping them through a vertical series of aerated chambers, or placing the compost in piles out in the open air and mixing it or turning it periodically.

Compound Leaf

A leaf composed of separate, smaller leaflets.

Comprehensive Asbestos Survey

See Asbestos Survey, Comprehensive.

Comprehensive Environmental Response, Compensation and Liability Act of 1980 (CERCLA)(42 USC 9601 et seq.)

CERCLA, known as "Superfund," is the federal law passed in 1980 and modified in 1986 by the Superfund Amendments and Reauthorization Act (SARA). CERCLA established a tax on certain chemical feed stocks to be used to fund the cleanup of abandoned hazardous waste sites. The Superfund trust was designed to provide immediate remedial action to investigate and clean up abandoned, or uncontrolled, highly contaminated sites. The federal government can then seek to recover these costs through negotiation or legal action against the contributors or sources of pollution. Under the act, EPA can pay for site cleanup when parties responsible for the contamination cannot be located or are unwilling or unable to perform the work; or take legal action to force parties responsible for the contamination to clean up the site or pay the federal government back for the costs of cleanup. EPA is authorized to implement the Act in all 50 states and U.S. territories. Superfund site identification, monitoring, and response activities in states are coordinated through the state environmental protection or waste management agencies. *See* CERCLA.

Comprehensive Environmental Response, Compensation, and Liability Information System (CERCLIS)

The EPA database that includes all sites that have been nominated for investigation by the Superfund program and the actions that have been taken at these sites. If the site investigation reveals contamination, the site is ranked and may be included on the National Priorities List for Superfund cleanup. Inclusion in the CERCLIS database does not necessarily mean that a property is a hazardous waste site. An emergency action may have been conducted there or a simple investigation that concluded that no further action was required.

Comprehensive Plan

An official public document adopted by a local government as a policy guide to decisions regarding social and physical development of a community. Plans typically cover private land uses, public facilities, and transportation. They are long range in nature and stress future planning direction over mitigating current existing problems.

Comprehensive Planning

Planning that incorporates all sources of information that impact or influence an issue or organization (and all levels of the organization) in developing future goals and objectives. Includes planning and management considerations of secondary impacts, resource recovery, and resource conservation strategies.

Compressed Air Environment, Hyperbaric Condition

A work site where the ambient pressure is greater than the atmospheric pressure at the entrance to the work site.

Compressed Gas

1) Any material or mixture having, in a container, an absolute pressure exceeding 40 psi at 70°F, or having an absolute pressure exceeding 104 psi at 130°F; or any liquid flammable material having a vapor pressure exceeding 40 psi absolute at 100°F according to the laws of chemical combination. 2) Gas whose volume has been reduced by pressure.

Compressed Gases in Solution

Nonliquefied compressed gases that are dissolved in a solvent.

Compression Chamber

See Hyperbaric Chamber.

Compressional Waves

Body waves, which along with shear waves, mainly cause high-frequency (greater than 1 hertz) vibrations, which are more efficient than low-frequency waves in causing low buildings to vibrate.

Compressive Strength

A material's ability to resist a force that tends to crush or buckle; maximum compressive load a specimen sustains divided by the specimen's original cross-sectional area.

Computer Assisted Tracking System (CATS)

A system developed by DOE to track and analyze individually identifiable concerns, findings, actions, verifications, and noteworthy practices for appraisals, audits, and surveys conducted by the department's Office of Environment, Safety, and Health.

Computer Codes

Systems of symbols and rules for representing data to a computer. For example, the most common codes used for the handling of data within a computer and for transmitting data are ASCII, BCD, and EBCDIC.

Computer Matching and Privacy Protection Amendments (CMPPA)
The amendments to the Privacy Act of 1974 promulgating agency procedures for the use and disclosure of computerized database matching programs on affected individuals and companies.

Computerized Accident/Incident Reporting System (CAIRS)
A DOE database containing all reported, type A, B, and C accident investigations.

CAIRS
See Computerized Accident/Incident Reporting System.

COMVAN
A term for an emergency communications van.

Concentration
The relative amount of a substance mixed with another substance. An example is 5 parts per million of carbon monoxide in air or 1 milligram/liter of iron in water.

Concentric Braced Frames
Braced frames in which the members are subjected primarily to axial forces.

Concept
A notion or statement of an idea, expressing how something might be done or accomplished, that may lead to an accepted procedure.

Concept of Operations
A verbal or graphic statement, in broad outline, of the organizational structure and general requirements for a coordinated federal response to an emergency. The concept of operations frequently is embodied in operation plans or a series of connected operations to be carried out simultaneously or in succession. The concept is designed to give an overall picture of the implementation steps re-

quired in the operation. It is included primarily to clarify purposes, "guesstimate" resource needs, and estimate timing and tactical requirements.

Concepts and Requirements
A DOE analytical methodology that asks, "Are the concepts and requirements of hazard analysis adequately defined?" The methodology includes consideration of related issues and topics such as determining safety goals/risks; performance goals/risks; safety analysis criteria including change analysis, analytical methods, scaling mechanisms, safety precedence sequence; procedures criteria; specification of safety requirements; information search needs; and life cycle analysis.

Conceptual Designs
Conceptual design encompasses those efforts to a) develop a project scope that will satisfy program needs; b) ensure project feasibility and attainable performance levels; c) develop reliable cost estimates and realistic schedules in order to provide a complete description of the project for congressional consideration; and d) develop project criteria and design parameters for all engineering disciplines, quantification of applicable codes and standards; quality assurance requirements, environmental studies, materials of construction, space allowances, energy conservation features, health safety, safeguards, and security requirements, and any other features or requirements necessary to describe the project.

Concrete Encasement
Placement of concrete around a sewer at its point of intersection with a potable waterline to provide a leakage barrier.

Condemnation
1) The process by which property of a private owner is taken or purchased, with compensation to the owner, under the right of eminent domain, taking of private property for public use. 2) The declaration by a governmental agency that a structure is unsafe for use and a menace to society.

Condensation

A polymerization reaction in which simple byproducts (for example, water) are formed.

Condensation Cloud

A mist or fog of minute water droplets that temporarily surrounds the fireball following a nuclear
(or atomic) detonation in a comparatively humid
atmosphere. The expansion of the air in the negative phase of the blast wave from the explosion
results in a lowering of the temperature, so that
condensation of water vapor present in the air
occurs and a cloud forms. The cloud is soon dis-
pelled when the pressure returns to normal and
the air warms up again. The phenomenon is similar to that used by physicists in the Wilson cloud
chamber and is sometimes called the cloud chamber effect.

Condensation Trail

A visible cloud streak, usually brilliantly white in
color, that trails behind a missile or other vehicle
in flight under certain conditions. Also called
contrails.

Condenser Stack Gases

The gaseous effluent evolved from the stack of
processes utilizing heat to extract mercury metal
from mercury ore.

Condition Assessment Surveys

Periodic DOE inspections of property using universally accepted methods and standards.

Condition Subsequent

A contract clause covering the occurrence of an
event that divests rights and duties (e.g., a fire
insurance policy clause excusing the insurer from
paying the policy if combustible materials are
found within 5 feet of the area where the fire
occurred).

Conditional Probability

The probability of an event that requires satisfy-
ing two or more conditions after one condition
has occurred.

Conditional Registration

Under special circumstances, the Federal Insecticide, Fungicide, and Rodenticide Act (FIFRA)
permits registration of pesticide products that is
"conditional" upon the submission of additional
data. These special circumstances include a finding by the EPA Administrator that a new product
or use of an existing pesticide will not significantly increase the risk of unreasonable adverse
effects. A product containing a new (previously
unregistered) active ingredient may be conditionally registered only if the Administrator finds that
such conditional registration is in the public interest, that a reasonable time for conducting the additional studies has not elapsed, and the use of the
pesticide for the period of conditional registration
will not present an unreasonable risk.

Conditionally Exempt Generators

Small quantity facilities that produce fewer than
220 pounds of hazardous waste per month. Exempt from most regulations, conditionally exempt
generators are required to determine whether their
waste is hazardous and to notify local waste management agencies. These generators may treat or
dispose of the waste on site or ensure that the
waste is sent to a permitted disposal or recycling
facility.

Conditions

According to DOE, any as-found state(s),
whether or not resulting from an event, that may
have adverse safety, health, quality assurance, security, operational, or environmental implications. A condition is more programmatic in
nature; for example, an error in analysis or calculation, an anomaly associated with design or performance, or an item indicating a weakness in the
management process are all conditions.

Cone of Depression (COD)

1) A depression in the groundwater table or potentiometric surface that has the shape of an inverted
cone and develops around a well from which
water is being withdrawn. It defines (in cross
section) the area of influence of a well and is also
called pumping cone and cone of drawdown. 2)

A lowering in the water table that develops around a pumped well.

CFEA

An acronym for Conference of Federal Environmental Engineers.

Conferences

A process that involves informal discussions between a federal agency and the Fish and Wildlife Service under Section 7(a)(4) of the Endangered Species Act regarding the impact of an action on proposed species or proposed critical habitat and recommendations to minimize or avoid the adverse effects.

Confidence

The chance of likelihood that a specified value is part of the population (if a specific value lies outside three standard deviations from the mean, then we have 99.70% confidence that this observation is different from the population since 99.70% of the population lies in that range). *See* Confidence Interval; Confidence Limit.

Confidence Interval

A range of values that has a specified probability (e.g., 95%) of containing a given parameter or characteristic. *See* Confidence; Confidence Limit.

Confidence Limit

The upper value of the confidence interval range (e.g. upper confidence limit). *See* Confidence Interval.

Confidential

A classification level that is applied to classified information, the unauthorized disclosure of which reasonably could be expected to cause damage to the national security.

Confidential Business Information (CBI)

1) Data in which a defendant/respondent has taken ample measures through the issuance and observance of company-wide policies and procedures to protect the confidentiality of that data, and the maintenance of such measures. 2) Information that is not and has not been readily available without the consent of other private persons by use of legitimate means. 3) Data that is likely to cause substantial harm to defendant/respondent's competitive position if disclosed. Includes the concept of trade secrecy and other related legal concepts that give (or may give) a business the right to preserve the confidentiality of business information and to limit its use or disclosure by others. The definition is meant to encompass any concept that authorizes a federal agency to withhold business information under 5 USC 552(b)(4), as well as any concept that requires EPA to withhold information from the public for the benefit of a business under 18 USC 1906. *See* Nonconfidential Business Data.

Confidential Commercial Information

Records provided to the government by a submitter that arguably contain material exempt from release under Exemption 4 of the Freedom of Information Act, 5 USC 552(b)(4), because disclosure could reasonably be expected to cause substantial competitive harm. For confidential commercial information submitted on or after January 1, 1988, the head of each executive department or agency shall, to the extent permitted by law, establish procedures to permit submitters of confidential commercial information to designate, at the time the information is submitted to the federal government or a reasonable time thereafter, any information the disclosure of which the submitter claims could reasonably be expected to cause substantial competitive harm. Such agency procedures may provide for the expiration, after a specified period of time or changes in circumstances, of designations of competitive harm made by submitters.

Confidential/Protected Information

Data and information submitted or otherwise provided to the Secretary of DOE or an agent of the Secretary or a PIA or SAA that fall within the definitions of a trade secret or confidential commercial or financial information are exempt from disclosure if the party submitting or providing the information so requests. However, the Secretary may disclose such information to any person requesting it after deletion of the portions that are exempt.

Confidential Risk Report

A report, based on site investigations, of the physical compliance status of an insurer or their property prior to issuance of a policy.

Configuration Management

In computer modeling and simulation, a discipline applying technical and administrative oversight and control to identify and document the functional requirements and capabilities of a model or simulation and its supporting databases, control changes to those capabilities, and document and report the changes.

Confined Aquifer

1) An aquifer bounded above and below by confining units of distinctly lower permeability than the aquifer media; or one containing confined groundwater. 2) An aquifer in which groundwater pressure is significantly greater than atmospheric pressure and its upper limit is the bottom of a bed of distinctly lower hydraulic conductivity than that of the aquifer itself.

Confinement

A form of barrier that is not designed to completely block releases to the environment. Confinement is determined by a designed flow through a filtered exhaust.

Confinement Areas

Areas having structures or systems from which releases of hazardous materials are controlled. The primary confinement systems are the process enclosures (glove boxes, conveyors, transfer boxes, other spaces normally containing hazardous materials), that are surrounded by one or more secondary confinement areas (operating area compartments).

Confinement Systems

The barrier and its associated systems (including ventilation) between areas containing hazardous

materials and the environment or other areas in the facility that are normally expected to have levels of hazardous materials lower than allowable concentration limits.

Confining Beds

Bodies of impermeable or distinctly less permeable material stratigraphically adjacent to one or more aquifers.

Confining Zones

A geological formation, group of formations, or part of a formation that is capable of limiting fluid movement above an injection zone.

Confiscation

The seizure of private property without compensation, usually for failure to pay taxes, or obtain the required permits, licenses, etc.

Confluent Growth

A continuous bacterial growth covering the entire filtration area of a membrane filter, or a portion thereof, in which bacterial colonies are not discrete.

Conformity

Compliance with existing rules, legislation, and agency mandates.

Congenital Anomalies

Birth defects.

Congressional Declaration of Purpose for Clean Air

The objectives set forth by Congress:

- a) to protect public health and welfare from any actual or potential adverse effect that in the Administrator's judgment may reasonably be anticipated to occur from air pollution or from exposures to pollutants in other media, which pollutants originate as emissions to the ambient air, notwithstanding attainment and maintenance of all national ambient air quality standards;

- b) to preserve, protect, and enhance the air quality in national parks, national wilderness areas, national monuments, national seashores, and other areas of special national or regional natural, recreational, scenic, or historic value;

- c) to ensure that economic growth will occur in a manner consistent with the preservation of existing clean air resources;

- d) to ensure that emissions from any source in any state will not interfere with any portion of the applicable implementation plan to prevent significant deterioration of air quality for any other state; and

- e) to ensure that any decision to permit increased air pollution in any area is made only after careful evaluation of all the consequences of such a decision and after adequate procedural opportunities for informed public participation in the decisionmaking process.

Congressional Declaration of Purpose for National Environmental Policy (NEPA)

The declaration set forth in Section 4331 of NEPA, recognizing the profound impact of man's activity on the interrelations of all components of the natural environment, particularly the profound influences of population growth, high-density urbanization, industrial expansion, resource exploitation, and new and expanding technological advances and recognizing further the critical importance of restoring and maintaining environmental quality to the overall welfare and development of man, and declaring that it is the continuing policy of the federal government, in cooperation with state and local governments, and other concerned public and private organizations, to use all practicable means and measures, including financial and technical assistance, in a manner calculated to foster and promote the general welfare, to create and maintain conditions under which man and nature can exist in productive harmony, and fulfill the social, economic, and other requirements of present and future generations of Americans.

Congressional Responsibility for National Environmental Policy

Congressional strategy, set forth in NEPA, to use all practicable means to improve and coordinate federal plans, functions, programs, and resources such that the nation may a) fulfill the responsibilities of each generation as trustee of the envi-

ronment for succeeding generations; b) ensure for all Americans safe, healthful, productive, and aesthetically and culturally pleasing surroundings; c) attain the widest range of beneficial uses of the environment without degradation, risk to health or safety, or other undesirable and unintended consequences; d) preserve important historic, cultural, and natural aspects of our national heritage, and maintain, wherever possible, an environment that supports diversity and variety of individual choice; e) achieve a balance between population and resource use which will permit high standards of living and a wide sharing of life's amenities; and f) enhance the quality of renewable resources and approach the maximum attainable recycling of depletable resources.

Conia

State of profound unconsciousness from which the patient cannot be aroused.

Coniferous Forest

A forest comprised primarily of evergreens, usually located in cool, dry climates.

Conjunctiva

The delicate mucous membrane that covers the exposed surface of the eyeball and lines the eyelids. *See* Conjunctivitis.

Conjunctive Decision Rule

A rule that establishes minimally acceptable levels on important decision criteria. Alternatives being assessed for their viability must then, at a minimum, meet these predefined rules on each criterion.

Conjunctivitis

Inflammation of the conjunctiva; can result in redness, irritation, and tearing of the eye. *See* Conjunctiva.

Connate Water

Refers to groundwater entrapped in the interstices, or voids, of a sedimentary or extrusive igneous rock at the time of its deposition. *See* Interstice.

Connected Piping

All underground piping including valves, elbows, joints, flanges, and flexible connectors attached to a tank system through which regulated substances flow. For the purpose of determining how much piping is connected to any individual underground storage tank (UST) system, the piping that joins two UST systems should be allocated equally between them.

Connectors

1) Flanged, screwed, welded, or other joined fittings used to connect two pipelines or a pipeline and a piece of equipment. 2) Flanged fittings that are not covered by insulation or other materials that prevent location of the fittings.

Consent Decree (CD)

1) A legal document, approved and issued by a judge, that formalizes an agreement reached between EPA and potentially responsible parties (PRPs) where PRPs will perform all or part of a cleanup action at a Superfund site; cease or correct actions or processes that are polluting the environment; or otherwise comply with regulations where the PRPs' failure to comply caused EPA to initiate regulatory enforcement actions. The consent decree describes actions to be taken by the potentially responsible parties and is subject to a public comment period. The Clean Water Act, Clean Air Act, Toxic Substances Control Act, and others all use consent decrees. 2) In a case settlement, the instrument whereby the defendant agrees to cease the actions that resulted in the case.

Consequence

The results or effects (especially projected exposure or exposure rates) of a release of hazardous material into the environment.

Consequence Assessment

The evaluation and interpretation of radiological or other hazardous substance measurements and other information to provide a basis for decision-making. Consequence assessments can include projections of offsite and secondary impacts.

Consequential Losses

Losses not directly due to an incident, but caused indirectly as a consequence of that incident; for example, spoilage of frozen foods is a loss consequent upon power failure.

Conservation

1) Using the materials of the environment in a wise or economical manner; usually associated with limited or irreplaceable resources and their preservation and management. Avoiding waste of, and renewing when possible, human and natural resources, including the protection, improvement, and use of natural resources according to principles that will ensure their highest economic or social benefits. 2) Preserving and renewing natural resources to ensure their highest economic or social benefit over the longest period of time.

Conservation Area Plan (CAP)

A resource conservation and utilization plan developed for a designated area of a state or states through a planning process and that includes one or more of the following elements: a) a land conservation element, the purpose of which shall be to control erosion and sedimentation; b) a water management element, the purpose of which shall be to provide for the conservation, utilization, and quality of water, including irrigation and rural water, supplies, the mitigation of floods and high water tables, construction, repair, and improvement of dams and reservoirs, improvement of agricultural water management, and improvement of water quality through control of nonpoint sources of pollution; c) a community development element, the purpose of which shall be the development of natural resources based industries, protection of rural industries from natural resource hazards, development of aquaculture, development of adequate rural water and waste disposal systems, improvement of recreation facilities, improvement in the quality of rural housing, provision of adequate health and education facilities, and satisfaction of essential transportation and communication needs; or d) other elements, the purpose of which may include energy conservation or protection of agricultural land, as appropriate, from conversion to other uses, or protection of fish and wildlife habitats.

Conservation District

Any district or unit of state or local government formed under state or territorial law for the express purpose of developing and carrying out a local soil and water conservation program. These districts or units are referred to as a "conservation districts," "soil conservation districts," "soil and water conservation districts," "resource conservation districts," "natural resource districts," "land conservation committees," or a similar name.

Conservation Planning Process

Ongoing planning efforts of any state, local unit of government, or local nonprofit organization to develop and carry out effective resource conservation and utilization plans for a designated area, including development of an area plan, goals, objectives, policies, implementation activities, evaluations and reviews, and the opportunity for public participation in such efforts. *See* Planning Process.

Conservation Recommendations

Suggestions regarding discretionary measures to minimize or avoid adverse effects of a proposed action on listed species or critical habitat or regarding the development of information.

Conservation Tillage

A soil management practice adaptable to a broad range of soil types and slopes throughout the country, that reduces soil erosion. Conservation tillage practices are supposed to result in better yields, greater land use flexibility, decreased fuel use, decreased labor and equipment costs, and the increased retention of soil moisture, making agricultural land more productive.

Conservator

A person who is trained and skilled in the theoretical and practical aspects of preventive conservation and of performing treatments necessary to prolong the physical and aesthetic life of museum objects.

Conserve, Conserving, and Conservation

Methods and procedures that include, but are not limited to, activities associated with scientific resources management such as research, census, law enforcement, habitat acquisition and maintenance, propagation, live trapping, and transplantation. In extraordinary cases where population pressures within a given ecosystem cannot be otherwise relieved, the term may include regulated takings.

Consolidated Aquifer

An aquifer made up of consolidated rock that has undergone solidification or lithification.

Consolidated Premanufacture Notices (PMN)

Any Premanufacture Notices submitted to EPA that cover more than one chemical substance (each being assigned a separate PMN number by EPA) as a result of a prenotice agreement with EPA.

Consolidation

The combining or merging of elements to perform a common or related function.

Constituents

Those chemical constituents listed in Appendix VIII to 40 CFR 261.

Constraints

1) Restrictions affecting freedom to act; boundaries or conditions that may dictate performance in other than the desired or ideal manner. Imposed conditions. 2) Conditional events that apply conditions or constraints to a basic logic gate or output event.

Construction

1) Preliminary planning to determine the economic and engineering feasibility and the public health and safety aspects of the project, the engineering, architectural, legal, fiscal, and economic investigations and studies, and any surveys, designs, plans, working drawings, specifications,the acquisition of all lands, easements, and rights-of-way necessary for the project, including lands for

disposal of dredged material, and relocations necessary for a project. 2) The erection or building of new structures and acquisition of lands or interests therein, or the acquisition, replacement, expansion, remodeling, alteration, modernization, or extension of existing structures. 3) The acquisition and installation of initial equipment necessary for the proper utilization and operation of a facility after completion of the project. Such equipment would include trucks, tractors, cranes, and other motorized vehicles or machinery required in connection with a) new, or newly acquired, structures; or b) the expanded, remodeled, altered, modernized, or extended part of existing structures. 4) Other action necessary for the carrying out the project, including inspection and supervision tasks.

Construction and Demolition Waste
Waste building materials, dredging materials, tree stumps, packaging, and rubble resulting from construction, remodeling, repair, and demolition operations on houses, commercial buildings, and other structures, and pavements. May contain lead, asbestos, or other hazardous materials.

Construction Project Planning
All activities performed after the initial identification of a project for the purposes of developing the project concept, reliable cost estimates, realistic performance schedules, and methods of performance.

Construction Projects
New facilities, facility additions, and facility alteration projects where engineering and design are required in their performance.

Construction Work
Work for construction, alteration, and/or repair, including painting and decorating. Construction includes new construction, reconstruction, remodeling, renovation, and replacement of facilities, or acquisition and installation of modular structures, and the performance of deferred maintenance of facilities.

Constructive Notice
Often called, "legal notice," the conclusive presumption that all persons have knowledge of the contents of a recorded instrument.

Consultant
A specialist in any field of activity (environmental consultant, engineering consultant, etc.), hired by an organization to recommend solutions to a problem.

Consultant Fire Protection Survey Program
The program under which fire protection surveys of principal DOE facilities are conducted for the Office of Operational Safety by fire protection engineers of selected contractors.

Consumer
A person or agency that uses information or intelligence produced by either its own staff or other agencies.

Consumer Commodities
Materials that are packaged and distributed in a form intended or suitable for sale through retail sales agencies or instrumentalities for consumption by individuals for the purposes of personal care or household use. This term also includes drugs and medicines.

Consumer Logistics
That part of logistics concerning reception of the initial product, storage, inspection, distribution, transport, maintenance (including repair and the serviceability), and disposal of material, and the provision of support and services. In consequence, consumer logistics includes material requirements determination, follow-up support, stock control, provision or construction of facilities (excluding any material element and those facilities needed to support production logistics activities), movement control, codification, reliability and defect reporting, storage, transport and handling safety standards, and related training.

Consumer Products

Articles, or component parts thereof, produced or distributed: 1) for sale to a consumer for use in or around a permanent or temporary household or residence, a school, in recreation, or otherwise; or 2) for the personal use, consumption or enjoyment of a consumer in or around a permanent or temporary household or residence, a school, in recreation, or otherwise. *See* 15 USC 2052 for exceptions.

Consumption

With respect to any substance, the amount of that substance produced in the United States, plus the amount imported, minus the amount exported to Parties of the Montreal Protocol. *See* Montreal Protocol.

Consumption Rate

The average quantity of an item consumed or expended during a given time interval, expressed in quantities by the most appropriate unit of measurement per applicable stated basis.

Consumptive Use

With respect to heating oil means consumed on the premises.

Contact Dermatitis

1) Allergic — a delayed-onset skin reaction caused by skin contact with a chemical to which the individual has been previously sensitized. 2) Irritant — inflammatory skin reaction caused by a skin irritant.

Contact Pesticide

A chemical that kills pests when it touches them, rather than by being eaten (stomach poison). Also, soil that contains the minute skeletons of certain algae that scratches and dehydrates waxy-coated insects.

Contact Print

A print made from a negative or a diapositive in direct contact with sensitized material.

Contact Rate

Amount of medium (e.g., ground water, soil) contacted per unit time or event (e.g. liters of water ingested per day).

Container

1) Portable devices in which a material is stored, transported, treated, disposed of, or otherwise handled. Any vessel, including tanks, cylinders, portable tanks and cargo tanks, used for transporting or storing any liquid or gas. 2) Any package, can, bottles, bag, barrel, drum, tank, or other containing device (excluding spray applicator tanks) used to enclose a pesticide or pesticide-related waste.

Container Anchorage Terminal

A sheltered anchorage with the appropriate facilities for the transshipment of containerized cargo from containerships to other vessels.

Container Assembly

An assembly consisting essentially of the container and fittings for all container openings, including shutoff valves, excess flow valves, liquid-level gaging devices, safety relief devices, and protective housing.

Containerships

Cargo vessels designed and constructed to transport, within specifically designed cells, portable tanks and freight containers that are lifted on and off with their contents intact.

Containment

1) To stop, hold, or surround or to cause through channeling activity a centralized front and to prevent the spreading or withdrawal of any part elsewhere. 2) Control of the expansion or propagation of a hazard that may result in loss of life or property; commonly used in response to fires and releases of hazardous substances. 3) A term signifying either the confinement of radioactive material in such a way that it is prevented from being dispersed into the environment or is only released at a specified rate, or the device used to effect such confinement.

Containment Coordinators

Individuals working under the direction of the on-scene coordinator/commander who is responsible for immediate containment of an emergency area.

Containment Storage Tanks

Storage tanks for contaminated water.

Containment Systems

The components of the packaging intended to retain the hazardous material during transport.

Contaminant

1) An undesirable foreign substance (usually chemical) nonexistent under normal conditions, or an unusually high concentration of a naturally occurring substance, in water, soil, or other environmental medium, that results in the degradation of the quality of the containing medium. 2) Any physical, chemical, biological, or radiological substance or matter that has an adverse affect on air, water, or soil. 3) A harmful, irritating or nuisance material or situation that is foreign to the environment it is found in. 4) A chemical or biological substance in a form that can be incorporated into, onto, or be ingested, and harms aquatic organisms, or users of the aquatic environment, and includes but is not limited to the substances on the 40 CFR 307(a)(1) list of toxic pollutants.

Contaminant Carriers

Dredged or fill materials that contain hazardous contaminants.

Contamination

1) The degradation of air, land, or water quality as a result of human activities through deposition of hazardous material in any place where it may make products or equipment unsuitable for some specific use. The deposit, absorption, or adsorption of biological or chemical agents on or by structures, areas, personnel, or objects. 2) Food and/or water made unfit for consumption by humans or animals because of the presence of environmental chemicals, radioactive elements, bacteria or organisms, the byproduct of the growth of bacteria or organisms, the decomposing

material (to include the food substance itself), or waste in the food or water. *See* Induced Radiation; Residual Radiation.

Contested

A term for a stipulation or settlement that is opposed in whole or part, by any of the parties to the proceeding in which such stipulation or settlement is proposed for adoption.

Contiguous Zone

The zone of the high seas, established by the United States under Article 24 of the Convention on Territorial Sea and Contiguous Zone, that is contiguous to the territorial sea and that extends 9 miles seaward from the outer limit of the territorial sea.

Continental United States

United States territory, including the adjacent territorial waters, located within North America between Canada and Mexico.

Contingency

An emergency caused by natural disasters, terrorists, subversives, or by required operations. Due to the uncertainty of the situation, contingencies require plans, rapid emergency response, and special procedures to ensure the safety and readiness of personnel, installations, and equipment. *See* Contingency Contracting.

Contingency Contracting

Task order type contracting performed in support of a contingency pursuant to the policies and procedures of the Federal Acquisition Regulatory System.

Contingency Costs

The costs that may be paid by investors after the initial investment, but which are not paid out of project revenues. Contingency costs may include such costs as audit fees, facility repairs, or annual insurance fees.

Contingency Plans

1) Plans for major contingencies that can reasonably be anticipated in principal geographic subareas. 2) Documents setting out an organized, planned, and coordinated course of action to be followed in case of a fire, explosion, or other accident that releases toxic chemicals, hazardous wastes, or radioactive materials that threaten human health or the environment. *See* National Oil and Hazardous Substances Contingency Plan.

Contingency Planning

1) The process of developing a set of alternative plans to fit a variety of potential future circumstances. 2) The development of plans for potential hazards involving requirements that can reasonably be expected in an area of responsibility. Contingency planning can occur anywhere within the range of operations and may be performed deliberately or under emergency response conditions. Contingency planning for joint operations is coordinated at the national level by assigning planning tasks and relationships among various agencies and apportioning or allocating them the staff and resources necessary to accomplish those tasks.

Contingency Planning Facilities List

A joint program of the Defense Intelligence Agency/Unified and Specified Command for the production and maintenance of current target documentation of all countries of contingency planning interest to U.S. military planners.

Contingent Effects

The effects, both desirable and undesirable, that are in addition to the primary effects associated with a release of hazardous materials.

Contingent Liability

The liability imposed on an individual, corporation, or partnership due to negligence and/or accidents caused by persons, for whose acts the first party may be held responsible by law; for example, a contractor's responsibility for work of a subcontractor.

Continuity of Government Emergency Management Teams

The DOE team predesignated to ensure the performance of essential DOE functions at designated locations and coordinate response to a condition caused by domestic or enemy attack involving a national security threat to the continuity of the federal government.

Continuity of Operations

The degree or state of being continuous in the conduct of functions, tasks, or duties necessary to accomplish an action or mission in carrying out a clean-up strategy. It includes the functions and duties of the lead agency, as well as the supporting functions and duties performed by the staff and others acting under the authority and direction of the agency.

Continuous Air Monitors

Instruments that collect airborne contamination and continuously count the activity collected on a filter medium. As concentrations rise above a set point, an audible and visual alarm is activated which continues until reset.

Continuous Discharge

A permitted release of pollutants into the environment that occurs without interruption, except for infrequent shutdowns for maintenance, process changes, etc.

Continuous Disposal

A method of tailings management and disposal in which tailings are dewatered by mechanical methods immediately after generation. The dried tailings are then placed in trenches or other disposal areas and immediately covered to federal standards.

Continuous Emission Monitoring System (CEMS)

The equipment used to sample, analyze, measure, and provide on a continuous basis a permanent record of emissions and flow (expressed in pounds per million British thermal units (lbs/mm Btu), pounds per hour (lbs/hr) or such other form as the Administrator of EPA may prescribe.

Continuous Emission Reduction System (CERS)
1) A technological process for production or operation by any source that is inherently low-polluting or nonpolluting. 2) A technological system for continuous reduction of the pollution generated by a source before such pollution is emitted into the ambient air, including precombustion cleaning or treatment of fuels.

Continuous Filament
An individual, small-diameter reinforcement that is flexible and indefinite in length.

Continuous Monitoring
The measurement of the air or water concentration of a specific contaminant on an uninterrupted, real-time basis by instrumental methods.

Continuous Strip Camera
A camera in which the film moves continuously past a slit in the focal plane, producing a photograph in one unbroken length by virtue of the continuous forward motion of the aircraft.

Continuous Strip Imagery
Imagery of a strip of terrain in which the image remains unbroken throughout its length, along the line of flight.

Continuous System
Any manufacturing or industrial system that operates 24 hours a day.

Continuous Wave (CW)
A constant, steady-state delivery of laser power.

Contour Interval
Difference in elevation between two adjacent contour lines.

Contour Line
A line on a map or chart connecting points of equal elevation.

Contour Plowing
Farming methods that break ground following the shape of the land in a way that discourages erosion.

Contract
An agreement, enforceable by law, between two or more competent persons, having for its object a legal purpose, wherein the parties are to act in a certain manner.

Contract Audit
A systematic review or examination by or on behalf of a government agency of a contractor's records or reports maintained or developed pursuant to a contract with the department.

Contract Audit Notice
A written notice of an agency's final actions upon the audit or examination of a contractor and that is formally issued to a contractor.

Contract Lab
1) Laboratories under contract to EPA that analyze soil, water, and waste samples taken from areas at or near Superfund sites. Developed for Superfund waste site samples to fill the need for legally defensible analytical results supported by a high level of quality assurance and documentation. 2) Laboratories under contract to EPA, that analyze samples taken from wastes, soil, air, and water or carry out research projects.

Contract Maintenance
The maintenance of material performed under contract by commercial organizations (including prime contractors) on a one-time or continuing basis, without distinction as to the level of maintenance accomplished.

Contract-Required Quantitation Limits
Chemical-specific levels that a CLP (Contract Laboratory Program) laboratory must be able to routinely and reliably detect and quantitate in specified sample matrices. May or may not be equal to the reported quantitation limit of a given chemical in a given sample.

Contract Rent

Payments in money or in kind for the right to use real property as required by the terms of the possessory interest agreement. It includes royalty payments and other rights to share in production, the value that the public owner is expected to realize from improvements erected at the expense of the possessor that will remain when the possessory interest terminates, and any other form of compensation paid or payable for the right to occupy the property. It does not, however, include payments for services such as utilities and janitorial labor or for the use of property not subject to the possessory interest.

Contract Specifications

A set of specifications prepared for an individual construction project, that contains design, performance, and material requirements for that project.

Contract Termination

As used in Department of Defense procurement, refers to the cessation or cancellation, in whole or in part, of work under a prime contract, or a subcontract thereunder, for the convenience of, or at the option of, the government, or due to failure of the contractor to perform in accordance with the terms of the contract (default).

Contract, Willful Noncompliance

A term meaning a Contractor knew or should have known of the requirement of the Scope of Work and failed to comply. However, when a contractor's compliance is impeded by a governmental entity with jurisdiction, such delays are usually given due consideration by the contracting officer.

Contracting Officers

Officials designated by an agency to enter into or administer contracts between the agency and contractors, and make contract-related determinations and findings, such as approving change orders or amendments.

Contracting Officer's Representative

A government employee designated in writing by the contracting officer to represent the contracting officer for administrative and technical functions regarding the contract between an agency and the contractor.

Contractor

1) A general, prime, specialty or subcontractor. 2) DOE prime contractors or subcontractors subject to the contractual provisions of DOE PR-50.704.2(a), or specific negotiated contract provisions indicating DOE's decision to enforce environmental protection, safety, and health protection requirements.

Contractor Employees

Persons employed by a contractor.

Contractor Self-Evaluation Report (CSER)

Formal reports prepared by the contractor summarizing the comparison of a training program to accreditation objectives and supporting criteria.

Contractual Liability

Liability assumed by contract or agreement, and that would not otherwise exist.

Contractual Relationship

For the purpose of environmental liability includes, but is not limited to, land contracts, deeds, other instruments transferring title or possession, unless, a) the real property on which the facility of concern is located was acquired by the defendant after the disposal or placement of a hazardous substance on, in, or at the facility; b) one or more of the circumstances described below is also established by the defendant by a preponderance of the evidence: 1) at the time the defendant acquired the facility the defendant did not know and had no reason to know that any hazardous substance was disposed of on, in, or at the facility; 2) defendant is a government entity; 3) defendant acquired the facility by inheritance or bequest. In addition to establishing the foregoing, the defendant must also establish that he or she had undertaken at the time of acquisition all appropriate inquiry into the previous ownership and uses of the property consistent with good commercial or customary practice in an effort to minimize liability.

If a defendant had actual knowledge of a release of a hazardous substance and then subsequently transferred ownership of the property to another person without disclosing such knowledge, that defendant is liable under Section 107(a)(1) of CERCLA and no defense under Section 107(b)(3) would be available to the defendant.

Contrails
Long, narrow clouds caused when high-flying jet aircraft disturb the atmosphere. *See* Condensation Trail.

Contributing Causes
Root causes or other factors contributing to the immediate cause of an accident or incident.

Contributory Negligence
1) Shared responsibility for the result of negligent practices. For example, a hazardous waste generator or its representative can be held accountable and/or liable for damages resulting from its negligent failure to inspect the vehicle transporting its wastes, if the vehicle is involved in an accident resulting in environmental damage, even though the accident itself may have been the fault of the transporter, the driver, or a third party. 2) The negligence attributed to the person or firm making a claim against an insured; a defense pleaded by the insured in a lawsuit.

Control
In mapping, charting, and photogrammetry, a collective term for a system of marks or objects on the earth, a map, or a photograph whose positions and/or elevations have been determined.

Control Barriers
1) Those barriers used to control energy flows, such as the insulation on an electrical cord. 2) Barriers used to control or contain a hazardous substance release.

Control Devices
1) Air pollution control equipment used to collect particulate matter emissions. 2) An enclosed combustion device, vapor recovery system, or flare. 3) Any piece of control hardware providing a means for human intervention in the control of a robot or robot system, such as an emergency stop-button, a start button, or a selector switch.

Control Group
A group of subjects observed in the absence of the exposure agent for comparison with exposed groups.

Control Methods and Technologies (CMT)
Methods and technologies for removal or destruction of pollutants before, during, or after combustion, and includes for new units siting requirements, and for existing units modification requirements, that minimize, on a site (or facility) specific basis, to the maximum extent practicable, potential risks to public health or the environment.

Control of Electromagnetic Radiation
In the event of attack, or imminent threat thereof, this national plan would minimize the use of electromagnetic radiation, such that it could not be used by hostiles to guide (or target) their aircraft, missiles, or other devices. The plan encompasses the United States, its territories, and the Panama Canal Zone.

Control Point
In making photo mosaics, a point located by ground survey with which a corresponding point on a photograph is matched as a check.

Control Program
The inherent set of control instructions that defines the capabilities, actions, and responses of the robot system. This program is usually not intended to be modified by the user.

Control Resources
Resources unaffected by the discharge of oil or release of the hazardous substance under investi-

gation. A control area or resource is selected for its comparability to the assessment area, or resource, and may be used for establishing the baseline condition and for comparison to injured resources.

Control Room

The area in a nuclear power plant from which most of the plant power production and emergency safety equipment can be operated by remote control.

Control Strategies

A combination of measures designated to achieve the aggregate reduction of emissions necessary for attainment and maintenance of national standards.

Control Substances

Chemical substances or mixtures or any other material other than a test substance that are administered to the test system in the course of a study for the purpose of establishing a basis for comparison with the test substance.

Control System Engineering

The branch of professional engineering that requires such education and experience as is necessary to understand the science of instrumentation and automatic control of dynamic processes; and requires the ability to apply this knowledge to the planning, development, operation, and evaluation of systems of control so as to ensure the safety and practical operability of such processes.

Control Systems

All elements comprising a system, including managements plans and policy, procedures, personnel, hardware, and facilities, as they relate to the control of worker and environmental safety within the system.

Control Techniques Guidelines (CTG)

A series of guidance documents issued by the EPA in lieu of regulations to assist states in defining reasonable available control technology (RACT) for major sources of volatile organic compounds (VOCs) that contribute to ozone levels in areas that violate the national ambient air quality standard for ozone.

Control Width, Earthquake

The maximum width of the zone containing mapped fault traces, including all faults that can be reasonably inferred to have experienced differential movement during Quaternary times and that join or can reasonably be inferred to join the main fault trace, measured within 10 miles along the fault's trend in both directions from the point of nearest approach.

Control Zones

Area at a hazardous materials incident, whose boundaries are based on safety and the degree of hazard, the Hot Zone, Decontamination Zone, and Support Zone are delineated. Each zone requires certain procedures be followed within its boundary.

Controlled Areas

1) Any locale where the activity of those within is controlled in order to protect individuals from exposure to radiation and radioactive materials. 2) Areas where workers might receive doses in excess of three-tenths of the occupational dose, equivalent limits during the anticipated working period and where appropriate controls (such as restricted access, individual assessment of dose and special health supervision) are accordingly applied.

Controlled Copies

Documents that are maintained on current basis by means of a formal transmittal and filing system.

Controlled Dangerous Air Cargo

Cargo regarded as highly dangerous and that may only be carried by cargo aircraft operating within specific safety regulations.

Controlled Effects, Nuclear Weapons
Nuclear weapons designed to achieve variation in the intensity of specific effects other than normal blast effect.

Controlled Map
A map with precise horizontal and vertical ground control as a basis. Scale, azimuth, and elevation are accurate. *See* Map.

Controlled Mosaic
A photo mosaic corrected for scale, rectified, and laid to ground control to provide an accurate representation of distances and direction. *See* Mosaic; Rectification; Uncontrolled Mosaic.

Controlled Reaction
A chemical reaction at temperature and pressure conditions that are maintained within safe limits to produce a desired product.

Controlled Route
A route, the use of which is subject to traffic or movement restrictions.

Controlled Shipping
Shipping that is controlled by the Military Sealift Command. Included in this category are Military Sealift Command ships (United States Naval Ships), government-owned ships operated under a general agency agreement, and commercial ships under charter to the Military Sealift Command. *See* Military Sealift Command.

Controller/Evaluator
An individual knowledgeable in emergency response procedures, functions, policies, requirements, practices; and the emergency response officer (ERO) who issues messages and data that execute emergency drill or exercise scenarios.

Controls
1) The implementation of management policies, standards, and procedures in achieving desired system performance and efficient work processes. Controls can be thought of as administrative barriers in both the prevention of accidents and incidents, and in their analysis and investigation. 2) When used with respect to nuclear reactors, means apparatus and mechanisms that, when manipulated, directly or indirectly affect the reactivity or power level of a reactor or status of an engineered safety feature.

CONUS
See Continental United States.

Convective
The transfer of heat or other atmospheric properties by massive motion, especially motion directed upward.

Convective Transport
The component of movement of heat or mass induced by thermal gradients in groundwater. *See* Advection.

Convention on International Trade in Endangered Species of Wild Fauna and Flora (CITES)
The international treaty established to protect endangered species, by banning and making it illegal to trade in these species across international boundaries, signed on March 3, 1973, and the appendices thereto.

Convention on Nature Protection and Wildlife Preservation
The convention agreement signed in 1940 that directs the Secretary of the U.S. Fish and Wildlife Service to cooperate with other parties to identify measures necessary to protect migratory birds and plants.

Conventional Filtration Treatment
A series of processes including coagulation, flocculation, sedimentation, and filtration resulting in substantial particulate removal. *See* Coagulation; Flocculation; Sedimentation; Filtration.

Conventional Mines
An open pit or underground excavation for the production of minerals.

Conventional Pollutants

Statutorily listed pollutants in the form of organic waste, sediment, acid, bacteria and viruses, nutrients, oil and grease, or heat. For the most part, the physical/chemical properties and exposure hazards of these substances are understood well by scientists.

Conventional Systems

Systems that have been traditionally used to collect municipal wastewater in gravity sewers and convey it to a central primary or secondary treatment plant prior to discharge to surface waters.

Convergence

See convergence factor; grid convergence; grid convergence factor; map convergence; true convergence.

Convergence Factor

The ratio of the angle between any two meridians on the chart to their actual change of longitude. *See* Convergence.

Convergence Zone

That region in the deep ocean where sound rays, refractured from the depths, return to the surface.

Conversion Angle

The angle between a circle (orthodromic) bearing and a rhumb line (loxodromic) bearing of a point, measured at a common origin.

Conversion Scale

A scale indicating the relationship between two different units of measurement. *See* Scale.

Converted Wetland

1) Wetlands converted to agricultural land. 2) Wetland that has been drained, dredged, filled, leveled, or otherwise manipulated (including any activity that results in impairing or reducing the flow, circulation, or reach of water) for the purpose or to have the effect of making the production of an agricultural commodity possible if: a) such production would not have been possible but for such action; and b) prior to the action the land was a wetland, and was neither highly erodible land nor highly erodible cropland. Wetland is not considered converted wetland if production of an agricultural commodity on such land during a crop year is possible as a result of a natural condition, such as drought; and is not assisted by an action of the producer that destroys natural wetland characteristics.

Conveyance

An instrument in writing by which some estate, interest, or title in real estate, is transferred from one person to another, such as a deed or mortgage.

Coolant

A liquid or gas used to reduce the heat generated by power production in nuclear reactors, electric generators, various industrial and mechanical processes, and automobile engines.

Cooling Tower

A structure that helps remove heat from water used as a coolant; e.g., in electric power generating plants.

Cooperative Agreement

A legal instrument EPA uses to transfer money, property, services, or anything of value to a recipient to accomplish a public purpose in which substantial EPA involvement is anticipated during the performance of the project.

Cooperative Logistics

The logistic support provided a foreign government/agency through its participation in the U.S. Department of Defense logistic system with reimbursement to the United States for support provided.

Cooperative Logistics Support Arrangements

The combining term for procedural arrangements (cooperative logistics arrangements) and implementing procedures (supplementary procedures) that together support, define, or implement cooperative logistic understandings between the

United States and a friendly foreign government under peacetime conditions.

Coordinate System

A method of land description using measurements from an intersection of a defined north/south axis and a defined east/west axis.

Coordinated Draft Plan

A plan for which a draft plan has been coordinated with the parties involved. It may be used for future planning and operations and may be implemented during an emergency. *See* Final Plan; Initial Draft Plan.

Coordinated Procurement Assignee

The agency or military service assigned purchase responsibility for all Department of Defense requirements of a particular federal Supply Group/class, commodity, or item.

Coordinated Universal Time (UTC)

An atomic time scale that is the basis for broadcast time signals. Coordinated Universal Time (UTC) differs from International Atomic Time by an integral number of seconds; it is maintained within 0.9 seconds of UT1 (i.e., Universal Time) by introduction of "leap seconds." The rotational orientation of the earth, specified by UT1, may be obtained to an accuracy of a tenth of a second by applying the UTC to the increment DUT1. The difference in Universal Time (DUT1) is determined by the equation UT1 - UTC; and refers to the time that is broadcast in code with the time signals. *See* International Atomic Time; Leap Second; Universal Time; ZULU Time.

Coordinates

Linear or angular quantities that designate the position that a point occupies in a given reference frame or system. Also used as a general term to designate the particular kind of reference frame or system such as plane rectangular coordinates or spherical coordinates. *See* Geographic Coordinates; Georef; Grid Coordinates.

Coordinating Authority

An individual assigned responsibility for coordinating specific functions or activities involving staff of two or more agencies or military services or two or more divisions within the same agency or service. The senior executive or individual has the authority to require consultation between the agencies involved, but does not have the authority to compel agreement. In the event that essential agreement cannot be obtained, the matter shall be referred to the appointing authority.

Coordination Processes

The coordination processes are the means by which significant environmental compliance issues will be resolved or disseminated to ensure timely development and consistent application of departmental environmental policy and guidance.

COPD

See Chronic Obstructive Pulmonary Disease.

Copepods

Small marine and freshwater crustaceans of the order Copepoda.

Coproduction

1) With respect to exports, a cooperative manufacturing arrangement (e.g., U.S. government or company with foreign government or company) providing for the transfer of production information that enables an eligible foreign government, international organization, or commercial producer to manufacture, in whole or in part, an item of U.S. defense equipment. Such an arrangement would include the functions of production engineering, controlling, quality assurance, and determination of resource requirements. This is normally accomplished under the provisions of a manufacturing license agreement per the U.S. International Traffic in Arms Regulation (ITAR) and could involve the implementation of a government-to-government memorandum of understanding. 2) A cooperative manufacturing arrangement (U.S. government or company with foreign government or company) providing for the transfer of production information that enables the receiving government, international or-

ganization, or commercial producer to manufac ture, in whole or in part, an item of defense equip ment. The receiving party could be an eligible foreign government, international organization, or foreign producer; or the U.S. government or a U.S. producer, depending on which direction the information is to flow.

Coproducts
A chemical substance produced for a commercial purpose during the manufacture, processing, use, or disposal of another chemical substance or mix ture.

Copy Negative
A negative produced from an original, not neces sarily at the same scale.

Coralline
Pertaining to or resembling coral; algae covered with a calcareous substance and forming stony deposits.

Core
The uranium-containing heart of a nuclear reac tor, where energy is released.

Core Melt Accidents
Reactor accidents in which fuel melts because of significant overheating.

Coriaceous
A term used to describe species with tough, leath erlike skins.

Cornea
Transparent membrane that covers the colored part of the eye.

Corneal Opacification
Clouding of the cornea.

Corolla
The inner portion of a flower.

Corporate Management Report and Plan (CMRP)
A document submitted to EPA, describing in full detail what actions have or will be taken to imple ment the findings of a Corporate Management Systems Report.

Corporate Management Systems Report (CMSR)
A fully integrated, stand-alone facilities audit re port, indicating comprehensive environmental compliance status.

Corrective Action
Any action taken in order to come into compli ance with any federal, state, or local statutory or regulatory requirement for the treatment, storage, or disposal of any hazardous waste.

Corrective Action Management Units (CAMU)
Large, land-based units that allow for the removal of waste from a smaller unit to another larger unit (if they are next to each other and there is no uncontaminated soil between them) without first undergoing treatment.

Corrective Action Plan (CAP)
A plan that identifies the actions required to cor rect, drill, or exercise issues or deficiencies. It also identifies a tasked manager and scheduled completion dates. These plans are typically re quired by state agencies charged with enforcing environmental cleanup actions.

Corrective Actions
EPA regulations that require corrective actions to encompass affected areas beyond the boundary of the facility, and corresponding evidence of finan cial responsibility. Corrective actions address re leases of hazardous waste or constituents regardless of when the source materials were em placed. The purpose is to limit the adverse im pacts of environmental hazards and to minimize the sensitivity of those consequences whenever possible.

Corrective Repair Maintenance

The repair of failed or malfunctioning equipment, systems, or facilities to restore the intended function or design condition. This maintenance does not result in a significant extension of the expected useful life.

Corresponding On-Shore Area

The on-shore attainment or nonattainment area that is closest to the source, unless the Administrator determines that another area with more stringent requirements with respect to the control and abatement of air pollution may reasonably be expected to be affected by such emissions.

Corrosion

The dissolving and wearing away of metal caused by a chemical reaction such as between water and the pipes that the water contacts, chemicals touching a metal surface, or contact between two metals.

Corrosion Engineering

The branch of professional engineering that requires such education and experience as is necessary to understand the environmental corrosion behavior of materials; and requires the ability to apply this knowledge by recommending procedures for control, protection, and cost effectiveness, resulting from the investigation of corrosion causes or theoretical reactions.

Corrosion Experts

People who, by reason of thorough knowledge of the physical sciences and the principles of engineering and mathematics acquired by a professional education and related practical experience, are qualified to engage in the practice of corrosion control on buried or submerged metal piping systems and metal tanks. Such people must be accredited or certified as being qualified by the National Association of Corrosion Engineers (NACE) or be registered professional engineers who have certification or licensing that includes education and experience in corrosion control of buried or submerged metal piping systems and metal tanks.

Corrosive

1) Able to cause destruction or rapid deterioration to the texture or substance of living tissue by chemical reaction. 2) A substance that reacts with the surface of a material causing it to deteriorate or wear away.

Corrosive Materials

Liquids or solids that cause visible destruction or irreversible alterations in human skin tissue at the site of contact, or in the case of leakage from its packaging, a liquid that has a severe corrosion rate on steel. Bromine and solid chloroacetic acid are examples of corrosive materials.

Cost-Benefit Analysis (CBA)

An economic method for estimating the desirability of a proposed project, in which the environmental advantages and disadvantages are defined in monetary terms, mitigation alternatives are discussed, and the totals compared.

Cost-Benefit Ratio

The ratio of total costs of a proposed project to total benefits, with both costs and benefits being discounted over the life of the project at an annual rate of interest. The difference between the two values is the present value of the net benefit to be had.

Cost Contract

1) A contract that provides for payment to the contractor of allowable costs, to the extent prescribed in the contract, incurred in performance of the contract. 2) A cost-reimbursement type contract under which the contractor receives no fee.

Cost-Effective Alternative

An alternative control or corrective method identified after analysis as being the best available in terms of reliability, permanence, and economic considerations. Although costs are one important consideration, when regulatory and compliance methods are being considered, such analysis does not require EPA to choose the least expensive alternative. For example, when selecting a method for cleaning up a site on the Superfund National Priorities List, EPA balances costs with the long-term effectiveness of the various methods proposed.

Cost-Effective Analysis
A procedure that is used to determine the most effective protection obtainable from fixed resources or, alternatively, to determine the least expensive protection for a given level of exposure.

Cost-Plus-Fixed-Fee Contract
A cost reimbursement type contract that provides for the payment of a fixed fee to the contractor. The fixed fee, once negotiated, does not vary with actual cost but may be adjusted as a result of any subsequent changes in the scope of work or services to be performed under the contract.

Cost Recovery
A legal process where potentially responsible parties (PRPs) who contributed to contamination at a Superfund site can be required to reimburse the Trust Fund for money spent during any cleanup actions by the federal government.

Cost Sharing Contract
A cost reimbursement type contract under which the contractor receives no fee but is reimbursed only for an agreed portion of its allowable costs.

Cost Sharing Payment
A payment made by the government to an owner or operator of a farm or ranch containing highly erodible cropland.

Cotyledon
In botany, a leaf of a plant embryo, being the first or one of the first to appear from a sprouting seed; in anatomy, the lobule of the placenta.

Council on Environmental Quality (CEQ)
The council created by the National Environmental Policy Act of 1969 to advise the president on environmental enforcement measures and objectives. Title II of the National Environmental Policy Act (NEPA) created the Council on Environmental Quality and defined its scope as a)

preparing an annual report on environmental quality and on existing and proposed federal efforts to improve environmental quality; b) appraising programs and activities of the federal government in the light of the national environmental policy; c) formulating and recommending national policies to promote environmental improvement; d) gathering and analyzing environmental information, making relevant studies, including monitoring trends in environmental quality; and e) advising the president.

Count, Radiation Measurement
The external indication of a device designed to enumerate ionizing events. It may refer to a single detected event or to the total registered in a given period of time. The term is often erroneously used to designate a disintegration, ionizing event, or voltage pulse.

Counterdrug (cd)
Those active measures taken to detect, monitor, and counter the production, trafficking, and use of illegal drugs.

Counterinsurgency
Military, paramilitary, political, economic, psychological, and civic actions taken by a government to defeat insurgency.

Countermeasures
That form of science that, by the employment of devices and/or techniques, has as its objective the impairment of the operational effectiveness of hazardous activity.

Country Cover Diagram
A small-scale index, by country, depicting the existence of air photography for planning purposes.

County Emergency Operations Plan
A plan required by Federal Emergency Management Agency (FEMA) regulations that describes actions a county will take to respond to emergency situations such as natural disasters, major fires, transportation incidents, or chemical releases.

Coupling, Impacts
The situation wherein if a person makes an error, there is an increased probability of an error immediately following. This can lead to chains of errors occurring. *See* Conditional Probability.

Course of Action (COA)
1) A plan that accomplishes, or is related to, the accomplishment of a mission. 2) The strategy adopted to accomplish a task or mission. 3) In military science,the recommended course of action includes the concept of operations, evaluation of supportability estimates of supporting organizations, and an integrated time-phased database of combat, combat support, and combat service support forces and sustainment. When approved, the course of action becomes the basis for the development of an operation plan or operation order.

Course of Action Development
In military science,the phase of the Joint Operation Planning and Execution System within the crisis action planning process that provides for the development of military responses and includes, within the limits of the time allowed, establishing force and sustainment requirements with actual units; evaluating force, logistic, and transportation feasibility; identifying and resolving resource shortfalls; recommending resource allocations; and producing a course of action via a commander's estimate that contains a concept of operations, employment concept, risk assessment, prioritized courses of action. *See* Course of Action; Crisis Action Planning.

Courses and Distances
A method of describing or locating real property. This description gives a starting point and the direction and length of lines to be run; practically indistinguishable from a metes and bounds description.

Covenant
A promise or agreement, usually in writing, whereby a party pledges or guarantees to another that something shall be done, or stipulates for the truth of certain facts.

Cover
Vegetation or other material providing protection as ground cover.

Cover Material
Soil used to cover compacted solid waste in a sanitary landfill.

Coverage
1) The ground area represented on imagery, photomaps, mosaics, maps, and other geographical presentation systems. 2) The summation of the geographical areas and volumes of aerospace under surveillance.

Covered Area
1) Any of the nine ozone nonattainment areas having a 1980 population in excess of 250,000 and having the highest ozone design value during the period 1987 through 1989. 2) An ozone nonattainment area classified as "Severe."

Covered Facility
A facility having one or more of the 366+ extremely hazardous substances in amounts higher than the quantity designated by EPCRA. These facilities must file reports with the State Emergency Response Commission (SERC) and Local Emergency Planning Commission (LEPC).

Covered Fleet
Ten or more motor vehicles that are owned or operated by a single entity. A covered fleet does not include motor vehicles held for lease or rental to the general public, motor vehicles held for sale by motor vehicle dealers (including demonstration vehicles), motor vehicles used for motor vehicle manufacturer product evaluations or tests, law enforcement and other emergency vehicles, or nonroad vehicles (including farm and construction vehicles).

Covert Operation
An operation that is so planned and executed as to conceal the identity of or permit plausible denial by the sponsor. A covert operation differs from a clandestine operation in that emphasis is placed

on concealment of identity of sponsor rather than on concealment of the operation. *See* Clandestine Operation; Overt Operation.

Covert Threats

Threats to a U.S. security interest caused by one or more individuals wishing to keep unfriendly actions and their identities from detection through the use of such tactics as stealth, guile, or deceit.

Covey

A group of birds; usually applied to game birds such as quail.

CPGAF

See Commission on Population Growth and the American Future.

CPL

An acronym for Confinement Protection Limits.

CPMPDW

An acronym for Convention on the Prevention of Marine Pollution.

CPSC

An acronym for Consumer Product Safety Commission.

CPVC

An acronym for chlorinated polyvinyl chloride.

Cr

See Chromium.

Cradle-to-Grave or Manifest System

A procedure in which hazardous wastes are identified as they are produced and are followed through further treatment, transportation, and disposal by a series of permanent, linkable, descriptive documents.

Crater

The pit, depression, or cavity formed in the surface of the earth by an explosion. It may range from saucer shaped to conical, depending largely

on the depth of burst. In the case of a deep underground burst, no rupture of the surface may occur. The resulting cavity is termed a camouflet.

Crater Depth

The maximum depth of the crater measured from the deepest point of the pit to the original ground level.

Crater Radius

The average radius of the crater measured at the level corresponding to the original surface of the ground.

Crawl Space

In some types of houses, that are constructed so that the floor is raised slightly above the ground, an area beneath the floor that allows access to utilities and storage space. Often used in conjunction with slab-on-grade or basement construction.

CRD

An acronym for Control Rod Drive.

CRDCS

An acronym for Control Rod Drive Control System.

CRDM

An acronym for Control Rod Drive Mechanism.

Credibility Assessments

Actions undertaken to determine the reliability or believability of expressed threats.

Credible Accidents

A DOE term for accidents with an estimated probability of occurrence greater than ten raised to the negative sixth power per year. Natural phenomena use separate probability criteria as stated in *Design and Evaluation Guidelines for Department of Energy Facilities Subjected to Natural Phenomena Hazards.*

Creep
The dimensional change in a material under physical load over time beyond instantaneous elastic deformation.

Crepuscular
A term meaning becoming active at twilight or before sunrise.

Crest
A tuft or ridge on the head of a bird or other animal.

CRGNSA
An acronym for Columbia River Gorge National Scenic Area Act.

Crisis Action Planning (CAP)
In military science, the Joint Operation Planning and Execution System process involving the time-sensitive development of joint operation plans and orders in response to an imminent crisis. Crisis action planning follows prescribed crisis action procedures to formulate and implement an effective response within the time frame permitted by the crisis.

Crisis Management Team (CMT)
Senior DOE personnel responsible for overall management of a declared emergency at the site when the EOC (emergency operations center) is activated.

Crisis Managers (CM)
The senior persons designated to assume command of operations in a particular emergency operations center (EOC) and authorized to direct the emergency management team assigned to that EOC. Also called team leaders.

Crisis Support Team (CST)
DOE contractors and managers, in the EOC after activation, who work support issues for the Incident Command Organization (ICO), initiate situation-dependent support activities, and provide necessary technical advice and resources to the CM and IC. The CST receives and works emergency-related issues and implements the directions of the CM.

Criteria
Descriptive factors taken into account by EPA in setting standards for various pollutants. These factors are used to determine limits on allowable concentration levels, and to limit the number of violations per year. For example, water quality criteria describe the concentration of pollutants that most fish can be exposed to for an hour without showing acute effects. When issued by EPA, the criteria provide guidance to the states on how to establish their standards.

Criteria Pollutants
The 1970 amendments to the Clean Air Act required EPA to set National Ambient Air Quality Standards for certain pollutants known to be hazardous to human health. EPA has identified and set standards to protect human health and welfare for six pollutants: ozone, carbon monoxide, total suspended particulates, sulfur dioxide, lead, and nitrogen oxide. It is on the basis of these criteria that standards are set or revised.

Criteria, Performance
1) Rules or tests, against which the quality of performance can be measured. They are most effective when expressed quantitatively. Fundamental criteria are contained in policies and objectives, as well as codes, standards, regulations, and recognized professional practices that DOE and DOE contractors are required to observer. 2) Descriptive factors taken into account by EPA in setting standards for various pollutants. These factors are used to determine limits on allowable concentration levels and to limit the number of violations per year. When issued by EPA, the criteria provide guidance to the states on how to establish their standards.

Critical Aquifer Protection Area (CAPA)
As defined in the Safe Drinking Water Act, a) all or part of an area located within an area for which an application of designation as a sole or principal source aquifer (pursuant to Section 1424(e)) has been submitted and approved by the Administra-

tor not later than 24 months after the date of enactment and that satisfies the criteria established by the Administrator; and b) all or part of an area that is within an aquifer designated as a sole source aquifer (SSA), as of the date of enactment of the Safe Drinking Water Act Amendments of 1986, and for which an areawide groundwater protection plan has been approved under Section 208 of the Clean Water Act (33 USC 1288) prior to June 19, 1986.

Critical Care Area
That area in a hospital designated for the treatment of severely ill patients.

Critical Endpoint
A term applied in the derivation of risk reference doses. A chemical may elicit more than one toxic effect (endpoint), even in one test animal, in tests of the same or different duration (acute, subchronic, and chronic exposure studies). The doses that cause these effects may differ. The critical endpoint used in the dose-response assessment is the one that occurs at the lowest dose. In the event that data from multiple species are available, it is often the most sensitive species that determines the critical endpoint.

Critical Facilities
Facilities such as those for radioactive material handling, processing, or storage and those facilities having high replacement value or vital importance to agency programs.

Critical Group
For a given radiation source, the members of the public whose exposure is reasonably homogeneous and is typical of individuals receiving the highest effective dose equivalent or dose equivalent (whichever is relevant) from the source.

Critical Habitat
1) The essential segment(s) of habitat that contains the unique combination of conditions (soils, vegetation, predator species, etc.) necessary for the continued survival of a endangered species. 2) The specific areas within the geographical area currently occupied by a species, at the time it is listed in accordance with the provisions of Section 1533 of the ESA, on which are found those physical or biological features essential to the conservation of the species, that may require special management considerations or protection. 3) Specific areas outside the geographical area occupied by a species at the time it is listed upon a determination by the Secretary that such areas are essential for the conservation of the species.

Critical Incident Technique
A method of identifying human errors and unsafe conditions that contribute to incidents and accidents within a given plant or system group. The method involves interviewing a representative sample of employees exposed to various hazards and having them describe unsafe behavior or conditions that they have observed in the past. The data is then tabulated into hazard categories to identify accident problem areas.

Critical Information
Information that is crucial and requires immediate attention. It is required to make decisions that will provide timely and appropriate response actions to a potential or actual hazard. It includes but is not limited to the following: a) strong indications of the imminent outbreak of any type of domestic or hazardous emergency; b) events within operating facilities where hazardous accidents and emergencies may pose synergistic and/or multiple chain reactions in and around a site, that may require modification of emergency response actions (i.e., storage of incompatible hazardous substances); and c) any indications of the release of nuclear, biological, or chemical agents or weapons.

Critical Item
An essential item that is in short supply or expected to be in short supply for an extended period. *See* Regulated Item.

Critical Jobs/Tasks
Jobs or tasks within an occupation that have been associated with major loss more frequently than others, or jobs identified as having the potential for a major loss.

Critical Mass
The smallest mass of fissionable material capable of supporting a self-sustaining chain reaction under specified conditions.

Critical Organs
1) Those organs or tissues, the irradiation or contamination of which will result in the greatest hazard to the health of an individual or his/her descendants. 2) The most exposed human organ or tissue exclusive of the integumentary system (skin) and the cornea.

Critical Path Method (CPM)
In planning and scheduling a complex series of interrelated project management operations, the sequence of events that is most critical as to the timing of successive project phases; the longest path of activities in a project management system.

Critical Pathways
1) The specific routes of transfer of hazardous substances from one environmental component to another (e.g., from one trophic level to another) that results in the greatest exposure of an applicable dose limit to a population group or an individual's whole body, organ, or tissue. 2) The dominant environmental pathways through which given substances and radionuclides reach critical groups.

Critical Period
The time of year when disturbances from normal timber operations are limited in areas where nesting endangered/threatened species or species of concern are located.

Critical Point
1) A key geographical point or position important to the success of an operation. 2) In time, a crisis or a turning point in a response operation. 3) A point where there is a change of direction of a release toward a populated area by wind, water, slope in topography, etc.

Critical Population Group
A population group showing the greatest fraction of an applicable radiation dose limit as a result of site releases.

Critical Safety Item (CSI)
A part, assembly, installation, or production system with one or more essential characteristics that, if not conforming to the design data or quality requirements, would result in an unsafe condition that could cause loss of resources, serious property damage, or serious injury to personnel.

Criticality
A term used in weapon and reactor physics to describe the state of a given fission system when the specific conditions are such that the mass of active material present is precisely a critical mass. Thus, the fission neutron production rate is a constant and is balanced by the combined rate of neutron loss and utilization so that the neutron population remains a constant. Supercriticality occurs when a greater than critical mass of active material is present and the neutron population increases rapidly. The importance of a criticality can result in intense penetrating radiation doses near the criticality and the potential release of mixed fission product radioactive materials to the building and the environment. Radiation doses near the criticality can be lethal in a short exposure time.

Criticality Accidents, Nuclear
1) Accidents resulting from criticality excursions. 2) Unplanned incidents where a series of faults and/or errors cause a very short-lived, uncontrolled nuclear chain reaction. *See* Criticality.

Criticality Alarm
A device incorporating a radiation detector and alarm circuitry placed at locations where significant quantities of fissile material are handled or stored. At a preset value, the device triggers alarms indicating high radiation is present at the detector probe and that a criticality accident may have occurred.

Criticality Excursions
Processes characterized by short releases of energy produced by uncontrolled nuclear chain reactions.

Criticality Incidents
Accidental, self-sustained atomic chain reactions. The conditions in which a system is capable of sustaining a nuclear chain reaction.

Critique
An evaluation process to assess the emergency response to a drill or exercise. Several types of critiques are typically conducted including, but not limited to, participant, controller, and evaluator critiques.

CRM
See Corrective Repair Maintenance. An acronym for Count Rate Meter.

Cross Connection
1) An unprotected physical connection between a potable water system used to supply water for drinking purposes and any source or system containing unapproved water or a substance that is not or cannot be approved as safe, wholesome, and potable. 2) A connection through which a supply of potable water could be contaminated or polluted, such as a connection between a supervised potable water supply and an unsupervised supply of unknown potability. Bypass arrangements, jumper connections, removable sections, swivel or changeover devices, or other devices through which backflow could occur, are considered cross connections.

Cross-Sectional Study
An epidemiologic study assessing the prevalence of a disease in a population. These studies are most useful for conditions or diseases that are not expected to have a long latent period and do not cause death or withdrawal from the study population. Potential bias in case ascertainment and exposure duration must be addressed when considering cross-sectional studies.

Crossover Analysis
An approach to cost analysis that shows the optimum volume of activity that should be used in alternative means of industrial manufacturing.

CRT
An acronym for Coolant Return Tank.

Crude Stocks
All stocks of domestic origin held at refineries and in transit thereto, except crude oil in transit from Alaska or any crude oil or product in transit by pipeline. Includes foreign stocks held at refineries after entry through customs for domestic consumption. After entry through customs for domestic consumption means the date of importation or the date of withdrawal specified on the U.S. Customs Service forms. Reporting of all stocks in custody of a refinery, regardless of ownership, is required.

Cruise Missile
A guided missile, the major portion of whose flight is conducted at approximately constant velocity. A cruise missile depends on the dynamic reaction of air for lift and upon propulsion forces to balance drag.

Crustaceans
Invertebrates that include shrimps, crabs, and other small marine species.

Cryogenic Liquid
Refrigerated liquefied gases having boiling points colder than 130°F at one atmosphere, absolute, such as liquid oxygen, nitrogen, argon.

Cryopedology
The scientific study of frozen ground.

Cryptology
The science that deals with hidden, disguised, or encrypted communications. It includes communications security and communications intelligence.

Crystallinity
The quality of having a molecular structure with atoms arranged in an orderly, three-dimensional pattern.

CS&R
See Codes, Standards, and Regulations.

CSA Tracking System
An OSHA computer application for a) tracking progress report due dates; b) recording progress report evaluations; c) recording actions to be taken and action dates; and d) tracking milestone abatement dates and monitoring abatement progress. The application consists of 7 files: 1) Corporation Master File; 2) Master Union File; 3) Facility File; 4) Facility Union File; 5) Progress Reports File; 6) Milestone File; and, 7) Milestone Abatement Activity File.

CSB
See Chemical Safety Board (CAA).

CSHIB
An acronym for Chemical Safety and Hazard Investigation Board. *See* Chemical Safety Board (CAA).

Ctenoid
A term meaning having narrow segments or spines resembling the teeth of a comb.

CTG
See Control Technique Guidelines.

CTSCZ
An acronym for Convention on the Territorial Sea and the Contiguous Zone.

Cubage
The number or sum resulting by multiplying the width of a thing by its height and by its depth or length.

Cubic Feet per Minute (cfm)
A measure of the volume of a substance flowing through air within a fixed period of time. With regard to indoor air, refers to the amount of air, in cubic feet, that is exchanged with indoor air in a minute's time, or an air exchange rate.

Cubic Foot per Second (cfs)
A unit of discharge for measurement of flowing liquid, equal to a flow of 1 cubic foot per second past a given section. Also called a second-foot.

Cullet
Waste glass recycled to a glass melting furnace.

Culm
The jointed stem of a grass or sedge.

Cultivating
Physical methods of soil treatment employed within established farming, ranching, and silviculture lands on farm, ranch, or forest crops to aid and improve their growth, quality or yield.

Cultivation, Relationship
A deliberate and calculated association with a person for the purpose of recruitment, networking, obtaining information, or gaining access for these or other purposes.

Cultural Eutrophication
Increasing rate at which water bodies "die" by pollution from human activities.

Cultural Landscape
A geographic area, including both cultural and natural resources, including the wildlife or domestic animals therein, that has been influenced by or reflects human activity or was the background for an event or person significant in human history. There are five types of cultural landscapes and they are not mutually exclusive:

- a) *Historic Scene* — a microenviron where a significant historic event occurred, frequently associated with structures or other tangible remains. Historic scenes are always present in historic parks though the integrity may be of questionable value;

- b) *Historic Site* — a site where an event or activity has imbued a particular piece of ground with significance warranting preservation of the historic appearance of the landscape, such as battlefields, landing sites, historic routes;

- c) *Historic Designed Landscape* — a landscape where form, layout, and use are more important than significant events or persons, and are the primary reasons for its preservation, although both may be relevant;

- d) *Historic Vernacular Landscape* — a landscape possessing a significant continuity of natural and manmade components that are united by human use and past events or aesthetically by plan or physical development; and

- e) *Ethnographic Landscape* — a landscape characterized by use by contemporary peoples, including subsistence hunting and gathering, religious or sacred ceremonies, and traditional meetings.

Cultural Park

A definable urban area that is distinguished by historic resources and land related to such resources and that constitutes an interpretive, educational, and recreational resource for the public at large.

Cultural Parks and Historic Conservation District Study

A comprehensive study and recommendations for a coordinated system of cultural parks and historic conservation districts that provide for the preservation, interpretation, development, and use by public and private entities of the prehistoric, historic, architectural, cultural, and recreational resources found in definable urban areas throughout the nation. The purpose of the study was to propose alternatives concerning the management and funding of such system by public and private entities and by various levels of government.

Cultural Resource Sites

Human-associated ruins of archaeologic significance.

Cultural Resource Specialist

A person trained in any one of the cultural resources fields, including anthropologists, archaeologists, ethnohistorians, architectural historians, archivists, curators, historians, historical archi-tects, historical landscape architects, and object conservators.

Cultural Resource Technician

Any one of various technically trained, skilled craftspersons who conducts cultural resources "hands on" work. These include preservation specialists, historical craftspersons, historical maintenance persons, and/or museum technicians.

Cultural Resources

Those tangible and intangible aspects of cultural systems, both past and present, that are valued by or representative of a given culture, or that contain information about a culture. Tangible cultural resources include, but are not limited to, sites, structures, districts, objects, and historic documents associated with or representative of peoples, cultures, and human activities and events, either in the present or in the past. Tangibles also include: plants, animals, and other natural resources culturally defined as food, manufacturing, and ceremonial items; naturally occurring or designated physical features, caves, mountain peaks, forest clearings, dance grounds, village sites, trails regarded as the sacred homes of deities, spirits, ancestors, and/or places of worship and ceremony. Certain cultural aspects are ethnographically documented for the Sioux in relation to the Black Hills, the Navajo, and Rainbow Bridge, and resources used by the Eskimo and native Hawaiian peoples in Alaskan and Hawaiian parks. Intangible cultural resources also include the primary written and verbal data for interpreting and understanding cultural features (family life, myth, folklore, ideology, folk song, and dance) that are renewable, and transmitted from generation to generation. Although material evidence of past cultures is finite, cultural resources in general are not, but are produced by each successive generation.

Cultural Resources Management

An umbrella term for activities affecting cultural resources; includes the preservation, use, protection, selective investigation of, or decision not to preserve prehistoric and historic remains. The term specifically includes the development of ways and means, including legislation and actions, to safeguard extant evidences, or to preserve records of the past.

Culture
1) A system of behaviors (including economic, religious, and social), values, ideologies, and social arrangements. For example, the culture of some people includes periodically moving in pursuit of subsistence (e.g., Eskimo) or wages (e.g., middle-class managers) and placing value on nuclear families (parents and children), wide-ranging social networks of friends, colleagues in various geographic areas, and condominiums. These features, in addition to tools and expressive elements such as graphic arts, help humans interpret their universe as well as deal with features of their environments, natural and social. Culture is learned and transmitted in a social context. Synonyms for culture include: life-ways, customs, traditions, social practices, and folkways. The terms "folk culture" and "folklike" might be used to describe aspects of the system that are unwritten, learned without formal instruction, and deal with expressive elements such as dance, song, music, and graphic arts. 2) Any organic growth developed intentionally by the provision of suitable nutrients and the proper environment. 3) Feature of the terrain that has been constructed by man. Included are such items as roads, buildings, and canals; boundary lines, and, in a broad sense, all names and legends on a map.

Cumulative Annual Effective Dose Equivalent
The sum of the annual effective dose equivalents recorded for an individual for each year of employment at DOE or DOE contractor facility since the effective date of this Order.

Cumulative Frequency, Probability
The frequency or probability that includes (or accumulates) all observations above or below specified values.

Cumulative Impact
The impact on the environment that results from the incremental impact of the action when added to other past, present, and reasonably foreseeable future actions regardless of what agency or person undertakes such other actions. Cumulative impacts can result from individually minor but collectively significant actions taking place over a period of time.

Cumulative Working Level Months (CWLM)
The sum of lifetime exposure to radon working levels expressed in total working level months.

Cuneate
A term referring to narrow wedge-shaped leaves that taper toward the base.

Curator
A person in charge of a collection of objects in a museum or other NPS repository of collections. The curator is a specialist in a field related to the collection and is responsible for the management of the collection, including acquisition and disposal, documentation and cataloging, preventive conservation, storage, access, interpretation and exhibition, including research and publication. Curators on park staffs who work directly with collections on a regular basis are known as "museum curators"; curators in other offices are known as "staff curators." In the NPS, curators are usually in charge of historic documents where there is no archivist.

Curb Weight
Weight of a ground vehicle including fuel, lubricants, coolant and on-vehicle material, excluding cargo and operating personnel.

Cure
To change the physical properties of a material irreversibly by chemical reaction via heat and catalysts, alone or in combination, with or without pressure.

Curie (Ci)
The former unit of radioactivity. One curie is 3.7×10^{10} power disintegrations per second. One gram of radium has 1 curie of radioactivity. It is named after Marie Curie (1867-1934), and has

since been replaced by the Becquerel (Bq): 1 Ci $= 3.7 \times 10^{10}$ Bq.

Current Assets

Cash or other assets or resources commonly identified as those that are reasonably expected to be realized in cash or sold or consumed during the normal operating cycle of the business.

Current Liabilities

Obligations whose liquidation is reasonably expected to require the use of existing resources properly classifiable as current assets or the creation of other current liabilities.

Curtail

To cease operations to the extent technically feasible to reduce emissions or other polluting activities.

Cusp

The fold or flap of a heart valve; also, a pointed end.

Custody

The responsibility for the control of, transfer and movement of, and access to, materials and components. Custody also includes the maintenance of accountability for samples, materials, and components.

Custody of Archaeological Resources

The regulations providing for a) the exchange between universities, museums, or other scientific or educational institutions, of archaeological resources removed from public lands and Native American lands; and b) the ultimate disposition of such resources and other resources removed pursuant to the Archaeological Preservation Act of 1960 or the Antiquities Act of 1906.

Cutaneous

A term meaning affecting the skin.

Cutie-Pie

A handheld instrument used to measure radiation levels.

CVCS

An acronym for Chemical Volume and Control System.

CVD

See Chemical Vapor Deposition.

CWA (Clean Water Act of 1977, 33 USC 121 et seq.)

The 1977 amendments to the Federal Water Pollution Control Act of 1972, that set the basic structure for regulating discharges of pollutants to waters of the United States. This law gave EPA the authority to set effluent standards on an industry-by-industry basis (technology-based) and continued the requirements to set water quality standards for all contaminants in surface waters. The CWA makes it unlawful for any person to discharge any pollutant from a point source into navigable waters unless a permit (NPDES) is obtained under the Act. The 1977 amendments focused on toxic pollutants. In 1987, the CWA was reauthorized and again focused on toxic substances, authorized citizen suit provisions, and funded sewage treatment plants (POTWs) under the Construction Grants Program. The CWA provides for the delegation by EPA of many permitting, administrative, and enforcement aspects of the law to state governments. In states with the authority to implement CWA programs, EPA still retains oversight responsibilities.

CWS

An acronym for Contaminated Water Storage.

CX

See Categorical Exclusion.

Cyanosis

Bluish discoloration of the skin and mucous membranes and fingernail beds caused by deficient oxygenation of the blood; usually evident when reduced hemoglobin (i.e., hemoglobin unable to carry oxygen) exceeds 5%.

Cybernetic Control Model
A system of control whereby deviations from standards are measured so that corrective actions can be instituted early to bring the system back into balance.

Cybernetics
A branch of learning that brings together theories and studies on communication and control in living organisms and machines.

Cycle
A series of events that occurs repeatedly in the same sequence.

Cyclone Collector
A device that uses centrifugal force to pull large particles from polluted air.

Cylinder
1) A pressure vessel designed for pressures higher than 40 psi absolute and having a circular cross section. 2) A pressure vessel constructed for and used in DOT service and having not over 1,000 pounds of water capacity (nominal). It does not include a portable tank, multiunit tank car tank, cargo tank, or tank car.

Cyme
A flat-topped flower cluster that blooms from the center toward the edges, and whose main axis is terminated by a flower.

Cyprinid
A small freshwater fish of the family Cyprinidae, that includes minnows, carps, and shiners.

Cytochrome P-448 and P-450
Enzymes found primarily in the liver and, to a lesser extent, in the lungs and other tissues that are integral in the metabolic activation and detoxification by biotransformation of many chemical substances.

Cytology
The scientific study of the structure and function of living cells.

Cytotoxicity
Producing a specific toxic action upon cells.

CZMA
See Coastal Zone Management Act of 1972.

D

d/m
An abbreviation for Drips per Minute.

D&D
See Decontamination and Decommissioning.

DA
An acronym for Direct Action; Damage Assessment.

Daily Cover
Cover material that is spread and compacted on the top and side slopes of compacted solid waste at least at the end of each operating day to control vectors, fire, moisture, and erosion and to ensure an aesthetic appearance.

Daily Instruction Logs
1) Logs containing temporary procedures before they become official. 2) Logs of daily activities conducted, or to be conducted.

Daily Movement Summary, Shipping
A tabulation of departures and arrivals of all merchant shipping (including neutrals) arriving or departing ports during a 24-hour period.

Damage
See Nuclear Damage (land warfare).

Damage Assessment
1) An appraisal of the effects of an environmental incident on the public health, safety, and welfare in an area or facility, to determine emergency response capability and to support planning for containment, recovery, and clean-up tasks. 2) The capability to estimate the damage to operations, facilities, and equipment as the result of an emergency.

Damage Control
In naval usage, measures necessary aboard ship to preserve and reestablish watertight integrity, stability, maneuverability, and offensive power; to control list and trim; to effect rapid repairs of materiel; to limit the spread of, and provide adequate protection from, fire; to limit the spread of, remove the contamination by, and provide adequate protection from, toxic agents; and to provide for care of wounded personnel. *See* Area Damage Control; Disaster Control.

Damage Criteria
The critical levels of various effects, such as blast pressure and thermal radiation, required to achieve specified levels of damage.

Damage Estimation
A preliminary appraisal of the potential effects of an incident.

Damage Radius
In naval mine warfare, the average distance from a ship within which a mine containing a given weight and type of explosive must detonate if it is to inflict a specified amount of damage.

Damage Threat

The probability that a target ship passing once through a minefield will explode one or more mines and sustain a specified amount of damage.

Damage Tolerance

A measure of the ability of structures to retain load-carrying capability after exposure to sudden loads.

Damages

Damages for injury or loss of natural resources as set forth in Section 107(a) or Section 111(b) of CERCLA.

Damping

Diminishing the intensity of vibrations.

Dams

Impoundment structures that completely span a navigable water of the United States and that may obstruct interstate waterborne commerce.

Dan

To mark a position or a sea area with dan buoys.

Dan Buoy

A temporary marker buoy used during minesweeping operations to indicate boundaries of swept paths, swept areas, known hazards, and other locations or reference points.

Danger

Potential for physical harm to people or damage to property.

Danger Area

1) A specified area above, below, or within which there may be potential danger. 2) In air traffic control, an airspace of defined dimensions within which activities dangerous to the flight of aircraft may exist at specified times. *See* Closed Area; Restricted Area.

Danger Tree

Any tree located on or adjacent to a utility right-of-way or facility that could damage utility facili-

ties should it fall where a) the tree leans toward the right-of-way, or b) the tree is defective because of any cause, such as heart or root rot, shallow roots, excavation, bad crotch, dead or with dead top, deformity, cracks or splits, or any other reason that could result in the tree or a main lateral of the tree falling.

Dangerous Cargo

Cargo that, because of its dangerous properties, is subject to special regulations for its transport. *See* Cargo.

Dangerous Materials

Explosives, flammables, oxidizing materials, corrosive liquids, compressed gases, poisons, radioactive materials, or a combination of other materials that could produce dangerous material.

Dangerous Propensity

A verified history of significant and/or repeated adverse operational act resulting in on-site and/or offsite contamination of property or the willful disregard for proper disposal of hazardous materials that supports a reasonable conclusion that a facility or individual may present a currently foreseeable and substantial threat to the environment, property, and to the public health, safety, and welfare.

Dangerously Exposed Waters

The sea area adjacent to a severely threatened coastline.

Darcy's Law

An empirically derived equation for the flow of fluids through porous media. It asserts that flow is laminar and inertia can be neglected, and that velocity of flow is directly proportional to hydraulic gradient (*See* Specific Discharge).

Data

Representation of facts, concepts, or instructions in a formalized manner suitable for communication, interpretation, or processing by humans or by automatic means. Any representations such as characters or analog quantities to which meaning is or might be assigned.

Data Call-In

A part of the Office of Pesticide Programs (OPP) process of developing key required test data, especially on the long-term, chronic effects of existing pesticides, in advance of scheduled Registration Standard reviews. Data Call-In is an adjunct of the Registration Standards program intended to expedite reregistration and involves the "calling in" of data from manufacturers.

Data Collection, Acquisition

The obtaining of information in any manner, including direct observation, liaison with official agencies, or solicitation from official, unofficial, or public sources.

Data Collection Agency

Any individual, organization, or unit that has access to sources of information and the capability of collecting information from them.

Data Collection Management

In intelligence usage, the process of converting intelligence requirements into collection requirements, establishing, tasking, or coordinating with appropriate collection sources or agencies, monitoring results and retasking, as required.

Data Collection Plan

A plan for collecting information from all available sources to meet intelligence requirements and for transforming those requirements into orders and requests to appropriate agencies. *See* Information Requirements.

Data Element

1) A basic unit of information built on standard structures having a unique meaning and distinct units or values. 2) In electronic recordkeeping, a combination of characters or bytes referring to one separate item of information, such as name, address, or age.

Data Item

A subunit of descriptive information or value classified under a data element. For example, the data element "military personnel grade" contains data items such as sergeant, captain, and colonel.

Data Journals

A journal, such as a personal diary, is a means of keeping track of events over a period of time. In environmental planning, a variety of such monitoring devices are used to obtain measurable data on facility/project activity and environmental compliance status. Journals are usually preorganized forms, divided by operations, area, and time. Most of the logging of data is done by the owner/operator's staff. Analysis of data can help determine compliance needs (both qualitative and quantitative) and other information, such as: kinds of facility/project activities; frequency of specific environmentally hazardous activities; uses of facility/project areas; use of equipment; areas of waste generation; areas of waste storage; areas of waste treatment; areas of waste disposal; sequential relationships among various activities; identification of participants in activities; record of interaction amongst individuals and work groups.

Data Link

The means of connecting one location to another for the purpose of transmitting and receiving data.

Data Mile

A standard unit of distance.

Data Quality Assessments

The requirements for data precision, accuracy, representativeness, completeness and comparability in Superfund are very strict. All monitoring entities (federal agencies, PRPs, states, etc.) should perform data reduction and validation in accordance with accepted procedures or as specified in EPA's CLP (Contract Laboratory Program) where applicable. Aspects of data quality that will be addressed are precision, accuracy, traceability of standards, traceability of data, methodology, reference or spiked samples, performance audits, and representativeness, comparability, and convenience.

Database
Information that is normally structured and indexed for user access and review. Databases may exist in the form of physical files (folders, documents, etc.) or formatted automated data processing system data files.

Date Line
See International Date Line.

Date of Agreement or Contract Award
The date the contract was signed by the party authorizing performance of work, or the date a Notice to Proceed was issued, whichever is earlier.

Date of Mailing
The date postmarked on the envelope if postage was prepaid and the envelope was properly addressed.

Datum
1) Any numerical or geometrical quantity or set of such quantities that may serve as reference or base for other quantities. Where the concept is geometric, the plural form is "datums" in contrast to the normal plural "data." 2) In geodetic terms, a reference surface consisting of five quantities: the latitude and longitude of an initial point, the azimuth of a line from that point, and the parameters of the reference ellipsoid.

Datum Level
A surface to which elevations, heights, or depths on a map or chart are related. *See* Altitude.

Datum Point
Any reference point of known or assumed coordinates from which calculation or measurements may be taken.

Dazzle
Temporary loss of vision or a temporary reduction in visual acuity. *See* Flash Blindness.

db
See Decibel.

DBE
See Design Basis Earthquakes.

DBF
See Design Basis Fires.

DBFL
See Design Basis Floods.

DBT
See Design Basis Tornadoes.

DC
See Direct Current; Double Check Valve Assembly.

DCG
An acronym for Derived Concentration Guide.

DCMD
An acronym for Demonstration Cities and Metropolitan Development Act of 1966.

DDEA
An acronym for Defense Dependents Education Act of 1978.

DDT (Dichloro-Diphenyl-Trichloroathane)
1) The first chlorinated hydrocarbon insecticide It has a half-life of 15 years and can collect in fatty tissues of certain animals. EPA banned registration and interstate sale of DDT for virtually all but emergency uses in the United States in 1972 because of its persistence in the environment and accumulation in the food chain. 2) An insecticide introduced in the 1940s and used widely because of its longlasting persistent nature. It is an organochlorine, with low toxicity as far as mammals are concerned, and is relatively inexpensive to manufacture. Its health effects to humans are not defined, but it is poisonous to other vertebrates, especially fish and, to some extent, birds. 3) A pesticide that causes eggshell

thinning in birds. Due to its negative impacts on wildlife, its use is restricted.

De Jure Boundary

An international or administrative boundary whose existence and legality is recognized; "by law."

De Facto Boundary

An international or administrative boundary whose existence and legality is not recognized, but which is a practical division between separate national and provincial administering authorities; "in fact."

De Minimis

Part of the maxim "de minimis non curat lex" (the law does not concern itself with trifles), sometimes used with reference to sources of radiation which a competent authority may decide to exempt from defined regulatory requirements because individual and collective effective dose equivalents received from them are both so low that they may be ignored.

De Minimis Rule (CAA)

A rule invoked when increased emissions of volatile organic compounds resulting from any physical change in, or change in the method of operation of, a stationary source does not exceed 25 tons when aggregated with all other net increases in emissions from the source over any period of 5 consecutive calendar years.

De Minimis Violations

Violations of standards that have no direct or immediate relationship to safety or health. Whenever de minimis conditions are found during an inspection, they are documented in the same way as any other violation but are not be included on the citation. The criteria for finding a de minimis violation is an employer complies with the clear intent of the standard but deviates from its particular requirements in a manner that has no direct or immediate relationship to employee safety or health. These deviations may involve distance specifications, construction material requirements, use of incorrect color, minor variations

from recordkeeping, testing, or inspection regulations, or the like.

Deaccession

A transaction whereby an object is removed from a museum collection according to established procedures.

Dead Loads

Nonvarying loads exerted by the weight of a mass at rest.

Dealer

Any person who is engaged in the sale or the distribution of new motor vehicles or new motor vehicle engines to the ultimate purchaser.

Debris

1) A term applied to the loose material arising from the disintegration of rocks and vegetative material, transportable by streams, ice, or floods. 2) Trash, ruins, and any accumulation of broken and detached matter, such as discarded household products and building materials.

Decantation

Separation of a liquid from solids, or from a liquid of higher density, by drawing off the upper layer after the heavier material has settled.

Decanting (Surface Decompression)

A method used for decompressing under certain circumstances. In this procedure the workers are brought to atmospheric pressure with a very high gas tension in the tissues and then immediately recompressed in a second and separate chamber or lock.

Decapod

A species descriptor for ten-legged arthropods.

Decay, Radioactive

The process whereby atoms of radioactive substances experience transformation into atoms of other elements with attendant emissions of penetration radiations (gamma ray) and some nuclear particles. Each radioactive substance has a unique decay rate, that may range from a fraction of a second to hundreds of years.

Decca

A radio phase-comparison system that uses master and slave stations to establish a hyperbolic lattice and, provide accurate ground position-fixing facilities.

Decent, Safe and Sanitary

1) Housing in sound, clean, and weathertight condition, in good repair and adequately maintained, in conformance with the applicable state and local building, plumbing, electrical, housing and occupancy codes or similar ordinances or regulations and, that meets the following minimum standards: each housekeeping unit shall include a kitchen with a fully usable sink, a stove or connection for a stove, a separate and complete bathroom, hot and cold running water in both bathroom and kitchen, an adequate and safe wiring system for lighting and other electrical services and heating as required by climatic conditions and local codes. 2) Each nonhousekeeping unit shall be in conformance with state and local code standards for boarding houses, hotels, and other dwellings for congregate living. When the term decent, safe, and sanitary is interpreted, under local, state or federal law, as establishing a higher standard, the elements of that higher standard, are usually adopted.

Deception

1) Those measures designed to mislead by manipulation, distortion, or falsification of evidence to induce a person or agency to react in a biased manner. 2) The three categories of deception are: a) physical means — activities and resources used to convey or deny selected information; b) technical means — material resources and their associated operating techniques used to convey or deny selected information through the deliberate radiation, reradiation, alteration, absorption, or reflection of energy; the emission or suppression of chemical or biological odors; and the emission or suppression of nuclear particles; c) administrative means — resources, methods, and techniques designed to convey or deny oral, pictorial, documentary, or other physical evidence.

Dechlorination

1) The partial or complete reduction of residual chlorine in a liquid by any chemical or physical process. 2) Removal of chlorine from a substance by chemically replacing it with hydrogen or hydroxide ions in order to detoxify the substances involved.

Decibel (dB)

A unit for measuring sound (noise) intensity. In general, a sound doubles in loudness for every increase of 10 decibels.

Deciduous

Means shedding or losing foliage at the end of a growing season, such as trees losing leaves in the fall.

Deciduous Stand

A plant community where deciduous trees or shrubs represent more than 50% of the total areal coverage of trees or shrubs.

Decision

A clear and concise statement of the alternative intended to be followed as the one most favorable to the successful accomplishment of the task.

Decision or Policy-Making Authority

The authority owners/operators possess whenever they: a) make a final decision; b) compel or prevent a decision either by reason of an exclusive power to initiate the decision or by reason of a veto that may or may not be overridden; c) make substantive recommendations that are, and over an extended period of time have been, regularly approved without significant amendment or modification by another person or entity; or d) vote on matters, appoint or hire people, obligate or commit to any course of action, or enter into any contractual agreement on behalf of their firm or agency. This authority does not include actions of the individuals that are solely secretarial or clerical.

Declassification

The determination that in the interests of national security, classified information no longer requires any degree of protection against unauthorized disclosure, coupled with removal or cancellation of the classification designation.

Declassify

To cancel the security classification of an item of classified matter.

Declination

The angular distance to a body on the celestial sphere measured north or south through 90° from the celestial equator along the hour circle of the body. Comparable to latitude on the terrestrial sphere. *See* Magnetic Declination; Magnetic Variation.

Decommissioning

The process of closing and securing a nuclear facility, or nuclear materials storage facility so as to provide adequate protection from radiation exposure and to isolate radioactive contamination from the human environment.

Decomposition

The breakdown of matter by bacteria and fungi. It changes the chemical makeup and physical appearance of materials. See graphic below.

Decomposition of Wastewater

1) The breakdown of organic matter in wastewater by bacterial action, either aerobic or anaerobic. 2) Transformation of organic or inorganic materials contained in wastewater through the action of chemical or biological processes.

Decompression Chamber

See hyperbaric chamber.

Decompression Sickness

A syndrome, including bends, chokes, neurological disturbances, and collapse, resulting from exposure to reduced ambient pressure and caused by gas bubbles in the tissues, fluids, and blood vessels.

Decontamination

1) The process of removing hazardous materials from exposed persons and equipment at a hazardous materials incident. 2) The removal of unwanted material (typically hazardous material) from facilities, soils, or equipment by washing, chemical action, mechanical cleaning, or other techniques. 3) The process of making any person, object, or area safe by absorbing, destroying, neutralizing, making harmless, or removing, chemical or biological agents, or by removing radioactive material clinging to or around it.

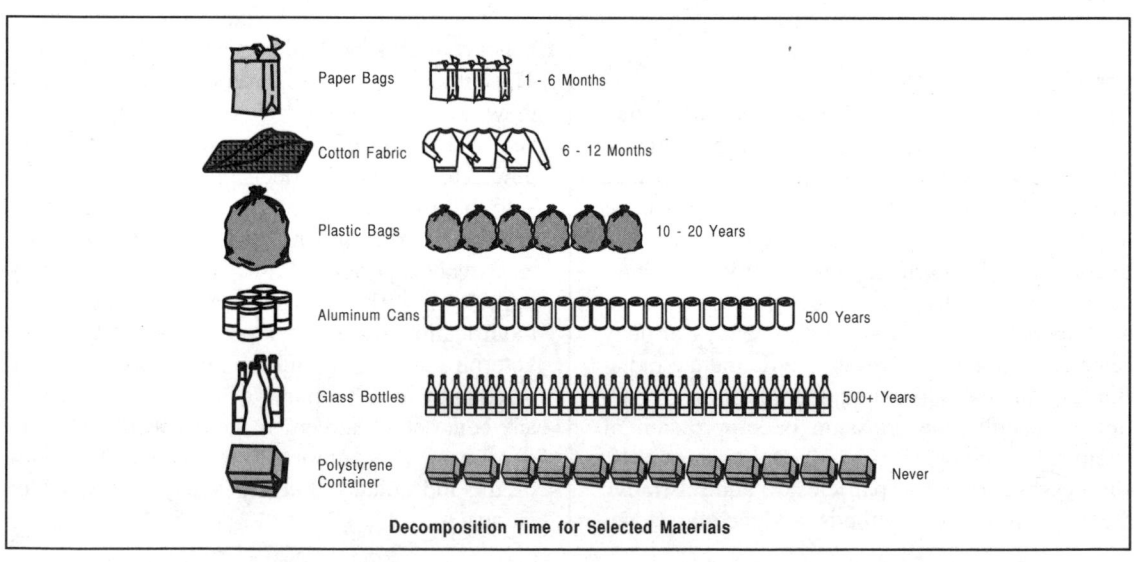

Paper Bags		1 - 6 Months
Cotton Fabric		6 - 12 Months
Plastic Bags		10 - 20 Years
Aluminum Cans		500 Years
Glass Bottles		500+ Years
Polystyrene Container		Never

Decomposition Time for Selected Materials

Decontamination Factor

The ratio of the initial level of contaminating hazardous material to the residual level achieved through the decontamination process.

Decontamination Station

A building or location suitably equipped and organized where personnel and material are cleansed of chemical, biological, or radiological contaminants.

Decontamination Zone

The area surrounding a chemical hazard incident (between the Hot Zone and the Support Zone) in which contaminants are removed from exposed victims.

Decumbent

A species descriptor that means growing along the ground but erect at the apex (tip).

Decussate

A species descriptor that means arranged on a stem in opposite pairs at right angles to those above and below.

Dedicated Fire Water Systems

Water storage and distribution systems that are available for, and used solely for, fire protection purposes, as opposed to a combined system that may be used for potable and process water supply in addition to fire protection.

Dedication

An appropriation of land to some public use, made by the owner, and accepted for such use by or on behalf of the public, as streets in a platted subdivision.

Deed

A legal instrument in writing, duly executed and delivered, whereby the owner of real property (grantor) conveys to another (grantee) some right to title or interest in or to real estate.

Deed Restriction

A provision in a deed controlling or limiting the use of the land.

Deep Dose Equivalent

As used in DOE Order 5400.5, means the dose equivalent in tissue at a depth of 1 cm deriving from external (penetrating) radiation.

Deep-Draft Harbor

A harbor that is authorized to be constructed to a depth of more than 45 feet, other than a project authorized by Section 202 the Water Resources Development Act.

Deep Eye Dose Equivalent

The dose equivalent at the respective depths of 0.007 cm, 1.0 cm, and 0.3 cm in tissue.

Deep Well Injection

A process by which waste fluids are injected deep below the surface of the earth.

Defat

To remove natural oils from the skin.

Default

The nonperformance of a duty; the omission or failure to perform a legal duty; failure to meet an obligation.

Default Bounding Accident (DBA)

An estimate of the maximum potential releases from any room, building, or group of buildings due to a specific incident at the site. This is the basis for initial response in situations where limited or no data on releases are available. All uses of DBA should be preceded by the accident category (such as "fire" or "criticality"), and followed by a specific clarifier (such as "room," "building," or "site") in order to minimize confusion. *See* Default Bounding Effect (DBE).

Default Bounding Effect (DBE)

An estimate of the maximum potential effect from the Default Bounding Accident (DBA). This is the basis for initial response in situations where limited or no data on releases or on meteorology are available. The DBE is based on the combination of the DBA for the affected area and the Worst-Case Meteorology at the site. The DBE includes the radiological and/or chemical exposure, as well as the Public Affairs Guidance (PAG) and/or Emergency Response Planning Guidance (ERPG) level. This allows the initial response Protective Action Recommendation (PAR) to be bounded at all times. *See* Default Bounding Accident.

Defects

Substandard physical conditions, either inherent in the material or created through another action or event.

Defense-Related Action

An agency action proposed to be carried out directly by a military department.

Defense Planning Guidance

A document, issued by the Secretary of Defense, that provides firm guidance in the form of goals, priorities, and objectives, including fiscal constraints, for the development of the Program Objective Memoranda by the military departments and Defense agencies. Also called DPG.

Defense Readiness Conditions

Graded warning codes, which when accompanied by a number, signify a different degree of defense readiness from normal operating status to maximum readiness.

Deficiency

An identified noncompliance with, or deviation from, an applicable requirement. Examples of the requirements are found in, but not limited to, federal or state regulations or statutes; DOE Orders; contractor or DOE facility operational procedures and administrative instructions; or any legally enforceable agreement, consensus or industry standard. Dependent on available funding or other resources, deficiencies will be corrected by the responsible organization(s). Corrective actions for deficiencies may be included in existing work packages or in planned work packages.

Deficiency Judgment

The difference between the indebtedness sued upon and the sale price of a mortgaged property in foreclosure, where the sale price is less than the indebtedness.

Deflagration

A rapid chemical reaction in which the output of heat is sufficient to enable the reaction to proceed and be accelerated without input of heat from another source. Deflagration is a surface phenomenon, with the reaction products flowing away from the unreacted material along the surface at subsonic velocity. The effect of a true deflagration under confinement is an explosion. Confinement of the reaction increases pressure, rate of reaction and temperature, and may cause transition into a detonation.

Defoliant

1) A herbicide that removes leaves from trees and growing plants. 2) A substance or mixture of substances intended for causing the leaves or foliage to drop from a plant, with or without causing abscission.

Defoliant Operation

The employment of defoliating agents on vegetated areas in support of military operations.

Defoliating Agent

A chemical that causes trees, shrubs, and other plants to shed their leaves prematurely.

Deforestation

The process of clearing forests.

Degradation

1) The process by which a chemical is reduced to a less complex form. 2) The process of decomposition. When applied to protective clothing, a molecular breakdown of material because of chemical contact; degradation is evidenced by visible signs such as charring, shrinking, or dissolving. Testing clothing material for weight changes, thickness changes, and loss of tensile strength will also reveal degradation.

Degradation Products

A substance resulting from the transformation of a pesticide by physical, chemical, or biochemical means.

Dehiscent

A species descriptor that means opening at the pores or splitting to release seeds within a fruit or pollen from an anther.

Delayed (Chronic) Health Hazards

A term related to "carcinogens" (as defined by 29 CFR 1910.1200) and other hazardous chemicals that cause an adverse effect to a target organ and which effect generally occurs as a result of long term exposure and is of long duration.

Delayed Compliance Orders

Orders issued by a government agency or by the Administrator to an owner or operator, postponing the date required under an applicable corrective action, mitigation, or implementation plan for compliance with any requirement of such plan.

Delegated State

A state (or other governmental entity) that has applied for and received authority to administer, within its territory, its state regulatory program as the federal program required under a particular federal statute. As used in connection with NPDES (National Pollutant Discharge Elimination System), Underground Injection Control (UIC) and Public Water Supply (PWS) programs, the term does not connote any transfer of federal authority to a state.

Delegation of Authority

The action by which a commander assigns part of his/her authority commensurate with the assigned task to a subordinate commander. While ultimate responsibility cannot be relinquished, delegation of authority carries with it the imposition of a measure of responsibility. The extent of the authority delegated must be clearly stated.

Delhi Process

Means for providing a (hazard) consensus from a group of people who are familiar with the (hazards) subject.

Delirium

A condition of extreme mental (and sometimes motor) excitement marked by defective perception, impaired memory, and a rapid succession of confused and unconnected ideas, often with illusions and hallucinations.

Delist

Use of the petition process to: a) have a chemical's toxic designation rescinded; b) remove a site from the National Priority List; or c) exclude a particular waste from regulation even though it is a listed hazardous waste.

Delisting Petitions

A petition to exclude a waste produced at a particular generating facility. The waste must not meet any of the criteria under which the waste was listed as hazardous waste or an acutely hazardous waste. Even after application of the petition to the Administrator and the waste is excluded, it still may be a hazardous waste by operation of Part 261 Subpart C. Procedures for application of a delisting petition are explained in 40 CFR 260.22. The regulatory intent of a delisting petition is to enable EPA to consider all factors in delisting wastes, not just those for which the waste was originally listed.

Delivery Forecasts

1) Periodic estimates of contract production deliveries used as a measure of the effectiveness of production and supply availability scheduling and as a guide to corrective actions to resolve procurement or production bottlenecks. 2) Estimates of deliveries under obligation against procurement from appropriated or other funds.

Delivery Requirements

The stipulation that requires that an item of material must be delivered in the total quantity required by the date required and, when appropriate, overpacked as required.

Delta P
A term meaning pressure difference.

Delta T
A term meaning temperature difference.

Dementia
A general deterioration of mental abilities.

Demersal
Species that inhabit the bottom or near bottom of the sea.

Demilitarized Zone
A defined area in which the stationing, or concentrating of military forces, or the retention or establishment of military installations of any description, is prohibited.

Demography
The study of age, sex, geographic distribution, rates of growth, movement patterns, etc. of human populations.

Demolition
1) The wreaking or taking out of any load-supporting structural member of a facility together with any related handling operations. 2) The destruction of structures, facilities, or material by use of fire, water, explosives, mechanical, or other means.

Demolition Chamber
Space intentionally provided in a structure for the emplacement of explosive charges.

Demonstration, Technology
The initial exhibition of a new technology process or practice or a significantly new combination or use of technologies, processes or practices, subsequent to the development stage, for the purpose of proving technological feasibility and cost effectiveness.

Demyelination
Destruction of the myelin sheath that surrounds and protects nerves.

Denervation Atrophy
Shrinkage or wasting of muscles due to loss of nerve supply.

Denitrification
1) The breakdown of nitrates by soil bacteria, resulting in the release of free nitrogen, under anaerobic conditions (like those found in water-logged soils, resulting in less fertile soil). 2) The anaerobic biological reduction of nitrate nitrogen to nitrogen gas.

Dense Fog Advisory
An alert given when fog reducing visibility to 1/4 mile or less is expected.

Density
1) The ratio of an item's weight to its volume or bulk, measured as mass per unit volume and expressed in pounds per gallon (lb/gal), pounds per cubic foot (lb/ft^3), and kilograms per cubic meter (kg/m^3). 2) In military warfare, the average number of mines per meter of minefield front.

Density Altitude
An atmospheric density expressed in terms of the altitude that corresponds with that density in the standard atmosphere.

Density Function
The value of the y-axis on a probability distribution curve. It is a measure of frequency of stated values on the x- axis.

Dentate
A species descriptor that means edged with tooth-like projections.

Denticulate
A species descriptor that means finely toothed.

Denudation
The wearing away of the land's surface by the combined impacts of weatherization and erosion.

Denuders
Horizontal or vertical containers that are part of a mercury chlor-alkali cell and in which water and alkali metal amalgams are converted to alkali metal hydroxide, mercury, and hydrogen gas in a short-circuited, electrolytic reaction.

Deny
To deny or restrict the use of any area for the present or future discharge of any dredged or fill material.

DEOA
An acronym for Department of Energy Organization Act of 1977.

Department
1) A major executive or administrative unit of the federal or state government. 2) A unit of the executive branch of the federal government that is headed by a member of the president's cabinet. Can also imply a unit of a municipal, county, or business entity.

Department Metric Coordinators
A person designated by the Assistant Secretary for Environment (DOE) to act as the department's central point of contact for metrication matters.

Department of Agriculture (DOA)
The federal agency established in 1889 to conduct farm-related educational and research programs; to administer federal agricultural-aid legislation; and to oversee various other programs and projects aimed at assisting farmers and ranchers.

Department of Commerce (DOC)
The federal agency established in 1913 to promote domestic and foreign trade matters.

Department of Defense Intelligence Information System
The aggregation of DOD personnel, procedures, equipment, computer programs, and supporting communications that support the timely and comprehensive preparation and presentation of intelligence and intelligence information to military commanders and national-level decisionmakers. Also called DODIIS.

Department of Energy (DOE)
The federal agency established in 1977 to control oil prices; coordinate energy research and development efforts; to set rates for oil and oil-related appliances; and to establish energy conservation standards.

Department of Energy Wastes
1) Radioactive waste generated by activities of the department (or its processors). 2) Waste for which DOE is responsible under law or contract. 3) Other waste for which the department is responsible. Such waste may be referred to as DOE waste.

Department of Housing and Urban Development (HUD)
The federal agency established at the beginning of the Johnson administration's Great Society (1965), to be responsible for national programs dealing with housing needs, urban renewal, and redevelopment.

Department of Justice (JD)
The federal agency created in 1870 to oversee other federal prosecuting agencies and to represent the federal government to the courts.

Department of Labor (DOL)
The federal agency created in 1913 to advance the health, safety, and welfare of workers and their working and employment conditions in general.

Department of Transportation (DOT)
The federal agency created in 1966 to foster a coordinated national transportation policy encompassing all modes except water transport. The regulatory body (federal or state) that establishes, monitors, and enforces transportation-related regulations, including those that govern shipment of hazardous wastes and hazardous materials.

Department of Treasury

The federal agency created in 1789 to impose, enforce, and collect taxes and customs duties; to enforce revenue and fiscal laws; to disburse federal funds; to manage public debt; and to manufacture money.

Department of the Air Force

The executive part of the Department of the Air Force at the seat of government and all field headquarters, forces, reserve components, installations, activities, and functions under the control or supervision of the Secretary of the Air Force. *See* Military Department.

Department of the Army (DA)

The executive part of the Department of the Army at the seat of government and all field headquarters, forces, reserve components, installations, activities, and functions under the control or supervision of the Secretary of the Army. *See* Military Department.

Department of the Navy

The executive part of the Department of the Navy at the seat of government; the headquarters, U.S. Marine Corps; the entire operating forces of the United States Navy, including naval aviation, and of the U.S. Marine Corps, including the reserve components of such forces; all field activities, headquarters, forces, bases, installations, activities, and functions under the control or supervision of the Secretary of the Navy; and the U.S. Coast Guard when operating as a part of the Navy pursuant to law. *See* Military Department.

Department Procurements

Contracts, grants, or cooperative agreements awarded by or for a government agency.

Departmental Intelligence

Intelligence that any department or agency of the federal government requires to execute its own mission.

Depleted Uranium

1) Source material uranium in which the isotope uranium-235 is less than 0.711 weight percent of the total uranium present. 2) Uranium containing less uranium-235 than the naturally occurring distribution of uranium isotopes. Depleted uranium does not include special nuclear material.

Depletion Allowance

A tax allowance extended to the owner of exhaustible resources based on an estimate of the permanent reduction in value caused by the removal of the resource.

Depletion Curve

In hydraulics, a graphical representation of water depletion from storage-stream channels, surface soil, and ground water. A depletion curve can be drawn for base flow, direct runoff, or total flow.

Deployment Planning

Planning that encompasses all activities from origin or home station through destination, specifically including intra-continental United States, inter-theater, and intra-theater movement legs, staging areas, and holding areas. ·

Deposition

Specific to air toxics, the adsorption on the respiratory tract surface of inhaled, gaseous, or particulate pollutants. Also, adsorption of a gaseous or particulate air pollutant at the surface of the ground, vegetation, or water.

Deposition Assessment

The EPA program established to identify and assess the extent of atmospheric deposition of hazardous air pollutants (and in the discretion of the Administrator, other air pollutants) to the Great Lakes, Chesapeake Bay, Lake Champlain, and coastal waters. As part of the program, the Administrator's tasks are to:

- a) monitor the Great Lakes, Chesapeake Bay, Lake Champlain, and coastal waters, including designing and deploying an atmospheric monitoring network for coastal waters;

- b) investigate the sources and deposition rates of atmospheric deposition of air pollutants (and their atmospheric transformation precursors);

- c) conduct research to develop and improve monitoring methods and to determine the relative contribution of atmospheric pollutants to total pollution loadings to the Great Lakes, Chesapeake Bay, Lake Champlain, and coastal waters;

- d) evaluate any adverse effects to public health or the environment caused by such deposition (including effects resulting from indirect exposure pathways) and assess the contribution of such deposition to violations of water quality standards established pursuant to the Federal Water Pollution Control Act (33 USC 1251 et seq.) and drinking water standards established pursuant to the Safe Drinking Water Act (42 USC 300f et seq.); and

- e) sample for such pollutants in biota, fish, and wildlife of the Great Lakes, Chesapeake Bay, Lake Champlain and coastal waters and characterize the sources of such pollutants.

Depositories
A disposal site, other than a processing site. *See* 40 CFR 192.01.

Depressed
A species descriptor that refers to the body form of a reptile that is flattened laterally.

Depression Angle
See Angle of Depression.

Depressurization
A condition that occurs when the air pressure inside a structure is lower than the air pressure outside. Depressurization can occur when household appliances that consume or exhaust house air, such as fireplaces or furnaces, are not supplied with enough makeup air. Radon containing soil gas may be drawn into a house more rapidly under depressurized conditions.

Depth
In maritime/hydrographic use, the vertical distance from the plane of the hydrographic datum to the bed of the sea, lake, or river. *See* Datum.

Depth Contour
A line connecting points of equal depth below the hydrographic datum. Also called bathymetric contour or depth curve.

Depth Curve
See Depth Contour.

Derived Limits
Values or quantities related to the primary or secondary limits by a defined model such that if the derived limits are not exceeded, it is most unlikely that the primary limits will be exceeded.

Derived Projection
Projecting risk from sources or calculations other than actual past experience.

Dermal
Pertaining to, or related, to the skin.

Dermal Toxicity
The ability of a pesticide or toxic chemical to poison people or animals by contact with the skin. *See* Contact Pesticide.

Dermatitis
Skin inflammation.

Dermis
The layer of the skin just below the epidermis or outer layer. The dermis has a rich supply of blood vessels, nerves, and skin structures.

DES
A synthetic estrogen, diethylstilbestrol is used as a growth stimulant in food animals. Formerly prescribed to prevent miscarriages. Residues in meat are thought to be carcinogenic.

Desalinization
Removing salt from ocean or brackish water.

Descriptive Names

Written indications on maps and charts, used to specify the nature of a feature (natural or artificial) shown by a general symbol.

Desert

A habitat with low rainfall and sparse vegetation.

Desiccant

A chemical agent that absorbs moisture; some desiccants are capable of drying out plants or insects, causing death. 2) A substance or mixture of substances intended for artificially accelerating the drying of plant tissue.

Desiccant Effect

Drying of the skin caused by removal of soluble oils.

Desiccation

The process of drying out; removal of moisture; drying.

Design Allowable

A limiting value for a material property that can be used to design a structural or mechanical system to a specified level of success with 95% statistical confidence. A-basis allowable — material property exceeds the design allowable 99 times out of 100. B-basis allowable — material property exceeds the design allowable 90 times out of 100.

Design Basis Accident (DBA)

Postulated accidents, or natural forces, and resulting conditions for which the confinement structure, systems, components and equipment must meet their functional goals. These safety class items are those necessary to ensure the capability to safely shut down operations, maintain the site in a safe shutdown condition, and maintain integrity of the final confinement barrier of radioactive or other hazardous materials; to prevent or mitigate the consequences of accidents; or to monitor releases that could result in potential offsite exposures.

Design Basis Earthquakes (DBE)

Earthquakes that are the most severe design basis accident of this type and that produce the vibratory ground motion for which safety class items are designed to remain functional.

Design Basis Fires (DBF)

Fires that are the most severe design basis accidents of this type. In postulating such fires, failure of aromatic and manual fire suppression provisions shall be assumed except for those safety class items/systems that are specifically designed to remain available (structurally or functionally) through the event.

Design Basis Floods (DBFL)

1) Floods that are the most severe design basis accidents of that type applicable to the area under consideration.

Design Basis Tornadoes (DBT)

Tornadoes that are the most severe design basis accident of that type applicable to the area under consideration.

Design Capacity

Anticipated operational occurrences (such as the loss of coolant flow) which are used to determine the specific design requirements for the reactor safety system.

Design Flood

1) The selected flood against which protection is provided, or eventually will be provided, by means of flood protective or control works. When a federal survey has been authorized the design flood is determined by the appropriate federal agency, in all other cases, it is determined by the responsible local agency. It is the basis for design and operation of a particular project after full consideration of flood characteristics, frequencies, and potentials, and economic and other practical considerations. 2) The flood (either observed or synthetic) chosen as the basis for the design of a hydraulic structure. *See* Design Basis Floods.

Designated Facility

A hazardous waste treatment, storage, or disposal facility that has received a) an EPA permit (or facility with interim status) in accordance with the requirements of Parts 270 and 124 of 40 CFR; b) a permit from a state authorized in accordance with Part 271 of 40 CFR; or, c) that is regulated under Section 261.6(c)(2) or Subpart F of Part 266 (precious metal recovery facilities) of 40 CFR, and that has been designated on the manifest by the generator pursuant to Section 262.20.

Designated Floodway

The channel of the stream and that portion of the adjoining flood plain required to reasonably provide for the passage of Design Flood, or the floodway between existing project levees.

Designated Nonfederal Representatives

Persons designated by a federal agency as its representatives to conduct informal consultation and/or to prepare any biological assessment.

Designated Pollutant

An air pollutant that is neither a criteria nor hazardous pollutant, as described in the Clean Air Act, but for which new source performance standards exist. The Clean Air Act does require states to control these pollutants, which include acid mist, total reduced sulfur (TRS), and fluorides.

Designated Unit

A unit of the National Wildlife Refuge System designated by the Secretary under Section 3911(a)(2) of the Wetlands Resources Act (WRA).

Designated Uses

Those water uses identified in state water quality standards which must be achieved and maintained as required under the Clean Water Act. Uses can include cold water fisheries, public water supply, or agriculture.

Designer Bugs

A popular term for microbes developed through biotechnology that can degrade specific toxic chemicals at their source in toxic waste dumps or in ground water.

Desired Ground Zero (DGZ)

The point on the surface of the earth at, or vertically below or above, the center of a planned nuclear detonation. *See* Actual Ground Zero; Ground Zero.

Desk Audit

A systematic process of observing and interviewing workers at their place of activity to measure and identify factors affecting compliance with quality control standards.

Desmid

A species descriptor for the a green, unicellular freshwater algae of the family Desmidiaceae that often forms chainlike colonies.

Desorption

See Sorption for a description of the reverse process.

Destruction

The total and irreversible loss of a natural resource. A direct or indirect alteration that appreciably diminishes the value of critical habitat for both the survival and recovery of a listed species. Such alterations include, but are not limited to, alterations adversely modifying any of those physical or biological features that were the basis for determining the habitat to be critical.

Destruction and Removal Efficiency (DRE)

A percentage that represents the number of molecules of a compound removed or destroyed in an incinerator. A DRE of 99.99% means that 9,999 molecules are destroyed for every 10,000 that enter.

Desulfurization

Removal of sulfur from fossil fuels to reduce pollution.

Detailed Operating Procedures

Working level documents to perform a task or job. Used to help avoid oversights and omissions and to ensure a proper sequence of work steps.

Detailed Photographic Report

A comprehensive analytical study written as a result of the interpretation of photography usually covering a single site, a facility, or facility complex, and of a detailed nature.

Detection Limits

The lowest amount that can be distinguished from the normal electronic noise of an analytical instrument.

Detention Dam

An impoundment structure used to detain small volumes of water periodically for short periods of time, i.e., for water sampling, to assess water quality prior to discharge, and for spill control.

Detention Pond

A manmade impoundment built for the temporary storage of excess storm water runoff so as to reduce the possibility of flood damage downstream.

Detention Time

The theoretical time required to displace the contents of a tank or unit at a given rate of discharge, represented by volume divided by rate of discharge.

Detergents

1) Synthetic washing agents that help to remove dirt and oil. Some contain compounds that kill useful bacteria and encourage algae growth when they are in wastewater that reaches receiving waters. 2) Gasoline additives that prevent the accumulation of deposits in engines or fuel supply systems.

Deterioration Limit

A limit placed on a particular product characteristic to define the minimum acceptable quality requirement for the product to retain its NATO code number.

Deterrence

The prevention from action by fear of the consequences. Deterrence is a state of mind brought about by the existence of a credible threat of unacceptable counteraction.

Deterrent Options

A course of action, developed on the best economic, environmental, political, and military judgment, designed to dissuade an adversary from a current course of action or contemplated operations.

Detonating Cord

A flexible fabric tube containing a high explosive designed to transmit the detonation wave.

Detonations

Violent chemical reactions within a chemical compound or mechanical mixture evolving heat and pressure. They are reactions that proceed through the reacted material toward the unreacted material at supersonic velocity. The result of the chemical reactions is the exertion of extremely high pressure on the surrounding medium, forming a propagating shock wave of supersonic velocity.

Detonator

1) A device containing a sensitive explosive intended to produce a detonation wave. 2) An explosive device used to initiate the detonation of other explosives.

Detour

Deviation from those parts of a route where movement has become difficult or impossible to ensure continuity of movement to a predetermined destination. The modified part of the route is known as a "detour."

Detoxification

Reduction of a chemical's toxic properties by means of biotransformation processes, to form a more readily excreted, or a less toxic chemical than the parent compound.

Detriment

The mathematical expectation of the harm (damage to health and other effects) incurred from the exposure of individuals or groups of persons in a human population to a radiation source, taking into account not only the probabilities but also the severity of each type of deleterious effect.

Detritus

1) Coarse debris carried by wastewater; commonly referred to as grit. 2) A species descriptor that refers to decomposing organisms that serve as a food supply to many species.

Deuterium

A nonradioactive isotope of hydrogen whose nucleus contains one neutron and one proton and is therefore about twice as heavy as normal hydrogen. Often referred to as heavy hydrogens.

Developer

A person, government unit, or company that proposes to build a hazardous waste treatment, storage, or disposal facility.

Developmental Reference Dose Values (RfD)

An estimate (with uncertainty spanning perhaps an order of magnitude or greater) of an exposure level for the human population, including sensitive subpopulations, that is likely to be without an appreciable risk of developmental effects. Developmental RfDs are used to evaluate the effects of a single event (generally 1 day) exposure.

Developmental Toxicity

Adverse effects on a developing organism that may result from exposure prior to conception (either parent), during prenatal development, or postnatally to the time of sexual maturation. Adverse developmental effects may be detected at any point in the life span of the organism. Major manifestations of developmental toxicity include death of the developing organism; induction of structural abnormalities (teratogenicity); altered growth; and functional deficiency.

Deviation

Departure from a norm.

Device

Any piece of control hardware, such as an emergency-stop button, a selector switch, a control pendant, a relay, a solenoid valve, or a sensor.

Dewatered

To remove the water from recently produced tailings, or other materials, by mechanical or evaporative methods such that the water content of the tailings does not exceed 30% by weight.

Dextral

1) A species descriptor that refers to the right side of a species. 2) In zoology, it means pertaining to a gastropod shell that has its aperture (opening) to the right when facing the observer with the apex (top) upward.

DFDP

An acronym for Defense Facility Decommissioning Program.

Diagrams

Geometric drawings used to explain a fact, a process, the sequence of an activity, or the composition of an element as associated with an accident or incident.

Diapause

A species descriptor that refers to a period during which growth or development is suspended, as in insects.

Diaphoresis

Excessive perspiration.

Diaphragms

Horizontal or nearly horizontal systems acting to transmit lateral forces to the vertical resisting elements. The term includes horizontal bracing systems.

Diaphragm Strut

The element of a diaphragm parallel to the applied load that collects and transfers diaphragm shear to vertical resisting elements or distributes loads within the diaphragm. Such members may take axial tension or compression.

Diapositive

A positive photograph on a transparent medium.

Diatom

A species descriptor that refers to minute unicellular or colonial (living in colonies) algae having siliceous cell walls consisting of two overlapping symmetrical parts.

Diatomaceous Earth (Diatomite)

A chalklike material (fossilized diatoms) used to filter out a solid waste in wastewater treatment plants, also used as an active ingredient in some powdered pesticides.

Diatomaceous Earth Filtration

A process resulting in substantial particulate removal in which a) a precoat cake of diatomaceous earth filter media is deposited on a support membrane (septum); and b) while the water is filtered by passing through the cake on the septum, additional filter media known as body food is continuously added to the feed water to maintain permeability.

Diazinon

An insecticide. In 1986, EPA banned its use on open areas such as sod farms and golf courses because it posed a danger to migratory birds who gathered on them in large numbers. The ban did not apply to its use in agriculture, or on lawns of homes and commercial establishments.

Dichasium

A species descriptor that refers to a flat-topped flower cluster having two lateral stems branching from the main axis.

Dichromatize

A species descriptor that means to become divided into parts or branches.

Dicofol

A pesticide used on citrus fruits.

Dictionary of Occupational Titles (DOT)

A reference published by the U.S. Employment Service, that alphabetically lists and defines over 20,000 job categories. It is the most referred to reference of its kind, and is used extensively by government agencies.

Dielectric Materials

Materials that do not conduct direct electrical current. Dielectric coatings are used to electrically isolate UST (Underground Storage Tank) systems from the surrounding soils. Dielectric bushings are used to electrically isolate portions of the UST system (e.g., tank from piping).

Diesel Oil

The oil fraction left after petroleum and kerosene have been distilled from crude oil.

Differential Cost Benefit Analysis (DCBA)

A procedure for optimization of radiation protection used to determine the point at which exposures have been decreased so far that any further decrease is considered less important than the additional necessary effort required to achieve it.

Differential Pressure

The difference in pressure between two points of a system, such as between the inlet and outlet of a pump.

Differential Settlement

Nonuniform settlement of land or the uneven lowering of it. A principal cause of damage and casualties resulting from earthquakes.

Differentiation

The process by which single cells grow into particular forms of specialized tissue, e.g., root, stem, leaf.

Diffraction Loading

The total force that is exerted on the sides of a structure by the advancing shock front of a nuclear explosion.

Diffuse Reflection

Reflection that takes place when different parts of a beam incident on a surface are reflected over a wide range of angles in accordance with Lambert's Law. The intensity will fall off as the inverse of the square of the distance away from the surface and also obey a Cosine Law of reflection.

Diffused-Air Aeration

Aeration produced in a liquid by air passing through a diffuser.

Diffused Air Process

A type of aeration that forces oxygen into sewage by pumping air through perforated pipes inside a holding tank and bubbling through the sewage.

Diffuser

A porous plate, tube, or other device through which air is forced and divided into minute bubbles for diffusion in liquids. Commonly made of carborundum, alundum, metal, or plastic.

Diffuser Plate

A porous plate used in aeration tanks to diffuse air or other gases in various water and wastewater treatment processes. *See* Diffuser.

Diffuser Tube

An air tube used in aeration tanks to diffuse air or other gases in various water and wastewater treatment processes. *See* Diffuser.

Diffusion

Movement of a chemical substance from areas of high concentration to areas of low concentration. Biologically, diffusion is an important means for toxicant deposition for gases and very small particles in the pulmonary region of the lungs.

Diffusion Coefficient

See Molecular Diffusion.

Diffusivity

In soil and water, the hydraulic conductivity divided by the differential water capacity, or the flux of water per unit gradient of moisture content, when other force fields are not present.

Digester

1) A tank in which sludge is placed to permit digestion to occur. 2) In wastewater treatment, a closed tank; in solid waste conversion, a unit in which bacterial action is induced and accelerated in order to break down organic matter and establish the proper carbon-to-nitrogen ratio. Also known as sludge digestion tank.

Digestion

1) The biochemical decomposition of organic matter in sludge, resulting in partial gasification, liquefaction, and mineralization of pollutants. 2) The process carried out in a digester.

Digitigrade

A species descriptor that means walking so that only the toes touch the ground.

DIH

An acronym for Differential in Hours.

Dike

1) A low wall that can act as a barrier to prevent a spill from spreading. 2) A concrete, metal, or compacted earth structure used to confine an accidental spill within an impounding area. 3) An embankment or ridge of either natural or man-made materials used to prevent the movement of liquids, sludges, solids, or other materials.

DIL

See Daily Instruction Logs.

Dilution

1) Disposal of wastewater or treated effluent by discharging it into a stream or body of water. 2) The use of water to lower the concentration or amount of a contaminant.

Dilution Ratio

The relationship between the volume of water in a stream and the volume of incoming water. It affects the ability of the stream to assimilate waste.

DIMIG

An acronym for Disintegrations per minute per gram.

Dimorphism

1) A species descriptor that means the occurrence of two distinct forms of the same parts, such as leaves, flowers, or stamens, in a single plant or in plants of the same kind. 2) In zoology, differing characteristics between male and female.

Dinocap

A fungicide used primarily by apple growers to control summer diseases. In 1986, EPA proposed restrictions on its use when laboratory tests found it caused birth defects in rabbits.

Dinoseb

A herbicide that is also used as a fungicide and insecticide. It was banned by EPA in 1986 because it posed the risk of birth defects and sterility.

Dioecious

A species descriptor that means having male and female flowers borne on separate plants.

Dioxins

Any of a family of compounds known chemically as dibenzo-p-dioxins. Concern about them arises from their potential toxicity and contamination in commercial products. Tests on laboratory animals indicate that they are one of the more toxic manmade chemicals known.

Dip-Sup

A type of surface faulting, the component of which is movement or slip that is parallel to the dip of the fault. The faulting may be normal or reverse displacement.

Diploid

1) The chromosome state in which each homologous chromosome is present in pairs. Normal human somatic (nonreproductive) cells are diploid (i.e., they have 46 chromosomes), whereas reproductive cells, with 23 chromosomes, are haploid. 2) A species descriptor that means having a homologous (genetically the same) pair of chromosomes for each characteristic except sex.

Diplopia

Double vision.

Direct Absorption Unit

A unit in which the refrigerant evaporator is in direct contact with the air to be conditioned.

Direct Bioassays

Assessments of radioactive material deposited in the body by detection of radiation emitted by the material in the body (in vivo measurement).

Direct Current (DC)

An electric current, such as that produced by a battery, in which the electrical potential does not change its sign and the voltage is often invariant with time. In direct currents, energy is carried by a continuous, unidirectional flow of electrons through a conductor.

Direct Discharger

A municipal or industrial facility that introduces pollution through a defined conveyance or system; a point source.

Direct Filtration

A series of processes including coagulation and filtration but excluding sedimentation resulting in substantial particulate removal.

Direct Precipitation

The water that falls directly into a lake or stream without passing through any land phase of the runoff cycle.

Direct Service Contract

A contract, wherein the contractor agrees to provide services directly to the public or to persons who are eligible for programs administered or supported by a government agency or department.

Directed Energy

An umbrella term covering technologies that relate to the production of a beam of concentrated electromagnetic energy or atomic or subatomic particles. Also called DE. *See* Directed-Energy Device; Directed-Energy Weapon.

Directed-Energy Device

A system using directed energy primarily for a purpose other than as a weapon. These devices may produce effects that could allow the device to be used as a weapon against certain threats, for example, laser range finders and designators used against sensors that are sensitive to light.

Directive

1) Generally, any communication that initiates or governs action, conduct, or procedure. 2) A military communication in which policy is established or a specific action is ordered. 3) A plan issued with a view to putting it into effect when directed, or in the event that a stated contingency arises.

Directly Ionizing Particles

Charged particles (electrons, protons, alpha particles, etc.) having sufficient kinetic energy to produce ionization by collision.

Director of Emergency Operations

The official with responsibility to coordinate the planning, development, and implementation of an overall, comprehensive, Emergency Management System.

Director

The Regional Administrator or the state Director, or an authorized representative. When there is no approved state program, and there is an EPA administered program, Director means the Regional Administrator. When there is an approved state program, Director normally means the state Director. In some circumstances, however, EPA retains the authority to take certain actions even when there is an approved state program. In such cases, the term Director means the Regional Administrator and not the state Director. The Director of the National Marine Fisheries Service, National Oceanic and Atmospheric Administration, Department of Commerce, or his/her authorized designee.

Disabling Injuries

Injuries that prevent a person from performing his/her regularly established job for one full day beyond the day of the accident; also called a lost-time injury.

Disaffected Person

A person who is alienated or estranged from those in authority or lacks loyalty to the government; a state of mind.

Disaster Control

Measures taken before, during, or after hostile action or natural or manmade disasters to reduce the probability of damage, minimize its effects, and initiate recovery. *See* Area Damage Control; Damage Control.

Discarded Materials

Solid waste materials that a) are not excluded by 40 CFR Part 261.4(a) or that are not excluded by variance granted under Parts 260.30 and 260.31; b) are abandoned; c) are recycled; or d) are considered inherently wastelike, as explained in 40 CFR Part 261.2(d).

Discharge

1) The release of any waste into the environment from a point source. Usually refers to the release of a liquid waste into a body of water through an outlet such as a pipe, but also refers to air emissions. 2) As defined by Section 311(a)(2) the of Clean Water Act, includes, but is not limited to, any spilling, leaking, pumping, pouring, emitting, emptying, or dumping of oil. 3) Substantial threats of discharge.

Discharge Area

An area of land where there is a net annual transfer of water from the ground water to surface water, such as to streams, springs, lakes, and wetlands.

Discharge of Dredged Material

Any addition of dredged material into the waters of the United States. The term includes, without limitation, the addition of dredged material to a specified discharge site located in waters of the United States and the runoff or overflow from a contained land or water disposal area.

Discharges of pollutants into waters of the United States resulting from the onshore subsequent processing of dredged material that is extracted for any commercial use (other than fill) are not included within this term are subject to Section 402 of Clean Water Act even though the extraction and deposit of such material may require a permit from the Corps of Engineers. The term does not include plowing, cultivating, seeding and harvesting for the production of food, fiber, and forest products (*See* 40 CFR 323.4 for the definition of these terms). The term also does not include de minimis, incidental soil movement occurring during normal dredging operations.

Discharge of Fill Material

The addition of fill material into waters of the United States. The term generally includes, without limitation, the following activities: placement of fill that is necessary for the construction of any structure in a water of the United States; the building of any structure or impoundment requiring rock, sand, dirt, or other material for its construction; site development fills for recreational, industrial, commercial, residential, and other uses; causeways or road fills; dams and dikes; artificial islands; property protection and/or reclamation devices such as riprap, groins, seawalls, breakwaters, and revetments; beach nourishment; levees; fill for structures such as sewage treatment facilities, intake and outfall pipes associated with power plants, and subaqueous utility lines; and artificial reefs. The term does not include plowing, cultivating, seeding and harvesting for the production of food, fiber, and forest products (*See* 40 CFR 323.4 for the definition of these terms).

Discharge of Pollutants

1) The addition of pollutants to navigable waters from any point source. 2) Any addition of pollutants to the waters of the contiguous zone or the ocean from any point source, other than from a vessel or other floating craft being used as a means of transportation. The term discharge includes either the discharge of a single pollutant or the discharge of multiple pollutants.

Discharge or Hazardous Waste Discharge

As defined by Section 311(a)(2) of the Clean Water Act, includes, but is not limited to, any accidental or intentional spilling, leaking, pumping, pouring, emitting, emptying, or dumping of oil or other hazardous substances into, or on, any land or water.

Discharge or Release to Water or Land

The direct or indirect transfer by any person in the course of doing business of any listed chemical to land or water in a manner that, if committed by the transferor, would pose a threat to public health and welfare. Discharge or release into water or onto land does not include the following: a) the sale, exchange or other transfer of a chemical to a solid waste disposal facility, or a hazardous waste facility provided that the disposal to such facility complies with all applicable state and federal statutes, rules, regulations, permits, requirements, and orders; b) the sale, exchange or other transfer of a chemical to any treatment works as defined in 33 United States Code Section 1292 provided that the discharge or release to such treatment works complies with all applicable standards and limitations imposed, and permits required, under federal law or an approved state program.

Discharge Point

The point within a disposal site at which dredged or fill material is released.

Discretionary Authority

The authority delegated to agency engineers to override provisions of nationwide permits, to add regional conditions, or to require individual permit applications.

Discrimination

Discharge, demotion, reduction in pay, coercion, restraint, threats, or other negative actions taken against an individual, or group, as a result of the individual's, or group's a)exercise of occupational safety and health rights; or b) race, creed, economic level, or color.

Dishonesty

1) The disposition, and intent, to deceive, cheat, steal or defraud. 2) An absence of integrity. 3) A lack of honesty; or 4) a crime resulting from dishonest conduct.

Disinfectant Contact Time

The time (T) in minutes that it takes for water to move from the point of disinfectant applications or the previous point of disinfectant residual measurement to a point before or at the point where residual disinfectant concentration (C) is measured (T in CT calculations). Refer to 40 CFR 141.2.

Disinfectants

Chemical or physical agents that kill pathogenic organisms in water. Chlorine is often used to disinfect sewage treatment effluent, water supplies, wells, and swimming pools.

Disinfected Wastewater

Wastewater in which chlorine or other disinfecting agents have been added to, during or after treatment, to destroy pathogenic organisms.

Disinfection

1) The process of killing the larger portion of microorganisms in, or on, a substance with a large probability that all pathogenic bacteria will be destroyed by the disinfecting agent used. 2) A process that inactivates pathogenic organisms in water by chemical oxidants or equivalent agents.

Disk

A species descriptor that means the round center of a ray flower, such as a daisy, around which petals are arranged.

Dispensing Unit

1) For natural gas, a stationary natural gas installation other than a bulk plant from which compressed natural gas (CNG) or liquid petroleum gas (LNG) is dispensed into fuel tanks or portable cylinders from a storage tank, bank of cylinders, compressor, or a distribution gas pipeline. 2) For LPG a stationary LPG installation other than a bulk plant from which a product is dispensed, for final utilization, into mobile fuel tanks or portable cylinders.

Dispersal

A species descriptor that refers to the migration of individuals from their home range.

Dispersants

1) Chemical agents used to break up concentrations of organic material such as spilled oil. 2) Chemical agents that emulsify, disperse, or solubilize oil into the water column or promote the surface spreading of oil slicks to facilitate dispersal of the oil into the water column.

Dispersed Site

A site selected to reduce concentration and vulnerability by its separation from other target sources or a recognized hazard area.

Dispersion

1) In chemical and biological operations, the spreading and mixing of chemical constituents in groundwater caused by diffusion and mixing due to microscopic variations in velocities within and between pores. 2) The dissemination of agents in liquid or aerosol form. 3) In airdrop operations, the scatter of personnel and/or cargo on a drop zone. 4) In shipping operations, the reberthing of a ship in the periphery of the port area or in the vicinity of the port for its own protection in order to minimize the risk of damage.

Dispersion Coefficient

A measure of the spreading of a flowing substance due to the nature of the porous medium and the specific substance or fluid properties, when interconnected channels are distributed at random in all directions. Also, the sum of the coefficients of mechanical dispersion and molecular diffusion in a porous medium.

Dispersion Error

The distance from the point of impact or burst of a round to the mean point of impact or burst.

Dispersion Model

A mathematical prediction of how pollutants from a discharge or emission source will be distributed in the surrounding environment under given conditions of wind, temperature, humidity, and other environmental factors. Models take into account a variety of mixing mechanisms that dilute effluents and transport them away from the point of emission.

Dispersion Resins

Resins manufactured in such a way as to form fluid dispersions when dispersed in a plasticizer or plasticizer/diluent mixtures.

Dispersion Technique

1) Any intermittent or supplemental control of air pollutants varying with atmospheric conditions. 2) Techniques that attempt to affect the concentration of a pollutant in the ambient air by a) using that portion of a stack that exceeds good engineering practice stack height; b) varying the rate of emission of a pollutant according to atmospheric conditions or ambient concentrations of that pollutant; or c) increasing final exhaust gas plume rise by manipulating source process parameters, exhaust gas parameters, stack parameters, or combining exhaust gases from several existing stacks into one stack, or other selective handling of exhaust gas streams so as to increase the exhaust gas plume rise. Refer to 40 CFR 61.100.

Dispersivity

The property of a porous medium and the specific substance or fluid that determines the dispersion characteristics of the contaminant in that medium by relating the components of pore velocity to dispersion coefficient. *See* Dispersion Coefficient.

Disposal

1) The discharge, deposit, injection, dumping, spilling, leaking, or placing of any solid waste or hazardous waste into or on any land or water so that such solid waste or hazardous waste or any constituent thereof may enter the environment or be emitted into the air or discharged into any waters, including ground waters. 2) Waste emplacement designed to ensure isolation of waste from the biosphere, with no intention of retrieval for the foreseeable future, and that requires deliberate action to regain access to the waste. 3) Final placement or destruction of toxic, radioactive, or other wastes; surplus or banned pesticides or other chemicals; polluted soils; and drums containing hazardous materials from removal actions or accidental releases. Disposal may be accomplished through use of approved secure landfills, surface impoundments, land farming, deep well injection, ocean dumping, or incineration. 4) To intentionally or accidentally discard, throw away, or otherwise complete or terminate the useful life of PCBs and PCB items.

Disposal includes spills, leaks, and other uncontrolled discharges of PCBs as well as actions related to containing, transporting, destroying, degrading, decontaminating, or confining PCBs and PCB items.

Disposal Areas

The regions within the perimeter of impoundments containing uranium by-product materials to which the post-closure requirements apply. Refer to 40 CFR 192.31 (f).

Disposal Facility

1) A facility or part of a facility at which hazardous waste is intentionally placed into, or on, any land or water, and at which waste will remain after closure. 2) A landfill, incinerator, or other facility, that receives waste for disposal. The facility may have one or many disposal methods

available for use. Does not include wastewater treatment.

Disposal Package
The primary container that holds, and is in contact with, solidified high-level radioactive waste, spent nuclear fuel, or other radioactive materials, and any overpacks that are emplaced at a repository.

Disposal Sites
Those portions of the waters of the United States where specific disposal activities are permitted and consist of a bottom surface area and any overlying volume of water. In the case of wetlands on which surface water is not present, the disposal site consists of the wetland surface area.

Disposal Systems, Nuclear
Any combination of engineered and natural barriers that isolate spent nuclear fuel or radioactive wastes after disposal.

Disposal Units
A discrete portion of the disposal site into which waste is placed for disposal. For near-surface disposal operations the unit is usually a trench.

Disposal Wells
Wells used for the disposal of waste into a subsurface stratum.

Disposer of PCB Waste
Any person who owns or operates a facility approved by the EPA for the disposal of PCB waste that is regulated for disposal under the requirements of 40 CFR 761, Subpart D.

Disposition
The movement and fate of chemicals in the body, including absorption, distribution, biotransformation, and excretion.

Dissolved Oxygen (DO)
Oxygen that is freely available in water to sustain the lives of fish and other aquatic organisms, and for the prevention of odors. Traditionally, the level of dissolved oxygen has been accepted as the single most important indicator of a water body's ability to support desirable aquatic life.

Dissolved Solids
Disintegrated organic and inorganic materials contained in water. Excessive amounts make water unfit to drink or use in industrial processes.

Distal
A species descriptor that means anatomically located far from the origin or line of attachment.

Distillation
The act of purifying liquids through boiling, so that the steam condenses to a pure liquid and the pollutants remain in a concentrated residue.

Distribute/Distribution in Commerce
To sell, import, introduce, or deliver for introduction into commerce, or to hold for sale or distribution after introduction.

Distribution
1) The transport of a substance through the body by physical means (e.g., active transport or diffusion). Distribution is dependent on the chemical properties of the toxicant or its metabolites and, to some extent, the route of exposure as well as physiologic variables. 2) In statistics, the frequency or manner in which observations of different value are distributed over the range of values. These values can be numbers, frequency, size, cost, etc.

Distribution Coefficient
The quantity of a solute absorbed per unit weight of a solid divided by the quantity dissolved in water per unit volume of water.

Distribution Reservoir
A reservoir, directly connected with the distribution system of the domestic water supply project, used primarily to care for fluctuations in demand that occur over short periods of from several hours to several days, or as local storage in case

of emergency such as a break in a main supply line or failure of pumping plant.

Distributor

A device used to apply liquid to the surface of a filter or contact bed. There are generally two types of distributors, fixed and movable. Fixed types may consist of perforated pipes, notched troughs, sloping boards, or sprinkler nozzles; movable types consist of rotating, reciprocating, or traveling perforated pipes or troughs applying a spray or a thin sheet of liquid.

Ditch Drain

A drainage structure or facility that will move water from an inside road ditch to an outside area.

Diurnal

A species descriptor for plants that open during daylight and close at night, or animals that are active during the day and sleep at night.

Divergent Windstorms

Includes downbursts, gust fronts, and downslope winds, and are characterized predominantly by a divergent flow field.

Diversity

A species descriptor that refers to the number of differing species in a habitat.

Divert

To change or turn the flow of a contaminant or spill; to alter course, mission, or destination; an illegal change or alteration of a water course to the detriment of downstream ecosystems.

Diving Chamber

See Hyperbaric Chamber.

Division

1) An organizational level having responsibility for operations within a defined geographic area. 2) In botany, a taxonomic grouping of organisms belonging to similar classes; the equivalent of phylum.

DMA

An acronym for Diagnosis of Multiple Alarms System.

DNA (Deoxyribonucleic Acid)

The molecule in which the genetic information for most living cells is encoded. The molecule is double stranded, with a "backbone" of phosphate and sugar (deoxyribose) to which the nucleotide bases are attached. The nucleotides form a ladderlike structure by hydrogen bonds such that adenine (A) pairs with thymine (T) and guanine (G) pairs with cytosine (C). The specific sequence of nucleotide bases defines the gene. Viruses, too, can contain DNA.

DNA Adduct

A lesion in the DNA formed by the covalent binding of an erogenous chemical to one of the nucleotide bases. DNA adducts are frequently the precursors to changes in the sequence of nucleotides (mutations). *See* DNA Crosslink.

DNA Crosslink

A lesion in the DNA formed by the covalent binding of an erogenous chemical to two nucleotide bases, one each on opposing strands of the DNA. DNA crosslinks usually prevent DNA replication and are lethal to cells attempting to divide. *See* DNA Adduct.

DNA Hybridization

Use of a segment of DNA, called a DNA probe, to identity its complementary DNA; used to detect specific genes. This process takes advantage of the ability of a single strand of DNA to combine with a complementary strand.

DNO

An acronym for Do Not Operate.

Doctrine

Fundamental principles by which the military forces or elements thereof guide their actions in support of national objectives. It is authoritative but requires judgment in application. *See* Joint Doctrine.

Documentation

Measured drawings, photographs, histories, or other media that depict historic sites, structures, or objects.

DOD Internal Audit Organizations

The following DOD organizations: the Army Audit Agency; Naval Audit Service; Air Force Audit Agency; and the Office of the Assistant Inspector General for Auditing, Office of the Inspector General, DOD.

DOE Accident Response Group Team Leaders

DOE senior officials who are responsible for all DOE field operations involved in responding to a nuclear weapon accident or significant incident in which the Department of Defense is the cognizant federal agency and a military person is the on-scene commander.

DOE Alternative

An administrative relief from DOE regulations that meets and provides equivalent health and safety protection.

DOE Contractors

Includes any prime contractors or subcontractors subject to the contractual provisions of 48 CFR 923.70, 48 CFR 970.23, or other contractual provisions where DOE has elected to enforce environment, safety, and health requirements by specific negotiated contract provisions.

DOE Emergency Operations Center (EOC)

The center located at DOE headquarters through which DOE's emergency management team coordinates the departmental response to an emergency.

DOE Factor Relationship and Sequence of Events (FRASE)

1) FRASE Categories — categories under which FRASE terms and phrases are grouped according to broader concepts. 2) FRASE Vocabulary — a controlled vocabulary designed for searching the narrative description fields of records on the SPMS.

DOE Offices

The various offices of the DOE, including, but not limited to, the following:

- Grand Junction Projects Office;
- NRS Office for Analysis and Evaluation of Operational Data;
- NRS Office of Inspection and Enforcement;
- Office of Defense Waste and Transportation Management;
- Office of Weapons Production;
- Albuquerque Operations Office;
- Chicago Operations Office;
- Idaho Operations Office;
- Nevada Operations Office;
- Oak Ridge Operations Office;
- Richland Operations Office;
- San Francisco Operations Office;
- Savannah River Operations Office;
- Office of the Assistant Secretary for Nuclear Energy;
- Office of the Assistant Secretary for Fossil Energy;
- Office of the Assistant Secretary for Defense Programs;
- Office of the Assistant Secretary for Conservation and Renewable Resources;
- Office of the Assistant Secretary for Environment, Safety, and Health;
- Office of Special Projects;
- Office of Environmental Restoration and Waste Management;
- Office of New Production Reactors;
- Office of Civilian Radioactive Waste Management;
- Office of Energy Research;
- Office of Basic Energy Sciences;
- Office of Health and Environmental Research;
- Program Enrichment Office;
- Regional Coordinating Offices;
- Sample Management Offices; etc.

DOE Operations

Those activities funded by DOE for which DOE has authority to enforce for environmental protection, safety, and health protection requirements.

DOE Programs

Organized sets of activities within a resource area having common objectives based on strategy set forth to meet assigned goals. It may include one or more projects and research and development activities in support of new, improved, or more efficient supply, or conservation systems or procedures.

DOE Property

All land, buildings, and structures (real property) and equipment, records, and supplies (personnel property) owned, or rented and leased from commercial sources by the U.S. government and subject to the administrative custody or jurisdiction of DOE.

DOE Representatives

Employees approved by the DOE Designating Official to a) work on standards committee assignments by reason of individual, professional, or technical expertise to further technical programmatic objectives of the department; b) serve as official spokespersons for the department on boards of directors governing as policy-developing bodies, including, for example, management boards of standards developing organizations.

DOE Sites

Either tracts owned by DOE or tracts leased or otherwise made available to the federal government under terms that afford to the Department of Energy rights of access and control substantially equal to those that the Department of Energy would possess if it were the holder of the fee (or pertinent interest therein) as agent of and on behalf of the government.

DOE Specification Packaging

General packaging designed to meet requirements established by DOT for hazardous materials.

DOJ

See U.S. Department of Justice.

DOMB

An acronym for Director of the Office of Management and Budget.

Domestic Crude Oil

1) A mixture of hydrocarbons that existed in liquid phase in underground reservoirs and remains liquid at atmospheric pressure after passing through surface separating facilities. 2) Petroleum produced in the 50 states or the outer continental shelf. Domestic crude includes synthetic hydrocarbons such as shale oil, tar sands oil, or heavy oil. Also, lease condensate moving to a refinery is included. Lease condensate is defined as natural gas liquid recovered from well gas (associated and nonassociated) in lease separators or field facilities. Drips are also included but topped crude oil and other unfinished oils are excluded. Natural gas liquids produced at natural gas processing plants and mixed with crude oil are likewise excluded where identifiable.

Domestic Emergencies

Emergencies affecting the public welfare and occurring within the 50 states, District of Columbia, Commonwealth of Puerto Rico, U.S. possessions and territories, or any political subdivision thereof, as a result of enemy attack, insurrection, civil disturbance, earthquake, fire, flood, or other public disasters or equivalent emergencies that endanger life and property or disrupt the usual process of government. The term "domestic emergency" includes any or all of the following emergency conditions:

- a) Civil Defense Emergencies — domestic emergency disaster situations resulting from devastation created by an enemy attack and requiring emergency operations during and following that attack. It may be proclaimed by appropriate authority in anticipation of an attack;

- b) Civil Disturbances — riots, acts of violence, insurrections, unlawful obstructions or assemblages, or other disorders prejudicial to public law and order. The term civil disturbance includes all domestic conditions requiring or likely to require the use of federal Armed Forces pursuant to the provisions of Chapter 15 of Title 10, United States Code;

- c) Major Disasters — any flood, fire, hurricane, tornado, earthquake, or other catastrophe that, in the determination of the president, is or threatens to be of sufficient severity and magnitude to warrant disaster assistance by the federal government under Public Law 606, 91st Congress (42 United States Code 58) to supplement the efforts and available resources of state and local governments in alleviating the damage, hardship, or suffering caused thereby; and,

- d) Natural Disasters — all domestic emergencies except those created as a result of enemy attack or civil disturbance.

Domestic Water Supply Reservoir

A reservoir used to impound or store water intended solely or primarily for domestic purposes.

Dominant

1) The species controlling an environment or ecosystem. 2) Trees with crowns extending above the general level of the crown cover and receiving full light from above and partly from the sides; crowns well developed but possibly somewhat crowded on the sides.

DOP

See Detailed Operating Procedures.

Doppler Radar

A radar system that differentiates between fixed and moving targets by detecting the apparent change in frequency of the reflected wave due to motion of target or the observer.

Doppler Effect

The phenomenon evidenced by the change in the observed frequency of a sound or radio wave caused by a time rate of change in the effective length of the path of travel between the source and the point of observation.

Dormant Season

That portion of the year when frosts occur. Refer to *U.S. Department of Interior, National Atlas 1970:110-111* for regional breakdowns.

Dorsal

A species descriptor that means situated at the rear of an animal, such as the dorsal fin in a fish.

Dorsoventral

A species descriptor that means extending from a dorsal (rear) to a ventral (front) surface.

Dorsum

A species descriptor referring to a part of an organ analogous to the back.

DOS

Term meaning Disk Operating System, refers specifically to the Microsoft computer operating systems marketed as IBM DOS, PC DOS, and MS-DOS. A program and group of utilities used to control a computer's disk drives, for information storage and retrieval, disk formatting, system configuration, automatic execution, etc.

Dose

1) A general term denoting the quantity of radiation or energy absorbed in a specified mass. 2) In terms of monitoring exposure levels, the amount of a toxic substance taken into the body over a given period of time. 3) In radiology, the quantity of energy or radiation absorbed. The amount of substances penetrating the exchange boundaries of organisms after contact. Doses are calculated from the intake and the absorption efficiency, and are usually expressed as mass of a substance absorbed into the body per unit body weight per unit time (e.g., mg/kg per day). Also, in radiology, the quantity of energy or radiation absorbed. *See* Absorbed Dose.

Dose Equivalents

1) Dose equivalent received by specified organs during a period of 1 calendar year that was the result of an uptake of a radionuclide by a person occupationally exposed. 2) The product of absorbed dose (D) in red (or gray) in tissue, a quality factor (Q), and other modifying factors (N) to account for differences in biological effectiveness due to the quality of radiation and its distribution in the body. Dose equivalent is expressed in units of rem (or sievert).

Dose Equivalent Index
For the purposes of radiation protection either the deep dose equivalent index, shallow dose equivalent index, or unrestricted dose equivalent index.

Dose Limit
The value of a quantity of radiation, or toxicity, that must not be exceeded.

Dose Rate Contour Line
A line on a map, diagram, or overlay joining all points at which the radiation, or toxicity, dose rate at a given time is the same.

Dose Rate Meters
Devices, instruments, or systems that can be used to measure or evaluate any quantity that can be related to the determination of either absorbed dose rate or dose equivalent rate.

Dose Response
A term referring to how an organism's response to a toxic substance changes as its overall exposure to the substance changes. For example, a small dose of carbon monoxide may cause drowsiness; a large dose may result in fatality.

Dose Upper Bounds
Dose levels established by a competent authority to constrain the optimization of protection for a given source or source type.

Dose-Response Evaluation
The process of quantitatively evaluating the toxicity information and characterizing the relationship between the dose of a contaminant administered or received and the incidence of adverse health effects in the exposed population. From the quantitative dose-response relationship, toxicity values are derived that are used in the risk characterization step to estimate the likelihood of adverse effects occurring in humans at different exposure levels.

Dose-Response Relationship
A relationship between a) the dose, often actually based on "administered dose" (i.e., exposure)

rather than absorbed dose; b) the extent of toxic injury produced by that chemical. Response can be expressed either as the severity of injury or proportion of exposed subjects affected. A dose-response assessment is one of the four steps in a risk assessment.

DOSEM
A master computer program to calculate offsite doses from accidental releases of plutonium, criticality products, depleted uranium, americium, or nonradioactive material.

Dosimeter
An instrument that measures exposure to radiation.

Dosimetry
1) In general, the measurement or modeling of the amount, rate, and distribution of a drug or toxicant especially as it pertains to producing a particular biological effect. 2) The measurement of radiation doses. 3) The theory and application of the principles and techniques involved in measuring and recording doses.

Dosimetry Processors
An individual or an organization that processes and evaluates personnel monitoring equipment in order to determine the radiation dose delivered to the equipment.

Dosing Tank
Any tank used in applying a dose; specifically used for intermittent application of wastewater to subsequent processes.

DOT
See U.S. Department of Transportation.

DOT Specifications
Regulations of the federal Department of Transportation published in 49 CFR Part 100-199.

DOT (Tank) Service

Service in which a pressure vessel is used, inspected and maintained in accordance with DOT regulations.

Double Check Valve Assembly (DCVA)

An assembly of at least two independently acting check valves including tightly closing shut-off valves on each side of the check valve assembly and test cocks available for testing the watertightness of each check valve.

Double Wash/Rinse

A minimum requirement to cleanse solid surfaces (both impervious and nonimpervious) two times with an appropriate solvent or other material in which PCBs are at least 5% soluble (by weight). The wash/rinse requirement does not mean the mere spreading of solvent or other aid over the surface, nor does the requirement mean a once-over wipe with a soaked cloth. Precautions must be taken to contain any runoff resulting from the cleansing and to properly dispose of wastes generated during the cleansing.

Downbursts

A strong downward current of air that induces an outward burst of damaging wind on or near the ground. Practically all downbursts occur beneath cumulonimbus clouds during their precipitation stages. Downburst winds are highly divergent, covering an area up to 30 miles long and 10 miles wide. The peak windspeed of downbursts is less than 180 mph. Due to a rapidly striking motion, the descending air successively hits the surface to burst out. Most downbursts are highly divergent but irrotational. However, some downbursts are rotational with a curved airflow identified as the "twisting downburst." Small tornadoes frequently form on the edge of a twisting downburst.

Downslope Wind

A hot (warm), dry downslope wind descending from its source region at high elevations. Usually downslope winds are nondivergent and irrotational. Can form over ice and/or snow.

Draft Hood

A device built into an appliance, or made a part of the vent connector from an appliance, that is designed to a) ensure the ready escape of the flue gases in the event of no draft, back draft, or stoppage beyond the draft hood; b) prevent a back draft from entering the appliance; and, c) neutralize the effect of stack action of the chimney or gas vent upon the operation of the appliance.

Draft Permits

Documents prepared under 40 CFR 124.6 indicating a tentative decision to issue or deny, modify, revoke and reissue, terminate, or reissue a permit. A notice of intent to terminate a permit and a notice of intent to deny a permit as discussed in 40 CFR 124.5, are types of draft permits. A denial of a request for modification, revocation, and reissuance or termination, as discussed in Part 124.5, is not a draft permit.

Drafting Break

The transferral of a whole section of an analytical diagram or tree to another location, in a technical document, for space convenience.

Drag Loading

The force on an object or structure due to transient winds accompanying the passage of a blast wave. The drag pressure is the product of the dynamic pressure and the drag coefficient that is dependent upon the shape (or geometry) of the structure or object. *See* Dynamic Pressure.

Drainage Basin

The land area from which water drains into a river or lake.

Drainage Facilities

Facilities constructed to control water, including, but not limited to, forks, inside ditches, waterbreaks, outsloping and rolling dips.

Drainage Structure

A structure installed to control, divert or to cross over water, including, but not limited to, culverts, bridges, and ditch drains.

Drainage System
Includes all the piping within or attached to the structure that conveys sewage or other liquid wastes to a drain outlet(s).

Drawdown
1) The vertical distance groundwater elevation is lowered, or the amount pressure head is reduced, due to the removal of groundwater. Also the decline in potentiometric surface caused by the withdrawal of water from a hydrogeologic unit. 2) Distance between the static water level and the surface of the cone of depression. 3) Lowering of the water table of an unconfined aquifer or the potentiometric surface of a confined aquifer caused by pumping of groundwater from wells.

Dredge and Fill Permit (404 Permit)
A regulatory permit issued by the Army Corp of Engineers (ACOE), required under Section 404 of the Federal Water Pollution Control Act Amendments of 1972 for all dredge and fill activities in any "navigable waters of the U.S."

Drinking Water Supply
As defined by Section 107(7) of CERCLA, means any raw or finished water source that is, or may be, used by a public water system (as defined in the Safe Drinking Water Act) or as drinking water by one or more individuals.

DRE
See Destruction and Removal Efficiency.

Dredged Materials
Materials that are excavated or dredged from waters of the United States.

Dredged Ocean Material
Any material excavated or dredged from the navigable waters of the United States.

Dredging
Removal of mud from the bottom of water bodies using a scooping machine. This disturbs the ecosystem and causes silting that can kill aquatic life. Dredging of contaminated muds can expose aquatic life to heavy metals and other toxins. Dredging activities may be subject to regulation under Section 404 of the Clean Water Act.

Drift
1) The movement of a pesticide during or immediately after application or use through air to a site other than the intended site of application or use. 2) In ballistics, a shift in projectile direction due to gyroscopic action that results from gravitational and atmospherically induced torques on the spinning projectile.

Drill Report
A report on the results and conclusions from the evaluation of the building emergency response will be prepared. A drill report clarifies which objectives were satisfactorily demonstrated and identifies issues or deficiencies.

Drills
1) Activities, either announced or unannounced, that test limited portions of an emergency plan. 2) Supervised, hands-on instruction periods intended to test, develop, and/or maintain a specific emergency response capability. Drills limit activities to specific components of emergency response and are often a component of a larger site-wide exercise.

Drinking Water Supplies
As defined by Section 101 (7) of CERCLA, any raw or finished water source that is or may be used by a public water system (as defined in the Safe Drinking Water Act) or as drinking water by one or more individuals.

Drive Power
The energy source or sources for the robot actuators.

Drone
A land, sea, or air vehicle that is remotely or automatically controlled. *See* Remotely Piloted Vehicle; Unmanned Aerial Vehicle.

Drop Zone

A specific area upon which airborne materials, fire suppressants and chemicals, equipment, or supplies are airdropped, to help contain a hazard.

Drums

Hollow, cylindrical containers. Typically, a metal cylindrical shipping container with a capacity of 12-110 gallons (45-416 liters) of liquid. Within the context of chemical engineering, drums are towers or vessels in a refinery into which heated products are conducted so that volatile portions can separate.

Drupe

A species descriptor for a fleshy fruit, such as a peach or plum, that usually has a single, hard seed.

Dry Caves

Long-term storage areas for irradiated elements that do not require cooling.

Dual Systems

Combinations of special or intermediate moment resisting space frames and shear walls or braced frames.

Dual Warning Phenomenology

Deriving warning information from two systems observing separate physical phenomena (e.g., radar/infrared or visible light/X-ray) associated with the same events to attain high credibility while being less susceptible to error.

Duct

A tube or conduit for conveying air to or from air conditioning or comfort-cooling equipment. Class 0 Air Ducts — air duct materials and connectors having a fire-hazard classification of zero. Class 1 Air Ducts — ducts of materials and connectors having a flame-spread rating of not over 25 without evidence of continued progressive combustion and a smoke-developed rating of not over 50. Class 2 Air Ducts — ducts of materials and connectors having a flame-spread rating of not over 50 without evidence of continued pro-

gressive combustion and a smoke-developed rating of not over 50 for the inside surface and not over 100 for the outside surface.

Duds

Bombs, grenades, or shells that fail to explode.

Due Process

In environmental issues, procedural due process relates to the methods that the government may use to enforce its laws; carry out its powers; in general, it provides all individuals and organizations with the right to receive notice of noncompliance and a reasonable opportunity to present objections or bring the situation into compliance. The legal right of due process is given to all persons by the U.S. Constitution.

Dump

1) Generally, a site used to dispose of solid wastes without environmental controls. Uncontrolled dumping is an illegal form of waste disposal, often resulting in the multiplication of disease-carrying organisms and pests, fires, air and water pollution, unsightliness, loss of habitat, and/or fines imposed upon the responsible parties. 2) In military terms, a temporary storage area, usually in the open, for bombs, ammunition, equipment, or supplies.

Dunning's Classification

A system of tree classification based on maturity of trees, age, position of tree crown in stand, shape of top, diameter, density of foliage and risk or susceptibility of tree to insect and other mortality where trees are classed as follows:

- Class 1 — Tree immature, 60 to 150 years of age, crown dominant or extending above general level of the crown cover, top pointed, d.b.h. up to 30 inches (76.2 cm), foliage dense and risk good;

- Class 2 — Tree immature, 60 to 150 years of age, crown codominant or equal to general level of the crown cover, top pointed, d.b.h. up to 24 inches (61.0 cm), foliage dense and risk good;

- Class 3 — Tree mature, 150 to 300 years of age, crown dominant or extending above general level of the crown cover, top rounded, d.b.h. 18 inches (45.7 cm) to 40 inches (101.6 cm), foliage moderately dense and risk fair to good;

- Class 4 — Tree mature, 150 to 300 years of age, crown codominant or equal to general level of the crown cover, top rounded and risk poor to fair;

- Class 5 — Tree overmature, over 300 years of age, crown dominant or extending above the general level of the crown cover, top flat, foliage thin, and risk poor;

- Class 6 — Tree immature, 60 to 150 years of age, crown intermediate to or suppressed by the general level of the crown cover, top pointed, d.b.h. 12 inches (30.5 cm) to 15 inches (38.1 cm), foliage moderately dense and risk fair to good; and

- Class 7 — Tree mature or overmature, over 150 years of age, crown intermediate or suppressed by the general level of the crown cover, top flat, d.b.h. rarely over 18 inches (45.7 cm), foliage sparse and risk poor.

Duress Systems
Systems that can covertly communicate a situation of duress to a security control center or other personnel who can notify a security control center.

Dust
1) Minute wind-blown soils and/or solid particulates resulting from human activities that are carried into the atmosphere, eventually settling due to gravity. 2) Mechanically produced solid particles in the air usually ranging in size from 0.1 microns to 25 microns. 3) Particles light enough to be suspended in air.

Dust Control
The control of dust by use of water or other materials.

Dust Devils
Rotating columns of air that form over dry ground heated by strong solar radiation. The direction of rotation is not unique, affected by the environmental flow field during the formation stage. Most dust devils are 72 mph or weaker. Occasionally 73 to 112 mph dust devils damage out-

buildings or garages. The central region of a dust devil is characterized by a descending motion and relatively clear air. Can form over ice and/or snow with snow rotating (snow devils).

Dustfall Jar
An open container used to collect large particles from the air for measurement and analysis.

Duty Officers, Emergency
Personnel with appropriate knowledge of emergency procedures to act as an intermediate crisis manager. Duty officers generally have a proscribed period of assigned duties.

DUVAS
An acronym for Derivative Ultraviolet Absorbtion Spectroscopy.

Dwelling Unit
One or more habitable rooms that are designed to be occupied by one family with facilities for living, sleeping, cooking, eating, and sanitation.

DWGNRA
An acronym for Delaware Water Gap National Recreation Area (WSRA).

Dynamic Equilibrium
A condition in which the amount of recharge to an aquifer equals the amount of natural discharge.

Dynamic Pressure
Pressure resulting from some medium in motion, such as the air following the shock front of a blast wave.

Dyscrasia
A blood disorder.

Dysphagia
Difficulty in swallowing.

Dyspnea
Shortness of breath; difficult or labored breathing.

Dysuria
Painful or difficult urination.

Dystrophic Lakes
Shallow bodies of water that contain much humus and/or organic matter; or contain many plants, but few fish, and are highly acidic.

E

E-glass
An abbreviation for electrical-glass, the borosilicate glass most often used for the glass fibers in conventional reinforced plastics.

E&CF
See Events and Causal Factors.

EA
See Environmental Assessment. An acronym for Emergency Actions.

Early Storage Reserve
The portion of the Strategic Petroleum Reserve that consists of petroleum products stored pursuant to the Energy Conservation Act.

Earth-Lined Channels
Open channel conveyance structures with sides and bottom constructed of naturally occurring earth materials.

Earthing
The process of making a satisfactory electrical connection between the structure, including the metal skin, of an object or vehicle, and the mass of the earth, to ensure a common potential with the earth. *See* Bonding.

Earthquake Resistant Bracing System
An anchoring system, bracing system, or other device designed and constructed, or represented as having been designed and constructed, for the purpose of protecting the health and safety of the occupants of and reducing damage to a mobile home or manufactured home in the event of an earthquake.

Earthquake Magnitude
A measure of the strain of an earthquake, or the strain energy released by it as calculated from the instrumental record made by the event on a calibrated seismograph.

Earthscan
An environmental news and information agency; partially funded by the United Nations Environmental Program, it publishes findings of major environmental problems. *See* United Nations Environmental Program.

Earthwork
The process of excavating, moving, storing, placing, and working any type of earth materials.

EAS
An acronym for Engineering Assistance Section.

Easement
A right or interest in the real property of another. The right to use another's land for a specific purpose, as a right of way.

Eastern Ozone Transport Region (EOTR)(CAA)

The single transport region for ozone, comprised of the states of Connecticut, Delaware, Maine, Maryland, Massachusetts, New Hampshire, New Jersey, New York, Pennsylvania, Rhode Island, Vermont, and the Consolidated Metropolitan Statistical Area that includes the District of Columbia, established by operation of law. Each state included within a transport region established for ozone must submit a state implementation plan or revision thereof to the Administrator that requires the following: a) that each area in such state that is in an ozone transport region, and that is a metropolitan statistical area or part thereof with a population of 100,000 or more comply with the provisions of the CAA pertaining to enhanced vehicle inspection and maintenance programs; and b) implementation of reasonably available control technology with respect to all sources of volatile organic compounds in the state covered by a current control techniques guideline.

EBWR

An acronym for Experimental Boiling Water Reactor.

ECC

See Emergency Control Center; Emergency Coordination Center.

Eccentric Braced Frames

Steel braced frame designs.

Ecofact

Evidence from the past that is used in reconstructing the natural environment; normally encompasses inorganic material and animal parts.

Ecological Factors

Any environmental element that impacts living organisms.

Ecological Balance

The condition of equilibrium among the predators, competitors, and other components of natural communities, such that their numbers remain fairly stable and their relative ecosystem remains in balance.

Ecological Impact

The effect that a manmade or natural activity has on living organisms and their nonliving (abiotic) environment.

Ecology

The study of the relationship of living things to one another and to the environment or the study of such relationships, especially the totality or pattern of interacting relationships. Research that includes all plant and animal species and their unique contributions to a particular habitat. Problems such as hazardous waste and depletion of resources are primary ecological considerations in real estate development.

Economic Potential

The total capacity of a nation to produce goods and services.

Economic Rent

The amount that would be paid in money or kind for the right to use real property if a) the contract rent were currently negotiated under the conditions that exist in a free and competitive market; and b) the fee owner paid property taxes on the value of the fee.

Economic Conservation

The management of environmental resources to obtain the highest and most feasible uses possible of natural resources.

Economic Poisons

Chemicals used to control pests and to defoliate cash crops such as cotton.

Economic Action

The planned use of economic measures designed to influence the policies or actions of another state, e.g., to impair the war-making potential of a hostile power or to generate economic stability within a friendly power.

Economic Mobilization

The process of preparing for and carrying out such changes in the organization and functioning of the national economy as are necessary to provide for the most effective use of resources in a national emergency.

Economic Justification

The ratio of the benefits of a project to its costs (benefit-cost ratio). Benefits and costs for both the applicant's service area and the total area affected by water distribution changes will be taken into account. The greatest economic justification is indicated by the largest benefit-cost ratio.

Economic Growth

The annual rate of change in the gross national product, relative to a given index year.

Economic Life

The period of time over which a property may be profitably used. It is reduced to a percent in the capitalization process. Example: 100% divided by 50 years equals 2% anticipated depreciation annually.

Ecosphere

1) The biosphere and all the ecological factors within it that influence organisms. 2) The "bio-bubble" that contains life on earth, in surface waters, and in the air. *See* Biosphere.

Ecosystem Research Program

A research program to improve understanding of the short-term and long-term causes, effects, and trends of ecosystems damage from air pollutants on ecosystems. The program includes the following elements: a) identification of regionally representative and critical ecosystems for research; b) evaluation of risks to ecosystems exposed to air pollutants, including characterization of the causes and effects of chronic and episodic exposures to air pollutants and determination of the reversibility of those effects; c) development of improved atmospheric dispersion models and monitoring systems and networks for evaluating and quantifying exposure to and effects of multiple environmental stresses associated with air pol-

lution; d) evaluation of the effects of air pollution on water quality, including assessments of the short-term and long-term ecological effects of acid deposition and other atmospherically derived pollutants on surface water (including wetlands and estuaries) and groundwater; e) evaluation of the effects of air pollution on forests, materials, crops, biological diversity, soils, and other terrestrial and aquatic systems exposed to air pollutants; and f) estimation of the associated economic costs of ecological damage that have occurred as a result of exposure to air pollutants.

Ecosystem

1) The interacting synergism of a biological community and its nonliving environmental surroundings; every plant, insect, aquatic animal, bird, or land species that forms a complex web of interdependency. 2) Interacting systems of biological communities and their nonliving environmental surroundings. A community of organisms that interact with each other and their environment. 3) An integrated unit in nature, sufficient unto itself with a balanced assortment of life forms, to be studied as a separate entity.

ECS

See Emergency Core Cooling System; Emergency Control Stations.

ECT

An acronym for Evaporator Condensate Tank.

Ectocone

An ecological community of mixed vegetation formed by the overlapping of adjoining communities.

ECW

An acronym for Effluent Cooling Water.

ECWD

An acronym for Effluent Cooling Water Drainage.

ED Charge

Enriched/depleted charge.

Edaphic Factors
Chemical, physical, and biological characteristics of soil that affect an ecosystem. A term pertaining to the soil as it affects living organisms.

EDB
An acronym for Ethylene Dibromide.

EDD
See Enforcement Decision Document.

Edema
Accumulation of an excessive amount of fluid in body cells or tissues; usually identified as swelling. Lung edema is the accumulation of fluid in the lung.

EDG
An acronym for Emergency Diesel Generator.

EED
In construction, an acronym for Electro-explosive Devices.

EEI
See Essential Elements of Information.

EEM
An acronym for Essential Equipment Monitor.

EEMS
An acronym for Enhanced Expanded Memory Specification. *See* Energy Emergency System.

EEMT
See Energy Emergency Teams.

EFC
An acronym for External Fission Counter.

Effect, No Effect, and Adverse Effect
Regional-level evaluations of the impacts of projects upon identified cultural resources. Criteria for determining effect are specifically defined. Procedures, that must be followed by all federal agencies on projects involving cultural resources,

are outlined in 36 CFR 800 (refer to Section 106 Process).

Effective Dose Equivalent Commitment (IAEA)
The infinite time integral of the per capita effective dose equivalent rate resulting from a given event, decision or defined finite portion of a practice for a specified population.

Effective Dose Equivalent
The summation of the products of the dose equivalent received by specified tissues of the body and a tissue-specific weighing factor. This sum is a risk-equivalent value and can be used to estimate the health-effects risk of the exposed individual. The tissue-specific weighing factor represents the traction of the total health risk resulting from uniform whole-body irradiation that would be contributed by that particular tissue. The effective dose equivalent includes the committed effective dose equivalent from internal deposition of radionuclides and the effective dose equivalent due to penetrating radiation from sources external to the body. Effective dose equivalent is expressed in units of rem (or sievert).

Effective Porosity
The amount of interconnected pore space through which fluids can pass, expressed as a percent of bulk volume. Part of the total porosity will be occupied by static fluid being held to the mineral surface by surface tension, hence, effective porosity should always be less than total porosity.

Effective Half-Life
The time required for a radioactive nuclide in a system to be diminished 50% as a result of the combined action of radioactive decay and biological elimination. Effective half-life equation: [biological half-life x radioactive half-life/biological half-life + radioactive half-life].

Effective Date
The date of promulgation in the Federal Register of an applicable standard or other regulation.

Effectiveness

How well a policy or program achieves its goals; it is also known as "impact." When evaluating the effectiveness of a simple program element, a single measure (perhaps a quantitative one) may be appropriate. Where a complex output or an entire program is being measured, however, more complex measures are essential. Some impacts may be measured only indirectly, by observing, for example, related changes in performance and behavior. Thus, the effectiveness of a policy intended to prevent trenching accidents might be evaluated by comparing the incidence rates for that type of accident in successive periods.

Effects of the Action

The direct and indirect effects of an action on the species or critical habitat, together with the effects of other activities that are interrelated or interdependent with that action, that will be added to the environmental baseline. The environmental baseline includes the past and present impacts of all federal, state, or private actions and other human activities in the action area, the anticipated impacts of all proposed federal projects in the action area that have already undergone formal or early Section 7 consultation, and the impact of state or private actions that are contemporaneous with the consultation in process. Indirect effects are those that are caused by the proposed action and are later in time, but still are reasonably certain to occur. Interrelated actions are those that are part of larger action and depend on larger action for their justification. Interdependent actions are those that have no independent utility apart from action under consideration.

Effects on Welfare

The known human effects of air pollution.

Effects

A general term meaning various types of environmental results or impacts, usually negative, including but not limited to: Acute Effects; Chilling Effect; Chronic Effects; Ecological Impacts; Effects on Welfare; Effects of the Action; Genetic Radiation Effects; Greenhouse Effect; Heat Island Effects; Ionizing Radiation Effects; Known Human Effects; Non-Stochastic Effects; Non-Stochastic Radiation Effects; Orthogonal Effects; P-Delta Effect; Somatic Radiation Effects; Stack Effect; Stochastic Effects; Radiation induced Hereditary Effects; Radiation Induced Genetic Effects; Stochastic Radiation Effects; Systemic Effects; Toxic Effects; Unacceptable Adverse Effects; Illnesses; and Injuries.

Efficiency

The relative results obtained in any operation in relation to the energy or effort required to achieve the results. It is the ratio of the total output to the total input, usually expressed as a percentage.

Efficiency Measures

A term that relates to productivity; that is, they tell how much is produced with a given amount of resources. Efficiency measures are essential to good management and are a necessary part of any evaluation system. Much of OSHA's monitoring activity focuses on efficiency questions, such as how many inspections are produced in a given time period, or with a given number of inspectors, or in a specific locality. Another sort of efficiency measure deals with such matters as the productivity of inspections in terms of serious violations found, or the prevalence of particular hazards in one industry versus another. Efficiency measures can serve as production objectives for managers, and thus they may become key indicators of organizational performance. Efficiency measures alone, however, are not sufficient for good management. Effectiveness measures are also necessary.

Efficiency Descriptor, Appliance

The ratio of the useful output to the total energy input, determined using test procedures and expressed for the following products in the following terms: a) for furnaces and direct heating equipment, annual fuel utilization efficiency; b) for room air conditioners, energy efficiency ratio; c) for central air conditioning and central air conditioning heat pumps, seasonal energy efficiency ratio; e) for water heaters, energy factor; and E) for pool heaters, thermal efficiency.

Efficiency, Counters

A measure of the probability that a count will be recorded when radiation is incident on a detector. Usage varies considerably so it is well to make sure that factors (window, transmission, sensitive volume, energy dependence, etc.) are included in a given case.

Effluent

Any gaseous or liquid waste fluid emitted by a source. A discharge from an exit that is relatively self-contained. Often referred to as pollution, a source of pollution, and/or pollutant discharges. 1) Treated or untreated air emissions or liquid discharges at a site or facility. 2) Airborne and liquid wastes deliberately discharged from a site or facility following such engineered waste treatment and all effluent controls, including on-site retention and decay, as may be provided. This term does not include solid wastes, wastes for shipment offsite, wastes that are contained (e.g., underground nuclear test debris) or stored (e.g., in tanks) or wastes that are to remain on-site through treatment or disposal. 3) Wastewater, treated or untreated, that flows out of a treatment plant, sewer, or industrial outfall. Generally refers to wastes discharged into surface waters.

Effluent Limitations

1) Restrictions established by a state or EPA on quantities, rates, and concentrations in wastewater discharges. 2) Limits on the amounts of pollutants that may be discharged by a facility; these limits are calculated so that water quality standards will not be violated even at low stream flows. 3) Any restriction established by the Administrator of EPA on quantities, discharge rates, and concentrations of chemical, physical, biological, and other constituents that are discharged from point sources, other than new sources, into navigable waters, the waters of the contiguous zone or the ocean.

Effluent Limitations Guidelines

Technical documents developed by EPA that set discharge limits for particular types of industries and specific pollutants. Any effluent issued by the Administrator pursuant to Section 304(b) of the CWA Act.

Effluent Monitoring

The collection and analysis of samples, or measurements of liquid and gaseous effluents for the purpose of characterizing and quantifying contaminants, assessing radiation exposures of members of the public, providing a means to control effluents at or near the point of discharge, and demonstrating compliance with applicable standards and permit requirements.

Effluent Standard

The maximum amount of a specified pollutant an effluent discharge is allowed to contain. For gaseous discharges. *See* Emission Standards.

Effluent Stream

See Gaining Stream.

Effluent Weir

A weir at the outflow end of a sedimentation basin or other hydraulic structure.

EFS

An acronym for Emergency Feedwater System.

EG

An acronym for Emergency (Diesel) Generators; Engine-Generators.

Egress

The act of departing from a point of access.

EHCI

See Emergency and Hazardous Chemical Inventory.

EIS Implementation Plans

Brief written plans that provide guidance for the preparation of a DOE Environmental Impact Statement (EIS) (including a Supplemental EIS). The plans record the results of the scoping process and outline the procedures by which an EIS is to be prepared.

EIS

An acronym for Environmental Impact Statements.

Ejector

A device for moving a fluid or solid by entraining it in a high velocity stream of air or water.

Ekistics

The study of the architectural, engineering, planning, sociological, etc., aspects of human settlement patterns.

Electric Energy

The energy associated with electric charges and their movements. Measured in watt-hours or kilowatt-hours (kWh). One watt-hour equals 860 calories.

Electric Utility

Any person, state agency, or federal agency, that sells electric energy.

Electric Utility Steam Generating Unit

Any fossil fuel fired combustion unit of more than 25 megawatts that serves a generator that produces electricity for sale. A unit that cogenerates steam and electricity and supplies more than one-third of its potential electric output capacity and more than 25 megawatts electrical output to any utility power distribution system for sale shall be considered an electric utility steam generating unit.

Electric Utility Steam Generating Units Study

A study of a) mercury emissions from electric utility steam generating units, municipal waste combustion units, and other sources, including area sources. Such study shall consider the rate and mass of such emissions, the health and environmental effects of such emissions, technologies that are available to control such emissions, and the costs of such technologies; b) hazards to public health reasonably anticipated to occur as a result of emissions by electric utility steam generating units of pollutants. The National Institute of Environmental Health Sciences conducts a related study to determine the threshold level of mercury exposure below which adverse human health effects are not expected to occur. Such study shall include a threshold for mercury concentrations in the tissue of fish that may be consumed without adverse effects to public health.

Electrical Engineering

The branch of professional engineering that embraces studies or activities relating to the generation, transmission, and utilization of electrical energy, including the design of electrical, electronic and magnetic circuits and the technical control of their operation and of the design of electrical gear. It is concerned with research, organizational, and economic aspects of the above.

Electrical Equipment

Underground equipment that contains dielectric fluid that is necessary for the operation of equipment such as transformers and buried electrical cable.

Electricity, Produced (kWh)

The total kilowatt-hours actually produced by all of the turbines of a particular turbine model contained within the wind project where the electricity is delivered to a wind power purchaser for sale during a specified reporting period.

Electro-Optics

The technology associated with those components, devices, and systems that are designed to interact between the electromagnetic (optical) and the electric (electronic) state.

Electro-Explosive Device

1) An explosive or pyrotechnic component that initiates an explosive, burning, electrical, or mechanical train and is activated by the application of electrical energy. 2) Devices containing some reaction mixture (explosive or pyrotechnic) that is electrically initiated. The output of the initiation is heat, shock, or mechanical action.

Electrodialysis

A process that uses electrical current applied to permeable membranes to remove minerals from water. Often used to desalinize salty or brackish water.

Electroexplosive Devices

See Electro-Explosive Device.

Electromagnetic Compatibility

The ability of systems, equipment, and devices that utilize the electromagnetic spectrum to operate in their intended operational environments without suffering unacceptable degradation or causing unintentional degradation because of electromagnetic radiation or response. It involves the application of sound electromagnetic spectrum management; system, equipment, and device design configuration that ensures interference-free operation; and clear concepts and doctrines that maximize operational effectiveness. Also called EMC.

Electromagnetic Environment

The resulting product of the power and time distribution, in various frequency ranges, of the radiated or conducted electromagnetic emission levels that may be encountered by a military force, system, or platform when performing its assigned mission in its intended operational environment. It is the sum of electromagnetic interference; electromagnetic pulse; hazards of electromagnetic radiation to personnel, ordnance, and volatile materials; and natural phenomena effects of lightning and p-static. Also called EME.

Electromagnetic Environmental Effects (E^3)

The impact of the electromagnetic environment upon the operational capability of military forces, equipment, systems, and platforms. It encompasses all electromagnetic disciplines, including electromagnetic compatibility/electromagnetic interference; electromagnetic vulnerability; electromagnetic pulse; electronic protection, hazards of electromagnetic radiation to personnel, ordnance, and volatile materials; and natural phenomena effects of lightning and p-static.

Electromagnetic Hardening

Action taken to protect personnel, facilities, and/or equipment by filtering, attenuating, grounding, bonding, and/or shielding against undesirable effects of electromagnetic energy.

Electromagnetic Pulse

The electromagnetic radiation from a nuclear explosion caused by Compton-recoil electrons and photoelectrons from photons scattered in the materials of the nuclear device or in a surrounding medium. The resulting electric and magnetic fields may couple with electrical/electronic systems to produce damaging current and voltage surges.

Electromagnetic Radiation

Radiation made up of oscillating electric and magnetic fields and propagated with the speed of light. Includes gamma radiation, X-rays, ultraviolet, visible, and infrared radiation, and radar and radio waves.

Electromagnetic Radiation Hazards

Hazards caused by a transmitter/antenna installation that generates electromagnetic radiation in the vicinity of ordnance, personnel, or fueling operations in excess of established safe levels or increases the existing levels to a hazardous level; or a personnel, fueling, or ordnance installation located in an area that is illuminated by electromagnetic radiation at a level that is hazardous to the planned operations or occupancy. These hazards will exist when an electromagnetic field of sufficient intensity is generated to: a) induce or otherwise couple currents and/or voltages of magnitudes large enough to initiate electroexplosive devices or other sensitive explosive components of weapon systems, ordnance, or explosive devices; b) cause harmful or injurious effects to humans and wildlife; c) create sparks having sufficient magnitude to ignite flammable mixtures of materials that must be handled in the affected area. Also called EMR Hazards, RADHAZ, HERO.

Electrometer
An instrument used to measure atmospheric electrical fields.

Electron
Negatively charged elementary particles that are a constituent of every neutral atom. An elementary particle with a rest mass of 9.1×10^{28} grams, bearing a negative electric charge, its mass is 0.00549 atomic mass units. Its unit of negative electricity equals 4.8×10^{-19} coulombs. Electrons orbit the atomic nucleus; their transfer or rearrangement between atoms underlies all chemical reactions. Either negative or positive electrons (sometimes called positrons) may be emitted from atomic nuclei during nuclear reactions; they are then called beta particles.

Electron Capture
A mode of radioactive decay involving the capture of an orbital electron by its nucleus. Capture from the particular electron shell is designated as "K-electron capture," "L-electron capture," etc.

Electron Capture Detector
A sensitive scientific device used to detect the presence of airborne chemical substances in the atmosphere.

Electron Volt
A unit of energy equivalent to the amount of energy gained by an electron in passing through a potential difference of 1 volt. Abbreviated eV. Larger multiple units of the electron volt frequently used are: a keV for thousand or kiloelectron volts, a MeV for million electron volts, and a BeV for billion electron volts.

Electronic Line of Sight
The path traversed by electromagnetic waves that is not subject to reflection or refraction by the atmosphere.

Electronic Observation
Using a number of audio and video electronic devices (i.e., still and time lapse photography, video recording, audio recording, seismographs, odometers) to monitor environmental transmutations at a specific facility and/or project site. The result is a detailed, permanent record of all events observed.

Electrostatic Precipitator
An air pollution control device that removes particles from a gas stream (smoke) after combustion occurs. The ESP imparts an electrical charge to the particles, causing them to adhere to metal plates inside the precipitator. Rapping on the plates causes the particles to fall into a hopper for disposal.

Element
Solid, liquid, or gaseous matter that cannot be further decomposed into simpler substances by chemical means. The atoms of an element may differ physically but do not differ chemically. *See* Chemical Elements (Section VI).

Element Isotopes
A term referring to element 104, 105, 106, 107, 108, and 109 isotopes that are radionuclides on the list of CERCLA hazardous substances.

Elemental Phosphorus Plants
Facilities that process phosphate rock to produce elemental phosphorus using pyrometallurgical techniques.

Elementary Neutralization Unit
A device that, 1) is used for neutralizing wastes that are hazardous wastes only because they exhibit the corrosivity characteristic defined in Section 261.22 of 40 CFR, or are listed in Subpart D of Part 261 of 40 CFR only for this reason; and 2) meets the definition of tank, container, transport vehicle, or vessel in Section 260.10 of 40 CFR.

Elements of Effective Environmental Audit Programs
Seven auditing elements are contained in EPA's published Environmental Auditing Policy Statement. 1) Top management commitment to environmental auditing and follow-up on audit results. 2) Independent and autonomous audit teams.

3) Adequate team staffing, expertise, and training. 4) Explicit goals, objectives, scope, resources, and frequency. 5) Planning process that collects, analyzes, interprets, and documents data in sufficient, reliable, relevant, and useful detail to achieve audit objectives. 6) Specific procedures to prepare terse written reports on audit findings, corrective actions, and implementation schedules. 7) A process that includes quality assurance/quality control methods to ensure accurate environmental audits.

Elements of National Power
All the means that are available for employment in the pursuit of national objectives.

Elevation
The vertical distance of a point or level on or affixed to the surface of the earth measured from mean sea level. *See* Altitude.

Elevator
A hoisting apparatus used as a material handling device.

Eleven Contiguous Western states
The states of Arizona, California, Colorado, Idaho, Montana, Nevada, New Mexico, Oregon, Utah, Washington, and Wyoming.

Eligible Apex Authority
Any sewerage authority or other unit of state or local government that on November 2, 1983, was authorized under court order to dump municipal sludge at the Apex site. No person may apply for a permit in relation to the dumping of, or the transportation for purposes of dumping, municipal sludge within the Apex unless that person is an eligible authority. *See* Apex.

Eligible Costs
The construction costs for wastewater treatment works upon which EPA grants are based.

Eligible Groundwater Project
A project that may include the purchase of land or easements, the construction or major rehabilita-

tion of facilities, or conducting of a feasibility study for a groundwater project.

Eligible Project Costs
Costs associated with engineering, land and easement acquisition, legal fees, preparation of the application to establish eligibility, environmental mitigation, a feasibility study conducted after establishing preliminary eligibility for a loan under this subchapter and reasonable construction costs. Costs that are not eligible include regular operation and maintenance costs, purchase of movable equipment not an integral part of the project, refinancing prior debt, and establishing a reserve fund.

Eligible Traffic
Traffic for which movement requirements are submitted and space is assigned or allocated. Such traffic must meet eligibility requirements specified in Joint Travel Regulations for the Uniformed Services and publications of the Department of Defense and military departments governing eligibility for land, sea, and air transportation, and be in accordance with the guidance of the Joint Chiefs of Staff.

Ellipsoid
Refers to a species with an ellipse-shaped surface.

Elutriation
1) The separation of lighter particles from heavier ones via a stream of air or fluid. Grain sizes can be analyzed separately by passing them through currents of water at different velocities. The principle also applies to the separation of materials in domestic waste management systems. 2) A process of sludge conditioning in which the sludge is washed with either fresh water or plant effluent to reduce the demand for conditioning chemicals and to improve settling or filtering characteristics of the solids.

ELWCR
An acronym for Erodible Land and Wetland Conservation and Reserve Program.

Elytral

The thickened, hard fore-wing of a beetle or a platelike respiratory structure on the dorsal surface of a scale worm.

Emarginate

Means having a notched tip.

Embedded Laser

A laser with an assigned class number higher than the inherent capability of the laser system in which it is incorporated, where the system's lower classification is appropriate to the engineering features limiting accessible emission.

Embolization

Obstruction of a blood vessel by a transported clot or other mass.

Embryo

1) An organism in the early stages of development; unhatched. 2) In humans and other mammals, the developing conceptus up to 8 weeks after fertilization of the egg. The stage in the developing organism at which organs and organ systems are developing. For humans, this involves the stage of development between the second through eighth weeks (inclusive) postconception. *See* Fetus.

Embryotoxicity

Any toxic effect on the conceptus as a result of prenatal exposure during the embryonic stages of development. These effects may include malformations and variations, altered growth, in utero death, and altered postnatal function.

Emergencies

1) Sudden and unexpected events requiring immediate remedial action. 2) Serious occurrences that require an increased alert status for on-site personnel and, in specified cases, for offsite authorities. 3) The detailed definitions and classifications of emergencies and appropriate emergency responses provided in DOE Order 5500.2A. The types of occurrences categorized as emergencies are specified in DOE Order 5000.3A.

Emergency Action Level (EAL)

Specific, predetermined, observable criteria used to detect, recognize and determine the emergency class of an operational emergency. An EAL can be an observable event, results of analysis, or another observed phenomenon that indicates entry into a particular emergency class.

Emergency and Hazardous Chemical Inventory (EHCI)

An annual report by facilities having one or more extremely hazardous substances or hazardous chemicals above certain weight limits, as specified in Section 311 and 312 of EPCRA.

Emergency and Hazardous Chemical Inventory Forms

Information on the inventory of hazardous chemicals required to be submitted by facility owners and operators pursuant to Section 312 of the Emergency Planning and Community Right-to-Know Act of 1986.

Emergency Briefing Centers

Facilities located within DOE headquarters for the purpose of briefing of management officials on emergencies.

Emergency Broadcasting System (EBS)

A communications system used to inform the public about an emergency and the protective actions to take. The EBS is a service of local radio and television stations, activated as needed and approved by a local emergency management agency.

Emergency, Chemical

A situation created by an accidental release or spill of hazardous chemicals that poses a threat to the safety of workers, residents, the environment, or property.

Emergency Condition
An urgent, nonroutine situation that requires the use of a pesticide(s) and shall be deemed to exist when a) no effective pesticides are available under FIFRA that have labeled uses registered for control of the pest under the conditions of the emergency; and b) no economically or environmentally feasible alternative practices that provide adequate control are available.

Emergency Control Center (ECC)
A facility from which designated management can immediately direct the response to an emergency. The ECC may be an office, conference room, or other predesignated location having communications and informational materials appropriate to carry on the necessary supportive functions of directing an emergency response.

Emergency Control Stations (ECS)
Locations within or near a designated critical facility or plant area for the purpose of maintaining control, orderly shutdown, and/or surveillance of operations and equipment during an emergency.

Emergency Coordination Center
A primary search and rescue facility suitably staffed by supervisory personnel and equipped for coordinating and controlling search and rescue operations. The facility may be operated unilaterally by personnel of a single agency (rescue coordination center), jointly by personnel of two or more agencies (joint rescue coordination center), or it may have a combined staff of personnel from two or more allied agencies at different levels (combined rescue coordination center).

Emergency Core Cooling System
Nuclear reactor system components (pumps, valves, heat exchangers, tanks, and piping) that are specifically designed to remove residual heat from the reactor fuel rods should the normal core cooling system fail.

Emergency Episode
See Air Pollution Episode.

Emergency Equipment
Any equipment that may be required to measure, control, or mitigate the consequences of, or in any way be involved in, an emergency.

Emergency Exposure
An incurred exposure received during abnormal exposure conditions in the interests of preventing serious injury or saving life or valuable property.

Emergency Exposure Guidance Level (EEGL)
The acceptable ceiling concentration for military and space personnel during a single emergency exposure lasting from 1 to 24 hours — an occurrence expected to be infrequent in the lifetime of the person.

Emergency Lock
A lock designed to hold and permit the quick passage of an entire shift of employees.

Emergency Management Coordination Committee
A group of senior-level representatives from appropriate organizations who collectively provide executive oversight and coordination of the Emergency Management System. The Emergency Management Coordination Committee is chaired by the Under Secretary.

Emergency Management Information System
A system designed under U.S. Department of Energy contract by Sandia National Laboratories for the processing and display of emergency information.

Emergency Management Organization (EMO)
The senior decisionmaking component of the Emergency Response Organization (ERO), comprised of the Crisis Manager (CM) and senior staff, including the Crisis Management Team (CMT)and the Crisis Support Team (CST).

Emergency Management System
A departmental program for the development, co-ordination, and direction of Emergency planning, preparedness, response, and readiness assurance. 1) Planning — The development and preparation of emergency plans and procedures and the determination of availability of resources to provide an effective response. 2) Preparedness — The training of personnel, acquisition of resources and facilities, and testing of emergency plans and procedures to ensure an effective response. 3) Response — The action(s) taken to cope with and minimize the effects of any emergency. 4) Readiness Assurance — The actions taken to provide assurance that headquarters, field elements, and facility contractors implement appropriate aspects of agency emergency management program policies and requirements.

Emergency Management Team Director
A predesignated senior official identified to direct an emergency management team.

Emergency Management, Teams
1) Federal Emergency Management Agency (FEMA) teams deployed to a radiological emergency scene by the FEMA director to make an initial assessment of the situation and then provide FEMA's primary response capability. 2) U.S. Department of Energy (DOE) teams designated to manage activities during emergencies involving DOE or requiring DOE assistance. 3) Teams of local and state fire, police, HazMat, paramedical, and medical personnel dispatched to the site of hazardous incidents.

Emergency Medical Services
The communications, transportation and medical and related services, such as first aid, rendered in response to the individual need for immediate medical care in order to reduce or prevent suffering and disability and reduce the incidence of death.

Emergency, Nonoperational
A significant accident, incident, event, or natural phenomenon that has, or could potentially affect people, property, or the environment; e.g., EMT response to a medical emergency, fire department, HazMat response to a limited acid spill. This type of emergency is classified below the level of an "Alert" and does not result in the automatic recall of the EMO or activation of the Emergency Operations Center (EOC).

Emergency, Operational
The most serious event consisting of any unwanted operational, civil, natural phenomenon, or security occurrence that has or could endanger or adversely affect people, property, or the environment.

Emergency Operations Center (EOC)
Facilities from which management and support personnel carry out emergency response activities. The EOC may be a dedicated facility or office, conference room, or other predesignated location having appropriate communications and informational materials to carry on the assigned emergency response mission and located, when possible, in a secure and protected location.

Emergency Operations Plan
A document prepared by a national park, in cooperation with its Regional Office, to guide the staff in how to prepare for emergencies and disasters; such plans are to protect cultural resources from effects and give them a priority in recovery from any disasters.

Emergency Order Authority
The powers of the Administrator of EPA to secure relief as may be necessary to abate a danger or threat, using orders enforceable in a district court of the United States and the jurisdiction to grant relief as the public interest and the equities of the case may require, when the Administrator determines that there may be an imminent and substantial endangerment to the human health or welfare or the environment because of an actual or threatened accidental release of a regulated substance.

Emergency Permits (RCRA; CFR)
A RCRA permit issued in accordance with Section 270.61.

Emergency Plan (EPLAN)

A plan that consists of a brief, clear, and concise description of the overall emergency system and organization, including designation of responsibilities, and descriptions of the procedures, including notifications (who and when), involved in coping with any or all aspects of a potential credible emergency.

Emergency Planning

The development and preparation of Emergency plans and procedures, and the determination and allocation of resources to provide an effective response.

Emergency Planning and Community Right-to-Know Act of 1986 (EPCRA, 42 USC 11011 et seq.)

An act requiring governors to establish emergency response commissions, emergency planning districts, and local emergency planning committees that are to develop rules, procedures, and response plans in the event of local emergencies at facilities considered hazardous, by their nature or the characteristics of materials and chemicals used. EPCRA establishes reporting requirements for owners and operators of facilities using hazardous chemicals; training programs; and public notification procedures. The law was designed to help local communities protect public health, safety, and the environment from chemical hazards. To implement EPCRA, Congress required each state to appoint a State Emergency Response Commission (SERC). The SERCs were required to divide their states into Emergency Planning Districts and to name a Local Emergency Planning Committee (LEPC) for each district. Broad representation by fire fighters, health officials, government and media representatives, community groups, industrial facilities, and emergency managers ensures that all necessary elements of the planning process are represented.

Emergency Planning, Preparedness, and Response Program (EPPRP)

An emergency program consisting of three major parts. 1) Planning — The development and preparation of emergency plans and procedures and the determination of availability of resources to provide an effective response. 2) Preparedness — The training of personnel, acquisition of resources and facilities, and testing of emergency plans and procedures to ensure an effective response. 3) Response — The action(s) taken to cope with and minimize the effects of an emergency.

Emergency Planning Zone (EPZ)

A geographic area surrounding a specific DOE facility for which special planning and preparedness efforts are carried out to ensure that prompt and effective protective actions can be taken to reduce or minimize the impact to on-site personnel, public health and safety, and the environment in the event of a major emergency.

Emergency Power

Auxiliary power systems that provide power to safety and security related equipment during periods of partial or total power failure of associated primary power system.

Emergency Powers

Those powers granted to the Administrator of EPA, whereby upon receipt of evidence that a pollution source or combination of sources (including moving sources) is presenting an imminent and substantial endangerment to public health or welfare, or the environment, may bring suit on behalf of the United States in the appropriate United States district court to immediately restrain any person causing or contributing to the alleged pollution to stop the emission of air pollutants causing or contributing to such pollution or to take such other action as may be necessary. If it is not practicable to ensure prompt protection of public health or welfare or the environment by commencement of such a civil action, the Administrator may issue such orders as may be necessary to protect public health or welfare or the environment.

Emergency Preparedness (EP)

The training of personnel, acquisition and maintenance of resources and testing of the plans, procedures, personnel and resources essential to ensure effective response to emergency situations.

Emergency Preparedness Coordinator

The local government official designated to be notified immediately of chemical emergencies (e.g., spills, chemical releases, explosions, or fires) under EPCRA.

Emergency Priority

A category of immediate mission request that takes precedence over all other priorities, e.g., an enemy breakthrough.

Emergency Procedures

Detailed instructions and guidance for carrying out emergency response actions.

Emergency Project

A project involving the removal, enclosure, or encapsulation of friable asbestos-containing material that was not planned but results from a sudden unexpected event.

Emergency Readiness Assurance Plan (ERAP)

A plan to ensure that Emergency plans, implementing procedures and resources are adequate and sufficiently exercised and evaluated.

Emergency Reference Levels

Intervention levels usually specified in advance by the competent authority or management for use in abnormal situations; if the value of the quantity of interest exceeds or is predicted to exceed a particular level, the appropriate remedial action may be taken.

Emergency Relocation Site

A site located where practicable outside a prime target area to which all or portions of a civilian or military headquarters may be moved. As a minimum, it is manned to provide for the maintenance of the facility, communications, and database. It should be capable of rapid activation, of supporting the initial requirements of the relocated headquarters for a predetermined period, and of

expansion to meet wartime requirements of the relocated headquarters.

Emergency Renovation Operations

Renovation operations that were not planned but result from a sudden, unexpected event. This term includes operations necessitated by non-routine failures of equipment.

Emergency Resources

Individuals, items of equipment or instrumentation, and specialized services that have been assembled, organized, or developed for the purpose of assisting in alleviating the consequences of an emergency.

Emergency Responder's Estimate

A logical process of reasoning by which a first responder considers all the circumstances affecting the hazardous situation and arrives at a decision as to a course of action to be taken to accomplish the medical, containment and clean-up efforts. A first responder's estimate that considers a hazardous situation in future terms, so as to require the making of assumptions, is called a first responder's long-range estimate of the situation.

Emergency Response

1) A response effort by employees from outside the immediate release area or by other designated responders (i.e., mutual-aid groups, local fire departments) to an occurrence that results, or is likely to result, in an uncontrolled release of a hazardous substance. Responses to incidental releases of hazardous substances where the substance can be absorbed, neutralized, or otherwise controlled at the time of release by employees in the immediate release area or by maintenance personnel are not considered to be emergency responses within the scope of this standard. 2) The implementation of planning and preparedness during an Emergency involving the effective decisions, actions and application of resources that must be accomplished to mitigate consequences and recover from an Emergency. 3) An organized response to an incident that is, or may pose, an emergency. Since every industry will experience

different kinds of emergencies, OSHA does not attempt to create a formula into which all emergencies will fit.

Emergency Response Command and Control

The exercise of authority and direction by a properly designated first responder over a combined response team in the accomplishment of the mission. Command and control functions are performed through an arrangement of personnel, equipment, communications, facilities, and procedures employed by a supervising first responder in planning, directing, coordinating, and controlling personnel and operations in the accomplishment of the response tasks.

Emergency Response Command and Control Systems

The facilities, equipment, communications, procedures, and personnel essential to a first responder for planning, directing, and controlling operations of assigned teams pursuant to the response mission.

Emergency Response Cycle

A decisionmaking process used to employ response teams. Within the cycle the general steps are: hazard detection and approach, location, identification, secure scene, obtain medical help (if necessary), site entry decisions, treatment execution, containment/clean-up assessment, and implementing corrective action.

Emergency Response Levels

Response levels associated with the following DOE-categorized emergencies: operational, energy, and continuity of government. Each level reflects the severity of the accident, based on the consequences or potential consequences of the accident. These levels are to be used by field elements in emergency planning and for reporting emergencies to DOE headquarters. *See* Emergency Action Level.

Emergency Response Organization (ERO)

The designated group(s) of personnel responsible for coping with and minimizing or mitigating the effects of any Emergency.

Emergency Response Planning Areas (ERPAs)

Subsections of the EPZ identified by the State of Colorado for which planning is required to ensure that prompt and effective actions can be taken to protect the health and safety of the public and the environment.

Emergency Response Planning Guidelines (ERPGs)

Values intended to provide estimates of concentration ranges where one might reasonably anticipate observing adverse effects as described in the definitions for ERPG-1, ERPG-2 and ERPG-3 as a consequence of exposure to the specific substance.

Emergency Response Posture

The disposition, strength, and condition of readiness of a response team as it affects its capabilities.

Emergency Response Program

A response program providing for specific actions to be taken in response to an accidental release of a regulated substance so as to protect human health and the environment, including procedures for informing the public and local agencies responsible for responding to accidental releases, emergency health care, and employee training measures.

Emergency Response Service Support

The essential capabilities, functions, activities, and tasks necessary to sustain all elements of emergency response in at all levels. It includes, but is not limited to, that support rendered by fire, police, medical, and government agency staff in ensuring the aspects of supply, maintenance, transportation, health services, and other services required by an existing or imminent hazardous condition are in a state of response readiness. Emergency response service support encompasses those activities that produce sustainment to all field operating staff responding to the hazard.

Emergency Response Service Support Area
An area that is organized to contain the necessary supplies, equipment, tools, and elements to provide the emergency response team with service support throughout the containment and clean-up operation.

Emergency Response Surveillance
A continuous, all-weather, day-and-night, systematic watch over the hazard area to provide timely information for monitoring the progress of containment and cleanup operations.

Emergency Response Survival
Those measures to be taken by individual members of an emergency response team when involuntarily separated from the team during a response action, including procedures relating to individual survival, hazard evasion, and conduct after coming in contact with hazardous constituents.

Emergency Response Teams (ERT)
Federal Emergency Management Agency (FEMA) teams deployed to a radiological emergency scene by the FEMA director to make an initial assessment of the situation and then provide FEMA's primary response capability.

Emergency Risk, Nuclear
A degree of risk where anticipated effects may cause some temporary shock, casualties, and may significantly reduce the unit's combat efficiency. *See* Moderate Risk, Nuclear; Negligible Risk.

Emergency Stop
The operation of a circuit using hardware-based components that overrides all other robot controls, removes drive power from the robot actuators, and causes all moving parts to stop.

Emergency Substitute
A product that may be used, in an emergency only, in place of another product, but only on the advice of technically qualified personnel of the nation using the product, who will specify the limitations.

Emergency Support Teams (EST)
Federal Emergency Management Agency (FEMA) headquarters teams that carry out notification, activation, and coordination procedures from the FEMA Emergency Information and Coordination Center (EICC). The emergency support teams are responsible for federal agency headquarters coordination, staff support of the FEMA director, and support of the senior FEMA official.

Emergency Systems
A general term referring to the various types of emergency systems and/or the system's functions currently in use. This includes, but is not limited to, the following system types or categories:

- backup systems;
- containment systems;
- duress systems;
- emergency core cooling system;
- emergency power system;
- emergency spray water system;
- emergency broadcast system;
- emergency management information system;
- emergency management systems;
- emergency cooling system;
- emergency feedwater system;
- emergency raw cooling water system;
- energy emergency system;
- explosion suppression system;
- fire protection systems;
- dedicated fire water systems;
- sprinkler system;
- fire alarm system;
- fire suppression system;
- intrusion alarm system (perimeter or interior);
- national warning system;
- plant protection system;
- radiation alarm system;
- reactor protection system;
- emergency core cooling system;

- safe shutdown system;

- sparger assemblies;

- supplementary safety system;

- surveillance systems;

- surveillance and nuclear detection systems;

- control systems;

- information systems.

Emergency Telecommunications Services

Telecommunications services directly supporting federal government activity responding to a presidentially declared disaster or emergency as defined in the Disaster Relief Act (42 USC Sec. 5122) and directly resulting from any of the following circumstances: a) state of crisis declared by the national command authorities; b) efforts to protect endangered U.S. personnel or property; c) enemy action, civil disturbance, natural disaster, or any other unpredictable occurrence that has damaged facilities whose uninterrupted operation is essential to national security emergency preparedness or the management of other ongoing crises; and d) certification by the head or director of a federal agency, commander of a unified/specified command, chief of a military service, or commander or major chief of a military command that a telecommunications service is so critical to protection of life and property or to the national security that it must be processed immediately.

Emergent Hydrophytes

Erect, rooted, herbaceous angiosperms that may be temporarily to permanently flooded at the base but do not tolerate prolonged inundation of the entire plant; e.g., bulrushes (*Scirpus* spp.), salt-marsh cordgrass.

Emergent Mosses

Mosses occurring in wetlands, but generally not covered by water.

Emesis

Vomiting.

Eminent Domain

1) The right of a government to take private property for public use upon the payment of just compensation. The legal processing by which the government exercises this right is called "condemnation proceedings." 2) Government taking-of, or forced acquisition-of, private land for public use, with compensation paid to the landowner.

Emission

1) A discharge into the air. *See* Effluent. 2) Act of giving off radiant energy by an atom or molecule. 3) Pollution discharged into the atmosphere from smokestacks, other vents, and surface areas of commercial or industrial facilities; from residential chimneys; and from motor vehicle, locomotive, or aircraft exhausts. 4) The release or discharge of a substance into the environment. Generally refers to the release of gases or particulates into the air.

Emission Factors

1) Emissions estimating techniques and methods established by the Administrator of EPA to quantify emissions of carbon monoxide (CO), volatile organic compounds (VOCs), and nitrogen oxides (NOx) from sources of such air pollutants (including area and mobile sources). Including emission factors for sources for which no such methods have previously been established. 2) The relationship between the amount of pollution produced and the amount of raw material processed. For example, an emission factor for a blast furnace making iron would be the number of pounds of particulates per ton of raw materials.

Emission Inventory

A list of air pollutants emitted into a community's atmosphere in amounts (usually tons) per day, by type of source. This inventory is the basis of establishing emission standards.

Emission Rate for Electric Utility Units

The annual sulfur dioxide or nitrogen oxides emission rate in pounds per million Btus, as reported in the National Acid Precipitation Assessment Program (NAPAP) Emissions Inventory,

Version 2, National Utility Reference File. For nonutility units, the term means the annual sulfur dioxide or nitrogen oxides emission rate in pounds per million Btus, as reported in the NA-PAP Emission Inventory, Version 2.

Emission Reductions Regulations

The regulations pertaining to various categories of consumer or commercial products that account for at least 80% of the VOC emissions, on a reactivity-adjusted basis, from consumer or commercial products in areas that violate the NAAQS for ozone. The regulations require the use of best available control technologies, and control or prohibit any activity, including the manufacture or introduction into commerce, offering for sale, or sale of any consumer or commercial product that results in emission of volatile organic compounds into the ambient air, with respect to regulated entities.

Emission Standard

The maximum allowable amount of a pollutant legally permitted to be discharged from a single, mobile, or stationary source.

1) The standards applicable to new or existing sources of hazardous air pollutants that require the maximum degree of reduction in emissions of the hazardous air pollutants (HAPs) subject to the CAA (including a prohibition on such emissions, where achievable) that the Administrator, taking into consideration the cost of achieving such emission reduction, and any non-air quality health and environmental impacts and energy requirements, determines is achievable for new or existing sources in the category or subcategory to which such emission standard applies, through application of measures, processes, methods, systems, or techniques including, but not limited to, measures that:

- a) reduce the volume of, or eliminate emissions of, such pollutants through process changes, substitution of materials, or other modifications;
- b) enclose systems or processes to eliminate emissions;

- c) collect, capture or treat such pollutants when released from a process, stack, storage, or fugitive emissions point;
- d) are design, equipment, work practice, or operational standards (including requirements for operator training, or certification); or
- e) are a combination of the above.

The maximum degree of reduction in emissions that is deemed achievable for new sources in a category or subcategory shall not be less stringent than the emission control that is achieved in practice by the best controlled similar source, as determined by the Administrator.

2) Requirements established by a state, local government, or the Administrator that limit the quantity, rate, or concentration of emissions of air pollutants on a continuous basis, including any requirements that limit the level of opacity, prescribe equipment, set fuel specifications, or prescribe operation or maintenance procedures for a source to ensure continuous emission reduction. The maximum amount of air polluting discharge legally allowed from a single source, mobile or stationary. These are legally enforceable regulations setting forth an allowable rate of emissions into the atmosphere, or prescribing equipment specifications for control of air pollution emissions. *See* Effluent.

Emissions Limitations

1) The specific numerical emission limitations for the following substances or mixtures: particulate matter (total and fine), opacity (as appropriate), sulfur dioxide, hydrogen chloride, oxides of nitrogen, carbon monoxide, lead, cadmium, mercury, and dioxins and dibenzofurans. Also includes emissions limitations on postcombustion concentrations of surrogate substances, parameters or periods of residence time in excess of stated temperatures with respect to pollutants other than those listed above.

2) Requirements established by a state, or the Administrator of EPA, that limit the quantity, rate, or concentration of emissions of air pollutants on a continuous basis, including any requirement relating to the operation or maintenance of a source to ensure continuous emission reduction.

Emissions Offsets

Emissions trading, by which the owner or operator of a new or modified major stationary source may comply with regulatory requirements in lieu of increased emissions of any air pollutant by obtaining emission reductions of such air pollutant from the same source or other sources in the same nonattainment area. A state may allow the owner or operator of a source to conduct emissions trading in another nonattainment area if a) the other area has an equal or higher nonattainment classification than the area in which the source is located; and b) emissions from such other area contribute to a violation of the national ambient air quality standard in the nonattainment area in which the source is located. Such emissions' trading reductions shall be, by the time a new or modified source commences operation, in effect and enforceable and shall ensure that the total tonnage of increased emissions of the air pollutant from the new or modified source shall be offset by an equal or greater reduction, as applicable, in the actual emissions of such air pollutant from the same or other sources in the area. *See* Emissions Trading.

Emissions Statement

A statement required by a state from the owner or operator of each stationary source of oxides of nitrogen or volatile organic compounds, for classes or categories of sources, showing the actual emissions of oxides of nitrogen and volatile organic compounds emitted from that source.

Emissions Trading

EPA policy that allows a plant complex with several facilities to decrease pollution from some facilities while increasing it from others, so long as total results are equal to or better than previous limits. Facilities where this is done are treated as if they exist in a bubble in which total emissions are averaged out. Complexes that reduce emissions substantially may "bank" their "credits" or sell them to other industries. *See* Emissions Offsets.

Emphysema

Chronic pulmonary disease characterized by loss of lung function due to destruction of many of the alveolar walls with resulting enlargement of the air spaces. The total epithelial area for gas exchange in the lungs is reduced in emphysema patients.

Empirical Correlates

Information that may appear to correlate with human performance, but without logical reason. An example is the postulated association of biorhythms with human performance.

Employee

For purposes of submitting a complaint under OSHA, an employee is either of the following: 1) A present employee of the employer about whose establishment the complaint is being made; or 2) A present employee of another employer if that employee is working at or near some other employer's workplace and is exposed to hazards of that workplace. Former employees are not considered employees for purposes of submitting a formal complaint. Former employees can only submit informal complaints.

Employee Interviews, Follow-Up

In emergency response, the interview conducted between the Incident Commander or designee, and affected site employees, contractors and/or visitors, for the purpose of obtaining information about an emergency.

Employee Interviews, Initial

Interviews conducted between responsible building management personnel and affected site employees, contractors, and/or visitors, for the purpose of obtaining detailed specific information on personnel accountability after evacuation and equipment or process status that could adversely affect Emergency response.

Employees' Representative

As defined by DOE, a person chosen by contractor employees to represent their occupational safety and health-related views, interests, and concerns. For purposes of access to an employee's bioassay, monitoring, or radiation exposure records, if the representative is not the recognized/certified collective bargaining agent, then he/she must have the employee's written authorization for such access.

Employer, Public Sector
The federal government, state, and every state agency, each county, city, district, and all public and quasi-public corporations and public agencies therein, every person including any public service corporation, that has any natural person in service, and the legal representative of any employer. The term includes, but is not limited to, any governmental entity that operates or administers schools, a department of health or human services, a library, a police department, a fire department, or similar public service agencies.

EMS
See Emergency Management System.

EMT
An acronym for Emergency Medical Technician.

Enabling Device
A manually operated device that when continuously activated, permits motion. Releasing the device stops robot motion and motion of associated equipment that may present a hazard.

Enabling Objective
A sub-objective that is written to support a main objective. An objective is a description of actions to be performed by participants and is usually performance based.

Encephalopathy
Any disease of the brain.

Enclosed Cab
An enclosure made of any combination of metal, glass, plastic, or other materials that prevents pesticide spray, dust, leaves, or branches from contacting employees.

Enclosed Laser Device
Any laser or laser system located within an enclosure that does not permit hazardous optical radiation emissions from the enclosure. The laser inside is termed an "embedded laser."

Enclosed Processes
A manufacturing or processing operation that is designed and operated so that there is no intentional release into the environment of any substance present during the operation. An operation with fugitive, inadvertent, or emergency pressure relief releases remains an enclosed process so long as measures are taken to prevent worker exposure to and environmental contamination from the releases.

Enclosures
A DOE term for primary confinement systems such as process systems, glove boxes, conveyors, hotcells, and canyons.

Encroachment
1) The illegal intrusion of a structure, part of a building, or obstruction over or upon a highway, sidewalk, or the property of another. 2) The use of either flood control project works, the waterway area of such project works, or the area covered by an adopted flood control plan.

Encumbrance
A claim, lien, charge, or liability attached to and binding upon real property, such as a judgment, mortgage, mechanics, lien, lien for unpaid taxes, right of way.

End Box Ventilation System
A ventilation system that collects mercury emissions from the end boxes, the mercury sump pumps, and their water collection systems.

End Boxes
A container(s) located on one or both ends of a mercury chlor-alkali electrolyzer that serves as a connection between the electrolyzer and denuder for rich and stripped amalgam.

Endangered Species
Animals, birds, fish, plants, or other living organisms in danger of extinction throughout all or a

significant portion of their native habitat or range, by manmade or natural changes in the environment, other than a species of the *Insecta* class determined to constitute a pest whose protection would present an overwhelming and overriding risk to man. Requirements for declaring a species endangered are contained in the Endangered Species Act (ESA). *See* Endangered Species Act of 1973.

Endangered Species Act of 1973 (ESA, 7 USC 136; 16 USC 460 et seq.)

The act encouraging states and other interested parties, through federal financial assistance and a system of incentives, to develop and maintain conservation programs that meet national and international standards for safeguarding the nation's heritage in fish, wildlife, and plants. The act provides a means whereby the ecosystems upon which these species depend can be conserved, and establishes a comprehensive act for the conservation of endangered and threatened species pursuant to the following: migratory bird treaties with Canada and Mexico; the Migratory and Endangered Bird Treaty with Japan; the convention on Nature Protection and Wildlife Preservation in the Western Hemisphere; the International Convention for the Northwest Atlantic Fisheries; the Convention on International Trade in Endangered Species of Wild Fauna and Flora (CITES); and other international agreements.

The U.S. and 70 other nations have established procedures to regulate the import and export of imperiled species and their habitat. The Fish and Wildlife Service works with U.S. Customs agents to stop the illegal trade of species, including the black rhino, African elephants, tropical birds and fish, orchids, and various corals. A species can be listed as "endangered" (threatened with extinction) throughout all or a significant part of its range, or "threatened" (likely to become endangered in the foreseeable future). As of 1993 the U.S. Fish and Wildlife Service (FWS) of the Department of Interior listed 632 endangered species (326 of which were plants) and 190 threatened species (78 of which were plants). Species include birds, insects, fish, reptiles, mammals, crustaceans, flowers, grasses, and trees. Anyone can petition FWS to include a species on this list or to prevent some activity, such as logging, mining, or dam building. The law prohibits any action, administrative or real, that results in a "taking" of a listed species, or adversely affects habitat. Likewise, import, export, interstate, and foreign commerce of listed species are all prohibited. EPA's decision to register a pesticide is based in part on the risk of adverse effects on endangered species as well as environmental fate (how a pesticide will effect habitat). Under FIFRA, EPA can issue emergency suspensions of certain pesticides to cancel or restrict their use if an endangered species will be adversely affected. Under a new program, EPA, FWS, and USDA are distributing hundreds of county bulletins that include habitat maps, pesticide use limitations, and other actions required to protect listed species.

Endangerment Assessment

A study conducted as a supplement to a remedial investigation to determine the nature and extent of contamination at a site on the National Priorities List (NPL) and the risks posed to public health and/or the environment. EPA or state agencies conduct the study when legal action is pending to require potentially responsible parties (PRPs) to perform or pay for the site cleanup. An endangered assessment supplements a remedial investigation.

Endemic

1) A term meaning confined to a given region, the region of origin; also relates to disease-causing organisms that are naturally restricted to a given area. 2) Relates to species that are native to a specific region; nonendemic species are called "exotic." 3) Present in a community or among a group of people (e.g. a disease prevailing continually in a region).

Endocrine

Pertaining to hormones or to the glands that secrete hormones into the blood.

Endogenous

1) Growing within a specific plant or animal, or growing within a specific geographic region. 2)

A level of respiration in which materials previously stored by a cell are oxidized.

Endosulfan

An organochlorine pesticide used to control mites, whose use has become restricted due to its harmful side effects on wildlife.

Endothelial

A term pertaining to the layer of flat cells lining the inner surface of blood and lymphatic blood vessels, and the surface lining of serosa and synovial membranes.

Endpoint

An observable or measurable biological or chemical event used in an index of the effect of a chemical on a cell, tissue, organ, organism, etc.

Energy

1) The capacity to do work and overcome resistance. A quantity that is conserved, although it may be exchanged among bodies and transformed from one form to another, converted between heat and work, or interconverted with mass. 2) The product of power (watts) and duration (seconds). Energy is generally measured in joules (J), where one watt second = one joule. Energy exists in many forms, including: electrical, acoustic, kinetic, thermal, biological, chemical (fossil fuels), and radiation.

Energy Audit

Any process that identifies and specifies the energy and cost savings that are likely to be realized through the purchase and installation of particular energy conservation measures or renewable-resource energy measures, including determination of the energy consumption characteristics of a building that a) identifies the type, size, and rate of energy consumption of such building and the major energy using systems of such building; b) determines appropriate energy conservation maintenance and operating procedures; and c) indicates the need, if any, for the acquisition and installation of energy conservation measures.

Energy Conservation Maintenance and Operating Procedure

Modifications in the maintenance and operations of a building, and any installations therein, that are designed to reduce energy consumption in such building and that require no significant expenditure of funds.

Energy Conservation Measures

An installation or modification of an installation in a building that is primarily intended to maintain or reduce energy consumption and reduce energy costs or allow the use of an alternative energy source, including, but not limited to, adding or increasing the following:

- insulation to a building structure and systems within the building;

- storm windows and doors, multiglazed windows and doors, heat absorbing or heat reflective glazed and coated windows and door systems, additional glazing, reductions in glass area, and other window and door system modifications;

- automatic energy control systems and load management systems;

- equipment required to operate variable steam, hydraulic, and ventilating systems adjusted by automatic energy control systems;

- solar space heating or cooling systems, solar electric generating systems, or any combination thereof;

- solar water heating systems;

- furnace or utility plant and distribution system modifications;

- caulking and weatherstripping;

- replacement or modification of lighting fixtures that replacement or modification increases the energy efficiency of the lighting system without increasing the overall illumination of a facility (unless such increase in illumination is necessary to conform to any applicable state or local building code);

- energy recovery systems;

- cogeneration systems that produce steam or forms of energy such as heat, as well as electricity for use primarily within a building or a complex of buildings owned by a school or hospital; and

- other measures as a grant applicant shows will save a substantial amount of energy and as are identified in an energy audit conducted pursuant to federal regulations.

Energy Conservation Project

An undertaking to acquire and to install one or more energy conservation measures in school or hospital facilities and technical assistance in connection with any such undertaking.

Energy Conservation Project Costs

Costs incurred in the design, acquisition, construction, and installation of energy conservation measures, including technical assistance costs.

Energy Conversion

The transformation of energy from one form to another.

Energy Dissipator

A device or material used to reduce the energy of flowing water.

Energy Efficiency

The ratio of the useful output of services from an article of industrial equipment to the energy use by such article, determined in accordance with test procedures under Section 6314 of the Energy Conservation Act (ECA).

Energy Efficiency Standard

A performance standard that prescribes a minimum level of energy efficiency or a maximum quantity of energy use for a covered product, determined in accordance with test procedures prescribed under the Energy Conservation Act (ECA).

Energy Emergencies

A DOE term for a condition or potential affecting the supply of energy or the energy infrastructure with significant potential impact on the national economy, national security, defense preparedness, or health and safety.

Energy Emergency Management System (EEMS)

The component of DOE's Emergency Management System (EMS) that defines the functional requirements of energy emergency management responsibilities assigned to the Office of International Affairs and Energy Emergencies (IE).

Energy Emergency Management Team (EEMT)

1) Teams established in accordance with DOE Order 5500.1A to manage and coordinate energy emergency responses. The EEMTs are composed of predesignated DOE individuals and chaired by the Deputy Assistant Secretary for Energy Emergencies (DAS/EE). EEMTs are activated at the outset of an energy emergency and serve as the local point for the development and coordination of energy emergency activities. 2) DOE teams predesignated to coordinate response to energy emergencies involving DOE or requiring DOE assistance.

Energy Flow

The transfer of energy from its source to some other point. In safety we are concerned with two types of energy flows: wanted energy flows-controlled (to do work) and unwanted energy flows-uncontrolled.

Energy Fluence Rate

The increment of energy fluence in a specified time interval.

Energy Flux

The quotient of dR by dt, where dR is the increment of radiant energy (dR) in the time interval dt.

Energy Management Systems (EMS)

Automated systems for monitoring and controlling energy-related systems and devices.

Energy Monitoring and Control System

An automated system for monitoring and controlling energy-related systems and devices.

Energy Recovery
To capture energy from waste through any of a variety of processes (e.g., burning). Many new technology incinerators are waste-to-energy recovery units.

Energy Savings
A reduction in the cost of energy, from a base cost established through historic use, utilized in an existing federally owned building or buildings or other federally owned facilities as a result of a) building improvements, altered operation and maintenance, or technical services; or b) the increased efficient use of existing energy sources by cogeneration or heat recovery.

Energy Source
Any electrical, mechanical, hydraulic, pneumatic, chemical, thermal, or other source.

Energy Survey
The procedure used to determine energy and cost savings likely to result from the use of appropriate energy-related maintenance and operating procedures and modifications, including the purchase and installation of particular energy-related equipment and the use of renewable energy sources.

Energy Technology Engineering Center, Canoga Park (ETEC)
The DOE facility founded in 1966 that provides management, engineering, testing, consultation, and project monitoring services for a wide range of DOE programs. The ETEC manages a reactor component testing program, in addition to providing engineering support, technical management, and monitoring for a number of DOE solar, conservation, geothermal, and fusion energy programs.

Energy Trace
Tracking an energy flow from its origin to any other place or object.

Energy Use
The quantity of energy directly consumed a) at a building or facility and measured in terms of energy delivered to the building or facility; b) by an article of industrial equipment at the point of use; and/or c) by a consumer product at point of use.

Enforcement
EPA, state, or local legal actions to obtain compliance with environmental laws, rules, regulations, or agreements and/or obtain penalties or criminal sanctions for violations. Enforcement procedures may vary, depending on the specific requirements of different environmental laws and related implementing regulatory requirements. Under CERCLA, for example, EPA will seek to require potentially responsible parties to clean up a Superfund site, or pay for the cleanup, whereas under the Clean Air Act the agency may invoke sanctions against cities failing to meet ambient air quality Standards that could prevent certain types of construction or federal funding. In other situations, if investigations by EPA and state agencies uncover willful violations, criminal trials and penalties are sought.

Enforcement Decision Document (EDD)
A public document that explains EPA's selection of a cleanup alternative at enforcement sites on the National Priorities List. Similar to a Record of Decision.

Enforcing Agency
The city, county, state, or other governmental agency responsible for issuing permits, conducting compliance inspections, and levying fines or other punitive measures for noncompliance.

Engineer
A professional person who applies the theories and principles of science and mathematics to design, develop, and/or analyze technical problems and solutions thereto. Evaluates the overall effectiveness of existing environmental control systems, analyzes and quantifies environmental impacts, as well as costs and compliance liabilities. Usually this person is required to have advanced education in his/her field of

specialization, and a license to practice engineering granted by a state regulatory agency.

Engineer-in-Training (EIT)

A person who has been granted a certificate as an engineer-in-training in accordance with a state's code.

Engineered Barriers

1) Manmade structures or devices that are intended to improve a land disposal facility's ability to comply with regulatory performance objectives. 2) Manmade components of a disposal system designed to prevent the release of radionuclides into the geologic medium involved. Such term includes the high-level radioactive waste form, high-level radioactive waste canisters, and other materials placed over and around such canisters.

Engineered Safety Features

1) Systems or design characteristics that are provided to prevent or mitigate the potential consequences of postulated design basis accidents. An engineered-safety-feature system is a safety class system. 2) Shutdown. Components or equipment designed to a) provide the capability to shutdown the facility and maintain it in a safe shutdown condition; b) ensure the integrity of the process system that provides a boundary against release of radioactive material (e.g., the integrity of the coolant pressure boundary in a reactor or a glove box in a process facility); c) prevent or mitigate the consequences of events or accidents that could result in potentially measurable offsite exposures.

Engineering Geologist

A person who studies the structure and composition of land and soil to determine the most feasible sites for the construction of roads, airfields, tunnels, dams, and other structures.

Engineering Control Zones

Areas under the control of the owner/operator that, upon detection of a hazardous waste release, can be readily cleaned up prior to the release of hazardous waste or hazardous constituents to groundwater or surface water.

Enriched Uranium

Uranium containing more uranium-235 than the naturally occurring distribution of uranium isotopes.

Enrichment

1) The process of increasing the concentration of fissionable uranium-235 in uranium from the naturally occurring level of about 0.7% to the concentration required to sustain fission in a nuclear reactor, generally about 3%. The principal method of enrichment is gaseous diffusion, but gaseous centrifugation is also receiving much attention, particularly abroad. 2) The addition of nutrients (e.g., nitrogen, phosphorus, carbon compounds) from sewage effluent or agricultural runoff to surface water. This process greatly increases the growth potential for algae and aquatic plants.

Enthalpy

The heat content of a body or system, defined by the following formula: $H = U + pV$. Where H = heat; U = internal energy; p = pressure; and V = volume.

Entisols

Soils without natural genetic horizons or with weakly developed horizons.

Entomology

The science and study of insects.

Environment

1) As defined by Section 101(8) of CERCLA, means: a) the navigable waters, the waters of the contiguous zone, and the ocean waters of which the natural resources are under the exclusive management authority of the United States under the Fishery Conservation and Management Act of 1976; and b) any other surface water, groundwater, drinking water supply, land surface or subsurface strata, or ambient air within the United States or under the jurisdiction of the United States. 2) The sum of all external conditions affecting the life, development, and sustenance of an organism. Includes water, air, and land and the interrelationship that exists among and between water, air, and

land and all living things. 3) The term is also used to denote various types and categories of environments, including, but not limited to: aquatic ecosystem; aquatic environment; benthic region; ecosphere; general environment; human environment; indoor climate; work environment; ambient; ecological impacts; ecosystems; habitats; lithosphere; natural and physical environment; socio-economic environment.

Environment Assessments

A DOE term for one of the three major assessments conducted as part of a Tiger Team Assessment. This type of assessment is concerned with both regulatory (i.e., externally enforced) requirements and DOE Orders (i.e., internally enforced requirements). DOE Tiger Team Environment Assessments specifically examine the following topic areas: air; soils/sediments/biota; surface water; groundwater; waste management; toxic and chemical materials; quality assurance environmental monitoring; radiation/radiologic materials; inactive waste sites; NEPA; and special issues (e.g. natural/cultural resources acts and executive orders.

Environment and Conservation Challenge Awards

The awards program established, in accordance with the goals and purposes of the National Environmental Policy Act of 1969, the Environmental Quality Improvement Act of 1970, and the National Environmental Education Act, for the purposes of recognizing outstanding environmental achievements by U.S. citizens, enterprises, or programs; providing an incentive for environmental accomplishment; promoting cooperative partnerships between diverse groups working together to achieve common environmental goals; and identifying successful environmental programs that can be replicated.

Environment, Safety, and Health Overview

An organized set of DOE activities to ensure that all aspects of environment, safety, and health-related activities at the program, project, and contractor level are adequately addressed. Such activities include a) establishing department-wide environment, safety, and health policies, requirements and standards; b) periodic and timely reviews of program and project documents, activities, actions, and plans; c) appraising the implementation of environment, safety and health programs at the headquarters, field, and contractor level as appropriate; and d) providing support, assistance, and guidance to headquarters program offices and field organizations.

Environment, Safety, and Health (ES&H) Program

Those DOE requirements, activities, and functions in the conduct of all DOE and DOE-controlled operations that are concerned with controlling air, water, and soil pollution; limiting the risks to the wellbeing of both operating personnel and the general public to acceptably low levels; and protecting property adequately against accidental loss and damage. Typical activities and functions related to this program include, but are not limited to, the following: environmental protection, occupational safety, fire protection, industrial hygiene, health physics, occupational medicine, process and facilities safety, nuclear safety, emergency preparedness, quality assurance, and radioactive and hazardous waste management.

Environmental Appropriations

Authorizations to make expenditures and to incur obligations for specific remediation purposes.

Environmental Assessment (EA)

1) A reviewing, verifying, decisionmaking tool, concerned with optimizing, prioritizing, weighing alternative strategies, and exposing problems and opportunities. 2) A preliminary, written, environmental analysis prepared pursuant to the National Environmental Policy Act to determine whether a federal action required by NEPA (see same) such as building airports or highways would significantly affect the environment and thus require preparation of a more detailed environmental impact statement or a Finding of No Significant Impact. A formal NEPA document, defined at 40 CFR 1508.9.

Environmental Audit (EA)

1) An independent assessment of a facility's compliance policies, practices, and controls. Many pollution prevention initiatives require an audit to determine where wastes may be minimized or eliminated or energy conserved. Many supplemental environmental projects that offset a penalty use audits to identify ways to reduce the harmful effects of a violation. 2) Documented assessments of a facility that monitor the progress of necessary corrective actions, to ensure compliance with environmental laws and regulations, and to evaluate field organization practices and procedures.

Environmental Budget

A comprehensive plan of financial operations embodying an estimate of proposed requirements for expenditure appropriations and provisions for maintaining, or obtaining, regulatory compliance over a given period and the means of financing such requirements.

Environmental Catastrophe

The hospitalization of five or more persons resulting from an accident or illness caused by an environmental hazard. These incidents include manmade and natural disasters (earthquakes, tidal waves, volcanos), or other occurrences causing significant damage.

Environmental Compliance Approach

Any one of the allowable methods by which the assessment, design, and/or implementation of an environmental investigation or abatement project may be demonstrated to be in compliance with an enforcing agency's (or multiple agencies) environmental regulations, ordinances, and policies. In general, two compliance approaches exist: 1) the performance compliance approach; and 2) the prescriptive compliance approach.

Environmental Condition

Any condition, including but not limited to, the state of preservation, contamination, actions of responsible parties, or regulatory standing of a site; or any condition, including but not limited to, the assessments, analytical analyses, or cleanup activities that affect a site.

Environmental Data, Analyses

The sorting, selecting, comparing, decomposing, screening, simulating, weighing, rating, testing, computing, and segregating of environmental planning and management facts and information.

Environmental Data, Collection

The method of conducting primary and secondary environmental research by questioning, interviewing, surveying, reading, field observation, database search, studying of literature, recording, mapping, photographing, and conducting laboratory experiments.

Environmental Data, Communication

The writing, illustrating, interacting, explaining, documenting, discussing, debating, and exchanging that result in the interpretation and dissemination of environmental information.

Environmental Data, Organization

A comprehensive process of arranging information by relating, ordering, ranking, merging, diagramming, categorizing, integrating, and composing facts into a rational, sequential, environmental report, application, or presentation.

Environmental Database

A collection of information specific to an environmental operation, governmental agency, business, organization, pollution/hazard category, etc.

Environmental Defense Fund (EDF)

A special interest coalition of attorneys and environmentalists formed to monitor environmental issues and, when necessary, take legal action to protect the environs.

Environmental Detection Limits

The smallest levels at which a radionuclide in an environmental medium can be unambiguously distinguished for a given confidence level using a particular combination of sampling and measurement procedures, sample volume, analytical detection limit, and processing procedure.

Environmental Documentation

Written documentation prepared and filed in accordance with the state and federal regulations. Environmental documentation includes, but is not limited to Notices of Exemption, draft and final Environmental Impact Reports, Assessments, Phase I/II/III Studies, Negative Declarations, Notices of Completion, Notices of Determination, Preliminary Assessments.

Environmental Education

The systematic instruction of individuals in subjects that will enhance their knowledge of the science, art, and law of environmental issues.

Environmental Effects on Public Welfare

A term that refers to, but is not limited to, environmental effects on: soils, water, crops, vegetation, manmade materials, animals, wildlife, weather, visibility, and climate, damage to and deterioration of property, and hazards to transportation, as well as effects on economic values and on personal comfort and well-being, whether caused by transformation, conversion, or combination with other air pollutants.

Environmental Engineer

A professional person who applies civil, mechanical, electrical, and/or chemical engineering principles to the control, elimination, and prevention of environmental hazards, such as air pollution, water pollution, and solid waste management. Usually this person is required to have advanced education in his/her field of specialization, and a license to practice engineering granted by a state regulatory agency.

Environmental Equity

Equal protection from environmental hazards for individuals, groups, or communities regardless of race, ethnicity, or economic status.

Environmental Fatality

A death resulting from an accident or illness; caused by or related to an environmental hazard.

Environmental Fatality/Catastrophe Investigations

Investigations and extensive interviews with witnesses to determine: the cause of the accident, the extent of damage, and the affected population; the effectiveness of emergency response actions; whether a violation of environmental, safety, or health standards caused the accident; what effect regulatory and OSHA standards had on the occurrence of the accident; and if standards and operating procedures could be revised to correct the hazardous condition(s) that led to the incident.

Environmental Fate

The destiny of a chemical or biological pollutant after release into the environment. Environmental fate involves temporal and spatial considerations of transport, transfer, storage, and transformation.

Environmental Finding

A relevant, written conclusion arrived at as a result of an environmental audit, environmental documentation review, or other assessment and is contained in the audit report, and/or Letter of Recommendations.

Environmental Fund

A sum of money or other resources segregated for the purpose of carrying on specific remediation activities or attaining certain objectives in accordance with public awareness goals, emergency response requirements, special interest objectives, project compliance limitations, etc., and constituting an independent fiscal and accounting entity.

Environmental Hazard

A condition capable of posing an unreasonable risk to air, water, or soil quality, or plant or animal life.

Environmental Health Assessment

An assessment of hazardous air pollutants conducted by an Interagency Task Force (ITF) that includes a) an examination, summary, and evaluation of available toxicological and epidemiological information for the pollutant to ascertain the levels of human exposure that pose a significant threat to human health and the associated acute, subacute, and chronic adverse health effects; b) a determination of gaps in available information related to human health effects and exposure levels; and c) where appropriate, an identification of additional activities, including toxicological and inhalation testing, needed to identify the types or levels of exposure that may present significant risk of adverse health effects in humans. *See* Interagency Task Force (ITF).

Environmental Health Effects Program

A research program on the short-term and long-term effects of air pollutants, including wood smoke, on human health.

Environmental Health Specialist

A public-sector employee who enforces public health and welfare standards, legislation and mandates regarding food, water, wastewater, and solid waste disposal. Advises on compliance and quality control measures for violations and unsafe conditions; usually plans and administers health regulations as an employee of a state government's health department.

Environmental Impact Analysis

The methodology or logical process by which the potential impact of a proposed development project on its immediate and more regional environs is analyzed. *See* Environmental Impact Assessment.

Environmental Impact Appraisal

An abbreviated document, based on an environmental review, that supports a negative declaration or no-impact finding, and that describes a proposed agency action, its expected impacts, and the basis for the conclusion that no significant impact is anticipated.

Environmental Impact Assessment (EIA)

The identification and evaluation of environmental consequences associated with a proposed project and the alternative mitigation measures to minimize those consequential impacts. This is a legal requirement for obtaining development permits in many states, and especially on projects with regional or national significance. All large projects conducted by federal agencies or receiving federal funding must complete this study. Synonymous with Environmental Assessment.

Environmental Impact Statement (EIS)

1) The formal written NEPA document resulting from an environmental impact analysis, required of federal agencies by the National Environmental Policy Act for major projects or legislative proposals significantly affecting the environment. A tool for decisionmaking, the EIS documents the environmental impacts of the proposed action; any unavoidable adverse effects; alternatives to the proposed action; the relationship between short-term and long-term productivity and enhancement of the environment; and any irreversible and irretrievable commitments of resources involved with the proposed action. 2) Documents defined at 40 CFR 1508.11 or a Supplemental EIS, prepared in accordance with the requirements of Section 102(2)(C) of NEPA, the CEQ Regulations, and DOE NEPA Guidelines.

Environmental Impairment Liability

A type of insurance coverage carried by hazardous waste generators and others involved in hazardous waste handling and disposal. Coverage typically provides funds for remediating environmental impairment or paying for damages resulting from the impairment. Not all such insurance policies include the same types of coverage, however, and some have specific exclusions for certain types of occurrences or releases.

Environmental Information Documents

Any written analysis prepared by an applicant, grantee, or contractor describing the environmental impacts of a proposed action.

Environmental Inspector

A person who conducts field investigations to obtain environmental data for use by governmental, environmental, engineering, and scientific disciplines to determine sources of pollution, extent of pollution, current environmental compliance status; recommends additional inspection or tests in the event of noncompliance findings. Usually conducts Phase I Environmental Inspections for a private firm or inspects for environmental compliance as a governmental staff member. *See* Environmental Technician.

Environmental Justice

The fair treatment of people of all races, cultures, and income and educational levels with respect to the development and enforcement of environmental laws, regulations, and policies. Fair treatment implies that no population should be forced to shoulder a disproportionate share of exposure to the negative effects of pollution due to lack of political or economic strength. *See* Environmental Equity.

Environmental Management

The management of resources, property, and all associated programs with an emphasis on environmental conservation and enhancement. Also, may be used to include those actions necessary to remediate situations where environmental conditions have already been negatively affected.

Environmental Mapping

A method of recording and displaying performance data in relation to an environmental setting. The planner notes activities and their frequencies at a site on facility maps, that, when completed, show operational behaviors. The data revealed from this technique include location of storage, treatment, shipping, disposal activities; frequency of the storage, treatment, shipping, disposal activities at varying locations; and vehicle, waste, personnel movement, the relation of people to the facility/project; and other recurrent patterns of operations.

Environmental Monitoring

The collection and analysis of samples or direct measurements of environmental media. Environmental monitoring consists of two major activities: effluent monitoring and environmental surveillance.

Environmental Noise

The intensity, duration, and the character of sounds from all sources.

Environmental Occurrence

Any sudden or sustained deviations from a regulated or planned performance at a site, facility, or operation that has environmental protection and compliance significance.

Environmental Planner

A professional who plans and designs the development of real property for projects, such as parks and other recreational facilities, airports, hospitals, commercial and residential subdivisions, and industrial sites. Compiles and analyzes data on site conditions such as geographic, demographic, physical, and natural site features (drainage etc.). Takes a lead role, as project manager, in the preparation of environmental impact assessments and statements, including the development of project alternatives and implementation plans. A multidisciplined person, usually with an advanced education in environmental planning and management, engineering, architecture, or urban planning. Synonymous with Environmental Specialist; Environmental Analyst. *See* Environmentalist; Environmental Engineer.

Environmental Protection Agency (EPA)

The federal agency established in 1970 to administer major laws to control and reduce contamination of air, water, and land systems. *See* EPA.

Environmental Protection Agency Glossary

The Environmental Protection Agency Glossary as included in the Agency's Information Resources Directory, an annual EPA publication that gives general reference and referral information of relevance to EPA's programs.

Environmental Protection Agency Grants for CAA Compliance
EPA grants to organizations of local elected officials with state transportation or air quality maintenance planning responsibilities for payment of the reasonable costs of developing SIP (State Implementation Plan) revisions. *See* State Implementation Plan.

Environmental Protection Standards
Specified sets of rules or conditions concerned with delineation of procedures, definition of terms, specification of performance, design, or operations, or measurements that define the quantity of emissions, discharges, or releases to the environment and the quality of the environment.

Environmental Quality
The properties and characteristics of the environment, either generalized or local, as they impinge on society and ecology.

Environmental Quality Standards
The maximum limits or concentrations of pollutants that are permitted in air, land, or water. Standards are based on the maximum acceptable levels considered safe to public health and welfare, wildlife, and the environment.

Environmental Release
Releases or hazardous spills resulting in chemical contamination.

Environmental Research
The systematic investigation and acquisition of information for the purpose of assessing, delineating, and characterizing the extent of contamination, developing mitigation plans, or contributing to specific site knowledge, or scientific advancement and includes the collection of data for inclusion in environmental reports and studies, and possible publication.

Environmental Research Geographic Location Information Act (ERGLIA)
The 1990 act established for the purpose of developing a database of environmental research articles indexed by geographic location comprised of important environmental research journals, conference proceedings, or other reference sources in which scientific research or engineering studies related to air, water, soil quality, pollution, or other environmental issues are routinely input.

Environmental Research Protocol
A written description of the proposed research activity that is submitted in contract documents for review and consideration and that is written in accordance with a specific scope of work or task requirement.

Environmental Researcher
The principal investigator or project director who has responsibility for conducting the research.

Environmental Response Team (ERT)
EPA's group of highly trained scientists and engineers based in Edison, NJ, and Cincinnati, OH, who provide around-the-clock technical backup and support to On-Scene Coordinators (OSCs), EPA regional offices, and states during all types of emergencies involving hazardous waste sites and spills of hazardous substances. The ERT's capabilities include multimedia sampling and analysis, hazard assessment, hazardous substance and oil spill cleanup techniques, and technical support.

Environmental Reviews
The process whereby an evaluation is undertaken by EPA to determine whether a proposed Agency action may have a significant impact on the environment and therefore require the preparation of the EIS.

Environmental Risk
Any potential for harm anticipated from adverse environmental impacts generating from, or migrating onto, a site that is greater than what might ordinarily be encountered in daily life or during the performance of routine work activities.

Environmental Sampling

The process of scientific evaluation of site specimens to determine existence of, classifications of, quantifications of, extent of, and intensities of a contaminant; may be used to classify type where no contamination exists, as in a soil sample, to determine the bearing pressure of soils in an area to be developed. Tests are usually a combination of field work followed by laboratory analyses.

Environmental Sampling Station

A permanent, high-volume air sampling filter system used primarily for sampling of normal releases to the environment.

Environmental Scientist

A person who conducts research studies to develop theories or methods of abating or controlling sources of environmental pollution, utilizing advanced knowledge of principles and concepts of various scientific and engineering disciplines.

Environmental Services

The various combinations of scientific, technical, and advisory activities (including modification processes, i.e., the influence of manmade and natural factors) required to acquire, produce, and supply information on the past, present, and future implications surrounding a site or project. In military science, services include analyses on states of space, atmospheric, oceanographic, and terrestrial surroundings for use in military planning and decisionmaking, or to modify those surroundings to enhance military operations.

Environmental Stress

Stress on a species caused by the dwindling of resources necessary to sustain the organism's survival.

Environmental Surveillance

The collection and analysis of samples, or direct measurements, of air, water, soil, foodstuff, biota, and other media for the purpose of determining compliance with applicable standards and permit requirements, assessing hazards and exposures of the public and assessing the effects, if any, on the local environment.

Environmental Surveys

Documented, multidiscipline assessments (with sampling and analysis) of a facility to determine environmental conditions and to identity environmental problem areas of environmental risk requiring corrective action.

Environmental Technician

A person who conducts tests to obtain environmental data for use by governmental, environmental, engineering and scientific disciplines to determine sources, types, and extent of pollution. *See* Environmental Inspector.

Environmental Tracking

Learning hazardous waste behavior by examining the physical traces of facility/project operations. Road wear, waste storage, waste deposit, haul routes, construction routes, staging areas, routes to containment/storage areas, etc., are all indications of daily operating activities and environmental "clues" that enable the planner to reconstruct the patterns of use in a specific environmental setting. All data must be verified and validated.

Environmental Unit

An environmental unit is that classification of the operations and materials requirements of the unit into appropriately identified waste streams deemed necessary or desirable for control of pollution prevention, waste minimization, and recycling operations. Except as otherwise provided by law, such units may be devised at the discretion of the facility owner/operator.

Environmentalist

An individual who plans, develops, and lobbies for standards and systems to improve the quality of air, water, food, work environs, wildlife protection, and other environmental factors. A person who promotes public awareness of the need to prevent, mitigate, and eliminate environmentally degrading practices. Some environmental interest groups bring class action suits against violators once considered beyond reproach. *See* Environmental Defense Fund.

Environmentally Sound Methods, Efforts, Actions, or Programs

A phrase that refers to the methods, efforts, actions or programs to prevent introductions or control infestations of aquatic nuisance species that minimize adverse impacts to the structure and function of an ecosystem and adverse effects on nontarget organisms and ecosystems and emphasize integrated pest management techniques and nonchemical measures.

Enzyme

A catalyst produced by living cells. All enzymes are proteins, but not all proteins are enzymes.

EOC

See Emergency Operations Center.

EOC Notification

A verbal or written notification that an occurrence has taken place, initial categorization/classification by a responsible individual has been accomplished, and initial response and mitigation actions are underway. Follow-up notifications will include more details of the occurrence to include the stability of the occurrence and any changes in severity.

EOC Notification Center

A communications facility within the EOC that is staffed 24 hours a day, 365 days a year. The EOCNC provides support to shift managers/supervisors in determining the categorization or classification of events and notifying offsite agencies.

EOCNO

An acronym for Emergency Operations Center Notification Officer.

EOD

See Explosive Ordnance Disposal.

Eon

1,000,000,000 years (one billion; 10^9).

EOP

An acronym for Emergency Operating Procedures.

EOR

An acronym for Enhanced Oil Recovery.

EOTR

See Eastern Ozone Transport Region (CAA).

EP Toxicity

Also known as Extraction Procedure (EP)for Toxicity Characteristics, EP Toxicity, or Extraction Procedure Toxicity. An analytical laboratory characterization using extraction procedures for determining primarily toxic metal concentrations and/or leaching potential. Recently replaced by a series of combined tests called Toxicity Characterization Leaching Procedure (TCLP).

EPA

An acronym for the U.S. Environmental Protection Agency; the agency that administers federal environmental policies, research, and regulations. EPA provides information on many environmental subjects including water pollution, hazardous and solid waste disposal, air and noise pollution, pesticides, and radiation. Main headquarters — 401 M Street S.W., Washington D.C. 20460.

EPA Hazardous Waste Number

1) The number assigned by EPA to each hazardous waste listed in Part 261, Subpart O, of 40 CFR and to each characteristic identified in Part 261, Subpart C, of 40 CFR. 2) Numbers assigned by the Environmental Protection Agency and used by industry; solid wastes are listed hazardous wastes from nonspecific sources in 40 CFR 261.31; solid wastes are listed hazardous wastes from specific sources in 40 CFR 261.32 unless they are excluded under 40 CFR 260.20 and 260.22 and are listed in Part 261, Appendix IX. Exclusions are for hazardous wastes from nonspecific and specific sources.

EPA Identification Number

The number assigned by EPA to each generator, transporter, and treatment, storage, or disposal facility.

EPA Program Offices

The program offices of the EPA, including, but not limited to a) the Office of Air and Waste Management, for air quality activities; b) the Office of Water and Hazardous Materials, for water quality activities and water supply activities; c) the Office of Pesticides, for environmental effects of pesticides; d) the Office of Solid Waste, for solid waste activities; e) the Office of Toxic Substances, for toxic substance activities; f) the Office of Radiation Programs, for radiation activities; and g) the Office of Noise Abatement and Control, for noise activities.

EPA Regions

The states and territories found in one of the ten regions of the United States.

EPAA

An acronym for Environmental Programs Assistance Act of 1984.

EPACT

An acronym for Environmental Protection Agency Control Techniques, and Control Technology documents.

EPCRA or EPCRTKA

See Emergency Planning and Community-Right-to-Know Act of 1986.

Ephemeris

A publication giving the computed places of the celestial bodies for each day of the year or for other regular intervals.

Epidemic

Widespread outbreak of a disease, or a large number of cases of a disease in a single community or relatively small area.

Epidemiologist

1) A person concerned with determining the causal factors of health problems, including issues such as acute and chronic disorders, communicable diseases, behavioral disorders, alcoholism, and drug abuse. 2) A medical scientist who studies the various factors involved in the incidence, distribution, and control of disease in a population.

Epidemiology

The study of epidemics and disease patterns, including the occurrence and distribution of diseases as they affect population, health-related states/events in human populations, along with the factors (e.g., age, gender, occupation, economic status) that influence distribution, and the application of this study to control health problems.

Epidermis

The outermost layer of the skin.

Epigenetic

Alterations in the expression of genes by mechanisms other than changes in the nucleotide sequence of DNA. The term has historically been used in the area of embryonic differentiation, but more recently has been used in describing a component of the formation of cancer.

Epiphyseal

Refers to part of the bone, often the end of a long bone, that develops separated from the main portion of the cartilage.

Epiphyte

A plant, such as certain orchids and ferns, that grows on another plant for mechanical support but not for nutrients; epiphytes are not considered parasites.

Episode, Pollution

An air pollution incident in a given area caused by a concentration of atmospheric pollution reacting with meteorological conditions that may result in a significant increase in illnesses or deaths.

Although most commonly used in relation to air pollution, the term may also be used in connection with other kinds of environmental events such as a massive water pollution situation.

Epithelial
Pertaining to the cell layer that covers all internal and external surfaces of the body, including the gastrointestinal, respiratory, and urinary tracts.

Epithet
A term referring to a descriptive substitute for the name of a species.

Epoch
A unit of geologic time subdivided into ages. Two or more epochs comprise a period.

EPPRP
See Emergency Planning, Preparedness, and Response Program.

EPZ
See Emergency Planning Zone.

Equilibrium
1) The state in which opposing forces are exactly counteracted or balanced. Types of equilibrium include acid-base, colloid, dynamic, homeostatic, and chemical. 2) Used in risk assessment of toxic air pollutants to generally describe the chemical equilibrium between a pollutant in the inhaled air and the level in the body. 3) In relation to radiation, the state at which the radioactivity of consecutive elements within a radioactive series is neither increasing nor decreasing. Equilibrium exists when the activity of all the progeny within a decay series is equal to the parent activity. For radon progeny, equilibrium is rarely achieved and the progeny activities are usually less than the radon activity.

Equipment Limitation
The term used when the use of timber harvesting equipment is to be limited for the protection of water quality, the beneficial uses of water, and/or other forest resources.

Equipment/Parts, Personal Protective
A term relating to various types of protective clothing and equipment used by workers in hazardous environments to prevent or minimize exposure to workplace or site hazards. Typical personal protective equipment includes items such as air masks, acid suits, lab coats, radiation suits, dust masks, goggles, safety glasses, side shields, fall protection devices, safety belts, safety lines, safety nets, flame retardant clothing, ankle protection, metatarsal protection, safety boots, safety shoes, shoe covers, metal shoe covers, gloves, wrist bands, bump caps, faceshields, hard hats, helmets, hoods, ear plugs, leggings, padding, and/or respirator(s).

Equipotential Line
1) Surface, or line, along which the potential is constant. 2) A contour line on the water table or potentiometric surface, along which the pressure head of groundwater in an aquifer is the same. 3) A line in a two-dimensional groundwater flow field such that the total hydraulic head is the same for all points along the line.

Equipotential Surface
A surface in a three-dimensional groundwater flow field such that the total hydraulic head is the same everywhere on the surface.

Equivalence Data
Chemical data or biological test data intended to show that two substances or mixtures are equivalent.

Equivalent Method
Any method of sampling and measuring the concentration of a contaminant, that has been demonstrated to the EPA Administrator's satisfaction to be, under specific conditions, an acceptable alternative to the normally used reference methods.

ER
An acronym for Office of Environmental Restoration and Waste Management; Office of Energy Research.

Era

After eon, an era is the second largest division of geologic time. Eras are divided into periods.

ERAB

An acronym for Energy Research Advisory Board.

Eradication

The total annihilation of a species throughout its range; the complete extinction of a species.

ERAP

See Emergency Readiness Assurance Plan.

ERDDAA

An acronym for Environmental Research, Development, and Demonstration Authorization Act of 1978.

ERGLIA

See the Environmental Research Geographic Location Information Act of 1990.

Ergonomics

A term referring to human factors or human factors engineering.

Ericoid Habitat

A term meaning occurring in association with an ericaceous (heath family) shrub layer.

ERL

See Emergency Reference Levels.

Erodibility Factor

The amount of soil that erodes from a standard experimental plot of bare soil under average conditions of slope, rainfall, etc. The factor varies with the physical characteristics of soil.

Erose

A species descriptor meaning irregularly notched, toothed, or indented.

Erosion

Gradual deterioration of land formations by the action of wind, water, or by the land-clearing/development practices related to farming, residential or industrial development, road building, or timber-cutting activities of humans. In the weathering process erosion is a natural geological function, but more often than not it is poor land management that strips the land of its topsoil, leaving it vulnerable to erosion by wind and water.

Erosion Control

The measures implemented to control and prevent soil erosion in an effort to preserve natural resources, control floods, prevent impairment of reservoirs, and maintain the navigability of rivers and harbors, protect public health, and public lands. Preventive measures include, but are not limited to, engineering operations, methods of cultivation, the growing of vegetation, and changes in use of land.

Erosion Hazard Rating

The rating derived from the procedure designed to evaluate the susceptibility of the soil within a given location to erosion.

ERP

See Emergency Response Program (CAA).

ERPG-1

A DOE term for the maximum airborne concentration below which it is believed that nearly all individuals could be exposed for up to 1 hour without experiencing other than mild transient adverse health effects or perceiving a clearly defined objectionable odor. *See* Emergency Response Planning Guidelines.

ERPG-2

A DOE term for maximum airborne concentration below which it is believed that nearly all individuals could be exposed for up to 1 hour without experiencing or developing irreversible or other serious health effects or symptoms that could impair their abilities to take protective action. *See* Emergency Response Planning Guidelines.

ERPG-3
A DOE term for the maximum airborne concentration below which it is believed that nearly all individuals could be exposed for up to 1 hour without experiencing or developing life threatening health effects. *See* Emergency Response Planning Guidelines.

Error Sampling
A well-defined, structured process employing experienced observers, defined deviations, and reproducible patterns of observation.

ERT
See Emergency Response Teams.

Erythema
A term meaning redness of the skin.

Erythroderma
A term meaning intense, widespread reddening of the skin.

ES&H
See Environment, Safety, and Health Program.

ESA
See the Endangered Species Act of 1973.

Escalation
An increase in scope or the hazard associated with an emergency, deliberate or unintentional.

ESD
See Emergency Shutdown Device.

ESEA
An acronym for Elementary and Secondary Education Act of 1965.

ESECA
See Energy Supply and Environmental Coordination Act of 1974 (15 USC 792(a)).

ESF
An acronym for Engineered Safety Features.

ESFAS
An acronym for Engineered Safety Features Actuation System.

ESMS
An acronym for Emission Standards for Moving Sources.

Esophageal Strictures
Narrowing of the esophagus that causes difficulty in swallowing; often due to scar formation following extensive burns.

Esophagus
The portion of the digestive canal extending from the throat to the stomach. Also referred to as the gullet.

ESP
An acronym for Electrostatic Precipitators; Environmentally Sound Prevention [Activities].

ESP Devices
Air pollution control devices that remove particles from a gas stream (smoke) after combustion occurs. The ESP imparts an electrical charge to the particles, causing them to adhere to metal plates inside the precipitator. Rapping on the plates causes the particles to fall into a hopper for disposal.

ESS
An acronym for Engagement Simulation Systems.

Essential Activities
Those activities necessary to prevent damage to Class A equipment and/or to prevent hazards to site personnel (HVAC surveillance and utility crews).

Essential Elements of Information (EEI)
The critical items of information regarding the enemy and the environment needed by the commander by a particular time to relate with other available information and intelligence in order to assist in reaching a logical decision.

Essential Experimental Populations

Experimental populations whose loss would be likely to appreciably reduce the likelihood of the survival of the species in the wild. All other experimental populations are to be classified as nonessential.

Essential Facilities

Structures that are necessary for emergency postearthquake operations.

Essential Industry

Any industry necessary to the needs of a striving economy. The term includes the basic industries as well as the necessary portions of those other industries that transform the crude basic raw materials into useful intermediate or end products, e.g., the iron and steel industry, the food industry, and the chemical industry.

Essential Personnel

Personnel required to maintain essential activities. These essential personnel are identified in position descriptions.

Established Federal Standard

Any operative occupational safety and health standard established by any agency of the United States and presently in effect, or contained in any act of Congress in force as of 1971.

Establishment

A single physical location where business is conducted or services or operations are performed. Where distinctly separate activities are performed at a single physical location, each activity shall be treated as a separate "establishment." Typically, an establishment refers to a field activity, installation, or facility.

Establishment Official

The highest ranking person at a federal establishment with authority over the establishment's working environment.

Estate

In real estate, refers to the degree, quantity, nature, and extent of interest that a person has in real property, such as a "fee simple absolute estate," an "estate for years."

Estate (Period to Period)

An interest in land where there is no definite termination date but the rental period is fixed at a certain sum per week, month, or year; often called a periodic tenancy.

Estimate, Military

1) An analysis of a foreign situation, development, or trend that identifies its major elements, interprets the significance, and appraises the future possibilities and the prospective results of the various actions that might be taken. 2) An appraisal of the capabilities, vulnerabilities, and potential courses of action of a foreign nation or combination of nations in consequence of a specific national plan, policy, decision, or contemplated course of action. 3) An analysis of an actual or contemplated clandestine operation in relation to the situation in which it is or would be conducted in order to identify and appraise such factors as available and needed assets and potential obstacles, accomplishments, and consequences.

Estimated Annual Operating Cost

The aggregate retail cost of the energy that is likely to be consumed annually in representative use of a consumer product, determined in accordance with Section 6293 of this title.

Estrus

A regularly recurring period of ovulation and sexual excitement in mammals other than humans.

Estuary

1) An inlet or indentation of the land that is subject to the tidal action of the sea; also the mouth of a river or creek, where fresh water mixes with salt water. 2) A complex ecosystem between a river and near-shore ocean waters where tidal action and river flow create a mixing of fresh and salt water. These brackish areas include bays,

mouths of rivers, salt marshes, wetlands, and lagoons and are influenced by tides and currents. These water ecosystems shelter and feed marine life, birds, and wildlife. *See* Wetlands.

ESW
An acronym for Emergency Service Water.

ETEC
See Energy Technology Engineering Center (Canoga Park).

Ethanol
An alcohol produced by fermentation or the hydrolysis of ethene (C_2H_4); it forms the basis of alcoholic beverages and is used as a solvent. It is also being used as an alternative fuel in modified engines, primarily on a research or experimental scale.

Ethnography
Part of the discipline of other ways of life (such as hunting, agriculture, strategies, family life, festivals).

Guided by anthropological concepts and studies of contemporary cultures in the participant observations, farming histories, and review of relevant cultures documentation (ethnohistories) and oral dissemination.

Ethnohistory
A systematic description of documents, related materials and anthropologic studies relating to the changes in cultural systems throughout time.

Ethnology
Systematic analysis of cultures, lives, and subsistence patterns.

Ethology
The study of animal behavior in the natural environment.

Ethylene Declared Plants
Any plant that produces ethylene declared by reaction of oxygen and hydrogen chloride with ethylene.

Ethylene Declared Purification
Any part of the process of ethylene declared production that follows ethylene declared formation, excluding product storage following the final finishing column.

Ethylene Dibromide (EDB)
A chemical used as an agricultural fumigant and in certain industrial processes. Extremely toxic and found to be a carcinogen in laboratory animals, EDB has been banned for most agricultural uses in the United States.

Etiologic Agents
Microorganisms, or toxins, that may produce human disease.

Euphoria
An intense and exaggerated feeling of well-being.

Euphotic Zone
The uppermost zone of a body of water, where sufficient light is transmitted for active photosynthesis to occur. This zone can be over 100 feet deep.

Euthanasia
The humane destruction of an animal accomplished by a method that involves instantaneous unconsciousness and immediate death or by a method that involves anesthesia, produced by an agent that causes painless loss of consciousness and death during such loss of consciousness.

Eutrophic Lakes
Shallow, murky bodies of water that have excessive concentrations of plant nutrients, such as nitrogen and phosphorus, causing excessive algal production. *See* Dystrophic Lakes.

Eutrophication

1) The enhancement of a body of water with plant nutrients, naturally or as a result of pollution, resulting in increased growth of aquatic plants, that reduces light intensity, produces or traps toxins, deoxygenates the water, raises the water level, and eventually kills fish and higher-ordered plants. 2) The slow aging process in a body of water, during which an increase of mineral and organic nutrients has reduced the oxygen, producing an aquatic environment that favors plants over animal life. During the later stages of eutrophication the water body is choked by abundant plant life as the result of increased amounts of nutritive compounds such as nitrogen and phosphorus. Human activities can accelerate the process.

Evacuation

1) The process of moving any person who is wounded, injured, or ill to and/or between medical treatment facilities. 2) The clearance of personnel, animals, or material from a given locality.

Evacuation, Controlled

Leaving an area or facility in an orderly, step-by-step fashion, directed by management. Actions should be taken to shut down equipment and remove/don protective gear as appropriate.

Evacuation, Immediate

Leaving an area or facility quickly using any available door — including alarmed doors — quickly and without taking time to put on, or take off, protective clothing or shut down equipment.

Evacuation of Dangerously Exposed Waters

The movement of merchant ships under naval control from severely threatened coastlines and dangerously exposed waters to safer localities. *See* Dangerously Exposed Waters; Severely Threatened Coastline.

Evacuation Policy

1) Command decision indicating the length in days of the maximum period of noneffectiveness that patients may be held within the command for treatment. Patients who, in the opinion of responsible medical officers, cannot be returned to duty status within the period prescribed are evacuated by the first available means, provided the travel involved will not aggravate their disabilities. 2) A command decision concerning the movement of civilians from the proximity of military operations for security and safety reasons and involving the need to arrange for movement, reception, care, and control of such individuals. 3) Command policy concerning the evacuation of unserviceable or abandoned material and including designation of channels and destinations for evacuated material, the establishment of controls and procedures, and the dissemination of condition standards and disposition instructions.

Evacuee

A civilian removed from a place of residence by official direction for reasons of personal security or the requirements of the military situation. *See* Displaced Person; Refugee.

Evaluation

1) The systematic comparison of a system's output or performance with its goals and objectives. Evaluation may range from the informal and simple (e.g., a survey of reactions to compliance inspector performance) to the formal and complex (e.g., a study of environmental/economic impacts on an industry). Evaluation usually refers to site, program, and/or policy assessments in terms of specific goals and objectives. 2) In intelligence usage, appraisal of an item of information in terms of credibility, reliability, pertinency, and accuracy. Appraisal or evaluation of items of information or intelligence is indicated by a standard letter-number system. The evaluation of the reliability of sources is designated by a letter from A through F, and the accuracy of the information is designated by numeral 1 through 6. These are two entirely independent appraisals, and these separate appraisals are indicated in accordance with the system indicated below. Thus, information adjudged to be "probably true" received from a "usually reliable source" is designated "B-2" or "B2," while information of which the "truth cannot be judged" received from a "usually reliable source" is designated "B-6" or "B6."

Evaluator, Response
A person knowledgeable in emergency response procedures, functions, policies, requirements, and practices who observes participant response to scenarios. The Evaluator determines compliance or noncompliance with applicable policies or procedures through the use of predetermined evaluation criteria.

Evaporation
The change from liquid to gas, due to latent heat from the ambient temperatures of surrounding medium.

Evaporation Pond
Shallow, artificial pond in which sewage sludge is pumped. After the sludge dries, it is either removed, incinerated, or buried under more sludge. Evaporation ponds are commonly used in connection with industrial wastewater disposal operations.

Evaporative Cooler
A device used for reducing the sensible heat of air for cooling, by the process of evaporation of water into an air stream.

Evaporative Emissions, Control
The EPA regulations applicable to evaporative emissions of hydrocarbons from all gasoline-fueled motor vehicles: 1) during operation; and 2) over 2 or more days of nonuse under ozone-prone summertime conditions. The regulations require the greatest degree of emission reduction achievable by means reasonably expected to be available for production during any model year to which the regulations apply, giving appropriate consideration to fuel volatility, and to cost, energy, and safety factors associated with the application of the appropriate technology.

Evaporimeter
A device used to measure the rate of evaporation of water.

Evapotranspiration
The combined loss of water from a land area, during a specified period of time, through evaporation from the soil and transpiration of plants. The sum of evaporation plus transpiration.

Evapotranspiration, Actual
The evaporation that actually occurs under given climatic and soil-moisture conditions.

Evapotranspiration, Potential
The evaporation that would occur under given climatic conditions if there were unlimited soil moisture.

Event
Any real-time occurrence or significant deviation from planned or expected behavior that could endanger or adversely affect people or the environment.

Event History Log
Documentation log kept during an emergency identifying events, actions, and times.

Events and Causal Factors
A term used to depict in logical sequence the necessary and sufficient events and causal factors for accident occurrence.

Evergreen Stand
A plant community where evergreen trees or shrubs represent more than 50% of the total areal coverage of trees and shrubs. The canopy is rarely without foliage; however, individual trees or shrubs may be bare.

Evidence
1) Something that tends to prove; grounds for belief. 2) In law, something legally presented before a court that bears on or establishes the point in question. The kinds of evidence are direct, circumstantial, and real.

Evolution
The continuous process of cumulative change in successive generations.

EWS
An acronym for Early Warning System.

Ex Parte Communication
An oral or written communication not on the public record with respect to which reasonable prior notice to all parties is not given, but does not include requests for status reports on any matter or proceeding.

Exaggerated Stereoscopy
See Hyperstereoscopy.

Excavation
1) In archaeology, the scientific examination of an artifact. It is important for a "by-layer" removal and study of a potentially significant site; a one meter by one meter size is the professional standard of archaeological recovery. 2) A manmade cavity or depression in the earth's surface, including its sides, walls, or faces formed by the removal of materials and producing unsupported earth conditions by reason of such removal. If installed forms or similar structures reduce the depth to width relationship, an excavation may become a trench.

Excavation Zone, UST
The volume containing the tank system and backfill material bounded by the ground surface, walls, and floor of the pit and trenches into which the UST (Underground Storage Tank) system is placed at the time of installation.

Exceedance
Violation of environmental protection standards by exceeding allowable limits or concentration levels.

Exceptional Transport
A load whose size, weight, or preparation entail special difficulties vis-a-vis the facilities or equipment of even one of the transport systems to be used.

Exceptions
An interim and maximum 180 day, nonrenewable, release from an OSHA standard.

Excess Emissions
Emissions of an air pollutant in excess of an emission standard.

Excess Property
The quantity of property in possession of any component of the DOD that exceeds the quantity required or authorized for retention by that component.

Excess Risk
An increased risk of disease above the normal background rate.

Exchange, Real Estate
A transaction in which title or interest in a property or facility are transferred between firms, or individuals in return for monetary, and/or other consideration.

Exchange Capacity
1) The amount of exchangeable ions, measured in milliequivalent per 100 grams of solid material at a given pH. 2) The total ionic charge of the adsorption complex active in the adsorption of ions.

Excimer (Excited Dimer)
A gas mixture used as the active medium in a family of lasers emitting ultraviolet light.

Excluded Ocean Material
Any dredged material discharged by the United States Army Corps of Engineers or discharged pursuant to a permit issued by the Secretary, any waste from a tuna cannery operation located in American Samoa or Puerto Rico discharged pursuant to a permit issued by the Administrator under Ocean Dumping Act.

Exclusion Areas
Security areas for the protection of classified matter where mere access to the area would result in access to classified matter.

Exclusionary Zoning

Any form of zoning ordinance that tends to exclude specific classes of persons or businesses from a particular district or area.

Exclusive Use

The enjoyment of a beneficial use of land or improvements, together with the ability to exclude from occupancy by means of legal process others who interfere with that enjoyment. Co-tenants may each make such use of land or improvements without impairing the other's right to use the property, as this constitutes but a single use jointly enjoyed. Exclusive use is not destroyed by one or more of the following: a) Multiple use by persons making different uses of the same property in such a manner that they do not prevent the enjoyment of coexisting rights held by others, as, for example, the development of mineral resources by one person and the enjoyment of recreational uses by others; b) Concurrent use when the extent of each party's use is limited by the other party's right to use the property at the same time, as, for example, when two or more parties each have the independent right to graze cattle on the same land; c) Alternating use when the duration of each party's use is limited, as, for example, the use of premises by a professional basketball team on certain days of each week and by a professional hockey team on certain other days; d) Persons lawfully passing over or taking things from the land; e) The existence of noninterfering easements, covenant rights, or servitudes in other persons or attached to other lands; f) Occasional trespassers.

Excretion

Elimination or discharge of excess and waste chemicals from the body. Chemicals may be excreted through feces, urine, exhaled breath, etc.

Execution Planning

The phase of the crisis action planning process in which an approved operation plan or other National Command Authorities-designated course of action is adjusted, refined, and translated into an operation order. Execution planning can proceed on the basis of prior deliberate planning, or it can take place under a "no plan" situation.

Exempt or Limited Quantities

Quantities of hazardous material that are so limited in magnitude that they are exempt from most requirements specified in the federal regulations.

Exempt Shipments of Plutonium

1) Plutonium shipments in any form designed for medical application. 2) Plutonium shipments that pursuant to rules promulgated by the Administrator of the Energy Research and Development Administration are determined to be made for purposes of national security, public health and safety, or emergency maintenance operations. 3) Shipments of small amounts of plutonium deemed by the Administrator of the Energy Research and Development Administration to require rapid shipment by air in order to preserve the chemical, physical, or isotopic properties of the transported item or material.

Exempt Solvent

Specific organic compounds that are not subject to requirements of regulation because they have been deemed by EPA to be of negligible photochemical reactivity.

Exempted Aquifer

1) Underground bodies of water defined in the Underground Injection Control program as aquifers that are sources of drinking water (although they are not being used as such) and that are exempted from regulations barring underground injection activities. 2) An aquifer or its portion that meets the criteria in the definition of "underground source of drinking water" but which has been exempted according to the procedures of 40 CFR 144.3.

Exercise

1) A scheduled and planned large-scale activity that tests the integrated capability and most aspects of the EP program associated with a particular DOE facility. 2) An action characterized by maneuvers, drills, and other repetitive operations; and carried out for testing, training, or discipline.

Exercise Report

A report on the results and conclusions from the evaluation of the Emergency response to an exercise scenario. The Drill Report identifies and classifies (as issues or deficiencies) findings and whether exercise objectives were met.

Exergonic

A term applied to chemical reactions that emit energy.

Exfiltration

The removal of personnel or citizens from areas under the influence of a hazardous condition.

Exfoliative Dermatitis

A skin condition that involves scaling or shedding of the superficial cells of the epidermis.

Exothermic Reaction

Chemical reaction that produces heat.

Exhaust Gases

Any offgases (the constituents of which may consist of any fluids, either as a liquid and/or gas) discharged directly or ultimately to the atmosphere that were initially contained in or were in direct contact with the equipment for which exhaust gas limits are prescribed in 40 CFR.

Exhaust System

All pipes, converters, and chambers through which the exhaust gas flows from the engine exhaust manifold outlet flange to the end of the tailpipe.

Existing Hazardous Waste Management (HWM) Facility

Facilities that were in operation or for which construction commenced on or before November 19, 1980. A facility has commenced construction if a) the owner or operator has obtained the federal, state, and local approvals or permits necessary to begin physical construction; and either b) a continuous on-site, physical construction program has begun; or c) the owner/operator has entered into contractual obligations that cannot be can-

celled or modified without substantial loss or for physical construction of the facility to be completed within a reasonable time.

Existing Injection Well

An injection well other than a new injection well.

Existing or New Major Fuel Burning Stationary Sources

A term that applies to existing or new major fuel burning stationary sources that a) have the design capacity to produce 250,000,000 Btus per hour (or its equivalent); and b) are not in compliance with the requirements of an applicable implementation plan or that are prohibited from burning oil or natural gas, or both, under any other authority of law.

Existing Portion

That land surface area of an existing waste management unit (included in the original RCRA Part A permit application) on which wastes have been placed prior to the issuance of a permit.

Existing Sources

Stationary sources that are not new sources.

Existing Stationary Facilities

Any of the following stationary sources of air pollutants, including any reconstructed source, that was not in operation prior to August 7, 1962, and was in existence on August 7, 1977, and has the potential to emit 250 tons per year or more of any air pollutant. In determining potential to emit, fugitive emissions, to the extent quantifiable, must be counted.

Existing Tank Systems

Tank systems used to contain an accumulation of regulated substances or for which installation has commenced on or before December 22, 1988. Installation is considered to have commenced if a) the owner or operator has obtained all federal, state, and local approvals or permits necessary to begin physical construction of the installation of the tank system; and b) if, 1) either a continuous on-site physical construction or installation program has begun; or, 2) the owner/operator has entered into contractual obligations that cannot be cancelled or modified without substantial loss or for physical construction at the site or installation of the tank system to be completed within a reasonable time.

Existing Tank System or Existing Component

A tank system or component that is used for the storage or treatment of hazardous waste and that is in operation or for which installation has commenced on or prior to July 14, 1986.

Existing Use

A use existing at the time of enactment of a statute (ordinance) that does not comply with the legislation and that as a matter of due process of law, must be permitted to continue for some reasonable period of time.

Exit

A continuous and unobstructed means of egress to a public way, and includes intervening doors, doorways, corridors, exterior exit balconies, ramps, stairways, smoke-proof enclosures, horizontal exits, exit passageways, exit courts, and yards.

Exoatmosphere

See Nuclear Exoatmospheric Burst.

Exogenous

Growing on the outside or exterior of a plant or animal.

Exosphere

The outermost layer of the earth's atmosphere, beyond the ionosphere.

Exotic

1) All species of plants and animals not naturally occurring, either presently or historically, in any ecosystem of the United States. 2) Plants or organisms that are not endemic to a region; non-native, introduced.

Exotic Species Restriction

The federal policy restricting agencies from introducing exotic species into the natural ecosystems on lands and waters that they own, lease, or hold for purposes of administration; including encouraging the states, local governments, and private citizens to prevent the introduction of exotic species into natural ecosystems of the United States.

Expansion Joints

Joints between parts of a structure to avoid distortion when subjected to movement and/or temperature change.

Expendable Property

Property that may be consumed in use or loses its identity in use and may be dropped from stock record accounts when it is issued or used.

Expendable Supplies

Supplies that are consumed in use, such as paint, fuel, cleaning and preserving materials, surgical dressings, drugs, medicines, or that lose their identity, such as spare parts, etc. Also called consumable supplies and material.

Experimental Populations

Introduced and/or designated populations (including any offspring arising solely therefrom) that have been so designated in accordance with the procedures of this subpart but only when, and at such times as the populations are wholly separate geographically from nonexperimental populations of the same species. Where part of an experimental population overlaps with natural populations of the same species on a particular occasion, but is wholly separate at other times, specimens of the experimental population will not be recognized as such while in the area of overlap. That is, experimental status will only be recognized outside the areas of overlap. Thus, such a population shall be treated as experimental only when the times of geographic separation are reasonably predictable; e.g., fixed migration patterns, natural or manmade barriers. A population is not treated as experimental if total separation will occur solely as a result of random and unpredictable events.

Experimental Start Date

The first date a test substance is applied to the test system.

Experimental Stewardship Program

The program that provides incentives to, or rewards for, the holders of grazing permits and leases whose stewardship results in an improvement of the range condition of lands under permit or lease. Such program shall explore innovative grazing management policies and systems that might provide incentives to improve range conditions.

These may include, but need not be limited to a) cooperative range management projects designed to foster a greater degree of cooperation and coordination between the federal and state agencies charged with the management of the rangelands and with local private range users; b) the payment of up to 50% of the amount due the federal government from grazing permittees in the form of range improvement work; c) such other incentives as he/she may deem appropriate.

Experimental Termination Date

The last date on which data are collected directly from a test system/study.

Expert Witness Fees

Recorded or billed costs incurred by an owner/operator or regulatory agency for an expert witness with respect to an environmental issue.

Exploitation

Taking full advantage of any information that has come to hand for tactical, operational, or strategic response purposes.

Exploration Shaft

A shaft created and used for the purpose of obtaining subsurface data.

Explosive

Any chemical compound, mixture, or device, of which the primary or common purpose is to function by explosion (i.e., with substantially instantaneous release of gas and heat) unless such compound, mixture, or device is otherwise specifically classified by the U.S. Department of Transportation. Classification of explosives by the U.S. Department of Transportation is as follows:

- Class A Explosives — Possessing detonating hazard, such as dynamite, nitroglycerin, picric acid, lead azide, fulminate of mercury, black powder, blasting caps, and detonating primers.

- Class B Explosives — Possessing flammable hazard, such as propellant explosives, including some smokeless propellants.

- Class C Explosives — Include certain types of manufactured articles that contain Class A or Class B explosives, or both, as components, but in restricted quantities.

Explosive Limits, Chemical

The amounts of vapor in air that form explosive mixtures. These limits are expressed as lower and upper values and give the range of vapor concentrations in air that will explode if an ignition source is present.

Explosive Mines

Metal or composition containers filled with a high explosive.

Explosive Ordnance

All munitions containing explosives, nuclear fission or fusion materials, and biological and chemical agents. These include bombs and warheads; guided and ballistic missiles; artillery, mortar, rocket, and small arms ammunition; all mines, torpedoes, and depth charges; demolition charges; pyrotechnics; clusters and dispensers; cartridge and propellant actuated devices; electro-explosive devices; clandestine and improvised explosive devices; and all similar or related items or components explosive in nature.

Explosive Ordnance Disposal

The detection, identification, on-site evaluation, rendering safe, recovery, and final disposal of unexploded explosive ordnance. It may also include explosive ordnance that has become hazardous by damage or deterioration.

Explosive Ordnance Disposal Incident

The suspected or detected presence of unexploded explosive ordnance, or damaged explosive ordnance, that constitutes a hazard to operations, installations, personnel, or material. Not included in this definition are the accidental arming or other conditions that develop during the manufacture of high explosive material, technical service assembly operations, or the laying of mines and demolition charges.

Explosive Ordnance Disposal Procedures

Those particular courses or modes of action taken by explosive ordnance disposal personnel for access to, diagnosis, rendering safe, recovery, and final disposal of explosive ordnance or any hazardous material associated with an explosive ordnance disposal incident.

- Access Procedures — Those actions taken to locate exactly and gain access to unexploded explosive ordnance.

- Diagnostic Procedures — Those actions taken to identify and evaluate unexploded explosive ordnance.

- Render Safe Procedures — The portion of the explosive ordnance disposal procedures involving the application of special explosive ordnance disposal methods and tools to provide for the interruption of functions or separation of essential components of unexploded explosive ordnance to prevent an unacceptable detonation.

- Recovery Procedures — Those actions taken to recover unexploded explosive ordnance.

- Final Disposal Procedures — The final disposal of explosive ordnance that may include demolition or burning in place, removal to a disposal area, or other appropriate means.

Explosive Ordnance Disposal Teams

Teams of trained explosive ordnance personnel. Responsibilities include identification, examination, and disposal of explosive ordnance.

Explosive Ordnance Disposal Unit

Personnel with special training and equipment who render explosive ordnance safe (such as bombs), make intelligence reports on such ordnance, and supervise the safe removal thereof.

Explosive Projectiles

Shells, projectiles, warheads, or rocket heads, loaded with explosives or bursting charges, with or without other materials, for use in cannons, guns, tubes, mortars or other firing or launching devices.

Explosive Torpedoes

Explosive torpedoes, such as those used in warfare, are metal devices containing a means of propulsion and a quantity of high explosives.

Explosives

Chemical compounds or mechanical mixtures that are unstable and, when subjected to heat, impact, friction, shock, or other suitable initiation stimulus, undergo a very rapid chemical change with the evolution of large volumes of highly heated gases that exert pressures in the surrounding medium. The term applies to materials that either detonate or deflagrate.

Explosives Activities

Functions (storage, handling, and processing) involving explosives from the manufacture or receipt of the explosives through the final shipping, configuration, including final storage but excluding the movement of explosives between explosives areas.

Explosives Bays

Locations (room, cubicle, cell, work area) containing a single type of explosives activity that affords the requirement protection for the appropriate hazard classification (Class I, II, III, IV) of the explosives activity involved. *See* Explosives Hazard Classes.

Explosives Buildings

Structures containing one or more explosives bays.

Explosives Hazard Classes

The level of protection required for any specific explosives activity, based on the hazard class (accident potential) for the explosives activity involved.

- *Explosives Hazard, Class I* — Those explosives activities involving a high potential for an accident that is unacceptable for the exposure of any personnel, thus requiring remote operations. In general, this would include activities where the energies that may interface with the explosives are approaching the upper limits of safety, and/or loss of control of the energy is likely to exceed the safety limits for the explosives involved. This category includes those research and development activities where the safety implications have not been fully characterized. Examples of Class I activities are screening, blending, pressing, extrusion, drilling of holes, dry machining, some wet machining, machining explosives and metal in combination, development of some new explosives or explosives processing methods, and explosives disposal.

- *Explosives Hazard, Class II* — Those explosives activities that involve a moderate potential for an accident because of type of explosives, condition of the explosives and/or nature of the operations involved. This category consists of activities where the accident potential is greater than Class III, but exposure of personnel performing contact operations is acceptable. Included are activities where energies that do or may interface with the explosives are normally well within the safety boundaries for the explosives involved but where loss of control of these energies might approach the safety limits of the explosives. Examples of Class II activities involving insensitive high explosives (IHE) are weighing, some wet machining, assembly and disassembly, and environmental testing (exposure of explosives samples to variations in temperature, humidity, etc.).

- *Explosives Hazard, Class III* — Those explosives activities that represent a low potential for an accident because of the type of explosives, the conditions of the explosives and/or the nature of the activity involved. Class III includes explosives activities where the accident potential of the operation being performed is not significantly different from explosives storage. Examples are normal handling, storage, packaging, unpackaging, and some inspection and nondestructive testing.

- *Explosives Hazard, Class IV* — Those explosives activities with insensitive high explosives (IHE) or IHE subassemblies that, although mass detonating, are so insensitive that there is negligible probability for accidental initiation or transition from burning to detonation. Explosions will be limited to pressure ruptures of containers heated in a fire. Although the fire hazards of IHE and IHE subassemblies are not as great as those of other explosives, it is classified as hazard class/division 1.3 (mass fire) to be consistent with DOD 6065.9. Most processing and storage activities with IHE and IHE subassemblies are class IV. However, some are found in Class I.

Explosivity

The characteristic of undergoing very rapid decomposition (or combustion) to release large amounts of energy.

Expose

To cause to ingest, inhale, contact via body surfaces, or otherwise come into contact with a hazardous chemical.

An individual may come into contact with a hazardous chemical through air, land, water, and consumer products, including occupational or workplace exposures.

Exposure

1) Contact of an organism with a chemical, physical, or biological agent. Exposure is quantified as the amount of the agent available at the exchange boundaries of the organism (e.g., skin, lungs, digestive tract) and available for absorption. The most common routes of exposure are through the skin, mouth, or by inhalation. 2) The amount of radiation or pollutant present in an environment that represents a potential health threat to the living organisms in that environment. 3) A measure of the ionization produced in air by x or gamma radiation. It is the sum of the electrical charges on all ions of one sign produced in air when all electrons liberated by photons in a volume element of air are completely stopped in air, divided by the mass of air in the volume element. The special unit of exposure is the roentgen.

Exposure Assessment

1) Measurement or estimation of the magnitude, frequency, duration, and route of exposure of ani-

mals or ecological components to substances in the environment. The exposure assessment also describes the nature of exposure and the size and nature of the exposed populations, and is one of four steps in risk assessment. 2) An assessment to determine the extent of exposure of, or potential for exposure of, individuals to petroleum from a release from an underground storage tank based on such factors as the nature and extent of contamination and the existence of or potential for pathways of human exposure including ground or surface water contamination, air emissions, and food chain contamination), the size of the community within the likely pathways of exposure, and the comparison of expected human exposure levels to the short-term and long-term health effects associated with identified contaminants and any available recommended exposure or tolerance limits for such contaminants.

Exposure Dose

The exposure dose at a given point is a measurement of radiation in relation to its ability to produce ionization. The unit of measurement of the exposure dose is the roentgen.

Exposure Event

An incident of contact with a chemical or physical agent. An exposure event can be defined by time (e.g., day, hour) or by the incident (e.g., eating a single meal of contaminated fish).

Exposure Pathways

The course a chemical or physical agent takes from the source to the exposed organism. An exposure pathway describes a unique mechanism by which an individual or population is exposed to chemicals or physical agents at or originating from the site. Each exposure pathway includes a source or release from a source, an exposure point, and an exposure route. If the exposure point differs from the source, a transport/exposure medium (e.g., air) or media (in cases of intermedia transfer) also is included.

Exposure Point

A point of potential contact between an organism and a chemical or physical agent.

Exposure Point Concentration

The concentration of a chemical at the exposure point.

Exposure Rate

The increment of exposure in a specified time interval.

Exposure Route

The way a chemical or physical agent comes in contact with an organism (i.e., by ingestion, inhalation, or dermal contact). Same as Exposure Pathways.

Extended or Renewed

The lengthening of the term of possession of an agreement by mutual consent or by the exercise of an option by either party to the agreement.

Extended Trails

Trails or trail segments that total at least 100 miles in length, except that historic trails of less than 100 miles may be designated as extended trails. While it is desirable that extended trails be continuous, studies of such trails may conclude that it is feasible to propose one or more trail segments that, in the aggregate, constitute at least 100 miles in length.

Extent of Damage

The visible plan area of damage, usually expressed in units of 1,000 square feet, in detailed damage analysis and in approximate percentages in immediate-type damage assessment reports; e.g., 50% structural damage.

External Corrosion

Corrosion of that portion of a metal structure (i.e., tank) that is exposed to external elements such as air, water, or soil.

External Inspection

An inspection of all visible external surfaces and appurtenances of an installed above, or underground, storage tank (pressure vessel).

Extinct

A species that has no surviving individuals.

Extirpate

A term that means to eliminate a population.

Extraction Plants

Facilities chemically processing beryllium ore to beryllium metal, alloy, or oxide, or performing any of the intermediate steps in these processes.

Extraction Sites

The places from which the dredged or fill material proposed for discharge is to be removed.

Extraction Zone

A specified drop zone used for the delivery of supplies and/or equipment by means of an extraction technique from an aircraft flying very close to the ground.

Extraordinary Nuclear Occurrences

Any event causing a discharge or dispersal of source, special nuclear, or byproduct material from its intended place of confinement in amounts offsite, or causing radiation levels offsite, that the Nuclear Regulatory Commission (NRC) determines to be substantial and that the commission determines has resulted or will probably result in substantial damages to persons offsite or property offsite. Any determination by the NRC that such an event has or has not, occurred shall be final and conclusive, and no other official or any court shall have power or jurisdiction to review any such determination. The NRC shall establish criteria in writing setting forth the basis upon which such determination shall be made.

Extrapolation

An estimate of response or quantity at a point outside the range of the experimental data. Also refers to the estimation of a measured response in a different species or by a different route than that used in the experimental study of interest (i.e., species-to-species, route-to-route, acute-to-chronic, high-to-low).

Extrathoracic

Situated or occurring outside the thorax (the part of the respiratory tract above the trachea).

Extreme High Water of Spring Tides

The highest tide occurring during a lunar month, usually near the new or full moon. This is equivalent to extreme higher high water of mixed semidiurnal tides.

Extreme Low Water of Spring Tides

The lowest tide occurring during a lunar month, usually near the new or full moon. This is equivalent to extreme lower low water of mixed semidiurnal tides.

Extreme Value

The largest observation during a given period of observation.

Extreme Value Projection

Risk projection based upon the worst event each period over a number of periods, such as the worst property damage case each 6 months over a period of 5 years.

Extremely Hazardous Substances

Any of the 400 plus chemicals or hazardous substances, identified by EPA on the basis of hazard or toxicity, and listed under SARA (Superfund Amendments and Reauthorization Act of 1986) Title III. The list is subject to revision.

Extremely Hazardous Waste

Any dangerous waste that persists in hazardous form for several years or more at a disposal site. It presents a significant environmental hazard, may be concentrated by living organisms through a food chain, or may affect the genetic makeup of humans or wildlife. It is highly toxic to humans or wildlife if disposed of in such quantities as would present an extreme hazard to humans or the environment.

Extremities

The hands and arms below the elbow or feet and legs below the knee.

Extrusion

An outcropping of igneous rocks at the earth's surface.

Eye Protection

A type of personal protective equipment that includes goggles, safety glasses, side shields, to protect the eyes and the area around the eyes. *See* Personal Protective Equipment.

F

F/S
An acronym for Frequency/Severity.

F-V
An acronym for Fussell-Vesely.

F40T12 Lamp
A nominal 40 watt tubular fluorescent lamp that is 48 inches in length, $1\frac{1}{2}$ inches in diameter, and conforms to ANSI standard C78.1-1978(R1984).

F96T12 Lamp
A nominal 75 watt tubular fluorescent lamp that is 96 inches in length, $1\frac{1}{2}$ inches in diameter, and conforms to ANSI standard C78.3-1978(R1984).

F96T12HO Lamp
A nominal 110 watt tubular fluorescent lamp that is 96 inches in length, $1\frac{1}{2}$ inches in diameter, and conforms to ANSI standard C78.1-1978(R1984).

FA
See Feasibility Assessment.

Fabric Filter
A cloth device that catches dust particles from industrial emissions.

Fabricating
Any processing of a manufactured product that contains commercial asbestos, with the exception of processing at temporary sites for the construction or restoration of facilities.

Fabricator
An individual or group who, without genuine resources, invent information or inflate or embroider over news for personal gain or for political purposes.

FACA
An acronym for the Federal Advisory Committee Act (5 USC).

Faceshield
A type of personal head protection equipment designed to protect the face and forehead.

Facies
The total characteristics of a rock regarding its texture, mineral, organic composition, form, and structure that, once defined, indicate its environment of origin, age, and history.

Facility
1) A real property entity, whose use is directed to a common purpose at a single location, consisting of one or more of the following: any building, structure, installation, equipment, pipe or pipeline (including any pipe into a sewer or publicly owned treatment works), well, pit, pond, lagoon, impoundment, ditch, landfill, storage container, motor vehicle, rolling stock, or aircraft. 2) Any site or area where a hazardous substance has been

deposited.   3) All contiguous land, structures, other appurtenances, and improvements on the land used for treating, storing, or disposing of hazardous waste. A facility may consist of several treatment, storage, or disposal operational units (e.g., one or more landfills, surface impoundments, or combinations of both). 4) Systems, buildings, utilities, services, and related activities, such as accelerators, storage areas, test loops, nuclear reactors, coal conversion plants, magnotohydrodynamics (MHD) experiments, windmills, radioactive waste disposal systems and burial grounds, testing laboratories, research laboratories, and accommodations for analytical examinations of irradiated and unirradiated components. Also includes pipelines, ponds, impoundments, landfills, motor vehicles, rolling stock, and aircraft.

Facility Audit Report (FAR)

Reports submitted by an audit firm to EPA, that:

- describe in detail the procedures followed during the audit, the type and condition of the facility itself, the regulatory history of the facility, and the facility's current compliance status;

- describe in detail each violation observed during the audit;

- provide any other information that in the judgment of the audit firm is pertinent to EPA's review; and

- list the relevant statutory and/or regulatory citation for each violation found, including locations and dates of the findings and any other relevant or appropriate information.

Facility Boundaries

Fences or other barriers that surround and prevent uncontrolled access to the facility or facilities.

Facility Components

Any pipe, duct, boiler, tank, reactor, turbine, or furnace at or in a facility; or any structural member of a facility.

Facility Mailing Lists

The mailing lists for facilities maintained by EPA.

Facility Managers

Individuals, or their designees usually but not always contractors, who have direct line responsibility for operation of a facility or group of related facilities, including authority to direct physical changes to the facility.

FACOSH

An acronym for Federal Advisory Council on Occupational Safety and Health.

Facsimile (FAX)

A system of telecommunication for the transmission of fixed images with a view to their reception in a permanent form.

Fact

Actuality, actual existence, event, objective reality. That which is perceived with the senses as real.

Factor Relationship and Sequence of Events Vocabulary

A controlled vocabulary designed for searching the narrative description fields of records on the Safety Performance Measurement System (SPMS).

Factory Mutual

A group of mutual insurers underwriting large highly protected properties. They place strong emphasis in and are experts on loss prevention engineering.

Facultative Anaerobic Bacteria

Bacteria that can adapt themselves to growth in the presence or absence of oxygen. Referred to as facultative bacteria.

Fahrenheit, G.D.

The German physicist, who defined a scale of measure for his alcohol thermometer in 1709 and used the same scale again in 1714 for his mercury thermometer. On this scale, water freezes at 32°F and boils at 212°F. This definition assumes that the atmospheric pressure is at a standard of 760mm of mercury pressure.

Fail-Safe

A design characteristic by which a unit or system will become safe and remain safe if a system or component fails or loses its activation energy.

Fail-Safe Interlock

An interlock where the failure of a single mechanical or electrical component of the interlock will cause the system to go into, or remain in, a safe mode.

Failed Element Monitors

Equipment monitors, including, but not limited to, low energy gamma monitors, 10-minute delay monitors, blanket gas activity monitors, gas chromatographs.

Failure Mode and Effect Analysis

A basic system safety technique wherein the kinds of failures that might occur and their effect on the overall product or system are considered.

Falcate

A species descriptor that means curved and tapering to a point.

Fallout

1) The settling of airborne solid and/or liquid particles to the ground; it occurs when the speed of their rise is less than that of the pull of gravity. The extent of suspended particulates falling to the ground can be measured by receptors placed on the ground. 2) The precipitation to earth of radioactive particulate matter from a nuclear cloud.

Fallout Contours

Lines joining points that have the same radiation intensity that define a fallout pattern, represented in terms of roentgens per hour.

Fallout Pattern

The distribution of fallout as portrayed by fallout contours.

Fallout Prediction

An estimate, made before and immediately after a nuclear detonation, of the location and intensity of militarily significant quantities of radioactive fallout.

Fallout Safe Height of Burst

The height of burst at or above which no militarily significant fallout will be reproduced as a result of a nuclear weapon detonation. *See* Types of Burst.

Fallout Wind Vector Plot

A wind vector diagram based on the wind structure from the surface of the earth to the highest altitude of interest.

Family

A species descriptor referring to a taxonomic category below "Order" and above "Genus" based on the grouping of related genera.

Fan Camera Photography

Photography taken simultaneously by an assembly of three or more cameras systematically installed at fixed angles relative to each other so as to provide wide lateral coverage with overlapping images. *See* Tri-Camera Photography.

Farm Tanks

Tanks located on a tract of land devoted to the production of crops or raising animals, including fish, and associated residences and improvements. Farm tanks must be located on farm property. "Farms" include fish hatcheries, rangeland, and nurseries with growing operations.

Fascicled

A species descriptor that means a bundlelike cluster of stems, flowers, or leaves.

Fasciculation

Muscle twitching.

Fatigue

The failure of a material's mechanical properties as a result of repeated stress.

Fatigue Strength

The maximum cyclical stress withstood for a given number of cycles before a material fails.

Fault Tree

An analytical tree used to determine fault. These may be used in accident/incident investigation or to determine accident potential before one has occurred.

Faults

Surfaces or zones of rock fracture along which there has been displacement.

Fauna

A species descriptor that refers to animal life.

FCA

An acronym for Flood Control Act of 1936.

FCF

An acronym for Fishermen's Contingency Fund.

FCPCS

An acronym for Federal Compliance with Pollution Control Standards.

FCs

See Fluorocarbons.

Fe

Iron.

Feasibility Assessment (FA)

A basic analysis that provides an initial determination of the viability of a proposed alternative for corrective action, mitigation, and site remediation purposes.

Feasibility, Plan Review Criterion

The determination of whether the assigned tasks could be accomplished by using available resources. *See* Acceptability of Plan Review Criterion.

Feasibility Study (FS)

1) A formal CERCLA document involving a process that emphasizes data analysis. The FS is undertaken by a lead agency (or responsible party if the responsible party will be developing a cleanup proposal) for developing, evaluating, and selecting remedial actions. The feasibility study is normally performed concurrently and in an interdependent fashion with the RCRA remedial investigation. The feasibility study uses data obtained during the remedial investigation. The data is used to define the objectives of the response action and to broadly develop remedial action alternatives. Finally, the feasibility study involves a detailed analysis of the limited number of alternatives that remain after the initial screening stage. The primary factors considered in screening and analyzing the alternatives are: public health, economics, engineering practicality, environmental impacts, and institutional/political issues. *See* Remedial Investigation/ Feasibility Study (RI/FS). 2) Processes undertaken by the lead agency (or responsible party if the responsible party will be developing a cleanup proposal) for developing, evaluating, and selecting remedial actions that emphasize data analysis. *See* 40 CFR 300.6 for additional explanation. 3) Analyses of the practicability of a proposal. The term can apply to a variety of proposed corrective or regulatory actions. 4) In research, a small-scale investigation of a problem to ascertain whether or not a proposed research approach is likely to provide useful data.

Feasibility Test

An operation plan review criteria to determine whether or not a plan is within the capacity of the resources that can be made available. *See* Logistic Implications Test.

Feasible

Capable of being accomplished in a successful manner within a reasonable period of time, taking into account economic, environmental, social, and technical factors. With regard to economic feasibility, the issue shall be whether the plan as revised could be conducted on a commercial basis within 3 years of the submission of the plan and not solely on the basis of whether extra cost is required to carry out the alternatives.

Feasible Alternatives
Chemical or nonchemical procedures that can reasonably accomplish the same functions with comparable effectiveness and reliability, taking into account economic, environmental, social, and technological factors and timeliness of control.

Feasible Mitigation Measure
A condition attached to the approval of an activity that if implemented would substantially reduce any adverse impact, taking into account economic, environmental, social, and technological factors and timeliness of control.

Feasible Water Treatment
Feasible actions with the use of the best technology, treatment techniques, and other means that the Administrator of EPA finds, after examination for efficacy under field conditions and not solely under laboratory conditions, are available (taking cost into consideration). Granular activated carbon is feasible for the control of synthetic organic chemicals. Each national primary drinking water regulation that establishes a maximum contaminant level shall list the technology, treatment techniques, and other means that the Administrator finds to be feasible for purposes of meeting such maximum contaminant level.

Feature
1) A nonportable object, not recoverable from its matrix (usually in an archaeological site) without destroying its integrity. Examples of features include rock paintings, hearths, and posts. 2) In cartography, any object or configuration of ground or water represented on the face of the map or chart.

Feature Line Overlap
A series of overlapping air photographs that follow the line of a ground feature, e.g., river, road, railway, etc.

Fecal Coliform Bacteria
Bacteria found in the intestinal tracts of mammals. Their presence in water or sludge is an indicator of pollution and possible contamination by pathogens.

Federal Agencies
Departments, agencies, corporations, or instrumentalities of the United States, including the United States Postal Service, the Federal National Mortgage Association, and the Federal Home Loan Mortgage Corporation.

Federal Air Quality Permit Requirements (FAQPR)
The permit program required by Section 7502(b)(6) of the CAA in accordance with regulations issued by the Administrator for the determination of baseline emissions in a manner consistent with the assumptions underlying the applicable approved state implementation plan, when the permitting agency determines that:

- by the time the source is to commence operation, sufficient offsetting emissions reductions have been obtained, such that total allowable emissions from existing sources in the region, from new or modified sources that are not major emitting facilities, and from the proposed source will be sufficiently less than total emissions from existing sources prior to the application for such permit to construct or modify a facility in accordance with reasonable further progress guidelines; or

- in the case of a new or modified major stationary source that is located in a zone (within the nonattainment area) identified by the Administrator, in consultation with the Secretary of Housing and Urban Development, as a zone to which economic development should be targeted, that emissions of such pollutant resulting from the proposed new or modified major stationary source will not cause or contribute to emissions levels that exceed the allowance permitted for such pollutant for such area from new or modified major stationary sources;

- the proposed source is required to comply with the lowest achievable emission rate;

- the owner/operator of the proposed new or modified source has demonstrated that all major stationary sources owned or operated by such person (or by any entity controlling, controlled by, or under common control with such person) in such state are subject to emission limitations and are in compliance, or on a schedule for compliance, with all applicable emission limitations and standards under this chapter;

- the Administrator has not determined that the applicable implementation plan is not being adequately implemented for the nonattainment area in which the proposed source is to be constructed or modified in accordance with regulatory requirements; and

- an analysis of alternative sites, sizes, production processes, and environmental control techniques for such proposed source demonstrates that benefits of the proposed source significantly outweigh the environmental and social costs imposed as a result of its location, construction, or modification.

Federal Benefit Program

Any program administered or funded by the federal government, or by any agent or state on behalf of the federal government, providing cash or in-kind assistance in the form of payments, grants, loans, or loan guarantees to individuals.

Federal Building

1) Any building in the United States that is controlled by the federal government for its use. 2) Any building to be constructed by, or for the use of, any federal agency that is not legally subject to state or local building codes or similar requirements. 3) Any building, structure, or facility, or part thereof, including the associated energy consuming support systems, that is constructed, renovated, leased, or purchased in whole or in part for use by the federal government and that consumes energy. 4) A collection of buildings, structures, or facilities and the energy consuming support systems for such collection.

Federal Coastline Intervention

Actions upon a determination of a grave and imminent danger to the coastline or related interests of the United States, such actions include a) re-moval or elimination of the threatened pollution damage; b) directly or indirectly undertake the whole or any part of any salvage or other action he/she could require or direct; and c) remove, and, if necessary, destroy the ship and cargo that is the source of the danger.

Federal Conservation of Migratory Nongame Birds

Research and conservation activities, in coordination with federal, state, international, and private organizations, to conserve migratory nongame birds under existing authorities provided by the Migratory Bird Treaty Act and Migratory Bird Conservation Act (MBTA/MBCA)(16 USC 701-715) and Section 8A of the Endangered Species Act (16 USC 1537a(e)) implementing the Convention on Nature Protection and Wildlife Preservation in the Western Hemisphere. These activities include:

- monitoring and assessing population trends and status of species, subspecies, and populations of all migratory nongame birds;

- identifying the effects of environmental changes and human activities on species, subspecies, and populations of all migratory nongame birds;

- identifying species, subspecies, and populations of all migratory nongame birds that, without additional conservation actions, are likely to become candidates for listing under the Endangered Species Act of 1973, as amended (16 USC 1531-1543);

- identifying conservation actions to ensure that species, subspecies, and populations of migratory nongame birds identified above do not reach the point at which the measures provided pursuant to the Endangered Species Act of 1973, as amended (16 USC 1531-1543) become necessary;

- identifying lands and waters in the United States and other nations in the Western Hemisphere whose protection, management, or acquisition will foster the conservation of species, subspecies, and populations of migratory nongame birds.

Federal Coordinating Officers

The individuals designated by the president or his/her representative to coordinate overall federal response activities under the Disaster Relief Act (DRA), Public Law 93-288.

Federal Facilities Compliance Agreement

An interagency agreement usually entered into between the United States Environmental Protection Agency and the head of an executive agency. The content of the Agreement generally pertains to environmental cleanup, ensuring that any environmental impacts associated with past and/or present activities at a federal facility are thoroughly and adequately investigated so that appropriate remedial response actions can be formulated, assessed, and implemented as each individual situation warrants.

Federal Facility

Any building, installation, structure, land, or public work owned by or leased to the federal government. Ships at sea, aircraft in the air, land forces on maneuvers, and other mobile facilities are not considered federal facilities. United States government installations located on foreign soil or on land outside the jurisdiction of the United States government are not considered federal facilities. *See* Federal Building; Federal Land.

Federal Facility Pollution Control Requirements

The requirements of each department, agency, and instrumentality of the executive, legislative, and judicial branches of the federal government, to be subject to, and comply with, all federal, state, interstate, and local requirements, administrative authority, and process and sanctions respecting the control and abatement of air pollution in the same manner, and to the same extent as any nongovernmental entity, whether substantive or procedural include the following: a) any recordkeeping or reporting requirement; b) any requirement respecting permits; c) any requirement to pay a fee or charge; d) any process and sanction, whether enforced in federal, state, or local courts; and e) any other requirement whatsoever. The President may exempt any emission source of any department, agency, or instrumentality in the executive branch from

compliance with such a requirement if he/she determines it to be in the paramount interest of the United States to do so, except that no exemption may be granted to extremely hazardous or life threatening sources.

Federal Field Exercises

Exercises of the Federal Radiological Emergency Response Plan (FRERP) involving federal agencies in support of the cognizant federal agency and state and local governments.

Federal Financial Assistance

Any form of loan, grant, guarantee, insurance, payment, rebate, subsidy, or any other form of direct or indirect federal assistance (other than general or special revenue sharing or formula grants made to states) approved by any federal officer or agency; or any loan made or purchased by any bank, savings and loan association, or similar institution subject to regulation by the Board of Governors of the Federal Reserve System, the Federal Deposit Insurance Corporation, the Comptroller of the Currency, the Federal Home Loan Bank Board, the Federal Savings and Loan Insurance Corporation, or the National Credit Union Administration.

Federal Implementation Plan

A plan (or portion thereof) promulgated by the Administrator of EPA to fill all or a portion of a gap or otherwise correct all or a portion of an inadequacy in a state implementation plan (SIP), and that includes enforceable emission limitations or other control measures, means or techniques (including economic incentives, such as marketable permits or auctions of emissions allowances), and provides for attainment of the relevant national ambient air quality standard.

Federal Insecticide, Fungicide, and Rodenticide Act of 1972 (FIFRA; 7 USC 135 et seq.)

The environmental pesticide control act requiring a five-phase registration process for pesticides to be used in connection with agricultural activities. Registration covers manufacturers as well as users, and outlines proper storage, use, handling, disposing, etc. The Act establishes penalties for improper use and violations. The primary focus of FIFRA is to provide federal control of pesticide distribution, sale, and use. EPA was given authority under FIFRA not only to study the consequences of pesticide usage but also to require users (farmers, utility companies, and others) to register when purchasing pesticides. Through later amendments to the law, users also must take exams for certification as applicators of pesticides. All pesticides used in the U.S. must be registered (licensed) by EPA. Registration ensures that pesticides will be properly labeled and that, if used in accordance with specifications, will not cause unreasonable harm to the environment.

Federal Land

All lands owned or controlled by the United States, including the Outer Continental Shelf, and any land in which the United States has reserved mineral interests, except lands a) held in trust for Native American Indians or Alaska natives; b) owned by Native American Indians or Alaska natives with federal restrictions on the title; c) within any area of the National Park System, the National Wildlife Refuge System, the National Wilderness Preservation System, the National System of Trails, or the Wild and Scenic Rivers System; or d) within military reservations.

Federal Land Managers

With respect to public lands, the Secretary of the department, or the head of any other agency or instrumentality of the United States, having primary management authority over such lands. In the case of any public lands or Native American Indian lands with respect to which no department, agency, or instrumentality has primary management authority, such term means the Secretary of the Interior. If the Secretary of the Interior consents, the responsibilities (in whole or in part) under the Archaeological Resources Protection Act (ARPA) of the Secretary of any department (other than the department of the Interior) or the head of any other agency or instrumentality may be delegated to the Secretary of the Interior with respect to any land managed by such other Secre-

tary or agency head, and in any such case, the term "federal land manager" means the Secretary of the Interior.

Federal Land Policy and Management Act of 1976 (FLPMA)

An act establishing federal policy regarding the retention, disposal, periodic inventorying, land-use planning, adjudication, and management of public lands in a manner that will protect and enhance the quality of aesthetic, historic, ecologic, physical environments, water, and wildlife habitats.

Federal Mining Inspector

Personnel of the Office of Surface Mining Reclamation and Enforcement and such additional personnel of the United States Geological Survey, Bureau of Land Management, or of the Mining Enforcement and Safety Administration so designated by the Secretary of the Department of Interior (DOI), or such other personnel of the Forest Service, Soil Conservation Service, or the Agricultural Stabilization and Conservation Service as arranged by appropriate agreement with the Secretary on a reimbursable or other basis.

Federal Modal Agencies
See Transportation Operating Agencies.

Federal Personnel

Officers and employees of the government of the United States, members of the uniformed services (including members of the Reserve), individuals entitled to receive immediate or deferred retirement benefits under any retirement program of the government of the United States (including survivor benefits).

Federal Radiological Emergency Response Plans (FRERP)

Comprehensive, coordinated plans broadly describing the entire federal government response to radiological emergencies in support of federal, state, and local government agencies.

Federal Radiological Monitoring and Assessment Centers (FRMAC)

Centers at or near the scene of a radiological incident that coordinates all offsite federal radiological monitoring and assessment activities. Information related to the offsite radiological impact of the accident is transmitted from the FRMAC to the cognizant federal agency and to the state(s).

Federal Radiological Monitoring and Assessment Plans (FRMAPs)

Plans contained in the Federal Radiological Emergency Response Plan for coordinating federal offsite radiological monitoring and assessment with that of the affected state(s).

Federal Response Centers (FRCs)

Centers established by the Federal Emergency Management Agency at locations identified in conjunction with the state that serves as a focal point for federal response team interactions with the state.

Federal Stock Number (FSN)

The Federal Stock Number of an item of supply consists of the applicable 4-digit class code number from the Federal Supply Classification plus a sequentially assigned 7-digit Federal Item Identification Number. The number shall be arranged as follows: 4210-196-5439. *See* National Stock Number. Note: Federal Stock Numbers were replaced by National Stock Numbers effective 30 September 1974.

Federal Transport Agencies

See Transportation Operating Agencies.

Federal Water Pollution Control Act (FWPCA)

Also known as the Clean Water Act, FWPCA is the federal statute that established regulatory and grant programs to "reach and maintain the chemical, physical, and biological integrity of the nation's waters."

The Act's most important provisions are those relating to the National Pollution Discharge Elimi-

nation System (NPDES); the Section 208 Areawide Waste Treatment Planning Program; dredge and fill permit requirements; and grants for Wastewater Treatment Facilities Planning. Additional goals of the Federal Water Pollution Act (FWPCA) and amendments (aka the Clean Water Act) are to eliminate the discharge of pollutants into navigable waters; provide interim goals for the protection and propagation of fish, shellfish, and wildlife and provide for recreation in and on water; establish policy that prohibits the discharge of toxic pollutants in toxic amounts; provide financial assistance to construct publicly owned treatment works; and establish programs for the control of nonpoint sources of pollution.

Federally Constructed Housing

Residential or multifamily housing that is constructed by the following: a) agencies of the federal government to provide dwelling accommodations for particular types or classes of persons under programs administered by such federal agencies (including all housing constructed by the department of Defense to provide dwelling accommodations for personnel of the armed services or for such personnel and their families); or b) agencies of a state or local government, with financial assistance in any form from the federal government, to provide dwelling accommodations for particular types or classes of persons under programs administered by such state or local agencies.

Federally Permitted Releases

As defined by Section 101(10) of CERCLA: 1) Discharges in compliance with a permit under Section 402 of the Federal Water Pollution Control Act and subject to a condition of such permit. 2) Discharges resulting from circumstances identified and reviewed and made part of the public record with respect to a permit issued or modified under Section 402 of the Federal Water Pollution Control Act and subject to a condition of such permit. 3) Continuous or anticipated intermittent discharges from a point source, identified in a permit or permit application under Section 402 of the Federal Water Pollution Control Act, that are caused by events occurring within the scope of relevant operating or treatment systems. 4) Discharges in compliance with a legally enforceable final permit issued pursuant to Section 3005(a) through (d) of the Solid Waste Disposal Act from a hazardous waste treatment, storage, or disposal facility when such permit specifically identifies the hazardous substances and makes such substances subject to a standard of practice, control procedure or bioassay limitation or condition, or other control on the hazardous substances in such releases. 5) Releases in compliance with a legally enforceable final permit issued pursuant to Section 3005 (a) through (d) of the Solid Waste Disposal Act from a hazardous waste treatment, storage, or disposal facility when such permit specifically identifies the hazardous substances and makes such substances subject to a standard of practice, control procedure or bioassay limitation or condition, or other control on the hazardous substances in such releases. 6) Any release in compliance with a legally enforceable permit issued under Section 102 or Section 103 of the Marine Protection, Research, and Sanctuaries Act of 1972. 7) Any injection of fluids authorized under federal underground injection control programs or state programs submitted for federal approval (and not disapproved by the Administrator of EPA) pursuant to part C of the Safe Drinking Water Act under Stion 111, Section 112, Title I Part C, Title 1 Part D, or state implementation plans submitted in accordance with Section 110 of the Clean Air Act (and not disapproved by the Administrator of EPA), including any schedule or waiver granted, promulgated, or approved under these sections. 8) Any injection of fluids or other materials authorized under state law for the purpose of:

- stimulating or treating wells for the production of crude oil, natural gas, or water;

- secondary, tertiary, or other enhanced recovery of crude oil or natural gas; or

- materials that are brought to the surface in conjunction with the production of crude oil or natural gas and that are reinjected;

9) The introduction of any pollutant specified in and in compliance with applicable pretreatment standards of Section 307(b) or (c) of the Clean Water Act and enforceable requirements in a pretreatment program submitted by a state or municipality for federal approval under Section 402 of such Act. 10) Any release of source, special nuclear, or by-product materials, as those terms are defined in the Atomic Energy Act of 1954, in compliance with a legally enforceable license, permit, regulation, or order issued pursuant to the Act. *See* 40 CFR 300.6.

Fee Area
Any area that was acquired in fee by the United States and is administered, either solely or primarily, by the Secretary of Interior through the United States Fish and Wildlife Service (USFWS).

Fee Simple, Absolute
Often called a fee or fee simple; the most comprehensive ownership of real property known to the law; the largest bundle of ownership rights in real estate.

Feed Grains
Corn, grain sorghums, and, if designated by the Secretary of Agriculture (DOA), barley, and if for any crop the producer so requests for purposes of having acreage devoted to the production of wheat considered as devoted to the production of feed grains. Feed grains shall include oats and rye and barley, if not designated by the Secretary, provided that acreages of corn, grain sorghums, and, if designated by the Secretary, barley, shall not be planted in lieu of acreages of oats and rye and barley if not designated by the Secretary.

Feed Materials Production Center
A DOE-owned manufacturing facility for the production of uranium metal used in U.S. defense programs.

Feedback
The two-way flow of information between personnel or organizations.

Feedback Loop
A continuous communication network used to achieve feedback.

Feedlot
A relatively small, confined area for the controlled feeding of animals that tends to concentrate large amounts of animal wastes that cannot be absorbed by the soil and, hence, may be carried to nearby streams or lakes by rainfall runoff.

Feedstock
Raw material supplied to a machine or processing plant from which other products can be made. For example, polyvinyl chloride and polyethylene are raw chemicals used to produce plastic tiles, mats, fenders, cushions, and traffic cones.

Feedwater
Water supplied to the reactor pressure vessel (in a Boiling Water Reactor) or the steam generator (in a Pressurized Water Reactor) that removes heat from the reactor fuel rods by boiling and becoming steam. The steam becomes the driving force for the plant turbine generator.

FEFGC
An acronym for Fuel Element Failure Gas Chromatograph.

Fellowship Award
Payments provided in accordance with an agency project to an individual who is devoting essentially full time to, study or research in the field in which such fellowship was awarded, in an institution of higher education, and is not engaging in gainful employment other than part-time employment in teaching, research, or similar activities.

FEMA (Federal Emergency Management Agency)
The agency responsible for providing a federal focus on emergency management in the United States. This includes natural disasters such as earthquakes, hurricanes, tornadoes, floods, technological calamities, and national security crises.

FEMA; P.O. Box 70274; Washington, DC 20024; 202/646-4600.

Femoral
A species descriptor that refers to the thigh.

Fence Line Concentration
Modeled or measured concentrations of air pollutants found at the boundaries of a property on which a pollution source is located. Usually assumed to be the nearest location at which an exposure of the general population could occur.

Fens
Types of wetlands that accumulate peat deposits. Fens are less acidic than bogs, deriving most of their water from groundwater rich in calcium and magnesium.

FERC
An acronym for Federal Energy Regulatory Commission.

Fermentation
Chemical reactions accompanied by living microbes that are supplied with nutrients and other critical conditions such as heat, pressure, and light that are specific to the reaction at hand.

Ferret
An aircraft, ship, or vehicle especially equipped for the detection, location, recording, and analyzing of electromagnetic radiation.

Ferry Vessels
Vessels that are limited in their use to the carriage of deck passengers or vehicles or both, operate on a short run on a frequent schedule between two points over the most direct water route, other than in ocean or coastwise service, and are offered as a public service of a type normally attributed to a bridge or tunnel. These types of vessels are common on the Puget Sound, in Seattle, WA, and other places.

Fertile
1) The ability to achieve conception and to produce offspring. For litter-bearing species, the number of offspring per litter is also used as a measure of fertility. Reduced fertility is sometimes referred to as subfertility. 2) Of a nuclide, capable of being transformed, directly or indirectly, into a fissile nuclide by neutron capture.

Fertilization
A species descriptor that means the union of a sperm and egg that stimulates growth of the embryo.

Fertilizers
Materials such as nitrogen and phosphorus that provide nutrients for plants. Commercially sold fertilizers may contain other chemicals or may be in the form of processed sewage sludge.

Fetotoxic
Having the ability to harm the fetus.

Fetus
The post-embryonic stage of the developing young. In humans, from the end of the second month of pregnancy up to birth.

FFCA
An acronym for Federal Facilities Compliance Agreement.

FHAR
An acronym for Fire Hazard Analysis Report.

FIANG
An acronym for Federal Inspector for Alaska Natural Gas (Transportation System).

Fibrosis
Formation of scar tissue in the lung or other tissues, usually as a result of inflammation occurring over a long period of time.

FICI
An acronym for Failed Instrument Component Inspection.

Fiduciary
1) Used as a noun — a person or entity who is in a position of trust in relation to another party, or in a confidential or trust position. For example, the fiduciary of an estate is the executor or administrator. 2) Used as an adjective — confidential, such as a confidential relationship. Fiduciary refers to the relationship of an agent to his/her principal.

Field Audits
Audits for verifying a) that operational aspects and procedures are in accordance with established protocols and adopted QA/QC plans; b) the collection of all samples including duplicates and field blanks; c) that documentation is in order and sufficient to establish the collection location of any sample collected; d) discrepancies that exist and initiating corrective action as appropriate; and e) or conducting tasks associated with collecting additional samples.

Field Command Posts
Designated areas at or near the scene of an emergency that are the collection centers for the on-scene commander and that are used for response, assessment, and communications to the emergency control center (ECC).

Field Control
A series of points whose relative positions and elevations are known. These positions are used in basic data in mapping and charting. Normally, these positions are established by survey methods, and are sometimes referred to as "trig control" or "trigonometrical net(work)." *See* Control Point.

Field Elements
A general term for any officially established DOE departmental components (excluding individual duty stations) located outside the Washington, DC, metropolitan area.

Field Facility/Building Emergency Plans
Plans prepared by DOE headquarters, field elements, field contractors, or offices under field element jurisdiction to guide response to specific

buildings or facilities (e.g., office buildings, process buildings, laboratories).

Field Gases

Feedstock gases entering the gas processing plant.

Field Laboratory Sample

Any material removed from a site or structure on which testing and analyses can be conducted to aid in ascertaining the presence, extent, or source of contaminants.

Field Level Exemptions

An interim releases from a mandatory DOE standard, granted by the field organization after a request for a temporary or permanent exemption. Such exemptions shall not exceed 180 days and are not renewable.

Field Monitoring

The use of sensitive detection equipment by trained personnel to perform measurements to determine the presence and levels of radioactive or other hazardous substance contamination at selected geographic locations in the offsite environment.

Field Observations

Watching people's behavior, or physical changes occurring in a specific environmental setting. It is the most direct and reliable means for an environmental planner to get information about the way a facility and its personnel operate. Two data objectives of field observation are assessing activities and inventorying environmental settings and features. The focus is to measure and detail facility/project activity, settings, work group interactions, and relationships.

Field Operations Plans

Documents that are prepared for either continuous or site specific data collection activities (air, water, pesticides, hazardous waste, etc.). Plans typically describe project organization and responsibilities, project description (objectives, scope, schedule of tasks and milestones, data usage, monitoring network/sampling and analysis design and rationale), data quality objectives, sampling procedures, calibration, analytical methods, documentation/data reporting, data assessment, audits, corrective action, reports, and safety.

Field Organizations

First line DOE field elements that carry the organizational responsibilities for a) managing and executing assigned programs; b) directing contractors who conduct the programs; and c)assuring that environment, safety, and health are integral parts of each program. *See* Field Elements.

Field Photography

Photography, other than large-format photography, intended for the purpose of producing documentation, cataloging, and inventorying the natural and built environment through various annotated and dated photos. Field photography is used for recording existing conditions to discern visible compliance status; studying selected site details, and sequential events such as the rate at which a leak spreads; and analyzing operational systems, as well as supplementing and verifying data.

Field Records

Notes of measurements taken, field photographs, and other recorded information intended for the purpose of producing documentation.

Field Sampling Plans

Plans that provide guidance for all fieldwork by defining in detail the sampling and data-gathering methods to be used on a project.

Field Sampling Team (FST)

The FST consist of two teams; one that identifies and quantifies radiological releases from a site during an emergency and one that identifies and quantifies HazMat releases during an emergency.

Field Site Emergency Plans

Plans prepared by field element contractors or other entities under field element jurisdiction to guide their responses for identified credible emergencies. *See* Field Elements; Field Organizations.

FIFRA
See Federal Insecticide, Fungicide and Rodenticide Act of 1972.

Fifty-Year Flood Flow
The magnitude of peak flow that one would expect to be equalled or exceeded, on the average, only once every 50 years. This flow is estimated by empirical relationships between precipitation and watershed characteristics and runoff and then modified by direct channel cross section measurements and local experience.

Filaments
Individual fibers of indefinite length used in tows, yarns, or roving.

Fill Materials
1) Materials used for the primary purpose of replacing an aquatic area with dry land or of changing the bottom elevation of a waterbody. The term does not include any pollutant discharged into the water primarily to dispose of waste, as that activity is regulated under Section 402 of the Clean Water Act. 2) Nonnative soils, construction materials, debris, etc. used to level ground prior to building activities. *See* Filling.

Fill Pipe
A fuel tank fill pipe, fill neck, fill inlet, and closure.

Filled by Pressure
A means of filling a pressure vessel whereby the quantity of compressed gas in the vessel at normal temperature is determined by a pressure gage or gages.

Filled by Volume
A means of filling a tank or cylinder whereby the volume of liquid in the vessel is determined by measuring the liquid level.

Filled by Weight
A means of filling a tank or cylinder whereby the amount of the product in the vessel is determined by weight.

Filler
A substance carried in an ammunition container such as a projectile, mine, bomb, or grenade. A filler may be an explosive, chemical, or inert substance.

Filling
Depositing dirt and mud or other materials into aquatic areas to create more dry land, usually for agricultural or commercial development purposes. Such activities often damage the ecology of the area.

Film Badges
Packets of photographic film used for the approximate measurement of radiation exposure for personnel monitoring purposes. Badges may contain two or more films of differing sensitivity, and they may contain filters that shield parts of the film from certain types of radiation.

Filter Feeding
A species descriptor that means in marine life, the process of filtering food from water through a siphoning organ.

Filters, Radiology
The two types of radiological filters are a) primary — shoots of material, usually metal, placed in a beam of radiation to remove, as far as possible, the less penetrating components of the beam; and b) secondary — sheets of material of lower atomic number, relative to that of the primary filter, placed in the filtered beam of radiation to remove characteristic radiation produced by the primary filter.

Filtration
A treatment process, under the control of qualified operators, for removing solid (particulate) matter from water by passing the water through porous media such as sand or a manmade filter.

The process is often used to remove particles that contain pathogenic organisms.

Fimbriate

A species descriptor that means fringed, as the edge of a petal or the opening of a duct.

Fin

A species descriptor pertaining to the portion of a fish's body that propels it or assists in swimming.

Final Authorizations

Approvals by EPA of a state program that has met the requirements of Section 3006(b) of RCRA (Resource Conservation and Recovery Act) and the applicable requirements of 40 CFR 271, Subpart A.

Final Closure

The closure of all hazardous waste management units at the facility in accordance with all applicable closure requirements so that hazardous waste management activities under Parts 264 and 265 of 40 CFR are no longer conducted at the facility unless subject to the provisions in Section 262.34.

Final Disposal Procedures

See Explosive Ordnance Disposal Procedures.

Final Plan

A plan for which drafts and addendums have been coordinated and approved and that has been signed by or on behalf of a competent authority.

Financial Assistance

Any form of loan, grant, guaranty, insurance, payment, rebate, subsidy, or any other form of direct or indirect federal assistance other than a) deposit or account insurance for customers of banks, savings and loan associations, credit unions, or similar institutions; b) the purchase of mortgages or loans by the Government National Mortgage Association, the Federal National Mortgage Association, or the Federal Home Loan Mortgage Corporation; c) assistance for environmental studies, planning, and assessments that are required incident to the issuance of permits or other authorizations under federal law; and d) assistance pursuant to programs entirely unrelated to development, such as any federal or federally assisted public assistance program or any federal seniors or disability insurance program.

Financial Assurance

A means (such as insurance, guarantee, surety bond, letter of credit, or qualification as a self-insurer) by the operator of a facility such as a landfill to ensure financial capability for cleaning up possible environmental releases and closure of that facility.

Financial Property Accounting

The establishment and maintenance of property accounts in monetary terms; the rendition of property reports in monetary terms.

Finding of No Significant Impact (FONSI)

1) A term used to describe the outcome of the RI/FS process when no adverse environmental effects have been identified. 2) A document, defined at 40 CFR 1508.13, prepared to record a departmental decision that the environmental impacts of an action considered in an environmental assessment will not have a significant effect on the human environment and that an environmental impact statement is not required for a proposed action.

Findings

1) Statements of fact concerning a condition that was investigated during an environmental audit or appraisal. They may be a simple statement of proficiency, or a description of a deficiency. 2) The results of an investigation; the salient, factual, and analytical highlights of an accident/incident. 3) DOE Tiger Team Assessments that include findings in Environmental and Management areas based on the following: a) observation of routine operations, emergency exercises, and the physical condition of the site and facilities; b) interviews with management, staff, operators, and craft personnel; and c) review of policy statements, records, procedures, and other relevant documents.

FIP
See Federal Implementation Plan (CAA).

Fire Hazards
Inherent hazards that include flammables, combustible liquids, pyrophorics, and oxidizers. Refer to 29 CFR 1910-1200.

Fire Protection
Protection from a broad range of fire risks normally included in the analysis conducted by fire protection engineers. These include some aspects of related perils such as explosion, windstorm, earthquake, lightning, and water damage. Fire prevention programs are a necessary part of fire protection programs. *See* Fire Protection Engineering.

Fire Protection Engineering
The branch of professional engineering that requires such education and experience as is necessary to understand the engineering problems relating to the safeguarding of life and property from fire and fire-related hazards; and requires the ability to apply this knowledge to the identification, evaluation, correction, or prevention of present or potential fire and fire related panic hazards in buildings, groups of buildings, or communities, and to recommend the arrangement and use of fire resistant building materials and fire detection and extinguishing systems, devices, and apparatus in order to protect life and property.

Fire Protection Systems
Systems designed to control or extinguish fires or to limit the extent of fire damage. These include a) automatic suppression systems such as sprinklers, Halo, or carbon dioxide systems; b) watchmen or automatic detection systems, water supplies, plus a fire department; c) fire walls and doors; and d) in the case of a facility, building separation with credit for water supplies plus an on-site fire department.

Fire Storm
A stationary mass fire, generally in built-up urban areas, generating strong, inrushing winds from all sides; the winds keep the fires from spreading while adding fresh oxygen to increase their intensity.

Firearms
All weapons capable of propelling a missile by means of an explosive charge, as well as all explosive ordnance, ESS equipment, chemical weapons, and pyrotechnic devices.

Fireball
The luminous sphere of hot gases that forms a few millionths of a second after detonation of a nuclear weapon and immediately starts expanding and cooling.

Fires
Four classifications of fires have been designated. 1) Class A — fires in ordinary combustible materials, such as wood, cloth, paper, rubber, and many plastics. 2) Class B — fires in flammable liquids, gases, and greases. 3) Class C — fires that involve energized electrical equipment where the electrical nonconductivity of the extinguishing media is of importance. When electrical equipment is de-energized, extinguishers for Class A or B fires typically may be used. 4) Class D — fires in combustible metals, such as magnesium, titanium, zirconium, sodium, and potassium.

First Aid
One-time treatment and subsequent observation of minor scratches, cuts, burns, splinters, and so forth, that do not typically require professional medical care.

First Attempt at Repair
To take rapid action for the purpose of stopping or reducing leakage of organic material to atmosphere using "best management practices."

First Draw
The water that comes out when a faucet in the kitchen or bathroom is first opened. This water is likely to have the highest level of lead contamination from plumbing materials.

First Federal Official

The first federal representatives of a participating agency of the National Response Team to arrive at the scene of a discharge or a release. These officials coordinate activities under this plan and may initiate, in consultation with the OSC, any necessary actions until the arrival of the predesignated OSC. A state with primary jurisdiction over a site covered by a cooperative agreement will act in the stead of the First Federal official for any incident at the site.

First Light

The beginning of morning nautical twilight; i.e., when the center of the morning sun is 12° below the horizon.

First Pass Effect

Reduction in a substance's systemic availability resulting from metabolism or excretion by the first major organ of contact with such capability after the absorption process. This phenomenon of removing chemicals after absorption before entering the general systemic circulation can occur in the lung or liver.

First Responder Team (FRT)

The first unit, usually fire or police, on the scene of a hazardous incident.

First Responder's Estimate of the Situation

The logical process of reasoning by which a first responder considers all the circumstances affecting the hazardous situation and arrives at a decision as to a course of action to be taken to accomplish the medical, containment, and cleanup efforts.

A first responder's estimate that typically considers a hazardous situation in future terms, and requires the making of assumptions, is called a first responder's long-range estimate of the situation.

Fish

1) Any of a wide variety of cold-blooded aquatic vertebrates that have typically an elongated somewhat spindle-shaped body terminating in a broad caudal fin, limbs in the form of fins when present

at all, and a 2-chambered heart by which blood is sent through thoracic gills to be oxygenated. 2) Finfish, mollusks, crustaceans, and all other forms of marine animal and plant life other than marine mammals, birds, and highly migratory species.

Fish and Wildlife

1) Any member of the animal kingdom, including without limitation any mammal, fish, bird (including any migratory, nonmigratory, or endangered bird for which protection is also afforded by treaty or other international agreement), amphibian, reptile, mollusk, crustacean, arthropod or other invertebrate, and includes any part, product, egg, or offspring thereof, or the dead body or parts thereof. 2) Wild vertebrate animals that are in an unconfined state, including, but not limited to, nongame fish and wildlife.

Fish and Wildlife Conservation

A term referring to the use of methods and procedures necessary to ensure to the maximum extent practicable, the well-being and enhancement of fish and wildlife and their habitats for the ecological, educational, aesthetic, cultural, recreational, and scientific enrichment of the public. These methods and procedures may include, but are not limited to, any activity associated with scientific resources management, such as: research, census, law enforcement, habitat acquisition, maintenance, development, information education, population manipulation, propagation, technical assistance to private landowners, live trapping, and transplantation.

Fish and Wildlife Service (FWS)

See U.S. Fish and Wildlife Service.

Fish Ladder

A species descriptor that means a device constructed by people that assists spawning fish to pass an obstruction, usually a dam.

Fish Restoration and Management Projects

Projects designed for the restoration and management of all species of fish that have material value in connection with sport or recreation in the marine and/or fresh waters of the United States. Projects include the following: a) research into problems of fish management and culture necessary to efficient administration affecting fish resources; b) the acquisition of such facts as are necessary to guide and direct the regulation of fishing by law, including the extent of the fish population, the drain on the fish supply from fishing and/or natural causes, the necessity of legal regulation of fishing, and the effects of any measures of regulation that are applied; c) the formulation and adoption of plans of restocking waters with food and game fishes according to natural areas or districts to which such plans are applicable, together with the acquisition of such facts as are necessary for the formulation, execution, and testing the efficacy of such plans; and d) the selection, restoration, rehabilitation, and improvement of areas of water or land adaptable as hatching, feeding, resting, or breeding places for fish, including acquisition, condemnation, lease, or gift of such areas or estates or interests, and the construction of such works including preliminary or incidental costs and expenses incurred.

Fishing Gear

Any commercial fishing vessel, and any equipment of such vessel, whether or not attached to such a vessel.

Fissile

Of a nuclide, easily undergoing nuclear fission (the splitting apart of the nuclei of atoms), as a result of interaction with slow neutrons.

Fissile Class I

Packages that may be transported in unlimited numbers and in any arrangement and that require no nuclear criticality safety controls during transportation. For purposes of nuclear criticality safety control, a transport index is not assigned to Fissile Class I packages. However, the external radiation levels may require a transport index number.

Fissile Class II

Packages that may be transported in any arrangement but in numbers that do not exceed a transport index of 50. For purposes of nuclear criticality safety control, individual packages may have a transport index of not less than 0.1 and not more than 10. However, the external radiation levels may require a higher transport index number but not to exceed 10. Such shipments require no nuclear criticality safety control by the shipper during transportation.

Fissile Class III

Shipments of packages that do not meet the requirements of Fissile Class I and II and that are controlled in transportation by special arrangements between the shipper and the carrier to provide nuclear criticality safety.

Fissile Classification

DOE's three classifications of a package or shipment of fissile materials according to the controls needed to provide nuclear criticality safety during transportation. *See* Fissile Class I to III.

Fissile Materials

1) Materials that consist of or contain one or more of the following fissile radionuclides: plutonium-238, plutonium-239, plutonium-241, uranium-233, uranium-235, neptunium-237, and curium-244. Fissile materials are classified according to the controls needed to provide nuclear criticality safety during transportation. 2) Regarding DOE Order 6430.1A, nuclides capable of undergoing fission by interaction with slow neutrons provided the effective thermal neutron production cross section, exceed the effective thermal neutron absorption cross section.

Fission

The process whereby the nucleus of a heavy element splits into (generally) two nuclei of lighter elements, with the release of substantial amounts of energy.

Fission Energy per Unit Mass of Uranium

The energy emitted by the fission of 1 gram atom of uranium-235, that equals 3.3×10^6 kilowatt hours. *See* Nuclear Fission.

Fission Products

1) A general term for the complex mixture of substances produced as a result of nuclear fission. 2) Nuclides produced either by fission or by the radioactive decay of nuclides formed by fission.

Fission to Yield Ratio

The ratio of the yield derived from nuclear fission to the total yield; it is frequently expressed in percent.

Fissionable Materials

Nuclides capable of sustaining a neutron induced fission chain reaction (e.g., uranium-233, uranium-235, plutonium-239, plutonium-238, plutonium-241, neptunium-237, americium-241, and curium-244).

Fissionable Materials Handlers

Individuals officially designated by management to manipulate or handle significant quantities of fissionable materials, or manipulate the controls of equipment used to produce, process, transfer, store, or package significant quantities of such materials.

Fissure

A fracture in a rock whose displacement is perpendicular to the break.

Fixed Assets

1) Assets of a permanent character having continuing value. 2) As used in military establishments, includes real estate and equipment installed or in use, either in productive plants or in field operations.

Fixed Capital Costs

The capital needed to provide all depreciable components.

Fixed Medical Treatment Facility

A medical treatment facility that is designed to operate for an extended period of time at a specific site.

Fixed Nuclear Facilities

Stationary nuclear installations that use or produce radioactive materials in their normal operations. These facilities include commercial nuclear power plants and other fixed facilities.

Fixed Port

Water terminals with an improved network of cargo-handling facilities designed for the transfer of oceangoing freight. *See* Port; Water Terminal.

Fixed Price Incentive Contract

A fixed price type of contract with provision for the adjustment of profit and price by a formula based on the relationship that final negotiated total cost bears to negotiated target cost as adjusted by approved changes.

Fixed Price Type Contract

A type of contract that generally provides for a firm price or, under appropriate circumstances, may provide for an adjustable price for the supplies or services being procured. Fixed price contracts are of several types so designed as to facilitate proper pricing under varying circumstances.

Fixed Sources

A stationary facility that converts fossil fuel into energy, such as steam, hot water, electricity.

Fixtures

1) Articles of personal property that have been installed in or attached to land or a building thereon, in a permanent manner, so that it is now considered to be a part of the real estate. 2) Any fixtures whose use or purpose directly applies to or augments the process of function of a profession, trade, or business.

Flagellum

A species descriptor that refers to whiplike extensions of unicellular organisms, usually used for locomotion.

Flame Field Expedients

Simple, handmade devices used to produce flame or illumination.

Flame-Resistant

Slow or unable to burn.

Flammable

1) The ability of a substance to ignite and burn. 2) Any material that can be ignited easily and that will burn rapidly.

Flammable Compressed Gases

Any flammable material having in the container a pressure that exceeds 40 psi at 100°F, is considered a flammable compressed gas. Acetylene, cyclopropane, and liquefied and nonliquefied hydrocarbon gas are examples of flammable compressed gases.

Flammable, Explosive Range

The range of gas or vapor concentration (percentage by volume in air) that will burn or explode if an ignition source is present. Limiting concentrations are commonly called the lower and upper explosive limits. Below the lower explosive limit, the mixture is too lean to burn; above the upper explosive limit, the mixture is too rich to burn.

Flammable Gas

A flammable gas is one with either of the following properties: 1) at atmospheric pressure and temperature forms a flammable mixture with air when present at a concentration of 13% or less (by volume) or that forms a range of flammable mixtures with air wider than 12% regardless of the lower limit, or 2) projects a flame more than 18 inches beyond the ignition source with valve opened fully, or the flame flashes back and burns at the valve with any degree of valve opening, when tested.

Flammable Liquid

1) According to the hazardous materials regulations, flammable liquids are liquids having the flash point below 100°F, except those liquids that meet the definition of a compressed gas, or a mixture having one or more components with a flash point of 100°F or higher that makes up at least 99% of the total volume of the mixture. 2) Liquids with a flash point above 20°F to and including 80°F as determined by Tagliabue's Open-Cup-Method. Liquid paint driers, petroleum distillates, pine oils, and liquid furniture polishes are examples of flammable liquids. When the flash point is 20°F or less it is termed an Extremely Flammable Liquid.

Flammable Solids

Any solid material, other than an explosive, that under conditions incident to transportation is liable to cause fires through friction, retained heat from manufacturing or processing, or that can be ignited readily, and when ignited, burns so vigorously and persistently as to create a serious transportation hazard. Included within this class are spontaneously combustible and water reactive materials. Wet hafnium metal, burnt fibers, and garbage tankage (containing less than 8% water) are examples of flammable solids.

Flank

A species descriptor that pertains to the side or lateral part of the body.

Flares

1) Devices that burn gaseous materials to prevent them from being released into the environment. Flares may operate continuously or intermittently and are usually found on top of a stack. Flares also burn off methane gas in a landfill. 2) Mechanical devices that use pyrotechnic materials to produce light for signaling, illuminating, or attracting attention.

Flash Blindness

Impairment of vision resulting from an intense flash of light. It includes temporary or permanent loss of visual functions and may be associated with retinal burns. *See* Dazzle.

Flash Burn

A burn caused by excessive exposure (of bare skin) to thermal radiation.

Flash Grenades

Devices that produce a brilliant flash (of about 2 million candle power) and a loud report (200 decibels at a distance of about 5 feet (1.5 meters)) without producing lethal fragmentation.

Flash Point

1) The minimum temperature at which a liquid gives off vapor within a test vessel in sufficient concentration to form an ignitable mixture with air near the surface of the liquid. 2) The lowest temperature at which a chemical will ignite. 3) The minimum temperature at which a substance gives off flammable vapor that will ignite if in contact with spark or flame.

Flashback

The movement of a flame to a fuel source; typically occurs via the vapor of a highly volatile liquid or by a flammable gas escaping from a cylinder.

Flat

A level landform composed of unconsolidated sediments — usually mud or sand. Flats may be irregularly shaped or elongate and continuous with the shore, whereas bars are generally elongate, parallel to the shore, and separated from the shore by water.

Fledgling

A species descriptor referring to the stage of development in birds when flight feathers are developed.

Flexible Response

The capability of emergency response teams for effective reaction to any hazardous situation with actions appropriate and adaptable to the circumstances existing.

Floating-Leaved Plant

A rooted, herbaceous hydrophyte with some leaves floating on the water surface. Plants such as yellow water lily (*Nuphar luteum*) that sometimes have leaves raised above the surface are considered floating-leaved plants or emergents, based on their site-specific growth patterns.

Floating Plant

A nonanchored plant that floats freely in the water or on the surface; e.g., water hyacinth (Eichhornia crassipes) or common duckweed (Lemna minor).

Floc

1) Small gelatinous masses formed in a liquid by the reaction of a coagulant additive through biochemical processes or agglomeration. 2) A clump of solids formed in sewage by biological or chemical action.

Flocculation

1) In wastewater treatment, the agglomeration of colloidal and finely divided suspended matter after coagulation by gentle stirring by either mechanical or hydraulic means. In biological wastewater treatment, where coagulation is not used, agglomeration may be accomplished biologically. 2) A process to enhance agglomeration or collection of smaller floc particles into larger, more easily settleable particles through gentle stirring by hydraulic or mechanical means. 3) The process by which clumps of solids in water or sewage are made to increase in size by biological or chemical action so that they can be separated from the water.

Flocculator

1) A mechanical device to enhance the formation of floc in a liquid. 2) An apparatus for the formation of floc in water and wastewater.

FLOCHK

An abbreviation for "flow check;" a computer code on a control computer that checks for fuel element failure.

Flocs

See Floc.

Floodplain

1) A somewhat level part of land adjacent to a river channel, formed by sediments deposited by

the river during repeated periods of flooding. 2) Lowlands adjoining inland and coastal waters and relatively flat areas and flood-prone areas of off-shore islands including, at a minimum, that area inundated by a 1% or greater chance flood in any given year. The base floodplain is defined as the 100-year (1.0%) floodplain. The critical action floodplain is defined as the 600-year (.02%) floodplain.

Floodway Encroachment Lines
The exterior limits of a designated floodway.

Floor Sweeps
Vapor collectors designed to capture vapors that are heavier than air and that collect along the floor.

Flora
A species descriptor for plants of a region or period.

Floriferous
A species descriptor that means bearing flowers.

Florology
The study of the creation of life and development of vegetative formations.

Flotation
The raising of suspended matter to the surface of the liquid in a tank as scum; by aeration, the evolution of gas, chemicals, electrolysis, heat, or bacterial decomposition, and the subsequent removal of scum by skimming.

Flow Charts
Schematic diagrams or outlines showing a succession of operations in an activity or system.

Flow Line
The general path that a particle of water follows under laminar flow conditions. Line indicating the direction followed by groundwater toward points of discharge. Flow lines are perpendicular to equipotential lines.

Flow Model
A computer model that calculates a hydraulic head field for the modeling domain using numerical methods to arrive at approximate solutions to the differential equation of groundwater flow.

Flow Net
A graphical representation of flow lines and equipotential lines for two-dimensional, steady-state groundwater flow.

Flow Path
The subsurface course a water molecule or solute flows in a given groundwater velocity field.

Flow Rates
The volume per time unit given to the flow of gases or other fluid substances that emerge from an orifice, pump, turbine, or, passes along a conduit or channel.

Flow-Through Process Tanks
Tanks that form an integral part of a production process through which there is a steady, variable, recurring, or intermittent flow of materials during the operation of the process. Flow-through process tanks do not include tanks used for the storage of materials prior to their introduction into the production process or for the storage of finished products or byproducts from the production process.

Flow Velocity
The volume of water flowing through a unit cross-sectional area of an aquifer. *See* Specific Discharge.

Flowmeter
A gauge that shows the speed of wastewater moving through a treatment plant. Also used to measure the speed of liquids moving through various industrial processes.

FLPMA
See Federal Land Policy and Management Act of 1976.

Flue Gas Scrubber

Equipment for removing ash and other by-products of combustion by the means of liquid sprays and/or filters (baffles), that effectively reduces the temperature of the solid and gaseous pollutants.

Flue Gas Desulfurization

1) A technology that uses a sorbent (lime-based filtering process) to remove sulfur dioxide from the gases produced by burning fossil fuels; sulfur dioxide reacts to the lime to produce a less harmful calcium sulfate. Flue gas desulfurization is the state-of-the-art technology in use by major SO_2 emitters. 2) The removal of sulfur oxides from exhaust gases of a boiler or industrial process; usually a wet scrubbing operation that concentrates hazardous materials in a slurry, requiring proper disposal.

Flue Gases

The gases coming out of a chimney after combustion in the burner it is venting. They can include nitrogen oxides, carbon oxides, water vapor, sulfur oxides, particles and many chemical pollutants.

Fluid Potential

The mechanical energy per unit mass of a fluid at any given point in space and time, with regard to an arbitrary state and datum.

Fluids

Materials or substances that flow or move whether in a semisolid, liquid, gas, or any other form or state, such as the following: combustible liquids, cryogenic liquids, flammable liquids, free liquids, free products, influents, natural gas liquids, pyrophoric liquids, viscous liquids.

Flumes

Natural or manmade channels that divert water.

Fluorescent Light Ballast

A device that electrically controls fluorescent light fixtures by providing a starting voltage and current and limiting the current during normal operation, includes a capacitor containing 0.1 kg or less of dielectric fluid, that may contain PCBs.

Fluorides

Gaseous, solid, or dissolved compounds containing fluorine that result from industrial processes; excessive amounts in food can lead to fluorosis.

Fluorocarbons (FCs)

Any of a number of organic compounds analogous to hydrocarbons in which one or more hydrogen atoms are replaced by fluorine. Once used in the United States as a propellant in aerosols, they are now primarily used in coolants and some industrial processes. FCs containing chlorine are called chlorofluorocarbons (CFCs). They are believed to be modifying the ozone layer in the stratosphere, thereby allowing more harmful solar radiation to reach the earth's surface.

Fluorosis

1) Accumulation of excessive fluoride in the body; characterized by increased bone density and mineral deposits in tendons, ligaments, and muscles. 2) An abnormal condition caused by excessive intake of fluorine, characterized chiefly by mottling of the teeth.

Flush

1) To open a cold-water tap to clear out all the water that may have been sitting for a long time in the pipes. In new homes, to flush a system means to send large volumes of water gushing through the unused pipes to remove loose particles of solder and flux. 2) To force large amounts of water through liquid to clean out piping or tubing, storage, or process tanks.

Flux

See Specific Discharge.

Fly Ash

1) Noncombustible residual particles from the combustion process, carried by flue gas. 2) Suspended particles, charred paper, dust, soot, and other partially oxidized matter carried in the products of combustion.

Flyway
The four administrative units used by the United States Fish and Wildlife Service and the states in the management of waterfowl populations.

FMEA
See Failure Mode and Effect Analysis.

FMPC
See Feed Materials Production Center.

Fog
A mist of sufficient concentration to obscure vision.

Fogging
Applying a pesticide by rapidly heating the liquid chemical so that it forms very fine droplets that resemble smoke or fog. It may be used to destroy mosquitoes, black flies, and similar pests.

FOIA
An acronym for Freedom of Information Act of 1966.

Foliaceous
A species descriptor that means having leaves, or leaflike structure.

Foliation
The layering in rocks caused by the parallel orientation of bands of minerals; characteristic of metamorphic rocks like slate.

Folklife
See Culture.

Follicle
A species descriptor that refers to a single-chambered fruit that splits along only one seam to release its seeds.

Follow-up, Medical
Constant or intermittent contact with a patient after diagnosis or therapy.

FONSI
See Finding of No Significant Impact.

Fontanelle
A species descriptor referring to the soft membranous intervals between the incompletely ossified cranial bones of a fetus or infant.

Food Chain
A species descriptor that refers to the interdependence of feeding organisms that prey upon lower or more vulnerable species; a sequence of organisms, each of which uses the next, lower member of the sequence as a food source. Frequently, if one species in a food chain is eliminated, all species within the chain are affected. For example, when farmers exterminated prairie dogs in the midwest, a dramatic decline in the black footed ferret occurred.

Food-Chain Crops
Crops grown for human consumption, and crops grown for feed for animals whose products are consumed by humans.

Food Stores
Fresh fruits or fresh vegetables or animal products. Those products that have been sterilized and canned such as canned milk or canned meats are exempt.

Foot Protection
A type of personal protective equipment such as: ankle protection, metatarsal protection, safety boats and shoes, rubber and metal shoe covers.

Forage Value Index
The weighted average estimate of the annual rental charge per head per month for pasturing cattle on private rangelands in the 11 western states of Montana, Idaho, Wyoming, Colorado, New Mexico, Arizona, Utah, Nevada, Washington, Oregon, and California.

Force Mains
Discharge lines from a sewage or stormwater lift station.

Forced Expiratory Volume (FEV)

The amount of air that can be forcefully exhaled in a specified time, usually one second (FEV1). A forced expiratory volume test provides an index of lung function.

Forced Vital Capacity (FVC)

The greatest amount of air that can be forcefully exhaled following maximum inhalation.

Foreign Commerce

Includes, among other things, any transaction a) between persons within one foreign country; b) between persons in two or more foreign countries; c) between a person within the United States and a person in a foreign country; or d) between persons within the United States, where the fish and wildlife in question are moving in any country or countries outside the United States.

Foreign Crude Oil

1) A mixture of hydrocarbons that existed in liquid phase in underground reservoirs and remain liquid at atmospheric pressure after passing through surface separating facilities. Lease condensate is also included. Lease condensate is natural gas liquids recovered from gas-well gas (associated and nonassociated) in lease separators for field facilities. Drips are also included but topped crude oil and other unfinished oils are excluded. Natural gas liquids produced at natural gas processing plants and mixed with crude oil are likewise excluded. 2) Petroleum produced outside the United States. Includes Athabasca hydrocarbons.

Forest and Rangeland Renewable Resources Planning Act of 1974 (FRRRPA)

The federal statute requiring the National Forest Service to carry out long-range planning for National Forest lands pursuant to principles established under the Multiple-Use Sustained-Yield Act and the National Environmental Policy Act. The law requires the Forest Service to prepare, maintain, and revise a renewable resource management program plan every 10 years, beginning 1980. The program must include an inventory of needs and opportunities for public and private investment in forestlands, to include a cost-benefit analysis and program prioritization.

Forest Management, Burning

The use of open fires, as part of a forest management practice, to remove forest debris or for forest management practices that include timber operations, silvicultural practices, or forest protection practices.

Forests, Reactor

Equipment located near top of reactor that checks for fuel element failure.

Form Lines

Lines resembling contours, but representing no actual elevations, that have been sketched from visual observation or from inadequate or unreliable map sources, to show collectively the configuration of the terrain.

Formal Complaint

A complaint submitted in writing either on an approved agency form (i.e., OSHA-7 Form) or in a letter; that alleges an imminent danger or a violation threatening physical harm (i.e., a hazard covered by a standard, ordinance, regulatory act, general duty clause) exists. This does not mean that the complaint must specify a particular law or standard; it need only specify a condition or practice that is hazardous, why it is hazardous; and be signed by at least one affected person.

Formal Consultation

A process between the U.S. Fish and Wildlife Service and the federal agency that commences with the federal agency's written request for consultation under Section 7 of the Endangered Species Act and concludes with the Service's issuance of the biological opinion under Section 7(b)(3) of the Act.

Formaldehyde

A colorless, pungent, irritating gas, CH_2O, used chiefly as a disinfectant and preservative and in synthesizing other compounds and resins.

Format

1) In photography, the size and/or shape of a negative or of the print therefrom. 2) In cartography, the shape and size of a map or chart.

Formation Fluid

Fluid present in a formation under natural conditions, as opposed to introduced fluids, such as drilling mud.

Formations

1) Bodies of rock characterized by a degree of lithologic homogeneity that is prevailingly, but not necessarily, tabular and is mappable on the earth's surface or traceable in the subsurface. 2) A body of rock of significant thickness that has characteristics making it distinguishable from adjacent rock unit.

Formatted Message Text

A message text composed of several sets ordered in a specified sequence, each set characterized by an identifier and containing information of a specified type, coded and arranged in an ordered sequence of character fields in accordance with the NATO message text formatting rules. It is designed to permit both manual and automated handling and processing. *See* Free Form Message Text.

Formerly Restricted Data

Information removed from the Restricted Data category upon a joint determination by the Department of Energy (or antecedent agencies) and Department of Defense that such information relates primarily to the military utilization of atomic weapons and that such information can be adequately safeguarded as classified defense information. (Section 142d, Atomic Energy Act of 1954, as amended.) *See* Restricted Data.

Formula Quantities

Strategic special nuclear material in any combination in a quantity of 5,000 grams or more computed by the formula, grams (grams contained U235) + 2.5 (grams U235 + grams plutonium).

Formulation

The substance or mixture of substances that is comprised of all active and inert ingredients in a pesticide.

FORTRAN

Formula Translation; a computer programming language.

Forward Aeromedical Evacuation

That phase of evacuation that provides airlift for patients between points within a hazard area, to the initial point of treatment, and to subsequent points of treatment.

Forward Slope

Any slope that descends toward a hazardous area.

Fossil

A species descriptor for an impression or cast of a plant or animal preserved in rock.

Fossil Fuel

1) Nonrenewable fuel resources derived from the incomplete decomposition of ancient organic remains (e.g., coal, crude oil, natural gas, and oil shales). 2) Natural gas, petroleum, coal, and any form of solid, liquid, or gaseous fuel derived from such materials for the purpose of creating useful heat.

Fossil Fuel and Wood Residue-Fired Steam Generating Unit (CAA; CFR)

A furnace or boiler used in the process of burning fossil fuel and wood residue for the purpose of producing steam by heat transfer.

Fostering

A species descriptor that refers to when the young of one species are raised by parents of a related species.

Foundations

Organizations or institutions established by endowment with provisions for future operations and maintenance.

Foundries
Facilities engaged in the melting or casting of beryllium metal or alloy.

404 Permit
See Dredge and Fill Permit.

Fowl Typhoid
The communicable disease of poultry caused by the bacteria Salmonella gallinarum.

FP
See Fission Products.

FPA
An acronym for the National Forest Products Association, 1619 Massachusetts Ave., N.W., Washington, DC 20036.

FPASA
An acronym for Federal Property and Administrative Services Act of 1949.

FPTS
An acronym for Fire Protection Tracking System.

FRACAS
An acronym for Failure Reporting Analysis and Corrective Action System.

Fracture
1) A general term for any break in a rock, that includes cracks, joints, and faults. 2) A rupture of the surface of a laminate because of external or internal forces, with or without complete separation.

Fracture Toughness
A measure of the damage tolerance of a material containing initial flaws or cracks.

Fragmentary Order
An abbreviated form of an operation order, usually issued on a day-to-day basis, that eliminates the need for restating information contained in a basic operation order. It may be issued in sections.

Frame
In photography, any single exposure contained within a continuous sequence of photographs.

Frank Effect Level (FEL)
A phrase related to biological responses to chemical exposures; the exposure level that produces an unmistakable adverse health effect (such as inflammation, severe convulsions, or death). *See* No-Observed-Adverse-Effect Level (NOAEL); No-Observed-Effect Level (NOEL).

FRASE
A DOE acronym for Factor Relationship and Sequence of Events.

Free Air Anomaly
The difference between observed gravity and theoretical gravity that has been computed for latitude and corrected for elevation of the station above or below the geoid, by application of the normal rate of change of gravity for change of elevation, as in free air.

Free Air Overpressure
The unreflected pressure, in excess of the ambient atmospheric pressure, created in the air by the blast wave from an explosion. *See* Overpressure.

Free Drop
The dropping of equipment or supplies from an aircraft without the use of parachutes.

Free Field Overpressure
See Free Air Overpressure.

Free-Flowing River or River Section
A river existing or flowing in natural condition without impoundment, diversion, straightening, rip-rapping, or other modification of the waterway.

Free-Form Message Text

A message text without prescribed format arrangements. It is intended for fast drafting as well as manual handling and processing. *See* Formatted Message Text.

Free Liquids

Liquids that readily separate from the solid portion of a waste under ambient temperature and pressure. Typically determined by paint filter test.

Free Product

Refers to regulated substances that are present as nonaqueous phase liquids (e.g., liquids not dissolved in water).

Freeboard

1) The vertical distance between the top of a tank or surface impoundment dike and the surface of the waste contained therein. 2) The height between the normal water surface elevation and the top of a hydraulic structure.

Freedom of Information Act of 1966 (FOIA; USC 552)

1) FOIA is the act that provides specifically that "any person" can make requests for government information. Citizens who make requests are not required to identify themselves or explain why they want the information they have requested. The position of Congress in passing FOIA was that the workings of government are "for and by the people" and that the benefits of government information should be made available to everyone. All branches of the federal government must adhere to the provisions of FOIA with certain restrictions for work in progress (early drafts), enforcement confidential information, classified documents, and national security information. 2) The federal act allowing public access to government documents and information.

Freezing Drizzle/Freezing Rain Advisory

A weather advisory issued when freezing rain or freezing drizzle, or both, is expected or imminent, and that will produce ice accumulations sufficient to break trees or power lines.

Freezing Point

The temperature at which crystals start to form as a liquid is slowly cooled; alternatively, the temperature at which a solid substance begins to melt as it is slowly heated.

Freight Consolidating Activity

A transportation activity that receives less than carload/truckload shipments of material for the purpose of assembling them into carload/truckload lots for onward movement to the ultimate consignee or to a freight distributing activity or other break bulk point. *See* Freight Distributing Activity.

Freight Containers

Reusable containers having a volume of 64 cubic feet or more, designed and constructed to permit being lifted with its contents intact and intended primarily for containment of package during transportation.

Freight Distributing Activity

A transportation activity that receives and unloads consolidated carloads/truckloads of less than carload/truckload shipments of material and forwards the individual shipments to the ultimate consignee. *See* Freight Consolidating Activity.

Frequency/Severity

Risk projection using all experience data from events of trivial consequences to the most serious events experienced by an organization or system under study.

Frequency Distribution

The relative frequency with which a variable quantity or variate assumes particular values.

Fresh Water

1) Water that generally contains less than 1,000 milligrams per liter of dissolved solids. 2) Water with salinity less than 0.5% dissolved salts.

FRGT

An acronym for Fast Response Gamma Thermometer.

Friable Asbestos Materials
Materials containing more than 1% asbestos by weight that by hand pressure can be crumbled, pulverized, or reduced to powder when dry.

Friable Asbestos-Containing Materials
1) Asbestos-containing materials applied on ceilings, walls, structural members, piping, duct work, or any other part of a building that when dry may be crumbled, pulverized, or reduced to powder by hand pressure. The term includes nonfriable asbestos-containing materials after such previously nonfriable asbestos-containing materials become damaged to the extent that when dry they may be crumbled, pulverized, or reduced to powder by hand pressure. 2) Asbestos insulation that is loose and capable of becoming airborne.

FRMAC Director
The manager of the Federal Radiological Monitoring and Assessment Center (FRMAC). Designated by Department of Energy in an emergency and by Environmental Protection Agency (EPA) in the recovery.

Frog
A species descriptor for a smooth-skinned amphibian, usually aquatic or semiaquatic.

Frontal Shield
A species descriptor that pertains to the area covering the forehead of birds.

FRRRPA
See Forest and Rangeland Renewable Resources Planning Act of 1974.

Fruit Dispersal
A species descriptor that means release of seeds or pollen.

FSAR
See Final Safety Analysis Report.

FTA
An acronym for Fault Tree Analysis; Federal Transit Act.

Fuel Economy Standard
The Corporate Average Fuel Economy Standard (CAFE) that went into effect in 1978. It was meant to enhance the national fuel conservation effort by slowing fuel consumption through a miles-per-gallon requirement for motor vehicles.

Fuel Efficiency
The proportion of potential heat in fuel that is effectively converted into energy.

Fuel Element(s)
A cluster of fuel rods (or plates). Also called a fuel assembly. Many fuel assemblies make up a reactor core.

Fuels
A term used to denote fossil fuels, coal, natural gas, petroleum, propellants, reactor fuel, solid-waste-derived fuel, etc.

Fuels and Vehicles Research (FVR)
An EPA program with special emphasis on the research and development of new and improved methods, having industry-wide application, for the prevention and control of air pollution resulting from the combustion of fuels. Program objectives are to:

1) conduct and accelerate research programs directed toward development of improved, cost-effective techniques for: a) control of combustion byproducts of fuels, b) removal of potential air pollutants from fuels prior to combustion, c) control of emissions from the evaporation of fuels, d) improving the efficiency of fuels combustion so as to decrease atmospheric emissions, and e) producing synthetic or new fuels that, when used, result in decreased atmospheric emissions;

2) provide for federal grants to public or nonprofit agencies, institutions, and organizations and to individuals, and contracts with public or private agencies, institutions, or persons;

3) determine, by laboratory and pilot plant testing, the results of air pollution research and studies in order to develop new or improved processes

and plant designs to the point where they can be demonstrated on a large and practical scale;

4) construct, operate, and maintain, or assist in meeting the cost of the construction, operation, and maintenance of new or improved demonstration plants or processes that have promise of accomplishing the intended purposes; and

5) study new or improved methods for the recovery and marketing of commercially valuable byproducts resulting from the removal of pollutants.

Fuel Tanks
Tanks other than cargo tanks, used to transport flammable or combustible liquid, or compressed gas for the purpose of supplying fuel for propulsion of the transport vehicle to which it is attached, or for the operation of other equipment on the transport vehicle.

Fugitive Emissions
1) Air pollutants released to the air other than those from stacks or vents; typically small releases from leaks in plant equipment such as valves, pump seals, flanges, sampling connections. 2) Emissions not caught by a capture system.

Full Participation Exercise
An exercise for a particular DOE or contractor-operated facility that demonstrates the integrated response capability of the facility emergency response organization (ERO), the DOE program office elements (both headquarters and field element) with responsibilities for emergency response along with those regional federal, state and local government agencies and provide support organizations that elect to participate.

Full-Scale Exercises
Exercises designed primarily for the purpose of validating the integrated emergency preparedness capability of a facility and state and local jurisdictions in an operational environment.

Full-Time Employees
Persons working 2,000 hours per year. A facility would calculate the number of full-time employees by totaling the hours worked during the calendar year by all employees, including contract employees, and dividing that total by 2,000 hours.

Fumes
1) Airborne solids generated by the condensation of vapors; particulates are usually metallic oxides less than 1 micrometer in size, and potentially toxic. 2) Tiny particles trapped in vapor in a gas stream. 3) Fine particles (typically of a metal oxide) dispersed in air that may be formed in various ways (e.g., condensation of vapors, chemical reaction). 4) Solid particles generated by condensation from the gaseous state, generally after volatilization of molten metals.

Fumigant
A pesticide that is vaporized to kill pests; used in buildings and greenhouses.

Function
A function is a group of services aimed at accomplishing a certain purpose or end.

Functional Appraisals
Documented reviews of ES&H specialty disciplines performed in accordance with written guidance and criteria to verity, by examination and evaluation of objective evidence at the facility and/or operation, that applicable elements of the program have been developed, documented, and effectively implemented in accordance with specific ES&H requirements and needs.

Functional Developmental Toxicity
The study of the causes, mechanisms, and manifestations of alterations or delays in functional competence of the organism or organ system following exposure to an agent during critical periods of development pre- and/or postnatally. This is a subset of development toxicity.

Functional Equivalent

A term used to describe EPA's decisionmaking process and its relationship to the environmental review conducted under the National Environmental Policy Act (NEPA). A review is considered functionally equivalent when it addresses the substantive components of a NEPA review.

Functional Units

DOE Logical and systematic groups of property that are necessary to support the site mission. A functional unit must be described in a breakdown structure for each he/she in order that it be properly identified and managed. Functional units will vary in size and scope within sites and from site to site, depending on the type or types of activities being carried out.

A functional unit will often comprise a total facility (e.g., laboratory, production plant, or utility) but may also be a portion of a facility (e.g., production line, shop, clean room, or tooling).

A functional unit is the basic entity for justifying individual projects and must be auditable in terms of mission requirements or performance standards.

Functionally Equivalent Components

Components that perform the same function or measurement and that meet or exceed the performance specifications of another component.

Functions

1) The appropriate or assigned duties, responsibilities, missions, or tasks of an individual, office, or organization.

Fund or Trust Fund

1) The Hazardous Substance Response Fund. 2) In the case of a hazardous waste disposal facility for which liability has been transferred, the Post-Closure Liability Fund established by CERCLA.

Fungi

1) Small nonchlorophyll-bearing plants without roots, stems, or leaves, that occur (among other places) in water, wastewater, or wastewater efflu-

ent and grow best in the absence of light. Their decomposition after death may cause disagreeable tastes and odors in water; in some wastewater treatment processes they are helpful, and in others, detrimental.

2) A group of organisms that are not photosynthetic, and that are usually nonmobile, filamentous, and multicellular such as:

- molds
- mildews
- yeasts
- mushrooms
- puffballs

Some of these organisms grow in the ground, others attach themselves to decaying trees and other plants, getting their nutrition from decomposing organic matter. Some cause disease, others stabilize sewage and break down solid wastes in composting.

3) Any nonchlorophyll-bearing thallophyte, that is, any nonchlorophyll-bearing plant of a lower order than mosses and liverworts, as for example, rust, smut, and bacteria, except those on or in living man or other animals and those on or in processed food, beverages, or pharmaceuticals.

Fungicides

Pesticides that are used to control, prevent, or destroy fungi.

Fungus

See Fungi.

Fuscous

A species descriptor that means dusky; dark gray or grayish brown.

Fusiform

A species descriptor that means tapering at each end; spindle shaped.

Fusion

1) The process whereby the nuclei of light elements combine to form the nucleus of a heavier

element, with the release of tremendous amounts of energy. 2) In intelligence usage, the process of examining all sources of intelligence and information to derive a complete assessment of activity.

FUSRAP

An acronym for Formerly Utilized Sites Remedial Actions Program.

Fuze

A device that initiates an explosive train. *See* Boresafe Fuze.

FVR

See Fuels and Vehicles Research (CAA).

FWCA

An acronym for Fish and Wildlife Conservation Act of 1980.

FWPCA

See Federal Water Pollution Control Act.

FWSRSA

An acronym for Farmington Wild and Scenic River Study Act (WSRA).

G

Gabbro
Dark, equigranular igneous rock that consists of calcic plagioclase, such as bytownite, and one or more dark minerals.

Gaining Stream
A stream or reach of a stream, the flow of which is increased by the inflow of groundwater. Also known as an effluent stream.

Galea
A species descriptor that means a helmet-shaped part, as in the upper part of certain plants and insects.

Gallons per Day (gpd)
A unit of measure; a measure of the withdrawal rate of a well.

Galvanize
Coating iron or steel with zinc to protect it against corrosion.

Game Fish
Species like trout, salmon, or bass, caught for sport. Many of them show more sensitivity to environmental change than "rough" fish.

Gamete
A mature male or female germ cell [sperm or ovum (egg)] usually possessing a haploid chromosome set and capable of initiating formation of a new diploid individual by fusion with a gamete from the opposite sex.

Gamma Multi-Hit Model
A dose-response model that can be derived under the assumption that the response is induced if the target site has undergone some number of independent biological events (hits).

Gamma Radiation
Gamma rays are true rays of energy in contrast to alpha and beta radiation. The properties are similar to X-rays and other electromagnetic waves. They are the most penetrating waves of radiant nuclear energy but can be blocked by dense materials such as lead. *See* Gamma Rays.

Gamma Rays
1) Penetrating, high-energy electromagnetic radiation emitted from atomic nuclei during a nuclear reaction. Gamma rays and very high energy X-rays differ only in origin. X-rays do not originate from atomic nuclei but are produced in other ways. 2) Electromagnetic radiation frequently accompanies alpha and beta emissions as radioactive materials decay.

Ganglia
1) In anatomy, a group of nerve cells located outside the brain or spinal cord in vertebrates. 2) In pathology, a cystic lesion resembling a cystlike tumor.

Gangrene
Death of tissue due to the lack of blood supply.

Gap, Imagery
Any space where imagery fails to meet minimum coverage requirements. This might be a space not covered by imagery or a space where the minimum specified overlap was not obtained.

Garbage
1) Waste material derived in whole or in part from fruits, vegetables, meats, or other plant or animal (including poultry) material, and other refuse of any character whatsoever that has been associated with any such material, including food scraps, table refuse, galley refuse, food wrappers or packaging materials, and other waste materials. 2) Wastes (animal and vegetable) resulting from the handling, storage, packaging, sale, preparation, cooking, and serving of food.

Garnetite
A contact metamorphic rock consisting primarily of garnet.

Gas
A physical state of matter in which the material has very low density and viscosity, and can expand and contract greatly in response to changes in temperature and pressure. A gas easily diffuses into other gases, readily and uniformly distributing itself throughout any container. Fluids that have neither independent shape or volume, and can be changed to the liquid or solid state only by the combined effect of pressure and temperature.

Gas-Cooled Fast Breeder Reactor
An alternative type of breeder reactor that uses gases instead of liquids as a coolant.

Gas Discharge Laser
A laser containing a gaseous lasing medium in a glass tube in which a constant flow of gas replenishes the molecules depleted by the electricity or chemicals used for excitation.

Gas Laser
A type of laser in which the laser action takes place in a gas medium.

Gas Volume Ratio
The limiting value for lithium target irradiation.

Gaseous Diffusion Plant
A nuclear power plant using a method of isotopic separation based on the fact that gas atoms or molecules with different masses will diffuse through a porous barrier (or membrane) at different rates. This method is used to separate uranium-235 from uranium-238; it requires large gaseous diffusion plants and enormous amounts of electric power.

Gasification
1) The transformation of soluble and suspended organic materials into gas during waste decomposition. 2) Conversion of solid material such as coal into a gas for use as a fuel.

Gasohol
A blend of alcohol and finished motor gasoline consisting of 90% or less finished motor gasoline, leaded or unleaded, and 10% or more alcohol (ethanol or methanol).

Gasoline
Leaded, unleaded, and unspecified gasoline.

Gasoline Vapor Recovery Requirements
The regulations enforced by states, and set forth by EPA, requiring all owners/operators of gasoline dispensing systems to install and operate a system for gasoline vapor recovery of emissions from the fueling of motor vehicles.

The Administrator issues guidance as appropriate as to the effectiveness of vapor recovery systems and the regulations typically apply only to facilities that sell more than 10,000 gallons of gasoline per month (50,000 gallons per month in the case of an independent small business marketer of gasoline. The effective dates are: a) six months after the adoption date, in the case of gasoline dispensing facilities for which construction commenced after November 15, 1990; b) one year after the adoption date, in the case of gasoline dispensing facilities that dispense at least 100,000 gallons of gasoline per month, based on average monthly sales for the 2-year period before the adoption date; or c) two years after the adoption date, in the case of all other gasoline dispensing facilities.

The adoption date refers to the date of adoption by the state of requirements for the installation and operation of a system for gasoline vapor recovery of emissions from the fueling of motor vehicles.

Gastrointestinal
Pertaining to the intestines and stomach.

Gastropods
A species descriptor for a mollusk of the class Gastropoda, including snails, slugs, and limpets, characteristically having a single, usually coiled shell and a ventral muscular mass serving as an organ of locomotion.

Gathering Lines
Pipelines, equipment, facilities, or buildings used in the transportation of oil or gas during oil or gas production or gathering operations.

Gauge Pressure (psig)
That pressure measured by a gauge and indicating the pressure exceeding atmospheric.

Gavage
Experimental exposure regimen in which a substance is administered to an animal into the stomach via a tube.

GDB
See Genome Database.

GDC
See General Design Criteria.

GDC Planning Board
The DOE advisory group of major headquarters and field organizations involved in the construction of facility acquisitions, that includes those organizations having planning, design, construction, environmental, safety and health, research, operations, and maintenance functions.

GDP
An acronym for Gaseous Diffusion Plant.

Geiger/Geiger-Mueller Counters
1) Handheld devices for counting charged particles by the ionization they produce; a nuclear scientist's basic tool for locating radioactive substances. 2) Electrical devices that detect the presence of certain types of radioactivity. 3) Highly sensitive gas-filled detectors and associated circuitry used for radiation detection and measurement.

GEMS
See Graphical Exposure Modeling System.

Gene
1) The simplest complete functional unit in a DNA molecule. A linear sequence of nucleotides in DNA that is needed to synthesize a protein and/or regulate cell function. A mutation in one or more of the nucleotides in a gene may lead to abnormalities in the structure of the gene product or in the amount of gene product synthesized. 2) A length of DNA that directs the synthesis of a protein.

Gene Library
A collection of DNA fragments from cells or organisms. So far, no simple way for sorting the contents of gene libraries has been devised. However, DNA pieces can be moved into bacterial cells where sorting according to gene function becomes feasible.

Genecology
The study of the genetics of plant and animal populations in relation to their environs.

General Cargo

Cargo without hazardous or dangerous properties and not requiring extra precautions for transport; e.g., boxes, barrels, bales, crates, packages, bundles, and pallets consisting of nonhazardous materials.

General Cargo Harbor

A harbor for which a project is authorized by Section 202 of the WRDA and any other harbor that is authorized to be constructed to a depth of more than 20 feet but not more than 45 feet.

General Design Criteria

Criteria used to ensure that the planning, design, and construction of facilities and systems, will be performed in a manner that will satisfy all applicable executive orders, laws, regulations, and best available technologies (BATs).

General Duty Clause

1) The mandates found in Executive Order 12196, and 29 CFR 1960.8, that require the head of each agency to furnish to each employee a workplace free from recognized hazards. 2) The OSHA mandates that require the owner/operator of any private sector facility to furnish to each employee a workplace free from recognized hazards. *See* General Employer Duties, OSHA.

General Emergencies

Emergency response levels that represent an event in progress or having occurred that involves actual or imminent substantial reduction of facility safety systems with potential for loss of containment or confinement integrity (e.g. release of large quantities of HazMat to the environs) or release of HazMat (radiological or nonradiological) in which offsite releases are occurring or are expected to occur that exceed PAG or ERPG exposure levels.

General Employee Duties, OSHA

OSHA mandates for employee compliance with occupational safety and health standards, rules, regulations, and orders applicable to his/her own actions and conduct.

General Employer Duties, OSHA

OSHA employer mandates to a) furnish to each employee a place of employment that is free from recognized hazards that are causing or are likely to cause death or serious physical harm to his/her employees; and b) comply with occupational safety and health standards promulgated under OSHA. *See* General Duty Clause.

General Environment

The total terrestrial, atmospheric, and aquatic environments outside sites within which any activity, operation, or process associated with the management and storage of spent nuclear fuel or radioactive waste is conducted.

General Map

A map of small scale used for general planning purposes. *See* Map.

General Permits

Permits applicable to a class or category of dischargers.

General Plant Projects

The means by which Congress annually provides funding for miscellaneous DOE construction items that are required during the fiscal year and that cannot be specifically identified beforehand.

General Public Knowledge

Knowledge that has been disseminated to the general public, including information in newspapers of general circulation or radio or television reports in the geographic area affected by the discharge. In order to demonstrate general public knowledge, it shall not be necessary to prove that any members of the public have actually acquired such knowledge but only that the information has been disseminated.

General Purchasing Agents

Agents who supervise, control, coordinate, negotiate, and develop the local procurement of supplies, services, and facilities by government agencies.

General Purpose Facilities Projects

Line item construction projects estimated to cost greater than 1.2 million and that are required to support the long-term administrative and technical needs of DOE-operated laboratories and facilities.

General Reporting Facility

A facility having one or more hazardous chemicals above the 10,000-pound Threshold Planning Quantity (TPQ). These facilities must file Material Safety Data Sheets and emergency inventory information with the SERC, LEPC, and local fire departments.

Generations, Photography

The preparation of successive positive/negative reproductions from an original negative/positive (first-generation). For example, the first positive produced from an original negative is a second-generation product; the negative made from this positive is a third-generation product; and the next positive or print from that negative is a fourth-generation product.

Generator, Pollution

1) Any owner/operator whose site activities, or processes, produces hazardous waste or whose actions first causes a hazardous waste to become subject to a regulation. 2) A facility or mobile source that emits pollutants into air or releases hazardous wastes into water or soil; any person who produces a hazardous waste that is listed by EPA and therefore subject to regulation. 3) A person (or an entity) who produces hazardous wastes by practice of the operations upon land that the person (or entity) controls. 4) Any person, by site location, whose act or process produces hazardous waste identified or listed in 40 CFR 261.

Generator or Producer Control of Land

Land that a generator of hazardous wastes owns, rents, leases, or operates.

Generic Exemptions

Temporary or permanent release from regulatory requirements, that extends beyond specific facilities and projects or applies to a category of facilities or action.

Generic Significance

Unusual occurrences that by their nature are capable of occurring at more than one specific facility, location, or site.

Genes

See Gene.

Genetic

Pertaining to characteristics that are passed by chromosomes from one generation to the next.

Genetic Engineering

A process of inserting new genetic information into existing cells in order to modify any organism for the purpose of changing specific characteristics.

Genetic Radiation Effects

Inheritable changes, chiefly mutations, produced by the absorption of ionizing radiations. On the basis of present knowledge these effects are purely additive, and there is no recovery.

Genome

A term used to refer to all the genetic material carried by a single gamete.

Genotoxic

A broad term that usually refers to a chemical that has the ability to damage DNA or the chromosomes. This can be determined directly by measuring mutations or chromosome abnormalities or indirectly by measuring DNA repair, sister-chromated exchange, etc. Mutagenicity is a subset of genotoxicity.

Genus

A species descriptor that refers to the principal subdivision of a family, such as the Cobra being a type of snake, that is a type of serpent, that is a type of reptile.

Geo
A combining term meaning earth, ground, or soil, that is used in connection with the terminology of various earth sciences and processes.

Geobotany
The science concerned with studying the global distribution of plants.

Geochemical Dispersion
1) Primary — the dispersion of elements deep within the earth. 2) Secondary — the dispersion of elements at or near the earth's surface.

Geochemistry
The study and science of the relationships of the elements and their isotopes, and the laws governing their distribution in the atmosphere, rocks, soils, and waters of the earth, and in biological materials.

Geodesy
1) The branch of applied mathematics that determines, through observation and measurement, the exact positions of points and the figures and areas of large portions of the earth's surface and the variations of terrestrial gravity. 2) The branch of surveying that takes into account the curvature of the earth.

Geodetic Datum
See Datum.

Geographic Coordinates
The quantities of latitude and longitude that define the position of a point on the surface of the earth with respect to the reference spheroid. *See* Coordinates.

Geographic Documentation
Geographic information that has been evaluated, processed, summarized, and published. *See* Geographic Information.

Geographic Information
Information concerning physical aspects, resources, and artificial features that is necessary for planning and operations.

Geographic Reference Points
A means of indicating position, usually expressed either as double letters or as codes established in operation orders, SOWs, or by other means.

Geography
1) The science concerned with delineating the earth. 2) In military science, the specialized field dealing with natural and manmade physical features that may affect the planning and conduct of military operations.

Geologic/Geological
A term meaning pertaining to geology. *See* Geology.

Geologic Repositories
A system that is intended to be used for, or may be used for, the disposal of radioactive wastes in excavated geologic media. A geologic repository includes a) a geologic repository operations area; and b) the portion of the geologic setting that provides isolation of the radioactive waste.

Geologic Resources
Those elements of the earth's crust such as soils, sediments, rocks, and minerals, including petroleum and natural gas, that are not included in the definitions of ground and surface water resources.

Geologic Strata
Layers of the earth's surface.

Geological Time
The system of time depicting the history of the earth since its creation into a sequence of definable episodes. The full history is divided into eras and subdivided into epochs.

Geology
The science concerned with the study of the origin, composition, structure, and history of the

earth, especially as these pertain to rocks, soils, sediments, minerals, etc. Subdivisions of geology include, but are not limited to, physical geology, economic geology, structural geology, mineralogy, mining, physiography, geomorphology, petrology, volcanology, paleontology, stratigraphic geology, and seismology.

Geometry

The branch of applied mathematics that determines the arrangement in space of the various components of an irradiation or measuring system. This designation includes positions and relevant parameters of source, detector, and any intervening absorber.

Geomorphologic Agent

A force causing change in land forms.

Geomorphology

The study of the form and evolution of the earth, specifically its surface and physical features and the relationship of these features to the geologic structures beneath them. It is an interpretive and descriptive science, in that it deals with the evolution of surface features as well as their morphology.

Geophysics

The science that studies the physics of the earth, including the fields of hydrology, meteorology, seismology, volcanology, magnetism, and geodesy.

Georef

1) A worldwide position reference system that may be applied to any map or chart graduated in latitude and longitude regardless of projection. It is a method of expressing latitude and longitude in a form suitable for rapid reporting and plotting. 2) An abbreviation for the World Geographic Reference System.

Geosere

The total plant succession of the geologic past.

Geosphere

The part of the earth that is not in the atmosphere, hydrosphere, or biosphere; the mineral nonliving part of the earth.

Geothermal Energy

An alternative means of energy whereby heat in a naturally occurring local anomaly (e.g., subsurface hot springs, hot dry rocks) is extracted via heat exchangers and used to heat water, that is then distributed via piping to nearby facilities. Sometimes used as a term denoting the change of temperature with increased depth into the earth's crust, expressed as degrees per unit of depth.

Geotechnical Engineering

The investigation and engineering evaluation of earth materials including soil, rock, groundwater, and manmade materials and their interaction with earth retention systems, structural foundations, and other civil engineering works. The practice involves application of the principles of soil mechanics and the earth sciences, and requires a knowledge of engineering laws, formulas, construction techniques, and performance evaluation of civil engineering works influenced by earth materials. Synonymous with "soil engineering."

Geotechnical Specialist (GTS)

A person registered by a state as a Certified Engineering Geologist, or a Registered Civil Engineer trained in soil mechanics, or an engineering geologist or civil engineer with a minimum of 3 years applicable experience working under the direct supervision of either a Certified Engineering Geologist or Registered Civil Engineer.

Germ Cell

A cell capable of developing into a gamete (ovum (egg) or sperm).

Germicide

Any compound that kills disease-causing microorganisms.

Gestation Period
The amount of time the developing young are carried within the body of the mother.

GGNS
An acronym for Grand Gulf Nuclear Station.

GIDEP
An acronym for Government Industry Data Exchange Program.

GIGO
An acronym for Garbage-In-Garbage-Out.

Gill Slits
A species descriptor that refers to the openings in the gill that permit water to enter.

Gills
The principal respiratory organs of a fish.

GJPO
An acronym for Grand Junction Projects Office.

Glabrous
A species descriptor that means having no hair; smooth.

Glacial
Pertaining to ice or its actions; frozen.

Glacial Boundary
The utmost extension of the outer margin of land-ice in any region.

Glacial Drift
A general term for unconsolidated sediment transported by glaciers and deposited directly onto land or in the sea.

Glaciate
To subject to glacial action; to cover with ice or a glacier.

Glass Melting Furnaces
Units comprising a refractory vessel in which raw materials are charged, melted at high temperature, refined, and conditioned to produce molten glass. These units include foundations, superstructure and retaining walls, raw material charger systems, heat exchangers, melter cooling systems, exhaust systems, refractory brick work, fuel supply and electrical boosting equipment, integral control systems and instrumentation, and appendages for conditioning and distributing molten glass to forming apparatuses.

Glaucoma
A disease of the eye characterized by abnormal and damaging high pressure inside the eye; usually due to a blockage of the channel that normally allows the outflow of fluid from the eye.

GLFC
An acronym for Great Lakes Fishery Commission.

Global Environmental Monitoring System (GEMS)
An organization established by the United Nations Environment Program as part of Earthwatch to monitor and collect data needed for environmental management issues. GEMS monitors climate, health, renewable resources, and waste transport.

Global Warming
See Climate Change; Greenhouse Effect.

Globose
A species descriptor that means spherical.

Glochidia
A parasitic larva, produced by freshwater mussels, that have hooks to attach to a host fish.

Glomerulus
A tuft formed of capillary loops that filter blood in the kidney. Part of the nephron, the basic structure of the kidney.

Glumes

A species descriptor that means a chaffy, basal bract on the spikelet of a grass.

Go, No-Go

The condition or state of operability of a component or system: "go," functioning properly; or "no-go," not functioning properly.

Goals

The long-term or short-term ends toward which an effort is directed.

GOCO

See Government-Owned Contractor-Operated Facilities.

Goggles

A type of personal protective equipment used for eye protection. *See* Personal Protective Equipment.

Gonad

A species descriptor that means testicle or ovary; an organ that produces reproductive cells.

Gonopodium

A species descriptor that means a penetrating organ used in copulation.

Gonopore

A species descriptor that means a reproductive aperture or pore.

Good Cause

A finding based upon a preponderance of the evidence that there is a factual basis and good reason for a specific decision that has been made.

Good Faith Contracting Effort

A concerted effort on the part of a potential contractor to seek out and consider minority/women owned and operated business enterprises as potential subcontractors, materials and equipment suppliers, or both, in order to meet the program participation goal.

Government-Owned Contract-Operated Ships

Those ships to which the U.S. government holds title and that the Military Sealift Command operates under a contract (i.e., nongovernment-manned). These ships are designated United States Naval Ships and use the prefix USNS. *See* Military Sealift Command; United States Naval Ship.

Government-Owned Contractor-Operated Facilities (GOCO)

Facilities owned or leased by DOE, or a contractor, for the account of DOE in connection with DOE prescribed contractual provisions, occupational safety and health standards pursuant to the authority in the Atomic Energy Act of 1954, as amended, the Energy Reorganization Act of 1974, and the Department of Energy Organization Act of 1977, for contractor employees working therein. A listing of these GOCO facilities is maintained by the Office of Operational Safety (EP-32). In the early 1990s these federal facilities included, but were not limited to Argonne National Laboratories; Energy Technology Engineering Center (Canoga Park); Idaho Chemical Processing Plant; Idaho National Engineering Laboratory; Inhalation Toxicology Research Institute; Lawrence Livermore National Laboratory; Lawrence Berkeley Laboratory; Los Alamos National Laboratory; Oak Ridge Gaseous Diffusion Plant; Oak Ridge National Laboratory; Pacific Northwest Laboratory; Portsmouth Gaseous Diffusion Plant; Rocky Flats Plant; Sandia National Laboratories; Stanford Linear Accelerator Center.

Government in the Sunshine Act (GSA)

An act setting forth procedures to comply with the public's right to the fullest practicable information regarding the decisionmaking processes of the federal government. Its purpose is to provide the public with such information while protecting the rights of individuals and the ability of the government to carry out its responsibilities.

Government Property

All government-owned or -leased property for which a department has responsibility, except the following: a) property furnished under contract requiring contractor assumption of the risk of loss or damage to government-furnished property; and b) property covered by a private insurance policy specifying a government department as the beneficiary.

Government Standards
Federal agency standards and specifications including proposed or recommended standards developed by federal agency personnel, outside groups under agency regulations, or by organizations or committees made up solely of government agency representatives.

Grab Sample
A single random sample of soil or of water taken without regard to time or flow.

Gradation
Bringing to a uniform grade or slope. The gradation of land by streams resulting in plains and valleys. The frequency distribution of various sized grains of sediment, soil, or other particulates.

Grade, Adjacent Ground Elevation
The lowest point of elevation of the finished surface of the ground, paving or sidewalk, within the area between the building and the property line, or when the property line is more than 5 feet from the building, between the building and a line 5 feet from the building.

Grade Beams
Reinforced concrete beams placed directly on the ground to provide the foundation for the superstructure.

Graded Approach
A DOE term pertaining to the depth of detail and magnitude of resources expended for maintenance elements. Graded approaches require that resources be tailored to, and commensurate with, the maintenance element's relative importance to safety, environmental compliance, safeguards and

security, programmatic importance, and/or other facility-specific requirements.

Gradient
The inclination of any slope, as of a stream, water table, or hillside, expressed as a percentage, or angle.

Grain Loading
The rate at which particles are emitted from a pollution source. Measurement is made by the number of grains per cubic foot of gas emitted.

Grandfather Clause
A provision in a zoning ordinance that permits the continuance of property uses existing at the time the ordinance was passed, even though such uses are banned by the ordinance. *See* Existing Use.

Granivorous
A species descriptor that means feeding on grain and seeds.

Granular Activated Carbon Treatment (GAC)
A filtering system often used in small water systems and individual homes to remove organics. GAC can be highly effective in removing elevated levels of radon from water.

Graphic
1) Any and all products of the cartographic and photogrammetric art. A graphic may be a map, chart, or mosaic or even a film strip that was produced using cartographic techniques. 2) Visual; easy to be seen.

Graphic Scale
A graduated line by means of which distances on the map, chart, or photograph may be measured in terms of ground distance. *See* Scale.

Graphical Exposure Modeling System (GEMS)
An interactive computerized management tool developed by the U.S. EPA that ties together several previously discrete tools into a coordinated sys-

tem, allowing for multiple types of analyses. These tools include environmental fate and transport models, chemical property estimation techniques, statistical analysis, and graphical and modeling programs.

Grate Siftings
The materials that fall from the solid waste fuel bed through the grate openings.

Graticule
1) In cartography, a network of lines representing the earth's parallels of latitude and meridians of longitude. 2) In imagery interpretation. *See* Reticle.

Graticule Ticks
In cartography, short lines indicating where selected meridians and parallels intersect.

Gravel
A mixture composed primarily of rock fragments 2 mm (0.08 inch) to 7.6 mm (3 inches) in diameter. Usually contains much sand. *See* Gradation; Grit.

Gravitational Head
A component of the total hydraulic head related to the position of a given mass of water relative to an arbitrary datum.

Gravitational Water
Water that moves into, through, or out of a soil or rock mass due to the influence of gravitational forces.

Gravity Extraction
The extraction of cargoes from aircraft by influence of their own weight.

Gray
The unit of absorbed dose; 1 Gy = 1 joule/kg.

Gray Water
Domestic wastewater composed of washwater from sinks, kitchen sinks, bathroom sinks and tubs, and laundry tubs.

Grazing Permit and Lease
Any document authorizing use of public lands or lands in national forests in the 16 contiguous western states for the purpose of grazing domestic livestock.

Great Lakes
Lake Ontario, Lake Erie, Lake Huron (including Lake St. Clair), Lake Michigan, Lake Superior, and the connecting channels (Saint Mary's River, Saint Clair River, Detroit River, Niagara River, and Saint Lawrence River to the Canadian border), and includes all other bodies of water within the drainage basin of such lakes and connecting channels, to the extent that those lakes are subject to the jurisdiction of the United States.

Great Lakes Monitoring Network
EPA's atmospheric deposition network used to monitor the atmospheric deposition of hazardous air pollutants (and other air pollutants), pursuant to the Great Lakes Water Quality Agreement. The network establish at least one facility capable of monitoring the atmospheric deposition of hazardous air pollutants in both dry and wet conditions, in each of the five Great Lakes.

Great Lakes Regional Coordination Panel
The panel comprised of the Aquatic Nuisance Species Task Force (ANSTF), the Great Lakes Commission (GLC), and Great Lakes representatives from federal, state, and local agencies and private environmental and commercial interests convened to a) identify priorities for the Great Lakes with respect to aquatic nuisance species; b) make recommendations to the Task Force regarding programs to carry out Section 4722(i) of the Aquatic Nuisance Prevention and Control Act (ANPCA); c) assist the Task Force in coordinating federal aquatic nuisance species program activities in the Great Lakes; d) coordinate, where possible, aquatic nuisance species program activities in the Great Lakes; e) provide advice to public and private individuals and entities concerning methods of controlling aquatic nuisance species; and f) submit annually a report to the Task Force describing activities within the Great Lakes re-

lated to aquatic nuisance species prevention, research, and control.

Great Plains Critical Lands Resource Conservation Program

The Secretary of Agriculture's authorization to formulate and carry out a program with owners and operators of land in the Great Plains area to reduce runoff, soil and water erosion, and otherwise to promote the conservation of soil and water resources in such area through the conversion of cropland from soil depleting uses to conserving uses including the production of soil conserving cover crops.

Greenbelt

Areas that may not be developed; generally serves as a buffer between pollution sources and concentrations of people. *See* Buffer Zone.

Greenhouse Effect

1) Global changes in climate and sea levels caused by a warming of the atmosphere due to the emission of gases that are transparent to incoming short-wave solar radiation and heat, but act to trap, absorb and/or reradiate certain long wavelengths. Incoming radiation is absorbed by materials at the earth's surface. The materials then begin to release radiation and heat back into the atmosphere that cannot pass through the layer of gases. 2) The warming of the earth's atmosphere caused by a build-up of carbon dioxide or other trace gases, it is believed by many scientists that this build-up allows light from the sun's rays to heat the earth but prevents a counterbalancing loss of heat. *See* Climate Change.

Greenwich Mean Time (GMT)

See Universal Time; ZULU Time.

Grenade Launchers

Gas pressure devices that propel grenades.

Grenades

Small metal or other containers designed to be thrown by hand or projected from a rifle. They are filled with an explosive or a liquid, gas, or solid material, such as a toxic gas or tear gas or an incendiary or smoke producing material with a bursting charge.

Grid

1) Two sets of parallel lines intersecting at right angles and forming squares; the grid is superimposed on maps, charts, and other similar representations of the earth's surface in an accurate and consistent manner to permit identification of ground locations with respect to other locations and the computation of direction and distance to other points. 2) A term used in giving the location of a geographic point by grid coordinates.

Grid Bearing

Bearing measured from grid north.

Grid Convergence

The horizontal angle at a place between true north and grid north. It is proportional to the longitude difference between the place and the central meridian. *See* Convergence.

Grid Convergence Factor

The ratio of the grid convergence angle to the longitude difference. In the Lambert Conical Orthomorphic projection, this ratio is constant for all charts based on the same two standard parallels. *See* Convergence; Grid Convergence.

Grid Coordinate System

A plane-rectangular coordinate system usually based on, and mathematically adjusted to, a map projection in order that geographic positions (latitudes and longitudes) may be readily transformed into plane coordinates and the computations relating to them may be made by the ordinary method of plane surveying. *See* Coordinates.

Grid Coordinates

Coordinates of a grid coordinate system to which numbers and letters are assigned for use in designating a point on a gridded map, photograph, or chart. *See* Coordinates.

Grid Interval

The distance represented between the lines of a grid.

Grid Magnetic Angle

The angular difference in direction between grid north and magnetic north. It is measured east or west from grid north. Grid magnetic angle is sometimes called grivation and/or grid variation.

Grid Navigation

A method of navigation using a grid overlay for direction reference. *See* Navigational Grid.

Grid North

The northerly or zero direction indicated by the grid datum of directional reference.

Grid Pattern

A design layout used by urban planners based on spacing streets at regular intervals and intersecting them at right angles. The system is further enhanced by alphabetizing street names in one direction and numbering them in ascending order in the other.

Grid Reference System

A system that uses a standard-scaled grid square, based on a point of origin on a map projection of the surface of the earth in an accurate and consistent manner to permit either position referencing or the computation of direction and distance between grid positions. *See* Grid.

Grid Ticks

Small marks on the neatline of a map or chart indicating additional grid reference systems included on that sheet. Grid ticks are sometimes shown on the interior grid lines of some maps for ease of referencing.

Grinder Pump

A mechanical device that shreds solids and raises the fluid to a higher elevation through pressure sewers.

Grit

The heavy suspended mineral matter 4mm (0.16 inch) to 8mm (0.32 inch) in diameter, such as sand, gravel, and cinders, present in water or wastewater. *See* Gravel.

Grit Chamber

A detention chamber or an enlargement of a sewer designed to reduce the velocity of flow of the liquid to permit the separation of mineral from organic solids by differential sedimentation.

Grit Collector

A device placed in a grit chamber to convey deposited grit to a point of collection.

Gross Alpha Particle Activity

Total activity due to emission of alpha particles. Used as the screening measurement for radioactivity generally due to naturally occurring radionuclides. Activity is commonly measured in picocuries.

Gross Beta Particle Activity

Total activity due to emission of beta particles. Used as the screening measurement for radioactivity from manmade radionuclides since the decay products of fission are beta particle and gamma ray emitters. Activity is commonly measured in picocuries. The total radioactivity due to beta particle emission as inferred from measurements on a dry sample.

Gross National Product (GNP)

The total value of all goods and services produced by a nation in a given year, usually the country's fiscal year. It is a convenient indicator of the level of economic activity, but because it fails to account for depreciation of stock, inventory, or other capital, it is only a general indication of activity.

Gross Weight

1) Weight of packaging plus the weight of its contents. 2) Weight of a vehicle, fully equipped and serviced for operation, including the weight of the fuel, lubricants, coolant, vehicle tools and

spares, crew, personal equipment, and load. 3) Weight of a container or pallet including freight and binding. *See* Net Weight.

Ground Control, Geodetic
A system of accurate measurements used to determine the distances and directions or differences in elevation between points on the earth. *See* Control Point; Field Control; Traverse.

Ground Cover
See Groundcovers.

Ground Cracks
Fractures induced by earthquake ground shaking and are a principal cause of damage and casualties. A partial or incomplete fracture.

Ground Failures
Landslides, lateral spreads, differential settlements, and ground cracks.

Ground Return
The reflection from the terrain as displayed and/or recorded as an image.

Ground Signals
A visual signal displayed on an airfield to give local air traffic rules information to flight crews in the air.

Ground Speed
The horizontal component of the speed of a contaminant plume relative to the earth's surface.

Ground Water
See Groundwater.

Ground Zero
The point on the surface of the earth at, or vertically below or above, the center of a planned or actual nuclear detonation. *See* Actual Ground Zero; Desired Ground Zero.

Groundcovers
Plants grown to keep soil from eroding.

Groundwater
1) Water that occupies pores and crevices in rock and soil, in a saturated zone or stratum beneath the surface of land or water. The upper limit of the groundwater is the water table. 2) The supply of fresh water found beneath the earth's surface, usually in aquifers, that is often used for supplying wells and springs. Because groundwater is a major source of drinking water there is growing concern over areas where leaching agricultural or industrial pollutants or substances from leaking underground storage tanks are contaminating groundwater.

Groundwater Barrier
Rock or artificial material with relatively low permeability that occurs below ground surface and impedes the movement of groundwater, causing a pronounced difference in the heads on opposite sides of the barrier.

Groundwater Basin
A term used to define a groundwater flow system that has defined boundaries and may include more than one aquifer underlain by permeable materials that are capable of storing or furnishing a significant water supply. The basin includes both the surface area and the permeable materials beneath it.

Groundwater, Confined
Groundwater within an aquifer that underlies a confining unit.

Groundwater Discharge
The flow of water released from the zone of saturation. *See* Groundwater Flow; Zone of Saturation.

Groundwater Discharge Area
The area in which groundwater is discharged to the land surface, surface water, or atmosphere. An area in which there are upward components of hydraulic head in the aquifer. Groundwater is flowing toward the surface in a discharge area and may escape as a spring, seep, or base flow, or by evaporation and transpiration.

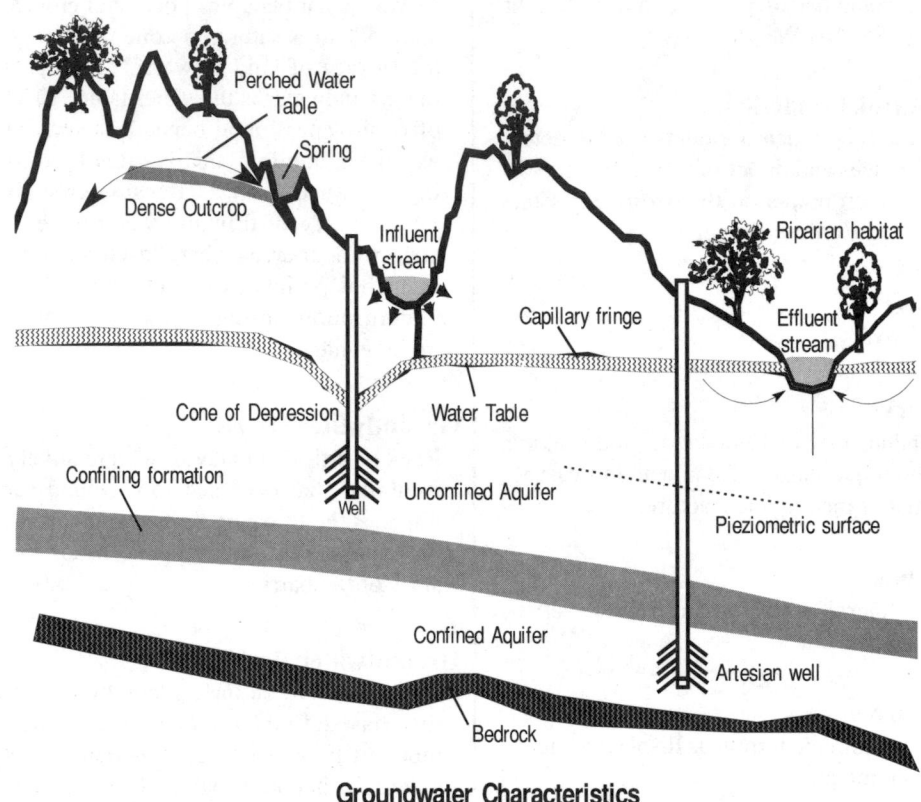

Groundwater Characteristics

Adapted from 'An Outline of Forest Hydrology', Univ. of Georgia Press, 1969.

Groundwater Discharge Velocity

Apparent velocity, calculated by Darcy's Law, that represents the flow rate at which water would move through an aquifer if the aquifer were an open conduit. Also known as "specific discharge."

Groundwater Divide

A ridge in the water table, or potentiometric surface, from which groundwater moves away at right angles in both directions. The line of highest hydraulic head in the water table or potentiometric surface.

Groundwater Flow

The direction and movement of water through openings in sediment and rock that occurs in the zone of saturation. *See* Zone of Saturation.

Groundwater Hydrology

The branch of science of hydrology that treats groundwater, its occurrences and motions, relationships and depletions; a study of the property of rocks that control groundwater movement and storage; methods of investigation and utilizations of groundwater. See figure above. *See* Hydrology.

Groundwater Model

A simplified conceptual or mathematical image of a groundwater system, describing the features essential to the purpose for which the model was developed and includes various assumptions pertinent to the system. Mathematical groundwater models can include numerical and analytical models, and are available as computerized software models and progams.

Groundwater Mound

Raised area in a water table or other potentiometric surface, created by groundwater recharge.

Groundwater Protection Advisory

A written statement containing advice for the use of a pesticide containing a listed hazardous chemical in its respective Groundwater or Pesticide Management Zone(s).

Groundwater Recharge

The process by which water is added to the saturated zone, or the volume of water added by the recharge process.

Groundwater Resources

Water in saturated zones or strata beneath the surface of land or water and the rocks or sediments through which groundwater moves. Includes groundwater resources that meet the definition of drinking water supplies.

Groundwater Runoff

Groundwater that is discharged into a stream channel as a spring or seepage water.

Groups

1) A term that refers to individuals assembled together through some unifying relationship or purpose. 2) Organizational levels having responsibility for a specified functional assignment at an incident, and subordinate to a branch. 3) Units of stratigraphic classification; a local or regional subdivision of a system, based on lithologic features. 4) Units or subdivisions of species classifications.

Growing Season

The frost-free period of the year.

Growth Management

Techniques used by local and state governments to control the amounts, types, locations, and rates of growth. Comprehensive plans, zoning ordinances, building permit moratoriums, and the requiring of complete infrastructure systems are common ways to implement growth management policies.

GRPA

An acronym for Genesee River Protection Act of 1989.

GSA

An acronym for Geothermal Steam Act of 1970; Government in the Sunshine Act.

GSDB

An acronym for Genome Sequence Database.

GSMFC

An acronym for Gulf States Marine Fisheries Compact.

Guarantor (CERCLA; USC)

Any person, other than the owner/operator, who provides evidence of financial responsibility for an owner/operator.

Guide Specification

1) A general specification; often referred to as a design standard or design guideline, that is a model standard and is suggested or required for use in the design of all of the construction projects of an agency. 2) Minimum requirements to be used as a basis for the evaluation of a national specification covering a fuel, lubricant or associated product proposed for standardization action.

Guideline on the Identification and Use of Air Quality Data Affected by Exceptional Events

The 1986 EPA guideline used by states as a general basis for reviewing ambient data. The guideline provides an overall criterion for determining whether an event is exceptional with regard to national standards. The steps in the evaluation procedure are:

- 1) a district (or the state board) identifies questionable data;

2) if a known event has occurred, the district gathers relevant data to document the occurrence;

3) if an event is only suspected, the district investigates available data for the possible event;

4) the district then submits to the Executive Officer a request for identifying the data as affected by an exceptional event and also provides supporting documentation; and

5) if the Executive Officer concurs with the district, he/she will identify the data as affected by an exceptional event.

If the district's request cannot be supported, it will be notified of the reasons. The Executive Officer will consider any additional data to support the request, but in the absence of any new evidence, will disapprove the request. After data are identified by the Executive Officer as affected by an exceptional event for state standards, the use or nonuse of the data for regulatory purposes will be determined through the public review process.

Guidelines

DOE or other government agency outlines or directions on how to conduct or control some program. As an example, DOE issues guidelines on keeping personnel radiation exposures "As Low as Reasonably Achievable." Guidelines normally do not have the legal impact of regulator's orders.

Guidelines for Carcinogenic Risk Assessment

The Administrator's revised guidelines for carcinogenic assessments based on the recommendations contained in the report of the National Academy of Sciences prepared pursuant to the CAA. *See* National Academy of Sciences Study.

Gular

A species descriptor that means pertaining to or located on the throat.

Gully

A relatively small watercourse or ditch eroded in the surface of the earth, typically in clay or unconsolidated material.

Gust Fronts

Lines of gusty wind moving out from a squall line or an area of severe thunderstorms. A gust front extends tons of miles parallel to the line of thunderstorms. At the leading age of a gust front, wind direction shifts abruptly from toward the storm (inflow) to away from the storm (outflow). The gustiness factor, the ratio of the total range of windspeed between gusts and lulls divided by the mean windspeed, is very large in gust fronts. Peak gusts are usually less than 113 mph.

GVR

See Gas Volume Ratio.

GVWR

An acronym for Gross Vehicle Weight Rating (CAA).

Gynaecandrous

A species descriptor that means staminate and pistallate flowers that are located on the same spike.

Gynoecium

A species descriptor that refers to the female reproductive organs of a flower; the pistil or pistils collectively.

Gypsum

Hydrated calcium sulfate; used extensively in the manufacture of wall paneling, plaster, paint, paper filters, etc.

Gyro-Magnetic Compass

A directional gyroscope whose azimuth scale is maintained in alignment with the magnetic meridian by a magnetic detector unit.

H

H&SM

An acronym for Health and Safety Manual.

H₂O₂

Hydrogen Peroxide.

H₂S

Hydrogen Sulfide.

HA

See Hazard Assessment (CAA).

Habitat

1) The places where a population (e.g., human, animal, plant, microorganism) lives and its surroundings, both living and nonliving. 2) The sum total of environmental conditions of a specific place occupied by an organism, population, or community; the dwelling place of a species with its particular environmental characteristics. 3) The locality and conditions that support the life of an organism.

Habitat Loss

The destruction of a natural habitat due to urban or agricultural development.

HABS

See Historic American Buildings Survey.

HABS Architectural Data Form

A one-page form intended to provide identifying information for accompanying HABS documentation.

HABS/HAER Inventory Card

A one-page form intended to provide identification. A contact print dry mounted on the form, a negative, and a separate contact sheet and index should be included with the inventory card.

HAC

See Hazard Assessment Center.

Hachuring

A method of representing relief upon a map or chart by shading in short disconnected lines drawn in the direction of the slopes.

Hacking

To release a captive-bred bird into the wild.

HAER

See Historic American Buildings Survey/Historic American Engineering Record.

Half-Life

1) The time required for a radioactive substance to lose half its energy. The half-life is a characteristic property of each radioactive species and is independent of its amount or condition. The effective half-life of a given isotope is the time in which the quantity in the body will decrease to

half as a result of both radioactive decay and biological elimination. 2) The time required for a pollutant to lose half its affect on the environment. For example, the half-life of DDT in the environment is 15 years, of radium, 1,580 years. *See* Atmospheric Half-Life; Biological Half-Life.

Half-Thickness

The thickness of absorbing material necessary to reduce by one half the intensity of radiation that passes through it.

Half-Value Layer

The thickness of any specified material necessary to reduce the intensity of an X-ray or gamma-ray beam to one half its original value. Same as half-thickness.

Halftone

Any photomechanical printing surface or the impression therefrom in which detail and tone values are represented by a series of evenly spaced dots in varying size and shape, varying in direct proportion to the intensity of the tones they represent. *See* Halftone Screen.

Halftone Screen

A series of regular spaced opaque lines on glass, crossing at right angles, producing transparent apertures between intersections. Used in a process camera to break up a solid or continuous tone image into a pattern of small dots. *See* Halftone.

Haline

A term used to indicate dominance of ocean salt.

Halite

Rock salt. An evaporite mineral that occurs together with other minerals.

Halocarbons

The chemical compounds CF_2Cl_2 and $CFCl_3$ and such other halogenated compounds as the Administrator of EPA determines may reasonably be anticipated to contribute to reductions in the concentration of ozone in the stratosphere.

Halocline

The boundary between two bodies of water that have different salinity characteristics.

Halogenated

Compounds that contain a halogen element (i.e., fluorine, chlorine, bromine or iodine).

Halogenated Organic Compounds

Compounds having a carbon-halogen bond.

Halogens

Extremely reactive elements that comprise Group VII of the periodic table: fluorine, chlorine, bromine, iodine, and astatine. Halogens react with metals to produce salts; chlorine reacts with sodium to produce sodium chloride (common table salt).

Halomorphic Soil

Soil that contains excessive amounts of salts or alkalis.

Halon

Bromine-containing compounds with long atmospheric lifetimes whose breakdown in the stratosphere cause depletion of ozone. Halons are used in fire fighting.

Hammermill

A high-speed machine that uses hammers and cutters to crush, grind, chip, or shred solid wastes.

Handle

A term that means mixing, loading, or applying, hazardous chemicals or maintaining, servicing, or cleaning contaminated equipment used in these activities.

Handover

The passing of response team control authority from one control agency to another control agency. Handover action may be accomplished between control agencies of separate levels of government when conducting joint operations or between control agencies within a single level. Handover action is complete when the receiving agency acknowledges assumption of control authority.

Haploid
Having half the number of normal chromosomes, or containing a single set of unpaired chromosomes. Gametes (specialized reproductive cells) are characterized as haploid. *See* Diploid.

Haplustolls
A well-drained, to moderately well-drained, darkly colored soil that is textured of loamy, very fine sand.

HAPs
See Hazardous Air Pollutants.

Harbor
1) A restricted body of water, an anchorage, or other limited coastal water area and its mineable water approaches, from which shipping operations are projected or supported. 2) Any channel or harbor, or element thereof, in the United States, capable of being utilized in the transportation of commercial cargo in domestic or foreign waterborne commerce by commercial vessels. The term does not generally include the following: a) an inland harbor; b) the Saint Lawrence Seaway; c) local access or berthing channels; d) channels or harbors constructed or maintained by nonpublic interests; and e) any portion of the Columbia River other than the channels on the downstream side of Bonneville Lock and Dam.

Harbor Operations and Maintenance
All operations, maintenance, repair, and rehabilitation, including maintenance dredging reasonably necessary to maintain the width and nominal depth of any harbor or inland harbor. The term does not include providing any lands, easements, rights-of-way, or dredged material disposal areas, or performing relocations required for project operations and maintenance.

Hard Compact
All earth material not classified as running soil.

Hard Conversion
The process of changing measurement language to nonequivalent metric units necessitating changes in the actual physical size and configuration of the part, product, or process that exceed those permitted by established measurement tolerance. Hard conversion allows for simplification and rationalization of size sequence.

Hard Hat
A type of head protection commonly used on construction sites, and in other facilities where a hazard may exist from falling objects. *See* Personal Protective Equipment.

Hard Water
Alkaline water containing dissolved salts that interfere with some industrial processes and prevent soap from lathering.

Hardened Site
A site, normally constructed under rock or concrete cover, designed to provide protection against the effects of conventional hazards. It may also be equipped to provide protection against the side effects of a nuclear attack and against a chemical or a biological attack.

Hardstand
1) A paved or stabilized area where vehicles are parked. 2) Open ground area having a prepared surface and used for storage and materials containment.

Hardware
1) The generic term dealing with physical items as distinguished from its capability or function such as equipment, tools, implements, instruments, devices, sets, fittings, trimmings, assemblies, subassemblies, components, and parts. The term is often used in regard to the stage of development, as in the passage of a device or component from the design stage into the hardware stage as the finished object. 2) In data automation, the physical equipment or devices forming a computer and peripheral components. *See* Software.

Harmonization

The process and/or results of adjusting differences or inconsistencies to bring significant features into agreement.

Harp

A failed fuel element container with cooling tubes along the side that resemble the strings of a harp.

Hatch List

A list showing, for each hold section of a cargo ship, a description of the items stowed, their volume and weight, the consignee of each, and the total volume and weight of material in the hold.

Hatchling

A species descriptor for a young animal that has just emerged from its shell.

HATS

An acronym for Hazard Abatement Tracking System.

Hazard

A situation, condition, or process that has the potential to adversely impact the health and safety of personnel, the public, the environment, or national security. Hazards are divided into three classes: a) Low — Hazards that present minor onsite and negligible offsite impacts to people, the environment or national security; b) Moderate — Hazards that present considerable potential onsite impacts to the people or the environment, but at most only minor offsite impact to people, the environment or national security. c) Catastrophic — Hazards with the potential for onsite and offsite impacts to large numbers of persons or with the potential for major impacts to the environment or national security.

Hazard Analysis

The functions, steps, and criteria for design and plan of work, that identity hazards, provide measures to reduce the probability and severity potentials, identify residual risks, and provide alternative methods of further control. The procedures involved in, a) identifying potential sources of release of hazardous materials from fixed facilities or transportation accidents; b) determining the vulnerability of a geographical area to a release of hazardous materials; and c) comparing hazards to determine which present greater or lesser risks to a community.

Hazard and Operability Study

A systematic technique for identifying hazards or operability problems throughout an entire facility. One examines each segment of a process and lists all possible deviations for normal operating conditions and how they might occur. The consequences on the process are assessed, and the means available to detect and correct the deviations are examined.

Hazard Assessment

1) An assessment of the potential effects of an accidental release of any regulated substance. The assessment includes an estimate of potential release quantities and a determination of downwind effects, including potential exposures to affected populations, and a previous release history of the past 5 years, including the size, concentration, and duration of releases, and shall include an evaluation of worst case accidental releases. The purpose of the assessment is to develop information and analyses on ways of preventing an occurrence and minimizing the consequences of accidental releases of extremely hazardous substances. Also includes recommendations with respect to the role of risk management plans in preventing accidental releases. 2) The determination of the overall effectiveness of force employment during military operations. The assessment is composed of three major components: a) battle damage assessment; b) munitions effects assessment; and c) reattack recommendation. The objective of a hazard assessment is to identify recommendations for the course of response operations. *See* Damage Assessment.

Hazard Assessment Center (HAC)

Located in the EOC (Emergency Operations Center), the HAC estimates impacts of releases to the public, coordinates radiological monitoring, models releases of radioactive and hazardous materials, and develops recommendations for Preliminary Assessments (PA) and Protective Action Recommendation (PARs) for the Crisis Support Manager (CSM).

Hazard Assessment, Research

A program of long-term research to develop and disseminate information on methods and techniques for hazard assessment that may be useful in improving and validating the procedures employed in the preparation of hazard assessments under the CAA.

Hazard Categories

Any of the following: a) Immediate (Acute) Health Hazard — highly toxic, toxic, irritant, sensitizer, corrosive, and other hazardous chemicals that cause an adverse effect to a target organ rapidly as a result of short term exposure and is of short duration; b) Delayed (Chronic) Health Hazard — carcinogens and other hazardous chemicals that cause an adverse effect to a target organ as a result of long term exposure and is of long duration; c) Fire Hazard — flammable, combustible liquid, pyrophoric, and oxidizer; and d) Sudden Release of Pressure — explosives and compressed gasses. Refer to 29 CFR 1910.1200.

Hazard Classifications

Alphabetical designations of the relative impact potential, or severity, that would probably occur if a loss-producing event resulted from a hazard. The three classifications are as follows: Class A — potential for permanent disability, loss of life, or body part, or extensive loss of structure, equipment or material. Class B — potential of serious injury or illness resulting in temporary disability or property damage that is disruptive. Class C — potential for minor injury or illness or nondisruptive property damage.

Hazard Communication Standard (HCS)

An OSHA regulation that requires chemical manufacturers, suppliers, and importers to assess the hazards of the chemicals they make, supply, or import, and to inform employers, customers, and workers of these hazards through a Material Safety Data Sheet. *See* Material Safety Data Sheets.

Hazard Identification

The process of determining whether exposure to a substance is causally related to an incidence and/or determining the severity of an adverse health effect (e.g., cancer, birth defects). Hazard identification involves gathering and evaluating data on the types of health injury or disease that may be produced by a chemical and on the conditions of exposure under which injury or disease is produced. It may also involve characterization of the behavior of a chemical within the body and the interactions it undergoes within organs, cells, or even parts of cells. Hazard identification is the first step in the risk assessment process.

Hazard Incident Control Point

A designated point close to a hazardous incident where emergency response teams rendezvous and establish control capability before initiating a tactical response.

Hazard Quotient

The ratio of a single substance exposure level over a specified time period (e.g., subchronic) to a reference dose for that substance derived from a similar exposure period.

Hazard Ranking System (HRS)

A scoring system used to evaluate potential risks to public health and the environment from releases or threatened releases of hazardous substances. The EPA and most states use the hazard ranking system to calculate a site score, from 0 to 100, based on the actual or potential release of hazardous substances from a site through air, surface water, or groundwater to affect people. This score is the primary factor used to decide if a hazardous waste site should be placed on the National Priorities List (NPL) and, if so, what ranking it should have compared to other sites on the list.

Hazard Zone

That area required by emergency responders for the conduct of medical support, hazard containment, and cleanup related operations.

Hazardous Air Pollutants (HAPs)

1) Air pollutants that are not covered by ambient air quality standards but which, as defined in the Clean Air Act, may reasonably be expected to cause or contribute to irreversible illness or death. Such pollutants include asbestos, beryllium, mercury, benzene, coke oven emissions, radionuclides, and vinyl chloride. 2) Air contaminants to which no ambient air quality standard is applicable and that causes, or contributes to, air pollution that may reasonably be anticipated to result in an increase in mortality or an increase in serious irreversible or incapacitating reversible, illness. Hazardous air pollutants are regulated by 40 CFR 61 (Regulations on National Emission Standards for Hazardous Air Pollutants). *See* Section IV: Hazardous Air Pollutant List.

Hazardous Air Pollution

Air pollution that may reasonably be anticipated to result in an increase in mortality or an increase in serious irreversible, or an incapacitating but reversible, illness.

Hazardous Chemical

EPA's designation for any hazardous material that requires a Material Safety Data Sheet. Such substances are capable of producing adverse physical effects (fire, explosion, etc.) or adverse health effects (cancer, dermatitis, etc.). Hazardous chemicals are further defined in 29 CFR 1910.1200, except that the term does not generally include the following:

- 1) any food, food additive, color additive, drug, or cosmetic regulated by the Food and Drug Administration;
- 2) any substance present as a solid in any manufactured item to the extent exposure to the substance does not occur under normal conditions of use;
- 3) any substance to the extent it is used for personal, family, or household purposes, or is present in the same form and concentration as a product packaged for distribution and use by the general public;
- 4) any substance to the extent it is used in a research laboratory or a hospital or other medical facility under the direct supervision of a technically qualified individual; or
- 5) any substance to the extent it is used in routine agricultural operations or is a fertilizer hold for sale by a retailer to the ultimate customer.

Hazardous Material

1) A substance or material of a particular quantity and form in commerce that may pose an unreasonable risk to health and safety or property. Materials include, but are not limited to, explosives, radioactive materials, etiologic agents, flammable liquids or solids, combustible liquids or solids, poisons, oxidizing or corrosive materials, and compressed gases. 2) Any material capable of posing an unreasonable risk to health, safety, and property during transportation and so designated in 49 CFR Part 172 and defined by Part 173. 3) Any solid, liquid, or gaseous material that is toxic, flammable, radioactive, corrosive, chemically reactive, or unstable upon prolonged storage in quantities that could pose a threat to life, property, or the environment. 4) Substances or materials, including a hazardous substance, that have been determined by the Secretary of Transportation to be capable of posing an unreasonable risk to health, safety, and property when transported in commerce, and that have been so designated in 40 CFR Part 260.10. 5) A hazardous waste as defined in 40 CFR Part 261.3.

Hazardous Materials Emergencies

Conditions or potential conditions that could result in the accidental release or loss of control of radioactive or toxic material.

Hazardous Materials Incident

The uncontrolled release or potential release of a hazardous material from its container into the environment.

Hazardous Materials Response Team

An organized group of employees, designated by the employer, who are expected to perform work to handle and control actual or potential leaks or spills of hazardous substances requiring possible close approach to the substance. The team members perform responses to releases or potential releases of hazardous substances for the purpose of control or stabilization of the incident. A "HazMat team" is not synonymous with "a fire department;" however, such a team may be a separate component of a fire department.

Hazardous Motion

Any motion that is likely to cause personal physical harm.

Hazardous Substance

The following are examples of "Listed Hazardous Substances and other Chemical Substances," "Extremely Hazardous Substances," "Regulated Substances," and "Toxic Substances" derived from CERCLA, RCRA, TSCA, and other environmental regulations. (*See* CERCLA Hazardous Substances; Hazardous Substances):

- Agent Orange
- Aldicarb
- Asbestos
- Commercial Asbestos
- Friable Asbestos
- Beryllium, Beryllium 7
- Cadmium
- Chlorinated Hydrocarbons
- Chlorofluorocarbons (CFCs)
- DDT
- Heptachlor
- Polychlorinated Biphenyls
- Polyvinyl Chloride
- Trichloroethylene (TCE)
- Chromium
- DES
- Diazinon
- Dinoseb
- Ethylene Dibromide
- Formaldehyde
- Lead
- Nitrogen Oxides (NOx)
- Nitric Oxides
- Nitrogen Dioxide (NO2)
- Phenols
- Phosphorus
- Radionuclides
- Alpha Decay Radioisotopes

- Radium-226
- Radon-222
- Thorium-230
- Uranium-238
- Beta Decay Radioisotopes
- Beta-Minus Decay Radioisotopes
- Antimony-125
- Cerium-144, Cerium-141
- Cesium-137, Cesium-134
- Cobalt-60, Cobalt-68
- Iodine-131
- Manganese-54
- Radium-228
- Ruthenium-103
- Strontium-90
- Tellurium-132
- Tritium
- Zinc-65
- Zirconium-95
- Element 104,105, 106, 107, 108, and 109 Isotopes
- Heavy Ion Decay Radioisotopes
- Isomeric Transition Isotopes
- Living Radioisotopes
- Thorium-232, Thorium-230
- Uranium-238

Hazardous Substance, UST System

An underground storage tank (UST) system that contains a hazardous substance defined in Section 101 of the Comprehensive Environmental Response, Compensation, and Liability Act of 1980 (but not including any substance regulated as a hazardous waste under Subtitle C) or any mixture of such substances and petroleum UST system.

Hazardous Substances

1) Materials that pose a threat to human health and/or the environment. Typical hazardous substances are toxic, corrosive, ignitable, explosive, or chemically reactive. 2) Any substance designated by EPA to be reported if a designated quantity of the substance is spilled in the waters of the United States or it otherwise emitted to the environment. 3) Materials, including their mixtures and solutions, that a) are listed in the Appendix to 40 CFR 172.101; b) are in a quantity, in one package, that equals or exceeds the reportable quantity (RQ) listed in the Appendix to 40 CFR 172.101; and c) when a mixture or solution are in a concentration by weight that equals or exceeds the con-

centration corresponding to the RQ of the material. 4) Any substance designated under 40 CFR 116 pursuant to the Clean Water Act. *See* Hazardous Substance.

Hazardous Substances List

The initial list of 100 substances that, in the case of an accidental release, are known to pose the greatest risk of causing death, injury, or serious adverse effects to human health or the environment. The list includes, but is not limited to, the list of extremely hazardous substances published under the Emergency Planning and Community Right-to-Know Act of 1986 (42 USC 110(01) et seq.). The initial list included chlorine, anhydrous ammonia, methyl chloride, ethylene oxide, vinyl chloride, methyl isocyanide, hydrogen cyanide, ammonia, hydrogen sulfide, toluene diisocyanate, phosgene, bromine, anhydrous hydrogen chloride, hydrogen fluoride, anhydrous sulfur dioxide, and sulfur trioxide.

Hazardous Substances List, Criteria

The criteria considered prior to including any substance on the List of Hazardous Substances. The criteria include, but may not be limited to, a) the severity of any acute adverse health effects associated with accidental releases of the substance; b) the likelihood of accidental releases of the substance; and c) the potential magnitude of human exposure to accidental releases of the substance.

Hazardous Waste

1) Any waste that contains a substance that is harmful to life. 2) As defined in RCRA, a solid waste, or combination of solid wastes, that because of its quantity, concentration, or physical, chemical, or infectious characteristics may cause or significantly contribute to an increase in mortality or an increase in serious irreversible, or incapacitating reversible illness; or pose a substantial present or potential hazard to human health or the environment when improperly treated, stored, transported, or disposed of or otherwise managed. 3) As defined by EPA, by-products of society that can pose a substantial or potential hazard to human health or the environ-

ment when improperly managed. Possesses at least one of four characteristics (ignitability, corrosivity, reactivity, or toxicity), or appears on special EPA lists. 4) Wastes that are identified or listed in 40 CFR 261.31 and 261.32.

Hazardous Waste Characteristics

The four categories used in defining hazardous waste are ignitability, corrosivity, reactivity, and toxicity (per RCRA).

Hazardous Waste Constituent

A constituent that caused the Administrator to list the hazardous waste in Part 261, Subpart D, of 40 CFR, or a constituent listed in Table 1 of Part 261.24 of 40 CFR.

Hazardous Waste Discharge

The accidental or intentional spilling, leaking, pumping, pouring, emitting, emptying, or dumping of hazardous waste into or on any land or water.

Hazardous Waste Facilities

All government owned or controlled contiguous land, structures, other appurtenances, and improvements on the land used for treating, storing, or disposing of hazardous waste. A facility may consist of several treatment, storage, or disposal operational units (e.g., one or more landfills, surface impoundments, or combinations).

Hazardous Waste Facility Permit

A two-phase permit process that treatment, storage and disposal companies handling hazardous materials (solid and/or liquid) must undergo to comply with EPA regulations that govern such aspects of facility locations, design, operating procedures, and closure. The initial phase or permit application places the facility on an Interim Status, during which EPA officials inspect the facility to determine existing compliance with EPA standards. If deemed in compliance with standards, the application is approved and a Part B Permit (final operating permit) is issued, based on the application as modified by provisions set forth by EPA.

Hazardous Waste Generation
The act or process of producing hazardous waste.

Hazardous Waste Generator
Any person whose act or process produces hazardous waste identified in 40 CFR 261. Generators are required to comply with strict regulations, depending on the volumes, types, and risk factors associated with their wastes. The regulations include, but are not limited to, waste sampling, testing, recordkeeping, storage requirements, shipping, and disposal requirements.

Hazardous Waste Management
The systematic control of the collection, source separation, storage, transportation, processing, treatment, recovery, and disposal of hazardous wastes.

Hazardous Waste Management Facilities
All contiguous land and structures, other appurtenances, and improvements on the land, used for treatment, storing, or disposing of hazardous waste. A facility may consist of several treatment, storage, or disposal operational units (for example, one or more landfills, surface impoundments, or combinations of them).

Hazardous Waste Management Unit
A permitted and contiguous area of land on or in which hazardous waste is placed, or the largest area in which there is significant likelihood of mixing hazardous waste constituents in the same area. Examples of hazardous waste management units include a surface impoundment, a waste pile, a land treatment area, a landfill cell, an incinerator, a tank and its associated piping and underlying containment system, and a container storage area. A container alone does not constitute a unit; the unit includes containers and the land on which they are placed.

Hazards Analysis
The procedures involved in a) identifying potential sources of release of hazardous materials from fixed facilities or transportation accidents; c) determining the vulnerability of a geographical area to a release of hazardous materials; and c) comparing hazards to determine that present greater or lesser risks to a community.

Hazards Identification
1) Providing information on which facilities have extremely hazardous substances, what those chemicals are, and how much there is at each facility. The process also provides information on how the chemicals are stored and whether they are used at high temperatures. 2) The process of determining whether exposure to an agent can cause an increase in the incidence of a particular adverse health effect (e.g., cancer, birth defect) and whether the adverse health effect is likely to occur in humans.

HazMat Employee
An individual who is employed by a HazMat employer and who, in the course of the individual's employment, a) loads, unloads, or handles hazardous materials; b) reconditions or tests containers, drums, and packages represented for use in the transportation of hazardous materials; c) prepares hazardous materials for transportation; d) is responsible for the safety of the transportation of hazardous materials; or e) operates a vehicle used to transport hazardous materials.

HazMat Employer
A person who a) transports, in commerce, hazardous materials; b) causes to be transported or shipped, in commerce, hazardous materials; c) reconditions or tests containers, drums, and packages represented for use in the transportation of hazardous materials; and d) utilizes one or more of its employees in connection with such activity. The term includes an owner/operator of a motor vehicle that transports, in commerce, hazardous materials, and any department, agency, or instrumentality of the United States, a state, a political subdivision of a state, or a Native American Indian tribe engaged in such activities.

HC
See Hydrocarbon.

HCF
An acronym for Hot Channel Factor.

HCPWT

An acronym for House [of Representatives] Committee on Public Works and Transportation.

HCS

See Hazard Communication Standard.

HDP

An acronym for High Delta Pressure.

Head Protection

A term for personal protective equipment, such as bump caps, faceshields, hard hats, helmets, and hoods. *See* Personal Protective Equipment.

Head Shields

The identifiable structures that arch over the lip in some nematodes (threadlike worms).

Head, Static

The height above a standard datum of the surface of a column of water (or liquid) that can be supported by the static pressure at a given point. The static head is the sum of the elevation head and the pressure head.

Head, Total

The sum of the elevation head (distance of a point above datum), the pressure head (the height of a column of liquid that can be supported by static pressure at the point), and the velocity head (the height to which the liquid can be raised by its kinetic energy). *See* Hydraulic Head.

Headquarters Coordinating Teams

The DOE group of representatives designated by program Secretarial Officers and other Headquarters officials created to assist the Assistant Secretary, Environmental Protection, Safety, and Emergency Preparedness in developing policy and guidance for the hazardous waste management program.

Heads of Field Operations

The top management officials of the operations (OPs) offices and other applicable field organizations. They are the senior officials who manage the day-to-day operations of DOE's facilities under their jurisdiction.

Heads of Headquarters Elements

DOE Senior Program Managers within the line organizational structure, such as the Assistant Secretaries for Conservation and Renewable Energy, Defense Programs, Fossil Energy, and Nuclear Energy and the Directors of Energy Research, Civilian Radioactive Waste Management, and Environmental Restoration and Waste Management. Also included are the Administrators of the Bonneville and Western Area Power Administrations.

Headwaters

The point on a nontidal stream above which the average annual flow is less than 5 cubic feet per second. The district engineer may estimate this point from available data by using the mean annual area precipitation, area drainage basin maps, and the average runoff coefficient, or by similar means. For streams that are dry for long periods of the year, district engineers may establish the "headwaters" as that point on the stream where a flow of 5 cubic feet per second is equaled or exceeded 50% of the time.

Health and Safety Study

Any study of any effect of a chemical substance or mixture on health or the environment or on both, including underlying data and epidemiological studies, studies of occupational exposure to a chemical substance or mixture, toxicological, clinical, and ecological studies of a chemical substance or mixture, and any test performed pursuant to TSCA.

Health Assessments

Preliminary assessments of the potential risk to human health posed by individual sites and facilities, based on such factors as the nature and extent of contamination, the existence of potential for pathways of human exposure including ground or surface water contamination, air emissions, and food chain contamination), the size and potential susceptibility of the community within the likely pathways of exposure, the comparison of expected human exposure levels to the short-term and long-term health effects associated with identified contaminants and any available recommended exposure or tolerance limits for such contaminants, and the comparison of existing morbidity and mortality data on diseases that may be associated with the observed levels of exposure. The assessment must include an evaluation of the risks to the potentially affected population from all sources of such contaminants, including known point or nonpoint sources other than the site or facility in question. The purpose of a health assessment is to help determine whether full-scale health or epidemiological studies and medical evaluations of exposed populations must be conducted.

Health Examinations
Examinations performed by a licensed medical physician on people to determine their physical condition and general health status.

Health Hazard, Chemical
A chemical, mixture of chemicals, or a pathogen for which there is statistically significant evidence based on at least one study conducted in accordance with established scientific principles that acute or chronic health effects may occur in exposed employees. This includes chemicals that are carcinogens, toxic or highly toxic agents, reproductive toxins, irritants, corrosives, sensitizes, hepatotoxins, nephrotoxins, neurotoxins, agents that act on the hematopoietic system, and agents that damage the lungs, skin, eyes, or mucous membranes. It also includes stress due to temperature extremes. Further definition of the terms used above can be found in Appendix A to 20 CFR 1910.1200.

Health Physicist
An individual engaged in the study of science concerned with recognition, evaluation, and control of health hazards.

Health Physics
The branch of radiological science dealing with the protection of personnel from harmful effects of ionizing radiation.

Heap-Leach Extraction
The application of chemical agents to ore stockpiles or mine walls for the extraction of the mineral content.

Heat-Distortion Temperature
Temperature at which a test bar deflects a certain amount under specified temperature and a stated load.

Heat Exchanger
Any device that transfers heat from one fluid (liquid or gas) to another or to the environment. For example, a pipe that passes water by hot rocks to warm the water, cool the rocks, or both.

Heat Input
The total gross calorific value (where gross calorific value is measured by ASTM Method D2015-66, D240-64, or D182-64) of all fuels burned.

Heat Island Effects
Domes of elevated temperatures over urban areas caused by structural and pavement heat fluxes, and pollutant emissions from the areas below the domes.

Heat Pump or Reverse Cycle
1) A refrigeration machine that is used for heating buildings rather than cooling them. An expanding refrigeration fluid removes heat from the outside air; the fluid is then compressed, and the heat resulting from compression is discharged to a heat exchanger into the surroundings to be heated. 2) A product that a) consists of one or more assemblies; b) is powered by single phase electric current; c) is rated below 65,000 Btus per hour; d) utilizes an indoor conditioning coil, compressors, and refrigerant-to-outdoor-air heat exchanger to provide air heating; and e) may also provide air cooling, dehumidifying, humidifying circulating, and air cleaning.

Heat Sink
The medium or location to which waste heat is discharged.

Heat Transfer
The exchange of heat between one material and/or liquid and another by conduction, convection, or radiation.

Heating Oils
Petroleum based oil that is typically used in the operation of heating equipment, boilers, or furnaces. Petroleum includes No.1, No.2, No.4-Light, No.4-Heavy, No.5-Light, No.5-Heavy, and No.6 technical grades of fuel oil; other residual fuel oils (including Navy Special Fuel Oil and Bunker C); and other fuels when used as substitutes for one of these fuel oils.

Heavy Duty Vehicle (HDV)
A truck, bus, or other vehicle manufactured primarily for use on the public streets, roads, and highways that has a gross vehicle weight in excess of 6,000 pounds. Such term includes any such vehicle that has special features enabling off-street or off-highway operation and use.

Heavy Liquids
A group of dense heavy liquids that usually have a specific gravity (SG) greater than 2.5.

Heavy Metals
A common hazardous waste category consisting of metallic elements with high atomic weights (e.g., mercury, chromium, cadmium, arsenic, lead), that can damage living things at low concentrations and tend to accumulate in the food chain.

Heavy Minerals
The accessory minerals of sedimentary rock that usually have a specific gravity greater than 2.8.

Heavy Snow Warning
Heavy snow accumulations of 6 inches or more in a 12-hour period or 8 inches or more in a 24-hour period, are imminent, or expected with near certainty.

Heavy Water
Deuterium oxide: that is, water in which all hydrogen atoms have been replaced by deuterium atoms.

Helicopter Support Team
A task organization formed and equipped for employment in a hazard zone to facilitate the landing and movement of people, equipment, and supplies, and to evacuate medical casualties.

Heliophobe
A plant that grows best in shady areas.

Heliophyte
A plant that grows best in sunny areas.

Heliothermic
Organisms that maintain a comparatively high body temperature by basking in the sun.

Helipad
A prepared area designated and used for takeoff and landing of helicopters.

Helium-Neon (HeNe) Laser
A laser in which the active medium is a mixture of helium and neon. Its wavelength is usually in the visible range. Used widely for alignment, recording, printing, and measuring.

HEM
See Human Exposure Model.

Hema or Hemo
A prefix, pertaining to blood.

Hemangiosarcoma
A malignant neoplasm characterized by rapidly proliferating, extensively infiltrating, anaplastic cells derived from blood vessels and lining blood-filled spaces.

Hematuria
Condition in which the urine contains an abnormal amount of blood or red blood cells.

Hemodialysis
Removal of soluble substances from the blood by their diffusion through a semipermeable membrane.

Hemoglobin
The oxygen-carrying protein in red blood cells.

Hemoglobinuria
Condition in which the urine contains an abnormal amount of hemoglobin.

Hemolysis
Destruction or dissolution of red blood cells in such a manner that hemoglobin is liberated into the medium in which the cells are suspended.

Hemolytic Anemia
Any anemia resulting from destruction of red blood cells.

Hemoptysis
The spitting of blood derived from hemorrhage in the lungs or bronchial tubes.

HEPA
See High Efficiency Particulate Air Filters.

Hepatic
Pertaining to the liver.

Hepato
Prefix, pertaining to the liver.

Hepatomegaly
Enlargement of the liver.

Heptachlor
An insecticide that was banned on some food products in 1975 and all of them in 1978. It was allowed for use in seed treatment until in 1983. More recently, it was found in milk and other dairy products in Arkansas and Missouri, as a result of illegally feeding treated seed to dairy cattle.

Herbaceous
With the characteristics of an herb; a plant with no persistent woody stem above ground; green and leaflike in appearance and texture.

Herbicide
A chemical (pesticide) used to kill or control the growth weeds; a chemical compound that will kill or damage plants. Almost 70% of all pesticides used by farmers and ranchers are herbicides. These chemicals have wide-ranging effects on nontarget species (other than those the pesticide is meant to control). *See* Anticrop Agent; Antiplant Agent.

Herbivores
A species descriptor for plant-eating animals.

Hermaphrodite
An organism, such as a worm, having male and female reproductive organs in the same individual.

Hermetically Sealed
Closed by fusion, gasketing, crimping, or equivalent means so that no gas or vapor can enter or escape.

Herpetology
The scientific study of reptiles.

Hertz, H.R.
The German physicist who defined a measure of frequency in cycles per second (cps).

Heterogeneity
The characteristic of a medium in which material properties vary from point to point.

Heteromorphic
Species possessing two sets of stamens (male reproductive organs in plants) of unequal length.

Heterostylous
A polymorphism of flowers that helps to prevent self-pollination by having various lengths of

styles and stamens between individuals of a species.

Heterotrophic Organisms

Consumers such as humans, animals, and decomposers (primarily bacteria and fungi)that are dependent on organic matter for food.

HEV

An acronym for Hybrid Electric Vehicle.

Hexapod

A species descriptor for six-legged arthropod.

HF

An acronym for Hydrogen Fluoride.

HFCVSTP

See Hydrogen Fuel Cell Vehicle Study and Test Program (CAA).

Hibernacula

A case, covering, or structure in which an organism remains dormant for the winter; the shelter of a hibernating animal.

High Air

Air pressure used to supply power to pneumatic tools and devices.

High Airburst

The fallout safe height of burst for a nuclear weapon that increases damage to or casualties on soft targets, or reduces induced radiation contamination at actual ground zero. *See* Types of Burst.

High Altitude Burst

The explosion of a nuclear weapon that takes place at a height in excess of 100,000 feet (30,000 meters). *See* Types of Burst.

High-Concentration PCBs

An item, article, or material that contains 500 ppm or greater PCBs, or those materials that EPA requires to be assumed to contain 500 ppm or greater PCBs in the absence of testing.

High-Contact Industrial Surface

A surface in an industrial setting that is repeatedly touched, often for long periods of time. Manned machinery and control panels are examples of these surfaces. High-contact industrial surfaces are generally made of impervious solid material. Examples of low-contact industrial surfaces include ceilings, walls, floors, roofs, roadways, and sidewalks in the industrial area, utility poles, unmanned machinery, concrete pads beneath structural building components, exterior structural components, indoor vaults, and pipes.

High-Contact Residential/Commercial Surface

A surface in a residential/commercial area that is repeatedly touched, often for long periods of time. Doors, wall areas below 6 feet, uncovered flooring, window sills, fencing, banisters, stairs, automobiles, and children's play areas, outdoor patios, and sidewalks, are examples of high-contact residential/commercial surfaces. Low-contact residential/commercial areas include interior ceilings, interior wall areas above 6 feet, roofs, asphalt roadways, wooden utility poles, unmanned machinery, concrete pads beneath electrical equipment, curbing, exterior structural components (e.g., aluminum/vinyl siding, cinder block, asphalt tiles), and pipes.

High-Density Polyethylene

A material that produces toxic fumes when burned. Used to make plastic bottles and other products.

High-Efficiency Boiler

A boiler that operates at a minimum of 50 million g-hours. If the boiler uses natural gas or oil as primary fuel, the carbon monoxide concentration in the stack would be 50 ppm or less and the excess oxygen would be at least 3% when PCBs are burned. If the boiler uses coal as the primary fuel, the carbon monoxide concentration in the stack would be 100 ppm or less and the excess oxygen would be at least 3% when PCBs are being burned.

High-Efficiency Particulate Air Filters
High-efficiency particulate air filters having a fibrous medium that produces a particle removal efficiency of at least 99.97% for 0.3-micrometer particles of dioctylphthalate (DOP) when tested in accordance with MIL-STD-282.

High Explosive Cargo
Cargo such as artillery ammunition, bombs, depth charges, demolition material, rockets, and missiles. *See* Cargo.

High Explosives
Explosive substances capable of mass detonation, and for which there is a significant probability of accidental initiation or transition from burning to detonation.

High-Grade Paper
Letterhead, dry copy papers, miscellaneous business forms, stationery, typing paper, tablet sheets, and computer printout paper and cards commonly sold as whiteledge, computer printout, and tab card grade by the wastepaper industry.

High-Level Wastes
1) Hot, intensely radioactive fuel wastes produced by the nuclear industry. Typically these wastes have an extremely long half-life, and due to their intense heat, must be kept cool in tanks of water for a decade or so, prior to attempting to move them to a final disposal site where they must remain separated from the environment for up to 1,000 years before their radioactive levels dissipate to safe levels. 2) The highly radioactive waste material that results from the reprocessing of spent nuclear fuel, including liquid waste produced directly in reprocessing and any solid waste derived from the liquid, that contains a combination of transuranic waste and fission products in concentrations requiring permanent isolation. 3) Waste generated in the fuel of a nuclear reactor, found at nuclear reactors or nuclear fuel reprocessing plants. It is a serious threat to anyone who comes near the wastes without shielding.

High Oblique
See Oblique Aerial Photograph.

High-Potential Historic Sites
Those historic sites related to a historic route, or sites in close proximity thereto, that provide opportunity to interpret the historic significance of a trail during the period of its major use. Criteria for consideration as high potential sites include historic significance, presence of visible historic remnants, scenic quality, and relative freedom from intrusion.

High-Potential Incidents (HIPO)
Incidents with a large potential of significant loss.

High-Potential Route Segments
Those segments of a trail that would afford high quality recreation experience in a portion of the route having greater than average scenic values or affording an opportunity to vicariously share the experience of the original users of a historic route.

High Radiation Area
Any area, accessible to individuals, in which there exists radiation originating in whole or in part within licensed material at such levels that a major portion of the body could receive, in any single hour, a dose in excess of 100 millirem.

High-Risk Personnel
Personnel who, by their position, assignment, or relative work environs, are likely to be exposed to a hazardous situation in the event of an industrial accident, failure in operations of one or more facility systems, or during the course of an emergency cleanup.

High Seas Emergency Action Authority
The authority given the Secretary of Commerce (DOC) in cases of extreme urgency. The Secretary may take measures rendered necessary by the urgency of the situation without the consultation or notification required under the Intervention on the High Seas Act or without the continuation of consultations already begun. Measures directed or conducted shall be proportionate to the damage, actual or threatened, to the coastline or related interests of the United States and may not go beyond what is reasonably necessary to prevent, mitigate, or eliminate that damage. In consider-

ing whether measures are proportionate to the damage, the Secretary shall, among other things, consider the following: a) the extent and probability of imminent damage if those measures are not taken; b) the likelihood of effectiveness of those measures; and c) the extent of the damage that may be caused by those measures.

High-Temperature Gas-Cooled Reactor (HTGR)

A reactor using blocks of graphite containing fissile and fertile material and cooled with helium. HTGR's are operated at a high temperature that permits conversion of heat to electricity with improved efficiency.

High Terrain Area

With respect to any emitting facility, any area having an elevation of 900 feet or more above the base of the stack of such facility. In high terrain areas emissions of sulfur oxides from facilities cannot (during any day on which the otherwise applicable maximum allowable increases are exceeded) cause or contribute to concentrations that exceed the following maximum allowable increases for such areas over the baseline concentration for such pollutant: 24-hr maximum = 62 mgcm; 3-hr maximum = 221 mgcm. *See* Low Terrain Area.

High Tide Line

The line of intersection of the land with the water's surface at the maximum height reached by a rising tide. The high tide line may be determined, in the absence of actual data, by a line of oil or scum along shore objects, a more or less continuous deposit of fine shell or debris on the foreshore or berm, other physical markings or characteristics, vegetation lines, tidal gages, or other suitable means that delineate the general height reached by a rising tide. The line encompasses spring high tides and other high tides that occur with periodic frequency but does not include storm surges in which there is a departure from the normal or predicted reach of the tide due to the piling up of water against a coast by strong winds such as those accompanying a hurricane or other intense storm.

High-Water Mark

A mark left on a beach by wave wash at the preceding high water. It does not necessarily correspond to the high-water line. Because it can be determined by simple observation, it is frequently used in place of the high-water line, that can be determined only by a survey. When so used, it is called the high-water line.

Highest and Best Use

The most profitable use to which the property is adapted and needed or the use that is likely to be in demand in the reasonably near future. A highest-and-best-use study may show that a parking lot in a downtown area should be replaced by an office building. Placing a value on this property based on present use would be erroneous.

Highly Erodible Land

Land that a) is classified by the Soil Conservation Service as class IV, VI, VII, or VIII land under the land capability classification system in effect on December 23, 1985; or b) has, or that if used to produce an agricultural commodity, would have an excessive average annual rate of erosion in relation to the soil loss tolerance level, as established by the Secretary, and as determined by the application of factors from the universal soil loss equation and the wind erosion equation, including factors for climate, soil erodibility, and field slope.

Highly Toxic

A term referring to any substance that falls within any of the following categories: a) produces death within 14 days in half or more than half of a group of 10 or more laboratory white rats each weighing between 200 and 300 grams, at a single dose of 50 milligrams or less per kilogram of body weight, when orally administered; or b) produces death within 14 days in half or more than half of a group of 10 or more laboratory white rats each weighing between 200 and 300 grams, when inhaled continuously for a period of 1 hour or less at an atmospheric concentration of 200 parts per million by volume or less of gas or vapor or 2 milligrams per liter by volume or less of mist or dust, provided such concentration is likely to be encountered by man when the substance is used in any reasonably foreseeable manner; or c) produces death within 14 days in half or more than half of a group of 10 or more rabbits tested in a dosage of 200 milligrams or less per kilogram of body weight, when administered by continuous contact with the bare skin for 24 hours or less. If available data on human experience with any substance indicate results different from those obtained on animals in the above-named dosages or concentrations, the human data shall take precedence.

Highway Route Controlled Quantity

A quantity within a single package that exceeds a) 3,000 times the Al value of the radionuclides for special form radioactive materials; b) 3,000 times the A2 value of the radionuclides for normal form radioactive materials; or c) 30,000 curies; whichever is least. Al means the maximum activity of special form radioactive materials permitted in a Type A package. A2 means the maximum activity of radioactive materials, other than special form or low specific activity radioactive materials, permitted in a Type A package.

Hill Shading

A method of representing relief on a map by depicting the shadows that would be cast by high ground if light were shining from a certain direction.

HIPO

See High-Potential Incidents.

Hispid

A species descriptor that means covered with stiff or rough hair, or bristles.

Histic

A term applied to soil layers that are high in organic carbon and undergo seasonal periods of water saturation.

Histograms

Pictorial representations of a distribution; barographs.

Histology

The discipline that deals with the structure of cells, tissues, and organs in relation to their function.

Historian

A specialist with advanced training in the research, interpretation, and writing of history. Historians serve as researchers, cultural resource managers, cultural resource specialists, and park interpreters.

Historic American Buildings Survey/Historic American Engineering Record

Programs that produce a thorough archival record of both buildings and engineering structures that comprise the heritage of the built environment of the United States. If the NPS substantially alters or demolishes a historic structure, HABS/HAER documentation standards must be met prior to construction activities.

Historic Conservation District

An urban area of one or more neighborhoods and that contains a) historic properties; b) buildings having similar or related architectural characteristics; c) cultural cohesiveness; d) any combination of the above.

Historic Designed Landscape

See Cultural Landscape.

Historic District

A geographically definable urban or rural area that possesses significant concentration, linkage, or continuity of historic sites, structures, or objects, unified historically or aesthetically by plan, physical developments, or similarity of use. A district also may be composed of individual elements by association or history. Historical units of the National Park System are ordinarily historic districts in themselves.

Historic Fabric

Material remains of a historic structure or object, whether original materials or materials incorporated in a subsequent historically significant period as opposed to materials utilized to maintain or restore the structure or object during a nonhistoric period.

Historic Preservation

The retention, by regulation or structural improvements, of historic sites and districts.

Historic Preservation Policy

The federal declaration, in cooperation with other nations and in partnership with the states, local governments, Native American Indian tribes, and private organizations and individuals to:

- use measures, including financial and technical assistance, to foster conditions under which our modern society and our prehistoric and historic resources can exist in productive harmony and fulfill the social, economic, and other requirements of present and future generations;

- provide leadership in the preservation of the prehistoric and historic resources of the United States and of the international community of nations;

- administer federally owned, administered, or controlled prehistoric and historic resources in a spirit of stewardship for the inspiration and benefit of present and future generations;

- contribute to the preservation of nonfederally owned prehistoric and historic resources and give maximum encouragement to organizations and individuals undertaking preservation by private means;

- encourage the public and private preservation and utilization of all usable elements of the nations historic built environment; and

- assist state and local governments and the National Trust for Historic Preservation in the United States to expand and accelerate their historic preservation programs and activities.

Historic Preservation Program

The Secretary of the Interior's program to expand and maintain a National Register of Historic Places composed of districts, sites, buildings, structures, and objects significant in American history, architecture, archaeology, engineering, and/or culture.

Historic Preservation Review Commission

A board, council, commission, or other similar collegial body that is established by state or local legislation, the members of which are appointed, unless otherwise provided, from among a) professionals in the disciplines of architecture, history, architectural history, planning, archaeology, or related disciplines, to the extent such professionals are available in the community concerned; and b) such other persons as have demonstrated special interest, experience, or knowledge in history, architecture, or related disciplines and as will provide for an adequate and qualified commission.

Historic Property

1) As referred to in a Programmatic Memorandum of Agreement (PMOA) with the Advisory Council on Historic Preservation (ACHP), the term would include all property, historic and prehistoric, on the List of Classified Structures, included on or eligible for the Register of Historic Places. All historic properties are managed in accordance with agency approved "Management Policies." 2) Any prehistoric or historic district, site, building, structure, or object included in, or eligible for inclusion on the National Register; such term includes artifacts, records, and remains that are related to such a district, site, building, structure, or object.

Historic Site

A distinguishable lot/property, with or without a structure; or an area of historic, prehistoric, or symbolic notoriety upon which an important historic or prehistoric event occurred, or which is directly connected with such events or persons, or that was the subject of an important historic or prehistoric activity.

Historic Structure

A constructed work, consciously created to serve some human act of nature or design. Examples are buildings, roads, railroad tracks, canals, nautical vessels, stockades, forts and cemeteries, ruins, fences, gardens, and monumental statuary.

Historic Vernacular Landscape
See Cultural Landscape.

Historical Archaeologist
A scientist with advanced training in historical archaeology and in the use of historical documents in the reconstruction of the past (*See* Anthropology); subdiscipline of archaeology concerned with the remains left by literate societies (in contrast, the distinction is not always clearcut). In the United States, historical archaeology generally deals with the evidences of European-American societies and with the evidences of aboriginal societies after the time of major cultural disruption or material change due to European-American contact.

Historical Architect
A specialist in the science and art of architecture with training in the methods and techniques of preserving prehistoric and historic structures. A historical architect has the understanding and skill to combine pertinent aspects of original historic construction methods and materials, with contemporary technology, engineering, cultural and aesthetic values, and physical fabric.

History
The study of the past through a written assessment of culture. The evidence from these writings are then placed in a chronological or topical sequence of preceding, contemporary, and subsequent events.

Histosols
Organic soils.

HIWAY
A line source model for gaseous pollutants.

HLFM
An acronym for High Level Flux Monitor.

HLLW
An acronym for High-Level Liquid Waste.

HLW
See High-Level Waste (same as High-Level Radioactive Waste).

HM
An acronym for Health Monitoring.

HOCs
See Halogenated Organic Compounds.

Hoist
In helicopters, the mechanism by which casualties or external loads may be raised or lowered vertically.

Holding Pond
A pond or reservoir, usually made of earth, built to store polluted runoff.

Holdings
The taxable value of locally assessable fixtures and the full cash value of locally assessable business personal property in a county.

Holdup, Nuclear Material
The nuclear material that is retained in process equipment at inventory time.

Holostomatous
A minute opening of a leaf or stem through which gases and water vapor pass.

Holotype
The specimen used as the basis of the original published description of a taxonomic species.

Home Use
Use in a household or its immediate environment.

Home Range
An area defined by the habitual movements of an animal.

Homeostasis

Maintenance of normal, internal stability in an organism by coordinated responses of the organ systems.

Homogeneity

The characteristic of a medium in which material properties are identical throughout.

Hood

Any air-intake device connected to a mechanical exhaust system for collecting vapors, fumes, smoke, dust, steam, heat, or odors from, at or near the equipment, place or area where generated, produced or released.

Hood Capture Efficiency

The emissions from a process that are captured by hood and directed into the control device, expressed as a percent of all emissions.

Hoop Stress

Circumferential stress in a cylindrically shaped part as a result of internal or external pressure.

Horizon

The apparent or visible junction of the earth and sky, as seen from any specific position. Also called the apparent, visible, or local horizon. A horizontal plane passing through a point of vision or perspective center. The apparent or visible horizon approximates the true horizon only when the point of vision is very close to sea level.

Horizontal Bracing Systems (HBS)

Horizontal truss systems that serve the same function as a diaphragm.

Horizontal Loading

Loading of items of like character and compatible materials in horizontal layers. *See* Loading.

Horizontal Stowage

The lateral distribution of unit equipment or categories of supplies so that they can be unloaded simultaneously from two or more holds.

Hormone

A chemical substance, formed in one organ or part of the body and carried in the blood to another organ or part where it alters the functional activity, and sometimes the structure, of one or more organs by its specific chemical activity.

Hospital

A medical treatment facility capable of providing in-patient care. It is appropriately staffed and equipped to provide diagnostic and therapeutic services, as well as the necessary emergency support services required to perform its functions. A hospital may, in addition, discharge the functions of a clinic.

Host

1) In genetics, the organism, typically a bacterium, into which a gene from another organism is transplanted. 2) In medicine, an animal infected by or parasitized by another organism.

Host Country

A nation in which representatives or organizations of another state are present because of government invitation and/or international agreement.

Host Defense Systems

A complex system that defends the body against biological or chemical agents. Often referred to with respect to the lungs where the system clears the lungs of microbes and particulate pollutants. Also refers to chemical defenses such as antioxidant substances that defend against oxidants such as ozone or nitrogen dioxide.

Host Fish

A fish on which mussel larvae reside until they are capable of surviving on their own.

Host Nation Support

Civil and/or military assistance rendered by a nation to foreign forces within its territory during peacetime, crises or emergencies, or war based on agreements mutually concluded between nations.

Hot Dry Rock

A body of rock that, because of a geothermal anomaly, is substantially hotter than the rock in the surrounding environs.

Hot Spot

A region, or spot, within a contaminated area/site in which the level of contamination is considerably greater than in neighboring/adjacent areas. *See* Hot Zone.

Hot Zone

The area immediately surrounding a chemical hazard incident, such as a spill, in which contamination or other danger exists.

Household or Domestic Waste

Solid waste, composed of garbage and rubbish, that normally originates from residential, private households, or apartment buildings. Domestic waste may contain a significant amount of toxic or hazardous waste from improperly discarded pesticides, paints, batteries, and cleaners.

HPCI

An acronym for High Pressure Coolant Injection.

HPCS

An acronym for High Pressure Core Spay.

HPIS

An acronym for High Pressure Injection System.

HPLC

An acronym for High Performance Liquid Chromatography.

HPMA

An acronym for the Hardwood Plywood Manufacturer's Association.

HS

See Hydrogen Sulfide.

HSA

An acronym for Historic Sites Act of 1935.

HSE

An acronym for Health, Safety, and Environment.

HSWA

An acronym for Hazardous and Solid Waste Amendments.

HTS

An acronym for High Temperature Superconductivity.

HUDA

An acronym for Housing and Urban Development Act.

Human Engineering

Designing hardware and equipment to effectively fit a wide range of human physical characteristics. *See* Ergonomics; Human Factors Engineering.

Human Environment

A comprehensive term for the natural and physical environment and the relationship of people with that environment. Economic or social effects alone are not intended to require preparation of an environmental impact statement. When an environmental impact statement is prepared and economic or social and natural or physical environmental effects are interrelated, then the environmental impact statement will address all of these effects on the human environment.

Human Equivalent Dose

The human dose of an agent expected to induce the same type and severity of toxic effect that an animal dose has induced.

Human Exposure Model (HEM)

A mathematical model used in exposure assessments for toxic air pollutants to quantify the number of people exposed to pollutants emitted by stationary sources and the pollutant concentrations they are exposed to. Input data include plant characteristics such as location, emission, and parameters, as well as Bureau of Census data used in the estimation of persons exposed, and appropriate meteorological data.

Human Factors

1) The biomedical, psycho-social, workplace environment, and engineering considerations pertaining to people in human-machine system. Some of these considerations are allocation of functions, task analysis, human reliability, training requirements, job performance aiding, personnel qualification and selection, staffing requirements, procedures, organizational effectiveness, and workplace environmental conditions. 2) The application of the human biological and psychological sciences in conjunction with the engineering sciences to achieve the optimum mutual adjustment of human beings and their work, the benefits being measured in terms of human efficiency and well-being. The principle disciplines involved are anthropometry, physiology, and engineering.

Human Factors Engineering (Ergonomics)

The application of knowledge about human performance capabilities and behavioral principles to the design, operation, and maintenance of human-machine systems so that personnel can function at their optimum level of performance. *See* Ergonomics; Human Engineering.

Human Performance

How a person functions, including both failure (errors) and success (reliability).

Human Reliability

The dependability of the human within a system.

Humanitarian and Civic Assistance

Assistance to the local populace provided by predominantly U.S. forces in conjunction with military operations and exercises. This assistance is specifically authorized by title 10, United States Code, Section 401, and funded under separate authorities. Assistance provided under these provisions is limited to the following: a) medical, dental, and veterinary care provided in rural areas of a country; b) construction of rudimentary surface transportation systems; c) well drilling and construction of basic sanitation facilities; and d) rudimentary construction and repair of public facilities. Assistance must fulfill unit training requirements that incidentally create humanitarian benefit to the local populace. *See* Humanitarian Assistance.

Humanitarian Assistance

Programs conducted to relieve or reduce the results of natural or manmade disasters or other endemic conditions such as hazardous releases, human pain, disease, hunger, or privation that might present a serious threat to life or that can result in great damage to or loss of property. Humanitarian assistance provided by U.S. forces is limited in scope and duration. The assistance provided is designed to supplement or complement the efforts of the host nation civil authorities or agencies that may have the primary responsibility for providing humanitarian assistance.

Humification

Microbial breakdown of organic matter in the soil to form humus.

Hummock

A low mound, ridge, or knoll.

Humults

Freely drained ultisols that have a high content of organic matter.

Humus

1) The dark-colored carboniferous residue in the soil resulting from the decomposed organic vegetable tissues of the plants originally growing there. Humus improves the texture of the soil and helps it to retain water. Similar residues are found in well-digested sledges and activated sludge. 2) Decomposed organic material.

Hunting Year

The 12-month period beginning on July 1 of any such year.

Hyaline

A species descriptor that means glossy or transparent appearance.

Hybrid

1) A cell or organism resulting from a cross between two unlike plant or animal cells or organisms. 2) An offspring produced by parents of different species; for example, a donkey and a horse produce a mule.

Hybrid Composite

A composite with two or more reinforcing fibers.

Hybridoma

A hybrid cell that produces monoclonal antibodies in large quantifies.

Hydration

The chemical addition of water to a compound.

Hydraulic Barrier

Modifications to a groundwater flow system that restrict or impede movement of contaminants.

Hydraulic Conductivity (K)

1) A proportionality constant relating hydraulic gradient to specific discharge, that for an isotropic medium and homogeneous fluid, equals the volume of water at the existing kinetic viscosity that will move in unit time under a unit hydraulic gradient through a unit area measured at right angles to the direction of flow. 2) The rate of flow of water in gallons per day through a cross section of 1 square foot under a unit hydraulic gradient, at the prevailing temperature (gpd/ft). In the International System of Units, the units are m/day/m or m/day. 3) A coefficient of proportionality describing the rate at which water can move through a permeable medium. The density and kinematic viscosity of the water must be considered in determining hydraulic conductivity.

Hydraulic Conductivity, Effective

The rate of water flow through a porous medium that contains more than one fluid, that should be specified in terms of both the fluid type, content, and existing pressure.

Hydraulic Fracturing

A general term, for the fracturing of rock in an oil or gas reservoir by pumping a fluid under high pressure into the well. The purpose is to produce artificial openings in the rock in order to increase permeability.

Hydraulic Gradient

1) Slope of a water table or potentiometric surface. More specifically, the change in static head per unit of distance in a given direction. 2) The rate of change in total head per unit of distance of flow in a given direction. 3) The change in total head with a change in distance in a given direction. The direction yields a maximum rate of decrease in head. The difference in hydraulic heads, divided by the distance along the flow path equals the hydraulic gradient (h_1-h_2 /L = i); or, the direction of groundwater flow due to changes in the depth of the water table.

Hydraulic Head

The height above a datum plane (such as mean sea level) of the column of water that can be supported by the hydraulic pressure at a given point in a groundwater system. The hydraulic head is equal to the distance between the water level in a well and the datum plane.

Hydraulic Lift Tanks

Tanks holding hydraulic fluid for a closed-loop mechanical system that uses compressed air or hydraulic fluid to operate elevators, and other similar devices.

Hydraulic Shoring

A shoring system using hydraulic cylinders, planks, rails, plywood or steel beams to support the excavated wall of trenches.

Hydraulic Structures

Structures for the conveyance and/or control of water under nonpressure open-channel flow.

Hydraulics

The branch of science or of engineering concerned with water or other fluids in motion.

Hydrazine (NH4)

The reactive chemical used in the production of explosives, chemicals, and rocket fuel.

Hydric Soil

Soil that, in its undrained condition, is saturated, flooded, or ponded long enough during a growing season to develop an anaerobic condition that supports the growth and regeneration of hydrophytic vegetation; soil that is wet long enough to periodically produce anaerobic conditions, thereby influencing the growth of plants. *See* Hydrophytic Vegetation.

Hydrocarbon (HC)

A compound containing only carbon and hydrogen. The fossil fuels are predominantly hydrocarbons, with varying amounts of organic compounds of sulfur, nitrogen, and oxygen, and some inorganic materials. Hydrocarbons contribute to air pollution problems like smog.

Hydrodynamic Dispersion

1) Spreading (at the macroscopic level) of the solute front during transport resulting from both mechanical dispersion and molecular diffusion. 2) The process by which groundwater containing a solute is diluted with uncontaminated groundwater as it flows through an aquifer. *See* Dispersion Coefficient.

Hydroelectric Power

The generation of electricity by way of a power plant in which the energy of falling water is converted into electricity by turning a turbine generator.

Hydrogen Bomb

See Thermonuclear Weapon.

Hydrogen Cyanide

A poisonous gas used in the production of nylon, pharmaceuticals, dyes, and some other polymers.

Hydrogen Fuel Cell Vehicle Study and Test Program (HFCVSTP)

An EPA sponsored program, in conjunction with the National Aeronautics and Space Administration and the Department of Energy, to study and test the development of a hydrogen fuel cell vehicle. The study and test program shall determine how best to transfer existing NASA hydrogen fuel cell technology into the form of a mass-producible, cost-effective hydrogen fuel cell vehicle. The study and test program includes a feasibility design study, the construction of a prototype, and a demonstration.

Hydrogen Gas Streams

Hydrogen streams formed in the chlor-alkali cell deluder.

Hydrogen-Ion Concentration

The weight of the hydrogen ion in moles per liter of solution, expressed as the pH value.

Hydrogen Sulfide (H2S)

1) A poisonous, stinky gas (smells like rotten eggs) used in chemical industries, in the manufacture of rayon, and in laboratory research. 2) Gas emitted during organic decomposition. Also a byproduct of oil refining and burning.

Hydrogen Sulfide Study

A study assessing the hazards to public health and the environment resulting from the emission of hydrogen sulfide associated with the extraction of oil and natural gas resources. The assessment includes a review of existing state and industry control standards, techniques and enforcement strategies. Comprehensive health and safety regulations with respect to the potential hazards of hydrofluoric acid and the uses of hydrofluoric acid in industrial and commercial applications to public health and the environment considering a range of events including worst-case accidental releases.

Hydrogeologic

Those factors that deal with subsurface waters and related geologic aspects of surface waters.

Hydrogeologic Feasibility

A determination by a registered geologist that water placed in the groundwater recharge facility will percolate to the groundwater zone intended to be recharged, and that water quality of that zone is compatible with the recharge water. For an in-lieu groundwater recharge project, hydrogeologic feasibility means a determination by a registered geologist that the proposed operation will result in recharge of the groundwater zone.

Hydrogeologic Parameters

Numerical parameters that describe the hydrogeologic characteristics of an aquifer such as porosity, permeability, and transmissivity.

Hydrogeologic Unit

Any soil or rock unit or zone that due to its hydraulic properties has a distinct influence on the storage or movement of groundwater.

Hydrogeology

The science that deals with the geology of groundwater, with particular emphasis on the chemistry and movement of water.

Hydrograph

A graphic display of the water level that measures the rate of flow over time. Measures the discharge, stage, velocity, available power, or other property of water over time.

Hydrographic Chart

A nautical chart showing depths of water, nature of bottom, contours of bottom and coastline, and tides and currents in a given sea or sea and land area.

Hydrographic Reconnaissance

Reconnaissance of an area of water to determine depths, beach gradients, the nature of the bottom, and the location of coral reefs, rocks, shoals, spills, and other manmade obstacles.

Hydrography

The science that deals with the measurements and description of the physical features of the oceans, seas, lakes, rivers, and their adjoining coastal areas, with particular reference to their use for navigational purposes.

Hydrological Cycle

The movement of water between bodies of water, land, and atmosphere by evaporation and precipitation, and the activity of humans, animals, and other living organisms. During the cycle, water evaporates from the seas, evaporates into the atmosphere, and falls as precipitation (rain) over land and sea. Rain that has fallen on the land eventually makes its way to rivers and streams that return it to the oceans completing the cycle. See figure on following page.

Hydrology

The science dealing with the properties, movement, and effects of water on the earth's surface, in the soil and rocks below, and in the atmosphere.

Hydrolysis

Decomposition or alteration of a chemical substance by water. In aqueous solutions of electrolytes, the reactions of cations with water to produce a weak base, or of anions with water to produce a weak acid.

Hydrophyte, Hydrophytic

Any plant growing in water or on a substrate that is at least periodically deficient in oxygen as a result of excessive water content.

Hydrophytic Vegetation

A plant growing in water; or a substrate that is at least periodically deficient in oxygen during a growing season as a result of excessive water content.

Hydrostatic Pressure

1) The pressure, expressed as a total quantity or per unit of area, exerted by a body of water at rest. 2) In the case of groundwater, the pressure generally due to the weight of water at higher levels in the same zone of saturation.

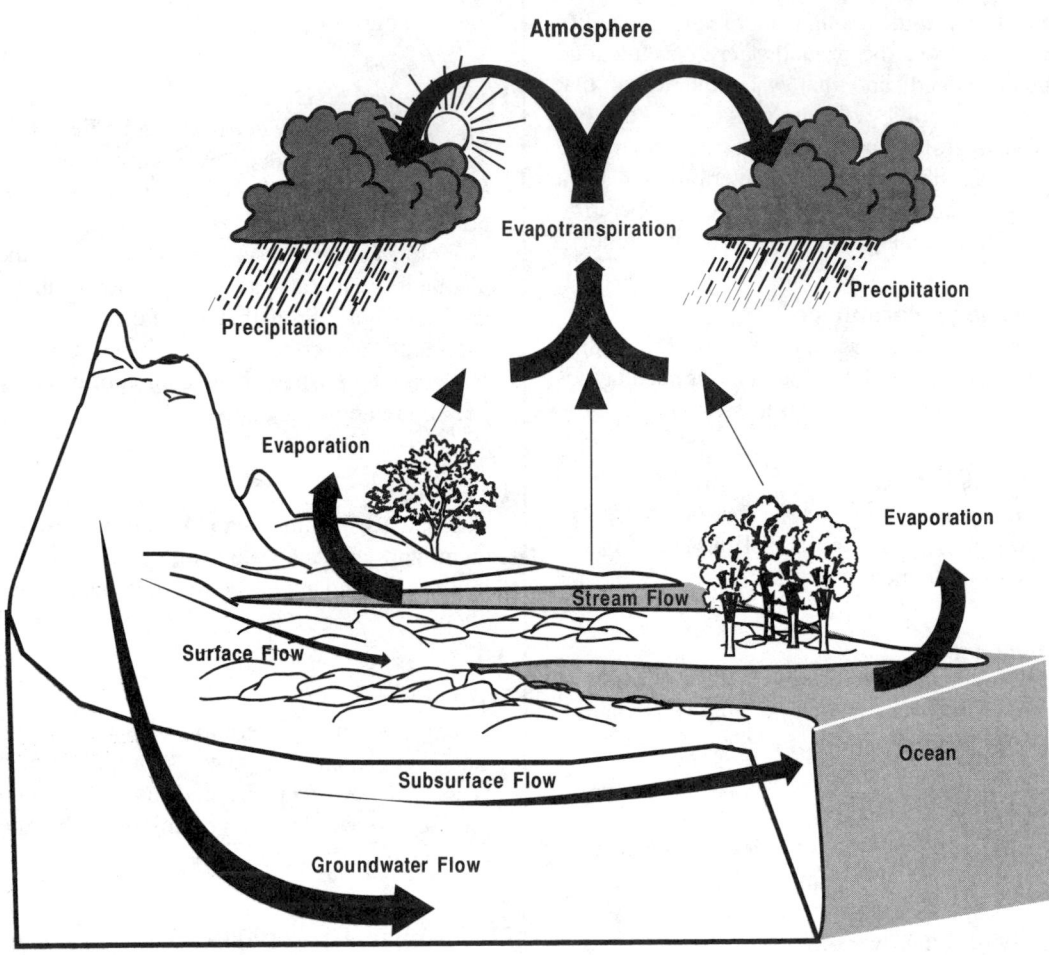

Hydrologic Cycle

Hydrostatic Sludge Removal
The discharge of sludge from hopper-bottomed sedimentation tanks by use of the hydrostatic pressure of the wastewater above the sludge outlet.

Hygrometer
An instrument used to measure the amount of moisture in the atmosphere.

Hygroscopic
Absorbing moisture from the air.

Hypanthium
The modified, often enlarged floral receptacle of various plants, having a cup-shaped or tubular form.

Hyper
A prefix pertaining to a higher than normal value.

Hyperbaric Chamber
1) A chamber in which employees are treated for decompression sickness and/or air embolism. It may also be used in preemployment physical ex-

aminations to determine the adaptability of the prospective employee to changes in pressure. 2) A chamber used to induce an increase in ambient pressure as would occur in descending below sea level, in a water or air environment. It is the only type of chamber suitable for use in the treatment of decompression sickness in flying or diving. Also called compression chamber; diving chamber; recompression chamber.

Hyperbilirubinemia
A condition in which an abnormally large amount of bilirubin is found in the blood. Jaundice becomes apparent when the level of bilirubin is double the normal level.

Hyperesthesia
Increased sensitivity to touch, pain, or other sensory stimuli.

Hyperfocal Distance
The distance from the lens to the nearest object in focus when the lens is focused at infinity.

Hypergolic Fuel
Fuel that will spontaneously ignite with an oxidizer, such as aniline with fuming nitric acid. It is used as the propulsion agent in certain missile systems.

Hyperhaline
A term used to characterize waters with salinity greater than 40%, due to ocean-derived salts. *See* Hypersaline.

Hyperpigmentation
An excess of pigment in a tissue or pan of the body.

Hyperplasia
The abnormal multiplication or increase in the number of normal cells in normal arrangement in a tissue.

Hyperreflexia
A condition in which the deep tendon reflexes are exaggerated.

Hypersaline
A term used to characterize waters with salinity greater than 40%, due to land-derived salts. *See* Hyperhaline.

Hypersensitivity
Exaggerated response by the immune system to an allergen. Sometimes used incorrectly in a non-immune sense to indicate increased susceptibility to the effects of a pollutant.

Hypersensitization
Increased sensitivity of the immune system; induced by initial exposure with subsequent exposures eliciting a greater than expected immunologic response.

Hypersonic
Of or pertaining to speeds equal to, or in excess of, five times the speed of sound. *See* Speed of Sound.

Hyperstereoscopy
Stereoscopic viewing in which the relief effect is noticeably exaggerated, caused by the extension of the camera base. Also called exaggerated stereoscopy.

Hypertension
Abnormally elevated arterial blood pressure; high blood pressure.

Hypertrophic
Denotes a body of water that has been grossly enriched with plant nutrients, usually due to the effects of pollution.

Hypertrophy
Enlargement of an organ due to increase in cell size with no change in the cell number. For example, liver hypertrophy occurs in mice exposed to chlorinated hydrocarbons or to phenobarbital.

Hyperventilation
Overventilation; increased rate of air exchange relative to metabolic carbon dioxide production

so that alveolar carbon dioxide pressure tends to fall below normal.

Hypo
A prefix pertaining to a less than normal value.

Hypocalcemia
A condition in which an abnormally low concentration of calcium ions is present in the blood.

Hypocenter
The point of impact directly beneath the center of a nuclear bomb explosion.

Hypogynous
Having floral parts or organs that are below and not in contact with the ovary.

Hypokalemia
A condition in which an abnormally low concentration of potassium ions is present in the blood.

Hypomagnesemia
A condition in which the plasma concentration of magnesium ions is abnormally low; may cause convulsions and concurrent hypocalcemia.

Hypophosphatemia
Condition in which an abnormally low concentration of phosphate is found in the blood.

Hypotension
Low arterial blood pressure.

Hypotonia
A condition in which there is a loss of muscle tone.

Hypoxemia
A condition in which inadequate oxygen is present in arterial blood, short of anoxia.

Hypoxia
Low oxygen content in a body tissue(s); below physiologic levels in air, blood, or body tissues.

I

IA

See Initial Assessment.

IAG

An acronym for Interagency Agreement.

IAPCT

An acronym for International Air Pollution Control Technologies (CAA). *See* Assessment of International Air Pollution Control Technologies.

ICIHSOP

An acronym for International Convention Relating to Intervention on the High Seas in Cases of Oil Pollution Casualties of 1969.

ICP/MS

An acronym for Inductively Coupled Plasma/Mass Spectrometer.

ICPP

An acronym for Idaho Chemical Processing Plant.

Idaho National Engineering Laboratory (INEL)

The DOE Research and Development and Field Facility established for the building and testing of nuclear reactors and support equipment. INEL reprocesses and recovers spent nuclear fuel from several test reactors, the nuclear naval fleet and other nuclear noncommercial reactors and processes liquid waste into the calcine form for inter-

mediate storage. INEL operates the Advanced Test Reactor and a radioactive waste management complex for storage and disposal of low-level waste and conducts associated programs in materials testing, isotope production, irradiation services and training and test support; in addition, INEL functions as the lead laboratory for the Multi-Megawatt Space Reactor program and Fusion Reactor Safety Research.

Idaho Operations Office

The DOE Idaho Operations Office, established in 1949, that administers the Idaho National Engineering Laboratory (INEL) and associated support facilities. Major program and project assignments include the following: nuclear materials production, defense waste and transportation management, energy conservation, alternate energy, remedial action, the Three Mile Island Program, and the Multi-Megawatt Space Reactor.

Identification Code (EPA I.D. Number)

The unique code assigned to each generator, transporter, and treatment, storage, or disposal facility by EPA to facilitate identification and tracking of hazardous waste. Superfund sites also have assigned I.D. numbers.

IDLH

See Immediately Dangerous to Life and Health.

IDS

An acronym for Integrated Database.

IEAEMM
An acronym for International Energy Agency Emergency Management Manual.

IEEE
An acronym for the Institute of Electrical and Electronic Engineers.

IFC
An acronym for Internal Fission Counter.

IFMIF
An acronym for International Fusion Materials Irradiation Facility.

IGCC
An acronym for Integrated Gasification Combined Cycle.

Igloo Space
An area in an earth-covered structure of concrete and/or steel designed for the storage of ammunition and explosives. *See* Storage.

Igneous
A term applied to rocks that were once molten and were formed by the solidification of magma. These rocks are classified according to silica content, grain size (gradation), and texture.

Ignitable/Ignitability
Capable of burning or causing a fire.

Igniter
A device designed to produce a flame or flash that is used to initiate an explosion.

Ignition Temperature
The minimum (auto ignition) temperature required to ignite gas or vapor without a spark or flame being present.

IH
See Industrial Hygiene.

IHSA
An acronym for Intervention on the High Seas Act.

IIRMP
An acronym for Interim Indoor Radon (and Radon Decay Product) Measurement Protocol.

IKC
An acronym for In-Kind Contribution; the matching of funds or other resources. *See* In-Kind Contributions.

ILRT
An acronym for Integrated Leak Rate Test.

ILS
See Integrated Logistics Support.

Image Motion Compensation
Movement intentionally imparted to film at such a rate as to compensate for the forward motion of an air or space vehicle when photographing ground objects.

Imagery
Collectively, the representations of objects reproduced electronically or by optical means on film, electronic display devices, or other media.

Imagery Intelligence (IMINT)
Information derived from the collection of data by visual photography, infrared sensors, lasers, electro-optics, and radar sensors such as synthetic aperture radar wherein images of objects are reproduced optically or electronically on film, electronic display devices, or other media.

Imagery Interpretation
1) The process of location, recognition, identification, and description of objects, activities, and terrain represented on imagery. 2) The extraction of information from photographs or other recorded images.

Imagery Interpretation Key

Any diagram, chart, table, list, or set of examples, etc., that is used to aid in the rapid identification of objects visible on imagery.

Immature

A species descriptor that means juvenile; in insects, the larval stage of development.

Immediate Acute Health Hazards (CERCLA, CFR)

Adverse effects to a target organ that generally occur rapidly as a result of short-term exposure to toxic substances, irritants, sensitizers, corrosives, and other hazardous chemicals. Effects are typically of short duration.

Immediate Causes

Practices or conditions that physically cause an accident or incident at a specific time and place.

Immediate Container, or True Container

The unit, drum, jar, plastic bag, or other receptacle or covering in which any environmental sample is collected for laboratory shipment.

Immediate Decontamination

Decontamination carried out by individuals upon becoming contaminated, to save life and minimize casualties. This may include decontamination of some personal clothing and/or equipment. *See* Decontamination Zone; Decontamination.

Immediate Release Area

The area, process, or machine that is creating the hazardous spill. The key factor that must be considered is the actual or estimated exposure or degree of danger to responders, other employees, neighbors, etc. In order to determine this, factors such as the size of the spill/release, the material of the spill, and the location of the incident (e.g., confined space) play a significant role. Planning must take place prior to any releases that pose an emergency. An employer must determine all likely potentials for emergencies using worst-case assumptions and plan response procedures ac-

cordingly; past history of emergencies at a site should be used as a guide.

Immediately Dangerous to Life and Health (IDLH)

1) The atmospheric concentration of a chemical that poses an immediate danger to the life or health of a person who is exposed but from which that person could escape without any escape-impairing symptoms or irreversible health effects. A companion measurement to the permissible exposure limit (PEL), IDLH concentrations represent levels at which respiratory protection is required. IDLH is expressed in parts per million (ppm) or mg/ml. 2) The maximum level to which a healthy individual can be exposed to a chemical for 30 minutes and escape without suffering irreversible health effects or impairing symptoms. *See* Level of Concern.

Immediately Dangerous to Life or Health Values

As defined in 29 Code of Federal Regulations Part 1926.103, a condition that either poses an immediate threat to life and health or an immediate threat of severe exposure to contaminants.

Imminent and Substantial Endangerment

A qualifying condition given to any solid or hazardous waste that, when applied, gives EPA the authority to take necessary actions to protect public health and the environment. This action may include but is not limited to restraining any person from handling, storage, treatment, transportation, or disposal of solid or hazardous wastes that meet this condition. The test for "imminent and substantial endangerment" places a heavy burden of proof on EPA and therefore, substantially limits EPA's authority to address disposal site problems.

Imminent Danger

Any condition or practice that is such that a hazard exists that could reasonably be expected to cause death or serious physical harm to employees (permanent or prolonged impairment of the body or temporary disablement requiring hospitalization), unless immediate actions are taken to mitigate the effects of the hazard and/or remove employees from the hazard.

Imminent Hazard
1) The existence of a condition that presents a substantial likelihood that death, serious illness, severe personal injury, or substantial endangerment to health, property, or the environment may occur before the reasonably foreseeable completion of an administrative hearing or other formal proceeding initiated to abate the risks of those effects. 2) Situations that exist when the continued use of a pesticide during the time required for cancellation proceeding would be likely to result in unreasonable adverse effects on the environment or will involve unreasonable hazard to the survival of a species declared endangered or threatened by the Secretary pursuant to the Endangered Species Act of 1973 (16 USC Section 1631 et seq.).

Imminent Safety Hazard
An imminent and unreasonable risk of death or severe personal injury.

Immiscible
The chemical property where two or more liquids or phases do not readily dissolve in one another such as oil and water.

Immune System
All internal structures and processes providing defense against disease-causing organisms (viruses, bacteria, fungi, parasites). Includes nonspecific defense mechanisms, such as interferon production, epithelial membranes and phagocytic cells, as well as specific immune responses of cells producing antibodies in response to antigens entering the body.

Immunodeficiency
A condition resulting from ineffective functioning of the immunological system. Immunodeficiency may be primary (due to a defect in the immune mechanism per se) or secondary (dependent upon another disease process or toxicant exposure).

Immunosuppression
Decrease of immunologic response, usually resulting from exposure to chemical, pharmacologic, physical, or immunologic agents.

Impact Area
An area having designated boundaries within the limits of which all hazards associated with contaminants will be released or impact.

Impact Assessment
See Environmental Impact Assessment (EIA).

Impact Strength
A material's ability to withstand shock loading as measured by the work done in fracturing a specimen.

Imperforate
A species descriptor that means having no opening.

Impermeability
The characteristic of geologic materials that limits their ability to transmit significant quantities of water under the pressure deviations normally found in the subsurface environment.

Impermeable
Not permitting passage or flows, as of groundwater through bedrock; impervious.

Impervious Rock
In hydrology, rock that does not permit the passage of liquid substances under subsurface pressures and conditions.

Impervious Solid Surfaces
Solid surfaces that are nonporous and thus will not absorb spilled PCBs within the short period of time required for cleanup under the PCB Spill Cleanup Policy. Impervious solid surfaces include, but are not limited to, metals, glass, aluminum siding, and enameled or laminated surfaces.

Implementation

To give practical effect to and ensure actual fulfillment by the establishment of concrete measures.

Implementation Plan, Compliance

Conformity to a state's implementation plan for eliminating or reducing the severity and number of violations of the national ambient air quality standards and achieving expeditious attainment of such standards; providing that such activities will not a) cause or contribute to any new violation of any standard in any area; b) increase the frequency or severity of any existing violation of any standard in any area; or c) delay timely attainment of any standard or any required interim emission reductions or other milestones in any area. Determinations of conformity are based on most recent estimates of emissions, as determined from the most recent population, employment, travel, and congestion estimates as determined by the metropolitan planning organization, regional council of governments, or other agency authorized to make such estimates.

Implementation Planning

Operational planning associated with the conduct of a continuing operation to attain defined objectives. At the national level, it includes the development of strategy and the assignment of strategic tasks to departments/agencies responsible for environmental enforcement activities. At lower levels, implementation planning prepares for the execution of assigned permitting and inspection tasks or related missions.

Implementation Plans

1) Documents outlining the steps to be taken to ensure compliance with environmental legislation within a specific time frame. These plans are required by various federal and state environmental protection statutes. 2) Concise descriptions of the approach, resources, and time period planned for implementing Orders that require such plans on a site-wide basis. The plan includes a description of the execution of environmental protection, safety, and health responsibilities and authorities by the field organization, and any proposed generic exemptions to parts of such DOE Orders. 3) Written plans that record the results of the scoping process and outline the procedures by which an environmental impact statement is to be prepared.

Implementing

Any activity related to the planning, developing, establishing, carrying-out, improving, or maintaining of environmental research and mitigation programs.

Implementing Agencies

EPA, or, a designated state or local agency responsible for carrying out an approved UST (Underground Storage Tank) program.

Implosion Weapon

A weapon in which a quantity of fissionable material, less than a critical mass at ordinary pressure, has its volume suddenly reduced by compression (a step accomplished by using chemical explosives) so that it becomes supercritical, producing a nuclear explosion.

Import

To land on, bring into, or introduce into, or attempt to land on, bring into, or introduce into, any place subject to the jurisdiction of the United States, whether or not such landing, bringing, or introduction constitutes an importation within the meaning of the customs laws of the United States.

Important Building

A building in which there may be a hazardous source of ignition under normal operating conditions.

Impounding Area

An area used to contain an accidental liquid spill through the use of dikes, berms, and/or topographic features.

Impoundment

1) The accumulation of water in a reservoir. 2) A body of water or sludge confined by a dam, dike, floodgate, or other barrier.

Imprint
Brief notes in the margin of a map giving all or some of the following: date of publication, printing, name of publisher, printer, place of publication, number of copies printed, and related information.

Improved Risk
Generally, an improved risk property that would qualify for complete insurance coverage by the Factory Mutual System, the Industrial Risk Insurers, and other industrial insurance companies that limit their insurance underwriting to the best protected class of industrial risk.

Improvised Nuclear Device (IND)
A device incorporating radioactive materials designed to result in the dispersal of radioactive material or in the formation of nuclear-yield reaction. Such devices may be fabricated in a completely improvised manner or may be an improvised modification to a U.S. or foreign nuclear weapon.

Impurities
Chemical substances that are unintentionally present with another chemical substance.

In-Extremis
A situation of such exceptional urgency that immediate action must be taken to minimize imminent loss of life or catastrophic degradation of the environment, including but not limited to, socioeconomic, political, or military situations.

In-Gas Service
Equipment that contains process fluid that is in the gaseous state at operating conditions.

In-Heavy Liquid Service
Equipment that is not in gas/vapor service or in light liquid service.

In-Kind Commodities
Commodities that are normally produced on land that is the subject of an agreement entered into under the Erodible Land and Wetland Conservation and Reserve Program.

In-Kind Contributions
Cash outlays and payments, or contributions of property or personnel services by non-governmental interests to share of the costs of hazard prevention and control activities, technologies, and related research programs.

In-Light Liquid Service
Equipment that contains a fluid for which: a) the vapor pressure of one or more of the components is greater than 0.3 kilopascals (KPa) at 20°C; b) the total concentration of the pure components having a vapor pressure greater than 0.3 KPa at 20°C is equal to or greater than 20% by weight; and c) the fluid is a liquid at operating conditions.

In Operation
Refers to a facility that is treating, storing, or disposing of hazardous waste.

In or Near Commercial Buildings
Within the interior of; on the roof of; attached to the exterior wall of; in the parking area serving; or within 30 meters of a nonindustrial building. Commercial buildings are typically accessible to employees and the general public. They include public assembly properties, educational properties, institutional properties, residential properties, stores, office buildings, and transportation centers (e.g., airport terminals, subway stations, bus or train stations).

In-Process Materials
Materials that are integral to the manufacturing or production processes and are needed to maintain continuity of operations. Other material that requires temporary location near the pertinent process areas in readiness for near-term use or for movement to other process areas may also be considered "in-process." For material involved in laboratory operations, analogous definitions are applied to determine eligibility for the "in-process" or "in-use" category and consequent exclusion from storage requirements of these criteria. *See* In-Use.

In-Process Wastewater

Any water that, during manufacturing or processing, comes into direct contact with vinyl chloride or polyvinyl chloride or results from the production or use of any raw material, intermediate product, finished product, by-product, or waste product containing vinyl chloride or polyvinyl chloride but which has not been discharged to a wastewater treatment process or discharged untreated as wastewater. Gasholder seal water is not in-process wastewater until it is removed from the gasholder.

In Situ

In the existing or original location; in place.

In Situ Extraction

Extraction of a mineral using chemical solutions, without removing the ore from its natural location.

In Situ Sampling Systems

Nonextractive samplers or in-line samplers.

In Situ Treatment

Treatment processes conducted in the existing or original location of the pollutant.

In Situ Volatization

The conversion of a chemical substance from a liquid or solid state to a gaseous or vapor state by the application of heat, by reducing pressure, or by a combination of these processes.

In-Use Materials

Materials that are integral to the manufacturing or production processes and are needed to maintain continuity of operations. Other materials that require temporary location near the pertinent process areas in readiness for near-term use or for movement to other process areas may also be considered "in-process." *See* In-Process Materials.

In Vacuum Service

Equipment that is operating at an internal pressure that is at least 5 kilopascals (kPa) below ambient pressure.

In VHAP Service

A piece of equipment that either contains or contacts a fluid (liquid or gas) that is at least 10% by weight a volatile hazardous air pollutant (VHAP) as determined according to the provisions of 40 CFR 61.246(d). The provisions of Section 61.245(d) also specify how to determine that a piece of equipment is not in VHAP service.

In Vinyl Chloride Service

A piece of equipment that either contains or contacts a liquid that is at least 10% vinyl chloride by weight or a gas that is at least 10% by volume vinyl chloride as determined according to the provisions of 40 CFR 61.67(h). The provisions of Section 61.67(h) also specify how to determine that a piece of equipment is not in vinyl chloride service.

In Vitro

1) Tests conducted outside the whole body in an artificially maintained environment, such as a test tube, culture dish, or bottle. 2) Any laboratory test using living cells taken from an organism.

In Vivo

Tests conducted within the living body of a plant or animal. In vivo tests are those laboratory experiments carried out on whole animals or human volunteers.

In VOC Service

1) A piece of equipment that contains or contacts a process fluid that is at least 10% VOC by weight (refer to 40 CFR 60.2 for complete definition of volatile organic compound and 40 CPR 60.485(d) to determine whether a piece of equipment is not in VOC service) and is not considered in heavy liquid service as defined in 40 CFR 60.481. 2) Equipment that contains or contacts a process fluid that is at least 10% volatile organic compounds by weight.

Inactive Portion

That portion of a facility that is not operated after the effective date of Part 261 of 40 CFR. Also known as Closed Portion. *See* Active Portion; Closed Portions.

Inactive Facilities

An area where a hazardous substance has been deposited, stored, disposed of, placed, or otherwise come to be located. It can be any building, structure, installation, equipment, pipe or pipeline (including any pipe into a sewer or publicly owned treatment works, well, pH, pond, lagoon, impoundment, ditch, landfill, storage container, motor vehicle, rolling stock, or aircraft. Excluded are areas that have a permit issued, or have been accorded interim status under Subtitle C of the Solid Waste Disposal Act of the Memorandum of Understanding between DOE and EPA for hazardous waste and radioactive mixed waste management, or operated under the provisions of DOE regulations.

Inactive Mines

Mines from which uranium ore has been previously removed but which are not active mines as of the effective date of the standard. Inactive mines that become active mines after the effective date of the standard are considered new sources under the provisions of Subparts A and B of 40 CFR 61.21.

Inactive Waste Disposal Sites

Disposal sites or portions of them where additional asbestos-containing waste material will not be deposited and where the surface is not disturbed by vehicular traffic.

Inadequate Warning Property

Characteristic (e.g., odor, irritation) of a substance that is not sufficient to cause a person to notice exposures, or releases.

Incapacitating Agent

An agent that produces temporary physiological or mental effects, or both, that will render individuals incapable of concerted effort in the performance of their assigned duties.

Incapacitating Illness or Injury (III)

The casualty status of a person whose illness or injury requires hospitalization but medical authority does not classify as very seriously ill or injured and the illness or injury makes the person physically or mentally unable to communicate. *See* Casualty Status.

Incentive Type Contract

A contract that may be of either a fixed price or cost reimbursement nature, with a special provision for adjustment of the fixed price or fee. It provides for a tentative target price and a maximum price or maximum fee, with price or fee adjustment after completion of the contract for the purpose of establishing a final price or fee based on the contractor's actual costs plus a sliding scale of profit or fee that varies inversely with the cost but which in no event shall permit the final price or fee to exceed the maximum price or fee stated in the contract. *See* Cost Contract; Fixed Price Type Contract.

Inch-Pound System of Units

The system of measurement units inch, pound, second, degrees Fahrenheight, and units derived from those, most commonly used in the United States. The inch-pound system is not to be confused with "Imperial System," that describes a related but not completely identical system currently in use in Great Britain and some other English speaking countries.

Incidence

The number of new cases of a disease within a specified time period. It is frequently presented as the number of new cases per 1,000, 10,000, or 100,000. The incidence rate is a direct estimate of the probability or risk of developing a disease during a specified time period.

Incidence Rate, WDL

The total number of days (away) entered in Columns 4 or 11 of the OSHA 200 Log used to calculate this rate. WDL = No. workdays lost x 200,000/total hours worked.

Incidence Rate, WDLR

The total number of days lost, due to restrictions that are entered in Columns 5 or 12 of the OSHA 200 Log used to calculate this rate. WDLR = No. of workdays restricted x 200,000/total hours worked.

Incident

1) Any deviation from normal operations or activities that has the potential to result in an emergency; an action likely to lead to grave consequences. 2) A failure of a control (e.g., barrier) without consequences. 3) An occurrence of an action or situation that is a separate unit of experience; a happening; something dependent on, or subordinate to, something else of greater or principal importance.

Incident Command Post (ICP)

A location within or near a designated facility or site area for the purpose of maintaining control, orderly shutdown, and/or surveillance of operations and equipment during an emergency.

Incident Command System (ICS)

1) The combination of facilities, equipment, personnel, procedures, and communications operating within a common organizational structure with responsibility for the management of assigned resources to effectively accomplish stated objectives pertaining to an incident. 2) An organizational scheme wherein one person, normally the Fire Chief, takes charge of an integrated, comprehensive emergency response. This commander is backed by an Emergency Operations Center that provides support, resources, communications, and advice.

Incident Commander (IC)

1) The person responsible for establishing and managing the overall operational plan at a hazardous material incident. The incident commander is responsible for developing an effective organizational structure, allocating resources, making appropriate assignments, managing information, and continually attempting to mitigate the incident. 2) The on-scene commander responsible for situation management in order to mitigate an emergency, ensure personnel safety, personnel accountability, and facilitate mitigating operations.

Incidental Taking

Takings that result from, but are not the purpose of, carrying out an otherwise lawful activity conducted by a federal agency or applicant.

Incineration

The destruction of certain types of solid, liquid, or gaseous wastes by controlled burning at high temperatures. Hazardous organic compounds are converted to ash, carbon dioxide, and water. Burning destroys organics, reduces the volume of waste, and vaporizes water and other liquids the wastes may contain. The residue ash produced may contain some hazardous material, such as noncombustible heavy metals, concentrated from the original waste. 2) Burning of certain types of solid, liquid, or gaseous materials. 3) A treatment technology involving destruction of waste by controlled burning of sludges to remove the water and reduce the remaining residues to a safe, non-burnable ash that can be disposed of safely on land, in some waters or in underground locations.

Incineration at Sea

Disposal of waste by burning at sea on specially designed incinerator ships.

Incineration Vessels

Vessels that carry hazardous substances for the purpose of incineration of such substances, so long as such substances or residues of such substances are on board.

Incinerators

1) Any enclosed engineered device using controlled flame combustion that neither meets the criteria for classification as a boiler nor is listed as an industrial furnace in Section 260.10 of 40 CFR. 2) An engineered device using controlled flame combustion to thermally degrade PCBs and PCB items. Examples of devices used for incineration include rotary kilns and high-temperature boilers. 3) A furnace for the routine burning of waste materials using controlled flame combustion, for the primary purpose of reducing the volume of the waste by removing combustible matter.

Incompatible Wastes

A hazardous waste that, due to its characteristics, is either unsuitable for placement in a particular device or facility because it may cause corrosion or decay to containment materials such as inner liners or tank walls. Or, is unsuitable for commingling with another waste or material under uncontrolled conditions because the commingling might produce heat or pressure; fire or pressure; fire or explosion; violent reaction; toxic dusts, mists, fumes, or gases; or flammable fumes or gases. A waste unsuitable for mixing with another waste or material because of reactivity hazards. Refer to 40 CFR 265 Appendix V.

Increments and Ceilings

The maximum allowable increases and maximum allowable concentrations for sulfur oxide and particulate matter. Each SIP must contain measures assuring that maximum allowable increases over baseline concentrations of, and maximum allowable concentrations of, such pollutant shall not be exceeded.

Increments of Progress

Steps toward compliance that will be taken by a specific source, including the following: a) date of submittal of the source's final control plan to the appropriate air pollution control agency; b) date by which contracts for emission control systems or process modifications will be awarded; or date by which orders will be issued for the purchase of component parts to accomplish emission control or process modification; c) date of initiation of on-site construction or installation of emission control equipment or process change; d) date by which on-site construction or installation of emission control equipment or process modification is to be completed; and e) date by which final compliance is to be achieved.

Incubation

A species descriptor that means keeping eggs warm until they hatch.

Incurred Losses

Losses that have happened; includes amounts paid and reserved for future payments.

Indefinite Delivery Type Contract

A task order type of contract used for procurement where the exact time and amount of service/product is not known at time of contracting.

Indemnify

To insure; to secure against loss or to reimburse an insured for loss.

Independent Audit Firm

A firm selected by EPA for the purpose of performing the Facility Compliance and Management Systems Audits. The firm must exercise the same independent judgment that a certified public accounting firm would be expected to exercise in auditing a publicly held corporation. The firm must:

a) not own stock in defendant/respondent facility, or any parent, subsidiary, or affiliated corporation;

b) have no history of participation in any prior contractual agreements with defendant/respondent or any parent, subsidiary, or affiliated corporation; and

c) have no other direct financial stake in the outcome of a facility compliance or management systems audit.

Independent Inspector

A person or other entity having no responsibility for the design, operations, or construction of the site or facility being inspected.

Independent Power Producer

Any person who owns or operates, in whole or in part, one or more new independent power production facilities.

Independent Safety Reviews

Reviews performed by personnel organizationally independent of the operating group and groups performing primary safety analysis. Other criteria for good independent review would include being financially independent of the operating group, no personal interest in review decisions, and using different analytical methods from those doing the primary safety analysis.

Index, Plant

Testing a plant for virus or viruslike disease infection by grafting with tissue from it to an indicator plant or by other means approved by the director.

Indian Governing Bodies

The governing bodies of tribes, bands, or groups of Native American Indians subject to the jurisdiction of the United States and recognized by the United States as possessing power of self government.

Indian Lands

Lands of Native American Indian tribes, or Native American Indian individuals, that are either held in trust by the United States or subject to a restriction against alienation imposed by the United States, except for any subsurface interests in lands not owned or controlled by a Native American Indian tribe or a Native American Indian individual.

Indian Tribal Law

Laws that extend to Native Americans certain exceptions to the protective measures of the Endangered Species Act, such as taking for sustenance limited quantities of endangered species.

Indian Tribe

1) The governing body of any Native American Indian tribe, band, nation, or other group that is recognized as a Native American Indian tribe by the Secretary of the Interior and for which the United States holds land in trust or restricted status for that entity or its members. Such term also includes any Native village corporation, regional corporation, and Native Groups established pursuant to the Alaska Native Claims Settlement Act (43 USC 1601 et seq.). 2) The Nez Perce Tribe, the Confederated Tribes and Bands of the Yakima Indian Nation, the Confederated Tribes of the Warm Springs of Oregon, and the Confederated Tribes of the Umatilla Indian Reservation. 3) Except in the case of RCRA, Native American Indian tribes, bands, nations, or other organized groups or communities, including any Alaska Native village but not including any Alaska Native regional or village corporation, that are recognized as eligible for the special programs and services provided by the United States to Native American Indians because of their status as Native American Indians and having a federally recognized governing body carrying out sub-

stantial governmental duties and powers over a defined area.

Indicator

In biology, an organism, species, or community whose characteristics show the presence of specific environmental conditions.

Indigenous

Native or original to a specific area.

Indirect Absorption Unit

A unit in which the refrigerant evaporator is not in direct contact with the air to be conditioned.

Indirect Discharge

The introduction of pollutants from a nondomestic source into a publicly owned wastewater treatment system. Indirect dischargers can be commercial or industrial facilities who must pretreat their wastes before discharge into local sewers.

Indirect Source

1) A pollution source, such as a regional mall, not actually releasing the emission itself but attracting mobile emissions and resulting in an increase in pollutants in its immediate vicinity. 2) A facility, building, structure, installation, real property, road, or highway that attracts, or may attract, mobile sources of pollution. Such term includes parking lots, parking garages, and other facilities subject to any measure for management of parking supply, including regulation of existing off-street parking but does not include new or existing on-street parking.

Indirect Source Regulations

A requirement under Section 110 of the Clean Air Act for preconstruction reviews by state agencies of all indirect sources above a certain size. If the construction or modification of an indirect source will violate air quality standards, the state can deny a construction permit.

Indirect Source Review Program (ISRP)
The facility-by-facility review of indirect sources of air pollution, including such measures as are necessary to ensure, or assist in assuring, that a new or modified indirect source will not attract mobile sources of air pollution, the emissions from which would cause or contribute to air pollution concentrations a) exceeding any national primary ambient air quality standard for a mobile source-related air pollutant after the primary standard attainment date; b) preventing maintenance of any such standard after such date.

Indirectly Ionizing Particles
Uncharged particles (neutrons, photons, etc.) that can liberate directly ionizing particles.

Individual
1) A citizen of the United States or an alien lawfully admitted for permanent residence. 2) A single member of a population.

Individual Generation Sites
Contiguous sites at or on which one or more hazardous wastes are generated. Individual generation sites, such as large manufacturing plants, may have one or more sources of hazardous waste but are considered single or individual generation sites if the sites or properties are contiguous.

Individual Protective Equipment
In nuclear, biological, and chemical operations, the personal clothing and equipment required to protect an individual from biological and chemical hazards and some nuclear effects. *See* Personal Protective Equipment.

Individual Risk
The increased risk for a person exposed to a specific concentration of a toxicant.

Indoor Air
Breathing air inside a habitable structure or conveyance, often highly polluted because of lack of exchange with fresh oxygen from outdoors. Solvents, smoke, paints, furniture glues, carpet padding, and other synthetic chemicals trapped inside the structure may often contribute to an unhealthy environment.

Indoor Air Pollution
Chemical, physical, or biological contaminants in indoor air.

Indoor Climate
Temperature, humidity, lighting, and noise levels in a habitable structure or conveyance. Indoor climate can affect indoor air pollution.

Indoor/Outdoor Ratio
The ratio of the indoor concentration of an air pollutant to the outdoor concentration of that pollutant.

Induced Environment
Any manmade or equipment-made environment that directly or indirectly affects the performance of man or material.

Induced Radiation
1) Radiation produced as a result of exposure to radioactive materials, particularly the capture of neutrons. Radiation produced within materials by nuclear reactions. 2) Radioactivity that is created when stable substances are bombarded by ionizing radiation. *See* Residual Radiation.

Indusia
A species descriptor that refers to an enclosing membrane, as that covering the sorus (spore cases) of a fern.

Industrial Buildings
Buildings directly used in manufacturing or technically productive enterprises. Access to these buildings is typically limited to employees only. Industrial buildings include those used directly in the production of power; manufacture of products; mining of raw materials; and storage of textiles, petroleum products, wood and paper products, chemicals, plastics, and metals.

Industrial Engineering

The branch of professional engineering that requires such education and experience as is necessary to investigate, to design, and to evaluate systems of persons, materials, and facilities for the purpose of economical and efficient production, use, and distribution. It requires the application of specialized engineering knowledge of the mathematical and physical sciences, together with the principles and methods of engineering analysis and design to specify, predict, and to evaluate the results to be obtained from such systems. Industrial engineering does not include the practice of civil, electrical, or mechanical engineering.

Industrial Equipment

1) Any article of equipment that: a) in operation consumes, or is designed to consume, energy; b) to any significant extent, is distributed in commerce for industrial or commercial use; and c) is not a covered product. The types of equipment referred to are as follows:

- compressors
- fans
- blowers
- refrigeration equipment
- air conditioning equipment
- electric lights
- electrolytic equipment
- electric arc equipment
- steam boilers
- ovens
- furnaces
- kilns
- evaporators and dryers

2) Physical apparatus used to perform industrial tasks, such as welders, conveyors, machine tools, fork trucks, turntables, positioning tables, or robots.

Industrial Furnace

Any of the following enclosed devices that are integral components of manufacturing processes and that use controlled flame devices to accomplish recovery of materials or energy:

- cement kilns
- lime kilns
- aggregate kilns
- phosphate kilns
- coke ovens
- blast furnaces
- smelting, melting, and refining furnaces (including pyrometallurgical devices such as reverberator furnaces, incinerators, foundry furnaces)
- titanium dioxide chloride process oxidation reactors;
- methane reforming furnaces; pulping liquor recovery furnaces
- combustion devices used in the recovery of sulfur values from spent sulfuric acid

The above list includes such other devices as the Administrator of EPA may, after notice and comment, add to this list on the basis of one or more of the following factors: a) the design and use of the device primarily to accomplish recovery of material products; b) the use of the device to burn or reduce raw materials to make material products; c) the use of the device to burn or reduce secondary materials as effective substitutes for raw materials, in processes using raw materials as principal feedstocks; d) the use of the device to burn or reduce secondary materials as ingredients in an industrial process to make a material product; e) the use of the device in common industrial practice to produce a material product; and other factors, as appropriate.

Industrial Heating Equipment

Any appliance, device, or equipment used, or intended to be used, in an industrial, manufacturing, or commercial occupancy for applying heat to any material being processed, but shall not include water heaters, boilers, or portable equipment used by artisans in pursuit of a trade.

Industrial Hygiene

The science and art devoted to the recognition, evaluation, and control of environmental factors or stresses arising in or from the workplace that may cause sickness, impaired heath and well-being, or significant discomfort and inefficiency among workers or those with whom they come into contact.

Industrial Mobilization

The transformation of industry from its peacetime activity to the industrial program necessary to support the national military objectives. It includes the mobilization of materials, labor, capital, production facilities, and contributory items and services essential to the industrial program. *See* Mobilization.

Industrial Petroleum Reserve

That portion of the Strategic Petroleum Reserve that consists of petroleum products owned by importers or refiners and acquired, stored, or maintained pursuant to the Energy Conservation Act (ECA).

Industrial Plant

Any fixed equipment or facility that is used in connection with, or as part of, any process or system for industrial production or output.

Industrial Preparedness Program

Plans, actions, or measures for the transformation of the industrial base, both government-owned and civilian-owned, from its peacetime activity to the emergency program necessary to support the national military objectives. It includes industrial preparedness measures such as modernization, expansion, and preservation of the production facilities and contributory items and services for planning with industry.

Industrial Property

Any contractor acquired or government-furnished property, including materials, special tooling, and industrial facilities, furnished or acquired in the performance of a contract or subcontract.

Industrial Robot System

A system that includes industrial robots, the end-effectors, and the devices and sensors required for the robots to be taught or programmed, or for the robots to perform the intended automatic operations, as well as the communication interfaces required for interlocking, sequencing, or monitoring the robots.

Industrial Source Complex (ISC) Model

A Gaussian dispersion model used to predict the movement of a plume of air pollution and concentrations the general population may be exposed to near a facility. There are two versions of the ISC model, short-term and long-term. This is a standard model used by the U.S. EPA and incorporates detailed source and emissions characteristics and appropriate meteorological data.

Industrial Use

Use for or in a manufacturing, mining or chemical process or use in the operation of factories, processing plants, and similar sites.

Industrial Waste

A term applied to any solid, semisolid, or liquid waste materials generated incidental to various manufacturing processes employed at industrial plants and establishments, that require disposal. These wastes can be divided into five categories:

- uncontaminated nondegradable factory refuse;
- inert process waste;
- flammable process waste;
- either acid or caustic; or
- indisputably toxic and hazardous waste.

INEL

See Idaho National Engineering Laboratory.

Inert Ingredient

Pesticide components such as solvents, carriers, and surfactants that are not active against target pests. Not all inert ingredients are innocuous.

Inertial Separator

A device that uses centrifugal force to separate waste particles.

Infectious Material

Any biological agent and other disease causing agent that after release into the environment and upon exposure, ingestion, inhalation, or assimilation into any person, either directly from the environment or indirectly by ingestion through food chains, will or may reasonably be anticipated to cause death, disease, behavioral abnormalities, cancer, genetic mutation, physiological malfunctions (including malfunctions in reproduction) or physical deformations in such persons or their offspring. Employers with employees engaged in emergency response activities involving infectious materials must comply with the requirements in 29 CFR 1910.120(q), and may also have to comply with the Bloodborne Pathogens standard, 29 CFR 1910.1030. If there is a conflict or overlap, the provision that is more protective of employee safety and health usually prevails.

Infectious Wastes

1) Equipment, instruments, utensils, and fomites of a disposal nature from the rooms of patients who are suspected to have or who have been diagnosed as having a communicable disease and must therefore be isolated as required by public health agencies. 2) Laboratory wastes, such as pathological specimens (for example, all tissues, specimens of blood elements, excreta, and secretions obtained from patients or laboratory animals) and disposable fomites (any substance that may harbor or transmit pathogenic organisms) attendant thereto. 3) Surgical operating room pathological specimens and disposable fomites attendant thereto and similar disposal materials from outpatient areas and emergency rooms.

Inferential Statistics

Analytical process that combines sampling, probability, and descriptive measures to predict outcomes or conclusions about the data of a facility/project. Primarily used by an environmental planner to test predictions and/or inferences made by others. In addition to testing hypotheses, inferential statistics is also used to measure correlations among variables; define values of one variable from the relationship between it and another variable, as in regression analysis; and, define confidence limits and degrees of independence of statistical inferences.

Infertile

Lacking fertility, the inability to conceive offspring. Infertility may be temporary or permanent; permanent infertility is termed sterility.

Infiltration

1) The downward entry of water into soil or rock. 2) The penetration of water through the ground surface into subsurface soil or the penetration of water from the soil into sewer or other pipes through defective joints, connections, or manhole walls. 3) A land application technique where large volumes of wastewater are applied to land, allowed to penetrate the surface and percolate through the underlying soil. *See* Percolation.

Infiltration Rate

The speed or rate at which a fluid penetrates soil or rock under specified conditions. The rate is determined by the permeability of the absorbing material or soil, the amount of vegetative cover, and the slope of the ground. The rate is expressed in depth of fluid per unit time or velocity.

Inflammation

A protective tissue response to injury that serves to destroy, dilute, or wall off both the injurious agent and the injured tissue. It is characterized by symptoms such as pain, heat, redness, swelling, and loss of function. Under some circumstances, it can be a toxic response due to local accumulations of cells and mediators.

Inflated

In botany, a term meaning hollow and enlarged.

Inflorescence

A species descriptor that means a flower cluster.

Inflow

1) Entry of extraneous rain water into a sewer system from sources other than infiltration, such as basement drains, manholes, storm drains, and street washing. 2) Wind direction shifting abruptly toward the storm (inflow) as opposed to wind moving away from the storm (outflow).

Influent

Water, wastewater, or other liquid flowing into a reservoir, basin, or treatment plant.

Informal Consultation

An optional process that includes all discussions, correspondence, etc., between the U.S. Fish and Wildlife Service and the federal agency or the designated nonfederal representative, prior to formal consultation (if required).

Information Box

A space on an annotated overlay, mosaic, map, etc., that is used for identification, reference, and scale information. *See* Reference Box.

Information Collection Plan

1) A plan for gathering data from all available sources to meet a specific research requirement. 2) A logical plan for transforming the essential elements of information into orders or requests to sources within a required time limit.

Information Cycle

The steps by which raw data is converted into information and made available to users. There are five steps in the cycle:

- *Planning and direction* — Determination of data requirements, preparation of a research plan, issuance of orders and requests to information repositories and agencies, and a continuous check on the productivity of data collection effort.

- *Collection* — Acquisition of information and the provision of this information to processing and/or production elements.

- *Processing* — Conversion of collected data into a form suitable to the production of information.

- *Production* — Conversion of data into various formats through the integration, analysis, evaluation, and interpretation of all source data and the preparation of information products in support of known or anticipated user requirements.

- *Dissemination* — Conveyance of information to users in suitable formats.

Information Database

The total holdings of data and finished information products at a given agency or organization.

Information Data Handling Systems

Systems that process and manipulate raw information and intelligence data as required. They are characterized by the application of general purpose computers, peripheral equipment, and automated storage and retrieval equipment for documents and photographs. While automation is a distinguishing characteristic of data handling systems, individual system components may be either automated or manually operated.

Information Estimate

The appraisal, expressed in writing or orally, of available data relating to a specific situation or condition with a view to determining alternative courses of action and the probability of their adoption.

Information File

In the Superfund program, a file that contains accurate, up-to-date documents on a Superfund site. The file is usually located in a public building such as a school, library, or city hall that is convenient to local residents.

Information Journal

A chronological log of data-collection activities covering a stated period, usually monthly or quarterly. It is an index of reports and letters that have been received and written; of important monitoring events that have occurred; and of actions that have been taken. The journal is a permanent and official record.

Information Maintenance

Data manipulation activities that include maintenance, collection, updating, revision, use, and/or dissemination.

Information Repository

A file containing current information, technical reports, and reference documents regarding a Superfund site. Information repositories are usually located in public buildings convenient for local residents to use such as an EPA office, city hall, or a public library.

Information Requirements

Those items of information regarding the environment that need to be collected and processed in order to meet the decisionmaking requirements of a requesting authority.

Informed Consent

The knowing consent of an individual or his/her legally authorized representative that is given without undue inducement or without any element of force, fraud, deceit, duress, or other form of constraint or coercion to participate in an activity. For consent to be "informed," the individual or his/her legally authorized representative must possess accurate and complete information about the environmental issues of concern.

Infrared Film

Film carrying an emulsion especially sensitive to "near-infrared." Used to photograph through haze, because of the penetrating power of infrared light; and in camouflage detection to distinguish between living vegetation and dead vegetation or artificial green pigment.

Infrared Imagery

That imagery produced as a result of sensing electromagnetic radiations emitted or reflected from a given target surface in the infrared position of the electromagnetic spectrum (approximately 0.72 to 1,000 microns).

Infrared Photography

Photography employing an optical system and direct image recording on film sensitive to near-infrared wavelengths (infrared film).

Infrared Radiation (IR)

1) Radiation emitted or reflected in the infrared portion of the electromagnetic spectrum. 2) Invisible electromagnetic radiation with wavelengths that lie within the range of 0.70 to 1000 um. These wavelengths are often broken up into regions: IR-A (0.7–1.4um), IR-B (1.4–3.0um) and IR-C (3.0–1000um).

Infrastructure

A term generally applicable to all fixed and permanent installations, fabrications, facilities, sewers, water lines, etc. *See* National Infrastructure.

Ingestion

Intake of material by way of the gastrointestinal system.

Ingestion Exposure Pathways

The pathways in which exposure occurs after ingestion of contaminated water or foods such as milk, fresh vegetables, or aquatic foodstuffs.

Ingestion Hazards

Hazards where a significant quantity of a toxic material may be ingested and subsequently absorbed due to the consumption of food or beverages (including drinking fountains). Where, for any substance, a serious hazard is determined to exist due to the potential of ingestion or absorption of the substance for reasons other than the consumption of contaminated food or drink (e.g., smoking materials contaminated with the toxic substance), the existence of a serious ingestion hazard will be considered, independent of measurements of airborne concentrations.

Ingress

The act of entering a site, structure, or area, through a point of access.

Inground Tank

A stationary storage device, whereby a portion of the tank wall is situated to any degree within the ground, preventing visual inspection of the external surface area of the tank that is underground.

Inhabited Building Distance

The minimum distance permitted between locations containing munitions and inhabited buildings, administrative areas, site boundaries, main power stations, and other facilities of vital or strategic nature.

Inhalation

Intake of material by way of the respiratory system (including the material that will eventually go to the intestinal system).

Inhalation LC 50

A concentration of a substance (measured as milligrams per liter of air, or parts per million parts of air) that is lethal to 50% of the test population of animals under test conditions as specified in TSCA Registration Guidelines.

Inhalation Toxicology Research Institute (ITRI)

A DOE Research and Development and Field Facility, established in 1960, to assess adverse human health effects associated with commercial energy technologies. The Institute investigates the degree to which the inhalation of by-products of energy technologies such as fugitive or operating emissions may harm the health of operators or the general public.

Inidator

An agent capable of starting but not necessarily completing the process of producing an abnormal, uncontrolled growth of tissue usually by altering a cell's genetic material. Initiated cells may or may not be transformed into tumors.

Initial Assessment (IA)

A preliminary assessment that provides a basic determination of the scope of a problem and viability of alternative proposed actions.

Initial Draft

A study that has been drafted and coordinated, and is ready for external coordination and/or approvals. It cannot be directly implemented by the issuing party, but it may form the basis for a corrective-action decision, or operation initiated by an agency in the event of an emergency. *See* Draft Plan.

Initial Radiation

The radiation, essentially neutrons and gamma rays, resulting from a nuclear burst and emitted from the fireball within 1 minute after burst. *See* Induced Radiation; Residual Radiation.

Initial Startup

Those activities subsequent to preoperational testing, starting with the initial loading of fuel and involving all actions taken, including tests to ensure a safe, orderly, incremental approach to predefined conditions of reactor operation.

Initiation of Negotiations

The initial written offer made by the acquiring entity to the owner of real property to be purchased, or the owner's representative.

Initiation of Procurement Action

That point in time when the approved document requesting procurement and citing funds is forwarded to the procuring activity.

Initiation Stimuli

Energy input to an explosive in a form potentially capable of initiating a rapid decomposition reaction. Typical initiation stimuli are heat, friction, impact, electrical discharge, and shock. Initiators are devices that provide initiation stimuli (e.g., detonators, squibs).

Injection

The forcing, under abnormal pressure, of sedimentary material (downward, upward, or laterally) into a pre-existing deposit or rock, either along some plane of weakness or into a crack or fissure (e.g., the transformation of wet sands and silts to a fluid state and their emplacement in adjacent sediments, producing structures, such as sandstone dikes or sand volcanoes). Also a sedimentary structure or rock formed by injection.

Injection Interval
That part of the injection zone in which the well is screened, or in which the waste is otherwise directly emplaced.

Injection Well
A well into which fluids are injected for purposes such as waste disposal, improving the recovery of crude oil, or solution mining.

Injection Zones
Geological formations, groups of formations, or parts of a formation receiving fluids through a well.

Injury
A term comprising such conditions as fractures, wounds, sprains, strains, dislocations, concussions, and compressions. In addition, it includes conditions resulting from extremes of temperature or prolonged exposure.

Acute poisonings, except those due to contaminated food, resulting from exposure to a toxic or poisonous substance are also classed as injuries.

Ink
Gadolinium nitrate, neutron absorber.

Inland Harbor
A navigation project that is used principally for the accommodation of commercial vessels and the receipt and shipment of waterborne cargoes on inland waters. The term does not include a) projects on the Great Lakes; b) projects that are subject to tidal influence; c) projects with authorized depths of greater than 20 feet; d) local access or berthing channels; and e) projects constructed or maintained by nonpublic interests.

Inland Search and Rescue Region
The inland areas of continental United States, except waters under the jurisdiction of the United States.

Inland Waters
For the purposes of classifying the size of discharges, those waters of the United States in the inland zone, waters of the Great Lakes, and specified ports and harbors on inland rivers.

Inland Zones
The environment inland of the coastal zone excluding the Great Lakes and specified ports and harbors of inland rivers. The term inland zone is used to delineate the area of federal responsibility for response actions. Precise boundaries are determined by agreement between the Environmental Protection Agency and the U.S. Coast Guard and are identified in federal regional contingency plans.

Inner Liner
Continuous layers of material placed inside tanks or containers that protect the construction materials of the tanks or containers from the contained waste or reagents used to treat the waste.

Innovation Diffusion
A structured, research-based, step-by-step process for developing acceptance of a new mode of behavior.

Innovative Technology
Designs, materials, or methods that the Secretary determines are previously undemonstrated or are too new to be considered standard practice.

Inocula/Inoculum
1) Bacteria placed in compost to start biological action. 2) A medium containing organisms that is introduced into cultures or living organisms.

Inorganic Arsenic
The oxides and other noncarbon compounds of the element arsenic included in particulate matter, vapors, and aerosols.

Inorganic Chemicals
Chemical substances of mineral origin, not of basically carbon structure.

Input Current
The root-mean-square (rms) current in amperes delivered to a fluorescent lamp ballast.

Insecticides
Pesticide compounds specifically used to kill or control the growth of insects.

Insectivore
A species descriptor for an organism that feeds primarily on insects.

Insects
Any of the numerous small invertebrate animals generally having the body more or less obviously segmented, for the most part belonging to the class insecta, comprising six-legged, usually winged forms, as for example, beetles, bugs, bees, flies, and to other allied classes of arthropods whose members are wingless and usually have more than six legs, as for example, spiders, mites, ticks, centipedes, and wood lice.

Insensitive High Explosives (IHE)
Explosive substances that, although mass detonating, are so insensitive that there is negligible probability of accidental initiation or transition from burning to detonation.

Insolation
The rate at which solar energy is received at the surface of the earth.

Inspected and Condemned
A term referring to structures or facilities inspected by government building or environmental inspectors that have been deemed unsound, unhealthful, or otherwise unfit for use or occupancy, due to an imminent structural or hazardous material threat to public health, safety, and welfare.

Inspection
Deliberate, systematic scrutiny, examination, or testing of activities or projects against established standards. An inspection may be a) routine, b) conducted pursuant to a complaint, c) a reinspection, or d) a follow-up inspection. Inspection of a structure, factory, plant, establishment, construction site, workplace, environment, or other area may include a physical inspection of systems, operating and maintenance procedures, logs, records, and/or site operations. *See* Environmental Inspector.

Inspection and Evaluation (I/E)
A documented review of the safeguards and security program activities, performed in accordance with written guidance and criteria, to verify by examination and evaluation of objective evidence that applicable protection measures have been developed, documented, and effectively implemented in accordance with current U.S. Department of Energy safeguards and security policies, standards, and procedures.

Inspection and Maintenance (I/M)
1) Activities to ensure proper emissions related operation of mobile sources of air pollutants, particularly automobile emissions controls. 2) Also applies to wastewater treatment plants and other antipollution facilities and processes.

Inspection Mark
A mark or statement, authorized by a regulatory agency, on a product or on the container of a product, indicating that the product has been inspected for wholesomeness by an inspector.

Inspector
Any inspector duly approved by an enforcing agency for a particular project.The project inspector shall be responsible for inspecting all work regulated by law, and contained in approved plans and specifications. A special inspector shall be responsible only for inspecting the work for which he/she was approved.

INST
See In Situ Treatment.

Installation
A grouping of facilities, located in the same vicinity, that support particular functions.

Installation Complex
In the Air Force, a combination of land and facilities comprised of a main installation and its non-contiguous properties (auxiliary air fields, annexes, and missile fields) that provide direct support to or are supported by that installation. Installation complexes may comprise two or more properties, e.g., a major installation, a minor installation, or a support site, each with its associated annex(es) or support property(ies).

Installation Inspector, UST
A person qualified, through professional education and experience in the physical sciences and engineering, to supervise the installation of tank systems.

Instar
A species descriptor that pertains to the stage between molts in insects; larval development stages.

Institutes
An organization existing for the promotion of a cause or discipline.

Institutional Control of Wastes
A period of time, assumed to be about 100 years, during which human institutions continue to control waste management facilities.

Institutional Solid Wastes
Solid wastes generated by educational, health care, correctional, and other institutional facilities.

Institutional Use
Use within the confines of, or on property necessary for the operation of, buildings such as hospitals, schools, libraries, auditoriums, and office complexes.

Instream Use
Water use taking place within a stream channel, e.g., hydroelectric power generation, navigation, water-quality improvement, fish propagation, recreation.

Instrument Meteorological Conditions (IMC)
Meteorological conditions expressed in terms of visibility, distance from cloud, and ceiling; less than minimums specified for visual meteorological conditions. *See* Visual Meteorological Conditions.

Insulating Material
Any material placed within or contiguous to a wall, ceiling, roof, or floor of a room or building, or contiguous to the surface of any appliance or its intake or outtake mechanism, for the purpose of reducing heat transfer or reducing adverse temperature fluctuations of the building room or appliance.

Insulation Design Density
The proven density for loose fill insulation other than cellulose that has been determined by the manufacturer to constitute the density whereby settlement of no more than 2% shall occur over the first 3 years, or no more than 4% over the first 15 years, of installation.

Insulation Manufacturer
Any person who either a) produces insulating material in the final composition either for use in the form sold or to be further dimensionally modified; or b) in the case of polyurethane, polyisocyanurate, and urea formaldehyde foam formed at the installation site, produces the primary components of the material. Does not include any building contractor or any other person whose sole activity is to install insulation at the installation site.

Insurance
Primary insurance, excess insurance, reinsurance, surplus lines insurance, and any other arrangement for shifting and distributing risk that is determined to be insurance under applicable state or federal law.

Insurgency

An organized movement aimed at the overthrow of a constituted government through use of subversion and armed conflict.

Intake

1) A measure of exposure expressed as the mass of substance in contact with the exchange boundary per unity body weight per unit time (e.g., mg/kg-day). Also termed the normalized exposure rate. 2) The amount of radioactive material taken into the body by inhalation, absorption through the skin, ingestion, or through open wounds.

Intangible Risks

Those risks for which it is usually not possible to determine dollar values, such as public opinion, employee morale.

Integral Vista

Views perceived from within the mandatory Class I federal area of specific landmarks or panoramas located outside the boundary of the mandatory Class I federal area.

Integrated Logistics Support (ILS)

A composite of all the support considerations necessary to ensure the effective and economical support of a system for its life cycle. It is an integral part of all other aspects of system acquisition and operation.

Integrated Material Management

The exercise of total Department of Defense management responsibility for a federal supply group/class, commodity, or item by a single agency. It normally includes computation of requirements, funding, budgeting, storing, issuing, cataloging, standardizing, and procuring functions.

Integrated Pest Management (IPM)

A mixture of pesticide and nonpesticide methods to control pests.

Integrated Risk Information System (IRIS)

An EPA database containing verified Reds (Reference Doses) and slope factors and up-to-date health risk and EPA regulatory information for numerous chemicals. IRIS is EPA's preferred source for toxicity information for Superfund.

Integrity

1) The authenticity of a property. 2) The survival of physical characteristics of an historic or prehistoric period.

Intelligence Operations

The variety of intelligence tasks that are carried out by various intelligence organizations and activities. Predominantly, it refers to either intelligence collection or intelligence production activities. When used in the context of intelligence collection activities, intelligence operations refer to collection, processing, exploitation, and reporting of information. When used in the context of intelligence production activities, it refers to collation, integration, interpretation, and analysis, leading to the dissemination of a finished product.

Intelligence Preparation, Environmental

An analytical methodology employed to reduce uncertainties concerning the hazard potential, environment, and terrain for all types of large scale emergency operations. Intelligence preparation builds an extensive database for each potential media in which a team may be exposed. The database is then analyzed in detail to determine the impact of the hazard, environment, and terrain on operations and presents it in graphic form. Intelligence preparation is a continuing process.

Intelligence Report (INTREP)

A specific report of information, usually on a single item, made at any level of command in tactical operations and disseminated as rapidly as possible in keeping with the timeliness of the information.

Intelligence System

Any formal or informal system to manage data gathering, to obtain and process the data, to interpret the data, and to provide reasoned judgments to decisionmakers as a basis for action. The term is not limited to intelligence organizations or services but includes any system, in all its parts, that accomplishes the listed tasks.

Intensity Factor

A multiplying factor used in planning activities to evaluate the foreseeable intensity or the specific nature of an operation in a given area for a given period of time.

Intention

An aim or design, to execute a specified course of action.

Intention Tremor

Trembling of the extremities during movement.

Interstitial Pneumonitis.

Inflammation of the alveolar walls and the spaces between them.

Intentional Introductions Policy Review

An aquatic nuisance species task force process, in consultation with state fish and wildlife agencies; other regional, state, and local entities; potentially affected industries; and other interested parties, to identify and evaluate approaches for reducing the risk of adverse consequences associated with intentional introduction of aquatic organisms into U.S. waters. *See* Aquatic Nuisance Species Task Force.

Inter Alia

Latin for "among other things."

Interagency Committee on Standards Policy

The committee established under the auspices of the Department of Commerce to coordinate and provide policy guidance to the heads of federal agencies on standards. It is comprised of representatives from the major federal departments and agencies that have an interest in standards. The Committee is chaired by the Deputy Assistant Secretary for Product Standards, Office of the As-

sistant Secretary for Productivity, Technology and Innovation, U.S. Department of Commerce.

Interagency Group on Energy Vulnerability (IG-EV)

The interagency forum chartered under the Senior Interagency Group for National Security Decision Directive (NSDD) 188, *Government Coordination for National Security Emergency Preparedness*. It consists of senior representatives with national security emergency preparedness responsibilities from departments and agencies. The IG-EV facilitates government-wide coordination of national policy issues relating to the vulnerability of U.S. energy systems in advance of crises and coordinates crisis assessments and response recommendations in an emergency.

Interagency Radiological Assistance Plan

See Federal Radiological Monitoring and Assessment Plans (FRMAP).

Interagency Task Force (ITF)

The task force comprised of representatives of the National Institute for Environmental Health Sciences, the Environmental Protection Agency, the Agency for Toxic Substances and Disease Registry, the National Toxicology Program, the National Institute of Standards and Technology, the National Science Foundation, the Surgeon General, and the Department of Energy.

The Interagency Task Force is chaired by a representative of the Environmental Protection Agency. Its mission is to evaluate hazardous air pollutants, to decide, on the basis of available information, its relative priority for preparation of environmental health assessments, based on reasonably anticipated toxicity to humans and exposure factors. The ITF must also complete environmental health assessments for each hazardous air pollutant by 1998.

Interbrood Intervals

A species descriptor that pertains to the period between producing young.

Interceptor Facility

A facility used to hold flows from main and trunk sewers and distribute them to a central plant for treatment and discharge.

Interceptor Sewers

Large sewer lines that, in a combined system, control the flow of the sewage to the treatment plant. In a storm, they allow some of the sewage to flow directly into a receiving stream, thus preventing an overload by a sudden surge of water into the sewers. They are also used in separate systems to collect the flows from main and trunk sewers and carry them to treatment points.

Interchart Relationship Diagram

A diagram on a map or chart showing names and/or numbers of adjacent sheets in the same or related series. Also called index to adjoining sheets. *See* Map Index.

Intercoastal Traffic

Sea traffic between the Atlantic, the Gulf of Mexico, and the Great Lakes; continental United States ports; and Pacific continental United States ports.

Interdepartmental Intelligence

Integrated departmental intelligence that is required by departments and agencies of the United States government for the execution of their missions but that transcends the exclusive competence of a single department or agency to produce.

Interdepartmental/Agency Support

Provision of logistic and/or administrative support in services or material by one or more military services to one or more departments or agencies of the United States government (other than military) with or without reimbursement.

Interdisciplinary Team

A group of persons convened for the purpose of preparing a site or facility environmental compliance plan. An interdisciplinary team shall include, but not be limited to, the client, a principal environmental investigator, a project manager, pertinent environmental specialists, and a staff member(s) of the lead regulatory agency(s).

Interest in Land

Any ownership or possessory right with respect to real property, including ownership in fee, an easement, a leasehold, and any subsurface or mineral rights.

Interface

1) A boundary or point common to two or more similar or dissimilar control systems, subsystems, or other entities against which or at which necessary information flow takes place. 2) The relationship between the work environment and one or more system components. Human performance is a function of the physical interfaces between people and equipment; the environments within which people or equipment work; the type and amount of training people receive; the accuracy and ease of use of the procedures people are given for guidance; and the effectiveness of the organizations in which people work.

Interfacility Transactions

Any letters, memos, contracts, or other communications between two or more offices or facilities owned and operated by defendant/respondent.

Interferences

A discharge that, alone or in conjunction with a discharge or discharges from other sources, both a) inhibits or disrupts the POTW, its treatment processes or operations, or its sludge processes, use or disposal; and b) therefore is a cause of a violation of any requirement of the POTW's NPDES permit (including an increase in the magnitude or duration of a violation) or of the prevention of sewage sludge use or disposal in compliance with the following statutory provisions and regulations or permits issued thereunder (or more stringent state or local regulations) — Section 405 of the Clean Water Act, the Solid Waste Disposal Act (including state regulations contained in any state sludge management plan prepared pursuant to Subtitle D of the SWDA), the Clean Air Act, the Toxic Substances Control

Act, and the Marine Protection, Research, and Sanctuaries Act.

Intergovernmental Liaison Staff (ILS)

Federal staff charged with maintaining effective, cooperative working relationships with states, local governments, and quasi-public entities (special districts).

Interim Actions

Actions that are within the scope of an ongoing Environmental Impact Statement and that an agency proposes to take before issuing a record of decision (ROD).

Interim Authorizations

Approval by EPA of a state hazardous waste program that has met the requirements of Section 3006(c) of RCRA and applicable requirements of 40 CFR Part 271, Subpart B.

Interim Dumping Measure

Any short-term method for the management of sewage sludge or industrial waste, that is used before implementation of an alternative system; and does not require a permit.

Interim Financing

Advance payments, partial payments, loans, discounts, advances, and commitments in connection therewith; and guarantees of loans, discounts, advances, and commitments in connection therewith; and any other type of financing necessary for both performance and termination of contracts.

Interim Permit Status

The period during which treatment, storage and disposal facilities coming under RCRA in 1980 are temporarily permitted to operate while awaiting denial or issuance of a permanent permit. Permits issued under these circumstances are usually called "Part A" or "Part B" permits.

Interlock

An arrangement whereby the operation of one control or mechanism brings about, or prevents the operation of another.

Intermediate Field Maintenance

That maintenance that is the responsibility of and performed by designated maintenance activities for direct support of using organizations. Its phases normally consist of the following: a) calibration, repair, or replacement of damaged or unserviceable parts, components, or assemblies; b) the emergency manufacture of nonavailable parts; and c) providing technical assistance to using organizations.

Intermediate Premanufacture Notices (PMNs)

Any PMN submitted to EPA for a chemical substance that is an intermediate in the production of a final product, provided that the PMN for the intermediate is submitted to EPA at the same time.

Intermediates

Chemical substances that are consumed, in whole or in part, in chemical reactions used for the intentional manufacture of other chemical substances or mixtures or that is intentionally present for the purpose of altering the rates of such chemical reactions.

Intermittent Control System (ICS)

A dispersion technique that varies the rate at which pollutants are emitted to the atmosphere according to meteorological conditions arid/or ambient concentrations of the pollutant, in order to prevent ground-level concentrations in excess of applicable ambient air quality standards. Such a dispersion technique is an ICS whether used alone, used with other dispersion techniques, or used as a supplement to continuous emission controls (i.e., used as a supplemental control system).

Intermittent Sampling

Periodic sampling for limited amounts of time throughout the course of a project or for a preset research time frame.

Intermodal Portable Tanks
A specific class of portable tanks designed primarily for international intermodal use.

Intermunicipal Agencies
Agencies established by two or more municipalities with responsibility for planning or administration of solid waste.

Internal Appraisals
Examinations and evaluations by the operating level (either federal or contractor) of those portions of its internal ES&H (Environment, Safety, and Health) program, including program plan implementation, and operations retained under its direct control.

Internal Audits
See Audit.

Internal Environment
The physical and chemical conditions inside a living organism; or the aesthetic and design conditions inside a built facility.

Internal Radiation
Nuclear radiation (alpha and beta particles and gamma radiation) resulting from radioactive substances in the body.

Internal Security
The state of law and order prevailing within a nation, agency, firm, or facility.

International Air Pollution
The endangerment of public health or welfare in foreign countries from pollution emitted in United States. Any foreign country so affected by such emission of pollutant or pollutants shall be invited to appear at any public hearing associated with any revision of the appropriate portion of the applicable implementation plan.

International Arms Control Organization
An appropriately constituted organization established to supervise and verify the implementation of arms control measures.

International Atomic Time
The time reference scale established by the Bureau International des Poids et Mesures on the basis of atomic clock readings from various laboratories around the world.

International Cooperation on Ocean Dumping
Effective international action and cooperation to ensure the protection of marine environments, and includes, governmental formulation, prevention, or support of specific proposals in the United Nations and other component international organizations for the development of appropriate international rules and regulations in support of the minimization and/or restriction of ocean dumping activities.

International Cooperative Logistics
Cooperation and mutual support in the field of logistics through the coordination of policies, plans, procedures, development activities, and the common supply and exchange of goods and services arranged on the basis of bilateral and multilateral agreements with appropriate cost reimbursement provisions.

International Date Line
The line coinciding approximately with the antimeridian of Greenwich, modified to avoid certain habitable land. In crossing this line there is a date change of one day. Also called date line.

International Energy Program
The agreement signed by the United States on November 18, 1974, including the annex entitled "Emergency Reserves," any amendment to such agreement that includes another nation as a party to such agreement, and any technical amendment to such agreement.

International Energy Program Allocation and Information Provisions
The provisions of the international energy program that relate to international allocation of petroleum products and to the information system provided in such program.

International Energy Supply Emergency

Any period beginning on any date that the president determines allocation of petroleum products to nations participating in the international energy program is required, and ending on a date on which he/she determines that such allocation is no longer required. Such a period may not exceed 90 days, but the president may establish one or more additional 90-day periods.

International Hydrological Decade

A 10-year cooperative scientific research program on the water problems of the world; planned and directed by UNESCO, from 1965 through 1975.

International Identification Code

In railway terminology, a code that identifies a military train from point of origin to final destination. The code consists of a series of figures, letters, or symbols indicating the priority, country of origin, day of departure, national identification code number, and country of destination of the train.

International Loading Gauge

The loading gauge upon which international railway agreements are based. A load whose dimensions fall within the limits of this gauge may move without restriction on most of the railways of continental western Europe. GIC is an abbreviation for "gabarit international de chargement," formerly called PPI.

International Logistics

The negotiating, planning, and implementation of supporting logistics arrangements between nations, their forces, and agencies. It includes furnishing logistic support (major end items, material, and/or services) to, or receiving logistic support from, one or more friendly foreign governments, international organizations, or military forces, with or without reimbursement.

It also includes planning and actions related to the intermeshing of a significant element, activity, or component of the military logistics systems or procedures of the United States with those of one or more foreign governments, international organizations, or military forces on a temporary or permanent basis. It includes planning and actions related to the utilization of United States logistics policies, systems, and/or procedures to meet requirements of one or more foreign governments, international organizations, or forces.

International Shipment

The transportation of hazardous materials into or out of the jurisdiction of the United States.

International System of Units (SI)

The system popularly known as the modernized metric system is a coherent system of units based upon and including the:

- meter (length)
- kilogram (mass)
- second (time)
- kelvin (temperature)
- ampere (electric current)
- cartel (luminous intensity)
- mole (amount of a substance).

The radian (plane angle) and the steradian (solid angle) are supplemental units of the system.

International Union for the Conservation of Nature and Natural Resources (IUCN)

An independent international agency founded in 1948, to promote and initiate scientifically based environmental conservation measures.

Interneural

In between nerves.

Interocular Distance

The distance between the centers of rotation of the eyeballs of an individual or between the oculars of optical instruments.

Interpretability

Suitability of aerial photography, for interpretation with respect to answering specific questions on ground features in terms of quality and scale. There are four general categories: 1) Poor — imagery is unsuitable for interpretation to answer adequately requirements on a given type of target; 2) Fair — imagery is suitable for interpretation to answer requirements on a given type of target but with only average detail; 3) Good — imagery is suitable for interpretation to answer requirements on a given type of target in considerable detail; and 4) Excellent — Imagery is suitable for interpretation to answer requirements on a given type of target in complete detail.

Interpretation
A stage in the information cycle in which the significance of data obtained is analyzed in relation to the current body of knowledge.

Interrogation
Systematic effort to procure information by direct questioning and control of a person, as opposed to interviewing in which the person is not under any control, and may or may not participate. *See* Interview, Intelligence.

Interspecies
A term that means between different species.

Interspecies Scaling Factors
Numerical values used in the determination of the equivalent doses between species, (e.g. frequently a known animal dose is scaled to estimate an equivalent human dose.) The U.S. EPA's cancer risk assessment guidelines (50 FR 33992) note that commonly used dosage scales include milligram per kilogram body weight per day, parts per million in soil or water or air, milligram per square meter body surface area per day, and milligram per kilogram body weight per lifetime. The guidelines for carcinogen assessment generally recommend using the surface area approach unless there is evidence to the contrary.

The dose as mg/kg of body weight/day is generally used to scale between species for noncancer effects of chemicals after dermal, oral, or parenteral exposure.

Interstate Agencies
1) Any agencies of two or more states established by or under an agreement or compact approved by the Congress, or any other agencies of two or more states or Native American Indian tribes having substantial powers or duties pertaining to the control of pollution as determined and approved by the Administrator of EPA under the "appropriate Act and regulations." 2) Agencies of two or more municipalities in different states, or agencies established by two or more states, with authority to provide for the management of solid wastes and serving two or more municipalities located in different states.

Interstate Air Pollution Control Agencies
1) Air pollution control agencies established by two or more states. 2) Air pollution control agencies of two or more municipalities located in different states.

Interstate Carrier, Water Supplies
Sources of water for drinking and sanitary use on planes, buses, trains, and ships operating in more than one state. These sources are federally regulated.

Interstate Commerce
Commerce between any state or territory and any place outside thereof, and commerce within the District of Columbia or within any territory not organized with a legislative body.

Interstate Pollution Abatement Notice (IPAN)
State Implementation Plan (SIP) requirements that require each major proposed new (or modified) source subject to regulation relating to significant deterioration of air quality or that may significantly contribute to levels of air pollution in excess of the national ambient air quality standards in any air quality control region outside the state in which such source intends to locate to a) provide written notice to all nearby states the air pollution levels of which may be affected by such source at least 60 days prior to the date on which commencement of construction is to be permitted by the state providing notice; and b) identify all major existing stationary sources that may pose negative air quality impacts.

Interstate Transport Commission (ITC)

A commission established on the Administrator's own motion or by petition from the governor of any state, when there is reason to believe that the interstate transport of air pollutants from one or more states contributes significantly to a violation of a national ambient air quality standard in one or more other states.

The transport commission is comprised of (at a minimum) each of the following members: a) the governor of each state in the region or the designee of each such governor; b) the Administrator or the Administrator's designee; c) the Regional Administrator (or the Administrator's designee) for each Regional Office for each Environmental Protection Agency Region affected by the transport region concerned; and d) an air pollution control official representing each state in the region, appointed by the governor. The transport commission's responsibilities are to assess the degree of interstate transport of the pollutant or precursors to the pollutant throughout the transport region, assess strategies for mitigating the interstate pollution, and recommend to the Administrator such measures as the Commission determines to be necessary to ensure that the plans for the relevant states meet the requirements of the CAA.

Interstate Waters

Waters that flow across or form part of state or international boundaries, e.g., the Great Lakes, the Mississippi River, or coastal waters.

Interstice

An opening or space in rock or soil that may be occupied by air, water, or other fluid; synonymous with void or pore.

Interstitial Monitoring

The continuous surveillance of the space between the walls of an underground storage tank.

Intersupraocular Scales

A species descriptor that means having scales above and between the eyes.

Intervenor

A person, group of persons, trade association, legal foundation, or public or private interest group who has been granted leave to intervene in any proceeding.

Intervention Levels

Levels usually specified in advance by the competent authority (IAEA) or management for use in abnormal situations; if the value of the quantity of interest exceeds or is predicted to exceed a particular level, the appropriate remedial action is typically taken. *See* Protective Actions Guides (PAGs); Emergency Reference Levels (ERLs).

Interview, Intelligence

To gather information from a person who is aware that information is being given and voluntarily gives it although there may be ignorance of the true connection and purposes of the interviewer.

Interviews, Environmental

The most common and most direct means of obtaining facility/project information. The purpose of conducting environmental interviews is to obtain specific environmental management and operations data on the facility and/or project, including management attitudes, operations activities, personnel tasks and competence, existing working/operating conditions, organization and perceptions of individuals participating as well as those of persons in the surrounding community.

Intra-Facility Transactions

Any letters, memos, contracts, or other communications between two or more locations or offices at a single facility owned and operated by defendant/respondent.

Intrabeam Viewing

The viewing condition whereby the eye is exposed to all or part of a direct laser beam or a specular reflection.

Intracoastal Sealift

Shipping used primarily for the carriage of personnel and/or cargo along a coast or into river ports to support operations within a given area.

Intraline Separation

The minimum quantity-distance separation allowed between explosives buildings on a DOE plant site unless equivalent protection to personnel and property is provided by building design and construction, or a barricade.

Intramuscular

Within the muscle; refers to injection.

Intransit Aeromedical Evacuation Facility

A medical facility, on or in the vicinity of an air base, that provides limited medical care for intransit patients awaiting air transportation. This type of medical facility is provided to obtain effective utilization of transport airlift within operating schedules. It includes "remain overnight" facilities, intransit facilities at aerial ports of embarkation and debarkation, and casualty staging facilities. *See* Aeromedical Evacuation Unit.

Intraperitoneal

Within the membrane surrounding the organs of the abdominal cavity; refers to injection.

Intraspecies

Within a particular species.

Intravascular

Within the blood vessels; refers to injection, usually into the veins (intravenous or IV).

Intrinsic Permeability

The relative ease with which a porous medium can transmit a liquid under a hydraulic or potential gradient. It is a property of the porous medium and is independent of the nature of the liquid or the potential field.

Introduced

1) A species descriptor indicating that a plant or animal has been brought in from outside a region; also called "exotic" or "nonnative." 2) The release, escape, or establishment of an exotic species into a natural ecosystem.

Intruder Barriers

A sufficient depth of cover over a waste that inhibits contact with the waste and helps to ensure that radiation exposures to an inadvertent intruder will meet the performance objectives, or engineered structures that provide equivalent protection to the inadvertent intruder.

Intrusion

A body of igneous rock that infiltrated preexisting rock, and the process by which it was formed.

Invasion

A species descriptor that means the migration of a species into a new area, usually to the detriment of organisms already living there.

Inventory Control

The phase of logistics that includes managing, cataloging, requirements determinations, procurement, distribution, overhaul, storage and disposal of material. Synonymous with material control, material management, and inventory management.

Inventory

The inventory of chemicals produced pursuant to Section 8(b) of the Toxic Substances Control Act (TSCA).

Inverse Square Law

The law that states the intensity of radiation at any distance from a point source varies inversely as the square of that distance.

Inversion

An atmospheric condition caused by a layer of warm air preventing the rise of cooling air trapped beneath it. This prevents the rise of pollutants that might otherwise be dispersed and can cause an air pollution episode.

Invertebrate
A species descriptor that refers to animals lacking backbones, such as insects.

Inverted Siphons
Pressure pipelines crossing under a highway or other obstruction.

Inverter
In electrical engineering, a device for converting direct current into alternating current. *See* Rectifier.

Investigation, Environmental
1) A general term for detailed, systematic searches to uncover the "who, what, when, where, why, and how" of environmental occurrences and to determine what corrective actions are needed in order to prevent a recurrence. 2) An authorized, systematized, detailed examination or inquiry to uncover facts and determine the truth of an environmental issue. This may include collecting, processing, reporting, storing, recording, analyzing, evaluating, producing, and disseminating site, or facility specific, environmental data.

Investigation Levels
Levels for the values of quantities (such as dose equivalent, intake, contamination per unit area) above which further investigations are considered to be justified by IAEA.

Investigation Report
A clear and concise written account of the results of an investigation.

Investment Costs
Program costs required beyond the development phase to introduce into operational use a new technology; to procure initial, additional, or replacement equipment for operations; or to provide for major modifications of an existing capability. They exclude research, development, test and evaluation, personnel, and Operation and Maintenance appropriation costs.

Involucre
A species descriptor that means a whorl of leaflike scales or bracts, beneath or around a flower or flower cluster.

IOAA
An acronym for Independent Offices Appropriation Act of 1952.

Ion
1) An electrically charged atom or group of atoms that can be drawn from wastewater during the electrodialysis process. 2) Any element or compound that has gained or lost an electron, so that it is no longer neutral electrically, but carries a charge.

Ion Exchange
Chemical reaction used in water or wastewater treatment processes in which mobile dehydrated ions of a solid are exchanged (with ions of like charge in solution).

Ion Exchange Treatment
A common water softening method often found on a large scale at water purification plants that remove some organics and radium by adding calcium oxide or calcium hydroxide to increase the pH to a level where the metals will precipitate out.

Ionization
1) The process of producing ions by the removal of electrons from, or the addition of electrons to, atoms or molecules. 2) The process where atoms acquire a net electrical charge due to the gain or loss of electrons.

Ionization Chamber
1) A device that measures the intensity of ionizing radiation. 2) An instrument designed to measure the quantity of ionizing radiation in terms of the charge of electricity associated with ions produced within a defined volume.

Ionizing Radiation

1) Radiation that can remove electrons from atoms, i.e., alpha, beta, and gamma radiation. 2) Any electromagnetic or particulate radiations capable of producing ions, directly or indirectly, in their passage through matter. 3) For the purposes of radiation protection, radiations capable of producing ion pairs in biological material(s).

Ionosphere

1) The layer of uppermost atmosphere where atoms tend to be ionized by incoming solar radiation. 2) That part of the atmosphere, extending from about 70 to 500 kilometers, in which ions and free electrons exist in sufficient quantities to reflect electromagnetic waves.

IPAN

See Interstate Pollution Abatement Notice (CAA).

IPRSF

An acronym for Interim Protocol for Radon Screening and Followup. *See* Radon; Radon Decay Products Measurements.

IRC

An acronym for the Internal Revenue Code of 1986.

IREP

An acronym for Interim Reliability Evaluation Program.

IRI

An acronym for Industrial Risk Insurers.

IRIS

See Integrated Risk Information System.

Iritis

Inflammation of the colored part of the eye (iris).

Irradiance (E)

Radiant flux (radiant power) per unit area incident upon a given surface. Units are in watts per square centimeter; sometimes referred to as power density, although not exactly correct.

Irradiated Food

Food that has been subject to brief radioactivity, usually by gamma rays, to kill insects, bacteria, and mold, and preserve it without refrigeration or freezing.

Irradiation

1) Exposure to radiation of wavelengths shorter than those of visible light (gamma, X-ray, or ultraviolet) for medical purposes, the destruction of bacteria in milk or other foodstuffs, or for inducing polymerization of monomers or vulcanization of rubber. 2) Exposure to ionizing radiation and electromagnetic waves.

Irreversible Commitment of Resources

Any commitment of resources that has the effect of foreclosing the formulation or implementation of any reasonable or prudent alternatives that would not violate Section 7(a)(2) of the Endangered Species Act.

Irrigation

Technique for applying water or wastewater to land areas to supply the water and nutrient needs of plants.

Irritant

Any noncorrosive substance that on immediate, prolonged, or repeated contact with normal living tissue will induce a local inflammatory reaction.

Irritating Materials

Irritating materials are liquid or solid substances that upon contact with fire or when exposed to air give off dangerous or intensely irritating fumes, but do not include any material classed as Poison Class A. Tear gas grenades, brombenzylcyanide, gas identification kits, and diphenylchlorarsine are examples of irritating materials.

Ischemia

Obstruction of blood flow (usually by arterial narrowing) that causes lack of oxygen and other bloodborne nutrients.

Ischemic Necrosis
Death of cells as a result of decreased blood flow to affected tissues.

Isochrone
A plotted line graphically connecting all points having the same time of travel for contaminants to move through the saturated zone and reach a well.

Isoconcentration
A graphic plot of points having the same contaminant concentration levels.

Isodose Rate Line
See Dose Rate Contour Line.

Isohyperthermic
An equally high temperature regime of soils (above 25° Celsius at 50 centimeters depth).

Isolated
A species descriptor that refers to a portion of a breeding population that is cut off from the rest of the population.

Isolation
An onsite PA that requires onsite personnel to either isolate the source of ventilation to buildings (if the building is so equipped) or to turn all ventilation systems off (both supply and exhaust), in order to reduce exposures to hazardous materials or radiological substances when exposures could be in excess of PAGs.

Isolation Zones
Areas surrounding a protected facility that have been cleared of any objects that could conceal vehicles or individuals, and that afford unobstructed observation of, or other means of detention of, entry into the area.

Isomer
One or two or more compounds having the same percentage composition but differing in the relative positions of the atoms within the molecule.

Isopleth
A line drawn on a map connecting points where the phenomenon being measured is equal.

Isopod
A species descriptor that refers to crustacean of the order Isopoda, that includes sow bugs and gribbles.

Isostatic
Being subject to equal pressure on all sides; hydrostatic equilibrium.

Isotherm
A line drawn on a map connecting points of equal temperature.

Isotope
1) A variation of an element that has the same atomic number but a different weight because of its neutrons. Various isotopes of the same element may have different radioactive behaviors. 2) Nuclides having the same number of protons in their nuclei, and hence having the same atomic number, but differing in the number of neutrons, and therefore also differing in the mass number. Almost identical chemical properties exist between isotopes of a particular element.

Isotopic Tracers
Isotopes or nonnatural mixtures of isotopes of an element that may be incorporated into a sample to make possible observation of the course of that element, alone or in combination, through a chemical, biological, or physical process.

Isotropic
Having uniform properties in all directions independent of the direction of load application.

Isotropy
A condition in which the properties of interest (usually hydraulic properties of the aquifer) are the same in all directions.

ISRP
See Indirect Source Review Program (CAA).

Issue

A significant deviation from an applicable requirement (i.e., federal or state regulation or statute, DOE Order, any legally enforceable agreement, consensus, or industry standard) applicable to facilities, personnel, or management. An issue may be a single or group of deficiencies that represent a negative trend. An issue may be generated from a group of deficiencies.

Issue Identification

1) The identification of a specific condition or practice. 2) The first step in the development of a Tiger Team Assessment finding, that includes collecting information on the following:

- the specific nature of the problem, issues, condition, or practice;

- detailed locations, as appropriate;

- the framework or perspective within which the problem or practice exists;

- the regulatory or performance standards being violated, met, or exceeded;

- supporting information describing the problem or practice, or events leading to the problem;

- information on actions being taken with respect to the problem or practice; and

- information regarding how the assessment team member learned of the problem or practice.

ISTEA

An acronym for Intermodal Surface Transportation Act of 1991.

Isthmus

A narrow strip of land, bordered by water on both sides, that links two larger bodies of land.

ISV

See Insitu Verification.

ITC

See Interstate Transport Commission (CAA).

Iteration

A repeated occurrence of similar evolutionary trends in successive generations of a group.

ITRI

See Inhalation Toxicology Research Institute.

IUCN Red Data Book

The official listing document of threatened species worldwide by the Swiss organization, International Union for Conservation of Nature and Natural Resources, now known as the World Conservation Union.

IWTF

See Inland Waterways Trust Fund.

Ix

See Ion Exchange.

J

Jacob's Staff
Used instead of a tripod for supporting a compass in difficult locations. The staff is a single, straight, pointed rod that is iron shod at the bottom and has a socket at the top.

Jargon
The set of words employed by a language, group, individual, or work, or in relation to a subject.

Jaundice
Yellowing of the skin and the whites of the eyes due to an accumulation of bile pigments (e.g., bilirubin) in the circulating blood.

Jet Propulsion Reaction
Propulsion in which the propulsion unit obtains oxygen from the air, as distinguished from rocket propulsion in which the unit carries its own oxygen-producing material. In connection with aircraft propulsion, the term refers to a gasoline or other fuel turbine jet unit that discharges hot gas through a tail pipe and a nozzle that provides a thrust that propels the aircraft. *See* Rocket Propulsion.

Jet Stream
A narrow band of high-velocity wind in the upper troposphere or in the stratosphere.

Jet Thrust Units
Class B explosives comprised of metal cylinders containing a mixture of chemicals capable of burning rapidly and producing considerable pressure. Jet thrust units are designed to be ignited by an electric igniter. They are used to assist airplanes in takeoff.

Job Classification
Evaluation of job content, required skills and risks, for the purposes of setting up wage brackets, operational procedures, and quality control standards.

Job Environment
All the physical, psychological, and social factors, circumstances, and relationships thereof, that surround, make up, and impact a firm and its employees.

Job Safety Analysis (JSA)
A systematic technique for the safety review of a job used to uncover inherent or potential hazards. A JSA includes five steps: 1) job identification; 2) breaking the job down into steps; 3) identifying the hazards and determining the necessary hazard controls; 4) applying controls; and 5) evaluating the controls.

Joint and Several Liability
A legal/insurance term used in the context of contribution to a hazardous waste site. Each contributor is considered "jointly and severally liable" for the entire site-cleanup costs regardless of the amount each actually contributed or the individual's ability to absorb the costs. Under

this concept, a PRP with considerable assets may be required to pay an amount of the cleanup assessment far beyond the valuation of its own contribution to the waste site.

Joint Contract
A contract in which two or more persons, or firms, are jointly liable or jointly entitled to performance under the contract.

Joint Doctrine
Fundamental principles that guide the employment of forces of two or more services in coordinated action toward a common objective. It will be promulgated by the Chairman of the Joint Chiefs of Staff, in coordination with the combatant commands, services, and Joint Staff.

Joint Force Meteorological and Oceanographic Forecast Unit (JFMU)
A flexible, transportable, jointly supported collective of meteorological and oceanographic personnel and equipment formed to provide the joint task force commander and joint force meteorological and oceanographic officer with full meteorological and oceanographic services.

Joint Force Meteorological and Oceanographic Officer (JMO)
The officer designated to provide direct meteorological and oceanographic support to the joint task force commander.

Joint Frequency Distribution
The result of a frequency analysis of the probability of the occurrence of two or more random events (e.g., hydrologic or meteorological parameters).

Joint Information Center
A DOE center established to coordinate the federal public information activities on scene. It may be co-located with the press activities of an affected facility or state and local authorities. Also known as Joint Public Information Center or Joint Information Bureau.

Joint Intelligence Architecture
A dynamic, flexible structure that consists of the National Military Joint Intelligence Center, the theater joint intelligence centers, and subordinate joint force joint intelligence centers. This architecture encompasses automated data processing equipment capabilities, communications and information flow requirements, and responsibilities to provide theater and tactical commanders with the full range of intelligence required for planning and conducting operations.

Joint Intelligence Center (JIC)
The intelligence center of the joint force headquarters. The joint intelligence center is responsible for providing and producing the intelligence required to support the joint force commander and staff, components, task forces and elements, and the national intelligence community. *See* Joint Intelligence Architecture.

Joint Intelligence Doctrine
Fundamental principles that guide in the preparation of information and the subsequent provision of intelligence to support military forces of two or more services employed in coordinated action. *See* Intelligence Doctrine.

Joint Intelligence Liaison Element
A liaison element provided by the Central Intelligence Agency in support of a unified command or joint task force.

Joint Logistics
The art and science of planning and carrying out logistics operations to support the protection, movement, maneuver, mission, and sustainment of operating forces of two or more services of the same nation.

Joint Movement Center
The center established to coordinate the employment of all means of transportation (including that provided by allies or host nations) to support the concept of operations. This coordination is accomplished through establishment of transportation policies within the assigned area of responsibility, consistent with relative urgency of need,

port and terminal capabilities, transportation asset availability, and priorities set by a joint force commander.

Joint Nuclear Accident Coordination Center (JNACC)

A joint U.S. Department of Energy (DOE) and Department of Defense (DOD) capability responsible for maintaining current information on the location of specialized DOE and DOD teams or organizations capable of providing nuclear weapons accidents assistance. The DOE and DOD elements of JNACC are also responsible for initiating actions to deploy response in the event of a nuclear weapon accident or significant incident. The DOE component is located at Kirkland Air Force Base, New Mexico, and the DOD component is located at Springfield, Virginia, Defense Nuclear Agency (DNA) Headquarters.

Joint Operation Planning

Joint operation planning activities exclusively associated with the preparation of operation plans, operation plans in concept format, and operation orders (other than the Single Integrated Operation Plan) for the conduct of military operations by the combatant commanders in response to requirements established by the Chairman of the Joint Chiefs of Staff. As such, joint operation planning includes contingency planning, execution planning, and implementation planning. Joint operation planning is performed in accordance with formally established planning and execution procedures. *See* Contingency Planning; Execution Planning; Implementation Planning; Joint Operation Planning and Execution System.

Joint Operation Planning and Execution System (JOPES)

A continuously evolving system that is being developed through the integration and enhancement of earlier planning and execution systems (Joint Operation Planning System and Joint Deployment System). It provides the foundation for conventional command and control by national- and theater-level commanders and their staffs. It is designed to satisfy their information needs in the conduct of joint planning and operations. JOPES

includes joint operation planning policies, procedures, and reporting structures supported by communications and automated data processing systems. JOPES is used to monitor, plan, and execute mobilization, deployment, employment, and sustainment activities associated with joint operations.

Joint Publication

A publication of joint interest prepared under the cognizance of Joint Staff directorates and applicable to the military departments, combatant commands, and other authorized agencies. It is approved by the Chairman of the Joint Chiefs of Staff, in coordination with the combatant commands, services, and Joint Staff. *See* Chairman of the Joint Chiefs of Staff Instruction; Joint Doctrine.

Joint Purchase

A method of purchase whereby purchases of a particular commodity for two or more departments are made by an activity established, staffed, and financed by them jointly for that purpose.

Joint Servicing

That function performed by a jointly staffed and financed activity in support of two or more agencies or military services.

Joint Staff

1) The staff of the commander of a unified or specified command, or of a joint task force, that includes members from each branch of the military. These members should be assigned in such a manner as to ensure that the commander understands the tactics, techniques, capabilities, needs, and limitations of the component parts of the force. Positions on the staff should be divided so that Service representation and influence generally reflect the Service composition of the force. 2) The staff under the Chairman of the Joint Chiefs of Staff as provided for in the National Security Act of 1947, as amended by the DOD Reorganization Act of 1986. The Joint Staff assists the Chairman, and subject to the authority, direction, and control of the Chairman, the other members of the Joint Chiefs of Staff and the Vice

Chairman in carrying out their responsibilities. *See* Staff.

Joint Strategic Planning System (JSPS)

The primary means by which the Chairman of the Joint Chiefs of Staff, in consultation with the other members of the Joint Chiefs of Staff and the combatant commanders, carries out his/her statutory responsibilities to assist the President and Secretary of Defense in providing strategic direction to the Armed Forces; prepares strategic plans; prepares and reviews contingency plans; advises the President and Secretary of Defense on requirements, programs, and budgets; and provides net assessment on the capabilities of the Armed Forces of the United States and its allies as compared with those of their potential adversaries.

Joint Tenancy

A type of co-ownership of real property, held by two or more persons, with all co-owners being equally entitled to the use, enjoyment, control, and possession of the land and with the right of survivorship.

Joint Venture

A relationship in which two or more firms combine their labor and resources for a single project undertaking and share the profits and losses equally unless otherwise agreed.

Joint Worldwide Intelligence Communications System (JWICS)

The sensitive compartmented information portion of the Defense Information System Network. It incorporates advanced networking technologies that permit point-to-point or multipoint information exchange involving voice, text, graphics, data, and video teleconferencing.

Joint Zone

In military science, an area established for the purpose of permitting friendly surface, air, and subsurface forces to operate simultaneously.

Jolly Balance

A torodial spring balance used primarily for measuring specific gravity by weighing a specimen twice; once when immersed in air and again when immersed in a liquid of known density.

JOPES

See Joint Operation Planning and Execution System.

Joule

A unit of energy or work that is equivalent to 1 watt-second or 0.239 calories. Named after James Prescott Joule (1818-1889).

Journeyman

A person who has either a) completed an accredited apprenticeship in his/her craft; or b) completed the equivalent of an apprenticeship in length and content of work experience and all other requirements in the craft that has workers classified as journeyman in the apprenticeable occupation.

JRCC

An acronym for Joint Rescue Coordination Center

JSA

See Job Safety Analysis.

JSPS

See Joint Strategic Planning System.

JTCG-ME

An acronym for Joint Technical Coordinating Group for Munitions Effectiveness.

JTTP

An acronym for Joint Tactics, Techniques, and Procedures.

Judgment

The final determination of the rights of the parties by a court in an action before it.

Judicial Officers (JO)

Permanent or temporary employees appointed by the Administrator of EPA, subject to the following conditions: a JO shall be a licensed attorney, shall not be employed in the Office of Enforcement or the Office of Water and Waste Management; and shall not participate in the consideration or decision of any case in which he/she performed investigative or prosecutorial functions, or that is tactually related to such a case. The Administrator may delegate any authority to act in an appeal of a given case under 40 CFR 124 to a JO who, in addition may perform other duties for EPA, provided such delegations shall not preclude a JO from referring any motion or case to the Administrator, when the JO decides such action would be appropriate.

Jurisdiction

The power of a governmental entity or court to review, permit, and determine compliance issues on specific types of project activities; the authority granted under a city's police powers to act over a particular activity.

Juvenile

Coming from the interior of the earth to the surface for the first time; new in origin or newly detected. Applied mostly to gases and waters.

JWICS

See Joint Worldwide Intelligence Communications System.

K

K Value

A measure of the erodibility of soils. *See* Erosion; Hydraulic Conductivity.

Kahawai

A Hawaiian word meaning "flowing stream." Usually refers to the stream bed, channel, and/or the bank areas that are covered in times of high water.

Kame

A general name for range of deposits formed by glacial drifts, comprised mostly of stratified sand and gravel.

Kansas City Plant (KCP)

A DOE Research and Development and Field Facility established in 1949. The plant is a highly diversified, technically oriented operation that embraces the full spectrum of work on nonnuclear products — from research on new materials to production of complex and reliable weapons components. Production activities are directed toward three basic areas: electrical and electronics work, including microelectronics; mechanical products; and plastic products.

Kaolinite

A common clay mineral that consists of sheets of tetrahedrally coordinated aluminum.

Karren

The furrows that occur from solution by rain wash on blocks of extremely pure limestone in karst areas. The furrows range from 3 centimeters wide by 15 centimeters long to 6 meters wide by 30 meters long.

Karst

Rough and uneven limestone topography of channels that have formed deep caverns, closed depressions or sinkholes, and underground drainage.

Karst Plain

A plain on which sinkholes, uvula, subterranean drainage, and other karst features have developed. Synonymous with karst topography.

Karst Terrain

An irregular limestone region with sinks, underground streams, and caverns.

Karst Topography

A type of terrain that is formed on limestone, gypsum, and other rocks by dissolution, and is characterized by sinkholes, caves, and underground drainage.

Katabatic Winds

Winds that flow down slopes that are cooled by radiation, the directions of which are controlled orographically. These winds result from the downward convection of cooled air.

Katamorphism
Metamorphism at or near the surface of the lithosphere, forming simple minerals from complex ones.

KCP
See Kansas City Plant.

Keel
A species descriptor that refers to a prominent ridge on the back of an animal.

Keelage
The charges paid by a ship entering into or remaining in certain ports.

Keratin
A species descriptor that means a tough, fibrous protein substance that forms the outer layer of epidermal structures (protective covering) such as hair, nails, horns, and hoofs.

Keratitis
Inflammation of the cornea.

Kerma
The sum of the initial kinetic energies of all charged ionizing particles liberated by uncharged ionizing particles divided by the mass of the material.

Kerogen
An insoluble organic material found in sedimentary rocks; the hydrocarbon contained in oil shales.

Kerosene
1) The petroleum fraction containing hydrocarbons that are slightly heavier than those found in gasoline and naphtha. 2) A petroleum distillate with a boiling point in the 300°F to 500°F range; generally a flash point higher than 100°F (by ASTM Method D56); an API gravity range from 40° to 46°; and a burning point in the range of 150°F to 175°F.

Kerosene Jet Fuel
A quality kerosene product with an average gravity of 40.7 API; a 10% distillation temperature of 400°F; and an end-point of 572°F [covered by ASTM Specification D1655 and Military Specification MIL-T-5624L (Grade JP-5 and JP-8)]. Used primarily as fuel for commercial turbojet and turboprop aircraft engines.

Key Compliance Area
An aspect of a company's operation that has direct bearing on statutory compliance with environmental regulations.

Key Facilities List
A register of selected command installations and industrial facilities of primary importance to the support of military operations or military production programs. It is prepared under the policy direction of the Joint Chiefs of Staff.

Key Position
A civilian position, public or private (designated by the employer and approved by the Secretary concerned), that cannot be vacated during a contract period, war, or national emergency.

Key Word
A computer term meaning a word affording a means of access to a particular part of the total databank.

Kickback
Payment by a contractor of a portion of a contract price to a public official to induce the awarding of the contract or to influence future contract awards and decisions.

Kill Probability
A measure of the probability of fatal destruction.

Kilo (k)
The prefix used to denote one thousand; 10.

Kiloton Weapon
A nuclear weapon, the yield of which is measured in terms of thousands of tons of trinitrotoluene

explosive equivalents, producing yields from 1 to 999 kilotons. *See* Megaton Weapon; Subkiloton Weapon.

Kilowatt (kW)
1,000 watts. A unit of power equal to 1,000 watts or to energy consumption at a rate of 1,000 joules per second. It is usually used for electrical power.

Kilowatt-Hour (kWh)
A unit of work or energy equal to one kilowatt in one hour. It is equivalent to 3.6 joules.

Kinematic Viscosity
The ratio of dynamic viscosity to mass density. It is obtained by dividing dynamic viscosity by the fluid density. Units of kinematic viscosity are expressed in square meters per second.

Kinesis
The unpredictable locomotory movement of an organism in response to a stimulus.

Kinetic Energy
The energy of motion; the ability of an object to do work because of its motion.

Kinetic Metamorphism
The deformation of rocks without chemical reconstitution.

Kinetic Rate Coefficient
A number that describes the rate at which a water constituent such as a biochemical oxygen demand or dissolved oxygen increases or decreases.

Kingdom
The highest taxonomic division into which organisms are classified, as either animals or plants. Some organisms not readily classified as plants or animals, such as amoebae and paramecium, are sometimes classified in a third kingdom called Protista.

Kings River Special Management Area
The area established in order to provide for public outdoor recreation use and enjoyment of certain areas within the Sierra National Forest and the Sequoia National Forest, to protect those areas' natural, archaeological, and scenic resources, and to provide for appropriate fish and wildlife management of the area. The special management area shall consist of the lands, waters, and interests therein within the area generally depicted on the map entitled *Boundary Map, Kings River Special Management Area*, dated April 1987.

Kintle
100 pounds in weight.

Klendusity
The ability of an organism to stay free from disease due to its pattern of growth.

Knot
Unit of speed equal to 1 nautical mile per hour. Frequently used to measure wind speeds, sea currents, ships, and aircraft motion.

Knowing and Willful Violation
A noncompliance situation in which a person a) makes any false material statement, representation, or certification in, or omits material information from, or knowingly alters, conceals, or fails to file or maintain any notice, application, record, report, plan, or other document required pursuant to this chapter to be either filed or maintained; b) fails to notify or report as required under any environmental regulation; or c) falsifies, tampers with, renders inaccurate, or fails to install any monitoring device or method required to be maintained.

Knowingly
Refers to knowledge of the fact that a discharge of, release of, or exposure to a listed hazardous substance is occurring, or a condition of noncompliance with environmental regulations exists. A person in the course of doing business who, through misfortune or accident and without design, intention, or negligence, commits an act or omits to do something that results in a discharge, release, or exposure is usually just as liable for remedying the situation, as a person who knowingly and willfully permits the condition. How-

ever, most enforcing agencies will levy much higher fines, and impose more stringent time frames on site remediation, on an owner/operator who knows he/she is in noncompliance.

Knowingly and Willingly
In reference to the violation of an environmental statute, that committed with knowledge, consciously, and intentionally; cognizant, thoughtfully.

Knowledge of Results
Having useful feedback on the operation so that the information is adequate and in the right form for proper interpretation to make decisions.

Knowledge
The fact or condition of knowing something with familiarity gained through experience or association.

Known
Generally understood; recognized or having an absolute responsibility to become familiar with, as applied to environmental compliance actions, required by law.

Known Human Effects
Commonly recognized human health effects of a particular substance or mixture as described either in the following: 1) scientific articles or publications abstracted in standard reference sources; or 2) the firm's product labeling of material safety data sheets (MSDS). However, an effect is not a "known human effect" if it was a) a significantly more severe toxic effect than previously described; b) a manifestation of a toxic effect after a significantly shorter exposure period or lower exposure level than described; and c) a manifestation of a toxic effect by an exposure route different from that described.

Known Precedents
The use of technical information and knowledge from past experience and existing data to assist in hazard or accident analysis. This knowledge could come from such sources as codes, manuals, and recommendations; written reports and case histories; lists of expertise (experts); and studies directed toward solutions of known problems.

Kraus Process
A modification of the activated sludge process in which aerobically conditioned supernatant liquor from anaerobic digesters is added to the activated sludge aeration tanks to improve the settling characteristics of the sludge and to add an oxygen resource in the form of nitrates.

Krill
Small marine creatures that serve as an important food supply to fish, whales, and birds.

Kuchler System
An approximation of the potential natural vegetation of the United States, established by A.W. Kuchler.

Kuleana
A Hawaiian word meaning a "small area of land."

L

Labeled Compounds

Compounds consisting, in part, of labeled molecules. By observations of radioactive or isotopic composition these compounds or their fragments may be followed through physical, chemical, or biological processes.

Labeling (USC)

All labels and all other written, printed, or graphic matter accompanying the pesticide or device at any time; or to which reference is made on the label or in literature accompanying the pesticide or device, except to current official publications of the Environmental Protection Agency, the United States Departments of Agriculture and Interior, the Department of Health and Human Services, state experiment stations, state agricultural colleges, and other similar federal or state institutions or agencies authorized by law to conduct research in the field of pesticides.

Labels (USC)

The written, printed, or graphic matter on, or attached to, the pesticide or device or any of its containers or wrappers.

Laboratory

A place equipped for experimental study in a science or for testing and analysis.

Laboratory Test

A procedure that is performed in an EPA and/or NVLAP approved laboratory and employs the principles of one or more of the fundamental sciences to detect, identify, measure, or enumerate any particular substance in a field laboratory sample.

Laboratory Audits

Evaluations to ensure that all the necessary quality control is being applied by a laboratory to deliver a quality product. Should allow the evaluators to determine that the organization and personnel are qualified to perform assigned tasks; adequate facilities and equipment are available; complete documentation, including chain-of-custody of sample is being implemented; proper analytical methodology is being used; adequate analytical quality control, including reference samples, control charts, and documented corrective action measures, is being provided; and acceptable data handling and documentation techniques are being used.

Lacrimation

Secretion and discharge of tears, especially in excess.

Lacustrine

A species descriptor that means living or growing in lakes.

Lagging

Boards that are joined, side-by-side, lining an excavation.

Lagoon
1) Shallow body of water, often separated from the sea by coral reefs or sandbars. 2) A shallow, artificial treatment pond where sunlight, bacterial action, and oxygen work to purify wastewater; a stabilization pond. An aerated lagoon is a treatment pond that uses oxygen to speed up the natural process of biological decomposition of organic wastes. A lagoon is regulated as a point source under the Clean Water Act if there is a direct surface water discharge. Some lagoons that discharge into groundwater also are regulated if they have a direct hydrogeologic connection to surface water. In other areas, lagoons were historically used to dump various liquid, solid, and hazardous wastes from manufacturing or industrial processes. These wastes typically flooded and polluted surrounding environs or seeped underground. Such lagoons are now regulated under RCRA but some must be cleaned up under Superfund. 3) A shallow pond used for storage of wastewaters or spent nuclear fuel rods.

Lahar
The mud flow of water-saturated volcanic ash, or the deposits of such ash and mud flows.

Lake Transition Line
The line closest to the watercourse or lake where riparian vegetation is permanently established.

Lake
1) A permanent natural body of water of any size, or an artificially impounded body of water having a surface area of at least one acre, isolated from the sea, and having an area of open water of sufficient depth and permanency to prevent complete coverage by rooted aquatic plants. 2) Standing bodies of open water that occur in a natural depression fed by one or more streams from which a stream may flow, that occur due to the widening or natural blockage or cutoff of a river or stream, or that occur in an isolated natural depression that is not a part of a surface river or stream. The term also includes standing bodies of open water created by artificially blocking or restricting the flow of a river, stream, or tidal area. The term does not typically include artificial lakes or ponds created

by excavating and/or diking dry land to collect and retain water for such purposes as stock watering, irrigation, settling basins, cooling, or rice growing.

Lamella
A species descriptor that means a thin scale, plate or layer, as found in the gills of a bivalve mollusk and in the gills of a mushroom.

Laminar Flow
1) Fluid flow where the head loss is proportional to the first power of the velocity; synonymous with streamline flow and viscous flow. The streamlines remain distinct and the flow directions at every point remain unchanged with time, as is characteristic of the movement of groundwater. 2) Type of flow in which the fluid particles follow paths that are smooth, straight, and parallel to the channel walls.

Lance
A mobile, storable, liquid propellant, surface-to-surface guided missile, with nuclear and nonnuclear capability; designed to support the Army corps with long-range fires.

Lanceolate
A species descriptor that means narrow and tapering at each end.

Land
Real property; the surface of the earth and that which is affixed to it permanently, that which is below it, and the space above it. Synonymous with "real property," "realty," and "real estate." Sometimes used to mean only the unimproved surface of the earth.

Land Application
Discharge of wastewater onto the ground for treatment or reuse. *See* Irrigation.

Land Conservation Element
The part of a conservation area plan under the Resource Conservation Act that sets forth meas-

ures to control erosion and sedimentation. *See* Conservation Area Plan.

Land Disposal

With respect to hazardous wastes, includes, but is not be limited to, any placement of such hazardous waste in a landfill, surface impoundment, waste pile, injection well, land treatment facility, salt dome formation, salt bed formation, or underground mine or cave, or placement in a concrete vault or bunker intended for disposal purposes.

Land Disposal Facilities

The land, buildings, and equipment that are intended to be used for the disposal of radioactive wastes into the subsurface of the land.

Land Disposal Restrictions (LDRs)

The 1984 amendments to RCRA that prohibits the disposal of hazardous wastes into or on the land; also called the "Land Ban."

Land Economics

That branch of economics that deals with the classification and utilization of land or real estate.

Land Effect

See Coastal Refraction.

Land Farming, of Waste

A disposal process in which hazardous waste deposited on or in the soil is naturally degraded by microbes.

Land Interchange

A land transfer in which the Secretary of Interior (DOI) and another person exchange titles to lands or interests in lands of approximately equal value where the Secretary finds that such a value determination can be made without a formal appraisal and under such regulations as the Secretary may prescribe.

Land Reclamation

1) The treatment of previously unusable land by filling, leveling, or cleanup activities until the land can be put to productive use. 2) The recov-

ery of land previously abandoned due to some form of natural resource damage.

Land Search

The search of terrain by earth-bound personnel.

Land Surface Owner

The person, persons, or corporation (the majority of the stock of which is held by a person or persons) who a) hold legal or equitable title to the land surface; b) have their principal place of residence on the land; or personally conduct farming or ranching operations upon a farm or ranch unit to be affected by surface coal mining operations; or receive directly a significant portion of their income, if any, from such farming or ranching operations.

Land Treatment Facilities

Facilities or parts of facilities at which hazardous wastes are applied onto or incorporated into the soil surface; such facilities are disposal facilities if the waste will remain after closure.

Land Use

The deployment of real property for any legal use, by its owner of record, or a lessee.

Land Use Authority

The powers of counties and cities to plan and control land use by virtue of their police powers, or other regulatory authority.

Land Use Ordinance

Any zoning ordinance adopted by a unit of local government to control development within its boundaries, and includes amendments to, revisions of, or variances from such ordinance.

Landfill

See Landfills.

Landfill Cells

1) Sites for disposal of solid waste in which compacted layers are covered with soil. 2) Discrete volumes of a hazardous waste landfill that use a liner to provide isolation of wastes from adjacent

cells or wastes. Examples of landfill cells are trenches and pits.

Landfills
1) Disposal sites for, primarily, nonhazardous solid waste. Refuse at sanitary landfills is spread and compacted and a cover of soil applied so that effects on the environment (including public health and safety) are minimized. Landfills are required to have liners and leachate treatment systems to prevent contamination of groundwater and surface waters. A municipal landfill disposes of domestic waste including garbage, paper, etc. This waste may include toxins that are used in the home, such as insect sprays and powders, engine oil, paints, solvents, and other materials. 2) Secure chemical landfills are disposal sites for hazardous waste. They are selected and designed to minimize the chance of release of hazardous substances into the environment. 3) Disposal facilities or part of a facility where waste is placed in or on land and that is not a land treatment facility, a surface impoundment, or an injection well.

Landmark
A feature, either natural or artificial, that can be accurately determined on the ground from a grid reference.

Landslides
Rock falls, avalanches, or slides as a result of an earthquake.

LANL
See Los Alamos National Laboratory.

Lap Joint
A joint made by bonding overlapped portions of two adherents.

Large-Format Photos
Photographs taken of historic buildings, sites, structures, or objects.

Large High-Voltage Capacitors
Capacitors that contain 1.36 kg (3 lbs.) or more of dielectric fluid and that operate at 2,000 volts (AC/DC) or above.

Large-Lot Storage
A quantity of material that will require four or more pallet columns stored to maximum height. Usually accepted as stock stored in carload or greater quantities.

Large Quantities
In transportation of radioactive materials, a quantity that exceeds the Type B quantity limits [49 CFR Part 173.389(b)]. Large quantities are subject to requirements for being carried on highways designated as preferred routes.

Large Quantity Generator
A person or facility that generates more than 2,200 pounds of hazardous waste per month. In 1989, only 1% of more than 20,000 generators fell into this category. Those generators produced nearly 97% of the nation's hazardous waste. These generators are subject to all requirements of RCRA.

Large-Scale Map
A map having a scale of 1:75,000 or larger. *See* Map.

Larva
A species descriptor that refers to a preadult form of a species that does not resemble the adult.

Laryngeal Edema
Swelling of the voice box due to fluid accumulation.

Laryngitis
Inflammation of the mucous membrane of the larynx.

Laryngospasm
Spasmodic closure of the vocal apparatus.

Larynx
The enlarged upper end of the trachea, below the root of the tongue commonly referred to as the voice box.

Laser Accessories
The hardware and options available for lasers, such as secondary gases, Brewster windows, Q-switches, and electronic shutters.

Laser
Originally an acronym for Light Amplification by Stimulated Emission of Radiation, the term refers to a cavity, with mirrors at the ends, filled with material such as crystal, glass, liquid, gas, or dye; a device that produces an intense beam of light with the unique properties of coherency, collimation, and monochromaticity.

Laser Controlled Area
See Controlled Area.

Laser Designator
A device that emits a beam of laser energy that is used to mark a specific place or object.

Laser Device
Either a laser or a laser system.

Laser Eye Safety Distance
The minimum distance required to protect the eye from corneal or retinal damage caused by a specific laser beam.

Laser Guided Weapon
A weapon that uses a seeker to detect laser energy reflected from a laser marked/designated target and through signal processing provides guidance commands to a control system that guides the weapon to the point from which the laser energy is being reflected.

Laser Medium
The active medium material used to emit the laser light and for which the laser is named.

Laser Rod
A solid-state, rod-shaped lasing medium in which ion excitation is caused by a source of intense light, such as a flash lamp. Various materials are used for the rod, the earliest of which was synthetic ruby crystal.

Laser Safety Officer (LSO)
One who has authority to monitor and enforce measure to the control of laser hazards and effect the knowledgeable evaluation and control of laser hazards.

Laser System
An assembly of electrical, mechanical, and optical components that includes a laser. Under the Federal Standard, a laser in combination with its power supply (energy source).

Lashing/Lashing Point
See Tie Down; Restraint of Loads.

Latency
The period of time between exposure to an injurious agent and the manifestation of a response.

Lateral Route
A route generally parallel to the forward edge of a hazard area, that crosses, or feeds into, axial routes.

Lateral
A species descriptor pertaining to the side of an animal.

Lateral Force Resisting System
The part of the structural system assigned to resist lateral forces.

Lateral Sewers
Pipes that run under city streets and receive the sewage from homes and businesses.

Lateral Spreads
Lateral movement of large blocks of soil on top of a liquefied subsurface layer. These lateral spreads, that break up in numerous fissures and

scarps, generally develop on gentle slopes, most commonly on those between 0.3° and 3°. Horizontal movements on lateral spreads commonly are as much as 10 to 15 feet, but, where slopes are favorable and the duration of ground shaking is long, lateral movement may be as much as 100 to 150 feet.

Latex Resins
Resins that are produced by a polymerization process that initiates from free radical catalyst sites and are sold undried. *See* Resin.

Lattice
A network of intersecting positional lines printed on a map or chart from which a fix may be obtained.

Lavage
A technique used to wash out a cavity such as the stomach or a portion of the lungs via a tube. This technique is commonly used clinically to remove toxic substances from the stomach. This procedure may also be used to obtain cell populations and fluids from the lung for experimental manipulation.

Lawrence Berkeley Laboratory (LBL)
A DOE Research and Development and Field Facility founded in 1931 to advance the development of the cyclotron invented by Ernest Lawrence. The major roles of LBL are to perform multidisciplinary research in the general and energy sciences; develop and operate unique national experimental facilities; educate and train the next generation of scientists and engineers; and foster productive relationships between LBL research programs and industry.

Lawrence Livermore National Laboratory (LLNL)
A DOE Research and Development and Field Facility established in 1952. LLNL is a scientific and technical resource for the nation's nuclear weapons program and other programs of national interest. LLNL's primary role is to perform the research, development, and testing associated with the nuclear design aspects of all phases of the nuclear weapon life cycle and associated national security activities. LLNL has developed expertise in inertial fusion, magnetic fusion, biomedical and environmental research, isotope separation, and applied energy technology.

LC 50, Median Lethal Concentration
The concentration of a chemical required to cause death in 50% of the exposed population when exposed for a specified time period, and observed for a specified period of time after exposure. Refers to inhalation exposure concentration in the context of air toxics (may refer to water concentration for tests of aquatic organisms or systems). *See* LD 50.

LCCA
An acronym for Lead Contamination Control Act of 1988.

LCCS
An acronym for Land Capability Classification System.

LCLO
An acronym for Lethal Concentration Low; the lowest concentration of a chemical required to cause death in some of the population after exposure for a specified period of time and observed for a specified period of time after exposure. Refers to inhalation time exposure in the context of air toxics (may refer to water concentration for tests of aquatic organisms or systems).

LDLO
An acronym for Lethal Dose Low; the lowest dose of a chemical required to cause death in some of the population after noninhalation exposure (e.g., injection, ingestion) for a specified observation period after exposure; the highest concentration of a toxic substance at which none of the test organisms die.

LD 50, Median Lethal Dose
The dose of a chemical required to cause death in 50% of the exposed population after noninhalation exposure (e.g., injection, ingestion) for a

specified observation period after exposure. The lower the LD 50, the more toxic the compound.

Leachate

1) A contaminated liquid resulting when water percolates, or trickles, through waste materials and collects component characteristics of those wastes. 2) Liquid (mainly water) that percolates through a landfill and has picked up dissolved, suspended, and/or microbial contaminants from the waste. Leaching may occur in farming areas, feedlots, and landfills, and may result in hazardous substances entering surface water, groundwater, or soil.

Leachate Collection System

A system that gathers leachate and pumps it to the surface for treatment.

Leaching

1) The removal of materials in solution from rock, soil, or waste. 2) The separation or dissolving out of soluble constituents from a porous medium by percolation of water. *See* Leachate.

Lead (Pb)

A heavy metal that is hazardous to health if breathed or swallowed. Its use in gasoline, paints, and plumbing compounds has been sharply restricted or eliminated by federal laws and regulations. *See* Heavy Metals.

Lead, Particulates

Suspended particulate matter containing lead (Pb).

Lead Agencies

1) The federal agency (or state agency operating pursuant to a contract or cooperative agreement executed pursuant to Section 104(d)(1) of CERCLA) that has primary responsibility for coordinating response action under this Plan. A federal lead agency is the agency that provides the On-Scene Coordinator (OSC)or Remedial Project Manager (RPM) as specified. In the case of a state as lead agency, the state shall carry out the same responsibilities delineated for OSCs/RPMs in this Plan (except coordinating and directing federal agency response actions). 2) The public agency that has the principal responsibility for carrying out or approving a project. If the project is to be carried out by a nongovernmental person, the Lead Agency shall be the public agency with the greatest responsibility for supervising or approving the project as a whole. Where a governmental department is the Lead Agency, it will prepare the environmental documents for the project, either directly or by contract, except as otherwise provided by department regulations.

Lead Authorized Officials

A federal or state official authorized to act on behalf of all affected federal or state agencies acting as trustees where there are multiple agencies, or an official designated by multiple tribes where there are multiple tribes, affected because of co-existing or contiguous natural resources or concurrent jurisdiction.

Lead-Based Paint

Any paint containing more than five-tenths of 1 per centum lead by weight (calculated as lead metal) in the total nonvolatile content of the paint, or the equivalent measure of lead in the dried film of paint already applied, or both.

Lead-Based Paint Abatement

Activities engaged in by workers, supervisors, contractors, inspectors, and planners who are engaged in the removal, disposal, handling, inspection, and transportation of lead-based paint and materials containing lead-based paint from public and private dwellings, public and commercial buildings, bridges, and other structures or superstructures where lead-based paint presents or may present an unreasonable risk to health or the environment.

Lead Free

1) A cooler in which each part or component that comes in contact with drinking water contains not more than 8% lead, except that no drinking water cooler that contains any solder, flux, or storage tank interior surface that may come in contact with drinking water shall be considered lead free

if the solder, flux, or storage tank interior surface contains more than 0.2% lead. The Administrator of EPA may establish more stringent requirements for treating any part or component of a drinking water cooler as lead free for purposes of this part whenever he/she determines that any such part may constitute an important source of lead in drinking water. 2) When used with respect to solders and flux refers to solders and flux containing not more than 0.2% lead. 3) When used with respect to pipes and pipe fittings refers to pipes and pipe fittings containing not more than 8.0% lead.

Lead-Lined Tank
A water reservoir container in a drinking water cooler that is constructed of lead or that has an interior surface that is not lead free.

Lead Mattes
Any molten solutions of copper and other metal sulfides produced by reduction of sinter product from the oxidation of lead sulfide ore concentrates.

Leaded Gasoline
1) Gasoline to which lead has been added to raise the octane level. 2) A complex mixture of relatively volatile hydrocarbons, with or without small quantities of additives, all of which have been blended to form a fuel suitable for use in spark ignition engines. Meets the detailed requirements for gasoline listed in ASTM D439 or Federal Specifications VV-G-1690B, to include no more than 10% boiling at 122°F under atmospheric pressure, with Reid vapor pressure ranging from 9 to 15 psi. The finished (marketable) leaded gasoline produced with the use of any lead additive, containing more than 0.05 grams of lead per gallon or more than 0.005 grams of phosphorus per gallon. The actual lead content of any given gallon, however, may vary as a function of the size of the producer and company specific EPA waiver provisions. For example, producers of 5,000 gallons or less per day may include 0.8 to 2.65 grams per gallon; large producers, 0.5 to 0.8 grams per gallon. This includes both premium and regular grades, depending on the oc-

tane rating; and excludes a) any blendstock until blending has been completed and the blendstock is incorporated in the finished leaded gasoline and no longer separately identified; and b) any alcohol to be used in the blending of gasohol.

Leak Detection System
1) A system capable of detecting the failure of either the primary or secondary containment structure or the presence of a release of hazardous waste or accumulated liquid in the secondary containment structure. A leak detection system must employ operational controls (daily visual inspections for releases into the secondary containment system of aboveground tanks) or consist of an interstitial monitoring device designed to continuously and automatically detect the failure of the primary or secondary containment structure or the presence of a release of hazardous waste into the secondary containment structure. 2) A system or technology capable of detecting leaks of hazardous constituents at the earliest practicable time.

Leak or Leaking
Any instance in which a PCB Article, PCB Container, or PCB Item has any PCBs on any portion of its external surface.

Leakage
The flow of water from one hydrogeologic unit to another. This may be natural, as through a somewhat permeable confining layer, or anthropogenic, as through an uncased well. It may also be the natural loss of water from artificial structures as a result of hydrostatic pressure.

Leaks
Holes or voids in the wall of an enclosure, capable of passing liquid or gas from one side of the wall to the other under action of pressure or concentration differential existing across the wall, independent of the quantity of fluid flowing.

Leaky Aquifer
An artesian, or water table, aquifer that loses or gains water through adjacent semipermeable confining units.

Leap Second

A second of time that is added to or removed from Coordinated Universal Time (UTC) to keep UTC within 0.9 seconds of UT1. Leap seconds are normally introduced at the end of June or December, if required. The decision to introduce a leap second is announced by the International Time Bureau (Bureau International de l'Heure, or BIH) approximately 8 to 10 weeks in advance. *See* Coordinated Universal Time; Universal Time.

Lease

1) An agreement under which a tenant receives the possession and use of real property for a certain period of time and the landlord receives the payment of rent and or the performance of other conditions. 2) An oral or written contract for the use, possession, and occupation of property.

Lease Storage Tank Facilities

Storage tanks used to accumulate crude oil from producing properties prior to first sale or shipment.

Leasehold

An estate or right in real property held under a lease.

Legal Description

A description recognized by law that is sufficient to locate and identify the property without oral testimony.

Legal Defense Costs

Any expenses that an insurer incurs in defending against claims of third parties brought under the terms and conditions of an insurance policy.

Legionella

A genus of bacteria, some species of which have caused a type of pneumonia called Legionnaires Disease.

Legume

A species descriptor that means a pod, such as a pea or bean, that splits into two valves with seeds attached to the lower edge of one of the valves.

LEHR

See Laboratory for Energy-Related Health Research.

Lemma

A species descriptor that means the outer, lower bract enclosing the flower in a grass spikelet.

Lens

A curved piece of optically transparent material that, depending on its shape, is used to either converge or diverge light.

Lens of Eye Dose Equivalents

The dose equivalent at the respective depths of 0.007 cm, 1.0 cm, and 0.3 cm in tissue.

Lenticels

A species descriptor that means small pores on the surface of stems of woody plants that allow the passage of gases to and from the interior tissue.

LEPC

See Local Emergency Planning Committee.

Lepidopterous

A species descriptor that means insects with four wings covered with small scales, including moths and butterflies.

Lesion

A pathologic or traumatic discontinuity of tissue or loss of function.

Less Than Adequate

A term meaning something does not meet minimum requirements.

Lessee

The party who possesses a right or estate in realty, holding under a lease; also commonly referred to as the tenant.

Lessor
The party who conveyed a right or estate in realty to the lessee under a lease; commonly referred to as the landlord.

LET
See Linear Energy Transfer.

Lethal
Deadly; fatal.

Lethal Concentration 50 (LC 50)
A concentration of a pollutant or effluent at which 50% of the test organisms die; a common measure of acute toxicity.

Lethal Concentration, Low
The lowest concentration of a chemical at which some test animals die following inhalation exposure.

Lethal Concentration, Median Level
A standard measure of toxicity. It tells how much of a substance is needed to kill half of a group of experimental organisms at a specific time of observation. *See* LD 50.

Lethal Dose
The dose of a toxicant that will kill 50% of the test organisms within a designated period of time. The lower the LD 50, the more toxic the compound.

Lethal Dose 50 (LD 50)
The dose of a toxicant that will kill 50% of test organisms within a designated period of time. The lower the LD 50, the more toxic the compound.

Lethal Dose, Low
The lowest dose of chemical at which some test animals die following exposure.

Lethal Dose of Radiation
The amount of ionizing radiation exposure required to cause death. A brief (within 4 days) whole body gamma exposure of 600 roentgens would be a lethal dose for most people.

Lethargy
A state of extreme tiredness or fatigue.

Letter of Credit
A written agreement, usually by a bank, in which the issuer agrees with the other contracting party, its customers, that the issuer will honor drafts drawn upon it by the person named in the letter as beneficiary. These instruments are governed nationally by Article 5 of the Uniform Commercial Code, and internationally by the Customs and Practices for Commercial Documentary Credits. The three major types of letters of credit are:

- *Commercial Letter* — the customer is the purchaser of goods sold by the beneficiary and the letter covers the purchase price of the goods;

- *Stand-by Letter* — a letter obtained instead of a guaranty contract requiring the issuer to honor drafts drawn by the beneficiary upon the issuer when the customer of the issuer fails to perform a contract between the customer and the beneficiary;

- *Document Based Letter* — a letter of credit that does not obligate the issuer to honor drafts unless they are accompanied by documents that are specified in the letter.

Letter of Permission
A type of individual permit issued in accordance with the abbreviated procedures of 33 CFR 325.2(e).

Leukemia
1) A progressive, malignant disease of the blood-forming tissues, marked by an excessive number of white blood cells and their precursors. 2) Progressive proliferation of abnormal leukocytes found in blood and blood-forming tissues and organs; due to cancer of the bone marrow cells that form leukocytes.

Leukocyte
White cell normally present in circulating blood.

Level of Concern (LOC)

The concentration of an Extremely Hazardous Substance in the air above which there may be serious irreversible health effects or death as a result of a single exposure for a relatively short period of time. LOCs are estimated by using 0.1 Immediately Dangerous to Life and Health (IDLH).

Levels of Compliance

The three DOE compliance categories are:

- *LEVEL 1* — does not comply with mandatory DOE requirement (DOE Orders), prescribed policies and standards, and documented accepted practice (the latter is a professional judgment based on the acceptance and applicability of national consensus standards not prescribed by DOE requirements);

- *LEVEL 2* — does not comply with recommended DOE references, standards, guidance, or with good practice (as derived from industry experience, but not based on national consensus standards); and

- *LEVEL 3* — has little or no compliance consideration; these concerns are based on professional judgment in pursuit of excellence in design or practice (i.e., these are improvements for their own sake, not deficiency-driven).

Levels of Potential Hazards

The three DOE potential hazard categories:

- *LEVEL 1* — has the potential for causing a severe injury or fatality, potentially fatal occupational illness, or loss of the facility;

- *LEVEL 2* — has the potential for causing minor injury, minor occupational illness, major property damage, or has the potential for resulting in or contributing to unnecessary exposure to radiation toxic substances; and

- *LEVEL 3* — has little potential for threatening safety, health, or property.

Levels of Protection

The four levels of protection prescribed for worker safety by EPA:

- *LEVEL A* — The level of protection EPA considers necessary for work in or entry into hazardous environments or contaminated sites where the potential for serious adverse occupational health effects are present. Includes sites contaminated with unknown materials, or sites where materials are known to exist that could cause both respiratory and dermal exposure effects. Level A protective equipment includes supplied-air positive pressure respirators and totally encapsulating full-body protective suits;

- *LEVEL B* — The protection level described by EPA that includes the maximum degree of respiratory protection, but a lesser degree of full-body and skin protection. Examples include airborne respirable contaminants that are very toxic, but not toxic through skin absorption;

- *LEVEL C* — The protection level described and required by EPA where known concentrations of airborne contaminants exist but are suitably protected against by air-purifying respirators and do not require skin protection; and

- *LEVEL D* — The protection level required and described by EPA where nuisance respiratory exposures and nonskin-absorbing contaminants exist. Respirators are required when air sampling and monitoring determine that hazards exist above the nuisance level.

Levy

A seizure of property by an officer of a court or governmental agency in execution of a judgment of the court or agency.

LGFSTF

See Liquefied Gaseous Fuels Spill Test Facility (CAA).

LHEAA

An acronym for Low-Income Home Energy Assistance Act of 1981.

Liabilities

Probable future sacrifices of economic benefits arising from present obligations to transfer assets or provide services to other entities in the future as a result of past transactions or events.

Liable

The standard of liability obtained under Section 311 of the Federal Water Pollution Control Act.

Liaison Officers

Federal agency officials sent to another agency or another emergency response facility to facilitate interagency communications and coordination.

Libel

Written or visual defamation without legal justification.

Library

A collection of books, journals, papers, and audio documents associated with a park, center, or regional office for general staff and visitor reference.

Licensed Materials

Source material, special nuclear material, or byproduct material received, possessed, used, or transferred under a general or specific license issued by the Atomic Energy Commission pursuant to regulations of the Atomic Energy Act.

Licensed Production

A direct commercial arrangement between a U.S. company and a foreign government, international organization, or foreign company, providing for the transfer of production information that enables the foreign government, international organization, or commercial producer to manufacture, in whole or in part, an item of U.S. defense equipment.

A typical license production arrangement would include the functions of production engineering, controlling, quality assurance and determining of resource requirements. It may or may not include design engineering information and critical materials production and design information.

A licensed production arrangement is accomplished under the provisions of a manufacturing license agreement per the U.S. International Traffic in Arms Regulation (ITAR).

Licensed Sites

Areas contained within the boundary of a location under the control of persons generating or storing uranium byproduct materials under a license issued by the Commission. These include such areas licensed by Agreement states, i.e., those states that have entered into an effective agreement under Section 274(b) of the Atomic Energy Act of 1954, as amended.

Licenses

Licenses issued under appropriate regulations, including licenses to operate production or utilization facilities, licenses to possess power reactor spent fuel in an independent spent fuel storage installation, etc.

Life Cycle

1) The sequence of events in the progression of an organism from birth to death. 2) The total phases through which an item passes from the time it is initially developed until the time it is either consumed in use or disposed of as being excess to all known material requirements.

Life Cycle Cost

1) The total costs of owning, operating, and maintaining a building over its useful economic life, including such costs as fuel, energy, labor, and replacement components, determined on the basis of a systematic evaluation and comparison of alternative building systems, except that in the case of leased buildings, where the life cycle costs are typically calculated over the effective remaining term of the lease. 2) All costs except the cost of personnel occupying the facility incurred from the time that space requirement is defined until that facility passes out of the government's hands.

Life Cycle Plans

An analysis and description of the major events and activities in the lite of a functional unit from planning through decommissioning and site restoration. The plan documents the history of the functional unit and forecasts future activities, including major line item and expense projects and their duration, relationships, and impact on life expectancy. The plan also describes maintenance practices and costs.

Life Safety/Disaster Warning (LS/DW) System

A public address system used to disseminate emergency warnings and information to a general Site population. Speakers on the system are located in occupied buildings onsite. Music is continuously played over the LS/DW System as a constant operational check in production buildings. Shift announcements are made daily for operability checks in nonproduction buildings.

Life Support Equipment

Equipment designed to sustain site employees throughout a hazardous working environment, optimizing their job effectiveness and affording a means of safe and reliable escape, decontamination, survival, and recovery in emergency situations.

Life-Threatening Environmental Situation

The circumstances in which the release of a hazardous substance requires immediate emergency response efforts in order to protect the public from serious danger or fatality.

Lifetime

Covering the lifespan of an organism (generally considered 70 years for humans).

Lift

In a sanitary landfill, a compacted layer of solid waste and the top layer of cover material.

Lifting Station

A mechanical device installed in a sewer or water system or other liquid-carrying pipeline that moves the liquid to a higher level.

Lifts

In a sanitary landfill, a compacted layer of solid waste and the top layer of cover material.

Light

The range of electromagnetic radiation frequencies detected by the eye, or the wavelength range from about 400 to 760 nanometers. The term is sometimes used loosely to include radiation beyond visible limits.

Light Filter

An optical element, such as a sheet of glass, gelatine, or plastic, dyed in a specific manner to selectively absorb light of certain colors.

Light-Water Reactor

A nuclear reactor in which ordinary water or light water is the primary coolant/moderator with slightly enriched uranium fuel. There are two commercial light-water reactor types — the boiling water reactor (BWR) and the pressurized water reactor (PWR).

Lightening

The operation (normally carried out at anchor) of transferring crude oil cargo from a large tanker to a smaller tanker, so reducing the draft of the larger tanker to enable it to enter port.

Lighterage

A small craft designed to transport cargo or personnel from ship to shore. Lighterage includes amphibians, landing craft, discharge lighters, causeways, and barges.

Lignite

A low-grade coal of a variety intermediate between peat and bituminous coal.

Lignite Coal

Consolidated lignitic coal having less than 8,300 Btus per pound, moist, and mineral matter free.

Limestone Scrubbing

A process in which sulfur gases moving toward a smokestack are passed through a limestone and water solution to remove sulfur before it reaches the atmosphere.

Limestones
Sedimentary rock composed of carbonates and calcite that can be categorized into three groups: 1) those formed by evaporation of aqueous solutions; 2) those formed by biochemically produced calcite from living organisms; and 3) those formed by contact with the fragments of preexisting limestone. Limestones are used as aquifers, reservoir rocks for hydrocarbons, building stone and aggregate, and as an ingredient for making cement.

Limit
1) In ANSI, the product of Accessible Emission Limit and Maximum Permissible Exposure Limit (MPEL). 2) The area of the limiting aperture (7mm for visible and near infrared lasers).

Limited Areas
Security areas for the protection of classified matter where guards, security inspectors, or other internal controls can prevent access by unauthorized persons to classified matter.

Limited Degradation
A policy that allows for some lowering of natural environmental quality to a given level beneath an established health standard.

Limited Evidence
According to the U.S. EPA carcinogen risk assessment guidelines, limited evidence is a collection of facts and accepted scientific inferences that suggests the agent may be causing an effect but the suggestion is not strong enough to be an established fact.

Limited Liability
Loss of contributed capital or investment as a maximum liability.

Limited Partnership
A partnership in which at least one partner has liability limited only to capital contributed to the enterprise; such partner usually has no part in the management of the partnership or its operations.

Limited Quantity
The maximum amount of hazardous material for which there is a specific labeling and packaging exception, when specified as such in a section applicable to a particular material, with the exception of Poison B materials.

Limited Responses
Responses to a request for radiological assistance that involves limited U.S. Department of Energy or other agency resources and does not require the formal field management structure.

Limiting Aperture
The maximum circular area over which radiance and radiant exposure can be averaged when determining safety hazards.

Limiting Device
A device that restricts the maximum envelope (space) by stopping or causing to stop all robot motion and is independent of the control program and the application programs.

Limiting Factor
1) An ecological factor that restricts the distribution or activity of an organism or biological community. 2) A condition, whose absence, or excessive concentration, is incompatible with the needs or tolerance of a species or population and that may have a negative influence on their ability to grow or even survive. 3) A factor or condition that, either temporarily or permanently, impedes mission accomplishment. Illustrative examples are transportation deficiencies, lack of in-place facilities, malpositioned response forces or material, extreme climatic conditions, distance, access.

Limits
The values of a quantity that must not be exceeded. Limits in radiation protection are as follows: primary, secondary, derived, authorized, operational.

Limnetic
Pertaining to the deeper, open waters of lakes or ponds.

Limnology

The study of the physical, chemical, meteorological, and biological aspects of fresh water.

Line Management

Those management positions whose responsibility is the accomplishment of the organization's primary mission(s), as distinguished from staff organization that supports the organization's primary mission(s).

Line Organizations

1) In DOE, that unbroken chain of command that extends from the Secretary through the Under Secretary, to the Program Senior Officials (PSO) who set program policy and plans and develop assigned programs, to the field organization managers who are responsible to the PSO for execution of these programs, to the contractors who conduct the programs. Environment, safety, and health are integral parts of each program. Accordingly, line management responsibility for ES&H functions flows from the Secretary through the Under Secretary, to the PSO, to the field organization managers, to the contractors. 2) The organization within a company or project responsible for accomplishing the primary goals.

Linear Energy Transfer

Of charged particles in a medium, the quotient of dE divided by dl, where dE is the energy lost by a charged particle in transversing a distance dl as a result of those collisions with electrons in which the energy loss is less than some specified value.

Linear Leaf

A species descriptor that means long, narrow leaf, characterized by parallel veins.

Linear Scale

See Graphic Scale; Scale.

Liner

1) A continuous layer of natural or manmade materials, beneath or on the sides of a surface impoundment, landfill, or landfill cells, that restricts the downward or lateral escape of hazardous waste, hazardous waste constituents, or leachate. 2) A liner designed, constructed, installed, and operated to prevent hazardous waste from passing into the liner at any time during the active life of the facility. 3) A liner designed, constructed, installed, and operated to prevent hazardous waste from migrating beyond the liner to adjacent subsurface soil, groundwater, or surface water at any time during the active life of the facility. 4) A relatively impermeable barrier designed to prevent leachate from leaking from a landfill. Liner materials include plastic and dense clay. 5) An insert or sleeve for sewer pipes to prevent leakage or infiltration.

Link

1) In communications, a general term used to indicate the existence of communications facilities between two points. 2) In military science, a maritime route, other than a coastal or transit route, that links any two or more routes.

Link-Lift Vehicle

The conveyance, together with its operating personnel, used to satisfy a movement requirement between nodes.

Link-Route Segments

Route segments that connect nodes wherein link-lift vehicles perform the movement function.

Liquefied Compressed Gases (LCG)

Gases that, under the charged pressure, are partially liquid at a temperature of 70°F.

Liquids (SWDA; RCRA; CFR)

Material that has a vertical flow of over 2 inches (50mm) within a three-minute period, or a material having one gram (1g) or more liquid separation, when determined in accordance with the procedures specified in ASTM D 4359-84, Standard Test Method for Determining Whether a Material is a Liquid or Solid, 1984 edition.

Lipid Solubility

The maximum concentration of a chemical that will dissolve in fatty substances; lipid soluble substances are insoluble in water. If a substance is lipid soluble it will very selectively disperse through the environment via living tissue.

Liquefaction

Changing a solid into a liquid. When seismic shear waves pass through a saturated granular soil layer, distorting its granular structure, this distortion causes some of the void spaces to collapse. Disruptions to the soil generated by these collapses cause transfer of the ground shaking load from grain-to-grain contacts to the pore water. This transfer of load increases pressure in the pore water, either causing drainage or, if drainage is restricted, a sudden buildup of pore-water pressures. When pore-water pressures reach a critical level (grain-to-grain stresses approach zero), the granular material suddenly behaves as a liquid rather than as a solid.

Liquefication, Coal

The conversion of coal into liquid hydrocarbons and related compounds by hydrogenation.

Liquefied Gaseous Fuels Spill Test Facility (LGFSTF)

An experimental research site for field testing hazardous air pollutants. The highest priority is given to those chemicals that would present the greatest potential risk to human health as a result of an accidental release a) from a fixed site; or b) related to the transport of such chemicals.

The purposes of LGSTF research are to a) develop improved predictive models for atmospheric dispersion that at a minimum describe dense gas releases in complex terrain including manmade structures or obstacles with variable winds, improve understanding of the effects of turbulence on dispersion patterns, and consider realistic behavior of aerosols by including physicochemical reactions with water vapor, ground deposition, and removal by water spray; b) evaluate existing and future atmospheric dispersion models by the development of a rigorous, standardized methodology for dense gas models, and the application of such methodology to current dense gas dispersion models using data generated

from field experiments; and c) evaluate the effectiveness of hazard mitigation and emergency response technology for fixed site and transportation related accidental releases of toxic chemicals. Models pertaining to accidental release are evaluated and improved periodically for their utility in planning and implementing evacuation procedures and other mitigative strategies designed to minimize human exposure to hazardous air pollutants released accidentally.

Liquefied Natural Gas (LNG)

Natural gas that has been liquefied by cooling to about 140°C. In this form, it occupies a relatively small volume.

Liquefied Petroleum Gas (LPG)

1) A gas comprised primarily of butane, propane, and pentane, sold in pressurized containers as bottled gas. 2) A finished petroleum hydrocarbon commodity, composed predominantly of propane, propylene, normal butane, isobutane, butylenes, or mixtures of these. It is normally stored and transported as a liquid under pressure and vaporizes, yielding a gaseous commodity, when released from pressure. It will include these materials in either the liquid or gaseous state. However, any product having a vapor pressure in excess of 215 psig at 100°F may require additional safeguards or regulations to provide the required safety.

Liquid-Crystal Polymers

A newer type of thermoplastic, melt processible, with high orientation in molding, improved tensile strength, and high-temperature capability.

Liquid Explosive

An explosive that is fluid at normal temperatures.

Liquid-Metal Fast Breeder Reactor (LMFBR)

A nuclear breeder reactor cooled by molten sodium in which fission is accompanied by fast neutron irradiation of uranium-238 giving rise to plutonium-242, a fissile material.

Liquid Propellant

Any liquid combustible fed to the combustion chamber of a rocket engine.

Liquid Traps

Sumps, well cellars, and other traps used in association with oil and gas production, gathering, and extraction operations (including gas production plants), for the purpose of collecting oil, water, and other liquids. These liquid traps may temporarily collect liquids for subsequent disposition or reinjection into a production or pipeline stream, or may collect and separate liquids from a gas stream.

Lis Pendens

A public notice, filed against specific lands, that an action at law is pending that may affect the title to the land.

List

1) EPA's list of violating facilities or lists of firms debarred from obtaining government contracts because they violated certain sections of the Clean Air or Clean Water Acts. The list is maintained by the Office of Enforcement and Compliance Monitoring. 2) The list of Endangered and Threatened Wildlife and Plants as found in federal regulations. 3) The list of National Historic Landmarks. 4) The list of Source Categories. 5) The list of Hazardous Air Pollutants (HAPs). 6) The list of Chemical Contaminants. 7) The list of High Probability Radon Areas. 8) Other environmental data lists.

List of Chemical Contaminants Found in Human Tissue

The list of all known chemical contaminants resulting from environmental pollution that have been found in human tissue including blood, urine, breast milk, and all other human tissue, and an explanation of what is known about the manner in which the chemicals entered into the environment and thereafter human tissue. In compiling the list, the Administrator of EPA, in consultation with National Institutes of Health, the National Center for Health Statistics, and the National Center for Health Services Research and Development, conducts an epidemiological study to demonstrate the relationship between levels of chemicals in the environment and in human tissue.

List of High Probability Radon Areas

The list identifying areas within the United States that the Administrator of EPA determines have a high probability of including schools that have elevated levels of radon. In compiling such a list, the Administrator shall make such determinations on the basis of, among other things, each of the following: a) geological data; b) data on high radon levels in homes and other structures nearby any such school; and c) physical characteristics of the school buildings.

List of National Historic Landmarks

The list of sites of national historic significance as of their initial listing in the Federal Register.

List of Source Categories

The Administrator's list of each category or subcategory of area sources that the Administrator finds presents a threat of adverse effects to human health or the environment (by such sources individually or in the aggregate) warranting regulation under the CAA. The list is based on actual or estimated aggregate emissions of a listed pollutant or pollutants, sufficient categories or subcategories of area sources to ensure that area sources representing 90% of the area source emissions of the 30 hazardous air pollutants that present the greatest threat to public health in the largest number of urban areas are subject to regulation. In addition to those categories and subcategories of sources listed for regulation, the Administrator may at any time list additional categories and subcategories of sources of hazardous air pollutants according to the same criteria. With respect to alkylated lead compounds, polycyclic organic matter, hexachlorobenzene, mercury, polychlorinated biphenyls, 2,3,7,8-tetrachlorodibenzofurans, and 2,3,7,8-tetrachlorodibenzo-p-dioxin, the Administrator shall, list categories and subcategories of sources assuring that sources accounting for not less than 90 per centum of the aggregate emissions of each such pollutant are subject to standards.

Listed Hazardous Wastes

Regulated wastes per Section 6921 of the Solid Waste Disposal Act (SWDA) as amended by the Resource Conservation and Recovery Act (RCRA). The Act sets forth a list of regulated contaminants, including compounds thereof, and maximum allowable concentrations, that have specific land disposal prohibitions.

Liquid Waste/CompoundMCL

Cyanides1,000 mg/l

Arsenic and/or compounds (as AS)   500 mg/l

Cadmium and/or compounds (as CD)   100 mg/l

Chromium VI and compounds (as Cr VI)   500 mg/l

Lead and/or compounds (as Pb)   500 mg/l

Mercury and/or compounds (as Hg)   20 mg/l

Nickel and/or compounds (as Ni)   134 mg/l

Selenium and/or compounds (as Se)   100 mg/l

Thallium and/or compounds (as Th)   130 mg/l.

Other liquid wastes listed by the Act include a) those with a pH of 2.0; b) those containing PCBs at 50 ppm; and c) wastes containing halogenated organic compounds in total concentrations of 1,000 mg/kg.

Listed Hazardous Substances

The elements and compounds and hazardous wastes appearing in Table 302.4 (40 CFR 302.4) are designated as hazardous substances under Section 102(a) of CERCLA.

Listed Species

Any species of fish, wildlife, or plant that has been determined to be endangered or threatened under Section 4 of the Act. Species are listed in 50 CFR 17.11-17.12.

Listed Wastes

Wastes listed as hazardous under RCRA but which have not been subjected to the Toxic Characteristics Listing Process because the dangers they present are considered self-evident.

Lithic

A term that means pertaining to stone, or lithium-based.

Lithification

The transmutation of sediment into sedimentary rock.

Lithium (Li)

Element No. 3 (symbol, Li; atomic weight 6.94); as found in nature, lithium consists of a mixture of two stable isotopes — lithium-6 (7.5%) and lithium-7 (92.4%). Lithium-6 is of interest as a possible fuel or source thereof for the generation of power from a controlled thermonuclear reaction.

Lithology

The study of rocks on the basis of their physical and chemical characteristics.

Lithosphere

1) A portion of earth that includes the crust and the upper part of the mantle, above the low-velocity zone. 2) The solid part of the earth below the surface, including any groundwater contained within it.

Litter

A basket or frame utilized for the transport of injured persons.

Littoral

A shore or coastal region.

Live-Bearing

A species descriptor that means giving birth to fully developed young; ovoviviparous.

Live Loads
A moving load or a load of variable force acting on a structure, in addition to its own weight.

LLD
See Lower Limit of Detection.

LLMW
An acronym for Low-Level Mixed Waste.

LLW
An acronym for Low-Level Wastes.

LLWDDD
An acronym for Low-Level Waste Disposal Development Demonstration.

LNG
See Liquified Natural Gas.

Load
1) The amount of power needed to be delivered at a given point on an electric system. 2) The total weight of passengers and/or freight carried on board a ship, aircraft, train, road vehicle, or other means of conveyance. *See* Allowable Load.

Load Factor
The strength-to-service-load ratio.

Load Growth
The growth in energy in power demands by a utility's customers.

Load Spreader
Material used to distribute the weight of a load over a given floor area to avoid exceeding designed stress.

Loading
1) The ratio of the biomass of gammarids (grams, wet weight) to the volume (liters) of test solution in either a test chamber or passing through it in a 24-hour period. 2) The process of putting personnel, material, and supplies on board ships, air-craft, trains, road vehicles, or other means of conveyance.

Loading Plan
All of the individually prepared documents that, taken together, present in detail all instructions for the arrangement of personnel, and the loading of equipment for one or more units or other special grouping of personnel or material moving by highway, water, rail, or air transportation. *See* Ocean Manifest.

Loading Site
An area containing a number of loading points.

Loads
A term referring to different types of loads including, but not limited to, a) dead load — the vertical load due to the weight of all permanent structural and nonstructural components of a unit such as walls, floors, and fixed service equipment; b) live load — the load superimposed by the use and occupancy of the unit not including the wind load, earthquake or dead load; and c) wind load — the lateral or vertical pressure or uplift on the unit due to wind blowing in any direction.

Lobed Leaf
A species descriptor that means characterized by rounded projections.

LOC
See Level of Concern.

LOCA
An acronym for Loss of Coolant Accident.

Local Agencies
Any local government agencies other than the state agencies, that are charged with responsibility for carrying out a portion of a plan or program.

Local Distribution Company
Any person: 1) engaged in the distribution of natural gas at retail, including any subsidiary or affiliate thereof engaged in the exploration and

production of natural gas; and 2) regulated, or operated as a public utility, by a state or local government or agency thereof.

Local Educational Agency
1) Any local educational agency as defined in the Elementary and Secondary Education Act of 1965 (20 U.S.C. 3381). 2) The owner of any private, nonprofit elementary or secondary school building. 3) The governing authority of any school operating under the Defense Dependents Education System provided for under the Defense Dependents Education Act of 1978.

Local Effect
A biological response occurring at the site of first contact between the toxic substance and the organism.

Local Emergency Planning Committee (LEPC)
A committee appointed by the state emergency response commission, as required by SARA (Superfund Amendments and Reauthorization Act) Title III to formulate a comprehensive emergency plan for its jurisdiction.

Local Governments
Any county, city, village, town, district, or political subdivisions of any state, Native American Indian tribe, or authorized tribal organization, or Alaska native village or organization, including any rural community or unincorporated town or village or any other public entity.

Local Health Agency
A county or city health authority.

Local Magnitude
The logarithm, to the base 10, of the amplitude in micrometers of the maximum amplitude of seismic waves that would be observed on a standard torsion seismograph at a distance of about 60 miles from the epicenter.

Local Organization
1) Any state, or political subdivision thereof; soil or water conservation district; flood prevention or control district; or combinations thereof; or any other agency having authority under state law to carry out, maintain, and operate works of improvement. 2) Any irrigation or reservoir company, water users' association, or similar organization having such authority and not being operated for profit that may be approved by the Secretary. 3) Any Native American Indian tribe or tribal organization, having authority under federal, state, or Native American Indian tribal law to carry out, maintain, and operate the works of improvement.

Local Procurement
The process of obtaining personnel, services, supplies, and equipment from local or indigenous sources.

Localized
A species descriptor that means found within a limited geographic area.

Loculicidal
A species descriptor that means a small cavity or compartment within an organ or part, such as a plant ovary.

LOCV
An acronym for Loss of Condenser Vacuum.

Log Culvert
A drainage structure consisting of logs or logs and fill material placed in a drainage in such a manner as to allow for the passage of water. Also commonly referred to as a "Humboldt" crossing.

Logic Trees
Diagrams, in the shape of a tree, using different geometrical symbols to aid a user in systematically portraying information in a logical sequence and showing relationships between elements of the tree. Trees may be positive or negative (fault tree).

Logical Correlates
Those performance indices and factors that correlate with ES&H performance in a logical manner. *See* Empirical Correlates.

Logistic Assessment
1) An evaluation of the logistic support required to support particular operations in response operations. 2) The actual and/or potential logistics support available for the conduct of military operations either within the theater of an incident, country, or area, or located elsewhere.

Logistic Estimate of the Situation
An appraisal resulting from an orderly examination of the logistic factors influencing contemplated courses of action to provide conclusions concerning the degree and manner of that influence.

Logistic Implications Test
An analysis of the major logistic aspects of a joint strategic plan and the consideration of the logistic implications resultant therefrom as they may limit the acceptability of the plan. The logistic analysis and consideration are conducted concurrently with the development of the strategic plan. The objective is to establish whether the logistic requirements generated by the plan are in balance with availabilities, and to set forth those logistic implications that should be weighed by the Joint Chiefs of Staff in their consideration of the plan. *See* Feasibility Test.

Logistic Support
The logistic services, material, and transportation required to support deployed forces based in the continental United States and/or worldwide .

Logistic Support, Medical
Medical care, treatment, hospitalization, evacuation, furnishing of medical services, supplies, material, and adjuncts thereto.

Logistical Control
Having the right people in the right place at the right time, working with the proper hardware, and in accordance with the proper procedures and management controls.

Logistics
The science of planning and carrying out the movement and maintenance of people, materials and equipment. In its most comprehensive sense, those aspects of military operations that deal with:

- design and development, acquisition, storage, movement, distribution, maintenance, evacuation, and disposition of material;

- movement, evacuation, and hospitalization of personnel;

- acquisition or construction, maintenance, operation, and disposition of facilities; and

- the acquisition or furnishing of services.

Logit Model
A dose-response model that can be derived under the assumption that the individual tolerance level is a random variable following the logit distribution.

Long-Term Contract
When used in relation to solid waste supply, contracts of sufficient duration to ensure the viability of a resource recovery facility (to the extent that such viability depends upon solid waste supply).

LOOP
An acronym for Loss of Offsite Power.

Lore
A species descriptor that means the area between a bird's eye and the base of the bill; the area between the snout and eye of a snake or a fish.

Los Alamos National Laboratory (LANL)
A DOE Research and Development and Field Facility, established in 1943 as part of the Manhattan Project during World War II to develop the world's first nuclear weapons.

LANL's primary mission is the application of science and technology to problems of national security, including the maintenance of a strong defense, the fulfillment of arms control commitments and the guarantee of a secure energy supply for the future. LANL also undertakes multidisciplinary fundamental and applied research.

Loss Control Management
The application of professional management techniques and skills to those program activities (e.g., risk avoidance, loss prevention, and loss reduction) specifically intended to minimize losses involved with undesired events resulting from the pure (nonspeculative) risks of business.

Loss Ratio
Used in insurance. A ratio calculated by dividing the amount of loss(es) by the amount of the premium(s). Normally expressed as a percentage of the premiums.

Losses
Measurable adverse reductions of chemical or physical qualities or viabilities of natural resources.

Lot
Specifically, a quantity of material all of which was manufactured under identical conditions and assigned an identifying lot number.

Lotic
A species descriptor that means pertaining to or living in moving water.

Love Seismic Waves
Types of surface waves having a horizontal motion that is shear or transverse to the direction of propagation. Its velocity depends only on density and rigidity modules, and not on bulk modules.

Low Air
Air supplied to pressurize working chambers and locks.

Low Airburst
The fallout safe height of burst for a nuclear weapon that maximizes damage to or casualties on surface targets. *See* Types of Burst.

Low-Concentration PCBs
Any fluid or material that is tested and found to contain less than 500 ppm PCBs or those PCB-containing materials that EPA requires to be assumed to be at concentrations below 500 ppm (untested mineral oil dielectric fluid).

Low-Income Community
A community with a population of less than 20,000 that is located in a county with a per capita income less than the per capita income of two-thirds of the counties in the United States.

Low-Income
A term that applies to income in relation to family size being at or below 125% of the poverty level determined in accordance with criteria established by the Director of the Office of Management and Budget; or is the basis on which cash assistance payments have been paid during the preceding 12-month period under titles IV and XVI of the Social Security Act (42 USC 601 et seq., 1381 et seq.) or applicable state or local law, or is the basis for eligibility for assistance under the Low-Income Home Energy Assistance Act of 1981.

Low-Level Radioactive Waste (LLRW)
1) Wastes less hazardous than most of those generated by a nuclear reactor. Usually generated by hospitals, research laboratories, and certain industries. 2) Radioactive waste not classified as HLW, TRU, spent fuel, or by-product material. 3) Radioactive wastes consisting of clothing and equipment from laboratory/industrial operations where radioactive substances have been used or tested, including building materials in facilities where these wastes have been stored. These wastes have relatively short half-lives, are suitable for disposal, and present no serious hazards to the public. The Department of Energy, Nuclear Regulatory Commission, and EPA share responsibilities for managing them. *See* Transuranic Waste; High-Level Wastes.

Low-Noise Emission Product
Any product that emits noise in amounts significantly below the levels specified in noise emission standards.

Low Oblique
See Oblique Air Photograph.

Low-Polluting Fuel
Methanol, ethanol, propane, or natural gas, or any comparably low-polluting fuel. In determining whether a fuel is comparably low-polluting, the Administrator of EPA considers both the level of emissions of air pollutants from vehicles using the fuel and the contribution of such emissions to ambient levels of air pollutants.

Low Specific Activity Materials
Any of the materials such as uranium or thorium ores (and physical or chemical concentrates of those ores); unirradiated, natural, or depleted uranium, or unirradiated natural thorium.

Low Sulfur Coal
Coal that, in a quantity necessary to produce one million British thermal units, does not contain sulfur or sulfur compounds the elemental sulfur content of which exceeds 0.6 pound. Sulfur content is determined after the application of any coal preparation process that takes place before sale of the coal by the producer.

Low Terrain Area
With respect to any emitting facility, any area having an elevation of 899 feet or less above the base of the stack of such facility. In low terrain areas emissions of sulfur oxides from facilities cannot (during any day on which the otherwise applicable maximum allowable increases are exceeded) cause or contribute to concentrations that exceed the following maximum allowable increases for such areas over the baseline concentration for such pollutant: 24-hr maximum = 36 mgcm; 3-hr maximum = 130 mgcm. *See* High Terrain Area.

Low Velocity Drop
A drop procedure in which the drop velocity does not exceed 30 feet per second.

Low-Velocity Zone (LVZ)
The zone within the earth where earthquake shock waves travel at slow rates. The bottom of the zone is at approximately 125 to 200 miles below the earth's surface.

Low Voltage
An electromotive force rated at 24 volts or less, supplied from a transformer, converter, or battery.

Lower Explosive Limit (LEL)
The concentration of a compound in air below which a flame will not propagate if the mixture is ignited.

Lower Limit of Detection
The smallest amount of a contaminant that can be distinguished in a sample by a given measurement procedure at a given confidence level.

Lower Respiratory Tract
The part of the respiratory tract below the larynx.

Lower Tier Crude Oil
Crude oil that is subject to the price ceiling established under 10 CFR Part 212.73.

Lowest Achievable Emission Rate (LAER)
The rate of emissions for any source, that reflects a) the most stringent emission limitation that is contained in the implementation plan of any state for such source unless the owner or operator of the proposed source demonstrates such limitations are not achievable; or b) the most stringent emissions limitation achieved in practice, that ever is more stringent. Application of this term does not permit a proposed new or modified source to emit pollutants in excess of existing new source standards. The use of the "lowest achievable emission rate" is required of new or modified sources locating in nonattainment areas (40 CFR 51.165).

Lowest-Observed-Adverse-Effect Level (LOAEL)
The lowest dose or exposure level of a chemical in a study at which there is a statistically or bio-

logically significant increase in the frequency or severity of an adverse effect in the exposed population as compared with an appropriate, unexposed control group.

Lowest-Observed-Effect Level (LOEL)
In a study, the lowest dose or exposure level at which a statistically or biologically significant effect is observed in the exposed population compared with an appropriate unexposed control group.

LPG
See Liquefied Petroleum Gas.

LPRS
An acronym for Low Pressure Recirculation System.

LPRSX
An acronym for Low Pressure Recirculation System Heat Exchanger.

LPSW
An acronym for Low Pressure Service Water.

LRSA
An acronym for the Lamprey River Study Act of 1991 (WSRA).

LSCRA
An acronym for Lower Saint Croix River Act of 1972 (WSRA).

Lubricating Oils
The fraction of crude oil that is sold for purposes of reducing friction in any industrial or mechanical device. Such term includes re-refined oil.

Luminaire
A complete lighting unit consisting of a fluorescent lamp or lamps, together with parts designed to distribute the light, to position and protect such lamps, and to connect such lamps to the power supply through the ballast.

Lung Classes
A classification scheme used to designate the clearance of inhaled radioactive materials from the lung. Materials are classified on the basis of their period of retention in the pulmonary region.

- "D" (Day) indicates a biological half-life of less than 10 days;
- "W" (Week), a half-life of 10 to 100 days; and
- "Y" (Year), a half-life greater than 100 days.

Lunular
A species descriptor that means crescent shaped.

Lurgi Process
The chief commercially available process for coal gasification. Having originated in Germany, this process has limited application in the United States because of problems of scaling up the size of operations and characteristics of U.S. coal.

LWC
An acronym for Lost Workday Cases.

LWCFA
An acronym for Land and Water Conservation Fund Act of 1965.

LWR
See Light-Water Reactor.

Lycaenid
A species descriptor that for a member of the family Lycaenidae; a heteroneuran lepidopteran insect, including moths and butterflies.

Lymphoma
Any abnormal growth (neoplasm) of the lymphoid tissues. Lymphoma usually refers to a malignant growth and thus is a cancer.

M

MAC
See Maximum Allowable Concentration (CAA).

Macrophage
A specialized cell of the immune system capable of engulfing and digesting foreign particles.

Macrophytes
Large aquatic plants.

Macrophytic Algae
Algal plants large enough either as individuals or communities to be readily visible without the aid of optical magnification.

MACS
An acronym for Mobile Air Conditioning Society.

Maculation
The spotted markings on a plant or animal, such as the spots on a leopard.

Magazine Vessels
Vessels used for receiving, storing, or dispensing of explosives.

Magazine
1) A mechanical device used to hold a predetermined number of cartridges in position for feeding into a weapon. 2) Buildings or structures, except an operating building, used for the storage of ammunition or explosives. A "first class" magazine is any structure, other than an explosives manufacturing building, used for the storage of more than 100 pounds of explosives. A "second class" magazine is a box, or other container, used for the storage of small quantities of explosives not exceeding 100 pounds.

Magma
Molten material comprised of silicates, water, and gases, that originates within the earth's lower crust or mantle. Magmas usually have temperatures that range from 700° to 1100° C. Magma is the principal cause of geothermal and hydrothermal anomalies. Magma that reaches the earth's surface is known as lava; as it solidifies it becomes igneous rocks. *See* Igneous.

Magneforming
Part of fabrication process of fuel subassemblies.

Magnetic Anomaly
A local change in the normal value of the earth's magnetic field, caused by the existence or nonexistence of magnetic minerals in rocks.

Magnetic Declination
The angle between the magnetic and geographical meridians at any place, expressed in degrees east or west to indicate the direction of magnetic north from true north. In nautical and aeronautical navigation, the term "magnetic variation" is used instead of "magnetic declination" and the angle is termed "variation of the compass" or "magnetic variation." Magnetic declination is not otherwise

synonymous with magnetic variation, which refers to regular or irregular change with time of the magnetic declination, dip, or intensity. *See* Magnetic Variation.

Magnetic Equator

A line drawn on a map or chart connecting all points at which the magnetic inclination (dip) is zero for a specified epoch. Also called aclinic line.

Magnetic North

The direction indicated by the north seeking pole of a freely suspended magnetic needle, influenced only by the earth's magnetic field.

Magnetic Variation

1) In navigation, at a given place and time, the horizontal angle between the true north and magnetic north measured east or west according to whether magnetic north lies east or west of true north. *See* Magnetic Declination. 2) In cartography, the annual change in direction of the horizontal component of the earth's magnetic field.

MAIC

An acronym for Maximum Allowable Increases in Concentrations (CAA).

Maintenance

1) All action taken to retain material in a serviceable condition or to restore it to serviceability. It includes inspection, testing, servicing, classification as to serviceability, repair, rebuilding, and reclamation. 2) All supply and repair action taken to keep a force in condition to carry out its mission. 3) The routine, recurring, and usual work for the preservation, protection, and keeping of any facility for its intended purposes in a safe and continually usable condition. 4) Performance of those adjustments or procedures specified in user information provided by the manufacturer with the laser or laser system, that are to be performed by the user to ensure the intended performance of the product.

Maintenance Area

A general locality in which are grouped a number of maintenance activities for the purpose of retaining or restoring material to a serviceable condition.

Maintenance Backlog

The amount of maintenance and repair work not accomplished at the end of the fiscal year that is needed or planned to sustain the assigned tasks.

Maintenance Management

The administration of a program utilizing such concepts as organization, plans, procedures, schedules, cost control, periodic evaluation, and feedback for the effective performance and control of maintenance with adequate provisions for interface with other concerned disciplines such as health, safety, environmental compliance, quality control, and security. All work done in conjunction with existing property is either maintenance (preserving), repair (restoring), service (cleaning and making usable), or improvements. The work to be considered under the DOE maintenance management program is only that for maintenance and repair.

Maintenance Plan

A narrative description of a site's maintenance program. The plan should be a real time document that is updated at least annually and that addresses all elements of a successful Maintenance program. The plan should describe the backlog and strategies to reduce the backlog, as well as the maintenance funding required to sustain the assigned mission. The maintenance plan should integrate individual maintenance activities addressed under each functional unit life cycle plan.

Major Construction Activities

Construction projects (or other undertakings having similar physical impacts) that are major federal actions significantly affecting the quality of the human environment as referred to in the National Environmental Policy Act (NEPA) (42 USC 4332).

Major Crude Oil Storer

A firm, other than a refiner or public storage facility, that owns or operates one or more tank farms and that stored more than 30,000 barrels of crude oil at any time during the current or preceding calendar year.

Major Development Actions

Any of the following a) subdivisions, partitions, and short plat proposals; b) any permit for siting or construction outside urban areas of multifamily residential, industrial, or commercial facilities, except such facilities as are included in the recreation assessment; c) the exploration, development, and production of mineral resources unless such exploration, development, or production can be conducted without disturbing the surface of any land within the boundaries of a special management area or is for sand, gravel, and crushed rock used for the construction, maintenance, or reconstruction of roads within the special management areas used for the production of forest products; and d) permits for siting or construction within a special management area of any residence or other related major structure on any parcel of land less than 40 acres in size.

Major Disaster

See Domestic Emergencies.

Major Discharges

Discharges of more than 10,000 gallons of oil to the inland waters or more than 100,000 gallons of oil to the coastal waters.

Major Emitting Facility

Any of the following stationary sources of air pollutants that emit, or have the potential to emit, 100 tons per year or more of any air pollutant from the following types of stationary sources:

- fossil-fuel fired steam electric plants of more than 200 and 50 million Btus per hour heat input,
- coal cleaning plants (thermal dryers),
- kraft pulp mills,
- portland cement plants,
- primary zinc smelters,
- iron and steel mill plants,
- primary aluminum ore reduction plants,
- primary copper smelters,
- municipal incinerators capable of charging more than fifty tons of refuse per day,
- hydrofluoric, sulfuric, and nitric acid plants,
- petroleum refineries,
- lime plants,
- phosphate rock processing plants,
- coke oven batteries,
- sulfur recovery plants,
- carbon black plants (furnace process),
- primary lead smelters,
- fuel conversion plants,
- sintering plants,
- secondary metal production facilities,
- chemical process plants,
- fossil-fuel boilers of more than 250 million Btus per hour heat input,
- petroleum storage and transfer facilities with a capacity exceeding 300,000 barrels,
- taconite ore processing facilities,
- glass fiber processing plants, and
- charcoal production facilities.

The term also includes any other source with the potential to emit 250 tons per year or more of any air pollutant. This term does not include new or modified facilities that are nonprofit health or education institutions that have been exempted by the state.

Major Emitting Facility, Permit Analysis

An analysis of the ambient air quality, climate and meteorology, terrain, soils and vegetation, and visibility at the site of the proposed major emitting facility and in the area potentially affected by the emissions from such facility for each pollutant regulated under the CAA that will be emitted from, or that results from the construction or operation of, such facility, the size and nature of the proposed facility, the degree of continuous emission reduction that could be achieved by such facility, and such other factors as may be relevant in determining the effect of emissions from a proposed facility on any air quality control region. The data is typically gathered over a period of one calendar year preceding the date of application for a permit.

The results of these analyses are made available at the time of the public hearing on the application for the facility's permit, and specifies with reasonable particularity each air quality model or models, necessary to take into account unique terrain or meteorological characteristics of an area potentially affected by emissions from the proposed permitted source.

Major Emitting Facilities, Preconstruction Requirements

The regulatory process for obtaining permits and approvals prior to construction that state no major emitting facility may be constructed in any area unless:

- a permit has been issued for such proposed facility setting forth emission limitations for such facility that conform to the requirements of the CAA;

- the proposed permit has been subject to a review and the required analysis has been conducted in accordance with regulations promulgated by the Administrator, and a public hearing has been held with opportunity for interested persons including representatives of the Administrator to appear and submit written or oral presentations on the air quality impact of such source, alternatives thereto, control technology requirements, and other appropriate considerations;

- the owner/operator of such facility demonstrates that emissions from construction or operation of such facility will not cause, or contribute to, air pollution in excess of any maximum allowable increase or maximum allowable concentration for any pollutant in any area — a) more than one time per year; b) national ambient air quality standard in any air quality control region; or c) any other applicable emission standard or standard of performance under the CAA;

- the proposed facility is subject to the best available control technology for each pollutant subject to regulation, emitted from, or that results from, such facility;

- the provisions with respect to protection of Class I areas have been complied with for such facility;

- there has been an analysis of any air quality impacts projected for the area as a result of secondary growth associated with such facility;

- the person who owns/operates, or proposes to own or operate, a major emitting facility for which a permit is required agrees to conduct such monitoring as may be necessary to determine the effect that emissions from any such facility may have, or is having, on air quality in any area that may be affected by emissions from such source; and

- in the case of a source that proposes to construct in a Class III area, emissions from which would cause or contribute to exceeding the maximum allowable increments applicable in a Class II area and where no standard has been promulgated subsequent to August 7, 1977, and the Administrator has approved the determination of best available technology.

The demonstration pertaining to maximum allowable increases does not apply to maximum allowable increases for Class II areas in the case of an expansion or modification of a major emitting facility whose allowable emissions of air pollutants, after compliance with other provisions, will be less than 50 tons per year and for which the owner/operator of such facility demonstrates that emissions of particulate matter and sulfur oxides will not cause or contribute to ambient air quality levels in excess of the national secondary ambient air quality standard for either of such pollutants.

In the case of a permit a facility must comply with emission limitations to ensure that emissions of sulfur oxides and particulates from such facility will not cause or contribute to concentrations of such pollutant that exceed the following maximum allowable increases over the baseline concentration for such pollutants: *Particulate matter*: Annual geometric mean = 19 mgcm; 24-hour maximum = 37 mgcm. *Sulfur dioxide*: Annual arithmetic mean = 20 mgcm; 24-hour maximum = 91 mgcm; 3-hour maximum = 325 mgcm.

Major Emitting Facilities, Study

The Administrator's (EPA) report to Congress on consequences of major emitting facilities with a potential to emit 250 tons per year or more. *See* Major Emitting Facility.

Major Facilities

Any RCRA, UIC, NPDES, or 404 facility or activity classified as such by the Regional Administrator, or, in the case of approved state programs, the Regional Administrator in conjunction with the state Director.

Major Gas Marketer

Any company that has sold natural gas to customers other than to gas utilities in a gross amount exceeding 10,000,000 standard cubic feet in any state during any one month of the preceding quarter, except any company that also qualifies as a major gas processor or producer.

Major Gas Processor

Any company that has processed natural gas in a state in a gross amount exceeding 50,000,000 standard cubic feet during any one month of the preceding quarter.

Major Life Activities

Activities such as caring for one's self, performing manual tasks, walking, seeing, hearing, speaking, breathing, learning, and holding gainful employment.

Major Modification

Modifications with respect to Prevention of Significant Deterioration and New Source Review under the Clean Air Act and refers to modifications to major stationary sources of emissions and provides significant pollutant increase levels below which a modification is not considered major.

Major Nuclear Power

Any nation that possesses a nuclear striking force capable of posing a serious threat to every other nation.

Major Oil Company

Any person who, individually or together with any other person with respect to which such person has an affiliate relationship or significant ownership interest, produced during a prior 6-month period specified by the Secretary, an average daily volume of 1,600,000 barrels of crude oil, natural gas liquids equivalents, and natural gas equivalents. One barrel of natural gas equivalent equals 5,626 cubic feet of natural gas measured at 14.73 pounds per square inch MSL and 60° Fahrenheit. One barrel of natural gas liquids equivalent equals 1.454 barrels of natural gas liquids at 60° Fahrenheit.

Major Petroleum Product Transporter

A firm that owns or operates a petroleum product pipeline, trucks, tankers, barges or railroad cars, and that transported 20,000 barrels of petroleum products during any one month of the current or preceding calendar year. End users that transport products only between facilities owned or leased by such end users for their own use shall not be considered major petroleum products transporters. Public storage facilities that transport petroleum product only between its owned and operated storage, terminalling, or warehousing operations shall not be considered major petroleum product transporters.

Major Petroleum Products Marketers Monthly Reports

Reports that contain specific information on motor gasoline (leaded, unleaded, unspecified), aviation fuels, distillates, and residual fuels (classified by sulfur content — fuels with a sulfur content greater than 0.5% sulfur and fuels with a sulfur content 0.5% or less). Report information is expressed in thousands of barrels and includes a) product inventory at the end of the month (e.g., inventories at refineries, public storage facilities, terminals, pipelines; excluding inventories at service stations and truck stops); b) products acquired during the month, categorized by refinery output and total imports.

Major Petroleum Products Storer

A person who received into storage 20,000 bbls of any combination of petroleum products during any month of the current or preceding calendar year, and that did not sell or export 20,000 bbls or more during any such month.

Major Port

Any port with two or more berths and facilities and equipment capable of discharging 100,000 tons of cargo per month from oceangoing ships. Such ports will be designated as probable nuclear targets. *See* Port.

Major PSD Modification

A "major modification" as defined in 40 CFR 52.21. *See* Major Modification.

Major PSD Stationary Source

A "major stationary source" as defined in 40 CFR 52.21(b)(1). *See* Major Stationary Source; Major Source.

Major Reconstruction

Structure or facility reconstruction other than that associated with normal or routine maintenance activities.

Major Release

A release of any quantity of hazardous substance(s), pollutant(s), or contaminant(s) that poses a substantial threat to public health or welfare or the environment or results in significant public concern.

Major Source

Any stationary source or group of stationary sources located within a contiguous area and under common control that emits, or has the potential to emit considering controls in the aggregate, 10 tons per year or more of any hazardous air pollutant or 25 tons per year or more of any combination of hazardous air pollutants. The Administrator of EPA may establish a lesser quantity, or in the case of radionuclides different criteria, for a major source than that specified in the previous sentence, on the basis of the potency of the air pollutant, persistence, potential for bioaccumulation, other characteristics of the air pollutant, or other relevant factors.

Major Stationary Source

In a nonattainment area, any stationary pollutant source that has a potential to emit more than 100 tons per year is considered a major stationary source. A term used to determine the applicability of Prevention of Significant Deterioration (PSD) and new source regulations (NSR). In PSD areas the cutoff level may be either 100 or 250 tons, depending upon the type of source. Refer to 42 USC 7491.

Make Safe

One or more actions necessary to prevent or interrupt complete functioning of the system; to disable a system. The necessary actions include the following: a) install (safety devices such as pins or locks); b) disconnect (hoses, linkages, batteries); c) bleed (accumulators, reservoirs); d) remove (explosive devices such as initiators, fuzes, detonators); e) intervene (as in welding, lockwiring).

Make-Up Water

Water used to supplement a system that due to its operating temperatures or other characteristics looses water due to evaporation, leakage, etc.

Malathion

A less toxic organophosphorus pesticide used to control grasshoppers, moths, mites, etc. This pesticide poses no problems to human health but has been known to be detrimental to fish and bee communities.

Male Reproductive Toxicity

The occurrence of adverse effects on the male reproductive system, that may result from exposure to environmental agents. The toxicity may be expressed as alterations to the male reproductive organs and/or the related endocrine system. The manifestation of such toxicity may include alteration in sexual behavior, fertility, pregnancy outcomes, or modifications in other functions that are dependent on the integrity of the male reproductive system.

Malformation

A permanent structural change in a developing organism that may adversely affect survival, development, or function.

Malfunction

A failure of a process to operate in a normal or usual manner such that contaminants are increased. Any sudden failures of pollution control equipment, monitoring equipment, etc.

Malignant

A condition of a neoplasm (tumor) in which it has escaped normal growth regulation and has demonstrated the ability to invade local or distant structures, thereby disrupting the normal architecture or functional relationships of the tissue system.

Mamma

A species descriptor that means an organ of female mammals that contains milk-producing glands.

Mammal

A species descriptor that means vertebrates that are warm-blooded, usually possess hair, and nourish their young on the mother's milk.

Management

1) All personnel above the level of job and task supervisors serving in a command role within the organizational structure. 2) The act or art of managing. This includes the executive function of planning, organizing, coordinating, directing, controlling and supervising any industrial or business projects or activities with responsibility for the results. 3) A process of establishing and attaining objectives to carry out responsibilities. Management consists of those continuing actions of planning, organizing, directing, coordinating, controlling, and evaluating the use of staff, money, materials, and facilities to accomplish objectives and tasks. Management is inherent in control, but it does not include as extensive authority and responsibility as executive authority.

Management and Organization Assessment

An assessment to evaluate the effectiveness and identify the strengths and weaknesses in DOE and site contractor management and administration of ES&H programs. A pragmatic "bottom up" assessment that is integrated with, and somewhat driven by, the findings identified by the concurrently performed Environment, Safety, and Health Assessment. Information/documents gathered in support of this assessment include: organization charts and functions; facility/site layout; description of operations; environmental survey; operations office and other appraisals; contract provisions; legislated federal and state requirements; past appraisal/inspection results/corrective actions; internal self-assessments/corrective actions; selected DOE and contractor policies, orders, and correspondence; incident reports; budgetary requests for corrective actions.

Management Appraisals

Documented determinations of managerial effectiveness in establishing and implementing ES&H program plans that conform to DOE policy requirements. These are based on analyses of functional appraisals, internal appraisals, and other information, and on the application of appropriate criteria. The appraisals are reviews and evaluations of management performance covering all ES&H disciplines and management responsibilities to ensure proper program balance.

Management Audit

Independent evaluation of environmental compliance policies, practices, and control technologies. The audit may include the need for a) formal corporate environmental compliance agenda, and means of implementation; b) environmental training programs; c) purchases of better equipment, enhanced operational procedures, and upgraded maintenance programs; d) budgeting and planning for efficient compliance measures; e) ongoing monitoring, recordkeeping, and reporting systems; and f) internal and community contingency plans, including hazard identification, risk assessments.

Management By Objective (MBO)

A management system wherein each manager establishes objectives (goals) consistent with the overall organizational objectives. The four basic steps in MBO include: 1) define the job (key responsibilities and duties); 2) define the expected results (objectives); 3) measure the results; and 4) appraisal (providing feedback on results and establishing necessary modification to objectives to achieve expected results during the next performance period).

Management Comment

A finding contained in an environmental audit report describing management practices at the site, facility, or organization audited as such practices relate to its current environmental compliance standing and operations activities.

Management, Hazardous Waste

The systematic control of the collection, source separation, storage, transportation, processing, treatment, recovery, and disposal of hazardous waste.

Management of Migration

Actions that are taken to minimize and mitigate the migration of hazardous substances, pollutants, or contaminants and the effects of such migration. These actions may be appropriate when the hazardous substances are no longer at or near the area where they were originally located or situations where a source cannot be adequately identified or characterized. Measures may include, but are not limited to, provision of alternative water supplies, management of the contamination, or treatment of a drinking water aquifer.

Management of Parking Supply

Any requirement providing that any new facility containing a given number of parking spaces shall receive a permit or other prior approval, issuance of which is to be conditioned on air quality considerations.

Management Oversight and Risk Tree

A formal, disciplined logic or decision tree to relate and integrate a wide variety of safety concepts systematically. As an accident analysis technique, it focuses on three main concerns: specific oversights and omissions, assumed risks, and general management system weaknesses.

Management Recommendation

A corrective action proposed by an environmental firm, or consultant to enable the owner/operator of the site or facility audited to better comply with appropriate environmental regulations.

Management Systems

The organizational structures and operating philosophies of companies, projects, or organizations. Management may follow a textbook model, such as Program Evaluation and Review Technique (PERT) or Management by Objectives (MBO), in their management system but the model is usually modified in philosophy and even more in actual operation.

Manatee Protection Areas

See Manatee Refuges or Sanctuaries.

Manatee Refuges or Sanctuaries

Areas in which the FWS has determined that certain waterborne activity would result in the taking of one or more manatees, or that certain waterborne activity must be restricted to prevent the taking of one or more manatees, including but not limited to a taking by harassment.

Mandatory Class I Federal Areas

1) Areas identified in 40 CFR 81, Subpart D. 2) Federal areas that may not be designated as other an Class I under 42 USC 7491 Section 169A.

Mandatory Standards

Standards adopted by an agency that define the minimum requirements that the agency and its contractors must comply with to the extent they apply to the activities being conducted.

Mandibles

A species descriptor that means the lower jaw in vertebrates; either the upper or lower part of the beak in birds; any one of several mouth parts in insects.

Mandibular

A species descriptor that means pertaining to the jaw.

Mandrel

The form around which resin-impregnated fiber or tape is wound to form structural shapes or tubes.

Mangrove

A species descriptor that means a tropical tree with exposed roots forming an interlocking mass; often vital to stabilizing shore lines.

Manifest

1) The shipping document EPA Form 8700-22 and, if necessary, Form 8700-22A, originated and signed by the generator in accordance with the instructions included in the appendix to Part 262 of the Resource Conservation and Recovery Act. The uniform shipping document is required by the EPA and establishes a tracking mechanism per RCRA. This tracking document follows the hazardous waste from point of generation to its final destination. Copies are maintained by the state where the wastes are generated, the destination state, the transporting company, and by the generator. Proper DOT shipping names, EPA waste codes, and other specific information are required. The manifest includes a statement that, when the generator signs the manifest, it certifies that it has done everything within its power to reduce the volume and/or toxicity of the hazardous waste. 2) The form used for identifying the quantity, composition, and the origin, routing, and destination of hazardous waste during its transportation from the point of generation to the point of disposal, treatment, or storage. 3) A document specifying in detail the passengers or items carried for a specific destination.

Manifest Document Number

The EPA twelve-digit identification number assigned to the generator plus a unique five-digit document number assigned to the Manifest by the generator for recording and reporting purposes.

Manmade Air Pollution

Air pollution that results directly or indirectly from human activities.

Manmade Beta Particle and Photon Emitters

All radionuclides emitting beta particles and/or photons listed in *Maximum Permissible Body Burdens and Maximum Permissible Concentration of Radionuclides in Air or Water for Occupational Exposure, NBS Handbook 69*, except the daughter products of thorium-232, uranium-235 and uranium-238.

Manmade Watercourse

A watercourse that is constructed and maintained to facilitate man's use of water and includes, but is not limited to, ditches and canals used for domestic, hydropower, irrigation, and other beneficial uses (manmade watercourses as defined do not include roadside drainage ditches).

Mantle

The uppermost part of the interior of the earth directly beneath the crust and above the core. The upper boundary of the mantle, known as the Mohorovicic Discontinuity, starts at about 30-45 miles beneath the surface and continues down to a depth of about 1790 miles to its lower boundary, the Gutenberg Discontinuity.

Manufacture

1) To produce, manufacture, or import into the customs territory of the United States for commercial purposes. 2) Regarding Toxic Chemicals, to produce, prepare, import, or compound a toxic chemical. Manufacture also applies to a toxic chemical that is produced coincidentally during the manufacture, processing, use, or disposal of another chemical or mixture of chemicals, including a toxic chemical that is separated from that other chemical or mixture of chemicals as a byproduct, and a toxic chemical that remains in that other chemical or mixture of chemicals as an impurity.

Manufacturers Formulation

A list of substances or component parts as described by the maker of a coating, pesticide, or other product containing chemicals or other substances.

Manufacturing Engineering
The branch of professional engineering that requires such education and experience as is necessary to understand and apply engineering procedures in manufacturing processes and methods of production of industrial commodities and products; and requires the ability to plan the practices of manufacturing, to research and develop the tools, processes, machines, and equipment, and to integrate the facilities and systems for producing quality products with optimal expenditure.

Manzanita
A species descriptor that means an evergreen shrub of Pacific North America bearing white or pink flowers in clusters.

Map
1) A graphic representation, usually on a plane surface, and at an established scale, of natural or artificial features on the surface of a part or the whole of the earth or other planetary body. The features are positioned relative to a coordinate reference system. 2) Drawings used to illustrate the physical relationships of elements of people, equipment, materials and environmental structures associated with an accident or incident. *See* Administrative Map, Chart Series, Chart Sheet, Controlled Map, General Map, Large-Scale Map, Map Chart, Map Series, Map Sheet, Medium-Scale Map, Planimetric Map, Situation Map, Small-Scale Map, Strategic Map, Tactical Map, Topographic Map, Traffic Circulation Map, Weather Map.

Map Chart
A representation of a land-sea area, using the characteristics of a map to represent the land area and the characteristics of a chart to represent the sea area, with such special characteristics as to make the map-chart most useful in military operations, particularly amphibious operations. *See* Map.

Map Convergence
The angle at which one meridian is inclined to another on a map or chart. *See* Convergence.

Map Index
A graphic key primarily designed to give the relationship between sheets of a series, their coverage, availability, and further information on the series. *See* Map.

Map Reference
A means of identifying a point on the surface of the earth by relating it to information appearing on a map, generally the graticule or grid.

Map Series
A group of maps or charts usually having the same scale and cartographic specifications, and with each sheet appropriately identified by producing agency as belonging to the same series.

Map Sheet
An individual map or chart either complete in itself or part of a series. *See* Map.

Mapping, Charting, and Geodesy (MC&G)
Maps, charts, and other data used for military planning, operations, and training. These products and data support air, land, and sea navigation; weapon system guidance; target positioning; and other military activities. These data are presented in the forms of topographic, planimetric, imaged, or thematic maps and graphics; nautical and aeronautical charts and publications; and, in digital and textual formats, gazetteers, that contain geophysical and geodetic data and coordinate lists.

Mapping Camera
See air cartographic camera.

MAP
See Mitigation Action Plan.

Margin
The difference between the net system generating capability and system maximum load requirements including net schedule transfers with other systems.

Margin of Exposure (MOE)
The ratio of the No-Observed-Adverse-Effect Level (NOAEL) to the estimated human exposure. The MOE was formerly referred to as the margin of safety (MOS).

Margin of Safety (MOS)
The term formerly applied to the margin of exposure concept. *See* Margin of Exposure (MOE).

Marginal Data
Explanatory information that clarifies, defines, illustrates, and/or supplements the primary portion of a study, or map sheet.

Marginal Weather
Weather that is sufficiently adverse to an operation so as to require the imposition of procedural limitations. *See* Adverse Weather.

Marine Protection, Research, and Sanctuaries Act (MPRSA)
An act that regulates dumping of all types of materials into ocean waters whose purpose is to prevent or strictly limit the dumping of any material that would adversely affect human health, welfare, or the marine environment, including ecological systems or economic potentialities. Transportation of wastes in and out of U.S. waters is one of the primary tasks of the Act.

Marine Sanitation Devices
Any equipment installed on board a vessel to receive, retain, treat, or discharge sewage and any process to treat such sewage.

Maritime Environment
The oceans, seas, bays, estuaries, islands, coastal areas, and the airspace above these, including amphibious objective areas.

Maritime Search and Rescue Region
The waters subject to the jurisdiction of the United States; the territories and possessions of the United States (except Canal Zone and the inland area of Alaska) and designated areas of the high seas.

Maritime Special Purpose Force (MSPF)
A task-organized force formed from elements of a Marine expeditionary unit (special operations capable) and naval special warfare forces that can be quickly tailored to a specific mission. The maritime special purpose force can execute on short notice a wide variety of missions in a supporting, supported, or unilateral role. It focuses on operations in a maritime environment and is capable of operations in conjunction with or in support of special operations forces. The maritime special purpose force is integral to and directly relies upon the Marine expeditionary unit (special operations capable) for all combat and combat service support.

Marked
The marking of PCB items and PCB storage areas and transport vehicles by means of applying a legible mark by painting, fixation of an adhesive label, or by any other method that meets the requirements of these regulations.

Market Value
1) The price, in terms of dollars, that a ready and able buyer, not forced to buy, would pay and that a ready and willing seller, not forced to sell, would accept, assuming further that both parties are fully informed, act reasonably, and have sufficient time to consider the transaction with due care. 2) The market value of real estate is the highest price, in terms of money, that a property will bring in a competitive and open market, allowing a reasonable time to find a purchaser who buys the property with knowledge of all the uses to which it is adapted, and for which it is capable of being used. Included in this definition are the following key points: a) market value is the highest price a property will bring versus the average price, or the lowest price; b) payment must be made in cash or its equivalent; c) both buyer and seller must act without undue pressure.

Market/Marketers
The processing or distributing in commerce, or the persons who process or distribute in commerce, used oil fuels to burners or other market-

ers, and may include the generators of the fuel if they market the fuel directly to the burner.

Marketable Title

A title that is free from reasonable doubt of defect and can be readily sold or mortgaged to a reasonably prudent purchaser, or a mortgage title free from material defects or grave doubts and reasonably free from possible litigation.

Marks

The descriptive name, instructions, cautions, or other information applied to PCBs and PCB items, or other objects subject to these regulations.

Marsh

A type of wetland that does not accumulate appreciable peat deposits and is dominated by herbaceous vegetation. Marshes may be either fresh or saltwater and tidal or nontidal. *See* Wetlands.

Marsupial

A species descriptor that means a mammal of the order Marsupialia, found mainly in Australia, that includes kangaroos, opossums, and wombats; set apart by urogenital and skeletal differences.

Marsupium

A species descriptor that means an external abdominal pouch in female marsupials that contains mammary glands (breasts) and that shelters the young; also, a temporary egg pouch in animals.

Mass Attenuation Coefficient

For a material for uncharged ionizing particles, the quotient of dN/N by pdi, where dN/N is the traction of particles that experience interactions in traversing a distance dl in a material of density p.

Mass Casualty

Any large number of casualties produced in a relatively short period of time, usually as the result of a single incident such as an aircraft accident, hurricane, flood, earthquake, or armed attack that exceeds local emergency support capabilities. *See* Casualty.

Mass Concrete

A large volume of cast-in-place concrete with dimensions large enough to require that measures be taken to cope with the generation of heat and attendant volume change and to minimize cracking.

Mass Energy Absorption Coefficient

For a material for uncharged ionizing particles the Mass Energy Absorption Coefficient is the product of the mass energy transfer coefficient and (1 - g), where g is the traction of the energy of secondary charged particles that is lost in the material.

Mass Median Aerodynamic Diameter (MMAD)

Median of the distribution of mass with respect to the aerodynamic diameter of a particle.

Mass Spectrometer

An instrument commonly used in the chemical analysis of organic compounds. It separates electrically charged particles by their mass.

Matching Program

Any computerized comparison of two or more automated systems of records or a system of records with nonfederal records for the purpose of establishing or verifying the eligibility of, or continuing compliance with statutory and regulatory requirements by, applicants for, recipients or beneficiaries of, participants in, or providers of services with respect to, cash or in-kind assistance or payments under federal programs.

Material Access Areas

Areas that contain a Category I quantity of special nuclear material and are specifically defined by physical barriers, located within a protected area, and subject to specific access controls.

Material Cognizance

Denotes responsibility for exercising supply management over items or categories of material.

Material Control

See Inventory Control.

Material Readiness

The availability of material required by an organization to support its activities or contingencies for disaster relief (flood, earthquake, etc.), or other emergencies.

Material Safety Data Sheets (MSDS)

1) Compilation of information required under the OSHA Communication Standard on the identity of hazardous chemicals, health, and physical hazards, exposure limits, and precautions. Section 311 of SARA (Superfund Amendments and Reauthorization Act) required facilities to submit MSDSs under certain circumstances. The sheet required to be developed is under 29 CFR 1910.1200(g). 2) Documents prepared by the chemical industry to transmit information about the physical properties and health effects of chemicals, and about emergency response plans.

Materials Handling

The movement of materials (raw materials, scrap, semifinished, and finished) to, through, and from productive processes; in warehouses and storage; and in receiving and shipping areas.

Materials Handling Equipment

Mechanical devices for handling of supplies with greater ease and economy.

Materials Lock

An air lock through which materials and equipment pass from one air pressure environment into another.

Materiel, Military

All items (including ships, tanks, self-propelled weapons, aircraft, and related spares, repair parts, and support equipment, but excluding real property, installations, and utilities) necessary to equip, operate, maintain, and support military activities without distinction as to its application for administrative or combat purposes. *See* Equipment; Personal Property.

Materiel Planning

A subset of Department of Defense logistic planning. It consists of a four-step process: 1) Requirements Definition — requirements for significant items must be calculated at item level detail (i.e., national stock number) to support sustainability planning and analysis. Requirements include unit roundout, consumption and attrition replacement, safety stock, and the needs of allies. 2) Apportionment — items are apportioned to the combatant commanders based on a global scenario to avoid sourcing of items to multiple theaters. The basis for apportionment is the capability provided by unit stocks, host nation support, theater prepositioned war reserve stocks and industrial base, and continental United States Department of Defense stockpiles and available production. Item apportionment cannot exceed total capabilities. 3) Sourcing — sourcing is the matching of available capabilities on a given date against item requirements to support sustainability analysis and the identification of locations to support transportation planning. Sourcing of any item is done within the combatant commander's apportionment. 4) Documentation — sourced item requirements and corresponding shortfalls are major inputs to the combatant commander's sustainability analysis. Sourced item requirements are translated into movement requirements and documented in the Joint Operation Planning and Execution System database for transportation feasibility analysis. Movement requirements for nonsignificant items are estimated in tonnage.

Matrices

Any multidimensional classification or chart.

Matrix

1) Solid framework of a porous material or system. 2) A material in which the fiber of a composite is imbedded; it can be plastic, metal, ceramic, or glass.

Matrix Organizations

Organizations wherein a project manager temporarily borrows the talent he/she needs on a specific project from another functional department. The project manager supervises the people borrowed during the loan period, not the functional department head.

Maverick

An air-to-surface missile with launch and leave capability. It is designed for use against stationary or moving small, hard targets such as tanks, armored vehicles, and field fortifications. Designated as AGM-65.

Maximal Effective Pressure

The highest effective a) peak incident pressure; b) incident plus dynamic pressure; or c) reflected pressure.

Maximum Allowable Concentration, Compliance (MACC)

The rules and orders promulgated by a state, and approved by the Administrator, for the purposes of determining compliance with the maximum allowable increases in ambient concentrations of an air pollutant. For determining compliance, the following concentrations of such pollutant are not taken into account: a) concentrations of such pollutant attributable to the increase in emissions from stationary sources that have converted from the use of petroleum products, or natural gas; b) the concentrations of such pollutant attributable to the increase in emissions from stationary sources that have converted from using natural gas by reason of a natural gas curtailment pursuant to the Federal Power Act (16 USC 791 et seq.); c) concentrations of particulate matter attributable to the increase in emissions from construction or other temporary emission-related activities; and d) the increase in concentrations attributable to new sources outside the United States over the concentrations attributable to existing sources that are included in the baseline concentration determined in accordance with the CAA.

Maximum Allowable Concentrations (MAC)

1) The maximum regulatory amount of a pollutant considered to be harmless to humans in their work environments under SDWA regulations. 2) The maximum allowable increase in concentrations over baseline concentrations for a pollutant

for each period of exposure equal to a) the concentration permitted under the national secondary ambient air quality standard; or b) the concentration permitted under the national primary ambient air quality standard, whichever concentration is lowest for the pollutant during a specific period of exposure. Synonymous with Maximum Contaminant Levels (MCLs).

Maximum Contaminant Level Goal

The maximum level of a contaminant in drinking water at which no known or anticipated adverse effect on the health of persons would occur, and that allows an adequate margin of safety. Maximum contaminant level goals are nonenforceable health goals.

Maximum Contaminant Levels (MCLs)

1) The maximum permissible regulatory level of a contaminant considered to be harmless to humans in their living and working environments. 2) The maximum permissible levels of a contaminant in water that is delivered to the free flowing outlet of the ultimate user of a public water system, except in the case of turbidity where the maximum permissible level is measured at the point of entry to the distribution system. Contaminants added to the water under circumstances controlled by the user, except those resulting from corrosion of piping and plumbing caused by water quality, are excluded from this definition. MCLs are enforceable standards.

Maximum Credible Accident (MCA)

In risk assessment, the MCA (for a DOE site) is a release of 100 grams of respirable plutonium particles that are dispersed into the site environment. An airplane crash is one of the MCA scenarios that may create a 100 gram release.

Maximum Efficient Rate of Production

The maximum rate of production of crude oil or natural gas, or both, that may be sustained without loss of ultimate recovery of crude oil or natural gas, or both, under sound engineering and economic principles.

Maximum Filling Density

The percent ratio of the weight of gas in the tank to the weight of water that the tank will hold. For determining the water capacity of the tank in pounds, the weight of a gallon (231 cubic inches) of water at 60° Fahrenheit in air is about 8.33 pounds.

Maximum Foreseeable Loss

The largest loss that could possibly happen under the worst circumstances.

Maximum Individual Risk (MIR)

The increased risk for a person exposed to the highest measured or predicted concentration of a toxicant.

Maximum Likelihood Estimate (MLE)

A statistical best estimate of the value of a parameter from a given data set.

Maximum Normal Operating Pressure

The maximum gauge pressure that is expected to develop in the containment vessel under the normal conditions of transport.

Maximum Permissible Concentration (MPC)

The concentration in air or water that would lead to an amount of radionuclide in the critical organ that would just deliver the maximum permissible dose rate to that organ. A phrase used in the conventional system of units. *See* Radioactivity Concentration Guide.

Maximum Permissible Dose (MPD)

The maximum dose of radiation that may be received by persons working with ionizing radiation, that will produce no detectable damage over the normal life span.

Maximum Permissible Exposure (MPE)

The level of laser radiation to which person may be exposed without hazardous effect or adverse biological changes in the eye or skin.

Maximum Permissible Level (MPL)

The maximum regulatory amount of contamination from radioactive substances considered to be harmless to humans in their work environments.

Maximum Possible Loss

1) In terms of fire hazards, the maximum possible loss that could occur in a single fire area assuming the failure of both automatic and manual fire extinguishing actions. 2) The largest loss that could possibly happen under the worst circumstances.

Maximum Probable Flood

A hypothetical flood (peak discharge, volume, and hydrography shape) that is considered to be the most severe reasonably possible, based on comprehensive hydro-meteorological application of probable maximum precipitation and other hydrological factors favorable for maximum flood runoff such as sequential storms and snowmelts.

Maximum Throughput

The maximum liquid volume that may be transported through a pipeline for an indefinite period without damaging any pipeline equipment.

Maximum Tolerated Dose (MTD)

The highest dose of a toxicant that causes toxic effects without causing death during a chronic exposure and that does not decrease the body weight by more than 10%.

Maximum Total Trihalomethane Potential (MTP)

The maximum concentration of total trihalomethanes produced in a given water containing a disinfectant residual after 7 days at a temperature of 25°C or above.

MBCA

An acronym for Migratory Bird Conservation Act of 1929.

MBE

See Minority Business Enterprise.

MBTA
See Migratory Bird Treaty Act of 1918.

MC&G
See Mapping, Charting, and Geodesy.

MCL
See Maximum Contaminant Levels.

MCLG
See Maximum Contaminant Level Goal.

MCLs
An acronym for Maximum Concentration Limits; Maximum Contaminant Levels. *See* Maximum Contaminant Levels; Maximum Allowable Concentrations.

Mean
The arithmetic average of all observations or values.

Mean Annual Loss
The average loss per year over a period of years. Sum of losses during a period, divided by years in the period.

Mean High Water
The average height of the high water over 19 years.

Mean Higher High Tide
The average height of the higher of two unequal daily high tides over 19 years.

Mean Lethal Dose
1) The amount of nuclear irradiation of the whole body that would be fatal to 50% of the exposed personnel in a given period of time. 2) The dose of chemical agent that would kill 50% of exposed, unprotected, and untreated personnel.

Mean Low Water
The average height of the low water over 19 years.

Mean Lower Low Water
The average height of the lower of two unequal daily low tides over 19 years.

Mean Point of Impact
The point whose coordinates are the arithmetic means of the coordinates of the separate points of impact/burst of a finite number of projectiles fired or released at the same aiming point under a given set of conditions.

Mean Sea Level
The average height of the surface of the sea for all stages of the tide; used as a reference for elevations.

Mean Tide Level
A plane midway between mean high water and mean low water.

Means of Emission Limitation
A system of continuous emission reduction including the use of specific technology or fuels with reduced pollution characteristics.

Measure of Energy Consumption
Energy use, energy efficiency, estimated annual operating cost, or other measures of energy consumption.

Measurements
The sizes, concentrations, or other values of areas, quantities, degrees, or capacities obtained by measuring.

Measures to Prevent Economic Disruption (MPED)
Actions necessary to prevent or minimize significant local or regional economic disruption or unemployment that would otherwise result from use by any source (or class or category) of a) coal or coal derivatives other than locally or regionally available coal; b) petroleum products; c) natural gas; or d) any combination of fuels to comply with the requirements of a state implementation plan. A rule or order issued to prohibit any such major fuel burning stationary source (or class or

category thereof) from using fuels other than locally or regionally available coal or coal derivatives to comply with implementation plan requirements.

Medical Device

As defined in the Federal Food, Drug, and Cosmetic Act (21 USC 321), any device, diagnostic product, drug, and drug delivery system that utilizes a Class I or Class II substance for which no safe and effective alternative has been developed, and approved.

Mechanical Aeration

Use of mechanical energy to inject air into water to cause a waste stream to absorb oxygen.

Mechanical Dispersion

The process whereby solutes are mechanically mixed during advective transport, caused by the velocity variations at the microscopic level; synonymous with hydraulic dispersion. The coefficient of mechanical dispersion is the component of mass transport flux of solutes caused by velocity variations at the microscopic level.

Mechanical Engineering

The branch of professional engineering that deals with engineering problems relating to generation, transmission, and utilization of energy in the thermal or mechanical form and also with engineering problems relating to the production of tools, machinery, and their products and to heating, ventilation, refrigeration and plumbing. It is concerned with the research, design, production, operational, organizational, and economic aspects of the above.

Mechanical Filter Respirator

A half-mask or full-face air purifying respirator with a filter usually consisting of cellulose or felt to trap particulate matter.

Mechanical Site Preparation

All site preparation activities undertaken by motorized heavy equipment to prepare an area for regeneration.

Mechanical Turbulence

Random irregularities of fluid motion in air caused by buildings or mechanical, nonthermal, processes.

Media

Specific environments of air, water, and soil, that are the subject of regulatory concern and activities.

Median Incapacitating Dose

The amount or quantity of chemical agent that when introduced into the body will incapacitate 50% of exposed, unprotected personnel.

Median Lethal Concentration

Concentration level at which 50% of the test animals die when exposed by inhalation for a specified time period.

Median Lethal Dose

Dose at which 50% of test animals die following exposure. Dose is usually given in milligrams per kilogram of body weight of the test animal.

Medical Evacuees

Personnel who are wounded, injured, or ill and must be moved to or between medical facilities.

Medical Exposure

Exposure of individuals resulting from their medical examination or treatment involving radiation.

Medical Intelligence

That category of intelligence resulting from collection, evaluation, analysis, and interpretation of foreign medical, bioscientific, and environmental information that is of interest to strategic planning and to military medical planning and operations for the conservation of the fighting strength of friendly forces and the formation of assessments of foreign medical capabilities in both military and civilian sectors.

Medical Treatment

Treatment, other than first aid, administered by a physician or by registered professional personnel under the guidance of a physician. Medical treatment does not include first aid treatment (one-time treatment and subsequent observation of minor scratches, cuts, burns, splinters, etc., that do not ordinarily require professional care) even though such care is provided by a physician or registered professional personnel.

Medical Treatment Facility

A facility established for the purpose of furnishing medical and/or dental care to eligible individuals.

Medical Wastes

1) Solid wastes that are generated in the diagnosis, treatment, or immunization of human beings or animals, in research pertaining thereto, or in the production or testing of biological matter. 2) Infectious agents; human blood and blood products; pathological wastes; sharps; body parts; contaminated bedding; surgical wastes and potentially contaminated laboratory wastes; dialysis wastes; and such additional medical items as the Administrator of EPA prescribes by regulation. This term does not include any hazardous waste identified or listed under Subtitle C (42 USC 6921 et seq.) or any household waste as defined in regulations under Subtitle C (42 USC 6921 et seq.).

Medium Atomic Demolition Munition

A low-yield, team-portable, atomic demolition munition that can be detonated either by remote control or a timer device.

Medium Discharges

Discharges of 1,000 to 10,000 gallons of oil to the inland waters or discharges of 10,000 to 100,000 gallons of oil to the coastal waters. Any oil discharge that poses a substantial threat to the public health or welfare or results in critical public concern shall be classified as a major discharge regardless of this quantitative measure.

Medium-Lot Storage

Generally defined as a quantity of material that will require one to three pallet stacks, stored to maximum height. Thus, the term refers to relatively small lots as distinguished from definitely large or small lots. *See* Storage.

Medium-Range Ballistic Missile

A ballistic missile with a range capability from about 600 to 1,500 nautical miles.

Medium-Scale Map

A map having a scale larger than 1:600,000 and smaller than 1:75,000. *See* Map.

MEF

See Major Emitting Facility.

Megaton Weapon

A nuclear weapon, the yield of which is measured in terms of millions of tons of trinitrotoluene explosive equivalents. *See* Kiloton Weapon; Subkiloton Weapon.

Megawatt (MW)

10^6 watts, 1,000 kilowatts, 1 million watts.

Meiosis

Cell and nuclear division in which the number of chromosomes is reduced from diploid (2n) to haploid (n). This process is characteristic of germ cell division in which two successive divisions of the nucleus produce four cells that contain half the number of chromosomes present in the somatic cells. Each of the four daughter cells obtain, at random, any one of the two copies of each chromosome from parent cell. These cells may mature to sperm or egg cells.

Melanistic

A species descriptor that means darkness of the skin, hair, or eyes resulting from high pigmentation (coloration).

Melanophore

A species descriptor that means a chromatophore (pigment-producing cell, or a pigmented animal cell that can change the color of the skin, as in some lizards) that contains melanin (a dark pigment).

Meltdown
A term used to describe the overheating of the core of a nuclear reactor to the extent that the radioactive fuel elements begin to melt.

Melting Point
The temperature that if exceeded will change a solid into a liquid; or the temperature at which the solid and liquid phases of a substance are in equilibrium at a given pressure.

MEPS
An acronym for Multimedia Environmental Pollutant Assessment System.

Mercury
The element mercury, a heavy metal, that can accumulate in the environment and is highly toxic if breathed or swallowed. Includes mercury in particulates, vapors, aerosols, and compounds. *See* Heavy Metals.

Mercury Chlor-Alkali Cells
Devices that are basically composed of an electrolyzer section and a denuder (decomposer) section and utilize mercury to produce chlorine gas, hydrogen gas, and alkali metal hydroxide.

Mercury Chlor-Alkali Electrolyzers
Electrolytic devices that are part of a mercury chlor-alkali cell and utilize a flowing mercury cathode to produce chlorine gas and alkali metal amalgam.

Mesic Distichlis Meadows
Well-drained grassy meadows.

Mesocone
A species descriptor that means protrusion in gastropods.

Mesohaline
A term used to characterize waters with salinity of 5 to 18%, due to ocean-derived salts.

Mesolithic
The time representing the developmental, versus chronological, transitional period in the growth of human societies between the Palaeolithic and Neolithic times.

Mesophyte/Mesophytic
Any plant growing where moisture and aeration conditions lie between extremes.

Mesosaline
A term used to characterize waters with salinity of 5 to 18%, due to land-derived salts.

Mesosaprobic
A term applied to a polluted body of water in which organic matter is undergoing rapid decomposition, due to the pollutant and a considerable reduction in oxygen levels.

Mesosphere
The part of the atmosphere that lies between the stratosphere and the thermosphere.

Mesozoic
The era of geological time comprising the Triassic, Jurassic, and Cretaceous periods, and occurring between the Paleozoic and the Cenozoic eras.

Metabolism
1) The biochemical reactions by which energy is made available for the use of an organism. Metabolism includes all chemical transformations occurring in an organism from the time a nutrient substance enters, until it has been utilized and the waste products eliminated. 2) Chemical process within an organism to release energy. 3) In toxicology, metabolism of a toxicant consists of a series of chemical transformations that take place within an organism. A wide range of enzymes act on toxicants, that may increase water solubility, and facilitate elimination from the organism. In

some cases, however, metabolites may be more toxic than their parent compound.

Metabolite

Any substance produced in or by biological processes and derived from a pesticide.

Metal-Matrix Composites

Materials in which continuous carbon, silicon carbide, or ceramic fibers are embedded in a metallic matrix material.

Metallurgical Coal

Coal with strong or moderately strong choking properties that contains no more than 8.0% ash and 1.25% sulfur, as mined, or after conventional burning.

Metallurgical Engineering

The branch of professional engineering, that requires such education and experience as is necessary to seek, understand, and apply the principles of the properties and behavior of metals in solving engineering problems dealing with the research, development, and application of metals and alloys; and the manufacturing practices of extracting, refining, and processing of metals.

Metamorphism

A transmutation in the texture and/or composition of a rock due to the effects of heat, pressure, or the addition of new materials.

Metamorphosis

Development from one stage of maturity to the next, usually with marked change in appearance.

Metaplasia

The abnormal transformation of an adult, fully differentiated tissue of one kind into a differentiated tissue of another kind.

Metastasis

The transfer of a disease, or its local manifestations, from one part of the body to another. In cancer, this relates to the appearance of neoplasms in parts of the body remote from the site of the primary tumor. This is a characteristic of malignancy.

Metatarsus

A species descriptor that means a part of the hind foot in four-legged animals or in the foot of birds.

Meteorological Data

Meteorological facts pertaining to the atmosphere, such as wind, temperature, air density, and other phenomena that affect military operations.

Meteorology

The study of the atmosphere, its structure, composition, and weather effects.

Metes and Bounds

A method of describing or locating real property, metes are measures of length and bounds are boundaries. This description starts with a well-marked point of beginning and follows the boundaries of the land until it returns once more to the point of beginning.

Methane (CH_4)

1) The lightest in the paraffinic series of hydrocarbons; colorless, odorless, and flammable. Its combustible characteristics make it a good fuel. 2) A colorless, nonpoisonous, flammable gas created by anaerobic decomposition of organic compounds. Methane forms the major portion of marsh gas and natural gas.

Methanol (CH_3OH)

An alcohol produced by the oxidation of methane, used as a solvent, a fuel, and as a component in the manufacture of synthetic resins.

Method 18

An EPA test method that uses gas chromatographic techniques to measure the concentration of individual volatile organic compounds in a gas stream.

Method 24

An EPA reference method to determine density, water content, and total volatile content (water and VOC) of coatings.

Method 25

An EPA reference method to determine the VOC concentration in a gas stream.

Method Quantification Limits

The minimum concentrations of substances that can be measured and reported.

Methodology

The technique or procedure used for site assessment, remediation, and compliance skills.

Metric System

The International System of Units (SI) as established by the General Conference on Weights and Measures in 1960 and as interpreted or modified for the United States by the Secretary of Commerce.

Metrication

An activity tending to increase the use of the International System of Units (SI). It may include metric training and the initiation or conversion to metric of new or existing measurement sensitive processes, software or hardware systems, and engineering standards.

Metrication Operating Committee

A committee of the Interagency Committee on Metric Policy, that serves as the vehicle for coordination of federal interagency metrication activities, and recommends policy guidance to the parent committee. The Metrication Operating Committee is comprised of representatives from the major federal departments and agencies who serve as their agencies' metric coordinators.

Metrology

The science of measurement, including the development of measurement standards and systems for absolute and relative measurements.

MFC

An acronym for Meteorological and Oceanographic Forecast Center.

MFL

See Maximum Foreseeable Loss.

MFWCS

An acronym for Main Feedwater and Condensate System.

mg/cm

An abbreviation for Micrograms per Centimeter.

MGD

See Million Gallons Per Day.

MgF$_2$

Magnesium Fluoride.

Mickey Leland National Urban Air Toxics Research Center (MLRC)

A Texas research facility capable of undertaking and maintaining research capabilities in the areas of epidemiology, oncology, toxicology, pulmonary medicine, pathology, and biostatistics. The National Urban Air Toxics Research Center is governed by a Board of Directors comprised of nine members, selected based on their respective academic and professional backgrounds and expertise in matters relating to public health, environmental pollution, and industrial hygiene. The duties of the Board of Directors are to determine policy and research guidelines, submit views from center sponsors and the public and issue periodic reports of center findings and activities. The Board of Directors is advised by a 13 member Scientific Advisory Panel. *See* Scientific Advisory Panel.

Microbes

Microscopic organisms such as algae, animals, viruses, bacteria, fungus, and protozoa, some of which cause diseases. *See* Microorganisms.

Microbial Pesticides

Microorganisms that are used to control a post. They are of low toxicity to man.

Microbursts

Small downbursts of wind with horizontal scales of less than the square root of 10 miles (3.16 miles). The mature life of microbursts is only a few to 10 minutes, making their detection and warning extremely difficult. The maximum windspeed of microbursts is less than 90 mph. Damage caused by microbursts is limited mostly to outbuildings and mobile homes.

Microclimate

The conditions immediately surrounding an organism, often differing significantly from the environment as a whole.

Microenvironment

The immediate local environment of an organism.

Micrograms per Cubic Meter (mg/m^3)

A unit of concentration that is numerically equal to the mass of a contaminant (in micrograms) present in a one cubic meter sample of air, measured at EPA reference conditions.

Micromort

Minimal mortality impact, a term meaning one in a million chance of death from environmental hazards.

Microorganisms

1) Any living organisms too small to see with the naked eye. 2) Bacteria, yeasts, simple fungi, algae, protozoans, and a number of other organisms that are microscopic in size. Most are beneficial but some produce disease. Others are involved in composting and sewage treatment.

Middle Distillate

One of the distillates obtained between kerosene and lubricating of oil fractions in the refining processes. These include light fuel oils and diesel fuel.

Migration

1) The movement of hazardous substances from the disposal site by means of air, surface water, or groundwater. 2) Regarding the ESA, the seasonal movement of animals from one territory to another.

Migratory Bird Treaty Act

The treaty of 1918 (16 USC 703 et seq.), providing legal protection of migratory birds; it also paved the way for cooperation in avian management between the U.S. and bordering countries.

Migratory Birds

All wild birds native to North America that are in an unconfined state and that are protected under the Migratory Bird Treaty Act (16 USC 703 et seq.), including ducks, geese, and swans of the family Anatidae, species listed as threatened or endangered under the Endangered Species Act (16 USC 1531 et seq.), and species defined as nongame under the Fish and Wildlife Conservation Act of 1980 (16 USC 2901-2912).

Migratory Waterfowl

The species enumerated in Paragraph (a) of Subdivision 1 of Article I of the treaty between the United States and Great Britain for the protection of migratory birds concluded August 16, 1916 (39 Statute 1702).

Milestones

1) Abatement-related activities, both interim and final, laid out in a mitigation plan or compliance agreement that must be accomplished in covered establishments by specified dates. 2) Important or critical events and/or activities that must occur in the project cycle in order to achieve the project objective(s).

Military Department

One of the departments within the Department of Defense created by the National Security Act of 1947, as amended. *See* Department of the Army; Department of the Navy; Department of the Air Force.

Military Geography

The specialized field of geography dealing with natural and manmade physical features that may affect the planning and conduct of military operations.

Military Intelligence Board (MIB)

A decisionmaking forum that formulates Defense intelligence policy and programming priorities. The Military Intelligence Board, chaired by the Director, Defense Intelligence Agency, who is dual-hatted as Director of Military Intelligence, consists of senior military and civilian intelligence officials of each Service, U.S. Coast Guard, each combat support agency, the Joint Staff/J-2/J-6, Deputy Assistant Secretary of Defense (Intelligence), Intelligence Program Support Group, National Military Intelligence Production Center, National Military Intelligence Collection Center, National Military Intelligence Support Center, and the combatant command J-2s.

Military Nuclear Power

A nation that has nuclear weapons and the capability for their employment.

Military Options

A range of military force responses that can be projected to accomplish assigned tasks. Options include one or a combination of the following: civic action, humanitarian assistance, civil affairs, and other military activities to develop positive relationships with other countries; confidence building and other measures to reduce military tensions; military presence; activities to convey threats to adversaries and truth projections; military deceptions and psychological operations; quarantines, blockades, and harassment operations; raids; intervention campaigns; armed conflict involving air, land, maritime, and strategic warfare campaigns and operations; support for law enforcement authorities to counter international criminal activities (terrorism, narcotics trafficking, slavery, and piracy); support for law enforcement authorities to suppress domestic rebellion; and support for insurgencies, counterinsurgency, and civil war in foreign countries.

Military Resources

Military and civilian personnel, facilities, equipment, and supplies under the control of a DOD component.

Military Sealift Command (MSC)

The U.S. Transportation Command's component command responsible for designated sealift service.

Mill

One-tenth of one cent; a tax rate of "one mill on the dollar" is the same as a rate of one-tenth of one percent of the assessed value of the property.

Milligrams/Liter (mg/l)

A measure of concentration used in the measurement of flu ids. Mg/l is the most common way to present a concentration in water and is roughly equivalent to parts per million.

Million Gallons per Day (MGD)

A measure of the withdrawal rate of a well; a measure of water flow.

Milliroentgen

A submultiple of the roentgen equal to one one-thousandth (1/1000) of a roentgen.

MILVAN

A military-owned demountable container, conforming to United States and international standards, operated in a centrally controlled fleet for movement of military cargo.

Mine

1) In land mine warfare, an explosive or other material, normally encased, designed to destroy or damage ground vehicles, boats, or aircraft, or designed to wound, kill, or otherwise incapacitate personnel. It may be detonated by the action of its victim, by the passage of time, or by controlled means. 2) In naval mine warfare, an explosive device laid in the water with the intention of damaging or sinking ships or of deterring shipping from entering an area. The term does not include devices attached to the bottoms of ships or to

harbor installations by personnel operating under-water, nor does it include devices that explode immediately on expiration of a predetermined time after laying.

Mine Disposal

The operation by suitably qualified personnel designed to render safe, neutralize, recover, remove, or destroy mines.

Mine-Mouth Plant

A steam-electric plant or coal gasification plant built close to a coal mine. It is usually associated with delivery of output via transmission lines or pipelines over long distances, as contrasted with plants located nearer load centers and at some distance from sources of fuel supply.

Mineral Feed

A commercial feed composed of a substance or mixture of substances intended to supply primarily mineral elements for animal nutrition.

Mineral Oil PCB Transformers

Any transformers originally designed to contain mineral oil as the dielectric fluid and that have been tested and found to contain 500 ppm or greater PCBs.

Mineral Recovery Remedial Activities

The general standards for remedial action, federal performance, and state participation, including the use of technology and the promulgation of standards to ensure the safe and environmentally sound stabilization of residual radioactive materials.

Mineral Soil

Soil composed of predominantly mineral rather than organic materials.

Mineral Water

Bottled drinking water containing more than 500 milligrams per liter of total dissolved solids and/or one or more chemical constituents in excess of the concentrations listed in the Federal Bottled Water Quality Standards, 21 CFR, Section 103.35 (d).

Miniature Boiler

A boiler that does not exceed any of the following limits:

- 16 inches inside diameter of shell;
- 5 cubic feet gross volume, exclusive of casing and insulation. (This volume includes the total volume of the steam and water containing parts of the boiler plus the volume of the combustion space and gas passages up to the point of attachment of the smokestack or chimney breaching);
- 20 square feet water heating surface;
- 100 psi maximum allowable working pressures.

Minimal Risk

A term meaning that the risk of harm anticipated at a specific site, facility, or location is not greater, considering probability and magnitude, than that ordinarily encountered in daily life or during the performance of routine work activities.

Minimization

Measures or techniques that reduce the amount of wastes generated during industrial production processes; this term also is applied to recycling and other efforts to reduce the volume of waste going to land fills. This term is interchangeable with waste reduction and waste minimization.

Minimize, Communications

A condition wherein normal message and telephone traffic is drastically reduced in order that messages connected with an actual or simulated emergency shall not be delayed.

Minimum Essential Equipment

That part of authorized allowances of equipment, clothing, and supplies needed to preserve the integrity of a response unit without regard to the performance of its cleanup mission. As used in response directives, minimum essential equipment should refer to specific items of both organizational and individual clothing and equipment.

Minimum Fragment Distance

The minimum distance required for the protection of personnel in the open, inhabited buildings, and public traffic routes from hazardous fragments.

Minimum Normal Burst Altitude

The altitude above terrain below which air defense nuclear warheads are not normally detonated.

Minimum Nuclear Safe Distance

The sum of the radius of safety and the buffer distance.

Minimum Requirements and Standards

The program content necessary to satisfy the policies and objectives of a directive.

Minimum Residual Radioactivity Weapon

A nuclear weapon designed to have optimum reduction of unwanted effects from fallout, rainout, and burst site radioactivity. *See* Salted Weapon.

Mining Overburden, Returned

Any material overlying an economic mineral deposit that is removed to gain access to that deposit and is then used for reclamation of a surface mine. Movement means that hazardous waste transported to a facility in an individual vehicle.

Mining Wastes

Residues resulting from the extraction of raw materials from the earth.

Minor Accidents

Any accidents that are not serious accidents or do not have high potential for being serious accidents.

Minor Discharges

Discharges to the inland waters of less than 1,000 gallons of oil or discharges to it coastal waters of less than 10,000 gallons of oil. Any oil discharge that poses a substantial threat to the public health or welfare or result in critical public concern shall be classified as a major discharge regardless of this quantitative measure.

Minor Drainage

The discharge of dredged or fill material incidental to connecting upland drainage facilities to waters of the United States, adequate to effect the removal of excess soil moisture from upland croplands. Construction and maintenance of upland (dryland) facilities, such as ditching and tiling, incidental to the planting, cultivating, protecting, or harvesting of crops.

Minor Installation

In the Air Force, a facility operated by an active, reserve, or Guard unit of at least squadron size that does not otherwise satisfy all the criteria for a major installation. This category includes Air Force stations; air stations; Air Reserve stations; and Air Guard stations. Examples of minor installations are active, reserve, or Air Guard flying operations that are located at civilian-owned airports. *See* Support Site.

Minor Port

A port having facilities for the discharge of cargo from coasters or lighters only. *See* Port.

Minor Releases

Releases of a quantity of hazardous substance(s), pollutant(s), or contaminant(s) that pose minimal threat to public health or welfare or the environment. *See* De Minimis Violations.

Minority Business Enterprise (MBE)

A business concern defined by ownership and control of at least 51% of the enterprise belonging to individuals from minority groups, including but not limited to, American Indians, Asians, Blacks, and Hispanics.

Minute Volume

The volume of air breathed per minute, usually liters/minute. The product of the tidal volume (the normal volume of air moved into and out of the lungs with each breath) and the respiratory rate.

Minuteman

A three-stage, solid propellant, ballistic missile that is guided to its target by an all-inertial guidance and control system. The missiles are equipped with nuclear warheads and designed for deployment in hardened and dispersed underground silos. With the improved third stage and the post-boost vehicle, the Minuteman III missile can deliver multiple independently targetable reentry vehicles and their penetration aids to multiple targets. Designated as LGM-30.

Miosis

Contraction of the pupil to the size of a pinpoint.

Miscellaneous Units

Hazardous waste management units where hazardous wastes are treated, stored, or disposed of and that is not a container, tank, surface impoundment, pile, land treatment unit, landfill, incinerator, boiler, industrial furnace, underground injection well with appropriate technical standards under 40 CFR Part 146, or unit eligible for a research, development, and demonstration permit under 270.65.

Miscible

Able to mix (but not chemically combine) in any ratio without separating into two phases (e.g., water and alcohol).

Misfires

Any cartridge, missile, or rocket that does not properly fire when triggered.

Mishaps

A synonym for accident. Used by some government organizations, including NASA and DOD.

Mission

1) The task, together with the purpose, that clearly indicates the action to be taken and the reason therefore. 2) In common usage, a duty assigned to an individual or unit; a task.

Mist

1) Liquid particles measuring 40 to 600 microns, that are formed by condensation of vapor. 2) Liquid condensation droplets dispersed in air. By comparison, "fog" particles are smaller than 40 microns.

Mitigation

1) Actions taken to prevent or reduce the severity of a hazard. 2) Measures taken to reduce adverse impacts on the environment.

Mitigation Action Plans

Documents that describe the plan for implementing commitments made in a DOE Environmental Impact Statement (EIS) and its associated record of decision (ROD) or in an Environmental Assessment/Finding of No Significant Impact (EA/FONSI) (where the FONSI is based, in significant part, on such a commitment) to mitigate adverse environmental impacts associated with an action.

Mitosis

Cellular and nuclear division that involves duplication of the chromosomes of a parent cell, and formation of two daughter cells. This type of cell division occurs in most somatic cells.

Mixed Liquor

A mixture of activated sludge and water containing organic matter undergoing activated sludge treatment in an aeration tank.

Mixed Wastes

1) Wastes that contain both radioactive and hazardous components as defined by the Atomic Energy Act (AEA) and the Resource Conservation and Recovery Act (RCRA), respectively. 2) Any waste that meets the definition of a hazardous waste and contains radioactive waste.

Mixing Zones

Limited volumes of water serving as zones of initial dilution in the immediate vicinity of a discharge point where receiving water quality may not meet quality standards or other requirements otherwise applicable to the receiving water. The mixing zone should be considered as a place where wastes and water mix and not as a place where effluents are treated.

Mixohaline

A term used to characterize water with salinity of 0.5 to 30%, due to ocean salts. *See* Brackish Waters.

Mixosaline

A term used to characterize waters with salinity of 0.5 to 30%, due to land-derived salts.

Mixtures

Any combinations of two or more chemical substances if the combination does not occur in nature and is not, in whole or in part, the result of a chemical reaction. Heterogeneous associations of substances where the various individual substances retain their identities and can usually be separated by mechanical means. Include solutions or compounds but do not include alloys or amalgams.

MLE

See Maximum Likelihood Estimate.

MLLA

An acronym for Mineral Lands Leasing Act of 1920.

MMPA

An acronym for Mining and Mineral Policy Act of 1970.

Mobile Command Vehicles

Vehicles designed specifically to support the on-scene commander with communications to the emergency operations center.

Mobile Fuel Tank

A vessel mounted on a vehicle or other readily portable device and used only to supply fuel to an internal-combustion engine or other equipment secured to the vehicle or device.

Mobile Source

See Mobile Sources.

Mobile Source-Related Air Toxics Study

The EPA study on the need for, and feasibility of, controlling emissions of toxic air pollutants that are unregulated under the CAA and associated with motor vehicles and motor vehicle fuels, that focuses on categories of emissions that pose the greatest risk to human health or about which significant uncertainties remain, including emissions of benzene, formaldehyde, and 1,3 butadiene.

Mobile Sources

Moving producers of air pollution, mainly forms of transportation such as cars, trucks, motorcycles, and airplanes.

Mobile Storage Tank

A tank installed on a trailer or semitrailer, and used temporarily to receive and store anhydrous ammonia. Temporarily means not more than 120 days.

Mobile Support Groups, Naval

Groups that provide logistic support to ships at anchorage; in effect, a naval base afloat although certain of its supporting elements may be located ashore.

Mobility Analysis

An in-depth examination of all aspects of transportation planning in support of operation plan and operation order development.

Mobilization

1) The act of assembling and organizing emergency response resources to support national objectives in time of emergency. 2) The movement of a hazard or the conversion of that hazard to a mobile form (such as plutonium oxide vapor in a fire) that can escape to the environment if no barriers confine the hazard. 3) The process by which Armed Forces are brought to a state of readiness for war or other national emergency. This includes activating all or part of the Reserve components as well as assembling and organizing

personnel, supplies, and material. Mobilization of the Armed Forces includes but is not limited to the following categories:

- *Selective Mobilization*—Expansion of the active Armed Forces resulting from action by Congress and/or the President to mobilize Reserve component units, individual ready reservists, and the resources needed for their support to meet the requirements of a domestic emergency that is not the result of an enemy attack.

- *Partial Mobilization* — Expansion of the active Armed Forces resulting from action by Congress (up to full mobilization) or by the President (not more than 1,000,000) to mobilize Ready Reserve component units, individual reservists, and the resources needed for their support to meet the requirements of a war or other national emergency involving an external threat to the national security.

- *Full Mobilization* — Expansion of the active Armed Forces resulting from action by Congress and the President to mobilize all Reserve component units in the existing approved force structure, all individual reservists, retired military personnel, and the resources needed for their support to meet the requirements of a war or other national emergency involving an external threat to the national security.

- *Total Mobilization* — Expansion of the active Armed Forces resulting from action by Congress and the President to organize and/or generate additional units or personnel, beyond the existing force structure, and the resources needed for their support, to meet the total requirements of a war or other national emergency involving an external threat to the national security.

Mobilization Exercise

An exercise involving, either completely or in part, the implementation of mobilization plans.

MOC

An acronym for Margin of Control. *See* Criticality.

Mock-Up

A model, built to scale, of a machine, apparatus, or system, used in studying the construction of, and in testing a new development, or in teaching personnel how to operate the actual machine, apparatus, or system.

Mode

In statistics, the most common or frequent observation or value.

Mode of Transportation

The various modes used for movement of substances, materials, and personnel. For each mode, there are several means of transport, such as inland surface transportation (rail, road, and inland waterway); sea transport (coastal and ocean); air transportation; and pipelines.

Model

A mathematical representation of a natural system intended to mimic the behavior of the real system, allowing description of empirical data and predictions about untested states of the system.

Model Plants

Descriptions of typical but theoretical plants used for developing economic, environmental impact, and energy impact analyses as support for regulations or regulatory guidelines.

These are imaginary plants, with features of existing or future plants used to estimate the cost of incorporating air pollution control technology as the first step in exploring the economic impact of a potential New Source Performance Standard (NSPS).

Modeling

An investigative technique using a mathematical or physical representation of a system or theory that accounts for all or some of its known properties. Models are often used to test the effect of changes of system components on the overall performance of the system.

Moderate Damage

See Nuclear Damage.

Moderate Risk, Nuclear

A degree of risk where anticipated effects are tolerable, or at worst a minor nuisance. *See* Emergency Risk; Negligible Risk.

Moderator

1) A material (e.g., graphite or water) used to reduce the kinetic energy of neutrons in a nuclear reactor. By slowing down neutrons to speeds at which they tend not to be absorbed by nonfissionable nuclei, the moderator prevents quenching of the chain reaction and permits the reactor to operate at low fuel enrichments. 2) A person selected to arbitrate or control the proceedings of a dispute. *See* Referee.

Modification

1) Any physical change in, or change in the method of operation of, a major source that increases the actual emissions of any hazardous air pollutant emitted by such source by more than a de minimis amount or that results in the emission of any hazardous air pollutant not previously emitted by more than a de minimis amount. 2) Any change made to structures, systems, components, or procedures during any phase of the life of the reactor project.

As applied to an active underground uranium mine, any major change in the method of operation or mining procedure that will result in an increase in the amount of radon-222 emitted to air.

Modified Hazard Ranking System

The methodology developed by DOE to rank sites containing hazardous substances and/or radionuclides.

Modified Solid Waste Incineration Unit

A solid waste incineration unit at which modifications have occurred. Modified indicates that a) the cumulative cost of the modifications, over the life of the unit, exceed 50% of the original cost of construction and installation of the unit (not including the cost of any land purchased in connection with such construction or installation) updated to current costs; or b) the modification is

a physical change in or changes in the method of operation of the unit that increases the amount of any air pollutant emitted by the unit for which standards have been established.

Modified Sources

Any physical changes in, or changes in the method of operation of, stationary sources that increase the emission rate of any pollutant for which a national standard has been promulgated under Part 50 of the CAA or that result in the emission of any such pollutant not previously emitted, except that routine maintenance, repair, and replacement is not considered a physical change. The following is not considered a change in the method of operation: a) an increase in the production rate, if such increase does not exceed the operating design capacity of the source; b) an increase in the hours of operation; and c) use of an alternative fuel or raw material.

Modifying Factor (MF)

A factor that is greater than zero and less than or equal to 10; used in the operational derivation of a reference dose. Its magnitude depends upon an assessment of the scientific uncertainties of the toxicological database not explicitly treated with standard uncertainty factors (e.g., number of animals tested). The default value for the MF is one.

Modulus

A measure of the ratio of load (stress) applied to the resultant deformation of a material, such as elasticity or shear.

Mogotes

A species descriptor that means small outcrop.

Molecular Diffusion

1) A process in which solutes are transported at the microscopic level due to variations in the solute concentrations within the fluid phases. 2) Dispersion of a chemical caused by the kinetic activity of the ionic or molecular constituents.

Molecular Hybridization Test
The use of a radioactive probe to test for the presence of a viroid.

Molecular Weight
The sum of the atomic weights of the atoms in a molecule; measured in daltons.

Mollusk
A species descriptor that means animals that have a muscular foot and a dorsal shell, such as snails and mussels.

Molt
A species descriptor that means to shed the outer covering.

Moment Magnitude
Derived from a seismic moment, the product of the surface area of the fault, the average displacement on the fault plane, and the rigidity of the material of the fault. After certain corrections, the moment magnitude can be calculated from measurements of long-period waves (200–300 seconds) that typically accompany great earthquakes.

Moment Resisting Space Frame
A space frame in which the members and joints are capable of resisting forces primarily by flexure.

Monitored Personnel Locator File
A DOE centralized file maintained at the System Safety Development Center in Idaho, that lists all monitored DOE and DOE contractor employed personnel and visitors who have had positive exposures. The file consists of identification information only (e.g., name, Social Security number, birth year, and employer organization or organization visited). The file is used to identify personnel work locations so that inquiries can be made to the reporting organization for official dose records.

Monitored Visitors
Nonemployees, including subcontractors, not classified as a "nonemployed radiation workers" visiting a facility that is operated by DOE or a DOE contractor under circumstances requiring that they be monitored for radiation exposure.

Monitored Workers
Employees of the reporting organization who work with, or are in the proximity of, ionizing radiation or radioactive material and who are monitored in accordance with DOE regulations.

Monitoring
1) Periodic or continuous surveillance or testing to determine the level of compliance with statutory requirements and/or pollutant levels in various media or in humans, animals, and other living things. 2) A set of observation and data collection methods to detect and measure deviations in current operations. 3) Actions intended to detect and evaluate radiological conditions.

Monitoring Coastal Waters
An assessment of a) the contribution of atmospheric deposition to pollution loadings in the Great Lakes, the Chesapeake Bay, Lake Champlain and coastal waters; b) the environmental and public health effects of any pollution that is attributable to atmospheric deposition to the Great Lakes, the Chesapeake Bay, Lake Champlain and coastal waters; c) the source or sources of any pollution to the Great Lakes, the Chesapeake Bay, Lake Champlain and coastal waters that is attributable to atmospheric deposition; d) whether pollution loadings in the Great Lakes, the Chesapeake Bay, Lake Champlain or coastal waters cause or contribute to exceedances of drinking water standards pursuant to the Safe Drinking Water Act (42 USC 300(f) et seq.) or water quality standards pursuant to the Federal Water Pollution Control Act (33 USC 1251 et seq.) or, with respect to the Great Lakes, exceedances of the specific objectives of the Great Lakes Water Quality Agreement; and e) a description of any revisions of the requirements, standards, and limitations pursuant to the CAA and other applicable federal laws as are necessary to ensure protection of human health and the environment.

The monitoring program takes into consideration the effects due to bioaccumulation and indirect exposure pathways.

Monitoring Systems

Any systems, required under the monitoring sections in applicable subparts, used to sample and condition (if applicable), to analyze, and to provide a record of emissions or process parameters.

Monitoring Wells

1) A well used to take water quality samples or to measure groundwater levels. 2) Wells drilled at a hazardous waste management facility or Superfund site to collect groundwater samples for the purpose of physical, chemical, or biological analysis to determine the amounts, types, and distribution of contaminants in the groundwater beneath the site. 3) Special wells drilled at specific locations on or off a hazardous waste site where groundwater can be sampled at various depths and studied to determine such things as the direction in which the groundwater flows and the types and amounts of contaminants present.

Monocarpic

A species descriptor that means producing a single fruit.

Monoclinous

A species descriptor that means having pistils and stamens in the same flower.

Monoclonal Antibodies

Molecules of living organisms that selectively find and attach to other molecules to which their structure conforms exactly. This could also apply to equivalent activity by chemical molecules.

Monocytic Leukemia

A form of bone marrow cancer characterized by an increase in the number of large, mononuclear white blood cells in tissues, organs, and the circulating blood.

Monoecious

A species descriptor that means having male and female reproductive organs in separate flowers on the same plant.

Monogamous

A species descriptor that means having one mate for life.

Monomer

A compound of relatively low molecular weight, that under certain conditions, either alone or with another monomer, forms various types and lengths of molecular chains called polymers or copolymers of high molecular weight.

Monophagous

A species descriptor that means eating only one kind of food.

Monophyletic

A species descriptor that means pertaining to a single phylum of plants or animals; derived from one source.

Monotypic

A species descriptor that means the only member of its genus.

Montane Forest

A forest located at the middle altitude of a mountain.

Monthly NEPA Reports

Documents submitted monthly to the Secretary that identify Environmental Assessments and Environmental Impact Statements that Secretarial Officers expect to forward for approval during the subsequent 3 months.

Montreal Protocol

The Montreal Protocol on Substances that Deplete the Ozone Layer, a protocol to the Vienna Convention for the Protection of the Ozone Layer, including adjustments adopted by parties thereto and amendments that have entered into force.

Monumentation

The act of setting a permanent survey control point.

Morbidity

The rate of incidence of disease in a population.

Morph

A species descriptor that means any individual of a polymorphic (the occurrence of different forms, stages, or color types in organisms of the same species) group.

Morphology

The biological study of the form or structure of cells, tissues, organs, or organisms; the study of the form and structure of living organisms.

Morphometry

Quantitative measure of morphology.

MORT

See Management Oversight and Risk Tree.

MORT Analysis

A DOE analytical process that addresses the factors involved in an incident/accident sequence and leads naturally to a) consideration of the management system factors and b) judgment whether the fault/failure potential was an assumed risk.

Mortality

The number of individual deaths in a population.

Mortgage

Classes of liens commonly given to secure advances on, or the unpaid purchase price of, real property, together with the credit instruments, if any, secured thereby.

Mosaic

An assembly of overlapping photographs that have been matched together to form a continuous photographic representation of a portion of the surface of the earth. *See* Controlled Mosaic; uncontrolled mosaic.

Mosaic Bones

A species descriptor that means bone tissue composed of somatic cells of genetically different types; this phenomenon is caused by gene or chromosome mutations.

Most Cost Effective Means

For the purposes of prioritizing eligible water conservation projects, the project with the greatest economic justification.

Motor Fuels

Petroleum or petroleum-based substances that are motor gasoline, aviation gasoline, No.1 or No.2 diesel fuel, or any grade of gasohol, and are typically used in the operation of a motor engine.

Motor Vehicle Emission and Fuel Standards

The standards applicable to the emission of any air pollutant from any class or classes of new motor vehicles or new motor vehicle engines, that in the EPA Administrator's judgment cause, or contribute to, air pollution that may reasonably be anticipated to endanger public health or welfare. Such standards shall be applicable to such vehicles and engines for their useful life, whether such vehicles and engines are designed as complete systems or incorporate devices to prevent or control such pollution. Effective for the model year 1998 and thereafter, emissions of oxides of nitrogen (NOx) from gasoline and diesel-fueled heavy duty trucks shall contain standards that provide that such emissions may not exceed 4.0 grams per brake horsepower hour (gbh).

Motor Vehicles

1) Self-propelled vehicles designed for transporting persons or property on a street or highway. 2) Vehicles, machines, tractors, trailers, or semitrailers, or any combinations thereof, propelled or drawn by mechanical power and used upon the highways in the transportation of passengers or property. They do not include a vehicle, locomotive, or car operated exclusively on a rail or rails, or a trolley bus operated by electric power derived from a fixed overhead wire, furnishing local passenger transportation similar to street-railway service.

MOU
See Memorandum of Understanding.

MOV
An acronym for Motor Operated Valves.

Movement
Means by which hazardous waste is transported to a facility in an individual vehicle.

Moving Map Display
A display in which a symbol, representing the vehicle, remains stationary while the map or chart image moves beneath the symbol so that the display simulates the horizontal movement of the vehicle in which it is installed. Occasionally the design of the display is such that the map or chart image remains stationary while the symbol moves across a screen. *See* Projected Map Display.

MPC
See Maximum Permissible Concentration.

MPD
See Maximum Permissible Dose.

MPL
See Maximum Possible Loss.

MPO
An acronym for Metropolitan Planning Organization.

MPPRCA
An acronym for Marine Plastic Pollution Research and Control Act of 1987.

MPRSA
An acronym for Marine Protection, Research, and Sanctuaries Act of 1972.

MPTDS
An acronym for Multiple Point Source Model with Terrain (MPTER), Deposition, and Settling [of pollutants].

MQL
An acronym for Method Quantification Limits.

Mrem
A one-thousandth part of a rem.

MRF
An acronym for Material Recovery Facility.

MRL
An acronym for Minimum-Risk Level.

MRS
An acronym for Moderator Recovery System; Monitored Retrievable Storage facility.

MRSA
An acronym for Merrimack River Study Act of 1990 (WSRA).

MSA
See Standard Metropolitan Statistical Area. An acronym for Major System Acquisition.

MSC
See Military Sealift Command.

MSDS
See Material Safety Data Sheets.

MTDDIS
An acronym for Mesoscale Transport Diffusion and Deposition Model for Industrial Sources.

MTSAA
An acronym for Multidiscipline Technical Safety Assurance Appraisal.

Muck Soils
Earth made from decaying plant materials.

Mucronate
A species descriptor that means a sharp tip of some plants and animal organs.

Mucronulate
A species descriptor that means having a sharp terminal point or spiny tip.

Mud Dump Site
The site and area located approximately 5¾ miles east of Sandy Hook, New Jersey.

Mud, Wet
Soft earth composed predominantly of clay and silt-fine mineral sediments less than 0.074 millimeter in diameter.

Mulches
Layers of material (wood chips, straw, loaves, etc.) placed around plants to hold moisture, prevent weed growth, protect the plants, and enrich the soil.

Multi-Employer Policy
An OSHA procedure for determining which establishment has responsibility for employee safety and health when more than one establishment has employees exposed to the same hazard.

Multi-Modal
In transport operations, a term applied to the movement of passengers and cargo by more than one method of transport.

Multi-Spectral Imagery
The image of an object obtained simultaneously in a number of discrete spectral bands.

Multifilament
A material consisting of many continuous filaments.

Multimedia Environment
All forms of the environment in which contaminants can be released; water, air, and land.

Multiple Impacts
Actions having multimedia effects on the environments air, land, water, special, and/or cultural resources or some combined impact in one or more of these media.

Multiple Use
1) The management of the public lands and their various resource values so that they are utilized in the combination that will best meet the present and future needs of the American people; making the most judicious use of the land for some or all of these resources or related services over areas large enough to provide sufficient latitude for periodic adjustments in use to conform to changing needs and conditions; the use of some land for less than all of the resources; a combination of balanced and diverse resource uses that takes into account the long-term needs of future generations for renewable and nonrenewable resources, including, but not limited to:

- recreation,
- range,
- timber,
- minerals,
- watershed,
- wildlife and fish,
- natural scenic,
- scientific and historical values, and
- harmonious and coordinated management of the various resources without permanent impairment of the productivity of the land and the quality of the environment with consideration being given to the relative values of the resources and not necessarily to the combination of uses that will give the greatest economic return or the greatest unit output.

2) Uses of land for more than one purpose (i.e., grazing of livestock, wildlife production, recreation, watershed, and timber production). Can also apply to use of bodies of water for recreational purposes, fishing, and water supply.

Multiple-Use Sustained-Yield Act (MUSYA)
A 1960 act authorizing the Secretary to Agriculture to cooperatively manage all the various renewable surface resources of the national forests to best suit the needs of the people. The focus is to develop and administer these resources for

multiple uses and sustained yields of forestry-related products and services

Multiple Warning Phenomenology

Deriving warning information from two or more systems observing separate physical phenomena associated with the same events to attain high credibility while being less susceptible to error.

Multistage Model

A mathematical function used to extrapolate the probability of incidence of disease from a bioassay in animals using high doses, to that expected to be observed at the low doses that are likely to be found in chronic human exposure. This model is commonly used in quantitative carcinogenic risk assessments where the chemical agent is assumed to be a complete carcinogen and the risk is assumed to be proportional to the dose in the low region.

Multivariate Statistics

Simultaneous examination and measurement of the relationship of several variables or multiple dimensions of variables. A highly complex procedure requiring numerous statistical iterations involving a computer. Statistical studies include the following: a) analysis of variance, classifying variation within a sample facility/project into separate components; b) factor analysis, measuring degrees of relatedness, dependency, of individual factors to common factors; and c) multidimensional scaling, that deals with data on a rank ordering or scaling methodology.

Municipal Solid Wastes

Garbage, refuse, sludges, wastes, and other discarded materials resulting from residential and nonindustrial operations and activities, such as household activities, office functions, and commercial housekeeping wastes.

Municipal Waste

Diverse waste items discarded by the residents and businesses of a particular incorporated city. The waste is typically comprised of paper, wood, yard wastes, food wastes, plastics, leather, rubber, and other combustible materials and noncombus-

tible materials such as metal, glass, and rock. Municipal waste is usually disposed of via incineration and/or landfilling. The term does not include industrial process wastes or medical wastes that are segregated from such other wastes, or combined wastes in which 30% or less of the total weight is comprised, in aggregate, of municipal waste.

Municipalities

Cities, towns, boroughs, counties, parishes, districts, or other public bodies created by or pursuant to state law, with responsibility for the planning or administration of solid waste management, or Indian tribes or authorized tribal organizations, or Alaska Native villages or organizations, and include any rural communities or unincorporated towns or villages or any other public entities for which an application for assistance is made by a state or political subdivision thereof.

Munition

A complete device charged with explosives, propellants, pyrotechnics, initiating composition, or nuclear, biological, or chemical material for use in military operations, including demolitions. Certain suitably modified munitions can be used for training, ceremonial, or nonoperational purposes. An explosive munition is any chemical compound or mechanical mixture that, when subjected to such stimuli as heat, impact, friction, or shock undergoes a very rapid chemical change that releases large volumes of highly heated gases that exert pressure in the surrounding medium. The term applies to materials that either detonate or deflagrate.

Museum Collection

An assemblage of objects, and/or natural history specimens collected according to a rational scheme and maintained so they can be preserved, studied, or interpreted for public benefit. Museum collections normally are kept in park museums, although they may also be maintained in archaeological and historic preservation centers. To be a museum collection, the assembled objects and specimens must be related to each other and to one or more themes.

Museum Object
A material thing possessing functional, aesthetic, cultural, symbolic, and/or scientific value. An object is usually movable by nature or design, such as a coin, a gun, a ceramic pot, a chair, a canoe, or an automobile. Museum objects include prehistoric and historic objects, artifacts, works of art, archival materials, and natural history specimens that are part of a museum collection. Elements, fragments, and components of structures may be designated museum objects if they are no longer part of the original structure. Large or immovable properties, such as monumental statuary, trains, nautical vessels, cairns, and rock paintings, are considered to be either structures or features of sites. Museum objects in the custody of the National Park Service are usually housed in park museum collections, universities, or archaeological and historic preservation centers.

MUSYA
See Multiple-Use Sustained-Yield Act.

Mutagen
See Mutagens.

Mutagenic
Ability to cause a permanent change in the structure of DNA. More specific than, but often used interchangeably with, genotoxic. *See* Genotoxic.

Mutagenicity
The property of a chemical that causes the genetic characteristics of an organism to change in such a way that future generations are permanently affected.

Mutagenesis
Any process by which cells are mutated.

Mutagens
Substances that can cause a change in genetic material.

Mutate
To bring about a change in the genetic constitution of a cell by altering its DNA.

Mutation
Changes in the composition of DNA, generally divided according to size into "gene mutations" (changes within a single gene) and chromosome mutations" (affecting larger portions of the chromosome, or the loss or addition of an entire chromosome). A "heritable mutation" is a mutation that is passed from parent to offspring and therefore was present in the germ cell of one of the parents. Somatic cell mutations may result in cancer.

Mutual Assent
One of the essential elements of a contract, often called "meeting of the minds"; the agreement of the parties to the contract, mutually consenting to be bound by the exact terms thereof.

Mutual Assistance Agreements
Agreements between contractors and the U.S. Department of Energy (DOE), and/or DOE and other government agencies or municipalities to share emergency response and techniques. Also known as Mutual Aid Agreements.

MUX
An acronym for Multiplexor.

MVEFS
See Motor Vehicle Emission and Fuel Standards (CAA).

MW
See Mixed Wastes; Megawatt.

Myalgia
Severe muscle pain.

Mycelium
A species descriptor pertaining to the vegetative part of a fungus consisting of a mass of branching, threadlike filaments called hyphae.

Mycorrhizae
A species descriptor that means the symbiotic (mutually beneficial) association of the mycelium (filaments) of a fungus with the roots of a plant.

Mydriasis
Dilation of the pupil.

Myelocytic Leukemia
A form of bone marrow cancer characterized by the presence of large numbers of granular white blood cells in tissues, organs, and the circulating blood.

Myocardial Ischemia
Insufficient oxygen supply to meet the metabolic demands of heart muscles.

Myocarditis
Inflammation of the muscles of the heart.

Myoclonus
Involuntary spasm or twitching of a muscle or group of muscles.

Myoglobin
The oxygen-transporting, pigmented protein of muscle; resembles blood hemoglobin in function.

Myoglobinuria
Presence of myoglobin in urine.

Myriapod
A species descriptor that means an arthropod, such as a centipede, with segmented bodies and many legs.

N

NO$_2$

See Nitrogen Dioxide.

NAAQS

See National Ambient Air Quality Standards.

NACOSH

An acronym for National Advisory Committee on Occupational Safety and Health.

Nacre

A species descriptor for mother-of-pearl. *See* Mollusk.

NAFEC

See National Association of Farmer Elected Committeemen.

NALR

See National Acid Lakes Registry (CAA).

Napalm

1) Powdered aluminum soap or similar compound used to gelatinize oil or gasoline for use in napalm bombs or flame throwers. 2) The resultant gelatinized substance.

NAPAP

See National Acid Precipitation Assessment Program (CAA).

Naphtha Jet Fuel

A fuel in the heavy naphtha boiling range with an average gravity of 52.8° API and 20% to 90% distillation temperatures of 290°F to 470°F and/or meeting Military Specification MIL-T-5624L (Grade JP-4). Used for turbojet and turboprop aircraft engines, primarily by the military. Excludes ram-jet and petroleum rocket fuels.

Narcosis

A disorder characterized by drowsiness or unconsciousness, caused by the action of a toxicant on the central nervous system.

NAS

An acronym for National Academy of Sciences.

NASA

See National Aeronautics and Space Administration.

Nasopharyngeal Region

The area including the nasopharynx, oropharynx, and nose. The pharynx is the cavity situated between the nasal cavities, mouth, and larynx, where it divides to form the trachea and the esophagus, which accept air and food, respectively.

Nasopharynx

Relating to the nasal cavity and that pan of the throat that lies above the level of the soft palate.

National Academy of Sciences Study

The study, analysis, and review of a) risk assessment methodology used by EPA to determine the carcinogenic risk associated with exposure to hazardous air pollutants from source categories and subcategories subject to the requirements of the CAA; and b) improvements in such methodology. The study includes, but is not limited to 1) the techniques used for estimating and describing the carcinogenic potency to humans of hazardous air pollutants; and 2) the techniques used for estimating exposure to hazardous air pollutants (for hypothetical and actual maximally exposed individuals as well as other exposed individuals). To the extent practicable, the Academy study was to include an evaluation of the methodology for assessing the risk of adverse human health effects other than cancer for which safe thresholds of exposure may not exist, including, but not limited to, inheritable genetic mutations, birth defects, and reproductive dysfunctions.

National Acid Lakes Registry (NALR)

The list, or registry, of all lakes that are known to be acidified due to acid deposition. Lakes are added to the registry as they become acidic or as data becomes available to show that they are acidic. Lakes are deleted from the registry as they become nonacidic.

National Acid Precipitation Assessment Program (NAPAP)

The acid precipitation research program set forth in the Acid Precipitation Act of 1980 (42 USC 8901 et seq.).

National Aeronautics and Space Administration (NASA)

The federal agency a) researches solutions to problems of flight within and outside of the earth's atmosphere; b) develops, constructs, tests, and operates aeronautical and space vehicles; c)conducts activities required for the exploration of space with manned and unmanned vehicles; and d) arranges for the most effective utilization of the scientific and engineering resources of the United States with other nations engaged in aeronautical and space activities for peaceful purposes.

National Ambient Air Quality Standards (NAAQS)

Maximum air pollutant standards that EPA set under the Clean Air Act for attainment by each state. The standards were to be achieved by 1975, along with state implementation plans (SIPs) to control industrial sources in each state. *See* Criteria Pollutants; State Implementation Plan; Emissions Trading.

National Ballast Water Control Studies

Studies conducted by the Aquatic Nuisance Species Task Force (ANSTF) on introduction of aquatic nuisance species by vessels. These studies include: a) a ballast exchange study that assesses the environmental effects of ballast water exchange on the diversity and abundance of native species in receiving estuarine, marine, and fresh waters of the United States and identifies areas within the waters of the United States and the exclusive economic zone, if any, where the exchange of ballast water does not pose a threat of infestation or spread of aquatic nuisance species in the Great Lakes and other waters of the United States; b) a biological study that determines whether aquatic nuisance species threaten the ecological characteristics and economic uses of waters of the United States other than the Great Lakes; and c) a shipping study that determines the need for controls on vessels entering waters of the United States, other than the Great Lakes, to minimize the risk of unintentional introduction and dispersal of aquatic nuisance species in those waters. The shipping study includes an examination of the degree to which shipping may be a major pathway of transmission of aquatic nuisance species in those waters; possible alternatives for controlling introduction of those species through shipping; and the feasibility of implementing regional versus national control measures.

National Capacity Variances

Nationwide variances based on inadequate treatment capacity. EPA included provisions within regulations for specific wastes that allows a variance from the land disposal restrictions. For example, the regulation on solvent wastes in 40 CFR 268.30 provides a 2-year variance on dilute mixtures of solvents and other wastes.

National Command Authorities (NCA)

The President and the Secretary of Defense or their duly deputized alternates or successors.

National Communications System (NCS)

The telecommunications system that results from the technical and operational integration of the separate telecommunications systems of the several executive branch departments and agencies having a significant telecommunications capability.

National Consensus Standard

Any occupational safety and health standard or modification thereof that a) has been adopted and promulgated by a nationally recognized standards-producing organization under procedures whereby it can be determined by the Secretary of Labor (DOL) that persons interested and affected by the scope or provisions of the standard have reached substantial agreement on its adoption; b) was formulated in a manner that afforded an opportunity for diverse views to be considered; and c) has been designated as such a standard by the Secretary, after consultation with other appropriate federal agencies.

National Contingency Plan (NCP)

The National Oil and Hazardous Substances Contingency Plan and revisions promulgated by EPA, pursuant to Section 105 of CERCLA and codified in 40 CFR Part 300. The scope plan includes a) Discharges or substantial threats of discharges of oil to or upon the navigable waters of the United States and adjoining shorelines; b) releases or substantial threats of releases of hazardous substances into the environment, and releases or substantial threats of releases of pollutants or contaminants that may present imminent and substantial danger to public health and welfare; c) establishing requirements for federal regional and federal local contingency plans; d) procedures for removal operations pursuant to Section 311 of the Clean Water Act (CWA); e) procedures for response operations pursuant to CERCLA: f) Designating trustees for natural resources (CERCLA); and g) national policies and procedures for using dispersants and other chemicals in removal and response actions.

National Defense Area (NDA)

An area established on nonfederal lands located within the United States or its possessions or territories for the purpose of safeguarding classified defense information or protecting DOD equipment and/or material. Establishment of a national defense area temporarily places such nonfederal lands under the effective control of the Department of Defense and results only from an emergency event. The senior DOD representative at the scene will define the boundary, mark it with a physical barrier, and post warning signs. The landowner's consent and cooperation will be obtained whenever possible; however, military necessity will dictate the final decision regarding location, shape, and size of the national defense area.

National Defense Reserve Fleet (NDRF)

1) Including the Ready Reserve Force, a fleet composed of ships acquired and maintained by the Maritime Administration (MARAD) for use in mobilization or emergency. 2) Less the Ready Reserve Force, a fleet composed of the older dry cargo ships, tankers, troop transports, and other assets in the MARAD's custody that are maintained at a relatively low level of readiness. They are acquired by MARAD from commercial ship operators under the provisions of the Merchant Marine Act of 1936; they are available only on mobilization or congressional declaration of an emergency. Because the ships are maintained in a state of minimum preservation, activation requires 30 to 90 days and extensive shipyard work for many.

National Emergency

A condition declared by the President or Congress by virtue of powers previously vested in them that authorize certain emergency actions to be undertaken in the national interest. Action to be taken may include partial, full, or total mobilization of national resources.

National Emissions Standards for Hazardous Air Pollutants (NESHAPS)

Emissions standards set by EPA for an air pollutant not covered by NAAQS that may cause an increase in deaths or in serious, irreversible, or incapacitating illness. Primary standards are designed to protect human health, secondary standards to protect public welfare.

National Environmental Policy Act of 1969 (NEPA)

The Act passed in 1970 (42 USC 4321 et seq.) requiring that the environmental impact of federal actions be considered. NEPA was one of the first laws ever written that established the broad national framework for protecting our environment. NEPA's basic policy is to ensure that all branches of government give proper consideration to the environment prior to undertaking any major federal action that significantly affects the environment. NEPA requirements are invoked when airports, buildings, military complexes, highways, parkland purchases, and other such federal activities are proposed. Environmental Assessments (EAs) and Environmental Impact Statements (EISs), which are assessments of the likelihood of impacts from alternative courses of action, are required from all federal agencies and are the most visible NEPA requirements. Since its adoption many agencies have created their own versions of NEPA [e.g., refer to DOE NEPA Guidelines, and relevant references from the Council on Environmental Quality Regulations (40 CFR Parts 1500-1508, as amended 7-1-86)].

National Environmental Policy Act Documents

Documents prepared pursuant to a requirement of NEPA or the Council on Environmental Quality Regulations (40 CFR parts 1500-1508, as amended 7-1-86). These documents include, but are not limited to, the following: an Environmental Impact Statement (EIS), an Environmental Assessment (EA), a Finding of No Significant Impact (FONSI), Notice of Intent [to prepare an EIS] (NOI), Record of Decision (ROD), Categorical Exclusion [determination] (CX).

National Historic Landmark

A site, structure, or object of national significance. The 1935 Historic Sites Act authorized the National Park Service to survey the nation for sites, buildings, or objects of national significance and to record and carry out necessary research on them. All National Historic Landmarks are entered ln the National Register of Historic Places.

National Historic Preservation Act

The federal law enacted in 1966, that authorizes federal assistance for historic preservation. The act established the National Register of Historic Places, and methods by which properties could be documented and nominated. Title II of the Act created the Advisory Council on Historic Preservation (ACHP).

National Infrastructure

Infrastructure provided and financed by a NATO member in its own territory solely for its own forces (including those forces assigned to or designated for NATO). *See* Infrastructure.

National Institute for Occupational Safety and Health (NIOSH)

The agency of the U.S. Department of Health and Human Services, established under Public Law 91.596 with major responsibility to undertake national occupational safety and health research and development activities. NIOSH provides research and evaluation studies of occupational injuries and hazardous substances in the workplace. These criteria are then used by OSHA for setting workplace safety standards. NIOSH is located at: 1600 Clifton Road, N.E.; Building 1, Room 3007; Atlanta, GA 30333; 1-800/356-4674.

National Intelligence

Integrated departmental intelligence that covers the broad aspects of national policy and national security, is of concern to more than one department or agency, and transcends the exclusive competence of a single department or agency.

National Intelligence Support Team (NIST)
A nationally sourced team composed of intelligence and communications experts from either Defense Intelligence Agency, Central Intelligence Agency, National Security Agency, or any combination of these agencies.

National Military Command System (NMCS)
The priority component of the Worldwide Military Command and Control System designed to support the National Command Authorities and Joint Chiefs of Staff in the exercise of their responsibilities.

National Objectives
The aims, derived from national goals and interests, toward which a national policy or strategy is directed and efforts and resources of the nation are applied.

National Oceanic and Atmospheric Administration (NOAA)
NOAA is the agency responsible for environmental satellite and data information, oceanic and atmospheric research, sustainable development, coastal management programs, cleanup of oil spills, the National Weather Service, and the National Marine Fisheries Service. NOAA is located at 14th and Constitution Ave., N.W., Rm. 6013; Washington, DC 20230; 202/482-6090.

National Oceanic and Atmospheric Administration (NOAA) Weather Radio
A service of the NOAA that provides continuous broadcasts of the latest weather information directly from the National Weather Service (NWS) offices, in Denver, CO. During severe weather conditions, NWS forecasters interrupt routine weather broadcasts and substitute special warning messages. The forecasters can also activate specially designed tone alert receivers that alert a listener to a warning message.

National Oil and Hazardous Substances Contingency Plan (NOHSCP/NCP)
The federal regulation that guides determination of the sites to be corrected under the Superfund program and the program to prevent or control spills into surface waters or other portions of the environment. *See* Superfund; National Contingency Plan (NCP).

National Park Service (NPS)
The branch of the Department of Interior responsible for the management and recording of historically significant sites, the Historic American Engineering Record (HAER), Historic Architectural Building Survey (HABS), and about 180 national park sites.

National Policy
A broad course of action or statements of guidance adopted by the government at the national level in pursuit of national objectives.

National Pollutant Discharge Elimination System (NPDES)
A permitting system established under the guidelines of the Clean Water Act applicable to any and all sources of discharge directly into rivers, lakes, or other surface waters. Permit holders are required to test and meet toxic pollutant effluent limitations prior to discharge of any wastewater. Pretreatment standards apply to discharge pollutants. NPDES requirements can be found in Section 402 of the Federal Water Pollution Act (FWPCA), also known as the Clean Water Act.

National Primary and Secondary Ambient Air Quality Standards (NAAQS)
The regulations prescribing a national primary ambient air quality standard and a national secondary ambient air quality standard for each air pollutant for which air quality criteria have been issued, that in the judgment of the Administrator of EPA, based on such criteria and allowing an adequate margin of safety, are requisite to protect the public health.

National Priorities List (NPL)
EPA's formal listing of the most serious uncontrolled or abandoned hazardous waste sites, many nominated by states, under guidelines established by the Comprehensive Environmental Response, Compensation, and Liability Act (CERCLA). NPL sites are those identified for possible long-

term remedial action under Superfund. A site must be on the NPL to receive money from the Trust Fund for remedial action. The list is based primarily on the score a site receives from the Hazard Ranking System (HRS). EPA is required to update the NPL at least once a year.

National Recreational Trails Advisory Committee

The 11-member advisory committee consists of members of government and recreational trail user organizations and represents the following recreational trail uses: hiking, cross-country skiing, off-highway motorcycling, snowmobiling, horseback riding, all-terrain vehicle riding, bicycling, and four-wheel driving. The advisory committee was established to a) review utilization of allocated moneys by states; b) establish and review criteria for trail-side and trail-head facilities that qualify for funding under this chapter; and c) make recommendations to the Secretary for changes in federal policy to advance the purposes of the National Trails System Act.

National Register of Historic Places

A record of sites, structures, or objects of national, state, or local significance. It was expanded by the 1966 Historic Preservation Act (HPA). To be eligible for inclusion on the National Register, properties can be publicly or privately owned but must meet the criteria found in 36 CFR 60 or 36 CFR 65. The program is administered by the National Park Service.

National Register or Register

See National Register of Historic Places.

National Response Center (NRC)

The federal center operated by the U.S. Coast Guard that receives and evaluates reports of oil and hazardous substance releases into the environment and immediately relays reports to a predesignated federal On-Scene Coordinator (OSC). The NRC operates a 24 hour a day, toll free number for reporting incidents: 1-800-424-8802.

National Response Team (NRT)

The NRT established pursuant to the National Contingency Plan (42 USC Section 9605), that includes representatives of thirteen (13) federal agencies with interests and expertise in various aspects of emergency response to pollution incidents, who coordinate federal responses to nationally significant pollution incidents and provide advice and technical assistance to the responding agencies. EPA serves as chair and the U.S. Coast Guard serves as vice- chair. The NRT is primarily a national planning, policy, and coordinating body and does not respond directly to incidents. The NRT provides policy guidance prior to an incident and assistance as requested by a federal On Scene Coordinator via a Regional Response Team during an incident. NRT assistance usually takes the form of technical advice, access to additional resources or equipment, or coordination with other RRTS.

National Security

Those aspects of national security as outlined in the Atomic Energy Act that could be affected adversely by fire, explosion, or other catastrophes.

National Security Areas (NSA)

Areas established on nonfederal or public accessible lands located within the United States. its possessions, or its territories for the purpose of safeguarding classified information or protecting DOE equipment and/or material. Establishment of an NSA temporarily places such nonfederal lands under the effective control of DOE and results only from an emergency event. The senior DOE representative having custody of the material at the scene will define the boundary, mark it with a physical barrier, and post warning signs. The landowner's consent and cooperation will be obtained whenever possible; however, operational necessity will dictate the final decision regarding location, shape, and size of NSA.

National Security Council (NSC)

A governmental body specifically designed to assist the President in integrating all spheres of national security policy. The President, Vice President, Secretary of State, and Secretary of Defense are statutory members. The Chairman of the Joint Chiefs of Staff; Director, Central Intelligence Agency; and the Assistant to the President for National Security Affairs serve as advisers.

National Security Information (NSI)

Information that has been determined pursuant to Executive Order 12356, NSI, or any predecessor order, to require protection against unauthorized disclosure and is so designated.

National Stock Number

The 13-digit stock number replacing the 11-digit Federal Stock Number. It consists of the 4-digit Federal Supply Classification code and the 9-digit National Item Identification Number. The National Item Identification Number consists of a 2-digit National Codification Bureau number designating the central cataloging office of the NATO or other friendly country that assigned the number and a 7-digit nonsignificant number. The number shall be arranged as follows: 9999-00-999-9999. *See* Federal Stock Number.

National Strategy

The comprehensive strategy to control emissions of hazardous air pollutants from area sources in urban areas. The objectives were to a) identify not less than 30 hazardous air pollutants that, as the result of emissions from area sources, present the greatest threat to public health in the largest number of urban areas and that are or will be listed; and b) identify the source categories or subcategories emitting such pollutants that are or will be listed.

When identifying categories and subcategories of sources, the Administrator took into considerations that sources accounting for 90% or more of the aggregate emissions of each of the 30 identified hazardous air pollutants are subject to standards pursuant to the CAA. The strategy included a schedule of specific actions to substantially reduce the public health risks posed by the release of hazardous air pollutants from area sources that will be implemented by the Administrator under the authority of the CAA or other laws, including, but not limited to the:

- Toxic Substances Control Act (15 USC 2601 et seq.),
- Federal Insecticide, Fungicide, and Rodenticide Act (7 USC 136 et seq.), and
- Resource Conservation and Recovery Act (42 USC 6901 et seq.)],
- or others enacted by the states.

The goal was to achieve a reduction in the incidence of cancer attributable to exposure to hazardous air pollutants emitted by stationary sources of not less than 75%, considering control of emissions of hazardous air pollutants from all stationary sources and resulting from measures implemented by the Administrator or by the states. The strategy also identified research needs in monitoring, analytical methodology, modeling or pollution control techniques and recommendations for changes in law that would further the goals and objectives of this subsection.

National Warning System (NAWAS)

The federal portion of the Civil Defense Warning System, used for the dissemination of warning and other emergency information from the warning centers or regions to warning points in each state.

National Wild and Scenic Rivers System

The system comprised of rivers that are a) authorized for inclusion therein by act of Congress; or b) designated as wild, scenic or recreational rivers by or pursuant to an act of the legislature of the state or states through which they flow, that are to be permanently administered as wild, scenic, or recreational rivers by an agency or political subdivision of the state or states concerned that are found by the Secretary of the Interior, upon application of the governor of the state or the governors of the states concerned, or a person or persons thereunto duly appointed, to meet the criteria established in this chapter and such criteria supplementary thereto as he/she may prescribe, and that are approved for inclusion in the system.

National Workforce Development Office (NWDO)

The EPA office responsible for developing environmental education programs, curricula, and materials for kindergarten through postgraduate levels. Operates an environmental employment program for people 55 and over. Oversees training programs and fellowships offered by EPA.

Nationally Recognized Testing Laboratory (NRTL)

A laboratory that has been recognized by the Department of Labor, Occupational Safety and Health Administration (OSHA) as meeting the requirements of 29 CFR 1910.7, and that test for safety, and list, label, or accept equipment or material. For example, Underwriters Laboratory (UL) is a NRTL.

Native

Indigenous; original to the region. Not introduced from another region; endemic.

Native Species

All species of plants and animals naturally occurring, either presently or historically, in any ecosystem of the United States.

Native Vegetation

Those plant species, communities, or vegetative associations that are endemic to a given area and that would normally be identified with a healthy and productive range condition occurring as a result of the natural vegetative process of the area.

Natural Background Radiation

The radiation in man's natural environment, including radiation originating outside the earth's atmosphere and radiation from the naturally occurring radioactive elements on earth. These elements may be found both in the environment and inside the bodies of men and animals.

Natural Barriers

Physical, chemical, and hydrological characteristics of the geological environment at the disposal site that, individually and collectively, act to retard or preclude waste migration.

Natural Conditions

Naturally occurring phenomena that reduce visibility as measured in terms of visual range, contrast, or coloration.

Natural Disaster

Any flood, high water, wind-driven water, drought, fire, hurricane, tornado, storm, etc. *See* Domestic Emergencies.

Natural Gas

1) Naturally occurring mixtures of hydrocarbon gases and vapors, the more important of which are methane, ethane, propane, butane, pentane, and hexane. The energy content of natural gas is usually taken as 1,032 Btu/cu ft. 2) A natural fuel containing primarily methane and ethane that occurs in certain geologic formations. 3) Naturally occurring mixtures of hydrocarbon gases and vapors, in gaseous or liquid form.

Natural Gas Liquids

Hydrocarbons, such as ethane, propane, butane, and pentane, that are extracted from field gas.

Natural Gas Processing Plants

Processing sites engaged in the extraction of natural gas liquids from field gas, fractionation of mixed natural gas liquids to natural gas products, or both.

Natural Phenomena

Exceptional, unusual, or abnormal natural occurrences.

Natural Phenomena Emergencies

Conditions caused by flood, earthquake, fire, storm, or other natural occurrences.

Natural Pollutant

A naturally occurring substance, that is considered a contaminant when it exists in excess quantities.

Natural Resource Damage Assessment

1) An assessment, based on the results of a Natural Resource Damage Preassessment Screen of a release, that a) establishes whether a natural resource injury has occurred and resulted from the release; b) quantifies the effects of the release in injury; and c) determines the financial compensation appropriate for the injury. 2) The process of collecting, compiling, and analyzing information, statistics, or data through prescribed methodologies to determine damages for injuries to natural resources.

Natural Resource Damage Preassessment Screens

Desk-top reviews of existing data that are triggered when a federal agency is notified by an On Scene Coordinator or other lead agency of a potential injury due to a release to a natural resource for which the agency is a trustee. These screens are to be completed as expeditiously as possible, with a minimal amount of field work, and provide a preliminary identification of the substance released, its source(s), initial estimates of the pathways for the purposes of identifying resources that may be impacted, and further identification of important resources that may justify further assessment.

Natural Resource Trustees

Any federal natural resources management agencies designated in the National Oil and Hazardous Substances Contingency Plan (NCP) and any state agencies designated by the governor of each state, pursuant to Section 107 of CERCLA, that may prosecute claims for damages under Section 107(f) or 111 (b) of CERCLA; or Native American Indian tribes, that may commence an action under Section 126(d) of CERCLA.

Natural Resources (CERCLA; CFR; USC)

Land, fish, wildlife, biota, air, water, groundwater, drinking water supplies, and other such resources belonging to, managed by, held in trust by, appertaining to, or otherwise controlled by the United States (including the resources of the fishery conservation zone established by the Fishery Conservation and Management Act of 1976), any

state or local government, any foreign government, any Indian tribe, or, if such resources are subject to a trust restriction on alienation, any member of a Native American Indian tribe. These natural resources have been categorized into the following five groups:

- 1) surface water resources,
- 2) groundwater resources,
- 3) air resources,
- 4) geologic resources, and
- 5) biological resources.

Natural Selection

The process of survival of the fittest, by which organisms that adapt to their environment survive while those that do not adapt disappear.

Natural Uranium

Uranium as found in nature; containing 0.7% uranium-235, 99.3% of uranium-238, and a trace of uranium-234. It is also called normal uranium.

Naturally Degradable Material

A material that, when discarded, will be reduced to environmentally benign subunits under the action of normal environmental forces, such as, among others, biological decomposition, photodegradation, or hydrolysis.

Naturally Occurring Background Levels

Ambient concentrations of chemicals that are present in the environment and have not been influenced by humans (e.g., aluminum, manganese).

Nautical Chart

See Hydrographic Chart.

Nautical Mile

A measure of distance equal to one minute of arc on the earth's surface. The United States has adopted the international equivalent of 1,852 meters or 6,076.11549 feet.

Nautical Plotting Chart

An outline chart, devoid of hydrographic information, of a specific scale and projection, usually portraying a graticule and compass rose, designed to be ancillary to standard nautical charts, and produced either as an individual chart or a part of a coordinated series.

Nautical Vessel

Any of the following three types of watercraft:

- Boats — a nautical vessel usually under 10 feet long, small enough to be treated as an object, and easily transported for management purposes; may include canal boats, canoes, and other small craft;

- Ships — a larger nautical vessel that is still intact, being treated as a historic structure such as a floating exhibit in a maritime museum; and

- Shipwrecks — remains of a ship found in its original underwater or terrestrial context.

Naval Base

A naval base primarily for support of the forces afloat, contiguous to a port or anchorage, consisting of activities or facilities for which the Navy has operating responsibilities, together with interior lines of communication and the minimum surrounding area necessary for local security. (Normally, not greater than an area of 40 square miles.) *See* Base Complex.

Naval District

A geographically defined area in which one naval officer, designated commandant, is the direct representative of the Secretary of the Navy and the Chief of Naval Operations. The commandant has the responsibility for the coordination of naval activities in the area.

Naval Mobile Environmental Team (NMET)

A team of naval personnel organized, trained, and equipped to support maritime special operations by providing weather, oceanography, mapping, charting, and geodesy support.

Naval Stores

Any articles or commodities used by a naval ship or station, such as equipment, consumable supplies, clothing, petroleum, oils, and lubricants, medical supplies, and ammunition.

Navigable Waters

Traditionally, waters sufficiently deep and wide for navigation by all, or specified sizes of vessels; nowadays, almost any surface water or groundwater body. Such waters in the United States come under federal jurisdiction and are included in certain provisions of the Clean Water Act.

Navigational Grid

A series of straight lines, superimposed over a conformal projection and indicating grid north, used as an aid to navigation. The interval of the grid lines is generally a multiple of 60 or 100 nautical miles. *See* Grid.

Navigation Head

A transshipment point on a waterway where loads are transferred between water carriers and land carriers. A navigation head is similar in function to a railhead or truckhead.

Navy Cargo Handling Force

The combined cargo handling units of the Navy, including primarily the Navy Cargo Handling and Port Group, the Naval Reserve Cargo Handling Training Battalion, and the Naval Reserve Cargo Handling Battalion. These units are part of the operating forces and represent the Navy's capability for open ocean cargo handling.

NAWCC

See North American Wetlands Conservation Council.

NAWFMP

See North American Waterfowl Management Plan of 1986.

NBC Defense
An acronym for Nuclear, Biological, and Chemical Defense [collectively]. *See* Nuclear Defense; Biological Defense; Chemical Defense.

NCA
See National Command Authorities.

NCO
See NEPA Compliance Officers.

NCP
See National Contingency Plan; National Oil and Hazardous Substances Contingency Plan.

NCR
See Nonconformance Report.

Nd:Glass Laser
A solid-state laser of neodymium (Nd) glass offering high power in short pulses. A neodymium doped glass rod used as a laser medium to produce 1064 nanometers of light.

Nd:YAG Laser
Neodymium (Nd) yttrium aluminum garnet; a synthetic crystal used as a laser medium to produce 1064 nanometers of light.

NDE
An acronym for Nondestructive Evaluation.

NDWAC
An acronym for National Drinking Water Advisory Council.

NIRA
An acronym for National Industrial Recovery Act of 1933.

NE
See Nuclear Energy.

Near Surface Disposal Facilities
Land disposal facilities in the upper 30 meters of the earth's surface (e.g., shallow land burial).

Neatlines
The lines that bound the body of a map, usually parallels and meridians. *See* Graticule.

Necessary Preconstruction Approvals or Permits
Those permits or approvals required by the permitting authority as a precondition to undertaking any activity under control by a regulatory agency. Construction, when used in connection with any source or facility, includes the modification of any source or facility.

Necrosis
1) Death of plant or animal cells. 2) Death of areas of tissue or bone, usually as individual cells, as groups of cells, or in localized areas. Necrosis can be caused by cessation of blood supply, physical agents such as radiation, or chemical agents. In plants, necrosis can discolor areas on the plant or kill it entirely.

Nectar
A species descriptor that refers to the secretion from plants that attracts pollinators.

Need to Know
A criterion used in security procedures that requires the custodians of classified information to establish, prior to disclosure, that the intended recipient must have access to the information to perform his/her official duties.

Needle-Leaved Deciduous Woody Gymnosperms
Trees or shrubs with needle-shaped or scalelike leaves that are shed during the cold or dry season.

Needle-Leaved Evergreen Woody Gymnosperms
Green, needle-shaped, or scalelike leaves that are retained by plants throughout the year.

Negative Declaration
A written announcement by a federal agency (having jurisdiction over a proposed real estate development project) stating that due to the lack

of significant adverse impacts, the agency has decided not to prepare an environmental impact statement for the project. The declaration must be issued 90 days prior to commencing with the project, and documentation for the finding must be available for public review.

Negligence

Failure to use the care, professionalism, and/or due diligence as a reasonably prudent and careful person would have used under similar circumstances. *See* Due Diligence.

Negligible Risk

A degree of risk where personnel are reasonably safe, and free from all but de minimis violations, producing little or no hazards.

Nematocide

A chemical agent that is destructive to nematodes (round worms or threadworms).

Nematodes

A species descriptor for invertebrate animals of the phylum nemathelminthes and class nematoda, that is, unsegmented round worms with elongated, fusiform, or saclike bodies covered with cuticle, and inhabiting soil, water, plants, or plant parts; may also be called nemas or eelworms.

Neodymium (Nd)

The rare earth element that is the active element in Nd:YAG and Nd:Glass lasers.

Neolithic

The late stone age, in which agricultural societies began to cultivate food crops and/or experiment with animal husbandry.

Neonatal

Newly born; in humans, up to 6 weeks of age.

Neoplasia

The pathologic process that results in the formation and growth of a tumor. *See* Neoplasm.

Neoplasm

A new and abnormal growth of tissue, such as a tumor.

NEP

See Nuclear Electric Propulsion.

NEPA

An acronym for the National Environmental Policy Act of 1969; the Act established to declare a national policy to encourage productive and enjoyable harmony between man and his/her environment, to promote efforts that will prevent or eliminate damage to the environment and biosphere and stimulate the health and welfare of man; to enrich the understanding of the ecological systems and natural resources important to the nation; and to establish a Council on Environmental Quality. *See* National Environmental Policy Act of 1969.

NEPA Compliance Guides

A collection of written guidance and reference material to assist government staff in both planning for and achieving compliance with NEPA and various related environmental statutes. The Guide, that is updated periodically, provides information on the NEPA process, the content of the NEPA documents, the substantive and timing relationships between NEPA reviews and review requirements of other environmental statutes, and timing relationships between the NEPA process and the development of agency actions.

NEPA Compliance Officers

Federal agency employees at program Offices and Operations Offices, and optionally at other offices, designated to coordinate, assist, and generally oversee the NEPA compliance activities in that office.

NEPA Documents

Environmental assessments, findings of no significant impact, notices of intent to prepare an environmental impact statement, record of decision, categorical exclusion determination, or any other documents prepared pursuant to a requirement of NEPA or the Council on Environmental

Quality Regulations (40 CFR Parts 1500-1508, as amended).

NEPA Status Reports
Reports on the status of existing or planned NEPA compliance activities, that are included in internal budget review documents (i.e., project data sheets or activity data sheets) prepared pursuant to agency orders and regulations.

Nephritis
Inflammation of the kidney.

Nephro
A prefix pertaining to the kidney.

Nephron
The structural and functional unit of the kidney, consisting of capillaries and tubes that adjust the composition of blood and form urine.

Nephrotoxic
Capable of damaging the kidney.

Neritic
A term applied to portions of the ocean that are lying over the Continental Shelf.

Nerve Agent
A potentially lethal chemical agent that interferes with the transmission of nerve impulses.

NESHAPS
See National Emissions Standards for Hazardous Air Pollutants.

Nesslerization
A method for determining the presence of ammonia from its reaction with a mercury complex in alkaline solution.

Nest Site
The geographic area and surrounding habitat that includes the nest tree(s), perch tree(s), screening tree(s), and replacement tree(s) of a bird species of special concern.

Nest Tree
A tree, snag, or other structure that contains the nest of a species of special concern.

Nester
A species that nests.

Net Explosive Weight
The weight of the energy-producing material in munitions.

Net Reserves
The recoverable quantity of an energy resource that can be produced and delivered.

Net Water Savings
A reduction in water demand on primary water sources, such as surface storage reservoirs and groundwater, that results in a net increase in the amount of water made available for use.

Net Weight
1) The weight of a ground vehicle without fuel, engine oil, coolant, on-vehicle material, cargo, or operating personnel. 2) A measure of weight referring only to the contents of a package, not including the weight of any packaging material.

Net Working Capital
Current assets minus current liabilities.

Net Worth
The excess of total assets over total liabilities as determined in accordance with generally accepted accounting principles, and is equivalent to owner's equity. Used in the specifications for the financial tests for closure, post-closure care, liability coverage, and in-kind contributions.

Neuropathy
1) Functional disturbances and/or pathological changes in the peripheral nervous system; a disease involving the cranial or spinal nerves.

Neurotoxicity
Ability to damage nerve tissue.

Neutralization

Decreasing the acidity or alkalinity of a substance by adding to it alkaline or acidic materials, respectively.

Neutralize

To render ineffective or unusable.

Neutron

An elementary particle with a mass slightly greater than that of a proton but without any electric charge. Neutrons are one of the constituents of the atomic nucleus, released during nuclear reactions, and can cause nuclear reactions including nuclear fission.

Neutron Induced Activity

Radioactivity induced in the ground or an object as a result of direct irradiation by neutrons.

Neutron Source

A radioactive material (decays by neutron emission) that can be inserted into a reactor to ensure that a sufficient quantity of neutrons is available to start a chain reaction and register on neutron detection equipment.

Nevada Operations Office (NOO)

The DOE Research and Development and Field Facility, established by the Atomic Energy Commission in 1962. The NOO is responsible for programs at the Nevada Test Site (NTS) and conducts all U.S. nuclear tests, including weapons development and weapons effects. NTS is an integral part of the NOO and does not operate as a separate entity. Located 65 miles northwest of Las Vegas, NTS was chosen as a continental proving ground in 1950 to reduce the expense and logistical problems of testing in the Pacific.

Through NOO site operations, its contractors have developed unique expertise in fields such as big hole drilling, mining and downhole diagnostics in support of the weapons development laboratories and the Department of Defense. Other programs and projects include: waste management; geologic, hydrologic, and seismic investi-

gations; biological and medical experiments; and the effects of liquid gaseous fuel spills.

New Chemical Substance

Chemical substances that are not included in the chemical substance list compiled and published under Section 8(b) [15 USCS 2607(b)].

New Facilities

See New Hazardous Waste Management Facility.

New Hazardous Waste Management Facility

A facility that began operation, or for which construction commenced, after October 21, 1976. *See* Existing Hazardous Waste Management Facilities.

New Motor Vehicle

A motor vehicle the equitable or legal title to which has never been transferred to an ultimate purchaser.

New Solid Waste Incineration Unit

A solid waste incineration unit the construction of which is commenced after the Administrator of EPA proposed requirements establishing emissions standards or other requirements that would be applicable to such unit or a modified solid waste incineration unit.

New Source

See New Sources.

New Source Performance Standards (NSPS)

Uniform national air emission and water effluent standards that limit the amount of pollution allowed from new sources or from existing sources that have been modified. NSPS standards include the following: a) emissions limitations and other requirements applicable to new units and guidelines (under the CAA), including requirements applicable to existing units; b) standards applicable to solid waste incineration units with capacity equal to or less than 250 tons per day combusting municipal waste and units combusting hospital waste, medical waste and infectious waste; and c) standards applicable to solid waste incineration units combusting commercial or industrial waste. In developing SOPs the Administrator, in consultation with representatives of the governors and of state air pollution control agencies considers information on:

- the quantity of air pollutant emissions that each such category will emit, or will be designed to emit;
- the extent to which each such pollutant may reasonably be anticipated to endanger public health or welfare; and
- the mobility and competitive nature of each such category of sources and the consequent need for nationally applicable new source standards of performance.

New Source Performance Standards are found in 40 CFR 60. These standards reflect the best system of emission reduction that (taking into account the cost of achieving such reduction) the EPA Administrator determines has been adequately demonstrated.

New Sources
1) Any stationary sources that are built or modified after publication of final or proposed regulations that prescribe a standard of performance that is intended to apply to that type of emission source. 2) Any building, structure, facility, or installation from which there is or may be a discharge of pollutants, the construction of which is commenced after the publication of proposed regulations prescribing a standard of performance under Section 306 of the Clean Air Act.

New Storage Facilities
Newly constructed facilities, or the conversion of existing facilities, or portions of existing facilities, for use as unirradiated enriched uranium storage facilities.

New Tailings
Uranium tailings produced after the promulgation of 40 CFR 61.251.

New Tailings Impoundment
Any location or structure at which uranium mill tailings are temporarily or permanently stored and that is placed in operation after the promulgation of 40 CFR 61.251.

New Tank Components
Systems or components that will be used for the storage or treatment of hazardous waste and for which installation, or construction, commenced after July 14, 1986. *See* Existing Tank Systems.

New Tank Systems
A tank system that will be used to contain an accumulation of regulated substances and for which installation commenced after December 22, 1988.

New Violation
Any statutory or regulatory violation not reported in a RCRA facility's inspection report.

New York Bight
The area comprised of the Hudson-Raritan Estuary and waters of the Atlantic Ocean (west of Montauk, Long Island, New York, to north of Cape May, New Jersey, and extending seaward to the edge of the Continental Shelf).

New York Bight Apex
The ocean waters of the Atlantic Ocean (northward of $40°10'N$ latitude and westward of $73°30'W$ longitude). Congress and the Administrator have determined that the New York Bight Apex is no longer a suitable location for the ocean dumping of municipal sludge. *See* Apex Site.

NFAWSR
An acronym for North Fork American Wild and Scenic River.

NFIA
An acronym for National Flood Insurance Act of 1968.

NFPA
An acronym for the National Fire Protection Association, located at 470 Atlantic Avenue, Boston, MA 02210.

NGPA

An acronym for Natural Gas Policy Act of 1978 (15 USC 3318).

NH₃

The chemical notation of anhydrous ammonia, a chemical compound composed of nitrogen and hydrogen. It is normally stored and transported as a liquid under pressure. However, in some large storage facilities it is refrigerated and stored at atmospheric pressure.

NHL

See National Historic Landmark.

NHPA

See National Historic Preservation Act of 1966.

NHPAA

An acronym for National Historic Preservation Act Amendments of 1980.

NHPDPA

An acronym for National Health Promotion and Disease Prevention Act of 1976.

Niche

The adaptive positioning of a species within the ecosystem.

NIEHS Studies/Research

NIEHS is an acronym for the National Institute of Environmental Health Sciences, the agency responsible for a program of basic research to identify, characterize, and quantify risks to human health from air pollutants. NIEHS Studies/Research is conducted primarily through a combination of university and medical school-based grants, as well as through intramural studies and contracts.

NIOSH

See National Institute for Occupational Safety and Health.

NIPCC

An acronym for the National Industrial Pollution Control Council (CAA).

NIST

An acronym for National Institute of Standards and Testing.

Nitrate

See Nitrates.

Nitrate Pollution

The contamination of fresh water caused by the leaching of nitrogen-based fertilizers from farmland. Nitrates are highly soluble in water, so this type of pollution is likely to occur after heavy rainfall, and can cause severe illness in infants and cows.

Nitrates

Compounds containing nitrogen that can exist in the atmosphere or as a dissolved gas in water and that can have harmful effects on humans and animals.

Nitric Acid Plants

Facilities producing nitric acid 30% to 70% in strength by either the pressure or atmospheric pressure process.

Nitric Oxides (NO)

Gasses formed by combustion under high temperature and high pressure in an internal combustion engine. It changes into nitrogen dioxide in the ambient air and contributes to photochemical smog.

Nitrification

The process whereby ammonia in wastewater is oxidized to nitrite and then to nitrate by bacterial or chemical reactions.

Nitrilotriacetic Acid (NTA)

A compound being used to replace phosphates in detergents.

Nitrite

1) An intermediate in the process of nitrification.
2) Nitrous oxide salts used in food preservation.

Nitrogen (N)

An odorless, colorless, chemically inactive gas that makes up about 80% of our atmosphere. It is an essential nutrient for plants and is used in fertilizers.

Nitrogen Dioxide (NO2)

A red-brown gas, odorless under atmospheric conditions; the result of nitric oxide combining with oxygen in the atmosphere. A major component of photochemical smog.

Nitrogen Oxide (NOx)

Chemical compounds of nitrogen (N) and oxygen (O). NOx is a major air pollutant, and a product of combustion from transportation and stationary sources and a major contributor to acid deposition and the formation of ground level ozone in the troposphere.

NOx results from incomplete combustion of fossil fuels, a primary source being from automobile exhausts; can be hazardous if concentrations are excessive.

Nitrogenous Wastes

Animal or vegetable residues that contain significant amounts of nitrogen.

NMHC

An acronym for Nonmethane Hydrocarbons (CAA).

NMHC, CO, NOx, PM Standards

The automobile regulations effective with respect to the model year 1994 and thereafter, applicable to emissions of nonmethane hydrocarbons (NMHC), carbon monoxide (CO), oxides of nitrogen (NOx), and particulate matter (PM) from light-duty trucks (LDTs) of up to 6,000 lbs. gross vehicle weight rating (GVWR) and light-duty vehicles (LDVs) that contain standards which provide that emissions from a percentage of each manufacturer's sales volume of such vehicles and

trucks shall comply with the levels specified in the implementation schedule in the following NMHC, CO, PM and NOx Emission tables:

NMHC, CO, and NOx Emission Standards for Light-Duty Trucks (LDTs) and Light-Duty Vehicles (LDVs)[1]

Vehicle Type	NMHC	CO	NOx	PM
LDTs/LDVs (0-3,750 lbs)				
(5 yrs/50,000 mi)	.25	3.4	.4*	
(10 yrs/100,000 mi)	.31	4.2	.6*	
LDTs/LDVs (3,751-5,750 lbs.)				
(5 yrs/50,000 mi)	.32	4.4	.7**	
(10 yrs/100,000 mi)	.40	5.5	.97	
LDTs Diesel (3,751-5,750 lbs.)				
(5 yrs/50,000 mi)	.32	4.4	.7***	
(11 yrs/120,000 mi)	.46	6.4	.98	.10
LDTs Over 5,750 lbs.				
(5 yrs/50,000 mi)	.39	5.0	1.1***	
(11 yrs/120,000 mi)	.56	7.3	1.53	.12

NMHC, CO, AND NOx Emission Standards Implementation Schedule

Vehicle Type	Model year	Percent[2]
LDVs & LDTs	1994	40
(0-5,750)**	1995	80
	after 1995	100
LDVs & LDTs	1996	50
(3,751 and up)	after 1996	100
(including Diesel)		

[1] Standards are expressed in grams per mile (gpm).

[2] Percentages in the table refer to a percentage of each manufacturer's sales volume.

*In the case of diesel-fueled LDTs (0-3,750 lvw) and light-duty vehicles, before the model year 2004, in lieu of the 0.4 and 0.6 standards for NOx, the applicable standards for NOx shall be 1.0 gpm for a useful life of 5 years or 50,000 miles (or the equivalent), whichever first occurs, and 1.25 gpm for a useful life of 10 years or 100,000 miles (or the equivalent) whichever first occurs.

**This standard does not apply to diesel-fueled LDTs (3,751-5,750 lbs. LVW).

***Not applicable to diesel-fueled LDTs.

NMOG

See Nonmethane Organic Gas (CAA).

NO
See Nitric Oxides.

No Action
A Preliminary Assessment (PA) decision that requires no action from members of the public or onsite personnel to reduce exposures to hazardous materials or radiological materials. This action is used primarily to clarify that PAs or PARs have been considered and found to be unnecessary.

No-Burn Day
Any day on which wood burning is prohibited by a state or local government.

No-Observed-Adverse-Effect Level (NOAEL)
1) The highest experimental dose at which there is no statistically or biologically significant increases in frequency or severity of adverse health effects, as seen in the exposed population compared with an appropriate, unexposed population. Effects may be produced at this level, but they are not considered to be adverse. 2) In dose-response experiments, the experimental exposure level representing the highest level tested at which no adverse effects were demonstrated.

No-Observed-Effect Level (NOEL)
In dose-response experiments, the experimental exposure level representing the highest level tested at which no effects at all were demonstrated.

NO₂
Nitrogen Dioxide.

NOAA
See National Oceanic and Atmospheric Administration.

NOAEL
See No-Observed-Adverse-Effect Level.

Nocturnal
A species descriptor that means active at night.

NOD
An acronym for Notice of Deficiency.

Node
A location in a mobility system where a movement requirement is originated, processed for onward movement, or terminated.

Nodulizing Kilns
Units in which phosphate rock is heated to high temperatures to remove organic material and/or to convert it to a nodular form.

NOEL
See No-Observed-Effect Level.

NOHSCP
See National Oil and Hazardous Substances Contingency Plan.

NOI
See Notice of Intent.

Noise Assessment Guidelines
Federal guidelines issued by HUD and used to determine the noise exposure of federally assisted residential projects.

Noise Pollution
Excessive noise in the built environment.

Noise Pollution Abatement
The use of noise suppression circuits and systems.

Noise Zoning
Separation or classification of areas according to the noise levels that result from typical operations and land uses in specific areas.

Nominal Depth
In relation to the stated depth for any navigation improvement project, the depth, including any greater depths that must be maintained for any harbor or inland harbor or element thereof included within such project in order to ensure the

safe passage at mean low tide of any vessel requiring the stated depth.

Nominal Filter
A filter capable of cutting off a nominated minimum percentage by weight of solid particles greater than a stated micron size.

Nominal Hazard Zone (NHZ)
The nominal hazard zone describes the space within which the level of the direct, reflected, or scattered radiation during normal operation exceeds the applicable maximum permissible exposure (MPE). Exposure levels beyond the boundary of the NHZ are below the appropriate MPE level.

Nominal Lamp Watts
The wattage at which a fluorescent lamp is designed to operate.

Nomograph
A diagram for the graphical solution of problems that involve formulas in two or more variables.

Non-Bulk Packaging
Packaging that has a) an internal volume of 460 liters (1 18.9 gallons) or less as a receptacle for a liquid; b) a capacity of 400 kilograms (881.8 pounds) or less as a receptacle for a solid; or c) a water capacity of 1,000 pounds (453.6 kilograms) or less as a receptacle for a gas.

Non-Community Water System
A public water system that is not a community water system, e.g., the water supply at a camp site or national park.

Non-Contact Cooling Water Pollutants
Pollutants present in water used for cooling that do not come into direct contact with any raw material, intermediate product, waste product or finished product.

Non-Detects
Chemicals that are not detected in a particular sample above a certain limit. This limit usually

will be the quantitation limit for the chemical in that sample.

Non-Emergency Respirator
A device designed to provide protection against atmospheres that are not immediately dangerous to life or health.

Non-Federal Agency
Any state or local government, or agency thereof, that receives records contained in a system of records from a source agency for use in a matching program.

Non-Fractionating Plants
Any gas plants that do not fractionate mixed natural gas liquids into natural gas products.

Non-Ionizing Electromagnetic Radiation
1) Radiation that does not change the structure of atoms but does heat tissue and may cause harmful biological effects. 2) Microwaves, radio waves, and low-frequency electromagnetic fields from high-voltage transmission lines.

Non-Isolated Intermediates
Any equipment through which chemical substances pass during a continuous flow process, but not including tanks or other vessels in which the substances are stored after their manufacture.

Non-Liquefied Compressed Gases
Gases, other than in solution, that under the charged pressure are entirely gaseous at a temperature of 70°F.

Non-Native
A species descriptor that means alien to an area; sometimes called "exotic"; not endemic.

Non-Nuclear Facilities
Facilities that meet neither the nuclear nor reactor facility definitions. Office buildings and nonradioactive hazardous waste storage facilities that are staffed by persons whose work does not involve hazardous quantities of radioactive material are examples of nonnuclear facilities.

Non-Operational Storage Tanks

Any underground storage tanks in which regulated substances will not be deposited or from which regulated substances will not be dispensed after the date of the enactment of the Hazardous and Solid Waste Amendments of 1984, enacted on November 8, 1984.

Non-PCB Transformers

Any transformers that contain less that 60 ppm PCB; except that any transformers that have been convened from a PCB Transformer or a PCB-Contaminated transformer cannot be classified as a non-PCB Transformer until reclassification has occurred, in accordance with the requirements of 40 CFR Part-761.

Non-Restricted Access Areas

Any areas other than restricted access, outdoor electrical substations, and other restricted access locations, as defined in this section. In addition to residential/commercial areas, these areas include unrestricted access rural areas (areas of low-density development and population where access is uncontrolled by either manmade barriers or naturally occurring barriers, such as rough terrain, mountains, or cliffs).

Non-Reusable Containers

Containers whose reuse is restricted.

Non-Stochastic Effects

Effects such as the opacity of the ions of the eye for which the severity of the effect varies with the dose, and for which a threshold may exist.

Non-Sudden Accidental Occurrences

Occurrences that take place over time and involve continuous or repeated exposure.

Non-Target Organisms

Those flora and fauna (including man) are not intended to be controlled, injured, killed, or detrimentally affected in any way by a pesticide.

Non-Transient Non-Community Water System

A public water system that is not a community water system and that regularly serves at least 25 of the same persons over 6 months per year.

NON

See Notification of Noncompliance.

Nonattainment Area(s)

For any air pollutant, an area that is shown by monitored data or that is calculated by air quality modeling (or other methods determined by the Administrator to be reliable) to exceed any national ambient air quality standards for the pollutant. Such term includes any area identified under subparagraphs (A) through (C) of Section 7407(d)(1) of the CAA.

Also considered a geographic area that does not meet one or more of the National Ambient Air Quality Standards (NAAQS) for the criteria pollutants designated in the Clean Air Act (CAA).

Nonattainment Classification and Attainment Dates

The five categories of ozone nonattainment areas: Marginal Area, Moderate Area, Serious Area, Severe Area, or Extreme Area (based on the design value for the area) and the attainment dates, pursuant to the CAA. Design values are calculated according to the interpretation methodology issued by the Administrator, and reiterated in the following table:

Nonattainment Classification and Attainment Dates

Area Class	Design Value*	Attainment date**
Marginal	0.121 up to 0.138	Nov. 15, 1993
Moderate	0.138 up to 0.160	Nov. 15, 1996
Serious	0.160 up to 0.180	Nov. 15, 1999
Severe	0.180 up to 0.280	Nov. 15, 2005
Extreme	0.280 and above	Nov. 15, 2010

*The design value is measured in parts per million (ppm).

**The primary standard attainment date is measured from November 15,1990.

Nonattainment Plan

The plan and provisions required to be submitted under the CAA to provide for the implementation of all reasonably available control measures as expeditiously as practicable (including such reductions in emissions from existing sources in the area as may be obtained through the adoption, at a minimum, of reasonably available control technology) and provide for attainment of the national primary ambient air quality standards.

The plan includes a comprehensive, accurate, current inventory of actual emissions from all sources of relevant pollutants in the planning area, including implementation procedures for conducting periodic revisions to ensure that the requirements of the CAA are met. The plan also identifies and quantifies emissions, if any, of any such pollutant or pollutants that will be allowed, from the construction and operation of major new or modified stationary sources in each planning area.

The plan must demonstrate to the satisfaction of the Administrator that the emissions quantified for this purpose will be consistent with the achievement of reasonable further progress and will not interfere with attainment of the applicable national ambient air quality standard by the applicable attainment date. Plan provisions include enforceable emission limitations, and such other control measures, means or techniques (including economic incentives such as fees, marketable permits, and auctions of emission rights), as well as schedules and timetables for compliance, as may be necessary or appropriate to provide for attainment of such standard in such area by the applicable attainment date specified in the CAA. Such plan shall provide for the implementation of specific contingency measures to be undertaken if the area fails to make reasonable further progress, or to attain the national primary ambient air quality standard by the attainment date applicable under the CAA.

Noncardiogenic Pulmonary Edema

An accumulation of an excessive amount of fluid in the lungs as a result of leakage from pulmonary capillaries, not due to heart failure.

Nonconfidential Business Data

Information excluded from Confidential Business Information treatment; data includes, but is not limited to, a) waste disposal facts including identities, quantities, and locations of such waste; b) information contained in or referred to in any manifest for any chemical disposed of on-site; c) monitoring data or analysis of such data pertaining to on-site disposal activities; d) state or federal permit applications; e) any data on planned improvements in the treatment, storage, or disposal of chemical wastes at any defendant/respondent owned facility; f) hydrogeologic or geologic data; g) groundwater monitoring data; h) any contingency plans, closure plans or post-closure plans; i) waste analysis plans; j) any training and/or inspection manuals and schedules; and k) any point source discharge or receiving water monitoring data.

Nonconventional Pollutant

Any pollutant that is not statutorily listed or that is poorly understood by the scientific community.

Nondestructive Inspection (NDI)

A process or procedure for determining material or part characteristics without permanently altering the test subject. Nondestructive testing is commonly used in conducting asbestos and lead-based paint surveys.

Nonfixed Radioactive Contamination

Radioactive contamination that can be readily removed from a surface by wiping with an absorbent material.

Nonfixed Medical Treatment Facility

A medical treatment facility designed to be moved from place to place, including medical treatment facilities afloat.

Nonflammable Compressed Gases

Any compressed gases that do not meet the definition as flammable compressed gases are considered as nonflammable compressed gases for the purpose of the hazardous materials regulations.

Nonformal Complaint

1) Any complaint, such as oral complaints filed by employees; unsigned written complaints. 2) Written and oral complaints filed by nonemployees (persons or groups other than current employees or their representatives). 3) Complaints of hazards not covered by a regulation, standard, or by the general duty clause. 4) Complaints of violations of regulations, such as recordkeeping violations (rather than of standards). 5) Complaints of violations of standards that are classified as de minimis.

Nongame Fish and Wildlife

Wild vertebrate animals that are in an unconfined state and that a) are not ordinarily taken for sport, fur, or food, except that if under applicable state law, any of such animals may be taken in some, but not all, areas of the state, any of such animals within any area of the state in which such taking is not permitted may be deemed to be nongame fish and wildlife; b) are not listed as endangered species or threatened species under the Endangered Species Act of 1973 (16 USC 1531-1543); and c) are not marine mammals.

Nonimpervious Solid Surfaces

Solid surfaces that are porous and are more likely to absorb spilled PCBs prior to completion of the cleanup requirements prescribed in this policy. Nonimpervious solid surfaces include, but are not limited to, wood, concrete, asphalt, and plasterboard.

Nonindigenous Species

Any species or other viable biological material that enters an ecosystem beyond its historic range, including any such organism transferred from one country into another.

Nonmethane Organic Gas (NMOG)

The sum of nonoxygenated and oxygenated hydrocarbons contained in a gas sample, including, at a minimum, all oxygenated organic gases containing five or fewer carbon atoms (i.e., aldehydes, ketones, alcohols, ethers); all known alkanes, alkenes, alkynes, and aromatics containing twelve or fewer carbon atoms. To demonstrate compliance with a NMOG standard, NMOG emissions are measured in accordance with the *California Nonmethane Organic Gas Test Procedures.*

Nonparametric Statistics

Statistical tests used, primarily, for environmental data that is hard to quantify and where the form of the facility/project is uncertain. Applies to data measured by rank ordering and prioritization, rather than quantification. Some nonparametric statistical tests are rank correlation coefficient, rank-sum test, and signed-rank test.

Nonpenetrating Radiation

A general term used to describe external radiations of such low penetrating power that the absorbed dose from exposures to humans is principally in the skin and does not reach other organs to any significant extent. It refers to alpha, beta, and very low energy gamma or X-ray radiations.

Nonpersistent Emergents

Emergent hydrophytes whose leaves and stems break down at the end of the growing season so that most aboveground portions of the plants are easily transported by currents, waves, or ice. The breakdown may result from normal decay or the physical force of strong waves or ice. At certain seasons of the year there are no visible traces of the plants above the surface of the water; e.g., wild rice (*Zizania aquatica*) and arrow arum (*Peltandra virginica*).

Nonpoint Sources

Pollution sources that are diffuse and do not have a single point of origin or are not introduced into a receiving stream from a specific outlet. Generalized discharge of waste into the air, or water, whose specific source cannot be located. The pollutants are generally carried off the land by stormwater runoff. The commonly used categories for nonpoint sources are: agriculture, forestry, urban, mining, construction, dams and channels, land disposal, and saltwater intrusion.

Nonprofit Organization

1) A nonprofit organization holding an exemption under Section 501(c) of Title 26. 2) A nonprofit association or nonprofit corporation, that is not controlled or owned by profitmaking corporations or business enterprises, and that is engaged in public or semipublic activity to further public health, safety, or welfare. 3) An organization that has current tax-exempt status under the laws of a state.

Nonrecurring Demand

A request by an authorized requisitioner to satisfy a material requirement known to be a one-time occurrence. This material is required to provide initial stockage allowances, to meet planned program requirements, or to satisfy a one-time project or maintenance requirement. Nonrecurring demands normally will not be considered by the supporting supply system in the development of demand-based elements of the requirements computation.

Nonrestricted Access Areas

Any area other than outdoor electrical substations and other restricted access locations. In addition to residential and commercial areas, these areas include unrestricted access rural areas (areas of low-density development and population where access is uncontrolled by either manmade or naturally occurring barriers, such as fences, rough terrain, mountains, or cliffs).

Nonroad Vehicle

A vehicle that is powered by a nonroad engine and that is not a motor vehicle or a vehicle used solely for competition.

Nonroad Engine

An internal combustion engine (including the fuel system) that is not used in a motor vehicle or a vehicle used solely for competition, or that is not subject to standards promulgated under Section 7411 or 7521 of the CAA.

Nonthreshold Toxicant

An agent considered to produce a toxic effect from any dose; any level of exposure is deemed to involve some risk. Usually used only in regard to carcinogenesis.

NORM

An acronym for Naturally Occurring Radioactive Materials.

Normal Form

1) Those materials that, by nature of their physical form or encapsulation, if released from their packaging might present some possibility of contamination as well as direct radiation. 2) Radioactive materials that have not been demonstrated to qualify as special form radioactive materials. *See* Special Form Radioactive Materials.

North American Waterfowl Management Plan (NAWFMP)

The plan signed by the Minister of the Environment for Canada and the Secretary of the Interior for the United States in May 1986.

North American Wetlands Conservation Council (NAWCC)

The nine-member council established to recommend wetlands conservation projects to the Migratory Bird Conservation Commission based on the following considerations: a) the extent to which the wetlands conservation project fulfills the purposes of the Wetlands Resources Act (WRA), the National Wetlands Priority Conservation Plan (NWPCP), or Agreement; b) the availability of sufficient nonfederal monies to carry out any wetlands conservation project and to match federal contributions; c) the extent to which any wetlands conservation project represents a partnership among public agencies and private entities; d) the consistency of any wetlands conservation project in the United States with the National Wetlands Priority Conservation Plan developed under the WRA; e) the extent to which any wetlands conservation project would aid the conservation of migratory nongame birds, other fish and wildlife and species that are listed, or are candidates to be listed, as threatened and endangered under the Endangered Species Act; f) the substantiality of the character and design of the wetlands conservation project; and g) the recommendations of any partnerships among public agencies and private entities in Canada, Mexico, or the United States that are participating actively in carrying out one or more wetlands conservation projects under the Act, the Plan, or Agreements made pursuant to the Act or Plan.

Northwest U.S.
The region comprised of the following states, and areas: Washington, Oregon, Idaho, Montana, Wyoming, northern Nevada, and southwestern Canada.

Not Seriously Injured (NSI)
The casualty status of a person a) whose injury may or may not require hospitalization; b) medical authority does not classify as very seriously injured, seriously injured, or as having an incapacitating illness or injury; and c) the person can communicate with officials. *See* Casualty Status.

Not Feasible to Prescribe or Enforce
As related to an emission standard means, any situation in which the Administrator of EPA determines that a) a hazardous air pollutant or pollutants cannot be emitted through a conveyance designed and constructed to emit or capture such pollutant, or that any requirement for, or use of, such a conveyance would be inconsistent with any federal, state, or local law; or b) the application of measurement methodology to a particular class of sources is not practicable due to technological and economic limitations.

Notice
A written notice indicating the taking of an adverse action or rejection during probationary period.

Notice of Availability (NOA)
A formal notice, published in the Federal Register, that announces the issuance and public availability of a draft or final Environmental Impact Statement. The Environmental Protection Agency Notice of Availability is the official public notification of an Environmental Impact Statement; a DOE Notice of Availability is an optional notice used to provide information to the public.

Notice of Intent (NOI)
1) A formal NEPA memorandum prepared by a federal agency, that states a draft environmental impact statement will be prepared and processed and that it will be circulated among federal, state, and local agencies, as well as any interested individuals. 2) A NEPA notice that briefly a) describes the proposed action and possible alternatives; b) describes an agency's proposed scoping process including whether, when, and where any scoping meeting(s) will be held; and c) state the name and address of a contact person within the agency who can answer questions about the proposed action and the environmental impact statement. 3) A document, defined at 40 CFR 1608.22, that announces the intent to prepare an Environmental Impact Statement for a proposed action.

Notice of Involvement
A brief notice published in the Federal Register and circulated to affected and interested persons and agencies, that describes a proposed floodplain/wetlands action and affords the opportunity for public review.

Notice of Violation (NOV)
A formal document completed by regulatory agencies as a result of established violations at or by a hazardous waste facility, transporter, or generator. This official notification is a legal document directing the violator to correct violations of existing environmental laws, and may include or be followed by fines.

Notification
The actions taken to notify cognizant agency officials of an occurrence, and the subsequent actions taken at successive levels within the agency to notify the violator of additional steps to be taken and senior officials within the agency of the occurrence.

Notification Report
A written notification submitted by the Operations Manager (or designee) within 24 hours of an occurrence that details known facts about the occurrence and actions taken.

NOV
    See Notice of Violation.

NOx
    See Nitrogen Oxide.

NOx Control
    A demonstration to the satisfaction of the Administrator that NOx control may be substituted for VOC control or may be combined with VOC control in order to maximize the reduction in ozone air pollution, pursuant to a state implementation plan, as revised. In accord with such, a lesser percentage of VOCs may be accepted as an adequate demonstration for purposes of the CAA.

NOx and VOC Study
    The EPA study on the role of ozone precursors in tropospheric ozone formation and control. The study examines the roles of NOx and VOC emission reductions, the extent to which NOx reductions may contribute (or be counterproductive) to achievement of attainment in different nonattainment areas, the sensitivity of ozone to the control of NOx, the availability and extent of controls for NOx, the role of biogenic VOC emissions, and the basic information required for air quality models.

NPAR
    An acronym for Nuclear Plant Aging Research Program.

NPCCI
    An acronym for Notification Procedures for Confidential Commercial Information.

NPDES
    A permit for the discharge of pollutants into the waters of the U.S. under the National Pollutant Discharge Elimination System pursuant to the Federal Clean Water Pollution Act.

NPL
    See National Priorities List (CERCLA).

NPRA
    An acronym for National Parks and Recreation Act of 1978.

NPRDS
    An acronym for Nuclear Plant Reliability Data System.

NRC
    See Nuclear Regulatory Commission; National Response Center.

NRC-Licensed Facilities
    Any facilities licensed by the Nuclear Regulatory Commission (NRC) or any agreement state, to receive title to, receive, possess, use, transfer, or deliver any source, byproduct, or special nuclear material, except facilities regulated by 40 CFR Parts 190, 191, or 192.

NRDC
    An acronym for Natural Resource Defense Council.

NRHP
    See National Register of Historic Places.

NRO
    An acronym for National Reconnaissance Office.

NRT
    See National Response Team; National Recreation Trail.

NRTAC
    See National Recreational Trails Advisory Committee.

NRTF
    An acronym for National Recreational Trails Fund.

NSAC
    An acronym for Nuclear Safety Analysis Center.

NSC
See National Security Council.

NSPKTR
A computer code to analyze probabilistic risk assessment (PRA) information; developed at the Brookhaven National Laboratory.

NSPS
See New Source Performance Standards.

NTA
See Nitrilotriacetic Acid.

Nth Country
A reference to additions to the group of powers possessing nuclear weapons; the next country of a series to acquire nuclear capabilities.

NTNCWS
An acronym for Nontransient Noncommunity Water System.

NTP
An acronym for Nuclear Thermal Propulsion.

NTS
An acronym for Nevada Test Site.

NTSA
An acronym for National Trails System Act.

NUATRC
See Mickey Leland National Urban Air Toxics Research Center.

Nuchal
A species descriptor that means pertaining to the neck; in insects, the dorsal region of the thorax.

Nuclear Accident
See Nuclear Incident; Nuclear Weapons Accident.

Nuclear Accident Dosimeter
A device containing several materials responsive to different amounts and energies of neutron and gamma radiation.

Nuclear Airburst
The explosion of a nuclear weapon in the air, at a height greater than the maximum radius of the fireball. *See* Types of Burst.

Nuclear Byproduct Material License
A license issued to a facility owner or operator by a federal agency pursuant to the conditions of the Atomic Energy Act of 1954 (as amended) or issued by an agreement state pursuant to appropriate state laws.

Nuclear Certifiable
Indicates a unit or vehicle possessing the potential of passing functional tests and inspections of all normal and emergency systems affecting the nuclear weapons.

Nuclear Certified Delivery Unit
Any level of organization and support elements that are capable of executing nuclear missions in accordance with appropriate bilateral arrangements and NATO directives. *See* Nuclear Delivery Unit.

Nuclear Certified Delivery Vehicle
A delivery vehicle whose compatibility with a nuclear weapon has been certified by the applicable nuclear power through formal procedures.

Nuclear Cloud
An all-inclusive term for the volume of hot gases, smoke, dust, and other particulate matter from the nuclear bomb itself and from its environment, that is carried aloft in conjunction with the rise of the fireball produced by the detonation of the nuclear weapon.

Nuclear Collateral Damage
Undesired damage or casualties produced by the effects from friendly nuclear weapons.

Nuclear Column

A hollow cylinder of water and spray thrown up from an underwater burst of a nuclear weapon, through which the hot, high-pressure gases formed in the explosion are vented to the atmosphere. A somewhat similar column of dirt is formed in an underground explosion.

Nuclear Commitment

A statement by a NATO member that specific forces have been committed or will be committed to NATO in a nuclear only or dual capable role.

Nuclear Criticality

A self-sustaining chain reaction; that is, the state in which the effective neutron multiplication constant of a system of fissionable material equals or exceeds unity.

Nuclear Criticality Safety

The prevention or termination of inadvertent nuclear criticality, mitigation of consequences, and protection against injury or damage due to an accidental nuclear ethicality.

Nuclear Damage

The three categories of nuclear damage are a) Light Damage — damage that does not prevent the immediate use of equipment or installations for which it was intended. Some repair by the user may be required to make full use of the equipment or installations; b) Moderate Damage — damage that prevents the use of equipment or installations until extensive repairs are made; and c) Severe Damage — damage that prevents use of equipment or installations permanently.

Nuclear Damage Assessment

The determination of the damage effect to population, facilities, and resources resulting from actual nuclear attack. It is performed during and after an attack. The operational significance of the damage is not evaluated in this assessment.

Nuclear Defense

The methods, plans, and procedures involved in establishing and exercising defensive measures against the effects of an attack by nuclear weapons or radiological warfare agents. It encompasses both the training for, and the implementation of, these methods, plans, and procedures. *See* NBC Defense; Radiological Defense.

Nuclear Emergency Search Teams

Groups of DOE and DOE contractor experts assigned responsibility to provide assistance without geographical limitations following a nuclear threat. Resources include radiation detection systems and personnel for searching and identifying lost or stolen nuclear weapons or special nuclear materials, responding to radiation dispersal threats, and providing assistance in disabling devices or mitigating their effects.

Nuclear Energy

All forms of energy released in the course of a nuclear fission or nuclear transformation.

Nuclear Energy Center Site

Any site large enough to support utility operations or other elements of the total nuclear fuel cycle, including, nuclear fuel reprocessing facilities, nuclear fuel fabrication plants, retrievable nuclear waste storage facilities, and uranium enrichment facilities.

Nuclear Energy Survey

A regional evaluation of natural resources (land, air, and water) available for use in connection with nuclear energy center sites, including:
a) estimates of future electric power requirements that can be served by each nuclear energy center site;
b) an assessment of the economic impact of each nuclear energy site; and consideration of any other relevant factors, including but not limited to population distribution, proximity to electric load centers and to other elements of the fuel cycle, transmission line rights-of-way, and the availability of other fuel resources;
c) an evaluation of the environmental impact likely to result from construction and operation of such nuclear energy centers, including an evaluation whether such nuclear energy centers will

result in greater or lesser environmental impact than separate siting of the reactors and/or fuel cycle facilities; and

d) consideration of the use of federally owned property and other property designated for public use, but excluding national parks, national forests, national wilderness areas, and national historic monuments.

Nuclear Engineering

The branch of professional engineering that encompasses, but is not limited to, the planning and design of the specialized equipment and process systems of nuclear reactor facilities; and the protection of the public from any hazardous radiation produced in the entire nuclear reaction process. These activities include all aspects of the manufacture, transportation, and use of radioactive materials. Nuclear engineers apply the principles of nuclear physics to the engineering utilization of nuclear phenomena for the benefit of mankind, and are primarily concerned with the protection of the public from the potential hazards of radiation and radioactive materials, including the interaction of radiation and nuclear particles with matter.

The field requires the application of specialized knowledge of the mathematical and physical sciences, together with the principles and methods of engineering design and nuclear analysis to specify, predict, and evaluate the behavior of systems involving nuclear reactions, and to ensure the safe, efficient operation of these systems, their nuclear products, and byproducts.

Nuclear Exoatmospheric Burst

The explosion of a nuclear weapon above the sensible atmosphere (above 120 kilometers) where atmospheric interaction is minimal. *See* Types of Burst.

Nuclear Facilities

Facilities whose operations involve radioactive materials in such form and quantity that a significant nuclear hazard potentially exists to the employees or the general public. Included are facilities that a) produce, process, or store radio-active liquid or solid waste, fissionable materials, or tritium; b) conduct separations operations; c) conduct irradiated materials inspection, fuel fabrication, decontamination, or recovery operations; or d) conduct fuel enrichment operations. Incidental use of radioactive materials in a facility operation (e.g., check sources, radioactive sources, and X- ray machines) does not require the facility to be included in this definition. Accelerators and reactors and their operations are not included.

Nuclear Facilities Incident Database

The database sponsored by DOE's Offices of Environment, Safety, and Health (ESH) and Defense Programs (DP) for the storage, analysis, and retrieval of reactor incident/event reports from the Savannah River Site (SRS) near Aiken, South Carolina.

Nuclear Fission

The splitting of large atomic nuclei into two or more new nuclear species, with the release of large amounts of energy.

Nuclear Fuel Cycle

The complete cycle of nuclear activities that includes mining, milling, conversion, enrichment, fuel fabrication, nuclear power plant operation, spent fuel storage, reprocessing (if applicable), and waste management operations.

Nuclear Fusion

A nuclear reaction where the nuclei of light atoms are fused to form heavier atoms with the release of energy. These reactions occur with the explosion of hydrogen bombs.

Nuclear Incident

An unexpected event involving a nuclear weapon, facility, or component, resulting in any of the following, but not constituting a nuclear weapon(s) accident: a) an increase in the possibility of explosion or radioactive contamination; b) errors committed in the assembly, testing, loading, or transportation of equipment, and/or the malfunctioning of equipment and material that could lead to an unintentional operation of all or part of the weapon arming and/or firing sequence, or which could lead to a substantial change in yield, or increased dud probability; and c) any act of God, unfavorable environment, or condition resulting in damage to the weapon, facility, or component within, or outside, the United States, resulting in bodily injury, sickness, disease, or death, or loss of or damage to property.

Nuclear Materials Management and Standards System
A reporting and analytical system used in safeguarding and managing nuclear materials.

Nuclear Poisons
1) Substances with large neutron cross sections. 2) Neutron absorbers in a reactor.

Nuclear Power Plant
Any device, machine, or assembly that converts fission nuclear energy into some form of useful power, such as electrical power; heat produced by a reactor makes steam to drive turbines that produce electricity.

Nuclear Radiation
Particulate and electromagnetic radiation emitted from atomic nuclei in various nuclear processes. The important nuclear radiations, from the environmental standpoint, are alpha and beta particles, gamma rays, and neutrons. All nuclear radiations are ionizing radiations, but the reverse is not true; X-rays for example, are included among ionizing radiations, but they are not nuclear radiations since they do not originate from atomic nuclei.

Nuclear Reactor
1) A facility in which fissile material is used in a self-supporting chain reaction (nuclear fission) to produce heat and/or radiation for both practical application and research and development. 2) A device, machine, or assembly that converts controlled fission nuclear energy of atoms of uranium-235 into some form of useful power, such as electrical power. The center of the thermal fission reactor is the core, that consists of a moderator in which a critical mass of fuel elements and regulatory rods are inserted. The moderator

slows down the escaping neutrons emitted by the uranium-235, without absorbing them, so they can alternatively bombard other uranium atoms, resulting in more fissions and releasing more neutrons, in a more or less self-perpetuating energy cycle. The energy is released as heat and other radiation. Reactors such as the fast-breeder reactor don't use moderators. *See* Liquid-Metal Fast Breeder Reactor.

Nuclear Regulatory Commission (NRC)
The federal agency responsible for permitting the construction and operation of nuclear reactors, and enforcing regulatory requirements for safety, pursuant to the Atomic Energy Act of 1954, as amended, and covered by provisions under Section 170(a) of that Act.

Nuclear Regulatory Commission Licensed Activities
Activities licensed pursuant to the Atomic Energy Act of 1954, as amended, and covered by provisions under Section 170(a) of that Act.

Nuclear Repository
Any system licensed by the NRC that is intended to be used for, or may be used for, the permanent deep geologic disposal of high-level radioactive waste and spent nuclear fuel, whether or not such system is designed to permit the recovery, for a limited period during initial operation, of any materials placed in such system. Such term includes both surface and subsurface areas at which high-level radioactive waste and spent nuclear fuel handling activities are conducted.

Nuclear Site Characterization
1) Siting research activities with respect to a test and evaluation facility at a candidate site. 2) Activities, whether in the laboratory or in the field, undertaken to establish the geologic condition and the ranges of the parameters of a candidate site relevant to the location of a repository, including borings, surface excavations, excavations of exploratory shafts, limited subsurface lateral excavations and borings, and insitu testing needed to evaluate the suitability of a candidate site for the location of a repository, but not including pre-

liminary borings and geophysical testing needed to assess whether site characterization should be undertaken.

Nuclear Test Facility

An at-depth, prototypic, underground cavity with subsurface lateral excavations extending from a central shaft that is used for research and development purposes, including the development of data and experience for the safe handling and disposal of solidified high-level radioactive waste, transuranic waste, or spent nuclear fuel.

Nuclear Threat Incidents

Situations involving the threatened, attempted, or actual theft, loss, unauthorized possession of source or special nuclear material, radioactive by-products, nuclear explosive devices, improvised devices (either separately or in combination with explosives), or radioactive dispersal devices, or the threatened use of said items.

Nuclear Transmutation

Artificially induced modification (nuclear reaction) of the constituents of certain nuclei, thus giving rise to different nuclides.

Nuclear Vulnerability Assessment

The estimation of the probable effect on population, facilities, and resources from a hypothetical nuclear attack.

Nuclear Waste

See High-Level Wastes; Low-Level Radioactive Waste.

Nuclear Weapon

A complete assembly (i.e., implosion type, gun type, or thermonuclear type), in its intended ultimate configuration that upon completion of the prescribed arming, fusing, and firing sequence, is capable of producing a nuclear reaction and release of energy.

Nuclear Weapons Accidents

Unexpected events involving nuclear weapons or radiological nuclear weapon components that re-sult in any of the following: a) accidental or unauthorized launching, firing, or use of a nuclear explosive; b) nuclear detonation; c) nonnuclear detonation/burning of a nuclear weapon; d) radioactive contamination; e) seizure, theft, or loss of a nuclear weapon or an actual component of a nuclear weapon; and f) public hazard, actual or implied.

Nuclear Winter

A term referring to the prediction by some scientists that smoke and debris rising from massive fires resulting from a nuclear war could enter the atmosphere and block out sunlight for weeks or months. The scientists making this prediction project a cooling of the earth's surface, and changes in climate that could, for example, negatively affect world agricultural and weather patterns.

Nuclear Yields

The energy released in the detonation of a nuclear weapon, measured in terms of the kilotons or megatons of trinitrotoluene required to produce the same energy release. Yields are categorized as a) very low — less than 1 kiloton; b) low — 1 kiloton to 10 kilotons; c) medium — over 10 kilotons to 50 kilotons; d) high — over 50 kilotons to 500 kilotons; and e) very high — over 500 kilotons.

Nucleon

The common name for a constituent particle of the atomic nucleus. It is applied to protons and neutrons, but it is intended to include any other particle that is found to exist in the nucleus.

Nucleus

The structure within the cell that contains the chromosomes and the nucleolus. The nucleus controls cellular function, both chemical reactions that occur in the cell, and reproduction of the cell. Also, the part of an atom containing protons and neutrons.

Nuclides

1) All nuclear species, both stable (about 270) and unstable (about 500), of the chemical elements, as

distinguished from the two or more nuclear species of a single chemical element that are called isotopes. 2) A species of atom characterized by a mass number, atomic number, and energy state of its nucleus, provided that the atom is capable of existing for a measurable time. 3) A species of atom characterized by the constitution of its nucleus.

Nuehal Hump
A species descriptor that means any hump on the nape of the neck.

Nuisance Dust
A dust not considered a direct contributable factor in lung disease.

Nuisance
A general term that includes, but is not limited to, a) any public nuisance known as common law or in equity jurisprudence; b) whatever is dangerous to human life or is detrimental to health; and c) whatever renders air, food, or drink unwholesome or detrimental to the health of human beings.

Nutrient
1) Any substance assimilated by living things that promotes growth. The term is generally applied to nitrogen and phosphorus in wastewater, but is also applied to other essential and trace elements. 2) A food substance that promotes growth.

NVLAP
An acronym for EPA's National Voluntary Laboratory Accreditation Program.

NWPA
An acronym for Nuclear Waste Policy Act.

NWPCP
An acronym for National Wetlands Priority Conservation Plan.

NWPS
An acronym for National Wilderness Preservation System.

NWRS
An acronym for National Wildlife Refuge System.

NWTRB
An acronym for Nuclear Waste Technical Review Board.

Nystagmus
Involuntary rapid (rhythmic or jerky) movements of the eyeballs.

O

O&M
See Operations and Maintenance.

O₃

O3
Ozone.

OAA
An acronym for Older Americans Act of 1965.

OACSEA
An acronym for Older Americans Community Services Employment Act.

Oak Ridge Operations Office
A DOE Research and Development and Field Facility, established under the Atomic Energy Commission in 1942. The principal programs of the Office are the production of nuclear weapon components in support of national defense programs, production of enriched uranium for defense requirements and for fueling nuclear power plants in the U.S. and abroad, processing of uranium materials and fuel cores for DOE's plutonium production reactors and extensive energy research and development in all DOE program areas. In addition, the Office provides assistance to local, state and federal government agencies and the private sector, and administers DOE contracts with universities in the Southeast. The Office reservation serves as a national environmental research site.

Oak Ridge Associated Universities (ORAU)
A private, not-for-profit association comprised of 55 colleges and universities. ORAU conducts research and educational programs in energy, health and the environment for DOE, member institutions of ORAU, other colleges and universities and private and governmental organizations.

Oak Ridge National Laboratory (ORNL)
The DOE Research and Development and Field Facility, founded in 1943. ORNL primarily supports the fission nuclear fuel cycle and development of magnetic fusion energy through scientific research and technology. In addition, ORNL identifies and solves generic research problems in energy technologies such as materials, separation techniques, chemical processes and biotechnology and is the major national source of stable and radioactive isotopes.

OAR
An acronym for Operation Assessment and Readiness.

OBA
See Operating Basis Accident.

OBE
See Operating Basis Earthquake.

OBES
An acronym for Office of Basic Energy Sciences.

Object Conservation

A term referring to the measures taken to prolong the life of a museum object. The primary goal is to preserve — in an unchanging, stabilized state — whatever still exists of an original object as much as possible. In the National Park Service, museum object conservation encompasses the following two functions a) preservation — the action taken to prevent damage and to minimize deterioration of an object by practicing preventive conservation or by performing a suitable treatment on an object itself; and/or b) restoration — the action that often refers to the attempt to return an object to its original appearance by removing accretions, later applied additions, and/or by replacing missing elements.

Oblanceolate

A species descriptor that means broader and rounded at the apex (tip) and tapering at the base.

Obligate Hydrophytes

Species that are found in wetlands (i.e., bogs, marshes, lakes).

Obligate Lacustrine Suckers

A species descriptor that means fish (suckers) that can survive only in lakes.

Obligate Nose Breathers

Animals that must breathe through the nose rather than through the mouth. Beyond the infant stage, humans may breathe either through the nose or mouth but this difference is significant when comparing effects between obligate nose breathers (e.g., rats, mice) and humans as the nasopharyngeal region can remove a proportion (often significant) of inhaled toxicants before they reach the lungs. When humans breathe through the mouth, early removal does not occur.

Oblique Air Photograph

An air photograph taken with the camera axis directed between the horizontal and vertical planes. Commonly referred to as an "oblique." "High oblique" is a photograph in which the apparent horizon appears. "Low oblique" is a photograph in which the apparent horizon does not appear.

Oblique Slip (USGS)

A combination of strike-slip and dip-slip fault movement; movement or slip that is intermediate in orientation between the dip-slip and the strike-slip. Also called a diagonal-slip fault.

Obliquity

The characteristic in wide-angle or oblique photography that portrays the terrain.

OBRA

An acronym for Omnibus Budget Reconciliation Act of 1990.

Observation Well

A well drilled in a selected location for the purpose of observing parameters such as water levels and pressure changes. A nonpumping well used to observe the elevation of the water table or the potentiometric surface. An observation well is generally of larger diameter than a piezometer and typically is screened or slotted throughout the thickness of the aquifer.

Observer

An individual who observes an emergency response drill or exercise and has no responsibility as a controller or evaluator. An observer has no interaction with any drill or exercise participant; any interaction with the conduct of a drill or exercise is through an identified controller.

Obsolescence

Impairment of desirability and usefulness of the property resulting from economic, functional, physical, fashion, or other changes.

Obstacle

Any obstruction designed or employed to disrupt, fix, turn, or block movement, and to impose additional losses in personnel response time and equipment deployment. Obstacles can exist naturally or can be manmade, or can be a combination of both.

Obstruction, Water Flow

Any dam, wall, wharf, embankment, levee, dike, pile, pump, abutment, projections, excavation, bridge, conduit, culvert, building, fence, rock, gravel, refuse, fill, house, barn, storage building, or other analogous structure or matter that may unduly impede, retard, or change the direction of the flow of water — either in itself, by catching or collecting debris carried by such water, or by placing the debris where the flow of the water would carry the debris downstream to the damage or detriment of either life or property.

OCAW

An acronym for Oil Chemical and Atomic Workers.

Occupational Doses

Exposure of individuals to radiation, or toxic substances a) in a restrictive area; or b) in the course of employment in which the individual's duties involve such exposure, provided that occupational dose shall not be deemed to include any exposure of an individual for the purpose of medical diagnosis or medical therapy of such individual.

Occupational Exposure

Exposure of a worker during a period of work.

Occupational Exposure Limit (OEL)

A generic term denoting a variety of values and standards, generally time-weighted average concentrations of airborne substances, to which a worker can be exposed during defined work periods.

Occupational Illnesses

Abnormal physical conditions or disorders of an employee, other than one resulting from an occupational injury, caused by exposure to environmental factors associated with employment. It includes, but may not be limited to, acute and chronic illnesses or diseases that may be caused by inhalation, absorption, ingestion, direct contact, or radiation.

Occupational Injuries

Any injuries, such as cuts, fractures, sprains, or amputations, that result from a work-related accident or from exposure to the work environment. In some cases, an employer may classify an exposure to chemicals or toxic agents as an injury when there is a single traumatic event associated with the exposure.

Occupational Medical Program

A program to a) ensure the health and safety of employees in their work environments through the application of occupational medical principles; b) determine the physical and mental fitness of employees to perform job assignments without undue hazard to themselves, fellow employees, or the public at large; c) ensure the early detection and treatment of employee illness or injuries by means of scheduled periodic health evaluations and unscheduled employee health visits; and d) contribute to the maintenance of employee health through the application of preventive medical measures, such as immunizations, alcohol and drug abuse programs, and health counseling.

Occupational Medicine

A specialty branch of the profession of medicine that deals with the health protection and health maintenance of employees, with special reference to job hazards, job stresses, and work environment hazards.

Occupational Safety and Health Administration (OSHA)

An agency of the U.S. Department of Labor, established under Public Law 91-596 with major responsibilities to promulgate, prescribe, and enforce occupational safety and health standards. OSHA issues standards and rules for safe and healthful working conditions, tools, equipment, facilities, and processes. Employers have the general duty of providing their workers a place of employment free from recognized hazards to safety and health, and must comply with OSHA standards. OSHA also conducts workplace inspections, and responds to complaints, to ensure standards are followed. OSHA headquarters are located at 200 Constitution Ave., N.W.; Washington, DC 20210; 202/219-8151.

Occupational Safety and Health Programs, Federal

The responsibilities of the head of each federal agency to establish and maintain an effective and comprehensive occupational safety and health program consistent with the standards promulgated under OSHA. Under the program the head of each agency must a) provide safe and healthful places and conditions of employment, consistent with the standards set under Section 655 of this Title; b) acquire, maintain, and require the use of safety equipment, personal protective equipment, and devices reasonably necessary to protect employees; c) keep adequate records of all occupational accidents and illnesses for proper evaluation and necessary corrective action; d) consult with the Secretary of Labor with regard to the adequacy as to form and content of records kept; and e) make an annual report to the Secretary with respect to occupational accidents and injuries and the agency's adopted health and safety program.

Occupational Safety and Health Standard

A standard that requires conditions, or the adoption or use of one or more practices, means, methods, operations, or processes, reasonably necessary or appropriate to provide safe or healthful employment and places of employment.

Occupiable Area

That portion of the gross area that is available for use by an occupant's personnel or furnishings, including space that is available jointly to the various occupants of the buildings, such as auditoriums, health units, and snack bars. Occupiable area does not include space in the building that is devoted to its operations and maintenance, including craft shops, gear rooms, and building supply storage and issue rooms. Ceiling-high corridors solely serving a single space assignment are occupiable. Occupiable area is computed by measuring from the occupant's side of ceiling-high corridor partitions or partitions enclosing mechanical, toilet, and/or custodial space to the inside finish of permanent exterior building walls or the face of the convector if the convector occupies at least 50% of the length of exterior wall. When computing occupiable area separated by partitions, measurements are taken from the center line of the partitions. In the context of occupied explosive areas, any work area to which personnel are assigned or any nonwork area where persons regularly congregate.

Occupied Nest

A nest currently being used by one or more adult birds with eggs or young present.

Occurrence

Any circumstance surrounding a condition or event that represents a) a problem or concern that could have a negative impact on safety, environment, health, quality, security, or operations; b) a failure, malfunction deficiency, deviation, defective item, or nonconformance associated with safety related material, equipment, processes, procedures or programs; or c) a deviation from standard requirements, procedures, or operations (including all safety, quality, environmental, and operational activities) in connection with any hazard or hazard-controlled operation.

Occurrence Reporting and Processing System (ORPS)

Both an interactive computer system designed to support DOE-owned or operated facilities for reporting and processing information concerning occurrences related to facility operations. ORPS is one of the actuarial modules available on the Safety Performance Measurement System (SPMS) maintained by DOE Idaho's System Safety Development Center (SSDC) at Idaho Falls, Idaho. The system provides a departmental mechanism for submission, collection, transmission, and analysis of occurrence reports as required by DOE Order 5000.3A.

Occurrence Reports

Written evaluations of an event or condition that are prepared in sufficient detail to enable the reader to assess their significance, consequences, or implications and to evaluate the actions being proposed or employed to correct the condition or to avoid recurrence.

Ocean Convoy

A convoy whose voyage lies, in general, outside the Continental Shelf.

Ocean Dumping Act

See Marine Protection, Research, and Sanctuaries Act (MPRSA).

Ocean Dumping Compliance/Enforcement Agreements (MPRSA)

Agreements set forth as a condition of issuing a permit, that authorizes a person to transport or dump sewage sludge or industrial waste, requiring that, before the issuance of such permit, the person and the state in which the person is located enter into an agreement with the Administrator of EPA that includes the following: a) a plan negotiated by the person, the state in which the person is located, and the Administrator that will, in the opinion of the Administrator, if adhered to by the person in good faith, result in the phasing out and termination of ocean dumping, and transportation for the purpose of ocean dumping, of sewage sludge and industrial waste, through the design, construction, and full implementation of an alternative system for the management of sewage sludge and industrial waste; b) a schedule that specifies reasonable dates by which the person shall complete the various activities that are necessary for the timely implementation of the alternative system;   c) timely notification requirements to the Administrator and the governor of the state of any problems the person has in complying with the schedule; d) ongoing evaluation requirements; e) fees and penalties the person is liable for; ; and f) authorization(s) for the person to use interim measures before completion of the alternative system. *See* Marine Protection, Research, and Sanctuaries Act (MPRSA).

Ocean Dumping Compliance/Enforcement Schedule (MPRSA)

A schedule included in a compliance agreement that establishes deadlines for a) the preparation of engineering designs and related specifications for the alternative systems, as applicable; b) compliance with appropriate federal, state, and local statutes, regulations, and ordinances; c) site and equipment acquisitions for such alternative system; d) construction and testing of such alternative system;   e) operation of such alternative system at full capacity; and f) other activities, including interim measures, that the Administrator of EPA considers necessary or appropriate. *See* Marine Protection, Research, and Sanctuaries Act (MPRSA).

Ocean Dumping Monitoring (MPRSA)

The Secretary of Commerce's (in coordination with the Coast Guard and the Administrator of EPA) comprehensive and continuing program of monitoring and research regarding the effects of the dumping of material into ocean waters or other coastal waters where the tide ebbs and flows or into the Great Lakes or their connecting waters. Including an evaluation of the short-term ecological effects and the socio-economic factors involved. *See* Marine Protection, Research, and Sanctuaries Act (MPRSA).

Ocean Dumping Research Program (MPRSA)

The EPA Administrator's program of research, investigations, experiments, training, demonstrations, surveys, and studies for the purpose of a) determining the means of minimizing or ending, ocean dumping of material that may unreasonably degrade or endanger human health, welfare, or amenities, or the marine environment, ecological systems, or economic potentialities, and developing disposal methods as alternatives to dumping; b) promoting coordination, and rendering financial and other assistance to appropriate public authorities, agencies, and institutions (whether federal, state, interstate, or local) and appropriate private agencies, institutions, and individuals in the conduct of related research and other activities. *See* Marine Protection, Research, and Sanctuaries Act (MPRSA).

Ocean Manifest

A detailed listing of the entire cargo loaded into any one ship showing all pertinent data that will readily identify such cargo and where and how the cargo is stowed.

Ocean Monitoring

The monitoring efforts established by the Administrator, in cooperation with the Under Secretary of Commerce for Oceans and Atmosphere, for monitoring environmental conditions a) at the New York Bight Apex site; b) at the 106-Mile Ocean Waste Dump Site; c) at a site at which industrial waste is dumped; and d) within the potential area of influence of the sewage sludge and industrial waste dumped at those sites. The program includes, but is not limited to, sampling of an appropriate number of fish and shellfish species and other organisms to assess the effects of environmental conditions on living marine organisms in these areas; and the use of satellite and other advanced technologies in conducting the ocean monitoring. *See* Marine Protection, Research, and Sanctuaries Act (MPRSA).

Ocean Waters

Those waters of the open seas lying seaward of the baseline from which the territorial sea is measured, as provided for in the Convention on the Territorial Sea and the Contiguous Zone (15 USC 1606). *See* Marine Protection, Research, and Sanctuaries Act (MPRSA).

Oceanic

A term applied to those parts of the world's oceans that are deeper than 200 meters.

Oceanography

The study of the sea, embracing and integrating all knowledge pertaining to the sea and its physical boundaries, the chemistry and physics of seawater, and marine biology.

OCM

An acronym for Operational Change Memos.

Ocreolae

A species descriptor that means sheafs composed of one or more stipules, enclosing the leafstalk.

OCRWM

See Office of Civilian Radioactive Waste Management.

OCS

See Outer Continental Shelf source.

OCSLA

An acronym for Outer Continental Shelf Lands Act of 1953.

OCSLAA

An acronym for Outer Continental Shelf Lands Act Amendments of 1978.

Ocular

Pertaining to the eye.

Odor Threshold

The lowest concentration of a vapor or gas that can be detected by smell.

OEL

See Occupational Exposure Limit.

OER

See Office of Energy Research.

Off-Gassing

Giving off a vapor or gas.

Off-Normal Occurrences

Abnormal or unplanned events or conditions that adversely affect, potentially affect, or are indicative of degradation in the safety, security, environmental, or health protection performance or operation of a facility.

Off-Road Vehicle

1) Any motorized vehicle designed for or capable of cross-country travel on or immediately over land, water, sand, snow, ice, marsh, swampland, or other natural terrain; except that such term excludes the following: a) any registered motorboat; b) any fire, military, emergency, or law enforcement vehicle when used for emergency

purposes, and any combat or combat support vehicle when used for national defense purposes; and c) any vehicle whose use is expressly authorized by the respective agency head under a permit, lease, license, or contract. 2) In terms of the ESA, vehicles designed to travel over rough terrain and, incidentally, often destroy wildlife.

Off-the-Shelf Item
An item that has been developed and produced to military or commercial standards and specifications, is readily available for delivery from an industrial source, and may be procured without change to satisfy a requirement.

Offer
A promise to act in a certain manner provided the other party will act in the manner requested.

Office
The directing headquarters of an enterprise or organization. A place where a particular kind of business is transacted or service is supplied.

Office of Air and Radiation (OAR)
The EPA office that administers air quality standards and planning programs of the Clean Air Act. Supervises the Office of Air Quality Planning and Standards in Durham, North Carolina, that develops national air standards and provides information on air pollution control. Administers the Air Pollution Technical Information Center, that publishes technical literature on air pollution.

Office of Chemical Control (OCC)
This EPA office selects and implements control measures for new and existing chemicals that pose a risk to human health and the environment. Oversees and manages the regulatory evaluation and decisionmaking process in the area of toxic substances. OCC evaluates alternative remediation control strategies under the Toxic Substances Control Act. The office also develops generic and chemical-specific rules for new chemicals.

Office of Civilian Radioactive Waste Management (OCRWM)
The DOE office established by the Nuclear Waste Policy Act of 1982 (42 USC 10224). The office has responsibility for the Nuclear Waste Fuel program and federal programs for a) recommending, constructing, and operating repositories for disposal of high-level radioactive waste and spent nuclear fuel; b) interim storage of spent nuclear fuel; c) monitored retrievable storage; and d) research, development, and demonstration regarding disposal of high-level radioactive waste and spent nuclear fuel.

Office of Conservation and Renewable Energy (OCRE)
The DOE office that manages programs designed to increase the production of renewable energy (including solar heat and electric energy, geothermal energy, and municipal waste energy) and to improve the energy efficiency of transportation, buildings, industrial and community systems, and related processes. These programs include support of high-risk, high-payoff research and development that would not otherwise be carried out by the private sector and dissemination of the results to a broad spectrum of private and public sector interests. The Assistant Secretary also has responsibility for administering statutorily mandated programs that provide assistance to conservation programs at the state level.

Office of Energy Research (OER)
The DOE office that advises the Secretary on the physical and energy research and development programs of the department, the use of multipurpose laboratories, education, and training for basic and applied research, and financial assistance and budgetary priorities for these activities. The Office manages the basic energy sciences, high energy physics, and fusion energy research programs; administers DOE programs supporting university researchers, funds research in mathematical and computational sciences critical to the use and development of supercomputers; and administers a financial support program for research and development projects not funded elsewhere in the department.

Office of Enforcement and Compliance Monitoring (OECM)

The EPA office that serves as the principal adviser to the Administrator (EPA) on enforcement of standards for air, water, toxic substances and pesticides, solid waste management, radiation, and noise control programs; investigates criminal and civil violations of environmental standards.

Office of Environment, Safety, and Health (OESH)

The DOE office responsible for ensuring that departmental programs are in compliance with environmental safety and health regulations and that environmental and safety impacts of programs receive management review.

Office of Environmental Restoration and Waste Management (OERWM)

The DOE office that provides program policy guidance and manages the assessment and cleanup of inactive waste sites and facilities, continues safe and effective waste management operations, and develops and implements an aggressively applied waste research and development program to provide innovative environmental technologies that yield permanent disposal solutions at reduced costs. The Director provides centralized management for the department for waste management operations, environmental restoration, and applied research and development programs and activities, including environmental restoration and waste management program policy and guidance to DOE operations offices in these areas.

Office of Federal Activities (OFA)

EPA's liaison office for all federal agencies. Manages National Environmental Policy Act environmental review of other agencies' projects and activities, EPA American Indian Program, and federal facilities compliance.

Office of Fossil Energy (OFE)

The DOE office responsible for research and development programs involving fossil fuels (coal, petroleum, and gas). The fossil energy program involves applied research, exploratory development, and limited proof-of-concept testing targeted to high-risk and high-payoff endeavors. The objective of the program is to provide the general technology and knowledge base that the private sector can use to complete development and initiate commercialization of advanced processes and energy systems. The program is principally executed through two Energy Technology Centers located in the field.

Office of Management and Budget (OMB)

The OMB evaluates, formulates, and coordinates management procedures and program objectives within and among federal departments and agencies. It also controls the administration of the federal budget, while routinely providing the President with recommendations regarding budget proposals and relevant legislative enactments.

Office of Mobile Sources (OMS)

The EPA office that enforces Clean Air Act provisions for mobile sources, including aircraft emission standards and automobile air pollution control programs.

Office of New Production Reactors (NPR)

The DOE office that manages and directs a program for the acquisition and construction of new production reactor capability to meet national security requirements.

Office of Nuclear Energy (NE)

The DOE office that administers the department's research and development programs associated with fission energy. This includes programs relating to nuclear reactor development, both civilian and naval; nuclear fuel cycle; space nuclear applications; and uranium enrichment. The office is also responsible for and manages the department's Remedial Action Program to treat or stabilize radioactive wastes and perform decontamination and decommissioning at DOE surplus sites. The office conducts technical analyses and provides advice concerning nonproliferation; assesses alternative nuclear systems and new reactor and fuel cycle concepts; and evaluates proposed advanced nuclear fission energy concepts and technical improvements for possible application to nuclear power plant systems.

Office of Pesticide and Toxic Substances (OPTS)

The EPA office that assesses the health and environmental hazards of chemical substances and mixtures. Collects information on chemical use, exposure, and effects; maintains inventory of chemical substances; reviews chemicals and regulates the manufacture, distribution, use and disposal of toxic chemicals. OPTS studies and makes recommendations for regulation of chemical substances under the Toxic Substances Control Act. OPTS is the office that compiles the national priorities list of substances subject to TSCA controls and regulates the use of toxic substances.

Office of Pesticide Programs (OPP)

The EPA office that conducts research and sets and enforces standards for pesticide manufacturing and use. Maintains nationwide accident report database system. OPP develops rules regarding pesticide labeling and descriptive literature.

Office of Policy, Planning, and Evaluation (OPPE)

The EPA office that coordinates agency planning, evaluation, and standard setting activities.

Office of Research and Development (ORD)

The EPA office that develops scientific databases to determine and support EPA standards and regulations; develops technology for environmental controls on industry.

Office of Solid Waste and Emergency Response (OSWER)

The EPA office that administers and enforces the Superfund Amendments (SARA) and the Resource Conservation and Recovery Act (RCRA), that manages the handling and disposal of hazardous wastes.

Office of Special Projects (OSP)

The DOE Tiger Team Assessment Program is implemented by the Office of Special Projects (OSP), that is within the Office of Environment, Safety, and Health (OESH). The OSP manages the staffing and conduct of the Tiger Team Assessments; ensures that the resulting assessment reports are completed, reviewed, revised and approved as necessary; provides liaison with other involved DOE and external entities; provides guidance to the Tiger Team Assessment process; maintains a database of Tiger Team roster, candidates, activities, and findings; and prepares summaries and trend analyses of Tiger Team findings.

Office of Stationary Source Compliance (OSSC)

The EPA office that administers Clean Air Act provisions for stationary sources, including steel, petroleum, coal-fire boilers and furnaces, electric utilities, natural gas, and other industrial air pollution standards.

Office of Wetlands Protection (OWP)

The EPA office that manages the dredge and fill program under Section 404 of the Clean Water Act, in cooperation with the Army Corps of Engineers (ACOE). The office also coordinates federal policies affecting wetlands and promotes public awareness about wetland preservation and management.

Official Information

Information that is owned by, produced for or by, or is subject to the control of the United States government.

Official Sample

A field sample taken by the director of a governmental agency or his/her agent for regulatory purposes.

Official Use

Use by an employee, agent, or designated representative of the federal government or one of its contractors in the course of his/her employment, agency, or representation.

Official Use Only

A designation identifying unclassified information that may be exempt from mandatory disclosure under the Freedom of Information Act (FOIA).

Officially Reportable Events

Events that require official notification to state and tribal governments as outlined in Section 103(c) of the Comprehensive Environmental Response, Compensation, and Liability Act of 1980; Title 40 CFR Part 117, Determination of Reportable Quantities for Hazardous Substances; Title 33 CFR Part 153.201, Notice of Discharge of Oil or Hazardous Substances; and Title 40 CFR Parts 110 and 112.

Offshore Facility

As defined by Section 101(17) of CERCLA and Section 311(a)(11) of the Clean Water Act, means any facility located in, on, or under any of the navigable waters of the U.S. and any facility that is subject to U.S. jurisdiction and is located in, on, or under any other waters, other than a vessel.

Offshore Patrol

A naval defense patrol operating in the outer areas of navigable coastal waters. It is a part of the naval local defense forces consisting of naval ships and aircraft and operates outside those areas assigned to the inshore patrol.

Offsite

Any site that is not on the subject site; the area beyond the boundaries of the site.

Offsite Coordination Center

Performs offsite liaison functions and oversees all site activities at the State Emergency Operations Center (SEOC). Primary communications link between onsite EOC and SEOC.

Offsite Event

An emergency that results for a site or facility, from an activity not taking place at the site/facility. This typically would involve a transportation accident of some kind (truck or train) involving hazardous materials destined for, originating from, or passing by the site.

Offsite Federal Support

Federal assistance in mitigating the offsite consequences of an emergency and protecting the public health and safety, including the assistance with determining and implementing public protective action measures.

Offsite Notification/Warning

An emergency notification and/or warning message issued to the state/local government and/or the public.

Offsite Waste Facility

A hazardous waste treatment, storage, or disposal area that is located at a place away from the generating site.

OHER

An acronym for Office of Health and Environmental Research.

Oil

As defined by the Clean Water Act, oil of any kind or in any form, including, but not limited to, petroleum, fuel oil, sludge, oil refuse, and oil mixed with wastes other than dredged spoil.

Oil and Gas Interest

Any oil or gas royalty or lease, or fractional interest therein, or certificate of interest or participation or investment contract relative to such royalties, leases or fractional interests, or any other interest or right that permits the exploration of, drilling for, or production of oil and gas or other related hydrocarbons or the receipt of such production or the proceeds thereof.

Oil Field Recovery Heater

A forced-circulation, once-through, water tube steam generator, used only in oil field thermal recovery operations, having no fired pressure parts larger than 4-inch pipe size and no other pressure part larger than 6-inch pipe size.

Oil Fingerprinting

A method that identifies sources of oil and allows spills to be traced back to their source.

Oil Importer

Any person who owns, at the first place of storage, any petroleum product imported into the United States.

Oil Manufacturer

Any person who re-refines or otherwise processes used oil to remove physical or chemical impurities acquired through use or who blends such re-refined or otherwise processed used oil with new oil or additives.

Oil Pollution Fund

The fund established by Section 311(k) of the Clean Water Act.

Oil Royalty, Federal

In-kind royalties from oil production on federal land as defined in the Energy Policy and Conservation Act (42 USC 6202(10)). Proceeds from the sale of federal royalty oil that is not otherwise required to be disposed of by the Mineral Lands Leasing Act (MLLA), are deposited into the Treasury of the United States.

Oil Shale

A sedimentary rock containing solid organic matter and kerogen from which oil can be obtained when the rock is heated to a sufficiently high temperature.

Oil Spill

An accidental or intentional discharge of oil that reaches bodies of water; can be controlled by chemical dispersion, combustion, mechanical containment, and/or adsorption.

Oiler

A naval or merchant tanker specially equipped and rigged for replenishing other ships at sea.

OL

An acronym for Operating Limit.

OLC

An acronym for On-Line Computer.

Olfactory Fatigue

Temporary loss of the sense of smell due to repeated or continued stimulation.

Oligohaline

A term to characterize water with salinity of 0.5% to 5.0% due to ocean-derived salts.

Oligosaline

A term to characterize water with salinity of 0.5% to 5.0% due to land-derived salts.

Oligosaprobic

A term applied to a polluted body of water in which organic matter is decomposing slowly, and the water has a relatively high oxygen content.

Oligotrophic Lakes

Deep clear lakes with low nutrient supplies. They contain little organic matter and have a high dissolved-oxygen level.

Oliguria

A condition in which abnormally small amounts of urine are produced.

Olivaceous

A species descriptor that means olive green in color.

OMB

See Office of Management and Budget.

Omnivore

A species that eats a large variety of foods.

On-Ground Tanks

Stationary devices designed to contain an accumulation of regulated substances and constructed of nonearthen materials (e.g., concrete, steel, plastic) that provide structural support and that are situated in such ways that the bottom of the tanks are on the same levels as the adjacent surrounding surfaces so that the external tank bottoms cannot be visually inspected.

On-Hand
A general term, referring to a quantity of an item that is physically available in a storage location and contained in the accountable property book records of an issuing activity.

On-Scene
The area surrounding an accident or incident site that is, or potentially could be, affected by the accident or incident. This area includes both the onsite and offsite areas.

On-Scene Coordinator (OSC)
1) The federal official predesignated by the Environmental Protection Agency or the U.S. Coast Guard to coordinate and direct federal responses under Subpart E and removals under Subpart F of the National Contingency Plan; or the Department of Defense (DOD) official designated to coordinate and direct the removal actions from releases of hazardous substances, pollutants, and/or from DOD vessels and facilities. 2) The person designated to coordinate the rescue and response efforts at a site. 3) Predesignated EPA, U.S. Coast Guard, or Department of Defense officials who coordinate and direct Superfund removal actions or Clean Water Act oil- or hazardous-spill corrective actions.

On-Scene Commanders
1) Officers or senior officials who command DOD and/or DOE operations at the scene of a DOD or DOE nuclear weapon accident or significant incident. 2) In the case of a security event, the officers or senior officials who command operations at the scene of the event.

On-Shore Facilities
1) As defined by Section 101(18) of CERCLA, any facility (including, but not limited to, motor vehicles and rolling stock) of any kind located in, on, or under any land or nonnavigable waters within the United States. 2) As defined by Section 311(a)(10) of the CWA, any facility (including, but not limited to, motor vehicles and rolling stock) of any kind located in, on or under any land within the U.S., except submerged land.

Oncogene
A naturally occurring gene that specifies the synthesis of a protein that is involved in normal cellular processes. Alterations in the structure or function of oncogenes are associated with the development of some cancers.

Oncogenesis
The origin and growth of a neoplasm.

Oncogenic
A substance that causes tumors, whether benign or malignant.

One-Hit Model
A mathematical model that assumes a single biological event can initiate a response.

Ongoing Projects
Activities for scientific purposes or to enhance the propagation or survival of threatened species that are not conducted in the course of a commercial activity initiated before the listing of the specified species.

Onsite
1) On the same or geographically contiguous property. May be divided by public or private right-of-way, provided the entrance and exit between the properties are at a crossroads intersection, and access is by crossing, as opposed to going along, the right-of-way. 2) Noncontiguous properties owned by the same person but connected by a right-of-way controlled by that person and to which the public does not have access are also considered onsite property. 3) Within the boundaries of a contiguous property unit.

Onsite Discharges
Airborne and liquid wastes discharged to onsite treatment or disposal systems, e.g., sewage lagoons, retention ponds, and cribs, for retention, settling, decay, or storage onsite.

Onsite Event

An emergency that results from an activity taking place within the site boundaries. This may include transportation accidents, but usually involves site operations, buildings, or tanks.

Onsite Facility

A hazardous waste treatment, storage, or disposal area that is located on the generating site.

Onsite Federal Support

Federal assistance that is the primary responsibility of the federal agency that owns, authorizes, regulates, or is otherwise deemed responsible for the radiological facility or material being transported (i.e., the cognizant federal agency). This response supports state and local efforts by supporting the owner or operator's efforts to bring the incident under control and thereby preventing or minimizing offsite consequences.

Onsite Technical Directors

Officials, selected by the U.S. Department of Energy (DOE) team leader or on-scene commander, who are responsible for directing the on-scene operations for the DOE team leader or on-scene commander for a nuclear weapons accident response.

Ontogenesis

The chain of development over the entire life history of a living organism.

Oocyte

The immature ovum.

Oostegites

A species descriptor that means plates on the thoracic limbs of certain crustaceans, forming a brood-pouch in which the young develop.

OOWSRA

See the Omnibus Oregon Wild and Scenic Rivers Act of 1988 (WSRA).

OP

See Ozone Protection.

Opacity

1) The amount of light obscured by particulate pollution in the air; clear window glass has zero opacity, a brick wall 100% opacity. Opacity is used as an indicator of changes in performance of particulate matter pollution control systems. 2) The degree to which emissions reduce the transmission of light.

Open Burning

The combustion of any material without the following characteristics a) control of combustion air to maintain adequate temperature for efficient combustion; b) containment of the combustion reaction in an enclosed device to provide sufficient residence time and mixing for complete combustion; c) control of emission of the gaseous combustion products. Uncontrolled fires in an open dump. *See* Incineration, Thermal Treatment.

Open Dump

1) An uncovered site used for disposal of waste without environ mental controls. 2) A solid waste land disposal site where wastes are disposed of in a manner that does not protect the environment, and where wastes are exposed to the elements. 3) Any facilities or sites where solid waste is disposed of which are not sanitary landfills that meet the criteria promulgated under statutory controls and that are not a facility for disposal of hazardous waste. *See* Dump.

Open Dump Inventory

The inventory of open dumps located in the United States that do not comply with EPA's *Criteria for Classification of Solid Waste Disposal Facilities and Practices*, listed in 40 CFR 257. The list is maintained and monitored by EPA's Office of Solid Waste.

Open-Ended Line

Any line, except pressure release lines, having one end in contact with process fluid and one end open to atmosphere, either directly or through an open valve.

Open-Ended Valve

Any valve, except pressure relief valves, having one side of the valve seat in contact with process fluid and one side open to atmosphere, either directly or through open piping.

Open Improved Storage Space

Open area that has been graded and hard surfaced or prepared with topping of some suitable material so as to permit effective material handling and containment operations. *See* Storage.

Open Spaces

Unimproved lands not designated as agricultural lands or forest lands. Open spaces include a) scenic, cultural, and historic areas; b) fish and wildlife habitat; c) lands that support plant species that are endemic to the scenic area or that are listed as rare, threatened or endangered species pursuant to state or Federal Endangered Species Acts; d) ecologically and scientifically significant natural areas; e) outstanding scenic views and sites; f) water areas and wetlands; g) archaeological sites, Native American Indian burial grounds and village sites, historic trails and roads, and other areas that are culturally or historically significant; h) potential and existing recreation resources; and i) federal and state wild, scenic, and recreation waterways.

Operable Unit

1) An action taken as one part of an overall site cleanup; a discrete part of the entire response action that decreases a release, threat of release, or pathway of exposure. For example, a carbon absorption system could be installed to stop rapidly spreading groundwater contaminants while a more comprehensive long-term remedial investigation/feasibility study is still underway. A number of operable units would be used during the course of a site cleanup project. A typical operable unit would be removing drums and tanks from the surface of a site. 2) A discrete part of the entire response action that decreases a release, threat of release, or pathway of exposure.

Operating Area Compartment

An area or series of areas that contain process enclosures, and/or their attendant equipment located within that area or series of areas.

Operating Basis Accident (OBA)

Maximum severity accident under which the plant structure, systems, and components are designed to either remain operable or be readily restored to operating condition. This is the highest severity event that the operating contractor may recover from without DOE approval.

Operating Basis Earthquake (OBE)

The operating basis earthquake that, considering the regional and local geology and seismology and specific characteristics of local subsurface material, could reasonably be expected to affect the plant site during the operating time of the plant; it is that earthquake that produces the vibratory growth motion for which those features of the nuclear power plant necessary for continued operation, without undue risk to the health and safety of the public, are designed to remain functional.

Operating Envelope

That portion of the restricted envelope (space) that is actually used by the robot while performing its programmed motions.

Operation Exposure Guide

The maximum amount of nuclear radiation that personnel may be permitted to receive while performing particular tasks.

Operational Accidents

Events stemming from technological and manmade hazards that present a potential risk to life, health, property, or the environment.

Operational Chain of Command

The chain of command established for a particular operation or series of continuing operations. *See* Chain of Command.

Operational Curtailment

A cessation of operations and the release of all but essential personnel at the site.

Operational Decontamination

Decontamination carried out by an individual and/or a team, restricted to specific parts of operationally essential equipment, material and/or working areas, in order to minimize contact and transfer hazards and to sustain operations. This may include decontamination of the individual beyond the scope of immediate decontamination, as well as decontamination of mission-essential spares and limited terrain decontamination. *See* Decontamination; Immediate Decontamination; Thorough Decontamination.

Operational Design Basis Accident (DBA)

Any design basis accident caused by an internal event. Direct causes are usually poor design or procedures, operator errors, equipment failures, or inadequate technical development (unknowns) that lead to the accident. The major accident categories are explosion, fire, nuclear criticality, leaks to the atmosphere, and leaks to the aquatic environment.

Operational Emergencies

Significant events involving DOE operations and activities that present a potential risk to life, health, property, or the environment.

Operational Emergency Management Teams (EMTs)

U.S. Department of Energy (DOE) teams predesignated to manage activities during operational emergencies involving DOE or requiring DOE assistance.

Operational Emergency Preparedness Management Plans (EPMPs)

Site-specific plans required by U.S. Department of Energy Order that identify emergency planning, preparedness, and response capabilities, personnel staffing, and equipment resources necessary to minimize emergency consequences to people, property, and the environment.

Operational Emergency Response Levels

Response levels to hazardous materials incidents, natural phenomena occurring at nuclear and non-nuclear facilities, safeguards and security incidents, Radiological Assistance Program requests for assistance, and nuclear weapon accidents or significant incidents. For hazardous material emergencies, the response levels are "unusual event," "alert," "site emergency," and "general emergency." For safeguards and security emergencies, response levels are "Alert III (CHARLIE)," "Alert II (BRAVO)," and "Alert I (ALPHA)." For Radiological Assistance Program emergencies, the response levels are "Radiological Assistance Program alert" and "Radiological Assistance Program emergency." Nuclear weapons accident or significant incident emergencies include all responses by the Accident Response Group; there are no specific response levels. May also be referred to as emergency action levels. *See* ALPHA; BRAVO; CHARLIE.

Operational Environment

A composite of the conditions, circumstances, and influences that affect the employment of military forces and bear on the decisions of the unit commander. Some examples are:

- *permissive environment* — an operational environment in which host country military and law enforcement agencies have control and the intent and capability to assist operations that a unit intends to conduct;

- *uncertain environment* — an operational environment in which host government forces, whether opposed to or receptive to operations that a unit intends to conduct, do not have totally effective control of the territory and population in the intended area of operations; and

- *hostile environment* — an operational environment in which hostile forces have control and the intent and capability to effectively oppose or react to the operations a unit intends to conduct.

Operational Life

Refers to the period beginning when installation of the tank system has commenced until the time the tank system is properly closed.

Operational Limits

Limits of any quantity specified by the management for a given radiation practice or source. These are equal to or lower than the authorized limits.

Operational Readiness Reviews

1) Structured methods for determining that a project, process, or facility are ready to operate and occupy and include, as a minimum, a review of the readiness of the plant and hardware, personnel, and procedures. 2) An evaluation of the operational capability and effectiveness of a team or any portion thereof. Reviews include a determination of compliance with applicable Environmental, Safety, and Health regulations.

Operational Safety Requirements

Requirements that define the conditions, safe boundaries, and bases thereof, and management or administrative controls required to ensure the safe operation of a nuclear facility.

Operationally Ready

A term applied to personnel who are available and qualified to perform assigned environmental tasks or response functions. May be used in a general sense or to express a level or degree of readiness.

Operations and Maintenance (O&M)

Activities conducted at a site after a response action occurs to ensure that the cleanup or containment system was installed correctly and is functioning properly.

Operations and Maintenance Plan (O&M Plan) for Asbestos-Containing Materials (ACM)

Written instructions to building maintenance personnel on activities to be conducted at a site to avoid or minimize fiber release during activities affecting the ACM. At a minimum the O&M plan should define a periodic inspection program and provide precautions to be taken when working on or near the ACM.

Operations, Environmental

1) Those activities funded by an agency, or owner/operator (O/O) of a facility for which the agency, or O/O has responsibility for environmental protection, safety, and health protection. 2) Activities conducted at a site after a Super fund site action is completed to ensure that the action is effective and operating properly. 3) Actions taken after construction to ensure that facilities constructed to treat wastewater will be properly operated, maintained, and managed to achieve efficiency levels and prescribed effluent limitations in an optimum manner.

Operations Section

The section responsible for all tactical operations at the site of an emergency incident.

Operations Security Measures

Methods and means to gain and maintain essential secrecy about critical information. The following categories apply:

- *action control* — the objective is to eliminate indicators or the vulnerability of actions to exploitation by adversary intelligence systems. Select what actions to undertake; decide whether or not to execute actions; and determine the "who," "when," "where," and "how" for actions necessary to accomplish tasks;

- *countermeasures* — the objective is to disrupt effective adversary information gathering or prevent their recognition of indicators when collected materials are processed. Use diversions, camouflage, concealment, jamming, threats, police powers, and force against adversary information gathering and processing capabilities; and

- *counteranalysis* — the objective is to prevent accurate interpretations of indicators during adversary analysis of collected materials. This is done by confusing the adversary analyst through deception techniques such as covers.

Operator of the Property

The person primarily responsible for the control or management of the property.

Operator

1) Owners or operators of any "facility or activity" subject to regulation under the Resource Conservation and Recovery Act (RCRA), Underground Injection Control (UIC), National Pollutant Discharge Elimination System (NPDES), or 404 programs. 2) Individuals designated by management to perform operations or conduct activities with radioactive materials at a nuclear facility. 3) Persons who control the use of an aircraft, vessel, or vehicle. 4) Any person who is senior management personnel or a corporate officer. Except in the case of knowing and willful violations, the term does not include any person who is carrying out his/her normal activities and who is acting under orders from the employer or a stationary engineer or technician responsible for the operation, maintenance, repair, or monitoring of equipment and facilities and who often has supervisory and training duties but who is not senior management personnel or a corporate officer. *See* Owner; Owner/Operator.

Operculum

A species descriptor that means a lid or flap covering an aperture, such as the gill cover in fish or the horny shell cover in snails.

Opisthotonos

Tetanic spasm in which the spine and extremities are bent up and forward so that a reclining body rests on the head and the heels.

Opportunistic

The term for a species that adapts its feeding habits to the most available food source.

Optic Atrophy

Shrinkage or wasting of the optic nerve that may lead to partial vision loss or blindness.

Optic Neuritis

Inflammation of the optic nerve.

Optical Cavity, Resonator

Space between the laser mirrors where lasing action occurs.

Optical Density

A logarithmic expression for the attenuation produced by an attenuating medium, such as an eye protection filter.

Optical Fiber

A filament of quartz or other optical material capable of transmitting light along its length by multiple internal reflection and emitting it at the end.

Optical Pumping

The excitation of the lasing medium by the application of light rather than electrical discharge.

Optical Radiation

Ultraviolet, visible, and infrared radiation (0.35-1.4 m) that falls in the region of transmittance of the human eye.

Optimum Interspersed Hydrogenous Moderation

The occurrence of hydrogenous material between containment vessels to such an extent that the maximum nuclear reactivity results.

Or Gate

A logic gate that produces an output when one or more of the input events occur.

Orbit Determination

The process of describing the past, present, or predicted position of a satellite in terms of orbital parameters.

Orbital Injection

The process of providing a space vehicle with sufficient velocity to establish an orbit.

Order

1) The whole or a part of a final disposition, whether affirmative, negative, injunctive, or declaratory in form, of an agency in a matter other than rule making but including licensing. 2) In DOD, a communication, written, oral, or by signal, that conveys instructions from a superior to a subordinate. In a broad sense, the terms "order"

and "command" are synonymous. However, an order implies discretion as to the details of execution whereas a command does not. 3) In terms of the ESA, a systematic grouping of organisms belonging to similar families. The order divides the class into animals that share many common characteristics.

Order to Comply with SIP (CAA)
The order issued by the Administrator of EPA upon finding that a) any person has violated or is in violation of any requirement or prohibition of an applicable state implementation plan or permit. At any time after the expiration of 30 days from the date on which such notice of a violation is issued, the Administrator may, without regard to the period of violation, 1) issue an administrative penalty order in accordance with the CAA, or 2) bring a civil action in accordance with the act; and b) violations of an applicable implementation plan or an approved permit program are so widespread that such violations appear to result from a failure of the state in which the plan or permit program applies to enforce the plan or permit program effectively. If the Administrator finds such failure extends beyond the 30th day after such notice (90 days in the case of such permit program), the Administrator gives public notice of such finding. During the period beginning with such public notice and ending when a state satisfies the Administrator that it will enforce its SIP or permit program, the Administrator may enforce any requirement or prohibition of such plan or permit program with respect to any person by 1) issuing an order requiring such person to comply with such requirement or prohibition; 2) issuing an administrative penalty order; or 3) bringing a civil action in accordance with the CAA.

Ordinary High Water Mark
That line on the shore established by the fluctuations of water and indicated by physical characteristics such as clear, natural line impressed on the bank, shelving, changes in the character of soil, destruction of terrestrial vegetation, the presence of litter and debris, or other appropriate means that consider the characteristics of the surrounding areas.

Ordinary Moment Resisting Space Frame
A moment resisting space frame not meeting special detailing requirements for ductile behavior.

Ordinary Transport
In railway terminology, a load whose size, weight or preparation does not entail special difficulties vis-a-vis the facilities or equipment of the railway systems to be used. *See* Exceptional Transport.

Ordnance
Explosives, chemicals, pyrotechnics, and similar stores, e.g., bombs, guns and ammunition, flares, smoke, napalm.

Organic
1) Referring to or derived from living organisms. 2) In chemistry, any compound containing carbon.

Organic Chemicals/Compounds
Animal or plant-produced substances containing mainly carbon, hydrogen, and oxygen.

Organic Matter
Carbonaceous waste contained in plant or animal matter and originating from domestic or industrial sources.

Organic Peroxide
An organic compound that may be considered a derivative of hydrogen peroxide where one or more of the hydrogen atoms have been replaced by organic radicals.

Organic Soil
Soil composed of predominantly organic rather than mineral material. *See* Histosols.

Organically Grown
Food, feed crops, and livestock grown within an intentionally diversified, self-sustaining agro-ecosystem. In practice, farmers build up nutrients in the soil using compost, agricultural wastes, and cover crops instead of synthetically derived fertilizers to increase productivity, rotate crops, weed mechanically, and reduce dramatically their de-

pendence on the entire family of pesticides. Farmers must be certified to characterize crops as organically grown and can only use approved natural and synthetic biochemicals, agents, and materials for three consecutive years prior to harvest. Livestock must be fed a diet that includes grains and forages that have been organically grown and cannot receive hormones, subtherapeutic antibiotics, or other growth promoters.

Organisms

Any living things, whether plant, mammal, bird, insect, reptile, fish, crustacean, aquatic or estuarine animal, or bacterium.

Organization of Petroleum Exporting Countries (OPEC)

An organization founded in 1960 to unify and coordinate petroleum policies of the members. OPEC headquarters are in Vienna, Austria. The members and the date of membership are:

Abu Dhabi (1967)	Algeria (1969)
Indonesia (1962)	Iran (1960)
Iraq (1960)	Kuwait (1960)
Libya (1962)	Nigeria (1971)
Qatar (1961)	Saudi Arabia (1960)
Venezuela (1960)	

Organization

1) A group of people with a more or less constant membership, a body of officers, a purpose, and usually, a set of regulations. The group will also exhibit an administrative and functional structure including established relationships of personnel through lines of authority and response with delegated and assigned duties. 2) In terms of the CAA, a legal entity, other than a government, established or organized for any purpose, and includes a corporation, company, association, firm, partnership, joint stock company, foundation, institution, trust, society, union, or any other association of persons.

Organochlorines

Organic chlorinated hydrocarbons used as the active ingredients in pesticides. They have proved very effective in controlling insects. Because of the harmful side effects many organochlorine insecticides have on wildlife, their use in many countries is being regulated.

Organogenesis

The development of specific body structures or organs from undifferentiated tissue. In humans, this relates primarily to post conception (weeks 2 through 8, inclusive).

Organoleptic

Affecting or involving an organ, especially a sense organ as of taste, smell, or sight.

Organomercury Fungicides

Poisonous chemical compounds containing mercury, primarily used as sprays and seed treatments to control fungal diseases in crops.

Organophosphates

1) Organophosphorus esters that inhibit cholinesterase. 2) Pesticide chemicals that contain phosphorus; used to control insects. They are short-lived, but some can be toxic when first applied.

Organophosphorus Pesticides

A group of less persistent pesticides of varying toxicity that break down rapidly and pose minimal threats to wildlife.

Organotins

Chemical compounds used in paints to protect the hulls of boats and ships, buoys, and dock pilings from marine organisms such as barnacles.

ORGDP

An acronym for Oak Ridge Gaseous Diffusion Plant.

Originating Medical Facility

A medical facility that initially transfers a patient to another medical facility.

ORM

See Other Regulated Material.

ORNL
See Oak Ridge National Laboratory.

ORPS
See Occurrence Reporting and Processing System.

Orthogonal Effects
The effects on a structure due to earthquake motions acting in directions other than parallel to the direction of resistance under consideration.

Orthomorphic Projection
A projection in which the scale, although varying throughout the map, is the same in all directions at any point, so that very small areas are represented by correct shape and bearings are correct.

OSC
See On-Scene Coordinator.

OSHA
An acronym for the Occupational and Safety Health Act of 1970 (29 USC 61 et seq.) and Occupational Safety and Health Administration. The law passed by Congress to ensure worker and workplace safety. Their goal was to make sure employers provide their workers a place of employment free from recognized hazards to safety and health, such as exposure to toxic chemicals, excessive noise levels, mechanical dangers, heat or cold stress, or unsanitary conditions.

In order to establish standards for workplace health and safety, the Act also created the National Institute for Occupational Safety and Health (NIOSH) as the research institution for the Occupational Safety and Health Administration (OSHA). OSHA is the division of the U.S. Department of Labor that over sees the administration of the Act and enforces federal standards in all 50 states. *See* Occupational Safety and Health Administration; Occupational Safety and Health Act.

OSHA Activities
The following list of program activities was adapted from OSHA's budget activity structure. OSHA's principal program areas are as follows:

- Safety Standards;
- Health Standards;
- Federal Inspections;
- State Programs;
- Discrimination Complaints;
- Other Compliance Programs;
- Science and Technology Support;
- Regulatory Analyses;
- Laboratories;
- Technical Data Center;
- Other Technical Support Activities;
- Health Response Team;
- Onsite Consultation Programs;
- New Directions Training Grants;
- Federal Agencies;
- Voluntary Protection;
- Training Institute;
- Information and Consumer Affairs;
- Bureau of Labor Statistics (BLS) Statistical Programs;
- Integrated Management Information Systems (IMIS);
- Statistical Studies;
- Office of Assistant Secretary;
- Policy and Legislation Analysis; and
- Administrative Programs.

The above list does not include all operations conducted by or within OSHA, and the list may be modified by the Office of Program Evaluation or at the request of managers.

OSHA Chemical Safety Management
The Safety Standard requiring employers to, at a minimum, a) develop and maintain written safety information identifying workplace chemical and process hazards, equipment used in the processes,

and technology used in the processes; b) perform a workplace hazard assessment, including, as appropriate, identification of potential sources of accidental releases, an identification of any previous release within the facility that had a likely potential for catastrophic consequences in the workplace, estimation of workplace effects of a range of releases, estimation of the health and safety effects of such range on employees; c) consult with employees and their representatives on the development and conduct of hazard assessments and the development of chemical accident prevention plans and provide access to these and other records required under the standard; d) establish a system to respond to the workplace hazard assessment findings, that shall address prevention, mitigation, and emergency responses; e) periodically review the workplace hazard assessment and response system; f) develop and implement written operating procedures for the chemical process including procedures for each operating phase, operating limitations, and safety and health considerations; g) provide written safety and operating information to employees and train employees in operating procedures, emphasizing hazards and safe practices; h) ensure contractors and contract employees are provided appropriate information and training; i) train and educate employees and contractors in emergency response in a manner as comprehensive and effective as that required by the regulation promulgated pursuant to Section 126(d) of the Superfund Amendments and Reauthorization Act of 1986 (Pub. L. 99-499); j) establish a quality assurance program to ensure that initial process related equipment, maintenance materials, and spare parts are fabricated and installed consistent with design specifications; k) establish maintenance systems for critical process related equipment including written procedures, employee training, appropriate inspections, and testing of such equipment to ensure ongoing mechanical integrity; l) conduct pre-startup safety reviews of all newly installed or modified equipment; m) establish and implement written procedures to manage change to process chemicals, technology, equipment, and facilities; and n) investigate every incident that results in or could have resulted in a major accident in the workplace, with any find-

ings to be reviewed by operating personnel and modifications made if appropriate.

OSHA Grants to States
Grants to assist states with designated agencies in a) identifying their needs and responsibilities in the area of occupational safety and health; b) developing state plans; or c) developing plans for 1) establishing systems for the collection of information concerning the nature and frequency of occupational injuries and diseases; 2) increasing the expertise and enforcement capabilities of their personnel engaged in occupational safety and health programs; or 3) otherwise improving the administration and enforcement of state occupational safety and health laws, including standards thereunder, consistent with the objectives of OSHA. The federal share for each state grant typically may not exceed 50% of the total cost to the state of such a program.

OSHA Standard Concerning Exposure to Bloodborne Pathogens
The final occupational health standard concerning occupational exposure to bloodborne pathogens, concerning occupational exposures to the hepatitis B virus, the human immunodeficiency virus, and other bloodborne pathogens.

OSHA Statistics Program
The Secretary's program of data collection, compilation, and analysis of occupational safety and health statistics on work-related injuries and illnesses that are disabling, serious, or significant injuries and illnesses, whether or not involving loss of time from work, other than minor injuries requiring only first aid treatment and that do not involve medical treatment, loss of consciousness, restriction of work or motion, or job transfers.

OSHRC
An acronym for Occupational Safety and Health Review Commission.

Osmosis
1) The flow of water through a semipermeable membrane from a solution of low concentration to a solution of higher concentration. The process

continues until solutions on either side of the membrane have equal concentrations. 2) The tendency of a fluid to pass through a permeable membrane such as the wall of a living cell into a less concentrated solution so as to equalize the concentrations on both sides of the membrane.

Ossify
A species descriptor that means to change into bone.

Osteosclerosis
Abnormal hardening or increase in density of the bone.

Ostracods
A species descriptor that means minute, chiefly freshwater crustaceans of the order Ostracoda that have a bivalve carapace (a shell with two hinged parts).

OSWER
See Office of Solid Waste and Emergency Response.

Other Regulated Material (ORM)
Any material that does not meet the definition of a hazardous material, other than a combustible liquid in packaging having a capacity of 110 gallons or less, and is specifically listed in the Table of Hazardous Materials (40 CFR 172.101) as an ORM. A material not listed in the Table of Hazardous Materials may also be considered an ORM. *See* Other Regulated Material ORM-A through ORM-E.

Other Regulated Material, ORM-A
An ORM-A material has an anesthetic, irritating, noxious, toxic, or other similar property and can cause extreme annoyance or discomfort to passengers and crews in the event of leakage during transportation. Phencapton, thiram, chloroform, and carbaryl are examples of Other Regulated Materials-A.

Other Regulated Material, ORM-B
An ORM-B material is capable of causing significant damage to a transport vehicle or vessel from leakage during transportation (includes a solid when wet with water). An ORM-B material will be so designated in the Table of Hazardous Materials (40 CFR 172.101), or be a liquid substance that has a corrosion rate exceeding 0.250 inch per year on aluminum at a test temperature of 130°F (40 CFR 173.500(a)(2)). Ammonium hydrogen fluoride (solid), chloroplatinic acid (solid), and barium oxide are examples of materials classed as ORM-B.

Other Regulated Material, ORM-C
Every material classed as an ORM-C will be so listed and identified in the Table of Hazardous Materials (40 CFR 172.101). An ORM-C material has other inherent characteristics not included within the ORM-A or ORM-B classes, but which renders the material unsuitable for shipment unless properly identified and prepared for transportation. One material considered in the Table of Hazardous Materials as an ORM-C is a magnetized material. A substance is considered to be a magnetized material if, when packaged for transport by air, it has a magnetic field strength of 0.002 gauss or more at a distance of 7 feet from any point of the surface of the package, or is of such a mass that it could affect the aircraft instruments, particularly the compasses. Petroleum coke, sawdust (when dry, clean, and free from oil), copra, castor beans and food (wet, mixed) are examples of materials classed as ORM-C.

Other Regulated Material, ORM-D
Materials, such as consumer commodities that would otherwise be subject to the hazardous materials regulations, that present a limited hazard during transportation because of their form, quantity, and packaging are classed as ORM-D; and ORM-D classification is only allowed when the material is granted an exception in a reference from the Table of Hazardous Materials. For example, a consumer commodity that contains a flammable solid and would ordinarily be classed as Flammable Solid, could be reclassified as an ORM-D material, provided the flammable solid is

inside containers each having a net weight of 1 pound or less, packed in strong outside packaging each having a net weight of 25 pounds or less.

Other Regulated Material, ORM-E

Materials that are not included in any other hazard class but that are hazardous wastes or hazardous substances and so designated by the Environmental Protection Agency's regulations (40 CFR 172.101).

Other Restricted Access (Nonsubstation) Locations

Areas other than electrical substations that are at least 0.1 kilometer (km) from a residential/commercial area and limited by manmade barriers (e.g., fences and walls) to substantially limited by naturally occurring barriers such as mountains, cliffs, or rough terrain. These areas generally include industrial facilities and extremely remote rural locations. [Areas where access is restricted but are less than 0.1 km from a residential/commercial area are considered to be residential/commercial areas].

Otherwise Protected Coastal Area

An undeveloped coastal barrier within the boundaries of an area established under federal, state, or local law, or held by a qualified organization, primarily for wildlife refuge, sanctuary, recreational, or natural resource conservation purposes.

Otherwise Use

Any use of a toxic chemical that is not covered by the terms "manufacture" or "process" and includes use of a toxic chemical contained in a mixture or trade name product. Relabeling or redistributing a container of a toxic chemical where no repackaging of the toxic chemical occurs does not constitute use or processing of the toxic chemical.

Outage

1) That space required to be left in the vessel to provide for expansion of the liquid by an increase of temperature. 2) For liquified natural gas (LNG), outage is that space required to be left in vessels filled by volume to provide for separation of the vapors resulting from boil-off of the liquid and also to provide for the expansion of the liquid with increase of temperature. 3) The amount by which a packaging falls short of being liquid full, usually expressed in percent by volume.

Outbound Traffic

Traffic originating in continental United States destined for overseas or overseas traffic moving in a general direction away from the continental United States.

Outdoor Electrical Substation

An outdoor, fenced-off, and restricted access area used in the transmission and/or distribution of electrical power. Outdoor electrical substations must restrict public access by being fenced or walled off. For purposes of the PCB Spill Cleanup Policy, outdoor electrical substations are defined as being located at least 0.1 km from a residential/commercial area. Outdoor fenced-off restricted access areas used in the transmission and/or distribution of electrical power that are located less than 0.1 km from a residential/commercial area are considered to be residential/commercial areas.

Outer Continental Shelf (OCS) Source

As defined in the CAA, any equipment, activity, or facility that a) emits or has the potential to emit any air pollutant; b) is regulated or authorized under the Outer Continental Shelf Lands Act (43 USC 1331 et seq.); and c) is located on the Outer Continental Shelf or in or on waters above the Outer Continental Shelf. Such activities include, but are not limited to, platform and drill ship exploration, construction, development, production, processing, and transportation. Emissions emanating from any vessel servicing or associated with an OCS source, including emissions while at the OCS source or en route to or from the OCS source within 25 miles of the OCS source, are considered direct emissions from the OCS source.

Outfall

The place where an effluent is discharged into receiving waters.

Outfall Sewer

A pipe that transports raw or treated sewage to its final point of discharge.

Outline Map

A map that represents sufficient geographic information to only permit the correlation of additional data placed upon it.

Outline Plan

A preliminary plan that outlines the salient features or principles of a course of action prior to the initiation of detailed planning.

Output Power

1) The energy per second measured in watts emitted from the laser in the form of coherent light. 2) Power — the rate of energy delivery expressed in watts (joules per second; i.e., 1 Watt = 1 joule x 1 second).

Outside Air

The air outside buildings and structures.

Outside Container

The outermost enclosure used in transporting a hazardous material other than a freight container; provides protection against the unintentional release of its contents.

Outter

An extreme value in a data set so far removed from the other values with which it is associated that the chance probability of its being a valid member of the group is very small. Such a questionable value may be eliminated from the group on the basis of further statistical investigations of the data set.

Overburden

The rock and soil cleared away before mining.

Overfill Releases

Releases that occur when a tank is filled beyond its capacity, resulting in a discharge of the regulated substance to the environment.

Overfire Air

Air forced into the top of an incinerator or boiler to fan the flames.

Overgrazing

A term referring to what occurs when animals feed too long in one area, causing destruction of vegetation and erosion of soil.

Overland Flow

A land application technique that cleanses wastewater by allowing it to flow over a sloped surface. As the water flows over the surface, the contaminants are removed and the water is collected at the bottom of the slope for reuse.

Overlap

1) In photography, the amount by which one photograph includes the same area covered by another, customarily expressed as a percentage. The overlap between successive air photographs on a flight line is called "forward overlap." The overlap between photographs in adjacent parallel flight lines is called "side overlap." 2) In cartography, that portion of a map or chart that overlaps the area covered by another of the same series.

Overlay

A printing or drawing on a transparent or semitransparent medium at the same scale as a map, chart, etc., to show details not appearing or requiring special emphasis on the original.

Overpressure

1) The pressure resulting from the blast wave of an explosion. It is referred to as "positive" when it exceeds atmospheric pressure and "negative" during the passage of the wave when resulting pressures are less than atmospheric pressure. 2) The peak incident pressure. 3) The incident plus dynamic pressure. 4) The reflected pressure.

Overprint

Information printed or stamped upon a map or chart, in addition to that originally printed, to show data of importance or special use.

Overseas

All locations, including Alaska and Hawaii, outside the continental United States.

Oversights and Omissions

Those things that are overlooked or left out of an organization's plans due to inadvertence, that cause delays, problems, or failures in achieving stated goals.

Overt Operation

An operation conducted openly, without concealment.

Overturn

The period of mixing (turnover), by top to bottom circulation, of previously stratified water masses. This phenomenon may occur in spring and/or fall, or after storms. It results in a uniformity of chemical and physical properties of the water at all depths.

Oviposition

A species descriptor that means to lay eggs.

Ovoid

A species descriptor that means egg shaped.

Ovotestis

A species descriptor that means the hermaphroditic (bisexual) reproductive glands of some gastropods.

Ovoviviparous

A species descriptor that means the condition in which eggs are hatched within the mother and born alive.

Ovum

A species descriptor that means the female reproductive cell or gamete (egg) in animals.

Owner/Operator (O/O)

1) The person or company who owns a facility or part of a facility; with a few exceptions the following definitions are applicable a) in the case of a hazardous substance that has been accepted for transportation by a common or contract carrier, the term owner or operator means the common carrier or other bona fide for hire carrier acting as an independent contractor during such transportation; b) in the case of a hazardous substance that has been delivered by common or contract carrier to a disposal or treatment facility the term owner or operator does not include such common or contract carrier; c) the term owner or operator does not include a unit of government that acquired ownership or control involuntarily through bankruptcy, tax delinquency, abandonment, or other circumstances in which the government involuntarily acquires title by virtue of its function as sovereign. Exclusions provided do not apply to any state or local government that has caused or contributed to the release or threatened release of a hazardous substance from the facility. State or local governments shall be subject to the provisions of RCRA in the same manner and to the same extent, both procedurally and substantively, as any nongovernmental entity. 2) In the case of the CAA, any person who owns, leases, operates, controls, or supervises a stationary source. *See* Owner; Operator.

Owner

1) Owners or operators of any facility subject to regulation under the Resource Conservation and Recovery Act (RCRA), Underground Injection Control (UIC), National Pollutant Discharge Elimination System (NPDES), or Section 404 programs. 2) In the case of an underground storage tank (UST) system in use on November 8, 1984, or brought into use after that date, persons who own an UST system used for storage, use, or dispensing of regulated substances; and in the case of any UST system in use before November 8, 1984, but no longer in use on that date, persons who owned such UST immediately before the discontinuation of its use. 3) Persons who own or operate a uranium mill or an existing tailings pile or a new impoundment. *See* Operator; Owner/Operator.

Ownership

Holding any of the following interests in a dwelling, or a contract to purchase one of the first six interests listed below. Those interests are: 1) a fee title; 2) a life estate; 3) a 50-year lease; 4) a lease with at least 20 years to run from the date of acquisition of the property; 5) a proprietary interest in a cooperative housing project that includes the right to occupy a dwelling; 6) a proprietary interest in a mobilehome; 7) a leasehold interest with an option to purchase. In the case of one who has succeeded to any of the foregoing interests by devise, bequest, inheritance, or operation of law, the tenure of ownership, but not occupancy, of the succeeding owner shall include the tenure of the preceding owner.

Oxidants

Substances containing oxygen that react chemically in the air to produce a new substance. For the purposes of this definition, oxidants include ozone, organic peroxides, and peroxyacyl nitrates, but not nitrogen dioxide. Atmospheric oxidant concentrations are to be measured with ozone as a surrogate by ultraviolet photometry, or by an equivalent method. The primary ingredient of photochemical smog.

Oxidation

1) The addition of oxygen that breaks down organic waste or chemicals such as cyanides, phenols, and organic sulfur compounds in sewage by bacterial and chemical means. 2) Oxygen combining with other elements. 3) The process in chemistry whereby electrons are removed from a molecule.

Oxidation Ponds

Manmade lakes or bodies of water in which waste is consumed by bacteria. It is used most frequently with other waste treatment processes. An oxidation pond is basically the same as a sewage lagoon.

Oxidizer

A gas, liquid, or solid material that may accelerate the combustion of other materials, primarily organics.

Oxidizing Materials

Substances that yield oxygen readily to stimulate the combustion of organic matter are considered as an oxidizing material for the purposes of the Hazardous Materials Regulations. Peracetic acid solution, nitric acid (over 40%), and sodium peroxide are all examples of oxidizing material.

Oxygen (O)

An odorless gas element that forms about 21% of the atmosphere and is essential to most living organisms; the most abundant of all elements; can be found in rocks, water, and air.

Oxygen Deficiency

1) Anywhere the oxygen concentration is below that level considered safe for human exposure (not less than 19.5%). 2) Concentrations of oxygen by volume below which atmosphere supplying respiratory protection must be provided.

Oxygenated Gasoline

Fuels containing such levels of oxygen as is necessary, in combination with other measures, to provide for attainment of the carbon monoxide national ambient air quality standard by the applicable attainment date and maintenance of the national ambient air quality standard thereafter.

Oxygenated Solvents

Organic solvents containing oxygen as part of their molecular structure. Alcohols and ketones are oxygenated compounds often used as paint solvents.

Ozonator

A device that adds ozone to water.

Ozone (O₃)

A colorless gas with a pungent odor, having the molecular form O_3, found in two layers of the atmosphere, the stratosphere and the troposphere. In the stratosphere (the atmospheric layer beginning 7 to 10 miles above the earth's surface), ozone is a form of oxygen found naturally that provides a protective layer shielding the earth from ultraviolet radiation's harmful heath effects on humans and the environment.

In the troposphere (the layer extending up 7 to 10 miles from the earth's surface), ozone is a chemical oxidant and major component of photochemical smog. Ozone can seriously affect the human respiratory system and is one of the most prevalent and widespread of all the criteria pollutants for which the Clean Air Act required EPA to set standards.

Ozone in the troposphere is produced through complex chemical reactions of nitrogen oxides, that are among the primary pollutants emitted by combustion sources; hydrocarbons, released into the atmosphere through the combustion, handling and processing of petroleum products; and sunlight.

Ozone Depletion

Destruction of the stratospheric ozone layer that shields the earth from ultraviolet radiation harmful to biological life. This destruction of ozone is caused by the breakdown of certain chlorine and/or bromine containing compounds (chlorofluorocarbons or halons) that break down when they reach the stratosphere and catalytically destroy ozone molecules.

Ozone-Depletion Potential (CAA)

The factors established by the Administrator of EPA to reflect the ozone-depletion potential of a substance, on a mass per kilogram basis, as compared to chlorofluorocarbon-11 (CFC-11). Factors are based upon a substance's atmospheric lifetime, the molecular weight of bromine and chlorine, and the substance's ability to be photolytically disassociated, and upon other factors determined to be an accurate measure of relative ozone-depletion potential.

Ozone Design Value (ODV) Study

The study of whether the methodology in use by the EPA, as of November 15, 1990, for establishing a design value for ozone provides a reasonable indicator of the ozone air quality of ozone nonattainment areas (CAA).

Ozone Layer

A layer of the atmosphere that absorbs energy from the sun's radiation preventing it from penetrating the atmosphere. When polluted, this layer is known as smog.

Ozonometer

An instrument used for measuring the amount of ozone in the air.

P

P-Delta Effect

The secondary effect on shears and moments of frame members induced by the vertical loads acting on the laterally displaced building frame.

PA

See Preliminary Assessment. Also an acronym for the Privacy Act of 1974.

Pacific Northwest Laboratory (PNL)

A DOE Research and Development and Field Facility, established in 1965. PNL has two principal missions. First, as a DOE multiprogram laboratory, PNL develops and deploys technology for energy security and national defense and transfers technology to enhance the international competitiveness of the United States. Second, as the research and development laboratory for the Hanford site, PNL provides advanced technology and environmental surveillance to support Hanford Operations.

Pack

To pack, repack, label, or relabel.

Packaged Laboratory Chemicals (PLC) or Lab-Pack Chemicals

The term used to describe reagent chemicals packaged in sizes of 1 gallon or smaller into DOT-specialized shipping containers for ultimate shipment to a TSD facility for landfill disposal or incineration.

Packaged Petroleum Product

A petroleum product (generally a lubricant, oil, grease, or specialty item) normally packaged by a manufacturer and procured, stored, transported, and issued in containers having a fill capacity of 55 United States gallons (or 45 imperial gallons, or 205 liters) or less.

Packaged Treatment Plant

A portable sewage treatment facility usually used as an interim means of sewage control, pending the construction of a permanent facility.

Packaging

1) One or more receptacles and wrappers and their contents excluding fissile material and other radioactive material, but including absorbent material, spacing structures, thermal insulation, radiation shielding, devices for cooling and for absorbing mechanical shock, external fittings, neutron moderators, nonfissile neutron absorbers, and other supplementary equipment. 2) The assembly of one or more containers and any other components necessary to ensure compliance with the minimum packaging and includes containers (other than freight containers or overpacks), cargo tanks, tank cars, and multiunit tanks.

Packed Tower

A pollution control device that forces dirty air through a tower packed with crushed rock or wood chips while liquid is sprayed over the packing material. The pollutants in the air stream either dissolve or chemically react with the liquid.

Packers
Devices lowered into a well to produce a fluid-tight seal.

Pad
Difference (padding) between operating value and operating limit.

PAG
See Protective Action Guide.

Pair Bond
A long-term relationship between a male and a female. Pair bond species mate for one or several breeding seasons while monogamous species mate for life.

Palea
A small, chafflike bract enclosing the flower of a grass spikelet.

Paleo
A prefix from the Greek word palois meaning "ancient."

Paleoecology
The study of flora and fauna of past environs, including their interrelationships.

Paleolithic
The preagricultural stage of development of human society, where food was obtained via hunting, fishing, and the gathering of wild plants; the early stone age.

Paleontology
Study of plants and past life forms in their historical contexts.

Paleozoic Era
The geologic time occurring between the Precambrian and the Mesozoic eras; composed of the Cambrian, Ordovician, Silurian, Devonian, Car-

boniferous, and Permian periods. The rocks formed during this era are called Paleozoic.

Pallet
A flat base for combining stores or carrying a single item to form a unit load for handling, transportation, and storage by materials handling equipment.

Palletized Unit Load
Quantity of any item, packaged or unpackaged, that is arranged on a pallet in a specified manner and securely strapped or fastened thereto so that the whole is handled as a unit.

Pallial
A species descriptor that means pertaining to the mantle (membrane between the body and shell) of a mollusk.

Palmate
A species descriptor that means having leaflets or lobes radiating from one point; resembling a palm.

Palmate Leaf
A species descriptor that means divided so as to radiate from one point like a hand.

Palynology
The study and analysis of pollen. Pollen grains are highly resistant to most forms of decomposition, and have unique characteristics that can lead to the identification of the species and era from which they come.

Pandemic
Widespread throughout an area, nation, or the world.

Panicle
A species descriptor that means a flower cluster that is loosely and irregularly branched.

Paniculate-Cymose
A species descriptor that means irregularly branched flower cluster blooming from the center.

Panoramic Camera
1) In aerial photography, a camera that, through a system of moving optics or mirrors, scans a wide area of the terrain, usually from horizon to horizon. The camera may be mounted vertically or obliquely within the aircraft, to scan across or along the line of flight. 2) In ground photography, a camera that photographs a wide expanse of terrain by rotating horizontally about the vertical axis through the center of the camera lens.

Papillae
A species descriptor that means a small, nipplelike projection.

Parallax Difference
The difference in displacement of the top of an object in relation to its base, as measured on the two images of the object on a stereo pair of photographs.

Parameter
A value that is a constant and consistent characteristic of a particular set of environmental data (e.g., the average number of cars per household).

Paraphrase
To change the phraseology of a message without changing its meaning.

Paraquat
An organic herbicide used to control weeds and grasses. A standard herbicide used to kill various types of crops, including marijuana. Used incorrectly, it is poisonous to humans; it kills plants on contact.

Pararescue Team
Specially trained personnel qualified to penetrate to the site of an incident by land or parachute, render medical aid, accomplish survival methods, and rescue survivors.

Parasite
An organism that extracts nutrients from another host organism.

Parasitic Stage
The period during the development of an organism in which it feeds on and is sheltered by a different organism (host).

Paratypes
A species descriptor that refers to a specimen other than the holotype that was collected before the original description but has been deemed one of the specimens upon which the original description was based.

PARD
An acronym for Protect as Restricted Data.

Parent Corporations
1) Corporations that directly own at least 50% of the voting stock of another corporation(s) (i.e., facility owners or operators), which are deemed "subsidiaries" of the parent corporations. 2) A separate and distinct corporation or entity that operates two or more firms.

Paresthesia
An abnormal sensation such as burning, prickling, or tingling.

Parietal
1) In anatomy, relating to either of the parietal bones, which are two large, irregularly quadrilateral bones that form, with the occipital bones, the sides and top of the skull. 2) In botany, attached to the ovary wall.

Parking Surcharge Regulations
Regulations imposing or requiring the imposition of any tax, surcharge, fee, or other charge on parking spaces, or any other area used for the temporary storage of motor vehicles.

Part A Permit/Part B Permit
See Interim Permit Status.

Parthenogenic
A species descriptor that means reproduction without contact between the sexual organs.

Partial Closure

The closure of a hazardous waste management unit in accordance with the applicable closure requirements of Parts 264 or 265 of 40 CFR at a facility that contains other active hazardous waste management units. For example, partial closure may include the closure of a tank (including its associated piping and underlying containment systems), a landfill cell, surface impoundment, waste pile, or other waste management unit, while other parts of the same facility continue in operation.

Partial Storage Monitoring

A periodic inspection of major assemblies or components for nuclear weapons, consisting mainly of external observation of humidity, temperatures, and visual damage or deterioration during storage. This type of inspection is also conducted prior to and upon completion of a movement.

Participant

Any individual, group of individuals, organization, association, partnership, or corporation taking part or intending to take part in a Commission proceeding. For the purpose of these rules the term participant does not include governmental entities nor any entity that, in the Commission's reasoned opinion, was established or formed by a governmental entity for the purpose of participating in a Commission proceeding.

Participant Observation

The primary field method of ethnographic anthropological research; involves the observance and recording of behaviors and activities while the researcher is resident in the community under study. The researcher participates in the daily rounds of life as much as possible. Participant observation is combined with other methods to obtain a broad, in-depth view of a group's culture.

Particle

A small mass of solid or liquid matter.

Particle Fluence

As used by the IAEA, the quotient of dN by da, where dN is the number of particles incident on an elementary sphere of cross-sectional area da.

Particle Flux

The quotient of dN by dt, where dN is the increment of particle number in the time interval dt.

Particulate Asbestos Materials

Finely dried particles of asbestos material.

Particulate Loading

The mass of particulates per unit volume of air or water.

Particulate Matter

1) Any airborne finely divided solid or liquid material with an aerodynamic diameter smaller than 100 micrometers. 2) Any finely divided solid or liquid material, other than uncombined water, as measured by the specified reference method. 3) Solid particles, such as the ash, that are released from combustion processes in exhaust gases at fossil-fuel plants.

Particulate Matter Emissions

All finely divided solid or liquid material, other than uncombined water, emitted to the ambient air as measured by applicable reference methods, or an equivalent or alternative method, specified in this chapter, or by a test method specified in an approved state implementation plan.

Particulates

A major category of airborne pollutants. Literally particles of dirt, dust, smoke, mist, or smog found in air emissions.

Parts per Billion (ppb)

A unit of measure commonly used to express low concentrations of contaminants. For example, a) if one drop of chlorine (Cl) is mixed in an olympic size swimming pool, the water will contain approximately 1 ppb of Cl; b) one ppb is comparable to one kernel of corn in a filled, 45-foot silo, 16 feet in diameter.

Parts per Million (ppm)
1) A unit of measure commonly used to express low concentrations of contaminants. For example, 1 ounce of Chlorine (Cl) in 1 million ounces of water is 1 ppm; one ppm is comparable to one drop of gasoline in a tankful of gas (full-size car). 2) A volumetric unit of gas concentration, that is numerically equal to the volume of a gaseous contaminant present in one million volumes of air.

Parts per Trillion (ppt)
One ppt is comparable to one drop of gasoline in a swimming pool covering the area of a football field 43 feet deep. *See* Parts per Million.

Parturition
A species descriptor that means pertaining to childbirth or labor.

Party or Parties
Any person on whose behalf an appearance has been filed in the proceeding; the appellant and the respondent and/or their representatives. A person or agency named or admitted as a party, or properly seeking and entitled as of right to be admitted as a party, in an agency proceeding, and a person or agency admitted by an agency as a party for limited purposes.

Passenger Aircraft
An aircraft that carries any person other than a crew member, company employee, an authorized representative of the United States, or a person accompanying the shipment.

Passenger Mile
A term for one passenger transported one mile. For air and ocean transport, use nautical miles; for rail, highway, and inland waterway transport in the continental United States, use statute miles.

Passenger Vessels
1) A vessel subject to any of the requirements of the International Convention for the Safety of Life at Sea, 1960, that carries more than 12 passengers. 2) A cargo vessel documented under the laws of the United States and not subject to the Convention, that carries more than 16 passengers. 3) A cargo vessel of any foreign nation that extends reciprocal privileges and is not subject to the Convention and that carries more than 16 passengers. 4) A vessel engaged in a ferry operation and that carries passengers.

Passerines
A species descriptor that means birds of the order Passerineformes, that includes perching birds and song birds, such as jays, blackbirds, finches, warblers, and sparrows.

Patent, Land
An instrument for conveyance of land owned by the government to an individual.

Pathogenic
Capable of causing disease.

Pathogens
1) Microorganisms that can cause disease in other organisms or in humans, animals, and plants. They may be bacteria, viruses, or parasites and are found in sewage, in runoff from animal farms or rural areas populated with domestic and/or wild animals, and in water used for swimming. Fish and shellfish contaminated by pathogens, or the contaminated water itself, can cause serious illnesses. 2) Any pathogenic- or disease-producing organisms; organisms that cause communicable diseases.

Pathological Waste
Primarily hospital and laboratory wastes that contain pathogens, whose disposal must be carefully regulated due to the inherent risks to the public health and welfare.

Patient
A sick, injured, wounded, or other person requiring medical/dental care or treatment.

Paucispiral

A species descriptor that refers to the growth lines on a snail's operculum occurring as a few, rapidly expanding spirals.

Payload

1) The sum of the weight of passengers and cargo that an aircraft can carry. *See* Load. 2) The load (expressed in tons of cargo or equipment, gallons of liquid, or number of passengers) that the vehicle is designed to transport under specified conditions of operation, in addition to its unladen weight.

Payments for Land Removed from Production for Conservation (RCA)

The Secretary of Agriculture's contracts to provide financial assistance in the form of payments to owners/operators of cropland located in counties where the soil normally freezes to a depth of at least 4 inches annually who remove such land from agricultural production for a period not to exceed 1 year for the purpose of installing enduring conservation measures that involve excavation of the soil. The payments under such contracts can not exceed an amount equal to the number of acres of cropland removed from agricultural production for such purpose multiplied by 50% of the typical annual rent, as determined by the Secretary, paid for similar land in the county. Financial assistance may not be provided without the approval of the soil and water conservation district board for the district in which the land is located.

PB

Polybutylene.

PCB and PCBs

1) Any chemical substance that is limited to the biphenyl molecule that has been chlorinated to varying degrees or any combination of substances that contain any such substance. 2) A group of toxic, persistent chemicals (polychlorinated biphenyls) used in transformers and capacitors for insulating purposes and in gas pipeline systems as a lubricant. Further sale of, or use of new, PCBs was banned by law in 1979. *See* Polychlorinated Biphenyls.

PCB Article

Any manufactured article, other than a PCB container, that contains PCBs and whose surface(s) has been in direct contact with PCBs. PCB articles include capacitors, transformers, electric motors, pumps, pipes, and any other manufactured item that a) is formed to a specific shape or design during manufacture; b) has end use function(s) dependent in whole or in part upon its shape or design during end use; and c) has either no change of chemical composition during its end use or whose changes of composition have no commercial purpose separate from that of the PCB article.

PCB Article Container/PCB Container

Any package, can, bottle, bag, barrel, drum, tank, or other device used to contain PCB articles or PCB equipment and whose surface(s) has not been in direct contact with PCBs.

PCB Equipment

Any manufactured item, other than a PCB container or PCB article container, that contains a PCB article or other PCB equipment (includes microwave ovens, electronic equipment, and fluorescent light ballasts and fixtures).

PCB Item

Any PCB article, PCB article container, PCB container, or PCB equipment that deliberately or unintentionally contains or has as a part of it any PCB or PCBs at a concentration of 50 ppm or greater.

PCB Transformer

Any transformer with dielectric fluid that contains 500 ppm PCB or greater concentration.

PCB Transformer Rupture

A violent or nonviolent break in the integrity of a PCB transformer caused by an overtemperature and/or overpressure condition that results in the release of PCBs.

PCB Waste Generator

Any person whose action or process produces PCBs that are regulated for disposal under 40 CFR 761 Subpart D, or whose action first causes PCBs or PCB items to become subject to the disposal requirements of Subpart D, or who has physical control over the PCBs when a decision is made that the use of the PCBs has been terminated and therefore is subject to the disposal requirements. Unless another provision specifically requires a site-specific meaning, "generator of PCB waste" includes all of the sites of PCB waste generation owned or operated by the person who generates PCB waste.

PCB Wastes

Those PCBs and PCB hems that are subject to the disposal requirements of 40 CFR 761.60. PCBs at concentrations of 500 ppm or greater must be disposed of in an incinerator that complies with 40 CFR 761.70.

PCB-Contaminated Electrical Equipment

Electrical equipment, including but not limited to transformers (including those used in railroad locomotives, etc.), capacitors, circuit breakers, reclosers, voltage regulators, switches (including sectionalizers and motor starters), electromagnets, and cable that contain PCBs at 50 ppm or greater, but less than 500 ppm. Oil-filled electrical equipment other than circuit breakers, reclosers, and cable whose PCB concentration is unknown must be assumed to be PCB-contaminated electrical equipment. Provisions permitting reclassification of electrical equipment containing PCBs at 500 ppm or greater PCBs to PCB-contaminated electrical equipment do exist.

PCC

An acronym for Primary Component Cooling.

pci/g

See Picocuries per Gram.

pci/l

See Picocuries per Liter.

PCLFC

An acronym for Projected Consequences of Less than Full Control.

PCMNA

An acronym for Provisions for Carbon Monoxide Nonattainment Areas (CAA).

PCNC

An acronym for Projected Consequences of No Control.

PCPS

See Pulverized-Coal Power System.

Peak Overpressure

The maximum value of overpressure at a given location that is generally experienced at the instant the shock (or blast) wave reaches that location. *See* Shock Wave.

Peak Positive Incident Pressure

The almost instantaneous rise from the ambient pressure caused by a blast wave's pressure disturbance.

Peaking Capacity

That part of a system's equipment that is prorated only during the hours of highest power demand.

Peaking Load

The greatest amount of all of the power loads on a system, or part thereof, that has occurred at one specified period of time.

PEARL

See Personnel Expertise and Resource Listing.

PECSS

An acronym for Poisoned Emergency Cooling System Sampling.

Pectin

A species descriptor that means colloidal substances found in ripe fruits, such as apples; pectin is used commercially to jell foods, drugs, and cosmetics.

Pectinase

A species descriptor that means a plant enzyme that catalyzes the hydrolysis of pectin.

Pectoral

A species descriptor that means in animals, pertaining to the chest muscle; in fish, the fin located nearest the head.

Pecuniary Liability

A personal, joint, or corporate monetary obligation to make good any lost, damaged, or destroyed property resulting from fault or neglect. It may also result under conditions stipulated in a contract or bond.

Pedicel

A species descriptor that means small stalks bearing a single flower.

Pedicellate

A species descriptor that means supported by a pedicel (small stalk).

Pedipalpi

A species descriptor that means appendages of an arachnid that are modified for sensory functions.

Pedology

The study of the morphology and distribution of soils.

Peduncle

1) In botany, a stalk or stem bearing a solitary flower. 2) In zoology, a starlike structure in invertebrate animals.

PEL

See Permissible Exposure Limit.

Pelage

A species descriptor that refers to the coat of a mammal consisting of hair, fur, wool or other soft covering as distinct from bare skin.

Pelagic

A species descriptor that means ocean-dwelling.

Penalty Assessment Criteria

The criteria used by the Administrator in determining the amount of any penalty to be assessed, and includes, in addition to such other factors as justice may require, the size of the business, the economic impact of the penalty on the business, the violator's full compliance history and good-faith efforts to comply, the duration of the violation as established by any credible evidence, payment by the violator of penalties previously assessed for the same violation, the economic benefit of noncompliance, and the seriousness of the violation. A penalty may be assessed for each day of violation.

Penalties for Failure to Comply with New Source Requirements

Penalties posed for noncompliance with any requirement or prohibition of the CAA relating to the construction of new sources or the modification of existing sources. The Administrator's penalties may include the following: a) issuance of an order prohibiting the construction or modification of any major stationary source in any area of noncompliance; b) issuance of an administrative penalty order; c) commencement of a civil action for a permanent or temporary injunction, or to assess and recover civil penalties up to $25,000 per day for each violation, or both; or d) commencement of a criminal action which upon conviction, is punishable by a fine pursuant to Title 18 or by imprisonment up to 5 years, or both.

Penalties for Knowing and Willful Violations

The penalties for such violations which, upon conviction, result in fines, imprisonment, or both. Under the CAA, any organization who knowingly releases listed hazardous air pollutants or extremely hazardous substances into the ambient air (or who knows at the time that they are placing others in imminent danger of death or serious bodily injury) are usually, upon conviction, punished by a fine of not more than $1,000,000 for each violation.

Pendent
A species descriptor that means hanging down, dangling, or suspended.

Pendulous
A species descriptor that means hanging loosely so as to swing or sway.

Penetrating Radiation
A general term used to describe external radiations with sufficient penetrating power that the absorbed dose from exposures to humans are delivered in significant quantities to tissues and organs other than the skin. It refers to most gamma radiation, X-radiation (excluding those with very low energy), and neutron radiation.

PEO
An acronym for Program Enrichment Office.

Peraeonal Segment
A species descriptor that means an individual segment of the shell in a sequence.

Peraeonal
A species descriptor that means a segment of a snail's shell.

Perceived Risk
1) A subjective assessment of a threat or hazard by a group of individuals, that may, or may not, bear any relationship to environmental facts and the statistical probability of an occurrence. 2) Risks as a person believes or understands them to be, whether actual or not. *See* Assessment of Risk.

Perched Water
Unconfined groundwater separated from an underlying main body of groundwater by an unsaturated zone.

Percoid
A species descriptor pertaining to the suborder of fish including perches, sunfishes, groupers, and grunts.

Percolation
1) The downward movement of water through the unsaturated zone; also defined as the downward flow of water in saturated or nearly saturated porous media at hydraulic gradients of 1.0 or less. 2) The act of water seeping or filtering through the soil without a definite channel. 3) The movement of water downward and radially through the sub-surface soil layers, usually continuing downward to the groundwater.

Percolation Pond
A basin into which the effluent from a sewerage treatment plant is pumped so that it may be absorbed into the ground for disposal and additional filtering.

Percolation Test
A soil test to determine if soil will take sufficient water seepage for use of septic tank.

Percutaneous Absorption
Passage of a substance through unbroken skin.

Performance Assessments
Systematic analysis of the potential risks posed by waste management systems to the public and environment and a comparison of those risks to established performance objectives.

Performance Bond
Cash or securities, deposited before a landfill operating permit is issued, that are held to ensure that all requirements for operating a landfill are performed. The money is returned to the owner after proper closure of the landfill is complete. If contamination or other problems appear at any time during operation, or upon closure, and are not addressed, the owner must forfeit all or part of the performance bond that is then used to cover costs of cleanup.

Performance Evaluation Samples

Reference samples provided to a laboratory for the purpose of demonstrating that the laboratory can successfully analyze the sample within limits of performance specified by the Agency. The true value of the concentration of the reference material is unknown to the laboratory at the time of the analysis.

Performance Objectives

Findings and concerns as stated within a Tiger Team Assessment are prefaced by a statement of the Performance Objective in each discipline area. Performance Objectives for Compliance Findings are derived from promulgated regulations and final DOE Orders, consent orders, agreements, and permit conditions. Performance Objectives for Best Management Practice Findings are derived from regulatory agency guidance, accepted industry practices, and professional judgment.

Performance Testing Laboratories

Calibration laboratories designated by the DOE Laboratory Accreditation Administrator to test dosimeters.

Performance-Based Training

A systematic approach to training that is based on tasks and the related knowledge and skills required for competent job performance.

Perianth

A species descriptor that means the outer envelope of a flower.

Peridotite

A species descriptor that means igneous rocks having a granitelike texture.

Periodicity

Recurring patterns of activity or behavior.

Periostracum

A species descriptor for the protective layer covering the outer portion of a mollusk shell.

Peripheral Nervous System

The portion of the nervous system outside of the brain and spinal cord, that includes sense organs and the nerves controlling the body.

Peripheral Neuropathy

A disorder of the peripheral nerves.

Periphyton

A species descriptor that means stationary organisms that live attached to surfaces projecting from the bottom of a freshwater environment.

Perishable Cargo

Cargo requiring refrigeration, such as meat, fruit, fresh vegetables, and medical department biological materials. *See* Cargo.

Permafrost

Permanently frozen subsoil; a permanently frozen layer of variable depth below the earth's surface in frigid regions.

Permanent Exemptions

Releases from mandatory standards. Such exemptions are not time-specified.

Permanent Partial Disabilities

Injuries other than death or permanent total disability that result in the loss, or complete loss of use, of any member or part of a member of the body or any permanent impairment of functions of the body or body pan. Loss disregards any pre-existing disability of the injured member or impaired body function.

Permanent Total Disabilities

Injuries other than death (from one accident) that permanently and totally incapacitate an employee, that deny gainful occupation, or result in the loss of use, or complete loss of, a) both eyes; b) one eye and one hand, arm, leg or foot; or c) any two of the following not on the same limb (hand, arm, foot, leg).

Permanent Variances

Releases from governmental ordinances, statutes, laws and regulatory standards. Such variances are not time-specified.

Permeability

The ability of a porous medium to transmit fluids under a hydraulic gradient. The property or capacity of a porous rock, sediment, or soil for transmitting a fluid. A measure of relative ease of fluid flow under unequal pressure; the rate at which liquids pass through soil or other materials in a specified direction.

Permeability Coefficient

The rate of flow of water through a unit cross-sectional area under a unit hydraulic gradient at the prevailing temperature adjusted to 15° C.

Permeation

The passage of chemicals, on a molecular level, through intact material such as protective clothing.

Permious

That property of a surface that allows water or other fluids to pass through.

Permissible Exposure Limit (PEL)

1) The maximum time-weighted average concentration mandated by the Occupational Safety and Health Administration (OSHA) to which workers may be repeatedly exposed for 8 hours per day, 40 hours per week without adverse health effects. 2) The regulatory exposure, inhalation or dermal, permissible exposure limit specified by OSHA, in 20 CFR Part 1910, Subparts G and Z.

Permit

1) An authorization, license, or equivalent control document issued by EPA or an approved state to implement the requirements of 40 CFR Parts 124, 270, and 274. 2) The whole or a part of an agency application, certificate, registration, charter, membership, statutory exemption or other form of permission or approval. 3) A document issued by a governmental entity to implement the require-

ments of a building, planning, or environmental regulation; e.g., a permit to build a structure, operate a wastewater treatment plant, or to operate a facility that may generate harmful emissions. Permits include RCRA "permit by rule" (Section 270.60), Underground Injection Control (UIC) Area Permit (Section 144.33), NPDES or 404 General Permit (Sections 270.61, 144.34, and 233.38). Permits do not include RCRA Interim Status (Section 270.70), UIC Authorization by Rule (Section 144.21), or any permit that has not yet been the subject of final agency action, such as a "draft permit" or a "proposed permit."

Permits Necessary to Begin Physical Construction

Permits and approvals required under federal, state, or local hazardous waste control statutes, regulations, or ordinances.

Permitting

An agency process respecting the grant, renewal, denial, revocation, suspension, annulment, withdrawal, limitation, amendment, modification, or conditioning of a permit.

Permitting Authorities

1) The District Engineer of the U.S. Army Corps of Engineers or such other individuals as may be designated by the Secretary of the Army to issue or deny permits under Section 404 of the Act; or the state Director of a permit program approved by EPA under Section 404(g) and Section 404(h) or his/her delegated representative. 2) Any governmental entity with police powers, home-rule authority, or authorization based upon enabling legislation.

Pershing

A mobile surface-to-surface inertially guided missile of a solid propellant type. It possesses a nuclear warhead capability and is designed to support the ground forces with the attack of long-range ground targets. Designated as MGM-31A.

Persistence

Refers to the length of time a compound, once introduced into the environment, stays there. A compound may persist for less than a second or indefinitely.

Persistency
In biological or chemical warfare, the characteristic of an agent that pertains to the duration of its effectiveness under determined conditions after its dispersal.

Persistent Emergent
Emergent hydrophytes that normally remain standing at least until the beginning of the next growing season.

Persistent Pesticides
Pesticides that do not break down chemically or break down very slowly and that remain in the environment after a growing season.

Person
As defined by Section 101(21) of CERCLA, means an individual, trust, firm, joint stock company, federal agency, consortium, joint venture, commercial entity, state, municipality, commission, political subdivision of a state, or any interstate body, and includes partnerships, firms, corporations, or associations.

Personal Property
1) Generally capitalizable property that can be moved, that is not permanently affixed to and part of real estate. Generally, items remain personal property if they can be removed without seriously damaging or diminishing the functional value of either the property or real estate. Examples of personal property are shop equipment and automated data-processing and peripheral equipment.
2) In military science, property of any kind or any interest therein, except real property, records of the federal government, and naval vessels of the following categories: surface combatants, support ships, and submarines.

Personal Protective Equipment (PPE)
Protective equipment, including but not limited to, anticontamination clothing such as acid suits, lab coats, radiation suits, and dust masks; eye protection such as goggles, safety glasses, safety glasses with side shields; fall protection devices such as safety belts, safety lines, and nets; flame retardant clothing; safety boots; shoe covers; gloves; hard hats; hearing protection; respirators; seat belts.

Personnel Dosimeters
Devices containing one or more radiation-responsive elements (e.g., film, thermoluminescent, nuclear track detector) and possibly one or more absorbers. A personnel dosimeter is worn to assess "whole body" dose equivalents. Specifically excluded are dosimeters expressly designed for extremities such as finger ring or wrist dosimeters.

Personnel Dosimetry Programs
Programs using personnel dosimeters to determine, record, report, and archive the dose equivalents received by personnel.

Personnel Expertise and Resource Listing
A database consisting of environmental, safety, and health (ES&H) personnel that is continually updated.

Personnel Monitoring Equipment
A device designed to be worn or carried by an individual for the purpose of estimating the dose received by the individual, such as a film badge, a pocket dosimeter, or a thermoluminescent dosimeter (TLD).

Personnel or Facility Personnel
All persons who work at, or oversee the operations of, a hazardous waste facility, and whose actions or failure to act may result in noncompliance. Refer to 40 CFR, Parts 264 or 265.

Personnel Reaction Time (Nuclear)
The time required by personnel to take prescribed protective measures after receipt of a nuclear strike warning.

Perspective Grid

A network of lines, drawn or superimposed on a photograph, to represent the perspective of a systematic network of lines on the ground or datum plane.

PERT

See Program Evaluation and Review Technique.

Pest

An insect, rodent, nematode, fungus, weed, or other form of terrestrial or aquatic plant or animal life or virus, bacterial or microorganism that is injurious to health or the environment.

Pesticide

See Pesticides.

Pesticide Safety Series

A series of leaflets that summarize health and safety aspects of various pesticides and groups of pesticides.

Pesticide Tolerance

The amount of pesticide residue allowed by law to remain in or on a harvested crop. By using various safety factors, EPA sets these levels well below the point where the chemicals might be harmful to consumers.

Pesticide-Related Wastes

All pesticide-containing wastes or byproducts that are produced in the manufacturing or processing of a pesticide and that are to be discarded but which, pursuant to acceptable pesticide manufacturing or processing operations, are not ordinarily a part of or contained within an industrial waste stream discharged into a sewer or the waters of a state.

Pesticides

Any substance or mixture of substances intended for preventing, destroying, repelling, or mitigating any pest, including insecticides, fungicides, and rodenticides. Also, any substance or mixture of substances intended for use as a plant regulator, defoliant, or desiccant. Pesticides can accumulate in the food chain and/or contaminate the environment if misused.

Pesticides, Ground-Based Application Equipment

Equipment that includes, but is not limited to hand sprayers, backpack sprayers, air-blast sprayers, field soil injection equipment, dusters, drills, granular applicators, ground-rig sprayers.

Pesticides, Reentry Interval

The period of time after a field is treated with a pesticide during which restrictions on entry are in effect to protect employees and the general public from potential exposure to hazardous levels of residue.

Petal

A species descriptor that means a segment of the corolla of a flower.

Petiole

1) In botany, the stalk by which a leaf is attached to the stem. 2) in zoology, the slender stalk like connection between the thorax and the abdomen in certain insects.

Petrel

A species descriptor that means seabirds of the order Procellariiformes, especially the storm petrel.

Petroleum

An oily flammable bituminous liquid that may vary from almost colorless to black; occurs in many places in the upper strata of the earth; is a complex mixture of hydrocarbons with small amounts of other substances, and is prepared for use as gasoline, naphtha, or other products by various refining processes.

Petroleum Coke

A solid residue; the final product of the condensation process in cracking. It consists probably of highly polycyclic aromatic hydrocarbons very poor in hydrogen. Calcination of petroleum coke can yield almost pure carbon or artificial graphite suitable for production of carbon or graphite electrodes, structural graphite, motor brushes, dry cells, etc.

Petroleum Engineering

The branch of professional engineering that embraces studies or activities relating to the exploration, exploitation, location, and recovery of natural fluid hydrocarbons. It is concerned with research, design, production, and operation of devices, and the economic aspects of the above.

Petroleum Intersectional Service

An intersectional or interzonal service in a theater of operations that operates pipelines and related facilities for the supply of bulk petroleum products to Army elements and other forces as directed.

Petroleum, Oils, and Lubricants (POL)

A broad term that includes all petroleum and associated products.

Petroleum Pipeline System

The system that transports petroleum products from refineries or bulk terminals to other terminals or interconnections with other pipelines. Usually does not include interconnections within a terminal facility or lines connecting public storage facilities to one another.

Petroleum Product

Crude oil, residual fuel oil, or any refined petroleum product (including any natural liquid and any natural gas liquid product).

Petroleum Refinery

Industrial plant that converts crude petroleum into the many petroleum fractions (e.g., asphalt, fuel oil, gasoline).

Petroleum Reserve

The Strategic Petroleum Reserve.

Petroleum Storage Facility

Any facility or geological formation that is capable of storing significant quantities of petroleum products.

Petroleum UST Systems

Underground storage tank systems that contain petroleum or a mixture of petroleum with de minimis quantities of other regulated substances. Such systems include those containing motor fuels, jet fuels, distillate fuel oils, residual fuel oils, lubricants, petroleum solvents, and used oils.

PETS

An acronym for Procedures for Evaluating Technical Specifications program.

PG

An acronym for Process Gas.

PGDP

An acronym for Paducah Gaseous Diffusion Plant.

pH

The means used to express the degree of acidity or alkalinity of a solution, with neutrality indicated as pH 7; the numerical scale increases with alkalinity and decreases with acidity. See pH Scale below.

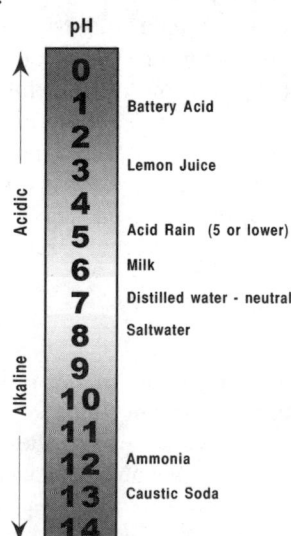

Phacelia
A gastric filament; functions to kill or paralyze live prey taken into the stomach of the species.

Phantoms
As used by the IAEA, mathematical or physical models used to simulate the radiation interaction characteristics of a human or animal body.

Pharmacokinetics
The field of study concerned with defining, through measurement or modeling, the absorption, distribution, metabolism, and excretion of drugs or chemicals in a biological system as a function of time.

Pharyngeal Teeth
A species descriptor that means teeth developed on the pharyngeal bone in many fishes.

Pharynx
Passageway for air from the nasal cavity to the larynx and for food from the mouth to the esophagus.

Phase I Environmental Site Assessment
An inspection process used to determine the environmental conditions at a specific site. At a minimum the Phase I process includes:

- a review of historical site records and available files and databases maintained by regulatory agencies at all levels of government;
- an analysis of special resource issues;
- field inspections of the subject site and adjacent properties for potential hazardous waste problems;
- site photography;
- a preliminary comprehensive asbestos survey;
- a final report regarding any potential issues of concern, with appendices that include maps, aerial photos, a 50 year title chain, and pertinent agency findings on, and immediately adjacent to, the subject site.

The Phase I inspection does not typically include sampling, monitoring, or other more detailed types of field/site investigations.

Phase II Environmental Site Assessment
An environmental process used to determine the extents of environmentally harmful chemical or solid wastes defined during a Phase I inspection, that pose a threat to public health. The Phase II process includes a) a review of the quantity and quality of Phase I data and site records; b) a review of available files and databases maintained by regulatory agencies at all levels of government; c) multiple field inspections to conduct site sampling and analysis of materials (or substances) on the subject site and adjacent properties; d) other monitoring as necessary, depending on specific site characteristics, including other more detailed types of field/site investigations.

Phase III Environmental Site Assessment
An environmental process used to mitigate the spread of environmentally harmful chemical or solid wastes sampled and analyzed during a Phase II inspection, that pose a threat to public health. The Phase III process includes a) preparation of a remedial investigation plan to control, neutralize, and mitigate the threat; b) site mobilization; c) multiple field tasks to implement the mitigation alternatives outlined in the remediation plan, and alleviate the hazard by whatever means is required based on the specific site characteristics; and/or, d) other more complex types of field/site construction procedures to limit the spread of the hazard, pending further investigations.

Phased Disposal
A method of tailings management and disposal that uses lined impoundments meeting the requirements of 40 CFR 192.32, no greater than 40 acres in area.

Phenology
The study of periodic biological occurrences and behavior, such as flowering, breeding, and migration.

Phenols
Organic compounds that are byproducts of petroleum refining, tanning, and textile, dye, and resin manufacturing. Low concentrations cause taste

and odor problems in water; higher concentrations can kill aquatic life and humans.

Phenophases
Leaf color change.

Phenotype
A species descriptor for organisms exhibiting similar environmentally and genetically observable appearances.

Pheromones
1) A hormonal chemical produced by members of a species that influences the behavior of other members of the same species. 2) Hormonal chemicals produced by females of a species to attract a mate.

Phoenix
A long-range air-to-air missile with electronic guidance/homing. Designated as AIM-54A.

Phonetic Alphabet
A military list of standard words used to identify letters in a message transmitted by radio or telephone. The following are the authorized words, listed in order, for each letter in the alphabet: ALPHA, BRAVO, CHARLIE, DELTA, ECHO, FOXTROT, GOLF, HOTEL, INDIA, JULIET, KILO, LIMA, MIKE, NOVEMBER, OSCAR, PAPA, QUEBEC, ROMEO, SIERRA, TANGO, UNIFORM, VICTOR, WHISKEY, X-RAY, YANKEE, and ZULU. *See* Operational Emergency Response Levels.

Phosphate Rocks
Ores from which phosphorus is extracted and that often contain low concentrations of uranium.

Phosphates
Certain chemical compounds containing phosphorus.

Phosphorus
An essential chemical food element that can contribute to the eutrophication of lakes and other water bodies. Increased phosphorus levels result from discharge of phosphorus-containing materials into surface waters.

Photic Zone
The upper water layer down to the depth of effective light penetration where photosynthesis balances respiration. This level (the compensation level) usually occurs at the depth of 1% light penetration and forms the lower boundary of the zone of net metabolic production.

Photochemical Oxidants
Air pollutants formed by the action of sunlight on oxides of nitrogen and hydrocarbons.

Photochemical Smog
Air pollution caused by chemical reactions of various pollutants emitted from different sources; ultraviolet radiation from the sun is thought to be significant to the reactions.

Photogrammetric Control
Control established by photogrammetric methods as distinguished from control established by ground methods. Also called minor control.

Photogrammetry
The science or art of obtaining reliable measurements from photographic images.

Photographic Coverage
The extent to which an area is covered by photography from one mission or a series of missions or in a period of time. Coverage, in this sense, conveys the idea of availability of photography and is not a synonym for the word "photography."

Photographic Panorama
A continuous photograph or an assemblage of overlapping oblique or ground photographs that have been matched and joined together to form a continuous photographic representation of the area.

Photographic Scale
The ratio of a distance measured on a photograph or mosaic to the corresponding distance on the

ground, classified as follows: a) very large scale – 1:4,999 and larger; b) large scale – 1:5,000 to 1:9,999; c) medium scale – 1:10,000 to 1:24,999; d) small scale – 1:25,000 to 1:49,999; and e) very small scale – 1:50,000 and smaller. *See* Scale.

Photomap

A reproduction of a photograph or photomosaic upon which the grid lines, marginal data, contours, place names, boundaries, and other data may be added.

Photon

A quantum of electromagnetic energy having properties of both a wave and a particle, but without mass or electric charge.

Photoperiod

The number of hours of light in a given day.

Photophobia

Abnormal sensitiveness to light, especially of the eyes.

Photosynthesis

1) The process by which plants convert light to chemical energy and synthesize organic compounds from inorganic compounds, such as carbon dioxide to oxygen. 2) The manufacture by plants of carbohydrates and oxygen from carbon dioxide and water in the presence of chlorophyll, using sunlight as an energy source.

Photovoltaic Conversion

Transformation of solar radiation directly into electricity by means of a solid-state device such as the single-crystal silicon solar cell. The physical phenomenon exhibited under certain circumstances by some materials in which a portion of the light energy striking the material is directly converted to electrical energy.

Photovoltaic System, Hybrid

A system of components that generates electricity from incident sunlight by means of the photovoltaic effect and, in conjunction with electronic and, if appropriate, optical, thermal, and storage de-

vices, provides electricity, as well as heat and/or light for individual, commercial, industrial, agricultural, or governmental use.

Phreatic Water

Groundwater. *See* the same.

PHSA

See Public Health Service Act.

Phyllite

A green, gray, or red metamorphic rock similar to slate.

Phylum

1) A species descriptor that distinguishes organisms by their bodily structure after first dividing organisms by their kingdoms. For example, sponges form one group within the phylum while mollusks and arthropods form two other groups. Vertebrates (animals with backbones) are grouped into a separate phylum, called a subphylum, that includes mammals and birds. 2) The divisions of the animal kingdom, synonymous to the division of plants.

Physical and Chemical Treatment

Processes generally used in large-scale wastewater treatment facilities. Physical processes may involve air-stripping or filtration. Chemical treatment includes coagulation, chlorination, or ozone addition. The term can also refer to treatment processes, treatment of toxic materials in surface waters and groundwaters, oil spills, and some methods of dealing with hazardous materials on or in the ground.

Physical Characteristics

Those characteristics of equipment that are primarily physical in nature, such as weight, shape, volume, waterproofing, and sturdiness. *See* Physical State.

Physical Construction

Excavation, movement of earth, erection of forms or structures, or similar activity to prepare a hazardous waste management (HWM) facility to accept hazardous waste.

Physical Harm
Injury and/or illness as well as adverse mental, neurological, or systemic effects resulting from an exposure or from circumstances encountered in the course of employment.

Physical Protection
The application of methods for preventing diversion of nuclear material or for detecting such diversion as it occurs.

Physical State
The state (solid, liquid, or gas) of a chemical under specific conditions of temperature and pressure. *See* Physical Characteristics.

Physically Separated
Set apart by distance, fences, walls, or similar obstructions.

Physiologically Based Pharmacokinetics
Pharmacokinetics based on measured physiological variables such as blood flows through organs, etc. *See* Pharmacokinetics.

Phytoplankton
1) Aquatic, microscopic plants. 2) The portion of the plankton community comprised of tiny plants (e.g., algae, diatoms).

Phytotoxic
Something that harms plants.

Picocurie
Measurement of radioactivity. A picocurie is one million millionth, or a trillionth, of a curie, and represents about 2.22 nuclear transformations per minute.

Picocuries per Liter (pci/l)
A unit of measure used for expressing levels of radon gas. *See* Picocurie.

Pictomap
A topographic map in which the photographic imagery of a standard mosaic has been converted into interpretable colors and symbols by means of a pictomap process.

Pictorial Symbolization
The use of symbols that convey the visual character of the features they represent.

Pier
1) A structure extending into the water approximately perpendicular to a shore or a bank and providing berthing for ships and that may also provide cargo-handling facilities. 2) A structure extending into the water approximately perpendicular to a shore or bank and providing a promenade or place for other use, as a fishing pier. 3) A support for the spans of a bridge. *See* Quay; Wharf.

Piezometric Surface
See Potentiometric Surface.

Pig
A container, usually lead, used to ship or store radioactive materials.

PIHSMP
An acronym for Protocol Relating to Intervention on the High Seas in Cases of Marine Pollution by Substances Other Than Oil (1973).

Pile, Nuclear
Fuel elements in a nuclear reactor; called a pile because the earliest reactors were piles of graphite and uranium blocks.

Pile, Waste
1) Any noncontainerized accumulation of solid, nonflowing hazardous waste that is used for treatment or storage. 2) The fuel element in a nuclear reactor. 3) A heap of waste.

Pilose
A species descriptor that means covered with fine, soft hair.

Pine Barrens Area

The Pinelands area in New Jersey, containing approximately 1,000,000 acres of pine-oak forest, extensive surface and groundwater resources, and a wide diversity of plant and animal species. The area provides significant ecological, natural, cultural, recreational, educational, agricultural, and public benefits. The area is depicted as the Pinelands National Reserve on the map entitled *Pinelands National Reserve Boundary Map* (NPS/80,011A; 1978).

Pinnate

A species descriptor that means having leaflets, lobes, or divisions in a featherlike arrangement on each side of a common axis, as in many compound leaves.

Pinnate Leaf

A species descriptor that means compound leaf with leaflets arranged in pairs along a stem.

Pinnatifid

A species descriptor that means having pinnately (arranged on either side of a common axis) cleft lobes or divisions.

Pioneer Plants

Herbaceous annual and seedling perennial plants that colonize bare areas as a first stage in secondary succession.

Pipeline

In logistics, the channel of support or a specific portion thereof by means of which material or personnel flow from sources of procurement to their point of use.

Pipeline Facilities

Pipe rights-of-way and any associated equipment, facilities, or buildings.

Pipeline Gathering System

A pipeline system that collects crude oil from lease storage facilities and delivers it to a crude oil pipeline system.

Pipeline Storage Tanks

Storage facilities owned by a pipeline firm and located at the points of origin and at terminals of pipeline segments and that are used to maintain normal pipeline operations.

Pistil

The seed-bearing organ of a flower.

Pitch

A residual petroleum product used in the manufacture of certain carbon fibers.

PJA

See Proper Job Analysis.

Placards

DOT-required signs that are affixed to the front, rear, and sides of all vehicles transporting hazardous materials and/or wastes. These signs must meet DOT specifications for size, color, and location on the vehicle and must be used according to predesigned hazard classification criteria based on the weight or volume of the particular materials being transported.

Placarded Cars

Rail cars that are placarded in accordance with requirements except those cars displaying only the Fumigation placards.

Plan

1) The National Oil and Hazardous Substances Pollution Contingency Plan published under Section 311(c) of the CWA and revised pursuant to Section 105 of CERCLA. 2) A drawing or set of drawings pertaining to one design for a unit distinguished by size, room configuration or type of construction, or pertaining to one typical system to be used in production models. The design drawings associated with a project include, but are not limited to, vicinity maps, site plans, foundation plans, floor plans, ceiling plans, roof plans, cross sections, interior elevations, exterior elevations and details. 3) Documents containing comprehensive procedures, regulations, or requirements for the purpose of achieving specific

objectives; a written document of goals, objectives, and future implementation strategies for a specific project or time frame.

Planimetric Map
A map representing only the horizontal position of features. Sometimes called a line map. *See* Map.

Planispiral
A species descriptor that means having a shell coiled in one plane.

Plankton
Tiny plants and animals that live in water.

Planned Renovation Operations
Renovation operations in which the amount of friable asbestos material that will be removed or stripped within a given period of time can be predicted. Individual nonscheduled operations are included, and a number of such operations can be predicted to occur during a given period of time based on operating experience.

Planned Special Exposure
An exposure in excess of recommended dose limits, authorized only infrequently under special circumstances during normal operations, when alternative procedures not involving such exposures cannot be used.

Planning
A basic function of management that involves goal-setting, objective-setting, and evaluation; that is, adjustment of objectives, goals, and organizational performance to reflect new policies and conditions. In this way, management can adapt an organization, to its environment, and ensure that it operates with optimal effectiveness and efficiency. At another level, it may require reassessment of all alternatives and resources devoted, or required, to implement a specific project/program. *See* Planning Process.

Planning Factor
A multiplier used in planning to estimate the amount and type of effort involved in a contemplated operation. Planning factors are often expressed as rates, ratios, or lengths of time.

Planning Process
According to the American Planning Association (APA), the process of planning involves the following: a) problem identification – studying the present, analyzing past trends, making projections for the future, and doing research; identifying rational alternative goals, solutions, and techniques; b) weighing competitive interests – working with the public and making recommendations; c) preparing plans and policies – implementing programs and projects; and d) monitoring – tracking the effectiveness of plans and programs.

Planning Zones
Areas for which planning is done to ensure that prompt and effective actions can be taken to protect emergency personnel, the public health and safety, and the environment in the event of a major emergency.

Planograph
A scale drawing of a storage area showing the approved layout of the area, location of bulk, bin, rack, and box pallet areas, aisles, assembly areas, walls, doorways, directions of storage, office space, wash rooms, and other support and operational areas.

Plant Community
A group of plant species that grow in stable association.

Plant Equipment
Personal property of a capital nature, consisting of equipment, furniture, vehicles, machine tools, test equipment, and accessory and auxiliary items, but excluding special tooling and special test equipment, used or capable of use in the manufacture of supplies or for any administrative or general plant purpose.

Plants
Members of the plant kingdom, including seeds, roots, and other parts thereof.

Plasma
An electrically neutral, partially ionized gas in which the motion of the constituent particles is dominated by electromagnetic interactions. The study of plasma motions is called magnetohydrodynamics (MUD).

Plasmid
A circular piece of DNA that exists apart from the chromosome and replicates independently of it. Bacterial plasmids carry information that renders the bacteria resistant to antibiotics. Plasmids are often used in genetic engineering to carry desired genes into organisms.

Plastic Range
The stress range in which a material will not fail when subjected to the action of a force, but will not recover completely so that a permanent deformation results when the force is removed.

Plastic Yielding
The point at which permanent deformation occurs when tensile stress is imposed on a material.

Plastic Zone
The region beyond the rupture zone associated with crater formation resulting from an explosion in which there is no visible rupture, but in which the soil is permanently deformed and compressed to a high density. *See* Rupture Zone.

Plastics
Nonmetallic compounds that result from a chemical reaction, and are molded or formed into rigid or pliable construction materials or fabrics.

Plastron
The ventral part of the shell of a sea turtle consisting typically of nine symmetrically placed bones overlaid by horny plates.

Plate Loss
A phenomena experienced in which there is a loss of scutes, lamina, or other than flat structure.

Platforms
Lower rigid portions of structures having a vertical combination of structural systems.

PLC
See Packaged Laboratory Chemicals.

Plecopteran Nymphs
The immature larval stage of a stonefly.

Pleistocene
Belonging to the geologic period characterized by northern glaciation and the appearance of early forms of humans.

Plenum
An air compartment that is part of an air-distribution system to which one or more ducts are connected. Two basic types are a) a furnace-supply plenum is a plenum attached directly to, or an integral part of, the air-supply outlet of the furnace; and b) a furnace-return plenum is a plenum attached directly to or an integral part of, the return inlet of the furnace.

PLFA
An acronym for Phospholipid Fatty Acids.

Plot Plan
1) A map, chart, or graph representing data of any sort. 2) A portion of a map or overlay on which are drawn the outlines of the areas covered by one or more photographs.

Plugging
1) The act or process of stopping the flow of water, oil, or gas into or out of a formation through a borehole or well penetrating that formation. 2) Stopping a leak or sealing off a pipe or hose.

Plugging and Abandonment Plans

Plans for the plugging and abandonment of wells; in accordance with applicable statutory and legal requirements.

Plugging Records

Systematic listings of permanent or temporary abandonment of water, oil, gas, test, exploration and waste injection wells, and may contain a well log, description of amounts and types of plugging material used, the method employed for plugging, a description of formations that are sealed and a graphic log of the well showing formation location, formation thickness, and location of plugging structures.

Plume

1) A visible or measurable discharge of a contaminant from a given point of origin; can be visible or thermal in water, or visible in the air as, for example, a plume of smoke. 2) The area of measurable and potentially harmful radiation leaking from a damaged reactor. 3) The distance from a toxic release considered dangerous for those exposed to the leaking fumes.

Plume Exposure Pathways

Principal exposure sources for pathways are a) whole-body external exposure (gamma radiation) and/or contact exposure to skin or eyes (hazardous substances) from contact with materials from the plume and from deposited material; b) inhalation and absorption of constituents in the passing plume.

Plume Search Array

A series of high-volume air samplers set out by a field sampling team (FST) at intervals across the path of a predicted plume. These samplers will be allowed to run for a set period of time and then retrieved and counted by the same or a different FST. The results will provide some indication of the quantity of release and the shape of the plume.

Plutonium (Pu)

A heavy, fissionable, radioactive, metallic element with atomic number 94. Plutonium-239 occurs in nature in trace amounts only. However, it can be produced as a byproduct of the fission reaction in a uranium-fueled nuclear reactor and can be recovered for future use.

Plutonium Processing and Handling Facilities

Facilities constructed primarily to process plutonium (including Pu 238) and handle substantial quantities of in-process plutonium where there is a possibility of a release to the environs under normal operations or design basis accident (DBA) conditions. *See* Design Basis Accident (DBA).

Plutonium Storage Facilities

Facilities constructed to store strategic quantities of plutonium.

PLWA

An acronym for Primary Light Water Addition.

PM

Particulate matter with an aerodynamic diameter less than or equal to a nominal 10 micrometers as measured by a reference method based on Appendix J of 40 CFR 50 and designated in accordance with or by an equivalent method designated in accordance with 40 CFR 53. *See* Particulate Matter.

PM Emissions

Finely divided solid or liquid materials, with an aerodynamic diameter less than or equal to a nominal 10 micrometers emitted to the ambient air as measured by an applicable reference method, or an equivalent or alternative method, or by a test method specified in an approved state implementation plan.

PM Standard

The standards effective with respect to model year 1994 and thereafter in the case of light-duty vehicles (LDV), and effective with respect to the model year 1995 and thereafter in the case of light-duty trucks (LDTs) of up to 6,000 pounds gross vehicle weight rating (GVWR), applicable to emissions of particulate matter (PM) from such vehicles and trucks that provide that such emissions from a percentage of each manufacturer's sales volume of such vehicles and trucks shall not exceed the following levels: for LDTs of up to 6,000 pounds GVWR (useful life period) = 5 years/50,000 miles, standard 0.08 gpm; 10 years/100,000 miles, standard 0.1 gpm. *See* NMHC, CO, PM, and NOx Standards.

PM_{10}
Particulate matter nominally 10m and less. *See* PM-10 Increments.

PM_{15}
Particulate matter nominally 15m and less. *See* PM-15 Increments.

PM-10 Increments
The maximum allowable emission increases in particulate matter with an aerodynamic diameter smaller than or equal to 10 micrometers.

PM-15 Increments
The maximum allowable emission increases in particulate matter with an aerodynamic diameter smaller than or equal to 15 micrometers.

PMA
See Power Marketing Administrations.

PMFC
An acronym for Pacific Marine Fisheries Compact.

Pneumonitis
Inflammation of the lungs.

PNL
An acronym for Pacific Northwest Laboratory.

Poikilocytosis
The presence of irregularly shaped red blood cells in the peripheral blood.

Point Designation Grid
A system of lines, having no relation to the actual scale, or orientation, drawn on a map, chart, or air photograph dividing it into squares so that points can be more readily located.

Point of Compliance
A vertical surface located at the hydraulically down gradient limit of the waste management area that extends down into the uppermost aquifer underlying the regulated units.

Point of Disinfectant Application
The point where the disinfectant is applied and water downstream of that point is not subject to recontamination by surface water runoff.

Point of Nearest Public Access
Locations inside or outside a site boundary where a member of the public could legally be (e.g., visitor center or public highway) without the specific knowledge of the owner/operator.

Point of Transfer
The location where connections and disconnections are made in order to transfer from one container to another, or where LPG is vented to the atmosphere in the course of transfer operation.

Point-of-Entry Treatment Devices
Treatment devices applied to the drinking water entering a house or building for the purpose of reducing contaminants in the drinking water distributed throughout the house or building.

Point-of-Use Treatment Devices
Treatment devices applied to a single tap used for the purpose of reducing contaminants in drinking water at that one tap.

Point Source
1) Any discernible, confined, and discrete conveyance, including, but not limited to, any pipe, ditch, ship, ore pit, channel, tunnel, conduit, well, landfill leachate, discrete fissure, container, rolling stock, factory smokestack, vessel, or other floating craft, from which pollutants are or may be discharged. This term does not include return flows from irrigated agriculture. 2) A stationary

location or fixed facility from which pollutants are discharged or emitted. *See* Nonpoint Source.

Poison

A substance that when taken by mouth, inhaled, or absorbed through the skin in small doses or low concentrations has a rapid action that often destroys life or seriously impairs the functions of organs or tissues.

Poison A

Extremely dangerous, Class A poisons are poisonous gases or liquids of such a nature that a very small amount of the gas or the vapor of the liquid mixed with air would be dangerous to life. Class A poisons include liquid bromoacetone, cyanogen gas, liquid nitrogen, peroxide, and phosphine.

Poison B

Class B poisons are not considered as dangerous as Class A poisons. This class includes those substances, liquid or solid, (including pastes and semisolids), other than Class A or "irritating material" that are known to be so toxic to man as to provide a hazard to health during transportation, or that in the absence of adequate data on human toxicity, are presumed to be toxic to man based on results with test animals (e.g., oral toxic testing). Arsenic acid (solid), and liquid chloropicrin are examples of Poison B materials.

POL

See Petroleum, Oils, and Lubricants.

Polar Coordinates

Coordinates derived from the distance and angular measurements from a fixed point (pole).

Polar Plot

The method of locating a target or point on the map by means of polar coordinates.

Polaris

An underwater/surface-launched, surface-to-surface, solid-propellant ballistic missile with inertial guidance and nuclear warhead. Designated as UGM-27. UGM-27A = 1,200 nautical mile range; UGM-27B = 1,500 nautical mile range; UGM-27C = 2,500 nautical mile range.

Police Power

The inherent right of a government, under the constitution, to enact such legislation as may be deemed necessary to protect and promote the health, safety, and general welfare of the public. Environmental legislation is supported by this theory.

Policies

1) Written statements that express the wisdom, philosophy, experience, and belief of an organization's senior managers for guidance toward attainment of stated goals. Lesser categories of guidance include practices or directives. 2) Standard methods of performing work or communicating, such as procedures (step-by-step methods of performing a task).

Policy and Policy Analysis

General principles, strategies, or rules. It is the basis for programs. For example, OSHA's health policy is a strategy to encourage employers to develop preventive health protection systems in their workplaces. This policy is implemented in part through voluntary protection programs and the consultation exemption program. Since policy implies and requires programming of resources (or it remains an abstraction), evaluations of policy requires that the impact of programs be evaluated in terms of overall policy goals. Through this process, operating policies and objectives are examined and evaluated against fundamental agency goals.

Pollen

1) A fine dust produced by plants. 2) The fertilizing element of flowering plants. 3) A natural or background air pollutant.

Pollination

The process by which pollen is transported to the female parts of a flower.

Pollutant

Any substance introduced into the environment that adversely affects the usefulness of a resource. Including, but not limited to:

- dredge spoil,
- solid waste,
- incinerator residue,
- filter backwash,
- sewage,
- garbage,
- sewage sludge,
- munitions,
- chemical wastes,
- biological materials, and
- radioactive materials (except those regulated under the Atomic Energy Act of 1954, as amended).

Examples of material not covered include radium and accelerator-produced isotopes, heat, wrecked or discarded equipment, rock, sand, cellar dirt, and industrial, municipal, and agricultural waste discharged into water. It also does not include a) sewage from vessels, or b) water, gas, or other material that is injected into a well to facilitate production of oil or gas, or disposal. *See* Pollutant/Contaminant.

Pollutant Discharge Elimination System (PDES)

Section 402 of the Clean Water Act, that establishes a permit for discharges to water and provides standards by which such permits may be granted.

Pollutant/Contaminant

1) As defined by Section 104(a)(2) of CERCLA, includes, but is not limited to, any element, substance, compound, or mixture, including disease causing agents, that after release into the environment and upon exposure, ingestion, inhalation, or assimilation into any organism, either directly from the environment or indirectly by ingesting through food chains, will or may reasonably be anticipated to cause death, disease, cancer, behavioral abnormalities, genetic mutation, physiologi-

cal malfunctions (including malfunctions in reproduction), or physical deformation in such organisms or their offspring. The term does not include petroleum, including crude oil or any fraction thereof, that is not otherwise specifically listed or designated as a hazardous substance under Section 101(14)(a) through (f) of CERCLA, nor does it include natural gas, liquified gas, or synthetic gas of pipeline quality. 2) As defined by Subpart F of the National Contingency Plan, the term pollutant or contaminant means any pollutant or contaminant that may present an imminent and substantial danger to public health or welfare. 3) As defined by the Clean Water Act, the term pollutant means dredged spoil, solid waste, incinerator residue, filter backwash, sewage, garbage, sludge, munitions, chemical wastes, biological materials, some radioactive materials, discarded equipment, rock, sand, dirt, and industrial, municipal, and agricultural waste discharged into water.

Pollutant Standard Index (PSI)

Measure of adverse health effects of air pollution levels in major cities.

Pollutant Study

The Administrator's study of hydrocarbons, carbon monoxide, petrochemical oxidants, and nitrogen oxide conducted to assess the impacts of those pollutants and promulgate regulatory controls to prevent the significant deterioration of air quality that would result from the emissions of such pollutants. The study purposes were to provide the following: a) specific numerical measures against which permit applications can be evaluated; b) a framework for stimulating improved control technology; c) protection of air quality values; and d) for fulfillment of the goals and purposes set forth in the CAA. Specific measures to fulfill goals and purposes contain air quality increments, emission limitations and density requirements, and other measures.

Pollution

1) The accumulation of wastes or byproducts of human activity. Pollution occurs when wastes are discharged in excess of the rate at which they can

be degraded, assimilated, or dispersed by natural processes. 2) Generally, the presence of matter or energy whose nature, location, or quantity produces undesired environmental effects. Under the Clean Water Act, the term is defined as the man-made or man-induced alteration of the physical, biological, and radiological integrity of water. 3) The disruption of an ecosystem by contaminants.

Pollution Liability

Liability for injuries or damage to persons, or property, arising from the release of hazardous substances or pollutants or contaminants.

Pollution, Overfishing, and Man-Induced Changes of Ocean Ecosystems Research

Under the Marine Protection, Research, and Sanctuaries Act (MPRSA), the scientific assessment of damages to the oceans natural resources from spills of petroleum or petroleum products. The research includes, but is not limited to, the following: a) the development and assessment of scientific techniques to define and quantify the degradation of the marine environment; b) the assessment of the capacity of the marine environment to receive materials without degradation; c) continuing monitoring programs to assess the health of the marine environment, including but not limited to the monitoring of bottom oxygen concentrations, contaminant levels in biota, sediments, and the water column, diseases in fish and shellfish, and changes in types and abundance of indicator species; and d) the development of methodologies, techniques, and equipment for disposal of waste materials to minimize degradation of the marine environment.

Pollution Prevention and Emissions Control Program (PPECP)

A basic engineering research and technology program to develop, evaluate, and demonstrate non-regulatory strategies and technologies for air pollution prevention. Strategies and technologies are developed with priority on those pollutants that pose a significant risk to human health and the environment, and with opportunities for participation by industry, public interest groups, scientists, and other interested persons.

The PPECP includes the following elements: a) improvements in nonregulatory strategies and technologies for preventing or reducing multiple air pollutants, including sulfur oxides, nitrogen oxides, heavy metals, PM-10 (particulate matter), carbon monoxide, and carbon dioxide, from stationary sources, including fossil fuel power plants; b) improvements in the relative cost effectiveness and long-range implications of various air pollutant reduction and nonregulatory control strategies such as energy conservation, including end-use efficiency, and fuel-switching to cleaner fuels; c) improvements in nonregulatory strategies and technologies for reducing air emissions from area sources; d) improvements in nonregulatory strategies and technologies for preventing, detecting, and correcting accidental releases of hazardous air pollutants; and e) improvements in nonregulatory strategies and technologies that dispose of tires in ways that avoid adverse air quality impacts.

Pollution Prevention Clearinghouse

The EPA Administrator's source reduction information clearinghouse that contains data on management, technical, and operational approaches to source reduction. The clearinghouse's purpose is to a) serve as a center for source reduction technology transfer; b) mount active outreach and education programs by the states to further the adoption of source reduction technologies; and c) collect and compile information reported by states receiving pollution prevention grants, on the operation and success of their source reduction programs.

Pollution Prevention Act of 1990 (PPA)

The Pollution Prevention Act (42 USC 13101 and 13102, 6602 et seq.) focuses industry, government, and public attention on reducing the amount of pollution produced through cost-effective changes in production, operation, and raw materials use. Opportunities for source reduction are often not realized because existing regulations and the industrial resources required for compliance, focus on treatment and disposal. Source reduction is fundamentally different and more desirable than waste management or pollution control. Pollution prevention also includes other practices that increase efficiency in the use of energy, water, or other natural resources, and protect our resource base through conservation. Practices include recycling, source reduction, and sustainable agriculture.

Polyacrylonitrile (PAN)
A product used as a base material in the manufacture of certain carbon fibers.

Polyandry
A species descriptor that means having an indefinite number of stamens (male reproductive organs).

Polybor
Sodium polyborate, neutron absorber mixed with Emergency Core Cooling System (ECCS) light water.

Polychlorinated Biphenyl (PCB)
1) Halogenated organic compounds limited to the biphenyl molecule that have been chlorinated to varying degrees. 2) Chemical substances that are limited to the biphenyl molecule that have been chlorinated to varying degrees or any combination of substances that contains such substance. 3) A group of toxic, persistent chemicals used in transformers and capacitors for insulating purposes and in gas pipeline systems as a lubricant. Further sale of PCBs for new use was banned by law in 1979. *See* PCB.

Polyelectrolytes
Synthetic chemicals that help solids to clump during sewage treatment.

Polyembryonic
A species descriptor that means having multiple embryos.

Polygamy
A species descriptor that means having more than one mate at the same time. More specifically, the female hatches more than one brood in a nesting season with different mates.

Polyhaline
A term used to characterize water with salinity of 18% to 30%, due to ocean salts.

Polymer
1) A high-molecular weight material formed by the joining together of many simple molecules (monomers). There may be hundreds or even thousands of the original molecules linked end to end and others cross-linked. Rubber and cellulose are naturally occurring polymers. Most resins are chemically produced polymers. 2) A basic molecular ingredient in plastic. 3) A very large molecule formed by combining a large number of smaller molecules, called monomers, in a regular pattern.

Polymerization
A chemical reaction in which the molecules of monomers are linked together to form polymers.

Polymorphism
A species descriptor that means the occurrence of different forms, stages, or color types in organisms of the same species.

Polysaline
A term used to characterize water with salinity of 18% to 30%, due to land-derived salts.

Polyvinyl Chloride (PVC)
A tough, environmentally indestructible plastic that releases hydrochloric acid when burned.

Polyvinyl Chloride Plants
Any plants where vinyl chloride alone or in combination with other materials is polymerized.

POM
An acronym for Polycyclic Organic Matter.

PONA
An acronym for Provisions for Ozone Nonattainment Areas.

Population

A group of interbreeding organisms of the same kind occupying a particular space. Generically, the number of humans or other living creatures in a designated area.

Population Dose Projections

Estimates of total radiation dose to which the population may be exposed.

Population Variability

The concept of differences in susceptibility of individuals within a population to toxicants due to variations such as genetic differences in metabolism and response of biological tissue to chemicals.

PORC

An acronym for Plant Oversight Review Committee.

Pore

See Interstice; Pore Space.

Pore Space

The total space in an aquifer medium not occupied by solid soil or rock particles. *See* Interstice.

Porosity

The ratio of the total volume of voids available for fluid transmission to the total volume of porous medium. Also the ratio of the volume of void spaces in a rock or soil mass to the total volume of the mass. Primary porosity refers to voids that were formed during the deposition or cementation of the material, whereas secondary porosity means voids formed after deposition or cementation, such as fractures.

Port

A place at which ships may discharge or receive their cargoes. It includes any port accessible to ships on the seacoast, navigable rivers or inland waterways. The term "ports" should not be used in conjunction with air facilities that are designated as aerial ports, airports, etc. *See* Major Port; Minor Port; Water Terminal.

Port Capacity

The estimated capacity of a port or an anchorage to clear cargo in 24 hours usually expressed in tons. *See* Beach Capacity; Clearance Capacity.

Port Evacuation of Cargoes

The removal of cargoes from a threatened port to alternative storage sites.

Port Evacuation of Shipping

The movement of merchant ships from a threatened port for their own protection.

Portable Air Tank

An air tank mounted with an air compressor on a towed vehicle.

Portable LNG Tank

A service tank not exceeding 2,000-gallon water capacity used to transport liquified natural gas (LNG) to its point of use.

Portable NH_3 Tank

A service tank not exceeding 1,200-gallon capacity used to transport anhydrous ammonia to its point of use.

Portable Tanks

Bulk packaging (except a cylinder having a water capacity of 1,000 pounds or less) designed primarily to be loaded into, or on, or temporarily attached to a transport vehicle or ship and equipped with skids, mountings, or accessories to facilitate handling of the tank by mechanical means.

Portal of Entry Effects

Biological response at the site of entry (e.g., the lungs, stomach) of a toxicant into the body.

Portland Cement

A mixture of lime- and clay-bearing materials that are calcined to form a clinker, that is then pulverized to form a fine powder for mortar concrete mixtures.

Poseidon

A two-stage, solid propellant ballistic missile capable of being launched from a specially configured submarine operating in either its surface or submerged mode. The missile is equipped with inertial guidance, nuclear warheads, and a maneuverable bus that has the capability to carry up to 14 reentry bodies that can be directed to as many as 14 separate targets. Designated as UGM-73A.

Posing an Exposure Risk, Food or Feed

Any locations where human food or animal feed products could be exposed to PCBs released from a PCB Item because the PCBs have a potential pathway to the food or feed. EPA considers human food or animal feed to include items regulated by the U.S. Department of Agriculture or the Food and Drug Administration (including additives). Food or feed is excluded from this definition if it is used or stored in private homes.

Position

A factual contention, legal contention, or specific recommendation by a party relating to an environmental issue to be addressed in a regulatory proceeding.

Positive Exposure

Any recorded exposure, corrected for background, greater than the established minimum detection limit of the monitoring device or the measuring technique employed.

Possessing a Reportable Source

Having physical possession of, or otherwise having control of, a reportable source of radiation.

Possession

1) Actual possession, constituting the occupation of land or improvements with the intent of excluding any occupation by others that interferes with the possessor's rights. 2) Constructive possession, occurs when a person, although he/she is not in actual possession of land or improvements, has a right to possession and no person occupies the property in opposition to such right.

Possessory Interest

An interest in real property that exists as a result of possession, exclusive use, or a right to possession or exclusive use of land and/or improvements unaccompanied by the ownership of a fee simple or life estate in the property. Such an interest may exist as the result of a) a grant of a leasehold estate, an easement, a profit, a prendre, or any other legal or equitable interest of less than freehold, regardless of how the interest is identified in the document by which it was created, provided the grant confers a right of possession or exclusive use that is independent, durable, and exclusive of rights held by others in the property; or b) actual possession by one intending to use the property to the exclusion of any other interfering use, irrespective of any semblance of actual title or right.

Post-Closure

The time period following the shutdown of a waste management or manufacturing facility. For monitoring purposes, this is often considered to be 30 years.

Post-Closure Plan

The plan for post-closure care prepared in accordance with the requirements of 40 CFR 264.117 through 264.120.

Post-Consumer Waste (PCW)

A material or product that has served the intended use and has been discarded for disposal or recovery after passing through the hands of a final user. PCWs are a part of the broader category "recycled materials."

Post-Emergency Response

That portion of an emergency response performed after the immediate threat of a release has been stabilized or eliminated and cleanup of the site has begun. If post emergency response is performed by an employer's own employees who were part of the initial emergency response, it is considered to be part of the initial response and not post-emergency response. However, if a group of an employer's own employees, separate from the group providing initial response, performs the cleanup operation, then the separate group of employees would be considered to be performing post-emergency response operations.

Post-Incident Activities

Those activities occurring after the cessation of an emergency where immediate health and/or safety hazards no longer exist; however, long-term recovery actions or monitoring functions may be required.

Post-Medical Disposition

The removal of a patient from a medical treatment facility by reason of return to service, transfer to another treatment facility, death, or other termination of medical care.

Post-Removal Site Control

Those activities that are necessary to sustain the integrity of a removal action following its conclusion. Post-removal site control may be a removal or remedial action under CERCLA. The term includes, but is not limited to, activities such as relighting gas flares, replacing filters, and collecting leachate.

Postcleithrum

A membrane-bone between the cleithrum and the supracleithrum in the pectoral girdle of a bony fish. These three bones are of dermal origin and are superimposed upon the original cartilaginous pectoral girdle that consists of the scapulae and coracoid.

Posterior

A species descriptor that means the rear or tail region of an animal.

Posterior Margin

A species descriptor that means toward the back end; used in reference to mussel/clam anatomy.

Posthypoxic Encephalopathy

Condition in which the brain has been damaged as a result of insufficient oxygen.

Postocular

A species descriptor that means behind the eyes.

Pot Furnaces

Glass making furnaces that contain one or more refractory vessels in which glass is melted by indirect heating. The openings of the vessels are in the outside wall of the furnace and are covered with refractory stoppers during melting.

Pot Life

The length of time a catalyzed thermosetting resin system retains a viscosity low enough for it to be suitable for processing.

Potable Water

1) Fresh water that is safe for human use and consumption. 2) Water that is free from disease producing organisms and injurious chemicals. It does not possess obnoxious tastes or odors, and is not turbid or colored to a degree that it is rendered repugnant to the consumer.

Potassium Iodide

A thyroid blocking agent that may be used in radiological events involving releases of radioiodine.

Potency

A comparative expression of chemical or drug activity measured in terms of the relationship between the incidence or intensity of a particular effect and the associated dose of a chemical, to a given or implied standard or reference.

Potential Energy

Energy that is not associated with motion — thus, that which is stored in chemical bonds and in water at high elevations is a form of potential energy.

Potential to Emit

The maximum capacity of a stationary source to emit a pollutant under its physical and operational design. Any physical or operational limitation on the capacity of a source to emit a pollutant. These limitations include restrictions on hours of operation of air pollution control equipment and changes in the type or amount of material combusted, stored, or processed, if the limitation or the effect it would have on emissions is federally enforceable. Secondary emissions do not count in determining the potential to emit of a stationary source.

Potentially Acceptable Site
Any site at which, after geologic studies and field mapping but before detailed geologic data gathering, the Department of Energy undertakes preliminary drilling and geophysical testing for identifying site location.

Potentially Responsible Party (PRP)
Any person, group of people, agencies, businesses, or combination of the same (such as owners, operators, generators, and transporters) who are potentially responsible for, or are contributing to, the contamination problems at a hazardous waste site. Whenever possible, EPA requires potentially responsible parties, through administrative and legal actions, to cleanup the hazardous waste sites they have contaminated.

Potentiometric Surface
A surface that represents the level to which water will rise in tightly cased wells. If the head varies significantly with depth in the aquifer then there may be more than one potentiometric surface. The water table is a particular potentiometric surface for an unconfined aquifer.

POTs
An acronym for potentiometers.

POTW
See Publicly Owned Treatment Works.

Pounds per Square Inch (psi)
The pressure of steam, air, water, or any fluids in relation to the square inch; i.e. one pound per square inch = 144 pounds per square foot = 0.07031 kilogram per square centimeter = 2.307 feet of water at 62°F = 27.68 inches of water at 62°F = 2.036 inches of mercury at 62°F = 0.068

atmospheres. *See* Section V: Data Conversion Factors.

Power
The rate at which work is done or energy is transformed. Power is measured in units of work per unit time; typical units are the horsepower and the watt.

Power Boiler
A steam boiler operated at pressure exceeding 15 psi.

Power Factor
The power input divided by the product of ballast input voltage and input current of a fluorescent lamp ballast, as measured under test conditions specified in ANSI standards.

Power Input
The power consumption in watts of a ballast and fluorescent lamp or lamps, as determined in accordance with the test procedures specified in ANSI Standard C82.2-1984.

Power Marketing Administrations (PMA)
The Alaska Power Administration; Bonneville Power Administration; Southwestern Power Administration; Southeastern Power Administration; and Western Area Power Administration. DOE markets energy in three forms: a) electricity produced by federal hydropower projects and acquired from thermal resources under the five PMAs; b) enriched uranium produced for domestic and international customers; and c) crude oil, petroleum products, and natural gas produced from the Naval Petroleum Reserves. The five PMAs market the power generated at all federal multipurpose water projects except those under the jurisdiction of the Tennessee Valley Authority. To carry out their responsibilities, the administrations contract for the sale and purchase of power; develop rates; construct, operate, and maintain transmission lines, substations, switchyards, and attendant facilities; conduct appropriate energy conservation programs; and oversee environmental reviews.

Power of Attorney
A legal instrument that authorizes another person to act, either a specific act or generally, in the stead of the person drawing the instrument.

Power Plant
A fossil-fuel fired electric generating unit that produces electric power for purposes of sale or exchange.

PP
An acronym for Plenum Pressure.

PPA
See Pollution Prevention Act of 1990.

ppb
See Parts per Billion.

PPECP
See Pollution Prevention and Emissions Control Program (CAA).

ppm
See Parts per Million.

PPMNA
An acronym for Provisions for Particulate Matter Nonattainment Areas.

ppt
See Parts per Trillion.

PRA
An acronym for Probabilistic Risk Assessment.

Practicable
Available and capable of being done after taking into consideration cost, existing technology, and logistics in light of overall project purposes.

Pre-Act Endangered Species Part
1) Any sperm whale oil, including derivatives thereof, that was lawfully held within the United States on December 28, 1973, in the course of a commercial activity. 2) Any finished scrimshaw product, if such product or the raw material for such product was lawfully held within the United States on December 28, 1973, in the course of a commercial activity.

Prearchitectural Program
A description of architectural and functional requirements for a building or remodeling project, during the conceptual or planning stage.

Precambrian
A species descriptor that means the oldest and most expansive of geological periods characterized by the appearance of primitive life forms.

Precious Metals
Uncommon and highly valuable metals characterized by their superior resistance to corrosion and oxidation. Included are gold, silver, and the platinum group metals (platinum, palladium, rhodium, iridium, ruthenium, and osmium).

Precipitate
A solid that separates from a solution because of some chemical or physical change.

Precipitation
Removal of solids from liquid waste so that the hazardous solid portion can be disposed of safely; removal of particles from airborne emissions.

Precipitators
Air pollution control devices that collect particles from an emission.

Precise Time
A time requirement accurate to within 10 milliseconds.

Precise Frequency
A frequency requirement accurate to within one part in 1,000,000,000 (one part in one billion).

Precision
The measurement of agreement of a set of replicate results among themselves without assumption of any prior information as to the true result.

Precision is assessed by means of duplicate/replicate sample analysis.

Precocial
A species descriptor that means pertaining to birds that are covered with down and capable of mobility when first hatched.

Precursor
In photochemical terminology, a compound such as a volatile organic compound (VOC) that "precedes" an oxidant. Precursors react in sunlight to form ozone or other photochemical oxidants.

Precursor Front
An air pressure wave that moves ahead of the main blast wave for some distance as a result of a nuclear explosion of appropriate yield and low burst height over a heat-absorbing (or dusty) surface. The pressure at the precursor front increases more gradually than in a true (or ideal) shock wave, so that the behavior in the precursor region is said to be nonideal.

Predator
A species descriptor that means an animal that hunts other animals for food.

Predisclosure Notification Procedures for Confidential Commercial Information
Procedures set forth by Executive Order 12600 (June 23, 1987, 52 Federal Register 23781), intended to improve the internal management of the federal government, with respect to the Freedom of Information Act (FOIA) and Confidential Information. The Order is not intended to create any right or benefit, substantive or procedural, enforceable at law by a party against the United States, its agencies, its officers, or any person.

Preferential Lane
The setting aside of one or more lanes of a street or highway on a permanent or temporary basis for the exclusive use of buses or carpools with three or more riders, or both, in an effort to promote ridesharing and to control the rate of traffic flow and subsequent emissions resulting therefrom.

Preferred Highway
A highway for shipment of highway route controlled quantities of radioactive materials so designated by a state routing agency, and any Interstate System highway for which an alternative highway has not been designated by such state agency.

Preferred Routes
A highway for shipment of highway route controlled quantities of radioactive materials so designated by a state routing agency, and any Interstate System highway for which an alternative highway has not been designated by such state agency.

Prehistory
The course of events in the period prior to recorded history.

Preinitiation
The initiation of the fission chain reaction in the active material of a nuclear weapon at any time earlier than that at which either the designed or the maximum compression or degree of assembly is attained.

Preliminary Assessment (PA)
The process of collecting and reviewing available information about a known or suspected hazardous waste site or release. EPA or states use this information to determine if the site requires further study. If further study is needed, a site inspection is conducted.

Preliminary Biological Opinion
An opinion issued as a result of an early consultation.

Preliminary Design
The preparation of preliminary planning and engineering studies, preliminary drawings, and outline specifications, life-cycle cost analysis, preliminary costs estimates, and scheduling for project completion. Preliminary design provides identification of long lead procurement items and

detailed descriptions of the services provided during preliminary design.

Preliminary Energy Audit

A determination of the energy consumption characteristics of a building, including the size, type, rate of energy consumption, and major energy-using systems of such building.

Preliminary Safety Analysis

Any safety analysis that is not based on final design information.

Premanufacture Notice (PMN)

A notice submitted by persons who intend to manufacture a new chemical substance in the United States for commercial purposes must submit a notice unless the substance is excluded under Section 720.30. If a person contracts with a manufacturer to manufacture or produce a new chemical substance, and the manufacturer manufactures or produces the substance exclusively for that person, and that person specifies the identity of the substance, and controls the total amount produced and the basic technology for the plant process; that person must submit the notice. If unclear who must report, EPA should be contacted to determine who must submit the notice. Only manufacturers that are incorporated, licensed, or doing business in the United States may submit a notice.

Premaxillae

A species descriptor that means bones located in front of and between the maxillary bones in the upper jaw of vertebrates.

Preparedness

The training of personnel, acquisition of resources and facilities, and testing of emergency plans and procedures to ensure effective responses.

PREPP

An acronym for Process Experimental Pilot Plant.

Prescribed Burning

The planned application of fire to vegetation on lands selected in advance of such application.

Prescribed Limits

Limits of any quantity specified by the competent authority for a given radiation practice or source. These are generally lower than the primary, secondary, or derived limits.

Prescribed Nuclear Stock

A specified quantity of nuclear weapons, components of nuclear weapons, and warhead test equipment to be stocked in special ammunition supply points or other logistical installations. The establishment and replenishment of this stockage is a command decision and is dependent upon the tactical situation, the allocation, the capability of the logistical support unit to store and maintain the nuclear weapons, and the nuclear logistical situation. The prescribed stockage may vary from time to time and among similar logistical support units.

Presence Sensing Safeguarding Device

A device designed, constructed and installed to create a sensing field or area to detect an intrusion into such field or area by contaminants or other materials.

Preservation

The act or process of applying measures to sustain the existing form, integrity and material of a structure, and/or the sustaining of the existing form and vegetative cover of a site. Preservation may include:

- cyclic work — the portion of maintenance activities such as tightening, adjusting, oiling;

- housekeeping — that portion of maintenance that removes undesirable or harmful deposits of soil in a manner that does the least amount of harm to the surface treated, repeated over short time intervals so that soil removal can be done with the gentlest and least radical methods;

- maintenance — the act or process of applying preservation treatments to a cultural resource. It includes housekeeping and routine and cyclic work scheduled to mitigate wear and deterioration without altering the appearance of the resource; repair or replacement-in-kind of broken or worn-out elements, parts, or surfaces so as to keep the existing appearance and function of a structure; work to moderate, prevent, or arrest erosion of archaeological sites; emergency stabilization work necessary to protect damaged historic fabric from additional damage; and actions taken to prevent damage and to minimize deterioration of a museum object by practicing preventive conservation or by performing a suitable treatment on an object itself; and

- stabilization — the act or process of applying measures designed to reestablish a weather-resistant enclosure and the structural stability of an unsafe or deteriorated structure while maintaining the essential form as it exists at present.

See Conservation; Object Conservation.

Preservation and Conservation of American Cultural Heritage, Report

A report on preserving and conserving the intangible elements of our cultural heritage such as arts, skills, folklife, and folkways.

This report was to take into account the view of public and private organizations, and to include recommendations for legislative and administrative actions by the federal government in order to preserve, conserve, and encourage the continuation of the diverse traditional prehistoric, historic, ethnic, and folk cultural traditions that underlie and are a living expression of our American heritage.

Preservation, Historic

The identification, evaluation, recordation, documentation, curation, acquisition, protection, management, rehabilitation, restoration, stabilization, maintenance and reconstruction, or any combination of the foregoing activities. *See* Preservation; Historic Preservation.

Preset Guidance

A technique of missile control wherein a predetermined flight path is set into the control mechanism and cannot be adjusted after launching.

Presidential CAA Review

The President's review of release prevention, mitigation, and response authorities of the various federal agencies, for the purposes of clarifying and coordinating agency responsibilities to ensure the most effective and efficient implementation measures are utilized by regulatory agencies, and to identify any deficiencies in authority or resources that may exist.

Presidential Selected Reserve Call-Up Authority

Provision of public law that provides the President a means to activate not more than 200,000 members of the Selected Reserve for 90 days to meet the support requirements of any operational mission without a declaration of a national emergency. It further grants the President authority to extend the original 90 days for an additional 90 days in the interest of national security. This authority has particular utility when used in circumstances in which the escalatory national or international signals of partial or full mobilization would be undesirable. Forces available under this authority can provide a tailored, limited-scope, deterrent, or operational response, or may be used as a precursor to any subsequent mobilization. *See* Mobilization.

Pressure

1) A measure of the application of force brought to bear on an object. 2) A force acting on a unit area. Usually shown as pounds per square inch (psi).

Pressure Altitude

An atmospheric pressure expressed in terms of altitude that corresponds to that pressure in the standard atmosphere.

Pressure Breathing

The technique of breathing that is required when oxygen is supplied directly to an individual at a pressure higher than the ambient barometric pressure.

Pressure Head

The hydrostatic pressure expressed as the height (above a measurement point) of a column of water that the pressure can support.

Pressure Releases

The emission of materials resulting from the system pressure being greater than the set pressure of the pressure relief device.

Pressure Sewers

A system of pipes in which water, wastewater, or other liquid is transported to a higher elevation by use of pumping force.

Pressure, Static

The pressure exerted by a fluid at rest.

Pressure Suit, Partial

A skin-tight suit that does not completely enclose the body but which is capable of exerting pressure on the major portion of the body in order to counteract an increased intrapulmonary oxygen pressure.

Pressure Suit, Full

A suit that completely encloses the body and provides a gas pressure, sufficiently above ambient pressure for maintenance of function.

Pressure Vessel

1) An unfired container, including cylinders, used for the storage or accumulation of any gas or liquid under pressure. This definition is not intended to include pressure chambers that are integral parts of such devices as pumps, motors, engines, clothes presses, flatwork ironers, tire molds, where the pressure-containing part is subjected to severe mechanical stresses. 2) A strong-walled container housing the core of most types of power reactors; it usually also contains the moderator, neutron reflector, thermal shield, and control rods.

Pressurized Water Reactor

A power reactor in which heat is transformed from the core to a heat exchanger by water kept under high pressure to prevent it from boiling. Steam is generated in a secondary circulation system. Many reactors producing electric power are pressurized water reactors.

Pretreatment

Methods used by industry and other nonhousehold sources of wastewater to minimize, eliminate, or alter the nature of wastewater pollutants from nondomestic sources before they are discharged into publicly owned treatment works (POTW).

Prevalence

The percentage of a population that is affected with a particular disease at a given time.

Preventable Heritable or Congenital Disorders

Any disorder or abnormality present at birth that is detectable by testing a newborn and for which effective means of prevention or amelioration exist.

Prevention

Measures taken to minimize the release of wastes to the environment.

Prevention of Accidental Releases

Regulations and programs authorized under the CAA to prevent the accidental release and to minimize the consequences of any such release of any listed substance or any other extremely hazardous substance. Owners/operators of stationary sources producing, processing, handling, or storing hazardous substances have a general duty to identify hazards that may result from such releases using appropriate hazard assessment techniques, to design and maintain a safe facility taking such steps as are necessary to prevent releases, and to minimize the consequences of accidental releases that do occur.

Prevention of Significant Deterioration (PSD)

Regulations promulgated by EPA governing source construction and modification in attainment areas to satisfy the nondegradation philosophy of the Clean Air Act (Section 160-169). State and/or federal permits are required that are intended to restrict emissions for new or modified sources in places where air quality is already better than required to meet primary and secondary ambient air quality standards. Each state is responsible for classifying its land areas into air quality categories, depending on degree of pollution.

Through the development of a state implementation plan (SIP) states will control all growth in those areas that would cause significant deterioration of air quality for suspended particulates, nitrogen oxide, and sulfur dioxide.

Prevention of Unintentional Introductions of Aquatic Nuisance Species
Regulations issued under the Aquatic Nuisance Prevention and Control Act (ANPCA), 16 USC Chapter 67, that a) apply to all vessels that carry ballast water and enter a United States port on the Great Lakes after operating on the waters beyond the exclusive economic zone; b) require a vessel to carry out exchange of ballast water on the waters beyond the exclusive economic zone prior to entry into any port within the Great Lakes; carry out an exchange of ballast water in other waters where the exchange does not pose a threat of infestation or spread of aquatic nuisance species in the Great Lakes and other waters of the United States, as recommended by the Aquatic Nuisance Species Task Force; or use environmentally sound alternative ballast water management methods if the Secretary determines that such alternative methods are as effective as ballast water exchange in preventing and controlling infestations of aquatic nuisance species. Requirements provide for sampling procedures to monitor compliance with the requirements of the regulations; encourage consultation with Canada; and provide for civil and criminal penalties for noncompliance. Requirements do not supersede those established under the Federal Water Pollution Control Act (33 USC 1251 et seq.). *See* Aquatic Nuisance Prevention and Control Act (ANPCA).

Preventive Conservation
That part of the preservation function of object conservation to prevent harm to an object before it occurs. This function includes actions that monitor and control a site's environment, improve storage methods, ensure periodic inspections of objects to ensure proper housekeeping procedures, maintain appropriate security measures, prevent damage from improper handling and transporting of objects, etc.

Preventive Maintenance
The care and servicing by personnel for the purpose of maintaining equipment and facilities in satisfactory operating condition by providing for systematic inspection, detection, and correction of incipient failures either before they occur or before they develop into major defects.

Prey
A species descriptor that means animals that are hunted by predators.

Prices Paid Index
Selected components from the Statistical Reporting Services Annual National Index of Prices Paid by Farmers for Goods and Services adjusted to reflect livestock production costs in the Western states include the following: fuels and energy, farm and motor supplies, autos and trucks, tractors and self-propelled machinery, other machinery, building and fencing materials, interest, farm wage rates, and farm services.

Primary Body Waves (USGS)
Waves that alternately push (compress) and pull (dilate) the material through which they travel. "P waves", or compressional waves, are the first waves to cause vibration in a building.

Primary Confinement Systems
Areas having structures or systems from which releases of hazardous materials are controlled. The primary confinement systems are the process enclosures (glove boxes, conveyors, transfer boxes, other spaces normally containing hazardous materials), that are surrounded by one or

more secondary confinement areas (operating area compartments).

Primary Coolants

Gases, liquids, or solids, or combinations of them, in contact with radioactive material, or, if the material is in special form, in contact with its capsule, and used to remove decay heat.

Primary Copper Smelter

Any installation or intermediate process engaged in the production of copper from copper-bearing materials through the use of pyrometallurgical techniques.

Primary Documents

Reports that are major, discrete portions of a remedial investigation/feasibility study or remedial design/remedial action.

Primary Drinking Water Regulation (PDWR)

A SDWA regulation that   a) applies to public water systems; b) specifies contaminants that, in the judgment of the Administrator, may have any adverse effect on the health of persons; c) specifies for each such contaminant either - 1) a maximum contaminant level, if, in the judgment of the Administrator, it is economically and technologically feasible to ascertain the level of such contaminant in water in public water systems, or 2) if, in the judgment of the Administrator, it is not economically or technologically feasible to so ascertain the level of such contaminant, each treatment technique known to the Administrator that leads to a reduction in the level of such contaminant sufficient to satisfy the requirements of 42 USC 300(g)(1); and d) contains criteria and procedures to ensure a supply of drinking water that dependably complies with such maximum contaminant levels; including quality control and testing procedures to ensure compliance with such levels and to ensure proper operation and maintenance of the system, and requirements as to the minimum quality of water that may be taken into the system and the siting for new facilities for public water systems.

Primary Emergency Plans

Plans prepared by DOE field offices to guide the response of field elements and contractors for major emergencies having departmental, national, or international implications.

Primary Emission Control Systems

Hoods, ducts, and control devices used to capture, convoy, and collect process emissions.

Primary Enforcement Responsibility

The primary responsibility for administration and enforcement of primary drinking water regulations (PDWR) and related requirements applicable to public water systems within a state. *See* Primary Drinking Water Regulation.

Primary Environmental Monitors

Monitoring equipment legally required to monitor ongoing discharges. In general, this term applies to monitors closest to the point of discharge that are used to determine if discharges are within specified limits. It also includes any equipment that actuates automatically in response to set level signals from such a monitor. It does not include equipment in general area, remediation, or compliance monitoring programs. Significant equipment in such programs will fit in the Class B Equipment definition. *See* Class B Equipment.

Primary Fuel

Fuel consumed in original production of energy, as contrasted to a conversion of energy from one form to another.

Primary Interest

Principal, although not exclusive, interest and responsibility for accomplishment of a given requirement, including responsibility for reconciling the activities of other agencies that possess collateral interest in the program.

Primary Limits

Values of dose equivalent and/or effective dose equivalent applying to an individual. In the case of a larger population the limit is taken to apply to the average dose in the critical group.

Primary Review Authority
The organization assigned by the lead agent to perform the actions and coordination necessary to develop and maintain the assigned joint publication under cognizance of the lead agent. *See* Lead Agency.

Primary Standard Attainment Date
The date specified in the applicable implementation plan for the attainment of a national primary ambient air quality standard for any air pollutant.

Primary Standards
National primary ambient air quality standards promulgated pursuant to Section 109 of the Clean Air Act.

Primary Treatment
The initial stage of treating wastewater, during which all solid matter is removed by skimming, settling, or filtering. At this stage essentially all floating or settable solids are mechanically removed by screening and sedimentation. Primary treatment results in the removal of about 30% of carbonaceous biochemical oxygen demand from domestic sewage.

Primate
A nonhuman member of the highest order of mammals, including prosimians, monkeys, and apes.

Prime Farmland
1) Land that is best suited (due to its characteristics) for the production of food, feed, forage, fiber, etc. 2) Land prescribed as such by the Secretary of Agriculture on the basis of moisture availability, temperature regime, chemical balance, permeability, surface layer composition, susceptibility to flooding, erosion characteristics, and that historically has been used for intensive agricultural purposes.

Principal Parallel
On an oblique photograph, a line parallel to the true horizon and passing through the principal point.

Principal Plane
A vertical plane that contains the principal point of an oblique photograph, the perspective center of the lens, and the ground nadir.

Principal Point
The foot of the perpendicular to the photo plane through the perspective center. Generally determined by intersection of the lines joining opposite collimating or fiducial marks.

Principal Scale
In cartography, the scale of a reduced or generating globe representing the sphere or spheroid, defined by the fractional relation of their respective radii. Also called nominal scale. *See* Scale.

Principal Vertical
On an oblique photograph, a line perpendicular to the true horizon and passing through the principal point.

Printing Size, Map or Chart
The dimensions of the smallest rectangle that will contain a map or chart, including all the printed material in its margin.

Priority, General
With reference to operation plans and the implementation tasks derived therefrom, an indication of relative importance rather than an exclusive and final designation of the order of accomplishment.

Priority of Laws
The existing relationship of federal laws to the law of a state, or political subdivision of a state. Generally speaking, no federal law may interfere with a state's right to protect, rehabilitate, preserve, and restore lands within its established boundary.

Priority Problem List
A management system wherein problems and deficiencies within an organization are categorized as to need for attention and importance, based on

input from the organization's line and staff managers.

PRISM

An acronym for Plant Risk Status Information Management System.

Private Applicator (USC)

1) Certified applicator who uses or supervises the use of a restricted material for the purpose of producing an agricultural commodity on property owned or rented by him/her or his/her employer. 2) A householder who uses or supervises the use of a restricted material, outside the confines of a residential dwelling for the purpose of controlling ornamental, plant or turf pests on residential property owed or rented by such householder. 3) A householder who uses or supervises the use of a restricted material not included in Section 6400(b) (federally restricted) within the confines of a residential dwelling owned or rented by such householder.

Privileged Information

Drill or exercise information that must be kept confidential from all participants in order to provide an accurate, nonbiased assessment of a facility's, or team's, emergency response capabilities.

Proandrous

A condition in which the stamens (male organ) of a flower mature before the pistil (female organ) is receptive.

Probability

A ratio of the number of times an event occurs divided by the number of times it is possible to occur. A probability of 1 means the event is certain. A probability of 0 means the event is impossible. A flipped coin has a probability of 0.5 of being heads (or tails).

Probability of Damage

The probability that damage will occur to a facility and persons in the immediate area expressed as a percentage or as a decimal.

Probability of Detection

The probability that the search object will be detected under given conditions if it is in the area searched.

Probability Sampling

A standard statistical methodology by which a sample is selected based on the theory of probability (a mathematical theory used to study the occurrence of random events).

Probable

A term used to qualify a statement made under conditions wherein the available evidence indicates that the statement is factual until there is further evidence in confirmation or denial.

Probable Causes

Causes attributed to an accident or incident as most likely in the absence of positive proof.

Probit Model

A dose-response model that can be derived under the assumption that individual tolerance is a random variable following logarithmic normal distribution.

Procedures

The written or established methods by which a company or organization operates to accomplish its objectives; a sequence of actions that collectively accomplish some desired task. Effective procedures include, but are not limited to the following characteristics: selection and training criteria, supervisory controls, clarity and adequacy, accuracy, emergency provisions and alternatives, cautions and warnings, event sequences, and communication interfaces.

Process Emissions

Inorganic arsenic emissions from copper converters that are captured directly at the source of generation.

Process for Commercial Purposes

The preparation of a chemical substance or mixture, after its manufacture, for distribution in commerce with the purpose of obtaining an immediate or eventual commercial advantage for the processor. Processing of any amount of a chemical substance or mixture is included. If a chemical substance or mixture containing impurities is processed for commercial purposes, then those impurities are also processed for commercial purposes.

Process of Consultation and Cooperation
1) A methodology by which the Secretary of Enegry (DOE) a) keeps the governor or governing body involved fully and currently informed about any potential economic or public health and safety impacts in all stages of the siting, development, construction, and operation of a test and evaluation facility; b) solicits, receives, and evaluates concerns and objections of such governor or governing body with regard to such test and evaluation facility on an ongoing basis; and c) works diligently and cooperatively to resolve such concerns and objections. 2) A methodology by which the state or affected Native American Indian tribe involved can exercise reasonable independent monitoring and testing of onsite activities related to all stages of the siting, development, construction, and operation of the test and evaluation facility, except that any such monitoring and testing shall not unreasonably interfere with onsite activities.

Process, Toxic Chemical
Preparation of a toxic chemical, after its manufacture, for distribution in commerce a) in the same form or physical state as, or in a different form of physical state from, that in which it was received by the person so preparing such substance; or b) as part of an article containing the toxic chemical. Process also applies to the processing of a toxic chemical contained in a mixture or trade name product.

Process Unit Shutdown
A work practice or operational procedure that stops production from a process unit or part of a process unit. An unscheduled work practice or operational procedure that stops production from a process unit or part of a process unit for less than 24 hours is not a process unit shutdown.

Process Units
Equipment assembled to produce a volatile hazardous air pollutant (VHAP) or its derivatives as intermediates or final products, or equipment assembled to use a VHAP in the production of a product.

Process Wastewater
Any water that, during manufacturing or processing, comes into direct contact with or results from the production or use of any raw material, intermediate product, finished product, byproduct, or waste product.

Process Wastewater Pollutants
Pollutants present in process wastewater.

Process Weight
The total weight of all materials, including fuel, used in a manufacturing process. It is used to calculate allowable particulate emissions rates.

Proclamation
A document published to the inhabitants of an area that sets forth the basis of authority and scope of activities of an agency in a given area and that defines the obligations, liabilities, duties, and rights of the population affected.

Procurement
The process of obtaining personnel, services, supplies, and equipment. *See* Central Procurement.

Procurement Items
Any devices, goods, substances, materials, products, or other items whether real or personal property that are the subject of any purchase, barter, or other exchange made to procure such items .

Procuring Agency
Any federal agency, or any state agency or agency of a political subdivision of a state that is using appropriated federal funds for such procurement, or any person contracting with any such agency

with respect to work performed under such contract.

Producing, Special Nuclear

1) To manufacture, make, produce, or refine special nuclear material. 2) To separate special nuclear material from other substances in which such material may be contained. 3) To make or to produce new special nuclear material.

Product Accumulator Vessels

Any distillate receivers, bottoms receivers, surge control vessels, or product separators in volatile hazardous air pollutant (VHAP) service that are vented to the atmosphere either directly or through a vacuum-producing system. Product accumulator vessels are in VHAP service if the liquids or the vapors in the vessel are at least 10% by weight VHAP.

Product Liability

Liability arising out of manufactured goods after they leave the premises. Applies to the manufacturer and those who handle or distribute the goods.

Production

The conversion of raw materials into products and/or components thereof, through a series of manufacturing processes. It includes functions of production engineering, controlling, quality assurance, and the determination of resources requirements.

Production Base

The total national industrial production capacity available for the manufacture of items to meet material requirements.

Production Facilities (AEA; ANL)

1) Any equipment or devices determined by rule of the Nuclear Regulatory Commission (NRC) to be capable of the production of special nuclear material in such quantity as to be of significance to the common defense and security, or in such manner as to affect the health and safety of the public. 2) Any important component part especially designed for such equipment or device as determined by the NRC.

Production Logistics

That part of logistics concerning research, design, development, manufacture, and acceptance of material. Production logistics include standardization and interoperability, contracting, quality assurance, initial provisioning, transportability, reliability and defect analysis, safety standards, specifications and production processes, trials and testing (including provision of necessary facilities), equipment documentation, configuration control, and modifications.

Professional Engineering

A general term that comprises the following branches of engineering practice and science: agricultural engineering, chemical engineering, civil engineering, control systems engineering, corrosion engineering, electrical engineering, fire protection engineering, industrial engineering, manufacturing engineering, mechanical engineering, metallurgical engineering, nuclear engineering, petroleum engineering, environmental engineering, safety engineering, and traffic engineering. *See* specific listings per type of engineering.

Progenitor

A species descriptor that means a direct ancestor or originator of the line of descent.

Program

1) A sequence of instructions to be executed by a computer. 2) A bundle of organizational resources (human, fiscal and technical) and a set of procedures, directed toward achieving specific objectives. 3) A state prepared plan for the conservation and management of all resident species that are deemed to be endangered or threatened, that includes goals, priorities, strategies, actions, and funding necessary to accomplish the objectives on an individual species basis.

Program Evaluation

An assessment of how efficiently and how effectively a program achieves its objectives. Program evaluation may stand alone or as an element of policy evaluation.

Program Evaluation and Review Technique (PERT)
A management system, originally developed on the U.S. Navy's Polaris Weapons Systems, used to analyze and control the timing aspects of a major project. In PERT, events leading to the accomplishment of a task or project are indicated by circles on a chart, with arrows showing the sequence and time between events. The critical path (the longest sequence) is typically highlighted.

Program Manager
The agency individual, or his/her designee designated by and under the direction of a senior official, who is directly involved in the operation of facilities under his/her cognizance, and with signature authority to provide technical direction to contractors.

Program of Nuclear Cooperation
Presidentially approved bilateral proposals for the United States to provide nuclear weapons and specified support to user nations who desire to commit delivery units to NATO in nuclear only or dual capable roles. After presidential approval in principle, negotiations will be initiated with the user nation to develop detailed support arrangements.

Program Offices
A DOE headquarters organization that is responsible for assisting and supporting field organizations in safety and health, administrative, management, and technical areas and reports to the cognizant program secretarial officer.

Program Organizations
DOE organization heads (Assistant Secretary, Administrator, or Director level) responsible for the decisionmaking and implementation of the department's programmatic or regulatory action requiring a National Environmental Policy Act review.

Program Senior Officials/Secretarial Officers
DOE program managers, including the Assistant Secretaries for Conservation and Renewable Energy; Fossil Energy; Nuclear Energy; Policy, Safety, and Environment; Defense Programs; and the Directors of Energy Research and Civilian Radioactive Waste Management. This definition also includes the Administrators of the Bonneville Power and Western Area Power Administrations.

Program Significant Delay
Any unplanned occurrence in any portion of a program conducted in accordance with approved requirements and procedures that results in recurring delays or events that significantly curtail operations or program processes.

Program Significant Cost
The monetary values necessary to repair, replace, or otherwise restore a facility/system/component to acceptable operation.

Programmatic Memorandum of Agreement (PMOA)
An agreement between the National Park Service (NPS), the Advisory Council on Historic Preservation (ACHP), and the National Conference of State Historic Preservation Officers (NCSHPO). Under Section 106 of the National Historic Preservation Act of 1966, as amended, the NPS must consult with the ACHP and the appropriate State Historic Preservation Officer (SHPO) whenever an action by the service will affect a historic property.

The PMOA establishes a procedure by which certain kinds of actions may proceed without detailed consultation, as long as those actions are generally approved by the Advisory Council and consistent with NPS-28 and with "Management Policies." Included are actions described in management plans concurred with by the Advisory Council, on preservation maintenance, and the energy management program. Compliance with the PMOA procedure satisfies NPS responsibilities under Section 106.

Programmatic NEPA Documents

Broad-scope Environmental Impact Statements or Environmental Assessments that identify and assess the environmental impacts of a DOE program; they may also refer to an associated NEPA document such as a Notice of Intent, record of decision, or findings of no significant impact. *See* NEPA Documents.

Progress Payment

Payment made as work progresses under a contract, upon the basis of costs incurred, of percentage of completion accomplished, or of a particular stage of completion. The term does not include payments for partial deliveries accepted by the government under a contract, or partial payments on contract termination claims.

Prohibit Specification (CWA; CFR)

To prevent the designation of an area as a present or future disposal site.

Project

A planned undertaking of something to be accomplished, produced, or constructed, having a finite beginning and a finite ending.

Project Design Criteria

Technical data and other project information developed during the project identification, conceptual design and/or preliminary design phases. They define the project scope, construction features and requirements, design parameters, applicable design codes, standards, and regulations; applicable health, safety, fire protection, safeguards, security, energy conservation, and quality assurance requirements; and other requirements. The project design criteria are normally consolidated into a document that provides the technical base for any further design performed after the criteria are developed. *See* Preliminary Design.

Project Managers

The managers responsible for a specific project assignment, as distinguished from line managers responsible for a general functional area.

Project Notification and Review System (PNRS)

See A-95 Review.

Project Proponent

The person who undertakes an activity that involves public agency financing or regulation.

Project Segment

An essential part or a division of a project, usually separated as a period of time, occasionally as a unit of work.

Projected Dose

An estimate of a toxicity, or radiation, dose that affected individuals could receive.

Projection

In cartography, any systematic arrangement of meridians and parallels portraying the curved surface of the sphere or spheroid upon a plane.

Proliferation, Nuclear Weapons

The process by which one nation after another comes into possession of, or into the right to determine the use of nuclear weapons, each potentially able to launch a nuclear attack upon another nation.

Promotion, Cell

The second hypothesized stage in a multistage process of cancer development. The conversion of initiated cells into tumorigenic cells.

Prompt Radiation

The gamma rays produced in fission and as a result of other neutron reactions and nuclear excitation of the weapon materials appearing within a second or less after a nuclear explosion. The radiations from these sources are known either as prompt or instantaneous gamma rays. *See* Induced Radiation; Residual Radiation.

Pronotum

A species descriptor that means plates covering the first segment of the thorax in insects.

Pronto
As quickly as possible.

Propaganda
Any form of communication in support of national objectives designed to influence the opinions, emotions, attitudes, or behavior of any group in order to benefit the sponsor, either directly or indirectly.

Propagules
A species descriptor that means portion of an organism capable of producing a new individual.

Propellant Plants
Any facilities engaged in the mixing, casting, or machining of propellants.

Propellants
1) Fuels and oxidizers physically or chemically combined that undergo combustion to provide rocket propulsion; the source that provides the energy required for propelling a projectile. 2) An explosive charge for propelling a projectile.

Proper Job Analysis
The breaking down of a job (task) into its component steps and the determination of downgrading incidents or problems and their controls associated with each step of that job. This is a tool to provide assurance that all important aspects of a job have been considered and evaluated in order to determine one unified procedure for doing the job the proper way.

Proper Job Instruction
An instructional technique employed by a supervisor when teaching a worker to do a new or different task for the first time, or when reviewing a task with an experienced worker. It involves telling, showing, testing and checking a worker to make sure he/she will perform the task properly.

Proper Shipping Name
The common name of a hazardous material.

Property
1) The rights of ownership; the right to use, possess, enjoy, and dispose of a thing in every legal way and to exclude everyone else from interfering with these rights. Property is generally classified into two groups: personal property and real property. 2) Anything that may be owned.

Property Line
A line, imaginary or otherwise, separating a property from adjoining property of public or private ownership.

Property Loss
The dollar cost of restoring damaged facilities or equipment to their original condition, whether or not such restoration actually occurs. In determining loss, the estimated damage to the building and contents shall include replacement cost, less salvage value, plus the cost of decontamination and cleanup. Effects upon program continuity, auxiliary costs of fire extinguishment, and consequent effects on related areas should be included if the effects can be determined.

Proposed Actions
Actions proposed by the federal agency or by a permit or license applicant, for which exemption is sought.

Proposed Critical Habitats
Habitats proposed in the Federal Register to be designated or revised as critical habitat under Section 4 of the Endangered Species Act (ESA) for any listed or proposed species.

Proposed Species
Any species of fish, wildlife, or plant that is proposed in the Federal Register to be listed under Section 4 of the Endangered Species Act.

Prosoma
A species descriptor that means the anterior (front) portion of the body of an invertebrate when primitive segmentation is not evident.

Prospective Client

Any person who requires environmental services but who is not yet aware of the need, or has not yet gone through the initial request for bid process.

Prostrate

A species descriptor that means growing flat along the ground.

Protected Areas

Areas encompassed by physical barriers (e.g., walls or fences), subject to access controls, surrounding a material access area or containing Category II special nuclear material.

Protection

The act or process of applying measures designed to affect the physical condition of a property by defending or guarding it from deterioration, loss or attack, or to cover or shield the property from danger or injury. In the case of structures, such treatment is generally of a temporary nature and anticipates future historic preservation treatment; in the case of archaeological sites, the protective measure may be temporary or permanent. Protection in its broadest sense also includes long-term efforts to deter or prevent vandalism, theft, arson, and other criminal acts against cultural resource information; description and synthesis of cultural resource information (describing the kinds of resources in a study area — sites, structures, and their associated objects) and summarizing their significance, frequently referred to as an overview, as in "cultural resource overview."

Protection of the Public Health and Welfare

Control of fire, explosion, or effects of hazards to minimize potential injury to the public and damage to property.

Protective Action (PA)

1) Physical measures, such as evacuation or sheltering, taken to prevent potential health hazards resulting from a release of HazMat to the environment from adversely affecting employees or the offsite population. PAs are taken at the direction of the state or local officials (offsite) or at the direction of the Crisis Manager or Incident Commander (onsite) that will lead to reduced exposures to HazMat. PAs are aimed at the general public or general Site population, and do not include the use of protective gear or exposure guidelines used by emergency response teams or Building Emergency Support Team. 2) Barriers of radiation-absorbing material, such as lead, concrete, plaster, plastic, that are used to reduce radiation exposure.

Protective Action Guide (PAG)

1) A chemical or radiation personnel exposure level or range beyond which protective actions should be considered. PAG values should reflect a balance of risks and costs to onsite personnel, public health and safety, and environment weighed against the benefits obtained from PAs. 2) Projected numerical dose values established by EPA, DOE, or states for individuals in the population. These values may trigger protective actions that would reduce or avoid the projected dose.

Protective Action Recommendation (PAR)

Timely recommendations to appropriate state or local authorities of PAs, such as sheltering and/or evacuation, for the general public.

Protective Clothing

Clothing especially designed, fabricated, or treated to minimize human body contact with hazardous materials and is separate from or in addition to normal wearing apparel. Clothing that protects personnel against hazards caused by extreme changes in physical environment, dangerous working conditions, or other environmentally related hazards. Protective clothing may include, but is not limited to, work clothing, chemical resistant boots, gloves, hats, hoods, and chemical resistant aprons.

Protective Force Personnel

Guards, security inspectors, couriers, authorized escorts, and personnel assigned to protective details, who are employed to protect the security interests of the DOE.

Protective Housing

A protective housing is a device designed to prevent access to radiant power or energy.

Protective Measures

Measures taken during an emergency for the purpose of preventing or minimizing hazards that are likely to develop if the actions were not taken.

Proteins

Complex nitrogenous organic compounds of high molecular weight that contain amino acids as their basic unit and are essential for growth and repair of animal tissue. Many proteins are enzymes.

Proteinuria

An excess of serum proteins in the urine.

Proton

A positively charged elementary particle having a mass roughly 1,840 times as great as an electron. The nucleus of an ordinary or light hydrogen atom. Protons are constituents of atomic nuclei and are emitted in some nuclear reactions. The atomic number (Z) of an atom is equal to the number of protons in its nucleus.

Protoplast

A membrane-bound cell from which the outer cell wall has been partially or completely removed. The term often is applied to plant cells.

Prototype

A model suitable for evaluation of design, performance, and production potential.

Protozoa

A species descriptor that means single-celled, usually microscopic organisms of the phylum or subkingdom Protozoa, that included the most primitive forms of animal life.

Protractile Premaxillaries

A species descriptor that means bones located in the upper jaw of vertebrates that are capable of being extended.

Proved Reserves

The estimated quantity of crude oil, natural gas, natural gas liquids, or coal, that analysis or geological and engineering data demonstrates with reasonable certainty to be recoverable from known oil, coal, or gas fields under existing economic and operating conditions.

PRP

See Potentially Responsible Party (CERCLA).

PRSA

An acronym for Pemigewasset River Study Act of 1989 (WSRA).

Pruritic

Pertaining to itching.

PSA

See Preliminary Safety Analysis.

PSD

See Prevention of Significant Deterioration (CAA).

PSD Permits

Permits issued under 40 CFR Part 52.21 or by an approved state. *See* Prevention of Significant Deterioration.

psi

See Pounds per Square Inch.

PSI

See Pollutant Standard Index.

psia

Pounds per square inch absolute.

psig

Pounds per square inch gauge.

PSS

An acronym for Probabilistic Safety Study.

Psychological Warfare (PSYWAR)

The planned use of propaganda and other psychological actions having the primary purpose of influencing the opinions, emotions, attitudes, and behavior of hostile foreign groups in such a way as to support the achievement of national objectives.

Psychosis

A mental disorder characterized by derangement of personality and loss of touch with reality.

PSYWAR

See Psychological Warfare.

PTP

See Peak-to-Peak Ratio.

Puberulent

A species descriptor that means covered with minute hairs or very fine down.

Pubescent

A species descriptor that means covered with short hairs or soft down; also, having reached puberty.

Public Affairs

1) Those public information and community relations activities directed toward the general public by the various elements of an agency. 2) Personnel involved in summarizing, coordinating, and providing the release of information to the news media in an emergency situation.

Public Aircraft

Aircraft used only in the service of a government or political subdivision. This does not include any government-owned aircraft engaged in carrying persons or property for commercial purposes.

Public and Commercial Building

Any building that is not a school building, except that the term does not include any residential apartment building of fewer than 10 units.

Public Comment Period

The time allowed for the members of an affected community to express views and concerns regarding an action proposed to be taken by EPA, such as a rulemaking, permit, or Superfund remedy selection.

Public Doses

The doses received by a member(s) of the public from exposure to radiation and to radioactive material released by a facility or operation, whether the exposure is within a DOE site boundary or offsite. A public dose does not include a dose received from occupational exposures, a dose received from naturally occurring "background" radiation, a dose received as a patient from medical practices, or a dose received from consumer products.

Public Entity

Includes the state, a county, city, city and county, district, public authority, public agency, and any other political subdivision or public corporation in the state when acquiring real property, or any interest therein, or ordering that acquired property be vacated, in any city or county for public use.

Public Environmental Information

All information and data resulting from any environmental research studies, surveys, experiments, or demonstration projects conducted or financed by a federal agency, that are not considered confidential business information and are made available to the public for review and/or duplication purposes.

Public Health Service Act (PHSA)

Also known as the Safe Drinking Water Act, the PHSA establishes the national primary drinking water regulations; research objectives; standards for maximum contaminant levels; penalties for noncompliance; and quality goals for state drinking water implementation plans and programs. The Act places primary enforcement responsibilities with the states, as well as regulations for state programs, program monitoring, record keeping, and time frames for compliance.

Public Hearings

Informal hearings to provide the public with the opportunity to give comments and to permit an exchange of information and opinion on a proposed rule.

Public Information

Government information for the guidance of the public and made public by each separate agency (through publication in the Federal Register). Guidance may include the following: a) descriptions of its central and field organization and the established places at which, the employees from whom, and the methods whereby, the public may obtain information, make submittals or requests, or obtain decisions; b) statements of the general course and method by which its functions are channeled and determined, including the nature and requirements of all formal and informal procedures available; c) rules of procedure, descriptions of forms available or the places at which forms may be obtained, and instructions as to the scope and contents of all papers, reports, or examinations; d) substantive rules of general applicability adopted as authorized by law, and statements of general policy or interpretations of general applicability formulated and adopted by the agency; e) each amendment, revision, or repeal of the foregoing; and f) information of a military nature, the dissemination of which through public news media is not inconsistent with security, and the release of which is considered desirable or nonobjectionable to the responsible releasing agency. Information reasonably available to the class of persons affected thereby is deemed published in the Federal Register when incorporated by reference therein with the approval of the Director of the Federal Register.

Public Information, Availability, and Freedom of Information

A term referring to each agency's responsibility to make available for public inspection and copying: a) final opinions, including concurring and dissenting opinions, as well as orders, made in the adjudication of cases; b) statements of policy and interpretations that have been adopted by the agency and are not published in the Federal Reg-

ister; and c) administrative staff manuals and instructions to staff that affect a member of the public; unless the materials are promptly published and copies offered for sale.

To the extent required to prevent a clearly unwarranted invasion of personal privacy, an agency may delete identifying details when it makes available or publishes an opinion, statement of policy, interpretation, or staff manual or instruction. Each agency, upon any request for records that a) reasonably describes such records; and b) is made in accordance with published rules stating the time, place, fees (if any), and procedures to be followed, shall make the records promptly available to any person.

This definition does not apply to matters that are a) specifically authorized under criteria established by an Executive order to be kept secret in the interest of national defense or foreign policy; b) related solely to the internal personnel rules and practices of an agency; c) specifically exempted from disclosure by statute; d) trade secrets and commercial or financial information obtained from a person and privileged or confidential; e) interagency or intraagency memoranda or letters that would not be available by law; f) personnel and medical files and similar files the disclosure of which would constitute a clearly unwarranted invasion of personal privacy; g) records or information compiled for law enforcement purposes; h) contained in or related to examination, operating, or condition reports prepared by, on behalf of, or for the use of an agency responsible for the regulation or supervision of financial institutions; or i) geological and geophysical information and data, including maps concerning wells.

Public Information Officers

DOE officers at headquarters and in the field responsible for preparing and coordinating the dissemination of public information in cooperation with other responding federal, state, and local agencies.

Public Involvement

The opportunity for participation by affected citizens in rulemaking, decisionmaking, and planning with respect to the public lands, including public meetings or hearings held at locations near the affected lands, or advisory mechanisms, or such other procedures as may be necessary to provide public comment in a particular instance.

Public Lands

1) Lands owned and administered by the United States as part of the national park system, the national wildlife refuge system, or the national forest system. 2) Lands, the fee title to which is held by the United States, other than lands on the Outer Continental Shelf and lands that are under the jurisdiction of the Smithsonian Institution. 3) Lands under the custody and control of the Secretary of the Interior and the Secretary of Agriculture, except Native American Indian lands. 4) Lands under the custody and control of the Tennessee Valley Authority that are situated in western Kentucky and Tennessee and are designated as "Land Between the Lakes." 5) Lands under the custody and control of the Secretary of Defense.

Public Notification

Warning signs. Television, radio, press notices, or other information measures used to advise the public of the health hazards associated with pollution, and to enhance public awareness of the measures that can be taken to prevent standards from being exceeded, including the ways in which the public can participate in regulatory and other efforts to improve environmental quality.

Public or Nonprofit Institution

An institution owned and operated by a state, a political subdivision of a state or an agency or instrumentality of either, or an organization exempt from income tax under Section 501(c)(3) of Title 26.

Public Rangelands

Lands administered by the Secretary of the Interior through the Bureau of Land Management or the Secretary of Agriculture through the National Forest Service in the sixteen contiguous western states on which there is domestic livestock grazing or that the Secretary concerned determines may be suitable for domestic livestock grazing.

Public Storage Facility

Public liquid bulk storage, terminalling, or warehousing operation for hire in which the owner or operator of the facility has no ownership interest in any of the materials stored on contract with its customers.

Public Traffic Route Distance

The minimum dimension permitted between locations containing munitions and any public street, road, highway, or passenger railroad (including roads on DOE-controlled land open to public travel).

Public Trustee

The public official in each country, whose office has been created by statute, to whom title to real property is conveyed by Trust Deed for the use and benefit of the beneficiary, who usually is the lender.

Public Use

A use for which property may be acquired by eminent domain.

Public Vessel

1) A vessel(s) owned by and being used in the public service of the United States. This does not include vessels owned by the United States and engaged in a trade or commercial service or vessels under contract or charter to the United States. 2) A vessel(s) owned or bareboat-chartered and operated by the United States, or by a state or political subdivision thereof, or by a foreign nation, except when such vessels are engaged in commerce.

Public Water System

Any water system that regularly supplies piped water to the public for consumption, serving at least an average of 25 individuals per day for at least 60 days per year, or has at least 15 service connections. The term includes any collection, treatment, storage, and distribution facilities under control of the operator of such system and used primarily in connection with the system, and any collection or pretreatment storage facilities not under such control that are used primarily in connection with the system.

Public Water System Program

A program for the adoption and enforcement of drinking water regulations (with such variances and exemptions from such regulations under conditions and in a manner that is not less stringent than the conditions under, and the manner in, which variances and exemptions may be granted.

Publicly Owned Preserves and Recreation Areas

Coastal Special Treatment Areas include those forested areas within the Coastal Zone within 200 feet (60.96 m) of all publicly owned preserved and recreation areas including national, state, regional, county, and municipal parks.

Publicly Owned Treatment Works (POTW)

1) Any device or system used in the treatment (including recycling and reclamation) of municipal sewage or industrial wastes of a liquid nature that is owned by a "state" or "municipality" (as defined by Section 502(4) of the Clean Water Act). The definition includes sewers, pipes, or other conveyances only if they convey wastewater to a POTW providing treatment. 2) A waste-treatment works owned by a state, unit of local government, or Native American Indian tribe, usually designed to treat domestic wastewaters.

Publicly Owned Treatment Works Studies

Studies to characterize emissions of hazardous air pollutants emitted by such facilities, to identify industrial, commercial, and residential discharges that contribute to such emissions and to demonstrate control measures for such emissions. Control measures may include pretreatment of discharges causing emissions of hazardous air pollutants and process or product substitutions or limitations that may be effective in reducing such emissions. The Administrator of EPA may prescribe uniform sampling, modeling and risk assessment methods for use in implementing the study.

Published Exposure Levels

Exposure limits published in *NIOSH Recommendations for Occupational Health Standards* (1986), incorporated by reference, or, if none is specified, the exposure limits published in the standards specified by the American Conference of Governmental Industrial Hygienists in their publication, *Threshold Limit Values and Biological Measure Indices for 1987-88* (1987).

PUEC

An acronym for Portsmouth Uranium Enrichment Complex.

Pullorum Disease

The communicable disease of poultry caused by the bacteria Salmonella pullorum.

Pulmonary Edema

Accumulation of extravascular fluid in the lungs that impairs gas exchange; usually due to either increased intravascular pressure or increased permeability of the pulmonary capillaries.

Pulmonary Region

The area of the respiratory system consisting of respiratory bronchioles and alveoli where gas exchange occurs.

Pulse

A discontinuous burst of laser, light, or energy, as opposed to a continuous beam. A true pulse achieves higher peak powers than that attainable in a continuous wave (CW) output.

Pulse Duration

The "on time of a pulsed laser," it may be measured in terms of millisecond, microsecond, or nanosecond as defined by half-peak-power points on the leading and trailing edges of the pulse.

Pultrusion

A continuous process for manufacturing composites in rods, tubes, and structural shapes having a constant cross section.

Pumped Storage

An arrangement in which water is pumped into a storage reservoir at a higher elevation when a surplus of electricity is being generated; during times of peak demand for electricity, this water is then used for the generation of electricity as in a hydroelectric power plant.

Pumping

Addition of energy (thermal, electrical, or optical) into the atomic population of the laser medium, necessary to produce a state of population inversion.

Pumping Station

Mechanical devices installed in sewer or water systems or other liquid-carrying pipelines that move the liquids to a higher level.

Pumping Test

1) A test that is conducted to determine aquifer or well characteristics. 2) A test made by pumping a well for a period of time and observing the change in hydraulic head in the aquifer. A pump test may be used to determine the capacity of the well and the hydraulic characteristics of the aquifer. Synonymous with aquifer test.

Pupa

A species descriptor that means the inactive stage in the metamorphosis (evolution) of many insects following the larval stage and preceding the adult form.

Pupal Stage

A species descriptor that means the nonfeeding period when larval tissues are reformed into adult structure inside a cocoon.

Pupation

A species descriptor that means to become a pupa (preadult).

Pupil

The circular opening in the center of the iris through which light rays enter the eye.

Purchase Description

A statement outlining the essential characteristics and functions of an item, service, or material required to meet the minimum needs of the government. It is used when a specification is not available or when specific procurement specifications are not required by an individual agency.

Purchasing Group

Any group of persons that has as one of its purposes the purchase of pollution liability insurance on a group basis.

Purchasing Office

Any installation or activity, or any division, office, branch, section, unit, or other organizational element of an installation or activity charged with the functions of procuring supplies or services.

PURPA

An acronym for the Public Utility Regulatory Policies Act of 1978.

PURPA Position

A factual contention, legal contention, or specific recommendation promoting one of the following PURPA purposes: a) conservation of energy supplied by electric utilities; b) optimization of the efficiency of use of facilities; or c) equitable rates to electric consumers.

Pustule

A species descriptor that means a small swelling; similar to a blister or pimple.

Putrescible

Able to rot quickly enough to cause odors and attract flies.

PV

An acronym for Photovoltaics.

PVC

See Polyvinyl Chloride.

Pyrolysis

Decomposition of a chemical by extreme heat.

Pyrophoric

Capable of igniting spontaneously on contact with air, at or below 130°F.

Pyrophoric-Igniting, Spontaneously

Emitting sparks when scratched or struck especially with steel.

Pyrophoric Liquids and Solids

Pyrophoric liquids are any liquids that ignite spontaneously in dry or moist air at or below 130° Fahrenheit.

A pyrophoric solid is any solid material, other than one classed as an explosive, that under normal conditions is liable to cause fires through friction, retained heat from manufacturing or processing, or that can be ignited readily and when ignited burns so vigorously and persistently as to create a serious transportation, handling, or disposal hazard. Included are simultaneously combustible and water-reactive materials.

Pyrophoric Materials

Materials that under normal conditions are liable to cause fires through friction, retained heat from manufacturing or processing, persistently as to create a serious transportation, handling or disposal hazard.

Pyrotechnic

A mixture of chemicals that when ignited is capable of reacting exothermically to produce light, heat, smoke, sound or gas, and may also be used to introduce a delay into an explosive train because of its known burning time. The term excludes propellants and explosives.

Pyrotechnic Delay

A pyrotechnic device added to a firing system that transmits the ignition flame after a predetermined delay.

Q

QAA
An acronym for Quality Assurance Acceptance.

QA/QC
See Quality Assurance/Quality Control.

QIC
An acronym for Quality Inspection Control.

ql
The symbol used to denote the 95% upper bound estimate of the linearized slope of the dose-response curve in the low dose region as determined by the multistage model.

Quadrangle
A tract of land in the USGS Survey System measuring 24 miles on each side of the square. Sometimes referred to as a "check."

Quadrant Elevation
1) The angle between the horizontal plane and the axis of the bore when the weapon is laid. 2) The algebraic sum of the elevation, angle of site, and complementary angle of site.

Quadrat
A sampling area, typically 1 square meter in size, used for studying the composition of an area of vegetation. As in archaeological studies the area is bounded by a frame subdivided with wires at right angles, overlaid on the ground.

Quadrat Major
A quadrat that includes the most significant findings in a study area.

Quadrat Method
International method for intensively studying environs within a prescribed area in an effort to gain a deeper insight into the wider area and its history. This method is conducted by bisecting an area with a multitude of connected quadrats, and provides a means of mapping exact locations of significant findings and data recovered during an intensive study of the area.

Quadrate
In zoology, a bone or cartilage of the skull joining the upper and lower jaws in birds, fish, reptiles, and amphibians.

Qualified Citizens Group
A nonprofit organization of citizens having an area based focus, that is not single-issue oriented and that can demonstrate a prior record of interest and involvement in goal-setting and research concerned with improving the quality of life, including plans to identify, protect, and enhance significant natural and cultural resources and the environment.

The group must demonstrate its capacity to employ the funds usefully, and have broad-based representation.

Qualified Citizens Group Grants

EPA grants made for the purpose of supporting and encouraging participation by qualified citizens groups in determining how scientific, technological, and social trends and changes affect the future environment and quality of life of an area, and for setting goals and identifying measures for improvement. A citizens group is only eligible for assistance if certified by the governor in consultation with the state legislature as a bona fide organization entitled to receive federal assistance to pursue the aims of this program. Grants made typically cannot exceed 75% of the estimated cost of a project or program, and no financial assistance provided can be used to support lobbying or litigation by any recipient group. *See* Qualified Citizens Groups.

Qualified Energy Conservation Measure

A cost effective measure, as identified by the Administrator in consultation with the Secretary of Energy, that increases the efficiency of the use of electricity provided by an electric utility to its customers.

Qualified Hydrologic Unit

A hydrologic unit in which the water quality has been significantly affected by acid mine drainage from coal mining practices in a manner that adversely impacts biological resources; and that contains lands and waters that are eligible pursuant to Section 1234 of the Surface Mining Control and Reclamation Act.

Qualified Incinerator

1) An incinerator approved under the provisions of Section 761.70 of TSCA. 2) A high-efficiency boiler approved under the provisions of Section 761.60(a)(3) — only PCBs in concentrations below 500 ppm can be destroyed in an approved high-efficiency boiler. 3) An incinerator approved under Section 3005(c) of the Resource Conservation and Recovery Act [42 USC 6925(c)] — only PCBs in concentrations below 50 ppm can be destroyed in a RCRA-approved incinerator. 4) Industrial furnaces and boilers that are identified in 40 CFR 260.10 and 40 CFR 266.41(b) when operating at their normal operating temperatures (this prohibits feeding fluids, above the level of detection, during either startup or shutdown operations).

Qualified Renewable Energy

Energy derived from biomass, solar, geothermal, or wind as identified by the Administrator in consultation with the Secretary of Energy.

Qualified Safety Engineer

A person who is qualified to make inspections or examinations of boilers or tanks according to the rules under which the vessel was constructed, and who holds a valid certificate of competency.

Qualifying Phase I Technology

A technological system of continuous emission reduction that achieves a 90% reduction in emissions of sulfur dioxide from the emissions that would have resulted from the use of fuels that were not subject to treatment prior to combustion.

Quality Assurance (DOE; ESH)

Involves all those planned and systematic actions necessary to provide adequate confidence that a facility, structure, system, or component will perform satisfactorily and safely in service. The goal of quality assurance is to ensure that a) research, development, demonstration, scientific investigations, and production activities are performed in a controlled manner; b) components, systems, and processes are designed, developed, constructed, tested, operated, and maintained according to engineering standards, quality practices, and Technical Specifications Operational Safety Requirements; and c) resulting technology data are valid and retrievable. Quality assurance includes quality control, that comprises all those actions necessary to control and verify the features and characteristics of a material, process, product, or service to specified requirements.

Quality Assurance Agency

A third-party entity approved by the department to conduct inspections and monitor quality assurance programs to determine compliance with approved plans and quality control manuals during the manufacture of mobile homes, commercial coaches, special purpose commercial coaches and recreational vehicles.

Quality Assurance Inspector

A person approved by the department and employed by an approved Quality Assurance Agency to conduct inspections and monitor quality assurance programs.

Quality Assurance Overviews

An organized set of activities performed as independent functions. Their purpose is to ensure that all aspects of quality related activities at the program, project, and contractor level of management are adequately addressed. Such activities include a) Periodic and timely reviews of program/project documents, activities, actions, and plans; b) review of new major procurements and management and operating contracts; c) review of extend/compete packages for management and operating contracts; and d) review of DOE Orders with relevance to the incorporation of the DOE quality assurance policy, where necessary.

Quality Assurance Plans

Documents that contain or reference the quality assurance elements established for an activity, group of activities, a scientific investigation, or a project and describes how conformance with such requirements is to be ensured for structures, systems, computer software, components, and their operation commensurate with a) the scope, complexity, duration, and importance to satisfactory performance; b) the potential impact on environment, safety, and health; and c) requirements for reliability and continuity of operation.

Quality Assurance/Quality Control (QA/QC)

1) A system of procedures, checks, audits, and corrective actions used to ensure that field work and laboratory analysis during the investigation and cleanup of Superfund sites meet established standards. 2) Quality Control, is considered routine monitoring and evaluation of performance against stated objectives for quality and quantity of work produced. It is distinct from agency-level evaluation of policies and programs. In many instances, quality control systems will ad-

dress both the efficiency and effectiveness dimensions of performance, but they do not assess the impacts of policies or whole programs.

Quality Assurance Records

Includes results of reviews, inspections, audits, and material analyses; monitoring of work performance; qualification of personnel, procedures, and equipment; and other documentation such as drawings, special reports, and corrective action reports.

Quality Assurance Units

Persons or organizational elements, except the study director, designated by testing facility management to perform the duties relating to quality assurance of varied studies.

Quality Control Manual

A manual developed by a manufacturer and approved by the department or a Design Approval Agency, that describes in detail a program of procedures, tests, and inspections to be performed by the manufacturer during the manufacturing process to ensure that all materials, systems, equipment and assemblies of a mobile home, commercial coach, special purpose commercial coach, or recreational vehicle comply with approved plans and regulations.

Quality Engineering

The branch of professional engineering that applies the principles of product and service quality evaluation and control in the a) planning, development, and operation of quality control systems; b) the application and analysis of testing and inspection procedures; and c) requires the ability to apply metrology and statistical methods to diagnose and correct improper quality control practices to ensure product and service reliability and conformity to prescribed standards.

Quality Factors

1) Principal modifying factors used to calculate the dose equivalent from an absorbed dose. 2) A factor that weights the absorbed dose, defined as a function of the collision-stopping power in water at the point of interest.

Quality of Water
The level of water quality as specified by the applicable state Water Quality Control Plan, including its water quality objectives, policies, and prohibitions.

Quantity Distances
Distances required for a specific level of protection for a particular hazard class/division of ammunition and explosives.

Quantum Evolution
Accelerated evolution resulting from a sudden shift from one environment to another distinctly different one, without any time for preadaptation.

Quantum Meruit
Court action for the value of services rendered by a defendant when no express contract regarding fees existed.

Quantum Valebant
Court action for the value of products sold by a defendant when no express contract regarding product costs existed.

Quarter Section
In U.S. and Canadian land surveying, a tract of land half a mile square containing 160 acres.

Quarterly Environmental Compliance Reports
Quarterly reports prepared by DOE facilities and sent to the appropriate Secretarial Officer(s) and to the Assistant Secretary for Environment, Safety and Health (EH-1) in response to the initiatives in SEN-7A-90. Quarterly environmental compliance reports include the status of the line organization's NEPA compliance activities.

Quartzipsamment
A sandy, quartz-based soil.

Quasi
Having the same characteristics of "as if." A modifier used to indicate that the subject is to be treated as though it were literally the same as the word that follows it.

Quasi-isotropic
Approximating isotropy by orientation of plies in several directions.

Quaternary
The geologic time frame since the end of the Pliocene era; ranked as the era following the Cenozoic era, or a period of the Cenozoic era following the Tertiary period.

Quay
A structure of solid construction along a shore or bank that provides berthing and that generally provides cargo-handling facilities. A similar facility of open construction is called a wharf. *See* Pier; Wharf.

Quebrada
A topographical term designating a canyon of rugged aspect; a fissurelike ravine; broken or uneven ground; a stream.

Quench Tank
A water-filled tank used to cool incinerator residue or hot materials from industrial processes.

Questionnaire
A written set of questions that generally calls for written responses; designed to elicit detailed data on facility activities, management attitudes, waste characteristics, compliance problems, etc. This is a quick, efficient and inexpensive method of obtaining a large quantity of varied environmental information from a broad cross section of persons affected by a facility/project. Two types of data can evolve from the use of questionnaires:

- factual data — that which an owner/operator knows about his/her own facility's and/or project's environmental characteristics, impacts, surroundings, and effects on others; and

- opinion data — includes potentially interested person's beliefs, values, environmental standards, viewpoints, and priorities.

For the purposes of environmental assessments, factual data and the identification of management systems and priorities are the primary information concerns.

Quick Clays

Clays that have lost their shear strength. Sometimes also called "sensitive" clays.

Quick Disconnect Device

A hand-operated device that provides a means for connecting and disconnecting an appliance or an appliance connector to a gas supply and that is equipped with an automatic means to shut off the gas supply when the device is disconnected.

Quick Ground

Ground in a loose disjointed state; soft watery strata (e.g., running sand, quicksand).

Quicklime

A calcinated material, primarily composed of calcium oxide or calcium oxide in combination with a lesser amount of magnesium oxide; it is capable of slaking with water.

Quicktrans

Long-term contract airlift service within the continental United States for the movement of cargo in support of the logistic system for the military services (primarily the Navy and Marine Corps) and Department of Defense agencies.

Quid Pro Quo

A term meaning "exchanging what for what," used as an early form of assessing contract performance and consideration.

Quiescence

A term used in seismology indicating a relatively long period of earthquake-free time.

Quiet Title Suit

An action in court to remove a defect, cloud, or suspicion regarding the legal rights of the owner to the parcel of real estate.

Quitclaim Deed

A deed in which the grantor warrants nothing. It conveys only the grantor's present interest in the real estate, if any.

QV

An acronym for Quality Verification.

R

R

See Roentgen.

R Value

The measure of the resistance of a material or building component to the passage of heat in [hour x feet^2 x °F] Btu.

R&D

See Research and Development.

R&PM

An acronym for Regulations and Procedures Manual (Publication-201).

R&QA

See Reliability and Quality Assurance.

RA

See Remedial Action. An acronym for Raker Act of 1913 (WSRA); Reclamation Act of 1902.

RAAS

An acronym for Remedial Action Assessment System.

Raceme

A species descriptor that means the arrangement of flowers singly along a common main stalk, as in the lily of the valley.

Rachis

A species descriptor that means the main stem of an inflorescence (flower cluster).

Rack

1) A device fixed in place, made of parallel bars evenly spaced, used to return or remove suspended or floating solids from wastewater. 2) In terms of the ESA, a species descriptor that means the antlers of mammals in the family *Cervidae*, including deer and moose.

RACM

See RACM and BACM Guidance.

RACM and BACM Guidance

EPA technical guidance on reasonably available control measures (RACM) and best available control measures (BACM) for urban fugitive dust, and emissions from residential wood combustion (including curtailments and exemptions from such curtailments) and prescribed silvicultural and agricultural burning. In issuing guidelines and making determinations, the Administrator (in consultation with the state) takes into account emission reductions achieved, or expected to be achieved.

RAD

A unit of absorbed dose of radiation, replaced by the gray. One radiation absorbed dose (RAD) of absorbed dose is equal to 0.01 joules per kilogram.

Radar Advisory

The term used to indicate that the provision of advice and information is based on radar observation.

Radar Imagery

Imagery produced by recording radar waves reflected from a given surface.

Radar Netting

The linking of several radars to a single center to provide integrated information.

Radar Netting Station

A center that can receive data from radar tracking stations and exchange this data among other radar tracking stations, thus forming a radar netting system.

RADIAC

An acronym derived from the words "radioactivity, detection, indication, and computation" and used as an all-encompassing term to designate various types of radiological measuring instruments or equipment.

Radial Displacement

On vertical photographs, the apparent "leaning out," or the apparent displacement of the top of any object having height in relation to its base. The direction of displacement is radial from the principal point on a true vertical, or from the isocentre on a vertical photograph distorted by tip or tilt.

Radiant Energy (Q)

Energy in the form of electromagnetic waves usually expressed in units of joules (watt-seconds). The energy (excluding rest energy) emitted, transferred, or received in the form of radiation.

Radiant Exposure (H)

The total energy per unit area incident upon a given surface. It is used to express exposure to pulsed laser radiation in units of J/cm^2. *See* Thermal Exposure.

Radiation (NIH; IAEA; NFI)

Any form of energy propagated as rays, waves, or streams of energetic particles. The term is frequently used in relation to the emission of rays from the nucleus of an atom. 1) The process by which energy in the form of electromagnetic radiation is emitted from matter. 2) The electromagnetic or particulate rays that are emitted from atoms or molecules as they undergo internal change. 3) The emission and propagation of energy through space or through a material medium in the form of waves; for instance, the emission and propagation of electromagnetic waves, or of sound and elastic waves. The term "radiation" or "radiant energy," when unqualified, usually refers to electromagnetic radiation. Such radiation commonly is classified according to frequency as Hertzian, infrared, visible (light), ultraviolet, X-ray, and gamma ray. 4) By extension, corpuscular emissions such as alpha and beta radiation, or rays of mixed or unknown type, as cosmic radiation.

Radiation Area

Any area, accessible to individuals, in which there exists radiation at such levels that an individual could receive in any 1 hour a dose to the whole body in excess of 5 millirems, or in any 5 consecutive days a dose in excess of 100 millirems.

Radiation Dose

The total amount of ionizing radiation absorbed by material or tissues, expressed in centigrays. The term radiation dose is often used in the sense of the exposure dose expressed in roentgens, that is a measure of the total amount of ionization that the quantity of radiation could produce in air. This could be distinguished from the absorbed dose, also given in rads, that represents the energy absorbed from the radiation per gram of specified body tissue. Further, the biological dose, in rems, is a measure of the biological effectiveness of the radiation exposure. *See* Absorbed Dose; Exposure Dose.

Radiation Dose Rate

The radiation dose (dosage) absorbed per unit of time. A radiation dose rate can be set at some particular unit of time (e.g., H + 1 hour) and would be called "H + 1 radiation dose rate."

Radiation Emergency Assistance Center/Training Sites

Multipurpose medical facilities located in Oak Ridge, Tennessee, prepared to deal with all types of radiation exposure emergencies and provide medical and health physics advice and assistance in radiological emergencies.

Radiation Exposure Module

A module of the Safety Performance Measurement System, divided into two databases; a locator file and a database containing the annual dose of all monitored DOE and DOE-contractor personnel.

Radiation Exposure State

The condition of a unit, or exceptionally an individual, deduced from the cumulative whole body radiation dose(s) received. It is expressed as a symbol that indicates the potential for future operations and the degree of risk if exposed to additional nuclear radiation.

Radiation Induced Genetic Effects

Changes induced by radiation in the genetic material of both somatic and germinal cells. Loosely used in radiation protection as a synonym for radiation induced hereditary diseases.

Radiation Induced Hereditary Effects

Stochastic effects that occur in the progeny of the exposed "individual."

Radiation Intensity

The radiation dose rate at a given time and place. It may be used, coupled with a figure, to denote the radiation intensity used at a given number of hours after a nuclear burst (e.g., RI-3 is a radiation intensity 3 hours after the time of burst).

Radiation Protection Officers

Technically competent DOE persons designated by management to supervise the application of radiation protection regulations and to provide advice on all relevant aspects of radiation protection.

Radiation Records Repositories

The DOE centralized database located at the System Safety Development Center, in Idaho, that contains statistical summaries of occupational radiation exposure information for activities associated with DOE operations. Individual occupational exposure records are maintained by DOE sites. The Radiation Records Repository also contains summary data submitted for the DOE predecessor agencies, the Atomic Energy Commission (AEC), and the Energy Research and Development Administration (ERDA) activities.

Radiation Safety (NCRP)

Safety measures concerned with the recognition, evaluation, and control of risks due to radiation exposure.

Radiation Scattering

The diversion of radiation (thermal, electromagnetic, or nuclear) from its original path as a result of interaction or collisions with atoms, molecules, or larger particles in the atmosphere or other media between the source of the radiation (e.g., a nuclear explosion) and a point at some distance away. As a result of scattering, radiation (especially gamma rays and neutrons) will be received at such a point from many directions instead of only from the direction of the source.

Radiation Shields

Materials interposed between a source of radiation and persons, or equipment or other objects, in order to attenuate the radiation.

Radiation Sickness

An illness resulting from excessive exposure to ionizing radiation. The earliest symptoms are nausea, vomiting, and diarrhea, that may be followed by loss of hair, hemorrhage, inflammation of the mouth and throat, and general loss of energy.

Radiation Standards
Regulations that set maximum exposure limits for protection of the public from radioactive materials.

Radiation Survey
An evaluation of the radiation hazards incident to the production, use, release, disposal, or presence of sources of radiation.

Radiation Units
Units of measure of radiations, radiation doses, and radioactivity.

Radiation Workers
Occupational workers whose job assignments require work on, with, or in the proximity of radiation-producing machines or radioactive materials, and/or who have the potential of being routinely exposed above 0.1 rem per year, that is the sum of the annual effective dose equivalent from external irradiation and the committed effective dose equivalent from internal irradiation.

Radio Frequency Radiation
See Nonionizing Electromagnetic Radiation.

Radio Tracking
Using an affixed transmitter to follow the movements of an animal.

Radioactive Articles
Radioactive articles are any manufactured instruments and articles such as an instrument, clock, electronic tube or apparatus, or similar instruments and articles having radioactive material as a component part.

Radioactive Contamination
Deposition of radioactive material in any place where it is not desired, and particularly in any place where its presence may be harmful. The harm may be vitiating the validity of an experiment or a procedure, or in actually being a source of excessive exposure to personnel.

Radioactive Contents
Radioactive contents are the radioactive material, together with any contaminated liquids or gases, within the package.

Radioactive Decay
Disintegration of the nucleus of an unstable nuclide by the spontaneous emission of charged particles and/or photons; the decrease in the radiation intensity of any radioactive material with respect to time.

Radioactive Decay Rate
The time rate of the disintegration of radioactive material generally accompanied by the emission of particles and/or gamma radiation.

Radioactive Effluent
Airborne or liquid radioactive materials that are discharged into the environment.

Radioactive Half-Life
Time required for a radioactive substance to lose 50% of its activity by decay. Each radionuclide has a unique half-life.

Radioactive Material Transportation Accidents
Incidents in which the conveyance transporting a radioactive material package is involved in an accident. Accidents are subsets of radioactive material transportation incidents and include a wide range of severities ranging from minor mishaps to the very severe. This definition is not limited by financial costs, injuries, or fatalities.

Radioactive Material Transportation Incidents
Events occurring during the course of transportation of radioactive materials (including loading, transport, unloading, and temporary storage) that result in actual or suspected release of radioactive material. The events may include fire, breakage, spillage, release or suspected release of radioactive material, excessive or suspected radiation, loss of possession, or accident conditions.

Radioactive Materials (SWDA; RCRA)

Any materials or combination of materials that spontaneously emit ionizing radiation; any material having a specific activity greater than 0.002 microcuries per gram. The term does not include any material that the Secretary of Energy (DOE) determines is of such low order of radioactivity that when transported does not pose a significant hazard to health or safety. There are sundry definitions provided within federal regulations pertaining to the various aspects of radioactive materials.

Radioactive Mixed Waste

Radioactive waste that also contains hazardous waste constituents. *See* Low-Level Radioactive Waste; Mixed Waste.

Radioactive Nuclide Intake

Amount of radioactive material introduced into the body by inhalation or ingestion, or through the skin. Also used to denote the process.

Radioactive Series (NCRP)

A succession of nuclides, each of which transforms by radioactive decay into the next until a stable nuclide results. The first member is called the parent and the subsequent members are called progeny, daughters, or decay products.

Radioactive Source Material

Uranium or thorium, or any combination thereof, in any physical or chemical form, except special nuclear material and ores that contain by weight less than 1/20th of 1% (0.05%) of uranium, thorium, or any combination thereof.

Radioactive Source Terms

Expressions used to disseminate information about the actual or potential release of radioactive material from a given source, that may include a specification of the composition, amount, rate, and modes of the release.

Radioactive Substances

Substances that emit radiation.

Radioactive Waste

1) Any waste that emits energy as rays, waves, or streams of energetic particles. Radioactive materials are often mixed with hazardous waste, usually from nuclear reactors, research institutions, or hospitals. 2) Solid or fluid materials of no value containing radioactivity; including discarded items such as clothing, containers, equipment, rubble, residues, or soils contaminated with radioactivity; or soils, rubble, equipment, or other items containing induced radioactivity such that the levels exceed safe limits for unconditional release. 3) Any waste that contains radioactive material in concentrations that exceed those listed in 10 CFR Part 20, Appendix B, Table 11 Column 2. 4) Solid, liquid, or gaseous material that contains radionuclides regulated under the Atomic Energy Act of 1954, as amended, and of negligible economic value considering costs of recovery.

Radioactive Waste Management

The systematic administration of activities that provide for the collection, storage, transportation, transfer, treatment, and disposal of radioactive waste.

Radioactivity

1) The property or characteristic of radioactive material to spontaneously "disintegrate" with the emission of energy in the form of radium. 2) The spontaneous emission of radiation, generally alpha or beta particles, often accompanied by gamma rays, from the nuclei of an unstable isotope. 3) The spontaneous decomposition of an atom accompanied by the release of energy. The unit of radioactivity is the curie.

Radioactivity Concentration Guide

The amount of any specified radioisotope that is acceptable in air and water for continuous consumption.

Radioactivity Decay Constant

For a radioactive nuclide in a particular energy state, the quotient of dP by dt, where dP is the probability of a given nucleus undergoing a spontaneous nuclear transition from that energy state in the time interval dt.

Radiobiology
The study of radiation effects on living things.

Radiographer
Any individual who performs radiographic operations or who, while in attendance at the site where radiographic operations are being performed, directly supervises such operations; and who is responsible to the user for assuring compliance with the requirements of radiation control regulations and license conditions.

Radiological Accidents
1) Loss of control of radioactive materials that present a potential hazard to personnel, public health, property, or environment. 2) Radiological accidents exceeding the established limit for exposure to ionizing radiation.

Radiological Assistance Program (RAP)
The program provides assistance to federal and state agencies and private entities in the event of an incident involving radioactive materials. The program also makes available a radiological assistance team of individuals to provide assistance to any DOE facility, common carrier, and law enforcement or other agencies for radiological incidents. *See* Radiological Assistance Teams (RATs).

Radiological Assistance Teams (RATs)
Teams dispatched to the site of a radiological incident by the DOE regional office responding to a radiological incident. Radiological Assistance Teams are located at DOE operations offices and national laboratories, most area offices, and associated contractor sites.

Radiological Defense
Defensive measures taken against the radiation hazards resulting from the employment of nuclear and radiological weapons.

Radiological Environment
Conditions found in an area resulting from the presence of a radiological hazard.

Radiological Monitoring
Periodic or continuous determination of the amount of ionizing radiation or radioactive contamination present in an occupied region as a safety measure for purposes of health protection. 1) Area monitoring is routine monitoring of the level of radiation or of radioactive contamination of any particular area, building, room, or equipment. 2) Personnel monitoring is monitoring of any part of an individual, his/her breath, excretions, or any part of his/her clothing.

Radiological Releases
Incidents in which radiological material (gas, liquid, and/or solid) are discharged into the biosphere in an unplanned manner.

Radiological Surveys
1) Evaluation of the radiation hazards incident to the production, use of, existence of radioactive materials or other sources of radiation under a specific set of conditions. Such evaluation customarily includes a physical survey of the disposition of materials and equipment, measurements or estimates of the levels of radiation that may be involved, and a sufficient knowledge of processes using or affecting these materials to predict hazards resulting from expected or possible changes in materials or equipment. 2) The directed effort to determine the distribution and dose rates of radiation in an area.

Radiological Transportation Incidents
Incidents that involve a transportation vehicle or shipment containing radioactive materials. *See* Transportation Incidents.

Radionuclide Barriers, Natural or Engineered
Structures that delay or prevent radionuclide migration from the source material.

Radionuclides
1) Hazardous substances and radioactive elements characterized according to their atomic mass and atomic number that can be manmade or naturally occurring. Radioisotopes can have a long life as soil or water pollutants, and are believed to have potentially mutagenic effects on the human body.

2) Nuclides with unstable ratios of neutrons to protons placing the nucleus in a state of stress. In an attempt to reorganize to a more stable state, they may undergo various types of rearrangement that involve the release of radiation. Radionuclides include, but may not be limited to: antimony-125, beryllium-7, cerium-134, cerium-137, cerium-141, cerium-144, cobalt-58, cobalt-60, element 104 isotopes, element 105 isotopes, element 106 isotopes, element 107 isotopes, element 108 isotopes, element 109 isotopes, iodine-131, manganese-64, radium-226, radium-228, radon-222, ruthenium-103, selenium-75, strontium-90, tellurium-132, thorium-230, thorium-232, tritium, uranium-238, zinc-65, and zirconium-95.

Radiotoxicity
A term referring to the potential of an isotope to cause damage to living tissue by absorption of energy from the disintegration of the radioactive material introduced into the body.

Radipose
A species descriptor that means a fleshy fin posterior to the dorsal.

Radius of Vulnerable Zone
The maximum distance from the point of release of a hazardous substance in which the airborne concentration could reach the level of concern under specified weather conditions.

RADM
An acronym for Regional Acid Deposition Model (CAA).

Radon
A colorless naturally occurring, radioactive, inert gaseous element formed by radioactive decay of radium atoms in soil or rocks. The radioactive gaseous element and its short-lived decay products produced by the disintegration of the element radium occurring in air, water, soil, or other media. Radon accumulating in residential basements and other areas of buildings without proper ventilation has been identified as a cause of lung cancer.

Radon Assessment and Mitigation (CAA)
The EPA Administrator's national assessment report to Congress conducted to a) identify the locations in the United States where radon is found in structures where people normally live or work, including educational institutions; b) assess the levels of radon gas that are present in such structures; c) determine the level of radon gas and radon daughters that poses a threat to human health and the extent of the threat to human health; d) determine methods of reducing or eliminating the threat to human health of radon gas and radon daughters; and e) include guidance and public information materials based on the findings or research of mitigating radon.

Radon Decay Products
A term used to refer collectively to the immediate products of the radon decay chain. These include Po-218, Pb-214, Bi-214, and Po-214, that have an average combined half-lives of about 30 minutes. *See* Radon Progeny.

Radon Flux
The number of radon atoms passing through a unit cross-sectional area per unit time.

Radon Gas and Indoor Air Quality Research Program
The research program established by the Administrator of EPA designed to:

- gather data and information on all aspects of indoor air quality in order to contribute to the understanding of health problems associated with the existence of air pollutants in the indoor environment;

- coordinate federal, state, local, and private research and development efforts relating to the improvement of indoor air quality; and

- assess appropriate federal government actions to mitigate the environmental and health risks associated with indoor air quality problems.

The program includes a) research and development concerning the identification, characterization, and monitoring of the sources and levels of indoor air pollution, including radon, that includes research and development relating to the measurement of various pollutant concentrations and their strengths and sources, high-risk building types, and instruments for indoor air quality data collection; b) research relating to the effects of indoor air pollution and radon on human health; c) research and development relating to control technologies or other mitigation measures to prevent or abate indoor air pollution (including the development, evaluation, and testing of individual and generic control devices and systems); d) demonstration of methods for reducing or eliminating indoor air pollution and radon, including sealing, venting, and other methods that the Administrator determines may be effective; e) research, to be carried out in conjunction with the Secretary of Housing and Urban Development, for the purpose of developing methods for assessing the potential for radon contamination of new construction (including, but not limited to, consideration of the moisture content of soil, porosity of soil, and radon content of soil), and design measures to avoid indoor air pollution; and f) the dissemination of information to ensure the public availability of the findings of the research activities.

Radon, High-Risk Areas

The list of areas within the United States that the Administrator of EPA, in consultation with federal departments and agencies, determines have a high probability of containing elevated levels of radon. determinations are made on the basis of:

- geological data;
- data on high radon levels in homes and other structures near any such federal building; and
- physical characteristics of the buildings.

Radon, Federal Buildings Study

The studies conducted by the head of each federal department or agency that owns a federal building for the purpose of determining the extent of radon contamination in such buildings. Such study shall include, in the case of a federal building using a nonpublic water source (such as a well or other groundwater), radon contamination of the water.

Radon Mitigation Demonstration Program (CAA)

The program established to test methods and technologies of reducing or eliminating radon gas and radon daughters where it poses a threat to human health. The program took into consideration demonstration programs underway in the Reading Prong of Pennsylvania, New Jersey, and New York and at other sites. The EPA Administrator is required to submit annual reports not later than February 1 of each year on the status of the demonstration program.

Radon Progeny

The short-lived radionuclides formed as a result of decay of radon. For radon-222, they consist of polonium-214 (RaC), polonium-218 (RaA), lead-214 (RaB), and bismuth-214 (RaC). Combined numbers of these radionuclides are reduced by one-half approximately every 30 minutes.

Radon Survey

A survey characterizing the extent of radon contamination in a building, facility, or site consisting of several structures. The survey includes testing from a representative sample of structures; any reliable testing data supplied by states, schools, or other parties; diagnostic and remedial efforts to reduce the levels of radon in such buildings; and the demonstrated expertise of the inspector conducting the survey regarding radon measurement and mitigation methods and other radon-related issues.

Radula

A species descriptor that means in mollusks, a flexible tonguelike organ with rows of horny teeth on the surface.

Railroad Emission Study

The study and investigation of emissions of air pollutants from railroad locomotives, locomotive engines, and secondary power sources on railroad rolling stock, in order to determine the extent to which such emissions affect air quality in air quality control regions throughout the United States, the technological feasibility and current state of technology for controlling such emissions, and the status and effect of current and proposed state and local regulations affecting such emissions.

Rainfall, Nuclear

The water that is precipitated from the base surge clouds after an underwater burst of a nuclear weapon. This rain is radioactive and presents an important secondary effect of such a burst.

Rainout

Radioactive material in the atmosphere brought down by precipitation.

RAM

See Reliability, Availability, and Maintainability; Radon Assessment and Mitigation.

RAMC

See Risk Assessment and Management Commission (CAA).

RAMCI

See Risk Assessment and Management Commission Investigation (CAA).

Ramping

A gradual, programmed increase/decrease in temperature or pressure to control the cure or cooling of composite parts.

Range

1) A 6-mile wide strip of land that runs in a north/south direction. Ranges are determined by government survey and are numbered in numerical order east or west of a principal meridian. 2) In terms of the ESA, the geographical area wherein a species resides. 3) The distance between any given point and an object or target. 4) Extent or distance limiting the operation or action of something, such as the range of an aircraft, ship, or gun. 5) The distance that can be covered over a hard surface by a ground vehicle, with its rated payload, using the fuel in its tank and the gasoline cans normally carried as part of the ground vehicle equipment.

Range Condition

The quality of the land reflected in its ability in specific vegetative areas to support various levels of productivity in accordance with range management objectives and the land use planning process, and relates to soil quality, forage values (whether seasonal or year round), wildlife habitat, watershed and plant communities, the present state of vegetation of a range site in relation to the potential plant community for that site, and the relative degree to which the kinds, proportions, and amounts of vegetation in a plant community resemble that of the desired community for that site.

Range Improvement

Any activity or program on or relating to rangelands that is designed to improve production of forage; change vegetative composition; control patterns of use; provide water; stabilize soil and water conditions; and provide habitat for livestock and wildlife. The term includes, but is not limited to, structures, treatment projects, and use of mechanical means to accomplish the desired results.

Range Improvement Burning

The use of open fires to remove vegetation for a wildlife, game or livestock habitat, or for the initial establishment of an agricultural practice on previously uncultivated land.

Range Masters

Individuals responsible for daily range operations; the range master ensures that the range is always safe and that only qualified firearms instructors conduct training activities.

Range Safety Officers

The designated and specifically trained individuals responsible for safety at a live firing range.

Range, Statistical

A measurement of the difference between two observations. The entire range is the difference between the smallest and largest value. Also related to the inner two quartile range that includes 60%

of all values (excluding the smallest 25% and the largest 26%).

Rangeland
Land on which the natural plant cover is primarily made up of native grasses, flowers, or shrubs valuable for feed.

RAP
An acronym for Remedial Action Program; Radiological Assistance Program.

Raptor
A species descriptor for a bird of prey.

Rasp
A machine that grinds waste into a manageable material and helps prevent odor.

Rated Load
The designed safe operating load for the equipment under prescribed conditions.

Rates
A term denoting units of measure such as absorbed dose rates, biological clearance rates, collective effective dose equivalent rates, contact rates, energy fluence rates, exposure rates, incidence rates, and lowest achievable emission rates.

Ratification
The declaration by which a nation formally accepts with or without reservation the content of a standardization agreement.

Rational Method
As applied to drainage design, the expression of peak discharge as equal to the product of rainfall intensity, drainage area, and a runoff coefficient depending on drainage basin characteristics.

Rationalization
Any action that increases effectiveness through more efficient or effective use of resources. Rationalization includes consolidation, reassignment of priorities to higher needs, standardization, spe-

cialization, mutual or improved interoperability, and greater cooperation.

Ratios
A term denoting units of measure such as critical temperature ratios, dilution ratios, gas volume ratios, loss ratios, and peak-to-peak ratios.

Raw Sewage
Untreated wastewater.

Raw Data
Any laboratory worksheets, records, memoranda, notes, or exact copies thereof, that are the result of original observations and activities of a study and are necessary for the reconstruction and evaluation of the report of that study. In the event that exact transcripts of raw data have been prepared (e.g., tapes that have been transcribed verbatim, dated, and verified accurate by signature), the exact copy or exact transcript may be substituted for the original source as raw data. Raw data may include photographs, microfilm or microfiche copies, computer printouts, magnetic media, including dictated observations, and recorded data from automated instruments.

Rayleigh Seismic Waves
Types of surface waves having a retrograde and elliptical motion at the free surface. These waves, along with love waves, mainly cause low-frequency vibrations that are more likely to make tall buildings vibrate. See Love Seismic Waves.

Rays
1) A species descriptor denoting the flat blades that encircle a flower disk. 2) In zoology, one of the bony spines supporting the membrane of a fish's fin. 3) A description for the color pattern or ridges on a shell.

RBE
See Relative Biological Effectiveness.

RBLC
An acronym for RACT/BACT/LAER Clearinghouse (CAA).

RCA
An acronym for Resource Conservation Act.

RCDPB
An acronym for Resource Conservation and Development Policy Board.

RCOG
An acronym for Regional Council of Governments.

RCRA Notifiers List
The EPA database that identifies companies that have notified the EPA (as required) that they generate, transport, treat, store, or dispose of hazardous wastes.

RCRA
See Resource Conservation and Recovery Act of 1976.

RCRIS
See Resource Conservation and Recovery Information System.

RCW
An acronym for Recirculated Cooling Water.

RD
See Remedial Design.

RDDT&E
An acronym for Research, Development, Demonstration, Testing, and Evaluation.

rDNA
See Recombinant DNA.

Re-Refined Oil
Used oil from which the physical and chemical contaminants acquired through previous use have been removed through a refining process.

Reaction Time
1) The elapsed time between the initiation of an action and the required response. 2) The time required between the receipt of an order directing an emergency response operation and the arrival of the initial members of the team concerned in the designated area.

Reactive
1) Materials that by themselves or in contact with water or other noncompatible materials are readily capable of detonation, explosive decomposition, or explosive reaction at normal temperatures and pressures. 2) Materials that are sensitive to mechanical or localized shock at normal temperatures and pressures.

Reactivity
1) The tendency of a substance to undergo chemical change. 2) Those hazardous wastes that are unstable and readily undergo violent chemical change but do not explode. 3) The ability of a substance to chemically interact with other substances.

Reactor
Any apparatus that is designed or used to sustain nuclear chain reactions in a controlled manner, including critical and pulsed assemblies and research, test, and power reactors. All assemblies designed to perform subcritical experiments that could potentially reach criticality are also to be considered reactors. Critical assemblies are special nuclear devices designed and used to sustain nuclear reactions. Critical assemblies may be subject to frequent core and lattice configuration changes and may be used often as mockups of reactor configurations. Therefore, requirements for modifications do not apply unless the overall assembly room is modified, a now assembly room proposed, or a new configuration not covered in previous safety evaluations.

Reactor Components
Various components of a nuclear reactor including, but not limited to: control rod drive control systems; pistol grip switches; coolant pumps; core(s); exhaust stacks; flux channel(s); fuel element(s); heat exchanger; ion exchange columns; electromechanical manipulator(s); neutron source; plutonium process hoods; pressure ves-

sel(s); reactor fuels; reactor wastes; sodium scrubber(s); reactor coolant systems; emergency spray water systems; and reactor protection systems.

Reactor Coolant System
The cooling system used to remove energy from the reactor core and transfer that energy either directly or indirectly to the steam turbine.

Reactor Opening Loss
The emissions of vinyl chloride occurring when a reactor is vented to the atmosphere for any purpose other than an emergency relief discharge as defined in 40 CFR 61.65(a).

Reactor Operations
All activities or functions involved in operating and using a reactor that, for purposes of this Order, begin with the initial loading of fuel in the reactor vessel and end with the removal of fuel to officially decommission or place the reactor in a standby status.

Reactor Projects
Activities that contribute to siting, designing, constructing, operating, or decommissioning a reactor, and those activities involving the operation or maintenance of operable and standby reactors, including shutdown reactors containing fuel.

Reactor Shutdown
Used as extra descriptor or as qualifier to reactor when the fact that reactor was in shutdown mode is significant to the severity of the incident.

Reactors, Chemical
Any vessels in which vinyl chloride is partially or totally polymerized into polyvinyl chloride.

Readily Available Inventories
Stocks and supplies of petroleum products that can be distributed or used without affecting the ability of the importer or refiner to operate at normal capacity; such term does not include minimum working inventories or other unavailable stocks.

Readily Accessible
Capable of being reached safely and quickly for operation, repair, or inspection without requiring those to whom ready access is requisite to climb over, or remove obstacles, or to resort to the use of portable access equipment.

Readiness Assurance
The actions taken to provide assurance that headquarters, field elements, and facility contractors implement appropriate aspects of U.S. Department of Energy (DOE) emergency management program policies and requirements as established by DOE order.

Readiness Planning
Operational planning required for emergency response operations. Its objective is the maintenance of high states of readiness for the deterrence of potential hazards. It includes planning activities that influence day-to-day operations and the response posture of teams. As such, its focus is on general capabilities and readiness rather than the specifics of a particular crisis, either actual or potential. The assignment of geographic responsibilities to team leaders, establishment of readiness standards and levels, development of deployment patterns, coordination of reconnaissance and medical assets and capabilities, and planning of joint exercises are examples of readiness planning. No formal joint planning system exists for readiness planning such as exists for contingency and execution planning.

Reaeration
The absorption of oxygen into water under oxygen deficient conditions.

Reagent Grade
Analytical reagent (AR) grade, ACS reagent grade, and reagent grade are synonymous terms for reagents that conform to the current specifications of the Committee on Analytical Reagents of the American Chemical Society (ACS).

Real Property

Includes a) land; b)the surface of the earth and whatever is erected, growing upon, or affixed to the land; c) that which is below land and the space above it; and d) equipment attached to and made part of buildings and structures (such as plumbing, electrical, heating, built-in cabinets, and elevators), but not movable equipment. The chief characteristics of real property are its immobility and tangibility. Synonymous with "land," "realty," and "real estate."

Real Time

Pertaining to the timeliness of data or information that has been delayed only by the time required for electronic communication. This implies that there are no noticeable delays.

Reasonable and Prudent Alternatives

Alternative actions identified during formal consultation that can be implemented in a manner consistent with the intended purpose of the action, that can be implemented consistent with the scope of the federal agency's legal authority and jurisdiction, that are economically and technologically feasible, and that would avoid the likelihood of jeopardizing the continued existence of listed species or resulting in the destruction or adverse modification of critical habitat.

Reasonable and Prudent Measures

Those actions the Director believes necessary or appropriate to minimize project impacts.

Reasonable Costs

1) Amounts that may be recovered for the cost of performing a damage assessment. Costs are reasonable when the injury determination, quantification, and damage determination phases have a well-defined relationship to one another and are coordinated; the anticipated increment of extra benefits in terms of the precision or accuracy of estimates obtained by using a more costly injury, quantification, or damage determination methodology are greater than the anticipated increment of extra costs of that methodology; and the anticipated cost of the assessment is expected to be less than the anticipated damage amount determined

in the injury, quantification, and damage determination phases. 2) A cost that is reasonable if, in its nature or amount, does not exceed that which would be incurred by a prudent person under the circumstances prevailing at the time the decision was made to incur the cost.

Reasonable Further Progress (RFP)(CAA)

Annual incremental reductions in emissions of the relevant air pollutant as are required by this part or may reasonably be required by the Administrator for the purpose of ensuring attainment of the applicable national ambient air quality standard by the applicable date.

Reasonable Further Progress Demonstration (RFPD)(CAA)

A demonstration that a state implementation plan (SIP), as revised, will result in VOC air emission reductions from the baseline emissions equal to the following amounts averaged over each consecutive 3-year period beginning 6 years after November 15, 1990, until the attainment date: a) at least 3% of baseline emissions each year; or b) an amount less than 3% of such baseline emissions each year, if the state demonstrates to the satisfaction of the Administrator (EPA) that the plan reflecting such lesser amount includes all measures that can feasibly be implemented in the area, in light of technological achievability.

Reasonable Progress

A judgment of compliance effort taking into account the costs of compliance, the time necessary for compliance, the environmental impacts of compliance, and the remaining useful life of the existing source or facility subject to the regulatory compliance requirement.

Reasonably Attributable

Attributable by visual observation or any other technique a state deems appropriate.

Reasonably Available Control Technology (RACT)

The lowest emissions limit that a particular source is capable of meeting by the application of control technology that is both reasonably available, as well as technologically and economically feasible. RACT is usually applied to existing sources in nonattainment areas and in most cases is less stringent than new source performance standards, devices, systems process modifications, or other apparatus or techniques that are reasonably available taking into account a) the necessity of imposing such controls in order to attain and maintain a national ambient air quality standard; b) the social, environmental, and economic impact of such controls; and c) alternative means of providing for attainment and maintenance of such standard. [This provision defines RACT for the purposes of 40 CFR 51.110(c)(2) and 51.341(b) only.]

Rebricking
Cold replacement of damaged or worn refractory parts of the glass melting furnace. Rebricking includes replacement of the refractories comprising the bottom, sidewalls, or roof of the melting vessel; replacement of refractory components in the heat exchanger; and replacement of refractory portions of the glass conditioning and distribution system.

Rebuild
To restore to the original specifications to the extent possible; the restoration of an item to a standard as nearly as possible to its original condition in appearance, performance, and life expectancy.

Receiver
An impartial person appointed to take possession of and manage property for the protection of all parties; a court appointed custodian.

Receiving Facility
A facility or operation where municipal or commercial waste is unloaded from a vessel.

Receiving Streams
Streams that receive outfall discharge of wastewater effluent.

Receiving Vessel
A tank or cylinder into which a product is being charged.

Receiving Waters
Oceans, lakes, rivers, and other bodies of water, and watercourses, into which wastewater or treated effluent is discharged.

Receptivity
The vulnerability of a target audience to particular psychological operations media.

Recharge (r)
The addition of water to the zone of saturation, usually by percolation from the soil surface (e.g., the recharge of an aquifer). Also, the amount of water added. Can be expressed as a rate (inches/year) or a volume.

Recharge Area
1) Area in which water reaches the zone of saturation by surface infiltration (e.g., an area where rainwater soaks through the earth to reach an aquifer). 2) An area in which there are downward components of hydraulic head in the aquifer. Infiltration moves downward into the deeper parts of an aquifer in a recharge area.

Recharge Basin
A basin or pit excavated to provide a means of allowing water to soak into the ground at rates exceeding those that would occur naturally.

Recharge Boundary
An aquifer system boundary that adds water to the aquifer. Streams and lakes are typical recharge boundaries.

Recipient Agency
Any agency, or contractor thereof, receiving records contained in a system of records from a source agency for use in a matching program.

Reciprocating Pump
A type of displacement pump consisting primarily of a closed cylinder containing a piston or

plunger, as the displacing mechanism, drawing liquid into the cylinder through an inlet valve and forcing it out through an outlet valve.

Reclaimed Water
Wastewater that as a result of treatment is suitable for uses other than potable use.

Reclamation
The recovery of natural resources previously abandoned due to some form of damage.

Reclamation Plan
A plan submitted by an applicant for a' permit under a state program or federal program that sets forth a plan for reclamation of the proposed surface coal mining operations pursuant to Section 1258 of the Surface Mining Control and Reclamation Act (SMCRA).

Recombinant Bacteria
A type of microorganism whose genetic makeup has been altered by deliberate introduction of new genetic elements. The offspring of these altered bacteria also contain these new genetic elements.

Recombinant DNA (rDNA)
The new DNA that is formed by combining pieces of DNA from different organisms or cells.

Recommendations
1) Technical opinions, not necessarily definitive, quantifiable or tied to an applicable requirement. 2) Specific methods and corrective actions believed feasible, logical, practical, and sufficient to fulfill the judgments of needs. In general, each need is expressed in two kinds of recommendations:

- 1) for correcting specific problems involved in the occurrence; and

- 2) for fixing systemic problems revealed during the investigation.

Recommended Maximum Contaminant Levels (RMCLs)
The maximum level of a contaminant in drinking water at which no known or anticipated adverse effect on human health would occur, and that includes an adequate margin of safety. Recommended levels are nonenforceable health goals. *See* Maximum Contaminant Levels.

Recompression Chamber
See Hyperbaric Chamber.

Reconnaissance Photography
Photography taken to obtain information on the current hazardous waste activities and operations at a specific site or facility, or to secure data concerning the meteorological, hydrographic, or geographic characteristics of a particular area, at a specific time. The primary purpose includes present and historic data collection efforts for later interpretation.

Reconstructed Source
An existing facility in which components are replaced to such an extent that the fixed capital cost of the new components exceed 50% of the capital cost that would be required to construct a comparable, entirely new facility. New source performance standards may be applied to sources that are reconstructed after the proposal of the standard if it is technologically and economically feasible to meet the standard.

Reconstruction
1) The act or process of reproducing by new construction the exact form and detail of a vanished structure, or any part thereof, as it appeared at a specific period of time. 2) The repair of damage to an existing approved building or an alteration of an existing nonconforming building to bring it into full conformance with the safety standards established by the policies and ordinances of an enforcing agency. 3) A situation that occurs when the fixed capital cost of the new component exceeds 60% of the fixed capital cost of a comparable entirely new source. For this definition, any final decision as to whether reconstruction has

occurred must be made in accordance with the provisions of 40 CFR 60.15(f)(1) through (3).

Record

Any item, collection, or grouping of information about an individual or company, that is maintained by an agency, including, but not limited to, his/her compliance history, financial transactions, and criminal or employment history, and that contains the name, or the identifying number, symbol, or other identifying particular assigned to the individual or company, such as a finger or voice print or photograph or tax identification number.

Also includes any report, document, writing, photograph, tape recording, or other electronic means of data collection and retention that pertains to defendant/respondent compliance with EPA, state and local governmental environmental rules and regulations.

Record Information

All forms (e.g., narrative, graphic, data, computer memory) of information registered in either temporary or permanent form so that it can be retrieved, reproduced, or preserved.

Record of Decision (ROD)

1) A public document that explains which cleanup alternative will be used at National Priorities List sites where the trust fund pays for the cleanup. The Record of Decision is based on information and technical analysis generated during the remedial investigation/feasibility study (RI/FS) and consideration of public comments and community concerns. 2) A concise public record of an agency's decision on a proposed action for which an environmental impact statement was prepared that includes the alternatives considered, the environmentally preferable alternative, factors balanced in the decision, and mitigation measures and monitoring to minimize harm. 3) A NEPA document prepared in accordance with the requirements of 40 CFR 1605.2, that provides a concise public record of the department's decision on a proposed action for which an Environmental Impact Statement was prepared, and identifies the alternatives considered in reaching the decision,

the environmentally preferable alternative(s), factors balanced by the department in making the decision, whether all practicable means to avoid or minimize environmental harm have been adopted, and if not, why they were not.

Recorded Doses

Those numbers (corrected for background), zero (minimal or negligible) and above, that are recorded as representing individuals' doses from external radiation sources or internally deposited radioactive materials determined in accordance with DOE requirements.

Recording

The act of writing or entering an instrument in a book of public record, usually in the office of the county clerk and recorder. Such recording constitutes notice to all persons of the rights or claims contained in the instrument. This type of notice is called "constructive notice" or "legal notice."

Recording Levels

Levels defined by the competent authority or the management for any of the quantities determined in the practice of radiation protection, above which recording of the information is taken to be necessary.

Recordkeeping, Inspections and Monitoring

The requirement for any person who owns or operates any polluting source, who manufactures pollution control equipment or process equipment, or who is subject to any environmental compliance requirement, on a one-time, periodic or continuous basis to a) establish and maintain records; b) prepare reports; c) install, use, and maintain monitoring equipment, and use audit procedures, or methods; d) sample such pollutants (in accordance with procedures or methods, at locations, and intervals, during periods and in such manner as the Administrator shall prescribe); e) keep records on control equipment parameters, production variables or other indirect data when direct monitoring of pollutants is impractical; f) submit compliance certifications in accordance with any agency's requirements; and g) provide such other information as the Administrator may reasonably require.

Recoverable

The capability or likelihood of being recovered from solid waste for a commercial or industrial use.

Recoverable Item

An item that normally is not consumed in use and is subject to return for repair or disposal.

Recovered Material

Waste material and byproducts that have been recovered or diverted from solid waste; does not apply to those materials and byproducts generated from, and commonly reused within, an original manufacturing process.

Recovered Resources

Material or energy recovered from solid waste.

Recovery

1) Improvement in the status of listed species to the point at which listing is no longer appropriate under the criteria set out in Section 4(a)(1) of the Endangered Species Act. 2) Actions taken after a site incident has been brought to a stable or shutdown condition to return the Site to normal operation.

Recovery Actions

Those actions taken after an emergency to restore the affected areas as nearly as possible to the pre-emergency condition.

Recovery Manager

The individual responsible for developing and implementing the approved recovery plan after an emergency has been terminated at the site. The recovery manager usually has close connections with, and strong operational knowledge of the affected facility or area.

Recovery Organization

The approved organization providing required expertise and abilities for returning areas affected by an emergency to normal operating conditions. The Recovery Organization structure may incorporate elements from many site organizations into a single unit.

Recovery Phase

The time period between terminating an emergency and resuming normal operations.

Recovery Plans

1) Plans developed to restore the affected area with federal assistance if needed. 2) Documents upon which actions of a Recovery Organization are based. It may include, but is not limited to, Integrated Work Control Programs (IWCPs), action plans to attain specific goals and materials, or service requests.

Recovery Turnover Package

The package containing a description of the Recovery Organization and a checklist to ensure that development of the Recovery Plan includes information from all necessary emergency and recovery-related organizations.

Recovery Zone (RZ)

A designated geographic area from which special operations forces can be extracted by air, boat, or other means.

Recreational River Areas

Those rivers or sections of rivers that are readily accessible by road or railroad, that may have some development along their shorelines, and that may have undergone some impoundment or diversion in the past.

Recreational Trail

A thoroughfare or track across land or snow, used for recreational purposes such as bicycling, cross-country skiing, day hiking, equestrian activities, jogging or similar fitness activities, trail biking, overnight and long-distance backpacking, snowmobiling, aquatic or water activity and vehicular travel by motorcycle, four-wheel drive or all-terrain off-road vehicles, without regard to whether it is a National Recreation Trail designated under

Section 4 of the National Trails System Act (NTSA)(16 USC 1243).

Rectangular Survey

See U.S. Government Survey System (USGSS).

Rectification

In photogrammetry, the process of projecting a tilted or oblique photograph on to a horizontal reference plane.

Rectifier

A device for converting alternating current into direct current. *See* Inverter.

Recurring Demand

A request by an authorized requisitioner to satisfy a material requirement for consumption or stock replenishment that is anticipated to recur periodically. Demands for which the probability of future occurrence is unknown are considered as recurring.

Recurring demands are considered by the supporting supply system in order to procure, store, and distribute material to meet similar demands in the future.

Recycle/Reuse

See Recycling.

Recycled Materials

Materials that can be utilized in place of raw or virgin materials in manufacturing a product.

These materials consist of items derived from post-consumer waste, industrial scrap, material derived from agricultural wastes and other items, all of which can be used in the manufacture of new products. See adjacent figure. *See* Recycling.

Recycled Oils

1) Any used oils that are reused, following their original use, for any purpose (including the purpose for which the oil was originally used). 2) Used oils from which physical and chemical contaminants acquired through use have been removed by re-refining or other processing, or any blend of oil, consisting of such re-refined or otherwise processed used oil and new oil or additives, with respect to which the manufacturer has determined, is substantially equivalent to new oil for a particular end use.

Recycled PCBs

Manufactured PCBs that appear in the processing of paper products or asphalt roofing materials as PCB-contaminated raw materials and that meet the following requirements: a) the concentration of Arocior PCBs in paper products leaving any manufacturing site or imported into the United States must have an annual average of less than 25 ppm with a 60 ppm maximum; b) there are no detectable concentrations of Arocior PCBs in asphalt roofing materials; c) the release of Arocior PCBs at the point at which emissions are vented

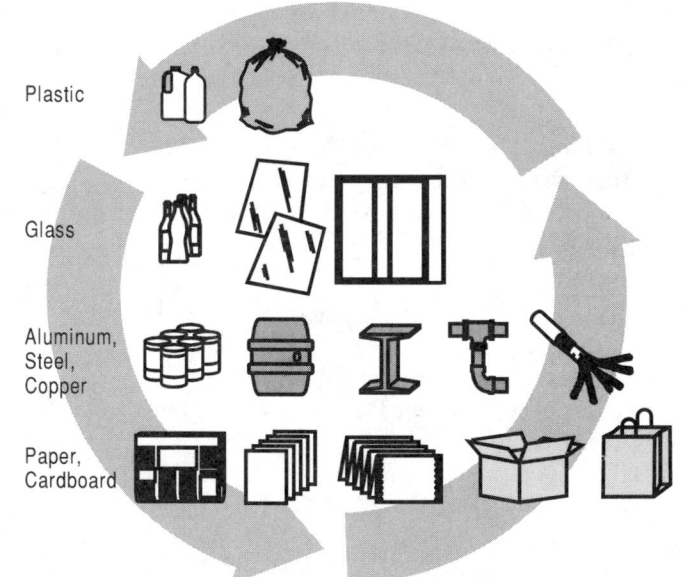

Plastic

Glass

Aluminum, Steel, Copper

Paper, Cardboard

Selected Recyclable Materials

to ambient air must be less than 10 ppm; d) the amount of Arocior PCBs added to water discharged from a processing site must at all times be less than 3 micrograms per liter (mg/l) for total Arociors (roughly 3 parts per billion); and e) disposal of any other process wastes above concentrations of 50 ppm PCB must be in accordance with Subpart D of 40 CFR 761.

Recycling
1) The reuse of materials ordinarily considered wastes, whether hazardous or nonhazardous; an operation in which a product or substance is passed through the same series of industrial processes, more than once. 2) The process of minimizing the generation of waste by recovering usable materials and objects in original or changed forms rather than discarding them as wastes. Examples are the recycling of paper, aluminum cans, and bottles. See figure on page 570.

Red Border
An EPA document that is undergoing final review before being submitted for final management decision.

Red Tide
A proliferation of a marine plankton that is toxic and often fatal to fish. This natural phenomenon may be stimulated by the addition of nutrients. A tide can be called red, green, or brown, depending on the coloration of the plankton.

Redds
The eggs deposited in one spawning season in fish.

Redeployment
The transfer of a group, unit, an individual, or supplies deployed in one area to another area, or to another location within the area, or to the zone of interior for the purpose of further employment.

Redesignation of Nonattainment Area
The five reasons by which the EPA can redesignate state nonattainment areas to attainment area are: 1) the Administrator determines that the area has attained the national ambient air quality standard (compliance); 2) the Administrator has fully approved the applicable implementation plan for the area (SIP approval); 3) the Administrator determines that the improvement in air quality is due to permanent and enforceable reductions in emissions resulting from implementation of the applicable implementation plan and applicable federal air pollutant control regulations and other permanent and enforceable reductions (prevention results); 4) the Administrator has fully approved a maintenance plan for the area (maintenance plan approval); and 5) the state containing such area has met all requirements applicable to the area (implementation compliance).

Redevelopment Agency
An agency established to facilitate improvements in designated areas. To accomplish this they engage in planning, lending, clearance, construction and reconstruction activities, expenditures for which are normally capitalized. Improvements are usually held by the agency for resale rather than agency use.

REDS
An acronym for Reactor Electric Distribution System.

Reduced Pressure Principle Backflow Prevention Device (RP)
A backflow preventer incorporating not less than two check valves, an automatically operated differential relief valve located between the two check valves, a tightly closing shut-off valve on each side of the check valve assembly, and equipped with necessary test cocks for testing.

Reduction
Chemical reaction in which an element gains an electron (has a decrease in positive valence).

Redundance, Planned
A planned duplication of controls to increase assurance of reliability.

Reentry

A planned activity for initial personnel reentry into previously evacuated areas of a site, and that may be conducted pre- or post-emergency response termination.

Reentry Interval

The period of time immediately following the application of a pesticide during which unprotected workers should not enter a field.

Referee

An impartial person selected or appointed to determine facts or arbitrate disputes, in the interest of all concerned parties.

Reference Box

The identification box placed in the margin of a map or chart that contains the series designation, sheet number, and edition number in a readily identified form.

Reference Datum

As used in the loading of aircraft, an imaginary vertical plane at or near the nose of the aircraft from which all horizontal distances are measured for balance purposes. Diagrams of each aircraft show this reference datum as "balance station zero."

Reference Dose (RfD)

An estimate (with uncertainty spanning perhaps an order of magnitude) of the daily exposure to the human population (including sensitive subpopulations) that is likely to be without deleterious effects during a lifetime. The RfD is reported in units of mg of substance/kg body weight/day for oral exposures, or mg of substance/m^3 of air breathed for inhalation exposures.

Reference Levels

The values of quantities that govern a particular course of action. Such levels may be established for any of the quantities determined in the practice of radiation protection; when they are reached or exceeded, all relevant information is considered and the appropriate action may be taken.

Reference levels are not to be confused with limits.

Reference Man/Woman

1) A hypothetical aggregation of human (male and female) physical and physiological characteristics arrived at by international consensus (ICRP Publication 23). These characteristics may be used by researchers and public health workers to standardize results of experiments and to relate biological insult from ionizing radiation to a common base. The "reference man/woman" is assumed to inhale 8,400 cubic meters of air in a year and to ingest 730 liters of water in a year. 2) A model of a hypothetical adult with the anatomical and physiological characteristics, used in dosimetry for radiation protection purposes.

Reference Methods

Methods of sampling and analyzing the ambient air for an air pollutant that are specified as reference methods in an appendix to 40 CFR 50, or a method that has been designated as a reference method in accordance with 40 CFR 53.

Reference Point

A prominent, easily located point in the terrain.

Reference Standards

Those guides or standards adopted by a government agency that the agency and its contractors should consider for guidance, as applicable, in addition to the mandatory standards.

Reference Substances

Any chemical substances or mixtures, or analytical standards, or materials other than a test substance, feed, or water, that are administered to or used in analyzing the test system in the course of a study for the purposes of establishing a basis for comparison with the test substance for known chemical or biological measurements.

Reference to Plat

A method of describing or locating real property by means of referring to a map of a subdivision usually recorded in the office of the county clerk and recorder.

Refiner
Any person who owns, operates, or controls the operation of any refinery.

Refiners Report
Periodic reports filed with the United States Department of Energy following instructions and definitions published by the DOE, and containing any supplemental information requested by a state.

Refinery
An industrial complex for processing crude oil by distillation and chemical reactions so as to produce a separate petroleum product. Typical crude fractions, from top to bottom or simple to complex, are a) ether, methane, and ethane (the gasolines); b) propane and butane c) kerosene, fuel oil, and lubricants; d) jelly paraffin, asphalt, and tar.

Refinery Fuel Use and Losses
All nonprocessing losses (e.g., spills, fire losses, contamination) by product. Reporting, by product, for fuel consumed at a facility for all purposes, is typically required.

Refinery Storage Facility
Storage located on a refinery site or operated in conjunction with a refinery and that primarily receives its petroleum product directly from a refiner.

Reflection
Energy diverted back from the interface of two media; the return of radiant energy (incident light) by a surface, with no change in wavelength. The reflection may be specular (i.e. direct) or diffuse according to the nature of the contact surfaces.

Reflex Arc Responses
Those involuntary responses to physical stimulus, such as the leg jerking when the knee is tapped in the right spot.

Reformulated Gasoline
Any gasoline that is certified by the Administrator under the CAA.

Refraction
The change of direction of propagation of any wave, such as an electromagnetic wave, when it passes from one medium to another in which the wave velocity is different. The bending of incident rays as they pass from one medium to another (e.g., air to glass).

Refractories
Nonmetallic materials having those chemical and physical properties that make them applicable for structures, or as components of systems, that are exposed to environments above 1,000°F.

Refrigerant
Any Class I or Class II substance used in a motor vehicle air conditioner, and/or any substitute substance.

Refrigerant Recycling Equipment
Equipment certified by the Administrator of EPA (or an independent standards testing organization approved by the Administrator) to meet the standards applicable to equipment for the extraction and reclamation of refrigerant from motor vehicle air conditioners.

Refuge Area
1) A coastal area considered safe from hazards to which merchant ships may be ordered to proceed when the shipping movement policy is implemented. 2) A wildlife preserve.

Refugia
Multiple places of protection or shelter (refuges).

Refugial Population
The plants or animals protected in a refuge.

Refuse
See Solid Waste.

Refuse Reclamation

Conversion of solid waste into useful products (e.g., composting organic wastes to make soil conditioners or separating aluminum and other metals for melting and recycling).

Regeneration

Manipulation of individual cells or masses of cells to cause them to develop into whole plants.

Region 1

EPA's Boston office serving the states of Connecticut, Maine, New Hampshire, Massachusetts, Rhode Island, and Vermont. The office is located at the John F. Kennedy Building, One Congress Street, Boston, Massachusetts 02203. Phone: (617) 565-3420.

Region 2

EPA's New York office serving the states and territories of New Jersey, New York, Puerto Rico, and the Virgin Islands. The office is located at the Jacobs K. Javits Building, 26 Federal Plaza, New York, New York 10278. Phone: (212) 264-2657.

Region 3

EPA's Philadelphia office serving the states of Delaware, Maryland, Pennsylvania, Virginia, West Virginia, and the District of Columbia. The office is located at 841 Chestnut Building, Philadelphia, Pennsylvania 19107. Phone: (215) 597-9800.

Region 4

EPA's Atlanta office serving the states of Alabama, Florida, Georgia, Kentucky, Mississippi, North Carolina, South Carolina, and Tennessee. The office is located at 345 Courtland Street, NE, Atlanta, Georgia 30365. Phone: (404) 347-4727.

Region 5

EPA's Chicago office serving the states of: Illinois, Indiana, Michigan, Minnesota, Ohio, and Wisconsin. The office is located at 77 West Jackson Boulevard, Chicago, Illinois 60604. Phone: (312) 353-2000.

Region 6

EPA's Dallas office serving the states of Arkansas, Louisiana, New Mexico, Oklahoma, and Texas. The office is located at the First Interstate Bank Tower at Fountain Place, 1445 Ross Avenue, Suite 1200, Dallas, Texas 75202. Phone: (214) 655-6444.

Region 7

EPA's Kansas City office serving the states of Iowa, Kansas, Missouri, and Nebraska. The office is located at 726 Minnesota Avenue, Kansas City, Kansas 66101. Phone: (913) 551-7000.

Region 8

EPA's Denver office serving the states of Colorado, Montana, North Dakota, South Dakota, Utah, and Wyoming. The office is located at One Denver Place, 999 18th Street, Suite 500, Denver, Colorado 80202. Phone: (303) 293-1603.

Region 9

EPA's San Francisco office serving the states and territories of Arizona, California, Hawaii, Nevada, American Samoa, and Guam. The office is located at 75 Hawthorne Street, San Francisco, California 94105. Phone: (415) 744-1305.

Region 10

EPA's Seattle office serving the states of Alaska, Idaho, Oregon, and Washington. The office is located at 1200 Sixth Avenue, Seattle, Washington 98101. Phone: (206) 553-4973.

Regional Administrator

The Regional Administrator for the EPA Region in which the facility is located, or a designee.

Regional Assistance Committees (RAC)

Regional committees chaired by a regional Federal Emergency Management Agency representative with members from numerous federal departments and agencies including the U.S. Department of Energy.

Regional assistance committees assist state and local government officials in the development of their radiological emergency response plans including reviewing plans and observing exercises.

Regional Coordinating Offices
DOE operations offices located at Oak Ridge, Savannah River, Albuquerque, Chicago, Idaho, Richland, and San Francisco that provide radiological assistance coordination, national contingency planning, and regional preparedness committee coordination.

Regional Frequency Analysis
An analysis that addresses the probability of the occurrence of two or more random hydrologic events.

Regional Office
One of the ten EPA Regional Offices.

Regional Petroleum Reserve
Portion of the Strategic Petroleum Reserve that consists of petroleum products stored pursuant to Section 6237 of the Energy Conservation Act (ECA).

Regional Response Team (RRT)
Representatives of federal, state, and local agencies who may assist in coordination of activities at the request of the On-Scene Coordinator or Remedial Project Manager before and during emergency, or Superfund, response actions. *See* On-Scene Coordinator.

Regions
Areas designated as air quality control regions (AQCR).

Register Marks
In cartography, designated marks, such as small crosses, circles, or other patterns applied to original copy prior to reproduction to facilitate registration of plates and to indicate the relative positions of successive impressions.

Registrant
Any manufacturer or formulator who obtains registration for a pesticide active ingredient or product.

Registration
Formal listing with EPA of a new pesticide before it can be sold or distributed in intrastate or interstate commerce. The product must be registered under the Federal Insecticide, Fungicide, and Rodenticide Act. EPA is responsible for registration (pre-market licensing) of pesticides on the basis of data demonstrating that they will not cause unreasonable adverse effects on human health or the environment when used according to approved label directions.

Registration Standards
Published reviews of all the data available on pesticide active ingredients.

Regolith
The layer of loose rock material resting on bedrock, and constituting the surface of most land.

Regularly Handle
A term that refers to employees who handle hazardous chemicals during any part of the day for more than 6 calendar days in any 30 consecutive day qualifying period beginning on the first day of handling.

Regulated Activities
Major Prevention of Significant Deterioration (PSD) stationary sources, or modifications to major PSD stationary sources.

Regulated Entities
1) Manufacturers, processors, wholesale distributors, or importers of consumer or commercial products for sale or distribution in interstate commerce in the United States. 2) Manufacturers, processors, wholesale distributors, or importers that supply products for sale or distribution in interstate commerce in the United States.

Regulated Item

Any item whose issue to a user is subject to control by an appropriate authority for reasons that may include cost, scarcity, technical or hazardous nature, or operational significance. Also called controlled item.

Regulated Substances

1) Chemicals, compounds, or materials the manufacture, generation, transportation, alteration, or disposition of which are regulated under any of the federal or state statutes. 2) A substance listed on the Hazardous Air Pollutant (HAP) list, or any other substance controlled by an environmental act, regulation, ordinance, or policy. *See* Hazardous Air Pollutants (HAPs).

Regulatory Deception

Actions executed to mislead governmental decisionmakers, causing them to derive and accept desired mitigation plans, capabilities, intentions, operations, or other activities that evoke actions that contribute to the originator's objectives. There are usually two types of regulatory deception.

- *Regulated Deception* — deception planned and executed to result in policies and actions that support the regulated individual or firm's objectives, policies, and strategic plans to avoid the costs of environmental compliance with specific regulations.

- *Regulator Or Department/Agency Deception* — deception planned and executed by government regulators, departments and agencies, about their systems, facilities, doctrine, tactics, techniques or service operations, or other activities that increase or maintain environmental hazards associated with noncompliance of specific environmental regulations/requirements.

Regulatory Organizations

1) Organizations responsible for the decisionmaking and implementation of a programmatic or regulatory action requiring a National Environmental Policy Act review. 2) Agencies responsible for enforcing environmental laws and regulations.

Rehabilitation

The act or process of returning a structure to a state of utility through repair or alteration that makes possible an efficient contemporary use while preserving those portions or features of the structure that are significant to its historical, architectural, and cultural values. *See* Preservation.

Reinforcement

A material added to the matrix to provide the required properties; ranges from short fibers through complex textile forms.

Reinforcement Ratio

The percentage of tension reinforcement in a reinforced concrete beam.

Related Energy Facility

Any necessary appurtenance to a storage facility, including pipelines, roadways, reservoirs, and salt brine lines.

Related Personal Property

Any personal property that, once installed, becomes an integral part of the real property in which it is installed or is related to, designed for, or specially adapted to the functional or productive capacity of the real property. The removal of related personal property would significantly diminish the economic value of the real property or the related personal property. Examples of related personal property are communications and telephone systems.

Relative Bearing

The direction expressed as a horizontal angle normally measured clockwise from the forward point of the longitudinal axis of a vehicle, aircraft, or ship to an object or body. *See* Bearing; Grid Bearing.

Relative Biological Effectiveness

1) For a particular living organism or part of an organism, the ratio of the absorbed dose of a reference radiation that produces a specified biological effect to the absorbed dose of the radiation of interest that produces the same biological effect.

2) The ratio of the number of rads of gamma (or X-ray) radiation of a certain energy that will produce a specified biological effect to the number of rads of another radiation required to produce the same effect.

Relative Light Output

The light output delivered through the use of a ballast divided by the light output delivered through the use of a reference ballast, expressed as a percent, as determined in accordance with the test procedures specified in ANSI Standard C82.2-1984.

Release

Any spilling, leaking, pumping, pouring, emitting, emptying, discharging, injecting, escaping, leaching, dumping, or disposing into the environment, including the abandonment or discarding of barrels, containers, and other closed receptacles containing any hazardous substance or pollutant or contaminant, but excludes the following: a) any release that results in exposure to persons solely within a workplace, with respect to a claim that such persons may assert against the employer of such persons; b) emissions from the engine exhaust of a motor vehicle, rolling stock, aircraft, vessel, or pipeline pumping station engine; c) release of source, byproduct, or special nuclear material from a nuclear incident, as those terms are defined in the Atomic Energy Act of 1954, if such release is subject to requirements with respect to financial protection established by the Nuclear Regulatory Commission, or for the purposes of any other response action, any release of source byproduct, or special nuclear material from any designated processing site; and d) the normal application of fertilizer.

Release Agents

Materials that are used to prevent cured matrix material from bonding to tooling.

Release Detection

Determining whether a release of a regulated substance has occurred from the underground storage tank (UST) system into the environment or into the interstitial space between the UST system and its secondary barrier or secondary containment around it.

Releases

1) Any spilling, leaking, pumping, pouring, emitting, emptying, discharging, injecting, escaping, leaching, dumping, or otherwise disposing of substances into the environment. This includes abandoning/discarding any type of receptacle containing substances, or the stockpiling of a reportable quantity of a hazardous substance in an enclosed containment structure. 2) Spills, leaks, emissions, discharges, escapes, leachings or disposings from an underground storage tank (UST) into groundwater, surface water, or subsurface soils. 3) With certain exceptions, any spilling, leaking, pumping, pouring, emitting, emptying, discharging, injecting, escaping, leaching, dumping, or disposing into the environment (including the abandonment or discarding of barrels, containers or other closed receptacles) of any hazardous substance, or CERCLA hazardous substance.

Relevant and Appropriate Requirements

Those federal requirements that, while not "applicable," are designed to apply to problems sufficiently similar to those encountered at CERCLA sites that their application is appropriate. Requirements may be relevant and appropriate if they would be "applicable" but for jurisdictional restrictions associated with the requirement. *See* Applicable or Relevant and Appropriate Requirements (ARARs).

Reliability and Quality Assurance

Involves all those planned and systematic actions necessary to provide adequate confidence that a facility, structure, system, or component will perform satisfactorily and safely in service. *See* Quality Assurance.

Reliability-Centered Maintenance

A maintenance system that determines the most effective maintenance activity, based on an analysis of an item failure modes, failure rates, and the importance of the item to the safety operation of the facility.

Reliability Diagram

In cartography, a diagram showing the dates and quality of the source material from which a map or chart has been compiled.

Relict

A species descriptor for a localized species or population that has survived from an earlier epoch.

Relief

1) Inequalities of evaluation and the configuration of land features on the surface of the earth that may be represented on maps or charts by contours, hypsometric tints, shading, or spot elevations. 2) The whole or a part of an agency grant of money, assistance, license, permit, authority, exemption, exception, privilege, or remedy. 3) The recognition of a claim, right, immunity, privilege, exemption, or exception; or the taking of other action on the application or petition of, and beneficial to, a person or firm.

Relief Valve

An automatic pressure relieving device actuated by the static pressure upstream of such device that opens further with the increase in pressure over the opening pressure. It is used primarily for liquid service.

Relief Valve Discharge

Any nonleak discharge through a relief valve. Relief valve discharge does not include discharges ducted to a control system from which the concentration of vinyl chloride in the exhaust gases does not exceed 10 ppm (average for 3-hour period), or equivalent as provided in 40 CFR 61.66.

rem (Roentgen Equivalent Man)

1) Unit of measure absorbed radiation dose; a unit of dose of any radiation to body tissue in terms of its estimated biological effects relative to an exposure of one roentgen of X-rays or gamma rays. For the purpose of this definition, any of the following is considered to be equivalent to a dose of one rem:

- an exposure of one roentgen due to X-ray or gamma radiation;
- a dose of one rad due to X-ray, gamma, or beta radiation;
- a dose of 0.1 rad due to neutrons or high energy protons;
- a dose of 0.05 rad due to particles heavier than protons and with sufficient energy to reach the lens of the eye; and
- an exposure of 14×10^6 neutrons per square centimeter.

2) The unit of dose equivalent from ionizing radiation to the human body, used to measure the amount of radiation to which a person or a part of a human has been exposed. *See* Radiation Exposure Module; Roentgen; Roentgen Equivalent Mammal/Man; Sievert.

Remanufacture

To upgrade or modify to the revised specifications of the manufacturer and applicable industry standards.

Remedial Action (RA)

1) The actual construction or implementation phase of a Superfund site cleanup that follows remedial design. The term includes, but is not limited to, offsite transport and offsite storage, treatment, destruction, or other means to secure disposition of offsite of hazardous substances and associated contaminated materials. Actions may include the costs of permanent relocation of residents and businesses and community facilities where the president determines that, alone or in combination with other measures, such relocation is more cost-effective than and environmentally preferable to transportation, storage, treatment, destruction, or offsite disposal of hazardous substances, or may otherwise be necessary to protect the public health or welfare.

The term implies other actions at the location of the release, such as:

- storage;
- confinement to perimeter protection using dikes, trenches, or ditches;
- clay cover;

- neutralization (chemical);
- cleanup of released hazardous substances or contaminated materials;
- recycling or reuse;
- diversion;
- destruction;
- segregation of reactive wastes;
- dredging or excavations;
- repair or replacement of leaking containers;
- collection of leachate and runoff;
- onsite treatment or incineration;
- provision of alternative water supplics; and
- any monitoring reasonably required to ensure that such actions to protect the public welfare and the environment are effective.

2) Those actions consistent with permanent remedy taken instead of, or in addition to, removal action in the event of a release or threatened release of a hazardous substance into the environment, to prevent or minimize the release of hazardous substances so that they do not migrate to cause substantial danger to present or future public health or welfare or the environment.

Remedial Design (RD)(RCRA)

1) An engineering phase that follows the Record of Decision (ROD) when technical drawings and specifications are developed for the subsequent remedial action at a site on the National Priorities List. 2) A phase of remedial action that follows the remedial investigation/feasibility study and includes development of enginecring drawings and specifications for a site cleanup.

Remedial Investigation/Feasibility Study (RI/FS)

Two distinct but related CERCLA studies, usually performed simultaneously, and together referred to as the "RI/FS." They are intended to gather the data necessary to determine the type and extent of contamination at a Superfund site; establish criteria for cleaning up the site; identify and screen cleanup alternatives for remedial action; and analyze in detail the technology and costs of the alternatives.

Remedial Investigation (RI)

In-depth studies designed to gather the data necessary to determine the nature and extent of contamination at a Superfund site; establish criteria for cleaning up the site; identify preliminary alternatives for remedial actions; and support the technical and cost analyses of the alternatives. The remedial investigation is usually done with the feasibility study. *See* Remedial Investigation/Feasibility Study.

Remedial Measures

Actions taken to reduce contaminant doses that might otherwise be received in abnormal exposure conditions. Remedial measures are sometimes called protective actions or countermeasures.

Remedial Project Manager (RPM)

The EPA, or state, official responsible for overseeing remedial response activities.

Remedial Response

A long-term action that stops or substantially reduces a release or threatened release of hazardous substances that is serious, but does not pose an immediate threat to public health and/or the environment.

Remedies

As defined by Section 101 (24) of CERCLA, those actions consistent with permanent remedy taken instead of, or in addition to, removal action in the event of a release or threatened release of a hazardous substance into the environment, to prevent or minimize the release of hazardous substances so that they do not migrate to cause substantial danger to present or future public health or welfare or the environment.

Remedy

1) The actual construction or implementation phase that follows the remedial design of the selected cleanup alternative at a site. 2) To prevent or minimize the release of hazardous substances so that they do not migrate to cause substantial danger to present or future public health or welfare or the environment.

Remote-Handled Transuranic Wastes

Packaged transuranic waste whose external surface dose rate exceeds 200 mrem per hour. Test specimens of fissionable material irradiated for research and development purposes only and not for the production of power or plutonium may be classified as remote-handled transuranic waste.

Remotely Piloted Vehicle

An unmanned vehicle capable of being controlled from a distant location through a communication link. It is normally designed to be recoverable. *See* Drone.

Remove or Removal

1) An immediate short-term action to address the cleanup or removal of released, or threatened to be released, hazardous substances from the environment. 2) Actions that may be necessary in the event of the threat of release of hazardous substances into the environment, including actions to monitor, assess, and evaluate the release or threat of release of hazardous substances, as well as the disposal of removed materials.

In addition, the term includes, but is not limited to, security fencing or other measures to limit access; provision of alternative water supplies; temporary evacuation and housing of threatened individuals not otherwise provided for; and any emergency assistance that may be provided for under Section 104(b) of the Disaster Relief Act of 1974.

Removal Action

Short-term immediate actions taken to address releases of hazardous substances that require expedited response. Removal actions may include any task necessary to prevent, minimize, or mitigate damage to the public health or welfare or to the environment, that may otherwise result from a release, or threat of release. *See* Cleanup.

Renal Toxicity

Ability to damage kidney cells; kidney toxicity.

Render Safe Procedures

See Explosive Ordnance Disposal Procedures.

Rendezvous

A prearranged meeting at a given time and location from which to begin an action or phase of an operation, or to which to return after an operation.

Renewable Energy Sources

Energy sources that are part of a renewable energy system or technology, and includes, but is not limited to, sources such as agriculture and urban waste, geothermal energy, solar energy, and wind energy.

Renewable-Resource Energy Measure

A measure that modifies any building or industrial plant, that involves changing, in whole or in part, the fuel or source of the energy used to meet the requirements of such building or plant from a depletable source of energy to a nondepletable source of energy; and that is likely to reduce energy costs (as calculated on the basis of energy costs reasonably projected over time) in an amount sufficient to enable a person to recover the total cost of purchasing and installing such measure (without regard to any tax benefit or federal financial assistance applicable thereto) within the period of a) the useful life of the modification involved, or b) 25 years after the purchase and installation of such measure, whichever is less. Such term does not include the purchase or installation of any appliance.

Renewable Resources Extension Act (RREA)

An extension program found in Subchapter III of the Forest and Rangeland Renewable Resources Planning Act (FRRRPA). The Act authorizes the Secretary of Agriculture, in cooperation with state officials, to provide educational programs that foster the recognition, understanding and resolution to problems dealing with renewable resources, by providing funds and technical assistance to a state's colleges and universities.

Renovation

Altering in any way one or more facility components. Operations in which load-supporting structural members are wrecked or taken out are excluded.

Rent

Money or other consideration given for the right of use, possession, and occupation of property.

Repair

The restoration of an item to serviceable condition through correction of a specific failure or unserviceable condition; repair to restore to operating condition after damage, malfunction, or wear. *See* Rebuild.

Repair Cycle

The stages through which a reparable item passes from the time of its removal or replacement until it is reinstalled or placed in stock in a serviceable condition.

Reparable Item

An item that can be reconditioned or economically repaired for reuse when it becomes unserviceable. *See* Recoverable Item.

Replacement

The substitution for an injured resource with a resource that provides the same or substantially similar services, when such substitutions are in addition to any substitutions made or anticipated as part of response actions and when such substitutions exceed the level of response actions determined appropriate to the site pursuant to the National Contingency Plan (NCP).

Replacement Factor

The estimated percentage of equipment or repair parts in use that will require replacement during a given period due to wearing out beyond repair, abandonment, pilferage, and other causes except catastrophes.

Replacement Value

The costs to replace something with like kind, quality, and capacity.

Replicate Samples

Samples prepared by dividing a sample into two or more separate aliquots. Laboratory duplicate samples are considered to be two replicates.

Reportable Occurrences

Events or conditions to be reported in accordance with the criteria defined in DOE Order 5000.3A.

Reportable Quantity (RQ)

The quantity of a hazardous substance that triggers reports under CERCLA. Reportable quantities are a) 1 pound, or b) for selected substances, an amount established by regulation either under CERCLA or under Section 311 of the Clean Water Act (CWA). Reportable quantities are measured over a 24-hour period. If a substance is released in amounts exceeding its RQ, the release must be reported to the National Response Center (NRC), the State Emergency Response Commission (SERC), and Community Emergency Coordinators (CEC) for areas likely to be affected.

Reportable Sources of Radiation

1) Radiation machines, when installed in such manner as to be capable of producing radiation. 2) Radioactive material contained in devices designed and manufactured for the purpose of detecting, measuring, gauging, controlling thickness, density, level, interface location, radiation, leakage or qualitative or quantitative chemical composition, for producing light or an ionized atmosphere, possessed pursuant to a regulatory permit/license.

Reported Significant Observations

A means of obtaining feedback from the work level on things that could contribute to an accident situation. Questionnaires are used to obtain reports on these observations. Similar to critical incident technique.

Repositories

Facilities for the permanent deep geological disposal of high level or transuranic waste.

Repowering (CAA)

Replacement of an existing coal-fired boiler with one of the following clean coal technologies: atmospheric or pressurized fluidized bed combustion, integrated gasification combined cycle, magnetohydrodynamics, direct and indirect coal-fired turbines, integrated gasification fuel cells, or as determined by the Administrator of EPA, in consultation with the Secretary of Energy, a derivative of one or more of these technologies, and any other technology capable of controlling multiple combustion emissions simultaneously with improved boiler or generation efficiency and with significantly greater waste reduction relative to the performance of technology in widespread commercial use as of November 15, 1990. The term also includes any oil and/or gas-fired unit that has been awarded clean coal technology demonstration funding as of January 1, 1991, by the DOE.

Representative Downwind Direction
During the forecast period, the mean surface downwind direction in the hazard area toward which the cloud travels.

Representative Downwind Speed
The mean surface downwind speed in the hazard area during the forecast period.

Representative, Employees
For purposes of submitting a complaint under OSHA, a representative of employees is any of the following: a) an authorized representative of the employee bargaining unit, such as a certified or recognized labor organization; b) an attorney acting for an employee; c) any other person acting in a bona fide representative capacity (e.g., a member of the employee's family or an elected official).

Representative Fraction
The scale of a map, chart, or photograph expressed as a fraction or ratio. *See* Scale.

Representative Insulation Sample
A sample of insulating material with the same characteristics (other than thickness) and using the same facing imposed on the insulating material manufactured for final use.

Representative Insulation Thickness
A thickness of insulating material at which the change in thermal performance per inch will vary no more than plus or minus 2% with increases in thickness.

Representative Sample
A sample of a universe or whole (e.g., waste pile, lagoon, groundwater) that can be expected to exhibit the average properties of the universe or whole.

Reprocessing
The dissolution of spent reactor fuel and separation of uranium, transuranic elements, and fission products; the processing of nuclear fuel (material), after its use in a reactor, to recover valuable material and to remove fission products.

Reproduction of Objects
The construction or fabrication of an accurate copy of an object. The object being reproduced may be too deteriorated or fragile to be displayed or otherwise used or may no longer exist. Reproduced objects are normally used as furnishings in historic structures or as equipment in living history programs.

Reproductive Toxicity
Harmful effects on fertility, gestation, or offspring, caused by exposure of either parent to a substance.

Request for Determination
A request made by any person to the office of administrative law, in accordance with the procedures specified in this article, to issue a determination as provided by government regulation, as to whether a state agency rule is a "regulation," as defined in the USC.

Required Strength
A term referring to the required strength to resist factored loads or related internal moments and forces.

Requirements
Something called for or demanded: a requisite or mandatory condition.

Requirements and Standards for PCBs

EPA's PCB spill cleanup policy requirements referring to both the procedural responses and numerical decontamination levels set forth as constituting adequate cleanup of PCBs. Standards refers to the maximum numerical decontamination levels.

Requisitioning Objective

The maximum quantities of material to be maintained on hand and on order to sustain current operations. It will consist of the sum of stocks represented by the operating level, safety level, and the order and shipping time or procurement lead time, as appropriate. *See* Level of Supply.

Reregistration

The re-evaluation and re-licensing of existing pesticides originally registered prior to current scientific and regulatory standards. EPA reregisters pesticides through its Registration Standards Program.

RESC

An acronym for Reactor Subcriticality.

Rescuer Protection Equipment

Gear necessary to prevent injury to workers responding to chemical incidents.

Research

All effort directed toward increased knowledge of natural phenomena and environment and toward the solution of problems in all fields of science. This includes basic and applied research.

Research and Development (R&D)

Theoretical analysis, exploration, experimentation or the extension of investigative findings and scientific or technical theories into practical application for experimental or demonstration purposes, including the experimental production and testing of models, prototype devices, materials and processes. Research and development does not include the internal or external administration of radiation of radioactive material to human beings.

Research Design

A synopsis, or planned approach to research objectives to be accomplished by the undertaking, including methods, procedures, and strategies for implementing a data recovery project and/or restoration program.

Research/Development Projects, Alternative Coal Mining Technologies (ACMT)

Under the Surface Mining Control and Reclamation Act (SMRCA), approved research, studies, surveys, experiments, demonstration projects, and training relating to a) the development and application of coal mining technologies that provide alternatives to surface disturbance and that maximize the recovery of available coal resources, including the improvement of present underground mining methods, methods for the return of underground mining wastes to the mine void, methods for the underground mining of thick coal seams and very deep seams; and b) safety and health in the application of such technologies, methods, and means.

Reservation

Any Native American Indian reservation or dependent Native American Indian community referred to in clause (a) or (b) of Section 1151 of Title 18; or any land selected by an Alaska Native village or regional corporation under the provisions of the Alaska Native Claims Settlement Act (43 USC 1601 et seq.').

Reserve Area

Any area of land withdrawn from the public domain and administered, either solely or primarily, by the Secretary of Interior through the U.S. Fish and Wildlife Service.

Reserve Generating Capacity

Extra capacity maintained to generate power in the event of unusually high demand or a loss, or unscheduled outage of regular generating capacity.

Reservoir

Any natural or artificial holding area used to store, regulate, or control water.

Reservoir Routing

A technique used in hydrology to compute the effect of reservoir inflow on reservoir outflow.

Resident Species

With respect to a state, a species that exists in the wild in that state during any part of its life.

Residential Areas

Those areas where people live or reside. Residential areas include housing and the property on which housing is located, as well as playgrounds, roadways, sidewalks, parks, and other similar areas within a residential community.

Residential Building

A structure or portion of a structure that provides facilities or shelter for human residency. The term does not include any multifamily residential structure more than three stories above grade.

Residential/Commercial Areas

Those areas where people live or reside or where people work in other than manufacturing or farming industries. Residential areas include housing and the property on which housing is located as well as playgrounds, roadways, sidewalks, parks, and other similar areas within a residential community. Commercial areas are typically accessible to both employees and the general public and include public assembly properties, institutional properties, stores, office buildings, and transportation areas.

Residential Development

The permitting for siting or construction of any residence or other related major structure.

Residential Solid Wastes

Garbage, rubbish, trash, and other solid waste resulting from the normal activities of households.

Residential Tanks

A tank located on property used primarily for dwelling purposes.

Residual Contamination

Contamination that remains after corrective actions have been taken to remove it. These actions may consist of nothing more than allowing the contamination to decay naturally (e.g., evapotranspiration).

Residual Disinfectant Concentration

The concentration of disinfectant measured in mg/l in a representative sample of water.

Residual Fuel Oil

A high viscosity fuel oil that must be heated before it can be pumped and handled conveniently. Used primarily in industry, in large commercial buildings, and for the generation of electricity. Includes Nos. 4, 5, and 6 fuel oils as defined in ASTM Specification D396 and Federal Specification VV-F-815C; Navy Special fuel oil in Military Specification IL-859E, including Amendment 2; and Bunker C fuel oil.

Residual Pollution

The amount of a pollutant remaining in the environment after a natural or technological process has taken place (e.g., the sludge remaining after initial wastewater treatment, or particulates remaining in air after the air passes through a scrubbing or other pollutant removal process).

Residual Radiation

Nuclear radiation caused by fallout, artificial dispersion of radioactive material, or irradiation that results from a nuclear explosion and persists longer than one minute after burst. *See* Contamination.

Residual Radioactive Material (UMTRCA)

1) Waste in the form of tailings resulting from the processing of ores for the extraction of uranium and other valuable constituents of the ores; and other waste (that the Secretary determines to be radioactive) at a processing site that relate to such processing, including any residual stock of unprocessed ores or low-grade materials. 2) Radioactive materials that are in or on soil, air, equipment, or structures as a consequence of past operations or activities.

Residual Radioactivity

Nuclear radiation that results from radioactive sources and that persists for longer than one minute. Sources of residual radioactivity created by nuclear explosions include fission fragments and radioactive matter created primarily by neutron activation, but also by gamma and other radiation activation. Other possible sources of residual radioactivity include radioactive material created and dispersed by means other than nuclear explosion. *See* Contamination; Induced Radiation.

Residual Risks

Risks remaining after the application of prevention, mitigation, and corrective actions.

Residual Volume

The volume of air remaining in the lungs after a maximal forceful exhalation.

Residues

Hazardous material remaining in a packaging, including a tank car, after its contents have been unloaded to the maximum extent practicable and before the packaging is either refilled or cleaned of hazardous material and purged to remove any hazardous vapors.

Resin

A material, generally a polymer, that has an indefinite and often high molecular weight and a softening or melting range and exhibits a tendency to flow when it is subjected to stress. Resins are used as the matrices to bind together the reinforcement material in composites.

Resin Grade

The subdivision of resin classification that describes it as a unique resin (i.e., the most exact description of a resin with no further subdivision).

Resistance

For plants and animals, the ability to withstand poor environmental conditions and/or attacks by chemicals or disease. The ability may be inborn or developed.

Resonator

The mirrors, or reflectors, making up the laser cavity including the laser rod or tube. The mirrors reflect light back and forth to build up amplification.

Resource

A person, thing, or action needed for living or to improve the quality of life.

Resource Conservation

Reduction of the amounts of solid waste that are generated, reduction of overall resource consumption, and utilization of recovered resources.

Resource Conservation and Development (RCD)

The program established under the Resource Conservation Act (RCA) to make available to states, local units of government, and local nonprofit organizations the technical and financial assistance necessary to operate and maintain a planning and implementation process needed to conserve and improve the use of land, develop natural resources, and improve and enhance the social, economic, and environmental conditions in rural areas of the United States.

Resource Conservation and Development Policy Board (RCDPB)

The board established within the Department of Agriculture to advise the Secretary regarding the administration of the provisions of the Resource Conservation Act (RCA), including the formulation of policies for carrying out conservation programs.

Resource Conservation and Recovery Act of 1976 (RCRA)

RCRA (42 USC 321 et seq.) is the federal statute enacted in 1976 regulating management of hazardous wastes to ensure "cradle-to-grave" (or generation to disposal) responsibility and tracking. The statute was enacted as a result of the realization that the improper disposal of hazardous wastes posed a significant threat to human health and the environment. RCRA authorizes EPA to list waste materials as hazardous wastes and to develop record keeping, labeling, and handling requirements for hazardous waste. Most of the regulations developed under RCRA concern the control of hazardous waste generators, transporters, and treatment, storage, and disposal facilities (TSDPS). The 1986 amendments to RCRA enabled EPA to address environmental problems that could result from underground tanks storing petroleum and other hazardous substances. RCRA focuses only on active and future facilities and does not address abandoned or historical sites. *See* CERCLA.

Resource Conservation and Recovery Activities

Includes, but is not limited to, all research, development, and demonstration projects on resource conservation or energy, or material, recovery from solid waste, and all technical or financial assistance for state or local planning for, or implementation of, projects related to resource conservation of energy or material, recovery from solid waste.

Resource Conservation and Recovery Information System (RCRIS)

EPA's database of RCRA sites. It includes small and large quantity hazardous waste generators, waste transporters, and waste treatment, storage, and disposal facilities.

Resource Recovery

The process of obtaining matter or energy from materials formerly discarded; recovery of material or energy from solid waste.

Resource Recovery Facility

Any facility at which solid waste is processed for the purpose of extracting, converting to energy, or otherwise separating and preparing solid waste for reuse.

Resource Recovery Systems

Solid waste management systems that provide collection, separation, recycling, and recovery of solid wastes, including disposal of nonrecoverable waste residues.

Resources

Personnel, funds, and major items of equipment available, or potentially available, for assignment to operational or emergency incident tasks.

Respective Agency Head, Public Land

The Secretary of the Interior, the Secretary of Defense, the Secretary of Agriculture, and the Board of Directors of the Tennessee Valley Authority, with respect to public lands under the custody and control of each.

Respirators

See Respiratory Protective Device (RPD).

Respiratory Depression

Slowing or cessation of breathing due to suppression of the function of the respiratory center in the brain.

Respiratory Protective Device (RPD)

A breathing device designed to protect the wearer from a hazardous atmosphere. A form of personal protective equipment, designed to protect workers from toxic exposure through inhalation routes.

Respiratory Rate

The frequency of a complete cycle of a breath, inhalation, and exhalations.

Respond

As defined by Section 101 (25) of CERCLA, respond means a removal, remedy, or remedial action.

Respondent

Any person named in a complaint, and alleged to be in violation of any environmental regulation, order, decision, or statute adopted, administered, or enforced by a public, or quasi-public, entity. The person or state agency from whose action or decision the appellant is seeking relief.

Response

As defined by Section 101(25) of CERCLA, removals, remedies, or remedial actions. Any actions taken to remove, remedy, or cleanup releases of hazardous substances involving either a short-term emergency removal action or a long-term remedial response. All such terms (including the terms removal and remedial action) include enforcement activities related thereto, such as a) removing hazardous materials from a site to an EPA approved and licensed hazardous waste facility for treatment, containment, and/or destruction; b) containing the waste safely onsite to eliminate further spreading and problems; c) destroying or treating the waste onsite using incineration or other technologies; and/or d) identifying and removing the source of groundwater contaminants and halting further absorption of the contaminants.

Response Actions
CERCLA-authorized actions involving either a short-term removal action or a long-term removal response that may include, but is not limited to, a) removing hazardous materials from a site to an EPA-approved hazardous waste facility for treatment, containment, or destruction; b) containing the waste safely onsite; c) destroying or treating the waste onsite; and d) identifying and removing the source of groundwater contamination and halting further migration of contaminants. Methods that protect human health and the environment from asbestos-containing material. *See* Cleanup.

Response Capability
The ability to achieve a specified emergency response objective. It includes four major components: personnel, modernization, readiness, and sustainability.

- Personnel — Numbers, size, and composition of the teams and members that comprise Emergency Response Teams (ERTs); e.g., agencies, police, fire, medical.

- Modernization — Technical sophistication of individuals, teams, systems, and equipments.

- Readiness — The ability of individuals, teams, systems, and/or equipment to deliver the results for which they were designed (includes the ability to deploy and employ without unacceptable delays).

- Sustainability — The ability to maintain the necessary level and duration of response activity to achieve cleanup objectives. Sustainability is a function of providing for and maintaining adequate levels of ready staff, material, and consumables necessary to support the emergency effort.

Response Organization
An organization prepared to provide assistance in an emergency (e.g., fire department; police; ERT).

Response Personnel
Staff attached to a response organization (e.g., HazMat team).

Response Plan Specifications
The fundamental requirements for an emergency response operation, providing in advance an outline of the concept, form, scope, setting, aim, objectives, personnel requirements, environmental safety implications, analysis arrangements, and implementation costs.

Response Readiness
Synonymous with operational readiness, with respect to actions or functions performed during emergency response cleanup.

Response Requirement
An established need justifying the timely allocation of resources to achieve a capability to accomplish approved emergency response objectives, missions, or implementation tasks.

Response Spectrum
The time internal from a step change in the input concentration at the instrument inlet to a reading of 90% (nominally equivalent to 2.2 time constants) of the ultimate recorded output.

Response Teams
A general term, used for the following types of technical or professional environmental, HazMat, and medical teams: airborne response teams, emergency support teams, emergency response teams, energy emergency teams, environmental

response teams, explosive ordnance disposal teams, hazardous material response teams, hostage negotiation teams, national response teams, nuclear emergency search teams, radiological assistance teams, regional response teams, special response teams, tactical response teams, and medical response teams.

Response Time

A term used to specify performance of a rapid action deluge fire protection system that represents the elapsed time between the initiation of the incident and water application to the material being protected.

Responsibility

1) The obligation to carry forward an assigned task to a successful conclusion. With responsibility goes authority to direct and take the necessary action to ensure success. 2) The obligation for the proper custody, care, and safekeeping of property or funds entrusted to the possession or supervision of an individual. *See* Accountability.

Responsible Party

As defined by the Toxic Substances Control Act, means the owner of the PCB equipment, facility, or other source of PCBs or the owner's designated agent (e.g., a facility manager or other responsible person). *See* Owner/Operator.

Responsiveness Summary

A summary of oral and/or written public comments received by EPA during a comment period on key EPA documents, and EPA's responses to those comments. The responsiveness summary is especially valuable during the Record of Decision (ROD) phase at a site on the National Priorities Listing when it highlights community needs and concerns for decisionmakers. *See* Record of Decision.

Restoration

Measures taken to return a site to pre-violation conditions; the act or process of accurately recovering the form and details of a structure and its setting as it appeared at a particular period of time by means of the removal of later work or by the replacement of missing earlier work.

Restoration, Management, and Protection, Wetlands/Habitat for Migratory Birds

The regulatory requirements of each federal agency responsible for acquiring, managing, or disposing of federal lands and waters, to do so in a cooperative effort to restore, protect, and enhance the wetland ecosystems and other habitats for migratory birds, fish, and wildlife within the lands and waters of each such agency.

Restraint of Loads

The process of binding, lashing, and wedging items into one unit or into its transporter in a manner that will ensure immobility during transit.

Restricted Area

1) An area (land, sea, or air) in which there are special restrictive measures employed to prevent or minimize exposure to hazards. 2) An area under military jurisdiction in which special security measures are employed to prevent unauthorized entry. 3) An area in which access is controlled by a licensee for purposes of protection of individuals from exposure to radiation and radioactive materials.

Restricted Dangerous Cargo

Cargo that does not belong to the highly hazardous category but which is dangerous and requires extra precautions in packing and handling, for transport.

Restricted Data

1) Data classified as confidential business or commercial information. *See* Confidential Business Information; Confidential Commercial Information 2) All DOE data (information) concerning the following: a) the design, manufacture, or use of atomic weapons; b) the production of special nuclear material; or c) the use of special nuclear material in the production of energy, but shall not include data declassified or removed from the restricted data category pursuant to Section 142 of the Atomic Energy Act.

Restricted-Use Pesticide (FIFRA)

A pesticide that is classified for restricted use under the provisions of Section 3(d)(1)(C) of the FIFRA. If the Administrator determines that the pesticide may generate cause, without additional regulatory restrictions, unreasonable adverse effects on the environment, including injury to the applicator, he/she shall classify the pesticide, or the particular use or uses to which the determination applies, for "restricted use," when that pesticide is applied a)in accordance with its directions for use, warnings, and cautions; b) for the uses for which the is registered, or for one or more of such uses; c) in accordance with a widespread and commonly recognized practice. Restricted-use pesticides may be applied only by trained, certified applicators or those under their direct supervision.

Restriction Enzymes

Enzymes that recognize certain specific regions of a long DNA molecule and then cut the DNA into smaller pieces.

Restrictive Lung Disease

Lung disease in which the expansion of the lung is restricted either because of alterations in the supportive structures of the lung (parenchyma) or because of disease of the pleura, the chest wall, or the neuromuscular apparatus. An example is fibrosis.

Restrictive Covenants

Restrictions in a deed by which the owner agrees to comply with certain predefined standards and refrain from doing other specified acts. Such covenants tend to cover exterior painting (requiring earthtones), fencing (materials and structural requirements), landscape maintenance standards.

Retailers, Chemical

A person who distributes in commerce a chemical substance, mixture, or article to ultimate purchasers who are not commercial entities.

Retaining Walls

Walls designed to maintain differences in ground elevations by holding back a bank of material.

Retention

The state of being held in a specific location; the traction of deposited material remaining in the body or in some organ of interest at any given time after deposition. Used to refer to the amount of an inhaled material that remains in the lung (pulmonary retention) or to the amount of a toxicant dose that remains in the body or body compartment for a specified period of time.

Retention Pond

A manmade impoundment with a permanent pool of water that is used to reduce stormwater flows at peak runoff.

Reticulate

A species descriptor that means marked with lines resembling a network, as in the veins of a leaf.

Retrices

A species descriptor that means having stiff tail feathers used for maneuvering during flight.

Retrobulbar Neuritis

Inflammation of the portion of the optic nerve behind the eyeball.

Retrofill

To remove PCB or PCB-contaminated dielectric fluid and to replace it with either PCB, PCB-contaminated, or non PCB dielectric fluid

Return Period

The average number of years within which a given event will be equaled or exceeded. Use to designate 50 or 100 year floods, etc.

Returned Sludge

Settled activated sludge returned to mix with incoming raw or primary settled wastewater.

Reverse Osmosis

A water treatment process used in small water systems by adding pressure to force water through a semipermeable membrane. Reverse osmosis removes most drinking water contaminants. Also used in wastewater treatment.

Large-scale reverse osmosis plants are now being developed.

Reviews
Inspecting or examining; critical evaluations using stated criteria; "reviews" of an analysis done by others.

Revolute
A species descriptor that means rolled back on the under surface from the tip, as in some leaves before they open.

Revolving Fund
A fund established to finance a cycle of operations to which reimbursements and collections are returned for reuse in a manner such as will maintain the principal of the fund (e.g., working capital funds, industrial funds, and loan funds).

RFA
An acronym for RCRA Facility Assessment.

RfD
See Reference Dose.

RFI
An acronym for RCRA Facility Inspection.

RFP
An acronym for Request for Proposal; Reasonable Further Progress (CAA).

RFPD
See Reasonable Further Progress Demonstration (CAA).

RFQ
An acronym for Request for Quote.

RHAA
An acronym for Rivers and Harbors Appropriation Act of 1899.

Rhinitis
Inflammation of the mucous membranes of the nasal passages.

Rhinorrhea
A discharge from the nasal mucous membrane.

Rhizomate
A species descriptor that means a rootlike, usually horizontal stem growing under or along the ground that sends out roots from its lower surface and leaves from its upper surface.

Rhomboidal
A species descriptor that means shaped like a parallelogram with unequal adjacent sides.

RI/FS
See Remedial Investigation/Feasibility Study.

RI
See Remedial Investigations.

RIAQRA
An acronym for the Radon Gas and Indoor Air Quality Research Act of 1986.

RIB
An acronym for Radioactive Ion Beam.

Ribonucleic Acid (RNA)
A molecule that carries the genetic message from DNA to a cell's protein-producing mechanisms; similar to, but chemically different from, DNA.

Richland Operations Office
A DOE Research and Development and Field Facility, established in 1943 as the Manhattan Project Plutonium Production Facility. The office manages the 562-square mile Hanford Site where a broad range of nuclear and nonnuclear energy programs are conducted under all DOE Secretarial Offices. The office provides continuing operation of nuclear production, chemical processing and waste management programs, including interim storage and ultimate disposal of high-level radioactive wastes, and manages advanced reactor

development programs. The office manages programs for facilities and site services and provide administrative and policy guidance to several operating and support service contractors.

Richter Magnitude (USGS)
The logarithm, to the base 10, of the amplitude in micrometers of the maximum amplitude of seismic waves that would be observed on a standard torsion seismograph at a distance of about 60 miles from the epicenter. Also called the local magnitude (ML).

Riffle
A rocky shoal or sandbar lying just below the surface of a river.

Right-of-Way (ROW)
An easement, lease, permit, or license to occupy, use, or pass over another's land; the strip of land used as roadbed by a railroad or used for a public purpose by other public utilities.

Right of Entry (CAA)
The Administrator of EPA or his/her authorized representative's right: a) of entry to, upon, or through any premises of any person who owns/operates any polluting source, who manufactures pollution control equipment or process equipment, who is subject to any environmental compliance requirement, or in which any records required to be maintained by law are located, and b) to at reasonable times, have access to and copy any records, inspect any facilities, monitoring equipment or methods required or used for determining the compliance status, and sample any pollutants that such person is required to sample.

Ringlemann Chart
A series of shaded illustrations used to measure the opacity of air pollution emissions. The chart ranges from light grey through black and is used to set and enforce emissions standards.

Riot Control Agent
A chemical that produces temporary irritating or disabling effects when in contact with the eyes or when inhaled.

Riot Control Operations
The employment of riot control agents and/or special tactics, formations, and equipment in the control of violent disorders.

RIP
An acronym for RCRA Implementation Plan.

Riparian
A term pertaining to the bank of a natural course of water.

Riparian Habitat
Areas adjacent to rivers and streams that have a high density, diversity, and productivity of plant and animal species relative to nearby uplands.

Riparian Rights
Entitlement of a land owner to the water on or bordering his/her property, including the right to prevent diversion or misuse of upstream waters. Generally, a matter of state law.

Riprap
Rock or other suitable material placed to prevent or reduce erosion.

Risk
A quantitative or qualitative expression of possible loss that considers both the probability that a hazard will cause harm and the consequences of that event. The probability of injury, disease, or death under specific circumstances. In quantitative terms, risk is expressed in values ranging from zero (representing the certainty that harm will not occur) to one (representing the certainty that harm will occur).

Risk Analysis
The quantification of the degree of risk.

Risk Assessment

1) An evaluation performed as part of the remedial investigation to assess conditions at a Superfund site and determine the risk posed to public health and/or the environment. 2) The qualitative and quantitative evaluation performed in an effort to define the risk posed to human health and/or the environment by the presence or potential presence and/or use of specific pollutants. 3) The scientific activity of evaluating the toxic properties of a chemical and the conditions of human exposure to it in order both to ascertain the likelihood that exposed humans will be adversely affected, and to characterize the nature of the effects they may experience. Risk assessments use specific chemical information plus risk factors such as the following:

- *Hazard identification* - The determination of whether a particular chemical is or is not causally linked to particular health effect(s);

- *Dose-response assessment* - The determination of the relation between the magnitude of exposure and the probability of occurrence of the health effects in question;

- *Exposure assessment* - The determination of the extent of human exposure;

- *Risk characterization* - The description of the nature and often the magnitude of human risk, including attendant uncertainty.

Risk Assessment and Management Commission (RAMC)

The 10-member commission established to develop a report and recommendations on the appropriate use of risk assessment and risk management in federal regulatory programs to prevent cancer or other chronic health effects that may result from exposure to hazardous substances. The commission was established pursuant to the Clean Air Act Amendments of 1990 (November 15, 1990), to make a full investigation of the policy implications and appropriate uses of risk assessment and risk management in regulatory programs under various federal laws and ceased to exist, approximately 9 months after the submission of their report. The report contained the results of all commission studies and investi-

gations, together with any appropriate legislative or administrative recommendations.

Risk Assessment and Management Commission Investigation (RAMCI)

The RAMC's investigation on the following:

a) the use and limitations of risk assessment in establishing emission or effluent standards, ambient standards, exposure standards, acceptable concentration levels, tolerances or other environmental criteria for hazardous substances that present a risk of carcinogenic effects or other chronic health effects and the suitability of risk assessment for such purposes;

b) the most appropriate methods for measuring and describing cancer risks or risks of other chronic health effects from exposure to hazardous substances considering such alternative approaches as the lifetime risk of cancer or other effects to the individual or individuals most exposed to emissions from a source or sources on both an actual and worst case basis, the range of such risks, the total number of health effects avoided by exposure reductions, effluent standards, ambient standards, exposures standards, acceptable concentration levels, tolerances and other environmental criteria, reductions in the number of persons exposed at various levels of risk, the incidence of cancer, and other public health factors;

c) methods to reflect uncertainties in measurement and estimation techniques, the existence of synergistic or antagonistic effects among hazardous substances, the accuracy of extrapolating human health risks from animal exposure data, and the existence of unquantified direct or indirect effects on human health in risk assessment studies;

d) risk management policy issues including the use of lifetime cancer risks to individuals most exposed, incidence of cancer, the cost and technical feasibility of exposure reduction measures and the use of site-specific actual exposure information in setting emissions standards and other limitations applicable to sources of exposure to hazardous substances; and

e) the degree to which it is possible or desirable to develop a consistent risk assessment methodology, or a consistent standard of acceptable risk, among various federal programs.

Risk Characterization

The final step of a risk assessment, that is a description of the nature and often the magnitude of human risk, including attendant uncertainty. *See* Risk Assessment.

Risk Communication

The process of exchanging information about levels or significance of health or environmental risk, between risk assessors, risk managers, the general public, news media, interest groups, etc.

Risk Factor

A characteristic (e.g., race, gender, age, obesity) or variable (e.g., smoking, exposure) associated with increased chance of toxic effects. Some standard risk factors used in general risk assessment calculations include average breathing rates, average weight, and average human life span.

Risk Management

The process of evaluating alternative regulatory and nonregulatory responses to risk and evaluating the risks associated with each, prior to selecting among them. The selection process necessarily requires the consideration of legal, technical, economic, and social factors.

Risk Retention Group

Any corporation or other limited liability association taxable as a corporation, or as an insurance company, formed under the laws of any state a) whose primary activity consists of assuming and spreading all, or any portion, of the pollution liability of its group members; b) that is chartered or licensed as an insurance company and authorized to engage in the business of insurance under the laws of any state; and c) that does not exclude any person from membership in the group solely to provide for members of such a group a competitive advantage over such a person.

Risk-Specific Dose

The dose corresponding to a specified level of risk.

River (WSRA)

A flowing body of water or estuary or a section, portion, or tributary thereof, including rivers, streams, creeks, runs, kills, rills, and small lakes.

River Basins

Land areas drained by a river and its tributaries.

Riverine Area

An inland or coastal area comprising both land and water, characterized by limited land lines of communication, with extensive water surface and/or inland waterways that provide natural routes for surface transportation and communications.

Riverine Operations

Operations conducted to cope with and exploit the unique characteristics of a riverine area. Joint riverine operations combine land, naval, and air operations, as appropriate, and are suited to the nature of the specific riverine area in which operations are to be conducted.

RMCLs

See Recommended Maximum Contaminant Levels.

RMDP

See Radon Mitigation Demonstration Program (CAA).

RNA

See Ribonucleic Acid.

Road Block

A barrier or obstacle used to block, or limit access to a site or the movement of vehicles along a route.

Road Capacity

The maximum traffic flow obtainable on a given roadway, using all available lanes, usually expressed in vehicles per hour or vehicles per day.

Road Hazard Sign

A sign used to indicate traffic hazards.

Road Net

The system of roads available within a particular locality or area.

ROADCHEM

A version of the ROADWAY computerized model to predict pollutant concentrations near roadways that includes chemical reactions of NO, NO_2, and O_3.

ROADWAY

A computerized model to predict pollutant concentrations near roadways.

Roadway Crown

The high point of a roadway cross section (usually at the centerline).

Roadways

Surfaces on which motor vehicles travel, including highways, roads, streets, parking areas, and driveways.

Roasting

The use of a furnace to heat arsenic plant feed material for the purpose of eliminating a significant portion of the volatile materials contained in the feed.

Rocket/Guided Missile Ammunition

Ammunition designed for launching from a tube, launcher, rails, trough, or other launching device, in which the propellant is explosive. It consists of an igniter, rocket motor, and projectile (warhead) either fused or unfused, containing high explosives or chemicals. Rocket ammunition may be shipped completely assembled or may be shipped unassembled in one outside container.

Rocket Motor Test Sites

Buildings, structures, facilities, or installations where the static test firing of a beryllium rocket motor and/or the disposal of beryllium propellant is conducted.

Rocket Propulsion

Reaction propulsion wherein both the fuel and the oxidizer, generating the hot gases expended through a nozzle, are carried as part of the rocket engine. Specifically, rocket propulsion differs from jet propulsion in that jet propulsion utilizes atmospheric air as an oxidizer whereas rocket propulsion utilizes nitric acid or a similar compound as an oxidizer.

ROD

See Record of Decision.

Rodenticide

A chemical pesticide or other agent used to destroy rats and other rodents or to prevent them from damaging food, crops, forage, etc.

Roentgen (R)

The unit of exposure dose of X-ray or gamma radiation. One roentgen is the exposure corresponding to ionization in the air of one electrostatic unit in charge of either sign in 0.001293 gram of air (2.58×10^{-4} Coulomb per kilogram of air). In field dosimetry, one roentgen is essentially equal to one rad.

Roentgen Equivalent Mammal/Man (rem)

One roentgen equivalent mammal is the quantity of ionizing radiation of any type that, when absorbed by man or other mammal, produces a physiological effect equivalent to that produced by the absorption of 1 roentgen of X-ray or gamma radiation.

Role Number

In the medical field, the classification of treatment facilities according to their different capabilities.

Roof-Top Ratio
Ratio of the flux at points ¼ and ¾ of the distance from the top to the bottom of the reactor core, used to position partial control rods correctly.

Root Cause Analysis
An analysis performed to determine the cause of part, system, and component failures.

Root Causes
1) Items that if corrected could prevent occurrence or reoccurrence of the situations and conditions that were found in an incident, and those specific/systemic factors that could cause or create conditions that may be less than adequate or could result in accidents or incidents. 2) A lack of adequate management control contributing to substandard practices or conditions (immediate causes) that result in accidents or incidents. Management control failures can result from the lack of adequate policy, inadequate policy implementation, lack of or insufficient risk evaluation, or inadequate resources.

Rosette
A species descriptor that means a circular cluster of leaves or other plant parts.

Rotational Windstorms
Tornadoes, waterspouts, and dust devils; characterized by a rotational flow field.

Rotifera
Minute, many-celled aquatic animals.

Rough Fish
Those fish, not prized for eating, such as gar and suckers. Most are more tolerant of changing environmental conditions than game species.

Roughing Filter
A wastewater filter of coarse material operated at a high rate to afford preliminary treatment measures.

Route Capacity
1) The maximum traffic flow of vehicles in one direction at the most restricted point on the route. 2) The maximum number of metric tons that can be moved in one direction over a particular route in one hour. It is the product of the maximum traffic flow and the average payload of the vehicles using the route.

Routes of Exposure
The means by which toxic agents gain access to an organism (e.g., ingestion, inhalation, dermal exposure, intravenous, subcutaneous, intramuscular, intraperitoneal administration). *See* Common Exposure Routes; Critical Pathways; Exposure Pathways; Ingestion Exposure Pathways; Plume Exposure Pathways.

Routine Use
With respect to the disclosure of information, the use of such data for a purpose that is compatible with the purpose for which it was collected.

Routine Wastes
Wastes generated due to normal operations and anticipated abnormal events.

RPAR
An acronym for Rebuttable Presumption Against Registration.

RPIS
An acronym for Real Property Inventory System.

rpm
An acronym for Revolutions per Minute.

RPM
See Remedial Project Manager. An acronym for Radial Power Monitor.

RPS
An acronym for Reactor Protection System; Radioisotope Power System.

RQ
See Reportable Quantity (TSCA).

RREA

See Renewable Resources Extension Act.

RRI

An acronym for RCRA Remedial Investigation.

RRT

See Regional Response Teams.

RSO

See Reported Significant Observations.

Rubbish

Solid waste, excluding food waste and ashes, from homes, institutions, and workplaces.

Rufous

A species descriptor that means reddish-brown color.

Rugose

A species descriptor that means having a rough and ridged surface, as in prominently veined leaves.

Rule

The whole or a part of an agency statement of general or particular applicability and future effect designed to implement, interpret, or prescribe law or policy or describing the organization, procedure, or practice requirements of an agency and includes the approval or prescription for the future of rates, wages, corporate or financial structures or reorganizations thereof, prices, facilities, appliances, services or allowances therefor or of valuations, costs, or accounting, or practices bearing on any of the foregoing.

Rule Making

An agency's process for formulating, amending, or repealing a rule.

Run

The net period of time during which an emission sample is collected. Unless otherwise specified, a run may be either intermittent or continuous within the limits of good engineering practice.

Runoff

1) That part of precipitation, snow melt, or irrigation water that runs off the land into streams or other surface water. It can carry pollutants from the air and land into the receiving waters. 2) Any rainwater, leachate, or other fluid that drains over land from any part of a facility.

Run-On

Any rainwater, leachate, or other liquid that drains over land onto any part of a facility.

Run with the Property

A concept stating that certain covenants in a deed to land are to pass along from owner to owner, so that whoever owns the land is bound by or entitled to the benefits thereof.

Running Soil

Earth material where the angle of repose is approximately zero, as in the case of soil in a nearly liquid state, or dry, unpacked sand that flows freely under slight pressure. Running material also includes loose or disturbed earth that can only be contained with solid sheeting.

RUP

See Restricted Use Pesticide (FIFRA).

Rupture, PCB Transformer

A hazardous or nonhazardous break in the integrity of a PCB transformer caused by over-heating and/or over-pressure conditions that result in the release of PCBs.

Rupture Zone

The region immediately adjacent to the crater boundary in which the stresses produced by the explosion have exceeded the ultimate strength of the medium. It is characterized by the appearance of numerous radial cracks of various sizes. *See* Plastic Zone.

Ruralization

The out-migration of people in large numbers from urban to rural environments. A characteristic of overcongested metropolitan areas. *See* Urbanization; Suburbanization.

RV
An acronym for Recreational Vehicle; Reactor Vessel.

RWQCB
An acronym for Regional Water Quality Control Board.

RWST
An acronym for Refueling Water Storage Tank.

S

S&A
An acronym for Sampling and Analysis.

S&M
An acronym for Surveillance and Maintenance.

S-Glass
Structural glass; a magnesia/alumina/silicate glass reinforcement designed to provide very high tensile strength.

S-Waves
See Secondary Body Waves.

SACWSRSA
An acronym for Sudbury, Assabet, and Concord Wild and Scenic River Study Act of 1990 (WSRA).

Safe
A condition wherein risks are as low as practicable and present no significant residual risk.

Safe Burst Height
The height of burst at or above which the level of fallout, or damage to ground installations, is at a predetermined acceptable level. *See* Types of Burst.

Safe Drinking Water Act (SDWA)
The SDWA of 1974 (43 USC 300) was established to protect the quality of drinking water in the United States. This law focuses on all waters actually or potentially designated for drinking use, whether from aboveground or underground sources. The Act authorized EPA to establish safe standards of purity and required all owners or operators of public water systems to comply with primary (health-related) standards. State governments, that assume this power from EPA, also encourage attainment of secondary standards (nuisance-related). *See* Public Health Service Act (PHSA).

Safe Mass
That mass of fissionable materials that is subcritical for all conditions to which it could reasonably be expected to be exposed, including processing, handling, storing, and procedural uncertainties.

Safe Shutdown Earthquake
An earthquake that is based upon an evaluation of the maximum earthquake potential considering the regional and local geology and seismology and specific characteristics of local subsurface material. It is that earthquake that produces the maximum vibratory ground motion for which certain structures, systems, and components are designed to remain functional.

Safe Work Permit (SWP)
A permit allowing employees to perform potential hazardous work, that outlines necessary safeguards, procedures, etc. An SWP usually requires several approval procedures before work can be-

gin. The form may have other names in different companies.

Safeguards
1) A barrier guard, device, or safety procedure designed for the protection of personnel. 2) A general term for integrated systems of physical protection, material accounting, and material control measures designed to date, prevent, detect, and respond to unauthorized possession, use, or sabotage of special nuclear materials. In practice, safeguards involve the development and application of techniques and procedures dealing with the establishment and continued maintenance of a system of activities including physical protection, quantitative knowledge of the location and use of special nuclear materials, and administrative controls and surveillance to ensure that procedures and techniques of the system are effective and are being carried out. Safeguards include the timely indication of possible diversion or credible assurances by audits and inventory verification that no diversion has occurred.

Safeguards and Security Alerts
Substantial alert actions put into effect when the head of a field office determines that conditions or information received warrants actions. These conditions are effected when additional safeguards and security measures are required at U.S. Department of Energy (DOE) or DOE-contractor or subcontractor facilities. There are three levels of action from preparatory (Level III) to maximum alert action (Level I).

Safeguards and Security Emergencies
Conditions in which there are potential or actual malevolent acts that create or appear likely to create a condition resulting in sabotage, bodily harm, unlawful access to DOE or DOE-contractor facilities, or the interruption or loss of vital services. Also included are special nuclear materials emergencies in which there is a situation involving stolen, lost, or unauthorized possession of source material, special nuclear material, or byproduct material of United States and/or foreign manufacture.

Safety
The control of accidental loss or injury.

Safety (Hazard) Analysis
1) The entire complex of safety (hazard) analysis methods and techniques ranging from relatively informal job and task safety analyses to large complex safety analysis studies and reports. 2) A documented process to systematically identify the hazards of a DOE Operation, to describe and analyze the adequacy of the measures taken to eliminate, control or mitigate identified hazards, and to analyze and evaluate potential accidents and their associated risks.

Safety Analysis Process
The identification of hazards, analysis of hazards control, and analysis of residual risk.

Safety Analysis Reports
DOE safety documents providing a concise but complete description and safety evaluation of the site, the design, normal and emergency operation, potential accidents, and predicted consequences of such accidents, and the means proposed to prevent such accidents or mitigate the consequences of such accidents.

Safety and Health Assessments
A DOE term for one of the three major assessments conducted as part of a Tiger Team Assessment. The Technical Safety Appraisal (TSA) process is a comprehensive, periodic review of field office operations conducted by DOE's Office of Safety Appraisals conducted on a site-specific basis. The primary components of this assessment are organization and administration, operations, maintenance, training and certification, auxiliary systems, emergency preparedness, technical support, security/safety interfaces, experimental activities, site/facility safety review, nuclear criticality safety, radiological protection, fire protection, packaging and transportation, quality verification, personnel protection, aviation safety, and medical services.

Safety and Health Concerns

A concern that addresses a situation that meets one or more of the following criteria: a) does not comply with a agency safety and health requirement or mandatory safety standard; b) threatens to compromise safe operations at a facility; or c) if properly addressed, would substantially improve a particular situation, even though that part of the operation was judged to have an acceptable margin of safety. Each concern is supported by several findings and has the characteristics of:

- being explicit;
- identifying the problem;
- being measurable (auditable); and
- being justifiable.

Each concern is also categorized by its seriousness, potential hazard consideration, and compliance consideration.

Safety and Health Directors

Individuals at the management level responsible for the overview and coordination of field, facility, occupational safety, and health programs.

Safety Appraisals

Determinations by external, independent reviewers of safety/loss control program effectiveness. The appraisal may be conducted as a management appraisal, a functional appraisal, or a comprehensive appraisal, that combines the previous two appraisals. A management appraisal is a review and evaluation of management performance covering all safety disciplines and management responsibilities to ensure proper safety/loss control program balance. A functional appraisal is a review of a safety specialty discipline (industrial safety, industrial hygiene, fire protection, etc.) to verify that applicable elements of the safety/loss control program have been developed, documented, and effectively implemented in accordance with specific safety/loss control requirements and needs.

Safety Barriers

Barriers used to prevent, control, or minimize the impact of unwanted hazards.

Safety Class Items

Systems, components, and structures, including portions of process systems, whose failure could adversely affect the environment or safety and health of the public. Determination of classification is based on analysis of the potential abnormal and accidental scenario consequences as presented in a Safety Analysis Report (SAR).

Safety Device/System

1) A device that prevents malfunctions. 2) Facility installed safety-related equipment that relates to processes, other major equipment, major personnel hazards, etc. It is not intended to include boundary ropes, chains, goggles, handrails, and any other of a host of minor items that could be included under literal compliance.

Safety Documents

Documents prepared specifically to ensure that the safety aspects of part or all of the activities conducted at a facility are formally and thoroughly analyzed, evaluated, and recorded.

Safety Engineering

The branch of professional engineering that requires such education and experience as is necessary to understand the engineering principles essential to the identification, elimination, and control of hazards to people and property; and requires the ability to apply this knowledge to the development, analysis, production, construction, testing, and utilization of systems, products, procedures and standards in order to eliminate or optimally control hazards.

Safety Fuze

A pyrotechnic contained in a flexible and weather-proof sheath burning at a timed and constant rate, used to transmit a flame to the detonator.

Safety Guides

Documents designated or recognized as an acceptable basis for criticality, safety, and response evaluations. These guides may be used as aids in establishing acceptable safety practices, and include material developed by the DOE, the EPA,

OSHA, NIOSH, professional societies, industrial organizations, and others.

Safety Height
See Altitude.

Safety Limits
Limits on important process variables that are necessary to provide reasonable protection to the integrity of certain physical barriers that guard against the uncontrolled release of contaminants or an accidental criticality.

Safety Officer
An individual responsible for monitoring and assessing safety hazards or unsafe situations, and developing measures for ensuring personnel safety, at a site or facility.

Safety Performance Measurement System (SPMS)
A collection of automated environmental, safety, and health (ES&H) information modules. SPMS is maintained for DOE by the System Safety Development Center (SSDC) at the Idaho National Engineering Laboratory (INEL) Computing Center.

Safety Precedence Sequence
A ranking of safety processes by their effectiveness. This system safety process is part of the Hazard Analysis Process.

Safety Procedure
An instruction, or procedure, designed for the protection of personnel.

Safety Reviews
Detailed examinations of the safety impact of proposed activities or ongoing activities during the siting, designing, constructing, operating, maintaining, modifying, or decommissioning of a hazardous waste management facility, that could affect health and safety. Documentation of the safety reviews serves to provide management with adequate identification of the safety issues and their possible implications, and also to allow others not directly involved in the program or review process to independently evaluate the completeness or adequacy of the review.

Safety Valve
An automatic pressure relieving device actuated by the static pressure upstream of such device and characterized by full opening pop action. It is used for gas or vapor service.

Safety Zone
In reference to the DOD, a term for land, sea, or air areas reserved for noncombat operations of friendly aircraft, surface ships, submarines, or ground forces.

Sagittal
A species descriptor relating to the structure that unites the two parietal bones of the skull.

Sale for Purposes Other than Resale
The sale of PCBs for purposes of disposal or for purposes of use except when use involves sale for distribution in commerce. PCB equipment that was first leased for purposes of use any time before July 1, 1979, is to be considered sold for purposes other than resale.

Saline
A general term for waters containing various dissolved salts. The term is typically restricted to inland waters where the ratios of the salts often vary; in the case of coastal waters where the salts are roughly in the same proportion as found in undiluted seawater the term haline is used. *See* Haline.

Salinity
1) The degree of salt in water. 2) The total amount of solid material in grams contained in 1 kg of water when all the carbonate has been converted to oxide, the bromine and iodine replaced by chlorine, and all the organic matter completely oxidized.

SALP

An acronym for Systematic Assessment of Licensee Performance.

Salt Water Intrusion

The invasion of fresh surface or groundwater by salt water. If the salt water comes from the ocean it may be called seawater intrusion. *See* Brackish Waters.

Salted Weapon

A nuclear weapon that has, in addition to its normal components, certain elements or isotopes that capture neutrons at the time of the explosion and produce radioactive products over and above the usual radioactive weapon debris.

Salts

Minerals that water picks up as it passes through the air, over and under the ground, and as it is used by households and industry.

Salvage

1) The recovery, through professional investigations and documentation, of significant data associated with cultural resources in lieu of in-place preservation of cultural resources. This generally involves the physical removal of portions of the resource and their preservation. Salvage studies must conform to agency standards of research; compliance with the PMOA or Section 106 is required prior to salvage. Once a standard technique in cultural resource management, salvage now constitutes a "last resort" far less desirable than preservation-in-place. The need for salvage usually results from a management action that will adversely affect cultural resources eligible for preservation. However, natural forces or visitor use may justify the application of salvage. *See* Section 106 Process and Program Memorandum of Agreement. 2) Property that has some value in excess of its basic material content but which is in such condition that it has no reasonable prospect of use for any purpose as a unit and its repair or rehabilitation for use as a unit is clearly impractical. 3) The saving or rescuing of condemned, discarded, or abandoned property, and of materi-

als contained therein for reuse, refabrication, or scrapping. 4) The utilization of waste materials.

Salvage Operation

A DOD term for a) the recovery, evacuation, and reclamation of damaged, discarded, condemned, or abandoned allied or enemy material, ships, craft, and floating equipment for reuse, repair, refabrication, or scrapping; b) naval salvage operations include harbor and channel clearance, diving, hazardous towing and rescue tug services, and the recovery of material, ships, craft, and floating equipment sunk off-shore or elsewhere stranded.

Salverform

A phenomenon in which a flower has united petals in which the calyx and corolla (perianth) are the same size, shape, and texture. The perianth extends from the center of the flower and the corolla has an elongated slender tube and a flared flat limb.

SAM

An acronym for Site Availability Mode.

Sampling

The process of taking a representative small portion or quantity of something for testing or analysis.

Sampling Area

The area delineated on a map accompanying an environmental investigation report showing areas sampled for by media type (e.g., soil, surface water, groundwater, asbestos, lead-based paint).

Sampling Plans

Documents that are prepared for either continuous or site specific data collection activities (e.g., air, water, pesticides, hazardous waste). The plan should describe project organization and responsibilities, project description (objectives, scope, schedule of tasks and milestones, data usage), monitoring network, sampling and analysis, design rationale, data quality objectives, sampling procedures, calibration, analytical methods, documentation/data reporting, field audits, corrective actions, and safety concerns.

SAN
See San Francisco Operations Office.

San Francisco Operations Office (SAN)
The DOE Research and Development and Field Facility established in 1952, to oversee defense and energy-related programs. It is responsible for the management, coordination, and support of programs and projects involving weapons research and development, basic research, and energy technologies. The office administers contracts for the operation of several laboratory and engineering facilities with a work force of approximately 20,000, including two major national laboratories. The office also manages field construction of major technical facilities.

Sanction
An agency's a) prohibition, requirement, limitation, or other condition affecting the freedom of a person; b) withholding of relief; c) imposition of penalty or fine; d) destruction, taking, seizure, or withholding of property; e) assessment of damages, reimbursement, restitution, compensation, costs, charges, or fees; f) requirement, revocation, or suspension of a permit; g) taking other compulsory or restrictive action.

Sand
Coarse-grained mineral sediments with diameters larger than 0.074 mm and smaller than 2 mm.

Sand Filters
Devices that remove some suspended solids from sewage. Air and bacteria decompose additional wastes filtering through the sand so that cleaner water drains from the bed.

Sandia National Laboratories (SNL)
A DOE Research and Development and Field Facility established in 1949 for the purposes of research, development, and engineering of nuclear weapon systems. The result of this office is the existence of a national stockpile of operational nuclear weapons that are strictly controlled. Sandia also conducts energy programs in fossil, solar, fission and basic energy sciences. The SNL group includes the Sandia National Laboratories-Albuquerque (SNLA) and Sandia National Laboratories-Livermore (SNLL).

Sanitary Engineering Structures
Tanks, reservoirs, and other structures commonly used in water and waste treatment works, where dense, impermeable concrete with high resistance to chemical attack is required.

Sanitary Landfill
1) A facility for the disposal of solid waste that meets the criteria published under Section 6944 of the Solid Waste Disposal Act. 2) A facility for the disposal of solid waste that meets the criteria published under Section 4004 (42 USC 6944). 3) A disposal facility employing an engineered method of disposing of solid wastes on land in a manner that minimizes environmental hazards by spreading the solid wastes in thin layers, compacting the solid wastes to the smallest practical volume, and applying cover material at the end of each working day. Such facilities must comply with the EPA *Guidelines for the Land Disposal of Solid Wastes* as prescribed in 40 CFR 241. *See* Landfill, Sanitary.

Sanitary Sewers
Underground pipes that carry off only domestic or industrial waste, not stormwater.

Sanitary Survey
An onsite review of the water sources, facilities, equipment, operation, and maintenance of a public water system to evaluate the adequacy of those elements for producing and distributing safe drinking water.

Sanitary Water
Water discharged from restrooms, showers, food preparation facilities, or other nonindustrial operations; also known as "gray water."

Sanitation
Control of physical factors in the human environment that could harm development, health, or survival.

Sanitize, Information
A term relating to the revision of a report or other document in such a fashion as to prevent identification of sources, or of the actual persons and places with which it is concerned, or of the means by which it was acquired. Usually involves deletion or substitution of names and other key details.

Sanitized, Information
A version of a document from which information claimed as trade secret or confidential has been omitted or withheld.

Saprophyte
A plant that lives on or derives nourishment from dead or decaying organic matter.

SAR
See Safety Analysis Reports.

SARA Title III Chemical Reporting
The EPA database from the Emergency Planning and Community Right-to-Know Act requirements that identifies a facility's chemical emissions, and the presence and amounts of hazardous chemicals maintained onsite.

SARA
See Superfund Amendments and Reauthorization Act of 1986.

Sarcoma
A malignant tumor arising in connective tissue and composed primarily of anaplastic cells resembling supportive tissue.

SAS
An acronym for Statistical Analysis System. *See* Multivariate Statistics.

SAS
An acronym for Semiannual Soils.

SASS
An acronym for Safety Assurance System Summary.

SAT
An acronym for Semi-Automatic Trim.

Saturated Zone
1) That part of the earth's crust in which all voids are filled with water. 2) That portion of the subsurface environment in which all voids (pores and cracks) are ideally filled with water under pressure greater than atmospheric. 3) The zone in which the voids in the rock or soil are filled with water at a pressure greater than atmospheric. The water table is the top of the saturated zone in an unconfined aquifer. *See* Zone of Saturation.

SAV
An acronym for Semiannual Vegetation.

Savanna
A dry, scrub-dominated grassland with areas of bare earth.

Savannah River Operations (SR)
A DOE Research and Development and Field Facility established in 1950. SR manages the Savannah River Site, a key DOE installation for nuclear materials production and research. The mission of the site is to produce tritium and plutonium for fabrication into weapons components for the nation's defense program. Plutonium-238 is produced as a long-lasting fuel source to generate electrical power and warm instruments during space exploration. Research in nuclear energy and ecology are conducted at the Savannah River Laboratory and Savannah River Ecology Laboratory. In 1972, SRS was designated the nation's first National Environmental Research Park, where scientists from other government agencies, private foundations and universities could use SRS land as a protected outdoor laboratory for long-term studies.

Savannah River Site (SRS)

The DOE site that conducts fuel and target fabrication, isotope production in nuclear reactors, chemical separations, waste management, and heavy-water extraction. Major facilities of the Savannah River Site include nuclear production reactors, two chemical separation plants, a fuel fabrication plant, waste management facilities, and extensive research and development facilities. *See* Savannah River Operations (SR).

SB

An acronym for Sediment Basin.

SC

An acronym for Safety Computer.

Scale

The ratio or fraction between the distance on a map, chart or photograph and the corresponding distance on the surface of the earth. *See* Conversion Scale; Graphic Scale; Photographic Scale; Principal Scale.

Scaling Law

A mathematical relationship that permits the effects of a nuclear explosion of given energy yield to be determined as a function of distance from the explosion (or from ground zero) provided the corresponding effect is known as a function of distance for a reference explosion, (e.g., of 1-kiloton energy yield).

Scheduled Maintenance

Periodic prescribed inspection and/or servicing of equipment accomplished on a calendar, mileage, or hours of operation basis.

SCANF

An acronym for Senate Committee on Agriculture, Nutrition, and Forestry.

Scanning Laser

A laser having a time-varying direction, origin, or pattern of propagation with respect to a stationary frame of reference.

SCAP

An acronym for Superfund Comprehensive Accomplishments Plan. *See* Comprehensive Environmental Response, Compensation and Liability Act (CERCLA).

Scarious

A species descriptor meaning thin, membranous, and dry.

Scavenger

An animal that feeds on dead animals killed by others.

SCDAA

An acronym for Soil Conservation and Domestic Allotment Act.

SCE

See Sister Chromatid Exchange.

Scenario

A blueprint for the execution of a emergency response drill or exercise. Scenarios consist of objectives, guidelines, timeliness sequence of events, supporting data and evaluation standards for conducting, and/or analyzing drills, exercises, and the potential occurrence of hazardous incidents.

Scenic River Area (WSRA)

Those rivers or sections of rivers that are free of impoundments, with shorelines or watersheds still largely primitive and shorelines largely undeveloped, but accessible in places by roads.

Scenic Easement (WSRA)

An area where rights to control the use of land (including the air space above such land) within the authorized boundaries of a component of the wild and scenic rivers system, for the purpose of protecting the natural qualities of a designated wild, scenic or recreational river.

SCENRUS

An acronym for Senate Committee on Energy and Natural Resources of the United States.

SCEPW
An acronym for Senate Committee on Environment and Public Works.

SCF
An acronym for Standard Cubic Foot.

Schedule and Timetable of Compliance
A schedule of required measures including an enforceable sequence of actions or operations leading to compliance with an environmental regulation, limitation, prohibition, or standard. *See* Schedule of Compliance (SOC).

Schedule of Compliance (SOC)
A schedule of remedial measures, including an enforceable sequence of actions or operations, leading to compliance with an applicable implementation plan, emission standard, emission limitation, or regulatory prohibition.

Schematics
Block functional diagrams showing the secession of functions or processes required to attain a desired output.

Scheme of Maneuver
The tactical plan to be executed by a task force in order to achieve assigned objectives.

Schools
1) Buildings housing classrooms, laboratories, dormitories, administrative facilities, athletic facilities, or related facilities operated in connection with a school. 2) Any elementary or secondary school as defined in Section 198 of the Elementary and Secondary Education Act of 1965 (20 USC 2854).

Science Advisory Board
The EPA office that advises the Administrator on the scientific and technical aspects of environmental problems and issues. Reviews and provides advice on agency programs, guidelines, protection standards, and 5-year plan for environmental research, development, and demonstration.

Scientific and Technical Intelligence
The product resulting from the collection, evaluation, analysis, and interpretation of scientific and technical information that covers a) developments in basic and applied research and in applied engineering techniques; and b) scientific and technical characteristics, capabilities, and limitations of all facility systems and materials, the research and development related thereto, and the production methods employed for their manufacture.

Scientific Advisory Panel
The 13 member panel, that assists the Board of Directors of the Mickey Leland National Urban Air Toxics Research Center in developing research agendas, reviewing proposals and applications, and awarding research grants. The panel includes scientists with relevant experience from the National Institute of Environmental Health Sciences, the Centers for Disease Control, the Environmental Protection Agency, the National Cancer Institute, and others. *See* Mickey Leland National Urban Air Toxics Research Center.

Scientific Support Coordinators (SSC)
Scientific and technical advisors in coastal and marine areas from the National Oceanic and Atmospheric Administration (NOAA) who serve as members of the federal On-Scene Coordinator's staff. Their capabilities include contingency planning, surface/ subsurface trajectory forecasting and hindcasting, resource risk analysis, and liaison to other scientists.

Sclera
The tough, white supporting tunic of the eyeball.

Sclerophyllous Forest
A term meaning characterized by thick hard foliage.

Sclerotization
The process by which the cuticle of an insect is hardened.

SCORPIO
A computer acronym for Subject Content Oriented Retriever for Processing Information On-line.

Scorpiod
A species descriptor meaning curved or curled like the tail of a scorpion.

SCRAM
1) Sudden shutting down of a nuclear reactor, usually by rapid insertion of control rods, either automatically or manually by the reactor operator. 2) A sudden or emergency shutting down of a nuclear reactor.

Scrap
Materials discarded from manufacturing operations that may be suitable for reprocessing.

Scrape
A shallow depression that serves as a nest.

Screening Count
A preliminary count of the permanent environmental sampling system filters, using a portable gross alpha counter. This count is used to determine whether a significant release plume has or has not passed over one of the permanent sampling stations.

Screening
Use of screens to remove coarse floating and suspended solids from sewage.

Scribing
In cartography, a method of preparing a map or chart by cutting the lines into a prepared coating.

Scrimshaw Product
Any art form that involves the substantial etching or engraving of designs upon, or the substantial carving of figures, patterns, or designs from, any bone or tooth of any marine mammal of the order Cetacea.

Scrub
A plant community characterized by scattered, low-growing trees and shrubs, interspersed with herbs, grasses, and patches of bare soil.

Scrubber
An air pollution device that uses a spray of water or reactant, or a dry process, to trap pollutants in emissions.

Scrubbing
A common method of reducing stack air emissions; removal of impurities by spraying a liquid that concentrates the impurities into waste.

SCT
An acronym for Spill Control Technology.

SCTI
An acronym for Sodium Components Test Installation.

Scute
A species descriptor meaning a horny, chitinous or bony external plate or scale, such as the shell of a turtle.

SDC
An acronym for Shutdown Cooling.

SDHX
An acronym for Shutdown Heat Exchanger.

SDS
An acronym for Shutdown Sequencer.

SDWA
See the Safe Drinking Water Act.

Sea-Air-Land Team (SEAL)
A naval force specially organized, trained, and equipped to conduct special operations in maritime and riverine environments.

SEAL Team
See Sea-Air-Land Team.

Sea Turtles

Those sea turtle species enumerated in 50 CFR 227.4, and any part(s), product(s), egg(s), or offspring thereof, or the dead body or part(s) thereof.

Sealed Source

Any hazardous substance or radioactive material that is permanently encapsulated in such manner that the contaminant material will not be released under the most severe conditions likely to be encountered by the source.

Search

Systematic reconnaissance of a defined area, so that all parts of the area have been visibly inspected.

Search and Rescue

The use of aircraft, surface craft, specialized rescue teams, and equipment to search for and rescue personnel in distress on land or at sea.

Search and Rescue Coordinator

The designated representative with overall responsibility and authority for operation of the joint rescue coordination center, and for joint search and rescue operations within the geographical area assigned.

Search and Rescue Incident Classification

Three emergency phases into which an incident may be classified, according to the seriousness of the incident and its requirement for response action:

- 1) uncertainty phase — Doubt exists as to the safety of property or personnel because of knowledge of possible difficulties or because of lack of information concerning hazard progress;

- 2) alert phase — Apprehension exists for the safety of property or personnel because of definite information that serious problems exist that do not amount to an emergency because of a continued lack of information concerning a potential or reported hazard; and

- 3) emergency phase — Immediate assistance is required because of a life threatening and/or

catastrophic, existing, or imminent, release or natural disaster.

Search and Rescue Mission Coordinator

A search and rescue controller selected by the search and rescue coordinator to direct a specific emergency rescue mission.

Search Radius

A radius centered on a datum point having a length equal to the total probable error plus an additional safety length to ensure a greater than 50% probability that the target is in the search area.

Seavan

Commercial- or government-owned (or leased) shipping containers that are moved via ocean transportation without bogey wheels attached (i.e., lifted on and off the ship).

Second Line Organization Level

The DOE element that is contractually or organizationally responsible for the work or job tasks being performed by an operating level. It may be an operations office, or an Assistant Secretary directly responsible for an energy technology center or a power administration.

Secondary Body Waves

Earthquake waves that shear the rock sideways at right angles to the direction of travel, producing an up-and-down and side-to-side oscillation like the snapping of a rope. P and S waves are the most damaging waves because buildings are more susceptible to damage from horizontal motion than from vertical motion.

Secondary Contamination

Transfer of a harmful substance from one body (primary body) to another (secondary body), permitting adverse effects to the secondary body.

Secondary Documents

Those reports that are discrete portions of primary documents and are typically input or feeder documents within the remedial investigation/feasibility study or remedial design/remedial action process.

Secondary Drinking Water Regulations

Regulations that apply to public water systems and that specify the maximum contaminant levels that, in the judgment of the Administrator of EPA, are requisite to protect the public welfare. Such regulations may apply to any contaminant in drinking water that a) may adversely affect the odor or appearance of such water and consequently may cause a substantial number of the persons served by the public water system to discontinue its use, or b) may otherwise adversely affect the public welfare. Such regulations may vary according to geographic and other circumstances.

Secondary Emissions

1) Emissions that occur as a result of the construction or operation of an existing stationary facility but do not come from the existing stationary facility. Secondary emissions may include, but are not limited to, emissions from ships or trains coming to or from the existing stationary facility. 2) Inorganic arsenic emissions that escape capture by a primary emission control system.

Secondary Environmental Monitoring

Environmental monitoring equipment or activities that, if degraded, will produce a more than minor disruption of a monitoring program. An example of a minor effect would be the failure of a unit whose place in the program is effectively duplicated by overlap between one or more other components. An example of a more than minor effect would be failure of sufficient units to preclude continued coverage, or the failure of a unit that provides the only coverage for large areas, such as a groundwater monitoring well.

Secondary Hood Systems

The equipment (including hoods, ducts, tans, and dampers) used to capture and transport secondary inorganic arsenic emissions.

Secondary Limits

Values of the dose equivalent indices (deep and shallow), in the case of external exposure, or of annual limits on intake, in the case of internal exposure, that can be used to obtain an indirect assessment of compliance with primary limit.

Secondary Maximum Contaminant Levels (SMCLs)

1) Contaminant levels that apply to public water systems and that, in the judgment of the Administrator of EPA, are requisite to protect the public welfare. 2) The maximum permissible levels of a contaminant in water that are delivered to the tree flowing outlet of the ultimate user of public water system. Contaminants added to the water under circumstances controlled by the user, except those resulting from corrosion of piping and plumbing caused by water quality, are excluded from this definition.

Secondary Recovery

Oil and gas obtained by the augmentation of reservoir energy; often by injection of air, gas, or water into a production formation.

Secondary Rescue Facilities

Local airbase-ready aircraft, crash boats, and other air, surface, subsurface, and ground elements suitable for rescue missions including government and privately operated units and facilities.

Secondary Road

A road supplementing a main road, usually wide enough and suitable for two-way all-weather traffic at moderate or slow speeds.

Secondary Standards

The national secondary ambient air quality standard promulgated pursuant to Section 109 of the Clean Air Act.

Secondary Treatment

The second step in most publicly owned waste treatment systems in which bacteria consume the organic parts of the waste. This treatment removes floating and settleable solids and about 90% of all oxygen-demanding substances and suspended solids. It is accomplished by bringing together waste, bacteria, and oxygen in trickling filters or in the activated sludge process. *See* Primary Treatment; Tertiary Treatment.

Secretary

The Secretary of a federal agency (e.g., Secretary of the Interior, Secretary of Energy, Secretary of Transportation, Secretary of Housing and Urban Development, Secretary of Agriculture, or Secretary of Commerce.

Secretary of a Military Department

The Secretary of the Air Force, Army, or Navy; or the Commandant of the Coast Guard when operating as a Department of Transportation Agency.

Section

An organizational level having functional responsibility for primary segments of incident operations, such as Operations, Planning, Logistics, and Administration.

Section 5 Notices

Any Premanufacture Notice (PMN), consolidated PMN, intermediate PMN, significant new use notice, exemption notice, or exemption application.

Section 106 Process

Refers to Section 106 of the National Historic Preservation Act of 1966, as amended, that requires the responsible federal agency officials to take into account the effect of any proposed undertaking upon cultural resources included in or eligible for inclusion in the National Register of Historic Places. It also requires the agency official to permit the Advisory Council on Historic Preservation (established by the Act) a reasonable opportunity to comment with regard to the undertaking.

Compliance with Section 106 is required for any federal, federally controlled, or federally licensed or permitted undertaking. The process is described in 36 CFR 800.4, "Agency Procedures." *See* National Historic Preservation Act (NHPA).

Sector

1) An area designated by boundaries within which a unit operates, and for which it is responsible. 2) One of the subdivisions of a coastal frontier. *See* Area of Influence.

Secure Automatic Communications Network

A data system designed to handle U.S. Department of Energy's normal requirements for secure message and data traffic within the continental United States and to exchange such traffic via the Department of Defense automatic digital network and that allows access to the Department of State Diplomatic Telecommunications System and the General Services Administration Advanced Record System.

Secure Chemical

See Landfills.

Secure Maximum Contaminant Level

The maximum permissible level of a contaminant in water that is delivered to the free-flowing outlet of the ultimate user of a water supply, the consumer, or of contamination resulting from corrosion of piping and plumbing caused by water quality.

Secured Enclosure

An enclosure to which casual access is impeded by an appropriate means (e.g., door secured by lock, magnetically or electrically operated, latch, or by screws).

Security

Activities through which DOE defines, develops, and implements its responsibilities, under the Atomic Energy Act of 1954, as amended, federal statutes, executive orders, and other directives, for the protection of Restricted Data and other classified information or matter, nuclear weapons and nuclear weapon components, and for the protection of department and departmental contractor facilities, property, and equipment. Security is also applied to special nuclear materials. When physical, personnel, and technical security are combined with material control and material accountability, the protection is referred to as safe-guards. *See* Safeguards.

Security Area

A physically defined space containing a depart-mental security interest and subject to physical protection and access controls.

Security Classification

A category to which national security information and material is assigned to denote the degree of damage that unauthorized disclosure would cause to national defense or foreign relations of the United States and to denote the degree of protec-tion required. There are three such categories:

- Top Secret — national security information or material that requires the highest degree of protection and the unauthorized disclosure of which could reasonably be expected to cause exceptionally grave damage to the national security. Examples of "exceptionally grave damage" include armed hostilities against the United States or its allies; disruption of foreign relations vitally affecting the national security; the compromise of vital national defense plans or complex cryptologic and communications intelligence systems; the revelation of sensitive intelligence operations; and the disclosure of scientific or technological developments vital to national security;

- Secret — national security information or material that requires a substantial degree of protection and the unauthorized disclosure of which could reasonably be expected to cause serious damage to the national security. Examples of "serious damage" include disruption of foreign relations significantly affecting the national security; significant impairment of a program or policy directly related to the national security; revelation of significant military plans or intelligence operations; and compromise of significant scientific or technological developments relating to national security; and

- Confidential — national security information or material that requires protection and that the unauthorized disclosure of which could reasonably be expected to cause damage to the national security.

Security Clearance

An administrative determination by competent authority that an individual is eligible, from a se-curity standpoint, for access to classified informa-tion or restricted areas.

SCCC

See Security Communications Control Center.

Security Communications Control Center (SCCC)

A continuously staffed operation located in Albu-querque, New Mexico, that is staffed, equipped, and operated by the Albuquerque Operations Of-fice to provide necessary communications and ac-tions to initiate immediate response to U.S. Department of Energy transportation safeguards system emergencies involving nuclear weapons, components and devices, and strategic quantities of government-owned special nuclear materials.

Security Events

Emergency conditions that threaten the security of personnel, property, or special nuclear material.

Security Facilities

Any facilities that have been approved by the DOE for generating, receiving, using, processing, storing, reproducing, transmuting, destroying, or handling special nuclear material or classified matter.

Security Interests

Any of the following that requires special protec-tion: classified matter, special nuclear material, security shipments, secure communications cen-ters, automatic data processing centers, or other systems including classified information, or DOE property.

Sediment

Topsoil, sand, and minerals washed from the land into water, usually after rain or snow melt. Sedi-ments collecting in rivers, reservoirs, and harbors can destroy fish and wildlife habitat and cloud the water so that sunlight cannot reach aquatic plants. Careless farming, mining, and building activities will expose sediment materials, allowing them to be washed off the land after rainfalls. Loss of topsoil from farming, mining, or building activities can be prevented through a variety of erosion-control techniques.

Sedimentation Tanks

Holding areas for wastewater where floating wastes are skimmed off and settled solids are removed for disposal.

Sedimentation

1) Letting solids settle out of wastewater by gravity during wastewater treatment. 2) Deposition of particles in the small airways of the lungs that occurs as gravity acts on particles in a downward direction and buoyancy and air resistance act in an upward direction. 3) The settling out of particles in the atmosphere due to their gravitational fall.

Seed Tree

A thrifty vigorous tree, 18 inches (45.7 cm) or larger, of commercial species showing evidence of seed bearing, with full crown, and free from damage caused by timber operations and hazard abatement that would impair seed productivity.

Seepage Water

Water flowing toward stream channels after infiltration into the ground.

Select Existing Drawings

Drawings of historic sites, structures or objects, whether original construction or later alteration; drawings that portray or depict the historic value or significance.

Selective Alpha Air Monitor (SAAM)

A continuous air monitoring instrument that will detect alpha particles and activate an alarm when other than normal levels are present.

Selective Pesticide

A chemical designed to affect only certain types of pests, leaving other plants and animals unharmed.

Selenodesy

The branch of applied mathematics that determines, by observation and measurement, the exact positions of points and the figures and areas of large portions of the moon's surface, or the shape and size of the moon.

Selenodetic

Of or pertaining to, or determined by selenodesy.

Self-Accelerating Decomposition Temperature (SADT)

The temperature at which a material (particularly organic peroxides) begins to become chemically active, generally releasing the energy of reaction in the form of heat, often producing enough heat to ignite combustible components or nearby materials, as a direct result of this thermochemical reaction. Some reactions are instantaneous and extremely violent.

Self-Assessment

A systematic evaluation of a facility maintenance program, including the activities and practices, utilizing the performance objectives and criteria from each element of a Facility Maintenance Management Program as defined by regulation or department policy.

Self-Contained Breathing Apparatus (SCBA)

A respiratory protective device designed for supplying a respirable atmosphere totally independent of the surrounding atmosphere. Designed for use in those areas considered immediately dangerous to life or health, as a result of toxic or unknown contamination or a lack of sufficient oxygen. Similar to gas-masks.

Self-Evaluation

A critical evaluation of a facility training program measured against the accreditation objectives and criteria.

Self-Insurance

Retention of risk. Generally refers to a planned program for financing or otherwise amortizing losses. A poor term because it is not insurance.

Sell

A term that includes offer for sale, expose for sale, possess for sale, exchange, barter, or trade.

Semiconfined Aquifer

An aquifer that is partially confined by a soil layer (or layers) of low permeability through which recharge and discharge can occur.

Semiannual

A 6-month period; the first semiannual period concludes on the last day of the last month during the 180 days following initial startup for new sources; and the first semiannual period concludes on the last day of the last full month during the 180 days after June 6, 1984, for existing sources.

Semiautomatic Firearms

A type of firearm that employs gas pressure or recoil force and mechanical spring action in ejecting the empty cartridge case after the first shot and loading the next cartridge from the magazine but that requires release and another pressure of the trigger for firing each successive shot.

Semiconductor Laser

A type of laser that produces its output from semiconductor materials.

Senescence

A term for the aging process. Sometimes used to describe lakes or other bodies of water in advanced stages of eutrophication.

Senior Federal Emergency Management Agency Officials

Officials appointed by the director of the Federal Emergency Management Agency (FEMA), or his/her representative, to direct FEMA response at the scene of a radiological emergency. The senior FEMA officials serve as the focal point for promoting the coordination of the federal response activities at the scene of an emergency.

Senior Management Officials

Officials with management responsibility for preparing environmental reports and studies, or the manager of environmental programs for the facility or establishments, or for the corporation owning or operating the facility or establishment, the person(s) responsible for compiling various reports under environmental regulatory requirements.

Senior Meteorological and Oceanographic Officer (SMO)

Meteorological and oceanographic officer responsible for assisting a military commander and staff in developing and executing operational meteorological and oceanographic service concepts.

Senior Reactor Operator

An individual certified by contractor management to operate or to direct the operation of a DOE-owned Category A reactor.

Senior Scientific Advisers

Senior scientists selected by the DOE team leader, Federal Radiological Monitoring and Assessment Center director, or on-scene commander to serve as his/her primary scientific or technical advisor. The person will have special technical expertise related to the radioactive source produced by the accident.

Senior Security Supervisors

Security contractor officials at an incident site who assume tactical control of the incident response.

Sensitive Compartmented Information (SCI)

All classified information and materials bearing intelligence community special access controls formally limiting access and dissemination. SCI does not include restricted data as defined in the Atomic Energy Act of 1954, as amended.

Sensitive Information

Information requiring special protection from disclosure that could cause embarrassment, compromise, or threats to security. The term may be applied to an agency, installation, person, position, document, material, or activity.

Sensitive Nuclear Material Production Information
1) Classified production rate or stockpile quantity information relating to plutonium, tritium, enriched lithium-6, and uranium-235 and uranium-233. 2) Laser separation technology.

Sensitization
An allergic condition that usually affects the skin or lungs. Once exposure to a substance has caused a reaction, the individual may be sensitized to that substance and further exposure even at low levels may elicit an adverse reaction.

Sensors
1) Devices that measure a physical quantity or the change in a physical quantity, such as temperature, pressure, flow rate, pH, or liquid level. 2) A type of equipment that detects, and may indicate, and/or record objects and activities by means of energy or particles emitted, reflected, or modified by objects. 3) A device that responds to physical stimuli (e.g., light, sound, magnetism, motion), and transmits the resulting signal or data for providing a measurement, operating a control, or both.

Sensory Neuropathy
Damage to the nerves that carry information about sensation (e.g., touch, pain, temperature) to the brain.

SEP
An acronym for Systematic Evaluation Program.

Sepal
A plant species descriptor for the green segments forming the calyx (outer covering) of a flower.

Separable Element
A portion of a project that: 1) is physically separable from other portions of the project and achieves hydrologic effects; or 2) produces physical or economic benefits, that are separately iden-tifiable from those produced by other portions of the project.

Separation Zone
An area between two adjacent horizontal or vertical areas into which units are not to proceed unless certain safety measures can be fulfilled.

Septic Tank
1) A watertight, covered receptacle designed to receive or process, through liquid separation or biological digestion, the sewage discharged from a building sewer. The effluent from such a receptacle is distributed for disposal through the soil, and settled solids and scum from the tank are pumped out periodically and hauled to a treatment facility. 2) An underground storage tank for wastes from homes having no sewer line to a municipal treatment plant. Waste goes from the home to the tank, where the organic waste is decomposed by bacteria. Solids and dead bacteria settle to the bottom as sludge while the liquid effluent portion flows out of the tank into the ground through drains. The sludge is pumped out periodically. Properly placed and maintained septic systems effectively treat domestic wastewater, while others are a major source of groundwater and surface water pollution.

Sequela
A condition that follows as a consequence of injury or disease.

SER
An acronym for Safety Evaluation Report.

SERC
See State Emergency Response Commission.

Sergeant
A mobile, inertially guided, solid-propellant, surface-to-surface missile, with nuclear warhead capability, designed to attack targets up to a range of 75 nautical miles.

Sericeous
A species descriptor that means covered with soft, silky hairs.

Serious Bodily Injury
An injury that involves a substantial risk of death, unconsciousness, extreme physical pain, protracted and obvious disfigurement or protracted loss or impairment of the function of a bodily member, organ, or mental faculty.

Serious Violations
An OSHA term for those violations having a substantial probability that death or serious physical harm could result and the employer could have had knowledge of the hazard with the exercise of reasonable diligence.

Seriously Ill or Injured (SII)
The casualty status of a person whose illness or injury is classified by medical authority to be of such severity that there is cause for immediate concern, but there is not imminent danger to life. *See* Casualty Status.

Seriously Wounded
A nonambulatory stretcher case.

Serosa
A membrane producing a serous secretion, or containing serum or a serumlike substance.

Serrate
A species descriptor that means having notched, toothlike projections.

Serrations
A species descriptor that means having a series of teeth or notches.

Service
1) The performance of adjustments, repair, or procedures on a nonroutine basis, required to return the equipment to its intended state. 2) The United States Fish and Wildlife Service or the National Marine Fisheries Service, as appropriate.

Service Connector
The pipe that carries tap water from the public water main to a building.

Service Environment
All external conditions, whether natural or induced, to which items of material are likely to be subjected throughout their life cycle.

Service Magazine
An auxiliary building of an operating line used for the intermediate storage of explosives within the operational plant area. The amount of explosives is normally limited to a maximum consistent with intraline separation from other explosives buildings based on the quantity of explosives in the service magazine.

Service Robots
Machines that extend human capabilities.

Sessile
1) In botany, stalkless and attached directly to the base. 2) In zoology, permanently attached, not free-moving.

Setback
Building offset from a property line, sidewalk, or street right-of-way.

SETS
An acronym for Statistical Export and Tabulation System.

Settleable Solids
1) Material heavy enough to sink to the bottom of a wastewater treatment tank. 2) Those solids suspended in wastewater that are determined to be settleable using Method 209E, Settleable Solids, *Standard Methods for Examination of Water and Waste Water*, 16th edition.

Settlement
An agreement between some or all of the parties to a proceeding on a mutually acceptable outcome to the proceedings. In addition to other parties to an agreement, settlements in applications must be

signed by the applicant and in complaints, by the complainant and defendant.

Settling Chamber
A series of screens placed in the way of flue gases to slow the stream of air, thus helping gravity to pull particles out of the emission into a collection area.

Settling Tank
A holding area for wastewater, where heavier particles sink to the bottom for removal and disposal.

Severe Winter Storm
A winter storm having the potential to severely disrupt the site operations and/or jeopardize the safety of the site personnel and visitors.

Severe Energy Supply Interruption
A national energy supply shortage that the President determines a) is, or is likely to be, of significant scope and duration, and of an emergency nature; b) may cause major adverse impact on national safety or the national economy; and c) results, or is likely to result, from the following: an interruption in the supply of imported petroleum products; an interruption in the supply of domestic petroleum products; sabotage or an act of God.

Sewage
1) The waste and wastewater produced by residential and commercial establishments and discharged into sewers. 2) The waste matter that passes through sewers.

Sewage Lagoon
See Lagoon.

Sewage Sludge
1) Any solid, semisolid, or liquid waste generated by a publicly owned wastewater treatment plant, the disposal of which is regulated under the Clean Water Act.

Sewer
1) The artificial conduit, usually underground, for carrying off wastewater and refuse. 2) A channel or conduit that carries wastewater and stormwater runoff from the source to a treatment plant or receiving waters. Sanitary sewers carry household, industrial, and commercial waste. Storm sewers carry runoff from rain or snow. Combined sewers are used for both purposes.

Sewerage
1) The system of sewers. 2) The entire system of sewage collection, treatment, and disposal.

SFCs
An acronym for Supercritical Fluids.

SFE
An acronym for Supercritical Fluid Extraction.

SFMP
An acronym for Surplus Facilities Management Program.

SG
See Steam Generator.

SGMAS
An acronym for Sea Grant Marine Advisory Services.

SGML
An acronym for Standard Generalized Markup Language.

SGTR
An acronym for Steam Generator Tube Rupture.

SGTS
An acronym for Standby Gas Treatment System.

SH
An acronym for Sleeve Housings.

Shaft Break Limit
Average assembly effluent temperature limit.

Shallow Dose Equivalents
The maximum dose equivalent within the spherical shell extending from a depth of 0.07 cm to a depth of 1 cm from the surface of a 30 cm diameter sphere, centered at this point and consisting of material equivalent to soft tissue with a density of $1 g/cm^3$.

Shallow Eye Dose Equivalents
The dose equivalent at the respective depths of 0.07 cm and 1.0 cm in tissue.

Shear Wall
A wall designed to resist lateral forces parallel to the plane of the wall (sometimes referred to as a vertical diaphragm or a structural wall).

Sheath
1) A species descriptor for protective covering, such as the tubular base of a leaf surrounding a stem. 2) A covering consisting of a smooth layer of wood placed over metal and secured to prevent any movement.

Sheet Explosive
Plastic explosive provided in a sheet form.

Sheet Piling
Closely spaced piles of wood, steel, or concrete driven vertically into the ground to obstruct the lateral movement of earth or water.

Sheetlines
Those lines defining the geographic limits of the map or chart detail.

Shelf Life
The length of time a material or substance, subject to deterioration or having a limited life that cannot be renewed, can be stored and continue to meet the specification requirements of its intended use. *See* Storage Life.

Shelter
1) A facility used to protect, house, and supply the essential needs of designated individuals during the period of an emergency. A shelter may or may not be specifically constructed for such use, depending on the type of emergency and the specific programmatic requirements. 2) A public announcement (PA) requiring onsite personnel or the public to move to and remain inside buildings, vehicles, or other structures in order to minimize exposures to radiological or otherwise hazardous substances. Doors and windows should be closed, and where possible, HVAC systems should be turned off.

Shelter Belt
A vegetative barrier with a linear configuration composed of trees, shrubs, and other approved perennial vegetation.

Shielding
1) Material of suitable thickness and physical characteristics used to protect personnel from radiation during the manufacture, handling, and transportation of fissionable and radioactive materials. 2) Obstructions that tend to protect personnel or materials from the effects of a nuclear explosion.

Shielding Materials
Any material that is used to absorb radiation and thus effectively reduce the intensity of radiation, and in some cases eliminate it. Lead, concrete, aluminum, water, and plastic are examples of commonly used shielding materials

Shillelagh
A missile system mounted on the main battle tank and assault reconnaissance vehicle for employment against enemy armor, troops, and field fortifications.

Shiner
A small, often silvery North American fish of the family Cyprinidae.

Shipping Container, or Outside Container
The box, bag, barrel, crate, or other receptacle or covering enclosing field samples packed in one or more immediate or true containers.

Shipping Papers

A shipping order, bill of lading, manifest, or other shipping document servicing a similar purpose and containing material and product information.

Shock Wave

The continuously propagated pressure pulse formed by the blast from an explosion in air, underwater, or underground. Also applies to the resultant surface and subsurface movements associated with earthquakes.

Shop Inspection

Inspection of tanks in a fabricator's shop, or at the job site during erection, as required by the ASME Code.

Shoring System

1) Temporary bracing of an existing building foundation to provide support during adjacent excavations. Also applies to supporting construction of above grade floors. 2) A temporary structure for the support of earth surfaces formed as a result of excavation work.

Short Title

A short, identifying combination of letters (acronym), and/or numbers assigned to a document or device for purposes of brevity and/or security.

Short-Term Exposure Limit (STEL)

1) A time weighted average that the American Conference of Government and Industrial Hygienists (ACGIH) indicates should not be exceeded any time during the work day. 2) The maximum concentration of a hazardous chemical or material allowed for a continuous 15-minute exposure period. There may be no more than four such exposures each day with at least 1 hour between exposures. The daily "threshold limit value-time weighted average" (TLV-TWA) may not be exceeded.

Short-Term Public Exposure Guidance Level (SPEGL)

The acceptable concentration for an unpredicted, single, short-term emergency exposure to the general public lasting from 1 to 24 hours. The SPEGL takes into account the wide range of susceptibility found in the general public, including sensitive populations such as children, the aged, persons with serious, debilitating diseases, and fetuses.

Shortfall

A lack of resources, equipment, personnel, material, or capability, reflected as the difference between the resources identified as a plan requirement and those apportioned, that would adversely affect the ability to accomplish its assignment.

Shotgun

Nonscientific term for the process of breaking up the DNA derived from an organism and then moving each separate and unidentified DNA fragment into a bacterium.

SHPO

See State Historic Preservation Officer.

SHPO Responsibilities

The tasks and responsibilities required to administer a State Historic Preservation Program, including, but not limited to a) conducting a comprehensive statewide survey of historic properties and maintaining an inventory of such properties in cooperation with federal, state, local governments, and private organizations and individuals; b) identifying and nominating eligible properties to the National Register; c) prepare and implement a comprehensive statewide historic preservation plan; d) administer the state program of federal assistance for historic preservation within the state; e) advise and assist, as appropriate, other agencies and local governments in carrying out their historic preservation responsibilities; f) cooperate with the Secretary, the Advisory Council on Historic Preservation, and other agencies, organizations, and individuals to ensure that historic properties are taken into consideration at all levels of planning and development; g) provide public information, education, training, and technical assistance relating to Historic Preservation Programs; and h) assisting local governments in the development of local historic preservation programs and certification pursuant to the NHPA.

SHPRB
See State Historic Preservation Review Board.

Shrub
A woody plant that at maturity is usually less than 6 m (20 feet) tall and generally exhibits several erect, spreading, or prostrate stems and has a bushy appearance; e.g., speckled alder (*Alnus rugosa*).

SHT
An acronym for Seal Head Tank.

Shutdown, Emissions
The cessation of operation of an affected source for any purpose.

Si
Periodic Element. *See* Silicon.

SI
See Site Inspection.

SIC Codes
The code numbers used for classification of economic activity in the Standard Industrial Classification Manual. *See* Standard Industrial Classification.

SICS
An acronym for Safety Injection Control System.

Side-Stream Extraction
The extraction of a mineral that is a byproduct of the principal mineral being extracted.

Sides, Walls, and Faces
The vertical or inclined earth surfaces formed as a result of excavation work.

Sidewinder
A solid-propellant, air-to-air missile with nonnuclear warhead and infrared, heat-seeking homer. The ground-to-air version is designated as "Chaparral."

Sierra Club
A special interest environmental organization with one of the largest memberships of all such environmental groups.

Sievert
A unit of ionizing radiation, equal to the amount that produces the same damage to humans as 1 roentgen of high-voltage X-rays. *See* rem.

Signal Words
The words used on a pesticide label to indicate the level of toxicity of the chemicals (e.g., Danger, Warning, Caution).

Significant Adverse Environmental Impact
A substantial, or potentially substantial, adverse change in any of the physical conditions (e.g., land, air, water, minerals, flora, fauna, ambient noise, and objects of historic or aesthetic significance) within an area affected by a proposed project. Economic or social changes in and of themselves are not typically considered significant impacts on the environment. A social or economic change related to a physical change may be considered a secondary, or causative, impact in determining whether the physical change is significant.

Significant Adverse Reactions
Reactions that may indicate a substantial impairment of normal activities, or long-lasting or irreversible damage to health or the environment.

Significant Deterioration
Pollution resulting from a new source in previously clean areas. *See* Prevention of Significant Deterioration.

Significant Economic Loss

A term referring to economic losses under emergency conditions, for productive activities, when profitability is greatly below expected profitability for that activity; or, when the value of public or private fixed assets is greatly below the expected value for those assets.

Significant Environmental Compliance Issues

Issues that are or have the potential of being precedent setting or controversial, and/or involve headquarters notification, concurrence, or approval.

Significant Exposure

Any exposure of human beings or the environment to PCBs as measured or detected by any scientifically acceptable analytical method.

Significant Financial Hardship

A term referring to both of the following issues: 1) an individual has or represents an interest not otherwise adequately represented, representation of which is necessary for a fair determination of the proceeding; and, 2) either the individual cannot afford to pay the costs of effective participation, including attorney's fees, expert witness fees, and other reasonable costs of participation and the cost of obtaining judicial review, or, in the case of a group or organization, the economic interest of the individual members of the group or organization is small in comparison to the costs of effective participation in the proceeding.

Significant Impairment

Visibility impairment that, in the judgment of the Administrator, interferes with management, protection, preservation, or enjoyment of the visitor's visual experience of the mandatory Class I federal area. This determination is made on a case-by-case basis taking into account the geographic extent, intensity, duration, frequency, and time of the visibility impairment, and how these factors correlate with a) times of restricted use of the mandatory Class I federal area, and b) the frequency and timing of natural conditions that reduce visibility.

Significant Incidents

An unexpected event involving nuclear weapons or radiological nuclear weapon components that result in any of the following: a) accidental or unauthorized launching, firing, or use of a nuclear explosive; b) nuclear detonation; c) nonnuclear detonation/burning of a nuclear weapon; d) radioactive contamination; e) seizure, theft, or loss of a nuclear weapon or an actual component of a nuclear weapon; and/or f) public hazard, actual or implied.

Significant Modification

A change to a nuclear facility that involves an unreviewed safety question.

Significant Municipal Facilities

Publicly owned sewage treatment plants that discharge a million gallons per day or more and are therefore considered by states to have the potential for substantial effect on the quality of receiving waters.

Significant Quantities

Masses of fissionable materials greater than a safe mass.

Significant Source of Groundwater

1) An aquifer that a) is saturated with water having less than 10,000 milligrams per liter of total dissolved solids; b) is found in 2,500 feet of the land surface; c) has a transmissivity greater than 200 gallons per day per foot, provided that any formation or part of a formation included within the source of groundwater has a hydraulic conductivity greater than 2 gallons per day per square foot; and d) is capable of continuously yielding at least 10,000 gallons per day to a pumped or flowing well for a period of at least a year. 2) An aquifer that provides the primary source of water for a community water system.

Significant Violations

Violations by point source dischargers of sufficient magnitude and/or duration to be a regulatory priority.

SII

See Seriously Ill or Injured.

Silicon Carbide Fiber

A reinforcing fiber with high strength and modulus; and density equal to that of aluminum. It is used in organic metal-matrix composites.

Silique

A long pod that is divided by a membranous partition and splits at both seams, such as the fruit of the mustards.

Silt

Fine particles of sand or rock that can be picked up by the air or water and deposited as sediment.

Siltation

The process of depositing silt.

Silvicultural System

The planned program of forest stand treatments during the life of a stand. It consists of a number of integrated steps conducted in logical sequence leading to or maintaining a forest stand of distinctive form for the level of management intensity desired.

Silviculture

1) The theory and practice of controlling the establishment, composition, and growth of forests.
2) Management of forest land for timber; sometimes contributes to water pollution, as in clearcutting.

Simulators

A computer or other piece of equipment that imitates or mimics the actions and reactions of a system or condition, showing the effects of various applied changes.

Single Department Purchase

A method of purchase whereby one government department buys commodities for another department or departments.

Single Failure

An occurrence that results in the loss of capability of a component to perform its intended safety function(s). Multiple failures (i.e., loss of capability of several components resulting from a single occurrence are considered to be a single failure). Systems are considered to be designed against an assumed single failure if a) neither a single failure of any active component; nor, b) a single failure of any passive component results in loss of the system's capability to perform its safety function(s).

Single Failure Analysis

Primary failure analysis to detect where a single failure could shut down a system or process.

Sinistral

A zoological term pertaining to a gastropod shell that has its aperture (opening) to the left when facing the observer with the apex (top) up.

Sinking

Controlling oil spills by using an agent to trap the oil and sink it to the bottom of the body of water where the agent and the oil are biodegraded.

Sinking Agents

Those additives applied to oil discharges to sink floating pollutants below the water surface.

SIP

See State Implementation Plan.

SIP Requirements

A term the refers to a state's implementation plan requirements, under the CAA, to contain emission limitations and such other measures as may be necessary, as determined by regulations, to prevent significant deterioration of air quality in each region (or portion thereof) designated as attainment or unclassifiable.

Siphon

An ESA term for a tubular organ, especially in aquatic invertebrates such as squids and clams, by which water is taken in or expelled.

SIS

An acronym for Special Isotope Separator.

Sister Chromatid Exchange (SCE)

The reciprocal exchange of chromosomal material between two chromatids (longitudinal subunits of a replicated chromosome). Increased SCE is indicative of genotoxic effects.

SIT

See Safety Injection Tank.

Site

1) The property on which a facility is located and any adjoining buffer zone. Roadways or areas serving functions other than that of the facility are usually not considered part of the site. 2) The area over which DOE has access control authority. A site may include many facilities of varying natures.

SITE

An acronym for Superfund Innovative Technology Evaluation. *See* Best Available Control Technology (BACT); Superfund Amendments and Reauthorization Act (SARA).

Site Area Emergency (SAE)

A term for events that are in progress or that have occurred which involve actual or likely major failures of facility functions needed for the protection of workers and the public; and/or actual malevolent acts resulting in major failure of protective systems. Any release of hazardous materials (radiological or nonradiological) that is expected to exceed appropriate protective action guides (PAG) or emergency response planning guidelines (ERPG) exposure levels onsite, but is not expected to exceed the appropriate PAGs or ERPGs offsite.

Site Boundaries

Well-marked boundaries of the property over which the owner/operator can exercise strict control without the aid of outside authorities.

Site Characterization

The program of exploration and research, both in the laboratory and in the field, undertaken to establish the geologic conditions and the ranges of those parameters of a particular site relevant to the procedures under this part. Site characterization includes borings, surface excavations, excavation of exploratory shafts, limited subsurface lateral excavations and borings, and insitu testing at depths needed to determine the suitability of the site for a geologic repository but does not include preliminary borings and geological testing needed to decide whether site characterization should be undertaken.

Site Closure and Stabilization

Those actions that are taken upon completion of operations that prepare the disposal site for custodial care and that ensure that the disposal site will remain stable and will not need ongoing active maintenance.

Site Development and Facility Utilization Plans

Formal written documents summarizing all of the various data necessary to plan for the most effective utilization and orderly future development and disposal of facilities at an individual site. Such planning shall be in accordance with site related program objectives and requirements and shall represent consolidated views of site management, the field organization, and the resource sponsor.

Site Drill

A drill involving activation of the EOC and its supporting FWCS.

Site Emergency

An emergency response level that represents an event in progress, or having occurred, that involves actual or likely major failures of facility functions that are needed for the protection of onsite personnel, the public health and safety, and the environment. Offsite releases of radioactive or other hazardous substances not exceeding protective action guidelines are occurring or are likely to occur. *See* Site Area Emergency.

Site Inspection (SI)

1) A technical phase that follows a preliminary assessment (PA) designed to collect more extensive information on a hazardous waste site. The information is used to score the site with the Hazard Ranking System to determine whether response action is needed or not. 2) The collection of information from a site to determine the extent and severity of hazards posed by the site. *See* Preliminary Assessment.

Site Plan Review

A process for which the purpose is to give a public entity control over the design and layout of private developments, whereby a proposed subdivision is reviewed, approved, and/or approved with modifications.

Site Quality Assurance Plan

A written document, associated with site sampling activities, that presents in specific terms the organization (where applicable), objectives, functional activities, and specific quality assurance (QA) and quality control (QC) activities designed to achieve the data quality goals of a specific project(s) or continuing operation(s). The QA Project Plan is prepared for each specific project or continuing operation (or group of similar projects of continuing operations). The QA Project Plan is typically prepared by the responsible program office, regional office, laboratory, contractor, recipient of an assistance agreement, or other organization.

Site Reconnaissance

A field investigation undertaken to obtain, by visual observation or other detection methods, information about the current hazardous waste activities and operations at a specific site or facility, or to secure data concerning the meteorological, hydrographic, or geographic characteristics of a particular area. *See* Site Inspection.

Site-Limited Intermediates

Intermediates that are manufactured, processed, and used only within a site and not distributed in commerce other than as an impurity or for disposal. *See* Intermediates.

Site-Specific Applications

A term that applies to a pesticide permit identifying the specific area to be treated, the size of that area, and the commodity(ies) or site(s) on that area to be treated.

Site-Specific Safeguards and Security Plan

A specific description of the systems and procedures implemented and planned to protect governmental security interests and other property.

Site-Wide NEPA Documents

Broad-scope Environmental Impact Statements or Environmental Assessments that identity and assess the individual and cumulative impact of the continuing and reasonably foreseeable future actions at a DOE site; they may also refer to an associated NEPA document such as a Notice of Intent, Record of Decision, or Finding of No Significant Impact.

Siting

The process of choosing a location for a facility.

Siting Research

Activities, including borings, surface excavations, shaft excavations, subsurface lateral excavations and borings, and insitu testing, to determine the suitability of a site for a test and evaluation facility.

Situation Assessment

An assessment produced by combining geography, weather, and threat data to provide a comprehensive projection of the situation for planning and decisionmaking purposes. *See* Assessment; Environmental Assessment.

Situation Map

A map showing the tactical or the administrative situation at a particular time.

Size Classes of Discharges

Size classes of oil discharges that are provided as guidance to the On-Scene Coordinator (OSC) and serve as the criteria for further actions. They are not meant to imply associated degrees of hazard to public health or welfare, nor are they a measure of environmental damage.

Size Classes of Releases
Refers to size classifications that are provided as guidance to the On-Scene Coordinator (OSC) for meeting pollution reporting requirements.

SJI
An acronym for the Steel Joist Institute.

SJP
See Standard Job Procedures.

Sketch Plan
A floor plan, generally not to exact scale, although often drawn from measurements, where the features are shown in proper relation and proportion to one another.

Skidding or Yarding
The movement of forest products from the point of felling to a landing.

Skimming
1) Using a machine to remove oil or scum from the surface of the water. 2) The removal of slag from the molten convener bath.

SLAC
See Stanford Linear Accelerator Center.

Slackwater
The period at high or low tide when there is no visible flow of water; an area in a sea or river unaffected by currents.

Slake
To become mixed with water so that a true chemical combination takes place, as in the slaking of lime.

Slanting
The incorporation, without appreciable extra cost or reduction in efficiency, of certain architectural and engineering features into new structures (ex-

cept temporary type) or portions of the structures to improve their ability to resist the effects of an incident and to offer protection to personnel and material.

Slated Items
Bulk petroleum and packaged bulk petroleum items that are requisitioned for overseas use by means of a consolidated requirement document, prepared and submitted through joint petroleum office channels. Packaged petroleum items are requisitioned in accordance with normal DOD requisitioning procedures.

SLCS
An acronym for Standby Liquid Control System.

SLFAA
An acronym for State and Local Fiscal Assistance Amendments of 1972.

SLI
An acronym for Sandia Laboratory Instruction.

Slick Surface Advisory
An advisory issued when precipitation or standing water is expected to freeze on sidewalks, parking lots, road surfaces, power lines or tree limbs, creating a hazard for travel and walking, or power loss or damage to the site property. This advisory is not used by the National Weather Service.

Slide Area Characteristics
A term for the two primary slide area types indicated by the following characteristics:

- Type 1 Shallow-Seated Landslide - An area where surface material (unconsolidated rock colluvium, and soil) has moved downslope along a relatively steep, shallow failure surface. The failure surface is generally steeper than 65 inches and less than 5 feet in depth. It is usually characterized by a) a scarp at the top; b) a concave sear below the scarp, where surface material has been removed; and sometimes c) a convex area at the bottom where slide material is deposited. Vegetation is usually disturbed (tilted trees), anomalous (younger, even-aged stand), or absent (bare soil). Minor bank slumps are excluded from this definition; and

- Type 2 Deep-Seated Landslide - An area where landslide material has moved downslope either as a relatively cohesive mass (rotational slides and translational block slides) or as an irregular, hummocky mass (earthflow). The failure surface is generally deeper than 5 feet and is usually well-exposed at the head scarp. Complex failures with rotational movement at the head and translational movement or earthflows downslope are common. Vegetation on rotational and translational slides is relatively undisturbed, although trees and shrubs may be pistol-butted or tilted. Deep-seated landslides may have intermediate tension cracks, scarps, and shallow slides superimposed throughout the slide mass. Deep-seated landslide risk is usually associated with cohesive soils.

Slide-Prone Areas
Areas susceptible to landslides due to their instability, slopes, and unstable soils. *See* Slide Area Characteristics.

Slightly Injured
A casualty that is a sitting or a walking case. *See* Casualty Status.

Slip Gauges
Gauges that have a probe that moves through the gas/liquid interface in a storage or transfer vessel and indicates the level of vinyl chloride in the vessel by the physical state of the material the gauge discharges.

Sloping
A method of excavation whereby the faces of an excavation or trench are laid back to provide protection from moving ground.

Sloughing
The process by which necrotic cells separate from the tissues to which they have been attached.

Slow Neutron
A low energy neutron, sometimes called a thermal neutron, with energy of about 0.025 electron volts in contrast to the energy of a fast neutron, that

may exceed 1,000 electron volts. These neutrons are very efficient in causing the fission of uranium-235.

Slow Sand Filtration
A treatment process involving passage of raw water through a bed of sand at low velocity (generally less than 0.4 meters/hour) that results in the substantial removal of chemical and biological contaminants.

Slow Speed Control
A mode of robotic motion control where the velocity of the robot is limited to allow persons sufficient time to either withdraw the hazardous motion or stop the robot.

Sludge
1) Any solid, semisolid, or liquid waste generated from a municipal, commercial, or industrial wastewater treatment plant, water supply treatment plant, or air pollution control facility exclusive of the treated effluent from a wastewater treatment plant; or the still bottom of a recycled/distilled material. 2) A semisolid residue from any of a number of air or water treatment processes or any other such waste having similar characteristics and effect. Sludge can be a hazardous waste.

Sludge Density Index
The reciprocal of the sludge volume index multiplied by 100.

Sludge Digestion
See Digestion.

Sludge Dryer
A device used to reduce the moisture content of sludge by heating to temperatures above 150°F (65°C) directly with combustion gases.

Sludge Index
See Sludge Volume Index.

Sludge Volume Index (SVI)

The ratio of the volume in milliliters of sludge settled from a 1,000-milliliter sample in 30 minutes to the concentration of mixed liquor in milligrams per liter multiplied by 1,000.

Slurry

A watery mixture of insoluble matter that results from some pollution control techniques.

Small Arms Ammunition

Fixed ammunition consisting of a) a metallic, plastic composition, or paper cartridge case; b) a primer; c) a propelling charge; d) with or without a bullet, projectile, shot, tear gas material, tracer components, incendiary compositions, or mixtures. It is further limited to ammunition designed to be fired from a pistol, revolver, role, or shotgun.

Small Business

A private firm that does not exceed a standard number of employees. The standard is promulgated by the Small Business Administration under Section 632(a) of Title 15 for the Standard Industrial Classification (SIC) code designated as its primary business activity.

Small Capacitors

Capacitors that contain less than 1.36 kilograms (3 pounds) of dielectric fluid. The following assumptions may be used if the actual weight of the dielectric fluid is unknown. Capacitors whose total volume is less than 1,639 cubic centimeters (100 cubic inches) may be considered to contain less than 1.36 kilograms (3 pounds) of dielectric fluid and a capacitors whose total volume is more than 3,278 cubic centimeters (200 cubic inches) must be considered to contain more than 1.36 kilograms (3 pounds) of dielectric fluid.

Capacitors whose volume is between 1,639 and 3,278 cubic centimeters may be considered to contain less then 1.36 kilograms (3 pounds) of dielectric fluid if the total weight of the capacitor is less than 4.08 kilograms (9 pounds).

Small Electric Utility

Any electric utility that owns or operates less than 200 megawatts of generating capacity as of the first year of the forecast period.

Small Gas Utility

Any gas utility that plans to deliver less than 25 billion cubic feet of gas in any year of the forecast period.

Small Manufacturers

A manufacturer of a chemical substance if its total annual sales, when combined with those of its parent company (if any) are less than $40 million. However, if annual production volume of a particular chemical substance at any individual site owned or controlled by the manufacturer is greater than 45,400 kilograms (100,000 pounds), the manufacturer shall not qualify as small for purposes of reporting on the production of that chemical at that site, unless the manufacturer's total annual sales, when combined with those of its parent company are less than $4 million, regardless of the quantity of chemicals produced by that manufacturer.

Small Quantities for Research and Development

Any quantity of PCBs that a) is originally packaged in one or more hermetically sealed containers of no more than 5.0 milliliters; and b) is used only for purposes of scientific experimentation or analysis or chemical research on, or analysis of PCBs, but not for research or analysis for the development of a PCB product.

Small Quantity Generators

RCRA generators who generate less than 1,000 kilograms of hazardous waste in a calendar month.

Small-Lot Storage

Generally a quantity of less than one pallet stack, stacked to maximum storage height. Thus, the term refers to a lot consisting of from one container to two or more pallet loads, but is not of sufficient quantity to form a complete pallet column.

Small-Scale Map

A map having a scale smaller than 1:600,000. *See* Map.

Small Source

A source that emits less than 100 tons of regulated pollutants per year, or any class of persons that the Administrator of EPA determines, through regulation, generally lacks technical ability or knowledge regarding control of air pollution.

SMCLs

See Secondary Maximum Contaminant Levels.

SMCRA

An acronym for Surface Mining Control and Reclamation Act.

Smear

A procedure in which a swab (e.g., a circle of filter paper) is rubbed on a surface and its radioactivity measured to determine if the surface is contaminated with loose radioactive material.

Smelter

A facility that melts or fuses ore, often with an accompanying chemical change, to separate the metal. Emissions are known to cause pollution. Smelting is the process involved.

SMO

See Senior Meteorological and Oceanographic Officer.

SMOA

See Superfund Memorandum of Agreement.

Smog

Air pollution associated with oxidants. *See* Photochemical Smog.

Smoke

Particles suspended in air after incomplete combustion of materials.

Smoke Grenades

Pyrotechnic devices capable of generating large amounts of smoke. While smoke grenades do not emit projectiles, they may emit fragments on actuation and may generate sufficient heat to cause fires and to injure personnel.

SMRSF

See Special Moment Resisting Space Frame.

SMSA

See Standard Metropolitan Statistical Area.

Snag

A standing dead tree or a standing section thereof, regardless of species.

SNL

See Sandia National Laboratories.

SNLA

An acronym for Sandia National Laboratories-Albuquerque.

SNLL

An acronym for Sandia National Laboratories-Livermore.

SNM

See Special Nuclear Materials.

SNM Vault

A penetration-resistant, windowless enclosure that has a) walls, floor, and coiling substantially constructed of materials that afford penetration resistance at least equal to that of 8-inch thick reinforced concrete; b) any openings greater than 96 square inches in area and over 6 inches in the smallest dimension protected by embedded steel bars at least 5/8 inches in diameter on 6-inch centers both horizontally and vertically; and c) a built-in combination locked steel door that in existing structures is at least 1-inch thick exclusive of bolt work and locking devices and that for new structures at least meets the Class 5 standards as set forth in FS AA-D-6008 of the Federal Specifications and Standards in 41 CFR 101. *See* Special Nuclear Materials.

Snow Advisory
An advisory issued when snowfall accumulations of 1 to 6 inches are expected.

Source Term
The amount of material available for release.

Special Nuclear Materials (SNM)
1) Plutonium-239, uranium-233, uranium-235, or any material artificially enriched by any of these elements. 2) Pursuant to the provisions of Section 51 of the Atomic Energy Act, any other material that the Nuclear Regulatory Commission determines to be special nuclear materials, not including source material.

SNRTA
An acronym for Symms National Recreational Trails Act of 1991.

SO$_2$
Sulfur Dioxide.

SOC
See Schedule of Compliance.

SOCs
See Synthetic Organic Chemicals.

Soft Detergents
Cleaning agents that break down in nature.

Soft Stories
Stories in which the lateral stiffness is less than 70% of the stiffness of the story above.

Soft Water
Any water that is not hard (i.e., does not contain a significant amount of dissolved minerals such as salts containing calcium or magnesium).

Software
1) A set of computer applications, programs, procedures, and associated documentation concerned with the operation of a data processing system (e.g., compilers, library routines, manuals, and circuit diagrams). 2) Any of the written programs, flow charts, etc., that are used to support the operation of computer equipment.

Soil
All vegetation, soils, and other ground media, including, but not limited to, sand, gravel, grass, and oyster shells. It does not include concrete and asphalt.

Soil Adsorption Field
A subsurface area containing a trench or bed with clean stones and a system of distribution piping through which treated sewage may seep into the surrounding soil for further treatment and disposal.

Soil and Water Conservation Practices (WPFPA)
Measures to conserve and develop the soil, water, woodland, wildlife, energy, and recreation resources of and enhance the water quality of lands within an area included in plans for works of improvement. Including, but not limited to, acquiring perpetual wetland or floodplain conservation easements to perpetuate, restore, and enhance the natural capability of wetlands and floodplains to retain excessive floodwaters, improve water quality and quantity, and provide habitat for fish and wildlife.

Soil Column
An insitu volume of soil down through which liquid wastes percolate from ponds, cribs, seepage basins, or trenches.

Soil Conditioner
An organic material like humus or compost that helps soil absorb water, build a bacterial community, and distribute nutrients and minerals.

Soil Gas

Gaseous elements and compounds that occur in the small spaces between particles of the earth and soil. Such gases can move through or leave the soil or rock, depending on changes in pressure.

Soil Injection

The emplacement of pesticides by ordinary tillage practices within the plow layer of a soil.

Soil Loss Equation

An equation used to determine the amount of soil that will erode from a unit area over a year, under varying conditions.

Soil Mechanics

The application of the laws of solid and fluid mechanics to soils and similar granular materials as a basis for design, construction, and maintenance of stable foundations and earth structures.

Soil Resistivity

The measured potential difference between two points in a naturally occurring soil between which a known electric current is passed.

Soil Shear Strength

The maximum resistance of a soil to shearing stresses.

Soil-Structure Resonance

The coincidence of the natural period of a structure with a dominant frequency in the ground motion.

Solar Absorption

The transformation of radiant energy to a different form of energy by the interaction of matter, depending on temperature and wavelength, typically resulting in a rise in temperature.

Solar Cell

A device that converts solar radiation to a current of electricity.

Solar Constant

The average intensity of solar radiation striking the earth's atmosphere. Measured on a plane perpendicular to the path of the radiation. Its value is 1.36 kilowatts per square meter.

Solar Energy

Energy that has recently originated in the sun, including direct and indirect solar radiation and intermediate solar energy forms such as wind, sea thermal gradients, products of photosynthetic processes, organic wastes, and others.

Solar Furnace

An optical device with large mirrors that focuses the rays from the sun upon a small focal point to produce extremely high temperatures.

Solar Heating and Cooling

The use of solar energy to provide portions of the total heating (including hot water) and cooling needs of a building. The term includes cooling by means of nocturnal heat radiation, by evaporation, or by other methods of meeting peakload energy requirements at nonpeakload times, as may be required under performance criteria prescribed by the Secretary of Housing and Urban Development utilizing the services of the Director of the National Institute of Standards and Technology, and in consultation with the Secretary of Energy, and the Administrator of the National Aeronautics and Space Administration.

Solar Spectrum

The total distribution of electromagnetic radiation emitted from the sun, minus those wavelengths that are absorbed by the atmosphere.

Solder

A metallic compound used to seal the joints between pipes or other metal pieces. Until recently, most solder contained 50% lead.

Sole-Source Aquifer

1) An aquifer that is the sole or principal source of drinking water, as established under Section 1424(e) of the SDWA, and that if contaminated

would create a significant hazard to public health. 2) An aquifer that supplies 50% or more of the drinking water of an area.

Solid Angle

The ratio of the area on the surface of a sphere to the square of the radius of that sphere. It is expressed in steradians (sr).

Solid Waste

1) Wastes as defined in Section 261.2 of 40 CFR, including, but not limited to the following:

- *Municipal Wastes* — paper, metal, food, glass, yard wastes (grass clippings, tree trimmings, etc.), wood, plastics, cloth and rubber, and other inert material;

- *Agricultural Wastes* — animal wastes (manure), crop and orchard residues (straw, stubble, leaves, hulls, vines, tree limbs, etc.), food processing wastes (animal parts, bones, fruit and vegetable pulp, seeds, skins, peelings, etc.), forest waste products (sawdust, wood edgings, etc.);

- *Mineral and Fossil-Fuel Wastes* — copper, iron and steel, bituminous coal, phosphate rock, lead, zinc, aluminum, etc.

2) As defined by RCRA, includes garbage, refuse, sludge from a waste treatment plant, water supply treatment plant or air pollution control facility; and other discarded material including solid, liquid, semi-solid, or contained gaseous materials resulting from industrial, commercial, mining, agricultural activities, and from community activities, but does not include solids or dissolved materials in irrigation return flows or industrial discharges that are point sources subject to permits under the Federal Water Pollution Control Act, or special nuclear or byproduct material as defined by the Atomic Energy Act.

3) As defined by the Solid Waste Disposal Act means any garbage, refuse, sludge from a waste treatment plant, water supply treatment plant, or air pollution control facility and other discarded material, including solid, liquid, semisolid, or contained gaseous material resulting from industrial, commercial, mining, and agricultural operations, and from community activities, but does not include solid or dissolved material in domes-

tic sewage, or solid or dissolved materials in irrigation return flows or industrial discharges that are point sources subject to permits under Section 1342 of Title 33, or source, special nuclear, or byproduct material as defined by the Atomic Energy Act of 1954. As defined above, solid waste is a catchall term that includes municipal, nonhazardous industrial, and hazardous waste.

Solid Waste Derived Fuel

A fuel that is produced from solid waste that can be used as a primary or supplementary fuel in conjunction with or in place of fossil fuels. The solid-waste derived fuel can be in the form of raw (unprocessed) solid waste, shredded (or pulped) and classified solid waste, gas or oil derived from pyrolyzed solid waste, or gas derived from the biodegradation of solid waste.

Solid Waste Disposal

The final placement of refuse that is not salvaged or recycled.

Solid Waste Disposal Act (SWDA)

An Act that establishes objectives to promote the protection of health and the environment and to conserve valuable material and energy resources by comprehensive and conscientious management of solid wastes. The Act promulgates guidelines for solid waste collection, transport, separation, recovery, and disposal practices and systems; and establishes the following: a) technical and financial assistance to state and local governments for the development of solid waste management plans; b) training grants; c) prohibitions on open dumping on public and private lands, and converting existing open dumps; d) quality control in hazardous waste management practices; e) requirements for minimizing the generation of hazardous waste at the sources; and f) methods of promoting process substitution, materials recovery, recycling, and reuse.

SWDA requires a cooperative effort among federal, state, and local governments in developing and implementing public waste management plans, projects, and programs. The original Act of 1965 provided for a national research and development program into improved methods of disposal, and for a program of technical and financial assistance to state and local governments.

Solid Waste Incineration Unit

A distinct operating unit of any facility that combusts any solid waste material from commercial or industrial establishments or the general public (including single and multiple residences, hotels, and motels). Such term does not include incinerators or other units required to have a permit under Section 3005 of the Solid Waste Disposal Act (42 USC 6925). The term "solid waste incineration unit" does not include the following:

- materials recovery facilities (including primary or secondary smelters) that combust waste for the primary purpose of recovering metals;

- qualifying small power production facilities, as defined in Section 796(17)(C) of Title 16, or qualifying cogeneration facilities, as defined in Section 796(18)(B) of Title 16, that burn homogeneous waste (such as units that burn tires or used oil, but not including refuse-derived fuel) for the production of electric energy or in the case of qualifying cogeneration facilities that burn homogeneous waste for the production of electric energy and steam or forms of useful energy (such as heat) that are used for industrial or commercial heating/cooling purposes; or

- air curtain incinerators provided that such incinerators only burn wood wastes, yard wastes and clean lumber and that such air curtain incinerators comply with opacity limitations to be established by the Administrator by rule.

Solid Waste Incineration Units, Performance Standards

A term for the guidelines promulgated pursuant to the CAA that require owners or operators of each solid waste incineration unit provide for compliance with emissions limitations, monitoring, training and certification (of solid waste incineration unit operators and high-capacity fossil fuel fired plant operators), obtaining/maintaining/reviewing permits, and conducting risk assessments. These guidelines contain provisions regarding the frequency of monitoring, test methods and procedures validated on solid waste incineration units, and the form and frequency of reports containing the results of monitoring and require that any monitoring reports or test results indicating an exceedance of any standard be reported separately and in a manner that facilitates review for purposes of enforcement actions.

Solid Waste Management (SWM)

1) The intentional, systematic control of the generation, storage, collection, treatment, transportation, separation, processing, recycling, and disposal of solid wastes. 2) Supervised handling of waste materials from their source through recovery processes to disposal.

Solid Waste Management Facility

1) Any resource recovery system or component thereof. 2) Any system, program, or facility for resource conservation. 3) Any facility for the collection, source separation, storage, transportation, transfer, processing, treatment or disposal of solid wastes, including hazardous wastes, whether such facility is associated with facilities generating such wastes or otherwise.

Solid Waste Management Unit (SWMU)

Any discernible waste management unit at a RCRA facility from which hazardous waste or constituents might migrate, irrespective of whether the unit was intended for the management of solid and/or hazardous waste. The definition includes the following: a) containers, tanks, surface impoundments, storage areas, waste piles, land treatment units, landfills, incinerators, underground injection wells, and other physical, chemical and biological units, including units defined as regulated units under RCRA; b) recycling units, wastewater treatment units, and other units that EPA has generally exempted from standards applicable to hazardous waste management units; and c) areas associated with production processes at facilities that have become contaminated by routine, systematic, and deliberate discharges of waste or constituents.

Solid Waste Planning

The planning or management activities associated with resource recovery and resource conservation measures.

Solidification and Stabilization

Removal of wastewater from a waste or changing it chemically to make the waste less permeable and susceptible to transport by water.

Solids

Materials that have a vertical flow of 2 inches (50 mm) or less within a 3-minute period, or a separation of 1 gram (1g) or less of liquid when determined in accordance with the procedures specified in ASTM D 4359-84 *Standard Test Method for Determining Whether a Material is a Liquid or Solid*, 1984 edition.

Solifluction

Freezing and thawing soil.

Solubility

The ability of one material to dissolve in or blend uniformly with another.

Soluble

Capable of being dissolved.

Solute Transport Model

A mathematical model used to predict the movement of solutes in an aquifer through time.

Solution

1) A mixture in which the components lose their identity and are uniformly dispersed. All solutions are composed of a solvent (water or other fluid) and the substance dissolved, called the solute. 2) A homogeneous mixture of two or more substances, usually liquid.

Solutions

Any homogeneous liquid mixture of two or more chemical compounds or elements that will undergo segregation under conditions normal to transportation.

Solvent

1) Any substance, most commonly water, but often an organic compound, that dissolves another substance. 2) A substance (usually liquid) capable of dissolving or dispersing one or more other substances.

Somatic Cells

All cells other than germ cells or gametes.

Somatic Radiation Effects

1) Radiation effects occurring in the exposed individual. 2) Effects of radiation limited to the exposed individual, as distinguished from genetic effects, that may also affect subsequent unexposed generations.

Sonar

A sonic device used primarily for the detection and location of underwater objects.

Sonic

Of or pertaining to sound or the speed of sound. *See* Speed of Sound.

SONMET

An acronym for Special Operations Naval Mobile Environment Team.

SOOE

See Study of Odors and Odorous Emissions.

Soot

Carbon dust formed by incomplete combustion.

SOP

An acronym for Standard Operating Power; Stratospheric Ozone Protection.

SOP

See Standard of Performance.

SOP or SOPs

See Standard Operating Procedure.

Sorption

1) Processes that remove solutes from the fluid phase and concentrate them on the solid phase of a medium; used to encompass absorption and adsorption. 2) The action of soaking up or attracting

substances; a process used in many pollution control systems.

Sound, Water
A body of water that is usually broad, elongate, and parallel to the shore between the mainland and one or more islands.

Source
1) Any buildings, structures, equipment, installations, or substance-emitting stationary activities that belong to the same industrial group, are located on one or more contiguous properties, are under the control of the same person (or persons under common control), and can potentially be the source of an accidental release. 2) Any building, structure, facility, or installation that emits or may emit any air pollutant. 3) Any source of an air pollutant except those emissions resulting directly from an internal combustion engine for transportation purposes or from a nonroad engine or nonroad vehicle as defined in Section 7550 of the CAA. 4) The originating location of toxic and/or hazardous chemicals or biological contaminants, wastes, or the point of emissions thereof.

Source Agency
Any agency that discloses records contained in a system of records to be used in a matching program, or any state or local government, or agency thereof, that discloses records to be used in a matching program.

Source Control Maintenance Measures
Measures intended to maintain the effectiveness of source control actions once such actions are operating and functioning properly, such as the maintenance of landfill caps and leachate collection systems.

Source Control Remedial Actions
Measures intended to contain hazardous substances or pollutants or contaminants inplace or eliminate potential contamination by transporting the hazardous substances, pollutants, or contaminants to a new location. Source control remedial actions may be appropriate if a) a substantial concentration or amount of hazardous substances, pollutants, or contaminants remain at or near the area where they are originally located; and b) inadequate barriers exist to retard migration of hazardous substances, pollutants, or contaminants into the environment. Source control remedial actions may not be appropriate if a) most hazardous substances, pollutants, or contaminants have migrated from the area where originally located; or b) if the lead agency determines that the hazardous substances, pollutants, or contaminants are adequately contained.

Source Materials
Materials that contain 0.05% or more of natural uranium, thorium, or any combination of the two.

Source Modification
Any physical change in, or change in the method of operation of, a stationary source that increases the amount of any air pollutant emitted by such source or that results in the emission of any air pollutant not previously emitted.

Source Reduction
1) The practice of reducing the amount of waste generated at the source of production. Examples include the redesign of processes to minimize waste volumes, the use of less hazardous or nonhazardous substitutes, and stack filtering and dewatering activities.

2) Any practice that: a) reduces the amount of any hazardous substance, pollutant, or contaminant entering any waste stream or otherwise released into the environment (including fugitive emissions) prior to recycling, treatment, or disposal; and b) reduces the hazards to public health and the environment associated with the release of such substances, pollutants, or contaminants. The term includes equipment or technology modifications, process or procedure modifications, reformulation or redesign of products, substitution of raw materials, and improvements in housekeeping, maintenance, training, or inventory control. Source reduction does not typically include any practice that alters the physical, chemical, or biological characteristics or the volume of a hazard-

ous substance, pollutant, or contaminant through a process or activity that itself is not integral to and necessary for the production of a product or the providing of a service.

3) Minimizing the generation, emission, or discharge of agricultural pollutants or wastes through the modification of agricultural production systems and practices. *See* Pollution Prevention Act (PPA).

Source Substitution
A condition that exists when two or more items possess such functional, physical, and/or chemical characteristics as to be equivalent in performance and durability, and are capable of being exchanged one for the other without alteration of the items themselves, or of adjoining items, except for adjustment, and without selection for fit and performance. *See* Compatibility.

Southeastern Power Administration
The Administration created by the Secretary of the Interior in 1950 to carry out functions assigned to the Secretary by the Flood Control Act of 1944, that pertain to the transmission and disposition of surplus electric power and energy generated at reservoir projects that are or may be under the control of the Department of the Army in the states of West Virginia, Virginia, North Carolina, South Carolina, Georgia, Florida, Alabama, Mississippi, Tennessee, and Kentucky.

Southwest
Geographic areas of Nevada, Utah, Colorado, New Mexico, Arizona, and Mexico.

Southwestern Power Administration
The Administration carries out the functions assigned to the Secretary by the Flood Control Act of 1944 in the states of Arkansas, Kansas, Louisiana, Missouri, Oklahoma, and Texas. It transmits and disposes of the electric power and energy generated at federal reservoir projects, supplemented by power purchased from public and private utilities in such a manner as to encourage the most widespread and economical use.

SOW
An acronym for Scope of Work or Statement of Work.

SOx
Sulfur oxides.

SP
An acronym for Suppression Pool.

SPA
An acronym for Shore Protection Act of 1988.

Space Frames
Three-dimensional structural systems without bearing walls composed of members interconnected so as to function as complete self-contained units with or without the aid of horizontal diaphragms or floor bracing systems.

Space Support Operations
Operations required to ensure that space control and support of terrestrial forces are maintained. They include activities such as launching and deploying space vehicles, maintaining and sustaining space vehicles while on orbit, and recovering space vehicles, if required.

Space Systems
All of the devices and organizations forming the space network. The network includes spacecraft, ground control stations, and associated terminals.

Space Weather
A term used to describe the environment and other natural phenomena occurring above 50 kilometers altitude.

Spacetrack
A global system of radar, optical and radiometric sensors linked to a computation and analysis center in the North American Air Defense Command combat operations center complex. The Spacetrack mission is detection, tracking, and cataloging of all manmade objects in orbit of the earth. It is the Air Force portion of the North

American Air Defense Command Space Detection and Tracking System. *See* Spadats; Spasur.

Spadats
A space detection and tracking system capable of detecting and tracking space vehicles from the earth, and reporting the orbital characteristics of these vehicles to a central control facility. *See* Spacetrack; Spasur.

Span of Detonation
That total period of time, resulting from a timer error, between the earliest and the latest possible atomic demolition munition detonation time.

- Early Time — The earliest possible time that an atomic demolition munition can detonate;
- Fire Time — That time the atomic demolition munition will detonate should the timers function precisely without error;
- Late Time — The latest possible time that an atomic demolition munition can detonate.

Sparger Assemblies
Direct flow of neutron poison and direct stream of heavy water into a bulk moderator to mix moderator and reduce temperature gradients, part of Safe Shutdown System (SSS) jets.

Sparrow
An air-to-air solid-propellant missile with nonnuclear warhead and electronic-controlled homing. Designated as AIM-7. The ship-launched surface-to-air version is designated as Sea Sparrow (RIM-7).

Spartan
A nuclear surface-to-air guided missile formerly deployed as part of the Safeguard ballistic missile defense weapon system. It is designed to intercept strategic ballistic reentry vehicles in the exoatmosphere.

Spasur
An operational space surveillance system with the mission to detect and determine the orbital elements of all manmade objects in orbit of the earth. The mission is accomplished by means of a continuous fan of continuous wave energy beamed vertically across the continental United States and an associated computational facility. It is the Navy portion of the North American Air Defense Command Space Detection and Tracking System. *See* Spacetrack; Spadats.

Spatulate
A species descriptor that means shaped like a spatular (broad, flat, flexible blade).

Spawning
The laying and fertilizing of fish eggs, often involving migration to stream headwaters.

SPC
An acronym for Suppression Pool Cooling.

SPCC
An acronym for Spill Prevention, Containment, and Countermeasures (CWA) or Spill Prevention, Control, and Countermeasure. *See* Spill Prevention Control and Countermeasures Plan; Remedial Action.

Special Access Program (SAP)
A sensitive program, approved in writing by a head of an agency with original top secret classification authority, that imposes need-to-know and access controls beyond those normally provided for access to confidential, secret, or top secret information. The level of controls is based on the criticality of the program and the assessed threat. The program may be an acquisition program, an intelligence program, or an operations and support program.

Special Aquatic Sites
Geographic areas, large or small, possessing special ecological characteristics of productivity, habitat, wildlife protection, or other important and easily disrupted ecological values. These areas are generally recognized as significantly influencing or positively contributing to the general overall environmental health or vitality of the entire ecosystem of a region. Refer to 40 CFR 230.10(a)(3).

Special Cargo

Cargo that requires special handling or protection, such as pyrotechnics, detonators, other hazardous materials/chemicals, and precision instruments.

Special Decompression Chamber

A chamber to provide greater comfort for employees when the total decompression time exceeds 75 minutes.

Special Form Radioactive Materials

1) Materials that are not dispersible because of their form (e.g., strongly encapsulated solids) and, therefore, present little or no possibility of contamination although they might present some direct radiation hazard (49 CFR Part 173.389 (g)). 2) Radioactive materials in either a massive solid form or totally encapsulated. 3) Radioactive materials that satisfy the following conditions: a) it is other than a single solid piece or is contained in a sealed capsule that can be opened only by destroying the capsule; b) the piece or capsule has at least one dimension not less than 5 millimeters; and c) satisfies the test requirements of 49 CFR Part 173.469. Special form encapsulations designed in accordance with the requirements of 49 CFR Part 173.389(g) in effect on June 30, 1983, and constructed prior to July 1, 1985, may continue to be used. Special form encapsulations designed or constructed after July 1, 1985, must meet the requirements of the CFR paragraph.

Special Hazards

Fuels, materials, components or situations that could increase the risks normally associated with accidents and could require special procedures, equipment, or extinguishing agents.

Special Management Areas (SMA)

Areas within the scenic area established pursuant to Section 544b of the Wild and Scenic Rivers Act (WSRA).

Special Moment Resisting Space Frame

A moment resisting space frame specially detailed to provide ductile behavior.

Special Nuclear Materials (SNM)

Plutonium, uranium-233, enriched uranium in uranium-233 or in uranium-235, or any material artificially enriched in any of the foregoing (but does not include source material) and any other material that, pursuant to the provisions of Section 51 of the Atomic Energy Act of 1954, as amended, has been determined to be special nuclear material.

Special Nuclear Materials Emergencies

Situations involving stolen, lost, or unauthorized possession of source material, special nuclear material, byproduct material of U.S. and/or foreign manufacture, improvised nuclear explosives, or radioactive dispersal devices or the threatened use of such items.

Special Nuclear Material Scrap

The various forms of special nuclear material generated during chemical and mechanical processing, other than recycle material and normal process intermediates, that are unsuitable for use in their present form, but all or some of which can be used after further processing.

Special Nuclear Material of Low Strategic Significance

This classification includes that material that is:

- less than a formula quantity of strategic special nuclear material, but more than 1,000 grams of uranium-235 (contained in uranium enriched to 20% or more in the U-235 isotope);

- more than 500 grams of uranium-233 or plutonium or in a combined quantity of more than 100 grams when computed by the equation, [grams minus (grams contained U-235) + 2(grams U-235 + grams plutonium)]; or

- 10,000 grams or more of uranium-235 (contained in uranium enriched to 10% or more but less than 20% in the U-235 isotope.

Special Operations Weather Team/Tactical Element (SOWT/TE)

A task-organized team of Air Force personnel organized, trained, and equipped to collect critical weather observations from data-sparse areas.

These teams are trained to operate independently in permissive or semipermissive environments, or as augmentation to other special operations elements in nonpermissive environments, in direct support of special operations.

Special Populations
Public groups located within the plume exposure emergency planning zone who, in the event the general public is instructed to evacuate, may require special transportation or protective provisions due to institutional confinement, lack of transportation, disability, or the need to staff certain industrial plants or public utilities.

Special Review
The regulatory process through which existing pesticides suspected of posing unreasonable risks to human health, nontarget organisms, or the environment are referred for review by EPA. The review requires an intensive risk/benefit analysis with opportunity for public comment. If the risk of any use of a pesticide is found to outweigh social and economic benefits, regulatory actions ranging from label revisions, to use-restrictions, to cancellation or suspended registration can be utilized.

Special Source of Groundwater
Those Class I groundwaters identified in accordance with the EPA's *Ground-Water Protection Strategy* (August 1984) that are a) within the controlled area encompassing a disposal system or are less than five kilometers beyond the controlled area; b) supplying drinking water for thousands of persons as of the date that the department chooses a location within that area for detailed characterization as a potential site for a disposal system; and c) irreplaceable in that no reasonable alternative source of drinking water is available to that population.

Special Treatment Areas
1) Specific areas that have been legally designated and described by the appropriate public agency or commission as wild and scenic rivers, scenic highways, and historical and archaeological sites (except old logging sites; abandoned rail-

road grades, mills or towns). 2) In ecological reserves, key habitat areas of endangered species of plants and animals; national, state, regional, county and municipal parks; and those areas within 200 feet, as measured along the surface of the ground from the established boundaries of such areas or the edge of the traveled surface of such highways.

The term is not intended to include any riding, hiking, or other recreational type trails.

Special Wastes
Nonhazardous solid wastes requiring handling other than that normally used for municipal solid waste.

Special Weapons
All weapons that are not normally issued to protective force personnel and include certain firearms, land mines, booby traps, and demolition changes.

Specially Designated Landfills
Landfills where complete long-term protection is provided for the quality of surface and subsurface waters from pesticides, pesticide containers, and pesticide-related wastes deposited therein, and against hazard to public health and the environment. Such sites should ideally be located and engineered to avoid direct hydraulic continuity with surface and subsurface waters, and any leachate or subsurface flow into the disposal area should be contained within the site unless treatment is provided. Monitoring wells are typically established and an ongoing sampling and analysis program conducted. The location of the disposal site should be permanently recorded in the appropriate local office of legal jurisdiction, and the facility must comply with Agency Guidelines for the Land Disposal of Solid Wastes as prescribed in 40 CFR Part 241.

Species
1) Any subspecies of fish or wildlife or plants, and any distinct population segment of any species of vertebrate fish or wildlife that interbreeds when mature. 2) A group of organisms with dis-

tinct characteristics that is capable of interbreeding and producing like offspring. 3) A basic taxonomic category. Excluded is any species of the class *Insecta* determined to constitute a pest, whose protection under the provisions of the Endangered Species Act would present an overwhelming and overriding risk to public health, safety, and welfare.

Species of Special Concern
Those species designated by the FWS, including, but not limited to: the bald eagle, golden eagle, great blue heron, great egret, northern goshawk, osprey, peregrine falcon, California condor, and great gray owl.

Specific Discharge
Apparent velocity, calculated by Darcy's Law, that represents the flow rate at which water would move through an aquifer if the aquifer were an open conduit. Also known as "groundwater discharge velocity."

Specific Gravity
1) The density (mass per unit volume) of a material divided by that of water at a standard temperature. 2) The ratio of the mass of a unit volume of a substance to the mass of the same volume of a standard substance (usually water) at a standard temperature.

Specific Ionization
The number of ion pairs per unit length of path of ionizing radiation in a medium (e.g., per centimeter at air or per micron of tissue).

Specific Performance
A remedy that the court will grant in certain cases, compelling the defendant to perform or carry out the terms of a valid, existing agreement or contract.

Specifications
Clear and accurate descriptions of the technical requirement for materials, products or services, that specifies the minimum requirement for quality and construction of materials and equipment necessary for an acceptable product. In general, specifications are in the form of written descriptions, drawings, prints, commercial designations, industry standards, and other descriptive references.

Specified Ports and Harbors
Those port and harbor areas on inland rivers, and land areas immediately adjacent to those waters, where the U.S. Coast Guard acts as predesignated "on-scene coordinator." Precise locations are determined by EPA/USCG regional agreements and identified in federal regional contingency plans.

Specimens
1) Materials derived from a test system for examination or analysis. 2) Any animal or plant, or any part, product, egg, or root, of any animal or plant.

Specs
See Specifications.

Spectrozonal Photography
A photographic technique whereby the natural spectral emissions of all objects are selectively filtered in order to image only those objects within a particular spectral band or zone and eliminate the unwanted backgrounds.

Speed of Sound
The speed at which sound travels in a given medium under specified conditions. The speed of sound at sea level in the International Standard Atmosphere is 1,108 feet/second, 658 knots, or 1,215 kilometers/hour. *See* Hypersonic; Sonic; Subsonic; Supersonic; Transonic.

Spent Fuel
Nuclear reactor fuel that has been used in a nuclear reactor and that contains large amounts of highly radioactive fission products. High-level radioactive waste.

Spent Materials
Any material that has been used and as a result of contamination can no longer serve the purpose for which it was produced without processing.

Spent Nuclear Fuel
Fuel that has been withdrawn from a nuclear reactor following irradiation, the constituent elements of which have not been separated by reprocessing.

Spike
A species descriptor that means a long flower cluster arranged along a stem.

Spiked Samples
Normal samples of material (gas, liquid, or solid) to which a known amount of some substance of interest is added. Spiked samples are used to check on the performance of a routine analysis or the recovery efficiency of an analytical method.

Spill
1) Intentional and unintentional spill, leak, and other uncontrolled discharge. 2) Any quantity of PCBs running off or about to run off the external surface of the equipment or other PCB source as well as the contamination resulting from those releases. The concentration of the spill is determined by the PCB concentration in the material spilled as opposed to the concentration of the material onto which the PCBs were spilled; if a spill of untested mineral oil occurs, the oil is presumed to contain PCBs greater than 50 ppm but less than 500 ppm. 3) The uncontrolled leaking of any environmentally hazardous substance onto land or water.

Spill Area
The area of soil on which visible traces of the spill can be observed plus a buffer zone of 1 foot beyond the visible traces. Any surface or object (e.g., concrete sidewalk or automobile) within the area of visible traces or on which visible traces of the spilled material can be observed is included in the spill area. This area represents the minimum assumed to be contaminated by PCBs in the absence of pre-cleanup sampling data; and it is the minimum area that must be cleaned.

Spill Boundaries
The actual area of contamination as determined by post-cleanup verification sampling or by pre-cleanup sampling to determine actual spill boundaries. EPA can require additional cleanup when necessary to decontaminate all areas within the spill boundaries to the level required in the PCB Spill Cleanup Policy.

Spill Control Technology Program
The program of testing and evaluation of technologies that may be utilized in responding to liquefied gaseous and other hazardous substance spills at the Liquefied Gaseous Fuels Spill Test Facility that threaten public health or the environment. In carrying out the program, a technology transfer program must be used that, at a minimum a) documents and archives spill control technology; b) investigates and analyzes significant hazardous spill incidents; c) develops and provides generic emergency action plans; d) documents and archives spill test results; e) develops emergency action plans to respond to spills; f) conducts training of spill response personnel; and g) establishes safety standards for personnel engaged in spill response activities.

Spill Prevention Control
Measures required under the Clean Water Act regulations (40 CFR 112.3) for both onshore and offshore facilities that have discharged or reasonably could be expected to discharge oil in harmful quantities.

Spill Prevention Control and Countermeasures Plan (SPCCP)
The plan covering the release of hazardous substances as defined in the Clean Water Act.

Spine
1) In zoology, the spinal column of a vertebrate. 2) In botany, a sharp-pointed, usually woody part extending from the stem of a plant.

Spiracle
A species descriptor that means a secondary gill slit positioned in front of the primary gill slits of fish.

Spirometry

The measurement of air volumes of the lungs (e.g., tidal volume, reserve volume).

SPMS

See Safety Performance Measurement System.

Spoil

1) The earth material that is removed in the formation of an excavation. 2) Dirt or rock that has been removed from its original location, destroying the composition of the soil in the process, as with strip-mining or dredging.

Spontaneously Combustible Materials

Solid substances (including sludges and pastes) that may undergo spontaneous heating or self-ignition under conditions normally incidental to transportation or that may, upon contact with the atmosphere, undergo an increase in temperature and ignite.

Spot Elevation

A point on a map or chart whose elevation is noted.

SPR

See Strategic Petroleum Reserve.

Sprawl

Unplanned development of open land.

Spring

A discrete place where groundwater flows naturally from rock or soil onto the land surface or into a surface-water body.

Spring Tide

The highest high and lowest low tides during the lunar month.

Sprint

A high acceleration, nuclear surface-to-air guided missile formerly deployed as part of the Safeguard ballistic missile defense weapon system. It is designed to intercept strategic ballistic reentry vehicles in the endoatmosphere.

SPS

See Safety Precedence Sequence.

Squamation

A species descriptor that refers to the arrangement of scales, as on a fish.

Squamous Cell Carcinoma

A malignant neoplasm derived from squamous epithelium.

Squib

A small pyrotechnic device that may be used to fire the igniter in a rocket. A squib is not the same as a detonator that explodes.

SQUIMP

An abbreviation for a computer code to analyze Probabilistic Risk Assessment (PRA) information; developed at the Idaho National Engineering Laboratory.

SR

An acronym for Savannah River Operations Office.

SRC

An acronym for Safety Review Committee.

SRIM

An acronym for Structural Reinforced Injection Molding.

SRO

See Senior Reactor Operator.

SRPA

An acronym for Small Reclamation Projects Act of 1956.

SRS

See Savannah River Site.

SRW

An acronym for Savannah River Water.

SS

An acronym for Shift Supervisor.

SSA

An acronym for the Social Security Act (42 USC).

SSDC

See System Safety Development Center.

SSFI

An acronym for Safety System Functional Inspection.

SSPS

An acronym for Solid State Protection System.

SSPSA

An acronym for Seabrook Station Probabilistic Safety Assessment.

SSR

An acronym for Secondary System Relief.

SSS

An acronym for Safe Shutdown System; Supplementary Safety System.

SST

An acronym for Single Shell Tanks.

Standby Power

A reserve power generator or supply with switching devices that will supply power to selected loads in the event of a normal power failure.

ST

An acronym for Sleeve Target.

STA

An acronym for Shift Technical Advisor; Small Tracts Act.

Staballoy

A term designating metal alloys made from high-density depleted uranium with other metals for use in kinetic energy penetrators for armor-piercing munitions. Several different metals such as titanium or molybdenum can be used for the purpose. The radioactivity of various staballoy metals is low and not considered to be a significant health hazard.

Stabilization

Conversion of the active organic matter in sludge into inert, harmless material.

Stabilization Ponds

See Lagoon.

Stable Air

A mass of air that is not moving normally, so that it holds rather than disperses pollutants.

Stable Costs

Costs incurred by a governmental, or quasi-governmental, entity as a result of implementing a mandated environmental (cost) program that, when reviewed over a 3-year period, has not fluctuated significantly.

Stack Effect

Used air, as in a chimney, that moves upward because it is warmer than the surrounding atmosphere.

Stack Gas

See Flue Gases.

Stack-Gas Desulfurization

Treating of stack gases to remove sulfur compounds.

Stacks

1) Chimneys or smokestacks; vertical pipes that discharge used air. 2) Points in a source designed to emit solids, liquids, or gases into the air, including a pipe or duct, but not including flares.

Stage

A directive to a field sampling team to go to a specific location and wait without sampling until further instructions are received.

Staging Area

In an incident command system (ICS), that location where incident personnel and equipment are assigned on an immediately available status.

Staging Bays

Bays within an operating building used to stage explosives in excess of a 4-hour supply. This practice is permissible as long as the bays are designed to provide Class II level of protection.

Stagnation

Lack of motion in a mass of air or water, that tends to hold pollutants.

Stamen

The pollen producing reproductive organ (male) of a flower, usually consisting of a filament and an anther.

Staminate

A species descriptor that means bearing stamens but lacking pistils.

Standard

1) An exact value, a physical entity, or an abstract concept, established and defined by authority, custom, or common consent to serve as a reference, model, or rule in measuring quantities or qualities, establishing practices or procedures, or evaluating results. 2) A fixed quantity or quality.

Standard Deviation

The square root of the average of the squares of the deviations from the mean.

Standard Industrial Classification (SIC)

The system of classification for business establishments set forth in the *Standard Industrial Classification Manual* (1972), Executive Office of the President, Office of Management and Budget, Washington, DC.

Standard Job Procedures

Tools for teaching the most systematic way to do a critical job consistently with maximum efficiency. *See* Proper Job Analysis.

Standard Metropolitan Statistical Area (SMSA)

A designation that applies to counties with at least one central city of 50,000 or more residents and any contiguous jurisdictions that are socially or economically integrated within the central city. The latest census lists the New York area as first, with a 1990 population of about 18.09 million people; the Los Angeles area as second, with a 1990 population of about 14.5 million. The 1990 combined population of these top two SMSA's, was greater than the total population of the next six SMSA's, combined. The following table represents the thirty largest SMSA's, listed by their principal central city:

30 LARGEST SMSA's*	
1) New York, NY	16) Minneapolis, MN
2) Los Angeles, CA	17) St. Louis, MO
3) Chicago, IL	18) Baltimore, MD
4) San Francisco, CA	19) Pittsburgh, PA
5) Philadelphia, PA	20) Phoenix, AZ
6) Detroit, MI	21) Tampa, FL
7) Boston, MA	22) Denver, CO
8) Washington D.C.	23) Cincinnati, OH
9) Dallas, TX	24) Milwaukee, WI
10) Houston, TX	25) Kansas City, MO
11) Miami, FL	26) Sacramento, CA
12) Atlanta, GA	27) Portland, OR
13) Cleveland, OH	28) Norfolk, VA
14) Seattle, WA	29) Columbus, OH
15) San Diego, CA	30) San Antonio, TX

*Source - The World Almanac and Book of Facts, 1993.

Standard of Performance (SOP)

1) As defined by the CAA, means a standard for emissions of air pollutants that reflects the degree of emission limitation achievable through the application of the best system of emission reduction that (taking into account the cost of achieving such reduction and any nonair quality health and environmental impact and energy requirements) the Administrator determines has been adequately demonstrated. 2) As defined by the USC, a requirement of continuous emission reduction, in-

cluding any requirement relating to the operation or maintenance of a source to ensure continuous emission reduction. 3) Any restriction established by the Administrator on quantities; rates; concentrations of chemical, physical, biological, and other constituents, that are or may be discharged from new sources into navigable waters, the waters of the contiguous zone, or the ocean.

Standard Operating Procedure (SOP)

1) A set of instructions covering those features of operations that lend themselves to a definite or standardized procedure without loss of effectiveness. The procedure is typically applicable in all instances unless ordered otherwise. 2) Formal written procedures officially adopted by the plant owner/operator and available on a routine basis to those persons responsible for carrying out the procedures. Also known as Standard Operating Procedures (SOPs).

Standard Parallel

A parallel on a map or chart along which the scale is as stated for that map or chart.

Standard Temperature

A temperature of 20°C (69°F).

Standard Wipe Test

For spills of high-concentration PCBs on solid surfaces, a cleanup to numerical surface standards and sampling by a standard wipe test to verify that the numerical standards have been met. This definition constitutes the minimum requirements for an appropriate wipe testing protocol. A standard-size template is used to delineate the area of cleanup; the wiping medium is a gauze pad or glass wool of known size that has been saturated with hexane. It is important that the wipe be performed very quickly after the hexane is exposed to air. EPA strongly recommends that the gauze (or glass wool) be prepared with hexane in the laboratory and that the wiping medium be stored in sealed glass vials until it is used for the wipe test. Further, EPA requires the collection and testing of field blanks and replicates.

Standardization

1) The process by which the Department of Defense achieves the closest practicable cooperation among the services and Defense agencies for the most efficient use of research, development, and production resources, and agrees to adopt, on the broadest possible basis, the use of a) common or compatible operational, administrative, and logistic procedures; b) common or compatible technical procedures and criteria; c) common, compatible, or interchangeable supplies, components, weapons, or equipment; and d) common or compatible tactical doctrine with corresponding organizational compatibility. 2) Formal methods officially adopted by an organization for use on a routine basis to carrying out work processes and procedures.

Standardized Data Reports

Forms used by environmental planners to economize the time and effort required to collect routine or repetitive data. Includes preorganized, preprinted data sheets and chapters; identification of the type of environmental research to be conducted and type of information to be collected; and provides blank spaces to input that data either manually or electronically. Primarily used to identify and tabulate routine information onsite conditions, facility use and capacity, applicable codes and compliance standards, status of permits, etc.

Standardized Mortality Ratio

The number of deaths, either total or cause-specific, in a given group expressed as a percentage of the number of deaths that could have been expected if the group has the same age and sex specific rates as the general population. Used in epidemiologic studies to adjust mortality rates to a common standard so that comparisons can be made among groups.

Standards

1) Prescriptive norms that govern action and actual limits on the amount of pollutants or emissions produced. EPA, under most of its responsibilities, establishes minimum standards. States are allowed to be more stringent. 2) Physi-

cal references used as a basis for comparison or calibration. 3) Concepts that have been established by authority, custom, or agreement to serve as a model or rule in the measurement of quality or the establishment of a practice or procedure.

Standards Information Management System

The system that provides access to two standards databases: 1) a set of general industrial standards developed by Argonne National Laboratory (ANL), and 2) a set of safety standards developed by Reynolds Electric and Engineering Company at the Nevada Test Site.

Standards-Developing Groups

Committees, subcommittees, associations, boards or other principal subdivisions of voluntary standards bodies, established for the purpose of developing, revising, or reviewing standards, and that are bound by the procedures of those bodies.

Standby

The condition when a reactor facility is neither operable nor declared excess, and documentary authorization exists to maintain the reactor for possible future operation.

Stanford Linear Accelerator Center (SLAC)

The DOE Research and Development and Field Facility that carries out experimental and theoretical research in high energy physics and developmental work in new techniques for particle acceleration and experimental instrumentation. The Center's main research instrument is a 2-mile-long linear electron accelerator, the largest in the world.

Startup

1) The setting in operation of a source for any purpose. 2) The setting in operation of a stationary source for any purpose. 3) Initial drive power application to an automated or computerized system after one of the following events, manufacture or modification, installation or reinstallation, programming or program editing, maintenance or repair. 2) The application of drive power to a robot/robotic system.

Starter Cartridges

According to the Hazardous Materials Transportation Act (HMTA), this classification includes Class B explosives that consist of plastic and/or rubber cases, each containing a pressed cylindrical block of propellant explosive and having in the top of the case a small compartment that encloses an electrical squib, small amounts of black powder, and smokeless powder, that constitutes an igniter. The starter cartridge is used to activate a mechanical starter for jet engines.

State

Any one of the United States, the District of Columbia, the Commonwealth of Puerto Rico, the U.S. Virgin Islands, Guam, American Samoa, and the Commonwealth of the Northern Mariana Islands.

State Agency Rule

Any state agency guideline, criterion, bulletin, manual, instruction, order, standard of general application, or other rule that has not been adopted as a regulation and filed with the Secretary of State pursuant to the Administrative Procedure Act, Chapter 3.5 of Title 2, Division 3, Part 1 of the Government Code.

State Air Quality Agency

A state agency designated to enforce and implement federal and state air quality laws. Usually located in the state's department of health.

State Air Quality Implementation Responsibility

Pursuant to the CAA, it is each state's primary responsibility for assuring air quality within the entire geographic area comprising such state by submitting an implementation plan for such state that will specify the manner in which national primary and secondary ambient air quality standards will be achieved and maintained within each air quality control region in such state. The governor of each state is required to submit to the Administrator a list of all areas (or portions thereof) in the state that are designated as a) nonattainment — any area that does not meet (or that contributes to ambient air quality in a nearby area that does not meet) the national primary or secondary ambient air quality standard for the pollutant; b) attainment — any area (other than an exempted area) that meets the national primary or secondary ambient air quality standard for the pollutant; or c) unclassifiable — any area that cannot be classified on the basis of available information as meeting or not meeting the national primary or secondary ambient air quality standard for the pollutant.

State Aquatic Nuisance Species Management Plans

A state-prepared a) comprehensive management plan submitted to the Aquatic Nuisance Species Task Force that identifies those areas or activities within a state for which technical and financial assistance is needed to eliminate or reduce the environmental, public health, and safety risks associated with aquatic nuisance species, particularly the zebra mussel; and/or b) a public facility management plan that is limited solely to identifying those public facilities within the state for which technical and financial assistance is needed to reduce infestations of zebra mussels. Each plan should identify the management practices and measures that will be undertaken to reduce infestations of aquatic nuisance species; describe state and local programs for environmentally sound prevention and control of the target aquatic nuisance species; identify federal activities that may be needed for environmentally sound prevention and control of aquatic nuisance species and a description of the manner in which those activities should be coordinated with state and local government activities; and present a schedule of implementing the plan, including a schedule objectives.

State Area Redesignation

The authority of states to redesignate areas as it deems appropriate to Class I or II areas. Areas that may be redesignated as Class I or II include a) an area that exceeds 10,000 acres in size and is a national monument, a national primitive area, a national preserve, a national recreation area, a national wild and scenic river, a national wildlife refuge, or a national lakeshore or seashore; and b)

a national park or national wilderness area established after August 7, 1977, that exceeds 10,000 acres in size. Area redesignations must be specifically approved by the governor of the state; cannot cause, or contribute to, concentrations of any air pollutant that exceed any maximum allowable increase or maximum allowable concentration permitted under the classification of any other area; and must comply with the provisions of the CAA. Prior to redesignation of any area, a public, and federal agency, notice providing a description and analysis of the health, environmental, economic, social, and energy effects of the proposed redesignation must be prepared and made available.

State Coordinating Officers

Officials designated by the governor of the affected state to work with the cognizant federal agency official and senior FEMA officials in coordinating the response effort of federal, state, local, volunteer, and private agencies.

State Coordination

The state-federal process by which a host state and, as appropriate, adjacent states are provided the opportunity to review and comment on an Environmental Assessment before approval.

State Emergency Response Commission (SERC)

The commission appointed by each state governor according to the requirements of SARA Title III, to oversee the administration of EPCRA at the state level. The SERC designates and appoints members to local emergency planning committees (LEPCs), designates emergency planning districts, supervises and coordinates LEPC's, and reviews emergency response plans for cities and counties.

State Energy Agency

The state agency responsible for developing state energy conservation plans, or, if no such agency exists, a state agency designated by the governor of such state to prepare and submit a state plan.

State/EPA Agreements

Agreements between the Regional Administrator and the state that coordinate EPA and state activities, responsibilities, and programs.

State Fish and Game Department

Any department or division of department of another name, or commission, or official or officials, of a state empowered under its laws to exercise the functions ordinarily exercised by a state fish and game department.

State Hazardous Wastes

Any waste defined as hazardous by a state. Pursuant to federal regulations, federal agencies are subject to and must comply with state requirements respective to solid and hazardous waste management.

State Historic Preservation Officer (SHPO)

An official within each state appointed by the governor to administer the State Historic Preservation Program. In addition, the SHPO has specific responsibilities relating to federal undertakings that affect cultural resources within the state.

State Historic Preservation Review Board (SHPRB)

A board, council, commission, or other similar collegial body established as provided in Section 470a(b)(1)(B) of the NHPA. The members of which are appointed by the State Historic Preservation Officer and a majority of the members are professionals qualified in the following and related disciplines: history, prehistoric and historic archaeology, architectural history, and architecture, and; that has the authority to a) review National Register nominations and appeals from nominations; b) review appropriate documentation submitted in conjunction with the Historic Preservation Fund; c) provide general advice and guidance to the State Historic Preservation Officer; and c) perform such other duties as may be appropriate.

State Implementation Plan (SIP)

An air quality maintenance and mitigation plan required under the Clean Air Act, to be developed by each state. Air quality programs and timetables for compliance with the act must be set forth in the SIPs (plans) to gain compliance with national primary and secondary ambient air quality standards.

SIPs provide for implementation, maintenance, and enforcement of primary standards in each air quality control region (or portion thereof) within a state. Each SIP plan must:

- include enforceable emission limitations and other control measures, means, or techniques (including economic incentives such as fees, marketable permits, and auctions of emissions rights), as well as schedules and timetables for compliance, as may be necessary or appropriate to meet the applicable requirements of the CAA;

- provide for establishment and operation of appropriate devices, methods, systems, and procedures necessary to monitor, compile, and analyze data on ambient air quality;

- include a program to provide for the enforcement of measures and regulation of the modification and construction of stationary sources within the areas covered by the plan as necessary to ensure that national ambient air quality standards are achieved, including a permit program;

- contain adequate provisions a) prohibiting, any source or other type of emissions activity within the state from emitting any air pollutant in amounts that will contribute significantly to nonattainment in, or interfere with maintenance by, any other state with respect to any such national primary or secondary ambient air quality standard, or interfere with measures required to be included in the applicable implementation plan for any other state to prevent significant deterioration of air quality or to protect visibility; and b) insuring compliance with the applicable requirements of Sections 7426 and 7415 of the CAA (relating to interstate and international pollution abatement);

- provide a) necessary assurances that the state (or, except where the Administrator deems inappropriate, the general purpose local government or governments, or a regional agency designated by the state or general purpose local governments for such purpose) will have adequate personnel, funding, and authority under state (and, as appropriate, local) law to carry out such implementation plan (and is not prohibited by any provision of federal or state law from carrying out such implementation plan or portion thereof); b) include requirements that the state comply with the requirements respecting state boards under Section 7428 of the CAA; and c) include necessary assurances that, where the state has relied on a local or regional government, agency, or instrumentality for the implementation of any plan provision, the state has responsibility for ensuring adequate implementation of such plan provision;

- require, as may be prescribed by the Administrator, a) the installation, maintenance, and replacement of equipment, and the implementation of other necessary steps, by owners or operators of stationary sources to monitor emissions from such sources; b) periodic reports on the nature and amounts of emissions and emissions-related data from such sources; and c) correlation of such reports by the state agency with any emission limitations or standards established pursuant to the CAA, that reports shall be available at reasonable times for public inspection;

- provide for authority comparable to that in Section 7603 of the CAA and adequate contingency plans to implement such authority;

- provide for revision of such plan from time to time as may be necessary to take account of revisions of such national primary or secondary ambient air quality standard or the availability of improved or more expeditious methods of attaining such standards;

- provide for the performance of air quality modeling; including requiring the owner/operator of each major stationary source to pay a fee sufficient to cover the reasonable costs of reviewing and acting upon any application for permit, and if the owner/operator receives a permit for such source, the reasonable costs of implementing and enforcing the terms and conditions of any such permit; and provide for consultation and participation by local political subdivisions affected by the plan.

State Mining Program
A program established by a state to regulate surface coal mining and reclamation operations, on lands within such state in accord with the require-

ments of the Surface Mining Control and Reclamation Act and regulations issued by the Secretary pursuant to this Act.

State Notification
The process by which a host state, as appropriate, and adjacent states are informed of an initial determination to prepare an Environmental Assessment or Environmental Impact Statement.

State Primary Drinking Water Regulation
A drinking water regulation of a state that is comparable to a national primary drinking water regulation.

State Regulation
A law, regulation, or other requirement of a state or its political subdivisions.

State Review of SIPs
Each state's review the provisions of its implementation plan that relate to major fuel burning sources and to determine, a) the extent to which compliance with requirements of such plan is dependent upon the use by major fuel burning stationary sources of petroleum products or natural gas; b) the extent to which such plan may reasonably be anticipated to be inadequate to meet the requirements of the CAA in such state on a reliable and long-term basis by reason of its dependence upon the use of such fuels; and c) the extent to which compliance with the requirements of such plan is dependent upon use of coal or coal derivatives that is not locally or regionally available.

State Routing Agencies
Entities authorized to use the state legal process to impose routing requirements, enforceable by state agencies, on carriers of radioactive materials without regard to intrastate jurisdictional boundaries. This term also includes Native American Indian tribal authorities that have police powers to regulate and enforce highway routing requirements within their lands.

State School Facilities Agency

An existing agency that is broadly representative of public institutions of higher education, non-profit institutions of higher education, public elementary and secondary schools, nonprofit elementary and secondary schools, public vocational education institutions, and nonprofit vocational education institutions.

State Wellhead Protection Program (SWPP)

The program to protect wellhead protection areas within a state's jurisdiction from contaminants that may have an adverse effects on the health and safety of the general public (SDWA, Subsection 142g(a)).

State-Designated Routes

Preferred routes selected in accordance with U.S. DOT Guidelines for Selecting Preferred Highway Routes for Highway Route Controlled Quantities of Radioactive Materials or an equivalent routing analysis that adequately considers overall risk to the public.

Statement of Negative Impact

A written statement by a federal agency that a proposed project will not have any adverse environmental impacts. *See* Negative Declaration.

Static Air Temperature

The temperature at a point at rest relative to the ambient air.

Static Water Level

The level of water in a well that is not being affected by withdrawal of groundwater.

Stationary Source

1) Fixed, nonmoving producers of pollution, mainly power plants and other facilities using industrial combustion processes. 2) Any buildings, structures, facilities, or installations that emit or may emit an air pollution for which a national standard is in effect.

Statistical Analysis

The use of numerical data and mathematical procedures to measure, differentiate, and correlate variables and variable data. Usually results in spreadsheets, tables, figures, graphs, charts, and other visuals representing the numerical data.

Statistical Data

Aggregate information pertaining to sites or facilities that is in such a form that it is not traceable back to the site or facility.

Statistical Export and Tabulation System (SETS)

The name of a computer code designed to simplify Boolean expressions, and assist in the development of CD-ROM applications.

Statistical Extrapolation

The methodology whereby an unknown value can be estimated by projecting the results of a probability sample to the universe from which the sample was drawn with a calculated precision (margin of error).

Statistical Record

A record in a system of records maintained for statistical research or reporting purposes only and not used in whole or in part in making any determination about an identifiable individual.

Statistically Significant Effect

In statistical analysis of data, a health effect that exhibits differences between a study population and a control group that are unlikely to have arisen by chance alone.

Statoconia

One of the calcareous granules found in the statocyst of certain animals.

Statocysts

1) In botany, a cell containing calcium carbonate in a fluid medium. 2) In zoology, a sensory vesicle containing calcium carbonate and that functions on the perception of the position of the body in space.

Statolith
A small, movable concentration of calcium carbonate.

Status Epilepticus
Severe seizures in which recovery does not occur between major episodes.

STC
An acronym for Single Strip Containers.

Steam Generator
The heat exchanger used in some reactor designs to transfer heat from the primary (reactor coolant) system to the secondary (steam) system. This design permits heat exchange with little or no contamination of the secondary system equipment.

Steam Power Plant
A plant in which the primary turbines connected to the generators are driven by steam.

Steep Slope
According to the Surface Mining Control and Reclamation Act (SMRCA), any slope above 20° or such lesser slope as may be defined by the regulatory authority after consideration of soil, climate, and other characteristics of a region or state.

STEL
See Short-Term Exposure Limit.

Stellate
A species descriptor that means shaped like a star; radiating from a center.

Stereographic Coverage
Photographic coverage with overlapping air photographs to provide a three-dimensional presentation of the picture; 60% overlap is considered normal and 53% is generally regarded as the minimum.

Sterilization
1) In pest control, the use of radiation and chemicals to damage body cells needed for reproduc-
tion. 2) The destruction of all living organisms in water or on the surface of various materials. In contrast, disinfection is the destruction of most living organisms in water or on surfaces.

STGWG
An acronym for State and Tribal Government Working Group.

STI
An acronym for Surveillance Test Internal.

Stiffness
The relationship of load to deformation for a particular material.

Stimulus-Mediation Response
The normal way, other than reflex arc response, that people respond to a stimulus. They receive a stimulus and mediate between the input and previous experience before responding.

Stimulus-Response
The type of response expected from most hardware wherein the response is consistently the same for a given input. Normally, people do not respond in this manner other than with a reflex arc response.

Stipulation
An agreement between some or all of the parties to a proceeding on the resolution of any issue of law or fact material to the proceeding.

Stipules
A species descriptor that means one of the usually small paired leaflike appendages at the base of a leaf or leafstalk.

STM
An acronym for Stack Tritium Monitor.

Stochastic Effects
1) Biological effects, the probability, rather than the severity, of which is a function of the magnitude of the radiation dose without threshold (i.e., stochastic effects are random in nature). Nonsto-

chastic effects are biological effects, the severity of which, in affected individuals, varies with the magnitude of the dose above a threshold value. 2) Radiation effects, the severity of which is independent of dose and the probability of which is assumed to be proportional to the dose without threshold at the low doses of interest in radiation protection.

Stoma
A species descriptor that means a minute opening of a leaf or stem through which gases and water vapor pass.

Stone
Rock fragments larger than 25.4 centimeters (10 inches) but less than 60.4 centimeters (24 inches).

Storage
1) Temporary holding of waste pending treatment or disposal.
2) Retention of high-level radioactive waste, spent nuclear fuel, or transuranic waste with the intent to recover such waste or fuel for subsequent use, processing, or disposal.
3) The containment of hazardous waste, either on a temporary basis or for a period of years, in such a manner as not to constitute disposal of such hazardous waste.
4) The retention of data in any form, usually for the purpose of orderly retrieval and documentation.
5) A device consisting of electronic, electrostatic, electrical, hardware, or other elements into which data may be entered, and from which data may be obtained as desired.

Storage methods include containers, tanks, waste piles, and surface impoundments. *See* Ammunition and Toxic Material Open Space; Bin Storage; Bulk Storage; Igloo Space; Large-Lot Storage; Medium-Lot Storage; Open Improved Storage Space; Open Unimproved Wet Space; Small-Lot Storage.

Storage Area Compartments
An area or series of areas that contain storage enclosures.

Storage Coefficient
The volume of water an aquifer releases from or takes into storage per unit surface (or subsurface) area per unit change in head. *See* Storativity.

Storage for Disposal
The temporary storage of PCBs that have been designated for disposal.

Storage Life
The length of time for which an item of supply including explosives, given specific storage conditions, may be expected to remain serviceable and safe. *See* Shelf Life.

Storativity (s)
A dimensionless term representing the volume of water an aquifer releases from or takes into storage per unit surface area of the aquifer per unit change in head. It is equal to the product of specific storage and aquifer thickness. In an unconfined aquifer, the storativity is equivalent to the specific yield. *See* Storage Coefficient.

STORET
Computer database acronym for storage and retrieval of water-related data.

Stories
The spaces between levels in buildings or storage areas.

Storm Sewer
A system of pipes (separate from sanitary sewers) that carries only water runoff from building and land surfaces.

Stormwater
Surface water runoff resulting from precipitation.

Stormwater Collection Systems
Piping, pumps, conduits, and any other equipment necessary to collect and transport the flow of surface water runoff resulting from precipitation, or from domestic, commercial, or industrial wastewater, to and from retention areas or any areas where treatment is designated to occur. The col-

lection of stormwater and wastewater does not include treatment except where incidental to conveyance.

Story Drift Ratio
The story drift divided by the story height.

Story Drift
The displacement of one level relative to the level above or below.

Story Shear
The summation of design lateral forces above the story under consideration.

Stowage
The act of placing hazardous materials on board a vessel.

Stowage Plan
A completed stowage diagram showing what material has been loaded and its stowage location in each hold, between-deck compartment, or other space in a ship, including deck space. Each port of discharge is indicated by colors or other appropriate means. Deck and between-deck cargo normally is shown in perspective, while cargo stowed in the lower hold is shown in profile, except that vehicles usually are shown in perspective regardless of stowage.

Stowage Factor
The number that expresses the space, in cubic feet, occupied by a long ton of any commodity as prepared for shipment, including all crating or packaging.

Strain
The elastic deformation of a material as a result of stress.

Strapping
1) An operation by which supply containers, such as cartons or boxes, are reinforced by bands, metal straps, or wire placed at specified intervals around them, drawn taut, and then sealed or clamped by a machine. 2) Measurement of stor-

age tanks and calculation of volume to provide tables for conversion of depth of product in linear units of measurement to volume of contents.

Strata
Single sedimentary beds or layers, regardless of thickness, that consist of generally the same kind of rock material.

Strategic Air Transport Operations
The carriage of passengers and cargo between hazardous incidents by means of scheduled service, special flight, air logistic support, or aeromedical evacuation.

Strategic Map
A medium scale map, or smaller, used for planning of operations, including the movement, concentration, and supply of response teams. *See* Map.

Strategic Material, Critical
A material required for essential uses in an emergency, the procurement of which in adequate quantity, quality, or time, is sufficiently uncertain, for any reason, to require prior provision of the supply thereof.

Strategic Petroleum Reserve (SPR)
The SPR was created by the Energy Policy and Conservation Act in December 1975. The objective of the SPR program is to stockpile crude oil to reduce the vulnerability of the United States to a severe energy emergency involving a disruption in its petroleum supplies. The term includes the Industrial Petroleum Reserve, the Early Storage Reserve, and the Regional Petroleum Reserve.

Strategic Special Nuclear Materials
Uranium-235 (contained in uranium enriched to 20% or more in the U-235 isotope), uranium-233, or plutonium.

Strategy
The art and science of developing and using political, economic, psychological, and environmental resources as necessary, to afford the

maximum support to policies, in order to increase probabilities and favorable outcomes and to lessen the chances of project or policy defeat.

Stratification
Separating into layers.

Stratofortress
An all-weather, intercontinental, strategic heavy bomber powered by eight turbojet engines. It is capable of delivering nuclear and nonnuclear bombs, air-to-surface missiles, and decoys. Its range is extended by in-flight refueling. Designated as B-52.

Stratosphere
1) The portion of the atmosphere that is 10 to 25 miles above the earth's surface. 2) The layer of the atmosphere above the troposphere in which the change of temperature with height is relatively small. *See* Atmosphere.

Stream
A natural or regulated water flowing in any channel natural or artificial. Streams can be perennial, flowing continuously; intermittent or seasonal, flowing only at certain times of the year; and ephemeral, flowing only in direct response to precipitation.

Stream and Lake Protection Zone
1) A required strip of land on each side of perennial streams, lakes, and those portions of intermittent streams that support trout at any time of the year, and downstream therefrom; to protect existing water quality and fish and wildlife habitat. The width of the zone is determined by on-the-ground investigations, that consider, a) soil type and permeability; b) the type or types, stabilizing effect, and amount of vegetative cover; and c) the slope of the land within the zone and its effectiveness in preventing sediment from reaching streams or lakes.

2) A strip of soil and vegetation along both sides of a stream or around the circumference of a lake defined as follows: a) approximately 150 feet (45.72 meters), as measured along the surface of the ground, from the stream or lake transition line of any stream or lake in areas with an extremely high Estimated Erosion Potential; b) approximately 100 feet (30.48 meters), as measured along the surface of the ground, from the stream or lake transition line of any stream or lake in areas with high "estimated erosion potential"; and c) approximately 50 feet (15.24 meters), as measured along the surface of the ground, from the stream or lake transition line of any stream or lake in areas with a moderate or low "estimated erosion potential."

Strength
The usable capacity of a structure or its members to resist load within the deformation limits.

Stress
The internal force that resists change in size or shape, expressed in force per unit area.

Striae
A species descriptor that means having many lines.

Stridor
A harsh, high-pitched respiratory sound often heard in acute respiratory obstruction.

Strike Slip
One of the three main types of surface faulting; in a fault, the component of the movement or slip that is parallel to the strike or perpendicular to the dip of the fault. Horizontal displacement parallel to the strike.

Strip, Asbestos
To take off friable asbestos materials from any part of a facility.

Strip-Cropping
Growing crops in a systematic arrangement of strips or bands that serve as barriers to wind and water erosion.

Strip-Mining

A process that uses machines to scrape soil or rock away from mineral deposits just under the earth's surface.

Strippers

Any vessels in which residual vinyl chloride is removed from polyvinyl chloride resin, except bulk resin, in the slurry form by the use of heat and/or vacuum. In the case of bulk resin, strippers include any vessel that is used to remove residual vinyl chloride from polyvinyl chloride resin immediately following the polymerization stop in the plant process flow.

Strong Sensitizer

A substance that will cause on normal living tissue through an allergic or photodynamic process a hypersensitivity that becomes evident on reapplication of the same substance and that is designated as such.

Structural Adhesive

An adhesive used for transferring loads between adherents.

Structural Bond

A bond joining load-bearing components of an assembly.

Structural Collapse

The failure of a structural component as a direct result of loss of structural integrity of the facility being subjected to various loadings.

Structural Engineering

The application of specialized civil engineering knowledge and experience to the design and analysis of buildings (or other structures) that are constructed or rehabilitated to resist forces induced by vertical and horizontal loads of a static and dynamic nature. This specialized knowledge includes familiarity with scientific and mathematical principles, experimental research data and practical construction methods and processes. The design and analysis shall include consideration of stability, deflection, stiffness and other structural phenomena that affect the behavior of the building (or other structure).

Structural Members

Load-supporting members of a facility, such as beams and load supporting walls; or any nonload-supporting member, such as ceilings and nonload-supporting walls.

Structure-Activity Relationship

Relationships of biological activity or toxicity of a chemical to its chemical structure or substructure.

Structures

Any fixed real property improvement constructed on or in the land that is not a building or utility (e.g., bridges, towers, and tanks). Typically denotes something constructed or built.

Strut

A structural member designed to resist forces in either tension or compression.

Studies

1) Written observations and/or analyses in detail (of a phenomenon, development, or question) usually within a restricted area with a view to some action. 2) Any in vivo or in vitro experiments in which test substances are studied prospectively in a test system under conditions to determine or help predict their fate, toxicity, metabolism, or other characteristics in humans, or other animals and plants. The term does not include studies utilizing human subjects or clinical studies. The term does not include basic exploratory studies carried out to determine whether a test substance has any potential utility.

Study and Report Concerning Economic Approaches to Controlling Air Pollution

A study and assessment of economic measures for control of air pollution that could strengthen effectiveness of existing methods of controlling air pollution, provide incentives to abate air pollution greater than that required by Clean Air Act, and serve as primary incentive for controlling air pollution problems not addressed by Clean Air Act.

Study Directors

Individuals responsible for the overall conduct of a study.

Study of Odors and Odorous Emissions

A study directed by the Administrator of EPA on the effects on public health and welfare of odors and odorous emissions, source of such emissions, technology or other measures available for control of such emissions, costs of such technology or measures, and costs and benefits of alternative measures or strategies to abate such emissions.

Study of Substances Discharged from Exhausts of Motor Vehicles

The Surgeon General's study to determine the amounts and kinds of such substances that, from the standpoint of human health, it is safe for motor vehicles to discharge into the atmosphere under the various conditions under which such vehicles operate.

Study on Regional Air Quality

A study of air quality in various areas throughout the country including the Gulf Coast region, such study is to include the analysis of liquid and solid aerosols and other fine particulate matter and the contribution of such substances to visibility and public health problems in such areas. In preparing this study the Administrator of EPA uses environmental health experts from the National Institutes of Health and other outside agencies and/or organizations.

Subacute Dietary LC 50

A concentration of a substance, expressed as parts per million, in food that is lethal to 50% of the test population of animals under specified test conditions.

Subbase

A layer of granular material located beneath the base course of a highway pavement.

Subchronic Exposure

Exposure to a substance spanning approximately 10% of the lifetime of an organism.

Subcommittee on Federal Response

A subcommittee of the Federal Radiological Preparedness Coordinating Committee formed to develop and test the Federal Radiological Emergency Response Plan. Most agencies that would participate in the federal radiological emergency response are represented on this subcommittee.

Subcutaneous

A method of exposure where the substance is injected beneath the skin.

Subgenus

A taxonomical category between a genus and a species.

Subgravity

A condition in which the resultant ambient acceleration is between 0 and 1G.

Subject Matter Experts

Individuals qualified, or previously qualified, and experienced in performing a particular task.

Subkiloton Weapon

A nuclear weapon producing a yield below 1 kiloton. *See* Kiloton Weapon; Megaton Weapon.

Submerged Cultural Resources

Historic, and prehistoric remains beneath the waters (both salt and fresh). Such resources are fully subject to the standards and procedures outlined in environmental law.

Submergent Plant

A vascular or nonvascular hydrophyte, either rooted or nonrooted, that lies entirely beneath the water surface, except for flowering parts in some species.

Submitter of Confidential Information

Any person or entity who provides confidential commercial information to the government. The term includes, but is not limited to, corporations, state governments, and foreign governments.

Subobjective

A preliminary objective that is written to support a main objective.

Subphylum

A subdivision of phylum composed of closely related groups of animals, such as vertebrates.

Subrhomboidal

A species descriptor that means less than rhomboidal in shape (like a parallelogram with unequal adjacent sides).

Subsidence

The lowering of the natural land surface in response to earth movements; lowering of fluid pressure; removal of underlying supporting material by mining or solidification of solids, either artificially or from natural causes; compaction due to wetting (hydrocompaction); oxidation of organic matter in soils; or added load on the land surface.

Subsistence

1) The traditional uses of natural, personal, or family consumption; for the making and selling of handicraft articles out of the nonedible byproducts of fish and wildlife resources taken for personal or family use or consumption and for customary trade (36 CFR 13.4d). 2) In general, subsistence activities are allowed only in those national parks where they are specifically authorized by law or treaty. Collecting of natural materials (but not taking animals) may be permitted. In the Alaskan and Pacific units of the National Park System, subsistence is the significant economic and cultural dependence on the harvest of wild natural resources by local rural residents through traditional hunting, fishing, and gathering activities. In the Southwest and elsewhere, subsistence also can include mixed agricultural, pastoral, and wild resource harvest techniques. 3)

The use of endangered or threatened wildlife for food, clothing, shelter, heating, transportation, and other uses necessary to maintain the life of the taker of the wildlife, or those who depend upon the taker to provide them with such subsistence, and includes selling any edible portions of such wildlife in native villages and towns in Alaska for native consumption within native villages and towns.

Subslabs

The concrete slab below the waterproofing membrane in a double-slab configuration. Also known as a structural slab, base slab, mud slab, or wearing slab.

Subsonic

Of or pertaining to speeds less than the speed of sound. *See* Speed of Sound.

Subspecies

A subgroup that may in outward appearance and behavior appear to be identical to other members of the species but which possess characteristics that are biologically different.

Substantial Business Relationships

The extent of business relationships necessary under applicable state law to make a guarantee contract issued incident to that relationship valid and enforceable. Substantial business relations must arise from a pattern of recent or ongoing business transactions, in addition to the guarantee itself, such that a currently existing business relationship between the guarantor and the owner or operator is demonstrated to the satisfaction of the applicable EPA Regional Administrator.

Substantial Contribution

1) A presentation made by an individual(s) that substantially assists an agency in the making of its order or decision because the order or decision had adopted in whole or in part one or more factual environmental contentions, legal contentions, or specific environmental policy or procedural recommendations presented by the individual(s). 2) A contribution clearly outside normally accepted or experienced bounds.

Substantial Drift
The quantity of pesticide outside of the area treated is greater than that which would have resulted had the applicator used due care.

Substantial Injury
A real and immediate physical injury or a resulting adverse physical condition of a substantial nature to one or more persons.

Substrate
The composition of a stream bed; the surface on which a plant grows or is attached.

Subterminal Mouth
A species descriptor that means located nearly at the end.

Subtropical
Regions bordering on the tropics.

Suburbinization
The development, or urbanization, of formerly rural areas due to the out-migration of large numbers of people from urban to rural and suburban environments. *See* Urbanization; Ruralization.

Subversion
Action designed to undermine the military, economic, psychological, or political strength or morale of a regime. *See* Unconventional Warfare.

Subversive Activity
Anyone lending aid, comfort, and moral support to individuals, groups, or organizations that advocate the overthrow of incumbent governments by force and violence is subversive and is engaged in subversive activity. All willful acts that are intended to be detrimental to the best interests of the government and that do not fall into the categories of treason, sedition, sabotage, or espionage will be placed in the category of subversive activity.

Subvortices
Spinning columns of air embedded inside a tornado, waterspout, or dust devil. A large wind-storm may be accompanied by several subvortices simultaneously. The travel of these subvortices is governed by the airflow in and around the parent storm.

Succession
Progressive changes in the composition of a plant community.

Succulent
A species descriptor for a plant having thick, fleshy leaves or stems that conserve moisture.

Sucker
1) In zoology, a chiefly North American fish having a thick-lipped mouth adapted for feeding by sucking. 2) In botany, a secondary shoot arising from the base of a trunk.

Sudden Accidental Occurrences
Occurrences that are not continuous or repeated in nature.

Sudden Releases of Pressure
A sudden, almost instantaneous release of pressure, gas, and heat when subjected to sudden shock or pressure or high temperature.

Suffrutescent
A species descriptor that means having a woody stem or base.

Suitability
The determination that a course of action will reasonably accomplish the identified objectives, mission, or task if carried out successfully.

Suitable
Capable of performing with safety the particular design function specified in the manufacturer's documentation.

Sulcus
A species descriptor that means narrow fissures separating cerebral convolutions (convex folds on the surface of the brain).

Sulfates

The water soluble fraction of suspended particulate matter containing the sulfate radical (SO_4) including but not limited to strong acids and sulfate salts.

Sulfur Dioxide (SO_2)

A major air pollutant resulting from the incomplete combustion of fossil fuels, especially high sulfur content coals. Sulfur dioxide is a colorless, irritating gas under atmospheric conditions.

Sulfuric Acid Plants

Any facilities producing sulfuric acid by the contact process by burning elemental sulfur, alkylation acid, hydrogen sulfide, or acid sludge. Does not include facilities where conversion to sulfuric acid is utilized primarily as a means of preventing emissions to the atmosphere of sulfur dioxide or other sulfur compounds.

Summation Gates

Special logic gates that require that an acceptable combination of input events be present to produce an output. Inputs can be present in varying proportions, as long as the sum of the inputs is adequate to generate an output.

Summit

The highest altitude above mean sea level that a projectile reaches in its flight from the gun to the target; the algebraic sum of the maximum ordinate and the altitude of the gun.

Sump

1) Any pit or reservoir that meets the definition of tank including the trenches connected to it that seek to collect hazardous waste for transport to hazardous waste storage, treatment, or disposal facilities. 2) A pit or tank that catches liquid runoff for drainage or disposal. A mechanism for removing water or wastewater from a sump or wet well. 3) Containment Sumps.

Sump Pump

See Sump.

Superclass

A taxonomic level between phylum and class; a combination of classes, such as fish.

Superelevation

The practice of elevating one side of a roadway over the other on curves in alignment.

Superfund

1) The program operated under the legislative authority of CERCLA and SARA that funds and carries out the EPA solid waste emergency and long-term removal remedial activities. These activities include establishing the National Priorities List, investigating sites for inclusion on the list, determining their priority level on the list, and conducting and/or supervising the ultimately determined cleanup and other remedial actions. 2) Nickname for the Comprehensive Environmental Response, Compensation and Liability Act, also referred to as the Trust Fund. *See* CERCLA.

Superfund Amendments and Reauthorization Act (SARA)

The 1986 modifications and amendments to the Comprehensive Environmental Response, Compensation and Liability Act (SARA, 42 USC 9601 et seq.). SARA reauthorized CERCLA to continue cleanup activities around the country. Several site specific amendments, definitions, clarifications, and technical requirements were added to the legislation, including additional enforcement authorities. Title III of SARA also authorized the Emergency Planning and Community Right-to-Know Act (EPCRA).

Superfund Memorandum of Agreement (SMOA)

A nonbinding, written document executed by an EPA Regional Administrator and the head of a state agency that may establish the nature and extent of EPA and state interaction during the removal, preremedial, remedial, and/or enforcement response process. The SMOA is not a site-specific document, although attachments may address specific sites. The SMOA generally defines the role and responsibilities of both the lead and support agencies.

Superfund State Contracts

A joint, legally binding agreement between EPA and a state to obtain the necessary assurances before a federal lead remedial action can begin at a site. In the case of a political subdivision-lead remedial response, a three-party Superfund state contract among EPA, the state, and the political subdivision thereof, is required before a political subdivision takes the lead for any phase of remedial response to ensure state involvement pursuant to Section 121(Q(l) of CERCLA. The Superfund state contract may be amended to provide the states CERCLA Section 104 assurances before a political subdivision can take the lead for remedial action.

Supernatant Liquor

The liquid in a sludge-digestion tank that lies between sludge at the bottom and scum floating near the top.

Supersonic

Of or pertaining to speed in excess of the speed of sound. *See* Speed of Sound.

Supervised Areas

Areas where radiation levels are such that annual exposure is most unlikely to exceed three-tenths of the occupational dose equivalent limits but may exceed one-tenth of those limits, and where special forms of supervision (such as area monitoring) are accordingly applied.

Supervisor

1) An individual officially designated by management to direct the activities of operators or fissionable materials handlers and to supervise the operation of equipment that handles, produces, processes, stores, packages, or uses radioactive material or significant quantities of fissionable materials. 2) An individual responsible for command of a project, program, division, group, etc.

Supplement Analyses

DOE documents that describe any changes in a proposed action that are relevant to environmental concerns, or any significant new circumstances and information relevant to environmental concerns and bearing on the proposed action or its impacts. A supplement analysis is used to determine whether a supplemental Environmental Impact Statement should be prepared (pursuant to 40 CFR 1502.9(c)), to support a decision to prepare a new Environmental Impact Statement, or to revise the Record of Decision.

Supplemental EIS

An environmental impact statement prepared to supplement a prior environmental impact statement, as provided at 40 CFR 1502.9(c).

Supplier of Water

Any person who owns or operates a public water system.

Supply Line

The piping, tubing, or hoses, including all related fittings, through which vapor or liquid passes between the first shut-off valve at the container and the final stage regulator or vaporizer.

Support Agencies

The agencies that provide the support agency coordinator to furnish necessary data and documents, and provide other assistance as requested by the On-Scene Coordinator (OSC) or the Remedial Project Manager (RPM). EPA, the USCG, another federal agency, or a state may be support agencies for a response action if operating pursuant to a contract executed under Section 104 of CERCLA or designated pursuant to a Superfund Memorandum of Agreement entered into pursuant to Subpart F of the NCP or other agreement. The support may also concur on decision documents.

Support Agency Coordinator

The official designated by the support agency, as appropriate, to interact and coordinate with the lead agency in response actions under the National Contingency Plan.

Support Site

In the Air Force, a facility operated by an active, reserve, or Guard unit that provides general support to the Air Force mission and does not satisfy the criteria for a major or minor installation. Examples of support sites are missile tracking sites, radar bomb scoring sites, Air Force-owned or contractor-operated plants and radio relay sites. *See* Installation Complex; Major Installation; Minor Installation.

Support Zone
That area beyond a Decontamination Zone that surrounds a chemical hazard incident in which medical care can be freely administered to stabilize victims.

Supporting Citation, Ingestion, and Absorption Hazards
Four primary considerations must be met to support an OSHA citation. 1) The potential for ingestion or absorption of the toxic material must exist. 2) The ingestion or absorption of the material must represent a health hazard. 3) The toxic substance must be of such a nature and exist in such quantities as to pose a serious hazard. The substance must be present on surfaces that have hand contact (such as lunch tables, cigarettes) or on other surfaces that, if contaminated, present the potential for ingestion or absorption of the toxic material (e.g., a water fountain). 4) Protective clothing or other abatement means would be effective in eliminating or significantly reducing exposure.

Supralabials
A species descriptor that means above the lip.

Supraoculars
A species descriptor that means above the eye.

Surface Area Scaling Factor
The intraspecies and interspecies scaling factor most commonly used for cancer risk assessments by the EPA to convert an animal dose to a human equivalent dose; milligrams per square meter surface area per day. Body surface area is proportional to basal metabolic rate; the ratio of surface area to metabolic rate tends to be constant from one species to another. Since body surface area is approximately proportional to an animal's body

weight to the 2/3 power, the scaling factor can be reduced to milligrams per (body weight)$^{2/3}$.

Surface Burst
See Types of Burst.

Surface Casings
The first string of well casing to be installed in the well.

Surface Coal Mining and Reclamation Operations
Surface mining operations and all activities necessary and incident to the reclamation of such operations. *See* Surface Coal Mining Operations.

Surface Coal Mining Operations
1) Activities conducted on the surface of lands in connection with a surface coal mine or subject to the requirements of the Surface Mining Control and Reclamation Act (SMCRA). Also, surface operations and surface impacts incident to an underground coal mine, the products of which enter commerce or the operations of which directly or indirectly affect interstate commerce. Such activities include excavation for the purpose of obtaining coal including such common methods as contour, strip, auger, mountaintop removal, box cut, open pit, and area mining, the uses of explosives and blasting, and in situ distillation or retorting, leaching (or other chemical or physical processing); and the cleaning, concentrating, or other processing or preparation, loading of coal for interstate commerce at or near the mine site.

2) Operations impacting areas on adjacent land, the use of which is incidental to any such activities. Also all lands affected by the construction resulting from or incident to mining activities, such as: a) new roads, or the improvement or use of existing roads to gain access to the site or for haulage; b) excavations; c) workings; d) impoundments; e) dams; f) ventilation shafts; g) entryways; h) refuse banks, dumps, stockpiles, overburden piles, spoil banks, culm banks; i) tailings; j) holes or depressions; k) repair areas; l) storage areas; m) processing areas; n) shipping areas; and o) other areas, upon which structures,

facilities, or other property or materials are sited on the surface. Such activities do not include the extraction of coal incidental to the extraction of other minerals where coal does not exceed 16 ⅔ per centum of the tonnage of minerals removed for purposes of commercial use or sale.

Surface Collecting Agents

Chemical agents that form a surface film to control the layer thickness of oil.

Surface Faulting

The lifting or tearing of the earth's surface by differential movement across a fault.

Surface Impoundment

1) A facility or part of a facility that is a natural topographic depression, manmade excavation, or dike area formed primarily of earthen materials (often lined with nonimpervious manmade materials), that is designed to hold an accumulation of liquid wastes or wastes containing free liquids, and that is not an injection well. 2) Treatment, storage, or disposal of liquid hazardous wastes in ponds. Examples of surface impoundments include holding, storage, and settling ponds, aeration pits, and lagoons.

Surface Pressure

The total load or force per unit area acting on a surface.

Surface-to-Surface Guided Missile

A surface-launched guided missile for use against surface targets.

Surface-to-Air Guided Missile

A surface-launched guided missile for use against air targets.

Surface Water

Bodies of water that are above ground, open to the atmosphere, and subject to surface runoff (e.g., rivers, lakes, reservoirs, ponds, streams, seas, estuaries), including all springs, wells, or other collectors directly influenced by surface water.

Surface Water Resources

The waters of the United States, including the sediments suspended in water or lying on the bank, bed, or shoreline and sediments in or transported through coastal and marine areas. This term does not include groundwater or water or sediments in ponds, lakes, or reservoirs designed for waste treatment under the Resource Conservation and Recovery Act of 1976 (RCRA), 42 USC, or the CWA, and applicable regulations.

Surface Wave Magnitude

Measures the amplitude of surface waves with a period of 20 seconds (a wavelength of about 38 miles) and are often dominant on the seismograms.

Surface Zero

See Ground Zero.

Surfactant

1) A surface-active compound used in detergents to promote lathering. 2) An agent that reduces surface tension (e.g., wetting agents, detergents, dispersing agents).

Surplus Facilities

DOE facilities or sites (including equipment) that have no identified or planned programmatic use and are contaminated with radioactivity to levels that require controlled access.

Surplus Property

Excess property not required for the needs and for the discharge of the responsibilities of all federal agencies, including the Department of Defense, as determined by the General Services Administration.

Surprise Dosage Attack

A chemical operation that establishes on target a dosage sufficient to produce the desired casualties before targets can mask or otherwise protect themselves.

Surrogates

Organic compounds that are similar to analytes of interest in chemical composition, extraction, and chromatography, but which are not normally found in environmental samples. These compounds are spiked into all blanks, standards, samples, and spiked samples prior to analysis. Percent recoveries are calculated for each surrogate.

Surveillance

1) All planned activities performed to ensure compliance with operational specifications established for a particular installation. 2) The systematic observation of aerospace, surface or subsurface areas, places, persons, or things, by visual, aural, electronic, photographic, or other means.

Surveillance and Nuclear Detection Systems

Research and development efforts for developing gamma ray and neutron detector arrays used in searching for or mapping nuclear material contamination in support of the Nuclear Emergency Search Team.

Surveillance System

A series of monitoring devices designed to determine environmental quality.

Survey Control Point

A survey station used to coordinate survey control.

Survey Photography

See Air Cartographic Photography.

Surveys

1) Any systematic collection of primary data. 2) The varying types of survey techniques that can be applied in obtaining environmental information: the cross section, the longitudinal, and the contrasting sample survey are the most common socio-environmental types, while the characteristics of the physical environs are determined through engineering surveys. 3) A comprehensive examination of policies, procedures, practices, facilities, and equipment, including field observation of actual conditions, within a stated broad scope.

Suspended Particulate Matter (PM 10)

Atmospheric particles, solid and liquid, except uncombined water as measured by a PM 10 sampler that collects 50% of all particles of 10 m aerodynamic diameter and that collects a declining fraction of particles as their diameter increases and an increasing fraction of particles as their diameter decreases, reflecting the characteristic of lung deposition. Suspended particulate matter (PM 10) is to be measured by the size selective inlet high volume (SSI) PM 10 sampler method in accordance with ARB Method P, as adopted on August 22, 1985, or by an equivalent PM 10 sampler method, for purposes of monitoring for compliance with the Suspended Particulate Matter (PM 10) standards.

Suspended Particulates

Minute solids (such as dust, dirt, sand, and residuals from incomplete combustion) that either float through, or are held in suspension in the air, and the atmosphere. These particulates can be minimized by filtering sources of emissions at the stack or by using field dewatering processes at onsite sources of emissions.

Suspended Solids

1) Small particles of solid pollutants that either float on the surface of, or are suspended in, water, wastewater, or other liquids, and that are largely removable by laboratory filtering processes. 2) The quantity of material removed from wastewater in a laboratory test, as prescribed in Standard Methods for the Examination of Water and Wastewater referred to as nonfilterable residue. *See* Total Suspended Solids.

Suspension

The act of suspending the use of a pesticide when EPA deems it necessary to do so in order to prevent an imminent hazard resulting from continued use of the pesticide. An emergency suspension takes effect immediately; under an ordinary suspension a registrant can request a hearing before the suspension goes into effect. Such a hearing process might take 6 months.

Suspension Culture
Individual cells or small clumps of cells growing in a liquid nutrient medium.

Suspicious Devices
Any devices or packages that arouse suspicion by sound, geographic location, or shape.

Sustainable Agriculture
Environmentally friendly methods of farming that allow the production of crops or livestock without damage to the farm as an ecosystem, including effects on soil, water supplies, biodiversity, or other surrounding natural resources. The concept of sustainable agriculture is an "intergenerational" one in which we pass on a conserved or improved natural resource base instead of one that has been depleted or polluted. Terms often associated with farms or ranches that are self-sustaining include low-input, organic, ecological, biodynamic, and permaculture.

Sustained Yield
The achievement and maintenance in perpetuity of a high-level annual or regular periodic output of the various renewable resources of the public lands consistent with multiple use.

Sutures
1) In biology, a seamlike joint or line of articulation, such as the line of dehiscence (an opening that releases seeds) in a seed or fruit. 2) In anatomy, the line of junction between two bones, especially the skull.

Swamp
A type of wetland that is dominated by woody vegetation and does not accumulate appreciable peat deposits. Swamps may be fresh or salt water and tidal or nontidal. *See* Wetlands.

SWAT
See Solid Waste Assessment Test.

SWDA
See Solid Waste Disposal Act.

Sweeping Gas Plenum
The removal of hydrogen, oxygen, and deuterium from a gas plenum.

SWMU
See Solid Waste Management Unit.

SWP Conditions
A designation for Safe Work Permit (SWP) conditions.

SWS
An acronym for Salt Water System; Service Water System.

SWSA
An acronym for Solid Waste Storage Area.

SWSRAAA
An acronym for Sipsey Wild and Scenic River and Alabama Addition Act of 1988 (WSRA).

Synergism
1) The cooperative interaction of two or more organisms, chemicals, or other phenomena producing a greater combined effect than the sum of their individual effects; chemicals or muscles in synergy enhance the effectiveness of one another beyond what an individual could have produced. 2) A pharmacologic or toxicologic interaction, with a combined result greater than the sum of the effect of each chemical alone.

Synonym
A name that is equivalent to or replaced by another name.

Synthetic Fuel
A fuel derived from feedstock such as coal, oil shale, tar sands, biomass, or natural gas.

Synthetic Natural Gas (SNG)

A manufactured gaseous fuel generally produced from naphtha or coal. Contains +95% methane, and has an energy content of 980 to 1,035 Btu's per standard cubic foot; almost equalling natural gas.

Synthetic Organic Chemicals (SOCs)

Manmade organic chemicals. Some SOCs are volatile, others tend to stay dissolved in water rather than evaporate out of it.

System

1) Any organized assembly of resources and procedures united and regulated by interaction or interdependence to accomplish a set of specific functions. 2) The assembly of equipment and appurtenances consisting essentially of the container or containers, major devices such as vaporizers, safety relief valves, excess flow valves, regulators, and connecting piping. 3) A generalized term used as a modifier to denote various engineering, environmental, informational, and operational systems including, but not limited to the following:

- Airborne Activity Confinement Systems
- Alternate Removal Systems
- Automatic Depressurization System
- Backup Systems
- Bearing Wall Systems
- Chemical Volume and Control System
- Chemical Hazards Emergency Management System
- Closed Vent Systems
- Confinement Systems
- Containment Systems
- Control Systems
- Control Rod Drive
- Control System
- Conventional Systems
- Cooling System
- Core Flood System
- Criticality Alarm System

- Disposal Systems
- Double Block and Blood System
- Drinking Water System
- Emergency Power System
- Emergency Broadcast System
- Emergency Systems
- Emergency Management Information System
- Energy Monitoring and Control Systems
- Engineered Barrier Systems
- Explosion Suppression System
- Explosion Suppression System
- Failure Reporting Analysis and Corrective Action System
- Fire Protection Systems
- Fire Suppression System
- Hazard Abatement Tracking System
- Hazardous Substance UST System
- Hazardous Ranking System
- High Pressure Injection System
- HVAC System
- Insitu Sampling Systems
- Integrated Risk Information System
- Lateral Force Resisting System
- Leachate Collection Systems
- Leak Detection Systems
- Management Systems
- Metric System
- Monitoring Systems
- Multimedia Environmental Pollutant Assessment System
- National Pollutant Discharge Elimination System
- National Warning System
- New Tank Systems
- Occurrence Reporting and Processing System
- Petroleum UST Systems
- Plant Protection System
- Primary Confinement Systems
- Primary Emission Control Systems

- Public Address System
- Raw Water System
- Reactor Coolant System
- Remedial Action Assessment System
- Remote Detection and Control Systems
- Resource Recovery Systems
- Safe Shutdown System
- Safety Performance Measurement System
- Safety Injection Control System
- Sanitary Treatment System
- Sewer System
- Stormwater Collection Systems
- Surveillance Systems
- Technical Information Systems
- Test Systems
- Unusual Occurrence Reporting System
- Ventilation System
- Wastewater Collection Systems
- Water Supply System

System Audits

Overall evaluations of projects to verify that sampling methodology is being performed in accordance with program requirement; to check on the use of appropriate QA/QC measures; to check methods of sample handling; to identify any existing quality problems; to check program documentation; to initiate corrective action if a problem is identified; to assess personnel experience and qualifications as required; to provide onsite debriefings for sampling personnel; and to provide written evaluations of the sampling program.

System Design

The preparation of an assembly of methods, procedures, or techniques united by regulated interaction to form an organized whole.

System Integrator

A company or business who either directly or through a subcontractor will assume responsibility for the design, build, and integration of an automated or computerized system, peripheral equipment, and other required ancillary equipment for a particular application.

System of Records

A group of any records under the control of an agency from which information is retrieved by the name of the individual or company or by some identifying number, symbol, or other identifying means particularly assigned to the individual (i.e., Social Security number, tax identification number).

System Safety

Safety analysis (usually specialized and sophisticated) applied as an adjunct to design of an engineered system.

System Safety Analyses

The formal analyses of a system and the interrelationships among its various parts (including plant and hardware, policies and procedures, and personnel) to determine the real and potential hazards within the system, and suggest ways to reduce and control those hazards.

System Safety Development Center (SSDC)

A DOE center located at the Idaho National Engineering Laboratory. Its functions include the development and application of new technologies, the implementation and analysis of safety information systems, the presentation of training seminars and workshops, and the publication and dissemination of SSDC documents.

System Safety Development Center Glossary

A glossary of terms and definitions as used by the System Safety Development Center in Idaho Falls, Idaho.

Systemic

Pertaining to or affecting the body as a whole or acting in a portion of the body other than the site of entry. Used to refer generally to noncancer effects. *See* Portal-of-Entry Effects.

Systemic Pesticide

A chemical that is taken up from the ground or absorbed through the surface and carried through the system of the organism being protected, making the organism toxic to pests.

Systems of Regulation

Any system or systems of regulation as the Administrator may deem appropriate, including requirements for registration and labeling, self-monitoring and reporting, prohibitions, limitations, or economic incentives (including marketable permits and auctions of emissions rights) concerning the manufacture, processing, distribution, use, consumption, or disposal of a product.

T

T&E
See Threatened and Endangered Species.

TA
An acronym for Test Authorizations.

Table of Allowance
An equipment allowance document that prescribes basic allowances of organizational equipment, and provides the control to develop, revise, or change equipment authorization inventory data.

Tacan
An ultrahigh frequency electronic air navigation system, able to provide continuous bearing and slant range to a selected station. The term is derived from tactical air navigation.

Tachycardia
Rapid heartbeat (typically greater than 100 beats per minute).

Tachypnea
Rapid breathing.

Tacit Arms Control Agreement
An arms control course of action in which two or more nations participate without any formal agreement having been made.

Tactical Aeromedical Evacuation
That phase of evacuation that provides airlift for patients from the hazard zone to points outside the zone, and between points within the communications zone.

Tactical Air Control Operations Team
A team of ground environment personnel assigned to certain allied tactical air control units/elements.

Tactical Information Processing and Interpretation System (TIPI)
A tactical, mobile, land-based, automated information-handling system designed to store and retrieve intelligence information and to process and interpret imagery or nonimagery data.

Tactical Map
A large-scale map used for tactical and administrative purposes. *See* Map.

Tactical Nuclear Weapon Employment
The use of nuclear weapons by land, sea, or air forces against opposing forces, supporting installations or facilities, in support of operations that contribute to the accomplishment of a military mission of limited scope, or in support of the military commander's scheme of maneuver, usually limited to the area of military operations.

Tactical Response Teams

Groups of one or more armed security inspectors who are specially trained and equipped to respond to security incidents. Also called Special Response Teams.

Tadpole

The larva of a frog or toad.

Taenioglossate

A species descriptor for long narrow tonguelike structure or a ribbon with toothlike structure.

Tagging

An emergency response procedure used to prioritize casualties, by need for medical attention based on the severity of exposure or injuries, at the scene of a hazardous incident or accident prior to triage. Generally, patients are tagged into three groups a) site fatalities or those who cannot be expected to survive even with treatments; b) those ambulatory or with minor injuries who will recover without treatment; and c) a medical priority group of those who need treatment in order to survive. *See* Triage.

Tailings

1) Residue of raw materials or waste separated out during the processing of crops or mineral ores. 2) The remaining portion of a metal-bearing ore after some or all of such metal, such as uranium, has been extracted.

Take

To harass, harm, pursue, hunt, shoot, wound, kill, trap, capture, or collect, or to attempt to engage in any such conduct.

TALM

An acronym for Temperature Alarm Monitor.

Tamper

1) To introduce a contaminant into a public water system with the intention of harming persons. 2) To otherwise interfere with the operation of a public water system with the intention of harming persons.

Tangible Net Worth

The tangible assets that remain after deducting liabilities; such assets would not include intangibles such as goodwill and rights to patents or royalties.

Tank

1) A stationary device, primarily designed to contain/store accumulations of hazardous liquid wastes. Typically constructed of nonearthen materials (e.g., wood, concrete, steel, plastic) that provide impervious surfaces and structural support. 2) A container, other than a cylinder in DOT service, used for the storage or accumulation of any liquid or gas under pressure. This definition is not intended to include pressure chambers that are integral parts of other devices, where the pressure-containing part is subjected to severe mechanical stresses.

Tank Configuration

Any cargo tank having a volumetric capacity of more than 1,000 gallons that can be used for the transportation of liquids. Tank configuration does not include a tank used to carry fuel necessary for the operation of the vehicle or equipment attached to a vehicle.

Tank Farm

A facility that is used for the storage of crude oils and that a) has total storage capacity of 20,000 barrels or more; b) is not located on a refinery site; c) that does not contain lease storage facilities; and d) is not a public storage facility. (e.g., airports and military bases).

Tank System

1) A hazardous waste storage or treatment tank and its associated ancillary equipment and containment system. 2) Underground storage tanks, connected underground piping, underground ancillary equipment, and containment systems, if any.

TAP

See Toxic Air Pollutants.

TAPPI

An acronym for Technical Association of Pulp and Paper Industry.

Taproot

The main root of a plant, usually stouter than the lateral roots and growing straight downward from the stem.

Tar Sands

Surface or near-surface sand or sandstone rocks that contain viscous natural hydrocarbons and/or heavy petroleum that cannot be recovered.

Target Audience

An individual or group selected for influence by means of psychological operations.

Target Compound List (TCL)

The list developed by EPA for Superfund site sample analyses. The TCL is a list of analytes (34 volatile organic chemicals, 66 semivolatile organic chemicals, 19 pesticides, 7 polychlorinated biphenyls, 23 metals, and total cyanide) for which every Superfund sample must be analyzed under the EPA Contract Laboratory Program.

Target Date

The date on which it is desired that an action be accomplished or initiated.

Target Organ System

An organ or functional system (e.g., respiratory, immune, excretory, reproductive systems) that demonstrates toxicity to a specific chemical; not necessarily the organ/system with the highest accumulation of the chemical, but rather that which elicits a toxic responses of concern.

Target Response, Nuclear

The effect on humans, material, and equipment of blast, heat, light, and nuclear radiation resulting from the explosion of a nuclear weapon.

Target Stress Point

The weakest point (most vulnerable to damage) on the critical damage point. Also called vulnerable node.

Tarsus

The distal segmented structure on the leg of an insect or arachnid; in vertebrates, the section of the foot between the leg and metatarsus.

Task Analysis

The systematic review of a collection of actions or behaviors necessary and sufficient to complete a given task. It includes an extremely thorough look at the individual elements and supplements comprising a task.

Task Force

A semipermanent organization of individuals, under one leader, formed for the purpose of carrying out a specific task or tasks.

Task Group

A subcomponent of a task force organized by the leader of the task force or a higher authority.

Task Organizing

The act of designing an operating force, support staff, or logistics package of specific size and composition to meet a unique task. Primary characteristics to examine in task-organizing include, but are not limited to, training, experience, equipage, sustainability, operating environment, hazard threat, and emergency mobility.

Task Unit

See Task Group.

Tautonym

A taxonomic designation, commonly used in zoology in which the genus and species names are the same.

Taxon

A group of organisms with common characteristics constituting one of the categories in taxonomic classification, such as phylum, order, or family.

Taxonomy
The science of classifying plants and animals into hierarchical groups; the science of classifying organisms; the systematic classification of a subject.

TBF
An acronym for Technical and Biological Feasibility.

TBFCA
An acronym for Technical and Biological Feasibility and Cost-effectiveness of Alternatives.

TBSCCW
An acronym for Turbine Building Secondary Closed Cooling Water.

TBSW
An acronym for Turbine Building Service Water.

TBT Paints
Paints containing tributylin. *See* Organotins.

Tc
Technetium.

TCC
An acronym for Transportation Component Command.

TCD
See Transportation Control Demonstration (CAA).

TCE
See Trichloroethylene.

TCM
See Transportation Control Measure (CAA).

TCP
See Tool Center Point.

TCSM
See Transportation Control Strategies and Measures (CAA).

TDLO
"Toxic dose low" is the lowest dose of a substance required to cause a toxic effect in some of the exposed population.

TDTOX
Tetradichloroxylene.

Team Search and Rescue
A specific task performed by emergency responders to effect the recovery of distressed personnel during hazardous emergency response operations.

Teams
1) A generalized term used as a modifier to denote various engineering, environmental, emergency response, medical, coordination, and program/task teams that consist of a number of persons associated together in work or activity. 2) A group of specialists or scientists functioning as a collaborative unit, including but not limited to management teams, accreditation review teams, crisis management teams, emergency management teams, headquarters coordinating teams, emergency response teams, environmental response teams, explosive ordnance disposal teams, hazardous materials response teams, national response teams, regional response teams, or tactical response teams.

TECHDOC
See Technical Documentation.

Technical Analysis
In imagery interpretation, the precise description of details appearing on imagery.

Technical Assistance Grant (TAG)
EPA grants of up to $50,000 for citizens' groups to obtain assistance in interpreting information related to cleanups at Superfund sites. Grants are used by such groups to hire technical advisors to

help them understand the site related information for the duration of response activities.

Technical Assistance Costs for Energy Conservation

The costs of carrying out a technical assistance program including costs incurred for the use of existing personnel or the temporary employment of other qualified personnel necessary for providing technical assistance.

Technical Assistance for Energy Conservation

Assistance, under rules promulgated by the Secretary (DOE), to states, units of local government, and public institutions (e.g., schools, hospitals) to conduct specialized studies identifying and specifying energy savings or energy cost savings that are likely to be realized as a result of a) modification or maintenance and operating procedures in a building, b) the acquisition and installation of one or more specified energy conservation measures in such building or c) both. Also, the planning or implementation of specific remodeling, renovation, repair, replacement, or insulation projects related to the installation of energy conservation measures in such building.

Technical Documentation (TECHDOC)

Visual information documentation (with or without sound as an integral documentation component) of an actual event made for purposes of evaluation. Typically, technical documentation contributes to the study of site, human or mechanical factors, procedures, and processes in the fields of medicine, science, logistics, research, development, environmental evaluation, laboratory analyses, and related investigations. *See* Visual Information Documentation.

Technical Evaluation

The study and investigations by a developing agency to determine the technical suitability of material, equipment, or a system, for use in accomplishing a stated environmental objective. *See* operational evaluation.

Technical Information

Information, including scientific information, that relates to environmental research, engineering, laboratory tests, report evaluations, production, operation, use, facility maintenance, and other supplies and equipment.

Technical Information Systems

Information systems established to detect deviations, determine rates and trends, initiate corrective actions, and ensure that project goals are attained. A technical information system usually consists of research-oriented persons, program persons, and others responsible for obtaining, handling, and providing technical information relevant to the work flow process in a communication network.

Technical Names

Recognized chemical names currently used in scientific and technical handbooks, journals, and texts. Generic descriptions authorized for use as technical names are organic phosphate compound, organic phosphorus compound, organic phosphate compound mixture, organic phosphorus compound mixture, methyl parathion, and parathion.

Technical Specification

A detailed description of technical requirements stated in terms suitable to form the basis for the actual design development and production processes of an item having the qualities specified in the operational characteristics.

Technical Support

Engineering, design, specialized inspections, planning, or other such project support.

Technically Qualified Individuals

A person or persons who, because of education, training, or experience, or a combination of these factors, is capable of understanding the health and environmental risks associated with a chemical substance that is used under his/her supervision; who is responsible for enforcing appropriate methods of conducting scientific experimentation, analysis, or chemical research to minimize such risks, and who is responsible for the safety assessments and clearances related to the procurement, storage, use, and disposal of the chemical substance as may be appropriate or required within the scope of conducting a research and development activity.

Technology-Based Standards

Effluent limitations applicable to direct and indirect sources that are developed on a category-by-category basis using statutory factors, not including water-quality effects.

Technosphere

The manmade or built environment.

Tectonic

A term applied to the warping, folding, and faulting of the earth's crust.

Tectonic Deformations

Geologic deformations that accompany surface faulting. The deformation may be local, affecting a narrow zone near a fault break, or it may involve differential vertical and horizontal movements over broad parts of the earth's crust.

TEG

Tetraethylene glycol

Telecommunication

Any transmission, emission, or reception of signs, signals, writings, images, and sounds or intelligence of any nature by wire, radio, visual, or other electromagnetic systems.

Telecommunications Center

A facility, normally serving more than one organization or terminal, responsible for transmission, receipt, acceptance, processing, and distribution of incoming and outgoing messages.

Teleconference

A conference between persons remote from one another but linked by a telecommunications system.

Telemetry Intelligence (TELINT)

Technical intelligence derived from the intercept, processing, and analysis of foreign telemetry. Telemetry intelligence is a category of foreign instrumentation signals intelligence.

Teleoperators

Robotic devices that are comprised of sensors and actuators for mobility and/or manipulation that are remotely controlled by a human operator.

Teleprocessing

The combining of telecommunications and computer operations interacting in the automatic processing, reception, and transmission of data and/or information.

Television Imagery

Imagery acquired by a television camera and recorded or transmitted electronically.

TELINT

See Telemetry Intelligence.

Temperature Gradient

At sea, a temperature gradient is the change of temperature with depth; a positive gradient is a temperature increase with an increase in depth, and a negative gradient is a temperature decrease with an increase in depth.

Temporarily Abandoned Areas

Mine areas in which further work is not intended for at least 6 months. Areas that function as escapeways, formerly used lunchrooms, shops, and transformer or pumping stations are not considered abandoned areas. Except for designated ventilation passageways designed to minimize the distance to vents, worked-out mine areas are considered temporarily abandoned areas for the purpose of this subpart if work is not intended in the area for at least 6 months.

Temporary Emergency Production Rate

The maximum rate of production for an oil field that a) is above the maximum efficient rate of production established for such field; and b) may be maintained for a temporary period of less than 90 days without reservoir damage and without significant loss of ultimate recovery of crude oil or natural gas, or both, from such field.

Temporary-Use Building
Any building for which the intended use is not for more than 3 years from the date of first occupancy.

Temporary Variances
A short-term release from an agency prescribed standard or regulation. Such variances usually do not exceed 1 year, except that in unusual cases a renewal may be granted, not to exceed an additional year.

Ten-to-the-Minus-Sixth (10^{-6})
Used in risk assessments to refer to the probability of risk. Literally means a chance of one in a million. Similarly, ten-to-the-minus-fifth (10^{-5}) means a probability of one in 100,000, and so on.

Tendril
A species descriptor that means a long, slender, coiling rootlike extension that attaches climbing plants to their surface.

Tensile Strength
The maximum tensile stress sustained by a material before it fails in a tension test.

Tent
A portable shelter installed onsite, made of fabric or plastic stretched over a supporting framework.

Tephigram
A diagram displaying temperature and entropy at different levels in the atmosphere.

Teratogen
A substance that causes malformation or serious deviation from normal development of embryos and fetuses.

Teratogenic
Having the ability to cause congenital anomalies.

Teratogenicity
The property of a chemical to cause structural or functional defects during the development of an organism.

Terete
A species descriptor that means cylindrical but usually slightly tapering at both ends.

Terminal
In biology, appearing at the end of a stem, branch or stalk.

Terminal Velocity
1) Hypothetical maximum speed a body could attain along a specified flight path under given conditions of weight and thrust if diving through an unlimited distance in air of specified uniform density. 2) Remaining speed of a projectile at the point in its downward path where it is level with the muzzle of the weapon.

Terminal Objective
The primary goal or purpose of an emergency drill or exercise, that requires enabling objectives to reliably test performance.

Terracing
Diking, built along the contour of sloping agricultural land, that holds runoff and sediment to reduce erosion.

Terrain Analysis
The collection, analysis, evaluation, and interpretation of geographic information on the natural and manmade features of the terrain, combined with other relevant factors, to predict the effect of the terrain on response operations.

Terrain Intelligence
Processed information on the significance of natural and manmade characteristics of an area.

Terrain Study
An analysis and interpretation of natural and manmade features of an area, their effects on re-

sponse operations, and the effect of weather and climate on these features.

Terrapin
A type of freshwater turtle.

Terrestrial
Living on land.

Terrestrial Environment
The earth's land area, including its manmade and natural surface and subsurface features, and its interfaces and interactions with the atmosphere and the oceans.

Territorial Seas
The belt of the seas measured from the line of ordinary low water along that portion of the coast that is in direct contact with the open sea and the line marking the seaward limit of inland waters, and extending seaward a distance of 3 miles.

Terrigenous
Derived from or originating on the land (usually referring to sediments) as opposed to material or sediments produced in the ocean (marine) or as a result of biologic activity (biogenous).

Territory
1) Any territory or possession of the United States, including the District of Columbia and the Commonwealth of Puerto Rico but excluding the Canal Zone. 2) An area that an animal will defend against intruders.

Terrorism
The calculated use of violence or threat of violence to inculcate fear; intended to coerce or to intimidate governments or societies in the pursuit of goals that are generally political, religious, or ideological. *See* Terrorist; Terrorist Groups.

Terrorist
1) An individual who uses violence, terror, and intimidation to achieve a result. 2) A person, or group of persons, who organize, conspire, or act in a manner that threatens or carries out violence

for the purpose of political coercion. *See* Terrorism.

Terrorist Act
Any potential or actual occurrence that creates or appears likely to create a condition resulting in sabotage, bodily harm, unlawful access to government facilities, or the interruption or loss of property or vital services.

Terrorist Group
Any element regardless of size or espoused cause, that repeatedly commits acts of violence or threatens violence in pursuit of its political, religious, or ideological objectives. *See* Terrorism.

Terrorist Response Plans
Plans for response to hostile action taken against the U.S. government or one of its primary contractors. Response plans may be written by contractor security organizations, DOE security organizations, local municipal and state organizations, or the Federal Bureau of Investigation (FBI).

Tertiary
1) The part of geologic time that extends from the end of the Cretaceous era to the beginning of the Pleistocene era; also refers to rock formed during this period. 2) The short flight feathers nearest the body on the inner edge of a bird's wing.

Tertiary Treatment
1) The third and usually final step in the sewage treatment process. Chemical methods and physical techniques are used to eliminate remaining soluble plant nutrients that could cause eutrophication if released into bodies of fresh water. 2) An enhancement of normal sewage treatment operations to provide water of potable quality using further chemical and physical treatment; the highest drinking water standard achieved in the U.S. 3) Advanced cleaning of wastewater that goes beyond the biological stage. It removes nutrients such as phosphorus and nitrogen and most BOD and suspended solids.

Test Mixtures
See Test Substances.

Test Reactor Facility
A prototypic, underground cavity with subsurface lateral excavations extending from a central shaft that is used for research and development purposes, including the development of data and experience for the safe handling and disposal of solidified high-level radioactive waste, transuranic waste, or spent nuclear fuel.

Test Substances
Substances or mixtures administered or added to a test system in a study, that substance or mixture is used to develop data to meet the requirements of a Toxic Substances Control Act (TSCA) Section 4(a) test rule, and/or is developed under a negotiated testing agreement or Section 6 rule/order to the extent the agreement, rule, or order references 40 CFR 792.3.

Test Systems
Any animals, plants, microorganisms, or subparts thereof, to which the test or control substance is administered or added for study. Test systems also include appropriate groups or components of the system not treated with the test or control substances.

Test Weight (tw)
Vehicle curb weight added to the gross vehicle weight rating (GVWR) and divided by two.

Testing Agency
An organization that a) is in the business of testing equipment and installations; b) is qualified and equipped for such experimental testing; c) is not under the jurisdiction or control of any manufacturer or supplier for any affected industry; d) maintains at least an annual inspection program of all equipment and installations currently listed or labeled; e) makes available a published directory showing current listings of manufacturer's equipment and installations that have been investigated, certified, and found safe for use in a specified manner and that are listed or labeled by the testing agency; and f) is approved by the department.

Testing Requirements
EPA's requirement for testing of substances or mixtures that may present an unreasonable risk of injury to health or the environment in order to develop data with respect to the health and environmental effects for which there is insufficient data and experience and that are relevant to a determination that the manufacture, distribution in commerce, processing, use, or disposal of such substance or mixture. For a more complete discussion see 15 USC 2603, *Testing of Chemical Substances and Mixtures*.

Testing Requirements Rule
The rule under 15 USC 2603, Section 4, Subsection (a), *Testing Requirements*, that includes a) identification of the chemical substance or mixture for which testing is required under the rule; b) standards for the development of test data for the substance or mixture; and c) with respect to chemical substances that are not new chemical substances and to mixtures, a specification of the period within which the persons required to conduct the testing shall submit their findings to the Administrator of EPA.

Tetany
A condition marked by involuntary muscle contractions or spasms.

Tetradynamous
A species descriptor that means having four long stamens and two short ones, as in the androecium of the Cruciferea.

Thallium (TI)
A metallic element used in alloys; its poisonous compounds are often used in pesticides.

Theoretical Arsenic Emissions Factor
The amount of inorganic arsenic, expressed in grams per kilogram of glass produced, as determined based on a material balance.

Thermal Conductivity
The ability of a material to conduct heat.

Thermal Crossover
The natural phenomenon that normally occurs twice daily when temperature conditions are such that there is a loss of contrast between two adjacent objects on infrared imagery.

Thermal Energy
The energy emitted from the fireball as thermal radiation. The total amount of thermal energy received per unit area at a specified distance from a nuclear explosion is generally expressed in terms of calories per square centimeter.

Thermal Exposure
The total normal component of thermal radiation striking a given surface throughout the course of a detonation; expressed in calories per square centimeter and/or megajoules per square meter.

Thermal Imagery
Imagery produced by sensing and recording the thermal energy emitted or reflected from the objects that are imaged.

Thermal Performance
The tested thermal conductivity, thermal conductance, or thermal resistance (R-value), as appropriate, of an insulating material.

Thermal Pollution
1) Discharge of heated water from industrial processes that can affect the life processes of aquatic organisms. 2) An increase in the temperature of water resulting from waste heat released by a thermal electric plant (e.g., pollution added to cooling waters and dispersed in a lake or river).

Thermal Pulse
The radiant power versus time pulse from a nuclear weapon detonation.

Thermal Radiation
1) The heat and light produced by a nuclear explosion. 2) Electromagnetic radiations emitted from a heat or light source as a consequence of its temperature; it consists essentially of ultraviolet, visible, and infrared radiations.

Thermal Reactor
A nuclear reactor in which the fission process is primarily propagated by thermal neutrons (neutrons that have been slowed down until they are in equilibrium with the moderator's atoms).

Thermal Stratification
The existence, as in a body of water, of a succession of differentiated thermal layers, each with different temperatures that decrease based on depth — with the coldest temperatures at the bottom, except beneath ice where inverse stratification occurs.

Thermal Treatment
The treatment of hazardous waste in a device that uses elevated temperatures as the primary means to change the chemical, physical, or biological character or composition of the hazardous waste. Examples of thermal treatment processes are incineration, molten salt, pyrolysis, calcination, wet air oxidation, and microwave discharge. *See* Incinerator.

Thermodynamics (Laws of)
1) Zeroth Law of Thermodynamics — two objects are considered to be in thermal equilibrium when no heat is exchanged between them when they are touching one another. 2) First Law of Thermodynamics — energy cannot be created or destroyed. 3) Second Law of Thermodynamics — when a free exchange of heat occurs between two bodies, heat transfer is always from the warmer to the cooler body. 4) Third Law of Thermodynamics — absolute zero degrees Kelvin (°K) can never be attained.

Thermograph
An instrument used to plot changes in temperature as a line on a rotating drum.

Thermoluminescent Dosimeters

Dosimeters made of crystalline materials that are capable of both storing a fraction of absorbed ionizing radiation and releasing this energy in the form of visible photons when heated. The amount of light released can be used as a measure of radiation exposure to these crystals.

Thermonuclear

An adjective referring to the process (or processes) in which very high temperatures are used to bring about the fusion of light nuclei, with the accompanying liberation of energy.

Thermonuclear Weapon

A weapon in which very high temperatures are used to bring about the fusion of light nuclei such as those of hydrogen isotopes (e.g., deuterium and tritium) with the accompanying release of energy. The high temperatures required are obtained by means of fission.

Thermoplastic

A plastic material that is capable of being repeatedly softened by application of heat and repeatedly hardened by cooling.

Thermoset

A plastic material that is capable of being cured by heat or catalyst into an infusible and insoluble material. Once cured, a thermoset cannot be returned to the uncured state.

Thermosphere

The part of the atmosphere where temperature increases with height.

THERP

An acronym for Technique for Human Error Rate Prediction.

Third Party Laboratory

A commercial lab or any laboratory approved by a governmental entity and having no vested interest in the laboratory findings of specific analyses.

Third World

A term coined in the 1940s to describe developing countries. The world was divided into three categories reflecting the socio-political environments present at the time. The First World consisted of countries with a free market society; the Second World was composed of all the socialist societies; and the Third World still remains as a means to describe countries whose societies are at a primary level. The term is no longer used with any regularity.

THM

See Trihalomethane.

Thoracic

A species descriptor that means situated near the thorax; the second or middle region in insects bearing the true legs and wings; in animals, the part of the body between the neck and the diaphragm.

Thorium (Th)

As found in nature, a naturally radioactive element with an atomic weight of approximately 232; atomic number 90. The fertile thorium-232 isotope is abundant and can be transmuted to fissionable uranium-233 by neutron irradiation and then used as nuclear reactor fuel.

Thorough Decontamination

Decontamination carried out, with or without external support, to reduce contamination on personnel, equipment, material, and/or working areas to the lowest possible levels, to permit the partial or total removal of individual protective equipment and to maintain operations with minimum degradation. This may include terrain decontamination beyond the scope of operational decontamination. *See* Decontamination; Immediate Decontamination; Operational Decontamination.

Threat Analysis

In antiterrorism, threat analysis is a continual process of compiling and examining all available information concerning potential terrorist activities by terrorist groups that could target a facility. A threat analysis will review the factors of a terrorist group's existence, capability, intentions, history, and targeting, as well as the security environment within which friendly forces operate. Threat analysis is an essential step in identifying probability of terrorist attack and results in a threat assessment.

Threat and Vulnerability Assessment
In antiterrorism, the pairing of a facility's threat analysis and vulnerability analysis.

Threat Identification and Assessment
The Joint Operation Planning and Execution System function that provides timely warning of potential threats to U.S. interests; intelligence collection requirements; the effects of environmental, physical, and health hazards, and cultural factors on friendly and enemy operations; and determines the enemy military posture and possible intentions.

Threatened and Endangered Species (T&E)
Any plant or animal species listed in Section 4 of the Endangered Species Act. *See* Endangered Species Act of 1973.

Threatened Illegal Discharges
The creation of a condition or the taking of an action that is intended to or will foreseeably create a substantial probability that an illegal discharge will occur.

Threatened Species
Any species that is likely to become an endangered species within the foreseeable future throughout all or a significant portion of its range.

Threats
Conditions that by their very nature pose harm or injury; something or someone intending to inflict evil, injury, or damage.

Three-Mile Island
The island site of the nuclear reactor that failed on March 28, 1979. Located in the Susquehanna River, near Harrisburg, Pennsylvania, a combination of human and mechanical error resulted in

water flooding the reactor building, the core overheated, and the nation lived in fear of a fuel meltdown for some 16 hours before the situation was finally brought under control. The event ended without harm to persons or property.

Threshold Limit Values (TLVs)
1) The maximum concentration of an airborne contaminant that workers can legally be subjected to in their daily working environments, without experiencing any adverse health effects. 2) A workplace exposure standard, assuming an exposure period of 8 hours per day, 40 hours per week. 3) The recommended exposure limit for specific contaminants as established by the American Conference of Governmental Industrial Hygienists (ACGIH). These values are constantly monitored and readjusted downward if medical research data indicates a previously set level is now determined harmful.

Threshold Toxicant
A substance showing an apparent level of effect that is a minimally effective dose, above which a response occurs; below that dose no response is expected.

Threshold Quantity
The toxicity, reactivity, volatility, dispersibility, combustibility, or flammability of a substance and the amount of the substance that, as a result of an accidental release, is known to cause or may reasonably be anticipated to cause death, injury, or serious adverse effects to human health.

Threshold Planning Quantity (TPQ)
1) A quantity designated for each chemical on the list of extremely hazardous substances that triggers notification by facilities to the state emergency response commission (SERC) that such facilities are subject to emergency planning under SARA Title III. 2) The amount of an extremely hazardous substance equal to or above which a facility must participate in SARA emergency planning. TPQs are provided in 40 CFR 365, Appendices A and B.

Thrombocytopenia
A condition in which there is an abnormally small number of platelets in the blood.

Thrombosis
Blood vessel clotting.

Thrum
A species descriptor that means loose ends or fringe.

Tidal Marsh
Low, flat marshlands traversed by channels and tidal hollows and subject to tidal inundation; normally, the only vegetation present are salt-tolerant bushes and grasses. *See* Wetlands.

Tidal Volume
The amount of air that is inhaled or exhaled during one breath; in humans, approximately 0.5 liter.

Tidal Waters
Those waters that rise and fall in a predictable and measurable rhythm or cycle due to the gravitational pulls of the moon and sun. Tidal waters end where the rise and fall of the water surface can no longer be practically measured in a predictable rhythm due to masking by hydrologic, wind, or other effects.

Tie Down
The fastening or securing of a load to its carrier by use of ropes, cables, or other means to prevent shifting during transport. Also used (as a noun) to describe the material employed to secure a load.

Tie Down Diagram
A drawing indicating the prescribed method of securing a particular item of cargo within a specific type of vehicle.

Tiering
Refers to the coverage of general matters in broader environmental impact statements, with subsequent narrower statements or environmental analyses incorporating by reference the general discussions and concentrating solely on the issues specific to the statement subsequently prepared.

Tiger Teams
Special DOE investigatory groups operating under the designated authority of the Tiger Team Assessment Program. Tiger team assessments are performed by teams at over 100 DOE operating facilities. The assessments were part of a ten-point initiative announced in 1989 by the Secretary of Energy, to conduct independent oversight compliance and management assessments of the ES&H programs at DOE facilities. Tiger Teams include individuals from the Department of Energy, Department of Energy Contractors, and private consulting organizations.

Tiger Team Assessment Program (TTAP)
A program to provide the Secretary of Energy with concise information on the a) current ES&H compliance status of each facility and associated vulnerabilities; b) root cause(s) for noncompliance; c) adequacy of DOE and site contractor ES&H management programs; d) response actions to address identified problem areas; and e) DOE-wide ES&H compliance trends and root causes.

Tiger Team Assessment Reports
The findings of a Tiger Team Assessment, documented in a written report. The Tiger Team Assessment Report contains individual findings (e.g. compliance findings, best management practices, and noteworthy practices), root causes, and requisite supporting documentation. The report typically does not include recommendations for corrective action. Broad recommendations as to how the findings and concerns should be acted upon by the relevant Program Senior Official are usually provided in the memorandum transmitting the final assessment report from the Assistant Secretary for Environment, Safety, and Health to the Secretary.

Tiger Team Assessments
Assessments that provide the Secretary of Energy with concise information on the following: a) current environment, safety and health (ES&H)

compliance status of each facility and associated vulnerabilities; b) root causes for noncompliance; c) adequacy of DOE and site contractor ES&H management programs; d) response actions to address identified problem areas; and e) input to evaluation of DOE-wide ES&H compliance trends.

The SOW for these assessments includes, but is not limited to: a) compliance with applicable federal, state, and local regulations, permits, agreements, and enforcement actions; b) compliance with DOE Order requirements for ES&H activities; c) adequacy of the facility's and the site contractor's ES&H management programs, including planning, organization, resources, training, and relationships with regulatory agencies; d) conformance with applicable "best" and accepted industry practices; and e) identification of root causes.

Tiltmeter
An instrument used to measure vertical changes in the slope of the ground's surface; these meters are used to predict imminent earthquake and volcanic activity.

Timberland
Forest land that is producing or capable of producing timber suitable for harvest.

Time and Material Contract
A contract providing for the procurement of supplies or services on the basis of direct labor hours at specified fixed hourly rates (which include direct and indirect labor, overhead, and profit), and material at cost.

Time Interval
Duration of a segment of time without reference to when the time interval begins or ends. Time intervals may be given in seconds of time or fractions thereof.

Time Loss (T/L) Analysis
The analysis of the amelioration process following an accident and the positive and negative effects of intervenors on the extent of the accident.

Time of Travel (TOT)
The time required for a contaminant to move in the saturated zone from a specific point to a well.

Time Specific Permit
1) A permit that specifies the date the intended action is to be completed by, or a permit with mandatory start dates and milestone requirements. 2) A pesticide permit that specifies the date the intended application is to commence or a permit with a notice of intent requirement. The pesticide use may commence within four days following such date if delays are caused by uncontrollable conditions such as adverse weather or unavailability of equipment. The commissioner shall require a notice of intent from either the grower, the grower's authorized representative, or the pest control operator when necessary to make the permit time and site specific.

Time Weighted Average (TWA)
1) Regarding air concentrations, the concentration of a substance in air that is measured by collecting it on a substrate at a known rate for a given period of time. 2) An approach to calculating the average exposure over a specified time period. TWA is used in determining threshold limit values; TLV-TWA is the time weighted average concentration for a normal 8-hour workday or 40-hour workweek, to which nearly all workers may be repeatedly exposed, day after day, without an adverse effect.

Timeline
The framework upon which the scenario is constructed. It provides the significant nonparticipant controlled events and the times at which they are planned to occur. These events are correlated to exercise messages.

Tinnitus
Ringing in the ears.

Tissue Equivalents
Materials whose absorbing and scattering properties for radiation of a given type and energy simulate those of a specified biological tissue.

Titration

A laboratory operation that forms the basis of volumetric analyses. A measured amount of a solution of one agent is added, a little bit at a time, to a fixed amount of another agent until they no longer react to one another, as the second agent is entirely consumed by the first.

TLD

See Thermoluminescent Dosimeters.

TLV

See Threshold Limit Values.

TNT Equivalent

A measure of the energy released from the detonation of a nuclear weapon, or from the explosion of a given quantity of fissionable material, in terms of the amount of TNT (trinitrotoluene) that could release the same amount of energy when exploded.

To Plan

The examination of feasible alternatives, review of alternatives, and reflection of this examination and review in choice of corrective actions, siting decisions, response measures, and other factors, together with associated implementation methods.

Toad

A warty-skinned, land frog.

TOC

An acronym for Total Organic Carbon.

Toilet Recirculating Chemical

A self-contained toilet in which waste is recirculated and chemically treated.

Tolerance

The permissible residue levels for pesticides in raw agricultural produce and processed foods. Whenever a pesticide is registered for use on a food or a feed crop, a tolerance (or exemption from the tolerance requirements) must be established. EPA establishes the tolerance levels, that are enforced by the Food and Drug Administration and the Department of Agriculture. Also used for engineering tolerances and clearances between parts.

Tolerance Dose

The amount of radiation that may be received by an individual within a specified period with negligible results.

Tolerance Limits

1) The criteria as to what is deemed acceptable in performance, significant error, or harmful energy. 2) The physical/environmental constraints beyond which a species cannot survive.

Tomahawk

An air-, land-, ship-, or submarine-launched cruise missile with three variants: land attack with conventional or nuclear capability, and tactical antiship with conventional warhead.

Tomentum

A species descriptor that means covering of closely matted woolen hairs.

Tomial

A species descriptor for the cutting edge of a bird's bill.

Ton

A unit of weight equal to 2,000 pounds (a short ton) in the United States, Canada, and South Africa, and 2,240 pounds (a long ton) in Great Britain. The metric ton equals 2,204.62 pounds.

Tool Center Point (TCP)

The origin of the tool coordinate system.

Tooling Resins

Plastic resins, chiefly epoxy and silicone, that are used as tooling aids.

Top Management

The individual manager or group of managers serving in a policymaking capacity for the total organization. These individuals also may be, and usually are, involved in policy implementation.

Topographic Map
A map that presents the vertical position of features in measurable form as well as their horizontal positions. *See* Map.

Topographic Surface
The boundary between the earth and the atmosphere; the zone richest with the growth and development of living things.

Topography
1) A description of the natural and artificial surface features of an area. 2) The physical features of a surface area including relative elevations and the position of natural and manmade features.

Topsoil
The surface layer of soil to a depth of about 1 foot.

Tornado
A violent local storm with whirling winds from 40 to over 300 mph. It appears as a rotating, funnel-shaped cloud that extends toward the ground from the base of a thunderstorm. A tornado varies from gray to black in color. These small, short-lived storms are the most violent of all atmospheric phenomena, and over a small area, are the most destructive.

Tornado Warning
A warning issued when a tornado has been reported or indicated on radar in a designated area.

Tornado Watch
An alert situation when conditions are favorable for tornado formation in a designated area.

Torpor
A species descriptor that means a state of inactivity.

Tort
1) A negligent or intentional wrong against another where the law will grant money damages in a civil action. 2) Legal wrongs arising from a duty owed to people generally, rather than specifically as by contract.

Tortoise
A land turtle.

Total Dissolved Solids
The total dissolved (filterable) solids as determined by use of the method specified in 40 CFR 136.

Total Dosage Attack
A chemical operation that does not involve a time limit within which to produce the required toxic level.

Total Exposure Points
Points of potential exposure to substances from more than one exposure pathway.

Total Pressure
The sum of dynamic and static pressures.

Total Recordable Cases (TRC)
The number of recordable injuries and illnesses per 200,000 total hours worked by all employees during the period covered. The 200,000 hours worked are equivalent to 100 full-time workers at 40 hours per week for 50 weeks. TRC = number of recordable injuries and illnesses times 200,000/total hours worked.

Total Suspended Solids (TSS)
A measure of the suspended solids in wastewater, effluent, or water bodies, determined by using tests for total suspended nonfilterable solids. *See* Suspended Solids.

Total Suspended Particulate Matter
Suspended atmospheric particles of any size, solid and liquid, except uncombined water. Total suspended particulate matter is measured by the high volume sampler method or by an equivalent

method for purposes of monitoring for compliance with the 24-hour sulfur dioxide (SO_2) standard.

Total Trihalomethanes (TTHM)

According to the Safe Drinking Water Act, the sum of the concentration in milligrams per liter of the trihalomethane per liter of the trihalomethane compounds, rounded to two significant figures.

Totally Enclosed Manner

1) Any process that will ensure that any exposure of human beings or the environment to any concentration of PCBs (polychlorinated biphenyls) will be insignificant (scientifically harmless). 2) Any manner that will ensure no exposure of human beings or the environment to any concentration of PCBs.

Totally Enclosed Treatment Facility

A facility for hazardous waste that is directly connected to an industrial production process and that is constructed and operated in a manner that prevents the release of any hazardous waste or any constituent thereof into the environment during treatment. An example is a pipe in which waste acid is neutralized.

Toughness

Tendency of a material to absorb work.

TOx

Tetradichloroxylene.

Toxic

1) Having properties of acute or chronic toxicity. 2) Harmful to living organisms, or having the ability to harm the body, especially by chemical means. 3) A characteristic of any substance (other than a radioactive substance) that has the capacity to produce personal injury or illness to humans through ingestion, inhalation, or absorption through any body surface.

Toxic Air Pollutants

The aggregate emissions of the following: benzene; 1,3 butadiene; polycyclic organic matter (POM); acetaldehyde; and formaldehyde.

Toxic Chemicals

Chemicals or chemical categories listed in 40 CFR 372.65, the release of which under certain conditions must be reported in accordance with Superfund Amendment and Reauthorization Act(SARA) Title III, Section 313.

Toxic Chemical, Biological, or Radiological Attack

An attack directed at personnel, animals, or crops, using injurious agents of radiological, biological, or chemical origin.

Toxic Chemical Release Form

The information form required to be submitted by facilities that manufacture, process, or use (in quantities above a specific amount) chemicals listed under SARA Title III.

Toxic Chemical Source Reduction and Recycling

Activities, measures, and reports on a facility that does the following:

- quantify chemicals entering any waste stream (or otherwise released into the environment) prior to recycling, treatment, or disposal;

- set goals and timetables on the amount of chemicals from the facility that are recycled (at the facility or elsewhere) during a calendar year, identify the percentage change from the previous year, and disseminate the process of recycling used;

- minimize by way of source reduction practices used, the amount of chemicals used during such year by categories (e.g., equipment, technology, process, or procedure modifications; reformulation or redesign of products; substitution of raw materials; improvement in management, training, inventory control, materials handling, or other general operational phases of industrial facilities);

- approximate the amount chemicals expected to be used for the next two calendar years, as a percentage change from the current amount;
- identify the techniques that were used to accomplish source reduction opportunities;
- quantify the amount of any toxic chemical released into the environment that resulted from a catastrophic event, remedial action, or other one-time event, and is not associated with production processes; and
- quantify the amount of chemicals from the facility that are treated, at the facility or elsewhere.

Toxic Clouds
Airborne masses of gases, vapors, fumes, or aerosols containing toxic materials.

Toxic Pollutants
1) Materials contaminating the environment that cause death, disease, and/or birth defects in organisms that ingest or absorb them. The quantities and length of exposure necessary to cause these effects can vary widely. 2) Any pollutant listed as toxic under 9307(a)(1) of TSCA.

Toxic Potential
The inherent ability of a substance to cause harm.

Toxic Release Inventory System (TRIS)
The EPA database of toxic substances/chemical waste spills and releases into the environment.

Toxic Substances
Chemicals or mixtures that may present an unreasonable risk of injury to health or the environment.

Toxic Substances Control Act (TSCA)
The 1976 federal statute (15 USC 2601 et seq.) designed to provide control over toxic chemicals before they reach commerce and industry. TSCA was enacted by Congress to test, regulate, and screen all chemicals produced or imported into the United States. Thousands of chemicals and their compounds are developed each year with unknown toxic or dangerous characteristics. To prevent tragic consequences, TSCA requires that any chemical that reaches the consumer marketplace be tested for possible toxic effects prior to commercial manufacture. Any existing chemical that poses health and environmental hazards is tracked and reported under TSCA. Procedures also are authorized for corrective action under TSCA in cases of cleanup of toxic materials contamination. TSCA supplements other federal statutes, including the Clean Air Act and the Toxic Release Inventory under EPCRA. The Act requires prenotification to EPA of all new chemicals prior to manufacturing, including all existing data on toxicity and other characteristics, so that the EPA can regulate or prohibit the use of the chemical if it is found to pose an unreasonable risk to human health and/or the environment.

Toxic Wastes
Solid, chemical, and liquid waste materials, generated incidental to manufacturing processes at a laboratory or industrial commercial site, that require disposal. These wastes can be categorized as either acid or caustic or as indisputably toxic and hazardous wastes. *See* Industrial Waste.

Toxicants
Poisonous agents that kill or injure animal or plant life.

Toxicity
The degree of danger posed by a substance to animal or plant life. *See* Acute Toxicity; Chronic Toxicity.

Toxicology
1) The study of poisonous plants and chemicals. 2) The science and study of poisons control. 3) The multidisciplinary study of toxicants, their harmful effects on biological systems and the conditions under which these harmful effects occur. The mechanisms of action, detection, and treatment of the conditions produced by toxicants are studied.

Toxic Agent
A poison formed as a specific secretion product in the metabolism of a vegetable or animal organism as distinguished from inorganic poisons. Such

poisons can also be manufactured by synthetic processes.

TPC
An acronym for Temporary Procedure Change.

TPL
An acronym for Transient Protection Limit.

TPQ
See Threshold Planning Quantity.

TRA
See Test Reactor Area.

Trace Elements
Essential elements necessary in extremely small amounts for proper functioning of metabolism in plants and animals. An absence of these elements could lead to disease and deformities.

Tracheitis
Inflammation of the membrane lining the trachea.

Tracheobronchial Region
The area of the lungs including the trachea (windpipe) and conducting airways (bronchi, bronchioles, and terminal bronchioles).

Tractor Roads and Skid Trails
Constructed trails or established paths used by tractors or other vehicles for skidding logs in going to and from landings.

Traffic Circulation Map
A map showing traffic routes and the measures for traffic regulation. It indicates the roads for use of certain classes of traffic, the location of traffic control stations, and the directions in which traffic may move.

Traffic Density
The average number of vehicles that occupy one mile or one kilometer of road space, expressed in vehicles per mile or per kilometer.

Traffic Engineering
The branch of professional engineering that requires such education and experience as is necessary to understand the science of measuring traffic and travel and the human factors relating to traffic generation and flow; and requires the ability to apply this knowledge to planning, operating, and evaluating streets and highways and their networks, abutting lands and interrelationships with other modes of travel, to provide safe and efficient movement of people and goods.

Traffic Flow
The total number of vehicles passing a given point in a given time. Traffic flow is expressed as vehicles per hour.

Traffic Management
The direction, control, and supervision of all functions incident to the procurement and use of freight and passenger transportation services.

Traffic Pattern
The traffic flow that is prescribed for aircraft landing at, taxiing on, and taking off from an airport. The usual components of a traffic pattern are upwind leg, crosswind leg, downwind leg, base leg, and final approach.

Trafficability
The capability of terrain to bear traffic. It refers to the extent to which the terrain will permit continued movement of any and/or all types of traffic.

Trafficking, Archaeological Resources
To sell, purchase, exchange, transport, receive, or offer to sell, purchase, or exchange, in interstate or foreign commerce, any archaeological resource excavated, removed, sold, purchased, exchanged, transported, or received in violation of any provision, rule, regulation, ordinance, or permit in effect under state or local law.

Trained Investigators
Individuals who have completed the Department of Energy Accident Investigation Workshop.

Training

1) The development of a skill or group of skills. Instruction in an art, profession, or occupation. 2) The process whereby an organization's employees, either individually or in groups, participate in a formalized program of instruction (with lesson plan, instructor, or instructional device) to acquire skills and knowledge for their current or future job performance. Training categories are as follows:

- Job-Required — Job-required training is designed to ensure adequate performance in a current assignment. This includes orientation training, training made necessary by new assignments or new technology, refresher training for the maintenance of ongoing programs, safety training, and training mandated by law or other state authority;

- Job-Related — Job-related training is designed to increase job proficiency or improve performance above the acceptable level of competency established for a specific job assignment;

- Upward Mobility — Upward mobility training is designed to provide career movement opportunity for employees within classifications designated as upward mobility per US Government Codes;

- Career-Related — Career-related training is designed to assist in the development of career potential and is intended to help provide an opportunity for self-development while also assisting in the achievement of a department's or the organization's mission. Career-related training may be unrelated to a current job assignment.

Training Aids

Any item that is developed and/or procured with the primary intent that it shall assist in training and the process of learning.

Training Program Accreditation Plan

An action plan developed following a thorough contractor self-evaluation and identification of training programs requiring accreditation. The Training Program Accreditation Plan identifies scope and resource needs for accomplishing accreditation for all programs at a facility.

Training Programs

Planned, organized sequences of activities designed to prepare individuals to perform their jobs, to meet a specific position or classification need, and to maintain or improve their performance on the job.

Training, Types and Sources

The various types of training and training resources, including:

- In-service Training — training sponsored and administered by an organization for employees of the organization, wherein the organization maintains a high degree of control over course content. Such training includes courses or activities that are a) designed and administered by organizational departments individually or in joint agreement; b) offered by the Department of Personnel Administration; and c) designed or contracted exclusively for the organization through private consultants or firms, accredited colleges or universities, or other nonorganizational entities.

- Out-Service Training — training sponsored by nonorganizational entities, that is open to the public as well as persons employed by the organization; and sponsoring entities, rather than the organization, maintains control over the course content. Such training includes courses or activities that are a) offered through accredited colleges or universities; b) conducted by private consultants or firms or other nonstate agencies.

- Individual Development Plans — written plans describing formal training or development programs in which the employee intends to participate and that is approved by the employee's supervisor.

Trajectory

See Ballistic Trajectory.

Transattack Period

In nuclear warfare, the period from the initiation of the attack to its termination.

Transfer of Development Rights

An aid to land-use planning; land development rights may be separated from the other rights of land ownership and transferred to local government authorities who use them to direct growth and public works projects, or to protect environmental features, historic sites, and open spaces.

Transfer Facility

Any transportation-related facility including loading docks, parking areas, storage areas, and other similar areas where shipments of hazardous waste are held during the normal course of transportation, excluding transport vehicles unless they are used for the storage of PCB waste.

Transfer Station Sites/Areas

Sites at which solid wastes are concentrated for transport to a processing facility or land disposal site. Transfer stations may be fixed or mobile.

Transformation

The process of placing new genes into a host cell, thereby inducing the host cell to exhibit functions encoded by the DNA.

Transmissive Faults/Fractures

Faults or fractures that have sufficient permeability and vertical extent to allow fluids to move between formations.

Transmissivity (t)

The rate at which water of the prevailing kinematic viscosity is transmitted through a unit width of the aquifer under a unit hydraulic gradient. It is equal to an integration of the hydraulic conductivities across the saturated part of the aquifer perpendicular to the flow paths. Transmissivity values are given in gallons per minute (gpm) through a vertical section of an aquifer 1 foot wide and extending the full saturated height of an aquifer under a hydraulic gradient of one in the English Engineering System. In the Standard International System of Units, transmissivity is given in cubic meters per day through a vertical section, of an aquifer 1 meter wide and extending the full saturated height of an aquifer under a hydraulic gradient of one. Transmissivity is a function of properties of the liquid, the porous media, and the thickness of the porous media.

Transmit

To physically deliver a letter, document, or other written instrument to the addressee or to deposit the written instrument into the United States mail or other mail delivery service.

Transonic

Of or pertaining to the speed of a body in a surrounding fluid when the relative speed of the fluid is subsonic in some places and supersonic in others. This is encountered when passing from subsonic to supersonic speeds and vice versa. *See* Speed of Sound.

Transpiration

The process by which water vapor is lost to the atmosphere from living plants. The term can also be applied to the quantity of water thus dissipated.

Transport

1) The movement of a hazardous substance by any mode, including pipeline. In the case of a hazardous substance that has been accepted for transportation by a common or contract carrier, the term transport or transportation shall include any "stoppage in transit" that is temporary and incidental to the transportation movement, including stops for the ordinary operating convenience of the carrier. Any such stoppage shall be considered as a continuity of movement and not as the storage of a hazardous substance. 2) The carriage and related handling of any material by a vessel, or by any other vehicle, including aircraft.

Transport Aircraft

Aircraft designed primarily for the carriage of personnel and/or cargo. Transport aircraft may be classed according to range, as follows:

- Short-range — not to exceed 1,200 nautical miles at normal cruising conditions (2,222 Km);

- Medium-range — between 1,200 and 3,500 nautical miles at normal cruising conditions (2,222 and 6,482 Km);

- Long-range — exceeds 3,500 nautical miles at normal cruising conditions (6,482 Km).

Transport, Hazardous Substances

The movement of a hazardous substance by any mode, including pipeline (as defined in the Pipeline Safety Act), and in the case of a hazardous substance that has been accepted for transportation by a common or contract carrier, the terms "transport" or "transportation" shall include any stoppage in transit that is temporary, incidental to the transportation movement, and at the ordinary operating convenience of a common or contract carrier, and any such stoppage shall be considered as a continuity of movement and not as the storage of a hazardous substance.

Transport Indices

The numbers placed on a package to designate a degree of control to be exercised by the carrier during transportation. The transport index to be assigned to a package of radioactive material shall be determined by whichever total is larger:

- the highest radiation dose rate in millirem per hour at 1 meter from any accessible external surface of the package; or

- the transport index of each Fissile Class II package is calculated by dividing the number 50 by the number of such Fissile Class II packages that may be transported together as determined under the limitations of 10 CFR 71.

The final number expressing the transport index is rounded up to the next higher tenth (e.g., 1.01 becomes 1.1).

Transport Vehicle

1) A motor vehicle or rail car used for the transportation of cargo by any mode. 2) A motor vehicle designed and used without modification to the chassis, to provide general transport service in the movement of personnel and cargo. *See* Vehicle.

Transportability

The capability of material to be moved by towing, self-propulsion, or carrier via any means, such as railways, highways, waterways, pipelines, oceans, and airways.

Transportation

The movement of hazardous waste by air, rail, highway, or water. *See* Transport.

Transportation, Hazardous

The movement of a hazardous substance by any mode, including pipeline (as defined in the Pipeline Safety Act), and in the case of a hazardous substance that has been accepted for transportation by a common or contract carrier, the terms "transport" or "transportation" include any "stoppage in transit" that is temporary, incidental to the transportation movement, and at the ordinary operating convenience of a common or contract carrier, and any such stoppage shall be considered as a continuity of movement and not as the storage of a hazardous substance.

Transportation Control Demonstration (TCD)

EPA required studies developed by states beginning November 15, 1996, and each third year thereafter, demonstrating whether current aggregate vehicle mileage, aggregate vehicle air emissions, congestion levels, and other relevant parameters are consistent with those used for the area's demonstration of attainment. In considering such measures, the state should ensure adequate access to downtown, other commercial, and residential areas and should avoid measures that increase or relocate emissions and congestion rather than reduce them.

Transportation Control Measure (TCM)

1) Emission reduction and transportation control measures related to criteria pollutants and their precursors, including, but not limited to:

- programs for improved public transit;

- restriction of certain roads or lanes to, or construction of such roads or lanes for use by, passenger buses or high occupancy vehicles;

- employer-based transportation management plans, including incentives;

- trip-reduction ordinances;

- traffic flow improvement programs that achieve emission reductions;

- fringe and transportation corridor parking facilities serving multiple occupancy vehicle programs or transit service;

- programs to limit or restrict vehicle use in downtown areas or other areas of emission concentration particularly during periods of peak use;

- programs for the provision of all forms of high-occupancy, shared-ride services;

- programs to limit portions of road surfaces or certain sections of the metropolitan area to the use of nonmotorized vehicles or pedestrian use, both as to time and place;

- programs for secure bicycle storage facilities and other facilities, including bicycle lanes, for the convenience and protection of bicyclists, in both public and private areas;

- programs to control extended idling of vehicles;

- programs to reduce motor vehicle emissions, that are caused by extreme cold start conditions;

- employer-sponsored programs to permit flexible work schedules;

- programs and ordinances to facilitate nonautomobile travel, provision and utilization of mass transit, and to generally reduce the need for single-occupant vehicle travel, as part of transportation planning and development efforts of a locality, including programs and ordinances applicable to new shopping centers, special events, and other centers of vehicle activity;

- programs for new construction and major reconstructions of paths, tracks or areas solely for the use by pedestrian or other nonmotorized means of transportation when economically feasible and in the public interest; and

- programs to encourage the voluntary removal from use and the marketplace of pre-1980 model year light duty vehicles and pre-1980 model light duty trucks.

2) Information on additional methods or strategies that will contribute to the reduction of mobile source related pollutants during periods in which any primary ambient air quality standard will be exceeded and during episodes for which an air pollution alert, warning, or emergency has been declared. 3) Information on other measures that may be employed to reduce the impact on public health or protect the health of sensitive or susceptible individuals or groups. 4) Information on the extent to which any process, procedure, or method to reduce or control such air pollutant may cause an increase in the emissions or formation of any other pollutant.

Transportation Control Strategies and Measure (TCSM)

According to CAA, any activity that would improve vehicular-related air quality impacts including, but not limited to, a) construction or restriction of certain roads or lanes solely for the use of passenger buses or high-occupancy vehicles; b) planning for requirements for employers to reduce employee work-trip-related vehicle emissions; c) highway ramp metering, traffic signalization, and related programs that improve traffic flow and achieve a net emission reduction; d) fringe and transportation corridor parking facilities serving multiple occupancy vehicle programs or transit operations; e) programs to limit or restrict vehicle use in downtown areas or other areas of emission concentration particularly during periods of peak use, through road use charges, tolls, parking surcharges, or other pricing mechanisms, vehicle restricted zones or periods, or other transportation-related programs as the Administrator, in consultation with the Secretary of Transportation, finds would improve air quality and would not encourage single-occupancy vehicle capacity.

Transportation Controls

Any plan, procedure, method, or arrangement, or any system of incentives, disincentives, restrictions, and requirements, that is designed to reduce the amount of energy consumed in transportation, except that the term does not include rationing of gasoline or diesel fuel.

Transportation Emergency

A situation created by a shortage of normal transportation capability and of a magnitude sufficient to frustrate military movement requirements, and that requires extraordinary action by the President or other designated authority to ensure continued movement of essential Department of Defense Traffic.

Transportation Incidents
Incidents that involve a transportation vehicle or shipment containing hazardous or radioactive materials.

Transportation Operating Agencies
Those federal agencies having responsibilities under national emergency conditions for the operational direction of one or more forms of transportation. Also called Federal Modal Agencies; Federal Transport Agencies.

Transportation System
All the land, water, and air routes and transportation assets of the United States.

Transportation Tank
A tank permanently installed on a truck, trailer, or semitrailer used to transport a product over the highway.

Transporters
People engaged in the offsite transportation of hazardous waste by air, rail, highway, or water.

Transports
Any movement of property by any mode, and any loading, unloading, or storage incidental thereto.

Transshipment Point
A location where material is transferred between vehicles.

Transuranic (TRU) Contaminated Materials
Materials that, without regard to source or form, contain certain alpha-emitting radionuclides with long half-lives.

Transuranic Elements
See Transuranic Nuclides.

Transuranic Nuclides
Elements that have atomic numbers greater than 92; all are radioactive, are products of artificial nuclear changes, and are members of the actinide group.

Transuranic Radionuclides
See Transuranic Nuclides.

Transuranic Wastes (TRU Waste)
1) Waste that is contaminated with alpha-emitting transuranic nuclides with half-lives greater than 20 years and concentrations greater than 100 nanocuries per gram. 2) TRU contaminated materials that have been declared as having no significant economic value or use. The following are not considered TRU wastes: a) high-level radioactive wastes; b) wastes that the DOE has determined, with the concurrence of the Administrator, do not need the degree of isolation required by regulation; or c) wastes that the Commission has approved for disposal on a case-by-case basis in accordance with 20 CFR Part 61.

Transverse
A term meaning extended or lying across.

Trap Tank
A tank mounted on wheels for off-highway use and having a capacity of 1200 gallons or less and used to transport LPG from a storage tank to a mobile fuel tank.

Trash-to-Energy Plans
Plans for putting waste back to work by burning trash to produce energy.

Travel Expenses
1) Per Diem Expenses — Per diem expenses consist of the charges and attendant expenses for meals and lodging and all charges for personal expenses incurred while on travel status. 2) Business Expenses — Business expenses consist of the charges for business phone calls and telegrams; emergency clothing, equipment or supply purchases; and all other charges necessary to the completion of official business. Any emergency purchase shall be explained, and if over $25 must be approved by the department head, deputy, or chief administrative officer.

Traverse

A method of surveying in which lengths and directions of lines between points on the earth are obtained by or from field measurements, and used in determining positions of the points.

Traverse Level

That vertical displacement above low-level air defense systems, expressed both as a height and altitude, at which aircraft can cross.

TRC

See Total Recordable Cases.

TRE

An acronym for Turbidity Removal Evaporator.

Treatability Studies

Studies in which a hazardous waste is subjected to a treatment process to determine a) whether the waste is amenable to the treatment process; b) what pretreatment, if any, is required; c) the optimal process conditions needed to achieve the desired treatment; d) the efficiency of a treatment process for a specific waste or wastes; and/or e) the characteristics and volumes of residuals from a particular treatment process. Also included in this definition, for the purpose of the 40 CFR 261.4 (e) and (f) exemptions, are liner compatibility, corrosion, and other material compatibility studies and toxicological and health effect studies.

Treatment

1) Any method, technique, or process designed to change the physical or chemical character of waste to render it less hazardous, safer to transport, store or dispose of, or reduce its volume. 2) The techniques or actions customarily applied in a specified situation. 3) When used in connection with hazardous waste, means any method, technique, or process, including neutralization, designed to change the physical, chemical, or biological character or composition of any hazardous waste so as to neutralize such waste or so as to render such waste nonhazardous, safer for transport, amenable for recovery, amenable for storage, or reduced in volume.

Treatment Facilities

Specific areas of land, structures, and equipment dedicated to waste treatment and related activities.

Treatment, Storage, and Disposal Facility (TSDF)

1) The name the EPA assigns to facilities that are licensed to transfer, treat, store, or dispose of regulated hazardous wastes under the Resource Conservation and Recovery Act (RCRA). A TSDF permit is the document assigned by regulators for specific locations; holders of TSDF permits do not necessarily perform actual final treatment or disposal services, but may just store wastes for eventual shipment. 2) A site where a hazardous substance is treated, stored, or disposed. TSD facilities are regulated by EPA and states under RCRA.

Treatment Technique Requirement

A requirement in a national primary drinking water regulation that specifies for a contaminant each treatment technique known to the Administrator that leads to a reduction in the level of such contaminant sufficient to satisfy the requirements of 40 CFR 141.

Treatment Technologies

Any unit operations or series of unit operations that alter the composition of a hazardous substance or pollutant or contaminant through chemical, biological, or physical means so as to reduce toxicity, mobility, or volume of contaminated materials being treated.

Treatment Zone

A soil area of the unsaturated zone of a land treatment unit within which hazardous constituents are degraded, transformed, or immobilized.

Tree

A woody plant that at maturity is usually 6m (20 feet) or more in height and generally has a single trunk, unbranched for 1 m or more above the ground, and a more or less definite crown (e.g., red maple (*Acer rubrum*) and northern white cedar (*Thuja occidentalis*).

Trench

An excavation made below the surface of the ground. In general, the depth is greater than the width at the bottom, but the width of a trench at the bottom is not greater than 15 feet.

Trench Jack

Screw or hydraulic type jacks used as cross bracing in a trench shoring system.

Trench Shield

A protective device that shields workers from the effect of ground movement and that can be moved along as work progresses.

Trending

An analysis of parts, systems, component surveillance, performance, and operating histories to determine such things as failure causes, operational effectiveness, cost-effectiveness, and other attributes.

Triage

The evaluation, classification, and medical screening of patients to determine their priority for treatment; the separation of a large number of casualties in emergency/disaster medical care into three groups a) those who cannot be expected to survive even with treatments; b) those who will recover without treatment; and c) the priority group of those who need treatment in order to survive.

Triangulation Station

A point on the earth, the position of which is determined by triangulation. Also called trig point.

Tribe

A taxonomic category between family and genus.

Trichloroethane

A solvent suspected of causing cancer in humans that is used in the electronics industry and as a dry-cleaning fluid.

Trichloroethylene (TCE)

A stable, low boiling colorless liquid, toxic by inhalation. TCE is used as a solvent, metal degreasing agent, and in other industrial applications.

Trichotomous

A species descriptor that means divided into three parts.

Trichotomously Branched

A species descriptor that means branched into three parts.

Trickling Filter

A coarse, biological treatment system in which wastewater is trickled over a bed of stones or other material covered with bacterial growth. The bacteria break down the organic waste in the sewage and produce clean water.

Trident

A general descriptive term for the seabased strategic weapon system consisting of the highly survivable nuclear-powered Trident submarine, long-range Trident ballistic missiles, and the integrated refit facilities required to support the submarine and missile subsystems as well as associated personnel.

Trident I

A three-stage, solid propellant ballistic missile capable of being launched from a Trident submarine either surfaced or submerged. It is sized to permit backfit into Poseidon submarines and is equipped with advanced guidance, nuclear warheads and a maneuverable bus that can deploy these warheads to separate targets. It is capable of carrying a full payload to 4,000 nautical miles with greater ranges achievable in reduced payload configurations. Designated as UGM-96A.

Trident II

A solid propellant ballistic missile capable of being launched from a Trident submarine. It is larger than the Trident I missile and will replace these missiles in Ohio-class submarines. It will provide the option to deploy a higher throw weight, more accurate, submarine-launched ballistic missile.

Tridentate
A species descriptor that means long, three-pronged fork.

Trigger Event
A report of an event or condition that initiates a hazard analysis or correction action function.

Trihalomethane (THM)
1) One of a family of organic compounds, named as derivatives of methane. THMs are generally the byproduct from chlorination of drinking water that contains organic material. 2) One of the family of organic compounds, named as derivatives of methane, wherein three of the four hydrogen atoms in methane are each substituted by a halogen atom in the molecular structure.

TRIP
An acronym for Toxic Release Inventory Program.

Tripartite Agreement
The agreement signed in March 1988 by the Director General for Ecological Conservation of Natural Resources of Mexico, the Director of the Canadian Wildlife Service, and the Director of the U.S. Fish and Wildlife Service.

Triple Rinse
The flushing of containers three times, each time using a volume of the normal diluent equal to approximately 10% of the container's capacity and adding the rinse liquid to the spray mixture or disposing of the by a method prescribed for disposing of the pesticide.

TRIS
See Toxic Release Inventory System.

Trismus
Lockjaw.

Tritium (T)
A manmade radioactive isotope of hydrogen with two neutrons and one proton in its nucleus. Because it is chemically identical to natural hydrogen, tritium can easily be taken into the body by any ingestion path. It decays by beta emission and has a radioactive half-life of about 12.5 years.

Troglobitic
A species descriptor that means cave-dwelling; in animals, a species that lives and completes its life cycle in caves and underground spaces, usually with small or absent eyes, attenuated appendages, and other adaptations to the subsurface environment.

Trophic Level
The nitrate and phosphate nutrient levels of a body of water.

Trophogenic Region
The upper region of a body of water where organic material is produced by photosynthesis.

Tropical Storm
A tropical cyclone in which the surface wind speed is at least 34 knots, but no more than 63 knots.

Tropopause
The boundary between the troposphere and the stratosphere, averaging about 10 miles over the equator, decreasing to about 4 miles over the poles; temperatures no longer decrease with height; the air is stagnant, and particulates cannot rise within it. The tropopause normally occurs at an altitude of about 25,000 to 45,000 feet (8 to 15 kilometers) in polar and temperate zones, and at 55,000 feet (20 kilometers) in the tropics. *See* Atmosphere.

Troposphere
The lowest level of the atmosphere where temperature decreases with height and where most weather phenomena occur; the area bounded by the earth's surface and the tropopause; the portion of the atmosphere between 7 miles and 10 miles

from the earth's surface where clouds form, convection is active, and mixing is continuous and more or less complete. *See* Atmosphere.

Tropospheric Scatter
The propagation of electromagnetic waves by scattering as a result of irregularities or discontinuities in the physical properties of the troposphere.

TRU
See Transuranic Nuclides.

TRU Wastes
See Transuranic Wastes.

True Bearing
The direction to an object from a point, expressed as a horizontal angle measured clockwise from true north.

True Convergence
The angle at which one meridian is inclined to another on the surface of the earth. *See* Convergence.

True Horizon
1) The boundary of a horizontal plane passing through a point of vision. 2) In photogrammetry, the boundary of a horizontal plane passing through the perspective center of a lens system.

True North
The direction from an observer's position to the geographic North Pole. The north direction of any geographic meridian.

Trust Fund
A fund set up under the Comprehensive Environmental Response, Compensation, and Liability Act (CERCLA Section 221) to help pay for cleanup of hazardous waste sites and to take legal action to force those responsible for the sites to clean them up.

TSA
An acronym for Technical Safety Appraisals.

TSCA
See Toxic Substances Control Act of 1976.

TSCANS
An abbreviation for computer code used for processing temperature data for alarm and rod reversal purposes.

TSCAT
An abbreviation for the saturation temperature used to calculate critical temperature ratios.

TSCATS
An abbreviation for an on-line TSCA test submission database.

TSCM
An acronym for Temperature Scram Circuit Monitor.

TSD
An acronym for Treatment, Storage, and Disposal.

TSDF
See Treatment, Storage, and Disposal Facility (RCRA).

TSS
See Total Suspended Solids.

Tsunamis
A series of waves of extremely long length and period typically caused by a sudden vertical displacement of a large area of the sea floor during an undersea earthquake.

TSUS
An acronym for Territorial Sea of the United States.

TTO
An acronym for Total Toxic Organics.

TTR
An acronym for Time to Repair.

Tubercle

1) In mussels a small raised area that limits water loss and prevents entry by microorganisms. 2) A species descriptor for a small knobby prominence on a plant or animal.

Tuberculation

A species descriptor that means having tubercles (small raised area in mussels that limits water loss).

Tubular Necrosis

Death of the cells lining the kidney tubules.

Tumor

An abnormal growth of tissue; a neoplasm.

Tunable Dye Laser

A laser whose active medium is a liquid dye, pumped by another laser or flash lamps, to produce various colors of light. The color of light may be tuned by adjusting optical tuning elements and/or changing the dye used.

Tundra

1) Treeless arctic and alpine regions, usually void of any vegetation other than certain types of mosses, herbaceous plants, and lichens. 2) A type of ecosystem dominated by lichens, mosses, grasses, and woody plants. Tundra is found at high latitudes (arctic tundra) and high altitudes (alpine tundra). Arctic tundra is underlain by permafrost and is usually very wet. *See* Wetlands.

Turbid

Muddy; comprised of sediment or foreign particles stirred up.

Turbidimeters

Devices that measure the amount of suspended solids in a liquid.

Turbidity

1) Haziness in air caused by the presence of particles and pollutants. 2) A cloudy condition in water due to suspended silt or organic matter. 3)

The cloudiness in a fluid caused by the presence of finely divided, suspended material.

Turbine Size (kW)

A turbine manufacturer's published kW rating, specified in units of miles per hour (mph) with wind speed shown in parentheses.

Turbulence

Irregular movement of air or fluids in which no defined path can be determined.

TVAA

An acronym for Tennessee Valley Authority Act of 1933.

TW

See Test Weight.

TWA

See Time Weighted Average.

TWF

An acronym for Transuranic Waste Facility.

TWTSF

An acronym for Transuranic Waste Treatment and Storage Facility.

Type A Assessments

Standard procedures for simplified assessments requiring minimal field observation to determine damages as specified in Section 301(c)(2)(A) of CERCLA.

Type B Assessments

Alternative methodologies for conducting assessments in individual cases to determine 0% type and extent of short-term and long-term injury and damages, as specified in Section 301(c)(2)(B) of CERCLA.

Type A Packaging

Packaging that is designed in accordance with the general packaging requirements and that is adequate to prevent the loss or dispersal of radioactive contents and to retain the efficiency of its radiation shielding properties if the package is subjected to the prescribed tests (49 CFR Part 173.398(b)) that represent the normal, rough handling conditions of transport.

Type B Packaging

Packaging radioactive material that meets the standards for Type A packaging and, in addition, meets the standards for the hypothetical accident conditions of transport as prescribed in 49 CFR Part 173.398(c).

Types of Burst

See Fallout Safe Height of Burst; High Airburst; High Altitude Burst; Low Airburst; Nuclear Airburst; Nuclear Exoatmospheric Burst; Safe Burst Height.

Types of Resin

Broad classifications of resin referring to the basic manufacturing processes for producing that resin, including, but not limited to, the suspension, dispersion, latex, bulk, and solution processes.

U

U.S. Armed Forces
A term used to denote collectively the regular components of the Army, Navy, Air Force, Marine Corps, and Coast Guard. *See* Armed Forces of the United States.

U.S. Citizen/Corporation
Any person who is a United States citizen by law, birth, or naturalization, any state, any agency of a state, or a group of states, or any corporation, partnership, or association organized under the laws of any state that has as its president or other chief executive officer and as its chairman of the board of directors, or holder of a similar office, a person who is a United States citizen by law, birth, or naturalization, and that has at least 75 per centum of the interest therein owned by citizens of the United States. Seventy-five per centum of the interest in the corporation shall not be deemed to be owned by citizens of the United States if:

- the title to 75 per centum of its stock is not vested in such citizens free from any trust or fiduciary obligation in favor of any person not a citizen of the United States;

- seventy-five per centum of the voting power in such corporation is not vested in citizens of the United States;

- through any contract or understanding it is so arranged that more than 25 per centum of the voting power may be exercised, directly or indirectly, in behalf of any person who is not a citizen of the United States; or

- if by any other means whatsoever control of any interest in the corporation in excess of 25 per centum is conferred upon or permitted to be exercised by any person who is not a citizen of the United States.

U.S. Civil Authorities
Elected and appointed public officials and employees who constitute the governments of the 50 states, District of Columbia, Commonwealth of Puerto Rico, U.S. possessions and territories, and political subdivisions thereof.

U.S. Coast Guard (USCG)
The federal agency responsible for port safety, maritime law enforcement, boating safety, search and rescue, aids to navigation, merchant marine safety, and environmental protection.

The Coast Guard works with EPA on marine protection programs, including regulating the transportation of hazardous cargoes, oil pollution cleanup, and marine salvage. Address: 2100 2nd Street, S.W., Washington, DC 20593; (202)267-1587.

U.S. Country Team
The senior, in-country, United States coordinating and supervising body, headed by the chief of the U.S. diplomatic mission, usually an ambassador, and composed of the senior member of each represented U.S. department or agency, as desired by the chief of the U.S. diplomatic mission.

U.S. Department of Energy (DOE)

DOE provides the framework for a comprehensive and balanced national energy plan through the coordination and administration of the energy functions of the federal government. The department is responsible for long-term, high-risk research and development of energy technology; the marketing of federal power; energy conservation; the nuclear weapons program; energy regulatory programs; and a central energy data collection and analysis program.

U.S. Department of Justice (DOJ)

The department responsible for all enforcement actions that must be filed in court, and organizing evidentiary and other documents to prepare for and conduct litigation. Litigation includes the protection, use, and development of the nation's natural resources and public lands, wildlife protection, Native American Indian rights and claims, cleanup of hazardous waste sites, acquisition of private property for federal use, and defense of environmental challenges to government programs and activities.

DOJ's Environment and Natural Resources Division is the nation's environmental lawyer and the largest environmental law firm in the country. Address: 10th and Constitution Ave., N.W., Washington, DC 20530; (202)514-2007.

U.S. Department of Labor (DOL)

DOL fosters, promotes, and develops the welfare of the wage earners of the United States, to improve the working conditions, and to advance their opportunities for profitable employment. The department administers a variety of federal labor laws guaranteeing workers' rights to safe and healthful working conditions, a minimum hourly wage and overtime pay, freedom from employment discrimination, unemployment insurance, and workers' compensation. It also protects workers' pension rights, provides for job training programs; helps workers find jobs; works to strengthen free collective bargaining; and keeps track of changes in employment, policies, and other national economic measurements.

U.S. Department of Transportation (DOT)

DOT establishes the nation's overall transportation policy. Under its umbrella there are nine administrations whose jurisdictions include highway planning, development, and construction; urban mass transit; railroads, aviation; and the safety of waterways, ports, highways, and oil and gas pipelines. Decisions made by the department in conjunction with the appropriate state and local officials strongly affect programs such as land planning, energy conservation, scarce resource utilization, and technological change. The department is also responsible for setting standards for safety and providing funds to plan, construct, and operate transportation systems (rail, highway, air, or water), and providing law enforcement and traffic management services for the nation's airspace and waterways. DOT regulates manufacturers of containers and transporters of hazardous materials. Address: 400 7th Street, S.W., Washington, DC 20590; (202)366-4570.

U.S. District Courts

The federal district courts of the United States and the United States courts of the Commonwealth of Puerto Rico, Guam, the U.S. Virgin Islands, the Canal Zone, and American Samoa.

U.S. Energy Information

All information in whatever form on a) fuel reserves, exploration, extraction, and energy resources (including petrochemical feedstocks) wherever located; b) production, distribution, and consumption of energy and fuels wherever carried on; and c) matters relating to energy and fuels, such as corporate structures and proprietary relationships, costs, prices, capital investment, and assets, and other matters directly related thereto, wherever they exist.

U.S. Environmental Protection Agency (EPA)

The federal agency established in 1970 by presidential Executive Order to bring together and coordinate parts of various government agencies involved with minimizing adverse environmental impacts and controlling pollution. The EPA protects and enhances our environment today and for future generations to the fullest extent possible under the laws enacted by Congress. The Agency's mission is to control and abate pollution in the areas of air, water, solid wastes, pesticides, radiation, and toxic substances. Its mandate is to mount an integrated, coordinated attack on environmental pollution in cooperation with state and local governments. When contacting EPA, it is best to start with your Regional Office. If the Regional Office is unable to assist you, your questions may be directed to EPA Headquarters in Washington, DC, at 401 M Street, S.W., Washington, DC 20460; (202)260-2080. *See* Region.

U.S. Firm

A corporation, partnership, limited partnership, or sole proprietorship that is incorporated or established under the laws of any of the United States with its principal place of business in the United States.

U.S. Fish and Wildlife Service (USFWS)

The branch of the U.S. Department of the Interior that is responsible for the protection of wildlife, wetlands habitats, and resource management.

U.S. Geological Survey (USGS)

An agency within the Department of the Interior responsible for conservation, geologic surveys, analyzing the quantity and quality of surface and groundwater and precipitation, and conducting research in geology and hydrology. Programs include extensive topographic and land-use mapping, energy and mineral resource assessments, evaluations of natural disasters, and space exploration. Address: 12201 Sunrise Valley Drive, Mail Stop 119, Reston, VA 22092; (703)648-4460.

U.S. Government Survey System (USGSS)

Often called the rectangular survey system; a method of describing or locating real property by reference to the government survey.

U.S. Military Service, Funded Foreign Training

Training that is provided to foreign nationals in United States Military Service schools and instal-

lations under authority other than the Foreign Assistance Act of 1961.

U.S. Roland

A short range, low-altitude, all-weather, Army air defense artillery surface-to-air missile system that is based upon the Roland III missile system.

UAV

See Unmanned Aerial Vehicle.

Ubiquitous Background Levels

Concentrations of chemicals that are present in the environment due to anthropogenic sources (e.g., industry, automobiles).

UCC

See Ultra Clean Coal.

UDSSP

An acronym for Upper Delaware Segment Special Provisions (WSRA).

UIC

See Underground Injection Control.

UL

An acronym for the Underwriters Laboratory.

Ullage

The amount by which a packaging falls short of being liquid full, usually expressed in percent by volume.

Ultimate Biochemical Oxygen Demand

1) The total quantity of oxygen required to satisfy completely the first-stage biochemical oxygen demand. 2) More strictly, the total quantity of oxygen required to satisfy completely both the first-stage and second-stage biochemical oxygen demands. *See* Biochemical Oxygen Demand.

Ultimate Purchaser

With respect to any new motor vehicle or new motor vehicle engine, the first person who in good faith purchases such new motor vehicle or new engine for purposes other than resale.

Ultisol
A type of mineral soil with an accumulation of silicate clay layers with an average soil temperature of 8° Celsius or higher.

Ultra Clean Coal (UCC)
Coal that has been washed, ground into fine particles, then chemically treated to remove sulfur, ash, silicone, and other substances; usually briquetted and coated with a sealant made from coal.

Ultramafic
Excessively rich in magnesium and iron.

Ultraviolet Imagery
That imagery produced as a result of sensing ultraviolet radiations reflected from a given surface.

Ultraviolet (UV) Radiation
Electromagnetic radiation with wavelengths between soft X-rays and visible violet light, often broken down into UV-A (315-400nm), UV-B (280-315nm), and UV-C (100-280nm).

Ultraviolet Rays
Radiation from the sun that can be useful or potentially harmful. UV rays from one part of the spectrum enhance plant life and are useful in some medical and dental procedures; UV rays from other parts of the spectrum to which humans are exposed (e.g., while getting a sun tan) can cause skin cancer or other tissue damage. The ozone layer in the atmosphere provides a protective shield that limits the amount of ultraviolet rays that reach the earth's surface.

Umbel
A species descriptor that means an umbrella-like flower cluster.

Umbo
In biology, a knob like protuberance, such as a prominence near the hinge of a bivalve shell.

Umbonate
A species descriptor that means knob like protuberance.

UMT
See Uranium Mill Tailings.

UMTA
An acronym for Urban Mass Transportation Act of 1964.

UMTRA
An acronym for Uranium Mill Tailings Remedial Action.

UMTRAP
An acronym for Uranium Mill Tailings Remedial Action Program.

UMTRCA
An acronym for Uranium Mill Tailings Radiation Control Act of 1978.

UNAAF
An acronym for Unified Action Armed Forces.

Unacceptable Adverse Effects
Impacts on an aquatic or wetland ecosystem that are likely to result in significant degradation of municipal water supplies (including surface or groundwater) or significant loss of or damage to fisheries, shell-fishing, or wildlife habitats or recreation areas.

Unaccounted For
An inclusive term applicable to personnel whose person or remains are not recovered or otherwise accounted for following a hazardous incident. Commonly used when referring to personnel who are killed in accidents, or in action (military), and whose bodies are not recovered. *See* Casualty; Casualty Category; Casualty Status.

UNAMAP
Computer acronym for User's Network for Applied Modeling of Air Pollution.

Unattached Fractions

The fractions of any short-lived daughter products of radon that are not attached to the ambient aerosol.

Unauthorized Excavation, Removal, Damage, Alteration, or Defacement (ARPA)

Regarding archaeological resources, means to illegally excavate, remove, damage, or otherwise alter or deface, or attempt to excavate, remove, damage, or otherwise alter or deface any archaeological resource located on public lands or Native American Indian lands unless such activity is pursuant to a permit.

Uncertain Environment

See Operational Environment.

Uncertainty

1) In the conduct of risk assessment (hazard identification, dose-response assessment, exposure assessment, risk characterization) the need to make assumptions or best judgments in the absence of precise scientific data creates uncertainties. These uncertainties, expressed qualitatively and sometimes quantitatively, attempt to define the usefulness of a particular evaluation in making a decision based upon the available data. 2) Non-quantifiable increases in accident probability resulting from the lack of a detailed, implementable, safety program (e.g., human factors review, hazard analysis, training). 3) Oversight and omissions in a management system. This may be termed descriptive uncertainty. A "degree of uncertainty" results from a quantitative inadequacy of estimation of a stated known factor.

Uncertainty Factor (UF)

One of several, generally 10-fold factors, applied to a NOAEL or a LOAEL to derive a reference dose (RfD) from experimental data. UFs are intended to account for a) the variation in the sensitivity among the members of the human population; b) the uncertainty in extrapolating animal data to humans; c) the uncertainty in extrapolating from data obtained in a less-than-lifetime exposure study to chronic exposure; and d) the uncertainty in using a LOAEL rather than a NOAEL for estimating the threshold region.

Unclassified Matter

Official matter that does not require the application of security safeguards, but the disclosure of which may be subject to control for other reasons. *See* Classified Matter.

Unconfined Aquifer

Conditions in which the upper surface of the zone of saturation forms a water table under atmospheric pressure.

Unconsolidated Aquifer

An aquifer made of loose material, such as sand or gravel that has not undergone lithification.

Uncontested

A stipulation or settlement that is filed concurrently by all parties to the proceeding in which such stipulation or settlement is proposed for adoption, or is not contested by any party to the proceeding within the comment period after service of the stipulation or settlement on all parties to the proceeding.

Uncontrolled Hazardous Waste Sites

Areas where an accumulation of hazardous waste create a threat to the health and safety of individuals or the environment or both. Some sites are found on public lands, such as those created by former municipal, county, or state landfills where illegal or poorly managed waste disposal has taken place. Other sites are found on private property, often belonging to generators or former generators of hazardous waste. Examples of such sites include, but are not limited to, surface impoundments, landfills and dumps.

Uncontrolled Mosaic

A mosaic composed of uncorrected photographs, the details of which have been matched from print to print, without ground control or other orientation. Accurate measurement and direction cannot be accomplished.

Uncontrolled Total Arsenic Emissions

The total inorganic arsenic in the glass melting furnace exhaust gas preceding any add-on emission control device.

Unconventional Warfare (UW)

A broad spectrum of military and paramilitary operations, normally of long duration, predominantly conducted by indigenous or surrogate forces who are organized, trained, equipped, supported, and directed in varying degrees by an external source. It includes guerrilla warfare and other direct offensive, low visibility, covert, or clandestine operations, as well as the indirect activities of subversion, sabotage, intelligence activities, and evasion and escape.

Uncorrected Violation

Any violation reported in a Facility Audit or Inspection Report that remains uncorrected for 60 days or more after the completion and submission of the audit/report.

Under Secretary

The Under Secretary of Commerce for Oceans and Atmosphere. The Under Secretary along with the Director serves as cochairperson of the Aquatic Nuisance Species Task Force (ANSTF) and is jointly responsible, and authorized to undertake activities necessary, for carrying out the National Ballast Water Control Program in consultation and cooperation with the other members of the ANSTF. *See* Aquatic Nuisance Species Task Force.

Underfire Air

Any fired or induced air, under control as to quantity and direction, that is supplied from beneath and that passes through solid waste fuel beds.

Underground Areas

Underground rooms, such as basements, cellars, shafts or vaults, providing enough space for physical inspection of the exterior of a tank situated on or above the surface of the floor.

Underground Coal Mine Development

The expansion of any existing underground coal mine in a manner designed to increase the rate of production of such mine, and the reopening of any underground coal mine that had previously been closed. Such term also includes construction of a coal preparation plant that is designed to reduce the sulfur content of coal produced from any coal mine.

Underground Injection

The subsurface emplacement of fluids through a bored, drilled, or driven well; or through a dug well where the depth is greater than the largest surface dimension. 2) A well injection. The term does not typically include the underground injection of natural gas for purposes of storage. *See* Injection Well.

Underground Injection Control (UIC)

1) A program under the Safe Drinking Water Act that regulates the use of wells to pump fluids into the ground; effective programs to prevent underground injection that endangers drinking water sources. Authorization of underground injection by permit issued by the state; includes inspection, monitoring, recordkeeping, and reporting requirements. 2) The program that provides grants to states under Section 1443(b) of SDWA, and sets forth regulations for injection wells.

Underground Injection Impact

An adverse impact that endangers drinking water sources, if such injection results in the presence of contaminants in underground water that supplies or can reasonably be expected to supply any public water system; and if the presence of such contaminants may result in system noncompliance with any national primary drinking water regulation, or may pose a threat to otherwise adversely affect the health of persons.

Underground Releases

Any below ground releases.

Underground Sources of Drinking Water

1) Aquifers or a portion of one that supplies any public water system; contains a sufficient quantity

of groundwater to supply a public water system; currently supplies drinking water for human consumption; contains fewer than 10,000 mg/l total dissolved solids; and/or that is not an exempted aquifer. 2) As defined in the UIC (Underground Injection Control) program, this term refers to aquifers that are currently being used as a source of drinking water, and those that are capable of supplying a public water system. They have a total dissolved solids content of 10,000 milligrams per liter or less, and are not exempted aquifers. *See* Exempted Aquifer.

Underground Storage Tank (UST)
1) Any one of a combination of tanks, including pipes that connect them, used to contain an accumulation of gasoline, or other petroleum products or chemical solutions and the volume of which is 10% or more beneath the surface of the ground. 2) A device whose entire surface area is totally below the surface of and covered by the ground. 3) A device meeting the definition of "tanks" in 40 CFR 260.10.

Underground Uranium Mines
Manmade underground excavations made for the purpose of removing material containing uranium for the principal purpose of recovering uranium.

Underground Water Source Protection Program
A program for the adoption and enforcement of a water source protection program and for keeping records and making required reports.

Underpinnings
Permanent supports replacing or reinforcing the older supports beneath a wall or column.

Undersea and Space Robots
The vehicles or platforms that transport the tools to the site. These vehicles are called remotely operated vehicles (ROVs) or autonomous undersea vehicles (AUVs); the feature that distinguishes them is, respectively, the presence or absence of an electronics tether that connects the vehicle and surface control station.

Undershell
A species descriptor that means plastron.

Undertaking
As referred to in preservation and environmental law and regulations, any federal, federally assisted, federally licensed, or federally sanctioned action, activity, or program. Undertakings include new and continuing projects and program activities that are a) directly undertaken by federal agencies; b) supported in whole or in part, directly or indirectly, by federal agencies; c) carried out pursuant to a federal lease, permit, license, approval, or other form of permission; or d) proposed by a federal agency for congressional authorization or appropriation. Undertakings may be either site-specific or nonsite-specific. Refer to 36 CFR 800.2(c).

Underwater Archaeology
The subdiscipline of archaeology that utilizes specialized skills and techniques to extend archaeological method and theory to submerged sites. This includes nautical archaeology that is specifically focused on shipwreck sites.

Underwater Demolition
The destruction or neutralization of underwater obstacles; this is normally accomplished by underwater demolition teams.

Underwater Demolition Team (UDT)
A specially trained and equipped team organized to a) make hydrographic reconnaissance of approaches to prospective landing beaches; b) effect demolition of obstacles and clearing mines in certain areas; c) locate, improve, and mark useable channels; d) secure channel and harbor clearance; e) acquire pertinent data during pre-assault operations, including military information; f) visually observe the hinterland to gain information useful to the landing force; and g) perform miscellaneous underwater and surface tasks within their capabilities.

Underwriter
An insurer.

Undeveloped Coastal Barrier

1) A depositional geologic feature (e.g., a bay barrier, tombolo, barrier spit, or barrier island) that is subject to wave, tidal, and wind energies, and protects landward aquatic habitats from direct wave attack. 2) All associated aquatic habitats, including the adjacent wetlands, marshes, estuaries, inlets, and nearshore waters; but only if such feature and associated habitats contain few man-made structures and these structures, and human activity on such feature and within such habitats do not significantly impede geomorphic and ecological processes.

Undue Economic Hardship

1) Substantial economic loss resulting from inability caused by regulatory enforcement to perform contracts with respect to species of fish and wildlife entered into prior to the date of publication in the Federal Register of a Notice of Consideration of such species as an endangered species. 2) Substantial economic loss to persons who, for the year prior to the Notice of Consideration of such species as an endangered species, derived a substantial portion of their income from the lawful taking of any listed species, which taking would be made unlawful under the ESA. 3) Curtailment of subsistence-taking (made unlawful under the ESA) by persons that are a) not reasonably able to secure other sources of subsistence; b) dependent to a substantial extent upon hunting and fishing for subsistence; and c) who must engage in such curtailed taking for subsistence purposes.

Undue Risks

Levels of identifiable risks that are unacceptable.

Undulate

A species descriptor that means moving in a smooth, wavelike motion.

UNEP

See United Nations Environmental Program.

UNESCO

See United Nations Educational, Scientific, and Cultural Organization.

Unexploded Explosive Ordnance

Explosive ordnance that has been primed, fused, armed, or otherwise prepared for action, and that has been fired, dropped, launched, projected, or placed in such a manner as to constitute a hazard to operations, installations, personnel, or materiel, and remains unexploded either by malfunction or design or for any other cause.

Unfinished Oils

Includes all oils requiring further processing. Oils that require only mechanical blending should not be reported as an unfinished oil.

Unfit-for-Use Tank System

A tank system determined through an integrity assessment or other inspection to be no longer capable of storing or treating hazardous waste without posing a threat of release of hazardous waste into the environment.

Ungulate

A species descriptor that means having hoofs.

Unidirectional (UD)

Refers to fibers that are oriented in the same direction, such as unidirectional fabric, teflon tape, or laminate.

Unified Action Armed Forces Publication

A UNAAF publication setting forth the principles, doctrines, and functions governing the activities and performance of the Armed Forces of the United States when two or more services or elements thereof are acting together.

Unified Dose Assessments

A functional capability to coordinate monitoring teams, collection of monitoring data, calculation of offsite radiation dose projections and used for the recommendation of protective actions for the plume and ingestion exposure emergency planning zones.

Uniform Building Code (UBC)

A building code published by the International Conference of Building Officials (ICBO).

Uniform Flow

A characteristic of a flow system where specific discharge has the same magnitude and direction at all points.

Uniform Mechanical Code (UMC)

The latest edition of the mechanical code as published by the International Association of Plumbing and Mechanical Officials (IAPMO).

Uniform Plumbing Code (UPC)

The latest edition of the plumbing code as published by the International Association of Plumbing and Mechanical Officials (IAPMO).

Uniformed Services

The Army, Navy, Air Force, Marine Corps, Coast Guard, National Oceanic and Atmospheric Administration, and Public Health Service. *See* Military Department.

Unilateral Arms Control Measure

An arms control course of action taken by a nation without any compensating concession being required of other nations.

Unintentional Introduction

An introduction of nonindigenous species that occurs as the result of activities other than the purposeful or intentional introduction of the species involved, such as the transport of nonindigenous species in ballast or in water used to transport fish, mollusks, or crustaceans for aquaculture or other purposes.

Uninterruptible Power Supplies

Power supplies that provide automatic, instantaneous power, without delay or transients, on failure of normal power. They can consist of batteries or full-time operating generators. They can be designated as standby or emergency power depending on the application. Emergency installations must meet the requirements specified for emergency power.

Unionids

A species descriptor that means freshwater mussels.

Unique Farmland

Land other than prime farmland that is used for the production of specific high-value food and fiber crops, such as citrus, nuts, olives, fruits, and vegetables.

Unique Habitat

The essential segment(s) of habitat that contains the unique combination of conditions (soils, vegetation, predator species, etc.) necessary for the continued survival of a endangered species.

Unirradiated Enriched Uranium

Naturally occurring uranium enriched with U-235 above its natural abundance of approximately 0.72% (weight percent) that has not been exposed to a neutron flux.

Uniserial

A species descriptor that means arranged in one row or in one sequence.

Unit

1) Any military element whose structure is prescribed by competent authority, such as a table of organization and equipment; specifically, part of an organization. 2) An organization title of a subdivision of a group in a task force. 3) A standard or basic quantity into which an item of supply is divided, issued, or used. In this meaning, also called unit of issue. 4) With regard to reserve components of the Armed Forces, denotes a Selected Reserve unit organized, equipped, and trained for mobilization to serve on active duty as a unit or to augment or be augmented by another unit.

Unit Cancer Risk

A measure of the probability of an individual's developing cancer as a result of exposure to a specified unit ambient concentration. For example, an inhalation unit cancer risk of 3.0×10^{-4} near a point source implies that if 10,000 people breathe a given concentration of a carcinogenic agent for 70 years, three of the 10,000 will develop cancer as a result of this exposure.

Unit Commitment Status
The degree of commitment of any unit designated and categorized as a force allocated to NATO.

Unit Load Devices
Types of freight containers, aircraft containers, aircraft pallets with nets, or aircraft pallets with nets over igloos.

Unit Masonry
Includes brick made of clay or shale, sand lime, and concrete; structural clay, concrete masonry units, solid load bearings, tile, load-bearing, and nonload-bearing, hollow load-bearing, and hollow nonload-bearing; natural stone and cast stone; ceramic glazed clay masonry, solid units, and hollow units; and prefaced concrete masonry units.

Unit of Local Government
1) The government of a county, municipality, or township, that is a unit of general purpose government of a state or the District of Columbia. 2) The recognized governing body of a Native American Indian tribe where the governing body performs substantial regulatory functions. 3) Any borough, parish, village, district, or other general purpose political subdivision of a state.

United Nations Environmental Program (UNEP)
The United Nations agency formed in 1972 to coordinate intergovernmental measures for environmental monitoring and protection. UNEP operates the Earthwatch program, that consists of the environmental monitoring system and the global resource information database. UNEP funds Earthscan, a remote environmental satellite sensing system. *See* Earthscan.

United Nations Educational, Scientific, and Cultural Organization (UNESCO)
A United Nations agency formed in 1945 to support and complement the efforts of member countries to promulgate education, scientific research and information, and international relations.

United States (U.S.)
The 50 states, the District of Columbia, the Commonwealth of Puerto Rico, the U.S. Virgin Islands, Guam, American Samoa, and the Commonwealth of the Northern Mariana Islands.

United States/Canadian Environment
The common environment along the 5,500 mile border between the United States and Canada.

United States/Canadian Negotiations on Air Quality
The negotiations on a cooperative agreement with the government of Canada aimed at preserving the mutual airshed of the United States and Canada so as to protect and enhance air resources; ensure the attainment and maintenance of air quality protection of public health and welfare; and take whatever diplomatic actions are necessary to reduce or eliminate any undesirable impact upon the United States and Canada resulting from air pollution from any source.

Unitized Load
A single item, or a number of items packaged, packed, or arranged in a specified manner and capable of being handled as a unit. Unitization may be accomplished by placing the item or items in a container or by banding them securely together. *See* Palletized Unit Load.

Units of Measure
Quantities adopted as standards of measurement for temperatures, doses, distances, areas, volumes, pressures, flow rates, ratios, deviations, time designations, toxicity, etc. Units of measure include, but are not limited to the following: activity per ton, body wave magnitude, british thermal unit, centimeters per second, cubic feet per minute, cubic yards, disintegrations per minute per gram, drips per minute, gallon, kilograms/per

time, kilometer, kilovolt, megawatt thermal, microcuries, micrograms/per volume, milliroentgen, million gallons per day, moment magnitude, parts per million, pounds/per time, microroentgon/per time, picocurie, picocuries per volume, square kilometers, and standard cubic foot. *See* Section V: Data Conversion Factors.

Universal Polar Stereographic Grid
A military grid prescribed for joint use in operations in limited areas and used for operations requiring precise position reporting. It covers areas between the 80 degree parallels and the poles.

Universal Time
A measure of time that conforms, within a close approximation, to the mean diurnal rotation of the earth and serves as the basis of civil timekeeping. Universal Time is determined from observations of the stars, radio sources, and also from ranging observations of the Moon and artificial earth satellites. The scale determined directly from such observations is designated Universal Time Observed (UTO); it is slightly dependent on the place of observation. When UTO is corrected for the shift in longitude of the observing station caused by polar motion, the time scale UT1 is obtained. When an accuracy better than one second is not required, Universal Time can be used to mean Coordinated Universal Time (UTC). Also called ZULU time. Formerly called Greenwich Mean Time.

Universal Transverse Mercator Grid (UTM Grid)
A grid coordinate system based on the transverse mercator projection, applied to maps of the earth's surface extending to 84°N and 80°S latitudes.

Univoltine
A term that means one flight season.

Unleaded Gasoline
A complex mixture of relatively volatile hydrocarbons, with or without small quantities of additives, all of which have been blended to form a fuel suitable for use in spark ignition engines.

Meets the detailed requirements for gasoline listed in ASTM D439 or Federal Specifications VV-G-1690B, to include no more than 10% boiling at 122°F under atmospheric pressure, with Reid vapor pressure ranging from 9 to 15 psi. Consists of finished (marketable) unleaded gasoline containing no more than 0.05 grams of lead per gallon and not more than 0.005 grams of phosphorus per gallon, regardless of the size of the producer. Includes both premium and regular grade, depending on the octane rating. Excluded are a) any blendstock until blending has been completed and the blendstock is incorporated in the finished unleaded gasoline and no longer separately identified; b) any alcohol to be used in the blending of gasohol.

Unlisted Hazardous Substances
Solid wastes, as defined in 40 CFR 261.2, that are not excluded from regulation as a hazardous waste under 40 CFR 261.4(b), is a hazardous substance under Section 101(14) of the Act if it exhibits any of the characteristics identified in 40 CFR 261.20 through 261.24.

Unmanned Aerial Vehicle (UAV)
A powered, aerial vehicle that does not carry a human operator, uses aerodynamic forces to provide vehicle lift, can fly autonomously or be piloted remotely, can be expendable or recoverable, and can carry a lethal or nonlethal payload. Ballistic or semiballistic vehicles, cruise missiles, and artillery projectiles are not considered unmanned aerial vehicles.

Unnecessary Duplication of Environmental Courses and Programs
That two local educational agencies or programs, including Regional Occupational Centers or Regional Occupational Programs offer the same environmental courses or programs to the same type of student population using similar operational characteristics as to prerequisites.

Unsaturated Zone or Zone of Aeration
The zone between the land surface and the water table, where the soil pores are not fully saturated, although some water may be present. It includes

the root zone, intermediate zone, and capillary fringe. In addition to water, the pore spaces contain air and other gases at less than atmospheric pressure. Saturated bodies, such as perched groundwater, may exist in the unsaturated zone, and water pressure within these may be greater than that of the atmosphere. *See* Vadose Zone.

Unspecified Motor Gasoline
Blending components in the gasoline range or finished gasoline blends, such as gasohol, that are not classified as leaded gasoline or unleaded gasoline.

Unstable Areas, Geologic
Areas consisting of slide areas or unstable soils, or by some or all of the following: a) hummocky topography consisting of rolling bumpy ground, frequent benches, and depressions; b) short irregular surface drainages that begin and end on the slope; c) tension cracks and head wall scarps indicating slumping are visible; d) slopes are irregular and may be slightly concave in upper half and convex in lower half as a result of previous slope failure; e) there may be evidence of impaired groundwater movement resulting in local zones of surface sag ponds with standing water, springs, or patches of wet ground. In addition, some or all of the following may be present: hydrophytic (wet site) vegetation prevalent; leaning, jackstrawed, or split trees are common; pistol-butted trees with excessive sweep may occur in areas of hummock topography.

Unstable Soils, Geologic
1) Unconsolidated, noncohesive soils (coarser-textured than loam) and colluvial debris including sands and gravels, rock fragments, or weathered granitics. Such soils are usually associated with a risk of shallow-seated landslides on slopes of 65% or more, having noncohesive soils less than 5 feet deep in an area where precipitation exceeds 4 inches in 24 hours in a 5-year recurrence interval. 2) Soils that increase and decrease in volume as moisture content changes. During dry weather, these materials become hard and rock-like exhibiting a network of polygonal shrinkage cracks and a blocky structure resulting from desication.

Some cracks may be greater than 5 feet in depth. These materials when wet are very sticky, dingy, shiny, and easily molded.

Unusual and Compelling State or Local Energy Interests
Interests that: 1) are substantially different in nature or magnitude than those prevailing throughout the United States generally; and 2) are such that the costs, benefits, burdens, and reliability of energy savings resulting from a state or local government regulation make such regulation preferable or necessary when measured against the costs, benefits, burdens, and reliability of alternative approaches to energy savings or production, including reliance on reasonably predictable market-induced improvements in efficiency of all products subject to the regulation.

Unusual Events
Emergency response levels that represent an event in progress or having occurred that normally would not constitute an emergency but which indicates a potential reduction of safety of a facility in which no potential exists for significant offsite release of radioactive or other hazardous substances.

Unusual Occurrence Reporting System (UORS)
A database of unusual occurrence reports submitted through a DOE reporting system.

Unusual Occurrence Reports (UOR)
Written evaluations of unusual occurrences that are prepared in sufficient detail to enable the reviewer to assess their significance, consequences, or implications and to determine the means of avoiding a recurrence with minimal additional inquiry.

Unusual Occurrences (UOs)
1) Unusual or unplanned events having programmatic significance such that they adversely affect or potentially affect the performance, reliability, or safety of a facility. 2) Nonemergency occurrences that have significant impact or potential for

impact on safety, environment, health, security, or operations.

Unutilized Natural Gas
Gas that is available in small remote fields and cannot be economically transported to natural gas pipelines, or gas the quality of which is so poor that extensive and uneconomic pretreatment is required prior to its introduction into the natural gas distribution system.

Unwarned Exposed
The vulnerability of friendly forces to nuclear weapon effects. In this condition, personnel are assumed to be standing in the open at burst time, but have dropped to a prone position by the time the blast wave arrives. They are expected to have areas of bare skin exposed to direct thermal radiation, and some personnel may suffer dazzle. *See* Warned Exposed; Warned Protected.

Unwarranted Failure to Comply
The failure of a permittee to prevent the occurrence of any violation of his/her permit due to indifference, lack of diligence, or lack of reasonable care, or the failure to abate any violation.

UORS
See Unusual Occurrence Reporting System.

Upgrades
Additions to, or retrofitting of, some systems such as cathodic protection, lining, or spill and overfill controls to improve the ability of an underground storage tank system to prevent the release of product.

Uplifts
1) Structurally high areas in the crust of the earth, produced by positive movements that raise or upthrust the rocks. They are the elevation of any extensive part of the earth's surface relative to some other parts. 2) In engineering, any force that tends to raise a structure and its foundation relative to its surroundings. They may be caused by pressure of adjacent ground, surface water, ex-

pansive soil under the base of the structure, or lateral forces such as wind.

Upper Bound Cancer Risk Assessment
A qualifying statement indicating that the cancer risk estimate is not a true value in that the dose-response modeling used provides a value that is not likely to be an underestimate of the true value. The true value may be lower than the upper bound cancer risk estimate and it may even be close to zero. This results from the use of a statistical upper confidence limit and from the use of conservative assumptions in deriving the cancer risk estimate.

Upper Respiratory Tract
The structures that conduct air into the lungs, including the nasal cavity, mouth, pharynx, and larynx.

Uppermost Aquifer
The geologic formation nearest the natural ground surface that is an aquifer, as well as lower aquifers that are hydraulically interconnected with this aquifer within the facility's property boundary.

UPS
See Uninterruptible Power Supplies.

Uptake
1) The quantity of radionuclide taken up by the systemic circulation (e.g., by absorption from compartments in the respiratory or gastrointestinal tracts). 2) The amount of radioactive material absorbed into the extracellular fluids. Also used to denote the process.

Uranium (U)
1) A radioactive element found in natural ores with an average atomic weight of about 238. Atomic number 92. 2) A radioactive heavy metal element used in nuclear reactors and the production of nuclear weapons. Term refers usually to U-238, the most abundant radium isotope, although a small percentage of naturally occurring uranium is U-236.

Uranium Byproduct Materials

The wastes produced by the extraction or concentration of uranium from any ore process primarily for a source material content. *See* Uranium Mill Tailings.

Uranium Mill Tailings

Defined under the Uranium Mill Tailings Radiation Control Act (UMTRCA) as naturally radioactive residue from the processing of uranium ore into yellowcake in a mill. Although the milling process recovers about 93% of the uranium, the residues, or tailings, contain several radioactive elements, including uranium, thorium, radium, polonium, and radon.

Uranium Mine Wastes Hazards Elimination Study

Under the UMTRCA, the Administrator's study to identify the location and potential health, safety, and environmental hazards of uranium mine wastes together with recommendations, if any, for a program to eliminate these hazards.

Uranium Processing, Affected Public Land

Under the UMTRCA, lands formerly under the jurisdiction of the Bureau of Land Management in the vicinity of processing sites in the following counties:

- Apache County in the state of Arizona;

- Mesa, Gunnison, Moffat, Montrose, Garfield, and San Miguel Counties in the state of Colorado;

- Boise County in the state of Idaho;

- Billings and Bowman Counties in the state of North Dakota;

- Grand and San Juan Counties in the state of Utah;

- Converse and Fremont Counties in the state of Wyoming; and

- any other county in the vicinity of a processing site, if no site in the county in which a processing site is located is suitable.

Uranium Processing Site

Under UMTRCA, any site, including the mill, containing residual radioactive materials at which all or substantially all of the uranium was produced for sale to any federal agency prior to January 1, 1971, under a contract with any federal agency, except in the case of a site at or near Slick Rock, Colorado, unless a) such site was owned or controlled as of January 1, 1978, or is thereafter owned or controlled, by any federal agency, or b) a license, issued by the Atomic Energy Commission or its predecessor agency under the Atomic Energy Act of 1954 (42 USC 2011 et seq.) or by a state as permitted under Section 274 of such Act (42 USC 2021) for the production at such site of any uranium or thorium product derived from ores is in effect on January 1, 1978, or is issued or renewed after such date. Also, any other real property or improvement thereon which a) is in the vicinity of such site, and b) is determined by the Secretary, in consultation with the Commission, to be contaminated with residual radioactive materials derived from such site.

Uranium Processing Sites, Initially Designated

The initial sites designated processing sites pursuant to UMTRCA. The initial group (as included in the act) consisted of sites at or near the following locations: Salt Lake City, Utah; Green River, Utah; Mexican Hat, Utah; Durango, Colorado; Grand Junction, Colorado; Rifle, Colorado (two sites); Gunnison, Colorado; Naturita, Colorado; Maybell, Colorado; Slick Rock, Colorado (two sites); Shiprock, New Mexico; Ambrosia Lake, New Mexico; Riverton, Wyoming; Converse County, Wyoming; Lakeview, Oregon; Falls City, Texas; Tuba City, Arizona; Monument Valley, Arizona; Lowman, Idaho; and Cannonsburg, Pennsylvania. The Secretary was charged with completing remedial action at the above listed sites, as well as designating all other processing sites within the United States that he/she determines requires remedial action to carry out the purposes of the UMTRCA.

Urban Fringe

The transitional stretch of land undergoing a transmutation from rural to urban uses, usually promulgated by a major or regional type project; an area where population density is too high for rural, yet still too sparse for urban, infrastructure development, and typical city services.

Urban Nodes

A planning concept whereby specific geographical areas are identified for development into centers of human work, shopping, and entertainment activities. This helps to consolidate infrastructure, transportation, and other services.

Urban Pattern

A term referring to the three basic types of spacial layouts, designs or patterns of development found in most cities throughout the world:

- Concentric Pattern — central business area surrounded by at least four concentric zones;

- Sector or Wedge Pattern — differing types of areas with different populations taper toward the central business district in a pie-like manner; and

- Multiple-Nuclei Pattern — multiple areas of population activity (e.g., regional malls) compete with the central business district and attract various types of development.

Urban Place

A developed area (incorporated or not) with a population of 2,500 or greater.

Urban Planner

A person who plans, designs, and implements solutions to the problems facing cities and towns in areas such as land use, transportation, housing, public facilities/infrastructure, and economic development. Besides physical and economic development, planners can specialize in policy planning, environmental protection and social research. The professional degree is a Master of Urban Planning (MUP). *See* Environmental Planner.

Urban Runoff

Stormwater from city streets and adjacent domestic or commercial properties that may carry pollutants of various kinds into the sewer systems and/or receiving waters.

Urbanization

The in-migration of people in large numbers from rural to urban environments. A characteristic of all industrialized countries.

Urea

A nitrogen-based (45%) fertilizer material made by reacting ammonia and carbon dioxide under pressure at high temperatures, without a catalyst. Urea is used in the manufacturing of plastics and in animal feeds; most urea is used in fertilizer applications or as a constituent in mixes.

Urea Formaldehyde Foam

A cellular plastic insulation material generated in a continuous stream by mixing the components that are a urea formaldehyde resin, air, and a foaming agent.

Uremia

A condition in which an abnormally high level of urea or other nitrogenous waste is found in the blood; due to kidney dysfunction.

Uronites

A species descriptor that means part of an abdominal appendage of some crustaceans.

Uropods

A species descriptor that means one pair of rear abdominal appendages of certain crustaceans, including lobsters and shrimp.

Urticaria

Hives.

Usable Storage Tank Capacity

The total liquid storage volume of a UST, less that volume which cannot be used for normal operations (i.e., less basic sediment and water, corrected to 60°F).

USATHMC

An acronym for U.S. Army Toxic and Hazardous Materials Center.

USCG
See U.S. Coast Guard.

USDA
See Department of Agriculture.

USDW
See Underground Sources of Drinking Water.

Used Oil
Any oil that has been refined from crude oil, has been used, and as a result of such use has been contaminated by physical or chemical impurities.

Useful Life
The time period in which a building element can be expected to perform effectively with proper maintenance.

USEPA
See Environmental Protection Agency; U.S. Environmental Protection Agency.

User Agencies
Government agencies or contractors thereof other than DOE that utilize facilities and equipment at DOE Government-Owned, Contractor-Operated (GOCO) sites. *See* Government-Owned, Contractor-Operated (GOCO).

User Network
A system of circuits or channels allocated to furnish communication paths between switching centers to provide communication service on a common basis to all connected stations or subscribers. It is sometimes described as a General Purpose Network.

USFWS
See U.S. Fish and Wildlife Service.

USGS
See U.S. Geological Survey.

UST
See Underground Storage Tank.

UST Systems
Underground storage tanks, connected underground piping, underground ancillary equipment, and containment system, if any. *See* Underground Tank Systems.

Ustic
A soil temperature regime common to subhumid and semiarid regions; moisture is limited; temperatures range between 5°C and 8°C at 50 cm depth.

UTC
An acronym for Coordinated Universal Time. *See* Universal Time.

Utility Plant Energy Conservation Measure
An installation or modification in a industrial facility that is primarily intended to maintain or reduce energy consumption and reduce energy costs or allow the use of alternative energy sources, including, but not limited to, a) furnace or utility plant and distribution system modifications; b) replacement burners, furnaces, boilers, or any combination thereof, that substantially increases the energy efficiency of the heating system; c) devices for modifying flue openings that will increase the energy efficiency of the heating system; d) electrical or mechanical furnace ignition systems that replace standing gas pilot lights; and e) utility plant system conversion measures including conversion of existing oil-fired and gas-fired boiler installations to alternative energy sources, including coal. *See* Energy Conservation Measure.

Utility Regulatory Commission (URC)
Any state agency or federal agency that has authority to fix, modify, approve, or disapprove rates for the sale of electric energy by any electric utility.

Utility Unit
1) A unit that serves a generator in any state that produces electricity for sale. 2) A unit that, during 1985, served a generator in any state that produced electricity for sale. Excluding units that cogencrate steam and electricity, unless the unit is

constructed for the purpose of supplying, or commences construction after November 15, 1990, and supplies, more than one-third of its potential electric output capacity and more than 25 megawatts electrical output to any utility power distribution system for sale.

Utilization Facilities

1) Any equipment or device, except an atomic weapon, determined by rule of the Nuclear Regulatory Commission (NRC) to be capable of making use of special nuclear material in such quantity as to be of significance to the common defense and security, or in such manner as to affect the health and safety of the public, or peculiarly adapted for making use of atomic energy in such quantity as to be of significance to the common defense and security, or in such manner as to affect the health and safety of the public. 2) Any important component part especially designed for such equipment or device as determined by the NRC.

Utilization of Older Americans

The Administrator's authorization to make grants to, or enter into cooperative agreements with, private nonprofit organizations designated by the Secretary of Labor under Title V of the Older Americans Act of 1965 (OAA), to utilize the talents of older Americans in programs administered by the Administrator for providing technical assistance to federal, state, and local environmental agencies on pollution prevention, abatement, and control projects. Funding may be made available from such programs or through Title V of the OAA and Title IV of the Job Training Partnership Act (JTPA).

UTM

An acronym for the Universal Transverse Mercator Grid System. *See* Grid System; Universal Transverse Mercator Grid System.

Utopianism

A type of planning based on the development of ideal futures, and assessments of the feasible methodologies that may be implemented to realize them.

Utricle

A species descriptor for a small, bladderlike, one-seeded fruit.

V

VAT

An acronym for Vinyl Asbestos Tile.

Vaccine

A dead, partial, or modified antigen used to induce immunity to certain infectious diseases.

Vacuum Filter

In wastewater treatment, a filter consisting of a cylindrical drum mounted on a horizontal axis, covered with a cloth filter, and revolving partially submerged in liquid. Vacuum pressure is maintained under the cloth for the larger part of a revolution to extract moisture. The cake is continuously scraped off.

Vadose Zone

The region between the ground surface and the water table, where soil is not waterlogged and most of the biological growth is concentrated.

VAHUDIA

An acronym for Veterans Affairs, Housing and Urban Development, and Independent Agencies Appropriations Act of 1990.

Validation

1) A process associated with the collection of information that provides official status to an identified hazard requirement and confirms that the planned corrective action requirement is appropriate for a situation. 2) The process of evaluating project planning, development, baselines, and proposed funding prior to inclusion of new projects or system acquisition or seeking increased funding for a prior project or system. It requires a review of project planning and conceptual development documentation, as well as discussion with the program or field element and principle contributing contractors to determine the source basis, procedures, and validity of proposed requirements, as well as scope, cost, schedule, finding, and so forth.

Value

The relationship between an object desired and a potential purchaser; the power of a good or service to command other goods or services in exchange.

In terms of real estate appraisal, value may be described as the present worth or future benefits arising from the ownership of property. For a property to have value in the real estate market, it must have the following four characteristics:

- Utility — the capacity to satisfy human needs and desires;

- Scarcity — a finite supply;

- Effective Demand — the need or desire for possession or ownership backed up by the financial means to satisfy that need; and

- Transferability — the transfer of ownership rights from one person to another with relative ease.

Value Engineering

An organized effort directed at analyzing the function of environmental systems, equipment, facilities, procedures, and supplies for the purpose of achieving the required function at the lowest total cost of effective ownership, consistent with requirements for performance, reliability, quality, and maintainability.

Values, Consequential

The consequences of risks or accidents that are nonmonetary and may be nonquantifiable or intangible, such as pain, humane consideration, pride, or employee or public opinion.

Valves

1) Mechanical devices by which the flow of material may be started, stopped, or regulated by a movable part that opens, shuts, or partially obstructs one or more ports or passageways. 2) In terms of the ESA, a species descriptor that refers to one of the paired hinged shells of mollusks; one of the sections into which a seed pod or fruit splits.

VAM

An acronym for Vibration and Acoustic Monitoring.

Van Pooling

An arrangement for the transportation of employees between their residences or other designated locations and their place of employment on a nonprofit basis in which the operating costs of such arrangement are paid for by the employees utilizing such arrangement.

Vannal

A species descriptor that means veins.

Vapor

The gas given off by substances that are solids or liquids at ordinary atmospheric pressure and temperatures (e.g., steam).

Vapor Capture System

Any combination of hoods and ventilation system that captures or contains organic vapors in order that they may be directed to an abatement or recovery device.

Vapor Density

The weight of a given volume of vapor or gas compared to the weight of an equal volume of dry air, both measured at the same temperature and pressure.

Vapor Dispersion

The movement of vapor plumes or clouds in air due to wind, gravity spreading, and mixing.

Vapor Plumes

Flue gases that are visible because they contain water droplets.

Vapor Pressure

A measure of the tendency of a liquid to become a gas at a given temperature; the pressure of the vapor (psig) in equilibrium with the liquid at a temperature of 100°F.

Vapor Recovery System

A system by which the volatile gases from gasoline are captured instead of being released into the atmosphere. Recovery systems may be required for gasoline stations in some cities and other nonattainment areas.

Vaporization

The change of a substance from a liquid to a gas.

Vaporizer-Burner

An integral vaporizer-burner unit, dependent upon the heat generated by the burner as the source of heat to vaporize the liquid used for dehydrators or dryers.

Vaporizers

1) LNG Vaporizer, a device used to convert liquified natural gas (LNG) from the liquid to a gaseous state by means of artificial or atmospheric heat. 2) LPG Vaporizer, a device used to convert

liquified petroleum gas (LPG) from the liquid to a gaseous state by means of artificial heat.

Variability
1) The manner in which the probability of damage to a specific site decreases with the distance from ground zero. 2) In a damage assessment, a mathematical factor introduced to average the effects of orientation, minor shielding, and uncertainty of response to the effects considered.

Variance
Government permission for a delay or exception in the application of a given law, ordinance, or regulation.

Variation
A divergency in the developing organism beyond the usual range of structural constitution that may not adversely affect survival or health. A specific category in the evaluation of developmental effects. *See* Malformation.

Variety
A closer taxonomic relationship than subspecies.

Vascular
Pertaining to blood vessels.

Vasoconstriction
Narrowing of a blood vessel resulting in decreased blood flow.

Vasodilation
Increased diameter of the blood vessels.

VDC
An acronym for Volts Direct Current.

Vectors
1) A physical quantity that cannot be described completely without referencing a direction. 2) An organism, often an insect or a rodent, that carries a parasite from one host to another. 3) An object that is used to transport genes into a host cell (vectors can be plasmids, viruses, or other bacte-

ria). 4) A gene is placed in the vector; the vector then infects the bacterium.

Vegetative Cover
Perennial grasses, legumes, forbs, shrubs, or trees with an expected life span of 5 or more years.

Vegetation Protection
Special measures to prevent damage to vegetation for the protection of water quality, the beneficial uses of water, and/or other natural resources.

Vehicle
A self-propelled, boosted, or towed conveyance for transporting a burden on land or sea or through air or space. *See* Air Cushion Vehicle; Remotely Piloted Vehicle; Transport Vehicle.

Vehicle, Alcohol Dual Energy
A vehicle that is capable of operating on alcohol and on gasoline or diesel fuel.

Vehicle, Alcohol Powered
A vehicle designed to operate exclusively on alcohol.

Vehicle Cargo
Wheeled or tracked equipment, including weapons, that require certain deck space, head room, and other definite clearance. *See* Cargo.

Vehicle, Natural Gas Dual Energy
A vehicle that is capable of operating on natural gas and on gasoline or diesel fuel.

Vehicle, Natural Gas Powered
A vehicle designed to operate exclusively on natural gas.

Velocity
Usually used when referring to wind, it is a term that describes wind speed and the direction of its flow.

Vent

1) The connection and piping through which gases enter and exit a piece of equipment. 2) A listed factory-made vent pipe and vent fittings for conveying products of combustion from a fuel-burning appliance to the outside atmosphere.

Vent Connector

Any pipe for conveying products of combustion from a fuel-burning appliance to a vent.

Venter

1) In anatomy, the abdomen or belly. 2) In biology, a swollen structure or part similar to a belly.

Ventilation

1) The act of admitting fresh air into a space in order to replace stale or contaminated air; achieved by blowing air into the space. 2) The movement of air between the lungs and the ambient air.

Ventilation, Adequacy

When specified for the prevention of fire during normal operation, ventilation shall be considered adequate when the concentration of the gas in a gas-air mixture does not exceed 25% of the lower flammable limit.

Ventilation, Suction

The act of admitting fresh air into a space in order to replace stale or contaminated air; achieved by blowing air into the space. Similarly, suction represents the admission of fresh air into an interior space by lowering the pressure outside of the space, thereby drawing the contaminated air outward.

Ventilation System

All equipment intended or installed for the purpose of supplying air to, or removing air from, any room or space by mechanical means, other than equipment that is a portion of any environmental heating, cooling, absorption, or evaporative cooling system.

Ventral

A species descriptor that means located at the lower side of a fish or a bird.

Ventricular Fibrillation

Rapid, tremulous movement of the ventricle that replaces normal contractions of the heart muscle; results in little or no blood being pumped from the heart.

Ventrum

A species descriptor that means anal region.

Venturi Meter

A differential meter for measuring the flow of water or other fluids through closed conduits or pipes, consisting of a venturi tube and one of several proprietary forms of flow-registering devices. The difference in velocity heads between the entrance and the contracted tube throat is an indication of the rate of flow.

Verification

1) Any action, including inspection, detection, and identification, taken to ascertain compliance with agreed corrective measures; the act of reviewing, inspecting, testing, checking, auditing, or otherwise determining and documenting whether items, processes, services, or documents conform to specified requirements. 2) In computer modeling and simulation, the process of determining that a model or simulation implementation accurately represents the developer's conceptual description and specifications. *See* Validation.

Vermiculation

A species descriptor that means wormlike marks; the condition of being worm eaten.

Vertebrate

Animals with a skull and spinal column made of bone or cartilage; an animal with a backbone.

Vertical Air Photograph
An air photograph taken with the optical axis of the camera perpendicular to the surface of the earth.

Vertical Load Carrying Space Frames
Space frames designed to carry all vertical (gravity) loads.

Vertical Loading
A type of loading whereby items of like character are vertically tiered throughout the holds of a ship, so that selected items are available at any stage of the unloading. *See* Loading.

Vertically Integrated Petroleum Company
Any person that through itself, or another person, is controlled by, controls, or under common control, is engaged in the production, refining, and marketing of petroleum products.

Vertigo
The sensation of spinning or revolving.

Very Seriously Ill or Injured (VSII)
The casualty status of a person whose illness or injury is classified by medical authority to be of such severity that life is imminently endangered. *See* Casualty Status.

Vesicant
An agent that produces blisters. *See* Blister Agent.

Vesiculation
The presence or formation of blisters. *See* Blister Agent.

Vessel
Includes every description of watercraft used or capable of being used as a means of transportation on the water.

Vessel Permit Application
An application for a permit required by the Shore Protection Act of 1988 made by the vessel owner/operator. The application includes a) the name, address, and telephone number of the vessel owner/operator; b) the vessels name and identification number; c) the vessels area of operation; d) the vessels transport capacity; e) a history of the types of cargo transported by that vessel during the previous year, including identifying the type of municipal or commercial waste transported as municipal waste, commercial waste, medical waste, waste of another character, any other information the Secretary may require, and an acknowledgment.

Vestigial
A species descriptor that means a rudimentary or degenerate structure.

Vesture
A species descriptor that means a covering, especially cloth.

VHAP
See Volatile Hazardous Air Pollutant.

Vibrating Reed Electrometers
Radiation monitors for air sampling for tritium.

Vibrissa
A species descriptor that means feather near the beak of an insectivorous (insect eating) bird.

VIDOC
See Visual Information Documentation.

Vignetting
A method of producing a band of color or tone on a map or chart, the density of which is reduced uniformly from edge to edge.

Villous
A species descriptor that means covered with fine, unmatted hair.

Vinyl Chloride
A colorless gas with the molecular form CH_2CHCl; chloroethene; a chemical compound, used in producing some plastics, that is believed to be carcinogenic.

Vinyl Chloride Monomer (Chloroethene)

A compound used in the manufacturing of PVC (polyvinyl chloride) piping and believed to cause cancer. The amount of this chemical used in PVC piping is strictly regulated.

Vinyl Chloride Purification

Includes any part of the process of vinyl chloride production that follows vinyl chloride formation.

Violation, Combining

The gathering of all instances of violations of a specific standard into one citation item during the inspection/ investigation of a single establishment or worksite. For the purpose of applying these guidelines in the construction industry, an establishment is normally the site of the construction job (e.g., the building site, the dam site). Where the construction site extends over a large geographical area (e.g., road building), the entire site shall be considered a single establishment; and all instances of the same violation with the same classification discovered during a single inspection shall normally constitute one alleged violation. *See* Violations, Grouping.

Violation, Criminal and Willful

A violation is criminal and willful if a) an owner/operator or representative was aware of the requirements of an environmental law, applicable standard or regulation, or comparable legal requirement (e.g., state or local law) and was also aware of a condition or practice in violation of those requirements; b) a business, corporation, or related entity committed a violation with plain indifference to the law where higher management officials were aware of an environmental requirement applicable to the company's business but made little or no effort to communicate the requirement to lower level supervisors and employees; c) company officials were aware of a continuing compliance problem but made little or no effort to avoid violations. In flagrant situations, willfulness can be found despite lack of knowledge of either a legal requirement or the existence of a hazard if the circumstances show that a facility/business owner would have placed

no importance on such knowledge even if he/she had possessed it.

Violation, General

A violation that is specifically determined not to be of a serious nature, but has a relationship to occupational safety and health of employees.

Violations, Grouping

The joining of violations of two or more specific standards under one citation item during the inspection/investigation of a single establishment or worksite. When a source of a hazard is identified which involves interrelated violations of different standards, the violations may be grouped into a single item if the agency representative believes that the violations are so closely related as to constitute a single hazardous condition. When two or more individual violations are found that, if considered individually represent other-than-serious violations, but if grouped create a substantial probability of death or serious physical harm, the violations may be grouped and alleged as a single serious violation. *See* Violations, Combining.

Violations of Air Contaminant Standards

Citations issued for exceeding air contaminant standards, when it has been established that an employee is being, or has been, exposed to a toxic substance in excess of the PEL established by OSHA standards. The violation is classified as serious or other-than-serious on the basis of the requirements in the *Chemical Information Manual*, OSHA Instruction CPL 2-2.43A, and the use of respiratory protection at the time of the violation. Classification of violations is dependent upon the determination that the illness is reasonably predictable at that exposure level, whether the illness is serious or other-than-serious and that the employer knew or could have known through reasonable diligence that a hazardous condition existed.

Violation, Regulatory

A violation, other than one defined as "serious" or "general," that pertains to permit, posting, recordkeeping, and reporting requirements as established by regulation or statute. For example, failure to obtain permit, failure to post citations or posters, failure to keep required records, failure to report industrial accidents.

Violation, Repeated

A violation that an owner/operator has corrected, or indicated correction of an earlier violation, for which a citation was issued, and upon a later inspection is found to have committed the same violation again within a period of 3 years immediately preceding the latter violation. For the purpose of considering whether a violation is repeated, a repeat citation issued to employers having fixed establishments (e.g., factories, terminals, stores) will be limited to the cited establishment; for employers engaged in businesses having no fixed establishments (e.g., construction, painting, excavation) a repeat violation will be based on prior violations cited within the same regulatory region.

Violation, Repeated versus Failure to Abate

A failure to abate situation exists when a condition previously cited has never been brought into compliance and is noted at a later inspection. If, however, the violation was not continuous (i.e., if it had been corrected and then reoccurred), the subsequent occurrence is a repeated violation.

Violation, Serious

A violation where there is a substantial probability that death or serious physical harm could result from an exposure exceeding an established permissible exposure limit or a condition that exists, or from one or more practices, means, methods, operations, or processes that have been adopted or are in use, in the place of employment unless the employer did not, and could not with the exercise of reasonable diligence, know of the presence of the violation.

Violation, Willful

A violation where the evidence shows either willful intent, plain indifference, or blatant disregard of the compliance requirements of an environmental law, applicable standard or regulation, or comparable legal requirement at the state or local level; or, even though the employer was not con-

sciously violating a safety law, he/she was aware that an unsafe or hazardous condition existed and made no reasonable effort to eliminate the condition. Knowledge of a hazard is obtained from such means as agency warnings, insurance company reports, safety committee or other internal reports, the occurrence of illnesses or injuries, media coverage, or, in some cases, complaints of employees or their representatives.

Virgin Materials

Raw materials, including previously unused copper, aluminum, lead, zinc, iron, or other metals or metal ores, any undeveloped resources that are, or with new technology will become, a source of raw materials.

Virus

1) The smallest form of microorganisms capable of causing disease. 2) Viruses of varied origin that are infectious to humans by airborne or waterborne transmission.

Viscosity

The cohesive force existing between particles of a fluid that causes the fluid to offer resistance to a relative sliding motion between the particles; the tendency of a material to resist flow.

Viscous Liquids

Liquid material that has a measured viscosity in excess of 2,500 centistokes at 25°C (77°F) when determined in accordance with the procedures specified in ASTM Method D 445-72.

Visibility Impairment Research (VIR)

Research to identify and evaluate sources and source regions of both visibility impairment and regions that provide predominantly clean air in Class I areas. The research includes a) expansion of current visibility related monitoring; b) assessment of current sources of visibility impairing pollution and clean air corridors; c) adaptation of regional air quality models for the assessment of visibility; and d) studies of atmospheric chemistry and physics of visibility.

Visibility Impairment

The reduction in visual range and atmospheric discoloration; any humanly perceptible changes in visibility including, reduction in visual range, contrast, and atmospheric discoloration.

Visibility Protection

The prevention of any future, and the remedying of any existing, impairment of visibility in mandatory Class I federal areas that impairment results from manmade air pollution. Activities include the following: a) identifying, characterizing, determining, quantifying, and measuring visibility impairment in federal areas; b) developing modeling techniques (or other methods) for determining the extent to which manmade air pollution may reasonably be anticipated to cause or contribute to such impairment; and c) implementing methods for preventing and remedying manmade air pollution and resulting visibility impairment. A Visibility Protection Report that identifies the classes or categories of sources and the types of air pollutants that, alone or in conjunction with other sources or pollutants, may reasonably be anticipated to cause or contribute significantly to impairment of visibility, is typically prepared.

Visibility Reducing Particles (VRB)

Atmospheric particles that significantly scatter or absorb light. The effect of these particles on light extinction is determined by instrumental monitoring of light scattering and absorption by ARB Method V, or equivalent method.

Visibility Transport Commission (VTC)

In conjunction with the CAA, the commissions established by the Administrator in Visibility Transport Regions (VTRs), comprised of (as a minimum) each of the following members: a) the governor of each state in the Visibility Transport Region, or the governor's designee; b) the Administrator or the Administrator's designee; and c) a representative of each federal agency charged with the direct management of each Class I area or areas within the Visibility Transport Region.

All representatives of the federal government are considered ex officio members.

The duties of the committee are to a) assess the scientific and technical data, studies, and other currently available information, including studies conducted pursuant to the CAA pertaining to adverse impacts on visibility from potential or projected growth in emissions from sources located in the Visibility Transport Region; and b) to prepare reports addressing:

- the establishment of clean air corridors, in which additional restrictions on increases in emissions may be appropriate to protect visibility in affected Class I areas;
- the imposition of the requirements affecting the construction of new major stationary sources or major modifications to existing sources in such clean air corridors specifically including the alternative siting analyses; and
- to promulgate regulations that address long range strategies for addressing regional haze that impairs visibility in affected Class I areas.

Visibility Transport Region (VTR)(CAA)

Areas where the EPA has reason to believe that the current or projected interstate transport of air pollutants from one or more states contributes significantly to visibility impairment in Class I areas located in the affected states.

Visible Emissions, Asbestos

Any emissions containing particulate asbestos material that are visually detectable without the aid of instruments. This does not include condensed uncombined water vapor.

Visible Radiation, Light

Electromagnetic radiation that can be detected by the human eye. It is commonly used to describe wavelengths that lie in the range between 400 nanometers and 700-780 nanometers.

Visual Information

Use of one or more of the various visual media with or without sound. Generally, visual information includes still photography, motion picture photography, video or audio recording, graphic arts, visual aids, models, display, visual presentation services, and the support processes.

Visual Information Documentation

Motion media, still photography, and audio recording of technical and nontechnical events while they occur, usually not controlled by the recording crew. Visual information documentation encompasses operational documentation, and technical documentation. Also called VIDOC. *See* Technical Documentation.

Visual Meteorological Conditions (VMC)

Weather conditions in which visual flight rules apply; expressed in terms of visibility, ceiling height, and aircraft clearance from clouds along the path of flight. When these criteria do not exist, instrument meteorological conditions prevail and instrument flight rules must be complied with. *See* Instrument Meteorological Conditions.

Visual Range

The distance at which a black object on the horizon has a 2% contrast with the horizon sky. This distance can be calculated from a measured light extinction coefficient (called Bext) by the formula: Vr = 3.912 divided by Bext.

Vital Activities

A term relating to the integrity of a national security program or a public health and safety function.

Vital Capacity

The maximal volume of air exhaled after the deepest inspiration without forced or rapid effort. In adult humans, generally 5 liters.

Vital Equipment

Equipment, systems, or components whose failure or destruction would cause unacceptable interruption to a national security program or harm to the health and safety of the public.

Vital Records

Records essential for maintaining the continuity of government activities during a national emergency.

Viviparous

1) In zoology, a species descriptor that means giving birth to living offspring that developed within the mother's body. 2) In botany, a species descriptor that means producing seeds that germinate before becoming detached from the parent plant.

VLF

An acronym for Very Low Flow.

VMC

See Visual Meteorological Conditions.

VNS

See Volumetric Neutron Source.

VOCs

See Volatile Organic Compounds.

Voids

Pockets of entrapped gas that have been cured into a laminate.

Volatile

The description of any substance that evaporates quickly; having a low boiling point (e.g., ether, chloroform, benzene); materials in a sizing or a resin formulation that can be vaporized at room or slightly elevated temperature.

Volatile Hazardous Air Pollutant (VHAP)

A regulated substance for which a standard for equipment leaks of the substance has been proposed and promulgated. Benzene and Vinyl chloride are VHAPs.

Volatile Organic Compound Study

The EPA study to determine the potential of VOCs to contribute to ozone levels that violate the national ambient air quality standard for ozone; and establish criteria for regulating consumer and commercial products or classes or categories thereof. In establishing study criteria, the Administrator takes into consideration each of the following: a) the uses, benefits, and commercial demand of consumer and commercial products; b) the health or safety functions (if any) served by such consumer and commercial products; c) those consumer and commercial products that emit highly reactive volatile organic compounds into the ambient air; d) those consumer and commercial products that are subject to the most cost-effective controls; and e) the availability of alternatives (if any) to such consumer and commercial products that are of comparable costs, considering health, safety, and environmental impacts.

Volatile Organic Compounds (VOCs)
1) Any organic compound that evaporates readily to the atmosphere, except for those designated by the EPA Administrator as having negligible photochemical reactivity. 2) Organic (carbon-containing) elements and compounds that evaporate readily into the atmosphere at normal temperatures. VOCs contribute significantly to photochemical smog production and certain health problems.

Volatile Synthetic Organic Chemicals (VSOCs)
Chemicals that tend to volatilize or evaporate from water.

Volatility
The relative rate of evaporation of materials to assume the vapor state.

Volcanic Dust
Fine pyroclastic ash particulates ejected by an explosive eruption. These fine particulates sometimes travel great distances before settling.

Volt
Named after Alessandro Volta (1745-1827), it is the SI unit of electric potential; the difference between two points on a wire conducting a constant current of 1 ampere when the power dissipated between the points equals 1 watt.

Voluntary Energy Performance Standards
Energy consumption goals met without specification of the methods, materials, and processes to be employed in achieving the goals, including statements of the requirements, criteria, and evaluation methods to be used, and any necessary recommendations or commentary.

Voluntary Standards
Standards that are established generally by private sector bodies and are available for use by any person or organization, private or governmental. Voluntary standards are also referred to as "industry standards" as well as "consensus standards" (standards developed under due process procedures) but do not include professional standards of personal conduct, private standards of individual firms, standards mandated by law, or standards of individual organizations for their internal use. *See* Voluntary Standards Bodies.

Voluntary Standards Bodies
Nongovernmental bodies that are broadly based, multimembered, domestic and multinational organizations, industry associations, and professional or technical societies that develop, establish, or coordinate voluntary standards activities.

VRE
See Vibrating Reed Electrometers.

VSII
See Very Seriously Ill or Injured.

VTC
See Visibility Transport Commission).

VTR
See Visibility Transport Region.

Vulnerability
The characteristics of a system that cause it to suffer a definite degradation (incapability to perform the designated mission) as a result of having been subjected to a certain level of effects in an unnatural (manmade) hazardous environment.

Vulnerability Analysis

An assessment of elements in the community that are susceptible to damage should a release of hazardous materials occur.

Vulnerable Zone

An area over which the airborne concentration of a chemical involved in an accidental release could reach the level of concern.

Vulnerable Zones Radius

The maximum distance from the point of release of a hazardous substance in which the airborne concentration could reach the level of concern under specified weather conditions.

W

WACC
An acronym for Waste Acceptance Criteria Committee.

Wading Crossing
See Deep Fording; Shallow Fording.

WAG
An acronym for Waste Area Grouping.

Waiver
The action taken by the department eliminating the need for the report required of the department when the agency is a party to or has joined in the petition for adoption.

Waler
A structural member in a horizontal or nearly horizontal position used for stiffening or securing other components of concrete forms, excavation sheeting, or similar temporary structures.

Walking Patient
A patient not requiring a litter while in transit; an ambulatory patient.

Wall, Bearing
A wall that supports any superimposed load in excess of 100 pounds per lineal foot.

Walleye
A guided air-to-surface glide bomb for the stand-off destruction of large semihard targets. It incor-

porates a contrast-tracking television system for guidance.

WAN
An acronym for Wide Area Network.

War Reserve, Nuclear
Nuclear weapons material stockpiled in the custody of the Department of Energy or transferred to the custody of the Department of Defense and intended for employment in the event of war.

Warehouse Chart
See Planograph.

Warned Exposed
The vulnerability of friendly forces to nuclear weapon effects. In this condition, personnel are assumed to be prone, with all skin covered, and with thermal protection — at least that provided by a two-layer summer uniform. *See* Unwarned Exposed; Warned Protected.

Warned Protected
The vulnerability of friendly forces to nuclear weapon effects. In this condition, personnel are assumed to have some protection against heat, blast, and radiation such as that afforded in closed armored vehicles or crouched in fox holes with improvised overhead shielding. *See* Unwarned Exposed; Warned Exposed.

Warning

A communication and acknowledgment of dangers implicit in a wide spectrum of activities by potential opponents ranging from routine defense measures to substantial increases in readiness and force preparedness and to acts of terrorism or political, economic, or military provocation.

Warning Area

See Danger Area.

Warning Order

A preliminary notice of an order or action that is to follow.

Waste

1) Any substance, solid, liquid, or gas, that remains as a residue or is an incidental byproduct of the use or manufacturing of a substance, that cannot be reused and/or disposed of in an environmentally safe manner. 2) Unwanted materials left over from a manufacturing process. 3) Refuse from places of human or animal habitation.

Waste, Database

A system for sharing hazardous waste information between generators and other firms to facilitate the transfer of wastes from the generator to firms that can use the wastes as raw materials.

Waste Containers

Receptacles for waste, including any liner or shielding material, that are intended to accompany the waste in disposal.

Waste Fund

The Nuclear Waste Fund established in Section 102(22)(c) of the AEA.

Waste Heat

Heat that is at temperatures close to the ambient air temperature and is of no value for production of power and is discharged to the environs.

Waste Holding Tank

A liquid tight tank for the temporary retention of body and/or liquid waste.

Waste Information Network (WIN)

An information network developed through the efforts of the national Hazardous Waste Remedial Actions Program (HAZRAP) in support of DOE's Office of Environmental Restoration and Waste Management. WIN is designed to promote information exchange among the DOE installations and waste management community through communications and database applications.

Waste Isolation Pilot Plant

A research and demonstration facility located at Carlsbad, New Mexico, intended to demonstrate safe disposal of radioactive waste in a deep geologic environment. A decision as to whether to convert the Waste Isolation Pilot Plant to a disposal facility for transuranic waste will be made after successful testing is demonstrated.

Waste Load Allocation

The maximum load of pollutants each discharger of waste is allowed to release into a particular waterway. Discharge limits are usually required for each specific water quality criterion being, or expected to be, violated.

Waste Management

The systematic administration of activities that provide for the collection, storage, transportation, transfer, processing, treatment, and disposal of waste.

Waste Management Processes

A term referring to the various processes and techniques used to manage waste, including, but not limited to, absorption (waste); aerobic treatment; biological treatment; chemical treatments; closed-loop recycling; coagulation; conventional filtration treatment; flocculation; granular activated carbon treatment; in situ treatment; incineration; ion exchange treatment; land farming (of waste); subsurface and near-surface land disposal; physical and chemical treatments; pretreatment; recycling; removal; retrofill; solidification and stabilization; tertiary treatment; thermal treatment; treatment, storage, and disposal; trenching; vertical tube storage treatment; waste minimization; wastewater treatment processes; and dumping.

Waste Material

Matter of any kind or description, including, but not limited to, dredged material, solid waste, incinerator residue, garbage, sewage, sewage sludge, munitions, radiological, chemical, and biological warfare agents, radioactive materials, chemicals, biological and laboratory waste, wreck or discarded equipment, rock, sand, excavation debris, and industrial, municipal, agricultural, and other waste. The term typically does not mean sewage from vessels, and oil is included only to the extent that such oil is taken onboard a vessel or aircraft for the purpose of dumping.

Waste Minimization Plan

A detailed comprehensive plan for implementing recycling and resource conservation at public/private facilities. These plans detail resources to be recycled, locations for material storage/pick-up, in-house program promotion efforts, and other implementation issues (e.g., recycling revenues generated into capital equipment resources).

Waste Oils

Incidental byproducts primarily derived from petroleum that include, but are not limited to, fuel oils, motor oils, gear oils, cutting oils, transmission fluids, hydraulic fluids, and dielectric fluids.

Waste Packages

The waste, waste container, and any absorbent that are intended for disposal as a unit. In the case of surface contaminated, damaged, leaking, or breached waste packages, any overpack shall be considered the waste container, and the original container shall be considered pan of the waste.

Waste Piles

1) Any noncontainerized accumulations of solid, nonflowing hazardous wastes that are used for treatment or storage. 2) Fuel elements in a nuclear reactor. 3) Heaps of waste.

Waste Source

A facility or vessel from which municipal or commercial waste is loaded onto a vessel, including any rolling stock or motor vehicles from which that waste is directly loaded.

Waste Treatment Plant

A facility containing a series of tanks, screens, filters, and other processes by which pollutants are removed from water.

Waste Treatment Stream

The continuous movement of waste from generator to treater and disposer.

Wastewater Collection Systems

Piping, pumps, conduits, and any other equipment necessary to collect and transport the flow of surface water runoff resulting from precipitation, or domestic, commercial, or industrial wastewater to and from retention areas or any areas where treatment is designated to occur. The collection of stormwater and wastewater does not include treatment except where incidental to conveyance.

Wasteful Manner

Any taking or method of taking that is likely to result in the killing or injury of endangered or threatened wildlife beyond those needed for subsistence purposes, or that results in the waste of a substantial portion of the wildlife, and includes without limitation the employment of a method of taking that is not likely to ensure the capture or killing of the wildlife, or that is not immediately followed by a reasonable effort to retrieve the wildlife.

Wasteload Allocation (WLA)

The portion of a stream's total assimilative capacity assigned to an individual discharger.

Wastes

1) Unwanted materials left over from a manufacturing process. 2) Refuse from places of human or animal habitation.

Wastes, Radioactive

Equipment and materials, from nuclear operations, that are radioactive and for which there are no further uses. Wastes are classified as high-level, having radioactive concentrations of hundreds to thousands of curies per gallon (or cubic foot); or low-level, in the range of 1 microcurie per gallon (or cubic foot).

Wastewater

The spent or used water of a community or industrial operation that contains dissolved or suspended matter. It may be a combination of the liquid-carried and water-carried wastes from residences, commercial buildings, industrial plants, and other sources, together with any groundwater, surface water, and stormwater.

Wastewater Decomposition

The transmutation of the organic or inorganic materials contained in wastewater through the action of chemical or biological processes.

Wastewater Lagoon

An impoundment area into which wastewater is discharged at a rate low enough to permit oxidation to occur without causing any substantial nuisances associated with odors and insects.

Wastewater Operations and Maintenance

Actions taken after construction to ensure that facilities constructed to treat wastewater will be properly operated, maintained, and managed to achieve efficiency levels and prescribed effluent levels in an optimum manner.

Wastewater Oxidation

The process where, through the agency of living organisms in the presence of oxygen, organic matter contained in wastewater is converted to a more stable or mineral form.

Wastewater Treatment Facilities Construction Grant

EPA grants for the construction of municipal wastewater treatment plants; to provide most of the cost for preliminary plans and feasibility studies, including the preparation of construction drawings, specifications, and eventual construction of a completely operational facility.

Wastewater Treatment Plant

A facility containing a series of tanks, screens, filters, and other processes by which pollutants are removed from water. Most treatments include chlorination to attain safe drinking water standards.

Wastewater Treatment Processes

Any processes that modify characteristics such as BOD, COD, TSS, and pH, usually for the purpose of meeting effluent guidelines and standards. Wastewater treatment processes include, but are not limited to, processes utilizing activated carbon, activated sludges, bar screens, comminution, conventional filtration treatments, oxidation ponds, and any process the purpose of which is to remove vinyl chloride from water. *See* Waste Management Processes.

Wastewater Treatment Tanks

Tanks that are designed to receive and treat influent wastewater through physical, chemical, or biological methods.

Wastewater Treatment Unit

A device that either a) is part of a wastewater treatment facility subject to regulation under either Section 402 or Section 307(b) of the Clean Water Act; b) receives, treats or stores an effluent wastewater that is a hazardous waste as defined in Section 261.3 of 40 CFR, or generates and accumulates a waste sludge that is a hazardous waste as defined in Section 261.3 of 40 CFR; or c) meets the definition of tank in Section 260.10 of 40 CFR.

Water

Clear, odorless, tasteless liquid that is essential for most plant and animal life; descends from clouds as rain and forms streams, lakes, and seas.

Water, Bulk Shipment
The bulk transportation of hazardous waste that is loaded or carried onboard a vessel without containers or labels.

Water Budget
An evaluation of all the sources of supply and the corresponding discharges with respect to an aquifer or a drainage basin.

Water Distribution System
1) With respect to mobile homes; all of the water supply piping within a mobile home park, extending from the main public supply or other source of supply to the lot outlets and including branch service lines, fittings, control valves, and appurtenances. 2) The potable water piping within or attached to a vehicle.

Water Dumping
The disposal of pesticides in or on lakes, ponds, rivers, sewers, or other water systems as defined in Public Law 92-500.

Water Jet
A high-pressure stream of water used for cutting organic composites.

Water Management Division Director
One of the directors of the Water Management Divisions within the regional offices of the EPA or this person's delegated representative.

Water Management Element
The part of a conservation area plan under the Resource Conservation Act (RCA) that sets forth measures to provide for the conservation, utilization, and quality of water, including irrigation and rural water, supplies, the mitigation of floods and high water tables, construction, repair, and improvement of dams and reservoirs, improvement of agricultural water management, and improvement of water quality through control of nonpoint sources of pollution. *See* Conservation Area Plan.

Water Pollution
The addition of sewage, industrial waste, and/or other harmful or objectionable material to water in concentrations and quantities sufficient enough to result in measurable degradation in water quality; the presence in water of enough harmful or objectionable material to damage the water's quality.

Water Pollution Control Act
A federal statute administered by EPA that regulates the discharge of pollutants into bodies of water.

Water Purveyor
A public utility, mutual water company, county water district, or municipality that delivers drinking water to customers.

Water Quality Criteria
Specific levels of water quality that, if reached, are expected to render a body of water suitable for its designated use. The criteria are based on specific levels of pollutants that would make the water harmful if used for consumption, recreational waters, fisheries and aquatic life, agricultural water, and industrial use.

Water Quality Standards (WQS)
1) State-adopted and EPA-approved ambient standards for water bodies. The standards cover the use of the water body and the water quality criteria that must be met to protect the designated use or uses. 2) The combination of a designated use and the maximum concentration of a pollutant that will protect that use for any given body of water.

Water Reactive Materials
Solid substances (including sludges and pastes) that, by interaction with water, are likely to become spontaneously flammable or to give off flammable or toxic gases in dangerous quantities.

Water Resistant
Having a degree of resistance to permeability by and damage caused by water in liquid form.

Water Solubility

The maximum concentration of a chemical compound that can result when it is dissolved in water. If a substance is water soluble it can very readily disperse through the environment.

Water Storage Tank

A tank designed for the purpose of storing potable water.

Water Suit

A G-suit in which water is used in the interlining thereby automatically approximating the required hydrostatic pressure-gradient under G forces.

Water Suppliers

Individuals or entities who own or operate a public water system.

Water Supply Connection

The fitting or point of connection in the vehicle water distribution system designed for connection to a water supply.

Water Supply System

The collection, treatment, storage, and distribution of potable water from source to consumer.

Water Table

1) The uppermost portion of groundwater whose level can vary based upon seasonal recharge and discharge rates. 2) The upper surface of the zone of saturation, where that surface is not formed by a confining unit and water pressure in the porous medium is equal to atmospheric pressure. 3) The surface between the vadose zone and groundwater. 4) That surface of a body of unconfined groundwater at which the pressure is equal to that of the atmosphere. 5) Generally, the level to which water will rise in a well (except artesian wells); the level of groundwater. The water table can be measured by installing shallow wells extending a few feet into the zone of saturation and then measuring the water level in those wells. No water table exists where that surface is formed by an impermeable body.

Water Terminal

A facility for berthing ships simultaneously at piers, quays, and/or working anchorages, normally located within sheltered coastal waters adjacent to rail, highway, air, and/or inland water transportation networks.

Water Tight

Of such tight construction or fit as to be impermeable to water except when under sufficient pressure to produce structural discontinuity.

Water User

Any person obtaining water from a public water supply.

Water Works Flood Improvements

Under the Watershed Protection and Flood Prevention Act (WPFPA), any undertaking for a) flood prevention (including structural and land treatment measures); b) the conservation, development, utilization, and disposal of water; or c) the conservation and proper utilization of land, in watershed or subwatershed area not exceeding 250,000 acres and not including any single structure that provides more than 12,500 acre-feet of floodwater detention capacity, and more than 25,000 acre-feet of total capacity.

Water-Reactive Material

A substance that readily reacts with water or decomposes in the presence of water, typically with substantial energy release.

Waterborne Disease Outbreaks

Significant occurrences of acute infections illness, epidemiologically associated with the ingestion of water from a public water system that is deficient in treatment, as determined by the appropriate local or state agency.

Waterbreak

A ditch, dike, or dip, or a combination thereof, constructed diagonally across roads, and firebreaks so that water flow is effectively diverted therefrom. Waterbreaks are synonymous with waterbars.

Watercourse

Any well-defined channel with distinguishable bed and bank showing evidence of having contained flowing water indicated by deposit of rock, sand, gravel, or soil, including but not limited to, streams, and manmade watercourses.

Watercourse and Lake Protection Zone

A strip of soil and vegetation, along both sides of a watercourse or around the circumference of a lake, where additional practices may be required for the protection of water quality, the beneficial uses of water, and other natural resources.

Waters of the United States

The navigable waters and the territorial sea of the United States.

Watershed

An area from which a stream or other body of water receives its makeup waters; land areas that drain into streams.

Watershed Protection and Flood Prevention Act of 1954 (WPFPA)

The Act establishing criteria for the formulation and justification of plans for works of improvement and criteria for the sharing of the cost of both structural and land-treatment measures that conform with the provisions of the Act and with policies established by or at the direction of the President for watershed protection, flood prevention, irrigation, drainage, water supply, and related water-resources development purposes.

Watt

A unit of power equal to the rate of energy use or conversion when one joule of energy is used or converted per second. *See* Joule.

Watt-Hour

The total amount of energy used in one hour by a device that uses one watt of power for continuous operation. Electrical energy is generally sold by the kilowatt-hour (kWh).

Wave

A formation of forces, landing ships, craft, amphibious vehicles or aircraft, required to beach or land about the same time. Can be classified as to type, function, or order (e.g., assault wave, boat wave, helicopter wave, numbered wave, on-call wave, scheduled wave).

Wavelength

The length of the light wave, usually measured from crest to crest, that determines its color. Common units of measurement are the micrometer (micron), the nanometer, and (earlier) the Angstrom unit.

WBE

See Women Business Enterprise.

WCCSA

An acronym for White Clay Creek Study Act of 1991 (WSRA).

Weapon Debris, Nuclear

The residue of a nuclear weapon after it has exploded; that is, materials used for the casing and other components of the weapon, plus unexpended plutonium or uranium, together with fission products.

Weaponeering

The process of determining the quantity of a specific type of lethal or nonlethal weapons required to achieve a specific level of damage to a given target, considering target vulnerability, weapon effect, munitions delivery accuracy, damage criteria, probability of kill, and weapon reliability.

Weapons of Mass Destruction

In arms control usage, weapons that are capable of a high order of destruction and/or of being used in such a manner as to destroy large numbers of people. Can be nuclear, chemical, biological, and radiological weapons, but excludes the means of transporting or propelling the weapon where such means is a separable and divisible part of the weapon.

Weather Central

An organization that collects, collates, evaluates, and disseminates meteorological information in such manner that it becomes a principal source of such information for a given area.

Weather Forecast

A prediction of weather conditions at a point, along a route, or within an area, for a specified period of time.

Weather Map

A map showing the weather conditions prevailing, or predicted to prevail, over a considerable area. Usually, the map is based upon weather observations taken at the same time at a number of stations. *See* Map.

Weather Minimum

The worst weather conditions under which aviation operations may be conducted under either visual or instrument flight rules. Usually prescribed by directives and standing operating procedures in terms of minimum ceiling, visibility, or specific hazards to flight.

Weather, VATB

A short form weather report, giving the following:

- V — Visibility in miles;
- A — Amount of clouds;
- T — Height of cloud top, in thousands of feet;
- B — Height of cloud base, in thousands of feet.

The reply is a series of four numbers preceded by the word "weather." An unknown item is reported as "unknown."

Weathering

The disintegration and material breakdown of rocks or other materials above the earth's surface over time. Occurs by wind, water, ice, or in combination with some chemical action.

Weatherization Materials

Building related equipment and materials, such as a) caulking and weatherstripping of doors and windows; b) furnace efficiency modifications including devices for minimizing energy loss through heating system, chimney, or venting devices; c) clock thermostats; d) ceiling, attic, wall, floor, and duct insulation; e) water heater insulation; f) storm windows and doors, multiglazed windows and doors, heat-absorbing or heat-reflective window and door materials; g) cooling efficiency modifications, including, but not limited to, replacement air-conditioners, ventilation equipment, screening, window films, and shading devices; and h) such other insulating or energy conserving devices or technologies as the Secretary may determine, after consulting with the Secretary of Housing and Urban Development, the Secretary of Agriculture, and the Director of the Community Services Administration.

Weatherized Warm Air Furnace

A furnace or boiler designed for installation outdoors, approved for resistance to wind, rain, and snow, and supplied with its own venting system.

Weeds

Plants that grow where they are not wanted.

Weibull Model

A dose-response model of the form $P(d) = 1-exp(-bd^m)$; where $P(d)$ is the probability of cancer due to a continuous dose rate d, and b and m are constants.

Weight and Balance Sheet

A sheet that records the distribution of weight in an aircraft and shows the center of gravity of an aircraft at takeoff and landing.

Weight of Evidence

1) The extent to which the available biomedical data support the hypothesis that a substance causes an effect in humans. For example, the following factors increase the weight of evidence that a chemical poses a hazard to humans: a) an increase in the number of tissue sites affected by the agent; b) an increase in the number of animal species, strains, sexes, and number of experiments and doses showing a response; c) the occurrence of a clear-cut dose-response relationship

as well as a high level of statistical significance in the occurrence of the adverse effect in treated subjects compared with untreated controls; and d) a dose-related shortening of the time of occurrence of the adverse effect. 2) An EPA classification system for characterizing the extent to which the available data indicate that an agent is a human carcinogen.

Weighting Factors

Tissue-specific factors that represent the fraction of the total health risk resulting from uniform, whole-body irradiation that could be contributed to that particular tissue. The weighting factors recommended by the ICRP (Publication 26) and used here are gonads (0.25), breasts (0.15), red bone marrow (0.12), lungs (0.12), thyroid (0.03), bone surfaces (0.03), remainder (0.30) ["Remainder" means the five other organs with the highest dose (e.g., liver, kidney, spleen, thymus, adrenal, pancreas, stomach, small intestine, or upper and lower large intestine, but excluding skin, lens of the eye, and extremities)]. The weighting factor for each of these organs is 0.06. *See* Weight of Evidence.

Weir

1) A diversion dam. 2) A device that has a crest and some side containment of known geometric shape, such as a rectangle, or trapezoid, and is used to measure the flow of liquid. Flow is related to the upstream height of water above the crest, to position of the crest with respect to the downstream water surface, and the geometry of the weir opening.

Well

Any shaft or pit dug or bored into the earth, generally of a cylindrical form, and often walled with bricks or tubing to prevent earth from caving in; a bored, drilled, or driven shaft or a dug hole, whose depth is greater than the largest surface dimension and whose purpose is to reach underground water supplies or oil, or to store or bury fluids below ground.

Well Field

An area containing two or more wells.

Well Injection

1) The subsurface emplacement of fluids through a bored, drilled, or driven well; or through a dug well, where the depth of the dug well is greater than the largest surface dimension. 2) The subsurface emplacement of fluids in a well. 3) Disposal of liquid wastes through a hole or shaft into a subsurface stratum.

Well Interference

1) The result of two or more pumping wells, the drawdown cones of which intercept. At a given location, the total well interference is the sum of the drawdowns due to each individual well. 2) The condition occurring when the area of influence of a water well comes into contact with or overlaps that of a neighboring well, as when two wells are pumping from the same aquifer or are located close to each other.

Well Monitoring

The measurement, by onsite instruments or laboratory methods, of the quality of water in a well.

Well Plug

A watertight and gastight seal installed in a bore hole or well to prevent movement of fluids.

Well Repairs/Workovers

Any reentries of an injection well; including, but not limited to, the pulling of tubular goods, cementing or casing repairs; and excluding any routine maintenance (e.g. resealing the packer at the same depth, or repairs to surface equipment).

Well Screen

A filtering device used to keep sediment from entering a water well.

Well Stimulation

Several processes used to clean the well bore, enlarge channels, and increase pore space in the interval to be injected thus making it possible for wastewater to move more readily into the formation, and includes surging, jetting, blasting, acidic, and hydraulic fracturing.

Well Yield

The volume of water discharged from a well in gallons per minute or cubic meters per day.

Wellhead

1) Oil or gas brought to the surface, ready for transportation to refineries or ships or pipelines. Wellhead costs usually refer to the cost of bringing the oil or gas from underground to the surface. 2) The physical structure, facility, or device at the land surface from or through which groundwater flows or is pumped from subsurface water-bearing formations.

Wellhead Protection Area (WHPA)

1) The surface and subsurface area surrounding a water well or well field, supplying a public water system, through which contaminants are reasonably likely to move toward and reach such water well or well field. The conceptual standards that form the basis for inclusion in a WHPA include, but are not limited to, distance, drawdown, time of travel, assimilative capacity, and flow boundaries. 2) A protected surface and subsurface zone surrounding a well or well field that supplies a public water system and through which contaminants could likely reach well water.

Wells

See Well.

WERF

An acronym for Waste Experimental Reduction Facility.

Western Area Power Administration (WAPA)

The administration responsible for the federal electric power-marketing and transmission functions in 15 central and western states, encompassing a geographic area of 1.3 million square miles. The administration sells power to 532 customers, consisting of cooperatives, municipalities, public utility districts, private utilities, federal and state agencies, and irrigation districts.

These wholesale power customers provide service to consumers in Arizona, California, Colorado, Iowa, Kansas, Minnesota, Montana, Nebraska, Nevada, New Mexico, North Dakota, South Dakota, Texas, Utah, and Wyoming. *See* Power Marketing Administrations.

Western States Acid Deposition Research (WSADR)

Under the CAA, annual and periodic assessment reports sponsored by the EPA on a) the occurrence and effects of acid deposition on surface waters located in that part of the United States west of the Mississippi River; b) the occurrence and effects of acid deposition on high elevation ecosystems (including forests, and surface waters); and c) the occurrence and effects of episodic acidification, particularly with respect to high elevation watersheds.

Research studies take into account data from the Western Lakes Survey, and other appropriate research and utilize predictive modeling techniques that take into account the unique geographic, climatological, and atmospheric conditions that exist in the western United States to determine the potential occurrence and effects of acid deposition due to any projected increases in the emission of sulfur dioxide and nitrogen oxides.

Wet Meadows

Natural areas except cutover timberland that are moist on the surface throughout most of the year and support aquatic vegetation, grasses, and forbs as their principal vegetative cover.

Wet Scrubbers

Absorption towers that are used to remove polluted gases from a waste gas stream by continuously wetting down fumes with a liquid.

Wetlands

1) Low-lying lands that are near bodies of water, periodically covered by fresh, brackish, or salt water, and largely covered by vegetation. 2) Land that has a predominance of hydric soils and is inundated or saturated by surface or groundwater at a frequency and duration sufficient to support hydrophytic vegetation and aquatic species that require saturated, or seasonally saturated, soil conditions for growth and reproduction.

Wetlands generally include swamps, marshes, bogs, estuaries, and other inland and coastal areas, and are federally protected.

Wetlands frequently serve as recharge/discharge areas and are known as "nature's kidneys" since they help purify water. Wetlands also have been referred to as natural sponges that absorb flood waters, functioning like natural tubs to collect overflow. Wetlands are important wildlife habitats, breeding grounds, and nurseries because of their biodiversity.

Many endangered species as well as countless estuarine and marine fish and shellfish, mammals, waterfowl, and other migratory birds use wetland habitat for growth, reproduction, food, and shelter. Wetlands are among the most fertile, natural ecosystems in the world since they produce great volumes of food (plant material); and they are subject to strict development restrictions.

The term does not typically include lands in Alaska identified as having high potential for agricultural development that have a predominance of permafrost soils. *See* Wetland Classification chart on page 735.

Wetlands Conservation Project
1) The obtaining of a real property interest in lands or waters, including water rights, if the obtaining of such interest is subject to terms and conditions that will ensure that the real property will be administered for the long-term conservation of such lands and waters and the migratory birds and other fish and wildlife dependent thereon. 2) The restoration, management, or enhancement of wetland ecosystems and other habitats for migratory birds and other fish and wildlife species if such restoration, management, or enhancement is conducted on lands and waters that are administered for the long-term conservation of such lands and waters and the migratory birds and other fish and wildlife dependent thereon. 3) In the case of projects undertaken in Mexico, includes technical training and development of infrastructure necessary for the conservation and management of wetlands and studies on the sustainable use of wetland resources.

Wetlands, Converted
Wetlands that have been drained, dredged, filled, leveled, or otherwise manipulated (including any activity that results in impairing or reducing the flow, circulation, or reach of water) for the purpose or to have the effect of making the production of an agricultural commodity possible if a) such production would not have been possible but for such action; and b) prior to the action, the land was a wetland and was neither highly erodible land nor highly erodible cropland. Wetland shall not be considered converted wetland if production of an agricultural commodity on such land during a crop year is possible as a result of a natural condition, such as drought; and is not assisted by an action of the producer that destroys natural wetland characteristics.

Wetlands of International Importance
Wetland areas defined by the IUCN and UNESCO as having global importance for environmental conservation and study.

Wetout
The saturation of all voids between strands and filaments of porous materials with resin.

Wetting Agent
A surface-active agent that promotes wetting by decreasing the cohesion within a liquid.

Wharf
A structure built of open rather than solid construction along a shore or a bank that provides cargo-handling facilities. A similar facility of solid construction is called a quay. *See* Pier; Quay.

What's Up
As used in air intercept, and response action, a DOD code meaning, "Is anything the matter?"

Wheel Load Capacity
The capacity of airfield runways, taxiways, parking areas, or roadways to bear the pressures exerted by aircraft or vehicles in a gross weight static configuration.

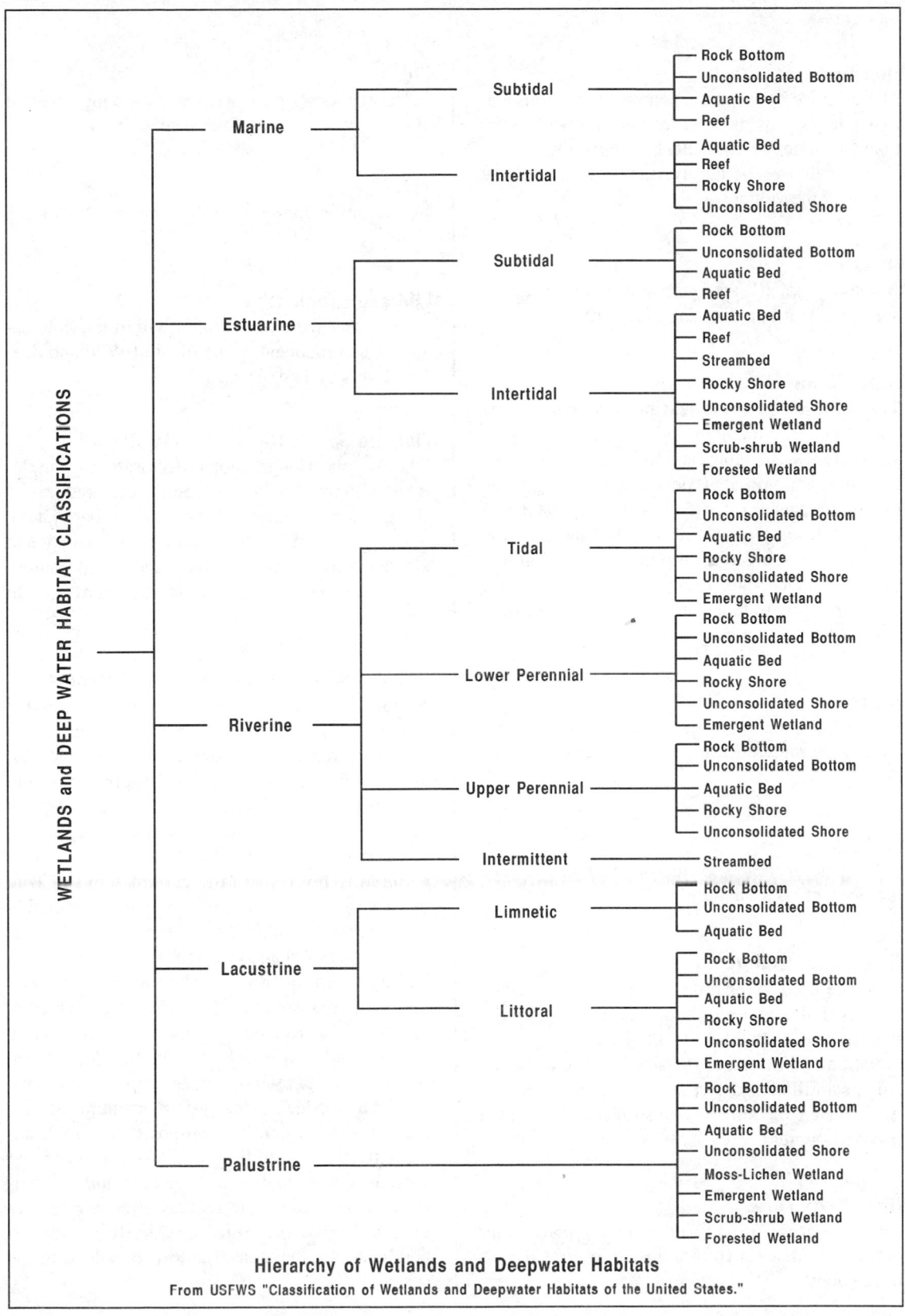

Hierarchy of Wetlands and Deepwater Habitats

From USFWS "Classification of Wetlands and Deepwater Habitats of the United States."

Wheelbase
The distance between the centers of two consecutive wheels. In the case of vehicles with more than two axles or equivalent systems, the successive wheelbases are all given in the order of front to rear of the vehicle.

Wheezing
Breathing noisily and with difficulty; usually a sign of spasm or narrowing of the airways.

While Giving Consideration
The selection of those feasible silvicultural systems, operating methods and procedures that substantially lessen significant adverse impact on the environment and that best achieve long-term, maximum sustained production of forest products, while protecting soil, air, fish and wildlife, and water resources from unreasonable degradation, and that evaluate and make allowance for values relating to range and forage resources, recreation and aesthetics.

Whiteout
Loss of orientation with respect to the horizon caused by sun reflecting on snow and overcast sky.

Whole Body
All organs or tissues exclusive of the integumentary system (skin) and the cornea.

Whole Body Counter
A device used to quantify and measure the radioactivity in the bodies of human beings or animals. It uses heavy shielding to keep out background radiation and measures the activity with ultrasensitive scintillation detectors and electronic equipment. This instrument is also referred to as an in-vivo counter.

Whole Body Dose
The dose of radiation received by the body in its entirety, as distinct from a dose to a limited area of the body.

Whorl
A species descriptor that means having three or more leaves radiating from a single point.

WHPP
An acronym for Waste Handling and Packaging Plant.

Wild and Scenic River
A river and the adjacent area within the boundaries of a component of the Natural Wild and Scenic Rivers system.

Wild and Scenic Rivers Act (WSRA)
The Act and Congressional declaration to implement a national wild and scenic rivers system, by designating the initial components of that system, and by prescribing the methods by which and standards according to which additional components may be added to the system from time to time.

Wild and Scenic Rivers, Additions Report
Regarding the Wild and Scenic Rivers Act (WSRA), the Senate or House document, or report, required to designate rivers to the national system. These documents and reports typically include maps and illustrations, that show among other things the area to be included; the characteristics that do or do not make the area a worthy addition to the system; the current status of land ownership and use in the area; the reasonably foreseeable potential uses of the land and water that would be enhanced, foreclosed, or curtailed if the area were included in the national wild and scenic rivers system; the federal agency (which in the case of a river that is wholly or substantially within a national forest, shall be the Department of Agriculture) by which it is proposed the area, should it be added to the system, be administered; the extent to which it is proposed that such administration, including the costs thereof, be shared by state and local agencies; and the estimated cost to the United States of acquiring necessary lands and interests in land and of administering the area, should it be added to the system.

Wild and Scenic Rivers, Comprehensive Management Plan

Regarding the Wild and Scenic Rivers Act (WSRA), the plan for protection of river values, boundary identifications, and classifications. The plan addresses resource protection, development of lands and facilities, user capacities, and other management practices necessary or desirable to achieve the purposes of the WSRA. Comprehensive management plans also provide for measures as may be necessary to control fire, insects, and diseases to fully protect the values for which the segment is designated as a wild river.

Wild and Scenic Rivers Maps

Regarding the Wild and Scenic Rivers Act (WSRA), the maps of all boundaries and descriptions of the classifications of designated river segments, and subsequent amendments to such boundaries, available for public inspection in the offices of the administering agency in the District of Columbia and in locations convenient to the designated river.

Wild and Scenic Rivers Regulations

Regarding the Wild and Scenic Rivers Act (WSRA), the regulations relating to the recreational and other uses of a river as may be necessary in order to protect the area comprising such river (including lands contiguous or adjacent thereto) from damage or destruction by reason of overuse and to protect its scenic, historic, aesthetic, and scientific values. Including regulations on the procedures and means to be utilized in the enforcement of such area's development and the preparation of area management plans.

Wild and Scenic Rivers System

Regarding the Wild and Scenic Rivers Act (WSRA), the component rivers, portions thereof, and adjacent land, designated as national wild and scenic rivers. The list includes the following:

1) Clearwater, Middle Fork, Idaho — The Middle Fork from the town of Kooskia upstream to the town of Lowell; the Lochsa River from its junction with the Selway at Lowell forming the Middle Fork, upstream to the Powell Ranger Station; and the Selway River from Lowell upstream to its origin;

2) Eleventh Point, Missouri — The segment of the river extending downstream from Thomasville to State Highway 142;

3) Feather, California — The entire Middle Fork downstream from the confluence of its tributary streams 1 kilometer south of Beckwourth, California;

4) Rio Grande, New Mexico - The segment extending from the Colorado state line downstream to the State Highway 96 crossing, and the lower 4 miles of the Red River;

5) Rogue, Oregon — The segment of the river extending from the mouth of the Applegate River downstream to the Lobster Creek Bridge;

6) Saint Croix, Minnesota and Wisconsin — The segment between the dam near Taylors Falls, Minnesota, and the dam near Gordon, Wisconsin, and its tributary, the Namekago, from Lake Namekago downstream to its confluence with the Saint Croix;

7) Salmon, Middle Fork, Idaho — From its origin to its confluence with the main Salmon River;

8) Wolf, Wisconsin — From the Langlade-Menominee County line downstream to Keshena Falls;

9) Lower Saint Croix, Minnesota and Wisconsin — The segment between the dam near Taylors Falls and its confluence with the Mississippi River;

10) Chattooga, North Carolina, South Carolina, Georgia — The segment from 0.8 miles below Cashiers Lake in North Carolina to Tugaloo Reservoir, and the West Fork Chattooga River from its junction with Chattooga upstream 7.3 miles, as generally depicted on the boundary map entitled *Proposed Wild and Scenic Chattooga River and Corridor Boundary* (August 1973);

11) Rapid River, Idaho — The segment from the headwaters of the main stem to the national forest boundary and the segment of the West Fork from the wilderness boundary downstream to the confluence with the main stem, as a wild river;

12) Snake River, Idaho and Oregon — The segment from Hells Canyon Dam downstream to Pittsburgh Landing, as a wild river; and the segment from Pittsburgh Landing downstream to an eastward extension of the north boundary of Section 1, township 5 north, range 47 east, Willamette meridian, as a scenic river;

13) Flathead , Montana — The North Fork from the Canadian border downstream to its confluence with the Middle Fork; the Middle Fork from its headwaters to its confluence to the South Fork; and the South Fork

from its origin to the Hungry Horse Reservoir, as generally depicted on the map entitled *Proposed Flathead Wild and Scenic River Boundary Location* (February 1976);

14) Missouri, Montana — The segment from Fort Benton 149 miles downstream to Robinson Bridge, as generally depicted on the boundary map entitled *Missouri Breaks Freeflowing River Proposal* (October 1975);

15) Obed, Tennessee — The segment from the western edge of the Catoosa Wildlife Management Area to the confluence with the Emory River; Clear Creek from the Morgan County line to the confluence with the Obed River, Daddys Creek from the Morgan County line to the confluence with the Obed River; and the Emory River from the confluence with the Obed River to the Nemo Bridge as generally depicted and classified on the stream classification map dated December 1973;

16) Pere Marquette, Michigan — The segment downstream from the junction of the Middle and Little South Branches to its junction with U.S. Highway 31 as generally depicted on the boundary map entitled *Proposed Boundary Location, Pere Marquette Wild and Scenic River*;

17) Rio Grande, Texas — The segment on the United States side of the river from river mile 842.3 above Mariscal Canyon downstream to river mile 651.1 at the Terrell-Val Verde County line;

18) Skagit, Washington — The segment from the pipeline crossing at Sedro-Woolley upstream to and including the mouth of Bacon Creek; the Cascade River from its mouth to the junction of its North and South Forks; the South Fork to the boundary of the Glacier Peak Wilderness Area; the Suiattle River from its mouth to the boundary of the Glacier Peak Wilderness Area at Milk Creek; the Sauk River from its mouth to its junction with Elliott Creek; the North Fork of the Sauk River from its junction with the South Fork of the Sauk to the boundary of the Glacier Peak Wilderness Area; as generally depicted on the boundary map entitled *Skagit River - River Area Boundary*;

19) Upper Delaware River, New York and Pennsylvania — The segment of the Upper Delaware River from the confluence of the East and West branches below Hancock, New York, to the existing railroad bridge immediately downstream of Cherry Island in the vicinity of Sparrow Bush, New York, as depicted on the boundary map entitled *The Upper Delaware Scenic and Recreational River* (April 1978);

20) Delaware, New York, Pennsylvania, and New Jersey — The segment from the point where the river crosses the northern boundary of the Delaware Water Gap National Recreation Area to the point where the river crosses the southern boundary of such recreation area; to be administered by the Secretary of the Interior;

21) American, California — The North Fork from a point 0.3 mile above Heath Springs downstream to a point approximately 1,000 feet upstream of the Colfax-Iowa Hill Bridge, including the Gold Run Addition Area, as generally depicted on the map entitled *Proposed Boundary Maps* contained in Appendix I of the document entitled *A Proposal: North Fork American Wild and Scenic River* (January 1978) published by the U.S. Forest Service, Department of Agriculture [to be designated as a wild river];

22) Missouri River, Nebraska, South Dakota — The segment from Gavins Point Dam, South Dakota, 59 miles downstream to Ponca State Park, Nebraska, as generally depicted in the document entitled *Review Report for Water Resources Development, South Dakota, Nebraska, North Dakota, Montana* (August 1977) prepared by the Division Engineer, Missouri River Division, Corps of Engineers;

23) Saint Joe, Idaho — The segment above the confluence of the North Fork of the Saint Joe River to Spruce Tree Campground, as a recreational river; the segment above Spruce Tree Campground to Saint Joe Lake, as a wild river, as generally depicted on the map entitled *Saint Joe River Corridor Map* (September 1978), on file with the U.S. Forest Service;

24) Salmon, Idaho — The segment of the main river from the mouth of the North Fork of the Salmon River downstream to Long Tom Bar in the following classes: A) the 46-mile segment from the mouth of the North Fork of the Salmon River to Corn Creek as a recreational river; and B) the 79-mile segment from Corn Creek to Long Tom Bar as a wild river; all as generally depicted on a map entitled *Salmon River* (November 1979), on file with the U.S. Forest Service;

25) Alagnak, Alaska — That segment of the main stem and the major tributary to the Alagnak, the Nonvianuk River, within Katmai National Preserve;

26) Alatna, Alaska — The main stem within the Gates of the Arctic National Park;

27) Aniakchak, Alaska — That portion of the river, including its major tributaries, Hidden Creek, Mystery Creek, Albert Johnson Creek, and North Fork Aniakchak River, within the Aniakchak National Monument and National Preserve;

28) Charley, Alaska — The entire river, including its major tributaries, Copper Creek, Bonanza Creek, Hos-

ford Creek, Derwent Creek, Flat-Orthmer Creek, Crescent Creek, and Moraine Creek, within the Yukon-Charley Rivers National Preserve;

29) Chilikadrotna, Alaska — That portion of the river within the Lake Clark National Park and Preserve;

30) John, Alaska — That portion within the Gates of the Arctic National Park;

31) Kobuk, Alaska — That portion within the Gates of the Arctic National Park and Preserve;

32) Mulchatna, Alaska — That portion within the Lake Clark National Park and Preserve;

33) Noatak, Alaska — The river from its source in the Gates of the Arctic National Park to its confluence with the Kelly River in the Noatak National Preserve;

34) North Fork of the Koyukuk, Alaska — That portion within the Gates of the Arctic National Park;

35) Salmon, Alaska — That portion within the Kobuk Valley National Park;

36) Tinayguk, Alaska — That portion within the Gates of the Arctic National Park;

37) Tlikakila, Alaska — That portion within the Lake Clark National Park;

38) Andreafsky, Alaska — That portion from its source, including all headwaters, and the East Fork, within the boundary of the Yukon Delta National Wildlife Refuge;

39) Ivishak, Alaska — That portion from its source, including all headwaters and an unnamed tributary from Porcupine Lake within the boundary of the Arctic National Wildlife Range;

40) Nowitna, Alaska — That portion from the point where the river crosses the west limit of township 18 south, range 22 east, Kateel River meridian, to its confluence with the Yukon River within the boundaries of the Nowitna National Wildlife Refuge;

41) Selawik, Alaska — That portion from a fork of the headwaters in township 12 north, range 10 east, Kateel River meridian to the confluence of the Kugarak River; within the Selawik National Wildlife Refuge;

42) Sheenjek, Alaska — The segment within the Arctic National Wildlife Refuge;

43) Wind, Alaska — That portion from its source, including all headwaters and one unnamed tributary in township 13 south, within the boundaries of the Arctic National Wildlife Refuge;

44) Alagnak, Alaska — Those segments or portions of the main stem and Nonvianuk tributary lying outside and westward of the Katmia National Park/Preserve and running to the west boundary of township 13 south, range 43 west;

45) Beaver Creek, Alaska — The segment of the main stem from the vicinity of the confluence of the Bear and Champion Creeks downstream to its exit from the northeast corner of township 12 north, range 6 east, Fairbanks meridian within the White Mountains National Recreation Area, and the Yukon Flats National Wildlife Refuge;

46) Birch Creek, Alaska — The segment of the main stem from the south side of Steese Highway in township 7 north, range 10 east, Fairbanks meridian, downstream to the south side of the Steese Highway in township 10 north, range 16 east;

47) Delta, Alaska — The segment from and including all of the Tangle Lakes to a point ½ mile north of Black Rapids;

48) Fortymile, Alaska — The main stem within the State of Alaska; O'Brien Creek; South Fork; Napoleon Creek, Franklin Creek, Uhler Creek, Walker Fork downstream from the confluence of Liberty Creek; Wade Creek; Mosquito Fork downstream from the vicinity of Kechumstuk; West Fork Dennison Fork downstream from the confluence of Logging Cabin Creek; Dennison Fork downstream from the confluence of West Fork Dennison Fork: Logging Cabin Creek; North Fork; Hutchison Creek; Champion Creek; the Middle Fork downstream from the confluence of Joooph Creek; and Joseph Creek;

49) Gulkana, Alaska — The main stem from the outlet of Paxon Lake in township 12 north, range 2 west, Copper River meridian to the confluence with Sourdough Creek; the south branch of the west fork from the outlet of an unnamed lake in Sections 10 and 15, township 10 north, range 7 west, Copper River meridian to the confluence with the west fork; the north branch from the outlet of two unnamed lakes, one in Sections 24 and 25, the second in Sections 9 and 10, township 11 north, range 8 west, Copper River meridian to the confluence with the west fork; the west fork from its confluence with the north and south branches downstream to its confluence with the main stem; the middle fork from the outlet of Dickey Lake in township 13 north, range 5 west, Copper River meridian to the confluence with the main stem;

50) Unalakleet, Alaska — The segment of the main stem from the headwaters in township 12 south, range

3 west, Kateel River meridian extending downstream approximately 65 miles to the western boundary of township 18 south, range 8 west;

51) Verde, Arizona — The segment from the boundary between national forest and private land in Sections 26 and 27, township 13 north, range 5 east, Gila Salt River meridian, downstream to the confluence with Red Creek, as generally depicted on a map entitled *Verde River - Wild and Scenic River* (March 1984), on file with the U.S. Forest Service;

52) Au Sable, Michigan — The segment of the main stem from the project boundary of the Mio Pond project downstream to the project boundary at Alcona Pond project as generally depicted on a map entitled *Au Sable River*, on file with the U.S. Forest Service;

53) Tuolumne, California — The main river from its sources on Mount Dana and Mount Lyell in Yosemite National Park to Don Pedro Reservoir consisting of approximately 83 miles as generally depicted on the proposed boundary map entitled *Alternative A* contained in the *Draft Tuolumne Wild and Scenic River Study and Environmental Impact Statement* published by the U.S. Department of the Interior and Department of Agriculture in May 1979;

54) Illinois, Oregon: The segment from the boundary of the Siskiyou National Forest downstream to its confluence with the Rogue River as generally depicted on a map entitled *Illinois River Study* and is also part of a report entitled *A Proposal: Illinois Wild and Scenic River*;

55) Owyhee, Oregon: The South Fork from the Idaho-Oregon state line downstream to Three Forks; the Owyhee River from Three Forks downstream to China Gulch; and the Owyhee River downstream from Crooked Creek to the Owyhee Reservoir as generally depicted on a map entitled *Owyhee, Oregon* (April 1984);

56) Horsepasture, North Carolina — The segment from Bohaynee Road (N.C. Hwy 281) downstream approximately 4.25 miles to where the segment ends at Lake Jocassee;

57) Cache la Poudre, Colorado — The following segments as generally depicted on the *Proposed Boundary Map* numbered FS-56 (March 1986), published by the U.S. Department of Agriculture;

58) Saline Bayou, Louisiana — The segment from Saline Lake upstream to the Kisatchie National Forest, as generally depicted on the *Proposed Boundary Map*, numbered FS-57 (March 1986);

59) Black Creek, Mississippi — The segment from Fairley Bridge Landing upstream to Moody's Landing as generally depicted on a map entitled *Black Creek Wild and Scenic River*, numbered FS-58 (March 1986);

60) Klickitat, Washington: The segment from its confluence with Wheeler Creek, Washington, near the town of Pitt, Washington, to its confluence with the Columbia River [to be classified as a recreation river];

61) White Salmon, Washington: The segment from its confluence with Gilmer Creek, Washington, near the town of BZ Corner, Washington, to its confluence with Buck Creek, Washington [to be classified as a scenic river];

62) Merced, California — The main stem from its sources (including Red Peak Fork, Merced Peak Fork, Triple Peak Fork, and Lyell Fork) on the south side of Mount Lyell in Yosemite National Park to a point 300 feet upstream of the confluence with Bear Creek, consisting of approximately 71 miles, and the South Fork of the river from its source near Triple Divide Peak in Yosemite National Park to the confluence with the main stem, consisting of approximately 43 miles, both as generally depicted on the map entitled *Merced River Wild and Scenic Rivers - Proposed* (June 1987);

63) Kings, California — The Middle Fork of the Kings River from its headwaters at Lake Helen between Muir Pass and Black Giant Mountain to its confluence with the main stem; the South Fork, Kings River from its headwaters at Lake 11599 to its confluence with the main stem; and the main stem of the Kings River from the confluence of the Middle Fork and the South Fork to the point at elevation 1,595 feet above mean sea level;

64) 1) North Fork Kern River, California — The segment of the main stem from the Tulare-Kern County line to its headwaters in Sequoia National Park, as generally depicted on a map entitled *Kern River Wild and Scenic River - Proposed* (June 1987); 2) South Fork Kern River, California - The segment from its headwaters in the Inyo National Forest to the southern boundary of the Domelands Wilderness in the Sequoia National Forest, as generally depicted on a map entitled *Kern River Wild and Scenic River - Proposed* (June 1987);

65) Bluestone, West Virginia — The segment in Mercer and Summers Counties, West Virginia, from a point approximately 2 miles upstream of the Summers and Mercer County line down to the maximum summer pool elevation (1,410 feet above mean sea level) of Bluestone Lake as depicted on the boundary map entitled *Bluestone Wild and Scenic River*, numbered WSR-BLU/20,000 (January 1987);

66) Sipsey Fork of the West Fork, Alabama — Segments of the Sipsey Fork and several tributaries; to be administered by the Secretary of Agriculture in the classifications indicated, as follows: A) Sipsey Fork from the confluence of Sandy Creek upstream to Forest Highway 26, as a scenic river; B) Sipsey Fork from Forest Highway 26 upstream to it origin at the confluence of Thompson Creek and Hubbard Creek, as a wild river; C) Hubbard Creek from its confluence with Thompson Creek upstream to Forest Road 210, as a wild river; D) Thompson Creek from its confluence with Hubbard Creek upstream to its origin in Section 4, township 8 south, range 9 west, as a wild river; E) Tedford Creek from its confluence with Thompson Creek upstream to Section 17, township 8 south, range 9 west, as a wild river; F) Mattox Creek from it confluence with Thompson Creek upstream to Section 36 of township 7 south, range 9 west, as a wild river; G) Borden Creek from its confluence with the Sipsey Fork upstream to Forest Road 208, as a wild river; H) Borden Creek from Forest Road 208 upstream to its confluence with Montgomery Creek, as a scenic river; I) Montgomery Creek from its confluence with Borden Creek upstream to the southwest quarter of the southwest quarter of Section 36, township 7 south, range 8 west, as a scenic river; J) Flannigan Creek from its confluence with Borden Creek upstream to Forest Road 208, as a wild river; K) Flannigan Creek from Forest Road 208 upstream to Section 4, township 8 south, range 8 west, as a scenic river; L) Braziel Creek from its confluence with Borden Creek upstream to Section 12, township 8 south, range 9 west, as a wild river; and M) Hogood Creek from its confluence with Braziel Creek upstream to the confluence with an unnamed tributary in Section 7, township 8 south, range 8 west, as a wild river;

67) Wildcat River, New Hampshire — A 14.51 mile segment including the following tributaries: Wildcat Brook, Bog Brook, and Great Brook (all as generally depicted on a map entitled *Wildcat River* (October 1987);

68) Big Marsh Creek, Oregon — The 15-mile segment from the northeast quarter of Section 15, township 26 south, range 6 east, to its confluence with Crescent Creek in the northeast quarter of Section 20, township 24 south, range 7 east, as a recreational river;

69) Chetco, Oregon — The 44.5-mile segment from its headwaters to the Siskiyou National Forest boundary;

70) Clackamas, Oregon — The 47-mile segment from Big Springs to Big Cliff;

71) Missouri River, Nebraska and South Dakota — The 39-mile segment from the headwaters of Lewis and Clark Lake to the Fort Randall Dam, to be administered by the Secretary of the Interior as a recreational river;

72) Crooked, Oregon — The 15-mile segment from the National Grassland boundary to Dry Creek;

73) Deschutes, Oregon — Those portions as follows: A) The 40.4-mile segment from Wickiup Dam to northern boundary of Sunriver at the southwest quarter of Section 20, township 19 south, range 11 east as a recreational river; to be administered by the Secretary of Agriculture; B) the 11-mile segment from the northern boundary of Sunriver at the southwest quarter of Section 20, township 19 south, range 11 east, to Lava Island Camp as a scenic river; to be administered by the Secretary of Agriculture; C) the 3-mile segment from Lava Island Camp to the Bend Urban Growth Boundary at the southwest corner of Section 13, township 18 south, range 11 east, as a recreational river; to be administered by the Secretary of Agriculture; D) the 19-mile segment from Oden Falls to the Upper End of Lake Billy Chinook as a scenic river; to be administered by the Secretary of the Interior; E) the 100-mile segment from the Pelton Reregulating Dam to its confluence with the Columbia River as a recreational river; to be administered by the Secretary of the Interior through a cooperative management agreement between the Confederated Tribes of the Warm Springs Reservation, and the state of Oregon;

74) Donner and Blitzen, Oregon — Those segments, including its major tributaries, as a wild river; to be administered by the Secretary of the Interior as follows: A) The 16.75-mile segment of the Donner and Blitzen from its confluence with the South Fork Blitzen and Little Blitzen; B) the 12.5-mile segment of the Little Blitzen from its headwaters to its confluence with the South Fork Blitzen; C) the 16.5-mile segment of the South Fork Blitzen from its headwaters to its confluence with the South Fork Blitzen; D) the 10-mile segment of Big Indian Creek from its headwaters to its confluence with the South Fork Blitzen; E) the 3.7-mile segment of Little Indian Creek from its headwaters to its confluence with Big Indi Creek; and F) the 13.25-mile segment of Fish Creek from its headwaters to its confluence with the Donner and Blitzen;

75) Eagle Creek, Oregon — The 27-mile segment from its headwaters below Eagle Lake to the Wallowa-Whitman National Forest boundary at Skull Creek;

76) Elk, Oregon — The 19-mile segment to be administered by the Secretary of Agriculture in the following classes: A) The 17-mile segment from the confluence of the North and South Forks of the Elk to Anvil Creek as a recreational river; and B) the 2-mile segment of the North Fork Elk from the falls to its confluence with the South Fork as a wild river;

77) Grande Ronde, Oregon — The 43.8-mile segment from its confluence with the Wallowa River to the Oregon-Washington state line;

78) Imnaha, Oregon. - Those segments, including the South Fork Imnaha; to be administered by the Secretary of Agriculture in the following classes: A) The 6-mile segment from its confluence with the North and South Forks of the Imnaha River to Indian Crossing as a wild river; B) the 58-mile segment from Indian Crossing to Cow Creek as a recreational river; C) the 4-mile segment from Cow Creek to its mouth as a scenic river; and D) the 9-mile segment of the South Fork Imnaha from its headwaters to its confluence with the Imnaha River as a wild river.

79) John Day, Oregon — The 147.5-mile segment from Service Creek to Tumwater Falls as a recreational river;

80) Joseph Creek, Oregon — The 8.6-mile segment from Joseph Creek Ranch, 1 mile downstream from Cougar Creek, to the Wallowa-Whitman National Forest boundary as a wild river;

81) Little Deschutes, Oregon — The 12-mile segment from its source in the northwest quarter of Section 15, township 26 south, range 6, 1/2 mile east to the north Section line of Section 12, township 26 south, range 7 east as a recreational river;

82) Lostine, Oregon — The 16-mile segment from its headwaters to the Wallowa-Whitman National Forest boundary; to be administered by the Secretary of Agriculture in the following classes: A) The 5-mile segment from its headwaters to the Eagle Cap Wilderness boundary as a wild river; and B) the 11-mile segment from the Eagle Cap Wilderness boundary to the Wallowa-Whitman National Forest boundary at Silver Creek as a recreational river;

83) Malheur, Oregon — The 13.7-mile segment from Bosonberg Creek to the Malheur National Forest boundary; to be administered by the Secretary of Agriculture in the following classes: A) The 7-mile segment from Bosonberg Creek to Malheur Ford as a scenic river; and B) the 6.7-mile segment from Malheur Ford to the Malheur National Forest boundary as a wild river;

84) McKenzie, Oregon — The 12.7-mile segment from Clear Lake to Scott Creek; to be administered by the Secretary of Agriculture in the following classes: A) The 1.8-mile segment from Clear Lake to the head of maximum pool at Carmen Reservoir as a recreational river; B) the 4.3-mile segment from a point 100 feet downstream from Carmen Dam to the maximum pool at Trail Bridge Reservoir as a recreational river; and C) the 6.6-mile segment from the developments at the base of the Trail Bridge Reservoir Dam to Scott Creek as a recreational river;

85) Metolius, Oregon — The 28.6-mile segment from the south Deschutes National Forest boundary to Lake Billy Chinook in the following classes: A) The 11.5-mile segment from the south Deschutes National Forest boundary (approximately 2,055.5 feet from Metolius Springs) to Bridge 99 as a recreational river; to be administered by the Secretary of Agriculture; B) the 17.1-mile segment from Bridge 99 to Lake Billy Chinook as a scenic river; by the Secretary of Agriculture, through a cooperative management agreement between the Secretary of the Interior and the Confederated Tribes of the Warm Springs Reservation, as provided in Section 1281(e) of the Act and Section 105 of the Omnibus Oregon Wild and Scenic Rivers Act of 1988: Provided, that the river and its adjacent land area will be managed to provide a primitive recreational experience;

86) Minam, Oregon — The 39-mile segment from its headwaters at the south end of Minam Lake to the Eagle Cap Wilderness boundary, 1/2 mile downstream from Cougar Creek, as a wild river;

87) North Fork Crooked, Oregon — The 32.3-mile segment from its source at Williams Prairie to 1 mile from its confluence with the Crooked River in the following classes: A) The 3-mile segment from its source at Williams Prairie to the Upper End of Big Summit Prairie as a recreational river; to be administered by the Secretary of Agriculture; B) the 3.7-mile segment from the Lower End of Big Summit Prairie to the bridge across from the Deep Creek Campground as a recreational river; to be administered by the Secretary of Agriculture; C) the 8-mile segment from the bridge across from the Deep Creek Campground to the Ochoco National Forest boundary, 1/2 mile from Lame Dog Creek as a scenic river; to be administered by the Secretary of Agriculture; D) the 1.5-mile segment from the Ochoco National Forest boundary to Upper Falls as a scenic river; to be administered by the Secretary of the Interior; E) the 11.1-mile segment from Upper Falls to Committee Creek as a wild river; to be administered by the Secretary of the Interior; and F) the 5-mile segment from Committee Creek to 1 mile from its confluence with the Crooked River as a recreational river;

88) North Fork John Day, Oregon — The 54.1-mile segment from its headwaters in the North Fork of the John Day Wilderness Area at Section 13, township 8 south, range 36 east, to its confluence with Camas Creek in the following classes: A) The 3.5-mile segment from its headwaters in the North Fork of the John Day Wilderness at Section 13, township 8 south, range 36 east, to the North Fork of the John Day Wilderness boundary as a wild river; to be administered by the Secretary of Agriculture; B) the 7.5-mile segment from the North Fork of the John Day Wilderness boundary to Trail Creek as a recreational river; to be administered by the Secretary of Agriculture; C) the 24.3-mile

segment from Trail Creek to Big Creek as a wild river; to be administered by the Secretary of Agriculture; D) the 10.5-mile segment from Big Creek to Texas Bar Creek as a scenic river; to be administered by the Secretary of Agriculture; and E) the 8.3-mile segment from Texas Bar Creek to its confluence with Camas Creek as a recreational river;

89) North Fork Malheur, Oregon — The 25.5-mile segment from its headwaters to the Malheur National Forest boundary as a scenic river; to be administered by the Secretary of Agriculture;

90) North Fork of the Middle Fork of the Willamette, Oregon — The 42.3-mile segment from Waldo Lake to the Willamette National Forest boundary; to be administered by the Secretary of Agriculture in the following classes: A) The 8.8-mile segment from Waldo Lake to the south section line of section 36, township 19 south, range 5 1/2 east as a wild river; B) the 6.5-mile segment from the south section line of section 36, township 19 south, range 5 1/2 east to Fisher Creek as a scenic river; and C) the 27-mile segment from Fisher Creek to the Willamette National Forest boundary as a recreational river;

91) North Fork Owyhee, Oregon — The 8-mile segment from the Oregon-Idaho state line to its confluence with the Owyhee River as a wild river; to be administered by the Secretary of the Interior;

92) North Fork Smith, Oregon — The 13-mile segment from its headwaters to the Oregon-California state line; to be administered by the Secretary of Agriculture in the following classes: A) The 6.5-mile segment from its headwaters to Horse Creek as a wild river; B) the 4.5-mile segment from Horse Creek to Baldface Creek as a scenic river; and C) the 2-mile segment from Baldface Creek to the Oregon-California state line as a wild river;

93) North Fork Sprague, Oregon — The 15-mile segment from the head of River Spring in the southwest quarter of section 15, township 35 south, range 16 east, to the northwest quarter of the southwest quarter of section 11, township 35 south, range 15 east, as a scenic river; to be administered by the Secretary of Agriculture;

94) North Powder, Oregon — The 6-mile segment from its headwaters to the Wallowa-Whitman National Forest boundary at River Mile 20 as a scenic river; to be administered by the Secretary of Agriculture;

95) North Umpqua, Oregon — The 33.8-mile segment from the Soda Springs Powerhouse to Rock Creek in the following classes: A) The 25.4-mile segment from the Soda Springs Powerhouse to the Umpqua National Forest boundary as a recreational river; to be administered by the Secretary of Agriculture; and B) the 8.4-mile segment from the Umpqua National Forest boundary to its confluence with Rock Creek as a recreational river; to be administered by the Secretary of the Interior;

96) Powder, Oregon — The 11.7-mile segment from Thief Valley Dam to the Highway 203 bridge as a scenic river; to be administered by the Secretary of the Interior;

97) Quartzville Creek, Oregon — The 12-mile segment from the Willamette National Forest boundary to slack water in Green Peter Reservoir as a recreational river; to be administered by the Secretary of the Interior;

98) Roaring, Oregon — The 13.7-mile segment from its headwaters to its confluence with the Clackamas River; to be administered by the Secretary of Agriculture in the following classes: A) The 13.5-mile segment from its headwaters to $\frac{1}{4}$ mile upstream of the mouth as a wild river; and B) the 0.2-mile segment from $\frac{1}{4}$ mile upstream of the mouth to its confluence with the Clackamas River as a recreational river;

99) Salmon, Oregon — The 33.5-mile segment from its headwaters to its confluence with the Sandy River in the following classes: A) The 7-mile segment from its headwaters to the south boundary line of section 6, township 4 south, range 9 east as a recreational river; to be administered by the Secretary of Agriculture: Provided, That designation and classification shall not preclude the Secretary from exercising discretion to approve the construction, operation, and maintenance of ski lifts, ski runs, and associated facilities for the land comprising the Timberline Lodge Winter Sports Area insofar as such construction does not involve water resources projects; B) the 15-mile segment from the south boundary line at section 6, township 4 south, range 9 east to the junction with the South Fork of the Salmon River as a wild river; to be administered by the Secretary of Agriculture; C) the 3.5-mile segment from the junction with the south fork of the Salmon River to the Mt. Hood National Forest boundary as a recreational river; to be administered by the Secretary of Agriculture; D) the 3.2-mile segment from the Mt. Hood National Forest boundary to Lymp Creek as a recreational river; to be administered by the Secretary of the Interior; and E) the 4.8-mile segment from Lymp Creek to its confluence with the Sandy River as a scenic river; to be administered by the Secretary of the Interior;

100) Sandy, Oregon — Those portions as follows: A) The 4.5-mile segment from its headwaters to the section line between sections 15 and 22, township 2 south, range 8 east as a wild river; to be administered by the Secretary of Agriculture; B) the 7.9-mile segment from the section line between sections 15 and 22, township 2 south, range 8 east to the Mt. Hood National Forest boundary at the west section line of section 26, town-

ship 2 south, range 7 east as a recreational river; to be administered by the Secretary of Agriculture; and C) the 12.5-mile segment from the east boundary of sections 25 and 36, township 1 south, range 4 east in Clackamas County near Dodge Park, downstream to the west line of the east half of the northeast quarter of section 6, township 1 south, range 4 east, in Multnomah County at Dabney State Park, the upper 3.8 miles as a scenic river and the lower 8.7 miles as a recreational river; both to be administered through a cooperative management agreement between the state of Oregon, the Secretary of the Interior and the Counties of Multnomah and Clackamas in accordance with Section 1281(e) of the WSRA;

101) South Fork John Day, Oregon — The 47-mile segment from the Malheur National Forest to Smokey Creek as a recreational river; to be administered by the Secretary of the Interior;

102) Squaw Creek, Oregon — The 15.4-mile segment from its source to the hydrologic Gaging Station 800 feet upstream from the intake of the McAllister Ditch, including the Soap Fork Squaw Creek, the North Fork, the South Fork, the East and West Forks of Park Creek, and Park Creek Fork;

103) Sycan, Oregon — The 59-mile segment from the northeast quarter of section 5, township 34 south, range 17 east to Coyote Bucket at the Fremont National Forest boundary;

104) Upper Rogue, Oregon — The 40.3-mile segment from the Crater Lake National Park boundary to the Rogue River National Forest boundary;

105) Wenaha, Oregon — The 21.55-mile segment from the confluence of the North Fork and the South Fork to its confluence with the Grande Ronde River;

106) West Little Owyhee, Oregon — The 51-mile segment from its headwaters to its confluence with Owyhee River as a wild river;

107) White, Oregon — The 46.5-mile segment from its headwaters to its confluence with the Deschutes River in multiple classes;

108) Rio Chama, New Mexico — The segment extending from El Vado Ranch launch site (immediately south of El Vado Dam) downstream approximately 24.6 miles to elevation 6,353 feet above mean sea level;

109) East Fork of Jemez, New Mexico — The 11-mile segment from the Santa Fe National Forest boundary to its confluence with the Rio San Antonio;

110) Pecos River, New Mexico — The 20.5-mile segment from its headwaters to the townsite of Tererro;

111) Smith River, California — The segment from the confluence of the Middle Fork Smith River and the North Fork Smith River to the Six Rivers National Forest boundary, including multiple segments of the mainstem and certain tributaries;

112) Middle Fork Smith River, California — The segment from the headwaters to its confluence with the North Fork Smith River, including the multiple segments of the mainstem and certain tributaries;

113) North Fork Smith River, California — The segment from the California-Oregon state line to its confluence with the Middle Fork Smith River, including multiple segments of the mainstem and certain tributaries;

114) Siskiyou Fork Smith River, California — The segment from its headwaters to its confluence with the Middle Fork Smith River, and multiple tributaries, thereto;

115) South Fork Smith River, California — The segment from its headwaters to its confluence with the main stem of the Smith River, and multiple creeks and tributaries, thereto;

116) Clarks Fork, Wyoming — (A) The 20.5-mile segment from the west boundary of section 3, township 56 north, range 106 west at the Crandall Creek Bridge downstream to the north boundary of section 13, township 56 north, range 104 west at Clarks Fork Canyon, wild river;

117) Niobrara, Nebraska — (A) The 40-mile segment from Borman Bridge southeast of Valentine downstream to its confluence with Chimney Creek and the 30-mile segment from the river's confluence with Rock Creek downstream to the State Highway 137 bridge, both segments to be classified as scenic and administered by the Secretary of the Interior. That portion of the 40-mile segment designated by this subparagraph located within the Fort Niobrara National Wildlife Refuge shall continue to be managed by the Secretary through the Director of the U.S. Fish and Wildlife Service. (B) The 25-mile segment from the western boundary of Knox County to its confluence with the Missouri River, including that segment of the Verdigre Creek from the north municipal boundary of Verdigre, Nebraska, to its confluence with the Niobrara.

Wild River Area

Regarding the Wild and Scenic Rivers Act (WSRA), those rivers or sections of rivers that are free of impoundments and generally inaccessible except by trail, with watersheds or shorelines essentially primitive and waters unpolluted. These represent vestiges of primitive America.

Wild Rodent

Wild ground squirrels, prairie dogs, chipmunks, rats, mice or any other members of the order Rodentia occurring in nature except muskrats and beavers.

Wild, Scenic, or Recreational River Area

Regarding the Wild and Scenic Rivers Act (WSRA), a free-flowing stream and the related adjacent land area that possesses one or more of the values referred to in Section 1271 of the Act. Every wild, scenic or recreational river in its free-flowing condition, or upon restoration to this condition, shall be considered eligible for inclusion in the national wild and scenic rivers system and, if included, shall be classified, designated, and administered as one of the following: wild river area; scenic river area; or recreational river area. *See* Wild River Area; Scenic River Area; and Recreational River Area.

Wilderness Area

Undeveloped federal land retaining its primeval character and influence, without permanent improvements or human habitation, that is protected and managed to preserve its natural conditions.

Wilderness Study

The Bureau of Land Management study of roadless areas of 5,000 acres or more and roadless islands of the public lands, identified as having wilderness characteristics described in the Wilderness Act of September 3, 1964.

Wildland Vegetation Management Burning

The use of prescribed burning conducted by a public agency, or through a cooperative agreement or contract involving a public agency, to burn land predominantly covered with chaparral, trees, grass, or standing brush.

Wildlife

Any member of the animal kingdom, including without limitation any mammal, fish, bird (in-cluding any migratory, nonmigratory, or endangered bird for which protection is also afforded by treaty or other international agreement), amphibian, reptile, mollusk, crustacean, arthropod or other invertebrate, and includes any part, product, egg, or offspring thereof, or the dead body or parts thereof.

Wildlife Conservation

Regarding the Wildlife Conservation Act (WCA), the practice of making decisions and implementing strategies to control wild animal populations and their environments, including influencing people to be cognizant of their impacts upon these resources.

Wildlife Conservation and Rehabilitation Program

Regarding the Wildlife Conservation Act (WCA), a program established to protect, conserve, and enhance wildlife, fish, and game resources to the maximum extent practicable on public lands subject to and consistent with any overall land use and management plans for the lands involved. Conservation and rehabilitation methods and procedures include, but are not limited to, all activities associated with scientific resources management such as protection, research, census, law enforcement, habitat management, propagation, live trapping and transplantation, and regulated taking in conformance with the provisions of the act.

Wildlife Conservation Plan

Regarding the Wildlife Conservation Act (WCA), a plan developed by a state for the conservation of fish and wildlife.

Wildlife Habitat

Areas that provide food, shelter, and living environs for wildlife.

Wildlife Management

The field concerned with wildlife conservation and management, including increasing populations of rare or endangered species, stabilizing certain wildlife populations, increasing or stabilizing species used for sport (hunting), and decreasing some species of harmful birds and mammals.

Wildlife Refuges
Areas designated for the protection of wild animals, within which hunting and fishing are either prohibited or strictly controlled.

Wildlife-Restoration Project
The selection, restoration, rehabilitation, and improvement of areas of land or water adaptable as feeding, resting, or breeding places for wildlife, including acquisition by purchase, condemnation, lease, or gift of such areas or estates or interests therein as are suitable or capable of being made suitable therefor, and the construction thereon or therein of such works as may be necessary to make them available for such purposes and also including such research into problems of wildlife management as may be necessary to efficient administration affecting wildlife resources, and such preliminary or incidental costs and expenses as may be incurred in and about such projects.

Wildlife Takings
Pursuing, hunting, shooting, capturing, collecting, or killing, or attempting to pursue, hunt, shoot, capture, collect, or kill a wildlife species, illegally.

Wilson Cloud
See Condensation Cloud.

WIN
See Waste Information Network.

Wind Abrasion
The process whereby wind-driven particulates abrade each other and any exposed surfaces they come into contact with.

Wind Chill Advisory
Public advisories given when low temperatures and strong winds will combine to produce wind chill values of 30°F or colder.

Wind Energy Research
A study relating to the use of lands in the area for purposes of wind energy research, to assess the impact of wind energy research activity on the value of the lands in the area and to develop permits for the use of such lands as a site for installation and field testing of an experimental wind turbine generating system.

Wind Gap
A pass or notch across a ridge or mountain that is not occupied by a stream. Such gaps have been abandoned by the streams that originally cut and occupied them.

Wind Profile
A graphic presentation of the way wind characteristics such as speed and direction influence one another, profiles vary with altitude.

Wind Project
A project with one or more wind turbine generators with a combined rated capacity of 100 kW or more, the electricity from which is sold to another party.

Wind Project Operator
Any developer or operator who directly receives payments for electricity from purchasers and/or consumers.

Wind Shear
A change of wind direction and magnitude.

Wind Velocity
The horizontal direction and speed of air motion.

Windbreak
A vertical structure designed and erected as a freestanding unit, the vertical surface of which is not more than 50% open.

Wind-Scoured Basins
Basins maintained or developed by deflation of the finer rock waste.

Window
English translation of German "Fenster" meaning the area of rocks exposed where erosion has broken through a thrust sheet to rocks below the fault.

Wingbar
A species descriptor for the white or light colored lines or bars on a bird's wing near the shoulder.

Winter Period
The seasonal period between October 15th and April 1st.

Winter Storm
A storm that includes snow, ice, low temperatures, winds, fog or any combination of these conditions.

Winter Storm Warning
A public advisory given when heavy snow accumulations of 6 inches or more in a 12-hour period or 8 inches or more in a 24-hour period are imminent or expected with near certainty. Strong winds produce much blowing and drifting of the snow under these conditions.

Winter Storm Watch
A public advisory given when one of the following conditions is anticipated in the near future: a) heavy snow accumulations of 6 inches or more in a 12-hour period or 8 inches or more in a 24-hour period; or b) falling or blowing snow with sustained winds or gusts of 35 mph or more producing reduced visibility or very low wind chills.

Winter Weather Advisories
The following advisories (with the noted exception), watches, and warnings are used by both the National Weather Service (NWS) and the Site Emergency Assessment (EA) Meteorologist. Advisories issued by the NWS are for the general geographic areas; those issued by the EA are specifically for the site.

Wipe Sampling
A sampling procedure used to establish the presence of a toxic material posing a potential absorption or ingestion hazard. Refer to the *OSHA Technical Manual* for sampling procedures.

WIPP
See Waste Isolation Pilot Plant.

Withdrawal, Land
Withholding an area of federal land from settlement, sale, location, or entry, under some or all of the general land laws, for the purpose of limiting activities under those laws in order to maintain other public values in the area or reserving the area for a particular public purpose or program; or transferring jurisdiction over an area of federal land, other than property governed by the Federal Property and Administrative Services Act, as amended (40 USC 472) from one department, bureau, or agency to another department, bureau, or agency.

Withdrawal Operation
A planned operation in which a response team in contact with a hazardous incident disengages from the emergency.

Withhold, Nuclear
The limiting of authority to employ nuclear weapons by denying their use within specified geographical areas or certain countries.

Witnesses
Persons who have first-hand knowledge of some fact related directly or indirectly to an accident or incident.

WMin
An acronym for Waste Minimization. *See* Waste Minimization Plan.

WMO
An acronym for Waste Management Operations.

WMO
See World Meteorological Organization.

WOG

An acronym for Water, Oil, or Gas Rating (as applied to valves and fittings).

Wollastonite Rock

A rock that resembles and is usually associated with marble. The wollastonite occurs in groups of needlelike or fibrous crystals, and calcite, diopside, homblende, and mica are commonly present.

Women Business Enterprise (WBE)

A business concern defined by ownership and control of at least 51% of the enterprise belonging to female individuals.

Wood Alcohol

See Methanol.

Wood Residue Value

Regarding the Wood Residue Utilization Act (WRUA), the projected value of wood residues as fuel or other merchantable wood products, as determined by the Secretary at the time of advertisement of the timber sales contract in accordance with appropriate appraisal and sale procedures.

Wood Residue Utilization Act (WRUA)

An extension program found in Subchapter III of the Forest and Rangeland Renewable Resources Planning Act. WRUA's purpose is to develop, demonstrate, and make available information on feasible methods with commercial implications to increase and improve resource utilization (in residential, commercial, and industrial or power plant applications) of wood residues resulting from timber harvesting, forest protection, and management activities on forest lands, and from the manufacture of wood products.

Wood Residues

Bark, sawdust, slabs, chips, shavings, mill trim, logging slash, down timber material, woody plants, and other wood products derived from wood processing and forest management operations. The term also includes, but is not limited to, standing live or dead trees that do not meet utilization standards because of size, species, merchantable volume, or economic selection criteria and that, in the case of live trees, are surplus to growing stock needs.

Wood Residues, Removal Cost

The projected cost of removal of wood residues from timber sales areas to points of prospective use, at the time of advertisement of a timber sales contract in accordance with appropriate appraisal and sale procedures.

Wood Treatment Facility

An industrial facility that treats lumber and other wood products for outdoor use. The process involves use of chromated copper arsenate and other toxic chemicals that are regulated as hazardous materials.

Wood-Burning Stove Pollution

Air pollution caused by emissions of particulate matter, carbon monoxide, total suspended particulates, and polycyclic organic matter from wood-burning stoves.

Woody Plant

A seed plant (gymnosperm or angiosperm) that develops persistent, hard, fibrous tissues, basically xylem (e.g., trees and shrubs).

Work

The process of conducting defined tasks or activities (e.g., historic research, site reconnaissance, laboratory analyses).

Work Clothing, Protective

A term that typically refers to long-sleeved shirts and long-legged trousers or a coverall type garment all of closely woven fabric or equivalent covering the body, including arms and legs. Protective work clothing does not necessarily cover the head, hands, or feet.

Work Environment

The surroundings in which systems operate. Includes all of the conditions that may affect one or more system components (e.g., temperature, humidity, noise, light, vibration, toxic materials, radioactive materials).

Work Processes
All of the components involved to get work done. Work processes consist of three major elements: a) procedures and management system control; b) hardware and equipment in the process; and c) personnel involved in the process.

Work Scope
An outline of definitive tasks (project specifications) that must be conducted to fulfill an environmental assessment or remediation requirement. The work scope is used to conduct cost and time estimates for a given project.

Worker Protection Standards
The OSHA Standards developed for the health and safety protection of employees engaged in hazardous waste operations. Such standards include, but are not be limited to, the following worker protection provisions:

- Site analysis — Requirements for a formal hazard analysis of the site and development of a site specific plan for worker protection.

- Training — Requirements for contractors to provide initial and routine training of workers before such workers are permitted to engage in hazardous waste operations that would expose them to toxic substances.

- Medical surveillance — A program of regular medical examination, monitoring, and surveillance of workers engaged in hazardous waste operations that would expose them to toxic substances.

- Protective equipment — Requirements for appropriate personal protective equipment, clothing, and respirators for work in hazardous waste operations.

- Engineering controls — Requirements for engineering controls concerning the use of equipment and exposure of workers engaged in hazardous waste operations.

- Maximum exposure limits — Requirements for maximum exposure limitations for workers engaged in hazardous waste operations, including necessary monitoring and assessment procedures.

- Informational program — A program to inform workers engaged in hazardous waste operations of the nature and degree of toxic exposure likely as a result of such hazardous waste operations.

- Handling — Requirements for the handling, transporting, labeling, and disposing of hazardous wastes.

- New technology program — A program for the introduction of new equipment or technologies that will maintain worker protection.

- Decontamination procedures — Procedures for decontamination; and

- Emergency response — Requirements for emergency response and protection of workers engaged in hazardous waste operations.

Working Capital Fund
A revolving fund established to finance inventories of supplies and other stores, or to provide working capital for industrial-type activities.

Working Condition A
Conditions where the annual exposures might exceed three-tenths of the dose equivalent limits.

Working Condition B
Conditions where it is most unlikely that the annual exposures will exceed three-tenths of the dose equivalent limits.

Working Conditions
Conditions under which workers are occupationally exposed to ionizing radiation.

Working Level
1) A unit of measure for documenting exposure to radon decay products. One working level is equal to approximately 200 picocuries per liter. 2) A unit for potential alpha energy concentration (i.e. the sum of the total energy per unit volume of air carried by alpha particles emitted during the complete decay of each atom and its progeny in a unit volume of air).

Working Level Month (WLM)
A unit of measure used to determine cumulative exposure to radon. A unit of exposure to air concentrations of potential alpha energy released from short-lived radon progeny. One working level month is defined as the cumulative exposure equivalent to exposure at one working level for a working month of 170 hours.

Works of Improvement
The facilities installed or being installed in accordance with an conservation area plan. *See* Conservation Area Plan.

Works of Improvement for Water Quality Management
Works that consist primarily of water storage capacity in reservoirs for regulation of streamflow, except that any such storage and water releases shall not be provided as a substitute for adequate treatment or other methods of controlling waste at the source, and shall be consistent with standards and regulations adopted by the Water Resources Council on federal cost sharing for water quality management.

World Conservation Strategy
A 1980 document, published by the International Union for Conservation of Nature and Natural Resources (IUCN), that analyzes issues of resource use and conservation; including issues of sustained economic development based on the use and conservation of resources.

World Geographic Reference System
See Georef.

World Health Organization (WHO)
A United Nations agency founded in 1948 as successor to the League of Nations Health Organization and the International Office of Public Health; its primary tasks are to control disease epidemics and promulgate international cooperation in improving the health of the world.

World Heritage Convention
The Convention Concerning the Protection of the World Cultural and Natural Heritage, approved by the Senate on October 26, 1973.

World Heritage Sites
Sites designated by the IUCN and UNESCO as having global importance for environmental conservation and study purposes.

World Meteorological Organization (WMO)
The international organization that promotes meteorological cooperation and the exchange of information. Through its commissions and committees, WMO promotes the development and standardization of methods, procedures, and techniques in the application of various meteorology problems.

World Wildlife Fund
See International Union for the Conservation of Nature and Natural Resources (IUCN).

Worldwide Terrain Areas
Regional subdivisions of surface terrain distinguished from one another based on landform and other natural environmental characteristics occurring at the surface, such as climate, soils, and vegetation. Eight classes of terrain are generally accepted to encompass the entire world, they are:

- flatplains - nearly level land;
- rolling & irregular - gently sloping, low relief;
- tablelands - upland plains interrupted by valleys or escarpments;
- plains - areas surrounded by hills or mountains;

- hills - moderate to steeply sloping areas;
- low mountain ranges - moderate to steeply sloping with low relief;
- high mountains - steeply sloping, with very high relief; and
- ice cap terrains - glacier ice surfaces.

Regional terrain characteristics play a major role in international urban and environmental program planning and development.

Worst-Case Meteorology

A worst-case estimate of transport and dispersion of potential releases from an incident at the site. It is the basis for initial response in situations where either limited data or no data on current meteorology are available, or where a dose model is not available. Worst-case meteorology is determined by the highest relative concentration to any single point offsite that persists for a duration equal to the time necessary for the Maximum Credible Accident (MCA), for any single point offsite, measured within the last 3 to 5 years.

WPFPA

See Watershed Protection and Flood Prevention Act of 1954.

WQS

See Water Quality Standards.

WRAP

An acronym for Waste Receiving and Processing Plant.

WRDA

An acronym for Water Resources Development Act of 1990.

Wreckage Locator Chart

A chart indicating the geographic location of all known aircraft wreckage sites, and all known vessel wrecks that show above low water or that can be seen from the air. It consists of a visual plot of each wreckage, numbered in chronological order, and cross referenced with a wreckage locator file containing all pertinent data concerning the wreckage.

Wrinkle

An imperfection in the surface of a laminate that looks like a crease or fold in one of the outer layers; it occurs in vacuum bag molding due to improper placement of the bag.

Writ of Execution

A writ or court order authorizing and directing an officer of the court, usually the sheriff, to carry into effect the judgment or decree of the court.

WRUA

See Wood Residue Utilization Act.

WSADR

See Western States Acid Deposition Research (CAA).

WSR

See Wild and Scenic River.

WYSIWYG

An acronym for "What You See Is What You Get!"

X

X-Axis

A horizontal axis in a system of rectangular coordinates; that line on which distances to the right or left (east or west) of the reference line are marked, especially on a map, chart, or graph.

X-Rays

Penetrating electromagnetic radiations having wave lengths shorter than those of visible light. They are usually produced by bombarding a metallic target with fast electrons in a high vacuum. In nuclear reactions it is customary to refer to photons originating in the nucleus as gamma rays, and those originating in the extranuclear part of the atom as X-rays. These rays are sometimes called roentgen rays after their discoverer, W.C. Roentgen.

X-Scale

On an oblique photograph, the scale along a line parallel to the true horizon.

Xenobiotic

A term for nonnatural or manmade substances found in the environment (i.e., synthetics, plastics).

Xenoblast

In metamorphic rock, crystal that is not bounded by its own faces but has its outlines impressed upon it by neighboring crystals.

Xenocryst

A crystal foreign to the rock in which it is enclosed.

Xenogamy

Cross-fertilization in plants.

Xenolith

An inclusion that has obviously been derived from some older formation genetically unrelated to the igneous rock itself, as, for example, a fragment of sandstone in granite.

Xenomorphic

A mineral of igneous rocks that is not bounded by its own crystal faces and that has its form impressed upon it by the adjacent minerals is xenomorphic.

Xenon

An atmospheric gas.

Xeric

Adaptable to extremely dry habitats.

Xeric Environ

A relatively dry environment.

Xeromorphy

Possessing features characteristic of a xerophyte.

Xerophyte

Any plant growing in a habitat in which an appreciable portion of the rooting medium dries to the wilting coefficient at frequent intervals. These plants are capable of enduring prolonged periods of drought and are typically found in very dry habitats (e.g., cactus).

Xeroseres

The temporary changes in a plant community in which pioneering or invading communities grow on dry and sterile ground, such as rock, sand, or clay during a gradual ecological succession.

XXX Form

A form for the Assessment of Effect on Cultural Resources; required for all proposed actions that may affect historic properties. In addition, it serves as an attachment to regional office correspondence on proposed actions requiring consultation under 36 CFR 800. The agreed-upon format for documentation of compliance with NPS policies and guidelines in accordance with the Programmatic Memoranda of Agreement (PMOA) between the Advisory Council on Historic Preservation and the National Conference of State Historic Preservation Officers.

Y

Y-Axis

A vertical axis in a system of rectangular coordinates; that line on which distances above and below (north or south) the reference line are marked, especially on a map, chart, or graph.

Y-Scale

On an oblique photograph, the scale along the line of the principal vertical, or any other line inherent or plotted, that, on the ground, is parallel to the principal vertical.

Y-12 Plant

A DOE research, development, and field facility built in 1943 as part of the Manhattan Project. The Oak Ridge Y-12 plant was established to separate uranium isotopes using the electromagnetic process. When the process was discontinued after World War II, the role of the Y-12 Plant changed to manufacturing, developmental engineering, and waste storage. The missions of the Y-12 Plant include production of nuclear weapon components and subassemblies, development and fabrication of test hardware for the weapon design laboratories, fabrication support for other energy systems plants, and support for federal agencies.

YAG

See Yttrium Aluminum Garnet.

Yaquina Head Outstanding Natural Area

The area established to protect the unique scenic, scientific, educational, and recreational values of certain lands in and around Yaquina Head, in Lincoln County, Oregon. The Bureau of Land Management area management requirements include the following: a) the conservation and development of the scenic, natural, and historic values of the area; b) the continued use of the area for purposes of education, scientific study, and public recreation that do not substantially impair the purposes for which the area is established; and c) the protection of the wildlife habitat of the area.

Yardangs

Peculiar forms carved by wind erosion usually from soft but coherent deposits. They consist of long sharp ridges separated by round-bottomed chutes or troughs.

Yarding

The movement of forest products from the point of felling to a landing.

Yaw

1) The rotation of a camera or a photograph coordinate system about either the photograph z-axis or the exterior z-axis. 2) The angle between the longitudinal axis of a projectile at any moment and the tangent to the trajectory in the corresponding point of flight of the projectile.

Yazoo

The phenomenon of a deferred tributary junction is another common feature where trunk streams have extensive flood plains.

Yeasts
A group of simple fungi, usually found in soils of orchards, vineyards, and other areas where the presence of sugars in soils promotes their growth.

Yellowcake
A product of uranium mills, concentrated in uranium content and suitable for shipment for further processing into fuel for reactors.

Yield
See Nuclear Yields.

Yield Point
The amount of pressure or stress a material can endure by deflecting, stretching, or bending without a greater load or breakage.

Young
A term applied to rivers that have just commenced to cut valleys, to topography that has suffered little erosion, and to drainage systems In an early state of development.

Young River
A river that is constantly able to erode its channel. This means its gradient is sufficiently steep for it to carry all the load brought to it by its tributaries and that there is energy to spare.

Young's Modulus
The ratio of normal stress to the corresponding strain for tensile or compressive stresses less than the proportional limit of the material.

Youth
The topographic condition or physiographic stage of a region soon after the beginning of stream erosion when main branches have well-developed narrow valleys but the areas between the streams are little modified.

Yttrium Aluminum Garnet (YAG)
A widely used solid-state crystal that is composed of yttrium and aluminum oxides that is doped with a small amount of the rare-earth neodymium.

Yucca
A large, organ-pipe, columnar-shaped tree cactus, native to desert areas throughout the southwestern United States.

Yucca Mountain Site
The candidate site in the state of Nevada recommended by the Secretary to the President in 1986.

Yusho
A disease detected in Japan (1968) caused by ingesting rice oil that had been seriously contaminated with PCBs from a faulty processing plant heat exchanger; rice oil disease.

Z

Z-List
OSHA's Toxic and Hazardous Substances Tables (Z-1, Z-2, and Z-3) of air contaminants (any material found in these tables is considered hazardous).

Z-Scale
On an oblique photograph, the scale used in calculating the height of an object. Also the name given to this method of height determination.

Zebra Mussel Program
A program of prevention, monitoring, control, education and research for the zebra mussel implemented in the Great Lakes and any other waters of the United States infested or likely to become infested by the zebra mussel, including a) research and development concerning the species life history, environmental tolerances and impacts on fisheries and other ecosystem components, and the efficacy of control mechanisms and means of avoiding or minimizing impacts; b) tracking the dispersal of the species and establishment of an early warning system to alert likely areas of future infestations; c) development of control plans in coordination with regional, state, and local entities; and d) provision of technical assistance to regional, state, and local entities to carry out the program.

ZEC
See Zone of Engineering Control.

Zectran
A synthetic carbamate insecticide.

Zener Diodes
Junction diodes and semiconductors.

Zeolite
Any of a large group of minerals that are hydrous silicates of aluminum with sodium and calcium, or rarely, with barium and strontium. Among the most common are natrolite, analcite, stilbite, and heulandite. In general they appear to he/she formed by alteration of feldspars and felspathoids and usually occur in basaltic lavas where they fill cavities and coat fractures and joint planes. Zeolites are usually colorless or white, sometimes red or yellow. They are of little economic importance but certain artificial zeolites are used in water-softening processes.

Zeolitization
The process by which the feldspars and other aluminosilicates of a rock are altered to zeolites.

Zero-Plated
A species descriptor referring to the lack of scutes, lamina, or other than flat structures.

Zero Point
The location of the center of a burst of a nuclear weapon at the instant of detonation. The zero point may be in the air, or on or beneath the surface of land or water, dependent upon the type

of burst, and it is thus to be distinguished from ground zero.

Zineb

An organic fungicide; the zinc salt of ethylenebis (dithiocarbamic acid).

Zigzag Folds

Folds that are angular in cross section.

Ziram

An organic fungicide; the zinc salt of di-methyldithiocarbamic acid.

Zircon

A common accessory mineral in siliceous igneous rocks, and in sedimentary rocks derived there-from.

ZOA

See Zone of Aeration.

Zobar

Trade name for a herbicide for translocated peren-nial weeds; polychlorobenzoic acid, diethylamine salt.

Zoic

In geology, a term used to denote rocks contain-ing fossils, or revealing evidence of contemporary plant or animal life; pertaining to or characterized by animal life. As a combining form the term is used in geology to designate the stage of life de-velopment or the characteristic life of certain long periods of time and the rocks formed during them (e.g., Mesozoic, Paleozoic).

Zonal Index

A measure of the strength of atmospheric pressure in a large geographic area of the world, usually expressed as a pressure difference.

Zonal Soil

Any of the great groups of soils having well-de-veloped soil characteristics that reflect the influ-ence of the active factors of soil genesis-climate and living organisms, chiefly vegetation.

Zonal Structure

1) A structure characterized by the arrangement of color, inclusions, etc., of a crystal in parallel or concentric layers, that usually follow the outline of the crystal, and mark the changes that have taken place during its growth. 2) A structure seen in certain crystals in the form of concentric zones of growth, generally due to a progressive change in the chemical composition of the magma from which they were formed.

Zone

1) A belt, layer, or series of layers of rock, regular or irregular, disposed horizontally, vertically, con-centrically, or otherwise, characterized by some particular property, action, or content (e.g., the zone of saturation, the Eohippus zone). 2) In crystallography, a series of faces on a crystal whose intersection lines are mutually parallel to each other and to a common line drawn through the center of the crystal, called the zone-axis. 3) In paleontology, the zone of paleontological stra-tigraphy based on two or more designated fossils. No fixed thickness or lithology is implied.

Zone I, Nuclear

A circular area, determined by using minimum safe distance I as the radius and the desired ground zero as the center, from which all armed forces are evacuated. If evacuation is not possible or if a commander elects a higher degree of risk, maximum protective measures will be required.

Zone II, Nuclear

A circular area (less Zone I), determined by using minimum safe distance II as the radius and the desired ground zero as the center, in which all personnel require maximum protection. Maxi-mum protection denotes that armed forces person-nel are in "buttoned up" tanks or crouched in foxholes with improvised overhead shielding.

Zone III, Nuclear

A circular area (less Zones I and II), determined by using minimum safe distance III as the radius and the desired ground zero as the center, in which all personnel require minimum protection. Minimum protection denotes that armed forces personnel are prone on open ground with all skin areas covered and with an overall thermal protection at least equal to that provided by a two-layer uniform.

Zone, Contiguous
The zone of the high seas, established by the United States under Article 24 of the Convention on Territorial Sea and Contiguous Zone, that is contiguous to the territorial sea and that extends 9 miles seaward from the outer limit of the territorial sea.

Zone, Convergence
That region in the deep ocean where sound rays, refractured from the depths, return to the surface.

Zone, Decontamination
The area surrounding a chemical hazard incident (between the hot zone and the support zone) in which contaminants are removed from exposed victims.

Zone, Exclusive Economic
The Exclusive Economic Zone of the United States established by Proclamation Number 5030, dated March 10, 1983, and the equivalent zone of Canada.

Zone, Hot
The area immediately surrounding a chemical hazard incident, such as a spill, in which contamination or other danger exists.

Zone, Low-Velocity (LVZ)
The zone within the earth where earthquake shock waves travel at slow rates. The bottom of the zone is at approximately 125 to 200 miles below the earth's surface.

Zone, Nominal Hazard (NHZ)
The nominal hazard zone describes the space within which the level of the direct, reflected, or scattered radiation during normal operation exceeds the applicable MPE. Exposure levels beyond the boundary of the NHZ are below the appropriate MPE level.

Zone, Photic
The upper water layer down to the depth of effective light penetration where photosynthesis balances respiration. This level (the compensation level) usually occurs at the depth of 1% light penetration and forms the lower boundary of the zone of net metabolic production.

Zone, Plastic
The region beyond the rupture zone associated with crater formation resulting from an explosion in which there is no visible rupture, but in which the soil is permanently deformed and compressed to a high density. *See* Rupture Zone.

Zone, Radius of Vulnerability
The maximum distance from the point of release of a hazardous substance in which the airborne concentration could reach the level of concern under specified weather conditions.

Zone, Recovery (RZ)
A designated geographic area from which special operations forces can be extracted by air, boat, or other means.

Zone, Rupture
The region immediately adjacent to the crater boundary in which the stresses produced by the explosion have exceeded the ultimate strength of the medium. It is characterized by the appearance of numerous radial cracks of various sizes. *See* Plastic Zone.

Zone, Support
The area beyond a decontamination zone that surrounds a chemical hazard incident in which medical care can be freely administered to stabilize victims.

Zone, Vulnerable
An area over which the airborne concentration of a chemical involved in an accidental release could reach the level of concern.

Zone of Aeration (ZOA)

A subsurface zone containing water under pressure less than that of the atmosphere. This zone is limited at its upper extent by the land surface and at its lower boundary by the water table, i.e., zone of saturation. *See* figure below.

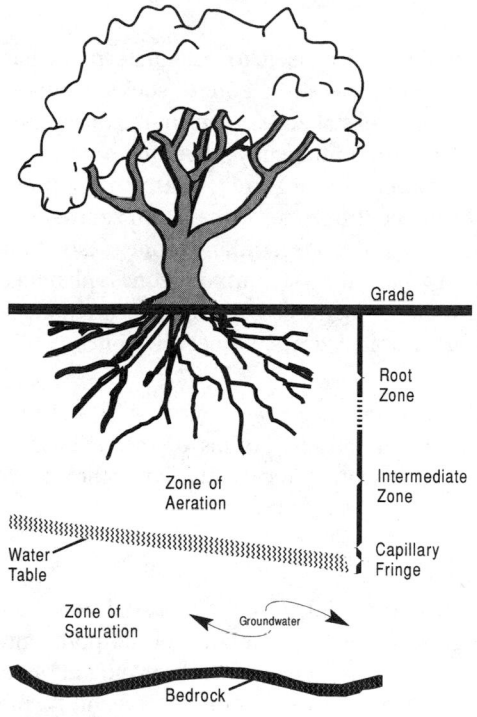

Hydrologic Zones

Zone of Cementation (ZOC)

The zone within the earth where rock grains become cemented together, mainly through the deposition of material leached out and carried down from the overlying belt.

Zone of Contribution (ZOC)

The area surrounding a pumping well that includes all areas or features that supply groundwater recharge to the well.

Zone of Deposition (ZOD)

The area in which continental glaciers deposit materials derived from the zone of erosion. It is usually covered with drift and has the general aspect of a plain.

Zone of Engineering Control (ZEC)

An area under the control of the owner/operator that, upon detection of a hazardous waste release, can be readily cleaned up prior to the release of hazardous waste or hazardous constituents to groundwater or surface water.

Zone of Erosion (ZOE)

The area from which continental glaciers have removed material by erosion; mostly a bare rock surface.

Zone of Flowage (ZOF)

The subsurface part of the earth in which the fracturing of rocks is prevented by pressure, and all deformation is due to subsurface flows. It includes the larger part of the earth, and underlies the zone of fracture, or that part of the earth's crust in which deformation may result in and be accomplished by fracture.

Zone of Fracture (ZOF)

The upper portion of the earth's crust in which rocks are deformed mainly by fracture. Also known as the zone of rock fracture.

Zone of Fracture and Flowage (ZFF)

The zone intermediate between the zone of fracture and the zone of flowage. It is the zone in which the strongest rocks behave as in the zone of rock fracture and the weakest as in the zone of rock flowage.

Zone of Incorporation (ZOI)

That area that, due to its characteristics (e.g., topography, hazardous pollutants) and proximity to a contaminated site must be included in remedial investigation, analysis, and implementation of cleanup measures.

Zone of Influence (ZOI)

The area surrounding a pumping well that is experiencing changes in the water table or potentiometric surfaces due to groundwater with-drawal.

Zone of Saturation (ZOS)
A subsurface zone in which all the interstices are filled with water under pressure greater than that of the atmosphere. This uppermost part of this zone is the water table, and above that is the zone of aeration. *See* Zone of Aeration.

Zone of Transport (ZOT)
The area surrounding a pumping well, bounded by an isochrone and/or isoconcentration contour, through which a contaminant may travel and reach the well.

Zone of Weathering
The level at which groundwater stands, the rocks are full of fractures, and are exposed to atmos-pheric agencies-moisture, carbon dioxide, oxy-gen, etc. The rocks tend to decay, to be converted into carbonates and hydroxides, and to form soils. Also known as the belt of weathering, the ZOW is where rock destruction occurs.

Zones, Confining
A geological formation, group of formations, or part of a formation that is capable of limiting fluid movement above an injection zone.

Zones, Control
Areas at a hazardous materials incident whose boundaries are based on safety and the degree of hazard; generally includes the hot zone, decon-tamination zone, and support zone. *See* Hot Zone; Decontamination Zone; Support Zone.

Zones, Disturbed
Those portions of controlled areas, the physical or chemical properties of which have changed as a result of underground facility construction or as a result of heat generated by the emplaced radioac-tive wastes such that the resultant change of prop-erties may have a significant affect on the performance of the geologic repository.

Zones, Emergency Planning
Areas for which planning is done to ensure that prompt and effective actions can be taken to pro-tect emergency personnel, the public health and safety, and the environment in the event of a ma-jor emergency.

Zones, General
A generalized term used to designate particular locations (e.g., aeration zones, suckled zones, buffer zones, coastal zones, confining zones, con-tiguous zones, contingency planning zones, dis-turbed zones, emergency planning zones, engineering control zones, excavation zones, flow zones, injection zones, inland zones, isolation zones, law hazard zones, mixing zones, planning zones, radiation zones, saturated zones, treatment zones, unsaturated zones, vulnerable zones).

Zones, Injection
Geological formations, groups of formations, or parts of a formation receiving fluids through a well.

Zones, Inland
The environment inland of the coastal zone ex-cluding the Great Lakes and specified ports and harbors of inland rivers. The term inland zone delineates the area of federal responsibility for response action. Precise boundaries are deter-mined by EPA/USCG (Environmental Protection Agency/U.S. Coast Guard) agreement and identi-fied in federal regional contingency plans.

Zones, Isolation
Areas surrounding a protected facility that have been cleared of any objects that could conceal vehicles or individuals, and that afford unob-structed observation of, or other means of deten-tion of, entry into the area.

Zones, Mixing
Limited volumes of water serving as zones of initial dilution in the immediate vicinity of a dis-charge point where receiving water quality may not meet quality standards or other requirements otherwise applicable to the receiving water. The mixing zone should be considered as a place

where wastes and water mix and not as a place where effluents are treated.

Zones, Vulnerable Radius

The maximum distance from the point of release of a hazardous substance in which the airborne concentration could reach the level of concern under specified weather conditions.

Zoning

1) Land-use controls that regulate development uses, densities, height, bulk, lot proportions, etc. They are enacted by local governmental entities under the enabling legislation of the state. Zoning constitutes an exercise of police powers and must bear a reasonable relation to the preservation of public health, safety, and welfare. A violation of a zoning ordinance can render title to the property unmarketable and may be sufficient grounds for rescission of a contract. 2) The systematic distribution of various types of metalliferous deposits that are related in origin. 3) Areas of metamorphosed rocks that exhibit zones in which a particular mineral or conglomeration of minerals are prevalent.

Zooecology

The branch of ecology concerned with the relationships between animals and their environments.

Zoogenic Deposit

A deposit formed through the deposition of animal remains.

Zoogenic Rock

A biogenic rock produced by animals or directly attributable to the activities of animals (e.g., shells, coral reefs).

Zoogeographer

A person who conducts global research and analysis on animal distribution, including their genetic and environmental evolutions.

Zoogeographic Region

A major portion of the world characterized by animal homogeneity.

Zoogeography

A science concerned with the global distribution of animals throughout time. A generalized science encompassing theories and techniques from botany, paleontology, physiology, animal morphology, zooecology, geography, and stratigraphy.

Zooglea

A jellylike matrix developed by bacteria. A major part of activated sludge floc and of trickling filter slimes. *See* Activated Sludge.

Zooglea Mass

The floc formed primarily by slime-producing bacteria in the activated sludge process or in biological beds.

Zoolite

A fossil animal.

Zooplankters

The tiny, floating, often microscopic aquatic animals eaten by fish.

Zooplankton

All of the aquatic animals composed of forms occurring suspended in water, with little or no powers of locomotion causing them to drift passively with water currents. In most aquatic habitats, the exact species of zooplankton present depends on environmental factors (e.g., sunlight, types of predators, depth of water, water temperature, and species competition).

ZOS

See Zone of Saturation.

ZOT

See Zone of Transport.

ZRL

An acronym for Zero Risk Level.

ZULU Time
See Universal Time.

Zygomorphic
Organisms that are bilaterally symmetrical and capable of being divided along a single longitudinal plane.

Zygotes
The cells formed through sexual union.

Zymogenous
A term relating to soil organisms that show a great increase in metabolic activity, including rate of reproduction, immediately following the introduction of organic material to the soil.

Section II

Environmental Acronyms and Abbreviations

A

A	— Ampere
A/E	— Architect/Engineer
A/G	— Air to Ground
A/NM	— Administrative/Network Management
A&R	— Air and Radiation
AA	— Agriculture Act of 1970
AA	— Antiquities Act of 1906
AAA	— American Anthropological Association
AACS	— Airborne Activity Confinement Systems
AAFES	— Army and Air Force Exchange System
AAG	— Association of American Geographers
AAIA	— Association of American Indian Affairs
AAR	— After-Action Report
AB	— Airbase
ABEL	— An abbreviation for an EPA computer model
ABN	— Airborne
ABOSFN	— Nominal Automatic Burnout Safety Factor
ABS-SC	— Automatic Backup Shutdown of the Safety Computer
AC	— Active Component
AC	— Alternating Current
ACAA	— Agricultural Conservation and Adjustment Administration
ACAA	— Automatic Chemical Agent Alarm
ACAPS	— Area Communications Electronics Capabilities
ACC	— Abnormal Condition Control
ACC	— Area Coordination Center
ACDMS	— Automated Control of Document Management Systems
ACDO	— Assistant Command Duty Officer
ACGIH	— American Conference of Governmental Industrial Hygienists
ACH	— Air Changes per Hour

ACHP	— Advisory Council on Historic Preservation
ACK	— Acknowledgment
ACL	— Allowable Cabin Load
ACL	— Alternate Concentration Level
ACLs	— Alternate Concentration Limits
ACM	— Asbestos-Containing Material
ACMT	— Alternative Coal Mining Technologies
ACO	— Administrative Consent Order
ACOC	— Area Communications Operating Center
ACOE	— Army Corps of Engineers
ACR	— Area Control Room
ACRR	— Annular Core Research Reactor
ACRS	— Advisory Committee on Reactor Safety
ACS	— Alternative Control Strategies
ACS	— American Chemical Society
ACT	— Activity
ACU	— American Conservation Union
ACV	— Air Cushion Vehicle
ADA	— Atomic Development Authority
ADABAS	— Adaptable Data Base Management System
ADC	— Agricultural Development Council
ADC	— Area Damage Control
ADCOM	— Air (Aerospace) Defense Command
ADCON	— Administrative Control
ADCP	— Acid Deposition Control Program
ADI	— Acceptable Daily Intake
ADM	— Action Description Memoranda
ADP	— Automated Data Processing
ADPE	— Automated Data Processing Equipment
ADPS	— Automatic Data Processing System
ADR	— Acid Deposition Report
ADR	— Alternative Dispute Resolution

ADS	— Activity Data Sheets
ADS	— Automatic Depressurization System
ADVCAP	— Advanced Capability
AE	— Aeromedical Evacuation
AEA	— Atomic Energy Act of 1954
AEAP	— As Expeditiously as Practicable
AEC	— Atomic Energy Commission
AECA	— Arms Export Control Act
AECC	— Aeromedical Evacuation Control Center
AECO	— Aeromedical Evaluation Control Officer
AED	— Air Enforcement Division
AEG	— Association of Engineering Geologists
AEL	— Accessible Emission Limit
AELT	— Aeromedical Evacuation Liaison Team
AEOD	— Office for Analysis and Evaluation of Operational Data
AEPS	— Aircrew Escape Propulsion System
AERL	— Air and Engineering Research Laboratory
AES	— Aeromedical Evacuation System
AES	— American Ethnological Society
AESC	— American Engineering Standards Committee
AFA	— American Forestry Association
AFB	— Air Force Base
AFC	— Automatic Frequency Control
AFCC	— Air Force Component Commander
AFCEE	— Air Force Center for Environmental Excellence
AFD	— Assign Fixed Directory
AFDC	— Air Force Doctrine Center
AFDIGS	— Air Force Digital Graphics System
AFDO	— Award Fee Determination Official
AFESC	— Air Force Engineering and Services Center
AFGE	— American Federation of Government Employees
AFI	— American Forest Institute

AFLC	— Air Force Logistics Command
AFM	— Air Force Manual
AFMLO	— Air Force Medical Logistics Office
AFMPC	— United States Air Force Military Personnel Center
AFOSI	— Air Force Office of Special Investigations
AFP	— Armed Forces Publication
AFR	— Air Force Regulation
AFRCC	— Air Force Rescue Coordination Center
AFRCE	— Air Force Regional Civil Engineers
AFRRC	— Armed Forces Radiological Research Center
AFS	— AIRS Facility Subsystem
AFSC	— Air Force Specialty Code
AFSPOC	— Air Force Space Operations Center
AFTAC	— Air Force Technical Applications Center
AFUG	— AIRS Facility Users Group
AFW	— Auxiliary Feedwater
AG	— Adjutant General (Army)
AG	— Air-Gap Separation
AG	— Attorney General
AGA	— American Gas Association
AGC	— Associate General Counsels
AGCA	— Associated General Contractors of America
AGI	— American Geological Institute
AGL	— Above Ground Level
AGS	— American Geographical Society
AGSS	— American Geographical and Statistical Society
AH	— Allowance Holder
AHA	— American Hospital Association
AHERA	— Asbestos Hazard Emergency Response Act
AHIP	— Army Helicopter Improvement Program
AHM	— Allowance Holder Monthly
AIA	— American Institute of Architects

AIA	— Asbestos Information Association
AIA	— Automatic Incident Actions
AIBS	— American Institute of Biological Sciences
AIC	— Acceptable Intake for Chronic Exposure
AICHE	— American Institute of Chemical Engineers
AICPA	— American Institute of Certified Public Accountants
AICUZ	— Air Installation Compatible Use Zones
AID	— Agency for International Development
AIF	— Atomic Industrial Forum
AIF	— Automated Installation Intelligence File
AIG	— Assistant Inspector General
AIHC	— American Industrial Health Council
AIP	— Agreement in Principle
AIP	— American Institute of Planners
AIP	— Auto Ignition Point
AIQC	— Antiterrorism Instructor Qualification Course
AIR	— Artificial Intelligence
AIR	— Air Interdiction
AIRS	— Aerometric Information Retrieval System
AIS	— Acceptable Intake for Subchronic Exposure
AIS	— Automated Information Systems
AISI	— American Iron and Steel Institute
AJBPO	— Area Joint Blood Program Office
AL	— Administrative Leave (Annual Leave)
ALA	— American Lung Association
ALAP	— As Low as Practicable
ALAPCO	— Association of Local Air Pollution Control Officials
ALARA	— As Low as Reasonably Achievable
ALC	— Application Limiting Constituent
ALCM	— Air Launched Cruise Missile
ALCOM	— United States Alaskan Command
ALCON	— All Concerned

ALEC	— American Legislative Exchange Council
ALERFA	— Alert Phase
ALI	— Annual Limit on Intake
ALJ	— Administrative Law Judge
ALLA	— Allied Long Lines Agency
ALMS	— Atomic Line Molecular Spectroscopy
ALNOT	— Alert Notice
ALOHA	— Areal Location of Hazardous Atmospheres
ALS	— Advanced Light Source
ALSS	— Advanced Logistic Support Site
AM	— Amplitude Modulation
AMA	— American Management Association
AMA	— American Medical Association
AMB	— Air Mobility Branch
AMBIENS	— Atmospheric Mass Balance of Industrially Emitted and Natural Sulfur
AMC	— Air Mobility Command
AMC	— American Mining Congress
AMC	— Army Material Command
AMD	— Air Management Division (Regional)
AMEMB	— American Embassy
AMH	— Automated Message Handler
AMMO	— Ammunition
AMOCO	— American Oil Company
AMOPS	— Army Mobilization Operations System
AMP	— Amplifier
AMPN	— Amplification
AMPS	— Automatic Mapping and Planning System
AMR	— Accreditation Maintenance Report
AMRAAM	— Advanced Medium-Range Air-to-Air Missile
AMS	— Administrative Management Staff
AMS	— Aerial Measuring System

AMS	— American Meteorological Society
AMS	— Army Map Service
AMSA	— Association of Metropolitan Sewage Agencies
AMSD	— Administrative and Management Services Division
AMTI	— Alternative Minimum Taxable Income
AMVER	— Automated Mutual-Assistance Vessel Rescue System
AN	— Alphanumeric
ANCA	— Allied Naval Communications Agency
ANCSA	— Alaska Native Claims Settlement Act
ANEC	— American Nuclear Energy Council
ANG	— Air National Guard
ANGTS	— Alaska Natural Gas Transportation System
ANILCA	— Alaska National Interest Lands Conservation
ANL-E	— Argonne National Laboratory (East)
ANL-W	— Argonne National Laboratory (West)
ANMC	— American National Metric Council
ANPCA	— Aquatic Nuisance Prevention and Control Act
ANPR	— Advance Notice of Proposed Ruling
ANRHRD	— Air, Noise, and Radiation Health Research Division
ANS	— American Nuclear Society
ANSI	— American National Standards Institute
ANSP	— Aquatic Nuisance Species Program
ANSS	— American Nature Study Society
ANSTF	— Aquatic Nuisance Species Task Force
ANZUS	— Australia-New Zealand-United States Treaty
AO	— Administrative Officer
AO	— Administrative Order
AO	— Area of Operations
AO	— Area Office
AO	— Auxiliary Offices
AO	— Awards and Obligations
AO	— Office of EPA's Administrator/Deputy Administrator

AO&M	— Administration, Operation, and Maintenance
AOAE	— Avoidance of Adverse Effect
AOB	— Advanced Operations Base
AOC	— Abnormal Operating Conditions
AOC	— Administrative Order on Consent
AOC	— Award of Contract
AOI	— Area of Interest
AOML	— Atlantic Oceanographic and Meteorological Laboratory
AOO	— Accounting Operations Office
AOR	— Area of Responsibility
AOS	— Audit Operations Staff
AOSS	— Aviation Ordnance Safety Supervisor
AOT	— Allowable Outage Time
AP	— Accounting Point
AP	— Average Power
APA	— Acid Precipitation Act of 1980
APA	— Administrative Procedure Act
APA	— Alaska Power Administration
APA	— American Planning Association
APC	— Armored Personnel Carrier
APCA	— Air Pollution Control Agency
APCD	— Air Pollution Control District
APDS	— Automated Procurement Documentation System
APE	— Area of Potential Effects
APEN	— Air Pollution Emissions Notice
APHA	— American Public Health Association
API	— American Paper Institute
API	— American Petroleum Institute
API	— Axial Power Indicator
APM	— Axial Power Monitors
APMRS	— Accident Prevention Measures for Regulated Substances
APORTS	— Aerial Ports

APP	— Accident Prevention Program
APPA	— American Public Power Association
APRHS	— Accident Prevention Regulations for Hazardous Substances
APRMP	— Accident Prevention Risk Management Plan
APRAC	— Urban Diffusion Model for Carbon Monoxide
APRP	— Acid Precipitation Research Program
APT	— Associated Pharmacologists and Toxicologists
APTF	— Acid Precipitation Task Force
APTI	— Air Pollution Training Institute
APTMD	— Air, Pesticides, and Toxics Management Division
APU	— Auxiliary Power Unit
APWA	— American Public Works Association
AQ-7	— Nonreactive Pollutant Modeling
AQAB	— Air Quality Advisory Board
AQCCT	— Air Quality Criteria and Control Techniques
AQCR	— Air Quality Control Region (CAA)
AQCTD/AP	— Air Quality and Chemical Tracking Division/Air Programs
AQD	— Air Quality Digest
AQDHS	— Air Quality Data Handling System
AQDM	— Air Quality Display Model
AQEL	— Air Quality and Emission Limitations
AQL	— Acceptable Quality Level
AQMA	— Air Quality Maintenance Area
AQMD	— Air Quality Management Division
AQMP	— Air Quality Maintenance Plan
AQSM	— Air Quality Simulation Model
AQTAD	— Air Quality Technical Assistance Demonstration
AR	— Analytical Reagent
AR	— Army Regulation
ARA	— Assistant Regional Administrator
ARAC	— Atmospheric Release Advisory Capability
ARAPT	— Alarm Response and Assessment Performance Test

ARARS	— Applicable or Relevant and Appropriate Requirements
ARB	— Air Resources Board
ARC	— Agency Ranking Committee
ARC	— American (National) Red Cross
ARCC	— American Rivers Conservation Council
ARCCC	— Accident Response Capabilities Coordinating Committee
ARCHIE	— Automated Resource for Chemical Hazard Incident Evaluation
ARD	— Air and Radiation Division
ARD	— Aquatic Resource Division
ARDC	— Air Research and Development Command
ARFOR	— Army Forces
ARG	— Accident Response Group
ARG	— American Resources Group
ARI	— Alternate Rod Insertion
ARIP	— Accidental Release Information Program
ARL	— Air Resources Laboratory
ARM	— Air Resources Management
ARM	— Antiradiation Missiles
ARNG	— Army National Guard
ARO	— Alternative Regulatory Option
ARPA	— Archaeological Resources Protection Act of 1979
ARPERCEN	— United States Army Reserve Personnel Center
ARPO	— Acid Rain Policy Office
ARPS	— Atmospheric Research Program Staff (ORD)
ARQ	— Automatic Request-Repeat
ARRDATE	— Arrival Date
ARRP	— Acid Rain Research Program
ARRPA	— Air Resources Regional Pollution Assessment Model
ARS	— Alternate Removal Systems
ART	— Accreditation Review Team
ARZ	— Auto-Restricted Zone
AS	— Area Source

ASA	— Atomic Security Agency
ASBPO	— Armed Services Blood Program Office
ASC	— Area Source Category
ASCC	— Air Standardization Coordinating Committee
ASCE	— American Society of Civil Engineers
ASCHE	— American Society of Chemical Engineers
ASCII	— American Standard Code for Information Interchange
ASCP	— American Society of Consulting Planners
ASD	— Administrative Services Division
ASD	— Analysis and Support Division
ASD	— Assistant Secretary of Defense
ASE	— Automated Stabilization Equipment
ASE	— Automotive Service Excellence
ASEE	— American Society for Environmental Education
ASF	— Aeromedical Staging Facility
ASG	— Area Support Group
ASHAA	— Asbestos School Hazard Abatement Act
ASHRAE	— American Society of Heating, Refrigeration and Air-Conditioning Engineers
ASI	— Assign and Display Switch Initialization
ASIWPCA	— Association of State and Interstate Water Pollution Control Administrators
ASKA	— Automatic System for Kinematic Analysis
ASMDHS	— Airshed Model Data Handling System
ASME	— American Society of Mechanical Engineers
ASMFC	— Atlantic States Marine Fisheries Compact
ASMRO	— Armed Services Medical Regulating Office
ASOC	— Air Support Operations Center
ASPA	— American Society of Public Administration
ASPPO	— Armed Service Production Planning Office
ASRL	— Atmospheric Sciences Research Laboratory
ASSETREP	— Transportation Assets Report

AST	— Aboveground Storage Tank
AST	— Assign Secondary Traffic Channels
ASTIP	— Army Scientific and Technical Information Program
ASTM	— American Society for Testing and Materials
ASTSWMO	— Association of State and Territorial Solid Waste Management Officials
ASWBPL	— Armed Services Whole Blood Processing Laboratories
ASWS	— Audubon Shrine and Wildlife Sanctuary
AT	— Antiterrorism
ATA	— Airport Traffic Area
ATA	— American Trucking Association
ATACMS	— Army Tactical Missile System
ATACO	— Air Tactical Actions Control Officer
ATACS	— Army Tactical Communications System
ATAF	— Allied Tactical Air Force (NATO)
ATBM	— Antitactical Ballistical Missile
ATC	— Area Training Center
ATD	— Air and Toxics Division
ATERIS	— Air Toxics Exposure and Risk Information System
ATGM	— Anti-Tank Guided Missile
ATH	— Assign Thresholds
ATH	— Air Transportable Hospital
ATM	— Assign Traffic Metering
ATMI	— American Textile Manufacturing Institute
ATP	— Allied Tactical Publication
ATP	— Antitampering Program
ATRMRD	— Air Toxics and Radiation Monitoring Research Division
ATRS	— Air, Toxics, and Radiation Staff
ATS	— Action Tracking System
ATS	— Applications Technology Satellite
ATSDR	— Agency for Toxic Substances and Disease Registry
ATTF	— Air Toxics Task Force

ATWS	— Anticipated Transient Without Scram
AUSA	— Assistant U.S. Attorney
AUSM	— Advanced Utility Simulation Model
AUV	— Autonomous Undersea Vehicles
AUX	— Auxiliary
AV	— Adjusted Volume
AV	— Air Vehicle
AV/VI	— Audiovisual/Visual Information
AVD	— Audio-Visual Division
AVL	— Assign Variable Location
AWACS	— Airborne Warning and Control System
AWADS	— Adverse Weather Aerial Delivery System
AWCAP	— Airborne Weapons Corrective Action Program
AWI	— Animal Welfare Institute
AWISE	— Association of Women in Science and Engineering
AWMD	— Air and Waste Management Division
AWN	— Automated Weather Network
AWOL	— Absent without Official Leave
AWPI	— American Wood Preservers Institute
AWRA	— American Water Resources Association
AWS	— Air Weather Service
AWS	— American Welding Society
AWSR	— Air Weather Service Regulation
AWWA	— American Water Works Association
AWWARF	— American Water Works Association Research Foundation
AWWUC	— American Water Works Utility Council
AZR	— Assign Zone Restriction

B

B/B	— Break Bulk
B&RC	— Budget and Reporting Code
BAAQMD	— Bay Area Air Quality Management District
BAC	— Best Available Controls
BAC	— Biotechnology Advisory Committee
BACER	— Biological and Climatological Effects Research
BACM	— Best Available Control Measures
BACT	— Best Available Control Technology
BAE	— Bureau of American Ethnology
BaP	— Benzo(a)Pyrene
BAP	— Benefits Analysis Program
BAQC	— Bureau of Air Quality Control
BARF	— Best Available Retrofit Facility
BART	— Bay Area Rapid Transit Authority
BART	— Best Available Retrofit Technology
BASI	— Best Available Scientific Information
BASIS	— Battelle's Automated Search Information System
BAT	— Best Available Technology
BAT	— Best Available Treatment
BATEA	— Best Available Technology Economically Achievable
BBC	— Balanced Biological Communities
bbl	— barrel
BBS	— Bulletin Board System
BC	— Bottom Current
BCC	— Blind Carbon Copy
BCCM	— Board for Certified Consulting Meteorologists
BCD	— Binary Coded Decimal
BCI	— Bit Count Integrity
BCL	— Battelle Columbus Laboratory

BCN	— Beacon
BCOC	— Base Cluster Operations Center
BCPT	— Best Conventional Pollutant Technology
BCT	— Best Conventional Technology
BD	— Budget Division
BDA	— Bomb or Battle Damage Assessment
BDAT	— Best Demonstrated Available Technology
BDC	— Blood Donor Centers
BDT	— Best Demonstrated Technology
BE	— Basic Encyclopedia
BEA	— Bureau of Economic Advisors
BEF	— Bottom End Fitting
BEJ	— Best Engineering Judgment
BEN	— An abbreviation for an EPA computer model
BEP	— Black Employment Program
BEP	— Building Emergency Plan
BEPA	— Building Emergency Program Administrator
BEPLAN	— Building Emergency Plan
BER	— Bit Error Ratio
BES	— Budget Estimate Submission
BEST	— Building Emergency Support Team
BETs	— Best Available Technology Economically Available
BeV	— Billion Electronvolts
BExC	— Benefits Exceed Costs
BFA	— Blank Fire Adapter
BFI	— Bottom Fitting Insert
BFPPS	— Bureau of Food, Pesticides and Product Safety
BFS	— Bulk Fuel System
BG	— Blanket Gas
BG	— Burial Ground
BG/ED	— Block Grant/Enumeration District
BI	— Brookings Institute

BIA	— Bureau of Indian Affairs
BID	— Background Information Document
BID	— Buoyancy Induced Dispersion
BIDE	— Basic Identity Data Element
BIF	— Boiler/Industrial Furnaces
BIFC	— Boise Interagency Fire Center
BIH	— Bureau International de l'Heure
BIT	— Binary Digit
BIT	— Boron Injection Tank
BIT	— Built-In Test
BITE	— Built-In Test Equipment
BIU	— Beach Interface Unit
BLCP	— Beach Lighterage Control Point
BLDREP	— Blood Report
BLM	— Bureau of Land Management
BLOB	— Biologically Liberated Organo-Beasties
BLP	— Buoyant Line and Point Source Model
BLS	— Bureau of Labor Statistics
BLVR	— Building Power Low Voltage Relay
BMP	— Best Management Practices
BMR	— Baseline Monitoring Report (CWA)
BNA	— Bureau of National Affairs
BNL	— Brookhaven National Laboratory
BOA	— Basic Ordering Agreement
BOC	— Base Operations Center
BOD	— Biological Oxygen Demand
BOF	— Basic Oxygen Furnace
BOM	— Bureau of Mines
BOP	— Balance of Plant
BOP	— Basic Oxygen Process
BOPF	— Basic Oxygen Process Furnace
BOR	— Bureau of Outdoor Recreation

BOR	— Bureau of Reclamation
BOR	— Burnout Risk
BOSF	— Burnout Safety Factor
BOSFN	— Nominal Burnout Safety Factor
BP	— Block Parity
BP	— Boiler Plate
BP	— Boiling Point
BPA	— Blanket Purchase Agreement
BPA	— Bonneville Power Administration
BPCT	— Best Practicable Control Technology
BPD	— Blood Products Depots
BPJ	— Best Professional Judgment (CWA)
BPS	— Bits per Second
BPT	— Best Practicable Treatment
BPT	— Best Practical Technology
BPV	— Back Pressure Valve
Bq	— Becquerel
BR	— Business Roundtable
BRAC	— Base Realignment and Closure
BRACC	— BRAC Commission
BRACs	— Base Realignment Contracts
BRC	— Base Recovery Course
BRC	— Below Regulatory Concern
BRS	— Bibliographic Retrieval Service
BS	— Bilateral Staff
BS&W	— Basic Sediment and Water
BSA	— Beach Support Area
BSO	— Benzene Soluble Organics
BST	— Bomb Search Team
BSU	— Blood Supply Unit
BTC	— Blood Transshipment Center
BTDR	— Building Time Delay Relay

BTF	— Biological Treatment Facility
Btu	— British Thermal Unit
Btuh	— Btu per Hour
BTSCP	— Brown Tree Snake Control Program
BTW	— Boundary Waters Treaty of 1909
BTZ	— Below the Treatment Zone
BU	— Bargaining Unit
BUBBLE	— Use of Alternative Emission Limits to Meet SIP/NSPS
BUD	— Benefits and Use Division
BULK	— Bulk Cargo
BVR	— Beyond Visual Range
BW	— Biological Warfare
BWR	— Boiling Water Reactor
BWS	— Bulk Water System
BWST	— Borated Water Storage Tank
BY	— Budget Year
BZ	— Buckled Zones
BZ	— Buffer Zone

C

°C	— Degrees Celsius (Centigrade)
C/O	— Carry Over Funds
C-B	— Chemical-Biological
C-E	— Communications-Electronics
C-Level	— Category Level
C&C	— Command and Control
C&D	— Charge and Discharge
C&LAT	— Cargo and Loading Analysis Table
C^2	— Command and Control
C^3	— Command, Control, and Communications

C^3CM	— Command, Control, and Communications Countermeasures
C^4	— Command, Control, Communications, and Computers
Ca	— Calcium
CA	— Citizen Act
CA	— Classification Act of 1949
CA	— Competition Advocate
CA	— Cooperative Agreement
CAA	— Clean Air Act
CAA	— Command Arrangement Agreements
CAA	— Compliance Assurance Agreement
CAAA	— Clean Air Act Amendments
CAB	— Civil Aeronautics Board
CAD	— Characterization and Assessment Division
CAD	— Computer-Aided Design
CAD	— Computer-Aided Drafting
CADPOS	— Communications and Data Processing Operations System
CADRS	— Concern and Deficiency Reporting System
CAE	— Council on Anthropology and Education
CAERP	— Community Awareness and Emergency Response Program
CAF	— Canadian Air Force
CAF	— Clean Alternative Fuels
CAFE	— Corporate Average Fuel Economy
CAFO	— Consent Agreement/Final Order
CAFP	— Clean Alternative Fuels Program
CAFMS	— Computer-Assisted Force Management System
CAG	— Carcinogen Assessment Group
CAG	— Civil Affairs Group
CAGI	— Compressed Air and Gas Institute
CAHR	— Containment Atmosphere Heat Removal
CAIMS	— Conventional Ammunition Integrated Management System
CAIR	— Comprehensive Assessment Information Rule
CAIRS	— Computerized Accident/Incident Reporting System

CAL	— Caliber
CALINE	— California Line Source Model
CAM	— Chemical Agent Monitor
CAM	— Computer Aided Manufacturing
CAM	— Crisis Action Module
CAMP	— Continuous Air Monitoring Program
CAMS	— Continuous Air Monitoring System
CAN	— Common Account Number
CANA	— Convalescent Antidote for Nerve Agent
CANUS	— Canada-United States
CAO	— Coordination of Atomic Operations
CAO	— Corrective Action Order
CAOO	— Cincinnati Accounting Operations Office
CAP	— Corrective Action Plan
CAP	— Cost Allocation Procedure
CAP	— Crisis Action Planning
CAP	— Criteria Air Pollutants
CAPA	— Critical Aquifer Protection Area
CAPCA	— Carolinas Air Pollution Control Association
CAPCOA	— California Air Pollution Control Officers Association
CAR	— Corrective Action Reporting
CARB	— California Air Resources Board
CARC	— Containment Air Recirculation and Cooling
CARP	— Contingency Alternate Route Plan
CARVER	— Criticality, Accessibility, Recuperability, Vulnerability, Effect, Recognizability
CAS	— Center for Automotive Safety
CAS	— Central Alarm Station
CAS	— Chemical Abstracts Service
CAS	— Comprehensive Asbestos Survey
CAS	— Condition Assessment Surveys
CASAC	— Clean Air Scientific Advisory Committee

CASLP   — Conference on Alternative State and Local Policies

CASPER   — Contact Area Summary Position Report

CASRN   — Chemical Abstract Service Registry Number

CAT   — Category

CAT   — Corrective Action Triggers

CAT   — Crisis Action Team

CATS   — Computer-Assisted Tracking System

CATS   — Corrective Action Tracking System

CAU   — Carbon Adsorption Unit

CB   — Chemical-Biological

CB   — Continuous Bubbler

CBA   — Chesapeake Bay Agreement

CBA   — Cost Benefit Analysis

CBB   — Chesapeake Bay Basin

CBBLS   — Hundreds of Barrels

CBD   — Central Business District

CBD   — Chemical, Biological Defense

CBFS   — Cesium Beam Frequency Standard

CBI   — Compliance Biomonitoring Inspection (CWA)

CBI   — Confidential Business Information

CBIA   — Coastal Barrier Improvement Act of 1990

CBMM   — Council of Building Materials Manufacturers

CBO   — Congressional Budget Office

CBOD-5   — Carbonaceous Biological Oxygen Demand 5

CBP   — Chesapeake Bay Program

CBP   — County Business Patterns

CBPO   — Consolidated Base Personnel Office

CBPS   — Chemical Biological Protective Shelter

CBR   — Chemical, Biological, and Radiological

CBRA   — Coastal Barrier Resources Act

CBRS   — Coastal Barrier Resources System

CBT   — Computer Based Training

CBTF	— Complementary Cumulative Distribution Function
CC	— Carbon Copy
CC	— Common Cause
CC/RTS	— Chemical Collection/Request Tracking System
CCA	— Competition in Contracting Act
CCA	— Contingency Capabilities Assessment
CCAA	— Canadian Clean Air Act
CCAP	— Center for Clean Air Policy
CCB	— Community Counter Terrorism Board
CCD	— Chemical Control Division
CCEA	— Conventional Combustion Environmental Assessment
CCEDR	— Cooper's Comprehensive Environmental Desk Reference
CCF	— Central Computing Facility
CCF	— Common Cause Failure
CCG	— Crisis Coordination Group
CCH	— Commerce Clearing House
CCHW	— Citizens Clearinghouse for Hazardous Wastes
CCID	— Confidential Chemicals Identification System
CCL	— Communications/Computer Link
CCMS	— Committee on the Challenges of a Modern Society
CCNR	— Consultative Committee for Nuclear Research
CCP	— Casualty Collection Point
CCP	— Composite Correction Plan (CWA)
CCS	— Chemical Coordination Staff
CCSA	— Containership Cargo Stowage Adapter
CCTP	— Clean Coal Technology Program
CCU	— Correspondence Control Unit
CCW	— Component Cooling Water
cd	— Counterdrug
Cd	— Cadmium
CD	— Consent Decree
CD	— Certification Division

CD	— Chlorinated Dibenzofuran
CD	— Climatological Data
CD	— Compliance Division
CD	— Counterdrug
CD-ROM	— Compact Disc Read Only Memory
CDBA	— Central Data Base Administrator
CDC	— Centers for Disease Control (HHS)
CDF	— Core Damage Frequency
CDHS	— Comprehensive Data Handling System
CDI	— Cargo Disposition Instructions
CDM	— Climatological Dispersion Model
CDM	— Collaborative Decisionmaking
CDM	— Comprehensive Data Management
CDMQC	— Climatological Dispersion Model with Calibration and Source Control
CDNS	— Climatological Data National Summary
CDP	— Census Designated Places
CDPH&E	— Colorado Department of Public Health and Environment
CDPM	— Crane Drip Pan Monitor
CDR	— Conceptual Design Report
CDR	— Continuous Data Recording
CDS	— Compliance Data System (CAA)
CE	— Combustion Engineering
CE	— Construction Entrance
CE	— Cost Effectiveness
CEA	— Comprehensive Economic Assessment
CEA	— Cooperative Enforcement Agreement
CEA	— Council of Economic Advisors
CEARC	— Canadian Environmental Assessment Research Council
CEARP	— Comprehensive Environmental Assessment and Response Program
CEB	— Chemical Element Balance
CEC	— Commission of European Communities
CEC	— Committee on Energy and Commerce

CEC	— Community Emergency Coordinator
CECATS	— CSB Existing Chemical Assessment Tracking System
CECR	— Center for Environmental Conflict Resolution
CED	— CERCLA Enforcement Division (OSWER)
CED	— Criminal Enforcement Division
CEDE	— Committed Effective Dose Equivalent
CEDREP	— Communications-Electronics Deployment Report
CEE	— Center for Environmental Education
CEEED	— Council on Environment, Employment, Economy and Development
CEEM	— Center for Energy and Environmental Management
CEF	— Civil Engineering File
CEG	— Common Equipment Group
CEG	— Controller/Evaluator Group
CEI	— Compliance Evaluation Inspection (CWA)
CEI	— Critical Employment Indicator
CEL	— Channel Effluent Limit
CELRF	— Canadian Environmental Law Research Foundation
CEM	— Combined Effects Munition
CEM	— Continuous Emission Monitoring (CAA)
CEMS	— Continuous Emission Monitoring System
CEO	— Chief Executive Officer
CEP	— Council on Economic Priorities
CEPP	— Chemical Emergency Preparedness Program
CEPW	— Committee on Environment and Public Works
CEQ	— Council on Environmental Quality
CEQA	— California Environmental Quality Act
CERCLA	— Comprehensive Environmental Response Compensation and Liability Act of 1980
CERCLIS	— Comprehensive Environmental Response, Compensation and Liability Information System
CERI	— Center for Environmental Research Information
CERS	— Continuous Emission Reduction System

CERT	— Certificate of Eligibles
CES	— Coast Earth Station
CESE	— Civil Engineering Support Equipment
CESG	— Communications Equipment Support Group
CESP	— Civil Engineering Support Plan
CESPG	— Civil Engineering Support Planning Generator
CEU	— Continuing Education Units
CExB	— Costs (of control) Exceed Benefits (of control)
CF	— Causeway Ferry
CF	— Conservation Foundation
CF	— Containment Failure
CF	— Contingency Fee
CF	— Coverage Factor
CF_4	— Carbon Tetrafluoride
CFA	— Cognizant Federal Agency
CFA	— Consumer Federation of America
CFC	— Chlorofluorocarbons
CFC	— Combined Forces Command
CFEE	— Conference of Federal Environmental Engineers
CFL	— Contingency Planning Facilities List
cfm	— Cubic Feet per Minute
CFM	— Chlorofluoromethane
CFR	— Code of Federal Regulations
CFS	— Core Fluid System
CFSG	— Citizen Forum on Self Government (NML)
CFT	— Core Fluid Tanks
CFV	— Clean Fuel Vehicles
CFWRU	— Cooperative Fishery and Wildlife Research Unit
CFWRDA	— Clarks Fork Wild and Scenic Designation Act of 1990
CGLSMP	— Coast Guard Logistic Support and Mobilization Plan
CG	— Center of Gravity
CG	— U.S. Coast Guard

CGCAP	— Coast Guard Capabilities Plan
CGL	— Comprehensive General Liability
CH	— Cargo Handling
CH	— Component Handling
CH	— Contact Handled
CHABA	— Committee on Hearing and Bio Acoustics
CHAMP	— Community Health Air Monitoring Program
CHAMPUS	— Civilian Health and Medical Program for the Uniformed Services
CHCSS	— Chief, Central Security Service
CHE	— Cargo Handling Equipment
CHEMS	— Chemical Hazards Emergency Management System
CHEMTREC	— Chemical Transportation Emergency Center
CHESS	— Community Health and Environmental Surveillance System
CHEMS	— Chemical Hazards Emergency Management System
CHIP	— Chemical Hazard Information Profile
CHIPS	— Chemical Hazard Information Profile System
CHOP	— Change of Operational Control
CHR	— Confinement Heat Removal
CHRIS	— Chemical Hazard Response Information System
CHSTR	— Characteristics of Transportation Resources
CHSTREP	— Characteristics of Transportation Resources Report
ci	— curie
CI	— Compression Ignition
CIA	— Central Intelligence Agency
CIAP	— Command Intelligence Architecture Plan
CIAQ	— Committee on Indoor Air Quality
CIBL	— Convective Internal Boundary Layer
CIBO	— Council of Industrial Boiler Owners
CIC	— Compensated Ion Chamber
CICA	— Competition in Contracting Act
CICIS	— Chemicals in Commerce Information System
CICS	— Customer Information Control System

CID	— Criminal Investigation Division
CIDRS	— Cascade Impactor Data Reduction System
CIF	— Consolidated Incinerator Facility
CIFC	— Committee on Interstate and Foreign Commerce
CIIA	— Committee on Interior and Insular Affairs
CIL	— Critical Items List
CILRT	— Containment Integrated Leak Rate Test
CIMI	— Committee on Integrity and Management Improvement
CIN	— Cargo Increment Number
CINC	— Commander in Chief
CIO	— Central Imagery Office
CIP	— Capital Improvement Project
CIP	— Catalog in Publication
CIP	— Communications Interface Processor
CIR	— Continuing Intelligence Requirement
CIRES	— Cooperative Institute for Research in Environmental Sciences
CIRM	— International Radio-Medical Center
CIRV	— Common Interswitch Rekeying Variable
CIRVIS	— Communications Instructions for Reporting Vital Intelligence Sightings
CIS	— Chemical Information System
CIS	— Commonwealth of Independent States
CIS	— Contracts Information System
CIT	— Critical Incident Technique
CITES	— Convention on International Trade in Endangered Species
CJCS	— Chairman of the Joint Chiefs of Staff
CJDA	— Critical Joint Duty Assignment
CJE	— Critical Job Element
CJO	— Chief Judicial Officer (OA)
CLC	— Capacity Limiting Constituents
CLDTMP	— A computer code to calculate cladding temperature limit
CLEANS	— Clinical Laboratory for Evaluation and Assessment of Noxious Substances

CLEVER	— Clinical Laboratory for Evaluation and Validation of Epidemiological Research
CLF	— Conservation Law Foundation
ClF$_3$	— Chlorine Trifluoride
CLIPS	— Chemical List Indexing and Processing System
CLIPS	— Communications Link Interface Planning System
CLP	— Certified Lab Program
CLP	— Contract Laboratory Program
CLPSB	— CINC Logistic Procurement Support Board
CLS	— Community Liaison Staff
CLS	— Contractor Logistic Support
CLSP	— Center for Law and Social Policy
cm	— Centimeter
cm/sec	— Centimeters per Second
Cm	— Mean Coverage Factor
CM	— Chairman's Memorandum
CM	— Construction Manager
CM	— Contract Manager
CM	— Core Melt
CM	— Corrective Measures
CM	— Crisis Manager
CMA	— Chemical Manufacturers Association
CMAS	— Cross-Media Analysis Staff
CMB	— Chemical Mass Balance
CMD	— Contracts Management Division
CMEP	— Critical Mass Energy Project
CMMF	— Committee on Merchant Marine and Fisheries
CMO	— Contract Management Office
CMP	— Communications Message Processor
CMPPA	— Computer Matching and Privacy Protection Amendments
CMRP	— Corporate Management Report and Plan
CMS	— Community Management Staff

CMS	— Corrective Measures Study
CMS	— Crisis Management System
CMSR	— Corporate Management Systems Report
CMT	— Control Methods and Technologies
CMT	— Crisis Management Team
CMTS	— Comments
CMTU	— Cartridge Magnetic Tape Unit
CN	— Counternarcotic
CNASP	— Chairman's Net Assessment for Strategic Planning
CNBCP	— Collective Nuclear, Biological, and Chemical Protection
CNC	— Condensation Nucleus Counter
CNCE	— Communications Nodal Control Element
CNG	— Coalition of Northeastern Governors
CNG	— Compressed Natural Gas
CNGB	— Chief, National Guard Bureau
CNPWP	— Convention on Nature Protection and Wildlife Preservation
CNO	— Chief of Naval Operations
CNR	— Composite Noise Rating
CNRR	— Containment Radioactivity Removal
CNTY	— Country
CNWDI	— Critical Nuclear Weapons Design Information
CO	— Carbon Monoxide
CO	— Change Order
CO	— Certificate of Occupancy
CO	— Commanding Officer
CO	— Contracting Officer
CO_2	— Carbon Dioxide
COA	— Commissioned Officers Association
COA	— Consideration of Alternatives
COA	— Course of Action
COB	— Close of Business
COBOL	— Common Business Oriented Language

COCA	— Consent Order and Compliance Agreement
COCO	— Contractor Owned, Contractor Operated
COD	— Certificate of Disposal, Certificate of Destruction
COD	— Chemical Oxygen Demand
COD	— Computer Operations Division
COD	— Cone of Depression
CODF	— Complementary Cumulative Distribution Function
COE	— Army Corps of Engineers
COG	— Compliance Order Guidance
COG	— Continuity of Government
COG	— Council of Governments
COGEMT	— Continuity of Government Emergency Management Team
COH	— Coefficient of Haze
COLA	— Cost of Living Adjustment
COLDS	— Cargo Offload and Discharge System
COM	— Collection Operations Management
COM	— Continuous Opacity Monitor
COMM	— Communications
COMP	— Component
COMPLEX	— Complex Terrain Screening Model
COMPTER	— An abbreviation for a multiple source air quality computer model
COMPUSEC	— Computer Security
COMSAT	— Communications Satellite
COMSEC	— Communications Security
COMTAC	— Tactical Communications
COMVAN	— Communications Van
CON	— Selected Contractor or "Awardee"
CONEXPLAN	— Contingency and Exercise Plan
CONOPS	— Concept of Operations
CONPLAN	— Operation Plan in Concept Format
CONUS	— Continental United States
COO	— Chicago Operations Office

COOP	— Continuity of Operations Plan
COPD	— Chronic Obstructive Pulmonary Disease
COPS	— Communications Operational Planning System
CORPS	— Army Corps of Engineers (same as ACOE; COE)
CORR	— Chemicals on Reporting Rules
COS	— Conservative Opportunity Society
COS	— Critical Occupational Specialty
COTS	— Commercial-Off-the-Shelf
COWPS	— Council on Wage and Price Stability
CP&I	— Coastal Patrol and Interdiction
CPA	— Certified Public Accountant
CPA	— Closest Point of Approach
CPAF	— Cost Plus Awards Fee
CPDD	— Control Programs Development Division
CPE	— Customer Premise Equipment
CPFF	— Cost Plus Fixed Fee
CPFL	— Contingency Planning Facilities List
CPG	— Contingency Planning Guidance
CPGAF	— Commission on Population Growth and the American Future
CPI	— Consumer Price Index
CPI	— Crash Position Indicator
CPIF	— Cost Plus Incentive Fee
CPL	— Chemistry and Physics Laboratory
CPL	— Confinement Protection Limits
CPM	— Certified Project Manager
CPM	— Civilian Personnel Manual
CPM	— Continuous Particle Monitor
CPM	— Critical Path Method
CPMPDW	— Convention on the Prevention of Marine Pollution
CPO	— Certified Project Officer
CPP	— Compliance Policy and Planning
CPR	— Cardiopulmonary Resuscitation

CPR	— Cardiovascular Pulmonary Resuscitation
CPR	— Center for Public Resources
CPR	— Coalition for Pesticide Reform
cps	— Cycles per Second
CPS	— Characters per Second
CPS	— Compliance Program and Schedule
CPSC	— Consumer Products Safety Commission
CPSDAA	— Compliance and Program Staff to the Deputy Assistant Administrator
CPVC	— Chlorinated Polyvinyl Chloride
CPU	— Central Processing Unit
Cr	— Chromium
CR	— Community Relations
CRA	— Classification Review Area
CRA	— Civil Rights Act
CRAM	— Control Random Access Memory
CRAVE	— Carcinogen Risk Assessment Verification Exercise
CRC	— CONUS Replacement Center
CRD	— Community Relations Division
CRD	— Control Rod Drive
CRDCS	— Control Rod Drive Control System
CRDM	— Control Rod Drive Mechanism
CRF	— Combustion Research Facility
CRGS	— Chemical Regulations and Guidelines System
CRGNSA	— Columbia River Gorge National Scenic Area Act
CRIF	— Cargo Routing Information File
CRITIC	— Critical Information
CRL	— Central Regional Laboratory
CRM	— Corrective Repair Maintenance
CRM	— Count Rate Meter
CROP	— Consolidated Rules of Practice
CRP	— Community Relations Plan

CRP	— Compliance Report and Plan
CRR	— Center for Renewable Resources
CRS	— Community Relations Staff (OEA)
CRSTER	— Single Source (CRSTER) Model
CRT	— Cathode Ray Tube
CRT	— Coolant Return Tank
CRTK	— Community Right-to-Know
CRTS	— Casualty Receiving and Treatment Ship
CS	— Compliance Staff (GAD)
CS	— Containment Spray
CS	— Contract Specialist
CS	— Controlled Space
CS&R	— Codes, Standards, and Regulations
CSA	— Chief of Staff, United States Army
CSA	— Chemical Safety Abstracts
CSAF	— Chief of Staff, United States Air Force
CSAM	— Computer Security for Acquisition Managers
CSB	— Chemical Safety Board
CSB	— Chemical Species Balance
CSD	— Criteria and Standards Division (OAR)
CSER	— Contractor Self-Evaluation Report
CSES	— Center for the Study of Earth from Space
CSG	— Council of State Governments
CSHEM	— Conference of State Health and Environmental Managers
CSHIB	— Chemical Safety and Hazard Investigation Board
CSI	— Chemical Substances Inventory
CSI	— Compliance Sampling Inspection (CWA)
CSI	— Critical Safety Item
CSI	— Critical Sustainability Item
CSIF	— Communications Service Industrial Fund
CSIN	— Chemical Substances Information Network
CSM	— Crisis Support Manager

CSMA	— Chemical Specialties Manufacturers Association
CSMP	— Continuous System Modeling Program
CSMPS	— Computerized Scientific Management Planning System
CSO	— Communications Support Organization
CSOA	— Combined Special Operations Area
CSP	— Crisis Staffing Procedures
CSPA	— Council of State Planning Agencies
CSPD	— Chemicals and Statistical Policy Division
CSPI	— Center for Science in the Public Interest
CSR	— Commander in Chief's (CINC's) Summary Report
CSRA	— Civil Service Reform Act
CSRL	— Center for the Study of Responsive Law
CSRS	— Civil Service Retirement System
CSS	— Clerical Support Staff
CSS	— Containment Spray System
CSS	— Coordinator Surface Search
CSSD	— Computer Services and Systems Division
CSSI	— Containment Spray System (Post-Accident Injection Phase)
CSSR	— Containment Spray System (Post-Accident Recirculation Phase)
CST	— Condensate Storage Tank
CST	— Crisis Support Team
CSWE	— Central Service Works Engineering
CT	— Counterterrorism
CT	— Current Transformer
CTD	— Control Technology Document
CTF	— Combined Task Force
CTG	— Commander, Task Group
CTG	— Control Technique Guidelines
CTID	— Communications Transmission Identifier
CTO	— Control Technology Office
CTOC	— Corps Tactical Operations Center
CTR	— Critical Temperature Ratio

CTSCZ	— Convention on the Territorial Sea and the Contiguous Zone
Cu	— Copper
CU	— Cubic Capacity
CUS	— Chemical Update System
CV	— Curriculum Vitae
CVBG	— Carrier Vessel Battle Group
CVCS	— Chemical Volume and Control System
CVD	— Chemical Vapor Deposition
CVN	— Carrier (Aircraft) Vessel, Nuclear
CVS	— Cardiovascular System
CVSD	— Continuous Variable Slope Delta
CW	— Continuous Wave
CW	— Chemical Warfare
CW	— Congress Watch
CWA	— Clean Water Act
CWAP	— Clean Water Action Project
CWC	— Composite Warfare Commander
CWGM	— Cooling Water Gamma Monitor
CWLM	— Cumulative Working Level Month
CWPD	— Conventional War Plans Division, Joint Staff (J-7)
CWR	— Calm Water Ramp
CWS	— Compressed Work Schedule
CWS	— Contaminated Water Storage
CWTC	— Chemical Waste Transportation Council
CX	— Categorical Exclusion
CY	— Calendar Year
CY	— Current Year
CZA	— Coastal Zone Authority
CZM	— Coastal Zone Management
CZMA	— Coastal Zone Management Act

D
—

D	— Absorbed Dose
d/m	— Drips per Minute
D/A	— Digital-to-Analog
D/C	— Down Converter
D&D	— Decontamination and Decommissioning
D&D	— Dial and Deliver
D&E	— Discharge and Exit
D&F	— Determination and Findings
DA	— Damage Assessment
DA	— Deputy Administrator
DA	— Department of Army
DA	— Designated Agent
DA	— Direct Action
DA	— DOE Design Agency
DA&M	— Director of Administration and Management
DAA	— Designated Approving Authority
DAA	— Deputy Assistant Administrator
DAC	— Derived Air Conservation
DACB	— Data Adapter Control Block
DACM	— Data Adapter Control Mode
DAIG	— Deputy Assistant Inspector General
DAMA	— Demand Assigned Multiple Access
DAMDF	— Durham Air Monitoring Demonstration Facility
DAO	— Department/Agency/Organization
DAP	— Division of Air Pollution
DAPSS	— Document and Personnel Security System
DAR	— Daily Activity Report
DAR	— Direct Assistance Request
DAR	— Distortion Adaptive Receiver

DARPA	— Defense Advanced Research Projects Agency
DART	— Disaster Assistance Response Team
DAS	— Direct Access Subscriber
DASA	— Department of the Army (DA) Staff Agencies
DASD	— Direct Access Storage Drive
DAS/EE	— Deputy Assistant Secretary/Energy Emergency
DASSS	— Decentralized Automated Service Support System
DAT	— Deployment Action Team
DATT	— Defense Attache
dB	— Decibel
dBA	— Noise Measurement Unit
DBA	— Data Base Administrator
DBA	— Default Basis Accident
DBA	— Default Bounding Accident
DBA	— Design Basis Accident
DBCP	— Dibromochloropropane
DBE	— Default Boundary Effect
DBE	— Design Basis Earthquake
DBF	— Design Basis Fires
DBFL	— Design Basis Floods
DBG	— Data Base Generation
DBI	— Defense Budget Issue
DBM	— Data Base Manager
DBMS	— Data Base Management System
DBOF-T	— Defense Business Operations Fund-Transportation
DBOS	— Data-Based Operating System
dBr	— Decibels Level Reference
DBT	— Design Basis Tornado
DC	— Direct Current
DCA	— Washington DC International Airport
DCA	— Document Control Assistant
DCAA	— Defense Contract Audit Agency

DCBA	— Differential Cost Benefit Analysis
DCC	— Damage Control Center
DCCC	— Defense Collection Coordination Center
DCCEP	— Developing Country Combined Exercise Program
dcf	— Dry cubic feet
DCG	— Derived Concentration Guide
DCH	— Direct Containment Heating
DCI	— Director of Central Intelligence
DCIS	— Data Call-In Staff (OPTS)
dcm	— Dry cubic meter
DCMA	— Dry Color Manufacturers Association
DCMC	— Office of Deputy Chairman, Military Committee
DCMD	— Demonstration Cities and Metropolitan Development Act
DCN	— Document Control Number
DCNO	— Deputy Chief of Naval Operations
DCO	— Delayed Compliance Order (CAA)
DCO	— Document Control Officer
DCP	— Discrimination Complaints Program
DCPA	— Defense Civil Preparedness Agency
DCPG	— Digital Clock Pulse Generator
DCPU	— Data Center Policy and Usage
DCR	— Design Change Request
DCR	— Document Control Register
DCS	— Defense Communications System
DCS	— Developing Countries Staff (OIA)
DCSCU	— Dual Capability Servo Control Unit
DCSLOG	— Deputy Chief of Staff for Logistics, U.S. Army
DCSOPs	— Deputy Chief of Staff for Operations and Plans, U.S. Army
DCSPER	— Deputy Chief of Staff for Personnel, U.S. Army
DCTN	— Defense Commercial Telecommunications Network
DCVA	— Double Check Valve Assembly
DD	— Deputy Director

DDA	— Designated Development Activity
DDEA	— Defense Dependents Education Act of 1978
DDI	— Deputy Director of Intelligence (CIA)
DDM	— Digital Data Modem
DDN	— Defense Data Network
DDO	— Director of Operations (CIA)
DDR&E	— Director of Defense Research and Engineering
DDS	— Defense Dissemination System
DDS	— Document Development Services
DDT	— Dichloro-dyphenyl-triachloroanthane
de	— Individual Drift Error
De	— Total Drift Error
DE	— Destruction Efficiency
DE	— Directed Energy
de max	— Maximum Drift Error
de min	— Minimum Drift Error
dea	— Aerospace Drift Error
DEA	— Drug Enforcement Administration
DEARAS	— Department of Defense Emergency Authorities Retrieval and Analysis System
DEC	— Department of Environmental Conservation
DECL	— Declassify
DEFCON	— Defense Readiness Condition
DEFSMAC	— Defense Special Missile and Astronautics Center
DEMARC	— Demarcation
DEO	— Director of Emergency Operations
DEOA	— Department of Energy Organization Act of 1977
DEP	— Deployed
DEPCJTF	— Deputy Commander, Joint Task Force
DEPMEDS	— Deployable Medical Systems
DEQ	— Department of Environmental Quality
DER	— Department of Environmental Resources

DERC	— Drill and Exercise Review Committee
DERS	— Digital Emergency Response System
DES	— Data Encryption Standard
DES	— Data Exchange System
DES	— Diethylstilbestrol
DESCOM	— Depot System Command (U.S. Army)
DEST	— Destination
DEW	— Directed-Energy Warfare
DF	— Dispersion Factor
DFDP	— Defense Facility Decommissioning Program
DFM	— Flow Monitor
DFR/E	— Defense Fuel Region, Europe
DFR/ME	— Defense Fuel Region, Middle East
DFSC	— Defense Fuel Supply Center
DFSP	— Defense Fuel Support Point
DFT	— Deployment for Training
DG	— Diesel Generator
DGZ	— Desired Ground Zero
DHHS	— Department of Health and Human Services
DHR	— Decay Heat Removal
DI	— Diagnostic Inspection (CWA)
DIA	— Defense Intelligence Agency
DIA	— Denver International Airport
DIAC	— Defense Intelligence Analysis Center
DIAR	— Defense Intelligence Agency Regulation
DICO	— Data Information Coordination Office
DIDHS	— Deployable Intelligence Data Handling System
DIDS	— Domestic Information Display System
DIG	— Deputy Inspector General
DIH	— Differential in Hours
DIL	— Daily Instruction Logs
DIMIG	— Disintegrations per Minute per Gram

DINET   — Defense Industrial Net

DIP   — Defense Improvement Project

DIP   — Dual In-Line Package

DIPC   — Defense Industrial Plant/Equipment Center

DIPSS   — Department of Integrated Personnel Service System

DIRM   — Directorate for Information and Resource Management

DIRNSA   — Director, National Security Agency

DIS   — Defense Investigative Service

DISA   — Defense Information Systems Agency

DISN   — Defense Information Systems Network

DJS   — Director, Joint Staff

DJSM   — Director, Joint Staff, memorandum

DLA   — Defense Logistics Agency

DLR   — Depot-Level Repairable

DLSA   — Defense Legal Services Agency

DMA   — Defense Mapping Agency

DMA   — Diagnosis of Multiple Alarms System

DMAHT   — Defense Mapping Agency Hydrographic/Topographic Center

DMAINST   — Defense Mapping Agency Instruction

dmax   — Maximum Drift Distance

DMB   — Datum Marker Buoy

DMC   — Data Mode Control

DME   — Distance Measuring Equipment

dmin   — Minimum Drift Distance

DMIS   — Duns Marketing Identification System

DML   — Data Manipulation Language

DMPI   — Designated Mean Point of Impact

DMR   — Discharge Monitoring Report (CWA)

DMR   — Document Modification Request

DMRIS   — Defense Medical Regulating Information System

DMRLS   — Data Management and Research Liaison Staff (OW)

DMS   — Defense Meteorological System

DMSO	— Directors of Major Staff Office
DMSP	— Defense Meteorological Satellite Program
DMSSC	— Defense Medical System Support Center
DMU	— Disk Memory Unit
DNA	— Defense Nuclear Agency
DNA	— Deoxyribonucleic Acid
DNBI	— Disease and Nonbattle Injury
DNO	— Do Not Operate
DNR	— Department of Natural Resources
DO	— Dissolved Oxygen
DOA	— Dead on Arrival
DOA	— Department of Agriculture
DOA	— Department of the Army
DOC	— Department of Commerce
DOD	— Department of Defense
DODD	— Department of Defense Directive
DODDS	— Department of Defense Dependent Schools
DODI	— Department of Defense Instruction
DODIIS	— Department of Defense Intelligence Information System
DOE	— Department of Ecology
DOE	— Department of Energy
DOES	— Disk-Oriented Engineering System
DOH	— Department of Health
DOH	— Department of Highways
DOI	— Department of Interior
DOIG	— Divisional Offices of the Inspector General
DOJ	— Department of Justice
DOL	— Department of Labor
DOLA	— Department of Local Affairs
DOM	— Day of Month
DOMB	— Director of the Office of Management and Budget
DOMS	— Director of Military Support

DON	— Department of the Navy
DOP	— Detailed Operating Procedures
DOS	— Department of State
DOS	— Disk Operating System
DOSEM	— An abbreviation for a computer model
DOT	— Department of Transportation
DOW	— Defenders of Wildlife
DOW	— DOW Chemical Company
DOY	— Day of Year
dp	— Parachute Drift
DP	— Differential Pressure
DP	— Defense Programs
DPA	— Deepwater Ports Act
DPC	— Domestic Policy Council
DPG	— Defense Planning Guidance
DPRB	— Defense Planning and Resources Board
DPS	— Data Processing System
DPSC	— Defense Personnel Support Center
DQO	— Data Quality Objective
DRA	— Deputy Regional Administrator
DRA	— Disaster Relief Act
DRB	— Defense Resources Board
DRC	— Deputy Regional Counsel
DRE	— Destruction and Removal Efficiency
DRMO	— Defense Reutilization Marketing Office
DRMS	— Defense Reutilization and Marketing Service
DS	— Dichotomous Sampler
DS	— Doctrine Sponsor
DSA	— Defense Special Assessment
DSAA	— Defense Security Assistance Agency
DSAP	— Data Self-Auditing Program
DSAR	— Defense Supply Agency Regulation

dscf	— Dry Standard Cubic Feet
dscm	— Dry Standard Cubic Meter
DSCS	— Defense Satellite Communications System
DSFM	— Division of the State Fire Marshall
DSN	— Defense Switched Network
DSNET	— Defense Secure Network
DSP	— Defense Support Program
DSPL	— Display System Programming Language
DSRS	— Data Storage and Retrieval System
DSS	— Data Systems Staff
DSS	— Decision Support System
DSS	— Domestic Sewage Study
DSSCS	— Defense Special Security Communications System
DSSO	— Data System Support Organization
DST	— Design Basis Tornadoes
DST	— Double-Shell Tank
DSTP	— Director of Strategic Target Planning
DT	— Detention Time
DTE	— Data Terminal Equipment
DTED	— Digital Terrain Elevation Data
DTMR	— Defense Traffic Management Regulation
DTO	— Division Transportation Office
DTS	— Defense Transportation System
DU	— Decision Unit
DUC	— Decision Unit Coordinator
DUSD	— Deputy Under Secretary of Defense
DUVAS	— Derivative Ultraviolet Absorbtion Spectroscopy
DVC	— Digital Voice Computer
DVITS	— Digital Video Imagery Transmission System
DW	— Drywell
DWGNRA	— Delaware Water Gap National Recreation Area
DWMP	— Defense Waste Management Plan

DWP   — Department of Water and Power

DWPF   — Defense Waste Processing Facility

DWS   — Drinking Water Standards

DWT   — Deadweight Tonnage

DWTM   — Office of Defense Waste and Transportation Management

DX   — Direct Exchange

DZ   — Drop Zone

DZST   — Drop Zone Support Team

E

E   — Irradiance

E   — Total Probable Error

E^3 — Electromagnetic Environmental Effects

E-MAIL   — Electronic Mail

E&CF   — Events and Causal Factors

E&DCP   — Evaluation and Data Collection Plan

E&E   — Evasion and Escape

E&H   — Environment and Health

E&M   — Ear and Mouth

E&S   — Error and Sensitivity

EA   — Electronic Attack

EA   — Emergency Actions

EA   — Emergency Assessment

EA   — Enforcement Agreement

EA   — Environmental Audit

EA   — Environmental Assessment

EAC   — Emergency Action Console

EAD   — Earliest Arrival Date

EAD   — Economic Analysis Division (OPPE)

EAD   — Energy and Air Division

EAD	— Evaluation and Analysis Division
EADS	— Environmental Assessment Data Systems
EAEC	— European Atomic Energy Community
EAF	— Electric Arc Furnace
EAG	— Exposure Assessment Group (ORD)
EAL	— Emergency Action Level
EAM	— Emergency Action Message
EAP	— Emergency Action Procedure
EAP-CJCS	— Emergency Action Procedures of the Chairman of the Joint Chiefs of Staff
EAR	— Environmental Auditing Roundtable
EAS	— Economic Analysis Staff
EAS	— Engineering Assistance Section
EB	— Emissions Balancing
EBCDIC	— Extended Binary Coded Decimal Interchange Code
EBS	— Emergency Broadcast System
EBWR	— Experimental Boiling Water Reactor
EC	— Environment Canada
EC	— European Community
ECAC	— Electromagnetic Compatibility Analysis Center
ECAD	— Existing Chemical Assessment Division
ECAO	— Environmental Criteria and Assessment Office
ECC	— Emergency
ECC	— Emergency Control Centers
ECC	— Executive and Congressional Communications (OA)
ECCI	— Emergency Core Cooling Injection
ECCM	— Electronic Counter-Countermeasures
ECCS	— Emergency Core Cooling System
ECE	— Economic Commission for Europe
ECHH	— Electro-Catalytic Hyper-Heaters
ECHO	— Each Community Helps Others
ECL	— Environmental Chemistry Laboratory

ECM	— Electronic Countermeasures
ECN	— Minimum Essential Emergency Communications Network
ECP	— Emergency Command Precedence
ECP	— Engineering Change Proposal
ECP	— Erosion Control Plan
ECP	— External Compliance Program (OCR)
ECRA	— Economic Cleanup Responsibility Act
ECS	— Emergency Control Station
ECS	— Emergency Core Cooling System
ECS	— Erosion Control Standard
ECSP	— Employee Counseling Services Program
ECT	— Evaporator Condensate Tank
ECTD	— Emission Control Technology Division
ECU	— Environmental Control Unit
ECU	— Environmental Crimes Unit
ECW	— Effluent Cooling Water
ECWD	— Effluent Cooling Water Drainage
ED	— Editorial Division (OEA)
ED	— Enforcement Division (OW)
ED	— Evaluation Directive
EDA	— Environmental Development Administration
EDB	— Energy Development Board
EDB	— Ethylene Dibromide
EDC	— Ethylene Dichloride
EDD	— Earliest Delivery Date
EDD	— Enforcement Decision Document
EDE	— Effective Dose Equivalent
EDF	— Environmental Defense Fund
EDG	— Emergency Diesel Generator
EDIS	— Engineering Data Information System
EDP	— Electronic Data Processing
EDPS	— Electronic Data Processing System

EDRS	— Enforcement Document Retrieval System
EDRS	— Engineering Data Retrieval System
EDS	— Electronic Data System
EDS	— Energy Data System
EDS	— Environmental Data Services
EDT	— Edit Data Transmission
EDZ	— Emission Density Zoning
EE	— Emergency Establishment
EEA	— Energy and Environmental Analysis
EEBD	— Emergency Escape Breathing Device
EEC	— Environmental Engineering Committee
EED	— Electro-Explosive Device
EED	— Equipment Engineering Department
EED	— Exposure Evaluation Division
EEGL	— Emergency Exposure Guidance Level
EEI	— Edison Electric Institute
EEI	— Essential Elements of Information
EEM	— Essential Equipment Monitor
EEMS	— Energy Emergency Management System
EEMS	— Enhanced Expanded Memory Specification
EEMT	— Energy Emergency Management Team
EEO	— Equal Employment Opportunity
EEOC	— Equal Employment Opportunity Commission
EEPROM	— Electronic Erasable Programmable Read-Only Memory
EER	— Excess Emission Report
EERF	— Eastern Environmental Radiation Facility
EERL	— Eastern Environmental Radiation Laboratory
EERU	— Environmental Emergency Response Unit
EESI	— Environment and Energy Study Institute
EESL	— Environmental Ecological and Support Laboratory
EETFC	— Environmental Effects, Transport and Fate Committee
EF	— Emission Factor

EF	— End Fitting
EF&P	— End Fitting Delta Pressure
EFC	— External Fission Counter
EFO	— Equivalent Field Office
EFS	— Emergency Feedwater System
EFTC	— European Fluorocarbon Technical Committee
EFTO	— Encrypt for Transmission Only
EG	— Emergency Generators
EG	— Engine-Generators
EGD	— Effluent Guidelines Division
EGR	— Exhaust Gas Recirculation
EHA	— Environmental Health Association
EHC	— Environmental Health Committee
EHCI	— Emergency and Hazardous Chemical Inventory
EHIS	— Emission History Information System
EHRS	— Environmental Health Research Staff
EHS	— Environmental Health Service
EIA	— Economic Impact Assessment
EIA	— Electronic Industries Association
EIA	— Energy Information Administration
EIA	— Environmental Impact Assessment
EIC	— Energy Information Center
EICC	— Emergency Information and Coordination Center
EIES	— Electronic Information Exchange System
EIL	— Environmental Impairment Liability
EIR	— Environmental Impact Report
EIR	— Exposure Information Report
EIS	— Emissions Inventory System (OAR)
EIS	— Environmental Impact Statement
EIS/AS	— Emissions Inventory System/Area Source
EIS/PS	— Emissions Inventory System/Point Source
EIT	— Engineer-in-Training

EKMA	— Empirical Kinetic Modeling Approach
ELBA	— Emergency Location Beacon
ELI	— Environmental Law Institute
ELINT	— Electronics Intelligence
ELR	— Environmental Law Reporter
ELT	— Emergency Locator Transmitter
ELVA	— Emergency Low Visibility Approach
ELWCR	— Erodible Land and Wetland Conservation and Reserve Program
EM	— Electron Microscope
EMAC	— Emergency Management Advisory Committee
EMAS	— Enforcement Management and Accountability System
EMC	— Electromagnetic Compatibility
EMCON	— Emission Control
EME	— Electromagnetic Environment
EMG	— Emergency Management Guide
EMI	— Electromagnetic Interface
EMO	— Emergency Management Organization
EMP	— Electromagnetic Pulse
EMR	— Electromagnetic Radiation
EMR	— Environmental Management Report
EMS	— Emergency Management System
EMS	— Emergency Medical Services
EMS	— Energy Emergency System
EMS	— Enforcement Management Subsystem
EMS	— Exposure Modeling System (OTS)
EMSD	— Environmental Monitoring Systems Division
EMSL	— Environmental Monitoring Support Laboratory
EMTs	— Emergency Management Team
EMT	— Emergency Medical Technician
EMTS	— Environmental Methods Testing Site
ENEA	— European Nuclear Energy Association
ENFOMAIN	— Enforcement Main Computer

EO	— Ethylene Oxide
EO	— Executive Order
EOC	— Emergency Operations Center
EOCNO	— Emergency Operations Center Notification Officer
EOD	— Engineering Operations Division (OAR)
EOD	— Entrance on Demand
EOD	— Explosives Ordnance Disposal
EOE	— Equal Opportunity Employer
EOF	— End of File
EOJ	— End of Job
EOM	— End of Message
EOP	— Emergency Operating Procedures
EOR	— Enhanced Oil Recovery
EOR	— End of Record
EOT	— Emergency Operations Team
EOTR	— Eastern Ozone Transport Region
EOY	— End of Year
EP	— Electrophotographic
EP	— Emergency Preparedness
EP	— Environmental Planner
EP	— Environmental Profiles
EP	— Essential Power
EP	— Execution Planning
EP	— External Programs
EP	— Extraction Procedure
EP TOX	— Extraction Procedure for Toxicity Characteristics
EPA	— Environmental Protection Agency
EPAA	— Environmental Programs Assistance Act
EPAAR	— Environmental Protection Agency Acquisition Regulations
EPACT	— Environmental Protection Agency's Control Techniques
EPC	— Economic Policy Council
EPCA	— Energy Policy and Conservation Act

EPCRA	— Emergency Planning and Community Right-to-Know Act
EPCRTKA	— Emergency Planning and Community Right-to-Know Act
EPDS	— Electronic Processing and Dissemination System
EPG	— Exercise Planning Group
EPI	— Environmental Policy Institute
EPIC	— Environmental Photographic Interpretation Center
EPIP	— Emergency Plan Implementing Procedure
EPLAN	— Emergency Plan
EPM	— Environmental Planning and Management
EPM	— Environmental Project Manager
EPM	— Environmental Protection Management
EPMPs	— Emergency Preparedness Management Plans
EPNL	— Effective Perceived Noise Level
EPO	— Emergency Planning Office
EPO	— Estuarine Programs Office (NOAA)
EPOW	— Extraction Procedure for Oily Wastes
EPPRP	— Emergency Planning, Preparedness, and Response Program
EPRI	— Electric Power Research Institute
EPS	— Emergency Preparedness Staff (OSWER)
EPTC	— Extraction Procedure Toxicity Characteristic
EPZ	— Emergency Planning Zone
eq	— Equal
EQ	— Environmental Qualification
EQB	— Environmental Quality Board
EQC	— Environmental Quality Council
ER	— Electro-Refining
ER	— Epidemiologic Research
ER	— Office of Energy Research
ER	— Office of Environmental Restoration and Waste Management
ERA	— Economic Regulatory Agency
ERA	— Equal Rights Amendment
ERAB	— Energy Research Advisory Board

ERAD	— Economic and Regulatory Analysis Division (OPPE)
ERAMS	— Environmental Radiation Ambient Monitoring System
ERAP	— Emergency Readiness Assurance Plan
ERB	— Environmental Review Board
ERC	— Emergency Response Commission
ERC	— Emission Reduction Credits
ERC	— Environmental Research Center
ERCS	— Emergency Response Cleanup Services
ERCS	— Emergency Response Contract Services
ERCWS	— Emergency Raw Cooling Water System
ERD	— Emergency Response Division (OSWER)
ERDA	— Energy Research and Development Administration
ERDDAA	— Environmental Research Development and Demonstration Authorization Act of 1978
ERGLIA	— Environmental Research Geographic Location Information Act
ERL	— Emergency Reference Levels
ERL	— Environmental Research Laboratory (ORD)
ERNS	— Emergency Response and Notification System
ERO	— Emergency Response Officer
ERO	— Emergency Response Organization
ERP	Emergency Response Program
ERP	— Enforcement Response Policy
ERPA	— Emergency Response Planning Area
ERPG	— Emergency Response Planning Guidelines
ERRD	— Emergency and Remedial Response Division
ERRIS	— Emergency and Remedial Response Information System
ERS	— Economic Research Service
ERT	— Emergency Response Team
ERT	— Environmental Response Team
ERTA	— Energy Research and Technology Administration
ERTAQM	— ERT Air Quality Model
ERV	— Emergency Relief Valve

ERWM	— Environment Restoration and Waste Management
ES	— Enforcement Strategy
ES	— Engineering Staff (OAR)
ES	— Ethnological Society
ES&H	— Environment, Safety, and Health Program
ESA	— Ecological Society of America
ESA	— Endangered Species Act
ESA	— Environmentally Sensitive Area
ESA	— Environmental Site Assessment
ESA	— Environmental Site Audit
ESA	— Extra Services Agreement
ESC	— Endangered Species Committee
ESCA	— Electron Spectroscopy for Chemical Analysis
ESCM	— Erosion and Sedimentation Control Measures
ESD	— Emergency Shutdown Device
ESD	— Emission Standards Division (OAR)
ESECA	— Energy Supply and Environmental Coordination Act of 1974
ESEA	— Elementary and Secondary Education Act
ESF	— Engineered Safety Features
ESFAS	— Engineered Safety Features Actuation System
ESH	— Environmental Safety and Health
ESMS	— Emission Standards for Moving Sources
ESO	— Enforcement Specialist Office (NEIC)
ESP	— Electrostatic Precipitators
ESP	— Environmentally Sound Prevention [activities]
ESS	— Engagement Simulation Systems
EST	— Emergency Service Team
ESW	— Emergency Service Water
ET	— Event Trend
ETA	— Energy Tax Act
ETA	— Estimated Time of Arrival
ETB	— End of Transmission Block

ETD	— Economics and Technology Division
ETD	— Estimated Time of Departure
ETEC	— Energy Technology Engineering Center (Canoga Park)
ETI	— Estimated Time of Intercept
ETIC	— Estimated Time for Completion
ETO	— Energy Technology Office
ETP	— Emissions Trading Policy
ETS	— Environmental Tobacco Smoke
ETSS	— Extended Training Service Specialist
ETXT	— End of Text Transmission
EUSC	— Effective United States Controlled Shipping
eV	— Electronvolt
EW	— Early Warning
EWCC	— Environmental Workforce Coordinating Committee
EWM	— Environmental and Waste Management
EWS	— Early Warning System
ExEx	— Expected Exceedance
EXORD	— Execute Order
EZ	— Extraction Zone

F

°F	— Degrees Fahrenheit
F/V	— Fishing Vessel
FA	— Feasibility Assessment
FAA	— Federal Aviation Administration
FAA	— Foreign Assistance Act
FACA	— Federal Advisory Committee Act
FACOSH	— Federal Advisory Council on Occupational Safety and Health
FAD	— Feasible Arrival Date
FAE	— Fuel Air Explosive

FALD	— Federal Agency Liaison Division (OEA)
FAME	— Framework for Achieving Managerial Excellence
FAPES	— Force Augmentation Planning and Execution System
FAR	— Facility Audit Report
FAR	— Federal Acquisition Regulations
FAR	— Federal Aviation Regulation
FAR	— Floor Area Ratio
FAS	— Frontera Audubon Society
FASB	— Financial Accounting Standards Board
FAST	— Fugitive Assessment Sampling Train
FATES	— FIFRA and TSCA Enforcement System
FAX	— Facsimile
FBC	— Fluidized Bed Combustion
FBI	— Federal Bureau of Investigation
FCA	— Flood Control Act of 1936
FCF	— Fisherman's Contingency Fund
FCs	— Fluorocarbons
FC	— Field Circular
FCC	— Federal Communications Commission
FCCU	— Fluid Catalytic Cracking Unit
FCO	— Federal Coordinating Officer
FCO	— Forms Control Officer
FCPCS	— Federal Compliance with Pollution Control Standards
FCQAS	— Financial Compliance and Quality Assurance Staff
FD	— Fire Department
FDA	— Food and Drug Administration
FDA	— Fuel Distribution Analyzer
FDAA	— Federal Disaster Assistance Administration
FDBM	— Functional Data Base Manager
FDC	— Fire Direction Center
FDF	— Fundamentally Different Factor
FDI	— Fault Detection Isolation

FDIC	— Federal Deposit Insurance Corporation
FDL	— Fast Deployment Logistics
FDO	— Fee Determination Official
FDO	— Flexible Deterrent Option
FDOS	— Floppy Disk Operating System
FDS	— Fault Detection System
FDSS	— Fault Detection Subsystem
Fe	— Periodic Element, Iron
FE	— Fugitive Emissions
FEC	— Federal Executive Council
FED-STD	— Federal Standard
FEDS	— Federal Energy Data System
FEFGC	— Fuel Element Failure Gas Chromatograph
FEGLI	— Federal Employee Group Life Insurance
FEI	— Federal Executive Institute
FEIS	— Final Environmental Impact Statement
FEIS	— Fugitive Emissions Information System
FEL	— Frank Effect Level
FEMA	— Federal Emergency Management Agency
FEPCA	— Federal Environmental Pesticides Control Act
FERA	— Federal Emergency Relief Administration
FERC	— Federal Energy Regulatory Commission
FERS	— Federal Employees Retirement System
FES	— Factor Evaluation System
FET	— Foundation on Economic Trends
FEV	— Forced Expiratory Volume
FEVI	— Front End Volatility Index
FEW	— Federally Employed Women
FEWS	— Followup Early Warning System
Ff	— Fatigue Correction Factor
FF	— Federal Facilities
FFAR	— Fuel and Fuel Additive Registration

FFCA	— Federal Facilities Compliance Agreement
FFCS	— Federal Facilities Compliance Staff (OEA)
FFDCA	— Federal Food Drug and Cosmetic Act
FFE	— Failed Fuel Element
FFF	— Firm Financial Facility
FFFSG	— Fossil Fuel Fired Steam Generator
FFIS	— Federal Facilities Information System
FFP	— Firm Fixed Price
FFTF	— Fast Flux Test Facility
FFTF	— Future Framework Task Force
FGD	— Flue Gas Desulfurization
FGMDSS	— Future Global Maritime Distress and Safety System
FHA	— Federal Highway Administration
FHA	— Federal Housing Administration
FHA	— Federal Housing Authority
FHAR	— Fire Hazard Analysis Report
FHSA	— Federal Hazardous Substances Act
FHWA	— Federal Highway Administration
FIANG	— Federal Inspector for Alaska Natural Gas
FIC	— Federal Information Center
FICA	— Federal Insurance Contributions Act
FICI	— Failed Instrument Component Inspection
FID	— Flame Ionization Detector
FID	— Foreign Internal Defense
FIDAF	— Foreign Internal Defense Augmentation Force
FIFO	— First In/First Out
FIFRA	— Federal Insecticide, Fungicide and Rodenticide Act
FIND	— Facility Index Directory (OIRM)
FINDS	— Facilities Index System
FIP	— Federal Information Plan
FIP	— Final Implementation Plan
FIPS	— Federal Information Procedures System

FIRCAP	— Foreign Intelligence Requirements Capabilities and Priorities
FISS	— Foreign Intelligence Security Service
FIST	— Fire Support Team
FIT	— Field Investigation Team
FIXe	— Navigational Fix Error
FLM	— Federal Land Manager
FLOCHK	— An abbreviation for a computer code
FLO/FLO	— Float On/Float Off
FLP	— Flash Point
FLPMA	— Federal Land Policy and Management Act
FLRA	— Federal Labor Relations Authority
FLRC	— Federal Labor Relations Council
FLSA	— Fair Labor Standards Act
FLTCINC	— Fleet Commander in Chief
FLTSAT	— Fleet Satellite
FLTSATCOM	— Fleet Satellite Communications
FM	— Frequency Modulation
FMAS	— Foreign Media Analysis Subsystem
FMC	— Federal Maritime Commission
FMCS	— Federal Mediation and Conciliation Service
FMD	— Financial Management Division (OARM)
FMEA	— Failure Mode and Effect Analysis
FMFIA	— Federal Managers Financial Integrity Act
FMFP	— Foreign Military Financing Program
FMFRP	— Fleet Marine Force Reference Publication
FML	— Flexible Membrane Liner
FMO	— Financial Management Officer
FMP	— Facility Management Plan
FMPC	— Feed Materials Production Center
FMS	— Financial Management System
FMSD	— Facilities Management and Services Division (OARM)
FMVCP	— Federal Motor Vehicle Control Program

FNOC — Fleet Numerical Oceanographic Command

FNS — Foreign Nation Support

FO — Facilities Office

FO — Fiber Optic

FOAE — Finding of Adverse Effect

FOC — Full Operational Capability

FOD — Foreign Object Damage

FOE — Friends of the Earth

FOF — Force-on-Force Performance Test

FOI — Freedom of Information

FOIA — Freedom of Information Act

FOIU — Fiber Optic Interface Unit

FONAE — Finding of No Adverse Effect

FONSI — Finding of No Significant Impact (NEPA)

FORAST — Forest Response to Anthropogenic Stress

FORSCOM — [U.S. Army] Forces Command

FORTRAN — Formula Translation

FOS — Fisheries Organization Society

FOSD — Field Operations and Support Division (OAR)

FOUO — For Official Use Only

FOV — Field of View

FP — Fine Particulate

FP — Fission Products

FPA — Federal Pesticide Act

FPA — Forest Products Association

FPASA — Federal Property and Administrative Services Act of 1949

FPC — Federal Power Commission

FPC — Field Press Censorship

FPD — Flame Photometric Detector

FPEIS — Fine Particulate Emissions Information System

FPI — Federal Prison Industries

FPM — Federal Personnel Manual

FPRS	— Federal Program Resources Statement
FPTS	— Fire Protection Tracking System
Fr	— French
FR	— Federal Register
FR	— Final Report
FR	— Final Rulemaking
FRA	— Federal Register Act
FRACAS	— Failure Rating Analysis and Corrective Action System
FRASE	— Factor Relationship and Sequence of Events
FRC	— Federal Records Center
FRC	— Federal Response Center
FRCC	— Front Range Community College
FRD	— Facility Requirements Division (OW)
FRDS	— Federal Reporting Data System
FREDS	— Flexible Regional Emissions Data System
FRERP	— Federal Radiological Emergency Response Plan
FRGT	— Fast Response Gamma Thermometer
FRM	— Federal Reference Methods
FRMAC	— Federal Radiological Monitoring and Assessment Center
FRMAP	— Federal Radiological Monitoring and Assessment Plan
FRN	— Final Rulemaking Notice
FRO	— Federal Register Office
FRRRPA	— Forest and Rangeland Renewable Resources Planning Act
FRS	— Formal Reporting System
FRT	— First Response Team
FRTIG	— Federal Retirement Thrift Investment Board
FS	— Feasibility Study
FS	— File Server
FS	— Forest Service
FSA	— Fire Support Area
FSA	— Food Security Act
FSAR	— Final Safety Analysis Report

FSB	— Forward Staging Report
FSC	— Fire Support Coordinator
FSCC	— Fire Support Coordination Center
FSCL	— Fire Support Coordination Line
FSE	— Fire Support Element
FSF	— Fuel Supply Facility
FSH	— Fuel Sleeve Housing
FSIP	— Federal Service Impasse Panel
FSN	— Federal Stock Number
FSO	— Fire Support Officer
FSS	— Federal Supply Schedule
FSSD	— Facilities and Support Service Division
FST	— Field Sampling Team
FSW	— Feet of Seawater
FSWA	— Federation of Sewage Works Associations
ft	— Foot or Feet
FTA	— Fault Tree Analysis
FTA	— Federal Transit Act
FTAAE	— Failure to Avoid Adverse Effects
FTC	— Federal Trade Commission
FTE	— Full Time Equivalent
FTP	— Federal Test Procedure
FTRG	— Fleet Tactical Readiness Group
FTS	— Federal Telecommunications System
FTS	— File Transfer System
FTT	— Full Time Temporary
FTX	— Field Training Exercise
FUA	— Fuel Use Act
FUDS	— Formerly Utilized Defense Sites
FURS	— Federal Underground (Injection Control) Reporting System
FUSRAP	— Formerly Utilized Sites Remedial Actions Program
FVC	— Filtered Vented Containment

FVC	— Forced Vital Capacity
FVMP	— Federal Visibility Monitoring Program
FVR	— Fuels and Vehicles Research
FW	— Feedwater
FW	— Weather Correction Factor
FWA	— Flow Weighted Average (Delta T)
FWC	— Functional Work Center
FWCA	— Fish and Wildlife Conservation Act of 1980
FWP	— Federal Women's Program (OCR)
FWPAC	— Federal Women's Program Advisory Committee (OCR)
FWPCA	— Federal Water Pollution Control Act
FWPCA	— Federal Water Pollution Control Administration
FWQA	— Federal Water Quality Association
FWRC	— Federal Water Resources Council
FWS	— Fish and Wildlife Service (DOI)
FWSRSA	— Farmington Wild and Scenic River Study Act
FY	— Fiscal Year
FYDP	— Future Years Defense Program
FZ	— Flow Zone

G

g	— gram
G/A	— Ground to Air
G-M	— Geiger-Muellor Counters
GA	— Geographical Association
GA	— Geologists Association
GA	— Grant Agreement
GAA	— General Agency Agreement
GAAP	— Generally Accepted Accounting Principles
GAC	— Granular Activated Carbon

GAD — Grants Administration Division (OARM)

gal — Gallon

GAO — Government Accounting Office

GB — Group Buffer

GB — Sarin (Nerve Agent)

gbh — Grams per Brake Horsepower Hour

GBL — Government Bill of Lading

GC — Gas Chromatography

GC — General Counsel

GC — Geneva Convention

GC^3A — Global Command, Control, and Communications Assessment

GC^4A — Global Command, Control, Communications, and Computer Assessment

GCEP — Gas Centrifuge Enrichment Plant

GCGLD — Grants, Contracts, and General Law Division

GCS — Ground Control Station

GD — Soman (Nerve Agent)

GDB — Genome Database

GDC — General Design Criteria

GDHS — Ground Data Handling System

GDIP — General Defense Intelligence Program

GDP — Gaseous Diffusion Plant

GDP — General Defense Plan

GDSS — Global Decision Support System

GE — General Emergency

GEI — Geographic Enforcement Initiative

GEMS — Global Environmental Monitoring System

GEMS — Graphical Exposure Modeling System

GENSER — General Service (Message)

GENTEXT — General Text

GEOCODES — Geographic Codes

GEOFILE — Geographic Location File

GEOIS	— Geographic Information System
GEOLOC	— Geographic Location Code
GEOREF	— Geographic Reference System
GEP	— Good Engineering Practice
GERT	— Graphical Evaluation and Review Technique
GET	— General Employee Training
GF	— General File
GFE	— Government-Furnished Equipment
GFP	— Government-Furnished Property
GGNS	— Grarid Guff Nuclear Station
GHz	— Gigahertz
GI	— Gastrointestinal
GIC	— International Loading Gauge
GICS	— Grant Information and Control System
GIDEP	— Government Industry Data Exchange Program
GIGO	— Garbage-In, Garbage-Out
GIS	— Geographical Information System
GIS	— Geoscience Information Society
GIS	— Global Indexing System
GIS	— Guidelines Implementation Staff (OW)
GJPO	— Grand Junction Projects Office
GLC	— Gas Liquid Chromatography
GLC	— Great Lakes Commission
GLERL	— Great Lakes Environmental Research Laboratory
GLFC	— Great Lakes Fishery Commission
GLNPO	— Great Lakes National Program Office
GLP	— Good Laboratory Practices
GLWQA	— Great Lakes Water Quality Agreement
GMA	— Grocery Manufacturers Association
GMCC	— Global Monitoring for Climatic Change
GMDSS	— Global Maritime Distress and Safety System
GMR	— Graduated Mobilization Response

GMT	— Greenwich Mean Time
GNP	— Gross National Product
GOCM	— Goals, Objectives, Commitments and Measures
GOCO	— Government Owned, Contractor Operated
GOES	— Geostationary Operational Environmental Satellite
GOGO	— Government Owned, Government Operated
GOMEET	— Goals, Objectives, Means, Ends, Effects and Timing
GOPO	— Government Owned, Privately Operated
GP	— Graphic Panel
GP	— Group
gpd	— Gallons per Day
GPO	— Government Printing Office
GPP	— General Plant Projects
GPS	— Global Positioning System
GPS	— Groundwater Protection Strategy
GPU	— Grapper Pick Up
gr	— grain
GRCA	— Ground Reference Coverage Area
GRGL	— Groundwater Residue Guidance Level
GRPA	— Genesee River Protection Act of 1989
GS	— General Schedule
GS	— Ground Speed
GSA	— General Services Administration
GSA	— Geothermal Steam Act of 1970
GSA	— Government in the Sunshine Act
GSDB	— Geonome Sequence Database
GSE	— Ground Support Equipment
GSM	— Ground Station Module
GSMFC	— Gulf States Marine Fisheries Compact
gt	— Gross Tons
GTF	— Grout Treatment Facility
GTM	— Gang Temperature Monitor

GTN	— Global Transportation Network
GTN	— Global Trends Network
GTR	— Government Transportation Request
GVP	— Gasoline Vapor Pressure
GVR	— Gas Volume Ratio
GVW	— Gross Vehicle Weight
GVWR	— Gross Vehicle Weight Rating
GW	— Groundwater
GW	— Guerrilla Warfare
GWC	— Global Weather Central
GWI	— Ground Water Institute
GWM	— Ground Water Monitoring
GWPMS	— Ground Water Policy and Management Staff
GWPS	— Ground Water Protection Standard
GWTF	— Ground Water Task Force (OSWER)

H

H&I	— Harassing and Interdicting
H&SM	— Health and Safety Manual, DOE PUB-3000
H_2O	— Water
H_2O_2	— Hydrogen Peroxide
H_2S	— Hydrogen Sulfide
HA	— Hatch Act
HA	— Hazard Assessment
HA	— Health Advisory
HA	— Humanitarian Assistance
HABS	— Historic American Building Survey
HAC	— Hazards Assessment Center
HAD	— Health Assessment Document
HAER	— Historic American Engineering Record

HAP   — Hazardous Air Pollutant

HAPEMS   — Hazardous Air Pollutants Enforcement Management

HAPPS   — Hazardous Air Pollutant Prioritization System

HARM   — High-Speed Anti-Radiation Missile

HATREMS   — Hazardous and Trace Emissions Monitoring System

HATS   — Hazard Abatement Tracking System

HAZ   — Hazardous Cargo

HazMat   — Hazardous Material

HAZRAP   — Hazardous Waste Remedial Actions Program

HB   — Health Benefits

HBEP   — Hispanic and Black Employment Programs

HBS   — Horizontal Bracing Systems

HC   — Hazardous Constituents

HC   — Hydrocarbons

HCA   — Hazardous Communications Act

HCA   — Humanitarian and Civic Assistance

HCCPD   — Hexachlorocyclopentadiene

HCF   — Hot Channel Factor

HCl   — Hydrogen Chloride

HCP   — Hardcopy Printer

HCP   — Hydrothermal Coal Process

HCPWT   — House Committee on Public Works and Transportation

HCS   — Hazard Communication Standard

HCS   — Helicopter Coordination Section

HD   — Harmonic Distortion

HDC   — Helicopter Direction Center

HDD   — Heavy Duty Diesel

HDGV   — Heavy Duty Gasoline (Powered) Vehicle

HDP   — High Delta Pressure

HDPE   — High Density Polyethylene

HDV   — Heavy Duty Vehicle

HE   — High Explosives

HE	— Human Error
HEAL	— Human Exposure Assessment Location
HECC	— House Energy and Commerce Committee
HED	— Hazard Evaluation Division (OPTS)
HEEP	— Health and Environmental Effects Profile
HEFOE	— Hydraulic Electrical Fuel Oxygen Engine
HEI	— Health Effects Institute
HELO	— Helicopter
HEM	— Human Exposure Model
HEMP	— High-Altitude Electromagnetic Pulse
HEMTT	— Heavy Expanded Mobile Tactical Truck
HEP	— Hispanic Employment Program (OCR)
HEPA	— High Efficiency Particulate Air Filters
HEPC	— Hydro-Electric Power Commission
HERD	— Health and Environmental Review Division (OPTS)
HERF	— Hazards of Electromagnetic Radiation to Fuel
HERL	— Health Effects Research Laboratory (ORD)
HERO	— Hazards of Electromagnetic Radiation to Ordnance
HERP	— Hazards of Electromagnetic Radiation to Personnel
HET	— Heavy Equipment Transporter
HEV	— Hybrid Electric Vehicle
HF	— High Frequency
HF	— Hydrogen Fluoride
HFCVSTP	— Hydrogen Fuel Cell Vehicle Study and Test Program
Hg	— Mercury
HHE	— Human Health and the Environment
HHS	— Health and Human Services
HI-VOL	— High Volume Sampler
HICAP	— High-Capacity Firefighting Foam Station
HIPO	— High Potential Incidents
HIWAY	— Line Source Model for Gaseous Pollutants
HIWS	— High-Level Waste and Standards

HLC	— High Level Caves
HLFM	— High Level Flux Monitor
HLLW	— High-Level Liquid Waste
HLW	— High-Level Wastes
HLZ	— Helicopter Landing Zone
HM	— Health Monitoring
HMIS	— Hazardous Materials Information System
HMMWV	— High Mobility Multipurpose Wheeled Vehicle
HMS	— Highway Mobile Source
HMT	— Hazardous Materials Table
HMTA	— Hazardous Materials Transportation Act
HMTR	— Hazardous Materials Transportation Regulations
HMW	— Health, Morale, and Welfare
HN	— Host Nation
HNS	— Host Nation Support
HOB	— Height of Burst
HOCs	— Halogenated Organic Compounds
HON	— Hazardous Organic NESHAPS
HOV	— High Occupancy Vehicle
HP	— Health Physics
HP	— Horsepower
HPA	— High Power Amplifier
HPCI	— High-Pressure Coolant Injection
HPCS	— High-Pressure Core Spray
HPIS	— High-Pressure Injection System
HPLC	— High-Performance Liquid Chromatography
HPMA	— Hardwood Plywood Manufacturers Association
HPMSK	— High-Priority Mission Support Kit
HPPP	— High-Pressure Pump Pad
HPRS	— High-Pressure Recirculation System
HPSI	— High-Pressure Spray (Post-Accident) Injection
HPSR	— High-Pressure Spray (Post-Accident) Recirculation

HPSW	— High-Pressure Service Water
HPV	— High-Priority Violator
hr	— hour
HQ	— Headquarters
HQCDO	— Headquarters Case Development Officer
HQDA	— Headquarters, Department of the Army
HQMC	— Headquarters, Marine Corps
HRC	— Human Resources Council
HRM	— Hoisting and Rigging Manual
HRPS	— High Risk Point Sources
HRS	— Hazard Ranking System
HRS	— Horizon Reference System
HRSD	— Hazardous Response Support Division
HRT	— Hostage Rescue Team
HRUP	— High Risk Urban Problem
HS	— Hydrogen Sulfide
HSA	— Historic Sites Act of 1935
HSC	— Health Services Command
HSDB	— Hazardous Substance Data Base
HSE	— Health, Safety, and Environment
HSED	— Hazardous Site Evaluation Division (OSWER)
HSEP	— Hospital Surgical Expansion Package (USAF)
HSL	— Hazardous Substance List
HSP	— Health and Safety Practices
HSRI	— Highway Safety Research Institute
HSS	— Health Service Support
HST	— Helicopter Support Team
HSWA	— Hazardous and Solid Waste Amendments
HT	— Hydrothermally Treated
HTA	— High Temperature Alarm
HTGR	— High Temperature Gas-Cooled Reactor
HTO	— Hazardous Tritium Oxides

HTP	— High Temperature and Pressure
HTS	— High Temperature Superconductivity
HTSA	— Highway Traffic Safety Administration
HU	— Hospital Unit
HUD	— Department of Housing and Urban Development
HUD	— Heads-Up Display
HUDA	— Housing and Urban Development Act
HUMINT	— Human Resources Intelligence
HUS	— Hardened Unique Storage
HVAA	— High-Value Airborne Assets
HVAC	— Heating, Ventilation, and Air Conditioning
HVIO	— High-Volume Industrial Organics
HW	— Hazardous Waste
HWDMS	— Hazardous Waste Data Management System (OSWER)
HWED	— Hazardous Waste Enforcement Division (OECM)
HWERL	— Hazardous Waste Engineering Research Laboratory
HWFW	— Half Wave/Full Wave
HWGTF	— Hazardous Waste Groundwater Task Force
HWLT	— Hazardous Waste Land Treatment
HWM	— Hazardous Waste Management
HWM	— High Water Mark
HWMD	— Hazardous Waste Management Division
HWRTF	— Hazardous Waste Restrictions Task Force (OW)
HWSS	— Hazardous Waste and Superfund Staff (ORD)
HWTC	— Hazardous Waste Treatment Council
HWVP	— Hanford Waste Vitrification Program
HX	— Heat Exchangers
Hz	— Hertz

I

I/E	— Inspection and Evaluation
I/M	— Inspection and Maintenance
I/O	— Input/Output
I&M	— Inspection and Maintenance
I&W	— Indication and Warning
IA	— Incident Actions
IA	— Information Association
IA	— Initial Assessment
IAAC	— Interagency Assessment Advisory Committee
IAC	— Instrumentation and Control
IAD	— Internal Audit Division
IADB	— Inter-American Defense Board
IADS	— Integrated Air Defense System
IAEA	— International Atomic Energy Agency
IAG	— Interagency Agreement
IAP	— Indoor Air Pollution
IAP	— Incentive Awards Program
IAP	— International Airport
IAPCT	— International Air Pollution Control Technologies
IAPMO	— International Association of Plumbing and Mechanical Officials
IARC	— International Agency for Research on Cancer
IATDB	— Interim Air Toxics Data Base
IAW	— In Accordance With
IBA	— Industrial Biotechnology Association
IBR	— Incorporation by Reference
IC	— Incident Commander
IC	— Incident Control
IC	— Isolation Condenser
ICAD	— Individual Concern and Deficiency

ICAO	— International Civil Aviation Organization
ICAP	— Inductively Coupled Argon Plasma
ICBE	— International Commission on Biological Effects
ICBM	— Intercontinental Ballistic Missile
ICBO	— International Conference of Building Officials
ICC	— Interstate Commerce Commission
ICE	— Industrial Combustion Emissions (Model)
ICE	— Internal Combustion Engine
ICECON	— Control of Ice Information
ICEDEFOR	— United States Forces, Iceland
ICIHSOP	— International Convention Relating to Intervention on the High Seas in Cases of Oil Pollution Casualties of 1969
ICMA	— International City Managers Association
ICO	— Incident Command Organization
ICON	— Imagery Communications and Operations Node
ICP	— Incident Command Post
ICP	— Incident Control Point
ICP	— Inductively Coupled Plasma
ICP/MS	— Inductive Coupled Plasma/Mass Spectrometer
ICPP	— Idaho Chemical Processing Plant
ICR	— Information Collection Request
ICRC	— International Committee of the Red Cross
ICRE	— Ignitable, Corrosive, Reactive, and/or Effluent
ICS	— Incident Command System
ICS	— Institute for Chemical Studies
ICS	— Intermittent Control Strategies
ICS	— Intermittent Control System (CAA)
ICS	— Internal Communications System
ICSAR	— Interagency Committee on Search and Rescue
ICU	— Interface Control Unit
ICWM	— Institute for Chemical Waste Management
ID	— Idaho Operations Office

ID	— Identification
IDAD	— Internal Defense and Development
IDB	— Integrated Data Base
IDCA	— International Development Cooperation Agency
IDCOR	— Industry Degraded Core Rulemaking Program
IDDF	— Intermediate Data Distribution Facility
IDHS	— Intelligence Data Handling System
IDLH	— Immediately Dangerous to Life and Health
IDS	— Integrated Database
IDS	— Interface Design Standards
IDSS	— Interoperability Decision Support System
IE	— Industrial Engineering
IE	— Office of Inspection and Enforcement
IEAEMM	— International Energy Agency Emergency Management Manual
IED	— Improved Explosives Devices
IEEE	— Institute of Electrical and Electronic Engineers
IEL	— Illustrative Evaluation Scenario
IEMD	— Integrated Environmental Management Division (OPPE)
IEMP	— Integrated Environmental Management Project
IEPD	— Industrial and Extractive Processes Division (ORD)
IES	— Institute for Environmental Studies
IFB	— Invitation for Bid
IFC	— Internal Fission Counter
IFCAM	— Industrial Fuel Choice Analysis Model
IFI	— Inspector Followup Items
IFMIF	— International Fusion Materials Irradiation Facility
IFPP	— Industrial Fugitive Process Particulate
IG	— Inspector General
IG-EV	— Interagency Group on Energy Vulnerability
IGA	— Intergovernmental Agreement
IGCC	— Integrated Gasification Combined Cycle
IGCI	— Industrial Gas Cleaning Institute

IGD	— Inspector General Division
IGFM	— Internal Gamma Flux Monitor
IGPS	— Global Positioning System
IGSM	— Interim Ground Station Module
IH	— Industrial Hygiene
IH	— Inner Housing
IH&S	— Industrial Hygiene and Safety
IHA	— Integrated Hazards Assessments
IHE	— Insensitive High Explosives
IHSA	— Intervention on the High Seas Act
III	— Incapacity, Illness, or Injury
IIR	— Imaging Infrared
IIRMP	— Interim Indoor Radon Measurement Protocol
IIS	— Inflationary Impact Statement
IJC	— International Joint Commission
IJC^3S	— Initial Joint Command and Control Communications System
IKC	— In-Kind Contribution
ILRT	— Integrated Leak Rate Test
ILS	— Integrated Logistics Support
ILS	— Intergovernmental Liaison Staff
ILSA	— Interstate Land Sales (Full Disclosure) Act
IMA	— Individual Mobilization Augmentee
IMC	— Instrument Meteorological Conditions
IMINT	— Imaginary Intelligence
IMIS	— Integrated Management Information System
IMD	— Information Management Division (OPTS)
IMM	— Intersection Midblock Model
IMO	— International Maritime Organization
IMOSAR	— IMO Search and Rescue Manual
IMP	— Implementation
IMPACT	— Integrated Model of Plumes and Atmosphere in Complex Terrain
IMPROVE	— Interagency Monitoring of Protected Visual Emissions

IMS	— Information Management Staff (OSWER)
IMSD	— Information Management and Services Division
in	— inch
INCNR	— Increment Number
IND	— Improvised Nuclear Device
INEL	— Idaho National Engineering Laboratory
INFOSEC	— Information Security
INMARSAT	— International Maritime Satellite
INPO	— Institute for Nuclear Power Operations
INPUFF	— Gaussian Puff Dispersion Model
INREQ	— Information Request
INST	— In Situ Treatment
INT	— Intermittent
INTAC	— Individual Terrorism Awareness Course
INTACS	— Integrated Tactical Communications System
INTREP	— Intelligence Report
INV	— Invalid
IO	— Immediate Office
IO	— Information Objectives
IO	— Information On-Line
IOAA	— Immediate Office of Assistant Administrator
IOAA	— Independent Offices Appropriation Act of 1952
IOAU	— Input/Output Arithmetic Unit
IOB	— Iron Ore Beneficiation
IOC	— Initial Operational Capability
IOGP	— Independent Oil and Gas Producers
IOM	— Installation, Operation, and Maintenance
IORV	— Inadvertently Opened Relief Valve
IOU	— I Owe You
IOU	— Input/Output Unit
IP	— EIS Implementation Plans
IP	— Inhalable Particulates

IP	— Initial Point
IPA	— Intelligence Production Agency
IPA	— Intergovernmental Personnel Act
IPA	— Intergovernmental Personnel Agreement
IPA	— Interstate Pollution Abatement Notice
IPCA	— Industrial Pest Control Association
IPDS	— Inland Petroleum Distribution System
IPE	— Individual Plant Examination
IPE	— Industrial Plant Equipment
IPL	— Integrated Priority List
IPM	— Inhalable Particulate Matter
IPM	— Integrated Pest Management
IPMPCS	— Integrated Pest Management and Program Coordination Staff
IPP	— Implementation Planning Program
IPP	— Industrial Preparedness Program
IPP	— Integrated Plotting Package
IPRSF	— Interim Protocol for Radon Screening and Followup
IPS	— Illustrative Planning Scenario
IPSP	— Intelligence Priorities for Strategic Planning
IR	— Incident Report
IR	— Information Requirement
IR	— Infrared
IRC	— Internal Revenue Code of 1986
IRC	— International Red Cross
IRDS	— Infrared Detection Set
IREP	— Interim Reliability Evaluation Program
IRG	— Interagency Review Group
IRI	— Industrial Risk Insurers
IRIS	— Instructional Resources Information System
IRIS	— Integrated Risk Information System
IRM	— Interim Remedial Measures (CERCLA)
IRMC	— Interagency Risk Management Council

IRO	— Insulated Uranium Oxide
IRP	— Installation Restoration Program
IRR	— Institute of Resource Recovery
IRR	— Integrated Readiness Report
IRS	— Intergovernmental Relations Staff (OEA)
IRS	— Intermedia Ranking Staff
IRS	— Internal Revenue Service
IRS	— International Referral System
IRSD	— Information and Regulatory Systems Division
IS	— Interim Status
ISA	— Inter-Service Agreement
ISAM	— Indexed Sequential (File) Access Method
ISC	— Industrial Source Complex
ISCL	— Interim Status Compliance Letter
ISCSTM	— Industrial Source Complex Short-Term Model
ISD	— Information Systems Division
ISD	— Instructional System Development
ISD	— Interim Status Document
ISDB	— Integrated Satellite Communications (SATCOM) Database
ISE	— Intelligence Support Element
ISE	— Ion-Specific Electrode
ISES	— International Solar Energy Society
ISF	— International Shipping Federation
ISMAP	— Indirect Source Model for Air Pollution
ISMMP	— Integrated CONUS Medical Mobilization Plan
ISO	— International Standards Organization
ISOO	— Information Security Oversight Office
ISR	— International Society of Radiology
ISRP	— Indirect Source Review Program
ISS	— Information System Staff (ORD)
ISS	— Interim Status Standards
ISSA	— Inter-Service Support Agreement

IST	— In Situ Treatment
IST	— Integrated System Test
ISTEA	— Intermodal Surface Transportation Efficiency Act
ISV	— In Situ Vitrification
ISW	— Institute for Solid Wastes
IT	— Inner Targets
ITAR	— International Traffic in Arms Regulation
ITC	— Interagency Testing Committee
ITC	— International Trade Commission
ITC	— International Transport Commission
ITD	— Industrial Technology Division (OW)
ITD	— Inhalation Toxicology Division
ITDP	— Individual Training and Development Plan
ITF	— Intelligence Task Force
ITF	— Interagency Task Force
ITP	— Individual Training Plan
ITRI	— Inhalation Toxicology Research Institute
ITV	— In-Transit Visibility
ITW/AA	— Integrated Tactical Warning/Attack Assessment
IUCN	— International Union for the Conservation of Nature and Natural Resources
IVTC	— International Visitors and Travel Coordinator
IWC	— In-Stream Waste Concentration (CWA)
IWCP	— Integrated Work Control Program
IWG	— Interagency Working Group
IWS	— Ionizing Wet Scrubber
IWTF	— Inland Waterways Trust Fund
Ix	— Ion Exchange

J

J	— Joule
JAARS	— Joint After-Action Reporting System
JADREP	— Joint Resource Assessment Database Report
JAG	— Judge Advocate General
JAI	— Joint Administrative Instruction
JAIEG	— Joint Atomic Information Exchange Group
JANAP	— Joint Army, Navy, Air Force Publication
JAO	— Joint Area of Operations
JAOC	— Joint Air Operations Center
JAPO	— Joint Area Petroleum Office
JBP	— Joint Blood Program
JBPO	— Joint Blood Program Office
JCAH	— Joint Commission on Accreditation for Hospitals
JCAT	— Joint Crisis Action Team
JCCC	— Joint Communications Control Center
JCCP	— Joint Casualty Collection Point
JCL	— Job Control Language
JCMC	— Joint Crisis Management Capability
JCMEB	— Joint Civil-Military Engineering Board
JCN	— Joint Communications Network
JCS	— Joint Chiefs of Staff
JCSC	— Joint Communications Satellite Center
JCSE	— Joint Communications Support Element
JCSM	— Joint Chiefs of Staff Memorandum
JD	— Department of Justice
JDC	— Joint Doctrine Center
JDD	— Joint Doctrine Division
JEC	— Joint Economic Committee
JEL	— Joint Electronic Library

JEM	— Joint Exercise Manual
JEPES	— Joint Engineer Planning and Execution System
JFAST	— Joint Flow and Analysis System Test
JFIP	— Japanese Facilities Improvement Project
JFMU	— Joint Force Meteorological and Oceanographic Forecast Unit
JFTR	— Joint Federal Travel Regulations
JFUB	— Joint Facilities Utilization Board
JIB	— Joint Information Bureau
JIC	— Joint Intelligence Center
JIEO	— Joint Interoperability Engineering Organization
JILE	— Joint Intelligence Liaison Element (CIA)
JIMPP	— Joint Industrial Mobilization Planning Process
JIOP	— Joint Interface Operational Procedures
JLC	— Justification for Limited Competition
JLOTS	— Joint Logistics Over-the-Shore
JLRSA	— Joint Long-Range Strategic Appraisal
JMAS	— Joint Manpower Automation System
JMC	— Joint Movement Center
JMO	— Joint Force Meteorological and Oceanographic Officer
JMO	— Joint Maritime Operations
JMP	— Joint Manpower Program
JMRO	— Joint Medical Regulating Office
JMTG	— Joint Military Terminology Group
JNACC	— Joint Nuclear Accident Coordination Center
JNCP	— Justification for Noncompetitive Procurement
JO	— Judicial Officers
JOA	— Joint Operations Area
JOC	— Joint Operations Center
JOFOC	— Justification for Other than Full and Open Competition
JOGS	— Joint Operation Graphics System
JOPES	— Joint Operation Planning and Execution System
JOTS	— Joint Operational Tactical System

JP	— Joint Publication
JPA	— Joint Permitting Agreement
JPD	— Joint Planning Document
JPEC	— Joint Planning and Execution Community
JPERSTAT	— Joint Personnel Status and Casualty Report
JPIC	— Joint Public Information Center
JPO	— Joint Petroleum Office
JPT	— Joint Planning Team
JRC	— Joint Reconnaissance Center
JRCC	— Joint Rescue Coordination Center
JRSC	— Joint Rescue Sub-Center
JRTC	— Joint Readiness Training Center
JS	— Joint Staff
JSA	— Job Safety Analysis
JSCAT	— Joint Staff Crisis Action Team
JSCC	— Joint Services Coordination Committee
JSD	— Jackson Structured Design
JSP	— Jackson Structured Programming
JSPD	— Joint Strategic Planning Document
JSPS	— Joint Strategic Planning System
JTA	— Joint Table of Allowances
JTB	— Joint Transportation Board
JTCG-ME	— Joint Technical Coordinating Group for Munitions Effectiveness
JTD	— Joint Table of Distribution
JTF	— Joint Task Force
JTIC	— Joint Transportation Intelligence Center
JTMD	— Joint Table of Mobilization Distribution
JTPA	— Job Training Partnership Act
JTR	— Joint Travel Regulations
JTTP	— Joint Tactics, Techniques, and Procedures
JWG	— Joint Working Group
JWICS	— Joint Worldwide Intelligence Communications System

K
—

K	— Hydraulic Conductivity
K	— Thousand
ºK	— degrees Kelvin
KAL	— Key Assets List
KAPP	— Key Assets Protection Program
kb	— Kilobits
kbps	— Kilobits per Second
KCP	— Kansas City Plant
KEK	— Key Encryption Key
keV	— Kilo Electronvolts
kg	— Kilogram
kg/yr	— Kilograms per Year
kHz	— Kilohertz
km	— Kilometer
KOR	— Knowing of Results
kt	— Kiloton(s)
kt	— Knot (Nautical Miles per Hour)
kV	— Kilovolt
KVG	— Key Variable Generator
kW	— Kilowatt
kWh	— Kilowatt-Hour
KWOC	— Keyword-Out-of-Context

L
—

l	— Liter
L	— Length
LA	— Lead Agent

LAD	— Latest Arrival Date
LAER	— Lowest Achievable Emission Rate
LAMP	— Lake Acidification Mitigation Project
LAN	— Local Area Network
LANL	— Los Alamos National Laboratory
LAO	— Limited Attack Option
LAT	— Latitude
LAW	— Light Antitank Weapon
lb	— Pound
LBL	— Lawrence Berkeley Laboratory
LBPS	— Lead-Based Paint Survey
lbs/year	— Pounds per Year
LC	— Lake Current
LC	— Liaison/Communicator
LC	— Liquid Chromatography
LC	— Locked Closed
LCCA	— Lead Contamination Control Act of 1988
LCCS	— Land Capability Classification System
LCD	— Local Climatological Data
LCE	— Logistics Capability Estimator
LCLO	— Lethal Concentration Low
LCO	— Limiting Condition for Operation
LCRS	— Leachate Control and Removal System
LD	— Lethal Dose
LD	— Light Duty
LD 50	— Low Dose, Fifty Percent Fatality
LDC	— London Dumping Convention
LDD	— Light Duty Diesel
LDIP	— Laboratory Data Integrity Program
LDLO	— Lethal Dose Low
LDPE	— Low Density Polyethylene
LDR	— Low Data Rate

LDRs	— Land Disposal Restrictions
LDRTF	— Land Disposal Restrictions Task Force
LDT	— Light Duty Truck
LDV	— Light Duty Vehicle
LED	— Light Emitting Diode
LEDET	— Law Enforcement Detachment (USCG)
LEGM	— Low Energy Gamma Monitor
LEHR	— Laboratory for Energy-Related Health Research
LEL	— Lower Explosive Limit
LEP	— Laboratory Evaluation Program
LEPC	— Local Emergency Planning Committee
LEPD	— Legal Enforcement Policy Division (OECM)
LER	— Licensee Event Report
LERTCON	— Alert Condition
LES	— Lincoln Laboratories Experimental Satellite
LET	— Linear Energy Transfer
LFA	— Lead Federal Agency
LFL	— Lower Flexibility Limit
LG	— Deputy Chief of Staff for Logistics
LGB	— Laser-Guided Bomb
LGFSTF	— Liquified Gaseous Fuels Spill Test Facility
LGM	— Laser-Guided Missile
LGW	— Laser-Guided Weapon
LHEAA	— Low-Income Home Energy Assistance Act of 1981
LIDAR	— Light Detection and Ranging
LIFO	— Last In/First Out
LIMB	— Limestone Injection Multi-staged Burner
LIMDIS	— Limited Distribution
LKP	— Last Known Position
LLD	— Lower Limit of Detection
LLMW	— Low Level Mixed Waste
LLRW	— Low Level Radioactive Waste

LLW	— Low-Level Radioactive Waste
LLWDDD	— Low Level Waste Disposal Development Demonstration
LMF	— Language Media Format
LMF	— Logical Mainframe
LMFBR	— Liquid-Metal Fast-Breeder Reactor
LMR	— Labor Management Relations
LNEP	— Low Noise Emission Product
LNG	— Liquified Natural Gas
LNO	— Liaison Officer
LNP	— Loss of Normal Power
LNRD	— Land and Natural Resources Division (DOJ)
LO	— Locked Open
LOA	— Lead Operational Authority
LOA	— Letter of Offer and Acceptance
LOAEL	— Lowest-Observed-Adverse-Effect Level
LOC	— Lines of Communications
LOC	— Level of Concern
LOC ACC	— Location Accuracy
LOCA	— Loss of Coolant Accident
LOCV	— Loss of Condenser Vacuum
LOE	— Level of Effort
LOEL	— Lowest-Observed-Effect Level
LOGSAFE	— Logistic Sustainment Analysis and Feasibility Estimator
LOI	— Loss-of-Input
LOIS	— Loss of Interim Status
LONG	— Longitude
LONGZ	— Long-Term Terrain Model
LOOP	— Loss of Offsite Power
LOP	— Line of Position
LOTA	— Loss of Target Accident
LP	— Legislative Proposal
LPCI	— Low-Pressure Coolant Injection

LPCR   — Low-Pressure Cooling Recirculation Phase
LPCS   — Low-Pressure Core Spray
LPG   — Liquified Petroleum Gas
LPI   — Low-Pressure Injection
LPI/D   — Low Probability of Intercept/Detection
lpm   — Liter per Minute
LPP   — Long Plenum Plugs
LPPP   — Low-Pressure Pump Pad
LPRS   — Low-Pressure Recirculation System
LPRSX   — Low-Pressure Recirculation System Heat Exchanger
LPSW   — Low-Pressure Service Water
LPU   — Line Printer Unit
LPV   — Laser-Protective Visor
LQG   — Large Quantity Generator (RCRA)
LRC   — Logistics Readiness Center
LRMS   — Low Resolution Mass Spectroscopy
LRO   — Labor Relations Officer
LRS   — Launch and Recovery Site
LRSA   — Lamprey River Study Act of 1991
LRTAP   — Long Range Transportation of Air Pollution
LS   — Lead Survey
LS/DW   — Life Safety/Disaster Warning
LSA   — Logistic Sustainability Analysis
LSCRA   — Lower Saint Croix River Act of 1972
LSD   — Laboratory Services Division (NEIC)
LSI   — Legal Support Inspection (CWA)
LSL   — Lump Sum Leave
LSO   — Laser Safety Officer
LSPT   — Limited Scope Performance Test
LST   — Low-Solvent Technology
LSV   — Logistics Support Vessel
LT   — Long Ton

LTA	— Less than Adequate
LTCS	— Long-Term Contracting Strategy
LTD	— Land Treatment Demonstration
LTOC	— Landing-Takeoff Cycle
LTOP	— Lease to Purchase
LTTP	— Long-Term Treatment Plan
LTU	— Land Treatment Unit
LUST	— Leaking Underground Storage Tanks
LUT	— Local User Terminal
LVS	— Logistics Vehicle System (USMC)
LVZ	— Low-Velocity Zone
LW	— Leeway
LWC	— Lost Workday Case
LWCFA	— Land and Water Conservation Fund Act of 1965
LWOP	— Lease with Option to Purchase
LWOP	— Leave without Pay
LWR	— Light Water Reactor
LZ	— Landing Zone
LZSA	— Landing Zone Support Area

M

m	— Meter
m/h	— Milliliters per Hour
M/T	— Measurement Tons
M-day	— Mobilization Day
M&O	— Management and Operations
M&R	— Maintenance and Repair
M&T	— Main and Trim
MABs	— Monoclonal Antibodies
MAC	— Management Advisory Committee

MAC — Maximum Allowable Concentration

MACs — Mobile Air Conditioning Society

MADCAP — Model of Advection, Diffusion and Chemistry for Air Pollutants

MAER — Maximum Allowable Emission Rate

MAG — Management Advisory Group

MAIC — Maximum Allowable Increases in Concentrations

MAO — Management and Operating Contractor for DOE Facility

MAP — Mitigation Action Plans

MAP^{3}S — Multistate Atmospheric Power Production Pollution Study

MAPPER — Maintaining, Preparing, and Producing Executive Reports

MAPSIM — Mesoscale Air Pollution Simulation Model

MARAD — Maritime Administration

MARC — Mining and Reclamation Council

MART — Maintenance Analysis and Review Technique

MAS — Military Agency for Standardization

MASF — Mobile Aeromedical Staging Facility

MASH — Mobile Army Surgical Hospital

MASINT — Measurement and Signature Intelligence

MAX — Maximum

Mb — Body Wave Magnitude

MBA — Materials Balance Area

MBBLs — Thousands of Barrels

MBC — Media Briefing Center

MBCA — Migratory Bird Conservation Act of 1929

MBDA — Minority Business Development Agency

MBE — Minority Business Enterprise

MBER — Minority Business Enterprise Representative

MBI — Major Budget Issue

MBO — Management by Objectives

mbs — Megabits per Second

MBTA — Migratory Bird Treaty Act of 1918

MC — Military Community

MC&G	— Mapping, Charting, and Geodesy
MCA	— Manufacturing Chemists Association
MCA	— Maximum Credible Accident
MCAS	— Marine Corps Air Station
MCC	— Motor Control Center
MCCDC	— Marine Corps Combat Development Command
MCD	— Municipal Construction Division (OW)
MCDS	— Management Control Data System
MCL	— Maximum Contaminant Level
MCLG	— Maximum Contaminant Level Goal
MCLS	— Maximum Concentration Limits
MCMG	— Marine Corps Meteorological Group
MCMU	— Mass Core Memory Unit
MCO	— Marine Corps Order
MCP	— Marine Corps Capabilities Plan
MCP	— Municipal Compliance Plan (CWA)
MCU	— Maintenance Communications Unit
MD	— Mail Drop
MD	— Management Division (Regional)
MDA	— Methylenedianilline
MDSD	— Monitoring and Data Support Division (OW)
MDSU	— Mobile Diving and Salvage Unit
MEA	— Munitions Effect Assessment
MED	— Manipulative Electronic Deception
MEDEVAC	— Medical Evacuation
MEDICO	— International Word for Radiomedical Situation
MEDINT	— Medical Intelligence
MEDPES	— Medical Planning and Execution System
MEDREGREP	— Medical Regulating Report
MEDS	— Meteorological Data System
MEDSOM	— Medical Supply, Optical, and Maintenance Unit
MEDSTAT	— Medical Status

MEF	— Major Emitting Facility
MEFS	— Midterm Energy Forecasting System
Meg	— Megabyte
MEK	— Methyl Ethyl Ketone
MEM	— Modal Emission Model
MEP	— Mobile Electric Power
MEP	— Multiple Extraction Procedure
MEPC	— Maritime Environment Protection Committee
MEPS	— Multimedia Environmental Pollutant Assessment System
MEQPT	— Major Equipment
MERL	— Municipal Environmental Research Laboratory
MERSAR	— Merchant Vessel Search and Rescue Manual
MESAR	— Minimum-Essential Security Assistance Requirements
MESOPAC	— Mesoscale Meteorological Preprocessor Program
MESOPLUME	— Mesoscale "Bent Plume" Model
MESS	— Model Evaluation Support System
MET	— Medium Equipment Transporter
METCON	— Control of Meteorological Information
METL	— Mission-Essential Task List
METS	— Metropolitan Emergency Telephone System
METSAT	— Meteorological Satellite
MeV	— Million Electronvolts
MF	— Modifying Factor
MF	— Multi-Frequency
MFBI	— Major Fuel Burning Installation
MFC	— Meteorological and Oceanographic Forecast Center
MFD	— Municipal Facilities Division (OW)
MFL	— Maximum Foreseeable Loss
MFO	— Multinational Force and Observers
MFTB	— Motor Freight Traffic Bureau
MFW	— Main Feedwater
MFWCS	— Main Feedwater and Condensate System

mg	— Milligram
Mg	— Megagram
mg/cm	— Milligram per Centimeter
mg/l	— Milligram per Liter
mg/kg	— Milligram per Kilogram
MG	— Motor Generator
MG-MA	— Motor Generator-Motor Alternator
mgallon	— Million Gallons
MGD	— Millions of Gallons per Day
MgF$_2$	— Magnesium Fluoride
MH	— Man Hours
MHD	— Magnetohydrodynamics
MHE	— Material Handling Equipment
MHW	— Mean High Water
MHz	— Megahertz
MI	— Movement Instructions
MIAC	— Maintenance Information and Control
MIB	— Military Intelligence Board
MIBK	— Methyl Isobutyl Ketone
MIC	— Methyl Isocyanate
MICE	— Management Information Capability for Enforcement
MICROMORT	— One in a Million Chance of Death from Environmental Hazards
MIDSD	— Management Information and Data Systems Division
MILDEP	— Military Department
MILES	— Multiple Integrated Laser Engagement System
MILOC	— Military Oceanography Group
MILSATCOM	— Military Satellite Communications
MILVAN	— Military Van
MIM	— Maintenance Instruction Manual
min	— Minute
MIPS	— Millions of Instructions per Second
MIR	— Maximum Individual Risk

MIS	— Management Information System
MIS	— Medical Information System
MIS	— Mineral Industry Surveys
MIS	— Minority Institutions
MISCAP	— Mission Capability
MISTT	— Midwest Interstate Sulfur Transformation and Transport
MITASK	— Mission Tasking
MITS	— Management Information Tracking System
MJ	— Megajoule
MJCS	— Joint Chiefs of Staff Memorandum
ml	— Milliliter
ML	— Magnitude Local
ML	— Meteorology Laboratory
MLE	— Maximum Likelihood Estimate
MLLA	— Mineral Lands Leasing Act of 1920
MLPP	— Multilevel Precedence and Preemption
MLRC	— Mickey Leland National Urban Air Toxics Research Center
MLRS	— Multiple Launch Rocket System
MLVSS	— Mixed Liquor Volatile Suspended Solids
MLW	— Mean Low Water
mm	— Millimeter
MMAD	— Mass Median Aerodynamic Diameter
MMD	— Mass Median Diameter
MMGRS	— Military Grid Reference System
MMI	— Man/Machine Interface
MMPA	— Mining and Mineral Policy Act of 1970
MMS	— Minerals Management Service (DOI)
MMT	— Million Metric Tons
MNCR	— Material Nonconformance Report
MNS	— Mission Needs Statements
MO	— Moment Magnitude
MO	— Month

MOA	— Memorandum of Agreement
MOAE	— Mitigation of Adverse Effect
MOB	— Main Operations Base
MOBILE	— Mobile Source Emissions Model
MOC	— Margin of Control
MOC	— Margin of Criticality
MOD	— Management and Organization Division (OARM)
MOD	— Manufacturers Operations Division (OAR)
MOD	— Marine Operations Division (OW)
MOD	— Memorandum of Decision
MOD	— Miscellaneous Obligation Document
MOD	— Minister (Ministry) of Defense
MODE	— Transportation Mode
MOE	— Margin of Exposure
MOGAS	— Motor Gasoline
MOI	— Memorandum of Intent
mol	— Mole
mol.wt.	— Mole Weight
MOP	— Memorandum of Policy
MOPP	— Mission-Oriented Protective Posture
MOR	— Memorandum of Record
MORT	— Management Oversight and Risk Tree
MOS	— Management Operations Staff
MOS	— Margin of Safety
MOS	— Military Occupational Specialty
MOU	— Memorandum of Understanding
MOV	— Motor Operated Valves
MP	— Melting Point
MPC	— Maximum Permissible Concentration
MPE	— Maximum Permissible Exposure
MPED	— Maximum Permissible Exposure Limit
MPEL	— Measures to Prevent Economic Disruption

MPD	— Maximum Permissible Dose
MPES	— Management Planning and Evaluation Staff
mph	— Miles per Hour
MPL	— Maximum Permissible Level
MPL	— Maximum Possible Loss
MPM	— Meters per Minute
MPO	— Metropolitan Planning Organization
MPPRCA	— Marine Plastic Pollution Research and Control Act of 1987
MPRS	— Management Planning and Reporting System
MPRSA	— Marine Protection, Research and Sanctuaries Act
MPTDS	— MPTER Model with Deposition and Settling of Pollutants
MPTER	— Multiple Point Source Model with Terrain
MQL	— Method Quantification Limits
mr/h	— Microroentgon per Hour
MRA	— Mountain Rescue Association
MRC	— Maintenance Requirement Card
MRC	— Major Regional Contingency
MRCI	— Maximum Rescue Coverage Intercept
Mrem	— One-Thousandth of a rem
MRF	— Material Recovery Facility
MRI	— Message Routing Indicator
MRI	— Midwest Research Institute
MRL	— Minimum-Risk Level
MRO	— Medical Regulating Office
MRR	— Minimum-Risk Route
MRS	— Moderator Recovery System
MRS	— Monitored Retrievable Storage Facility
MRSA	— Materiel Readiness Support Agency
MRSA	— Merrimack River Study Act of 1990
MRU	— Mountain Rescue Unit
ms	— Milliseconds
MS	— Mail Stop

MS	— Management Staff (OPTS)
MS	— Mass Spectrometry
MS	— Multilateral Staff (OIA)
MS-DOS	— Microsoft-Disk Operating System
MSA	— Major System Acquisition
MSA	— Metropolitan Statistical Area
MSAM	— Multi-Keyed Indexed Sequential File Access Method
MSC	— Military Sealift Command
MSCA	— Multi-Site Cooperative Agreement
MSD	— Management Systems Division (OPPE)
MSD	— Marginal Support Date
MSDS	— Material Safety Data Sheet
MSEE	— Major Source Enforcement Effort
MSG	— Monosodium Glutamate
MSHA	— Mine Safety and Health Administration (DOL)
MSIS	— Model State Information System
MSIV	— Main Steam Isolation Valve
MSL	— Mean Sea Level
MSPF	— Maritime Special Purpose Force
MSRs	— Management Systems Reviews
MSS	— Management Support Staff (OPTS)
MT	— Measurement Ton
MTB	— Materials Transportation Bureau
MTBE	— Methyl Tertiary Butyl Ether
MTBF	— Mean Time Between Failures
MTD	— Maximum Tolerated Dose
MTDDIS	— Mesoscale Transport Diffusion and Deposition Model for Industrial Sources
MTE	— Measurement and Test Equipment
MTF	— Medical Treatment Facility
MTG	— Media Task Group
MTI	— Maintenance Team Inspection

MTON	— Measurement Ton(s)
MTP	— Maximum Total Trihalomethane Potential
MTR	— Materials Test Reactor
MTP	— Mission Tasking Package
MTS	— Management Tracing System (OW)
MTSAA	— Multidiscipline Technical Safety Assurance Appraisal
MTSL	— Monitoring and Technical Support Laboratory
MTT	— Mobile Training Team
MTU	— Mobile Treatment Unit
MTX	— Message Text Format
MU	— Mulching
MUD	— Magnetohydrodynamics
MUL	— Department of Defense Master Urgency List
MUP	— Master of Urban Planning
MUST	— Medical Unit, Self-Contained, Transportable
MUSYA	— Multiple-Use Sustained-Yield Act of 1960
MUX	— Multiplexor
mV	— Millivolt
MVA	— Multivariate Analysis
MVAPCA	— Motor Vehicle Air Pollution Control Act
MVEL	— Motor Vehicle Emissions Laboratory
MVEFS	— Motor Vehicle Emission and Fuel Standards
MVI/M	— Motor Vehicle Inspection/Maintenance
MVICSA	— Motor Vehicle Information and Cost Savings Act
MVMA	— Motor Vehicle Manufacturers' Association
MVPCB	— Motor Vehicle Pollution Control Board
MVRS	— Marine Vapor Recovery System
MVS	— Multiple Virtual Storage System
MVTS	— Motor Vehicle Test Station
MW	— Megawatt
MW	— Mixed Wastes
MW	— Molecular Weight

MWC	— Municipal Waste Combustor
MWF	— Medical Working File
MWG	— Model Work Group
MWL	— Municipal Waste Leachate
MWMF	— Mixed Waste Management Facility
MWO	— Maintenance Work Order
MWR	— Morale, Welfare, and Recreation
MYDP	— Multi-Year Development Plans

N

N	— Newton
N/A	— Not Applicable
N/A	— Not Available
NO$_2$	— Nitrogen Dioxide (NO$_2$)
NA	— Nucleic Acid
NA	— National Archives
NA	— Nonattainment
NAA	— Nonattainment Area
NAAB	— National Architectural Accrediting Board
NAAG	— National Association of Attorney Generals
NAAQS	— National Ambient Air Quality Standards (CAA)
NAAS	— National Air Audit System (OAR)
NAC	— National Asbestos Council
NACA	— National Agricultural Chemicals Association
NACE	— National Association of Corrosion Engineers
NACO	— National Association of Counties
NACOA	— National Advisory Committee on Oceans and Atmosphere
NACOSH	— National Advisory Committee on Occupational Safety and Health
NACRS	— National Asbestos-Contractor Registration System
NACSI	— National Communications Security (COMSEC) Instruction

NADB	— National Aerometric Data Bank (OAR)
NADP	— National Atmospheric Deposition Program
NADPSC	— National ADP Service Center
NAE	— National Academy of Engineering
NAF	— Nonappropriated Fund
NAFEC	— National Association of Farmer Elected Committeemen
NAIS	— Neutral Administrative Inspection Scheme
NAK	— Negative Acknowledgment
NALD	— Nonattainment Areas Lacking Demonstrations
NALR	— National Acid Lakes Registry
NAMA	— National Air Monitoring Audit
NAMS	— National Air Monitoring Station
NANCO	— National Association of Noise Control Officials
NAPA	— National Academy of Public Administration
NAPAP	— National Acid Precipitation Assessment Program
NAPBN	— National Air Pollution Background Network
NAPCTAC	— National Air Pollution Control Techniques Advisory Committee
NAR	— National Asbestos Registry
NARA	— National Air Resources Act
NARA	— National Archives and Records Administration
NAS	— National Academy of Sciences
NAS	— National Audubon Society
NASA	— National Aeronautics and Space Administration
NASN	— National Air Sampling Network
NAT	— Nonair-Transportable (Cargo)
NATICH	— National Air Toxics Information Clearinghouse
NATO	— North Atlantic Treaty Organization
NATS	— National Air Toxics Strategy
NAVAIDS	— Navigational Aids
NAVATAC	— Navy Antiterrorism Analysis Center
NAWAS	— National Warning System
NAWC	— National Association of Water Companies

NAWCC	— North American Wetlands Conservation Council
NAWF	— North America Wildlife Foundation
NAWFMP	— North American Waterfowl Management Plan of 1986
NBAR	— Non-Binding Allocation of Responsibility
NBC	— Nuclear, Biological, and Chemical
NBS	— National Bureau of Standards
NC	— Normally Closed
NC^3A	— Nuclear Command, Control, and Communications Assessment
NCA	— National Coal Association
NCA	— National Command Authorities
NCA	— Noise Control Act
NCAA	— NATO Civil Airlift Agency
NCAC	— National Clean Air Coalition
NCAF	— National Clean Air Fund
NCAPC	— National Center for Air Pollution Control
NCAQ	— National Commission on Air Quality
NCAR	— National Center for Atmospheric Research
NCASI	— National Council of the Paper Industry for Air and Stream Improvements
NCC	— National Climatic Center
NCC	— National Computer Center
NCF	— Network Control Facility
NCF	— No Containment Failure
NCHF	— Navy Cargo Handling Force
NCHRP	— National Cooperative Highway Research Program
NCHS	— National Center for Health Statistics (NIH)
NCI	— National Cancer Institute
NCIC	— National Crime Information Center
NCL	— National Consumers League
NCLAN	— National Crop Loan Assessment Network
NCLP	— National Contract Laboratory Program
NCM	— National Coal Model

NCM	— Notice of Commencement of Manufacture
NCMAG	— National Computer (Center) Management Advisory Group
NCMP	— Navy Capabilities and Mobilization Plan
NCO	— NEPA Compliance Officer
NCO	— Noncommissioned Officer
NCOIC	— Noncommissioned Officer-in-Charge
NCP	— National Contingency Plan (CERCLA)
NCR	— Noncompliance Report (CWA)
NCR	— Nonconformance Report
NCRIC	— National Chemical Response and Information Center
NCS	— National Communications System
NCS	— National Compliance Strategy
NCSHPO	— National Conference of State Historic Preservation Officers
NCSL	— National Conference of State Legislatures
NCSORG	— Naval Control of Shipping Organization
NCT	— Network Control Terminal
NCVECS	— National Center for Vehicle Emissions Control and Safety
NCWM	— National Conference of Weights and Measures
NCWQ	— National Commission on Water Quality
NDA	— National Defense Area
NDC	— Naval Doctrine Command
NDCS	— National Drug Control Strategy
NDD	— Negotiation Decision Document
NDDN	— National Dry Deposition Network
NDE	— Nondestructive Evaluation
NDHQ	— National Defence Headquarters, Canada
NDI	— Nondestructive Inspection
NDIA	— New Denver International Airport
NDIRA	— Nondispersive Infrared Analysis
NDMC	— NATO Defense Manpower Committee
NDMS	— National Disaster Medical System
NDP	— National Disclosure Policy

NDPD	— National Data Processing Division
NDRF	— National Defense Reserve Fleet
NDS	— National Dioxin Study
NDS	— National Disposal Site
NDT	— Nondestructive Test
NDWAC	— National Drinking Water Advisory Council
NE	— Nuclear Energy
NEA	— National Energy Act
NEA	— Northeast Asia
NEA	— Nuclear Energy Agency
NEC	— National Electrical Code
NECRMP	— Northeast Corridor Regional Modeling Project
NEDA	— National Environmental Development Association
NEDS	— National Emissions Data System (CAA)
NEEC	— National Environmental Enforcement Council
NEEJ	— National Environmental Enforcement Journal
NEIC	— National Enforcement Investigations Center
NEMA	— National Electrical Manufacturers' Association
NEO	— Noncombatant Evacuation Operation
NEP	— National Energy Plan
NEP	— National Estuary Program
NEP	— Nuclear Electric Propulsion
NEPA	— National Environmental Policy Act
NER	— National Emissions Report (OAR)
NERA	— National Economic Research Associates
NEREP	— Nuclear Execution and Reporting Plan
NERO	— National Energy Resources Organization
NEROS	— Northeast Regional Oxidant Study
NESCAUM	— Northeast States for Coordinated Air Use Management
NESHAPS	— National Emission Standard for Hazard Air Pollutants
NEST	— Nuclear Emergency Search Team
NETS	— Nationwide Emergency Telecommunications System

NETTING	— Emission Trending Used to Avoid PSD/NSR Permit Review Requirements
NEW	— Net Explosive Weight
NFA	— National Fire Academy
NFA	— No Flow Assemblies
NFA	— No-Fire Area
NFAN	— National Filter Analysis Network
NFAWSR	— North Fork American Wild and Scenic River
NFIA	— National Flood Insurance Act of 1968
NFMA	— National Forest Management Act
NFPA	— National Fire Protection Association
NFS	— National Forest Service
NFWF	— National Fish and Wildlife Foundation
ng	— Nanogram
NGA	— National Governors Association
NGA	— Natural Gas Association
NGPA	— Natural Gas Policy Act of 1978
NGO	— Nongovernmental Organization
NGPA	— Natural Gas Policy Act
NGS	— National Geographic Society
NGWIC	— National Ground Water Information Center
NHIS	— National Health Interview Survey
NHL	— National Historic Landmark
NHPA	— National Historic Preservation Act
NHPAA	— National Historic Preservation Act Amendments of 1980
NHPDPA	— National Health Promotion and Disease Prevention Act of 1976
NHS	— National Historical Society
NHTSA	— National Highway Traffic Safety Administration (DOT)
NHWP	— Northeast Hazardous Waste Project
NHZ	— Nominal Hazard Zone
NICS	— National Institute for Chemical Studies
NIEHS	— National Institute of Environmental Health Sciences

NIEI	— National Indoor Environmental Institute
NIH	— National Institutes of Health
NIM	— National Impact Model
NIMBY	— Not in My Backyard
NIOSH	— National Institute of Occupational Safety and Health
NIPCC	— National Industrial Pollution Control Council
NIPDWR	— National Interim Primary Drinking Water Regulations
NIRA	— National Industrial Recovery Act of 1933
NIS	— Noise Information System
NISP	— Nuclear Weapons Intelligence Support Plan
NIST	— National Intelligence Support Team
NIST	— National Institute of Standards and Testing
NITEP	— National Incinerator Testing and Evaluation Program
NLA	— National Lime Association
NLAP	— National Lab Audit Program
NLC	— National League of Cities
NLETS	— National Law Enforcement Teletype System
NLM	— National Library of Medicine
NLT	— Not Later Than
NLT	— Not Less Than
NLU	— Normal Latch Up
nm	— Nanometer
NM	— Nautical Mile
NMC	— National Meteorological Center
NMCS	— National Military Command System
NMET	— Naval Mobile Environmental Team
NMFS	— National Marine Fisheries Service (DOC)
NMHC	— Nonmethane Hydrocarbons
NML	— National Municipal League
NMOC	— Nonmethane Organic Compounds
NMOG	— Nonmethane Organic Gas
NMP	— National Municipal Policy

NMR	— News Media Representative
NMR	— Nuclear Magnetic Resonance
NMS	— National Military Strategy
NMS	— Nuclear Material Safeguards
NMSA	— NATO Mutual Support Act
NNC	— Notice of Noncompliance
NNPSPP	— National Nonpoint Source Pollution Program
NO	— Nitric Oxides
NO	— Normally Open
NO_2	— Nitrogen Dioxide
NOA	— New Obligation Authority
NOA	— Notice of Availability
NOA	— Nuclear Quality Assurance
NOAA	— National Oceanic and Atmospheric Administration
NOAEL	— No Observed Adverse Effect Level
NOC	— Notice of Commencement
NOD	— Notice of Decision
NOD	— Notice of Deficiency (RCRA)
NOEL	— No Observed Effect Level
NOHSCP	— National Oil and Hazardous Substances Contingency Plan
NOI	— Notice of Intent
NON	— Notice of Noncompliance (TSCA)
NOO	— Nevada Operations Office
NOP	— Nuclear Operations
NOPES	— Non-Occupational Pesticide Exposure Study
NOPO	— Nuclear Operations Planning Office
NORA	— National Oil Recyclers Association
NORAD	— North American Aerospace Defense Command
NORM	— Naturally Occurring Radioactive Materials
NORM	— Normal
NOS	— Not Otherwise Specified
NOV	— Notice of Violation

NOx	— Nitrogen Oxide
NPA	— National Planning Association
NPAA	— Noise Pollution and Abatement Act
NPAR	— Nuclear Plant Aging Research Program
NPCCI	— Notification Procedures for Confidential Commercial Information
NPDES	— National Pollution Discharge Elimination System
NPDWR	— National Primary Drinking Water Regulations
NPES	— Nuclear Planning and Execution System
NPIC	— National Photographic Interpretation Center
NPIRS	— National Pesticide Information Retrieval System
NPL	— National Priorities List
NPM	— National Program Manager
NPN	— National Particulate Network
NPOL	— Nuclear Pollution
NPP	— Nuclear Power Plants
NPR	— New Production Reactor
NPR	— Notice of Proposed Rulemaking
NPRA	— National Parks and Recreation Act of 1978
NPRDS	— Nuclear Plant Reliability Data System
NPS	— National Park Service
NPS	— National Permit Strategy
NPS	— Nuclear Planning System
NPSH	— Not Positive Suction Head
NPUG	— National Prime User Group
NR	— National Register
NRA	— National Recreation Area
NRC	— National Referral Center
NRC	— National Register Criteria
NRC	— National Research Council
NRC	— National Response Center
NRC	— Non-Reusable Container
NRC	— Nuclear Regulatory Commission

NRDC	— Natural Resources Defense Council
NRDM	— Nuclear Weapons (NUWEP) Reconnaissance Data Manual
NREL	— National Renewable Energy Laboratory
NRFI	— Not Ready for Issue
NRHP	— National Register of Historic Places
NRL	— Nuclear Weapons (NUWEP) Reconnaissance List
NRO	— National Reconnaissance Office
NRPB	— National Research and Planning Board
NRPM	— Nuclear Weapons (NUWEP) Reconnaissance Planning Manual
NRR	— NRC Office of Nuclear Reactor Regulation
NRT	— National Recreation Trail
NRT	— National Response Team
NRT	— Near-Real-Time
NRTAC	— National Recreation Trails Advisory Committee
NRTF	— National Recreation Trails Fund
NRTL	— Nationally Recognized Testing Laboratory
NRWA	— National Rural Water Association
NRZ	— Non-Return-to-Zero
NS	— Noxious Substances
NS	— Nuclear Safety
NS/EP	— National Security and Emergency Preparedness
NSA	— National Security Agency
NSA	— National Security Areas
NSAC	— Nuclear Safety Analysis Center
NSC	— National Security Council
NSCS	— National Security Council System
NSDD	— National Security Decision Directive
NSEP	— National Security Emergency Preparedness
NSF	— National Sanitation Foundation
NSF	— National Science Foundation
NSF	— National Strike Force
NSI	— National Security Information

NSI	— Not Seriously Injured
NSIDC	— National Snow and Ice Data Center
NSM	— National Search and Rescue (SAR) Manual
NSN	— National Stock Number
NSNF	— Nonstrategic Nuclear Forces
NSO	— Nonferrous Smelter Order (CAA)
NSP	— National Search and Rescue Plan
NSPE	— National Society for Professional Engineers
NSPKTR	— An abbreviation for a computer code
NSPS	— New Source Performance Standards (CAA)
NSR	— New Source Review (CAA)
NSS	— Non-Self-Sustaining
NSSCS	— Non-Self-Sustaining Containership
NSTL	— National Space Technology Laboratory
NSWMA	— National Solid Waste Management Association
NSWS	— National Surface Water Survey
NTA	— Nitrilotriacetic Acid
NTC	— National Training Center
NTDS	— Naval Tactical Data System
NTE	— Not to Exceed
NTG	— Nuclear Test Gage
NTIS	— National Technical Information Service
NTN	— National Trends Network
NTNCWS	— Non-Transient Non-Community Water System
NTP	— National Toxicological Program
NTP	— Nuclear Thermal Propulsion
NTS	— Nevada Test Site
NTSA	— National Trails System Act
NTSB	— National Transportation Safety Board
NUATRC	— [Mickey Leland] National Urban Air Toxics Research Center
NUCA	— National Utility Contractors' Association
NUDET	— Nuclear Detonation

NURF	— NAPAP Utility Reference File
NUWEP	— Policy Guidance for the Employment of Nuclear Weapons
NV	— Nevada Operations Office
NVLAP	— National Voluntary Laboratory Accreditation program
NVPP	— National Vehicle Population Poll
NW	— Not Waiverable
NWA	— National Water Alliance
NWC	— Nuclear Weapons Complex
NWDO	— National Workforce Development Office
NWF	— National Wildlife Federation
NWPA	— Nuclear Waste Policy Act
NWPCP	— National Wetlands Priority Conservation Plan
NWPS	— National Wilderness Preservation System
NWRC	— National Weather Records Center
NWREP	— Nuclear Weapons Report
NWRS	— National Wildlife Refuge System
NWS	— National Weather Service
NWTRB	— Nuclear Waste Technical Review Board

O

O/O	— Owner or Operator
O/B	— Outboard
O&M	— Operation and Maintenance
O_3	— Ozone
OA	— Objective Area
OA	— Office of Audits
OA	— Office of the Administrator (EPA)
OAA	— Older Americans Act of 1965
OACSEA	— Older Americans Community Services Employment Act

OADEMQA	— Office of Acid Deposition, Environmental Monitoring, and Quality Assurance
OADR	— Originating Agency's Determination Required
OAE	— Operational Area Evaluation
OALJ	— Office of the Administrative Law Judges (OA)
OAQPS	— Office of Air Quality Planning and Standards
OAR	— Office of Air and Radiation
OAR	— Operation Assessment and Readiness
OARM	— Office of Administration and Resources Management
OASD	— Office of the Assistant Secretary of Defense
OBA	— Operating Basis Accident
OBA	— Oxygen Breathing Apparatus
OBE	— Operating Basis Earthquake
OBES	— Office of Basic Energy Sciences
OBFS	— Offshore Bulk Fuel System
OBRA	— Omnibus Budget Reconciliation Act of 1990
OBST	— Obstacle
OC	— Object Class
OC	— Office of the Comptroller
OCAPO	— Office of Compliance Analysis and Program Operations
OCAW	— Oil Chemical and Atomic Workers
OCC	— Offsite Coordination Center
OCC	— Office of Chemical Control
OCCA	— Ocean Cargo Clearance Authority
OCDM	— Offshore and Coastal Dispersion Model
OCE	— Office of Criminal Enforcement (OECM)
OCEANCON	— Control of Oceanographic Information
OCESL	— Office of Criminal Enforcement and Special Litigation
OCI	— Office of Criminal Investigation (OECM)
OCIL	— Office of Community and Intergovernmental Liaison
OCIR	— Office of Community and Intergovernmental Relations
OCJCS	— Office of the Chairman of the Joint Chiefs of Staff

OCL	— Office of Congressional Liaison (OEA)
OCM	— Office of Compliance Monitoring (OPTS)
OCM	— Operational Change Memos
OCONUS	— Outside the Continental United States
OCOP	— Outline Contingency Operation Plan
OCP	— Operational Configuration Processing
OCR	— Office of Civil Rights (AO)
OCR	— Office of Community Relations
OCR	— Optical Character Recognition
OCRE	— Office of Conservation and Renewable Energy
OCRWM	— Office of Civilian Radioactive Waste Management
OCS	— Outer Continental Shelf
OCSLA	— Outer Continental Shelf Lands Act of 1953
OCSLAA	— Outer continental Shelf Lands Act Amendments of 1978
OD	— Office of the Director
OD	— Operations Division (NEIC)
ODA	— Office of the Deputy Administrator
ODC	— Office of Defense Cooperation
ODR	— Office of Defense Representative
ODV	— Ozone Design Value
ODW	— Office of Drinking Water (OW)
OE	— Office of Enforcement
OEA	— Office of External Affairs
OEC	— Office of Energy Conservation
OECD	— Organization of Economic Cooperation and Development
OECM	— Office of Enforcement and Compliance Monitoring
OEET	— Office of Environmental Engineering and Technology
OEL	— Occupational Exposure Limit
OEM	— Office of Emergency Management
OEMT	— Operational Emergency Management Team
OEP	— Office of Emergency Preparedness
OEP	— Office of Energy Planning

OEP	— Office of Enforcement Policy (OCAPO)
OEPER	— Office of Environmental Processes and Effects Research
OEQC	— Office of Environmental Quality Control
OER	— Office of Energy Research
OER	— Office of Exploratory Research (ORD)
OERR	— Office of Emergency and Remedial Response
OERWM	— Office of Environmental Restoration and Waste Management
OES	— Office of Executive Support (AO)
OESH	— Office of Environment, Safety, and Health
OET	— Office of Emergency Transportation
OF	— Optional Form
OFA	— Office of Federal Activities
OFDA	— Office of Foreign Disaster Assistance
OFE	— Office of Fossil Energy
OFP	— Office of Federal Policy
OFPPA	— Office of Federal Procurement Policy Act
OFR	— Office of the Federal Register
OFSPS	— Office of Federal Statistical Policy and Standards
OGA	— Other Government Agencies
OGC	— Office of General Counsel
OGR	— Office of Government Relations
OGWP	— Office of Ground-Water Protection
OH	— Outer Housing
OH	— Overhead
OHD	— Occupational Health Division
OHEA	— Office of Health and Environmental Assessment (ORD)
OHER	— Office of Health and Environmental Research
OHMTADS	— Oil and Hazardous Materials Technical Assistance Data System
OHR	— Office of Health Research
OHRM	— Office of Human Resources Management
OHSS	— Occupational Health and Safety Staff (OA)
OI	— Office of Investigations

OIA	— Office of International Activities
OIC	— Officer in Charge
OICC	— Operational Intelligence Coordination Center
OIG	— Office of the Inspector General (OEA)
OIL	— Office of Intergovernmental-Liaison (OEA)
OILSR	— Office of Interstate Land Sales Registration
OIRA	— Office of Information and Regulatory Affairs
OIRM	— Office of Information Resources Management (OARM)
OL	— Operating Limit
OLA	— Office of Legislative Analysis (OEA)
OLC	— On-Line Computer
OLD	— On-Line Tests and Diagnostics
OM	— Occupational Medicine
OM	— Operating Method
OMA	— Office of Military Affairs (CIA)
OMB	— Office of Management and Budget
OMC	— Office of Military Cooperation
OMEP	— Office of Marine and Estuarine Protection (OW)
OMPC	— Office of Municipal Pollution Control (OW)
OMS	— Office of Mobile Sources (OAR)
OMSE	— Office of Management Systems and Evaluation (OPPE)
OMTA	— Office of Management and Technical Assessment
ONDCP	— Office of National Drug Control Policy
OO	— Operations Office (ORD)
OOS	— Out-of-Service
OOWSRA	— Omnibus Oregon Wild and Scenic Rivers Act of 1988
OP	— Operating Plan
OP	— Operating Procedure
OP	— Ozone Protection
OPA	— Office of Policy Analysis (OPPE)
OPA	— Office of Pubic Affairs (OEA)
OPAC	— Overall Performance Appraisal Certification

OPAR	— Office of Policy Analysis and Review (OAR)
OPAR	— Operation Plans Assessment Report
OPBE	— Office of Planning, Budgeting and Evaluation
OPCEN	— Coast Guard Operations Center
OPCOM	— Operational Command (NATO)
OPD	— Office of Program Development (OAR)
OPDS	— Offshore Petroleum Discharge System
OPEC	— Oil Producers' Economic Cartel
OPEC	— Organization of Petroleum Exporting Countries
OPLAN	— Operational Plan
OPLAW	— Operational Law
OPM	— Office of Program Management (OSWER)
OPM	— Operations per Minute
OPME	— Office of Program Management and Evaluation (OPTS)
OPMO	— Office of Program Management Operations (OPTS/OAR)
OPMS	— Office of Program Management and Support (OSWER)
OPMT	— Office of Program Management and Technology (OSWER)
OPP	— Office of Pesticide Programs (OPTS)
OPPE	— Office of Policy, Planning, and Evaluation
OPPI	— Office of Policy, Planning and Information (OSWER)
OPPM	— Office of Policy and Program Management (OSWER)
OPR	— Office of Primary Responsibility
OPREP	— Operational Report
OPs	— Operations
OPTS	— Office of Pesticides and Toxic Substances
OPZONE	— Operation Zone
OR	— Operational Readiness
ORAU	— Oak Ridge Associated Universities
ORC	— Office of Regional Counsel
ORC	— Operations Review Committee
ORD	— Office of Research and Development
ORD	— Operational Requirements Document

ORD	— Ordinance
ORG	— Origin
ORGDP	— Oak Ridge Gaseous Diffusion Plant
ORI	— Ocean Resources Institute
ORM	— Other Regulated Material (ORM-A through ORM-E)
ORNL	— Oak Ridge National Laboratory
ORO	— Oak Ridge Operations Office
ORO	— Office of Regional Operations
ORPM	— Office of Research Program Management (ORD)
ORPS	— Occurrence Reporting and Processing System
ORS	— Office of Regulatory Support
ORSSA	— Office of Regulatory Support and Scientific Analysis
ORV	— Off-Road Vehicle
OS	— Operating System
OS/VS	— Operating System/Virtual Storage
OSC	— On-Scene Coordinator
OSC	— Options Selection Committee
OSD	— Office of the Secretary of Defense
OSDBU	— Office of Small and Disadvantaged Business Utilization
OSE	— On Scene Endurance
OSHA	— Occupational Safety and Health Act
OSHA	— Occupational Safety and Health Administration
OSHRC	— Occupational Safety and Health Review Commission
OSI	— Operational Subsystem Interface
OSP	— Office of Special Projects
OSP	— Operational Safety Procedures
OSR	— Office of Standards and Regulations (OPPE)
OSR	— Operational Safety Requirements
OSS	— Office of Strategic Services
OSSC	— Office of Stationary Source Compliance
OSSM	— Office of Safety Surface Mining (DOI)
OST	— Office of Science and Technology

OSTP   — Office of Science and Technology Policy

OSW   — Office of Solid Waste (OSWER)

OSWER   — Office of Solid Waste and Emergency Response

OT   — Overtime

OTA   — Office of Technology Assessment (Congress)

OTC   — Over the Counter

OTD   — Office of Technology Development

OTH   — Over the Horizon

OTP   — Office of Territorial Programs

OTS   — Office of Toxic Substances (OPTS)

OUST   — Office of Underground Storage Tanks (OSWER)

OUT   — Outsize Cargo

OVE   — On-Vehicle Equipment

OVER   — Oversize Cargo

OW   — Office of Water

OWCP   — Office of Workers' Compensation Programs (DOL)

OWEP   — Office of Water Enforcement and Permits (OW)

OWP   — Office of Wetlands Protection (OW)

OWPE   — Office of Waste Programs Enforcement (OSWER)

OWR   — Omega West Reactor

OWRS   — Office of Water Regulations and Standards (OW)

Ox   — Total Oxidants

OY   — Operating Year

OYG   — Operating Year Guidance

OZIPP   — Ozone Isopleth Plotting Package

OZIPPM   — Modified Ozone Isopleth Plotting Package

P
___

P&A   — Precision and Accuracy

P&ID   — Piping and Instrumentation Drawing

Pa	— Pascal
PA	— Preliminary Assessment
PA	— Privacy Act of 1974
PA	— Production Agency
PA	— Property Administrator
PA	— Protective Action
PA	— Public Affairs
PA	— Public Announcement
PAA	— Priority Abatement Areas
PAAT	— Public Affairs Assist Team
PACE	— Professional Association of Consulting Engineers
PAD	— Planning and Analysis Division (OW)
PADRE	— Particle Analysis and Data Reduction
PAG	— Protective Action Guide
PAG	— Public Affairs Guidance
PAGM	— Permit Applicants Guidance Manual
PAH	— Polycyclic Aromatic Hydrocarbon
PAI	— Performance Audit Inspection (CWA)
PAIR	— Preliminary Assessment Information Rule
PAL	— Point, Area, and Line Source Air Quality Model
PALDS	— PAL Model with Deposition and Settling of Pollutants
PAN	— Peroxyacetyl Nitrate
PAN	— Pollution Abatement Notice
PAO	— Public Affairs Officer
PAR	— Performance Assessment Report
PAR	— Population at Risk
PAR	— Preparedness Assessment Report
PAR	— Protective Action Recommendation
PARD	— Protect as Restricted Data
PARS	— Precision and Accuracy Reporting System
PAS	— Policy Analysis Staff
PASS	— Procurement Automated Source System

PAT	—	Permit Assistance Team
PAT	—	Public Affairs Team
PATS	—	Plant Action Tracking System
PAX	—	Passengers
Pb	—	Periodic Element, Lead
PB	—	Polybutylene
PBA	—	Production Base Analysis
PBB	—	Polybromated Biphenyls
PBD	—	Program Budget Decisions
PBF	—	Power Burst Facility
PBL	—	Planetary Boundary Layer
PBLSQ	—	The Lead Line Source (PBLSQ) Model
Pc	—	Cumulative Probability of Detection
PC	—	Personal Computer
PC	—	Planned Commitment
PC	—	Position Classification
PC	—	Pulverized Coal
PC-LITE	—	Processor, Laptop Imagery Transmission Equipment
PCA	—	Principal Component Analysis
PCA	—	Pollution Control Agency
PCB	—	Polychlorinated Biphenyl
PCBs	—	Polychlorinated Biphenyls
PCC	—	Primary Component Cooling
PCC	—	Primary Control Center
PCCW	—	Pubic Citizens Congress Watch
PCDD	—	Polychlorinatcd Dibenzodioxin
PCDF	—	Polychlorinated Dibenzofuran
PCE	—	Pollution Control Equipment
PCF	—	Personnel Control Facilities
pci/l	—	Picocuries per Liter
pci/g	—	Picocuries per Gram
PCIE	—	Presidents Council on Integrity and Efficiency in Government

PCLFC	— Projected Consequences of Less Than Full Control
PCMD	— Procurement and Contract Management Division
PCMNA	— Provisions for Carbon Monoxide Nonattainment Areas
PCNC	— Projected Consequences of No Control
PCON	— Potential Contractor
PCP	— Pentachlorophenol
PCPS	— Pulverized-Coal Power System
PCs	— Personal Computers (IBM Compatibles)
PCS	— Permit Compliance System
PCS	— Power Conversion System
PCW	— Post-Consumer Waste
PCZ	— Physical Control Zone
Pd	— Drift Compensated Parallelogram Pattern
PD	— Permits Division (OW)
PD	— Position Document
PD	— Presidential Directive
PD	— Probability of Damage
PD	— Probability of Detection
PD	— Procedures Description
PDB	— Plant Damage Bin
PDC	— Program Development Computer
PDED	— Program Development and Evaluation Division (OW)
PDM	— Program Decision Memorandum
PDM	— Power Density Monitor
PDMS	— Pesticide Document Management System (OPP)
PDR	— Particulate Data Reduction
PDS	— Protected Distribution System
PDWR	— Primary Drinking Water Regulation
PE	— Professional Engineer
PE	— Program Element
PEAD	— Presidential Emergency Action Document
PEARL	— Personnel Expertise and Resource Listing

PEAS   — Policy and External Affairs Staff
PECSS   — Presorted Emergency Cooling System Sampling
PED   — Program Evaluation Division
PEDB   — Planning and Execution Data Base
PEFOS   — Program Evaluation and Field Operations Staff
PEI   — Principal Environmental Investigator
PEL   — Permissible Exposure Limit
PEL   — Personal Exposure Limit
PEO   — Program Enrichment Office
PEP   — Personnel Exchange Program
PEPE   — Prolonged Elevated Pollution Episode
PERO   — President's Emergency Relief Organization
PERT   — Program Evaluation and Review Technique
PES   — Planning and Evaluation Staff
PES   — Preparedness Evaluation System
PETS   — Procedures for Evaluating Technical Specifications Program
PF   — Paved Flume
PFD   — Personal Flotation Device
PFLT   — Paint Filter Liquids Test
PFR   — Phase Failure Relays
PFSS   — Pesticide Farmworker Safety Staff (OPTS)
PG   — Processed Gas
PGD   — Policy and Grants Division (OPTS)
PGDP   — Paducah Gaseous Diffusion Plant (Paducah)
PH1   — Phase I Environmental Inspection
PH2   — Phase II Environmental Inspection
PH3   — Phase III Environmental Inspection
PHA   — Preliminary Hazards Assessment
PHC   — Principal Hazardous Constituent
PHF   — Procedure History File
PHO   — Public Hazard Office
PHS   — Public Health Service

PHSA	— Public Health Service Act
PI	— Preliminary Injunction
PI	— Public Information
PIAT	— Public Information Assist Team
PIC	— Products of Incomplete Combustion
PIC	— Public Information Center
PICO	— Pacific Islands Contact Office
PID	— Photoionization Detector
PIDD	— Planned Inactivation or Discontinued Date
PIGS	— Pesticides in Groundwater Strategy
PIHSMP	— Protocol Relating to Intervention on the High Seas in Cases of Marine Pollution by Substances other than Oil
PIM	— Public Information Meeting
PIN	— Personnel Identification Number
PIN	— Procurement Information Notice
PIPQUIC	— Program Integration Project Queries Use in Interactive Command
PIPS	— Plans Integration Partitioning System
PIRG	— Public Interest Research Group
PIRU	— Public Information Reference Unit
PIS	— Public Information Specialist
PITS	— Project Information Tracking System
PJA	— Proper Job Analysis
PJI	— Proper Job Instruction
PKG-POL	— Packaged Petroleum, Oils, and Lubricants
PL	— Public Law
PLC	— Packaged Laboratory Chemicals
PLFA	— Phospholipid Fatty Acids
PLIRRA	— Pollution Liability Insurance and Risk Retention Act
PLS	— Program Liaison Staff
PLUVUE	— Plume Visibility Model
PLWA	— Primary Light Water Addition

PM	— Particulate Matter
PM	— Preventive Maintenance
PM	— Project Manager
PM10	— Particulate Matter, 10 Millimeters and Less
PM15	— Particulate Matter, 15 Millimeters and Less
PMA	— Power Marketing Administration
PMD	— Personnel Management Division
PMD	— Planning and Management Division
PMEL	— Pacific Marine Environment Laboratory
PMEL	— Precision Mechanics and Electronics Laboratory
PMF	— Probable Maximum Flood
PMFC	— Pacific Marine Fisheries Compact
PMIP	— Presidential Management Intern Program
PMIS	— Personnel Management Information System
PMN	— Premanufacture Notice
PMO	— Program Management Office
PMOA	— Programmatic Memorandum of Agreement
PMOS	— Program Management and Operations Staff
PMR	— Pollutant Mass Rate
PMRS	— Performance Management and Recognition System
PMS	— Planning and Management Staff
PMS	— Program Management Staff
PMSD	— Program Management and Support Division
PMSO	— Program Management and Support Office
PMSS	— Policy and Management Support Staff
PN	— Pseudonoise
PNAH	— Polynuclear Aromatic Hydrocarbons
PNL	— Pacific Northwest Laboratory
PNRS	— Project Notification and Review System
PO	— Program Operations
PO	— Project Officer
PO	— Purchase Order

POA — Program Office Approvals

POAS — Psychological Operations Automated System

POAT — Psychological Operations Assessment Team

POC — Point of Contact

POC — Program Office Contacts

POD — Probability of Detection

POGO — Privately Owned, Government Operated

POHC — Principal Organic Hazardous Constituent

POL — Petroleum, Oils, and Lubricants

POLAD — Political Advisor

POM — Polycyclic Organic Matter

POM — Program Objective Memorandum

POMO — Program Operations and Management Office

PONA — Provisions for Ozone Nonattainment Areas

PORC — Plant Overnight Review Committee

PORTS — Portsmouth Gaseous Diffusion Plant

PORV — Power Operated Relief Valve

POS — Probability of Success

POS — Program Operations Staff (ORD)

POSS — Program Operations Support Staff (OARM)

POTS — Potentiometers

POTW — Publicly Owned Treatment Works

POV — Privately Owned Vehicle

pp — Plenum Pressure

PP — Program Planning

PPA — Pesticide Producers Association

PPA — Planned Program Accomplishment

PPA — Pollution Prevention Act of 1990

PPAG — Proposed Public Affairs Guidance

ppb — Parts per Billion

PPBS — Planning, Programming, and Budgeting System

PPBS — Program Planning and Budget Staff (OGC)

PPC	— Project Planning and Control
PPE	— Personal Protective Equipment
PPECP	— Pollution Prevention and Emissions Control Program
PPIC	— Pollution Prevention Information Clearinghouse
ppm	— Parts per Million
PPMAP	— Power Planning Modeling Application Procedure
PPMNA	— Provisions for Particulate Matter Nonattainment Areas
PPP	— Pollution Prevention Plan
PPRS	— Program Planning and Review Staff
PPSP	— Power Plant Siting Program
ppt	— Parts per Trillion
PPT	— Permanent Part Time
PR	— Preliminary Review
PR	— Primary Zone
PR	— Procurement Request
PRA	— Paperwork Reduction Act
PRA	— Planned Regulatory Action
PRA	— Probabilistic Risk Assessment
PRC	— Populace and Resources Control
PRD	— Pesticides Regulation Division
PREPP	— Process Experimental Pilot Plant
PRG	— Program Review Group
PRISM	— Plant Risk Status Information Management System
PRM	— Presidential Review Memorandum
PRM	— Prevention Reference Manuals
PROPIN	— Proprietary Information
PROVORG	— Providing Organization
PRP	— Potentially Responsible Party (CERCLA)
PRSA	— Permigewasset River Study Act of 1989
PRT	— Pararescue Team
PRU	— Pararescue Unit
PRV	— Pressure Regulator Valve

PS	— Palentological Society
PS	— Planning Staff (OPTS) (ORD)
PS	— Point Source
PS	— Protection Strategy
PSA	— Preliminary Safety Analysis
PSA	— Professional Services Agreement
PSAM	— Point Source Ambient Monitoring
PSD	— Planning Systems Division
PSD	— Prevention of Significant Deterioration
PSD	— Program Systems Division (OIRM)
PSE	— Peculiar Support Equipment
PSE	— Program Subelement
psi	— Pounds (or Pressure) per Square Inch
PSI	— Pollutant Standard Index
psia	— Pounds per Square Inch Absolute
psig	— Pressure per Square Inch Gauge
PSM	— Point Source Monitoring
PSO	— Program Secretarial Officer
PSO	— Program Senior Officials
PSPD	— Permits and State Program Division (OSWER)
PSR	— Primary System Relief
PSS	— Personnel Security Staff (OEA)
PSS	— Probabilistic Safety Study
PSS	— Program Support Staff
PSYWAR	— Psychological Warfare
PT	— Part Time
PTAT	— Pesticides, Toxics and Air Team (ORD)
PTE	— Potential to Emit
PTFE	— Polytetrafluoroethylene (Teflon)
PTMAX	— Singlestack Meteorological Model in EPA UNAMAP Series
PTMTP	— Multistack Meteorological Model in EPA UNAMAP Series
PTP	— Peak-to-Peak Ratio

PTPLU — Point Source Gaussian Diffusion Model

PTSD — Pesticides and Toxic Substances Division

PTSED — Pesticides and Toxic Substances Enforcement Division

PUB — Publication

PUC — Public Utilities Commission

PUEC — Portsmouth Uranium Enrichment Complex

PURPA — Public Utility Regulatory Policies Act of 1978

Pv — Photovoltaics

PV — Project Verification

PVC — Polyvinyl Chloride

pW — Picowatt

PW — Process Water

PWA — Process Waste Assessment

PWGM — Process Water Gamma Monitor

PWR — Pressurized Water Reactor

PWS — Public Water Supply

PWS — Public Water System (SDWA)

PWSS — Public Water Supply System (SDWA)

PY — Prior Year

PZ — Pickup Zone

Q

QA — Quality Assurance

QA/QC — Quality Assurance/Quality Control

QAA — Quality Assurance Acceptance

QAC — Quality Assurance Coordinator

QAMIS — Quality Assurance Management and Information System

QAMS — Quality Assurance Management Staff (ORD)

QAO — Quality Assurance Officer (OAR)

QAPPs — Quality Assurance Project Plans

QAT   — Quality Assurance Team
QC   — Quality Control
QCA   — Quiet Communities Act
QCI   — Quality Control Index
QCP   — Quiet Community Program
QDR   — Quality Deficiency Report
QF   — Quality Factor
QIC   — Quality Inspection Control
QMPs   — Quality Management Plans
QNCR   — Quarterly Noncompliance Report
QRE   — Quick Reaction Element
QTY   — Quantity
QV   — Quality Verification

R

R   — Radius of Search
R   — Roentgen
R&D   — Research and Development
R&PM   — Regulations and Procedure Manual, PUB-201
R&QA   — Reliability and Quality Assurance
RA   — Raker Act of 1913 (WSRA)
RA   — Reasonable Alternative
RA   — Reclamation Act of 1902
RA   — Regional Administrator (EPA)
RA   — Regulatory Alternatives
RA   — Regulatory Analysis
RA   — Remedial Action
RA   — Resource Allocation
RA   — Risk Analysis
RA   — Risk Assessment

RAAS   — Remedial Action Assessment System

RAC   — Regional Asbestos Coordinator

RAC   — Regional Assistance Committees

RAC   — Response Action Contracts

RACM   — Reasonable Available Control Measures

RACT   — Reasonably Available Control Technology

RAD   — Radiation Absorbed Dose

RADHAZ   — Radiation Hazard

RADIAC   — Radioactivity, Detection, Indication, and Computation

RADM   — Random (Walk) Advection and Dispersion Model

RADM   — Regional Acid Deposition Model

RAF   — Royal Air Force (UK)

RAM   — Radon Assessment and Mitigation

RAM   — Random Access Memory

RAM   — Reliability, Availability, and Maintainability

RAM   — Urban Air Quality Model for Point and Area Sources in EPA UNAMAP Series

RAMC   — Risk Assessment and Management Commission

RAMCI   — Risk Assessment and Management Commission Investigation

RAMP   — Remedial Action Master Plan

RAMP   — Rural Abandoned Mine Program

RAMS   — Regional Air Monitoring System

RAOC   — Rear Area Operations Center

RAP   — Radon Action Program

RAP   — Radiological Assistance Program

RAP   — Remedial Accomplishment Plan

RAP   — Remedial Action Program

RAPP   — Remedial Action Projects Program (JCS)

RAPS   — Regional Air Pollution Study

RARG   — Regulatory Analysis Review Group

RAST   — Recovery Assistance, Securing, and Traversing

RAT   — Relative Accuracy Test

RATs	— Radiological Assistance Team
RB	— Red Border
RBC	— Reactor Building Cooling
RBCCW	— Reactor Building Closed Cooling Water
RBCLCW	— Reactor Building Closed Loop Cooling Water
RBE	— Relative Biological Effectiveness
RBFC	— Reactor Building Fan Coolers
RBLC	— RACT/BACT/LAER Clearinghouse
RBS	— Reactor Building Spray
RBSI	— Reactor Building Spray Injection
RBSVS	— Reactor Building Standby Ventilation System
RC	— Regional Counsel
RC	— Responsibility Center
RCA	— Radiological Control Area
RCA	— Resource Conservation Act
RCA	— Responsibility Center A
RCA	— Riot Control Agent
RCB	— Responsibility Center B
RCB	— Retrieval Containment Building
RCC	— Radiation Coordinating Council
RCC	— Rescue Coordination Center
RCD	— Resource Conservation and Development
RCDO	— Regional Case Development Officer
RCDPB	— Resource Conservation and Development Policy Board
RCIC	— Reactor Core Isolation Cooling
RCM	— Reliability-Centered Maintenance
RCM	— Responsibility Center Monthly
RCMLs	— Recommended Maximum Contamination Level
RCOG	— Regional Council of Governments
RCP	— Reactor Coolant Pump
RCP	— Research Centers Program (ORD)
RCRA	— Resource Conservation and Recovery Act of 1976

RCRIS   — Resource Conservation and Recovery Information System

RCS   — Reactor Coolant System

RCSI   — Reactor Coolant System Integrity

RCT   — Radiological Control Technician

RCU   — Rate Changes Unit

RCW   — Recirculated Cooling Water

RD   — Registration Division (OPTS)

RD   — Remedial Design

RD&D   — Research, Demonstration and Development

RDD   — Required Delivery Date (at Destination)

RDDT&E   — Research, Development, Demonstration, Testing and Evaluation

RDF   — Refuse-Derived Fuel

rDNA   — Recombinant DNA

RDT&E   — Research, Development, Test and Evaluation

RDU   — Regional Decision Unit

RE   — Reasonable Efforts

RE   — Reportable Event

REA   — Rural Electrification Administration

REAC/TS   — Radiological Emergency Assistance Center/Training Site

READ   — Regulatory and Economics Analysis Division

REAG   — Reproductive Effects Assessment Group (ORD)

RECON   — Reconnaissance

RED   — RCRA Enforcement Division (OSWER)

REDAC   — Remote Detection and Control

REDS   — Reactor Electric Distribution System

REE   — Rare Earth Elements

REEP   — Reasonable Extra Efforts Program

REEP   — Review of Environmental Effects of Pollutants

REF   — Reference

REHR   — Reactor Heat Removal

REIC   — Radiation Effects Information Center

REL   — Relative

rem	— Roentgen Equivalent Man
REM	— Radiation Exposure Module
REMPC	— Remedial Planning Contractor
REP	— Reasonable Efforts Program
REPOL	— Reporting Emergency Petroleum, Oils, and Lubricants
REPS	— Regional Emissions Projection System
RERP	— Radiological Emergency Response Plan
RESA	— Real Estate Settlement Act
RESC	— Reactor Subcriticality
RFA	— RCRA Facility Assessment
RFA	— Regulatory Flexibility Act
RFA	— Restricted Fire Area
RFB	— Request for Bid
RFC	— Request for Comments
RfD	— Reference Dose
RFD	— Reference Dose Values
RFETS	— Rocky Flats Environmental Technology Site
RFFO	— Rocky Flats Field Office
RFI	— RCRA Facility Inspection
RFI	— Remedial Facility Investigation
RFI	— Request for Information
RFP	— Reasonable Further Progress
RFP	— Request for Proposal
RFPO	— Reasonable Further Progress Demonstration
RFQ	— Request for Quote
RFS	— Request for Service
RFW	— Request for Waiver
RG	— Regulatory Guide
RGS	— Research Grants Staff (ORD)
RH	— Remote Handled
RHA	— Rural Housing Alliance
RHAA	— Rivers and Harbors Appropriation Act of 1899

RHR — Residual Heat Removal

RI — Reconnaissance Inspection (CWA)

RI — Remedial Investigation

RI — Routing Indicator

RI/FS — Remedial Investigation/Feasibility Study (CERCLA)

RIA — Regulatory Impact Analysis

RIA — Regulatory Impact Assessment

RIAQRA — Radon Gas and Indoor Air Quality Research Act of 1986

RIB — Radioactive Ion Beam

RIC — Radon Information Council

RIC — Research Triangle Park (RTP) Information Center

RID — Regulatory Integration Division (OPPE)

RIF — Reduction in Force

RIG — Risk-Based Inspection Guide

RIM — Regulatory Information Memorandum

RIM — Regulatory Interpretation Memorandum

RIM — Relative Importance Measure

RIP — RCRA Implementation Plan

RIS — Regulatory Innovations Staff (OPPE)

RISC — Regulatory Information Science Center (OMB)

RJE — Remote Job Entry

RM — Recovery Manager

RMA — Records Management Officer

RMAO — Resources Management and Administrative Office (OW)

RMC — Resource Management Committee (CSIF)

RMCG — Reactor Materials Control Group

RMCL — Recommended Maximum Contaminant Level

RMDHS — Regional Model Data Handling System

RMDP — Radon Mitigation Demonstration Program

RMIS — Resources Management Information System

rms — Root Mean Square

RMS — Resource Management Staff (OSWER)

RNA	— Ribonucleic Acid
RO	— Reactor Operator
RO	— Regional Office
RO	— Remains Open
ROA	— Restricted Operations Area
ROADCHEM	— ROADWAY Version with Chemical Reactions of NO, NO_2 and O_3
ROADWAY	— Model for Pollutant Concentrations Near Roadways
ROC	— Record of Communication
ROC	— Required Operational Capability
ROD	— Record of Decision
ROD	— Report of Discrepancy
ROG	— Reactive Organic Gases
ROI	— Radiological Operating Instructions
ROLLBACK	— Proportional Pollutant Reduction Model
ROM	— Read Only Memory
ROM	— Regional Oxidant Model
ROM/BIOS	— Read Only Memory with Basic Computer In/Out Services
ROP	— Regional Oversight Policy
ROPA	— Record of Procurement Action
ROVs	— Remotely Operated Vehicles
ROW	— Right-of-Way
ROZ	— Restricted Operations Zone
RP	— Reduced Pressure
RP	— Release Point
RP	— Responsible Party
RP	— Respirable Particulates
RPAR	— Rebuttable Presumption Against Registration (FIFRA)
RPD	— Respiratory Protective Device
RPIO	— Responsible Planning and Implementation Officer
RPIS	— Real Property Inventory System
rpm	— Revolutions per Minute
RPM	— Radial Power Monitor

RPM	—	Reactive Plume Model
RPM	—	Remedial Project Manager
RPO	—	Regional Planning Officer
RPO	—	Regional Program Office
RPS	—	Radioisotope Power System
RPS	—	Reactor Protection System
RPS	—	Remedial Planning Staff (OSWER)
RPT	—	Recirculation Pump Trip
RPTOR	—	Reporting Organization
RPTS	—	Regional Priority Tracking System
RPV	—	Reactor Pressure Vessel
RPV	—	Remotely Piloted Vehicle
RQ	—	Reportable Quantity
RQMT	—	Requirement
RRC	—	Regional Response Center
RRDF	—	Roll-On/Roll-Off Discharge Facility
RREA	—	Renewable Resources Extension Act
RRF	—	Ready Reserve Force
RRI	—	RCRA Remedial Investigation
RRMT	—	Reactor and Reactor Material Technology
RRS	—	Radiological Research Society
RRT	—	Regional Response Team
RRT	—	Requisite Remedial Technology
RS	—	Requirement Submission
RSE	—	Removal Site Evaluations
RSG	—	Reference Signal Generator
RSI	—	Rationalization, Standardization, and Interoperability
RSKERL	—	Robert S. Kerr Environmental Research Laboratory
RSMD	—	Resource Systems Management Division (OC)
RSO	—	Reported Significant Observations
RSPA	—	Research and Special Programs Administration
RSS	—	Reactor Safety Study

RSS	— Regional Services Staff (ORD)
RSS	— Remote Sensing Society
RSSMAP	— Reactor Safety Study Methodology Application Program
RSSR	— Reactor Building Spray Recirculation
RT	— Regional Total
RT	— Rough Terrain
RTCH	— Rough Terrain Container Handler
RTCM	— Reasonable Transportation Control Measures
RTD	— Reactor Technology Department
RTD	— Rapid Transit District
RTD	— Return to Duty
RTDM	— Rough Terrain Diffusion Model
RTECS	— Registry of Toxic Effects of Chemical Substances
RTFL	— Rough Terrain Forklift
RTM	— Regional Transport Model
RTP	— Research Triangle Park
RTR	— Real Time Radiography
RTR	— Roof-Top Ratio
RU	— Rescue Unit
RUP	— Restricted Use Pesticide (FIFRA)
RV	— Reactor Vessel
RV	— Recreational Vehicle
RVC	— Reactor Volume Control
RVP	— Reid Vapor Pressure
RW	— River Water
RW	— Office of Civilian Radioactive Waste Management (DOE)
RWA	— Regional Water Authority
RWE	— Reactor Works Engineering
RWIS	— Raw Water Intake Structure
RWL	— Reactor Water Level
RWQCB	— Regional Water Quality Control Board
RWST	— Refueling Water Storage Tank

RX   — Reactors

RZ   — Radiation Zone

RZ   — Recovery Zone

S
---

s   — Second

S/I   — Site Inspection

S/R   — Safety/Relief

S&A   — Surveillance and Analysis

S&A   — Sampling and Analysis

S&E   — Salaries and Expenses

S&F   — Store-and-Forward

S&M   — Surveillance and Maintenance

S&S   — Safeguards and Security

S&T   — Scientific and Technical

SO_2 — Sulfur Dioxide

SA   — Sunshine Act

SAAM   — Selective Alpha Air Monitor

SAB   — Science Advisory Board (AO)

SAC   — Suspended and Canceled Pesticides (FIFRA)

SACWRSA   — Sudbury, Assabet, and Concord Wild and Scenic River Study

SADA   — Science Assistant to the Deputy Assistant

SADT   — Self-Accelerating Decomposition Temperature

SAE   — Site Area Emergency

SAE   — Society of Automotive Engineers

SAEWG   — Standing Air Emissions Work Group (OAR)

SAH   — Society of American Historians

SAIC   — Special Agents in Charge (NEIC)

SAIP   — Systems Acquisition and Implementation Program

SAL   — Small Arms Locker

SALP	— Systematic Assessment of Licensee Performance
SAM	— Site Availability Mode
SAM	— Surface-to-Air Missile
SAMAC	— Standing AIRS Management Advisory Committee (OAR)
SAMS	— School of Advanced Military Studies
SAMWG	— Standing Air Monitoring Work Group
SAN	— San Francisco Operations Office (DOE)
SANE	— Sulfur and Nitrogen Emissions
SANSS	— Structure and Nomenclature Search System
SAP	— Scientific Advisory Panel
SAP	— Special Access Program
SAPO	— Subarea Petroleum Office
SAR	— Safety Analysis Report
SAR	— Search and Rescue
SAR	— Start Action Request
SARA	— Superfund Amendments and Reauthorization Act
SARMIS	— Search and Rescue Management Information System
SAROAD	— Storage and Retrieval of Aerometric Data
SARTEL	— Search and Rescue (SAR) Telephone
SAS	— Semiannual Soils
SAS	— Special Ammunition Storage
SAS	— Statistical Analysis System
SASD	— Strategies and Air Standards Division (OAR)
SASS	— Safety Assurance System Summary
SASS	— Source Assessment Sampling System
SAT	— Security Alert Team
SAT	— Semi-Automatic Trim
SATCOM	— Satellite Communications
SAV	— Semiannual Vegetation
SAW	— Surface Acoustic Wave
SAWMA	— Soil and Water Management Association
SB	— Sediment Basin

SBA	— Small Business Act
SBA	— Small Business Administration
SBO	— Small Business Ombudsman (OSDBU)
SBRPT	— Subordinate Reporting Organization
SC	— Safety Computer
SC	— Search and Rescue (SAR) Coordinator
SC	— Sierra Club
SC	— Steering Committee
SCAB	— South Coast Air Basin
SCANF	— Senate Committee on Agriculture, Nutrition, and Family
SCAP	— Superfund Comprehensive Accomplishments Plan
SCBA	— Self-Contained Breathing Apparatus
SCC	— Source Classification Code
SCC	— Standards Coordinating Committee
SCCC	— Security Communications Control Center
SCDAA	— Soil Conservation and Domestic Allotment Act
SCE	— Sister Chromatid Exchange
SCENRUS	— Senate Committee on Energy and Natural Resources of the United States
SCEPW	— Senate Committee on Environment and Public Works
SCF	— Standard Cubic Foot
SCFM	— Standard Cubic Feet per Minute
SCG	— Standby Diesel Generator
SCI	— Sensitive Compartmented Information
SCI	— Society of Chemical Industries
SCLDF	— Sierra Club Legal Defense Fund
SCOC	— Systems Control and Operations Concept
SCORPIO	— Subject Content Oriented Retriever for Processing Information On-line
SCP	— System Change Proposal
SCR	— Selective Catalytic Reduction
SCRAM	— An abbreviation for scrammble

SCRC	— Superfund Community Relations Coordinator
SCRP	— Superfund Community Relations Plan
SCRP	— Superfund Community Relations Program
SCS	— Soil Conservation Service
SCS	— Supplementary Control Strategy
SCS	— Supplementary Control System
SCSA	— Soil Conservation Society of America
SCSP	— Storm and Combined Sewer Program
SCT	— Spill Control Technology
SCTI	— Sodium Components Test Installation
SCUD	— Surface-to-Surface Missile System
SCW	— Service Clarified Water
SCWO	— Supercritical Water Oxidation
SD	— Special District
SDBUS	— Small and Disadvantaged Business Utilization Specialist
SDC	— Shutdown Cooling
SDG	— Scenario Development Group
SDG	— Special District Government
SDHX	— Shutdown Heat Exchanger
SDIO	— Strategic Defense Initiative Organization
SDLS	— Satellite Data Link Standards
SDN	— System Development Notification
SDO	— Staff Duty Officer
SDS	— Shutdown Sequencer
SDWA	— Safe Drinking Water Act
SEA	— State Enforcement Agreement
SEAL	— Sea-Air-Land Team
SEAS	— Strategic Environmental Assessment System
SEB	— Source Evaluation Board
SEC	— Second
SEC	— Senior Enforcement Counsel (OECM)
SECDEF	— Secretary of Defense

SECSTATE — Secretary of State

SECTRANS — Secretary of Transportation

SEDP — Site Evacuation and Decontamination Plan

SEE — Senior Environmental Employment

SEE — Society of Environmental Engineers

SEIA — Socioeconomic Impact Analysis

SEL REL — Selective Release

SEM — Scanning Electron Microscope

SEOC — State Emergency Operations Center

SEOP — State Emergency Operations Plan

SEP — Special Emphasis Program (OCR)

SEP — Systematic Evaluation Program

SEPWC — Senate Environment and Public Works Committee

SER — Safety Evaluation Report

SERC — State Emergency Response Commission

SERE — Survival, Evasion, Resistance, Escape

SERER — Survival, Evasion, Resistance, Escape, Recovery

SERI — Solar Energy Research Institute

SERS — SES and Executive Resources Staff (OHRM)

SES — Secondary Emissions Standard

SESA — Solar Energy Society of America

SETS — Site Enforcement Tracking System

SETS — Statistical Export and Tabulation System

SFA — Spectral Flame Analyzers

SFCs — Supercritical Fluids

SFCP — Shore Fire Control Party

SFE — Supercritical Fluid Extraction

SFFAS — Superfund Financial Assessment System

SFG — Special Forces Group

SFIREG — State FIFRA Issues Research and Evaluation Group

SFMP — Surplus Facilities Management Program

SFO — Servicing Finance Office

SG	— Steam Generator
SGMAS	— Sea Grant Marine Advisory Services
SGML	— Standard Generalized Markup Language
SGTR	— Steam Generator Tube Rupture
SGTS	— Standby Gas Treatment System
SH	— Sleeve Housings
SH	— Support Hospital
SHAPE	— Supreme Headquarters Allied Powers Europe
SHD	— Special Handling Designator
SHF	— Soil and Health Foundation
SHORAD	— Short-Range Air Defense
SHORTZ	— Short-Term Terrain Model
SHPO	— State Historic Preservation Officer
SHPRB	— State Historic Preservation Review Board
SHT	— Seal Head Tank
Si	— Silicon
SI	— International System of Units
SI	— Site Identification
SI	— Site Inspection
SI	— Special Intelligence
SIC	— Standard Industrial Classification
SICEA	— Steel Industry Compliance Extension Act
SICS	— Safety Injection Control System
SIGINT	— Signal Initialization
SIMMS	— Single Inline (Computer) Memory Modules
SIMS	— Secondary Ion-Mass Spectrometry
SIMS	— Standards Information Management System
SIP	— State Implementation Plan (CAA)
SIR	— Serious Incident Report
SIS	— Science Integration Staff (OPTS)
SIS	— Special Information Systems
SIS	— Special Isotope Separator

SIT	— Safety Injection Tank
SITE	— Superfund Innovative Technology Evaluation
SJA	— Staff Judge Advocate
SJI	— Steel Joist Institute
SJP	— Standard Job Procedures
SJS	— Secretary, Joint Staff
SL	— Sea Level
SLAC	— Standard Linear Accelerator Center
SLAMS	— State/Local Air Monitoring Station
SLB	— Shallow Land Burial
SLBM	— Sea-Launched Ballistic Missile
SLCS	— Standby Liquid Control System
SLD	— Special Litigation Division (OECM)
SLFAA	— State and Local Fiscal Assistance Amendments of 1972
SLI	— Sandia Laboratory Instruction
SLPD	— State and Local Planning Division
SLSM	— Simple Line Source Model
SMA	— Special Management Areas
SMC	— Selection and Monitoring Chassis
SMCLs	— Secondary Maximum Contaminant Levels
SMCRA	— Surface Mining Control and Reclamation Act
SME	— Subject Matter Expert
SMIO	— Search and Rescue Mission Information Officer
SMO	— Senior Meteorological and Oceanographic Officer
SMO	— Strategic Mobility Office
SMOA	— Superfund Memorandum of Agreement
SMRP	— Surface Mining and Reclamation Program
SMRSF	— Special Moment Resisting Space Frame
SMSA	— Standard Metropolitan Statistical Area
SNA	— System Network Architecture
SNAAQS	— Secondary National Ambient Air Quality Standards
SNAP	— Significant Noncompliance Action Program

SNARL	— Significant No Adverse Reaction Level
SNARL	— Suggested No Adverse Response Level
SNC	— Significant Noncompliers
SNG	— Synthetic Natural Gas
SNL	— Sandia National Laboratories
SNLA	— Sandia National Laboratories-Albuquerque
SNLL	— Sandia National Laboratories-Livermore
SNM	— Special Nuclear Materials
SNM	— System Notification Message
SNRTA	— Symms National Recreational Trails Act of 1991
SNUR	— Significant New Use Rule (TSCA)
SO	— Safety Observer
SO_2	— Sulfur Dioxide
SOC	— Schedule of Compliance
SOCMA	— Synthetic Organic Chemical Manufacturers Association
SOCMI	— Synthetic Organic Chemical Manufacturing Industry
SOCs	— Synthetic Organic Chemicals
SOE	— Special Operations Executive
SOE	— Stationary Operating Engineer
SOG	— Special Operations Group
SOLAS	— Safety of Life at Sea
SOLE	— Special Operations Liaison Element
SOM	— Start of Message
SOMPF	— Special Operations Mission Planning Folder
SONMET	— Special Operations Naval Mobile Environment Team
SOOE	— Study of Odors and Odorous Emissions
SOP	— Shift Operating Procedures
SOP	— Standard of Performance
SOP	— Standard Operating Power
SOP	— Standard Operating Procedures
SOPs	— Standard Operating Procedures
SORTS	— Status of Resources and Training System

SORV	— Stuck-Open Relief Valve
SOSR	— Suppress, Obscure, Secure, and Reduce
SOTDAT	— Source Test Data
SOV	— Single Occupancy Vehicle
SOW	— Scope of Work
SOW	— Statement of Work
SOWT/TE	— Special Operations Weather Team/Tactical Element
SOx	— Sulfur Oxides
SP	— Suppression Pool
SPA	— Shore Protection Act of 1988
SPAB	— Society for the Protection of Ancient Buildings
SPAD	— Special Programs and Analysis Division (OEA)
SPC	— Suppression Pool Cooling
SPCC	— Spill Prevention, Containment, and Countermeasures
SPCC	— Spill Prevention, Control, and Countermeasures
SPCCP	— Spill Prevention, Control, and Countermeasures Plan
SPD	— State Programs Division (OW)
SPE	— Secondary Particulate Emissions
SPEC	— Society for Pollution and Environmental Control
Specs	— Specifications
SPEGL	— Short-Term Public Exposure Guidance Level
SPF	— Structured Programming Facility
SPI	— Strategic Planning Initiative
SPLMD	— Soil-Pore Liquid Monitoring Device
SPM	— Senior Project Manager
SPMS	— Safety Performance Measurement System
SPMS	— Special Purpose Monitoring Stations
SPMS	— Strategic Planning and Management System
SPOC	— Search and Rescue Points of Contact
SPOC	— Single Points of Contact
SPP	— Standard Practice Procedures
SPR	— Strategic Petroleum Reserve

SPR III	— Sandia Pulse Reactor III
SPS	— Safety Precedence Sequence
SPS	— State Permit System
SPSC	— System Planning and System Control
SPSS	— Statistical Package for the Social Sciences
SPUR	— Software Package for Unique Reports
SQBE	— Small Quantity Burner Exemption (RCRA)
SQG	— Small Quantity Generator (RCRA)
SQUIMP	— An abbreviation for a computer code
Sr	— Steradians
SR	— Savannah River Operations Office
SR	— Special Reconnaissance
SRB	— Software Release Bulletin
SRBM	— Short-Range Ballistic Missile
SRC	— Safety Review Committee
SRC	— Solvent Refined Coal
SRC	— Survival Recovery Center
SRIM	— Structural Reinforced Injection Molding
SRM	— Standard Reference Method
SRO	— Senior Reactor Operator
SRPA	— Small Reclamation Projects Act of 1956
SRS	— Savannah River Site
SRU	— Search and Rescue Unit
SRU	— System Resource Unit
SRV	— Safety/Relief Valve
SRW	— Savannah River Water
SS	— Shift Superintendent
SS	— Shift Supervisor
SS	— Socioeconomic Status
SS	— Superfund Surcharge
SSA	— Social Security Act (42 USC)
SSA	— Sole Source Aquifer

SSAC	— Soil Site Assimilated Capacity
SSC	— Scientific Support Coordinator
SSCD	— Stationary Source Compliance Division
SSCRA	— Soldiers and Sailors Civil Relief Act
SSD	— Standard Support Document
SSDC	— System Safety Development Center
SSEIS	— Standard Support and Environmental Impact Statement
SSEIS	— Stationary Source Emissions and Inventory System
SSFI	— Safety System Functional Inspection
SSI	— Size Selective Inlet
SSM	— Surface-to-Surface Missile
SSMI	— Special Sensor Microwave Imagery
SSMS	— Spark Source Mass Spectroscopy
SSN	— Social Security Number
SSO	— Source Selection Official
SSO	— Support Services Office
SSOMI	— Safety System Outage Modification Inspection
SSPS	— Solid State Protection System
SSPSA	— Seabrook Station Probabilistic Safety Assessment
SSR	— Secondary System Relief
SSS	— Safe Shutdown System
SSS	— Selective Service System
SSS	— Strategic Studies Staff (OPPE)
SSS	— Supplementary Safety System
SST	— Single Shell Tanks
SSURO	— Stop Sale, Use, and Removal Order (FIFRA)
ST	— Sleeve Target
STA	— Shift Technical Advisor
STA	— Small Tracts Act
STA	— Special Treatment Area (Coastal Commission)
STANAG	— Standardization Agreement (NATO)
STAPP	— State and Territorial Air Pollution Program

STAR	— State Acid Rain (Projects)
STARC	— State Area Coordinators
START	— Superfund Technical Assessment and Response Team
STC	— Single Strip Container
STCAC	— Scientific Technical Careers Advisory Committee
std	— Standard
STEL	— Short-Term Exposure Limit
STGWG	— State and Tribal Government Working Group
STI	— Surveillance Test Interval
STIN	— Scientific and Technical Information Network
STM	— Stack Tritium Monitor
STOD	— Special Technical Operations Division
STON	— Short Ton(s)
STORET	— Storage and Retrieval of Water Related Data
STP	— Sewage Treatment Plant
STP	— Standard Temperature and Pressure
STR	— Strength
STU	— Secure Telephone Unit
SU	— Search Unit
SUP	— Standard Unit of Processing
SURE	— Sulfate Regional Experiment Program
SURG	— Surgeon
SV	— Sampling Visit
SVC	— Service(s)
SVI	— Sludge Volume Index
SWA	— Southwest Asia
SWAT	— Solid Waste Assessment Test
SWAT	— Special Weapons and Tactics
SWC	— Settlement with Conditions
SWDA	— Solid Waste Disposal Act
SWE	— Society of Women Engineers
SWERD	— Solid Waste and Emergency Response Division (OGC)

SWGR	— Switchgear Room
SWIE	— Southern Waste Information Exchange
SWMU	— Solid Waste Management Unit
SWP	— Safety Work Permit
SWPP	— State Wellhead Protection Program
SWS	— Salt Water System
SWS	— Service Water System
SWSA	— Solid Waste Storage Area
SWSRAAA	— Sipsey Wild and Scenic River and Alabama Addition Act
SYS	— System
SYSCON	— Systems Control
SYSOP	— System Operator

T

T	— Ton (short)
T/L	— Time/Loss Analysis
T/V	— Tank Vessel
TO	— Technical Order
T&B	Top and Bottom
T&DE	— Test and Diagnostic Equipment
T&E	— Test and Evaluation
T&E	— Threatened and Endangered Species
T&M	— Time and Materials
TA	— Test Authorizations
TA/CP	— Technology Assessment/Control Plan
TAD	— Time Available for Delivery
TAFPD	— Technical Assessment and Fraud Prevention Division
TAFT	— Technical Assistance Field Team
TAG	— Technical Assistance Grant
TALM	— Temperature Alarm Monitor

TALMS	— Tunable Atomic Line Molecular Spectroscopy
TAMAC	— Toxic Air Monitoring (Technical) Advisory Committee
TAMS	— Toxic Air Monitoring System
TAN	— Test Area North
TAO	— TSCA Assistance Office (OPTS)
TAP	— Technical Assistance Program
TAP	— Toxic Air Pollutant
TAP	— Training Accreditation Program
TAPDS	— Toxic Air Pollutant Data System
TAPPI	— Technical Association of Pulp and Paper Industry
TAT	— Technical Assistance Team
TB	— Turbine Building
TBD	— To be Determined
TBF	— Technical and Biological Feasibility
TBFCA	— Technical and Biological Facility and Cost Effectiveness of Alternatives
TBM	— Tactical Ballistic Missile
TBP	— To be Published
TBSCCW	— Turbine Building Secondary Closed Cooling Water
TBSL	— To be Supplied Later
TBSW	— Turbine Building Service Water
TBT	— Tributyltin
TBTC	— Transportable Blood Transshipment Center
TBV	— Turbine Block Valve
Tc	— Technetium
TC	— Target Concentration
TC	— Technical Center
TC	— Thermocouple(s)
TC	— Tidal Current
TCC	— Transportation Component Compound
TCD	— Transportation Control Demonstration
TCDD	— Tetrachlorodibenzodioxin

TCDF	— Tetrachlorodibenzofurans
TCE	— Trichloroethylene
TCL	— Target Compound List
TCLP	— Toxicity Characteristic Leachate Procedure
TCM	— Transportation Control Measure
TCMD	— Transportation Control and Movement Document
TCN	— Transportation Control Number
TCP	— Tool Center Point
TCP	— Transportation Control Plan
TCRP	— Transit Cooperative Research Program
TCSEC	— Trusted Computer System Evaluation Criteria
TCSM	— Transportation Control Strategies and Measure
TD	— Time Delay
TD	— Total Drift
TDA	— Table of Distribution and Allowance
TDBM	— Technical Data Base Management
TDLO	— Toxic Dose Low
TDR	— Transfer of Development Rights
TDS	— Total Dissolved Solids
TDTOX	— Tetradichloroxylene
TDY	— Temporary Duty
TEAM	— Total Exposure Assessment Methodology
TEC	— Technical Evaluation Committee
Tech	— Technical
TECHCON	— Technical Control
TECHDOC	— Technical Documentation
TEG	— Tetraethylene Glycol
TEGD	— Technical Enforcement Guidance Document
TELINT	— Telemetry Intelligence
TELNET	— Telecommunication Network
TENCAP	— Tactical Exploitation of National Capabilities Program
TERC	— Total Environmental Restoration Contract

TERCOM	— Terrain Contour Matching
TEU	— Twenty-Foot Equivalent Unit
TF	— Task Force
TFCS	— Treasury Financial Communications System
TFE	— Transportation Feasibility Estimator
TFR	— Temporary Flight Restrictions
TG	— Task Group
TGIF	— Thank God It's Friday!
TGO	— Total Gross Output
THC	— Total Hydrocarbons
THERP	— Technique for Human Error Rate Prediction
THM	— Trihalomethane
THREATCON	— Terrorist Threat Condition
TI	— Temporary Intermittent
TI	— Threat Identification
TIBL	— Thermal Internal Boundary Layer
TIC	— Technical Information Coordinator
TIFF	— Tagged Image File Format
TIM	— Technical Information Manager
TIP	— Transportation Improvement Program
TIPI	— Tactical Information Processing and Interpretation System
TIR	— Total Indicated Runout
TIS	— Technical Information Staff
TITC	— TSCA Interagency Testing Committee
TL	— Team Leader
TLAM	— Tomahawk Land-Attack Missile
TLC	— Traffic Load Control
TLCF	— Teleconference
TLD	— Thermoluminescent Dosimeter
TLV	— Threshold Limit Value
TM	— Technical Manual
TMG	— Timing

TMO	— Transportation Management Office
TMP	— Telecommunications Management Program
TNT	— Trinitrotoleuene
TO	— Task Order
TOA	— Table of Allowance
TOA	— Trace Organic Analysis
TOC	— Tactical Operations Center
TOC	— Total Organic Carbon
TOC	— Total Organic Compound
TOD	— Time of Day
TOR	— Terms of Reference
TOT	— Time of Travel
TOX	— Tetradichloroxylene
TP	— Technical Publication
TPC	— Temporary Procedure Change
TPD	— Toxics and Pesticides Division (ORD)
TPH	— Triphenyltin Hydroxide
TPI	— Technical Proposal Instructions
TPL	— Technical Publications List
TPL	— Transient Protection Limit
TPO	Technical Programs Office
TPQ	— Threshold Planning Quantity
TPSIS	— Transportation Planning Support Information System
TPT	— Tactical Petroleum Terminal
TPTRL	— Time-Phased Transportation Requirements List
TQM	— Total Quality Management
TRA	— Technical Review Authority
TRA	— Test Reactor Area
TRAC	— Terrain Responsive Atmospheric Code
TRADOC	— U.S. Army Training and Doctrine Command
TRAM	— Transient Muitiplexor
TRB	— Transit Research Board

TRC	— Technical Review Committee
TRC	— Total Recordable Cases
TRD	— Technical Resources Document
TRE	— Turbidity Removal Evaporator
TRIP	— Toxic Release Inventory Program
TRIS	— Toxic Release Inventory System
TRLN	— Triangle Research Library Network
TRO	— Temporary Restraining Order
TROPO	— Troposphere
TRS	— Total Reduced Sulfur
TRU	— Transuranic
TRU	— Transuranic Nuclides
TS	— Technical Specifications
TS	— Training Services
TSA	— Technical Safety Appraisal
TSA	— Technical Systems Audit
TSC	— Toxic Substances Coordinator
TSCA	— Toxic Substances Control Act
TSCANS	— An abbreviation for a TSCA computer code
TSCAT	— An abbreviation for a TSCA computer code
TSCATS	— The Online TSCA Test Submission Database
TSCC	— Toxic Substances Coordinating Committee
TSCM	— Temperature Scram Circuit Monitor
TSD	— Technical Support Division
TSD	— Technical Support Document
TSD	— Treatment, Storage and Disposal
TSDF	— Treatment, Storage, and Disposal Facility
TSDG	— Toxic Substances Dialogue Group
TSH	— Target Sleeve Housing
TSM	— Transportation System Management
TSO	— Time Sharing Option
TSP	— Teleprocessing Services Program

TSP	— Total Suspended Particulates
TSS	— Technical Support Staff
TSS	— Timesharing System
TSS	— Terminal Security System
TSS	— Total Suspended Solids
TSSP	— Tactical Satellite Signal Processor
TSUS	— Territorial Seas of the United States
TT&C	— Telemetry, Tracking, and Commanding
TTAP	— Tiger Team Assessment Program
TTFA	— Target Transformation Factor Analysis
TTHM	— Total Trihalomethane
TTO	— Total Toxic Organics
TTR	— Time to Repair
TUM	— Training User's Manual
TVA	— Tennessee Valley Authority
TVAA	— Tennessee Valley Authority Act of 1933
TW	— Test Weight
TWA	— Time Weighted Average
TWC	— Total Water Current
TWF	— Transuranic Waste Facility
TWMD	— Toxics and Waste Management Division
TWTSF	— Transuranic Waste Treatment and Storage Facility
TX	— Transmitter
TZ	— Treatment Zone

U

U	— Uranium
UAM	— Urban Airshed Model
UAPSP	— Utility Acid Precipitation Study Program
UAQI	— Uniform Air Quality Index

UARG	— Utility Air Regulatory Group
UAV	— Unmanned Aerial Vehicle
UBC	— Uniform Building Code
UBOD	— Ultimate Biological Oxygen Demand
UCC	— Ultra Clean Coal
UCNI	— Unclassified Controlled Nuclear Information
UCP	— Unified Command Plan
UCR	— Unit Cancer Risk
UCT	— Underwater Construction Team
UD	— Unidirectional
UDC	— Unit Descriptor Code
UDMH	— Unsymmetrical Dimethyl Hydrazine
UDSSP	— Upper Delaware Segment Special Provisions
UDT	— Underwater Demolition Team
UEL	— Upper Explosive Limit
UEPM	— Urban and Environmental Planning and Management
UF	— Uncertainty Factor
UF_4	— Uranium Tetrafluoride
UF_6	— Uranium Hexafluoride
UFL	— Upper Flammability Limit
UFSAR	— Updated Final Safety Analysis Report
UGM	— Underwater Guided Missile
UIC	— Underground Injection Control (SDWA)
UK	— United Kingdom
UL	— Underwriters Laboratory
ULP	— Unfair Labor Practice
UMC	— Uniform Mechanical Code
UMIB	— Urgent Marine Information Broadcast
UMP	— Upward Mobility Program
UMT	— Uranium Mill Tailings
UMTA	— Urban Mass Transportation Administration
UMTRA	— Uranium Mill Tailings Remedial Action

UMTRAP	— Uranium Mill Tailings Remedial Action Program
UMTRCA	— Uranium Mill Tailings Radiation Control Act
UN	— United Nations
UNAAF	— Unified Action Armed Forces
UNAMAP	— User's Network for Applied Modeling of Air Pollution
UNC	— United Nations Command
UNDRO	— United Nations Disaster Relief Office
UNEP	— United Nations Environment Program
UNESCO	— United Nations Educational, Scientific, and Cultural Organization
UNITAF	— Unified Task Force
UNO	— Unit Number
UNODIR	— Unless Otherwise Directed
UNON	— Unless Otherwise Noted
UNSC	— United Nations Security Council
UOs	— Unusual Occurrences
UOR	— Unusual Occurrence Report
UORS	— Unusual Occurrence Reporting System
UP	— Urban Planner
UPL	— Uniform Plumbing Code
UPS	— Uninterruptible Power Source
URC	— Utility Regulatory Commission
URDB	— User Requirements Database
U.S.	— United States
USA	— United States Army
USACOM	— United States Atlantic Command
USAF	— United States Air Force
USAFEP	— United States Air Forces Europe Pamphlet
USAFR	— United States Air Force Reserve
USAID	— United States Agency for International Development
USAISC	— United States Army Information System Command
USAITAC	— United States Army Intelligence Threat Analysis Center

USAMMA	— United States Army Medical Materiel Agency
USASOC	— United States Army Special Operations Command
USATHMC	— U.S. Army Toxic and Hazardous Materials Center
USBM	— United States Bureau of Mines
USBS	— United States Bureau of Standards
USC	— Unified Soil Classification
USC	— United States Code
USCENTCOM	— United States Central Command
USCG	— United States Coast Guard
USDA	— United States Department of Agriculture
USDW	— Underground Sources of Drinking Water
USEPA	— United States Environmental Protection Agency
USERC	— United States Environment and Resources Council
USERID	— User Identification
USEUCOM	— United States European Command
USFJ	— United States Forces Japan
USFK	— United States Forces Korea
USFORAZORES	— United States Forces Azores
USFS	— United States Forest Service
USFWS	— United States Fish and Wildlife Service
USG	— United States Government
USGS	— United States Geological Survey (DOI)
USGSS	— United States Government Survey System
USH	— Universal Sleeve Housing
USIA	— United States Information Agency
USLO	— United States Liaison Officer
USMC	— United States Marine Corps
USMCR	— United States Marine Corps Reserve
USMILGP	— United States Military Group
USMILREP	— United States Military Representative
USMTF	— United States Message Text Format
USMTM	— United States Military Training Mission

USN	— United States Navy
USNMR	— United States National Military Representative
USNR	— United States Navy Reserve
USNS	— United States Naval Ship
USPACAF	— United States Air Forces, U.S. Pacific Command
USPACFLT	— United States Pacific Fleet
USPACOM	— United States Pacific Command
USPS	— United States Postal Service
USRADS	— Ultrasonic Ranging and Data System
USSOCOM	— United States Special Operations Command
USSS	— United States Signals Intelligence System
UST	— Underground Storage Tank
UT	— Universal Time
UTC	— Coordinated Universal Time
UTC	— Unit Type Code
UTM Grid	— Universal Transverse Mercator Grid System
UTO	— Unit Table of Organization
UTO	— Universal Time Observed
UTP	— Urban Transportation Planning
UV	— Ultraviolet
UV	— Undervoltage
UVEPROM	— Ultraviolet Erasable Programmable Read Only Memory
UW	— Unconventional Warfare
UZM	— Unsaturated Zone Monitoring

V

V	— Volt
VA	— Veterans Administration
VAC	— Volts Alternating Current

VAHUDIA	— Veterans Affairs, Housing and Urban Development, and Independent Agencies Appropriations Act of 1990
VAM	— Vibration and Acoustic Monitoring
VAT	— Value Added Tax
VAT	— Vinyl Asbestos [Floor] Tile
VATB	— Visibility, Amount of Clouds, Height of Cloud Top, Height of Cloud Base
VCM	— Vinyl Chloride Monomer
VCP	— Vitrified Clay Pipe
VDC	— Volts Direct Current
VDR	— Voice Digitization Rate
VDSD	— Visual Distress Signaling Device
VDU	— Visual Display Unit
VE	— Visual Emissions
VEH	— Vehicular Cargo
VEO	— Visible Emission Observation
VERTREP	— Vertical Replenishment
VHAP	— Volatile Hazardous Air Pollutant
VHF	— Very High Frequency
VHS	— Vertical and Horizontal Spread Model
VHT	— Vehicle-Hours of Travel
VHT	— Very High Temperature
VI	— Visual Information
VIDOC	— Visual Information Documentation
VIP	— Very Important Person
VIP	— Visual Information Processor
VIP	— Vulnerability Impact
VIR	— Visibility Impairment Research
VIS	— Site Visitation
VISTTA	— Visibility Impairment from Sulfur Transformation and Transport in the Atmosphere
VKT	— Vehicle Kilometers Traveled
VLF	— Very Low Flow

VLFC	— Very Low Flow Constant
VM	— Volt Meter
VMC	— Visual Meteorological Conditions
VMT	— Vehicle Miles Traveled
VNS	— Volumetric Neutron Source
VOCs	— Volatile Organic Compounds
vol	— Volume
VOR	— Very High Frequency Omnidirectional Range Station
VOST	— Volatile Organic Sampling Train
VOX	— Voice Actuation (Keying)
VP	— Vapor Pressure
VRB	— Visibility Reducing Particles
VRE	— Vibrating Reed Electrometers
VS&PT	— Vehicle Summary and Priority Table
VSI	— Visual Site Inspection
VSII	— Very Serious Ill or Injured
VSOCs	— Volatile Synthetic Organic Compounds
VSS	— Vital Safety System
VSS	— Volatile Suspended Solids
VTC	— Video Teleconferencing
VTC	— Visibility Transport Commission
VTR	— Visibility Transport Region
VTS	— Vertical Tube Storage
VU	— Volume Unit

W

W	— Watt
WA	— Work Assignment
WACC	— Waste Acceptance Criteria Committee
WADTF	— Western Atmospheric Deposition Task Force

WAG	— Waste Area Grouping
WAN	— Wide Area Network
WAP	— Waste Analysis Plan (RCRA)
WAPA	— Western Area Power Administration
WASTE	— An abbreviation for a computer database
WATCHCON	— Watch Condition
WB	— Wet Bulb
WB	— World Bank
WBE	— Women Business Enterprise
WC	— Wind Current
WCA	— Wildlife Conservation Act
WCC	— Washington Computer Center
WCCSA	— White Clay Creek Study Act of 1991
WD	— Water Division (OGC)
WDL	— Work Days Lost
WDLR	— Work Days Lost Restricted
WDROP	— Distribution Register of Organic Pollutants in Water
WED	— Water Enforcement Division
WENDB	— Water Enforcement National Data Base
WERF	— Waste Experimental Reaction Facility
WERL	— Water Engineering Research Laboratory
WETM	— Weather Team
WG	— Wage Grade
WG	— Work Group
WGS	— World Geodetic System
WHC	— Westinghouse Hanford Company
WHO	— World Health Organization (UN)
WHPA	— Wellhead Protection Area
WHPP	— Waste Handling and Packaging Plant
WHWT	— Water and Hazardous Waste Team
WIC	— Washington Information Center
WICEM	— World Industry Conference on Environmental Management

WIPP	— Waste Isolation Pilot Plant
WIN	— Waste Information Network
WL	— Warning Letter
WL	— Working Levels
WLA	— Wasteload Allocation
WLD	— Water and Land Division
WLG	— Washington Liaison Group
WLM	— Working Level Month
WM	— Waste Management
WMAC	— Waste Management Advisory Council
WMD	— Waste Management Division
WMED	— Waste Management and Economics Division
WMin	— Waste Minimization
WMO	— Waste Management Operations
WMO	— World Meteorological Organization
WMP	— War and Mobilization Plan
WMP	— Waste Minimization Plan
WMS	— Workforce Management Staff
WOG	— Water, Oil, Gas Rating
WORM	— Write Once Read Many
WPA	— Water Jet Propulsion Assembly
WPA	— Well Protection Act
WPB	— Coast Guard Patrol Boat
WPCF	— Water Pollution Control Federation
WPFPA	— Watershed Protection and Flood Prevention Act of 1954
WPI	— Wholesale Price Index
WPM	— Words per Minute
WPN	— Weapon(s)
WPO	— Water Policy Office (OW)
WPS	— Wildlife Preservation Society
WRA	— Wetlands Resource Act
WQS	— Water Quality Standards

WRAP	— Waste Receiving and Processing Plant
WRC	— Water Resources Council
WRDA	— Water Resources Development Act of 1990
WRI	— World Resources Institute
WRUA	— Wood Residue Utilization Act
WS	— Work Scope
WSADR	— Western States Acid Deposition Research
WSESRB	— Weapon System Explosive Safety Review Board
WSF	— Water Soluble Fraction
WSR	— Wild and Scenic River
WSRA	— Wild and Scenic Rivers Act
WSTB	— Water Science and Technology Board
WT	— Gross Weight
WT	— Watertight
WTCA	— Water Terminal Clearance Authority
WTPS	— Water, Toxics and Pesticides Staff
WTSHRD	— Water and Toxic Substances Health Research Division
WWCCS	— Worldwide (Military) Command and Control System
WWEMA	— Waste and Wastewater Equipment Manufacturers Association
WWF	— World Wildlife Fund
WWMS	— Water and Waste Management Staff
WYSIWYG	— What You See Is What You Get!

X/Y/Z

XXX	— Form for Assessment of Effect on Cultural Resources
YAG	— Yttrium Aluminum Garnet
ZBB	— Zero Base Budgeting
ZHE	— Zero Headspace Extractor
Zn	— Periodic Element, Zinc
ZEC	— Zone of Engineering Control

ZFF	— Zone of Fracture and Flowage
ZOA	— Zone of Aeration
ZOC	— Zone of Cementation
ZOC	— Zone of Contribution
ZOD	— Zone of Deposition
ZOE	— Zone of Erosion
ZOF	— Zone of Flowage
ZOF	— Zone of Fracture
ZOI	— Zone of Incorporation
ZOI	— Zone of Influence
ZOS	— Zone of Saturation
ZOT	— Zone of Transport
ZOW	— Zone of Weathering
ZPSS	— Zion Probabilistic Safety Study
ZRL	— Zero Risk Level
ZS	— Zoological Society
ZSS	— Zero Sum Society
Zt	— Total Available Effort
ZULU	— Time Zone Indicator for Universal Time

Phase I Environmental Site Assessment

PHASE I ENVIRONMENTAL SITE ASSESSMENT
with
COMPREHENSIVE ASBESTOS SURVEY

Silverpoint Office Building
6666 Summit Street
Silverpoint, Colorado
Property I.D. No: 1098

prepared for
Urbanetics Partners
120 16th Street, Suite 300
Denver, CO 80202
Attn: Mr. John Doe

prepared by
LTR ENVIRONMENTAL, INC.
7600 E. Arapahoe Road, Suite 114
Englewood, Colorado 80112
PH: (303) 843-9079/FAX (303) 843-9094

Final Date: June 26, 1995

Submitted by

André R. Cooper
President and CEO

All environmental deliverables should be accompanied by a cover sheet. Here is a typical sheet utilized by LTRE for its Phase Is. Client, date, and project identification are imperative.

TABLE OF CONTENTS

A typical table of contents with a listing of the minimum types of exhibits that should be included in a Phase I ESA, as appropriate.

SITE MAPS	SITE PHOTOS
AERIAL PHOTOS	REGULATORY DATABASE SEARCH
LUST SITE RECORDS	DATA REFERENCES
LABORATORY ANALYSES	CHAIN OF CUSTODY FORM
LAB & INSPECTOR'S CERTIFICATIONS	

PHASE I ENVIRONMENTAL SITE ASSESSMENT

Silverpoint Office Building
6666 Summit Street
Silverpoint, Colorado

EXECUTIVE SUMMARY

A Phase I Environmental Site Assessment (ESA) was completed by LTR Environmental, Inc. (LTRE) for the Office building located at 6666 Summit Street in Silverpoint, Colorado. This work was performed for Urbanetics Partners of Frisco, Colorado. This Phase I ESA was conducted in accordance with the Resolution Trust Corporation's (RTC) scope of work for environmental assessments (January 1993). Investigation activities included agency interviews, site inspections, asbestos sampling and analyses, property transaction reviews, and local and state governmental records reviews.

The subject property is identified as a 3724 square foot office building located at 6666 Summit Street and described as in the County of Grand Tax Assessor's Map Recorded in book 1039, pages 12 through 13. Based on the age of the current structure a Comprehensive Asbestos Survey was conducted to determine the presence of asbestos containing materials, per scope. Twenty-one samples were taken of the eleven homogenous groups identified on-site. All samples were analyzed, and all friable samples were found not to contain asbestos. One nonfriable roof mastic material was confirmed to contain asbestos.

The surrounding area is primarily low density resort residential, with commercial establishments along Arapahoe Boulevard approximately 700 feet west of the site. Immediately north of the site lies parking areas that serve commercial/retail operations. There was no evidence collected during this ESA which would indicate that the site has been adversely affected by environmental hazards from commercial operations in the site vicinity. No industrial facilities are located in the site area. No special resources were identified on or immediately adjacent to the site. LTRE contacted the CO Regional Water Quality Control Board, the Grand County Public Works Department, and the Tri-County Public Health Investigations Division concerning the LUST sites in the site vicinity. Copies of Site Investigation data are included in the Appendices.

ESA-1

All Phase I ESA deliverables should be accompanied by an executive summary, or synopsis of the salient facts of the study. This summary should provide the reader with the who, what, where, and nature of the potential environmental issues of concern, if any.

The SOW should be reiterated in the Phase I ESA to inform readers not familiar with the contract of the actual tasks contracted for. Often, the SOW is provided by the client and in such instances should be followed exactly, in other cases we suggest using boilerplate SOWs.

1.0 SCOPE of SERVICES

LTRE performed a Phase I ESA, including photographic inspection of the site and facilities, and adjacent properties. Phase I site reconnaissance tasks were completed by Mr. Andre Cooper, M.S., on June 6, 1995. The Comprehensive Asbestos Survey was conducted by Mr. Peter McSimmons, AHERA and Colorado Certified Asbestos Inspector (see certifications in the appendices), on June 6, 1995.

Historical records and regulatory database searches were conducted to obtain information on past land-use activities that may have been environmentally significant.

The Phase I ESA and Asbestos Survey services provided were as follows.

Site History

To conduct tasks related to reconstruction the site's history, LTRE:

- researched available deed and title information to identify owners who may have used the property for industrial and/or hazardous waste handling activities;

- obtained and reviewed aerial photographs of the site and adjacent properties to determine current uses that may have an environmental impact on the site;

- obtained and reviewed governmental records (site plans, permits, etc.) available to identify use, generation, storage, treatment, and/or disposal of hazardous materials. or release incidents which may impact or have impacted the site;

- reviewed available reports and other documentation from government agencies, on the site and adjacent lands;

- interviewed site area representatives to identify any additional areas of concern.

Environmental Database Searches

To conduct tasks related to environmental database searches, LTRE identified, obtained, and reviewed state, federal, and local databases and records to discover if the site, or any adjacent sites have posed an environmental hazard in the past, or currently pose such a threat. A Database Report is included in the appendices.

Database and information researched included the following:

ESA-2

Federal Records Searched

NATIONAL PRIORITIES LIST (NPL) — The U.S. Environmental Protection Agency (EPA) listing of federal Superfund sites. The NPL is a list of sites that have been evaluated using the Hazard Ranking System, and that have been determined to pose an imminent threat to human health or the environment.

CERCLIS — EPA database of known, alleged, or potential hazardous waste sites that have been, or require investigation under CERCLA. For sites that have been investigated, site status is given, sites not investigated are potentially eligible for inclusion on the NPL.

RCRIS (Resource Conservation and Recovery Information System) - Database of sites that generate, store, transport, treat, and/or dispose of hazardous wastes. Sites that fall into these categories are required to submit a notification of hazardous waste activity to EPA. RCRA facilities are classed in the following categories: Large or Small Quantity waste generators.

RCRA — TSD Sites (Treatment, Storage, and Disposal), companies which have reported that they treat, store, and/or dispose of hazardous waste; and RCRA Transport Sites, companies which have reported that they transport hazardous wastes.

State Records Searched

The office responsible for maintaining information regarding environmental hazards in the state, is the Colorado Department of Health and Environment (CDPHE). The following is a list of the state records reviewed for this audit.

Hazardous Waste Sites and Solid Waste Disposal Sites   CDPHE database for the identification and location of current and historical sites that engage in solid waste collection, transport, separation, recovery, and/or disposal activities.

Underground Storage Tank Records (USTs) — CDPHE database for identification and locations of sites that maintain underground tanks that contain regulated (usually petroleum related) substances.

Leaking Underground Storage Tank Records (LUSTs) — CDPHE database for identification and locations of sites that maintain underground tanks that contain regulated (usually petroleum related) substances, with reported leaks.

Here is a listing of the typical records that must be searched. States may have their own names for various databases, but the content is similar.
The importance of stating what it is you're going to do, and what databases you're going to search before you do it cannot be overemphasized as it constitutes your Phase I ESA project plan!

ESA-3

Site Reconnaissance tasks are conducted on-site as well as on adjacent sites and sites in the immediate vicinity that may pose a negative impact on the subject site.

Be careful when bidding on Comprehensive Asbestos Surveys in other states; many have their own licensing requirements in addition to AHERA Certification.

Site Reconnaissance

A reconnaissance visit to the site was made to inspect physical facilities, identify site drainage patterns, and make other observations. The Project Manager for this site investigation was Andre Cooper. The following tasks were conducted:

- visual inspection of the site and surrounding properties was conducted. The inspection was conducted to identify potential USTs, ASTs, potential sources of ACMs, PCBs, or other hazardous chemicals;

- exterior site analysis and photographs to identify potential hazards from on-site and off-site property uses;

- visual surface investigations to reveal evidence of spills (stained soils or concrete), and vegetative stress.

COMPREHENSIVE ASBESTOS SURVEY

As mentioned above, a Comprehensive Asbestos Survey was conducted on the Summit Street site.

The Comprehensive Asbestos Survey and inspection included:

- visual inspections of the building units to determine the presence of suspect asbestos-containing building materials either friable or non-friable;

- identification of locations of homogeneous areas of suspect asbestos-containing materials from which samples were to be obtained;

- collection of bulk samples of suspect ACMs;

- provide diagrams of the inspected buildings which illustrate sample collection locations;

- provide selected photographs of the types of suspect materials sampled;

- bulk-sample testing and analyses by a NVLAP certified laboratory;

- provide a written summary of the asbestos inspection.

ESA-4

Special and Cultural Resources

Visual observations and records investigations for special and cultural resources were conducted in the following areas:

Air Quality	Archaeological Resources
Biotic and Wildlife Habitats	Coastal Zones
Unique Farmlands	Historic Resources
Land Use	Threatened Endangered Species
Socio Economic Impacts	Transportation
Recreation Areas	Wetlands
Wildlife	Wild and Scenic Rivers

2.0 PROPERTY INFORMATION

The pertinent asset information is:

Property Name:	Silverpoint Office Building
Property Address:	6666 Summit Street, Silverpoint, CO
Property No:	1098
Financial Institute:	First National Bank
Institution No:	RTC# 7380
Property Firm:	Urbanetics Partners
Property Mgr:	John Doe
Property Mgr:	Roger Moreland
Owner:	Janet Jammes (per Tax Records)

The legal description for 6666 Summit Street is: Lot 12 in Block 21, Tract 14, in the city of Silverpoint, county of Grand, state of Colorado, as per map recorded in book 1039, pages 12 through 13 of maps, in the office of the County Recorder of said county,

ESA-5

A brief discussion of each potential special resource should be included in the Phase I ESA, even if the statement is no more than an acknowledgment that the issue is not applicable to the subject site.

Note: All property data has been sanitized for this sample.

except therefrom an undivided one-half interest in and to all oil, gas and minerals, and all oil, gas and mineral rights upon and under the above described lands....as reserved in deed from First National Bank of Grand, recorded in Book 206, Page 19, Official Records.

According to records reviewed at the Tax Assessor's Office the property is also known as:

Parcel No.1234-0985-065.

3.0 SITE LOCATION and DESCRIPTION

Legal descriptions should be obtained from the client and verified with the assessor. Site location and description data is typically a combination of data contained in prior appraisals, zoning/building plans and maps, and data obtained during site reconnaissance.

The property is located on the north side of Summit Street about one-half block east of Arapahoe Boulevard in the city of Silverpoint, Grand County, Colorado (see maps in Appendix B). Most development in the area is a mix of office, low to medium density residential, and retail complexes that line Arapahoe Boulevard to the west. No industrial facilities were identified in the immediate area.

The subject lot and structure are rectangularly shaped. The site is terraced above neighboring properties to the north and east. Residential properties abut the site to the east, with the Summit Street right-of-way to the south and retail facilities beyond. The north and west sides of the site are also retail operations. The lot is zoned for office/commercial use and consists of a two story, wood frame building, with covered parking areas at grade. According to information obtained from the asset management firm, the total floor area of the structure is about 3,724 square feet.

On the day of our investigation the building is divided into six (6) units. The tenants and approximate square footage of their units were as follows:

Unit	Tenant	Approx. Sq Ft.*
1	Watt Property Management	630
2	Rolling Ski Apparel	380
3	Travel Agency	575
4	Specialty Vacations	1050
5	City-Wide Environmental	575
6	Independent Realtors, Inc.	205

*Square footage approximated from property manager's notes. Common area square footage are not included.

The building was constructed in 1980. The Certificate of Occupancy was dated May 12, 1980.

ESA-6

Besides the physical building improvements, the remainder of the lot is asphalt paved for tenant parking. During the site visit, a visual survey of the building and property was conducted for the presence of conditions which could indicate environmental impacts (e.g., open containers, tanks, etc.).

One open, partially filled, drum of oil wastes was identified on-site. The property manager indicated someone had illegally abandoned the barrel on-site some time ago. No signs of past or present leaks were observed around the oil barrel, and no other adverse conditions were noted.

Adjacent Properties

As noted earlier, each of the abutting lots to the north, south, and west (along Arapahoe Boulevard), are low to medium density commercial/retail. To the east is low density residential.

No major industrial facilities were observed on either aerial photo (1991 or 1965), and none were identified on the day of our site reconnaissance.

There was no evidence collected during this ESA which would indicate that the site has been adversely affected by any of its' adjacent properties.

Due to the commercial/retail nature of the Arapahoe Boulevard corridor, records indicated the presence of five (5) facilities with active USTs (in place) within 0.25 miles of the property. These facilities were primarily auto sales and service related businesses.

4.0 SITE HISTORY

Bob Vinces, the on-site property manager, was interviewed in person. Mr. Vinces indicated he was unaware of any environmental hazards at the site. Conversations with the City of Silverpoint's Building and Planning Department personnel, revealed no environmental issues of concern. The same was true of LTRE's discussions with County Engineers, located at the permitting center. Computer printouts of site specific records from the County's Tax Assessor Office are contained in the appendices. The results of these interviews are included throughout this study.

Based upon these interviews there was no indication of industrial usage, fires, solid waste disposal, hazardous materials storage, and/or disposal activities at the site. However, during our review of previous business licenses issued to the site address LTRE discovered a permit for a paint stripping operation had been issued in February 1976.

Site history research is to accomplish one primary task:
to identify conclusively whether any hazardous uses have occurred on or immediately adjacent to the subject site.

ESA-7

Site history tasks are accomplished by reviewing historic directories, ownership records, aerial photos, permits, topographic maps, site plans, and conducting interviews with private and public entities, such as fire and health departments, land owners/managers in the vicinity, etc.

As the site is totally developed, and the current structure was built in 1980, no physical indications of this previous site use were discovered on the day of our inspection. Across Summit Street to the south of the site LTRE personnel noticed a paint/furniture refinishing business. The manager wasn't in, and no evidence of hazardous disposal practices were evident on the day of our investigation.

Likewise environmental liens, or government notifications, relating to violations of environmental laws with respect to the site or abutting properties were not identified.

Based upon review of topographic maps (U.S. Geological Survey (USGS) 7.5 minute series Grand, Colorado quadrangle), property transaction records, and aerial photographs the usage of the site has been primarily commercial and retail.

Historic aerial photos for 1991 and 1965 were available at the City Engineering and Mapping Department (see appendices).

The 1991 aerial photo shows the 9,375 square foot rectangular shaped lot with the 3,724 square foot (rectangular) building as it was on the day of our investigation. The scale of this photo (1"=100') easily displays the predominance of single-family residential to the east, and commercial/retail to the west along Arapahoe Boulevard.

In the 1965 aerial photo, the site is undeveloped and covered with vegetation, while the single-family residential areas to the east were fairly developed, the Arapahoe Boulevard corridor to the west was less developed than it is today.

Based upon the site visit, interviews with local and state officials, and review of federal, state and local files, evidence of current or prior releases of petroleum or hazardous materials/wastes was not found on the property.

Evidence of prior site usage with respect to agricultural operations involving pesticides/herbicides was not identified.

Property transaction records, in the form of assessor's records, were reviewed at the Tax Assessor and Recorders Offices at City Hall, Grand, Colorado, on February 18, 1995.

See appendices for copy of Tax Assessors current records for this site.

A summary 50-year Chain of Title for this property is presented on the following page.

ESA-8

Table 1

SILVERPOINT OFFICE BUILDING
Silverpoint, Colorado
PROPERTY TRANSACTION RECORDS

Date	Owner
12/31/91	Pat Johnson
12/31/84	Vance Crimper
08/08/80	Janet Marianna
05/23/79	Bob & Jean Clellan
09/12/78	Ken Howardson
05/23/77	Shirley Krambs
08/18/76	Peter Randall
02/24/47	Kenneth Howardson
12/21/45	A.B. Dunsaker Company
As of 45'	CO. Construction Company

In general a synopsis of property ownership obtained from the County Tax Assessor should be sufficient; however on large sites containing dozens of acres that have been platted and replatted, sold and bartered, it can become a major task.

As the site area around the structure is paved with cement and asphalt no indications of previous site usage, potential storage and disposal, or other potentially hazardous operations were noticed on the day of our investigation.

5.0 REGULATORY REVIEW

At the request of LTRE, government records were reviewed at Grand County and CEQA offices, on February 26, 1994. This review included Spill and Incident Reports, Underground Storage Tank (UST) records, Resource Conservation and Recovery Act (RCRA) generator and handlers files, RCRA sites files, Comprehensive Environmental Recovery, Compensation, and Liability Information System (CERCLIS) sites, as well as hazardous waste sites and solid waste disposal sites. Regulatory database searches were conducted for all sites found within a one mile radius of the subject site. The regulatory database search is included in the appendices.

ESA-9

Based upon these file reviews, the following information was noted:

- The site and immediately abutting properties were not included on any regulatory database listing.

- Due to the commercial/retail nature of the Arapahoe Boulevard corridor, records indicated the presence of five (5) facilities with active USTs (in place) within 0.25 miles of the property. These facilities were primarily auto sales and service related businesses. Eight LUST sites were reported within .5 miles of the site.

- No RCRA Transporters were identified within 1.0 mile of the site.

- RCRA cleanup files did not contain sites located within 1.0 mile of the site.

- RCRA treatment, storage, or disposal facilities were not identified within 1.0 mile of the property.

- The site and immediately abutting properties were not listed as RCRA hazardous waste generators/handlers. Four small and very small quantity generators where identified within approximately 1/4 mile of the site.

- Three RCRA Large Quantity (hazardous waste) generators were identified within 1/4 mile of the site.

- No Superfund (or potential superfund) sites were identified within 1.0 mile of the site.

- No National Priority List (NPL) sites were identified within 1.0 miles of the property.

6.0 SITE INVESTIGATION and REVIEW of HAZARDS

Topography

According to the topographic maps by the U.S. Geological Survey (USGS) 7.5 minute series Grand, Colorado quadrangle, (Scale 1:24,000, 1964, photorevised 1981), and the City of Silverpoint's 5' Contour, Silverpoint Datum Topographical Map (1"=200') the site is located at an elevation of about 5150' above mean sea level. Site specific topography is relatively flat. Local area topography is sloping to the east. Topography in the general vicinity is about 220' at its highest point, southwest of the site.

To avoid making your clients analyze a full search, a summary of your database findings in list format should always be included .
The site investigation and hazard review portion of your Phase I ESA report is the largest, and requires the most work.

ESA-10

Geology/Soils

Geologic maps delineating areas underlain by Quaternary sedimentary deposits, Tertiary and pre-tertiary sedimentary rock, and pre-tertiary plutonic and metamorphic rock have been prepared for five alluvial basins in the Grand region. The subject site lies in an area of the Grand basin which is comprised of undifferentiated medium-grained Pleistocene alluvium.

The soils are compact to very dense, moderately drained, moderately sorted, moderately permeable sand containing lenses of small gravel, silt, and clay. Chiefly marine in origin; with some nonmarine units. Locally contains freshwater pelecypod and gastropod shells and extinct vertebrate fossils. Maximum thickness is unknown, but reports studied for this assessment indicate these soils are more than 60 inches thick (Holguin, Fahan & Assocs., 1990). These soils have excessive natural drainage, rapid subsurface permeability, very slow runoff, and moderate to high wind erosion characteristics.

Seismology

The subject site is located within a fault zone. The site lies midway between the Sopero fault to the east and the western Avon fault. Numerous small earthquakes have been detected near the Sopero fault, which is a single strand with Strikes at N. 25° W. Dips 77° W. at surface, 82° W. at depth. Length 7 km. Records indicate that this fault has not been the source of a known damaging earthquake.

The Avon Hills fault has had numerous small earthquakes near and west of its fault trace, which is several echelon strands locally in a zone as wide as 2km. Strikes at N. 20 to 60° W. The valley segment generally unexposed. Dips 70° SW. in subsurface of Avon Hills, although exposed subsidiary fault dips 75° N.E. Total length at least 80 km. Records also indicate that this fault has not been the source of a known damaging earthquake.

Upon investigation of the site, no exterior signs of earthquake damage were observed at the site, or in the immediate site vicinity. However, the site is in an earthquake prone region. The primary seismologic hazards associated with the Silverpoint area include earthquake damage, and its resulting fires, and tsunamis which might result in the erosion of, and pollution of, lake areas.

Exposed fault traces represent roughly planar surfaces of shear that result from opposing movements of adjoining rock masses; along the plate boundary, this movement results from widespread, generally north-south compressive strain.

ESA-11

Each potentially hazardous issue must be discussed in its own paragraph and be detailed enough to enable you and the reader to ascertain whether any adverse impacts may exist.

The shearing is resisted by a frictionlike process that permits either an intermittent impulsive slip (rupture), which causes earthquakes, or a continuous slow movement (creep), which may occur without detectable earthquakes. Metropolitan southern Colorado lies along the broad boundary between two of the earth's moving crustal plates.

This area exhibits prominent alignments of earthquake epicenters that coincide with and directly reflect the fault locations and movements. There have been 3 damaging earthquakes in the region in the past 180 years, and essentially all urbanized areas lie within range of one or more of these damaging earthquakes.

Information on the Levels and Scopes of (Environmental) Risk for the Silverpoint Area is included in the appendices (Table HM-1 of the Silverpoint General Plan).

Hydrology

Water encountered in excavating for buildings can cause serious problems both during and after construction. The water table in most of the Silverpoint area is low enough that it poses no constraint on development. The site lies in the West Slope Groundwater Basin. Groundwater in the site area was reported to be about 135 feet .

The office site is not within a floodplain. A 1993 groundwater monitoring report conducted at the Gas Station located at 1129 Arapahoe Boulevard indicated "the direction of groundwater flow remained toward the southwest." As this site is approximately .35 miles to the north of the subject site it is uncertain whether flows at the subject site are the same.

The natural groundwater flow direction in the site vicinity has been changed by the West Coast Barrier Project, which has created a groundwater mound intended to prevent the incursion of saline water into productive aquifers.

The project is an injection system combined with drawdown in inland pumping wells and can disrupt natural flow directions. The line of injection wells is located approximately .75 miles west of the site area and therefore the current groundwater flow in the site vicinity is unknown (ARC Assocs., 1989).

According to a 1993 report by Engineering of Silverpoint, the site lies near the boundary of the zone in which groundwater contains over 250 ppm chloride, which is too saline for domestic use if untreated.

ESA-12

The specific data presented in this Phase I ESA hazard discussion are for illustrative purposes only, and even though the study is based upon an actual Phase I, data presented do not reflect the actual conditions of our subject site.

Chemicals and Raw Materials

Record reviews and personal interviews indicate that the site had a tenant that performed paintstripping onsite. The exact location of this tenant in relation to the site structure is unknown, however it is believed the tenant stored and used hazardous chemical materials. Subsurface investigations would be the only way to determine whether this tenant negatively impacted the site. A petroleum refinery is located within the City of Silverpoint area but is not within 1.0 miles of the site.

PCBs

Evidence of transformers, capacitors, hydraulic equipment, polychlorinated biphenyls (PCBs), or automotive or industrial batteries was not observed on site during the site visit or reported in the historical record.

Radon

The first level of the structure is dedicated to parking areas, and discussions with the City of Silverpoint Planning Department indicated that there was no history of elevated radon gas levels in the immediate site area.

Lead-Based Paint

All painted surfaces are relatively new. Based on the office use of the structure LTRE does not recommend that a lead-based paint survey be performed at this property. No exterior signs of blistering or peeling were observed.

Hazardous Substances

Based upon the site visit, interviews with local and state officials, and review of federal, state and local files, evidence of current or prior release of petroleum or hazardous materials/wastes was not found on the property. The RCRA Generators identified within one mile of the site are summarized in the appendices. Although, four small and very small quantity hazardous waste generators and three large quantity generators have been identified in the vicinity, no reports of adverse impacts to the subject property have been identified.

Environmental litigations or administrative actions related to released or threatened releases of hazardous substances or petroleum products are not known to exist in regard to the site or abutting properties.

The issues discussed here should always be researched when conducting Phase I site assessments.

ESA-13

Make discussions of the hazardous categories presented here a part of your standard SOW; other issues may come into play on site specific instances, but in general a thorough investigation will be accomplished, by following this guide.

Landfills

No solid waste landfills were reported on, or adjacent to, the property.

Pits, Sumps, Drywells, and Catchbasins

Based upon observations and data collected during this survey the site does not contain private wells, a septic system, sumps, or groundwater monitoring wells.

Storm Water Drainage

Surface water drainage across the site appears to travel from south to north. Regionally, surface water drainage is northeast to southwest, toward the Pacific Ocean.

Asbestos Containing Materials

An asbestos inspection of the interior and exterior areas of the Silverpoint Office Building was conducted on February 17, 1994, to determine the presence of friable and non-friable suspect asbestos-containing materials. Friable asbestos is defined by EPA in AHERA, 40 CFR Part 763, as materials that can be "crushed, crumbled and reduced to powder by hand pressure." Any material that does not meet this definition is classified as nonfriable.

Bulk samples of suspected ACMs were collected, numbered, and submitted for laboratory testing and analyses. The Comprehensive Asbestos Survey was conducted by a State of Colorado and AHERA Accredited Asbestos Inspector.

Tasks included the sampling and laboratory analysis of 21 bulk-samples. The results of laboratory analysis and our inspection findings are included in this study. All known suspect asbestos-containing materials were sampled, reanalyzed, and found not to contain asbestos.

A detailed discussion of the asbestos inspection is provided in section 7.0 (Comprehensive Asbestos Survey). Laboratory findings and asbestos inspector certifications are included in the appendices.

Onsite ASTs and USTs

According to state/city records, site reconnaissance findings and database searches conducted, USTs/ASTs were not identified on-site.

ESA-14

Offsite Tanks

The database report in the appendices lists the UST facilities within 1.0 mile of the site. The nearest facilities with underground storage tanks are located at 707 N Arapahoe Boulevard (Earl's Edsels - 4 USTs), and 708 N Arapahoe Boulevard (Super Paint - 1 UST). Both of these sites are approximately 2.5 blocks north of the subject site. Five UST sites were identified within .25 mile of the site. These sites account for a total of 16 tanks; 15 of the tanks are primarily used for petroleum products such as, diesel, unleaded gas, and oil. Although underground storage tanks (USTs) have been identified within the site vicinity, barring unforeseen disasters, it is unlikely that they will adversely impact the subject property due to their distance from the site and the nature of their operations.

Leaking Underground Storage Tanks (LUSTs)

LUST Site data is maintained by several different agencies in the State of Colorado. The primary agency records researched for this study include records from the Grand County Fire Department; the Colorado Regional Water Quality Board-Grand Region; the Colorado Department of Health and Environmental Services-Public Health Investigations Agency.

LTRE contacted each of the aforementioned agencies regarding this study. Some of these agencies, particularly the Regional Water Quality Board, are a month or so behind in scheduling appointments for records review and LTRE's time was impacted accordingly. Nevertheless, due to the numerous tank removal projects, replacements, and closures occurring statewide, these agencies are requiring site cleanup reports (SCRs) at most LUST sites.

Many SIs have been completed, or are in the process of being completed. The SCR process includes, but is not limited to, soil and/or groundwater testing, monitoring, and/or corrective action.

Corrective action may include simple overexcavation to full soil and groundwater remediation.

A database search of all LUST sites within .5 miles of the subject site was conducted (see appendices). Eight facilities, within .5 miles of the site, were identified on the State's LUST list. Three are gasoline service stations.

Eight leaks have been reported in the area since 1986.

Subsurface groundwater contamination is extremely important in Phase I ESA, due to the inherent risks to water supplies and the public health, safety, and welfare.

ESA-15

The following LUST sites were identified and agency files were researched for each. The two closest facilities were:

- Bill's Auto Repair, 707 N Arapahoe Boulevard, Silverpoint, CO. In June of 1990, a 2,000 gallon UST, which contained gasoline was removed. Analytical test on soils taken from the bottom of the excavation revealed petroleum related product leaks impacting soil. The cause was listed as unknown. The gradient of this LUST site in relation to the subject site is unknown. A preliminary investigation was completed June 1992 (see appendices). The assessment indicated probable cause of contamination as historic. Soil tests were conducted. The assessment indicated soil contamination in excess of regulatory action levels was present. No information regarding further action was on file, hence, current contaminant levels are unknown. As the site is .10 miles northwest of the subject site, and definitive information on groundwater flow direction was unavailable, LTRE considers this LUST site to be a "Moderate Risk" to the subject property.

- Avon Plaza, 125 Arapahoe Boulevard, Silverpoint, CO. On 3/15/90 a 500 gallon UST, which contained oil was removed. Analytical test on soils taken from the bottom of the excavation revealed, oil leaks had impacted soils on site. The cause was listed as unknown. The gradient of this LUST site in relation to the subject site is unknown. A preliminary investigation was completed June 1992 (see appendices). Soil tests were conducted. The assessment indicated soil contamination in excess of action levels, set forth by the State of Colorado. The assessment indicated contamination was confined to the LUST site property and corrective actions should be taken (e.g. excavation). No information regarding further action was on file, hence, current contaminant levels are unknown. As the site is .23 miles southwest of the subject site, and the site appears to be downgradient (definitive information on gradient was unavailable), LTRE considers this LUST site to be a "Low Risk" to the subject property.

Another reason groundwater contamination is so important is the costs required for cleanup actions are typically substantial and time frames are long.

Onsite and offsite LUST sources must be investigated, and their potential impacts assessed.

Other LUST sites defined and researched are:

Site Name	Status	Impact
Bob's Station, 6229 Arapahoe	Monitoring	Low Risk
Tire Store, 6200 Arapahoe	Final Closure Report	Low Risk
Station #A65, 6119 Arapahoe	No Further Action	No Impact
BPI, 400 Arapahoe	Unknown	Low Risk
Station #2446, 6002 Silverpoint	Monitoring	Low Risk

ESA-16

Copies of site investigations and/or agency LUST site data records are included in the appendices. Agency records on the first site were not up to date on the dates of our investigations - current status of this site was unavailable.

LTRE recommends the client follow up with the Regional Water Quality Control Board and the County Public Works Department, periodically to ascertain the current status of Quarterly Monitoring and the Site Investigation (SI) status for three of the eight LUST sites defined in the vicinity of the site. (Sites identified by name.)

7.0 COMPREHENSIVE ASBESTOS SURVEY

Introduction

Asbestos is a naturally occurring mineral. Because of its properties of incombustibility, noise absorption, and its resistance to electrical current, corrosion and bacterial attack, asbestos was used in a large number of building products intended for fireproofing, acoustical soundproofing, and heating and cooling system insulation. Prolonged exposure to airborne asbestos fibers has been known to cause environmental hazards to those exposed. In response, federal, state and local governments have been focusing ever-increasing attention on the presence of asbestos-containing materials (ACMs) in buildings. As a result a maze of overlapping statutes, ordinances and regulations have been adopted governing the use, handling, treatment, removal and disposal of ACMs.

In 1973, EPA banned the use of sprayed-on or trowled-on friable materials. By 1979, sprayed-on ACMs were no longer allowed in building construction. Asbestos-containing materials (ACM) have been used extensively in many schools, public buildings, and private residences. Over three thousand products have been identified as asbestos-containing materials. Many of these products have application as building materials.

The Environmental Protection Agency (EPA) recently estimated the friable (easily crumbled with hand pressure) asbestos could be found nationally in approximately 31,000 schools and 733,000 other public and private buildings.

Three forms of asbestos are typically found in buildings. They are:

- surfacing materials;
- thermal system insulation;
- miscellaneous forms.

A breakdown of the above forms of asbestos follows.

ESA-17

Due to site confidentiality actual LUST site data could not be included for our sample. In all multifamily residential and school buildings constructed prior to 1979 a Comprehensive Asbestos Survey should always be conducted.

- *Surfacing materials* include sprayed-on or trowled-on materials applied to surfaces for acoustical or fire protective purposes. Included in this category are decorative, sprayed ceiling material, some plasters, and structural fire proofing;

- *Thermal system insulation* refers to the insulation used on pipes, fittings, boilers, breaching, tanks and ducts. This material is used to minimize the diffusion of heat;

- The *miscellaneous* category of asbestos materials contains all other materials. This group includes vinyl asbestos floor tile, ceiling tiles, cement-asbestos board (transite), linoleum, heat resistant gaskets, and roofing materials.

The mere presence of asbestos in a building does not constitute a health hazard. To become a potential health risk, the asbestos must be disturbed through maintenance, repair, renovation, demolition, or daily activity. At that time small microscopic fibers are released into the air. These microscopic fibers pose the potential health risk. If they are inhaled and become lodged in the alveolar sacs of the lung, the body defense mechanisms attempt to remove or destroy them.

The quality that made asbestos desirable as a construction material is that it is almost indestructible. Therefore the majority of the fibers inhaled over a lifetime remain in the tissues of the lung.

Although the exact mechanisms are not understood, asbestos exposure has been linked to several diseases. Among these are lung cancer, the debilitating asbestosis, cancers of the esophagus, stomach, colon, and the rare chest cancer called mesothelioma.

In structures other than multifamily or school related the CAS can be at the option of the client, based upon state regulations, and may or may not be required.

Interviews

Current tenants, city building, county planning, and property management officials were interviewed in person.

The current property manager was interviewed regarding his knowledge of suspect ACMs and the presence of as-built construction documents. Reportedly, there were no as-builts available and he had no knowledge of asbestos being present on-site.

ESA-18

Construction Documents

On the date of our inspection as-built documents were not available from the property manager or City Building Department. Silverpoint, Colorado is an incorporated city in Grand County. In efforts to review all available plans, specifications, and other construction documentation to identify phases of construction; locations and functions of building mechanical systems; inaccessible areas; and locations of suspect materials; LTRE visited the City of Silverpoint, and the Grand County Planning, Building, and Development departments.

The City would not release copies of original construction documents without the express written permission of the owner and/or architect. Hence, as mentioned above, construction documents revealing material specifications were not available on the day of our inspection.

Inaccessible Areas

All building areas were accessible on the day of our inspection.

Bulk-Sampling Protocol

Bulk samples were collected in order to obtain samples that are, in the opinion of the inspector, representative of each type of suspected material. Each bulk sample was given an identification number, photographs were taken of selected materials being sampled and the material was quantified. Photographs taken during the asbestos inspection are enclosed.

Two (2) suspect asbestos-containing roofing materials were identified; they are, brown asphalt shingles and black roof penetration sealant. Bulk samples of these suspect ACMs were not collected during the asbestos inspection.

In the professional opinion of the inspector, the collection of these bulk samples would compromise and possibly breach the structural integrity of the roofing material(s) and the sample results would not warrant such damage. It should be noted that many roofing felts and cements do contain asbestos.

Currently NESHAPs, 40 CFR Part 61, classifies these materials as Category I Nonfriable ACM. Materials of this category may be maintained in place until renovation or demolition requires that they be removed. At that time, they may be removed and disposed of as "construction waste" in a landfill approved for this material.

The CAS should follow a standardized format based upon the requirements of the state regulatory body, AHERA protocol, and client needs based on property type and disposition or remodeling plans, if any.

ESA 19

*The standardized
CAS format.*

Friable and Nonfriable Condition of ACMs

Each material from which bulk samples were collected was classified according to the condition of the material. Information pertaining to the conditions of the materials sampled are provided in the bulk sample collection/chain of custody forms which are enclosed.

Sample Collection

A total of twenty-1.0 (21) bulk samples of suspect ACMs were collected. All of the samples were analyzed. Pertinent information relating to the sampled materials was recorded onto bulk sample collection/ chain-of-custody forms.

Bulk samples, bulk sample collection/chain-of-custody forms which indicate the sample collection locations are in the appendices.

Sample Diversity/Homogenous Areas

A total of 11 homogenous areas were identified during our inspection. Suspected ACMs sampled included: ceiling materials, wall materia, duct wrap, roofing, linoleum, mastic, joint tape, and vinyl floor tile.

Homogenous areas and sample identification for suspect ACMs are included on the bulk sample collection form.

Previous Sampling

To LTRE's knowledge no previous asbestos sampling activity has occurred at the site.

EPA Asbestos Test Method

Asbestos samples were analyzed using EPA Test Method Number 600/MA-82-020 - Polarized Light Microscopy (PLM).

Sample Disposition

Arrangements have been made for ARC Science Laboratory, Inc., to hold samples at its Denver, Colorado, offices for a period of sixty days for additional point sampling. After that time samples will be destroyed.

ESA-20

Sampling Results and Recommendations

Twenty-one (21) bulk samples of suspect asbestos-containing building materials were collected and analyzed to determine their asbestos content. All samples were analyzed. All friable materials tested were found not to contain asbestos.

One nonfriable roof mastic sample tested positive for more than a trace of asbestos:

Asbestos Analytical Findings			
Sample No.	Description	Findings	Condition
6666R1	roof mastic, gray	22% chrysotile	nonfriable, good

CAS findings in total amounts of asbestos-containing materials and a synopsis of sampling results and recommendations must always be included in the survey.

The above material is located on the roof area between sheets of asphalt roofing and along parapet walls where asphalt roof material is sealed to the structure.

The total area of roofing is approximately 3,400 square feet. The area of the gray roof mastic is approximately 430 linear feet.

- As this material was in good shape, and as it is a nonfriable material, it should be maintained in place. Due to the nature and location of this ACM no special operations and maintenance plans or additional work should be required at the site.

Typically, if only nonfriable materials are identified, an Operations and Maintenance Plan is preferred over abatement.

However, if the roof is to be demolished or renovated a state certified asbestos contractor should be utilized.

Laboratory results are included in the appendices.

No asbestos hazard existed at this site on the day of our investigation. LTRE believes the number of samples collected and analyzed is sufficient to draw this conclusion.

No additional analytical work for ACM hazards is required at the site.

ESA-21

Table 2- Homogenous Areas

Silverpoint Office Building — Asbestos Survey

Homogenous Area	Material	Condition	Category
1 - Unit E	ceiling tile perforated	good	friable
2 - Unit E	wall joint tape	good	nonfriable
3 - Unit E	wallboard	good	nonfriable
4 - Unit E	duct insulation	good	friable
5 - Unit E	ceiling tile, type 2	good	friable
6 - Unit E	wall material	good	nonfriable
7 - Unit E	wall material, block	good	nonfriable
8 - Roof	gray mastic	good	nonfriable
9 - Roof	rollroofing, top layer	good	nonfriable
10 - Roof	rollroofing, lower felt	good	nonfriable
11 - Roof	hot mop coating	good	nonfriable
12 - Exterior	stucco material	good	friable
13 - Exterior	garage sheetrock	good	nonfriable
14 - Exterior	first floor wallboard	good	nonfriable
15 - Common	restroom, floor tile	good	nonfriable
16 - Unit C	wall material, joint tape	good	nonfriable
17 - Unit C	wall material, wallboard	good	friable
18 - Unit C	ceiling tile, 2'x4'	good	friable

ESA-22

Preparing a table of laboratory findings is the best way to present CAS sampling analyses and results.

Always check the SOW to determine if you must use a NVLAP certified lab to run your samples.

8.0 SITE INVESTIGATION and REVIEW of SPECIAL RESOURCES

Based upon discussions with The Nature Conservancy (TNC), and the Advisory Council on Historic Preservation (ACHP) the property does not fall within their review guidelines. No special resource issues were identified on, or adjacent to the subject site.

> Historic Resources (Historic Preservation Act) — The site is of recent construction and has no historic significance.
>
> Archaeological Resources (Archaeological Resources Protection Act) — There are no known archaeological resources on or adjacent to the site.
>
> Biotic Communities and Wildlife Habitats (Endangered Species Act) — There are no aquatic refuges, shrubby grasslands, herbaceous woodlands, woody wetlands, woodlands/forests, or other type of habitat areas on or adjacent to the site.
>
> Farmlands (Farmlands Protection Act) — Historical records and aerial photos show no evidence of prior site usage with respect to agricultural operations.
>
> Coastal Zones and Barriers (Coastal Zone Management Act) — Due to the inland location of the site, this issue is irrelevant.
>
> Recreational Areas — No major public recreation areas are on or adjacent to, the site.
>
> Land Use (Federal Land Policy and Management Act) — Land uses in the area are a mix of residential, and commercial. The site is compatible with its surrounding area and there are no environmental consequences.
>
> Sole Source Aquifers (Safe Drinking Water Act) — Federally designated sole source aquifers were not identified within the site area's groundwater basin.
>
> Wetlands — No protected wetland areas are on, or immediately adjacent to, the site. There are no designated wild and scenic rivers in close proximity to the site.

Special Resources should always be discussed in Phase I ESA even if only to acknowledge that they are not appropriate to the subject site.

ESA-23

This section is of utmost importance. So many studies present the facts but do not interpret them. Don't let yours be one of those.

Here is where you tell the client what should be done based on your findings. If some of this section seems redundant that is because often times your client will only see this page. It must reiterate the potential hazards and courses of action that are identified throughout the study.

9.0 SUMMARY AND RECOMMENDATIONS

Based upon site survey observations, interviews, and historic and present usage of the property, it appears that the site has been utilized primarily as an office/commercial property since its construction in 1980. Record reviews and personal interviews did not indicate that the site was used to store, dispose of, or manage hazardous materials.

Based on the age of the current structure a Comprehensive Asbestos Survey was conducted to determine the presence of asbestos containing materials, per scope. Twenty-one samples were taken of the eleven homogenous groups identified on-site. All samples were analyzed, and all friable samples were found not to contain asbestos. One nonfriable roof mastic material was confirmed to contain asbestos.

The surrounding area is primarily low density residential, with commercial establishments along Arapahoe Boulevard approximately 100 feet west of the site. Immediately north of the site lies parking areas that serve commercial/retail operations. There was no evidence collected during this ESA which would indicate that the site has been adversely affected by environmental hazards from commercial operations in the site vicinity.

No industrial facilities are located in the site area. Based upon the study findings LTRE's recommendations are as follows:

- 1) As none of the friable suspect ACMs contained asbestos, and the nonfriable material confirmed to contain asbestos was exterior to the structure, and all materials appeared to be in good condition on the day of our inspection, we recommend the roof mastic be maintained in place. As the material is not in a high contact area no special maintenance plans or additional work is required at the site. However, if the roof will be impacted by future remodeling/demolition, a state certified asbestos contractor should be consulted.

- 2) The client should follow up with the Regional Water Quality Control Board and the County Public Works Department, periodically to ascertain the current status of Quarterly Monitoring and the Site Investigation (SI) status for three of the eight LUST sites defined in the vicinity of the site. Based upon data collected during the site visit, interviews, and file reviews, the environmental risk is expected to be very low for the site.

There were no other concerns identified during the site investigation.

ESA-24

10.0 WARRANTS

This warranty is in lieu of all other warranties either express or implied. Conclusions set forth in this report are based upon, and limited by, the government data and other information available to LTRE.

While LTRE has used reasonable care to avoid reliance upon faulty, or incomplete information, LTRE is not able to verify the accuracy of all data and information provided by governmental entities and third parties. Therefore, LTRE is not responsible for any conclusion contained in this report that is based, in whole or in part, upon inaccurate data obtained from third parties.

The information herein is for the exclusive use of Urbanetics Partners and LTRE. LTRE is not responsible for use of this information by any other parties.

It should be noted that all surface environmental assessments are inherently limited in the sense that conclusions are drawn and recommendations developed from information obtained from limited research and site evaluation at a specific time. The passage of time may result in a change in environmental circumstances at this site and surrounding properties. Or hazardous materials beneath the surface or covered by debris may be present, but undetectable, during a site investigation.

Verification of subsurface conditions, including the hazard potential of buried or covered debris is beyond the scope of this investigation.

All asbestos and lead-based paint surveys are inherently limited in the sense that conclusions are drawn and recommendations developed from information obtained from limited site sampling at a specific time. The passage of time may result in deterioration and/or damage to nonfriable asbestos-containing materials, or a lead-based paint may be used in areas where these materials did not exist and/or areas where no sampling was conducted.

The work performed in conjunction with this assessment and the sampling data developed are intended as a description of available information on the dates and locations given.

LTRE does not provide professional legal, or title insurance services and makes no guarantee, explicit or implied, that the listing which was reviewed represented a comprehensive delineation of past site ownership or tenancy.

ESA-25

Warrants are vital to your Phase I ESA. The client must understand that right after you leave someone may dump wastes; or a LUST may occur next door; or a government employee didn't know of the hazardous spill that occurred yesterday, because his/her boss still had the file; or a multitude of other circumstances.

APPENDICES

*Due to the confi-
dential nature of
the Phase I ESA
presented herein
and the fact that
photos, maps, and
lab data may lead
to the actual identi-
fication of a site,
only summaries of
the first two appen-
dices are included
for your review.**

Appendix A   Regulatory Database Summary Sheet*

Appendix B   Data References*

Appendix C   Aerial Photos

Appendix D   Site Photos

Appendix E   Site Maps

Appendix F   Lust Site Records

Appendix G   Laboratory Analyses — Asbestos

Appendix H   Chain Of Custody Forms

Appendix I   Lab and Inspector's Certifications

Note: To complete the Phase I ESA all of the above Appendices would have to be obtained and included in the study.

REGULATORY DATABASE SUMMARY				
PROPERTY INFORMATION			**CLIENT INFORMATION**	
Silverpoint Offices Silverpoint, CO			LTRE Englewood, CO	
Environmental Risk Distribution Summary				
Agency/Database	1/8 mile	1/4 mile	1/2 mile	1 mile
EPA	NPL Sites designated for Superfund clean-up by the US EPA	0	0	0	0
EPA	CERCLIS Sites under review by U.S. EPA	0	0	0	0
EPA	RCRIS Facilities that treat, store, of dispose of Haz Waste	0	0	0	0
State	LUST Site with leaking underground storage tanks	2	6	0	0
State	SWLF Sites permitted as solid waste landfills, incinerators, or transfer stations	0	0	0	0
State	UST Sites with registered Underground Storage Tanks	2	3	0	0
State	ERNS Sites with previous hazardous materials spills	0	0	0	0
State	RCRIS Sites that generate large or small quantities of hazardous waste	3	4	0	0

Legend: **NPL** - National Priorities List; **UST** - Underground Storage Tank; **ERNS** - Emergency Response Notification System; **RCRIS** - Resource Conservation & Recovery Information System ; **LUST** - Leaking Underground Storage Tank; **CERCLIS** - Comprehensive Environmental Response, Compensation, and Liability Information System.

LIMITATION OF LIABILITY Customer proceeds at its own risk in choosing to rely on these records prior to proceeding with any transaction.

Sample environmental database summary.

DATA REFERENCES

QUADRANGLE MAP

United States Geological Survey, 1966, 7.5 Minute Series Topographic Map, Grand Quadrangle, Colorado, Photorevised 1981.

PLANS, STUDIES, & REPORTS REVIEWED

City of Silverpoint General Plan, 1988.

State of the City's Environment, Environmental Quality Board, 1990.

Urban Ecology, Silverpoint, Department of City Planning, June, 1990.

Evaluating Seismology Hazards in the Silverpoint Region — An Earth Science Perspective, US Geological Survey, Professional Paper 1360, 1985.

Conservation Plan, Silverpoint, Colorado, Silverpoint Department of City Planning, December, 1973.

Open Space Plan, Silverpoint, Colorado, Silverpoint Department of City Planning, June, 1973.

Soils Investigation, Bill's Auto Repair, Environmental Assocs., 1992.

Environmental Assessment, Bill's Auto Repair, Environmental Assocs., 1993.

Groundwater Monitoring Report, Bill's Auto Repair, Environmental Assocs., 1993.

Site Assessment, Bill's Auto Repair, Environmental Assocs. 1990.

Phase II Assessment/Subsurface Site Investigation Plan, Bill's Auto Repair, Environmental Assocs., 1992/1993.

AERIAL PHOTOGRAPHS

Public Works Department, Mapping Division, Silverpoint, CO, 1965, 1990.

ASSESSORS DATA & MAPS

Tax Assessors Office, Grand County, CO, 1991.

Brief Overview of typical data references utilized to conduct the Sample Phase I Environmental Site Assessment.

Section IV

Hazardous Air Pollutants (HAPs) List (CAA)

Hazardous Air Pollutants (HAPs) List (CAA)

CAS NO.	CHEMICAL NAME	CAS NO.	CHEMICAL NAME
75070	Acetaldehyde	532274	2-Chloroacetophenone
79061	Acrylamide	108907	Chlorobenzene
79107	Acrylic acid	510156	Chlorobenzilate
107131	Acrylonitrile	67663	Chloroform
107051	Allyl chloride	107302	Chloromethyl methyl ether
92671	4-Aminobiphenyl	126998	Chloroprene
62533	Aniline	1319773	Cresols/Cresylic acid
90040	o-Anisidine	95487	o-Cresol
1332214	Asbestos	108394	m-Cresol
71432	Benzene	106445	p-Cresol
92875	Benzidine	98828	Cumene
98077	Benzotrichloride	94757	2,4-D, salts and esters
100447	Benzyl chloride	3547044	DDE
92524	Biphenyl	334883	Diazomethane
117817	Bis(2-ethylhexyl)phthalate (DEHP)	132649	Dibenzofurans
542881	Bis(chloromethyl)ether	96128	1,2-Dibromo-3-chloropropane
75252	Bromoform	84742	Dibutylphthalate
106990	1,3-Butadiene	106467	1,4 Dichlorobenzene(p)
156627	Calcium cyanamide	91941	3,3-Dichlorobenzidene
105602	Caprolactam	111444	Dichloroethyl ether (Bis(2-chloroethyl)ether)
133062	Captan	542756	1,3-Dichloropropene
63252	Carbaryl	62737	Dichlorvos
75150	Carbon disulfide	111422	Diethanolamine
56235	Carbon tetrachloride	121697	N,N-Diethyl aniline (N,N-Dimethylaniline)
463581	Carbonyl sulfide	64675	Diethyl sulfate
120809	Catechol	119904	3,3-Dimethoxybenzidine
133904	Chloramben	60117	Dimethyl aminoazobenzene
57749	Chlordane	119937	3,3 -Dimethyl benzidine
7782505	Chlorine	79447	Dimethyl carbamoyl chloride
79118	Chloroacetic acid	68122	Dimethyl formamide

CAS NO.	CHEMICAL NAME	CAS NO.	CHEMICAL NAME
57147	1,1-Dimethyl hydrazine	7647010	Hydrochloric acid
131113	Dimethyl phthalate	7664393	Hydrogen fluoride
77781	Dimethyl sulfate	123319	Hydroquinone
534521	4,6-Dinitro-o-cresol, and salts	78591	Isophorone
51285	2,4-Dinitrophenol	58899	Lindane (all isomers)
121142	2,4-Dinitrotoluene	108316	Maleic anhydride
123911	1,4-Dioxane (1,4-Diethyleneoxide)	67561	Methanol
122667	1,2-Diphenylhydrazine	72435	Methoxychlor
106898	Epichlorohydrin	74839	Methyl bromide (Bromomethane)
106887	1,2-Epoxybutane	74873	Methyl chloride (Chloromethane)
140885	Ethyl acrylate	71556	Methyl chloroform
100414	Ethyl benzene	78933	Methyl ethyl ketone (2-Butanone)
51796	Ethyl carbamate (Urethane)	60344	Methyl hydrazine
75003	Ethyl chloride (Chloroethane)	74884	Methyl iodide (Iodomethane)
106934	Ethylene dibromide (Dibromoethane)	108101	Methyl isobutyl ketone (Hexone)
107062	Ethylene dichloride (1,2-Dichloroethane)	624839	Methyl isocyanate
107211	Ethylene glycol	80626	Methyl methacrylate
151564	Ethylene imine (Aziridine)	1634044	Methyl tert butyl ether
75218	Ethylene oxide	101144	4,4-Methylene bis(2-chloroaniline)
96457	Ethylene thiourea	75092	Methylene chloride
75343	Ethylidene dichloride (1,1-Dichloroethane)	101688	Methylene diphenyl diisocyanate
50000	Formaldehyde	101779	4,4 -Methylenedianiline
76448	Heptachlor	91203	Naphthalene
118741	Hexachlorobenzene	98953	Nitrobenzene
87683	Hexachlorobutadiene	92933	4-Nitrobiphenyl
77474	Hexachlorocyclopentadiene	100027	4-Nitrophenol
67721	Hexachloroethane	79469	2-Nitropropane
822060	Hexamethylene-1,6-diisocyanate	684935	N-Nitroso-N-methylurea
680319	Hexamethylphosphoramide	62759	N-Nitrosodimethylamine
110543	Hexane	59892	N-Nitrosomorpholine
302012	Hydrazine	56382	Parathion

CAS NO.	CHEMICAL NAME	CAS NO.	CHEMICAL NAME
82688	Pentachloronitrobenzene	79016	Trichloroethylene
87865	Pentachlorophenol	95954	2,4,5-Trichlorophenol
108952	Phenol	88062	2,4,6-Trichlorophenol
106503	p-Phenylenediamine	121448	Triethylamine
75445	Phosgene	1582098	Trifluralin
7803512	Phosphine	540841	2,2,4-Trimethylpentane
7723140	Phosphorus	108054	Vinyl acetate
85449	Phthalic anhydride	593602	Vinyl bromide
1336363	Polychlorinated biphenyls (Aroclors)	75014	Vinyl chloride
1120714	1,3-Propane sultone	75354	Vinylidene chloride
57578	beta-Propiolactone	1330207	Xylenes (isomers and mixture)
123386	Propionaldehyde	95476	o-Xylenes
114261	Propoxur (Baygon)	108383	m-Xylenes
78875	Propylene dichloride	106423	p-Xylenes
75569	Propylene oxide		

Compounds and Miscellaneous Substances

CAS NO.	CHEMICAL NAME
75558	1,2-Propylenimine (2-Methylaziridine)	
91225	Quinoline	0	Antimony Compounds
106514	Quinone	0	Arsenic Compounds (inorganic)
100425	Styrene	0	Beryllium Compounds
96093	Styrene oxide	0	Cadmium Compounds
1746016	2,3,7,8-Tetrachlorodibenzo-p-dioxin	0	Chromium Compounds
79345	1,1,2,2-Tetrachloroethane	0	Cobalt Compounds
127184	Tetrachloroethylene (Perchloroethylene)	0	Coke Oven Emissions
7550450	Titanium tetrachloride	0	Cyanide Compounds[1]
108883	Toluene	0	Glycol ethers[2]
95807	2,4-Toluene diamine	0	Lead Compounds
584849	2,4-Toluene diisocyanate	0	Manganese Compounds
95534	o-Toluidine	0	Mercury Compounds
8001352	Toxaphene (chlorinated camphene)	0	Fine mineral fibers[3]
120821	1,2,4-Trichlorobenzene	0	Nickel Compounds
79005	1,1,2-Trichloroethane	0	Polycylic Organic Matter[4]
		0	Radionuclides (including radon)[5]
		0	Selenium Compounds

NOTES TO HAPS LIST

For all listings above which contain the word "compounds" and for glycol ethers, the following applies: Unless otherwise specified, these listings are defined as including any unique chemical substance that contains the named chemical (i.e., antimony, arsenic, etc.) as part of that chemical's infrastructure.

1 X CN where X = H or any other group where a formal dissociation may occur. For example KCN or Ca(CN)$_2$.

2 Includes mono- and di- ethers of ethylene glycol, diethylene glycol, and triethylene glycol R-(OCH$_2$CH$_2$)$_n$- OR where: n = 1, 2, or 3; R = alkyl or aryl groups; R = R, H; or groups which, when removed, yield glycol ethers with the structure — R-(OCH$_2$CH)$_n$-OH. Polymers are excluded from the glycol category.

3 Includes mineral fiber emissions from facilities manufacturing or processing glass, rock, or slag fibers (or other mineral derived fibers) of average diameter 1 micrometer or less

4 Includes organic compounds with more than one benzene ring, and which have a boiling point greater than or equal to 100°C.

5 A type of atom which spontaneously undergoes radioactive decay.

REVISION OF THE (HAPs) LIST

The Administrator shall periodically review the list established by this subsection and publish the results thereof and, where appropriate, revise such list by rule, adding pollutants which present, or may present, through inhalation or other routes of exposure, a threat of adverse human health effects (including, but not limited to, substances which are known to be, or may reasonably be anticipated to be, carcinogenic, mutagenic, teratogenic, neurotoxic, which cause reproductive dysfunction, or which are acutely or chronically toxic) or adverse environmental effects whether through ambient concentrations, bioaccumulation, deposition, or otherwise, but not including releases subject to regulation under subsection (r) of this section as a result of emissions to the air. No air pollutant which is listed under section 7408(a) of this title may be added to the list under this section, except that the prohibition of this sentence shall not apply to any pollutant which independently meets the listing criteria of this paragraph and is a precursor to a pollutant which is listed under section 7408(a) of this title or to any pollutant which is in a class of pollutants listed under such section. No substance, practice, process or activity regulated under subchapter VI of this chapter shall be subject to regulation under this section solely due to its adverse effects on the environment.

PETITIONS TO MODIFY HAPs LIST

Beginning at any time after 6 months after November 15, 1990, any person may petition the Administrator to modify the list of hazardous air pollutants under this subsection by adding or deleting a substance or, in case of listed pollutants without CAS numbers (other than coke oven emissions, mineral fibers, or polycyclic organic matter) removing certain unique substances. Within 18 months after receipt of a petition, the Administrator shall either grant or deny the petition by publishing a written explanation of the reasons for the Administrator's decision. Any such petition shall include a showing by the petitioner that there is adequate data on the health or environmental effects of the pollutant or other evidence adequate to support the petition. The Administrator may not deny a petition solely on the basis of inadequate resources or time for review.

ADDITIONS TO THE LIST

The Administrator shall add a substance to the list upon a showing by the petitioner or on the Administrator's own determination that the substance is an air pollutant and that emissions, ambient concentrations, bioaccumulation or deposition of the substance are known to cause or may reasonably be anticipated to cause adverse effects to human health or adverse environmental effects.

DELETIONS FROM THE LIST

The Administrator shall delete a substance from the list upon a showing by the petitioner or on the Administrator's own determination that there is adequate data on the health and environmental effects of the substance to determine that emissions, ambient concentrations, bioaccumulation or deposition of the substance may not reasonably be anticipated to cause any adverse effects to the human health or adverse environmental effects. The Administrator shall delete one or more unique chemical substances that contain a listed hazardous air pollutant not having a CAS number (other than coke oven emissions, mineral fibers, or polycyclic organic matter) upon a showing by the petitioner or on the Administrator's own determination that such unique chemical substances that contain the named chemical of such listed hazardous air pollutant meet the deletion requirements above. The Administrator must grant or deny a deletion petition prior to promulgating any emission standards pursuant to subsection (d) of this section applicable to any source category or subcategory of a listed hazardous air pollutant without a CAS number listed under subsection (b) of this section for which a deletion petition has been filed within 12 months of November 15, 1990. If the Administrator determines that information on the health or environmental effects of a substance is not sufficient to make a determination required by this subsection, the Administrator may use any authority available to the Administrator to acquire such information.

TEST METHODS

The Administrator may establish, by rule, test measures and other analytic procedures for monitoring and measuring emissions, ambient concentrations, deposition, and bioaccumulation of hazardous air pollutants. The PSD provisions of the CAA do not apply to the HAPs list.

Section V

Data Conversion Factors

Data Conversion Factors

Multiply an existing factor *(A)* in units represented in the left column, by the number *(B)* in the center to arrive at an equivalent factor in units represented in the right column *(C)*.

Multiply (A)	By (B)	To Obtain (C)
• Acres	160	square rods
• acres	4840	square yards
• acres	43,560	square feet
• Acres Inches	27,154	gallons
• Acres Inches per Hour	452	gpm
• Atmospheres	14,696	lbs per square inch
• atmospheres	76.0	centimeters mercury
• atmospheres	29.92	inches mercury
• atmospheres	33.90	feet of water
• atmospheres	1.0333	kgs per square cm
• atmospheres	14.70	lbs per square inch
• atmospheres	1.058	tons per square foot
• Barrels- (Oil)	42	gallons
• barrels-(beer)	31.5	gallons
• barrels-(wine)	31.0	gallons

BIG NUMBERS

Million =1,000,000 = Thousand Thousand
Billion =1,000,000,000 = Thousand Million
Trillion =1,000,000,000,000 = Million Million
Quadrillion =1,000,000,000,000,000 = Million Billion

• Btus	0.2520	kilogram-calories
• Btus	778.2	foot-pounds
• Btus	3.927×10^{-4}	horsepower-hours
• Btus	107.5	kilogram-meters
• Btus	2.928×10^{-4}	kilowatt-hours
• Btus per Minute	12.96	foot-lbs. per second
• Btus per minute	0.02356	horsepower
• Btus per minute	0.1757	kilowatts

Multiply (A)	By (B)	To Obtain (C)
• Btus per minute........................	17.57....................	watts
• Centares...............................	1.........................	square meters
• Centigrams	0.01.....................	grams
• Centiliters	0.01.....................	liters
• Centimeters............................	0.3937...................	inches
• centimeters............................	0.03281..................	feet
• centimeters............................	0.01.....................	meters
• centimeters............................	10	millimeters
• Centimeters Mercury	0.01316.................	atmospheres
• centimeters mercury...................	0.4461...................	feet of water
• centimeters mercury...................	136.0....................	kgs per square meter
• centimeters mercury...................	27.85....................	lbs per square foot
• centimeters mercury...................	0.1934...................	lbs per square inch
• Centimeters per Second...............	1.969....................	feet per minute
• centimeters per second	0.03281..................	feet per second
• centimeters per second	0.036....................	kilometers per hour
• centimeters per second	0.6......................	meters per minute
• centimeters per second	0.2237...................	miles per hour
• centimeters per second	3.728×10^{-4}...........	miles per minute
• Centimeters/Second/Second	0.03281..................	feet per second/second
• Cubic Centimeters	3.531×10^{-5}...........	cubic feet
• cubic centimeters	6.102×10^{-2}............	cubic inches
• cubic centimeters	10^{-6}....................	cubic meters
• cubic centimeters	1.308×10^{-6}.............	cubic yards
• cubic centimeters	2.642×10^{-4}...........	gallons
• cubic centimeters	10^{-3}....................	liters
• cubic centimeters	2.113×10^{-3}.............	pints (liquid)
• cubic centimeters	1.057×10^{-3}.............	quarts (liquid)
• Cubic Feet.............................	2.832×10^{4}.............	cubic centimeters
• cubic feet.............................	1728	cubic inches
• cubic feet.............................	0.02832..................	cubic meters
• cubic feet.............................	0.03704..................	cubic yards
• cubic feet.............................	7.48052..................	U.S. gallons

Multiply (A)	By (B)	To Obtain (C)
• cubic feet	6.23	imperial gallons
• cubic feet	28.32	liters
• cubic feet	59.84	pints (liquid)
• cubic feet	29.92	quarts (liquid)
• Cubic Feet per Minute	472	cubic cms per second
• cubic feet per minute	0.1247	gallons per second
• cubic feet per minute	0.4720	liters per second
• cubic feet per minute	62.43	lbs. water per minute
• Cubic Feet per Second	0.646317	million gallons per day
• cubic ft per second	448.831	gallons per minute
• Cubic Foot Water	62.4	pounds
• cubic foot water	998.4	ounces
• cubic foot water	28.315	kilograms
• Cubic Inches	16.39	cubic centimeters
• cubic inches	5.787×10^{-4}	cubic feet
• cubic inches	1.639×10^{-5}	cubic meters
• cubic inches	2.143×10^{-5}	cubic yards
• cubic inches	4.329×10^{-3}	gallons
• cubic inches	1.639×10^{-2}	liters
• cubic inches	0.03463	pints (liquid)
• cubic inches	0.01732	quarts (liquid)
• Cubic Meters	10^6	cubic centimeters
• cubic meters	35.31	cubic feet
• cubic meters	61,023	cubic inches
• cubic meters	1.308	cubic yards
• cubic meters	264.2	U.S. gallons
• cubic meters	220	imperial gallons
• cubic meters	10	liters
• cubic meters	2113	pints (liquid)
• cubic meters	1057	quarts (liquid)
• Cubic Yards	7.646×10^5	cubic centimeters
• cubic yards	27.0	cubic feet
• cubic yards	46,656	cubic inches

Multiply (A)	By (B)	To Obtain (C)
• cubic yards	0.7646	cubic meters
• cubic yards	202.0	gallons
• cubic yards	764.6	liters
• cubic yards	1616	pints (liquid)
• cubic yards	807.9	quarts (liquid)
• Cubic Yards per Minute	0.45	cubic feet per second
• cubic yards per minute	3.367	gallons per second
• cubic yards per minute	12.74	liters per second
• Decigrams	0.1	grams
• Deciliters	0.1	liters
• Decimeters	0.1	meters
• Degrees (angle)	60	minutes
• degrees (angle)	0.01745	radians
• degrees (angle)	3600	seconds
• Degrees per Second	0.01745	radians per second
• degrees per second	0.1667	revolutions per minute
• degrees per second	0.002778	revolutions per second
• Dekagrams	10	grams
• Dekaliters	10	liters
• Dekameters	10	meters
• Drams	27.34375	grains
• drams	0.0625	ounces
• drams	1.771845	grams

ENERGY

Multiply (A)	By (B)	To Obtain (C)
• Btus	1054	joules
• Calories	4.184	joules
• Kilowatt Hours	3.60×10^6	joules

Multiply (A)	By (B)	To Obtain (C)
• Fathoms	6	feet
• Feet	30.48	centimeters
• feet	12	inches

Multiply (A)	By (B)	To Obtain (C)
• feet	0.3048	meters
• feet	3	yards
• Feet of Water	0.02950	atmospheres
• feet of water	0.8826	inches of mercury
• feet of water	0.03048	kilograms/sq cm
• feet of water	62.43	lbs per square foot
• feet of water	0.4335	lbs per square inch
• Feet per Minute	0.5080	cms per second
• feet per minute	0.01667	feet per second
• feet per minute	0.01829	kilometers per hour
• feet per minute	0.3048	meters per minute
• feet per minute	0.01136	miles per hour
• Feet per Second per Second	30.48	cms/second/second
• feet per second per second	0.3048	meters/second/second
• Foot-Pounds	1.286×10^{-3}	Btus
• foot-lbs	5.050×10^{-7}	horsepower hrs
• foot-lbs	3.241×10^{-4}	kilogram–calories
• foot-lbs	0.1383	kilogram–meters
• foot-lbs	3.766×10^{-7}	kilowatt–hours
• Foot-Pounds per Minute	1.286×10^{-3}	Btus per minute
• foot-lbs per minute	0.01667	ft-lbs per second
• foot-lbs per minute	3.030×10^{-5}	horsepower
• foot-lbs per minute	3.241×10^{-4}	kg.-calories per minute
• foot-lbs per minute	2.260×10^{-5}	kilowatts
• Foot-Pounds per Second	7.717×10^{-2}	Btus per minute
• foot-lbs per second	1.818×10^{-3}	horsepower
• foot-lbs per second	1.945×10^{-2}	kg.-calories per minute
• foot-lbs per second	1.356×10^{-3}	kilowatts
• Gallons	3785	cubic centimeters
• gallons	0.1337	cubic feet
• gallons	231	cubic inches
• gallons	3.785×10^{-3}	cubic meters
• gallons	4.951×10^{-3}	cubic yards

Multiply (A)	By (B)	To Obtain (C)
• gallons	128	fluid ounces
• gallons	3.785	liters
• gallons	8	pints (liquid)
• gallons	4	quarts (liquid)
• Gallons, U.S.	0.83267	imperial gallons
• Gallons, Imperial	1.20095	U.S. gallons
• gallons, imperial	277.3	cubic inches
• gallons, imperial	0.16	cubic feet
• gallons, imperial	4.546	liters
• gallons, imperial	0.00454	cubic meters
• Gallons Water (U.S.)	8.3453	pounds
• gallons water (U.S.)	3.785	kilograms
• Gals Water (IMPERIAL)	10.02	pounds
• gals water (imperial)	4.54	kilograms
• Gallons per Minute	2.228×10^{-3}	cubic feet per second
• gallons per minute	0.06308	liters per second
• gallons per minute	8.0208	cubic feet per hour
• Gals Water per Minute	6.0086	tons of water per day
• Gigawatts	10	terawatts
• gigawatts	10^{-3}	megawatts
• gigawatts	10^{-6}	kilowatts
• gigawatts	10^{-9}	watts
• Grains (Troy)	0.06480	grams
• grains (troy)	0.04167	pennyweights (troy)
• grains (troy)	2.0833×10^{-3}	ounces (troy)
• Grains per U.S. Gallon	17.118	parts per million
• grains per U.S. gallon	142.86	pounds per million
• Grains per Imperial Gal.	14.286	parts per million
• Grams	980.7	dynes
• grams	15.43	grains
• grams	10^{-3}	kilograms
• grams	10	milligrams
• grams	0.03527	ounces

Multiply (A)	By (B)	To Obtain (C)
• grams	0.03215	ounces (troy)
• grams	2.205×10^{-3}	pounds
• Grams per Centimeter	5.600×10^{-3}	pounds per inch
• Grams per Cubic Cm	62.43	pounds per cubic foot
• grams per cubic cm	0.03613	pounds per cubic inch
• Grams per Liter	58.417	grains per gallon
• grams per liter	8.345	pounds per 1000 gals.
• grams per liter	0.062427	pounds per cubic foot
• grams per liter	1000	parts per million
• Hectograms	100	grams
• Hectoliters	100	liters
• Hectometers	100	meters
• Hectowatts	100	watts
• Horsepower	42.44	Btus per Minute
• horsepower	33,000	ft-pounds per minute
• horsepower	550	ft-pounds per second
• horsepower	1.014	horse-power (metric)
• horsepower	10.68	kg.-calories per minute
• horsepower	0.7457	kilowatts
• horsepower	745.7	watts
• Horsepower (Boiler)	33,479	Btus per Hour
• horsepower (boiler)	9.803	kilowatts
• Horsepower-Hrs	2547	Btus
• horsepower-hrs	1.98×10^{6}	foot-pounds
• horsepower-hrs	641.7	kilogram-calories
• horsepower-hrs	2.7377×10^{5}	kilogram-meters
• horsepower-hrs	0.7457	kilowatt-hours
• Inches	2.540	centimeters
• inches	25.4	millimeters
• inches	.0254	meters
• inches	.0833	feet
• Inches of Mercury	0.3342	atmospheres
• inches of mercury	1.133	feet of water

Multiply (A)	By (B)	To Obtain (C)
inches of mercury	0.03453	kilograms/sq. cmr
inches of mercury	70.73	pounds per square ft
inches of mercury	0.4912	pounds per square inch
Inches of Water	0.002458	Atmospheres
inches of water	0.07355	inches of mercury
inches of water	0.002540	kilograms per sq cm
inches of water	5.204	pounds per square ft
inches of water	0.03613	pounds per square inch
Kilograms (kgs.)	980,665	dynes
kilograms	2.205	pounds (lbs.)
kilograms	1.102×10^{-3}	tons (short)
Kilograms	10	grams
Kilograms per Meter	0.6720	pounds per foot
Kilograms per Square Cm	0.9678	atmospheres
kilograms per square cm	32.81	feet of water
kilograms per square cm	28.96	inches of mercury
kilograms per square cm	2048	pounds per square foot
kilograms per square cm	14.22	pounds per sq inch
Kilograms per Square Millimeter	10^6	kilograms per sq meter
Kiloliters	10	liters
Kilometers (kms.)	10^5	centimeters
kilometers	3281	feet
kilometers	10	meters
kilometers	0.6214	miles
kilometers	1094	yards
Kilometers per Hour	27.78	centimeters per second
kilometers per hour	54.68	feet per minute
kilometers per hour	0.9113	feet per second
kilometers per hour	0.5396	knots
kilometers per hour	16.67	meters per minute
kilometers per hour	0.6214	miles per hour
Kilometers per Hr per Second	27.78	cms/second/second
kilometers per hour per second	0.9113	feet per second/second

Multiply(A)	By (B)	To Obtain (C)
• kilometers per hour per second	0.2778	meters/second/second
• Kilowatts (kw.)	56.92	Btus per minute
• kilowatts	4.425×10^4	foot-lbs. per minute
• kilowatts	737.6	foot-lbs. per second
• kilowatts	1.341	horsepower
• kilowatts	14.34	kg.-calories per minute
• kilowatts	10	watts
• kilowatts	10^{-3}	megawatts
• kilowatts	10^{-6}	gigawatts
• kilowatts	10^{-9}	terawatts
• Kilowatt-Hours	3413	Btus
• kw-hrs.	2.655×10^6	foot-pounds
• kw-hrs.	1.341	horsepower-hours
• Liters	10	cubic centimeters
• liters	0.03531	cubic feet
• liters	61.02	cubic inches
• liters	10^{-3}	cubic meters
• liters	1.308×10^{-3}	cubic yards
• liters	0.2642	gallons
• liters	2.113	pints (liquid)
• liters	1.057	quarts (liquid)
• Liters per Minute	5.886×10^{-4}	cubic ft per second
• liters per minute	4.403×10^{-3}	gals per second
• Megawatts	10^6	watts
• megawatts	10	kilowatts
• megawatts	10^{-3}	gigawatts
• megawatts	10^{-6}	terawatts
• Meters	100	centimeters
• meters	3.281	feet
• meters	39.37	inches
• meters	10^{-3}	kilometers
• meters	10	millimeters
• meters	1.094	yards

Multiply (A)	By (B)	To Obtain (C)
• Meters per Minute	1.667	cms per second
• meters per minute	3.281	feet per minute
• meters per minute	0.05468	feet per second
• meters per minute	0.06	kilometers per hour
• meters per minute	0.03728	miles per hour
• Meters per Second	196.8	feet per minute
• meters per second	3.281	feet per second
• meters per second	3.6	kilometers per hour
• meters per second	0.06	kilometers per minute
• meters per second	2.237	miles per hour
• meters per second	0.03728	miles per minute
• Metric Tons	2204.6	pounds
• metric tons	1.1023	short tons
• Microns	10^{-6}	meters
• Miles	1.609×10^5	centimeters
• miles	5280	feet
• miles	1.609	kilometers
• miles	1760	yards
• Miles per Hour (mph)	44.70	centimeters per second
• miles per hour	88	feet per minute
• miles per hour	1.467	feet per second
• miles per hour	1.609	kilometers per hour
• miles per hour	0.8684	knots
• miles per hour	26.82	meters per minute
• Miles per Minute	2682	centimeters per second
• miles per minute	88	feet per second
• miles per minute	1.609	kilometers per minute
• miles per minute	60	miles per hour
• Milliers	10	kilograms
• Milligrams	10^{-3}	grams
• Milliliters	10^{-3}	liters
• millimeters (mm)	0.1	centimeters
• millimeters	0.03937	inches

Multiply (A)	By (B)	To Obtain (C)
milligrams per liter	1	parts per million
million gallons per day	1.54723	cubic ft per second
miner's inches	1.5	cubic ft per minute
minutes (angle)	2.909×10^{-4}	radians
Ounces	16	drams
ounces	137.5	grains
ounces	0.0625	pounds (lbs.)
ounces	28.349527	grams
ounces	0.9115	ounces (troy)
ounces	2.790×10^{-5}	tons (long)
ounces	2.835×10^{-5}	tons (metric)
Ounces, Troy	480	grains
ounces, troy	20	pennyweights
ounces, troy	0.083333	pounds (troy)
ounces, troy	31.103481	grams
ounces, troy	1.09714	ounces, avoir.
Ounces (Fluid)	1.805	cubic inches
ounces (fluid)	0.02957	liters
Ounces per Sq Inch	0.0625	pounds per sq inch
Parts per Million (ppm)	0.0584	grains per U.S. gallon
parts per million	0.07016	grains/imperial gallon
parts per million	8.345	pounds/million gallon
Pennyweights (Troy)	24	grains
pennyweights (troy)	1.55517	grams
pennyweights (troy)	0.05	ounces (troy)
pennyweights (troy)	4.1667×10^{-3}	lbs. (troy)
Pints	0.4732	liters
Pounds (Avoir.)	16	Ounces
pounds (avoir.)	256	drams
pounds (avoir.)	7000	grains
pounds (avoir.)	0.0005	tons (short)
pounds (avoir.)	453.5924	grams
pounds (avoir.)	1.21528	pounds (troy)

Multiply (A)	By (B)	To Obtain (C)
• pounds (avoir.)	14.5833.................	ounces (troy)
• pounds (avoir.)	0.454....................	kilograms
• Pounds (Troy)	5760	grains
• pounds (troy)......................	240	pennyweights (troy)
• pounds (troy)......................	12	ounces (troy)
• pounds (troy)......................	373.24177...............	grams
• pounds (troy)......................	0.822857................	pounds (avoir.)
• pounds (troy)......................	13.1657.................	ounces (avoir.)
• pounds (troy)......................	3.6735×10^{-4}	tons (long)
• pounds (troy)......................	4.1143×10^{-4}	tons (short)
• pounds (troy)......................	3.7324×10^{-4}	tons (metric)
• Pounds of Water	0.01602.................	cubic feet
• pounds of water	27.68...................	cubic inches
• pounds of water	0.1198..................	U.S. gallons
• pounds of water	0.10....................	imperial gallons
• Pounds of Water per Minute	2.670×10^{-4}	cubic feet per second
• Pounds per Cubic Foot...............	0.01602.................	grams/cubic centimeter
• pounds per cubic ft	16.02...................	kilograms/cubic meter
• pounds per cubic ft	5.787×10^{-4}	lbs. per cubic inch
• Pounds per Cubic Inch	27.68...................	grams/cubic centimeter
• pounds per cubic inch...............	2.768×10^{4}	kilograms/cubic meter
• pounds per cubic inch...............	1728	lbs. per cubic foot
• Pounds per Foot	1.488...................	kilograms per meter
• Pounds per Inch	178.6...................	grams per centimeter
• Pounds per Square Foot (psf)	0.01602.................	feet of water
• pounds per square foot...............	4.883×10^{-4}	kilograms/sq. cm
• pounds per square foot...............	6.945×10^{-4}	lbs. per square inch
• Pounds per Square Inch (psi)..........	0.06804.................	atmospheres
• pounds per square inch	2.307...................	feet of water
• pounds per square inch	2.036...................	inches of mercury
• pounds per square inch	0.07031.................	kilograms/sq. cm
• Quarts (Dry)	67.20...................	cubic inches
• Quarts (Liquid)	57.75...................	cubic inches

Multiply (A)	By (B)	To Obtain (C)
Quintal, Argentina	101.28	pounds
Quintal, Brazil	129.54	pounds
Quintal, Castille, Peru	101.43	pounds
Quintal, Chile	101.41	pounds
Quintal, Mexico	101.47	pounds
Quintal, Metric	220.46	pounds
Temp. (°C) + 273.15	1	absolute temp. in °K
temp. (°C) + 17.78	1.8	temperature in °F
temp. (°F) + 460	1	absolute temp. in °R
temp. (°F) −32	0.5555555	temperature in °C
Tons (Long)	2240	pounds
tons (long)	1016	kilograms
tons (long)	1.120	tons (short)
Tons (Metric)	10	kilograms
tons (metric)	2205	pounds
Tons (Short)	2000	pounds
tons (short)	32000	ounces
tons (short)	907.18486	kilograms
tons (short)	2430.56	pounds (troy)
tons (short)	0.89287	tons (long)
tons (short)	29166.66	ounces (troy)
tons (short)	0.90718	tons (metric)
Tons of Water per Day	83.333	pounds water/hour
tons of water per day	0.16643	gallons per minute
tons of water per day	1.3349	cubic feet per hour
Watts	0.05692	lbs. water per hour
watts	44.26	foot-lbs. per minute
watts	0.7376	foot-lbs per second
watts	1.341×10^{-3}	horsepower
watts	0.01434	kg.-calories/minute
watts	10^{-3}	kilowatts
watts	10^{-6}	megawatts
watts	10^{-9}	gigawatts

Multiply (A)	By (B)	To Obtain (C)
watts	10^{-12}	terawatts
Watt-Hours	3.415	Btus
watt-hours	2656	foot-pounds (lbs.)
watt-hours	1.341×10^{-3}	horsepower hrs
watt-hours	0.8605	kilogram-calories
watt-hours	367.2	kilogram-meters
watt-hours	10^{-3}	kilowatt-hours

Abbreviations for Frequently Used Units of Measure

cfm	cubic feet per minute		kg	kilograms
cfs	cubic feet per second		kwh	kilowatt hours
ci	cubic inches		mgd	million gallons per day
cms	centimeters		mph	miles per hour
cy	cubic yards		mps	meters per second
cym	cubic yards per minute		p	pressure
fpm	feet per minute		pcf	pounds per cubic foot
fps	feet per second		ppt	parts per trillion
gpm	grams per mile		ppth	parts per thousand
gal	gallons		psf	pounds per square foot
gpd	gallons per day		psi	pounds per square inch
gpg	grams per gallon		rpm	revolutions per minute
h	heat		rps	revolutions per second
hp	horsepower		tw	test weight
in	inches		u	internal energy
keV	kilovolts		v	volume

Section VI

Chemical Elements

Chemical Elements

Ac	Actinium	Dy	Dysprosium
Ag	Silver (Argentum)	Er	Erbium
Al	Aluminum	Es	Einsteinium
Am	Americium	Eu	Europium
Ar	Argon	F	Fluorine
As	Arsenic	Fe	Iron (Ferrum)
At	Astatine	Fm	Fermium
Au	Gold (Aurum)	Fr	Francium
B	Boron	Ga	Gallium
Ba	Barium	Gd	Gadolinium
Be	Beryllium	Gm	Germanium
Bi	Bismuth	H	Hydrogen
Bk	Berkelium	He	Helium
Br	Bromine	Hf	Hafnium
C	Carbon	Hg	Mercury (Hydrargyrum)
Ca	Calcium	Ho	Holmium
Cd	Cadmium	In	Indium
Ce	Cerium	Ir	Iridium
Cf	Californium	I	Iodine
Cl	Chlorine	K	Potassium
Cm	Curium	Kr	Krypton
Co	Cobalt	La	Lanthanum
Cr	Chromium	Li	Lithium
Cs	Caesium (Cesium)	Lu	Lutetium
Cu	Copper (Cuprum)	Lw	Lawrencium

Mg	Magnesium		Rn	Radon
Mn	Manganese		Ru	Ruthenium
Mo	Molybdenum		S	Sulphur
Mv	Mendelevium		Sb	Antimony (Stibium)
N	Nitrogen		Sc	Scandium
Na	Sodium (Natrium)		Se	Selenium
Nb	Niobium		Si	Silicon
Nd	Neodymium		Sm	Samarium
Ne	Neon		Sn	Tin (Stannium)
Ni	Nickel		Sr	Strontium
No	Nobelium		Ta	Tantalum
Np	Neptunium		Tb	Terbium
O	Oxygen		Tc	Technetium
Os	Osmium		Te	Tellurium
P	Phosphorus		Th	Thorium
Pa	Protactinium		Ti	Titanium
Pb	Lead (Plumbum)		Tl	Thallium
Pd	Palladium		Tm	Thulium
Pm	Promethium		U	Uranium
Po	Polonium		V	Vanadium
Pr	Praseodymium		W	Tungsten (Wolfram)
Pt	Platinum		Xe	Xenon
Pu	Plutonium		Y	Yttrium
Ra	Radium		Yb	Ytterbium
Rb	Rubidium		Zn	Zinc
Re	Rhenium		Zr	Zirconium
Rh	Rhodium			

Section VII

Environmental Protection Agency Data

EPA Offices, Programs, and Regional Contact Data

■ EPA HEADQUARTERS, WATERSIDE MALL (WSM), 401 M ST., SW, WASHINGTON, DC 20460

The Environmental Protection Agency (EPA) was established in the executive branch as an independent agency pursuant to Reorganization Plan No. 3 of 1970. The EPA was created to administer federal environmental policies, research, and regulations. EPA provides information on many environmental subjects including water pollution, hazardous and solid waste disposal, air and noise pollution, pesticides, and radiation. In addition, EPA coordinates and supports research and anti-pollution activities by state and local governments, and other private and public groups and institutions. EPA also monitors and oversees the projects and activities of other federal agencies, when an agency's actions may pose negative impacts to the environment. In addition to WSM there are eight other headquarters locations:

- ■ Fairchild Building (FC), 499 South Capitol Street, SW, Washington, DC 20460

- ■ Judiciary Square (JS), 501 3rd Street, Washington DC 20005

- ■ Weststory Building (WSB), 607 14th Street, NW, 5th Floor, Washington, DC 20005

- ■ Crystal Mall II (CM-2), 1921 Jefferson Davis Highway, Arlington, VA 22202

- ■ Crystal Gateway (CG-1), 1235 Jefferson Davis Highway, Arlington, VA 22202

- ■ Crystal Station (CS-1), 2800 Crystal Drive, Arlington, VA 22202

- ■ Rosslyn Building (ROSS), 1550 Wilson Boulevard, Rosslyn, VA 22209

- ■ Analytical Chemistry Section (ACS), Bldg. 306 - BARC E, Beltsville, MD 20705

- ■ SDC SAIC Building, 200 North Glebe Road, Arlington, VA 22203

EPA Offices

■ OFFICE of the ADMINISTRATOR (AO) — (202) 260-4700

Provides overall supervision to the agency. The Administrator is directly responsible to the President of the United States, and is assisted by the Deputy Administrator and the staff offices listed below. The Office of Small/Disadvantaged Business Utilization which promotes utilization of small, small disadvantaged, minority and women owned firms in the contracting process, is located in the AO. This office sponsors training and networking seminars and EPA's Mentor-Protege Program.

AO offices and divisions include: Affirmative Action and Special Emphasis; Administrative Law Judges; Civil Rights; Communications Planning; Congressional Liaison; Executive Support; Legislative Analysis; Operations and Analysis; Press Relations; Public Liaison; Regional Operations; Science Advisory Board; and the Division of State and Local Relations.

■ OFFICE of ADMINISTRATION and RESOURCES MANAGEMENT (OARM) — (202) 260-4083

Primary responsibility for policy and procedures governing natural and human resources management, environmental equity, environmental health and safety, administrative services, systems development, information management, data processing, and procurement. OARM offices and divisions include: Acquisition Management; Administration and Resource Management; Administrative Systems; Budget; Comptroller; Contracts management; Employee Participation and Communications; Environmental Equity; Facilities Management; Financial Management; Grants Administration; Procurement Operations; Human Resources Management; Information Resources Management and Services; Management and Organization; National Data Processing; Policy, Research and Development; Policy, Training and Oversight; Public Information Center; Safety, Health and Environmental Management; and the Superfund/RCRA Procurement Operations Division.

■ OFFICE of AIR and RADIATION PROGRAMS (OAR) — (202) 260-1993

Administers air quality standards and planning programs of the Clean Air Act. Supervises the Office of Air Quality Planning and Standards in Durham, North Carolina, which develops national air standards and provides information on air pollution control. Administers the Air Pollution Technical Information Center, which publishes technical literature on air pollution.

OAR includes the offices of stationary and mobile sources — Office of Mobile Sources enforces Clean Air Act provisions for mobile sources, including aircraft emission standards and automobile air pollution control programs — Office of Stationary Source Compliance administers Clean Air Act provisions for stationary sources, including steel, petroleum, coal-fire boilers and furnaces, electric utilities, natural gas, and other industrial air pollution standards. In addition the following offices and divisions are located within the OAR: Acid Rain; Air Quality Management; Atmospheric Programs; Criteria and Standards; Emission Planning and Strategies; Engineering Operations; Field Operations and Support; Indoor Air; and Radon.

■ OFFICE of ENFORCEMENT (OE) — (202) 260-2532

Principal adviser to the administrator on enforcement of standards for air, water, toxic substances and pesticides, solid waste management, radiation, and noise control programs. Investigates criminal and civil violations of environmental standards. Includes Office of Federal Activities which is the liaison office for all federal agencies and manages National Environmental Policy Act environmental reviews of other agencies' projects and activities, the EPA American Indian Program, and federal facilities compliance.

OE offices and divisions include: Air Enforcement; Civil Enforcement; Compliance Analysis and Program Operations; Criminal Enforcement and Investigations; Enforcement and Compliance; Federal Facilities Enforcement; Laboratory Services; National Enforcement Investigations; Pesticides and Toxic Substances Enforcement; Planning and Management; Program Operation; RCRA Enforcement; Special Programs and Analysis; Strategic Planning and Prevention; Superfund Enforcement; and Water Enforcement.

■ OFFICE of GENERAL COUNSEL (OGC) — (202) 260-8880

Provides legal services to all offices and divisions with respect to EPA programs and activities; provides legal opinions, counsel, and litigation support. OGC also assists in the formulation and administration of policies and programs. OGC offices and divisions include: Contracts, Claims and Property Law; Cross-Media Analysis and Review; Grants and Intergovernmental Relations; Inspector General; International Activities; Management and Administration; Pesticides and Toxic Substances; and a Water Division.

■ OFFICE of INSPECTOR GENERAL (OIG) — (202) 260-8970.

Conducts audits and investigations relating to programs and operations of EPA. Provides leadership and coordination to detect fraud and abuse and enhance agency efficiency. Advises senior management and Congress of serious abuses and deficiencies relating to EPA programs, policies, and operations. The OIG is comprised of the Mid-Atlantic; Eastern Field; Southern Field; and Western Field divisional offices.

■ OFFICE of INTERNATIONAL ACTIVITIES (OIA) — (202) 260-4304

Develops policies and procedures for the direction of EPA's international programs and activities. The agency conducts ongoing evaluations, and is charged with taking the lead in solving complex international environmental problems and protecting the global environment.

■ OFFICE OF PESTICIDES and TOXIC SUBSTANCES (OPTS) — (202) 260-2906

Studies and makes recommendations for regulation of chemical substances under the Toxic Substances Control Act. Compiles national priorities list of substances subject to the act. Controls and regulates use of toxic substances. OPTS assesses the health and environmental hazards of chemical substances and mixtures; collects information on chemical use, exposure, and effects; and maintains an inventory of chemical substances. OPTS includes the offices of Chemical Control and Pesticide Programs.

The Office of Chemical Control selects and implements control measures for new and existing chemicals that pose a risk to human health and the environment. Oversees and manages the regulatory evaluation and decisionmaking process in the area of toxic substances. Evaluates alternative remediation control strategies under the Toxic Substances Control Act. Develops generic and chemical-specific rules for new chemicals. Reviews chemicals and regulates the manufacture, distribution, use, and disposal of toxic chemicals.

The Office of Pesticide Programs conducts research, sets and enforces standards for pesticide manufacturing and use, maintains nationwide accident report database system, and develops rules regarding pesticide labeling and descriptive literature.

■ OFFICE of POLICY, PLANNING, and EVALUATION (OPPE) — (202) 260-4020

Coordinates agency planning, evaluation, and standard setting activities. The office is primarily responsible for policy and economic analysis standards and regulations planning. OPPE includes the following offices and divisions: Climate Change; Economic Analysis and Innovation; Policy Analysis; Program Evaluation; Regulatory Management and Evaluation; Strategic Planning and Environmental Data; Strategic Planning and Management; Waste and Chemical Policy; and the Water and Agricultural Policy Division.

■ OFFICE OF RESEARCH AND DEVELOPMENT (ORD) — (202) 260-9139

Develops scientific databases to determine and support EPA standards and regulations. Develops technology for environmental controls on industry. ORD includes the following offices and divisions: Research and Development; Air and Energy Engineering Research Lab; Atmospheric Research and Exposure Assessment Lab; Environmental Criteria and Assessment; Environmental Engineering and Technology Demonstration; Environmental Monitoring Systems Lab; Environmental Processes and Effects Research; Environmental Research Lab; Exploratory Research; Health Effects Research; Health Research; Modeling, Monitoring Systems and Quality Assurance; Program and Policy Coordination; Risk Reduction Engineering Lab; and the Office of Science, Planning, and Regulatory Evaluation.

■ OFFICE of SOLID WASTE and EMERGENCY RESPONSE (OSWER) — (202) 260-4610

Administers and enforces the Superfund Act (SARA) and the Resource Conservation and Recovery Act (RCRA), which manages the handling and disposal of hazardous wastes. OSWER's responsibilities include: development of guidelines and standards for land disposal of hazardous wastes and USTs; technical assistance in the development, management, and operation of solid waste management activities; and analyses on the recovery of useful energy from solid waste. OSWER includes the following offices and divisions: CERCLA and RCRA Enforcement; Hazardous Site Control; Hazardous Site Evaluation; Implementation; Permits and State Programs; Policy and Standards; Program Management and Support; Solid Waste; Waste Management; Superfund Revitalization; Technology Innovation; and Underground Storage Tanks Division.

■ OFFICE of WATER (OW) — (202) 260-7818.

Develops national programs, technical policies, and regulations relating to drinking water, water quality and groundwater; environmental and pollution source standards development; and wetlands protection. In addition, the OW provides technical direction, support, and evaluation of regional water quality activities; enforcement of standards; training in the field of water quality; economic and long-term environmental analysis; and marine and estuarine protection. OW includes the Office of Wetlands Protection which manages the dredge and fill program, under Section 404 of the Clean Water Act; coordinates federal policies affecting wetlands; and promotes public awareness about wetland preservation and management. OW offices and divisions include: Drinking Water Standards; Engineering and Analysis; Health and Ecological Criteria; Municipal Support; Oceans and Coastal Protection; Permits; Standards and Applied Science; Technical Support; Wastewater Enforcement and Compliance; and Wetlands, Oceans and Watersheds.

EPA Regional Offices

Region 1

Environmental Protection Agency
One Congress Street, Boston, Massachusetts
02203
(617) 565-3420

Connecticut	Maine
New Hampshire	Massachusetts
Rhode Island	Vermont

Region 2

Environmental Protection Agency
26 Federal Plaza, Suite 900, New York, New
York 10278
(212) 264-2657

New Jersey	New York
Puerto Rico	Virgin Islands

Region 3

Environmental Protection Agency
841 Chestnut Building
Philadelphia, Pennsylvania 19107
(215) 597-9800

Delaware	Maryland
Pennsylvania	West Virginia
District of Columbia	Virginia

Region 4

Environmental Protection Agency
345 Courtland Street, NE
Atlanta, Georgia 30365
(404) 347-4727

Alabama	Florida
Georgia	Kentucky
Mississippi	North Carolina
South Carolina	Tennessee

Region 5

Environmental Protection Agency
77 West Jackson Boulevard
Chicago, Illinois 60604
(312) 353-2000

Illinois	Indiana
Michigan	Minnesota
Ohio	Wisconsin

Region 6

Environmental Protection Agency
First Interstate Tower at Fountain Place
1445 Ross Avenue, 12th Floor, Suite 1200
Dallas, Texas 75202
(214) 655-6444

Arkansas		Louisiana
New Mexico	Oklahoma	Texas

Region 7

Environmental Protection Agency
726 Minnesota Avenue
Kansas City, Kansas 66101
(913) 551-7000

Iowa	Kansas
Missouri	Nebraska

Region 8

Environmental Protection Agency
One Denver Place
999 18th Street, Suite 500
Denver, Colorado 80202
(303) 293-1603

Colorado	Montana
North Dakota	South Dakota
Utah	Wyoming

Region 9

Environmental Protection Agency
75 Hawthorne Street
San Francisco, California 94105
(415) 744-1305

Arizona	California
Hawaii	Nevada
American Samoa	Guam

Region 10

Environmental Protection Agency
1200 Sixth Avenue
Seattle, Washington 98101
(206) 553-4973

Alaska	Idaho
Oregon	Washington

Section VIII

Environmental Jargon Finder (Topic Index)

ENVIRONMENTAL
JARGON FINDER

Topic Index

AIR QUALITY and RELATED ISSUES

Acceptability of Plan Review Criterion
Accessible Emission Level
Accidental Release
Acid Deposition
Acid Deposition Report
Acid Precipitation Research Program
Acid Precipitation Task Force
Acid Rain
Adequacy of Operation Plan Review Criterion
Adverse Effect
Adverse Environmental Effect
Adverse Impact on Visibility
Adverse Modifications
Adverse Weather
Advisory
Aerosol
Afterwinds
Air
Air-Breathing Missile
Air Changes Per Hour
Air Contaminants
Air-Gap Separation
Air-Handling Unit
Air Mass
Air Monitoring
Air Pollutant
Air Pollution
Air Pollution Control Agency
Air Pollution Control Technology Information
Air Pollution Episode
Air Pollution Planning and Control Grants
Air Priorities Committee
Air Purification Devices
Air Quality
Air Quality Control Region
Air Quality Criteria
Air Quality Maintenance Area
Air Quality Maintenance Plan
Air Quality Monitoring
Air Quality Monitoring Program
Air Quality Planning
Air Quality Remediation Program
Air Quality Standard
Air Resources
Airborne Particulates
Airborne Radioactive Material
Airborne Release

Airborne Response Teams
Airshed
Allowable Emissions
Ambient Air
Ambient Air Quality Standards
Ambient Air Standard
Ambient Temperature
Applicable or Relevant and Appropriate
  Requirements
Applicable Requirements
Applicable Standards and Limitations
Approved Programs
Approved States
Area Source
Area Source Program
Areas of Critical Environmental Concern
Aromatic
Assessment of International Air Pollution
  Control Technologies
Atmosphere
Atmosphere Gases
Atmospheric Dispersion
Atmospheric Environment
Atmospheric Half-life
Atmospheric Pressure
Atmospheric Release Advisory Capability
Atmospheric Residence Time
Attainment Area
Attainment Demonstration
Attainment of Carbon Monoxide Levels
Attainment of Ozone Levels
Attainment of PM-10 Levels

Barometer
Barometric Altitude
BART
Baseline
Baseline Concentration
Baseline Data
Baseline Emissions
Baseline Vehicles
Below Regulatory Concern
Best Available Control Technology
Best Available Retrofit Technology
Best Available Technology
Best Available Technology Economically
  Achievable
Biosphere
Blizzard Warning

Stable Air
State Agency Rule
State Air Quality Agency
State Air Quality Implementation
 Responsibility
State Area Redesignation
State Implementation Plan
State Review of SIPs
Stationary Sources
Stratosphere
Study and Report Concerning Economic
 Approaches to Controlling Air Pollution
Study of Substances Discharged from Exhausts
 of Motor Vehicles
Study of Odors and Odorous Emissions
Study on Regional Air Quality
Substantial Drift
Sulfur Dioxide
Sulfuric Acid Plants
Suspended Particulates
Systems

Threshold Limit Values
Toxic Air Pollutants
Toxic Clouds
Transpiration
Tropical Storm
Troposphere
Tropospheric Scatter
Turbulence

United States/Canadian Negotiations on Air
 Quality

Ventilation
Ventilation, Adequacy
Ventilation System
Violations of Air Contaminant Standards
Visibility Impairment
Visibility Protection
Visibility Reducing Particles
Visibility Transport Region
Visibility Transport Commission
Visible Emissions, Asbestos
VOCs
Volatile Hazardous Air Pollutant
Volatile Organic Compound Study
Volatile Organic Compounds
Volcanic Dust

Wilson Cloud
Wind Abrasion
Wind Chill Advisory
Wind Energy Research
Wind Profile
Wind Project
Wind Shear
Wind Velocity
Windbreak
Winter Storm
Winter Storm Warning
Winter Storm Watch
Winter Weather Advisories
Wood-Burning Stove Pollution
World Meteorological Organization

BIOLOGICAL/CHEMICAL PROCESSES and RELATED ISSUES

Abiotic
Ablative
Absorb
Absorbed Dose
Absorbed Dose Rate
Absorption
Absorption, Chemical
Absorption Hazards
Absorption, Human
Absorption, Radiation
Absorption, Waste
Absorptive Capacity
Acaricide
Acceptable Daily Intake
Acceptable Quality Level
Acetic Acid
Acetone
Acetylcholine
Acid
Acid Deposition
Acid Dipping
Acrylic Fiber
Acrylic Resins
Act of God
Act of Nature
Actinmycetes
Actinoids
Activated Carbon
Activated Sludge

Activated Sludge Process
Active Immunity
Active Ingredient
Acute
Acute Dermal LD 50
Acute Effect
Acute Exposure
Acute LD 50
Acute Oral LD 50
Acute Radiation Dose
Acute Toxicity
Additive
Additive and Synergistic Effects
Adenoma
Adhesion
Administered Dose
Adsorption
Adulterants
Adulteration
Aeration
Aerial Plankton
Aerobic
Aerobic Treatment
Aerodynamic Diameter
Aetiology
Agency for Toxic Substances and Disease
  Registry (ASTDR)
Agent Orange
Agglutination
Aggregate Risk
Aggressive Biological Treatment Facility
Alachlor
Alanine
Alar
Albumin
Albuminuria
Alcohol
Aldicarb
Aldrin
Algae
Alkali
Alkaline
Alkalinity
Alkylation
Allergen
Alpha Particles
Alpha Rays
Altered Growth
Altitude Sickness

Alveolar
Alveolar Ducts
Alveolar Macrophage
Alveolar Ventilation
Alveoli
Amino Acids
Anemia
Aneuploidy
Anhydrous
Anisocytosis
Anisotropic
Anoxia
Antagonism
Anti-Microbial Agents
Antibodies
Anticrop Agent
Anticrop Operation
Antidote
Antigen
Antimateriel Agent
Antiplant Agent
API Scale
Aplastic Anemia
Apnea
Apomixis
Applied Dose
Arrhythmia
Asbestos
Asbestosis
Asphyxia
Asphyxiants
Asphyxiation
Asthma
Aspiration Pneumonia
Ataxia
Atelectasis
Atopy
Atrophy
ATSDR
Attractant

Background Count
Background Level
Background Radiation
Bacteria
Bactericide
Beneficial Organisms
Benzene
Beryllium(Be)

Beryllium Alloys
Beryllium Propellants
Bioaccumulation
Bioaccumulative
Bioassay
Bioassay Procedures
Bioavailability
Biochemical
Biochemical Oxygen Demand
Biochemicals
Biocides
Bioclimatology
Bioconcentration
Bioconversion
Biodegradable
Biodiversity
Bioecology
Bioengineering
Biological Additives
Biological Agent
Biological Ammunition
Biological Assessments
Biological Clearance Rate
Biological Control
Biological Defense
Biological Environment
Biological Half-Life
Biological Half-Time
Biological Magnification
Biological Monitoring
Biological Operation
Biological Opinion
Biological Oxidation
Biological Oxygen Demand
Biological Pesticides
Biological Processes
Biological Resources
Biological Treatment
Biological Warfare
Biological Weapon
Biologically Significant Effect
Biology
Biomagnification
Biomass
Biometeorology
Biometrics
Biomonitoring
Bioremediation
Biosphere

Biostabilizers
Biota
Biotechnology
Biotic Communities
Biotic Factors
Biotic Index
Biotic Potential
Biotic Pyramid
Biotransformation
Bismaleimide
Blister Agent
Blood Agent
BOD
BOD Load
BOD 5
Body Content
Body System(s)
Bronchi
Bronchial
Bronchial Epithelium
Bronchiectasis
Bronchiole
Bronchitis
Bronchorrhea
Bronchospasm
Burning Agents

Cancer
Carbamates
Carbon Absorbers
Carbon Absorption
Carbon Dioxide
Carbon Monoxide
Carbonate
Carboxyhemoglobin
Carcinogen
Carcinogen Risk Assessment Verification
  Workgroup
Carcinogenic
Carcinogenic Process
Carcinoma
Cardiac Dysrhythmia
Case-Control Study
Cataract
Category of Chemical Substances
Category of Mixtures
Centers for Disease Control and Prevention
Central Nervous Systems
Cerebellar Abnormalities

Cerebellum
Cerebral Infarctions
Cerebrum
Chemexfoliation
CFCs
Chemical Abstract Service
Chemical Agent
Chemical Agent Cumulative Action
Chemical Ammunition
Chemical Ammunition Cargo
Chemical, Biological, and Radiological
  Operation
Chemical Defense
Chemical Dose
Chemical Engineering
Chemical Formula
Chemical Hazards Emergency Management
  System
Chemical Lot
Chemical Mixture
Chemical Monitoring
Chemical Operations
Chemical Oxygen Demand
Chemical Processes
Chemical Processing
Chemical Processor
Chemical Protective Clothing
Chemical Reaction
Chemical Safety and Hazard Investigation
  Board
Chemical Safety Board
Chemical Standards for the Development of
  Test Data
Chemical Substance
Chemical Survey
Chemical Treatment
Chemical Vapor Deposition
Chemical Warfare
Chemical Warfare Agent
Chemical Warfare Weapons
Chemical Waste Landfill
Chemicals of Potential Concern
Chemoreception
Chemosterilant
CHEMS
CHESS
Chloramines
Chlorinated Hydrocarbons
Chlorinated Solvent

Chlorination
Chlorination Chamber
Chlorinators
Chlorine
Chlorofluorocarbons
Chlorosis
Chromium
Chromosome
Chromosome Abnormality
Chronic Effect
Chronic Exposure
Chronic Obstructive Pulmonary Disease
Chronic Radiation Dose
Chronic Reference Dose Value
Chronic Toxicity
Ciliated Epithelial Cell
Cirrhosis
Clastogenic
Coagulation
Coliform Index
Coliform Organisms
Collective Effective Dose Equivalent
Collective Effective Dose Equivalent Rate
Collective Nuclear, Biological and Chemical
  Protection
Colloids
Committed Effective Dose Equivalent
Complete Carcinogen
Composite Sample
Compost
Composting
Compressed Gas
Compressed Gases in Solution
Congenital Anomalies
Conjunctiva
Conjunctivitis
Contact Dermatitis
Contaminant
Contamination
Contingent Effects
Convective
Convective Transport
Conventional Pollutant
Corneal Opacification
Corrosion
Corrosive
Corrosive Materials
Cotyledon
Counterdrug

Critical Organs
Critical Pathways
Cryogenic Liquid
Crystallinity
Cyanosis
Cytochrome P-448 and P-450
Cytology
Cytotoxicity

DDT (Dichloro-Diphenyl-Trichloroathane)
Dechlorination
Decomposition
Decomposition of Wastewater
Defoliant
Defoliant Operation
Defoliating Agent
Degradation
Delayed Chronic Health Hazards
Delirium
Dementia
Demyelination
Denervation Atrophy
Denitrification
Dermal Toxicity
Dermatitis
Dermis
Desiccant
Desiccant Effect
Desiccation
Detergents
Detoxification
Deuterium
Developmental Toxicity
Diaphoresis
Diazinon
Dichasium
Dicofol
Digestion
Dilution
Dilution Ratio
Dinocap
Dinoseb
Dioxins
Diplopia
Direct Bioassays
Disinfectants
Disinfected Wastewater
Disinfection
Dispersants

Dispersion
Dispersion Coefficient
Dispersion Error
Dispersion Model
Dispersion Resins
Dispersivity
Dissolved Oxygen
Dissolved Solids
Diuresis
DNA (Deoxyribonucleic Acid)
DNA Adduct
DNA Crosslink
DNA Hybridization
Dose Equivalents
Dose Equivalent Index
Dose-Response Evaluation
Dose Limit
Dose Response
Dose-Response Relationship
Dose Upper Bounds
Dosimetry
Dyscrasia
Dysphagia
Dyspnea
Dysuria

Edaphic Factors
Edema
Effective Dose Equivalent
Effective Half-Life
Elutriation
Embolization
Embryo
Embryotoxicity
Emesis
Emphysema
Encephalopathy
Endemic
Endosulfan
Endothelial
Enthalpy
Entomology
Environmental Stress
Enzyme
EP Toxicity
Epidemic
Epidemiology
Epidermis
Epigenetic

Epiphyseal

Epithelial

Erythema

Erythroderma

Esophageal Strictures

Esophagus

Ethanol

Ethylene Dibromide

Etiologic Agents

Euphoria

Evolution

Excretion

Exergonic

Exfoliative Dermatitis

Explosive Limits, Chemical

Explosives

Explosivity

Expose

Exposure

Exposure Assessment

Exposure Dose

Exposure Event

Exposure Pathways

Exposure Point

Exposure Point Concentration

Exposure Rate

Exposure Route

Extrathoracic

Extremely Hazardous Substances

Facultative Anaerobic Bacteria

Fecal Coliform Bacteria

Fermentation

Fertilizers

Fetotoxic

Fetus

Fibrosis

Fissile

Fissile Class I

Fissile Class II

Fissile Class III

Fissile Classification

Fissile Materials (CFR)

Fission

Fission Products

Flash Point

Floc

Flue Gas Desulfurization

Fluids

Fluorides

Fluorocarbon

Fluorosis

Fumes

Fumigant

Functional Developmental Toxicity

Fungi

Fungus

Fusion

Gamete

Gamma Radiation

Gangrene

Gasification

Gasohol

Gastrointestinal

Gene

Gene Library

Genetic

Genetic Engineering

Genetic Radiation Effects

Genome

Genotoxic

Geochemistry

Germ Cell

Germicide

Gestation Period

Glaciate

Glaucoma

Gross Alpha Particle Activity

Gross Beta Particle Activity

Guidelines for Carcinogenic Risk Assessment

Gypsum

Habitat

Halocarbons

Halocline

Halogenated

Halogenated Organic Compounds

Halogens

Halomorphic Soil

Halon

Hazardous Chemical

Health Hazard, Chemical

Hema or Hemo

Hemangiosarcoma

Hematuria

Hemodialysis

Hemoglobin

Hemoglobinuria
Hemolysis
Hemolytic Anemia
Hemoptysis
Hepatic
Hepato
Hepatomegaly
Herbicide
Heterogeneity
Highly Toxic
Homeostasis
Homogeneity
Hormone
Host
Human Equivalent Dose
Human Exposure Model
Hybrid
Hybrid Composite
Hybridoma
Hydration
Hydrazine
Hydrocarbon
Hydrogen Cyanide
Hydrogen-Ion Concentration
Hydrogen Sulfide
Hydrolysis
Hyperbilirubinemia
Hyperesthesia
Hyperplasia
Hyperpigmentation
Hyperreflexia
Hypersensitization
Hypertension
Hyperventilation
Hypocalcemia
Hypokalemia
Hypomagnesemia
Hypophosphatemia
Hypotension
Hypoxemia
Hypoxia

Immediately Dangerous to Life and Health
Immediately Dangerous to Life or Health
  Values
Immune System
Immunodeficiency
Immunosuppression
Impurities

In Situ Volatization
In Vitro
In Vivo
Incapacitating Agent
Infectious Material
Infectious Wastes
Inflammation
Ingestion
Ingestion Exposure Pathways
Ingestion Hazards
Inhalation
Inhalation LC 50
Inhalation Toxicology Research Institute
Inocula/Inoculum
Inorganic Arsenic
Inorganic Chemicals
Intake
Intramuscular
Intravascular
Irritant
Irritating Materials
Ischemia
Ischemic Necrosis
Isomer

Jaundice

Keratitis
Kerosene
Kinematic Viscosity
Kinesis
Kinetic Rate Coefficient

Laboratory
Laboratory Test
Laboratory Audits
Lacrimation
Laryngeal Edema
Laryngitis
Laryngospasm
Larynx
LD 50, Median Lethal Dose
Lead
Lead-Based Paint
Legionella
Lens of Eye Dose Equivalents
Lesion
Lethal
Lethal Concentration 50

Lethal Concentration, Low
Lethal Concentration, Median Level
Lethal Dose
Lethal Dose 50
Lethal Dose, Low
Lethal Dose of Radiation
Lethargy
Leukemia
Leukocyte
Lifetime
Lignite
Liquefied Compressed Gases
Liquids
Lipid Solubility
Liquefied Natural Gas
Liquefied Petroleum Gas
List of Chemical Contaminants Found in
  Human Tissue
Lowest-Observed-Adverse-Effect Level
Lowest-Observed-Effect Level
Lymphoma

Male Reproductive Toxicity
Malformation
Malignant
Manifests
Margin of Exposure
Maximum Individual Risk
Maximum Likelihood Estimate
Maximum Permissible Concentration
Maximum Permissible Dose
Maximum Permissible Exposure
Maximum Permissible Level
Maximum Tolerated Dose
Median Incapacitating Dose
Median Lethal Concentration
Median Lethal Dose
Meiosis
Mercury Chlor-Alkali Cells
Mercury Chlor-Alkali Electrolyzers
Metabolism
Metabolite
Metaplasia
Metastasis
Methane
Methanol
Method Quantification Limits
Microbes
Microbial Pesticides

Microenvironment
Microorganisms
Miosis
Mitosis
Mixtures
Monomer
Morbidity
Mulches
Mutagenic
Mutagenesis
Mutagens
Mutate
Mutation
Myalgia
Mydriasis
Myelocytic Leukemia
Myocardial Ischemia
Myocarditis
Myoclonus
Myoglobin

Narcosis
Nasopharyngeal Region
Nasopharynx
Natural Background Radiation
Natural Gas
Natural Gas Liquids
Natural Pollutant
Natural Selection
Natural Uranium
Naturally Degradable Material
Naturally Occurring Background Levels
Necrosis
Nematocide
Neodymium
Neonatal
Neoplasia
Neoplasm
Nephritis
Nephron
Nephrotoxic
Nerve Agent
Neuropathy
Neurotoxicity
Neutralization
Neutralize
Nitrates
Nitric Oxides
Nitrification

Nitrilotriacetic Acid
Nitrite
Nitrogen
Nitrogen Dioxide
Nitrogen Oxide
Nitrogenous Wastes
No-Observed-Adverse-Effect Level
No-Observed--Effect Level
Noncardiogenic Pulmonary Edema
Nonmethane Organic Gas
NOx
Nuclear Poisons
Nuclear Radiation
Nucleon
Nucleus
Nuclides
Nutrient
Nystagmus

Occupational Doses
Occupational Exposure
Occupational Medicine
Odor Threshold
Off-Gassing
Office of Chemical Control
Office of Pesticide and Toxic Substances
Oil
Olfactory Fatigue
Oncogene
Oncogenesis
Oncogenic
Ontogenesis
Optic Atrophy
Optic Neuritis
Organic
Organic Chemicals/Compounds
Organic Matter
Organic Peroxide
Organic Soil
Organically Grown
Organisms
Organochlorines
Organogenesis
Organoleptic
Organomercury Fungicides
Organophosphates
Organophosphorus Pesticides
Organotins
OSHA Chemical Safety Management

OSHA Standard, [...] Bloodborne Pathogens
Osteosclerosis
Oxidants
Oxidation
Oxidizer
Oxidizing Materials
Oxygen
Oxygen Deficiency
Oxygenated Gasoline
Oxygenated Solvents
Ozone
Ozone Depletion

Packaged Laboratory Chemicals
Paresthesia
Particle
Particle Flux
Particle Fluence
Particulates
Parts per Billion
Parts per Million
Parts per Trillion
Pathogenic
Pathogens
PCB and PCBs
Pedology
Percutaneous Absorption
Peripheral Nervous System
Peripheral Neuropathy
Permissible Exposure Limit
Persistence
Pesticide Tolerance
Pesticides
Petroleum
pH
Pharmacokinetics
Pharynx
Phenols
Phosphates
Phosphorus
Photochemical Oxidants
Photochemical Smog
Photon
Physical and Chemical Treatment
Physiologically Based Pharmacokinetics
Plasmid
Plutonium
Pneumonitis
Poikilocytosis

Poison
Pollutant
Polychlorinated Biphenyl
Polyelectrolytes
Polyvinyl Chloride
Posing an Exposure Risk, Food or Feed
Positive Exposure
Posthypoxic Encephalopathy
Preliminary Assessment
Preliminary Biological Opinion
Prescribed Limits
Preventable, Heritable, or Congenital Disorders
Proteins
Proteinuria
Proton
Pruritic
Published Exposure Levels
Pullorum Disease
Pulmonary Edema
Pulmonary Region
Pulse
Pulse Duration
Pyrolysis
Pyrophoric
Pyrophoric Liquids
Pyrotechnic

Quality of Water
Quench Tank

Radiant Exposure
Radiation
Radiation Dose
Radiation Dose Rate
Radioactive Materials
Radioactive Nuclide Intake
Radioactive Wastes
Radionuclides
Radiotoxicity
Radon
Radon Decay Products
Radon Progeny
Re-Refined Oil
Reaction Time
Reactive
Reactivity
Reagent Grade
Recombinant Bacteria
Recombinant DNA

Recorded Doses
Recycled Oils
Recycled PCBs
Recycling
Reference Levels
Reformulated Gasoline
Refrigerant
Relative Biological Effectiveness
Release Agents
Releases
Relevant and Appropriate Requirements
REM
Renal Toxicity
Reproductive Toxicity
Residual
Residual Contamination
Residual Disinfectant Concentration
Residual Risks
Residues
Resin
Respiratory Depression
Respiratory Protective Device
Respiratory Rate
Restricted Dangerous Cargo
Restricted-Use Pesticide
Restriction Enzymes
Restrictive Lung Disease
Retailers, Chemical
Reference Dose
Retrobulbar Neuritis
Rhinitis
Rhinorrhea
Rhizomate
Rhomboidal
Ribonucleic Acid
Riot Control Agent
Rodenticide
Roentgen
Roentgen Equivalent Mammal/Man
Routes of Exposure

Saline
Salinity
Salts
Sclerotization
Secondary Contamination
Secondary Drinking Water Regulations
Secondary Limits
Secondary Maximum Contaminant Levels

Secondary Standards
Secondary Treatment
Secure Chemical
Secure Maximum Contaminant Level
Secured Enclosure
Sedimentation Tanks
Sedimentation
Seepage Water
Selective Pesticide
Selenodesy
Selenodetic
Sensory Neuropathy
Separation Zone
Serrate
Serrations
Sewage Sludge
Sewage Lagoon
Shallow Dose Equivalents
Shallow Eye Dose Equivalents
Shelf Life
Short-Term Exposure Limit
Short-Term Public Exposure Guidance Level
Significant Adverse Reactions
Significant Exposure
Significant Impairment
Significant Quantities
Silicon Carbide Fiber
Silique
Silt
Siltation
Silvicultural System
Sinking Agents
Sludge
Sludge Digestion
Sludge Dryer
Sludge Volume Index
Soft Detergents
Soil Adsorption Field
Solifluction
Solubility
Soluble
Solution
Solvent
Somatic Radiation Effects
Sorption
Source Materials
Source Reduction
Source Substitution
Spent Fuel

Spent Materials
Spent Nuclear Fuel
Spill Control Technology Program
Spill Prevention Control
Spill Prevention Control and Countermeasures
  Plan
Spoil
Spontaneously Combustible Materials
Squamation
Squamous Cell Carcinoma
Stabilization Ponds
Stack-Gas Desulfurization
Standard Wipe Test
Statoconia
Statocysts
Statolith
Status Epilepticus
Sterilization
Stimulus-Mediation-Response
Stimulus-Response
Stochastic Effects
Storage Coefficient
Storativity
Strong Sensitizer
Structural Adhesive
Sub-Rhomboidal
Subacute Dietary LC 50
Subchronic Exposure
Subcutaneous
Subgenus
Suffrutescent
Sulfates
Sulfur Dioxide
Sulfuric Acid Plants
Supernatant Liquor
Supporting Citation, Ingestion and Absorption
  Hazards
Synthetic Fuel
Synthetic Natural Gas
Synthetic Organic Chemicals
Systemic
Systemic Pesticide

Target Compound List
Target Organ System
TDLO
TDTOX
Teratogen
Teratogenicity

Test Mixtures
Test Substances
Thallium
Thoracic
Thorium
Thorough Decontamination
Threshold Limit Values
Threshold Planning Quantity
Threshold Quantity
Threshold Toxicant
Thrombocytopenia
Thrombosis
Tinnitus
Tissue Equivalents
TNT Equivalent
Toilet Recirculating Chemical
Tolerance
Tolerance Dose
Tolerance Limits
Total Dosage Attack
Total Exposure Points
Total Trihalomethanes
TOx
Toxic
Toxic Chemicals
Toxic Chemical, Biological, or Radiological
  Attack
Toxic Chemical Release Form
Toxic Chemical Source Reduction and
  Recycling
Toxic Clouds
Toxic Pollutants
Toxic Potential
Toxic Release Inventory System
Toxic Substances
Toxic Substances Control Act
Toxic Wastes
Toxicants
Toxicity
Toxicology
Toxin Agent
Trace Elements
Tracheitis
Tracheobronchial Region
Transpiration
Transuranic Contaminated Materials
Transuranic Elements
Transuranic Nuclides
Transuranic Wastes

Treatment
Trichloroethane
Trichloroethylene
Trickling Filter
Trihalomethane
Triple Rinse
Trismus
Tritium
Tubular Necrosis
Tumor
Types of Resin

Ubiquitous Background Levels
Ultimate Biochemical Oxygen Demand
Ultra Clean Coal
Umbonate
Unacceptable Adverse Effects
Uncontrolled Total Arsenic Emissions
Unfinished Oils
Ungulate
Unified Dose Assessments
Unirradiated Enriched Uranium
Unit Cancer Risk
Unleaded Gasoline
Unlisted Hazardous Substances
Unmanned Aerial Vehicle
Unspecified Motor Gasoline
Unutilized Natural Gas
Upper Bound Cancer Risk-Assessment
Upper Respiratory Tract
Uranium By-Product Materials
Uranium Mill Tailings
Uranium Mine Wastes Hazards Elimination
  Study
Uranium Processing Site
Urea
Urea Formaldehyde Foam
Uremia

Vaccines
Vapor Recovery System
Vaporization
Vaporizer-Burner
Vaporizers
Vapors
Vascular
Vasoconstriction
Vermiculation
Vesicant

Vesiculation
Vinyl Chloride
Vinyl Chloride Monomer
Viscosity
Viscous Liquids
Volatile Organic Compounds
Volatile Synthetic Organic Chemicals

Waste Oils
Wastewater Oxidation
Wastewater Treatment Processes
Water Solubility
Water-Reactive Material
Waterborne Disease Outbreaks
Whole Body
Whole Body Dose

Xenobiotic
Xenomorphic
Xenon
Xeromorphy

Yellowcake
Yttrium Aluminum Garnet

Zectran
Zeolitization
Zineb
Ziram
Zobar
Zygomorphic
Zymogenous

EMERGENCY RESPONSE, MANMADE, and NATURAL DISASTERS

Accident
Accident Prevention Measures for Regulated
  Substances
Accident Prevention Program
Accident Prevention Regulations for
  Hazardous Substances
Accident Prevention Risk Management Plan
Accident Prone Situation
Accident Response Capabilities Coordinating
  Committee
Accident Response Groups

Accident Scenario
Accident Site
Accident Types
Accidental Occurrences
Accidental Release
Accidents, Explosive
Act of God
Act of Nature
Acute
Acute Exposure
Adverse Environmental Effect
Adverse Weather
Adversely Affect
Advisory
Aeromedical Evacuation
Aeromedical Evacuation Control Center
Aeromedical Evacuation System
Aeromedical Evacuation Unit
Airborne Response Teams
Aircraft Accidents
Aircraft Incidents
Airway
Airway Resistance
Ambulatory Patient
Anticontamination Clothing
Arrhythmia
As Low as Reasonably Achievable
Automatic Incident Actions
Aversion Response
Awareness Barrier Physical and/or Visual
Awareness Signal

Battle Damage Assessment
Battle Damage Repair
Bird Strike
Blizzard Warning
Blowing Snow Advisory
Bomb Damage Assessment
Bomb Disposal Unit
Bomb Incidents
Bomb Threats
Building Emergency Support Team
Building Emergency Program Administrator
Building Emergency Plan

Casualty
Casualty Category
Casualty Status
Catastrophic Collapses

Emergency, Operational
Emergency Operations Center
Emergency Operations Plan
Emergency Order Authority
Emergency Permits
Emergency Plan
Emergency Planning
Emergency Planning and Community
  Right-to-Know Act
Emergency Planning, Preparedness, and
  Response Program
Emergency Planning Zone
Emergency Plans
Emergency Powers
Emergency Preparedness
Emergency Preparedness Coordinator
Emergency Priority
Emergency Procedures
Emergency Projects
Emergency Readiness Assurance Plan
Emergency Reference Levels
Emergency Relocation Site
Emergency Renovation Operations
Emergency Resources
Emergency Responder's Estimate
Emergency Response
Emergency Response Command and Control
Emergency Response Cycle
Emergency Response Levels
Emergency Response Organization
Emergency Response Planning Areas
Emergency Response Planning Guidelines
Emergency Response Posture
Emergency Response Program
Emergency Response Service Support
Emergency Response Service Support Area
Emergency Response Surveillance
Emergency Response Survival
Emergency Response Teams
Emergency Support Teams
Emergency Systems
Emergency Telecommunications Services
Energy Emergencies
Energy Emergency Management Teams
Energy Emergency System
Energy Emergency Teams
Environmental Catastrophe
Environmental Fatality

Environmental Fatality/Catastrophe
  Investigations
Environmental Hazard
Escalation
Exercise
Explosive Ordnance
Explosive Ordnance Disposal
Explosive Ordnance Disposal Incident
Explosive Ordnance Disposal Teams
Explosive Ordnance Disposal Unit
Explosive Projectiles
Explosive Torpedoes
Explosives
Explosives Activities
Explosives Bays
Explosives Buildings
Explosives Hazard Classes
Exposure Pathways
Exposure Point
Exposure Point Concentration
Exposure Rate
Exposure Route
Extent of Damage

Fallout
Fallout Contours
Fallout Pattern
Fallout Prediction
Fallout Safe Height of Burst
Fallout Wind Vector Plot
Federal Response Centers
Field Facility/Building Emergency Plans
Fifty-Year Flood Flow
Fire Hazards
Fire Protection
Fire Protection Engineering
Fire Protection Systems
Fire Storm
First Aid
First Federal Official
First Responder Team
First Responder's Estimate of the Situation
Flammable

General Emergencies

Habitat Loss
Hazard Analysis
Hazard and Operability Study

National Warning System
Natural Disaster
Natural Resource Damage Assessment
NBC Defense
Nuclear Accident
Nuclear Airburst
Nuclear Cloud
Nuclear Collateral Damage
Nuclear Damage
Nuclear Damage Assessment
Nuclear Defense
Nuclear Emergency Search Teams
Nuclear Incident
Nuclear Threat Incidents
Nuclear Vulnerability Assessment
Nuclear Weapon
Nuclear Weapons Accidents
Nuclear Winter

Occurrences
Off-Site Coordination Center
Off-Site Event
Off-Site Federal Support
Off-Site Notification/Warning
On-Scene
On-Scene Coordinator
On-Scene Commanders
On-Site Event
On-Site Facility
On-Site Federal Support
On-Site Technical Directors
Operating Basis Accident
Operating Basis Earthquake
Operational Accidents
Operational Design Basis Accident
Operational Decontamination
Operational Emergencies
Operational Emergency Response Levels
Operational Emergency Management Teams
Operational Emergency Preparedness
  Management Plans

Pararescue Team
Permissible Exposure Limit
Post-Emergency Response
Post-Incident Activities
Post-Medical Disposition
Post Removal Site Control
Primary Emergency Plans

Radiation Emergency Assistance
  Center/Training Site
Radioactive Material Transportation Accidents
Radioactive Material Transportation Incidents
Radiological Transportation Incidents
Regional Response Team
Respirators
Respiratory Depression
Respiratory Protective Device
Respiratory Rate
Response
Response Actions
Response Capability
Response Organization
Response Personnel
Response Plan Specifications
Response Readiness
Response Requirement
Response Teams
Response Time
Routes of Exposure

Search
Search and Rescue
Search and Rescue Coordinator
Search and Rescue Incident Classification
Search and Rescue Mission Coordinator
Search Radius
Self-Contained Breathing Apparatus
Senior Federal Emergency Management
  Agency Officials
Significant Incidents
Site Area Emergency
State Emergency Response Commission
Subcommittee on Federal Response

Terrorism
Terrorist
Terrorist Act
Terrorist Group
Terrorist Response Plans
Transportation Emergency
Transportation Incidents
Trigger Event

Unusual Occurrence

Vulnerability
Vulnerability Analysis

Vulnerable Zone

Weapons of Mass Destruction

Zone, Decontamination
Zone, Hot
Zone, Nominal Hazard
Zone, Radius of Vulnerability
Zone, Recovery
Zone, Support
Zone, Vulnerable
Zones, Emergency Planning

ENERGY and RELATED ISSUES

Average Annual Energy Use
Aviation Fuels
Aviation Gasoline

Bonneville Power Administration
British Thermal Unit

Clean Alternative Fuels
Clean Alternative Fuels Program
Clean Fuel Vehicle

Directed-Energy Device

Electric Energy
Electric Utility
Electric Utility Steam Generating Unit
Electricity, Produced
Energy
Energy Audit
Energy Conservation Maintenance and
  Operating Procedure
Energy Conservation Measures
Energy Conservation Project
Energy Conversion
Energy Efficiency
Energy Efficiency Standard
Energy Emergencies
Energy Emergency Management System
Energy Flow
Energy Fluence Rate
Energy Flux
Energy Management Systems
Energy Monitoring and Control System

Energy Recovery
Energy Savings
Energy Source
Energy Survey
Energy Technology Engineering Center,
  Canoga Park
Energy Trace
Energy Use

Fission Energy per Unit Mass of Uranium
Fossil Fuel
Fossil Fuel and Wood Residue-Fired Steam
  Generating Unit
Fuel Economy Standard
Fuel Efficiency
Fuel Element(s)
Fuels
Fuels and Vehicles Research

Geothermal Energy

Hydroelectric Power
Hydrogen Fuel Cell Vehicle Study and Test
  Program
Hypergolic Fuel

Independent Power Producer
Interagency Group on Energy Vulnerability
International Energy Program
International Energy Program Allocation and
  Information Provisions
International Energy Supply Emergency

Joule

Kilowatt
Kilowatt-Hour
Kinetic Energy
Kinetic Rate Coefficient

Linear Energy Transfer
Liquefied Natural Gas
Liquefied Petroleum Gas
Low-Polluting Fuel

Major Nuclear Power
Major Oil Company
Major Petroleum Product Transporter
Major Petroleum Products Storer

Mass Energy Absorption Coefficient
Measure of Energy Consumption
Megawatt
Motor Fuels
Motor Vehicle Emission and Fuel Standards

Naphtha Jet Fuel
Nuclear Energy
Nuclear Energy Center Site
Nuclear Energy Survey
Nuclear Fuel Cycle
Nuclear Power Plant
Nuclear Reactor
Nuclear Transmutation

Office of Conservation and Renewable Energy
Office of Energy Research
Office of Fossil Energy
Office of New Production Reactors
Office of Nuclear Energy
Output Power

Potential Energy
Power Boiler
Power Factor
Power Input
Power Marketing Administrations
Power Plant
Preliminary Energy Audit
Primary Fuel

Radiant Energy
Reactor
Reactor Operations
Reactor Projects
Refiner
Refinery
Refinery Fuel Use and Losses
Refinery Storage Facility
Related Energy Facility
Renewable Energy Sources
Renewable-Resource Energy Measure

Severe Energy Supply Interruption
Solar Absorption
Solar Cell
Solar Constant
Solar Energy
Solar Furnace

Solar Heating and Cooling
Solid Waste Derived Fuel
Southeastern Power Administration
Southwestern Power Administration
Spent Nuclear Fuel
Standby
Steam Power Plant
Synthetic Fuel
Synthetic Natural Gas

Technical Assistance for Energy Conservation
Thermal Energy
Trash-to-Energy Plans

Uninterruptible Power Supplies
Unusual and Compelling State or Local Energy
 Interests
Utility Plant Energy Conservation Measure

Vehicle, Alcohol Dual Energy
Vehicle, Natural Gas Dual Energy
Voluntary Energy Performance Standards

Western Area Power Administration
Wind Energy Research

ENVIRONMENTAL PROFESSIONS, PROFESSIONALS, and RELATED ISSUES

Agricultural Engineering
Agronomy
Approved Medical Practitioners
Arboriculture
Arborist
Archaeology
Architectural and Engineering Services
Architectural Conservation
Architectural Conservator
Architectural Historian
Architecture
Archivist
Autecology
Aviation Medicine

Bioclimatology
Bioecology
Bioengineering

Biogeography
Biology
Biometeorology
Biometrics
Biotechnology

Chemical Engineering
Conservator
Contractor
Crisis Managers
Crisis Support Team
Cultural Resource Specialist
Cultural Resource Technician
Curator

Developer

Ecology
Emergency Management Team Director
Emergency Management, Teams
Emergency Preparedness Coordinator
Emergency Response Teams
Emergency Support Teams
Energy Emergency Management Team
Engineer
Engineer-in-Training
Engineering Geologist
Entomology
Environmental Engineer
Environmental Health Specialist
Environmental Inspector
Environmental Planner
Environmental Researcher
Environmental Response Team
Environmental Scientist
Environmental Technician
Environmentalist
Epidemiologist
Epidemiology
Ergonomics
Ethnography
Ethnohistory
Ethnology
Ethology
Evaluator, Response
Explosive Ordnance Disposal Teams

Federal Coordinating Officers
Federal Land Managers

Federal Mining Inspector
Field Photography
Field Sampling Team
Fire Protection Engineering
First Federal Official
First Responder Team
Florology

Genecology
General Purchasing Agents
Geobotany
Geochemistry
Geodesy
Geography
Geology
Geometry
Geomorphology
Geophysics
Geotechnical Engineering
Geotechnical Specialist
Groundwater Hydrology

Hazard Assessment, Research
Hazardous Materials Response Team
HazMat Employer
Histology
Historian
Historic Preservation
Historical Archaeologist
Historical Architect
History
Human Engineering
Human Factors Engineering
Hydraulics
Hydrogeology
Hydrography
Hydrology

Imagery
Independent Audit Firm
Independent Inspector
Industrial Engineering
Industrial Hygiene
Inspector

Journeyman
Judicial Officers

Laser Safety Officer

Lead Authorized Officials
Liaison Officers
Lithology
Logistic Support, Medical
Logistics

Mapping, Charting, and Geodesy
Materials Handling
Mechanical Engineering
Medical Treatment
Medical Treatment Facility
Metallurgical Engineering
Meteorology
Metrology
Military Geography
Mobile Support Groups- Naval
Morphology
Morphometry

Nonparametric Statistics
Nuclear Engineering

Occupational Medicine
Oceanography
On-Scene Coordinator
On-Scene Commanders
Onsite Technical Directors
Owner/Operator

Paleoecology
Paleontology
Palynology
Pedology
Petroleum Engineering
Phenology
Photogrammetry
Production Logistics
Professional Engineering
Program Manager
Program Offices
Project Managers
Project Proponent

Qualified Safety Engineer
Quality Assurance Inspector
Quality Engineering

Radiobiology
Radiographer

Radiological Assistance Teams
Reconnaissance Photography

Safety and Health Directors
Safety Engineering
Safety Officer
Scientific Advisory Panel
Scientific Support Coordinators
Search and Rescue Coordinator
Structural Engineering
Survey Photography
System Integrator

Third Party Laboratory
Toxicology
Traffic Engineering
Trained Investigators

Underwater Archaeology
Underwater Demolition Team
Underwriter

Value Engineering

Weaponeering
Wind Project Operator

Zooecology
Zoogeographer
Zoogeography

GEOLOGIC, HYDROLOGIC, and LAND ISSUES

Aquifer
Aquifer Recharge Area
Aquifer System
Artesian Aquifer
Artesian Well

Background Soil pH
Bank
Basalt
Basin
Beach
Beach Capacity
Beachhead
Bedrock

Groundwater Flow
Groundwater Hydrology
Groundwater Model
Groundwater Mound
Groundwater Protection Advisory
Groundwater Recharge
Groundwater Resources
Groundwater Runoff
Gypsum

Halomorphic Soil
Hard Compact
Headwaters
Hill Shading
Hot Dry Rock
Humification
Hydration
Hydraulic Barrier
Hydraulic Fracturing
Hydraulic Conductivity
Hydraulic Gradient
Hydraulic Head
Hydric Soil
Hydrodynamic Dispersion
Hydrogeologic
Hydrogeologic Parameters
Hydrogeologic Unit
Hydrogeology
Hydrological Cycle
Hydrology

Igneous
Impermeable
Impervious Rock
Impervious Solid Surfaces
Inactive Mines
Infiltration
Injection Well
Injection Zones
Inland Harbor
Inland Waters
Inland Zones
In Situ
In Situ Extraction
In Situ Volatization

Kahawai
Kame
Kaolinite

Karst
Karst Topography

Lagoon
Lahar
Lake
Lake Transition Line
Land
Land Conservation Element
Land Disposal
Land Disposal Facilities
Land Economics
Land Effect
Land Farming, of Waste
Land Reclamation
Land Search
Land Treatment Facilities
Land Use
Land Use Authority
Land Use Ordinance
Landfill
Landfill Cells
Landmark
Landslides
Lignite
Lignite Coal
Limestones
Lithic
Lithification
Lithology
Lithosphere
Low Sulfur Coal
Low Terrain Area

Magma
Magnetic Declination
Magnetic Equator
Magnetic Variation
Mantle
Map
Map Reference
Map Series
Map Sheet
Mapping, Charting, and Geodesy
Marsh
Maximum Probable Flood
Mesolithic
Mesozoic
Metallurgical Coal

Mine
Mine Disposal
Mineral Recovery Remedial Activities
Mineral Soil
Mineral Water
Mixohaline
Mixosaline
Monitoring Wells
Muck Soils

Natural Uranium
Neolithic
Nonimpervious Solid Surfaces

Oblique Slip
Obliquity
Observation Well
Oil Shale
Oligotrophic Lakes
Operating Basis Earthquake
Organic Soil

Paleoecology
Paleolithic
Paleontology
Paleozoic Era
Permeability
Permeability Coefficient
Permious
Phosphate Rocks
Pleistocene
Pore
Pore Space
Porosity

Quadrangle
Quadrant Elevation
Quadrat
Quadrat Method
Qualified Hydrologic Unit
Quaternary
Quick Clays
Quick Ground
Quicklime

Range
Rangeland
Real Property
Recharge Area

Recharge Basin
Reclamation
Reservation
Reserve Area
Reservoir
Right-of-Way
Riprap
River Basins
Running Soil

Saturated Zone
Sediment
Sedimentation
Semiconfined Aquifer
Separation Zone
Silt
Siltation
Soil
Soil Adsorption Field
Soil and Water Conservation Practices
Soil Column
Soil Conditioner
Soil Injection
Soil Loss Equation
Soil Mechanics
Soil Resistivity
Soil Shear Strength
Soil-Structure Resonance
Stone
Strata
Stratification
Stream
Stream and Lake Protection Zone
Surface Faulting
Surface Impoundment
Swamp

Tar Sands
Tectonic
Tectonic Deformations
Terracing
Terrain Analysis
Tidal Marsh
Tidal Waters
Timberland
Topographic Map
Topographic Surface
Topography
Topsoil

Transmissive Faults/Fractures
Trench

U.S. Geological Survey
Unconfined Aquifer
Unconsolidated Aquifer
Underground Areas
Underground Coal Mine Development
Underground Injection
Underground Sources of Drinking Water
Underground Uranium Mines
Uplift
Unsaturated Zone
Unstable Areas, Geologic
Unstable Soils, Geologic

Well Field
Well Interference
Well Monitoring
Well Yield
Wellhead
Wellhead Protection Area
Wells
Wet Meadows
Wetlands
Wollastonite Rock

Xeric

Young River

Zonal Soil
Zonal Structure
Zone, Convergence
Zone, Low-Velocity
Zone, Rupture
Zone of Aeration
Zone of Cementation
Zone of Contribution
Zone of Deposition
Zone of Erosion
Zone of Flowage
Zone of Fracture
Zone of Fracture and Flowage
Zone of Saturation
Zone of Transport
Zone of Weathering
Zoogenic Deposit
Zoogenic Rock

| HAZARDOUS MATERIALS ISSUES

Asbestos-Containing Waste Materials
Banned Hazardous Substance
Beryllium Containing Wastes
Bulky Wastes
CERCLA Hazardous Substances
Certified Wastes
Characteristic, Waste
Chemical Warfare Agent
Chemical Waste Landfill
Chemicals of Potential Concern
Class I and Class II Substances
Classified Wastes
Comprehensive Environmental Response,
  Compensation, and Liability Act

Discharge
Discharge of Pollutants
Discharge or Hazardous Waste Discharge
Discharge or Release to Water or Land
Discharge Point
Disposer of PCB Waste

Emergency and Hazardous Chemical Inventory
Emergency Planning and Community
  Right-to-Know Act
EP Toxicity
EPA Hazardous Waste Number
EPA Identification Number
Existing Hazardous Waste Management
  Facility
Extremely Hazardous Substances
Extremely Hazardous Waste
Federal Insecticide, Fungicide, and
  Rodenticide Act

Fly Ash
Fissionable Materials
Fissionable Materials Handlers
Fumigant

Hazard
Hazard Analysis
Hazard and Operability Study
Hazard Assessment
Hazard Assessment Center
Hazard Assessment, Research
Hazard Categories

Hazard Classifications
Hazard Communication Standard
Hazard Identification
Hazard Incident Control Point
Hazard Quotient
Hazard Ranking System
Hazard Zone
Hazardous Air Pollutants
Hazardous Air Pollution
Hazardous Chemical
Hazardous Material
Hazardous Materials Emergencies
Hazardous Materials Incident
Hazardous Materials Response Team
Hazardous Motion
Hazardous Substance
Hazardous Substance, UST System
Hazardous Substances
Hazardous Substances List
Hazardous Substances List, Criteria
Hazardous Waste
Hazardous Waste Constituent
Hazardous Waste Discharge
Hazardous Waste Facilities
Hazardous Waste Facility Permit
Hazardous Waste Generation
Hazardous Waste Generator
Hazardous Waste Management
Hazardous Waste Management Facilities
Hazardous Waste Management Unit
Hazards Analysis
Hazards Identification
HazMat Employer
High Explosive Cargo
High Explosives
High-Level Wastes

Incompatible Wastes
Industrial Waste
Infectious Material
Infectious Wastes

List of Source Categories
Listed Hazardous Substances
Listed Hazardous Wastes
Listed Wastes
Low-Level Radioactive Waste

Major Release

Management, Hazardous Waste
Materials Handling
Maximum Contaminant Level Goal
Maximum Contaminant Levels
Medical Wastes
Mining Wastes
Minor Releases
Mixed Wastes
Modified Hazard Ranking System

National Oil and Hazardous Substances
  Contingency Plan
Nitrogenous Wastes
Nuclear Waste

Office of Civilian Radioactive Waste
  Management
Office of Environmental Restoration and
  Waste Management

Pathological Waste
PCB Waste Generator
PCB Wastes
Pesticide-Related Wastes
Pesticides
Pile, Waste
Piles, Nuclear
Plutonium
Plutonium Processing and Handling Facilities
Plutonium Storage Facilities
Pollution Prevention Act

Radioactive Substances
Radioactive Waste
Radioactive Waste Management
Regularly Handle
Regulated Activities
Regulated Entities
Regulated Item
Regulated Substances
Relevant and Appropriate Requirements
Reliability and Quality Assurance
Remote-Handled Transuranic Wastes

Secondary Recovery
Significant Modification
Significant Quantities
Significant Violations
Solid Waste Disposal Act

Special Wastes
State Hazardous Wastes
Superfund Amendments and Reauthorization
  Act

Toxic Pollutants
Toxic Potential
Toxic Release Inventory System
Toxic Substances
Toxic Substances Control Act
Toxic Wastes
Toxicants
Toxicity
Toxicology
Toxin Agent
Transport, Hazardous Substances
Transportation, Hazardous
Transuranic Wastes

Uncontrolled Hazardous Waste Sites
Unlisted Hazardous Substances
Uranium Mill Tailings
Uranium Byproduct Materials
Uranium Mine Wastes Hazards Elimination
  Study

Volatile Hazardous Air Pollutant

Waste
Waste Containers
Waste-Database
Waste Fund
Waste Heat
Waste Holding Tank
Waste Information Network
Waste Isolation Pilot Plant
Waste Load Allocation
Waste Management
Waste Material
Waste Minimization Plan
Waste Oils
Waste Packages
Waste Piles
Waste Source
Waste Treatment Plant
Waste Treatment Stream

REGULATORY ENTITIES, REGULATIONS, CODES, STANDARDS, and PROGRAMS

Aquatic Nuisance Species Task Force
Aquatic Nuisance Prevention and Control Act
Archaeological Resources Protection Act
Asbestos Standards
ASHRAE
ASME
ASME Code
ASMFC
Atomic Energy Act
Atomic Energy Commission
Authorized Agency Representative
AWWA Standard

Boards

Categorical Pretreatment Standards
Chemical Safety and Hazard Investigation
  Board
Chemical Standard for the Development of
  Test Data
Clean Air Act
Clean Water Act
Coastal Barriers Task Force
Coastal Zone Management Act
Code of Federal Regulations
Codes, Standards, and Regulations
Cognizant Federal Agencies
Comprehensive Environmental Response,
  Compensation, and Liability Act

Data Collection Agency
Department
Department of Agriculture
Department of Commerce
Department of Energy
Department of Energy Wastes
Department of Housing and Urban
  Development
Department of Justice
Department of Labor
Department of the Air Force
Department of the Army
Department of the Navy
Department of Transportation
Department of Treasury

International Hydrological Decade
International Identification Code
International Loading Gauge
International Logistics
International Shipment
International System of Units
International Union for the Conservation of
  Nature and Natural Resources
Interagency Committee on Standards Policy
Interdepartmental/Agency Support
Interdepartmental Intelligence
Intermunicipal Agencies

Local Agencies
Local Educational Agency
Local Emergency Planning Committee
Local Governments
Local Health Agency
Local Organization

Mandatory Standards
Marine Protection, Research, and Sanctuaries
  Act
Matching Program
Migratory Bird Treaty Act
Military Intelligence Board
Minimum Requirements and Standards
Multiple-Use Sustained-Yield Act

National Consensus Standard
National Environmental Policy Act
National Historic Preservation Act
National Priorities List
National Recreational Trails Advisory
  Committee
National Register or Register
National Security Council
National Workforce Development Office

Occupational Safety and Health Administration
Occupational Safety and Health Programs,
  Federal
Occupational Safety and Health Standard
Ocean Dumping Act

Permit
Permitting Authorities
Pollution Prevention Act
Primary Standards

Procuring Agency
Program
Program Offices
Program Organizations
Programmatic Memorandum of Agreement
Public Health Service Act

Quality Assurance Agency

Radiation Standards
Redevelopment Agency
Reference Standards
Regional Assistance Committees
Regional Coordinating Offices
Regional Office
Regions
Registration Standards
Regulated Activities
Regulated Entities
Regulatory Organizations
Renewable Resources Extension Act
Resource Conservation and Development
  Policy Board
Respective Agency Head, Public Land

Safe Drinking Water Act
Science Advisory Board
Scientific Advisory Panel
Secretary
Senior Scientific Advisers
Solid Waste Disposal Act
Source Agency
Standard
Standard Industrial Classification
Standard Job Procedures
Standard Metropolitan Statistical Area
Standards Information Management System
Standards-Developing Groups
State
State Agency Rule
State Air Quality Agency
State Coordination
State Emergency Response Commission
State Energy Agency
State/EPA Agreements
State Historic Preservation Review Board
State Implementation Plan
State Mining Program
State Primary Drinking Water Regulation

State Regulation
State Routing Agencies
State School Facilities Agency
State Wellhead Protection Program
Superfund Amendments and Reauthorization
 Act
Support Agencies

Technology-Based Standards
Testing Agency
Toxic Substances Control Act

U.S. Armed Forces
U.S. Civil Authorities
U.S. Country Team
U.S. Coast Guard
U.S. Department of Energy
U.S. Department of Justice
U.S. Department of Labor
U.S. Department of Transportation
U.S. District Courts
U.S. Environmental Protection Agency
U.S. Fish and Wildlife Service
U.S. Geological Survey
Unit of Local Government
United Nations Educational, Scientific, and
 Cultural Organization
United Nations Environmental Program
United States

Violation, General
Violations, Grouping
Violation, Regulatory
Violation, Repeated
Voluntary Energy Performance Standards
Voluntary Standards
Voluntary Standards Bodies

Water Pollution Control Act
Watershed Protection and Flood Prevention Act
Wild and Scenic Rivers Act
Wood Residue Utilization Act
Worker Protection Standard

SPECIAL and CULTURAL
RESOURCES ISSUES

Adjoining Flood Plain

Advisory Council on Historic Preservation
Affected Indian Tribe
Affected Persons
Affected Tribal Council
Alaskan Native
American Indian
Antarctic "Ozone Hole"
Antennae, Wildlife Species
Aquatic
Aquatic Environment
Aquatic Nuisance Prevention and Control Act
Aquatic Nuisance Species
Aquatic Nuisance Species Control
Aquatic Nuisance Species Monitoring
Aquatic Nuisance Species Program
Aquatic Nuisance Species Task Force
Aquatic Nuisance Task Force Objectives
Aquifer
Aquifer Recharge Area
Aquifer System
Aquifer Test
Archaeological Clearance
Archaeological Excavation and Removal
 Permit
Archaeological Resource
Archaeological Resources Protection Act
Archaeological Site
Archaeology
Architectural Conservation
Architectural Conservator
Architectural Historian
Area Affected by Outer Continental Shelf
 Activities
Artesian Aquifer
Artesian Well
Attractive Nuisance
Authentic Native Articles of Handicrafts and
 Clothing

Beach
Beachhead
Biogeographical Province
Biotic Potential
Biotic Pyramid
Bottom Lands
Brown Tree Snake Control Program

California Tidelands
Catchment Area

Qualified Hydrologic Unit

Range
Range Condition
Range Improvement
Raptor
Recharge
Recharge Area
Recharge Basin
Recharge Boundary
Renewable Energy Sources
Resource Conservation
Restoration
Restoration, Management, and Protection,
  Wetlands/Habitat for Migratory Birds
River
River Basins
Riverine Area

Silvicultural System
Sole Source Aquifer
Special Management Areas
Spring
Spring Tide
State Aquatic Nuisance Species Management
  Plans
State Fish and Game Department
State Historic Preservation Officer
State Historic Preservation Review Board
State Wellhead Protection Program
Submerged Cultural Resources
Sustainable Agriculture

T&E
Taxonomy
Technosphere
Terrain Analysis
Terrain Intelligence
Terrain Study
Terrapin
Terrestrial
Terrestrial Environment
Territorial Seas
Terrigenous
Territory
Threatened and Endangered Species
Threatened Species

Unauthorized Excavation, Removal, Damage,
  Alteration, or Defacement
Unconfined Aquifer
Underwater Archaeology
Uppermost Aquifer

Vegetation Protection
Visual Range

Wild and Scenic River
Wild and Scenic Rivers Act
Wild and Scenic Rivers Maps
Wild and Scenic Rivers Regulations
Wild and Scenic Rivers System
Wild River Area
Wild, Scenic or Recreational River Area
Wilderness Area
Wildland Vegetation Management Burning
Wildlife
Wildlife Conservation
Wildlife Conservation and Rehabilitation
  Program
Wildlife Conservation Plan
Wildlife Habitat
Wildlife Management
Wildlife Refuges
Wildlife-Restoration Project
Wildlife Takings
World Wildlife Fund
Worldwide Terrain Areas

Xeric Environ

Zebra Mussel Program
Zooecology
Zoolite
Zooplankters
Zooplankton
Zygomorphic
Zygotes
Zymogenous

WATER RESOURCES and RELATED ISSUES

Aqueous
Aquifer Test
Areawide Wastewater Treatment Management

Auxiliary Water Supply
Ballast Water
Best Management Practices
Blackwater
Boiling Water Reactor
Brackish Waters

Capillary Water
Chesapeake Bay and Lake Champlain
  Monitoring
Clean Water Act
Close Reflection by Water
Coastal Waters
Coefficient of Storage
Community Water Systems
Connate Water

Dangerously Exposed Waters
Decomposition of Wastewater
Dedicated Fire Water Systems
Detention Pond
Dewatered
Disinfected Wastewater
Domestic Water Supply Reservoir
Drinking Water Supplies
Dystrophic Lakes

Eligible Groundwater Project
Eutrophic Lakes
Evacuation of Dangerously Exposed Waters
Evaporation Pond
Extreme Low Water of Spring Tides
Extreme High Water of Spring Tides

Feasible Water Treatment
Federal Water Pollution Act
Feedwater
Free-Flowing River or River Section

Gravitational Water
Gray Water
Great Lakes
Great Lakes Monitoring Network
Great Lakes Regional Coordination Panel
Groundwater
Groundwater Resources

Hard Water
Headwaters

Heavy Water
High Tide Line
High-Water Mark
Holding Pond
In-Process Wastewater
Inland Waters
Interstate Carrier, Water Supplies
Interstate Waters

Kings River Special Management Area

Lagoon
Lahar
Lake
Lake Transition Line
Light-Water Reactor

Manmade Watercourse
Maximum Total Prihalomethane Potential
Mean High Water
Mean Lower Low Water
Mean Low Water
Mean Point of Impact
Mean Sea Level
Mean Tide Level
Mineral Water
Monitoring Coastal Waters

National Acid Lakes Registry
National Acid Precipitation Assessment
  Program
National Ballast Water Control Studies
National Pollutant Discharge Elimination
  System
Net Water Savings
Nitrate Pollution
Non-Community Water System
Non-Contact Cooling Water Pollutants
Non-Transient Non-Community Water System
NPDES

Obstruction, Water
Ocean Waters
Oligotrophic Lakes
Ordinary High Water Mark
Oxidation Ponds

Particulate Loading
Perched Water